University Physics

Volume 3

XanEdu

Printed in the United States of America

ISBN: 978-1-50669-825-0

530 Great Road
Acton, MA 01720
800-562-2147
www.xanedu.com

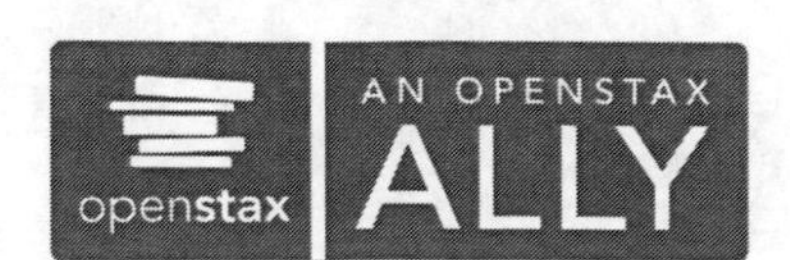

University Physics Volume 3

SENIOR CONTRIBUTING AUTHORS

SAMUEL J. LING, TRUMAN STATE UNIVERSITY

JEFF SANNY, LOYOLA MARYMOUNT UNIVERSITY

WILLIAM MOEBS, PHD

OpenStax
Rice University
6100 Main Street MS-375
Houston, Texas 77005

To learn more about OpenStax, visit https://openstax.org.
Individual print copies and bulk orders can be purchased through our website.

PRINT BOOK ISBN-10	**1-938168-18-6**
PRINT BOOK ISBN-13	**978-1-938168-18-5**
PDF VERSION ISBN-10	**1-947172-22-0**
PDF VERSION ISBN-13	**978-1-947172-22-7**
ENHANCED TEXTBOOK ISBN-10	**1-947172-22-0**
ENHANCED TEXTBOOK ISBN-13	**978-1-947172-22-7**
Revision Number	**UP3-2016-002(05/18)-MJ**
Original Publication Year	**2016**

OpenStax

OpenStax provides free, peer-reviewed, openly licensed textbooks for introductory college and Advanced Placement® courses and low-cost, personalized courseware that helps students learn. A nonprofit ed tech initiative based at Rice University, we're committed to helping students access the tools they need to complete their courses and meet their educational goals.

Rice University

OpenStax, OpenStax CNX, and OpenStax Tutor are initiatives of Rice University. As a leading research university with a distinctive commitment to undergraduate education, Rice University aspires to path-breaking research, unsurpassed teaching, and contributions to the betterment of our world. It seeks to fulfill this mission by cultivating a diverse community of learning and discovery that produces leaders across the spectrum of human endeavor.

Foundation Support

OpenStax is grateful for the tremendous support of our sponsors. Without their strong engagement, the goal of free access to high-quality textbooks would remain just a dream.

Laura and John Arnold Foundation (LJAF) actively seeks opportunities to invest in organizations and thought leaders that have a sincere interest in implementing fundamental changes that not only yield immediate gains, but also repair broken systems for future generations. LJAF currently focuses its strategic investments on education, criminal justice, research integrity, and public accountability.

The William and Flora Hewlett Foundation has been making grants since 1967 to help solve social and environmental problems at home and around the world. The Foundation concentrates its resources on activities in education, the environment, global development and population, performing arts, and philanthropy, and makes grants to support disadvantaged communities in the San Francisco Bay Area.

Calvin K. Kazanjian was the founder and president of Peter Paul (Almond Joy), Inc. He firmly believed that the more people understood about basic economics the happier and more prosperous they would be. Accordingly, he established the Calvin K. Kazanjian Economics Foundation Inc, in 1949 as a philanthropic, nonpolitical educational organization to support efforts that enhanced economic understanding.

Guided by the belief that every life has equal value, the Bill & Melinda Gates Foundation works to help all people lead healthy, productive lives. In developing countries, it focuses on improving people's health with vaccines and other life-saving tools and giving them the chance to lift themselves out of hunger and extreme poverty. In the United States, it seeks to significantly improve education so that all young people have the opportunity to reach their full potential. Based in Seattle, Washington, the foundation is led by CEO Jeff Raikes and Co-chair William H. Gates Sr., under the direction of Bill and Melinda Gates and Warren Buffett.

The Maxfield Foundation supports projects with potential for high impact in science, education, sustainability, and other areas of social importance.

Our mission at The Michelson 20MM Foundation is to grow access and success by eliminating unnecessary hurdles to affordability. We support the creation, sharing, and proliferation of more effective, more affordable educational content by leveraging disruptive technologies, open educational resources, and new models for collaboration between for-profit, nonprofit, and public entities.

The Bill and Stephanie Sick Fund supports innovative projects in the areas of Education, Art, Science and Engineering.

Table of Contents

PREFACE

Welcome to *University Physics*, an OpenStax resource. This textbook was written to increase student access to high-quality learning materials, maintaining highest standards of academic rigor at little to no cost.

About OpenStax

OpenStax is a nonprofit based at Rice University, and it's our mission to improve student access to education. Our first openly licensed college textbook was published in 2012 and our library has since scaled to over 25 books used by hundreds of thousands of students across the globe. OpenStax Tutor, our low-cost personalized learning tool, is being used in college courses throughout the country. The OpenStax mission is made possible through the generous support of philanthropic foundations. Through these partnerships and with the help of additional low-cost resources from our OpenStax partners, OpenStax is breaking down the most common barriers to learning and empowering students and instructors to succeed.

About OpenStax's resources

Customization

University Physics is licensed under a Creative Commons Attribution 4.0 International (CC BY) license, which means that you can distribute, remix, and build upon the content, as long as you provide attribution to OpenStax and its content contributors.

Because our books are openly licensed, you are free to use the entire book or pick and choose the sections that are most relevant to the needs of your course. Feel free to remix the content by assigning your students certain chapters and sections in your syllabus in the order that you prefer. You can even provide a direct link in your syllabus to the sections in the web view of your book.

Instructors also have the option of creating a customized version of their OpenStax book. The custom version can be made available to students in low-cost print or digital form through their campus bookstore. Visit your book page on OpenStax.org for more information.

Errata

All OpenStax textbooks undergo a rigorous review process. However, like any professional-grade textbook, errors sometimes occur. Since our books are web based, we can make updates periodically when deemed pedagogically necessary. If you have a correction to suggest, submit it through the link on your book page on OpenStax.org. Subject matter experts review all errata suggestions. OpenStax is committed to remaining transparent about all updates, so you will also find a list of past errata changes on your book page on OpenStax.org.

Format

You can access this textbook for free in web view or PDF through OpenStax.org, and for a low cost in print.

About *University Physics*

University Physics is designed for the two- or three-semester calculus-based physics course. The text has been developed to meet the scope and sequence of most university physics courses and provides a foundation for a career in mathematics, science, or engineering. The book provides an important opportunity for students to learn the core concepts of physics and understand how those concepts apply to their lives and to the world around them.

Due to the comprehensive nature of the material, we are offering the book in three volumes for flexibility and efficiency.

Coverage and scope

Our *University Physics* textbook adheres to the scope and sequence of most two- and three-semester physics courses nationwide. We have worked to make physics interesting and accessible to students while maintaining the mathematical rigor inherent in the subject. With this objective in mind, the content of this textbook has been developed and arranged to provide a logical progression from fundamental to more advanced concepts, building upon what students have already learned and emphasizing connections between topics and between theory and applications. The goal of each section is to enable students not just to recognize concepts, but to work with them in ways that will be useful in later courses and future careers. The organization and pedagogical features were developed and vetted with feedback from science educators dedicated to the project.

VOLUME I

Unit 1: Mechanics

Chapter 1: Units and Measurement

Chapter 2: Vectors

Chapter 3: Motion Along a Straight Line

Chapter 4: Motion in Two and Three Dimensions

Chapter 5: Newton's Laws of Motion

Chapter 6: Applications of Newton's Laws

Chapter 7: Work and Kinetic Energy

Chapter 8: Potential Energy and Conservation of Energy

Chapter 9: Linear Momentum and Collisions

Chapter 10: Fixed-Axis Rotation

Chapter 11: Angular Momentum

Chapter 12: Static Equilibrium and Elasticity

Chapter 13: Gravitation

Chapter 14: Fluid Mechanics

Unit 2: Waves and Acoustics

Chapter 15: Oscillations

Chapter 16: Waves

Chapter 17: Sound

VOLUME II

Unit 1: Thermodynamics

Chapter 1: Temperature and Heat

Chapter 2: The Kinetic Theory of Gases

Chapter 3: The First Law of Thermodynamics

Chapter 4: The Second Law of Thermodynamics

Unit 2: Electricity and Magnetism

Chapter 5: Electric Charges and Fields

Chapter 6: Gauss's Law

Chapter 7: Electric Potential

Chapter 8: Capacitance

Chapter 9: Current and Resistance

Chapter 10: Direct-Current Circuits

Chapter 11: Magnetic Forces and Fields

Chapter 12: Sources of Magnetic Fields

Chapter 13: Electromagnetic Induction

Chapter 14: Inductance

Chapter 15: Alternating-Current Circuits

Chapter 16: Electromagnetic Waves

VOLUME III

Unit 1: Optics

Chapter 1: The Nature of Light

Chapter 2: Geometric Optics and Image Formation

Chapter 3: Interference

Chapter 4: Diffraction

Unit 2: Modern Physics

Chapter 5: Relativity

Chapter 6: Photons and Matter Waves

Chapter 7: Quantum Mechanics

Chapter 8: Atomic Structure

Chapter 9: Condensed Matter Physics

Chapter 10: Nuclear Physics

Chapter 11: Particle Physics and Cosmology

Pedagogical foundation

Throughout *University Physics* you will find derivations of concepts that present classical ideas and techniques, as well as modern applications and methods. Most chapters start with observations or experiments that place the material in a context of physical experience. Presentations and explanations rely on years of classroom experience on the part of long-time physics professors, striving for a balance of clarity and rigor that has proven successful with their students. Throughout the text, links enable students to review earlier material and then return to the present discussion, reinforcing connections between topics. Key historical figures and experiments are discussed in the main text (rather than in boxes or sidebars), maintaining a focus on the development of physical intuition. Key ideas, definitions, and equations are highlighted in the text and listed in summary form at the end of each chapter. Examples and chapter-opening images often include contemporary applications from daily life or modern science and engineering that students can relate to, from smart phones to the internet to GPS devices.

Assessments that reinforce key concepts

In-chapter **Examples** generally follow a three-part format of Strategy, Solution, and Significance to emphasize how to approach a problem, how to work with the equations, and how to check and generalize the result. Examples are often followed by **Check Your Understanding** questions and answers to help reinforce for students the important ideas of the examples. **Problem-Solving Strategies** in each chapter break down methods of approaching various types of problems into steps students can follow for guidance. The book also includes exercises at the end of each chapter so students can practice what they've learned.

Conceptual questions do not require calculation but test student learning of the key concepts.

Problems categorized by section test student problem-solving skills and the ability to apply ideas to practical situations.

Additional Problems apply knowledge across the chapter, forcing students to identify what concepts and equations are appropriate for solving given problems. Randomly located throughout the problems are **Unreasonable Results** exercises that ask students to evaluate the answer to a problem and explain why it is not reasonable and what assumptions made might not be correct.

Challenge Problems extend text ideas to interesting but difficult situations.

Answers for selected exercises are available in an **Answer Key** at the end of the book.

Additional resources

Student and instructor resources

We've compiled additional resources for both students and instructors, including Getting Started Guides, PowerPoint slides, and answer and solution guides for instructors and students. Instructor resources require a verified instructor account, which you can apply for when you log in or create your account on OpenStax.org. Take advantage of these resources to supplement your OpenStax book.

Community Hubs

OpenStax partners with the Institute for the Study of Knowledge Management in Education (ISKME) to offer Community Hubs on OER Commons – a platform for instructors to share community-created resources that support OpenStax books, free of charge. Through our Community Hubs, instructors can upload their own materials or download resources to use in their own courses, including additional ancillaries, teaching material, multimedia, and relevant course content. We encourage instructors to join the hubs for the subjects most relevant to your teaching and research as an opportunity both to enrich your courses and to engage with other faculty.

To reach the Community Hubs, visit www.oercommons.org/hubs/OpenStax (https://www.oercommons.org/hubs/OpenStax) .

Partner resources

OpenStax partners are our allies in the mission to make high-quality learning materials affordable and accessible to students and instructors everywhere. Their tools integrate seamlessly with our OpenStax titles at a low cost. To access the partner resources for your text, visit your book page on OpenStax.org.

About the authors

Senior contributing authors

Samuel J. Ling, Truman State University
Dr. Samuel Ling has taught introductory and advanced physics for over 25 years at Truman State University, where he is currently Professor of Physics and the Department Chair. Dr. Ling has two PhDs from Boston University, one in Chemistry and the other in Physics, and he was a Research Fellow at the Indian Institute of Science, Bangalore, before joining Truman. Dr. Ling is also an author of *A First Course in Vibrations and Waves*, published by Oxford University Press. Dr. Ling has considerable experience with research in Physics Education and has published research on collaborative learning methods in physics teaching. He was awarded a Truman Fellow and a Jepson fellow in recognition of his innovative teaching methods. Dr. Ling's research publications have spanned Cosmology, Solid State Physics, and Nonlinear Optics.

Jeff Sanny, Loyola Marymount University
Dr. Jeff Sanny earned a BS in Physics from Harvey Mudd College in 1974 and a PhD in Solid State Physics from the University of California–Los Angeles in 1980. He joined the faculty at Loyola Marymount University in the fall of 1980. During his tenure, he has served as department Chair as well as Associate Dean. Dr. Sanny enjoys teaching introductory physics in particular. He is also passionate about providing students with research experience and has directed an active undergraduate student research group in space physics for many years.

William Moebs, Formerly of Loyola Marymount University
Dr. William Moebs earned a BS and PhD (1959 and 1965) from the University of Michigan. He then joined their staff as a Research Associate for one year, where he continued his doctoral research in particle physics. In 1966, he accepted an appointment to the Physics Department of Indiana Purdue Fort Wayne (IPFW), where he served as Department Chair from 1971 to 1979. In 1979, he moved to Loyola Marymount University (LMU), where he served as Chair of the Physics Department from 1979 to 1986. He retired from LMU in 2000. He has published research in particle physics, chemical kinetics, cell division, atomic physics, and physics teaching.

Contributing authors

Stephen D. Druger
Alice Kolakowska, University of Memphis
David Anderson, Albion College
Daniel Bowman, Ferrum College
Dedra Demaree, Georgetown University
Edw. S. Ginsberg, University of Massachusetts
Joseph Trout, Richard Stockton College
Kevin Wheelock, Bellevue College
David Smith, University of the Virgin Islands
Takashi Sato, Kwantlen Polytechnic University
Gerald Friedman, Santa Fe Community College
Lev Gasparov, University of North Florida
Lee LaRue, Paris Junior College
Mark Lattery, University of Wisconsin
Richard Ludlow, Daniel Webster College
Patrick Motl, Indiana University Kokomo
Tao Pang, University of Nevada, Las Vegas
Kenneth Podolak, Plattsburgh State University

Reviewers

Salameh Ahmad, Rochester Institute of Technology–Dubai
John Aiken, University of Colorado–Boulder
Raymond Benge, Terrant County College

Gavin Buxton, Robert Morris University
Erik Christensen, South Florida State College
Clifton Clark, Fort Hays State University
Nelson Coates, California Maritime Academy
Herve Collin, Kapi'olani Community College
Carl Covatto, Arizona State University
Alejandro Cozzani, Imperial Valley College
Danielle Dalafave, The College of New Jersey
Nicholas Darnton, Georgia Institute of Technology
Ethan Deneault, University of Tampa
Kenneth DeNisco, Harrisburg Area Community College
Robert Edmonds, Tarrant County College
William Falls, Erie Community College
Stanley Forrester, Broward College
Umesh Garg, University of Notre Dame
Maurizio Giannotti, Barry University
Bryan Gibbs, Dallas County Community College
Lynn Gillette, Pima Community College–West Campus
Mark Giroux, East Tennessee State University
Matthew Griffiths, University of New Haven
Alfonso Hinojosa, University of Texas–Arlington
Steuard Jensen, Alma College
David Kagan, University of Massachusetts
Sergei Katsev, University of Minnesota–Duluth
Jill Leggett, Florida State College–Jacksonville
Alfredo Louro, University of Calgary
James Maclaren, Tulane University
Ponn Maheswaranathan, Winthrop University
Seth Major, Hamilton College
Oleg Maksimov, Excelsior College
Aristides Marcano, Delaware State University
James McDonald, University of Hartford
Ralph McGrew, SUNY–Broome Community College
Paul Miller, West Virginia University
Tamar More, University of Portland
Farzaneh Najmabadi, University of Phoenix
Richard Olenick, The University of Dallas
Christopher Porter, Ohio State University
Liza Pujji, Manakau Institute of Technology
Baishali Ray, Young Harris University
Andrew Robinson, Carleton University
Aruvana Roy, Young Harris University
Gajendra Tulsian, Daytona State College
Adria Updike, Roger Williams University
Clark Vangilder, Central Arizona University
Steven Wolf, Texas State University
Alexander Wurm, Western New England University
Lei Zhang, Winston Salem State University
Ulrich Zurcher, Cleveland State University

1 | THE NATURE OF LIGHT

Figure 1.1 Due to total internal reflection, an underwater swimmer's image is reflected back into the water where the camera is located. The circular ripple in the image center is actually on the water surface. Due to the viewing angle, total internal reflection is not occurring at the top edge of this image, and we can see a view of activities on the pool deck. (credit: modification of work by "jayhem"/Flickr)

Chapter Outline

Introduction

Our investigation of light revolves around two questions of fundamental importance: (1) What is the nature of light, and (2) how does light behave under various circumstances? Answers to these questions can be found in Maxwell's equations (in **Electromagnetic Waves (http://cnx.org/content/m58495/latest/)**), which predict the existence of electromagnetic waves and their behavior. Examples of light include radio and infrared waves, visible light, ultraviolet radiation, and X-rays. Interestingly, not all light phenomena can be explained by Maxwell's theory. Experiments performed early in the twentieth century showed that light has corpuscular, or particle-like, properties. The idea that light can display both wave and particle characteristics is called *wave-particle duality*, which is examined in **Photons and Matter Waves**.

In this chapter, we study the basic properties of light. In the next few chapters, we investigate the behavior of light when it interacts with optical devices such as mirrors, lenses, and apertures.

1.1 | The Propagation of Light

Learning Objectives

By the end of this section, you will be able to:

- Determine the index of refraction, given the speed of light in a medium
- List the ways in which light travels from a source to another location

The speed of light in a vacuum *c* is one of the fundamental constants of physics. As you will see when you reach **Relativity**, it is a central concept in Einstein's theory of relativity. As the accuracy of the measurements of the speed of light improved, it was found that different observers, even those moving at large velocities with respect to each other, measure the same value for the speed of light. However, the speed of light does vary in a precise manner with the material it traverses. These facts have far-reaching implications, as we will see in later chapters.

The Speed of Light: Early Measurements

The first measurement of the speed of light was made by the Danish astronomer Ole Roemer (1644–1710) in 1675. He studied the orbit of Io, one of the four large moons of Jupiter, and found that it had a period of revolution of 42.5 h around Jupiter. He also discovered that this value fluctuated by a few seconds, depending on the position of Earth in its orbit around the Sun. Roemer realized that this fluctuation was due to the finite speed of light and could be used to determine *c*.

Roemer found the period of revolution of Io by measuring the time interval between successive eclipses by Jupiter. **Figure 1.2**(a) shows the planetary configurations when such a measurement is made from Earth in the part of its orbit where it is receding from Jupiter. When Earth is at point *A*, Earth, Jupiter, and Io are aligned. The next time this alignment occurs, Earth is at point *B*, and the light carrying that information to Earth must travel to that point. Since *B* is farther from Jupiter than *A*, light takes more time to reach Earth when Earth is at *B*. Now imagine it is about 6 months later, and the planets are arranged as in part (b) of the figure. The measurement of Io's period begins with Earth at point A' and Io eclipsed by Jupiter. The next eclipse then occurs when Earth is at point B', to which the light carrying the information of this eclipse must travel. Since B' is closer to Jupiter than A', light takes less time to reach Earth when it is at B'. This time interval between the successive eclipses of Io seen at A' and B' is therefore less than the time interval between the eclipses seen at *A* and *B*. By measuring the difference in these time intervals and with appropriate knowledge of the distance between Jupiter and Earth, Roemer calculated that the speed of light was 2.0×10^8 m/s, which is 33% below the value accepted today.

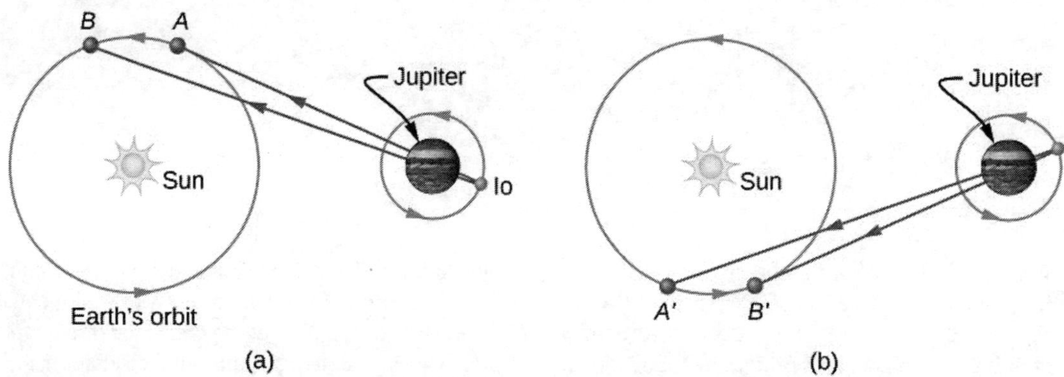

Figure 1.2 Roemer's astronomical method for determining the speed of light. Measurements of Io's period done with the configurations of parts (a) and (b) differ, because the light path length and associated travel time increase from *A* to *B* (a) but decrease from A' to B' (b).

The first successful terrestrial measurement of the speed of light was made by Armand Fizeau (1819–1896) in 1849. He placed a toothed wheel that could be rotated very rapidly on one hilltop and a mirror on a second hilltop 8 km away (**Figure 1.3**). An intense light source was placed behind the wheel, so that when the wheel rotated, it chopped the light beam into a succession of pulses. The speed of the wheel was then adjusted until no light returned to the observer located behind the wheel. This could only happen if the wheel rotated through an angle corresponding to a displacement of $(n + ½)$ teeth, while the pulses traveled down to the mirror and back. Knowing the rotational speed of the wheel, the number of teeth on the wheel, and the distance to the mirror, Fizeau determined the speed of light to be 3.15×10^8 m/s, which is only 5% too high.

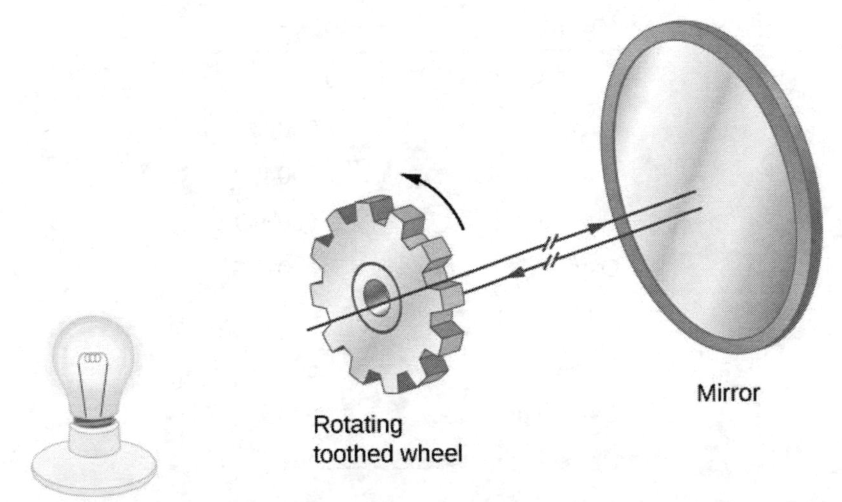

Figure 1.3 Fizeau's method for measuring the speed of light. The teeth of the wheel block the reflected light upon return when the wheel is rotated at a rate that matches the light travel time to and from the mirror.

The French physicist Jean Bernard Léon Foucault (1819–1868) modified Fizeau's apparatus by replacing the toothed wheel with a rotating mirror. In 1862, he measured the speed of light to be 2.98×10^8 m/s, which is within 0.6% of the presently accepted value. Albert Michelson (1852–1931) also used Foucault's method on several occasions to measure the speed of light. His first experiments were performed in 1878; by 1926, he had refined the technique so well that he found c to be $(2.99796 \pm 4) \times 10^8$ m/s.

Today, the speed of light is known to great precision. In fact, the speed of light in a vacuum c is so important that it is accepted as one of the basic physical quantities and has the value

$$c = 2.99792458 \times 10^8 \text{ m/s} \approx 3.00 \times 10^8 \text{ m/s} \tag{1.1}$$

where the approximate value of 3.00×10^8 m/s is used whenever three-digit accuracy is sufficient.

Speed of Light in Matter

The speed of light through matter is less than it is in a vacuum, because light interacts with atoms in a material. The speed of light depends strongly on the type of material, since its interaction varies with different atoms, crystal lattices, and other substructures. We can define a constant of a material that describes the speed of light in it, called the **index of refraction** n:

$$n = \frac{c}{v} \tag{1.2}$$

where v is the observed speed of light in the material.

Since the speed of light is always less than c in matter and equals c only in a vacuum, the index of refraction is always greater than or equal to one; that is, $n \geq 1$. **Table 1.1** gives the indices of refraction for some representative substances. The values are listed for a particular wavelength of light, because they vary slightly with wavelength. (This can have important effects, such as colors separated by a prism, as we will see in **Dispersion**.) Note that for gases, n is close to 1.0. This seems reasonable, since atoms in gases are widely separated, and light travels at c in the vacuum between atoms. It is common to take $n = 1$ for gases unless great precision is needed. Although the speed of light v in a medium varies considerably from its value c in a vacuum, it is still a large speed.

Medium	***n***
Gases at $0°C$, 1 atm	
Air	1.000293
Carbon dioxide	1.00045
Hydrogen	1.000139
Oxygen	1.000271
Liquids at $20°C$	
Benzene	1.501
Carbon disulfide	1.628
Carbon tetrachloride	1.461
Ethanol	1.361
Glycerine	1.473
Water, fresh	1.333
Solids at $20°C$	
Diamond	2.419
Fluorite	1.434
Glass, crown	1.52
Glass, flint	1.66
Ice (at $0°C$)	1.309
Polystyrene	1.49
Plexiglas	1.51
Quartz, crystalline	1.544
Quartz, fused	1.458
Sodium chloride	1.544
Zircon	1.923

Table 1.1 Index of Refraction in Various Media For light with a wavelength of 589 nm in a vacuum

Example 1.1

Speed of Light in Jewelry

Calculate the speed of light in zircon, a material used in jewelry to imitate diamond.

Strategy

We can calculate the speed of light in a material v from the index of refraction n of the material, using the equation $n = c/v$.

Solution

Rearranging the equation $n = c/v$ for v gives us

$$v = \frac{c}{n}.$$

The index of refraction for zircon is given as 1.923 in **Table 1.1**, and c is given in **Equation 1.1**. Entering these values in the equation gives

$$v = \frac{3.00 \times 10^8 \text{ m/s}}{1.923} = 1.56 \times 10^8 \text{ m/s}.$$

Significance

This speed is slightly larger than half the speed of light in a vacuum and is still high compared with speeds we normally experience. The only substance listed in **Table 1.1** that has a greater index of refraction than zircon is diamond. We shall see later that the large index of refraction for zircon makes it sparkle more than glass, but less than diamond.

1.1 Check Your Understanding Table 1.1 shows that ethanol and fresh water have very similar indices of refraction. By what percentage do the speeds of light in these liquids differ?

The Ray Model of Light

You have already studied some of the wave characteristics of light in the previous chapter on **Electromagnetic Waves (http://cnx.org/content/m58495/latest/)** . In this chapter, we start mainly with the ray characteristics. There are three ways in which light can travel from a source to another location (**Figure 1.4**). It can come directly from the source through empty space, such as from the Sun to Earth. Or light can travel through various media, such as air and glass, to the observer. Light can also arrive after being reflected, such as by a mirror. In all of these cases, we can model the path of light as a straight line called a **ray**.

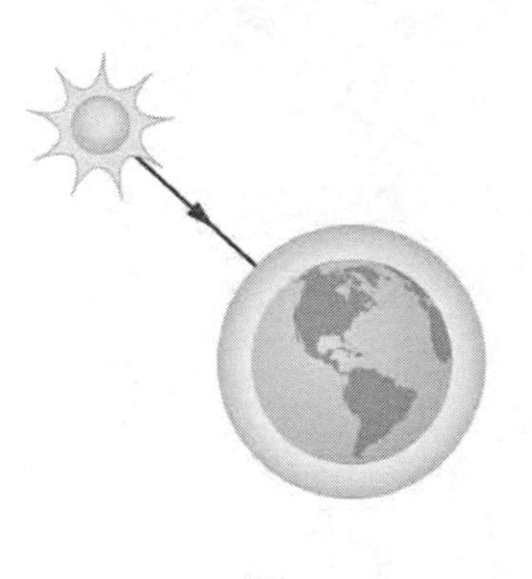

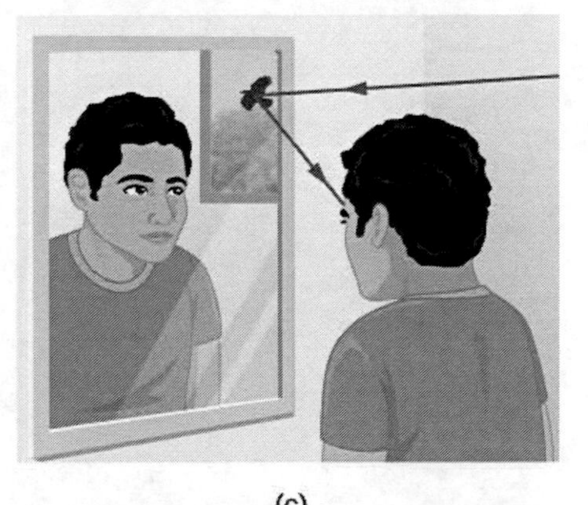

(a) (b) (c)

Figure 1.4 Three methods for light to travel from a source to another location. (a) Light reaches the upper atmosphere of Earth, traveling through empty space directly from the source. (b) Light can reach a person by traveling through media like air and glass. (c) Light can also reflect from an object like a mirror. In the situations shown here, light interacts with objects large enough that it travels in straight lines, like a ray.

Experiments show that when light interacts with an object several times larger than its wavelength, it travels in straight lines and acts like a ray. Its wave characteristics are not pronounced in such situations. Since the wavelength of visible light is less than a micron (a thousandth of a millimeter), it acts like a ray in the many common situations in which it encounters objects larger than a micron. For example, when visible light encounters anything large enough that we can observe it with unaided eyes, such as a coin, it acts like a ray, with generally negligible wave characteristics.

In all of these cases, we can model the path of light as straight lines. Light may change direction when it encounters objects (such as a mirror) or in passing from one material to another (such as in passing from air to glass), but it then continues in a straight line or as a ray. The word "ray" comes from mathematics and here means a straight line that originates at some point. It is acceptable to visualize light rays as laser rays. The *ray model of light* describes the path of light as straight lines.

Since light moves in straight lines, changing directions when it interacts with materials, its path is described by geometry and simple trigonometry. This part of optics, where the ray aspect of light dominates, is therefore called **geometric optics**. Two laws govern how light changes direction when it interacts with matter. These are the *law of reflection*, for situations in which light bounces off matter, and the *law of refraction*, for situations in which light passes through matter. We will examine more about each of these laws in upcoming sections of this chapter.

1.2 | The Law of Reflection

Learning Objectives

By the end of this section, you will be able to:

- Explain the reflection of light from polished and rough surfaces
- Describe the principle and applications of corner reflectors

Whenever we look into a mirror, or squint at sunlight glinting from a lake, we are seeing a reflection. When you look at a piece of white paper, you are seeing light scattered from it. Large telescopes use reflection to form an image of stars and other astronomical objects.

The **law of reflection** states that the angle of reflection equals the angle of incidence, or

$$\theta_r = \theta_i \tag{1.3}$$

The law of reflection is illustrated in **Figure 1.5**, which also shows how the angle of incidence and angle of reflection are measured relative to the perpendicular to the surface at the point where the light ray strikes.

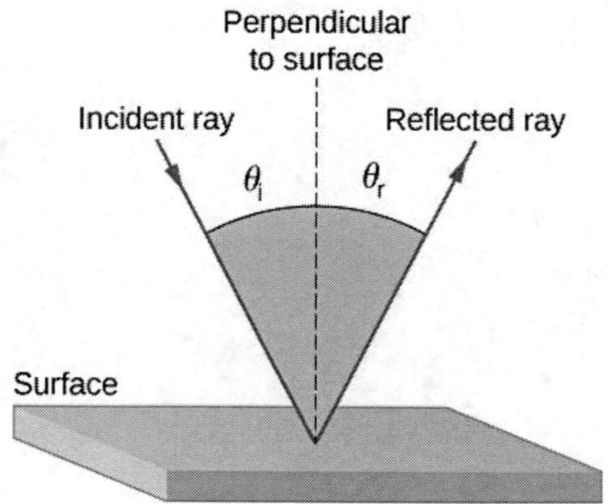

Figure 1.5 The law of reflection states that the angle of reflection equals the angle of incidence— $\theta_r = \theta_i$. The angles are measured relative to the perpendicular to the surface at the point where the ray strikes the surface.

We expect to see reflections from smooth surfaces, but **Figure 1.6** illustrates how a rough surface reflects light. Since the light strikes different parts of the surface at different angles, it is reflected in many different directions, or diffused. Diffused light is what allows us to see a sheet of paper from any angle, as shown in **Figure 1.7**(a). People, clothing, leaves, and walls all have rough surfaces and can be seen from all sides. A mirror, on the other hand, has a smooth surface (compared with the wavelength of light) and reflects light at specific angles, as illustrated in **Figure 1.7**(b). When the Moon reflects from a lake, as shown in **Figure 1.7**(c), a combination of these effects takes place.

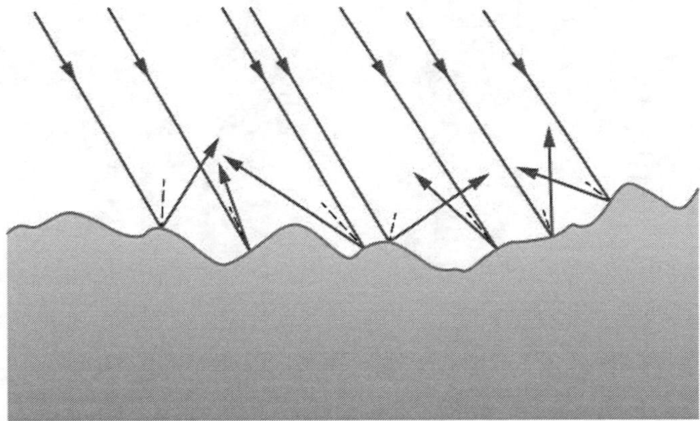

Figure 1.6 Light is diffused when it reflects from a rough surface. Here, many parallel rays are incident, but they are reflected at many different angles, because the surface is rough.

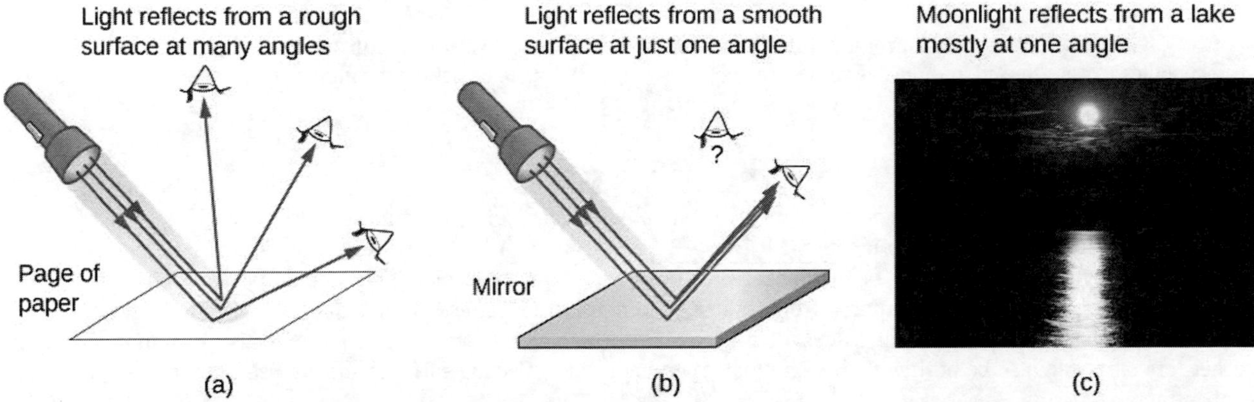

Figure 1.7 (a) When a sheet of paper is illuminated with many parallel incident rays, it can be seen at many different angles, because its surface is rough and diffuses the light. (b) A mirror illuminated by many parallel rays reflects them in only one direction, because its surface is very smooth. Only the observer at a particular angle sees the reflected light. (c) Moonlight is spread out when it is reflected by the lake, because the surface is shiny but uneven. (credit c: modification of work by Diego Torres Silvestre)

When you see yourself in a mirror, it appears that the image is actually behind the mirror (Figure 1.8). We see the light coming from a direction determined by the law of reflection. The angles are such that the image is exactly the same distance behind the mirror as you stand in front of the mirror. If the mirror is on the wall of a room, the images in it are all behind the mirror, which can make the room seem bigger. Although these mirror images make objects appear to be where they cannot be (like behind a solid wall), the images are not figments of your imagination. Mirror images can be photographed and videotaped by instruments and look just as they do with our eyes (which are optical instruments themselves). The precise manner in which images are formed by mirrors and lenses is discussed in an upcoming chapter on Geometric Optics and Image Formation.

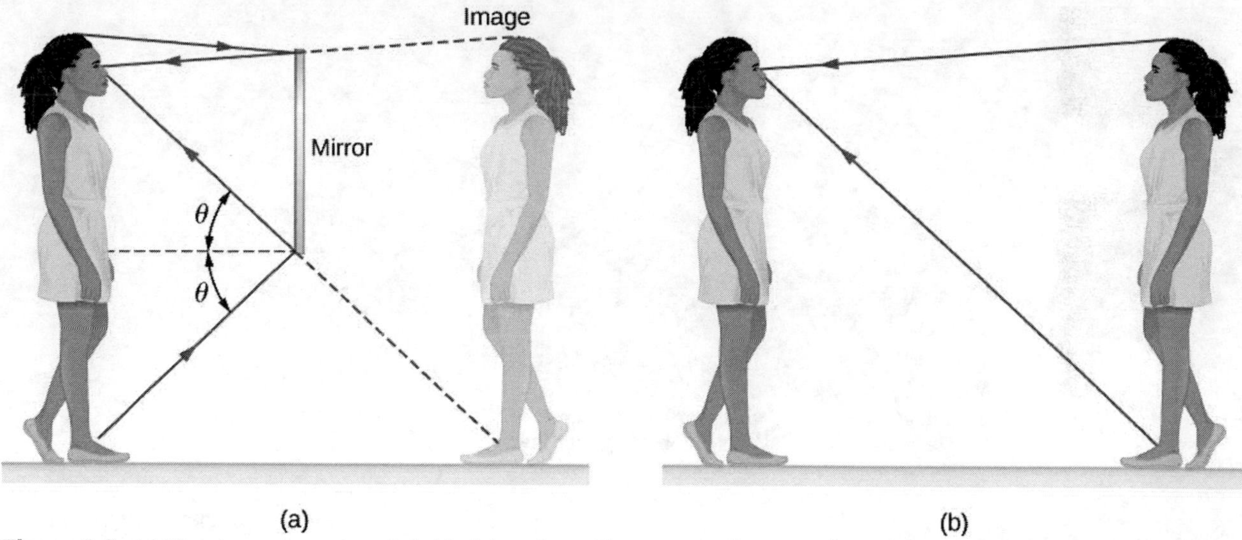

Figure 1.8 (a) Your image in a mirror is behind the mirror. The two rays shown are those that strike the mirror at just the correct angles to be reflected into the eyes of the person. The image appears to be behind the mirror at the same distance away as (b) if you were looking at your twin directly, with no mirror.

Corner Reflectors (Retroreflectors)

A light ray that strikes an object consisting of two mutually perpendicular reflecting surfaces is reflected back exactly parallel to the direction from which it came (**Figure 1.9**). This is true whenever the reflecting surfaces are perpendicular, and it is independent of the angle of incidence. (For proof, see at the end of this section.) Such an object is called a **corner reflector**, since the light bounces from its inside corner. Corner reflectors are a subclass of retroreflectors, which all reflect rays back in the directions from which they came. Although the geometry of the proof is much more complex, corner reflectors can also be built with three mutually perpendicular reflecting surfaces and are useful in three-dimensional applications.

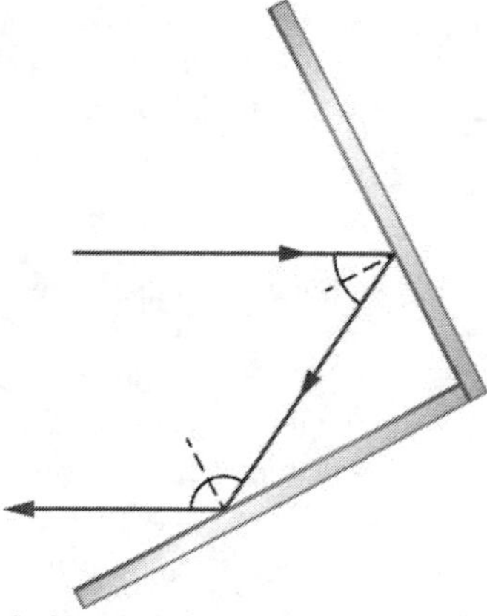

Figure 1.9 A light ray that strikes two mutually perpendicular reflecting surfaces is reflected back exactly parallel to the direction from which it came.

Many inexpensive reflector buttons on bicycles, cars, and warning signs have corner reflectors designed to return light in the direction from which it originated. Rather than simply reflecting light over a wide angle, retroreflection ensures high visibility if the observer and the light source are located together, such as a car's driver and headlights. The Apollo astronauts placed a true corner reflector on the Moon (**Figure 1.10**). Laser signals from Earth can be bounced from that corner reflector to measure the gradually increasing distance to the Moon of a few centimeters per year.

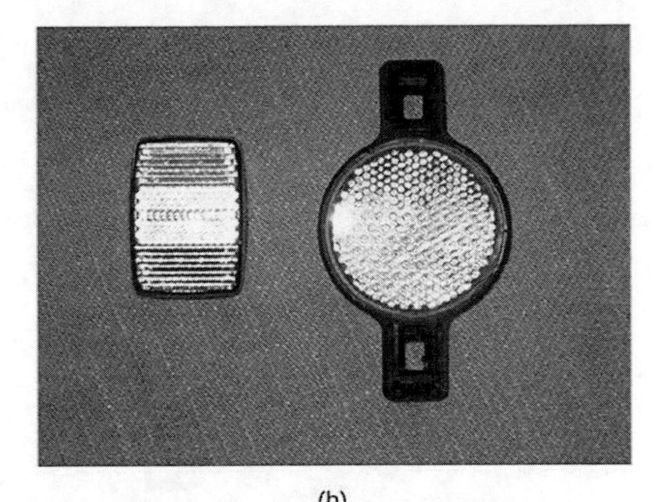

(a) (b)

Figure 1.10 (a) Astronauts placed a corner reflector on the Moon to measure its gradually increasing orbital distance. (b) The bright spots on these bicycle safety reflectors are reflections of the flash of the camera that took this picture on a dark night. (credit a: modification of work by NASA; credit b: modification of work by "Julo"/Wikimedia Commons)

Working on the same principle as these optical reflectors, corner reflectors are routinely used as radar reflectors (**Figure 1.11**) for radio-frequency applications. Under most circumstances, small boats made of fiberglass or wood do not strongly reflect radio waves emitted by radar systems. To make these boats visible to radar (to avoid collisions, for example), radar reflectors are attached to boats, usually in high places.

Figure 1.11 A radar reflector hoisted on a sailboat is a type of corner reflector. (credit: Tim Sheerman-Chase)

As a counterexample, if you are interested in building a stealth airplane, radar reflections should be minimized to evade detection. One of the design considerations would then be to avoid building $90°$ corners into the airframe.

1.3 | Refraction

Learning Objectives

By the end of this section, you will be able to:

- Describe how rays change direction upon entering a medium
- Apply the law of refraction in problem solving

You may often notice some odd things when looking into a fish tank. For example, you may see the same fish appearing to be in two different places (**Figure 1.12**). This happens because light coming from the fish to you changes direction when it leaves the tank, and in this case, it can travel two different paths to get to your eyes. The changing of a light ray's direction (loosely called bending) when it passes through substances of different refractive indices is called **refraction** and is related to changes in the speed of light, $v = c/n$. Refraction is responsible for a tremendous range of optical phenomena, from the action of lenses to data transmission through optical fibers.

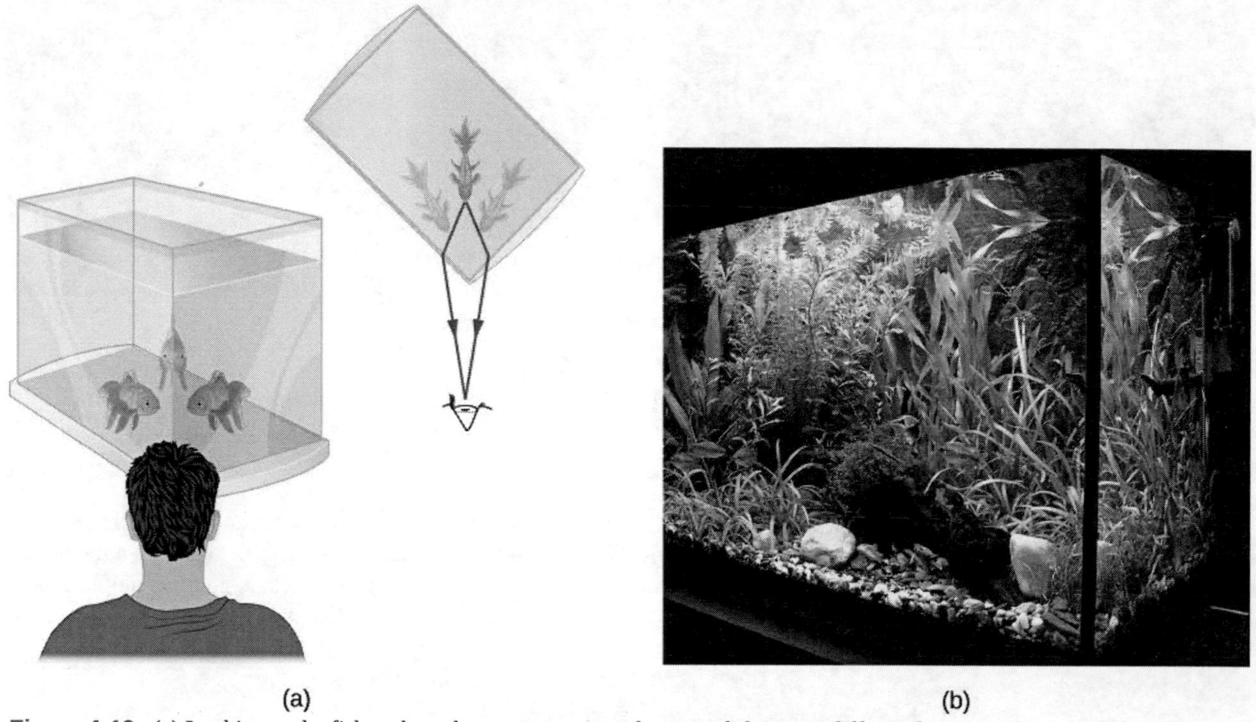

Figure 1.12 (a) Looking at the fish tank as shown, we can see the same fish in two different locations, because light changes directions when it passes from water to air. In this case, the light can reach the observer by two different paths, so the fish seems to be in two different places. This bending of light is called refraction and is responsible for many optical phenomena. (b) This image shows refraction of light from a fish near the top of a fish tank.

Figure 1.13 shows how a ray of light changes direction when it passes from one medium to another. As before, the angles are measured relative to a perpendicular to the surface at the point where the light ray crosses it. (Some of the incident light is reflected from the surface, but for now we concentrate on the light that is transmitted.) The change in direction of the light ray depends on the relative values of the indices of refraction (The Propagation of Light) of the two media involved. In the situations shown, medium 2 has a greater index of refraction than medium 1. Note that as shown in Figure 1.13(a), the direction of the ray moves closer to the perpendicular when it progresses from a medium with a lower index of refraction to one with a higher index of refraction. Conversely, as shown in Figure 1.13(b), the direction of the ray moves away from the perpendicular when it progresses from a medium with a higher index of refraction to one with a lower index of refraction. The path is exactly reversible.

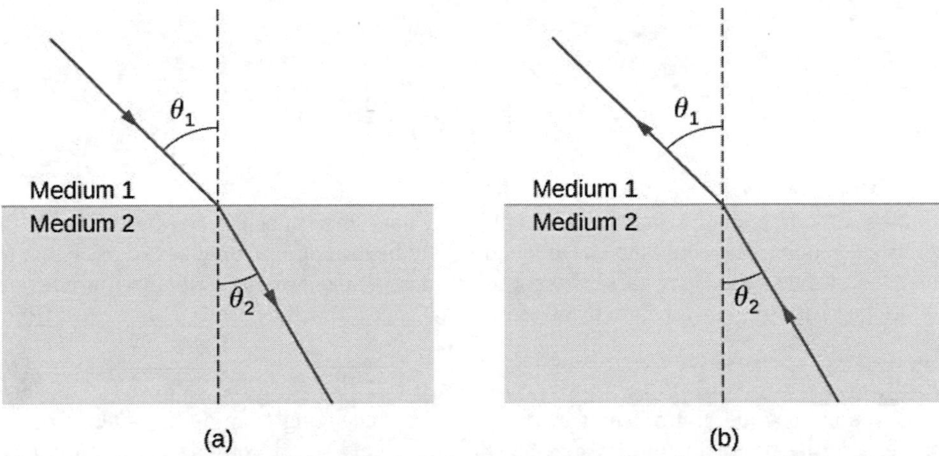

Figure 1.13 The change in direction of a light ray depends on how the index of refraction changes when it crosses from one medium to another. In the situations shown here, the index of refraction is greater in medium 2 than in medium 1. (a) A ray of light moves closer to the perpendicular when entering a medium with a higher index of refraction. (b) A ray of light moves away from the perpendicular when entering a medium with a lower index of refraction.

The amount that a light ray changes its direction depends both on the incident angle and the amount that the speed changes. For a ray at a given incident angle, a large change in speed causes a large change in direction and thus a large change in angle. The exact mathematical relationship is the **law of refraction**, or Snell's law, after the Dutch mathematician Willebrord Snell (1591–1626), who discovered it in 1621. The law of refraction is stated in equation form as

$$n_1 \sin\theta_1 = n_2 \sin\theta_2. \tag{1.4}$$

Here n_1 and n_2 are the indices of refraction for media 1 and 2, and θ_1 and θ_2 are the angles between the rays and the perpendicular in media 1 and 2. The incoming ray is called the incident ray, the outgoing ray is called the refracted ray, and the associated angles are the incident angle and the refracted angle, respectively.

Snell's experiments showed that the law of refraction is obeyed and that a characteristic index of refraction n could be assigned to a given medium and its value measured. Snell was not aware that the speed of light varied in different media, a key fact used when we derive the law of refraction theoretically using Huygens's principle in **Huygens's Principle**.

Example 1.2

Determining the Index of Refraction

Find the index of refraction for medium 2 in **Figure 1.13**(a), assuming medium 1 is air and given that the incident angle is $30.0°$ and the angle of refraction is $22.0°$.

Strategy

The index of refraction for air is taken to be 1 in most cases (and up to four significant figures, it is 1.000). Thus, $n_1 = 1.00$ here. From the given information, $\theta_1 = 30.0°$ and $\theta_2 = 22.0°$. With this information, the only unknown in Snell's law is n_2, so we can use Snell's law to find it.

Solution

From Snell's law we have

$$\begin{aligned} n_1 \sin\theta_1 &= n_2 \sin\theta_2 \\ n_2 &= n_1 \frac{\sin\theta_1}{\sin\theta_2}. \end{aligned}$$

Entering known values,

$$n_2 = 1.00\frac{\sin 30.0°}{\sin 22.0°} = \frac{0.500}{0.375} = 1.33.$$

Significance

This is the index of refraction for water, and Snell could have determined it by measuring the angles and performing this calculation. He would then have found 1.33 to be the appropriate index of refraction for water in all other situations, such as when a ray passes from water to glass. Today, we can verify that the index of refraction is related to the speed of light in a medium by measuring that speed directly.

Explore **bending of light (https://openstaxcollege.org/l/21bendoflight)** between two media with different indices of refraction. Use the "Intro" simulation and see how changing from air to water to glass changes the bending angle. Use the protractor tool to measure the angles and see if you can recreate the configuration in **Example 1.2**. Also by measurement, confirm that the angle of reflection equals the angle of incidence.

Example 1.3

A Larger Change in Direction

Suppose that in a situation like that in **Example 1.2**, light goes from air to diamond and that the incident angle is $30.0°$. Calculate the angle of refraction θ_2 in the diamond.

Strategy

Again, the index of refraction for air is taken to be $n_1 = 1.00$, and we are given $\theta_1 = 30.0°$. We can look up the index of refraction for diamond in **Table 1.1**, finding $n_2 = 2.419$. The only unknown in Snell's law is θ_2, which we wish to determine.

Solution

Solving Snell's law for $\sin\theta_2$ yields

$$\sin\theta_2 = \frac{n_1}{n_2}\sin\theta_1.$$

Entering known values,

$$\sin\theta_2 = \frac{1.00}{2.419}\sin 30.0° = (0.413)(0.500) = 0.207.$$

The angle is thus

$$\theta_2 = \sin^{-1}(0.207) = 11.9°.$$

Significance

For the same $30.0°$ angle of incidence, the angle of refraction in diamond is significantly smaller than in water ($11.9°$ rather than $22.0°$—see **Example 1.2**). This means there is a larger change in direction in diamond. The cause of a large change in direction is a large change in the index of refraction (or speed). In general, the larger the change in speed, the greater the effect on the direction of the ray.

1.2 Check Your Understanding In **Table 1.1**, the solid with the next highest index of refraction after diamond is zircon. If the diamond in **Example 1.3** were replaced with a piece of zircon, what would be the new angle of refraction?

1.4 | Total Internal Reflection

Learning Objectives

By the end of this section, you will be able to:

- Explain the phenomenon of total internal reflection
- Describe the workings and uses of optical fibers
- Analyze the reason for the sparkle of diamonds

A good-quality mirror may reflect more than 90% of the light that falls on it, absorbing the rest. But it would be useful to have a mirror that reflects all of the light that falls on it. Interestingly, we can produce total reflection using an aspect of refraction.

Consider what happens when a ray of light strikes the surface between two materials, as shown in Figure 1.14(a). Part of the light crosses the boundary and is refracted; the rest is reflected. If, as shown in the figure, the index of refraction for the second medium is less than for the first, the ray bends away from the perpendicular. (Since $n_1 > n_2,$ the angle of refraction is greater than the angle of incidence—that is, $\theta_2 > \theta_1$.) Now imagine what happens as the incident angle increases. This causes θ_2 to increase also. The largest the angle of refraction θ_2 can be is $90°$, as shown in part (b). The **critical angle** θ_c for a combination of materials is defined to be the incident angle θ_1 that produces an angle of refraction of $90°$. That is, θ_c is the incident angle for which $\theta_2 = 90°$. If the incident angle θ_1 is greater than the critical angle, as shown in Figure 1.14(c), then all of the light is reflected back into medium 1, a condition called **total internal reflection**. (As the figure shows, the reflected rays obey the law of reflection so that the angle of reflection is equal to the angle of incidence in all three cases.)

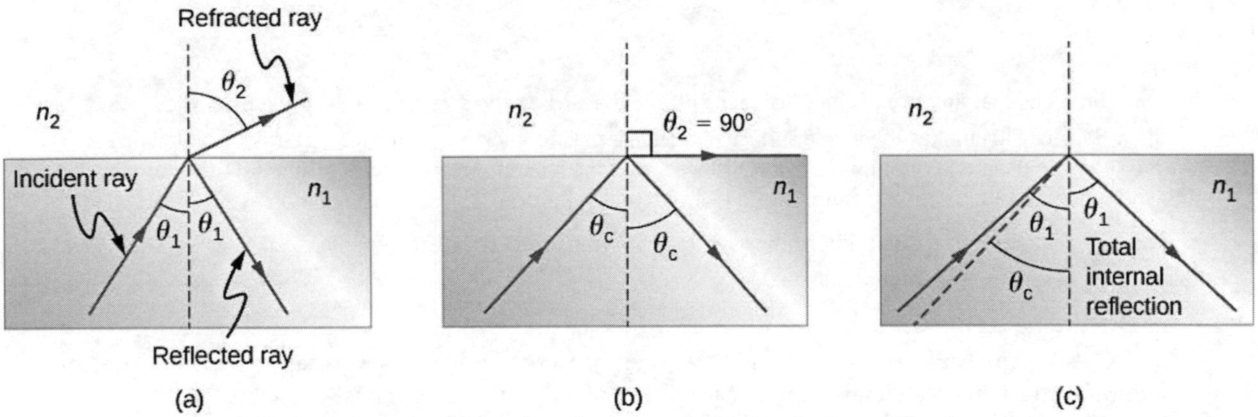

Figure 1.14 (a) A ray of light crosses a boundary where the index of refraction decreases. That is, $n_2 < n_1$. The ray bends away from the perpendicular. (b) The critical angle θ_c is the angle of incidence for which the angle of refraction is $90°$. (c) Total internal reflection occurs when the incident angle is greater than the critical angle.

Snell's law states the relationship between angles and indices of refraction. It is given by

$$n_1 \sin\theta_1 = n_2 \sin\theta_2.$$

When the incident angle equals the critical angle $(\theta_1 = \theta_c)$, the angle of refraction is $90°$ $(\theta_2 = 90°)$. Noting that $\sin 90° = 1,$ Snell's law in this case becomes

$$n_1 \sin\theta_1 = n_2.$$

The critical angle θ_c for a given combination of materials is thus

$$\theta_c = \sin^{-1}\left(\frac{n_2}{n_1}\right) \text{ for } n_1 > n_2. \tag{1.5}$$

Total internal reflection occurs for any incident angle greater than the critical angle θ_c, and it can only occur when the second medium has an index of refraction less than the first. Note that this equation is written for a light ray that travels in medium 1 and reflects from medium 2, as shown in **Figure 1.14**.

Example 1.4

Determining a Critical Angle

What is the critical angle for light traveling in a polystyrene (a type of plastic) pipe surrounded by air? The index of refraction for polystyrene is 1.49.

Strategy

The index of refraction of air can be taken to be 1.00, as before. Thus, the condition that the second medium (air) has an index of refraction less than the first (plastic) is satisfied, and we can use the equation

$$\theta_c = \sin^{-1}\left(\frac{n_2}{n_1}\right)$$

to find the critical angle θ_c, where $n_2 = 1.00$ and $n_1 = 1.49$.

Solution

Substituting the identified values gives

$$\theta_c = \sin^{-1}\left(\frac{1.00}{1.49}\right) = \sin^{-1}(0.671) = 42.2°.$$

Significance

This result means that any ray of light inside the plastic that strikes the surface at an angle greater than $42.2°$ is totally reflected. This makes the inside surface of the clear plastic a perfect mirror for such rays, without any need for the silvering used on common mirrors. Different combinations of materials have different critical angles, but any combination with $n_1 > n_2$ can produce total internal reflection. The same calculation as made here shows that the critical angle for a ray going from water to air is $48.6°$, whereas that from diamond to air is $24.4°$, and that from flint glass to crown glass is $66.3°$.

1.3 Check Your Understanding At the surface between air and water, light rays can go from air to water and from water to air. For which ray is there no possibility of total internal reflection?

In the photo that opens this chapter, the image of a swimmer underwater is captured by a camera that is also underwater. The swimmer in the upper half of the photograph, apparently facing upward, is, in fact, a reflected image of the swimmer below. The circular ripple near the photograph's center is actually on the water surface. The undisturbed water surrounding it makes a good reflecting surface when viewed from below, thanks to total internal reflection. However, at the very top edge of this photograph, rays from below strike the surface with incident angles less than the critical angle, allowing the camera to capture a view of activities on the pool deck above water.

Fiber Optics: Endoscopes to Telephones

Fiber optics is one application of total internal reflection that is in wide use. In communications, it is used to transmit telephone, internet, and cable TV signals. **Fiber optics** employs the transmission of light down fibers of plastic or glass. Because the fibers are thin, light entering one is likely to strike the inside surface at an angle greater than the critical angle and, thus, be totally reflected (**Figure 1.15**). The index of refraction outside the fiber must be smaller than inside. In fact, most fibers have a varying refractive index to allow more light to be guided along the fiber through total internal refraction. Rays are reflected around corners as shown, making the fibers into tiny light pipes.

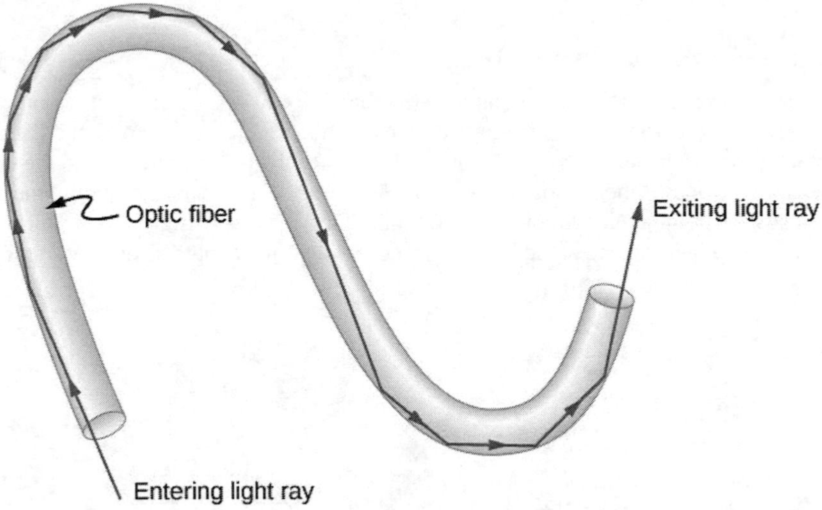

Figure 1.15 Light entering a thin optic fiber may strike the inside surface at large or grazing angles and is completely reflected if these angles exceed the critical angle. Such rays continue down the fiber, even following it around corners, since the angles of reflection and incidence remain large.

Bundles of fibers can be used to transmit an image without a lens, as illustrated in **Figure 1.16**. The output of a device called an endoscope is shown in **Figure 1.16**(b). Endoscopes are used to explore the interior of the body through its natural orifices or minor incisions. Light is transmitted down one fiber bundle to illuminate internal parts, and the reflected light is transmitted back out through another bundle to be observed.

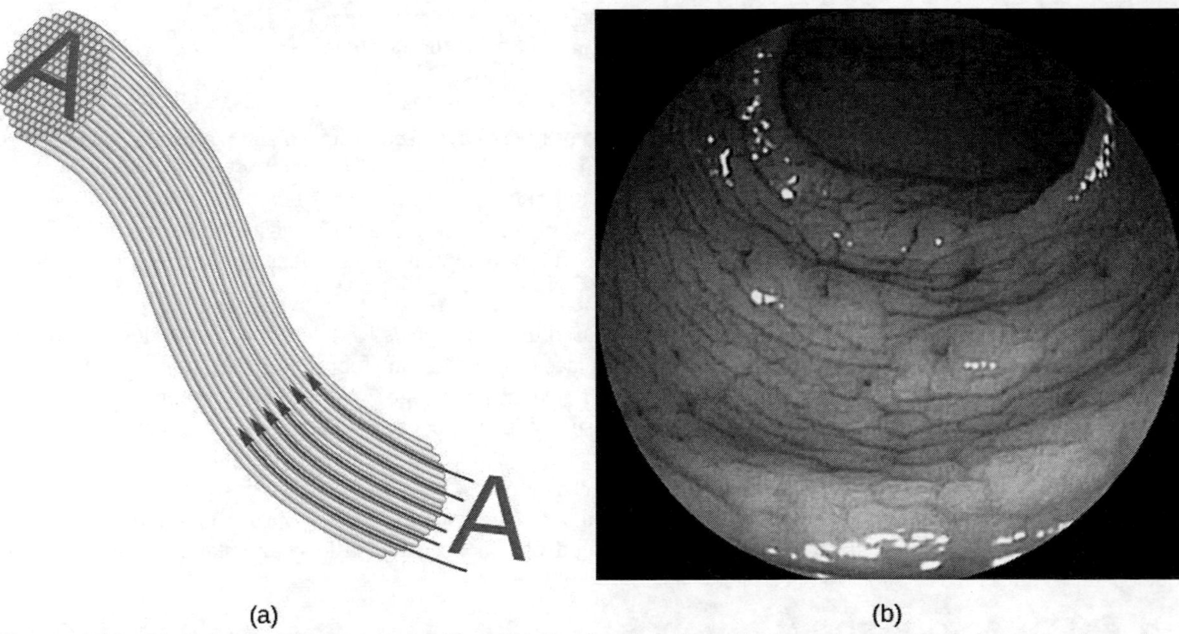

Figure 1.16 (a) An image "A" is transmitted by a bundle of optical fibers. (b) An endoscope is used to probe the body, both transmitting light to the interior and returning an image such as the one shown of a human epiglottis (a structure at the base of the tongue). (credit b: modification of work by "Med_Chaos"/Wikimedia Commons)

Fiber optics has revolutionized surgical techniques and observations within the body, with a host of medical diagnostic and therapeutic uses. Surgery can be performed, such as arthroscopic surgery on a knee or shoulder joint, employing cutting tools attached to and observed with the endoscope. Samples can also be obtained, such as by lassoing an intestinal polyp for external examination. The flexibility of the fiber optic bundle allows doctors to navigate it around small and difficult-to-reach regions in the body, such as the intestines, the heart, blood vessels, and joints. Transmission of an intense laser beam to burn away obstructing plaques in major arteries, as well as delivering light to activate chemotherapy drugs, are becoming commonplace. Optical fibers have in fact enabled microsurgery and remote surgery where the incisions are small and the surgeon's fingers do not need to touch the diseased tissue.

Optical fibers in bundles are surrounded by a cladding material that has a lower index of refraction than the core (**Figure 1.17**). The cladding prevents light from being transmitted between fibers in a bundle. Without cladding, light could pass between fibers in contact, since their indices of refraction are identical. Since no light gets into the cladding (there is total internal reflection back into the core), none can be transmitted between clad fibers that are in contact with one another. Instead, the light is propagated along the length of the fiber, minimizing the loss of signal and ensuring that a quality image is formed at the other end. The cladding and an additional protective layer make optical fibers durable as well as flexible.

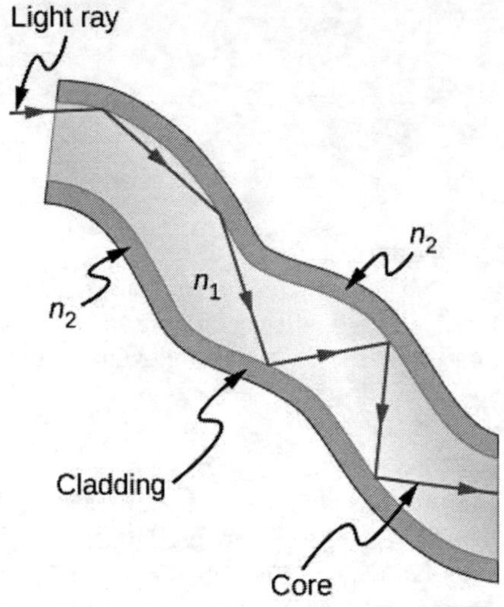

Figure 1.17 Fibers in bundles are clad by a material that has a lower index of refraction than the core to ensure total internal reflection, even when fibers are in contact with one another.

Special tiny lenses that can be attached to the ends of bundles of fibers have been designed and fabricated. Light emerging from a fiber bundle can be focused through such a lens, imaging a tiny spot. In some cases, the spot can be scanned, allowing quality imaging of a region inside the body. Special minute optical filters inserted at the end of the fiber bundle have the capacity to image the interior of organs located tens of microns below the surface without cutting the surface—an area known as nonintrusive diagnostics. This is particularly useful for determining the extent of cancers in the stomach and bowel.

In another type of application, optical fibers are commonly used to carry signals for telephone conversations and internet communications. Extensive optical fiber cables have been placed on the ocean floor and underground to enable optical communications. Optical fiber communication systems offer several advantages over electrical (copper)-based systems, particularly for long distances. The fibers can be made so transparent that light can travel many kilometers before it becomes dim enough to require amplification—much superior to copper conductors. This property of optical fibers is called low loss. Lasers emit light with characteristics that allow far more conversations in one fiber than are possible with electric signals on a single conductor. This property of optical fibers is called high bandwidth. Optical signals in one fiber do not produce undesirable effects in other adjacent fibers. This property of optical fibers is called reduced crosstalk. We shall explore the unique characteristics of laser radiation in a later chapter.

Corner Reflectors and Diamonds

Corner reflectors (**The Law of Reflection**) are perfectly efficient when the conditions for total internal reflection are satisfied. With common materials, it is easy to obtain a critical angle that is less than $45°$. One use of these perfect mirrors is in binoculars, as shown in **Figure 1.18**. Another use is in periscopes found in submarines.

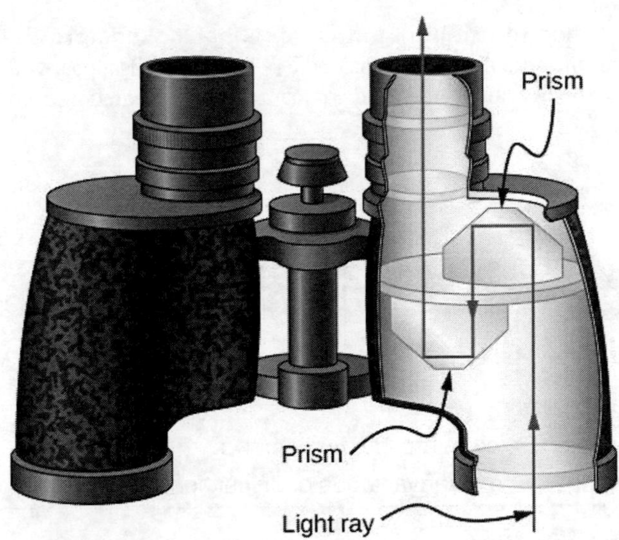

Figure 1.18 These binoculars employ corner reflectors (prisms) with total internal reflection to get light to the observer's eyes.

Total internal reflection, coupled with a large index of refraction, explains why diamonds sparkle more than other materials. The critical angle for a diamond-to-air surface is only $24.4°$, so when light enters a diamond, it has trouble getting back out (**Figure 1.19**). Although light freely enters the diamond, it can exit only if it makes an angle less than $24.4°$. Facets on diamonds are specifically intended to make this unlikely. Good diamonds are very clear, so that the light makes many internal reflections and is concentrated before exiting—hence the bright sparkle. (Zircon is a natural gemstone that has an exceptionally large index of refraction, but it is not as large as diamond, so it is not as highly prized. Cubic zirconia is manufactured and has an even higher index of refraction (≈ 2.17), but it is still less than that of diamond.) The colors you see emerging from a clear diamond are not due to the diamond's color, which is usually nearly colorless. The colors result from dispersion, which we discuss in **Dispersion**. Colored diamonds get their color from structural defects of the crystal lattice and the inclusion of minute quantities of graphite and other materials. The Argyle Mine in Western Australia produces around 90% of the world's pink, red, champagne, and cognac diamonds, whereas around 50% of the world's clear diamonds come from central and southern Africa.

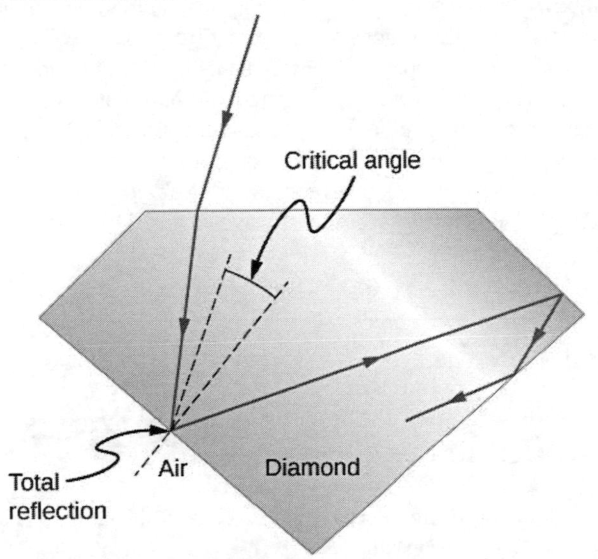

Figure 1.19 Light cannot easily escape a diamond, because its critical angle with air is so small. Most reflections are total, and the facets are placed so that light can exit only in particular ways—thus concentrating the light and making the diamond sparkle brightly.

Explore refraction and reflection of light (https://openstaxcollege.org/l/21bendoflight) between two media with different indices of refraction. Try to make the refracted ray disappear with total internal reflection. Use the protractor tool to measure the critical angle and compare with the prediction from Equation 1.5.

1.5 | Dispersion

Learning Objectives

By the end of this section, you will be able to:

- Explain the cause of dispersion in a prism
- Describe the effects of dispersion in producing rainbows
- Summarize the advantages and disadvantages of dispersion

Everyone enjoys the spectacle of a rainbow glimmering against a dark stormy sky. How does sunlight falling on clear drops of rain get broken into the rainbow of colors we see? The same process causes white light to be broken into colors by a clear glass prism or a diamond (Figure 1.20).

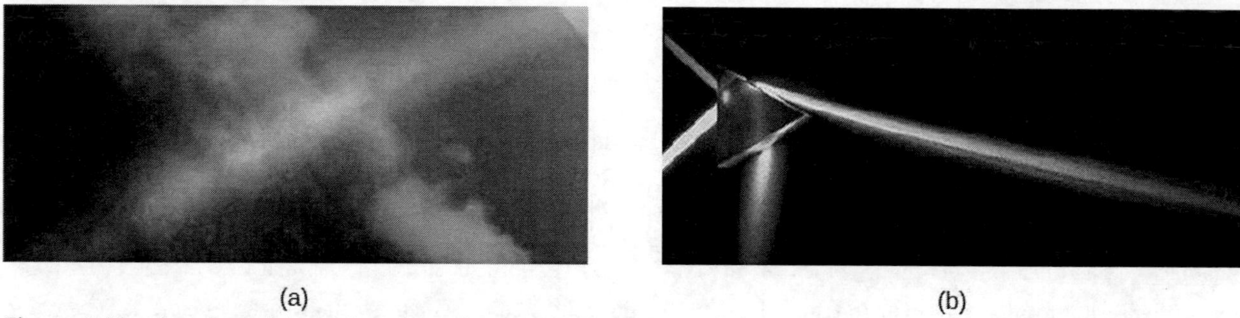

(a) (b)

Figure 1.20 The colors of the rainbow (a) and those produced by a prism (b) are identical. (credit a: modification of work by "Alfredo55"/Wikimedia Commons; credit b: modification of work by NASA)

We see about six colors in a rainbow—red, orange, yellow, green, blue, and violet; sometimes indigo is listed, too. These colors are associated with different wavelengths of light, as shown in Figure 1.21. When our eye receives pure-wavelength light, we tend to see only one of the six colors, depending on wavelength. The thousands of other hues we can sense in other situations are our eye's response to various mixtures of wavelengths. White light, in particular, is a fairly uniform mixture of all visible wavelengths. Sunlight, considered to be white, actually appears to be a bit yellow, because of its mixture of wavelengths, but it does contain all visible wavelengths. The sequence of colors in rainbows is the same sequence as the colors shown in the figure. This implies that white light is spread out in a rainbow according to wavelength. **Dispersion** is defined as the spreading of white light into its full spectrum of wavelengths. More technically, dispersion occurs whenever the propagation of light depends on wavelength.

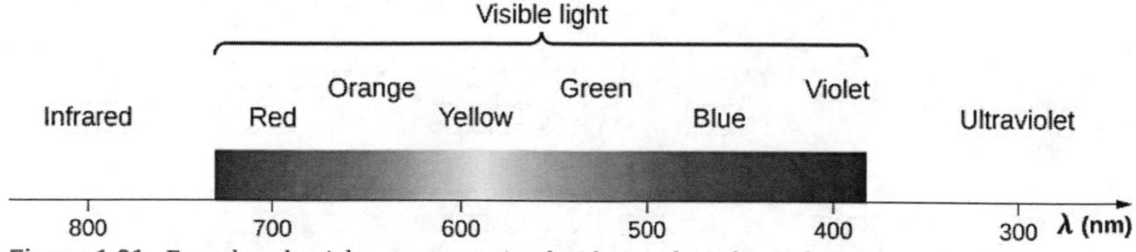

Figure 1.21 Even though rainbows are associated with six colors, the rainbow is a continuous distribution of colors according to wavelengths.

Any type of wave can exhibit dispersion. For example, sound waves, all types of electromagnetic waves, and water waves can be dispersed according to wavelength. Dispersion may require special circumstances and can result in spectacular displays such as in the production of a rainbow. This is also true for sound, since all frequencies ordinarily travel at the same speed. If you listen to sound through a long tube, such as a vacuum cleaner hose, you can easily hear it dispersed by interaction with the tube. Dispersion, in fact, can reveal a great deal about what the wave has encountered that disperses its wavelengths. The dispersion of electromagnetic radiation from outer space, for example, has revealed much about what exists between the stars—the so-called interstellar medium.

Nick Moore's video (https://openstaxcollege.org/l/21nickmoorevid) discusses dispersion of a pulse as he taps a long spring. Follow his explanation as Moore replays the high-speed footage showing high frequency waves outrunning the lower frequency waves.

Refraction is responsible for dispersion in rainbows and many other situations. The angle of refraction depends on the index of refraction, as we know from Snell's law. We know that the index of refraction n depends on the medium. But for a given medium, n also depends on wavelength (Table 1.2). Note that for a given medium, n increases as wavelength decreases and is greatest for violet light. Thus, violet light is bent more than red light, as shown for a prism in Figure 1.22(b). White light is dispersed into the same sequence of wavelengths as seen in Figure 1.20 and Figure 1.21.

Medium	Red (660 nm)	Orange (610 nm)	Yellow (580 nm)	Green (550 nm)	Blue (470 nm)	Violet (410 nm)
Water	1.331	1.332	1.333	1.335	1.338	1.342
Diamond	2.410	2.415	2.417	2.426	2.444	2.458
Glass, crown	1.512	1.514	1.518	1.519	1.524	1.530
Glass, flint	1.662	1.665	1.667	1.674	1.684	1.698
Polystyrene	1.488	1.490	1.492	1.493	1.499	1.506
Quartz, fused	1.455	1.456	1.458	1.459	1.462	1.468

Table 1.2 Index of Refraction n in Selected Media at Various Wavelengths

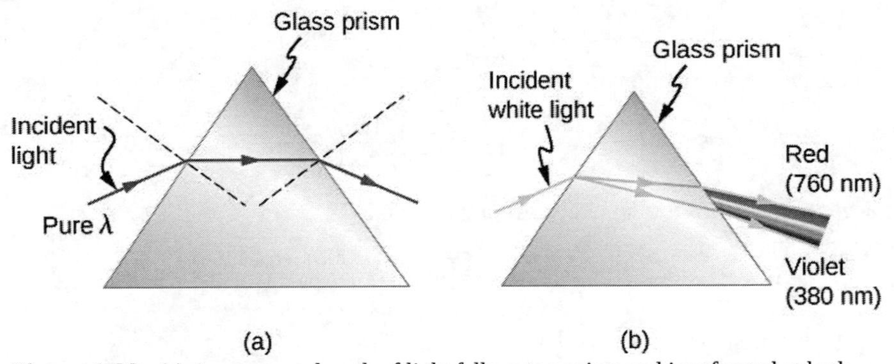

Figure 1.22 (a) A pure wavelength of light falls onto a prism and is refracted at both surfaces. (b) White light is dispersed by the prism (shown exaggerated). Since the index of refraction varies with wavelength, the angles of refraction vary with wavelength. A sequence of red to violet is produced, because the index of refraction increases steadily with decreasing wavelength.

Example 1.5

Dispersion of White Light by Flint Glass

A beam of white light goes from air into flint glass at an incidence angle of $43.2°$. What is the angle between the red (660 nm) and violet (410 nm) parts of the refracted light?

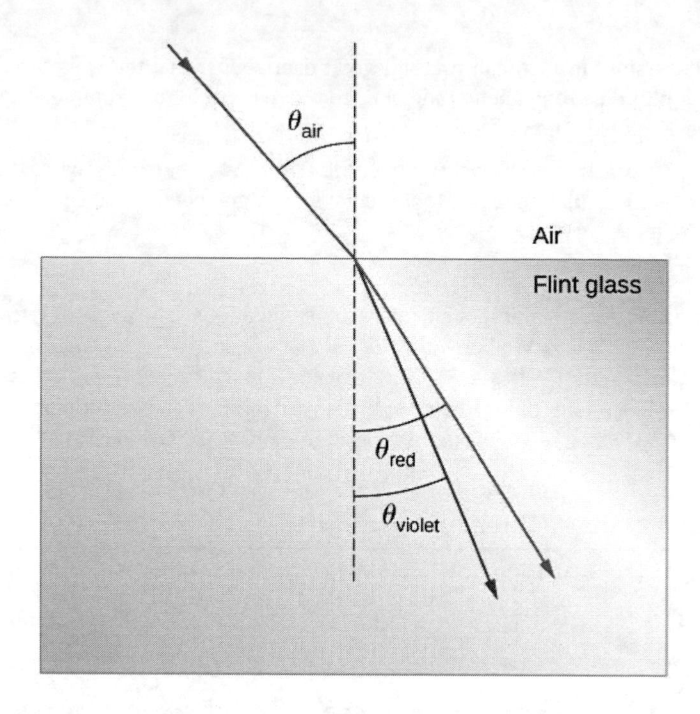

Strategy

Values for the indices of refraction for flint glass at various wavelengths are listed in **Table 1.2**. Use these values for calculate the angle of refraction for each color and then take the difference to find the dispersion angle.

Solution

Applying the law of refraction for the red part of the beam

$$n_{\text{air}} \sin \theta_{\text{air}} = n_{\text{red}} \sin \theta_{\text{red}},$$

we can solve for the angle of refraction as

$$\theta_{\text{red}} = \sin^{-1}\left(\frac{n_{\text{air}} \sin \theta_{\text{air}}}{n_{\text{red}}}\right) = \sin^{-1}\left[\frac{(1.000) \sin 43.2°}{(1.662)}\right] = 27.0°.$$

Similarly, the angle of incidence for the violet part of the beam is

$$\theta_{\text{violet}} = \sin^{-1}\left(\frac{n_{\text{air}} \sin \theta_{\text{air}}}{n_{\text{violet}}}\right) = \sin^{-1}\left[\frac{(1.000) \sin 43.2°}{(1.698)}\right] = 26.4°.$$

The difference between these two angles is

$$\theta_{\text{red}} - \theta_{\text{violet}} = 27.0° - 26.4° = 0.6°.$$

Significance

Although 0.6° may seem like a negligibly small angle, if this beam is allowed to propagate a long enough distance, the dispersion of colors becomes quite noticeable.

1.4 Check Your Understanding In the preceding example, how much distance inside the block of flint glass would the red and the violet rays have to progress before they are separated by 1.0 mm?

Rainbows are produced by a combination of refraction and reflection. You may have noticed that you see a rainbow only when you look away from the Sun. Light enters a drop of water and is reflected from the back of the drop (**Figure 1.23**). The light is refracted both as it enters and as it leaves the drop. Since the index of refraction of water varies with wavelength, the light is dispersed, and a rainbow is observed (**Figure 1.24**(a)). (No dispersion occurs at the back surface, because the law of reflection does not depend on wavelength.) The actual rainbow of colors seen by an observer depends on the myriad rays being refracted and reflected toward the observer's eyes from numerous drops of water. The effect is most spectacular when the background is dark, as in stormy weather, but can also be observed in waterfalls and lawn sprinklers. The arc of a rainbow comes from the need to be looking at a specific angle relative to the direction of the Sun, as illustrated in part (b). If two reflections of light occur within the water drop, another "secondary" rainbow is produced. This rare event produces an arc that lies above the primary rainbow arc, as in part (c), and produces colors in the reverse order of the primary rainbow, with red at the lowest angle and violet at the largest angle.

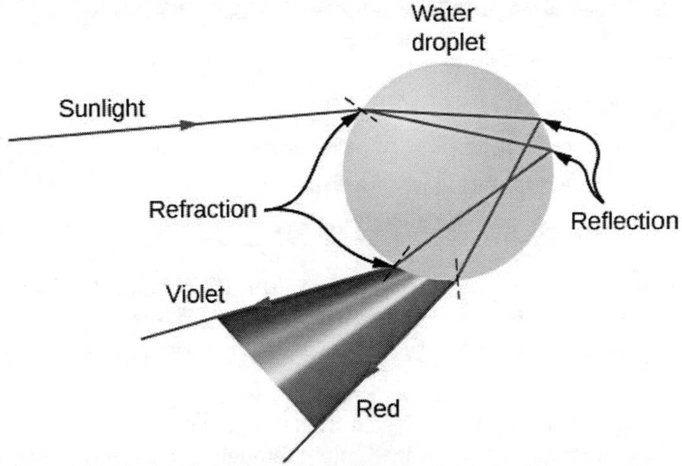

Figure 1.23 A ray of light falling on this water drop enters and is reflected from the back of the drop. This light is refracted and dispersed both as it enters and as it leaves the drop.

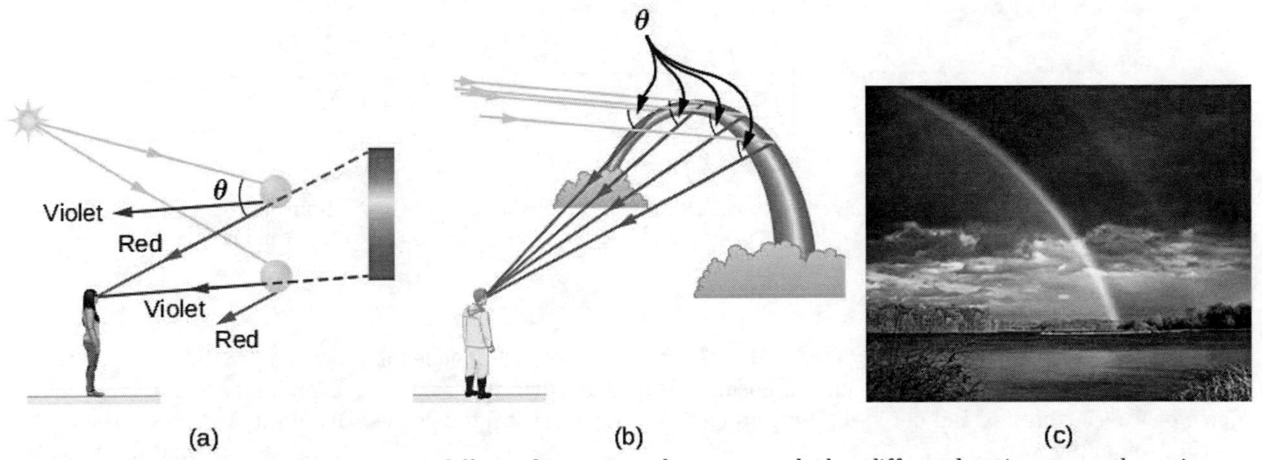

Figure 1.24 (a) Different colors emerge in different directions, and so you must look at different locations to see the various colors of a rainbow. (b) The arc of a rainbow results from the fact that a line between the observer and any point on the arc must make the correct angle with the parallel rays of sunlight for the observer to receive the refracted rays. (c) Double rainbow. (credit c: modification of work by "Nicholas"/Wikimedia Commons)

Dispersion may produce beautiful rainbows, but it can cause problems in optical systems. White light used to transmit messages in a fiber is dispersed, spreading out in time and eventually overlapping with other messages. Since a laser produces a nearly pure wavelength, its light experiences little dispersion, an advantage over white light for transmission of information. In contrast, dispersion of electromagnetic waves coming to us from outer space can be used to determine the amount of matter they pass through.

1.6 | Huygens's Principle

Learning Objectives

By the end of this section, you will be able to:

- Describe Huygens's principle
- Use Huygens's principle to explain the law of reflection
- Use Huygens's principle to explain the law of refraction
- Use Huygens's principle to explain diffraction

So far in this chapter, we have been discussing optical phenomena using the ray model of light. However, some phenomena require analysis and explanations based on the wave characteristics of light. This is particularly true when the wavelength is not negligible compared to the dimensions of an optical device, such as a slit in the case of *diffraction*. Huygens's principle is an indispensable tool for this analysis.

Figure 1.25 shows how a transverse wave looks as viewed from above and from the side. A light wave can be imagined to propagate like this, although we do not actually see it wiggling through space. From above, we view the wave fronts (or wave crests) as if we were looking down on ocean waves. The side view would be a graph of the electric or magnetic field. The view from above is perhaps more useful in developing concepts about **wave optics**.

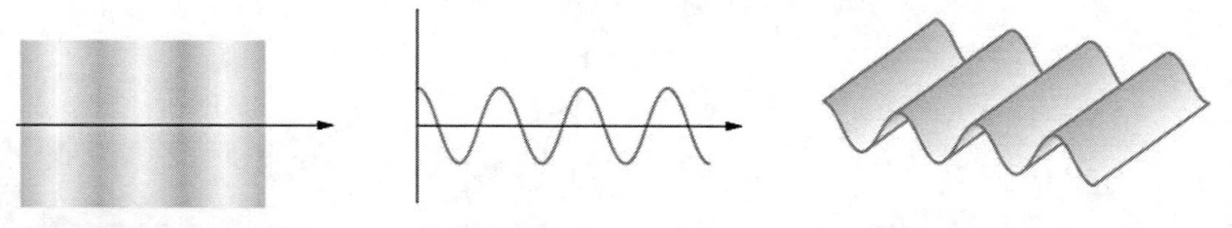

Figure 1.25 A transverse wave, such as an electromagnetic light wave, as viewed from above and from the side. The direction of propagation is perpendicular to the wave fronts (or wave crests) and is represented by a ray.

The Dutch scientist Christiaan Huygens (1629–1695) developed a useful technique for determining in detail how and where waves propagate. Starting from some known position, **Huygens's principle** states that every point on a wave front is a source of wavelets that spread out in the forward direction at the same speed as the wave itself. The new wave front is tangent to all of the wavelets.

Figure 1.26 shows how Huygens's principle is applied. A wave front is the long edge that moves, for example, with the crest or the trough. Each point on the wave front emits a semicircular wave that moves at the propagation speed v. We can draw these wavelets at a time t later, so that they have moved a distance $s = vt$. The new wave front is a plane tangent to the wavelets and is where we would expect the wave to be a time t later. Huygens's principle works for all types of waves, including water waves, sound waves, and light waves. It is useful not only in describing how light waves propagate but also in explaining the laws of reflection and refraction. In addition, we will see that Huygens's principle tells us how and where light rays interfere.

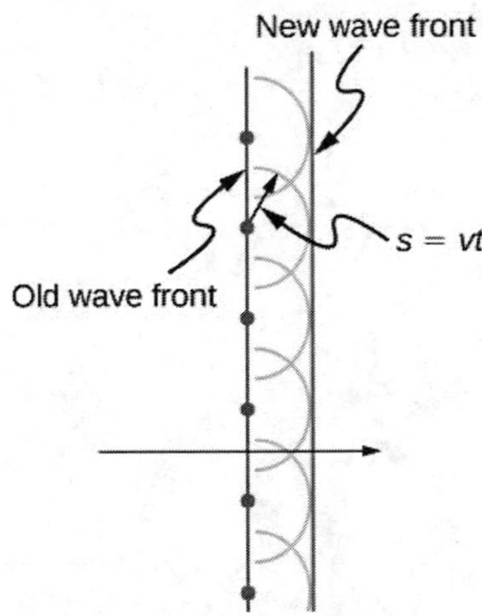

Figure 1.26 Huygens's principle applied to a straight wave front. Each point on the wave front emits a semicircular wavelet that moves a distance $s = vt$. The new wave front is a line tangent to the wavelets.

Reflection

Figure 1.27 shows how a mirror reflects an incoming wave at an angle equal to the incident angle, verifying the law of reflection. As the wave front strikes the mirror, wavelets are first emitted from the left part of the mirror and then from the right. The wavelets closer to the left have had time to travel farther, producing a wave front traveling in the direction shown.

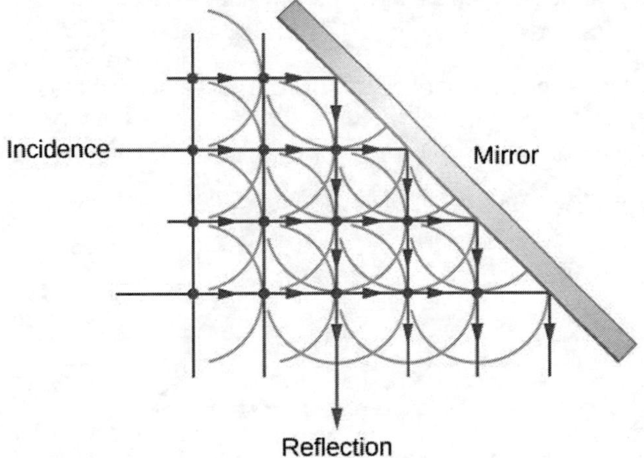

Figure 1.27 Huygens's principle applied to a plane wave front striking a mirror. The wavelets shown were emitted as each point on the wave front struck the mirror. The tangent to these wavelets shows that the new wave front has been reflected at an angle equal to the incident angle. The direction of propagation is perpendicular to the wave front, as shown by the downward-pointing arrows.

Refraction

The law of refraction can be explained by applying Huygens's principle to a wave front passing from one medium to another (**Figure 1.28**). Each wavelet in the figure was emitted when the wave front crossed the interface between the media. Since the speed of light is smaller in the second medium, the waves do not travel as far in a given time, and the new wave front changes direction as shown. This explains why a ray changes direction to become closer to the perpendicular when light slows down. Snell's law can be derived from the geometry in **Figure 1.28** (**Example 1.6**).

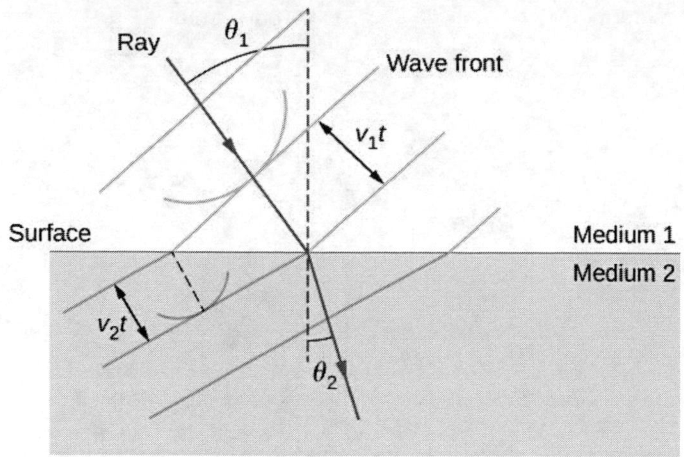

Figure 1.28 Huygens's principle applied to a plane wave front traveling from one medium to another, where its speed is less. The ray bends toward the perpendicular, since the wavelets have a lower speed in the second medium.

Example 1.6

Deriving the Law of Refraction

By examining the geometry of the wave fronts, derive the law of refraction.

Strategy

Consider **Figure 1.29**, which expands upon **Figure 1.28**. It shows the incident wave front just reaching the surface at point A, while point B is still well within medium 1. In the time Δt it takes for a wavelet from B to reach B' on the surface at speed $v_1 = c/n_1$, a wavelet from A travels into medium 2 a distance of $AA' = v_2 \Delta t$, where $v_2 = c/n_2$. Note that in this example, v_2 is slower than v_1 because $n_1 < n_2$.

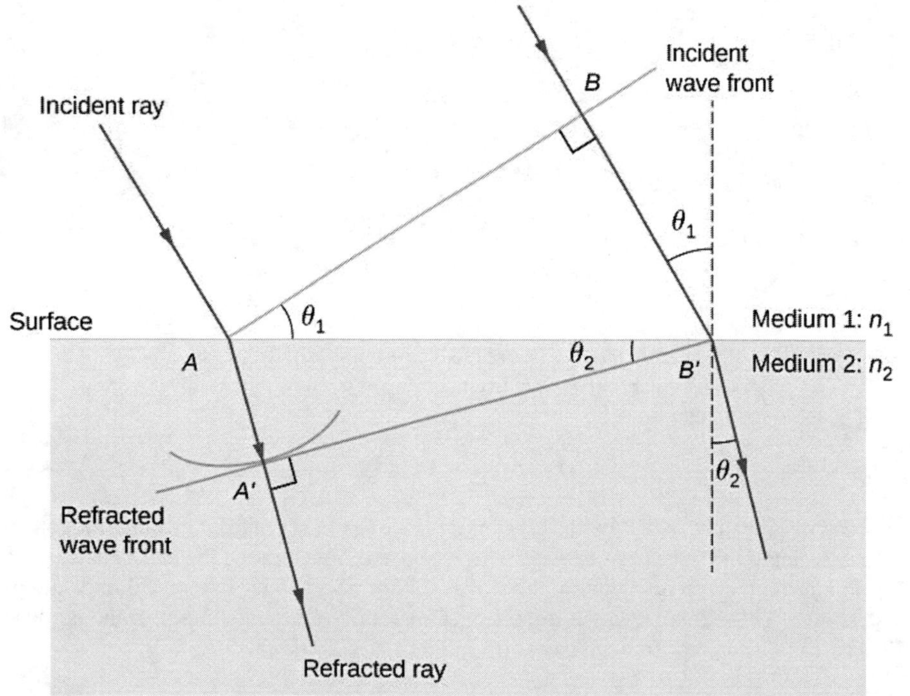

Figure 1.29 Geometry of the law of refraction from medium 1 to medium 2.

Solution

The segment on the surface AB' is shared by both the triangle ABB' inside medium 1 and the triangle $AA'B'$ inside medium 2. Note that from the geometry, the angle $\angle BAB'$ is equal to the angle of incidence, θ_1. Similarly, $\angle AB'A'$ is θ_2.

The length of AB' is given in two ways as

$$AB' = \frac{BB'}{\sin\theta_1} = \frac{AA'}{\sin\theta_2}.$$

Inverting the equation and substituting $AA' = c\Delta t/n_2$ from above and similarly $BB' = c\Delta t/n_1$, we obtain

$$\frac{\sin\theta_1}{c\Delta t/n_1} = \frac{\sin\theta_2}{c\Delta t/n_2}.$$

Cancellation of $c\Delta t$ allows us to simplify this equation into the familiar form

$$n_1 \sin\theta_1 = n_2 \sin\theta_2.$$

Significance

Although the law of refraction was established experimentally by Snell and stated in **Refraction**, its derivation here requires Huygens's principle and the understanding that the speed of light is different in different media.

1.5 Check Your Understanding In **Example 1.6**, we had $n_1 < n_2$. If n_2 were decreased such that $n_1 > n_2$ and the speed of light in medium 2 is faster than in medium 1, what would happen to the length of AA'? What would happen to the wave front $A'B'$ and the direction of the refracted ray?

This **applet (https://openstaxcollege.org/l/21walfedaniref)** by Walter Fendt shows an animation of reflection and refraction using Huygens's wavelets while you control the parameters. Be sure to click on “Next step” to display the wavelets. You can see the reflected and refracted wave fronts forming.

Diffraction

What happens when a wave passes through an opening, such as light shining through an open door into a dark room? For light, we observe a sharp shadow of the doorway on the floor of the room, and no visible light bends around corners into other parts of the room. When sound passes through a door, we hear it everywhere in the room and thus observe that sound spreads out when passing through such an opening (**Figure 1.30**). What is the difference between the behavior of sound waves and light waves in this case? The answer is that light has very short wavelengths and acts like a ray. Sound has wavelengths on the order of the size of the door and bends around corners (for frequency of 1000 Hz,

$$\lambda = \frac{c}{f} = \frac{330\text{ m/s}}{1000\text{ s}^{-1}} = 0.33\text{ m},$$

about three times smaller than the width of the doorway).

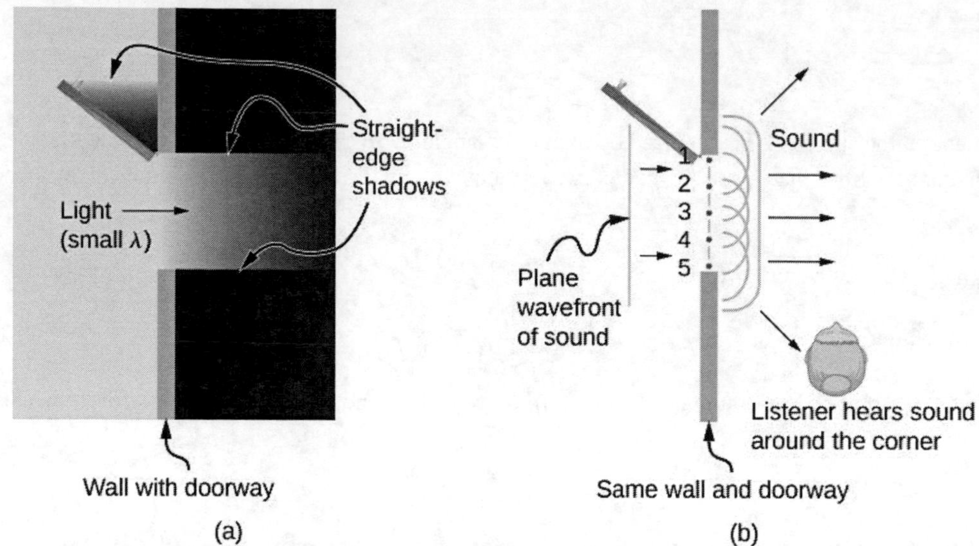

Figure 1.30 (a) Light passing through a doorway makes a sharp outline on the floor. Since light's wavelength is very small compared with the size of the door, it acts like a ray. (b) Sound waves bend into all parts of the room, a wave effect, because their wavelength is similar to the size of the door.

If we pass light through smaller openings such as slits, we can use Huygens's principle to see that light bends as sound does (**Figure 1.31**). The bending of a wave around the edges of an opening or an obstacle is called diffraction. Diffraction is a wave characteristic and occurs for all types of waves. If diffraction is observed for some phenomenon, it is evidence that the phenomenon is a wave. Thus, the horizontal diffraction of the laser beam after it passes through the slits in **Figure 1.31** is evidence that light is a wave. You will learn about diffraction in much more detail in the chapter on **Diffraction**.

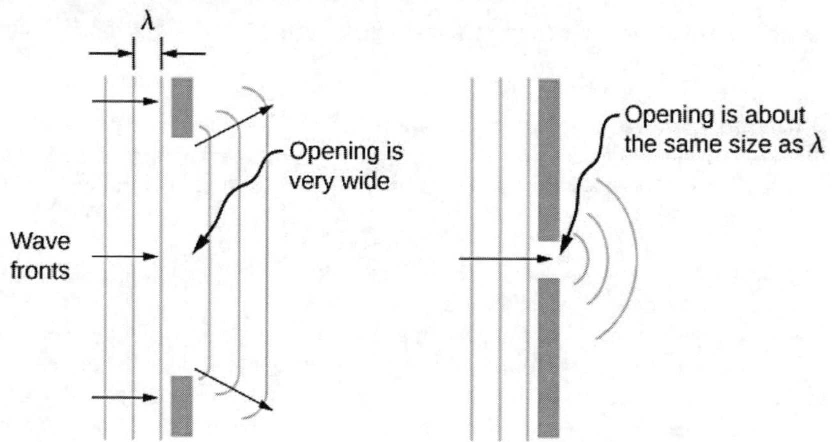

Figure 1.31 Huygens's principle applied to a plane wave front striking an opening. The edges of the wave front bend after passing through the opening, a process called diffraction. The amount of bending is more extreme for a small opening, consistent with the fact that wave characteristics are most noticeable for interactions with objects about the same size as the wavelength.

1.7 | Polarization

Learning Objectives

By the end of this section, you will be able to:

- Explain the change in intensity as polarized light passes through a polarizing filter
- Calculate the effect of polarization by reflection and Brewster's angle
- Describe the effect of polarization by scattering
- Explain the use of polarizing materials in devices such as LCDs

Polarizing sunglasses are familiar to most of us. They have a special ability to cut the glare of light reflected from water or glass (**Figure 1.32**). They have this ability because of a wave characteristic of light called polarization. What is polarization? How is it produced? What are some of its uses? The answers to these questions are related to the wave character of light.

(a) (b)

Figure 1.32 These two photographs of a river show the effect of a polarizing filter in reducing glare in light reflected from the surface of water. Part (b) of this figure was taken with a polarizing filter and part (a) was not. As a result, the reflection of clouds and sky observed in part (a) is not observed in part (b). Polarizing sunglasses are particularly useful on snow and water. (credit a and credit b: modifications of work by "Amithshs"/Wikimedia Commons)

Malus's Law

Light is one type of electromagnetic (EM) wave. As noted in the previous chapter on **Electromagnetic Waves (http://cnx.org/content/m58495/latest/)** , EM waves are *transverse waves* consisting of varying electric and magnetic fields that oscillate perpendicular to the direction of propagation (**Figure 1.33**). However, in general, there are no specific directions for the oscillations of the electric and magnetic fields; they vibrate in any randomly oriented plane perpendicular to the direction of propagation. **Polarization** is the attribute that a wave's oscillations do have a definite direction relative to the direction of propagation of the wave. (This is not the same type of polarization as that discussed for the separation of charges.) Waves having such a direction are said to be **polarized**. For an EM wave, we define the **direction of polarization** to be the direction parallel to the electric field. Thus, we can think of the electric field arrows as showing the direction of polarization, as in **Figure 1.33**.

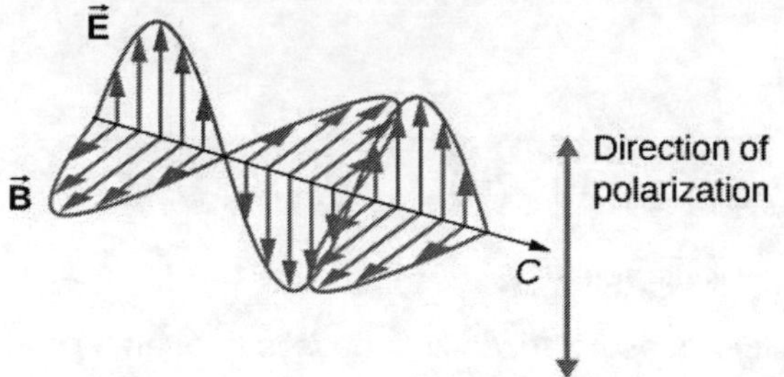

Figure 1.33 An EM wave, such as light, is a transverse wave. The electric ($\vec{\mathbf{E}}$) and magnetic ($\vec{\mathbf{B}}$) fields are perpendicular to the direction of propagation. The direction of polarization of the wave is the direction of the electric field.

To examine this further, consider the transverse waves in the ropes shown in Figure 1.34. The oscillations in one rope are in a vertical plane and are said to be **vertically polarized**. Those in the other rope are in a horizontal plane and are **horizontally polarized**. If a vertical slit is placed on the first rope, the waves pass through. However, a vertical slit blocks the horizontally polarized waves. For EM waves, the direction of the electric field is analogous to the disturbances on the ropes.

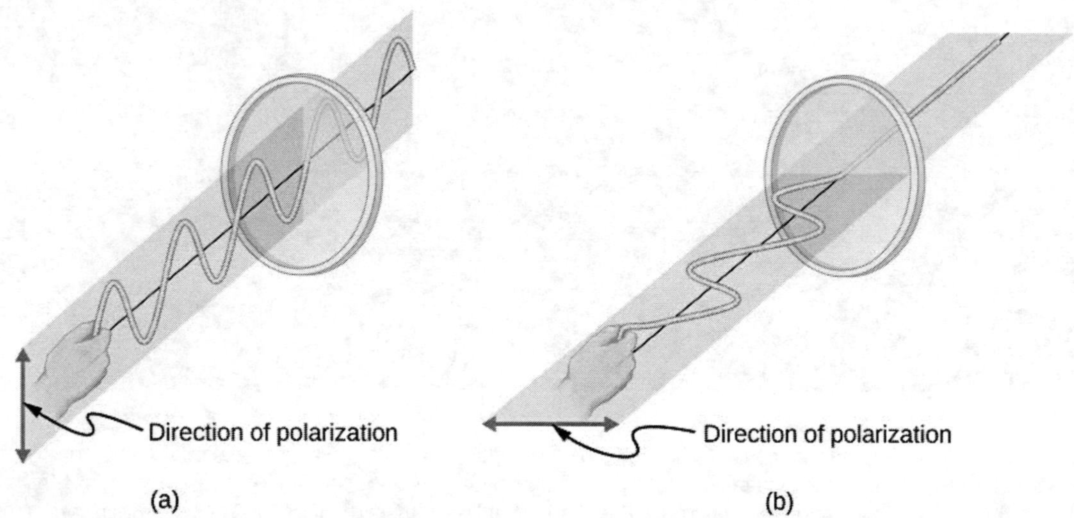

Figure 1.34 The transverse oscillations in one rope (a) are in a vertical plane, and those in the other rope (b) are in a horizontal plane. The first is said to be vertically polarized, and the other is said to be horizontally polarized. Vertical slits pass vertically polarized waves and block horizontally polarized waves.

The Sun and many other light sources produce waves that have the electric fields in random directions (Figure 1.35(a)). Such light is said to be **unpolarized**, because it is composed of many waves with all possible directions of polarization. Polaroid materials—which were invented by the founder of the Polaroid Corporation, Edwin Land—act as a polarizing slit for light, allowing only polarization in one direction to pass through. Polarizing filters are composed of long molecules aligned in one direction. If we think of the molecules as many slits, analogous to those for the oscillating ropes, we can understand why only light with a specific polarization can get through. The axis of a polarizing filter is the direction along which the filter passes the electric field of an EM wave.

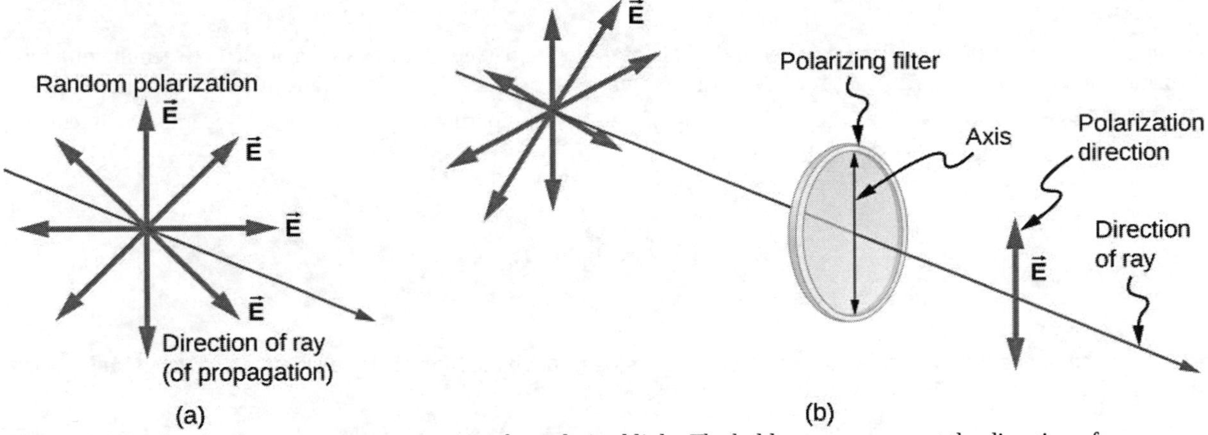

Figure 1.35 The slender arrow represents a ray of unpolarized light. The bold arrows represent the direction of polarization of the individual waves composing the ray. (a) If the light is unpolarized, the arrows point in all directions. (b) A polarizing filter has a polarization axis that acts as a slit passing through electric fields parallel to its direction. The direction of polarization of an EM wave is defined to be the direction of its electric field.

Figure 1.36 shows the effect of two polarizing filters on originally unpolarized light. The first filter polarizes the light along its axis. When the axes of the first and second filters are aligned (parallel), then all of the polarized light passed by the first filter is also passed by the second filter. If the second polarizing filter is rotated, only the component of the light parallel to the second filter's axis is passed. When the axes are perpendicular, no light is passed by the second filter.

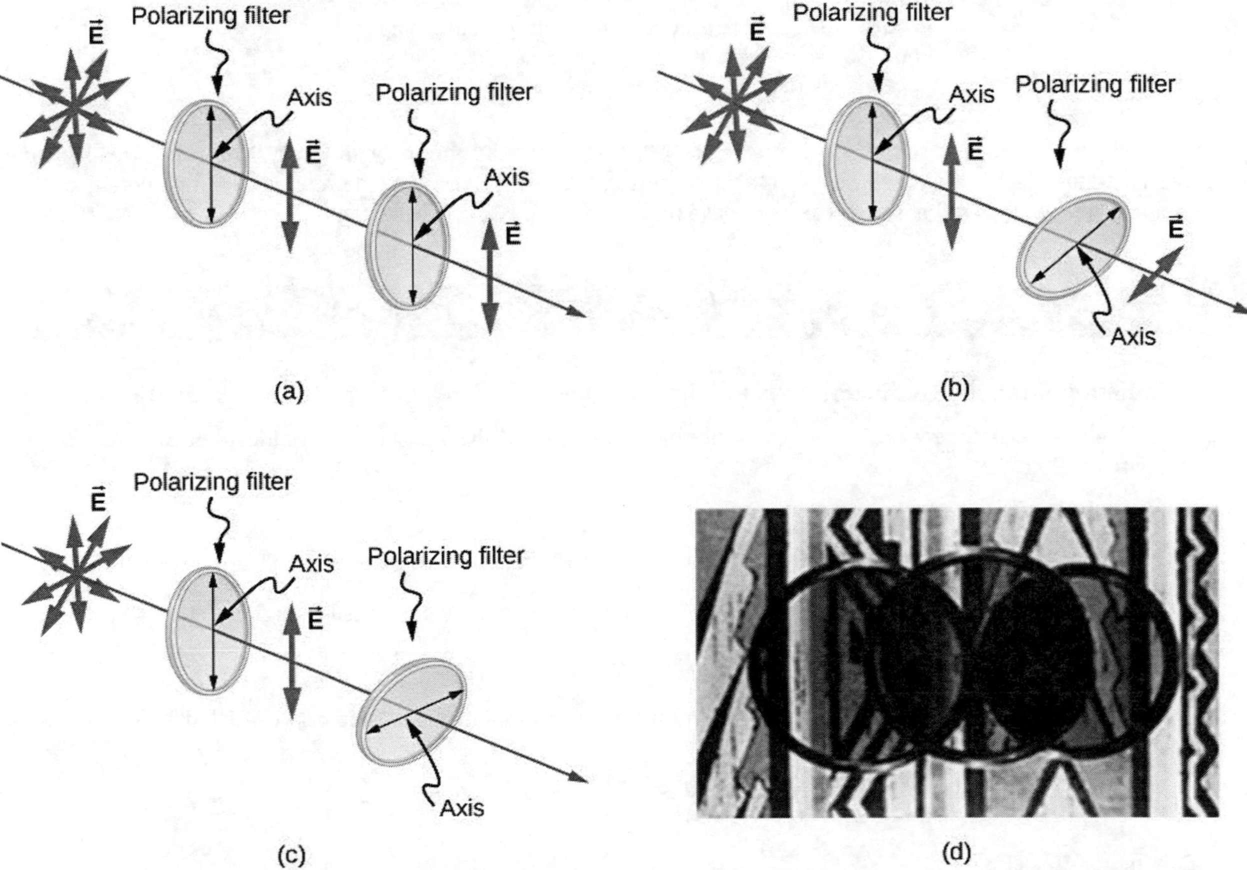

Figure 1.36 The effect of rotating two polarizing filters, where the first polarizes the light. (a) All of the polarized light is passed by the second polarizing filter, because its axis is parallel to the first. (b) As the second filter is rotated, only part of the light is passed. (c) When the second filter is perpendicular to the first, no light is passed. (d) In this photograph, a polarizing filter is placed above two others. Its axis is perpendicular to the filter on the right (dark area) and parallel to the filter on the left (lighter area). (credit d: modification of work by P.P. Urone)

Only the component of the EM wave parallel to the axis of a filter is passed. Let us call the angle between the direction of polarization and the axis of a filter θ. If the electric field has an amplitude *E*, then the transmitted part of the wave has an amplitude $E\cos\theta$ (**Figure 1.37**). Since the intensity of a wave is proportional to its amplitude squared, the intensity *I* of the transmitted wave is related to the incident wave by

$$I = I_0 \cos^2 \theta \tag{1.6}$$

where I_0 is the intensity of the polarized wave before passing through the filter. This equation is known as **Malus's law**.

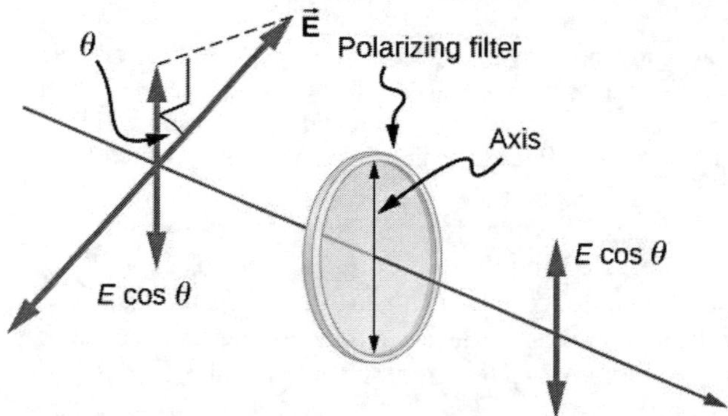

Figure 1.37 A polarizing filter transmits only the component of the wave parallel to its axis, reducing the intensity of any light not polarized parallel to its axis.

This **Open Source Physics animation (https://openstaxcollege.org/l/21phyanielefie)** helps you visualize the electric field vectors as light encounters a polarizing filter. You can rotate the filter—note that the angle displayed is in radians. You can also rotate the animation for 3D visualization.

Example 1.7

Calculating Intensity Reduction by a Polarizing Filter

What angle is needed between the direction of polarized light and the axis of a polarizing filter to reduce its intensity by 90.0%?

Strategy

When the intensity is reduced by 90.0%, it is 10.0% or 0.100 times its original value. That is, $I = 0.100\, I_0$. Using this information, the equation $I = I_0 \cos^2 \theta$ can be used to solve for the needed angle.

Solution

Solving the equation $I = I_0 \cos^2 \theta$ for $\cos\theta$ and substituting with the relationship between *I* and I_0 gives

$$\cos\theta = \sqrt{\frac{I}{I_0}} = \sqrt{\frac{0.100\, I_0}{I_0}} = 0.3162.$$

Solving for θ yields

$$\theta = \cos^{-1} 0.3162 = 71.6°.$$

Significance

A fairly large angle between the direction of polarization and the filter axis is needed to reduce the intensity to

10.0% of its original value. This seems reasonable based on experimenting with polarizing films. It is interesting that at an angle of $45°$, the intensity is reduced to 50% of its original value. Note that $71.6°$ is $18.4°$ from reducing the intensity to zero, and that at an angle of $18.4°$, the intensity is reduced to 90.0% of its original value, giving evidence of symmetry.

1.6 Check Your Understanding Although we did not specify the direction in **Example 1.7**, let's say the polarizing filter was rotated clockwise by $71.6°$ to reduce the light intensity by 90.0%. What would be the intensity reduction if the polarizing filter were rotated counterclockwise by $71.6°$?

Polarization by Reflection

By now, you can probably guess that polarizing sunglasses cut the glare in reflected light, because that light is polarized. You can check this for yourself by holding polarizing sunglasses in front of you and rotating them while looking at light reflected from water or glass. As you rotate the sunglasses, you will notice the light gets bright and dim, but not completely black. This implies the reflected light is partially polarized and cannot be completely blocked by a polarizing filter.

Figure 1.38 illustrates what happens when unpolarized light is reflected from a surface. Vertically polarized light is preferentially refracted at the surface, so the reflected light is left more horizontally polarized. The reasons for this phenomenon are beyond the scope of this text, but a convenient mnemonic for remembering this is to imagine the polarization direction to be like an arrow. Vertical polarization is like an arrow perpendicular to the surface and is more likely to stick and not be reflected. Horizontal polarization is like an arrow bouncing on its side and is more likely to be reflected. Sunglasses with vertical axes thus block more reflected light than unpolarized light from other sources.

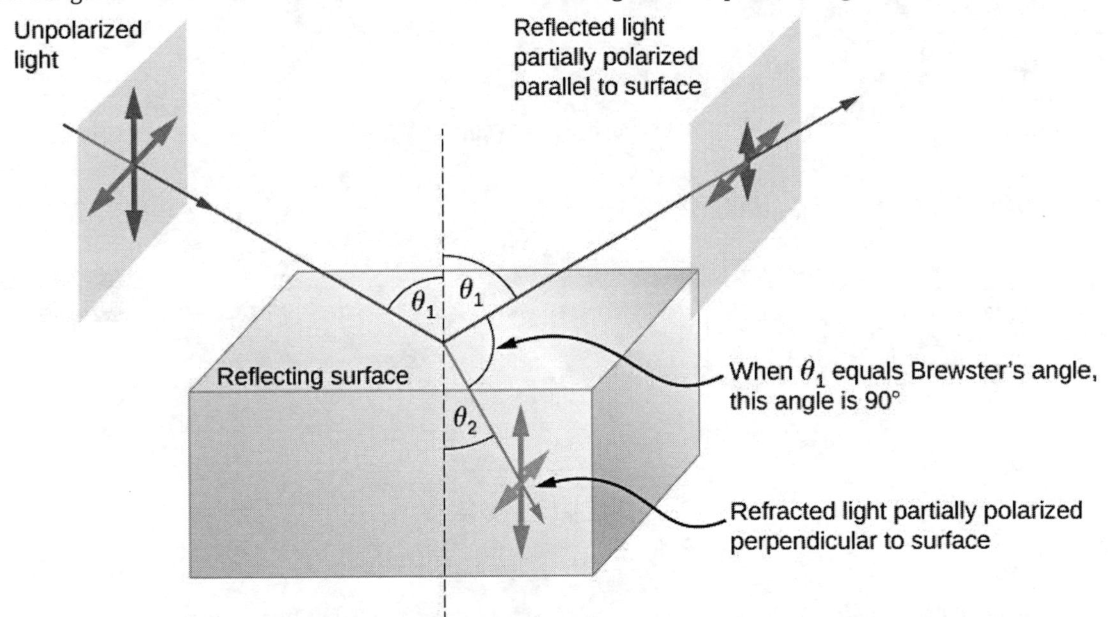

Figure 1.38 Polarization by reflection. Unpolarized light has equal amounts of vertical and horizontal polarization. After interaction with a surface, the vertical components are preferentially absorbed or refracted, leaving the reflected light more horizontally polarized. This is akin to arrows striking on their sides and bouncing off, whereas arrows striking on their tips go into the surface.

Since the part of the light that is not reflected is refracted, the amount of polarization depends on the indices of refraction of the media involved. It can be shown that reflected light is completely polarized at an angle of reflection θ_b given by

$$\tan\theta_b = \frac{n_2}{n_1} \tag{1.7}$$

where n_1 is the medium in which the incident and reflected light travel and n_2 is the index of refraction of the medium that forms the interface that reflects the light. This equation is known as **Brewster's law** and θ_b is known as **Brewster's angle**, named after the nineteenth-century Scottish physicist who discovered them.

This **Open Source Physics animation (https://openstaxcollege.org/l/21phyaniincref)** shows incident, reflected, and refracted light as rays and EM waves. Try rotating the animation for 3D visualization and also change the angle of incidence. Near Brewster's angle, the reflected light becomes highly polarized.

Example 1.8

Calculating Polarization by Reflection

(a) At what angle will light traveling in air be completely polarized horizontally when reflected from water? (b) From glass?

Strategy

All we need to solve these problems are the indices of refraction. Air has $n_1 = 1.00$, water has $n_2 = 1.333$, and crown glass has $n_2' = 1.520$. The equation $\tan\theta_b = \frac{n_2}{n_1}$ can be directly applied to find θ_b in each case.

Solution

a. Putting the known quantities into the equation

$$\tan\theta_b = \frac{n_2}{n_1}$$

gives

$$\tan\theta_b = \frac{n_2}{n_1} = \frac{1.333}{1.00} = 1.333.$$

Solving for the angle θ_b yields

$$\theta_b = \tan^{-1} 1.333 = 53.1°.$$

b. Similarly, for crown glass and air,

$$\tan\theta_b' = \frac{n_2'}{n_1} = \frac{1.520}{1.00} = 1.52.$$

Thus,

$$\theta_b' = \tan^{-1} 1.52 = 56.7°.$$

Significance

Light reflected at these angles could be completely blocked by a good polarizing filter held with its axis vertical. Brewster's angle for water and air are similar to those for glass and air, so that sunglasses are equally effective for light reflected from either water or glass under similar circumstances. Light that is not reflected is refracted into these media. Therefore, at an incident angle equal to Brewster's angle, the refracted light is slightly polarized vertically. It is not completely polarized vertically, because only a small fraction of the incident light is reflected, so a significant amount of horizontally polarized light is refracted.

1.7 Check Your Understanding What happens at Brewster's angle if the original incident light is already 100% vertically polarized?

Atomic Explanation of Polarizing Filters

Polarizing filters have a polarization axis that acts as a slit. This slit passes EM waves (often visible light) that have an electric field parallel to the axis. This is accomplished with long molecules aligned perpendicular to the axis, as shown in **Figure 1.39**.

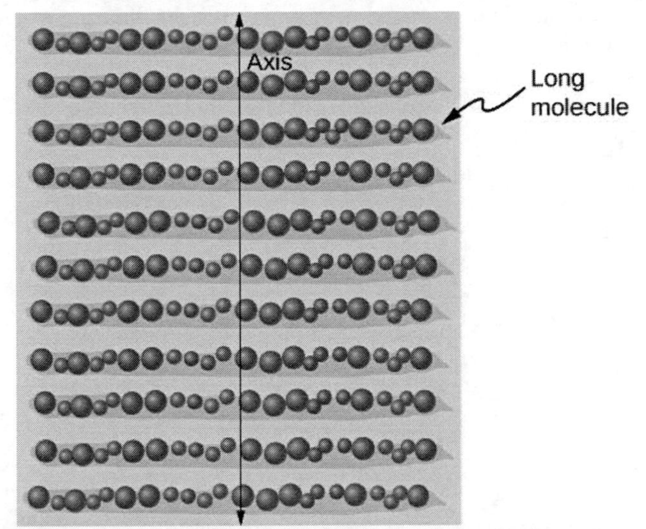

Figure 1.39 Long molecules are aligned perpendicular to the axis of a polarizing filter. In an EM wave, the component of the electric field perpendicular to these molecules passes through the filter, whereas the component parallel to the molecules is absorbed.

Figure 1.40 illustrates how the component of the electric field parallel to the long molecules is absorbed. An EM wave is composed of oscillating electric and magnetic fields. The electric field is strong compared with the magnetic field and is more effective in exerting force on charges in the molecules. The most affected charged particles are the electrons, since electron masses are small. If an electron is forced to oscillate, it can absorb energy from the EM wave. This reduces the field in the wave and, hence, reduces its intensity. In long molecules, electrons can more easily oscillate parallel to the molecule than in the perpendicular direction. The electrons are bound to the molecule and are more restricted in their movement perpendicular to the molecule. Thus, the electrons can absorb EM waves that have a component of their electric field parallel to the molecule. The electrons are much less responsive to electric fields perpendicular to the molecule and allow these fields to pass. Thus, the axis of the polarizing filter is perpendicular to the length of the molecule.

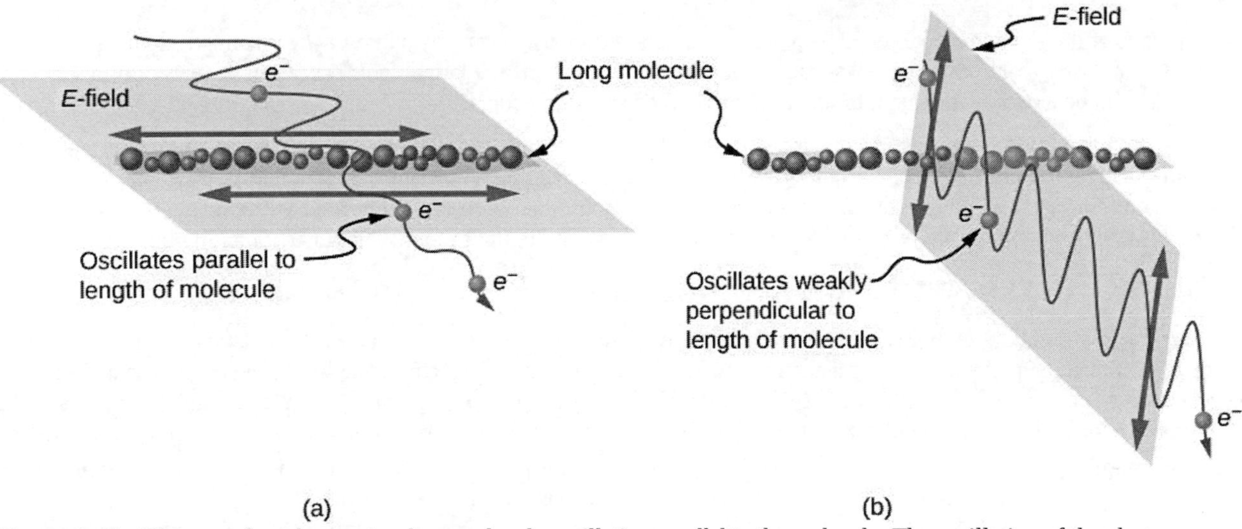

Figure 1.40 Diagram of an electron in a long molecule oscillating parallel to the molecule. The oscillation of the electron absorbs energy and reduces the intensity of the component of the EM wave that is parallel to the molecule.

Polarization by Scattering

If you hold your polarizing sunglasses in front of you and rotate them while looking at blue sky, you will see the sky get bright and dim. This is a clear indication that light scattered by air is partially polarized. **Figure 1.41** helps illustrate how this happens. Since light is a transverse EM wave, it vibrates the electrons of air molecules perpendicular to the direction that it is traveling. The electrons then radiate like small antennae. Since they are oscillating perpendicular to the direction of the light ray, they produce EM radiation that is polarized perpendicular to the direction of the ray. When viewing the light along a line perpendicular to the original ray, as in the figure, there can be no polarization in the scattered light parallel to the original ray, because that would require the original ray to be a longitudinal wave. Along other directions, a component of the other polarization can be projected along the line of sight, and the scattered light is only partially polarized. Furthermore, multiple scattering can bring light to your eyes from other directions and can contain different polarizations.

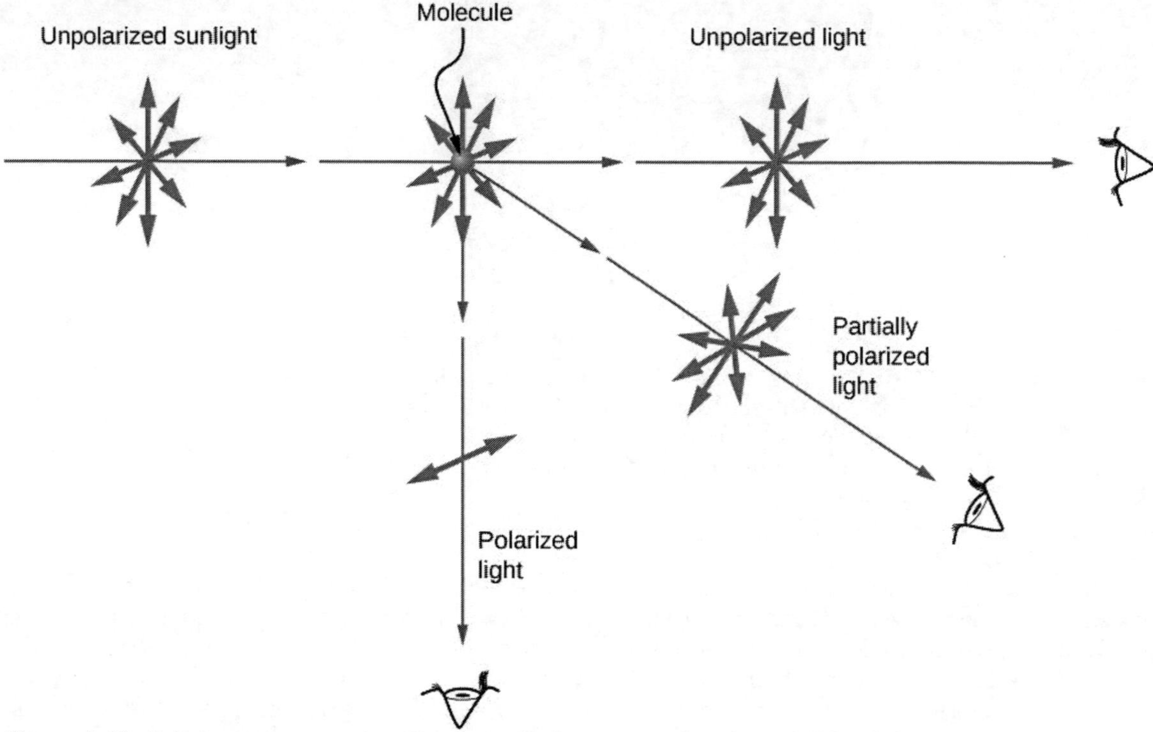

Figure 1.41 Polarization by scattering. Unpolarized light scattering from air molecules shakes their electrons perpendicular to the direction of the original ray. The scattered light therefore has a polarization perpendicular to the original direction and none parallel to the original direction.

Photographs of the sky can be darkened by polarizing filters, a trick used by many photographers to make clouds brighter by contrast. Scattering from other particles, such as smoke or dust, can also polarize light. Detecting polarization in scattered EM waves can be a useful analytical tool in determining the scattering source.

A range of optical effects are used in sunglasses. Besides being polarizing, sunglasses may have colored pigments embedded in them, whereas others use either a nonreflective or reflective coating. A recent development is photochromic lenses, which darken in the sunlight and become clear indoors. Photochromic lenses are embedded with organic microcrystalline molecules that change their properties when exposed to UV in sunlight, but become clear in artificial lighting with no UV.

Liquid Crystals and Other Polarization Effects in Materials

Although you are undoubtedly aware of liquid crystal displays (LCDs) found in watches, calculators, computer screens, cellphones, flat screen televisions, and many other places, you may not be aware that they are based on polarization. Liquid crystals are so named because their molecules can be aligned even though they are in a liquid. Liquid crystals have the property that they can rotate the polarization of light passing through them by $90°$. Furthermore, this property can be turned off by the application of a voltage, as illustrated in **Figure 1.42**. It is possible to manipulate this characteristic quickly and in small, well-defined regions to create the contrast patterns we see in so many LCD devices.

In flat screen LCD televisions, a large light is generated at the back of the TV. The light travels to the front screen through millions of tiny units called pixels (picture elements). One of these is shown in **Figure 1.42**(a) and (b). Each unit has three cells, with red, blue, or green filters, each controlled independently. When the voltage across a liquid crystal is switched off, the liquid crystal passes the light through the particular filter. We can vary the picture contrast by varying the strength of the voltage applied to the liquid crystal.

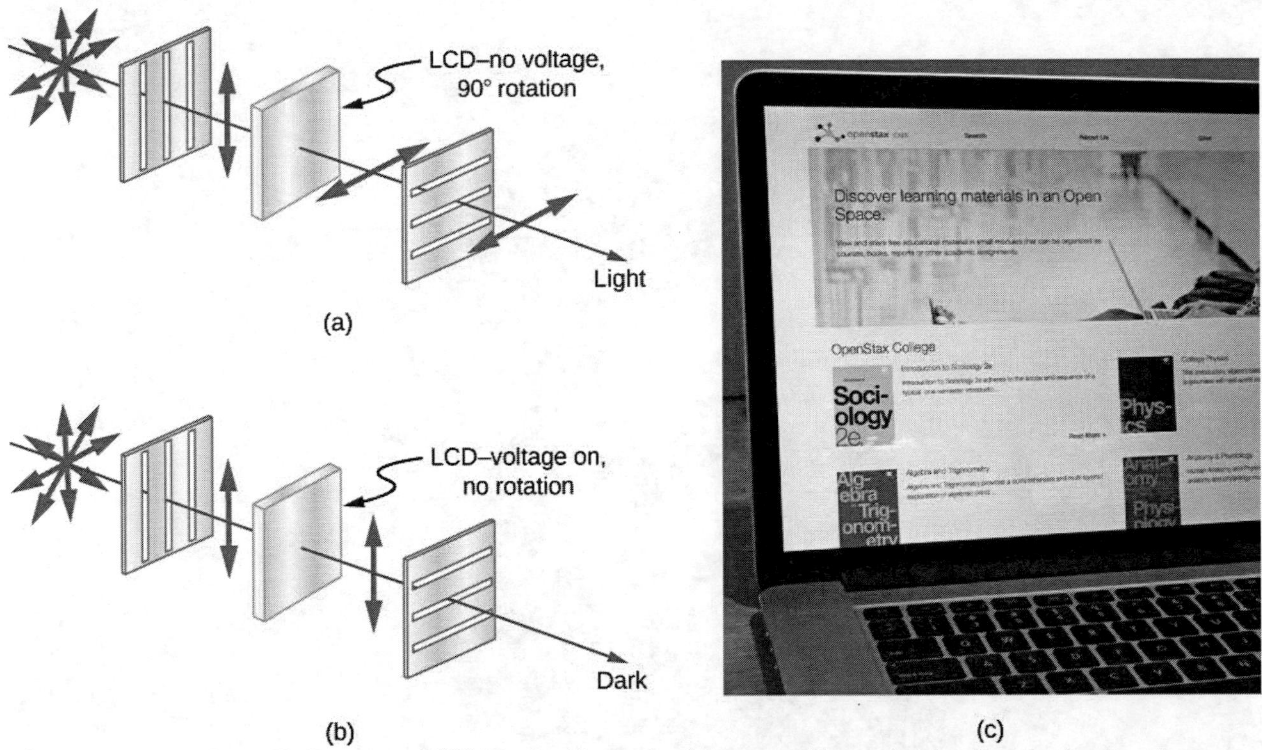

Figure 1.42 (a) Polarized light is rotated $90°$ by a liquid crystal and then passed by a polarizing filter that has its axis perpendicular to the direction of the original polarization. (b) When a voltage is applied to the liquid crystal, the polarized light is not rotated and is blocked by the filter, making the region dark in comparison with its surroundings. (c) LCDs can be made color specific, small, and fast enough to use in laptop computers and TVs. (credit c: modification of work by Jane Whitney)

Many crystals and solutions rotate the plane of polarization of light passing through them. Such substances are said to be **optically active**. Examples include sugar water, insulin, and collagen (**Figure 1.43**). In addition to depending on the type of substance, the amount and direction of rotation depend on several other factors. Among these is the concentration of the substance, the distance the light travels through it, and the wavelength of light. Optical activity is due to the asymmetrical shape of molecules in the substance, such as being helical. Measurements of the rotation of polarized light passing through substances can thus be used to measure concentrations, a standard technique for sugars. It can also give information on the shapes of molecules, such as proteins, and factors that affect their shapes, such as temperature and pH.

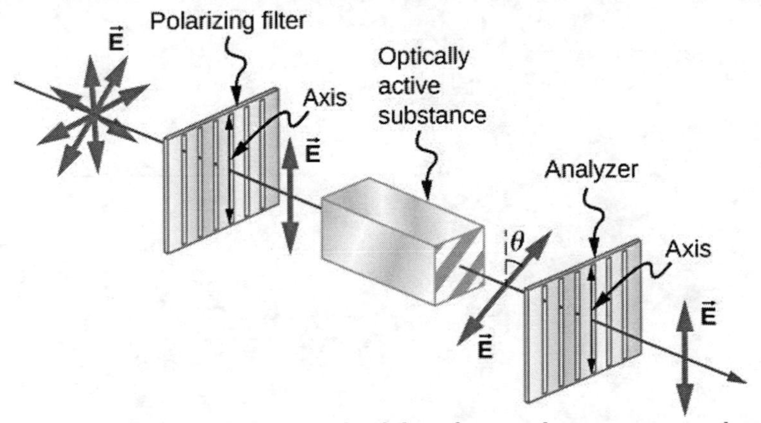

Figure 1.43 Optical activity is the ability of some substances to rotate the plane of polarization of light passing through them. The rotation is detected with a polarizing filter or analyzer.

Glass and plastic become optically active when stressed: the greater the stress, the greater the effect. Optical stress analysis on complicated shapes can be performed by making plastic models of them and observing them through crossed filters, as seen in **Figure 1.44**. It is apparent that the effect depends on wavelength as well as stress. The wavelength dependence is sometimes also used for artistic purposes.

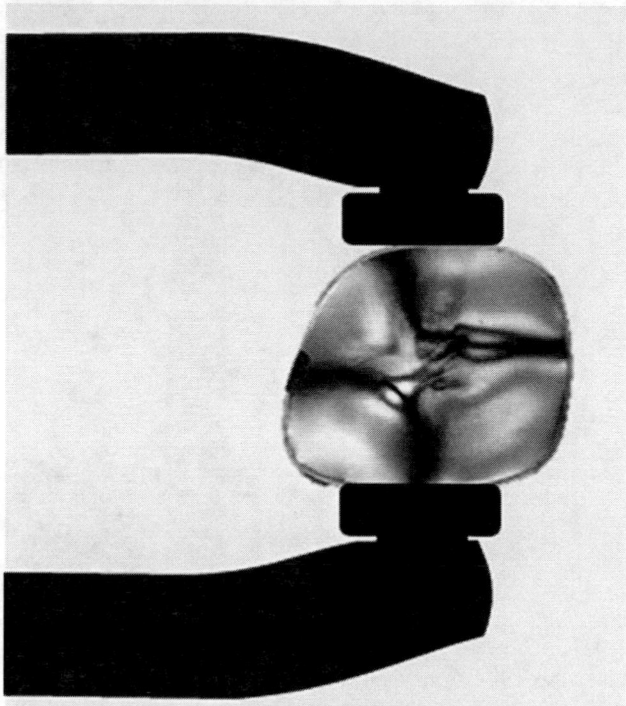

Figure 1.44 Optical stress analysis of a plastic lens placed between crossed polarizers. (credit: “Infopro”/Wikimedia Commons)

Another interesting phenomenon associated with polarized light is the ability of some crystals to split an unpolarized beam of light into two polarized beams. This occurs because the crystal has one value for the index of refraction of polarized light but a different value for the index of refraction of light polarized in the perpendicular direction, so that each component has its own angle of refraction. Such crystals are said to be **birefringent**, and, when aligned properly, two perpendicularly polarized beams will emerge from the crystal (Figure 1.45). Birefringent crystals can be used to produce polarized beams from unpolarized light. Some birefringent materials preferentially absorb one of the polarizations. These materials are called dichroic and can produce polarization by this preferential absorption. This is fundamentally how polarizing filters and other polarizers work.

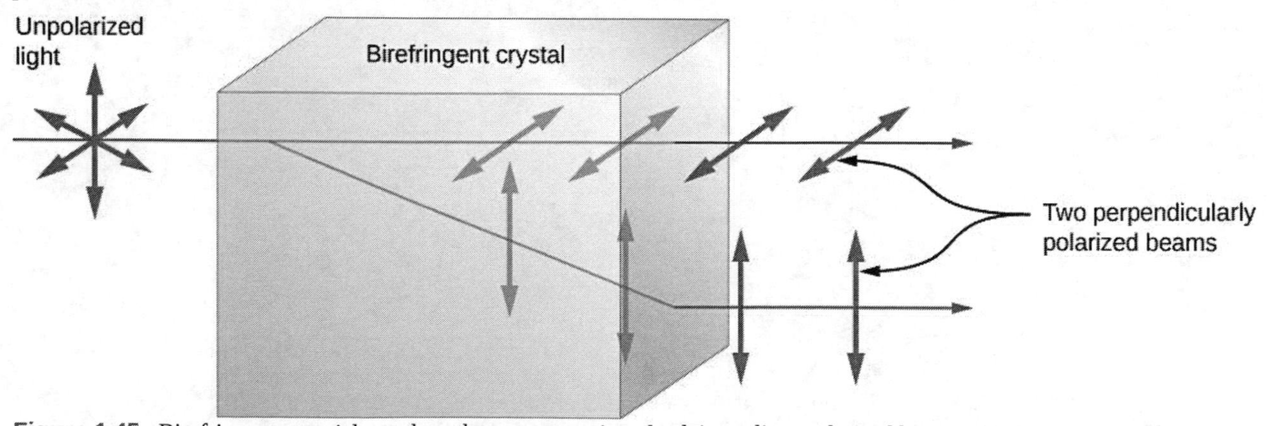

Figure 1.45 Birefringent materials, such as the common mineral calcite, split unpolarized beams of light into two with two different values of index of refraction.

CHAPTER 1 REVIEW

KEY TERMS

birefringent refers to crystals that split an unpolarized beam of light into two beams

Brewster's angle angle of incidence at which the reflected light is completely polarized

Brewster's law $\tan\theta_b = \frac{n_2}{n_1}$, where n_1 is the medium in which the incident and reflected light travel and n_2 is the index of refraction of the medium that forms the interface that reflects the light

corner reflector object consisting of two (or three) mutually perpendicular reflecting surfaces, so that the light that enters is reflected back exactly parallel to the direction from which it came

critical angle incident angle that produces an angle of refraction of $90°$

direction of polarization direction parallel to the electric field for EM waves

dispersion spreading of light into its spectrum of wavelengths

fiber optics field of study of the transmission of light down fibers of plastic or glass, applying the principle of total internal reflection

geometric optics part of optics dealing with the ray aspect of light

horizontally polarized oscillations are in a horizontal plane

Huygens's principle every point on a wave front is a source of wavelets that spread out in the forward direction at the same speed as the wave itself; the new wave front is a plane tangent to all of the wavelets

index of refraction for a material, the ratio of the speed of light in a vacuum to that in a material

law of reflection angle of reflection equals the angle of incidence

law of refraction when a light ray crosses from one medium to another, it changes direction by an amount that depends on the index of refraction of each medium and the sines of the angle of incidence and angle of refraction

Malus's law where I_0 is the intensity of the polarized wave before passing through the filter

optically active substances that rotate the plane of polarization of light passing through them

polarization attribute that wave oscillations have a definite direction relative to the direction of propagation of the wave

polarized refers to waves having the electric and magnetic field oscillations in a definite direction

ray straight line that originates at some point

refraction changing of a light ray's direction when it passes through variations in matter

total internal reflection phenomenon at the boundary between two media such that all the light is reflected and no refraction occurs

unpolarized refers to waves that are randomly polarized

vertically polarized oscillations are in a vertical plane

wave optics part of optics dealing with the wave aspect of light

KEY EQUATIONS

Speed of light	$c = 2.99792458 \times 10^8 \text{ m/s} \approx 3.00 \times 10^8 \text{ m/s}$
Index of refraction	$n = \frac{c}{v}$
Law of reflection	$\theta_r = \theta_i$

Law of refraction (Snell's law)	$n_1 \sin\theta_1 = n_2 \sin\theta_2$
Critical angle	$\theta_c = \sin^{-1}\left(\frac{n_2}{n_1}\right)$ for $n_1 > n_2$
Malus's law	$I = I_0 \cos^2\theta$
Brewster's law	$\tan\theta_b = \frac{n_2}{n_1}$

SUMMARY

1.1 The Propagation of Light

- The speed of light in a vacuum is $c = 2.99792458 \times 10^8$ m/s $\approx 3.00 \times 10^8$ m/s.
- The index of refraction of a material is $n = c/v$, where v is the speed of light in a material and c is the speed of light in a vacuum.
- The ray model of light describes the path of light as straight lines. The part of optics dealing with the ray aspect of light is called geometric optics.
- Light can travel in three ways from a source to another location: (1) directly from the source through empty space; (2) through various media; and (3) after being reflected from a mirror.

1.2 The Law of Reflection

- When a light ray strikes a smooth surface, the angle of reflection equals the angle of incidence.
- A mirror has a smooth surface and reflects light at specific angles.
- Light is diffused when it reflects from a rough surface.

1.3 Refraction

- The change of a light ray's direction when it passes through variations in matter is called refraction.
- The law of refraction, also called Snell's law, relates the indices of refraction for two media at an interface to the change in angle of a light ray passing through that interface.

1.4 Total Internal Reflection

- The incident angle that produces an angle of refraction of $90°$ is called the critical angle.
- Total internal reflection is a phenomenon that occurs at the boundary between two media, such that if the incident angle in the first medium is greater than the critical angle, then all the light is reflected back into that medium.
- Fiber optics involves the transmission of light down fibers of plastic or glass, applying the principle of total internal reflection.
- Cladding prevents light from being transmitted between fibers in a bundle.
- Diamonds sparkle due to total internal reflection coupled with a large index of refraction.

1.5 Dispersion

- The spreading of white light into its full spectrum of wavelengths is called dispersion.
- Rainbows are produced by a combination of refraction and reflection, and involve the dispersion of sunlight into a continuous distribution of colors.
- Dispersion produces beautiful rainbows but also causes problems in certain optical systems.

1.6 Huygens's Principle

- According to Huygens's principle, every point on a wave front is a source of wavelets that spread out in the forward direction at the same speed as the wave itself. The new wave front is tangent to all of the wavelets.
- A mirror reflects an incoming wave at an angle equal to the incident angle, verifying the law of reflection.
- The law of refraction can be explained by applying Huygens's principle to a wave front passing from one medium to another.
- The bending of a wave around the edges of an opening or an obstacle is called diffraction.

1.7 Polarization

- Polarization is the attribute that wave oscillations have a definite direction relative to the direction of propagation of the wave. The direction of polarization is defined to be the direction parallel to the electric field of the EM wave.
- Unpolarized light is composed of many rays having random polarization directions.
- Unpolarized light can be polarized by passing it through a polarizing filter or other polarizing material. The process of polarizing light decreases its intensity by a factor of 2.
- The intensity, *I*, of polarized light after passing through a polarizing filter is $I = I_0 \cos^2 \theta$, where I_0 is the incident intensity and θ is the angle between the direction of polarization and the axis of the filter.
- Polarization is also produced by reflection.
- Brewster's law states that reflected light is completely polarized at the angle of reflection θ_b, known as Brewster's angle.
- Polarization can also be produced by scattering.
- Several types of optically active substances rotate the direction of polarization of light passing through them.

CONCEPTUAL QUESTIONS

1.1 The Propagation of Light

1. Under what conditions can light be modeled like a ray? Like a wave?

2. Why is the index of refraction always greater than or equal to 1?

3. Does the fact that the light flash from lightning reaches you before its sound prove that the speed of light is extremely large or simply that it is greater than the speed of sound? Discuss how you could use this effect to get an estimate of the speed of light.

4. Speculate as to what physical process might be responsible for light traveling more slowly in a medium than in a vacuum.

1.2 The Law of Reflection

5. Using the law of reflection, explain how powder takes the shine off of a person's nose. What is the name of the optical effect?

1.3 Refraction

6. Diffusion by reflection from a rough surface is described in this chapter. Light can also be diffused by refraction. Describe how this occurs in a specific situation, such as light interacting with crushed ice.

7. Will light change direction toward or away from the perpendicular when it goes from air to water? Water to glass? Glass to air?

8. Explain why an object in water always appears to be at a depth shallower than it actually is?

9. Explain why a person's legs appear very short when wading in a pool. Justify your explanation with a ray diagram showing the path of rays from the feet to the eye of an observer who is out of the water.

10. Explain why an oar that is partially submerged in water appears bent.

1.4 Total Internal Reflection

11. A ring with a colorless gemstone is dropped into water.

The gemstone becomes invisible when submerged. Can it be a diamond? Explain.

12. The most common type of mirage is an illusion that light from faraway objects is reflected by a pool of water that is not really there. Mirages are generally observed in deserts, when there is a hot layer of air near the ground. Given that the refractive index of air is lower for air at higher temperatures, explain how mirages can be formed.

13. How can you use total internal reflection to estimate the index of refraction of a medium?

1.5 Dispersion

14. Is it possible that total internal reflection plays a role in rainbows? Explain in terms of indices of refraction and angles, perhaps referring to that shown below. Some of us have seen the formation of a double rainbow; is it physically possible to observe a triple rainbow?

(credit: "Chad"/Flickr)

15. A high-quality diamond may be quite clear and colorless, transmitting all visible wavelengths with little absorption. Explain how it can sparkle with flashes of brilliant color when illuminated by white light.

1.6 Huygens's Principle

16. How do wave effects depend on the size of the object with which the wave interacts? For example, why does sound bend around the corner of a building while light does not?

17. Does Huygens's principle apply to all types of waves?

18. If diffraction is observed for some phenomenon, it is evidence that the phenomenon is a wave. Does the reverse hold true? That is, if diffraction is not observed, does that mean the phenomenon is not a wave?

1.7 Polarization

19. Can a sound wave in air be polarized? Explain.

20. No light passes through two perfect polarizing filters with perpendicular axes. However, if a third polarizing filter is placed between the original two, some light can pass. Why is this? Under what circumstances does most of the light pass?

21. Explain what happens to the energy carried by light that it is dimmed by passing it through two crossed polarizing filters.

22. When particles scattering light are much smaller than its wavelength, the amount of scattering is proportional to $\frac{1}{\lambda}$. Does this mean there is more scattering for small λ than large λ? How does this relate to the fact that the sky is blue?

23. Using the information given in the preceding question, explain why sunsets are red.

24. When light is reflected at Brewster's angle from a smooth surface, it is 100% polarized parallel to the surface. Part of the light will be refracted into the surface. Describe how you would do an experiment to determine the polarization of the refracted light. What direction would you expect the polarization to have and would you expect it to be 100%?

25. If you lie on a beach looking at the water with your head tipped slightly sideways, your polarized sunglasses do not work very well. Why not?

PROBLEMS

1.1 The Propagation of Light

26. What is the speed of light in water? In glycerine?

27. What is the speed of light in air? In crown glass?

28. Calculate the index of refraction for a medium in which the speed of light is 2.012×10^8 m/s, and identify the most likely substance based on **Table 1.1**.

29. In what substance in **Table 1.1** is the speed of light 2.290×10^8 m/s?

30. There was a major collision of an asteroid with the Moon in medieval times. It was described by monks at Canterbury Cathedral in England as a red glow on and around the Moon. How long after the asteroid hit the Moon, which is 3.84×10^5 km away, would the light first arrive on Earth?

31. Components of some computers communicate with each other through optical fibers having an index of refraction $n = 1.55$. What time in nanoseconds is required for a signal to travel 0.200 m through such a fiber?

32. Compare the time it takes for light to travel 1000 m on the surface of Earth and in outer space.

33. How far does light travel underwater during a time interval of 1.50×10^{-6} s?

1.2 The Law of Reflection

34. Suppose a man stands in front of a mirror as shown below. His eyes are 1.65 m above the floor and the top of his head is 0.13 m higher. Find the height above the floor of the top and bottom of the smallest mirror in which he can see both the top of his head and his feet. How is this distance related to the man's height?

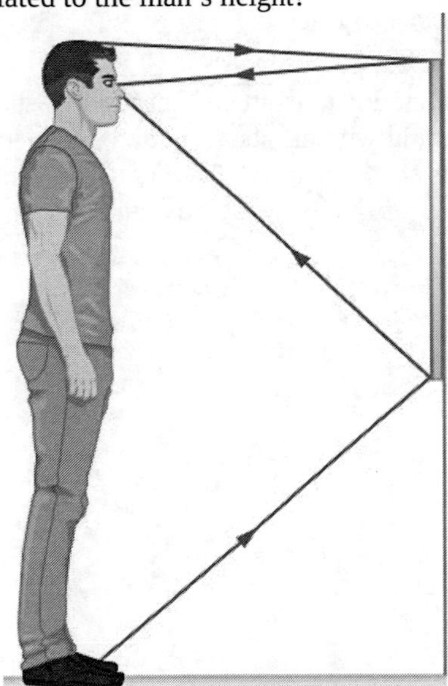

35. Show that when light reflects from two mirrors that meet each other at a right angle, the outgoing ray is parallel to the incoming ray, as illustrated below.

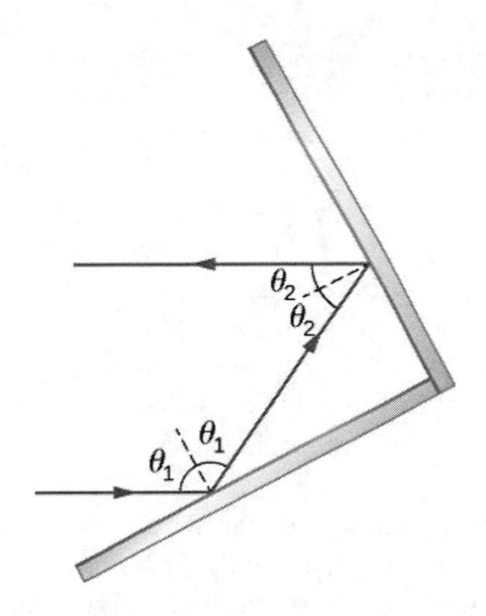

36. On the Moon's surface, lunar astronauts placed a corner reflector, off which a laser beam is periodically reflected. The distance to the Moon is calculated from the round-trip time. What percent correction is needed to account for the delay in time due to the slowing of light in Earth's atmosphere? Assume the distance to the Moon is precisely 3.84×10^8 m and Earth's atmosphere (which varies in density with altitude) is equivalent to a layer 30.0 km thick with a constant index of refraction $n = 1.000293$.

37. A flat mirror is neither converging nor diverging. To prove this, consider two rays originating from the same point and diverging at an angle θ (see below). Show that after striking a plane mirror, the angle between their directions remains θ.

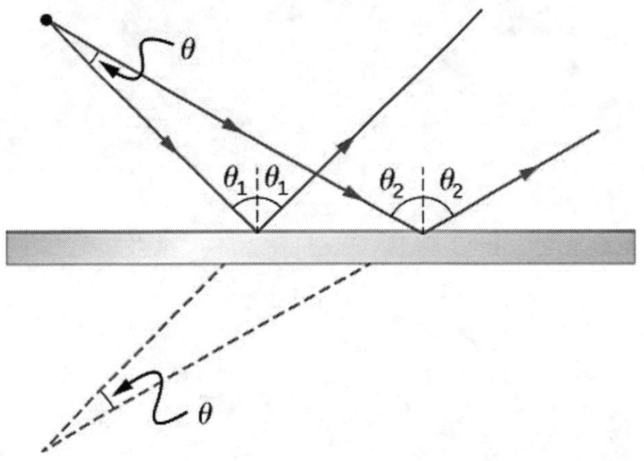

1.3 Refraction

Unless otherwise specified, for problems 1 through 10, the indices of refraction of glass and water should be taken to be 1.50 and 1.333, respectively.

38. A light beam in air has an angle of incidence of $35°$ at the surface of a glass plate. What are the angles of reflection and refraction?

39. A light beam in air is incident on the surface of a pond, making an angle of $20°$ with respect to the surface. What are the angles of reflection and refraction?

40. When a light ray crosses from water into glass, it emerges at an angle of $30°$ with respect to the normal of the interface. What is its angle of incidence?

41. A pencil flashlight submerged in water sends a light beam toward the surface at an angle of incidence of $30°$. What is the angle of refraction in air?

42. Light rays from the Sun make a $30°$ angle to the vertical when seen from below the surface of a body of water. At what angle above the horizon is the Sun?

43. The path of a light beam in air goes from an angle of incidence of $35°$ to an angle of refraction of $22°$ when it enters a rectangular block of plastic. What is the index of refraction of the plastic?

44. A scuba diver training in a pool looks at his instructor as shown below. What angle does the ray from the instructor's face make with the perpendicular to the water at the point where the ray enters? The angle between the ray in the water and the perpendicular to the water is $25.0°$.

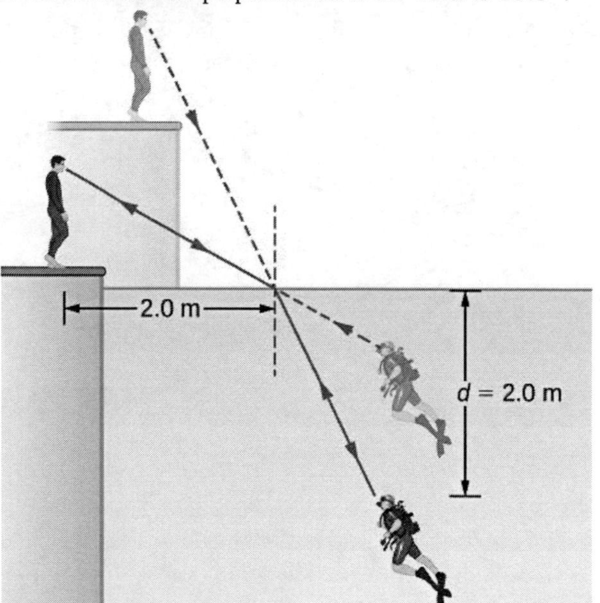

45. (a) Using information in the preceding problem, find the height of the instructor's head above the water, noting that you will first have to calculate the angle of incidence. (b) Find the apparent depth of the diver's head below water as seen by the instructor.

1.4 Total Internal Reflection

46. Verify that the critical angle for light going from water to air is $48.6°$, as discussed at the end of **Example 1.4**, regarding the critical angle for light traveling in a polystyrene (a type of plastic) pipe surrounded by air.

47. (a) At the end of **Example 1.4**, it was stated that the critical angle for light going from diamond to air is $24.4°$. Verify this. (b) What is the critical angle for light going from zircon to air?

48. An optical fiber uses flint glass clad with crown glass. What is the critical angle?

49. At what minimum angle will you get total internal reflection of light traveling in water and reflected from ice?

50. Suppose you are using total internal reflection to make an efficient corner reflector. If there is air outside and the incident angle is $45.0°$, what must be the minimum index of refraction of the material from which the reflector is made?

51. You can determine the index of refraction of a substance by determining its critical angle. (a) What is the index of refraction of a substance that has a critical angle of $68.4°$ when submerged in water? What is the substance, based on **Table 1.1**? (b) What would the critical angle be for this substance in air?

52. A ray of light, emitted beneath the surface of an unknown liquid with air above it, undergoes total internal reflection as shown below. What is the index of refraction for the liquid and its likely identification?

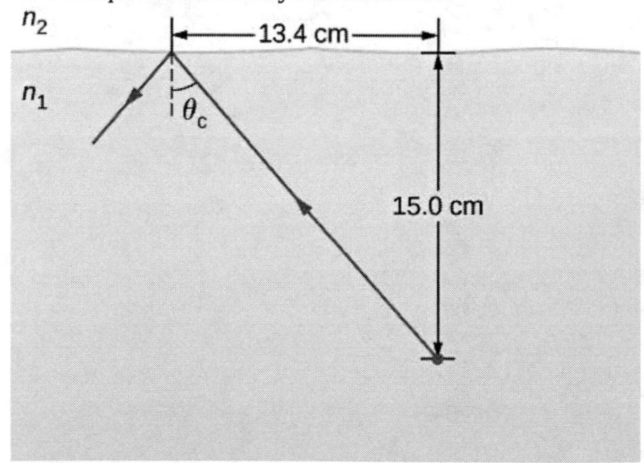

53. Light rays fall normally on the vertical surface of the glass prism ($n = 1.50$) shown below. (a) What is the largest value for ϕ such that the ray is totally reflected at the slanted face? (b) Repeat the calculation of part (a) if the prism is immersed in water.

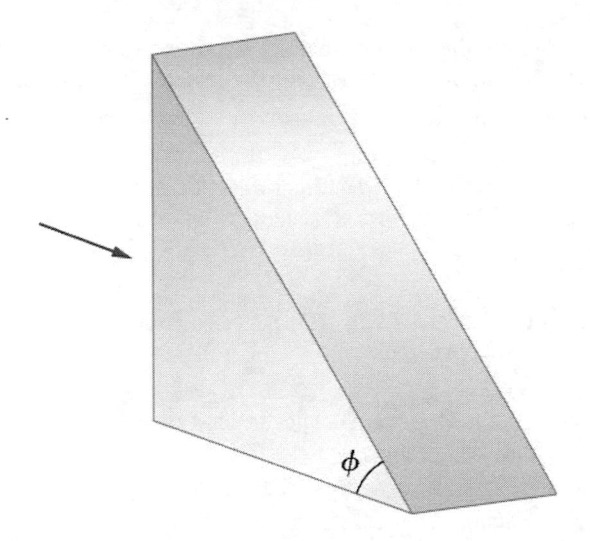

1.5 Dispersion

54. (a) What is the ratio of the speed of red light to violet light in diamond, based on **Table 1.2**? (b) What is this ratio in polystyrene? (c) Which is more dispersive?

55. A beam of white light goes from air into water at an incident angle of $75.0°$. At what angles are the red (660 nm) and violet (410 nm) parts of the light refracted?

56. By how much do the critical angles for red (660 nm) and violet (410 nm) light differ in a diamond surrounded by air?

57. (a) A narrow beam of light containing yellow (580 nm) and green (550 nm) wavelengths goes from polystyrene to air, striking the surface at a $30.0°$ incident angle. What is the angle between the colors when they emerge? (b) How far would they have to travel to be separated by 1.00 mm?

58. A parallel beam of light containing orange (610 nm) and violet (410 nm) wavelengths goes from fused quartz to water, striking the surface between them at a $60.0°$ incident angle. What is the angle between the two colors in water?

59. A ray of 610-nm light goes from air into fused quartz at an incident angle of $55.0°$. At what incident angle must 470 nm light enter flint glass to have the same angle of refraction?

60. A narrow beam of light containing red (660 nm) and blue (470 nm) wavelengths travels from air through a 1.00-cm-thick flat piece of crown glass and back to air again. The beam strikes at a $30.0°$ incident angle. (a) At what angles do the two colors emerge? (b) By what distance are the red and blue separated when they emerge?

61. A narrow beam of white light enters a prism made of crown glass at a $45.0°$ incident angle, as shown below. At what angles, θ_R and θ_V, do the red (660 nm) and violet (410 nm) components of the light emerge from the prism?

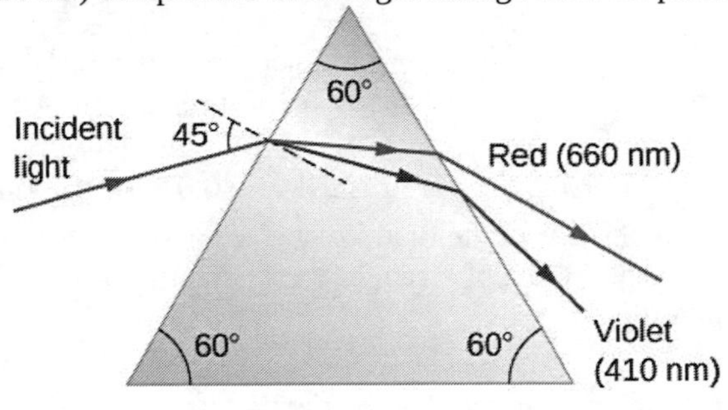

1.7 Polarization

62. What angle is needed between the direction of polarized light and the axis of a polarizing filter to cut its intensity in half?

63. The angle between the axes of two polarizing filters is $45.0°$. By how much does the second filter reduce the intensity of the light coming through the first?

64. Two polarizing sheets P_1 and P_2 are placed together with their transmission axes oriented at an angle θ to each other. What is θ when only 25% of the maximum transmitted light intensity passes through them?

65. Suppose that in the preceding problem the light incident on P_1 is unpolarized. At the determined value of θ, what fraction of the incident light passes through the combination?

66. If you have completely polarized light of intensity $150\ W/m^2$, what will its intensity be after passing through a polarizing filter with its axis at an $89.0°$ angle to the light's polarization direction?

67. What angle would the axis of a polarizing filter need to make with the direction of polarized light of intensity $1.00\ kW/m^2$ to reduce the intensity to $10.0\ W/m^2$?

68. At the end of **Example 1.7**, it was stated that the intensity of polarized light is reduced to 90.0% of its original value by passing through a polarizing filter with its axis at an angle of $18.4°$ to the direction of polarization. Verify this statement.

69. Show that if you have three polarizing filters, with the second at an angle of $45.0°$ to the first and the third at an angle of $90.0°$ to the first, the intensity of light passed by the first will be reduced to 25.0% of its value. (This is in contrast to having only the first and third, which reduces the intensity to zero, so that placing the second between them increases the intensity of the transmitted light.)

70. Three polarizing sheets are placed together such that the transmission axis of the second sheet is oriented at $25.0°$ to the axis of the first, whereas the transmission axis of the third sheet is oriented at $40.0°$ (in the same sense) to the axis of the first. What fraction of the intensity of an incident unpolarized beam is transmitted by the combination?

71. In order to rotate the polarization axis of a beam of linearly polarized light by $90.0°$, a student places sheets P_1 and P_2 with their transmission axes at $45.0°$ and $90.0°$, respectively, to the beam's axis of polarization. (a) What fraction of the incident light passes through P_1 and (b) through the combination? (c) Repeat your calculations for part (b) for transmission-axis angles of $30.0°$ and $90.0°$, respectively.

72. It is found that when light traveling in water falls on a plastic block, Brewster's angle is $50.0°$. What is the refractive index of the plastic?

73. At what angle will light reflected from diamond be completely polarized?

74. What is Brewster's angle for light traveling in water that is reflected from crown glass?

75. A scuba diver sees light reflected from the water's surface. At what angle relative to the water's surface will this light be completely polarized?

ADDITIONAL PROBLEMS

76. From his measurements, Roemer estimated that it took 22 min for light to travel a distance equal to the diameter of Earth's orbit around the Sun. (a) Use this estimate along with the known diameter of Earth's orbit to obtain a rough value of the speed of light. (b) Light actually takes 16.5 min to travel this distance. Use this time to calculate the speed of light.

77. Cornu performed Fizeau's measurement of the speed of light using a wheel of diameter 4.00 cm that contained 180 teeth. The distance from the wheel to the mirror was 22.9 km. Assuming he measured the speed of light accurately, what was the angular velocity of the wheel?

78. Suppose you have an unknown clear substance immersed in water, and you wish to identify it by finding its index of refraction. You arrange to have a beam of light enter it at an angle of $45.0°$, and you observe the angle of refraction to be $40.3°$. What is the index of refraction of the substance and its likely identity?

79. Shown below is a ray of light going from air through crown glass into water, such as going into a fish tank. Calculate the amount the ray is displaced by the glass (Δx), given that the incident angle is $40.0°$ and the glass is 1.00 cm thick.

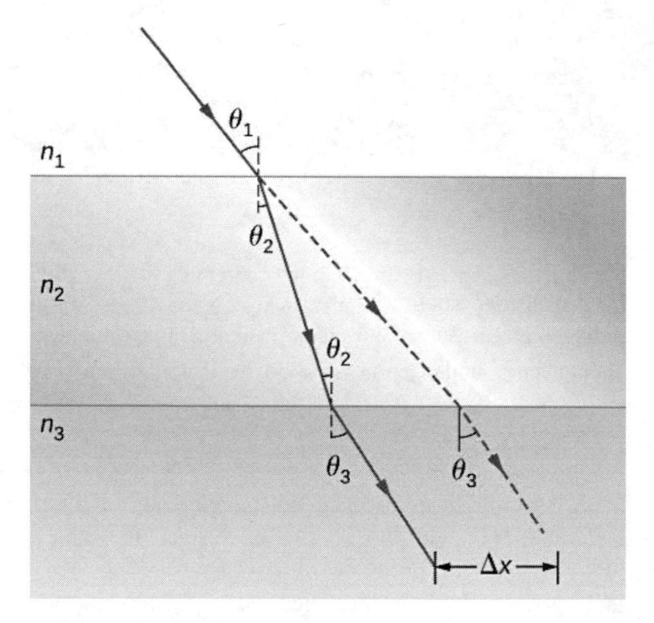

80. Considering the previous problem, show that θ_3 is the same as it would be if the second medium were not present.

81. At what angle is light inside crown glass completely polarized when reflected from water, as in a fish tank?

82. Light reflected at $55.6°$ from a window is completely polarized. What is the window's index of refraction and the likely substance of which it is made?

83. (a) Light reflected at $62.5°$ from a gemstone in a ring is completely polarized. Can the gem be a diamond? (b) At what angle would the light be completely polarized if the gem was in water?

84. If θ_b is Brewster's angle for light reflected from the top of an interface between two substances, and θ_b' is Brewster's angle for light reflected from below, prove that $\theta_b + \theta_b' = 90.0°$.

85. Unreasonable results Suppose light travels from water to another substance, with an angle of incidence of $10.0°$ and an angle of refraction of $14.9°$. (a) What is the index of refraction of the other substance? (b) What is unreasonable about this result? (c) Which assumptions are unreasonable or inconsistent?

86. Unreasonable results Light traveling from water to a gemstone strikes the surface at an angle of $80.0°$ and has an angle of refraction of $15.2°$. (a) What is the speed of light in the gemstone? (b) What is unreasonable about this result? (c) Which assumptions are unreasonable or inconsistent?

87. If a polarizing filter reduces the intensity of polarized light to 50.0% of its original value, by how much are the electric and magnetic fields reduced?

88. Suppose you put on two pairs of polarizing sunglasses with their axes at an angle of $15.0°$. How much longer will it take the light to deposit a given amount of energy in your eye compared with a single pair of sunglasses? Assume the lenses are clear except for their polarizing characteristics.

89. (a) On a day when the intensity of sunlight is $1.00\ \text{kW/m}^2$, a circular lens 0.200 m in diameter focuses light onto water in a black beaker. Two polarizing sheets of plastic are placed in front of the lens with their axes at an angle of $20.0°$. Assuming the sunlight is unpolarized and the polarizers are 100% efficient, what is the initial rate of heating of the water in $°\text{C/s}$, assuming it is 80.0% absorbed? The aluminum beaker has a mass of 30.0 grams and contains 250 grams of water. (b) Do the polarizing filters get hot? Explain.

CHALLENGE PROBLEMS

90. Light shows staged with lasers use moving mirrors to swing beams and create colorful effects. Show that a light ray reflected from a mirror changes direction by 2θ when the mirror is rotated by an angle θ.

91. Consider sunlight entering Earth's atmosphere at sunrise and sunset—that is, at a $90.0°$ incident angle. Taking the boundary between nearly empty space and the atmosphere to be sudden, calculate the angle of refraction for sunlight. This lengthens the time the Sun appears to be above the horizon, both at sunrise and sunset. Now construct a problem in which you determine the angle of refraction for different models of the atmosphere, such as various layers of varying density. Your instructor may wish to guide you on the level of complexity to consider and on how the index of refraction varies with air density.

92. A light ray entering an optical fiber surrounded by air is first refracted and then reflected as shown below. Show that if the fiber is made from crown glass, any incident ray will be totally internally reflected.

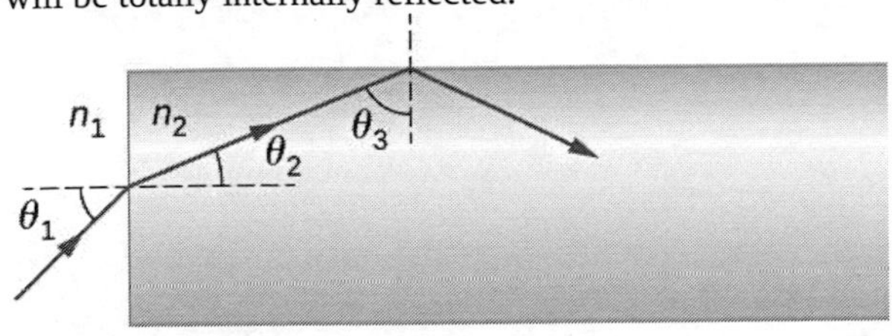

93. A light ray falls on the left face of a prism (see below) at the angle of incidence θ for which the emerging beam has an angle of refraction θ at the right face. Show that the index of refraction n of the glass prism is given by

$$n = \frac{\sin \frac{1}{2}(\alpha + \phi)}{\sin \frac{1}{2}\phi}$$

where ϕ is the vertex angle of the prism and α is the angle through which the beam has been deviated. If $\alpha = 37.0°$ and the base angles of the prism are each $50.0°$, what is n?

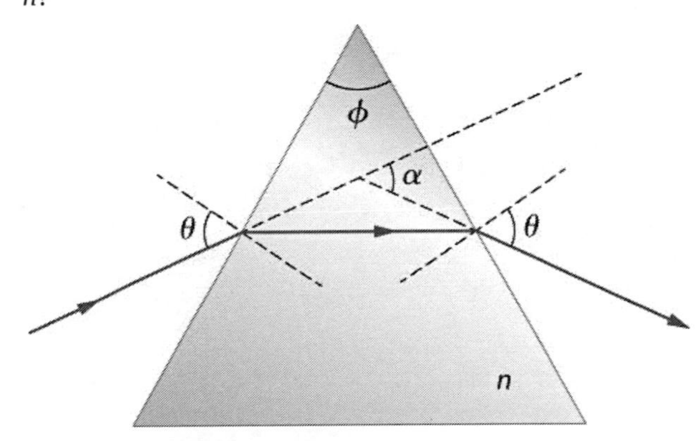

94. If the apex angle ϕ in the previous problem is $20.0°$ and $n = 1.50$, what is the value of α?

95. The light incident on polarizing sheet P_1 is linearly polarized at an angle of $30.0°$ with respect to the transmission axis of P_1. Sheet P_2 is placed so that its axis is parallel to the polarization axis of the incident light, that is, also at $30.0°$ with respect to P_1. (a) What fraction of the incident light passes through P_1? (b) What fraction of the incident light is passed by the combination? (c) By rotating P_2, a maximum in transmitted intensity is obtained. What is the ratio of this maximum intensity to the intensity of transmitted light when P_2 is at $30.0°$ with respect to P_1?

96. Prove that if I is the intensity of light transmitted by two polarizing filters with axes at an angle θ and I' is the intensity when the axes are at an angle $90.0° - \theta$, then $I + I' = I_0$, the original intensity. (*Hint:* Use the trigonometric identities $\cos 90.0° - \theta = \sin \theta$ and $\cos^2 \theta + \sin^2 \theta = 1$.)

2 | GEOMETRIC OPTICS AND IMAGE FORMATION

Figure 2.1 *Cloud Gate* is a public sculpture by Anish Kapoor located in Millennium Park in Chicago. Its stainless steel plates reflect and distort images around it, including the Chicago skyline. Dedicated in 2006, it has become a popular tourist attraction, illustrating how art can use the principles of physical optics to startle and entertain. (credit: modification of work by Dhilung Kirat)

Chapter Outline

Introduction

This chapter introduces the major ideas of geometric optics, which describe the formation of images due to reflection and refraction. It is called "geometric" optics because the images can be characterized using geometric constructions, such as ray diagrams. We have seen that visible light is an electromagnetic wave; however, its wave nature becomes evident only when light interacts with objects with dimensions comparable to the wavelength (about 500 nm for visible light). Therefore, the laws of geometric optics only apply to light interacting with objects much larger than the wavelength of the light.

2.1 | Images Formed by Plane Mirrors

Learning Objectives

By the end of this section, you will be able to:

- Describe how an image is formed by a plane mirror.
- Distinguish between real and virtual images.
- Find the location and characterize the orientation of an image created by a plane mirror.

You only have to look as far as the nearest bathroom to find an example of an image formed by a mirror. Images in a **plane mirror** are the same size as the object, are located behind the mirror, and are oriented in the same direction as the object (i.e., "upright").

To understand how this happens, consider **Figure 2.2**. Two rays emerge from point *P*, strike the mirror, and reflect into the observer's eye. Note that we use the law of reflection to construct the reflected rays. If the reflected rays are extended backward behind the mirror (see dashed lines in **Figure 2.2**), they seem to originate from point *Q*. This is where the image of point *P* is located. If we repeat this process for point P', we obtain its image at point Q'. You should convince yourself by using basic geometry that the image height (the distance from *Q* to Q') is the same as the object height (the distance from *P* to P'). By forming images of all points of the object, we obtain an upright image of the object behind the mirror.

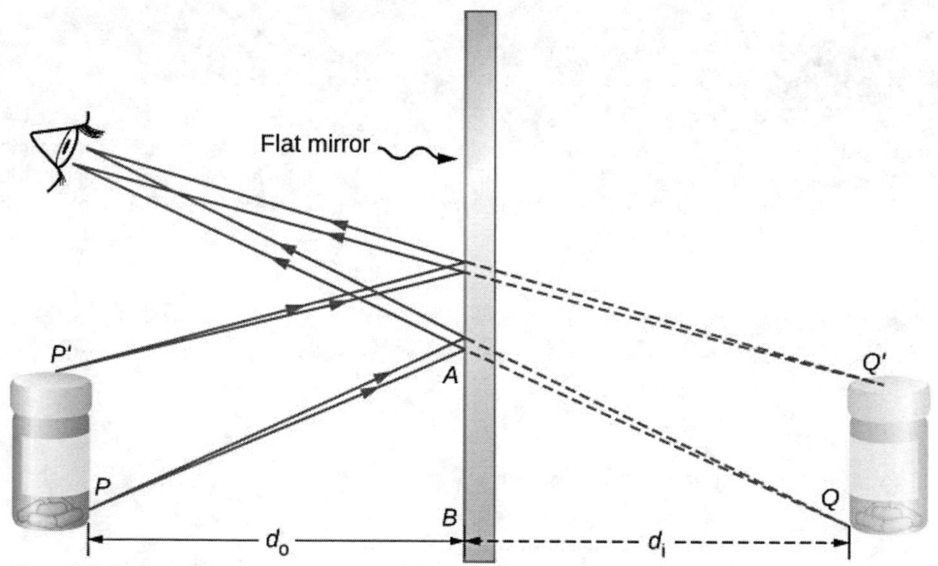

Figure 2.2 Two light rays originating from point *P* on an object are reflected by a flat mirror into the eye of an observer. The reflected rays are obtained by using the law of reflection. Extending these reflected rays backward, they seem to come from point *Q* behind the mirror, which is where the virtual image is located. Repeating this process for point P' gives the image point Q'. The image height is thus the same as the object height, the image is upright, and the object distance d_o is the same as the image distance d_i. (credit: modification of work by Kevin Dufendach)

Notice that the reflected rays appear to the observer to come directly from the image behind the mirror. In reality, these rays come from the points on the mirror where they are reflected. The image behind the mirror is called a **virtual image** because it cannot be projected onto a screen—the rays only appear to originate from a common point behind the mirror. If you walk behind the mirror, you cannot see the image, because the rays do not go there. However, in front of the mirror, the rays behave exactly as if they come from behind the mirror, so that is where the virtual image is located.

Later in this chapter, we discuss real images; a **real image** can be projected onto a screen because the rays physically go through the image. You can certainly see both real and virtual images. The difference is that a virtual image cannot be projected onto a screen, whereas a real image can.

Locating an Image in a Plane Mirror

The law of reflection tells us that the angle of incidence is the same as the angle of reflection. Applying this to triangles *PAB* and *QAB* in **Figure 2.2** and using basic geometry shows that they are congruent triangles. This means that the distance *PB* from the object to the mirror is the same as the distance *BQ* from the mirror to the image. The **object distance** (denoted d_o) is the distance from the mirror to the object (or, more generally, from the center of the optical element that creates its image). Similarly, the **image distance** (denoted d_i) is the distance from the mirror to the image (or, more generally, from the center of the optical element that creates it). If we measure distances from the mirror, then the object and image are in opposite directions, so for a plane mirror, the object and image distances should have the opposite signs:

$$d_o = -d_i. \tag{2.1}$$

An extended object such as the container in **Figure 2.2** can be treated as a collection of points, and we can apply the method above to locate the image of each point on the extended object, thus forming the extended image.

Multiple Images

If an object is situated in front of two mirrors, you may see images in both mirrors. In addition, the image in the first mirror may act as an object for the second mirror, so the second mirror may form an image of the image. If the mirrors are placed parallel to each other and the object is placed at a point other than the midpoint between them, then this process of image-of-an-image continues without end, as you may have noticed when standing in a hallway with mirrors on each side. This is shown in **Figure 2.3**, which shows three images produced by the blue object. Notice that each reflection reverses front and back, just like pulling a right-hand glove inside out produces a left-hand glove (this is why a reflection of your right hand is a left hand). Thus, the fronts and backs of images 1 and 2 are both inverted with respect to the object, and the front and back of image 3 is inverted with respect to image 2, which is the object for image 3.

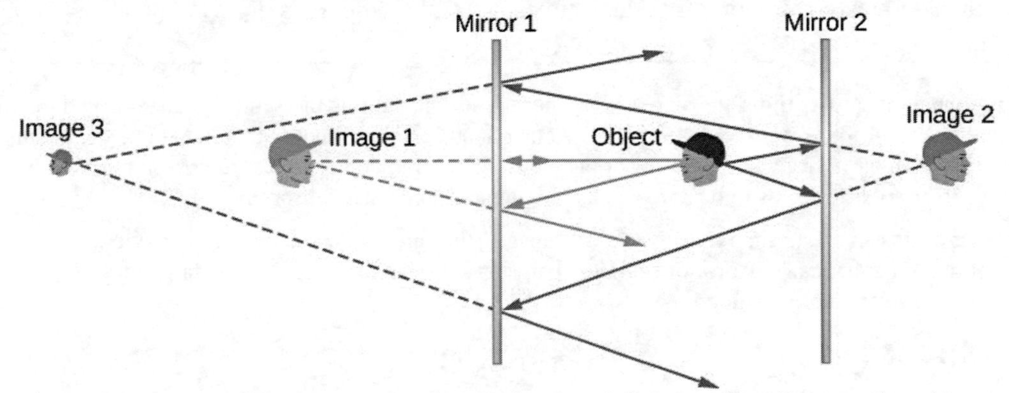

Figure 2.3 Two parallel mirrors can produce, in theory, an infinite number of images of an object placed off center between the mirrors. Three of these images are shown here. The front and back of each image is inverted with respect to its object. Note that the colors are only to identify the images. For normal mirrors, the color of an image is essentially the same as that of its object.

You may have noticed that image 3 is smaller than the object, whereas images 1 and 2 are the same size as the object. The ratio of the image height with respect to the object height is called **magnification**. More will be said about magnification in the next section.

Infinite reflections may terminate. For instance, two mirrors at right angles form three images, as shown in part (a) of **Figure 2.4**. Images 1 and 2 result from rays that reflect from only a single mirror, but image 1,2 is formed by rays that reflect from both mirrors. This is shown in the ray-tracing diagram in part (b) of **Figure 2.4**. To find image 1,2, you have to look behind the corner of the two mirrors.

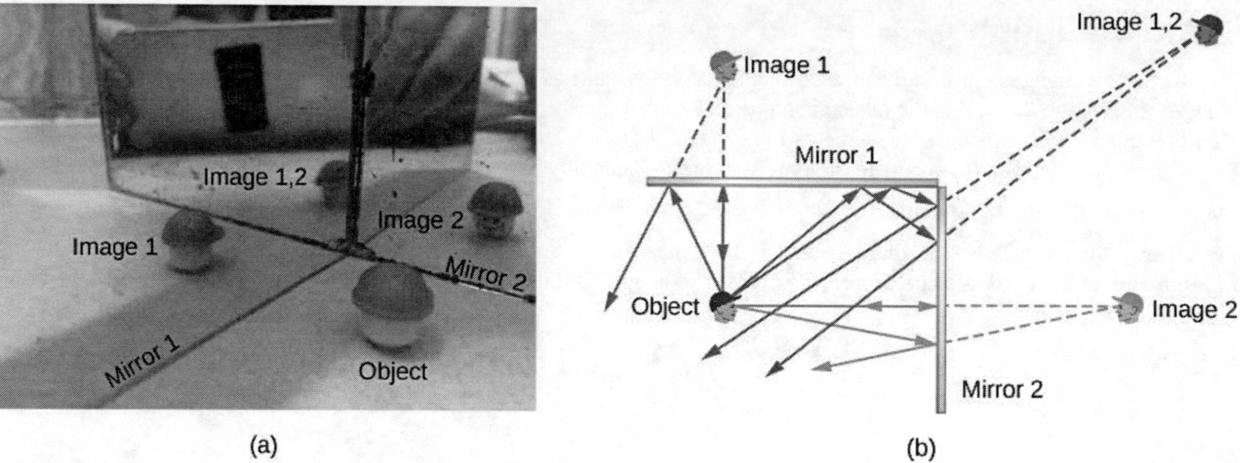

Figure 2.4 Two mirrors can produce multiple images. (a) Three images of a plastic head are visible in the two mirrors at a right angle. (b) A single object reflecting from two mirrors at a right angle can produce three images, as shown by the green, purple, and red images.

2.2 | Spherical Mirrors

Learning Objectives

By the end of this section, you will be able to:

- Describe image formation by spherical mirrors.
- Use ray diagrams and the mirror equation to calculate the properties of an image in a spherical mirror.

The image in a plane mirror has the same size as the object, is upright, and is the same distance behind the mirror as the object is in front of the mirror. A **curved mirror**, on the other hand, can form images that may be larger or smaller than the object and may form either in front of the mirror or behind it. In general, any curved surface will form an image, although some images make be so distorted as to be unrecognizable (think of fun house mirrors).

Because curved mirrors can create such a rich variety of images, they are used in many optical devices that find many uses. We will concentrate on spherical mirrors for the most part, because they are easier to manufacture than mirrors such as parabolic mirrors and so are more common.

Curved Mirrors

We can define two general types of spherical mirrors. If the reflecting surface is the outer side of the sphere, the mirror is called a **convex mirror**. If the inside surface is the reflecting surface, it is called a **concave mirror**.

Symmetry is one of the major hallmarks of many optical devices, including mirrors and lenses. The symmetry axis of such optical elements is often called the principal axis or **optical axis**. For a spherical mirror, the optical axis passes through the mirror's center of curvature and the mirror's **vertex**, as shown in Figure 2.5.

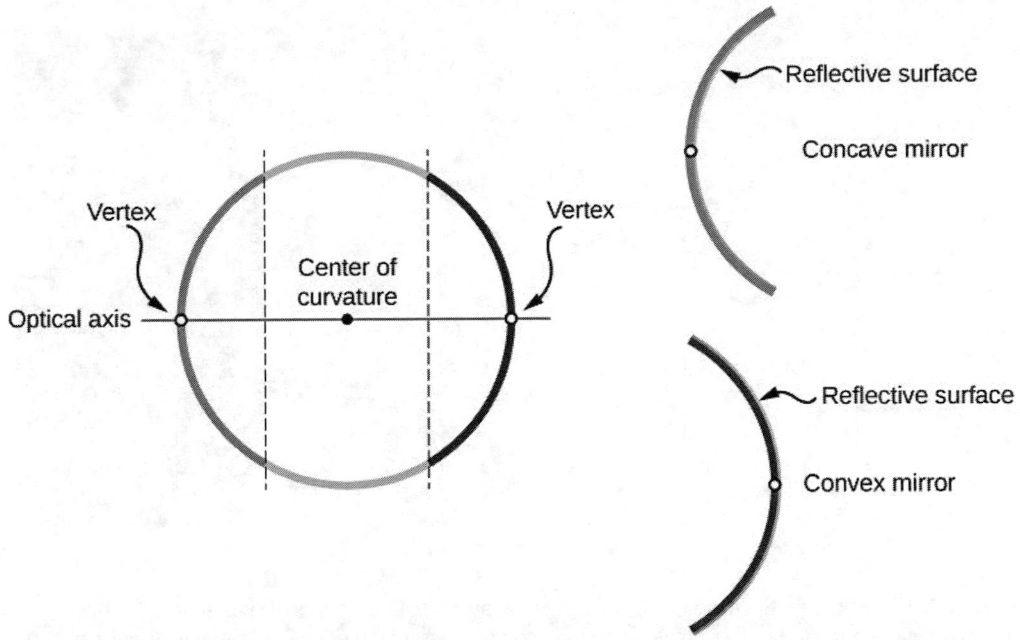

Figure 2.5 A spherical mirror is formed by cutting out a piece of a sphere and silvering either the inside or outside surface. A concave mirror has silvering on the interior surface (think “cave”), and a convex mirror has silvering on the exterior surface.

Consider rays that are parallel to the optical axis of a parabolic mirror, as shown in part (a) of Figure 2.6. Following the law of reflection, these rays are reflected so that they converge at a point, called the **focal point**. Part (b) of this figure shows a spherical mirror that is large compared with its radius of curvature. For this mirror, the reflected rays do not cross at the same point, so the mirror does not have a well-defined focal point. This is called spherical aberration and results in a blurred image of an extended object. Part (c) shows a spherical mirror that is small compared to its radius of curvature. This mirror is a good approximation of a parabolic mirror, so rays that arrive parallel to the optical axis are reflected to a well-defined focal point. The distance along the optical axis from the mirror to the focal point is called the **focal length** of the mirror.

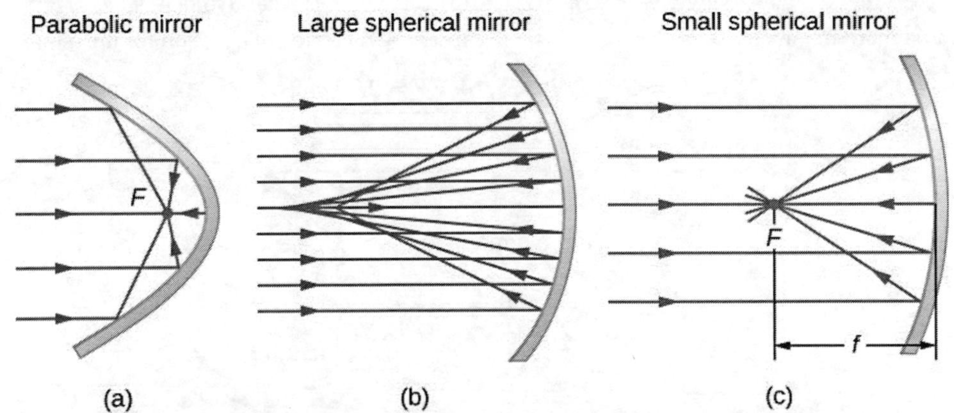

Figure 2.6 (a) Parallel rays reflected from a parabolic mirror cross at a single point called the focal point F. (b) Parallel rays reflected from a large spherical mirror do not cross at a common point. (c) If a spherical mirror is small compared with its radius of curvature, it better approximates the central part of a parabolic mirror, so parallel rays essentially cross at a common point. The distance along the optical axis from the mirror to the focal point is the focal length f of the mirror.

A convex spherical mirror also has a focal point, as shown in Figure 2.7. Incident rays parallel to the optical axis are reflected from the mirror and seem to originate from point F at focal length f behind the mirror. Thus, the focal point is virtual because no real rays actually pass through it; they only appear to originate from it.

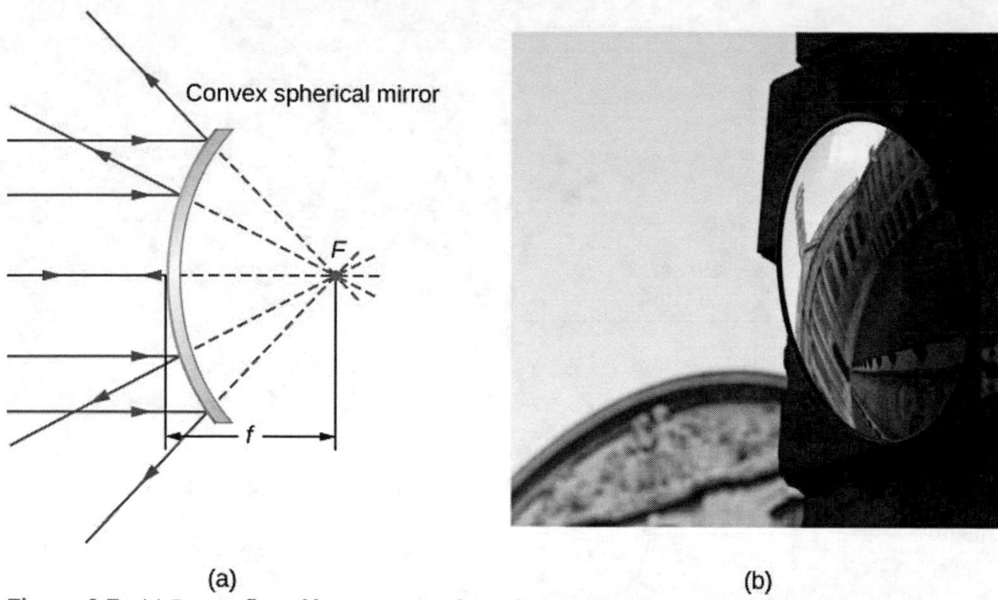

Figure 2.7 (a) Rays reflected by a convex spherical mirror: Incident rays of light parallel to the optical axis are reflected from a convex spherical mirror and seem to originate from a well-defined focal point at focal distance f on the opposite side of the mirror. The focal point is virtual because no real rays pass through it. (b) Photograph of a virtual image formed by a convex mirror. (credit b: modification of work by Jenny Downing)

How does the focal length of a mirror relate to the mirror's radius of curvature? **Figure 2.8** shows a single ray that is reflected by a spherical concave mirror. The incident ray is parallel to the optical axis. The point at which the reflected ray crosses the optical axis is the focal point. Note that all incident rays that are parallel to the optical axis are reflected through the focal point—we only show one ray for simplicity. We want to find how the focal length *FP* (denoted by *f*) relates to the radius of curvature of the mirror, *R*, whose length is $R = CF + FP$. The law of reflection tells us that angles *OXC* and *CXF* are the same, and because the incident ray is parallel to the optical axis, angles *OXC* and *XCP* are also the same. Thus, triangle *CXF* is an isosceles triangle with $CF = FX$. If the angle θ is small (so that $\sin\theta \approx \theta$; this is called the "small-angle approximation"), then $FX \approx FP$ or $CF \approx FP$. Inserting this into the equation for the radius *R*, we get

$$R = CF + FP = FP + FP = 2FP = 2f$$

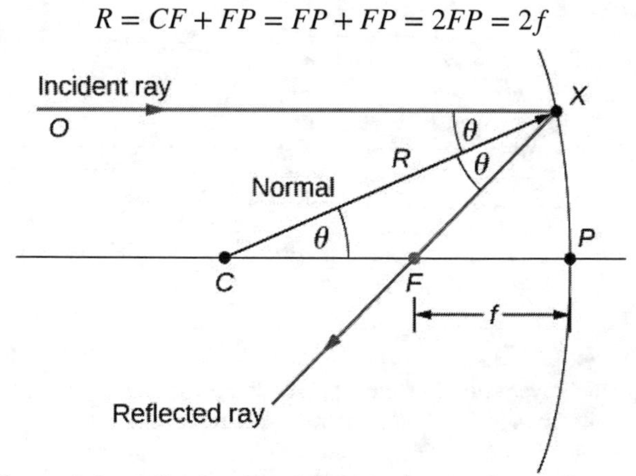

Figure 2.8 Reflection in a concave mirror. In the small-angle approximation, a ray that is parallel to the optical axis *CP* is reflected through the focal point *F* of the mirror.

In other words, in the small-angle approximation, the focal length f of a concave spherical mirror is half of its radius of curvature, *R*:

$$f = \frac{R}{2}. \tag{2.2}$$

In this chapter, we assume that the **small-angle approximation** (also called the paraxial approximation) is always valid. In this approximation, all rays are paraxial rays, which means that they make a small angle with the optical axis and are at a distance much less than the radius of curvature from the optical axis. In this case, their angles θ of reflection are small angles, so $\sin\theta \approx \tan\theta \approx \theta$.

Using Ray Tracing to Locate Images

To find the location of an image formed by a spherical mirror, we first use ray tracing, which is the technique of drawing rays and using the law of reflection to determine the reflected rays (later, for lenses, we use the law of refraction to determine refracted rays). Combined with some basic geometry, we can use ray tracing to find the focal point, the image location, and other information about how a mirror manipulates light. In fact, we already used ray tracing above to locate the focal point of spherical mirrors, or the image distance of flat mirrors. To locate the image of an object, you must locate at least two points of the image. Locating each point requires drawing at least two rays from a point on the object and constructing their reflected rays. The point at which the reflected rays intersect, either in real space or in virtual space, is where the corresponding point of the image is located. To make ray tracing easier, we concentrate on four "principal" rays whose reflections are easy to construct.

Figure 2.9 shows a concave mirror and a convex mirror, each with an arrow-shaped object in front of it. These are the objects whose images we want to locate by ray tracing. To do so, we draw rays from point *Q* that is on the object but not on the optical axis. We choose to draw our ray from the tip of the object. Principal ray 1 goes from point *Q* and travels parallel to the optical axis. The reflection of this ray must pass through the focal point, as discussed above. Thus, for the concave mirror, the reflection of principal ray 1 goes through focal point *F*, as shown in part (b) of the figure. For the convex mirror, the backward extension of the reflection of principal ray 1 goes through the focal point (i.e., a virtual focus). Principal ray 2 travels first on the line going through the focal point and then is reflected back along a line parallel to the optical axis. Principal ray 3 travels toward the center of curvature of the mirror, so it strikes the mirror at normal incidence and is reflected back along the line from which it came. Finally, principal ray 4 strikes the vertex of the mirror and is reflected symmetrically about the optical axis.

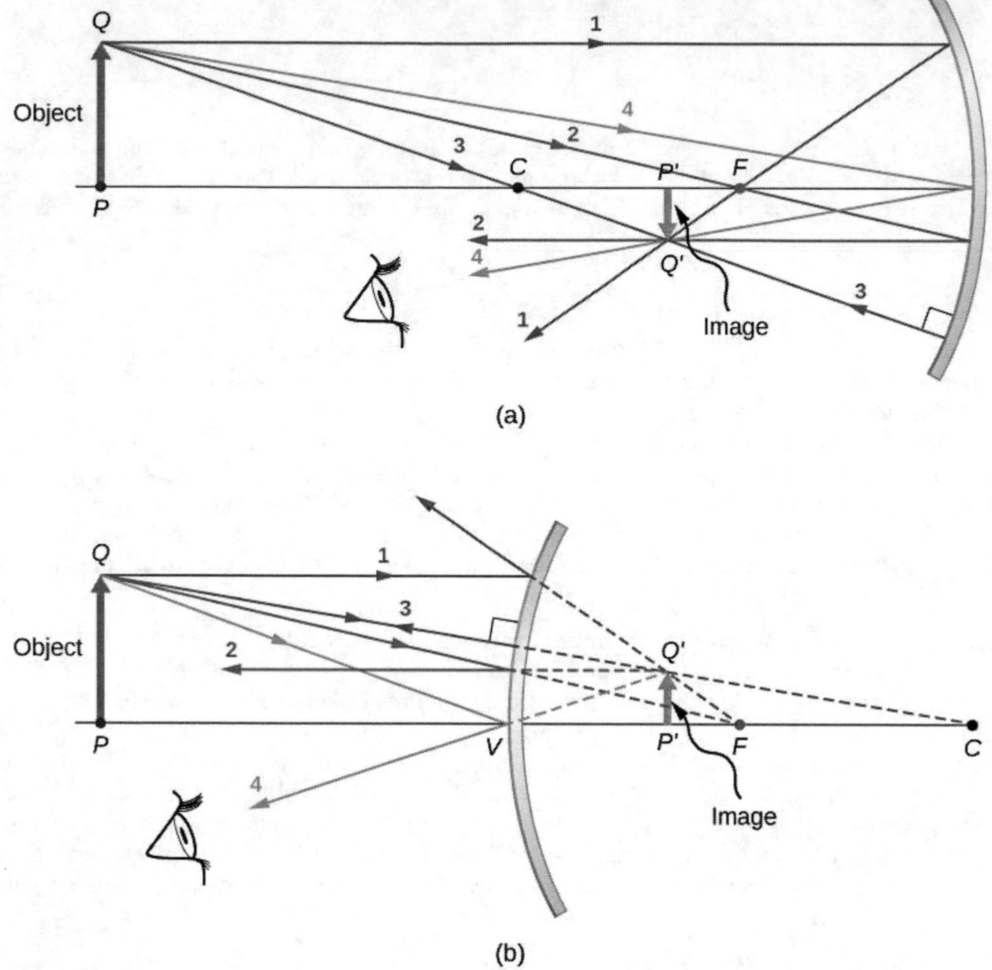

Figure 2.9 The four principal rays shown for both (a) a concave mirror and (b) a convex mirror. The image forms where the rays intersect (for real images) or where their backward extensions intersect (for virtual images).

The four principal rays intersect at point Q', which is where the image of point Q is located. To locate point Q', drawing any two of these principle rays would suffice. We are thus free to choose whichever of the principal rays we desire to locate the image. Drawing more than two principal rays is sometimes useful to verify that the ray tracing is correct.

To completely locate the extended image, we need to locate a second point in the image, so that we know how the image is oriented. To do this, we trace the principal rays from the base of the object. In this case, all four principal rays run along the optical axis, reflect from the mirror, and then run back along the optical axis. The difficulty is that, because these rays are collinear, we cannot determine a unique point where they intersect. All we know is that the base of the image is on the optical axis. However, because the mirror is symmetrical from top to bottom, it does not change the vertical orientation of the object. Thus, because the object is vertical, the image must be vertical. Therefore, the image of the base of the object is on the optical axis directly above the image of the tip, as drawn in the figure.

For the concave mirror, the extended image in this case forms between the focal point and the center of curvature of the mirror. It is inverted with respect to the object, is a real image, and is smaller than the object. Were we to move the object closer to or farther from the mirror, the characteristics of the image would change. For example, we show, as a later exercise, that an object placed between a concave mirror and its focal point leads to a virtual image that is upright and larger than the object. For the convex mirror, the extended image forms between the focal point and the mirror. It is upright with respect to the object, is a virtual image, and is smaller than the object.

Summary of Ray-Tracing Rules

Ray tracing is very useful for mirrors. The rules for ray tracing are summarized here for reference:

- A ray travelling parallel to the optical axis of a spherical mirror is reflected along a line that goes through the focal point of the mirror (ray 1 in **Figure 2.9**).

- A ray travelling along a line that goes through the focal point of a spherical mirror is reflected along a line parallel to the optical axis of the mirror (ray 2 in **Figure 2.9**).
- A ray travelling along a line that goes through the center of curvature of a spherical mirror is reflected back along the same line (ray 3 in **Figure 2.9**).
- A ray that strikes the vertex of a spherical mirror is reflected symmetrically about the optical axis of the mirror (ray 4 in **Figure 2.9**).

We use ray tracing to illustrate how images are formed by mirrors and to obtain numerical information about optical properties of the mirror. If we assume that a mirror is small compared with its radius of curvature, we can also use algebra and geometry to derive a mirror equation, which we do in the next section. Combining ray tracing with the mirror equation is a good way to analyze mirror systems.

Image Formation by Reflection—The Mirror Equation

For a plane mirror, we showed that the image formed has the same height and orientation as the object, and it is located at the same distance behind the mirror as the object is in front of the mirror. Although the situation is a bit more complicated for curved mirrors, using geometry leads to simple formulas relating the object and image distances to the focal lengths of concave and convex mirrors.

Consider the object *OP* shown in **Figure 2.10**. The center of curvature of the mirror is labeled *C* and is a distance *R* from the vertex of the mirror, as marked in the figure. The object and image distances are labeled d_o and d_i, and the object and image heights are labeled h_o and h_i, respectively. Because the angles ϕ and ϕ' are alternate interior angles, we know that they have the same magnitude. However, they must differ in sign if we measure angles from the optical axis, so $\phi = -\phi'$. An analogous scenario holds for the angles θ and θ'. The law of reflection tells us that they have the same magnitude, but their signs must differ if we measure angles from the optical axis. Thus, $\theta = -\theta'$. Taking the tangent of the angles θ and θ', and using the property that $\tan(-\theta) = -\tan\theta$, gives us

$$\left.\begin{array}{l}\tan\theta = \dfrac{h_o}{d_o}\\[2ex] \tan\theta' = -\tan\theta = \dfrac{h_i}{d_i}\end{array}\right\}\frac{h_o}{d_o} = -\frac{h_i}{d_i} \text{ or } -\frac{h_o}{h_i} = \frac{d_o}{d_i}. \tag{2.3}$$

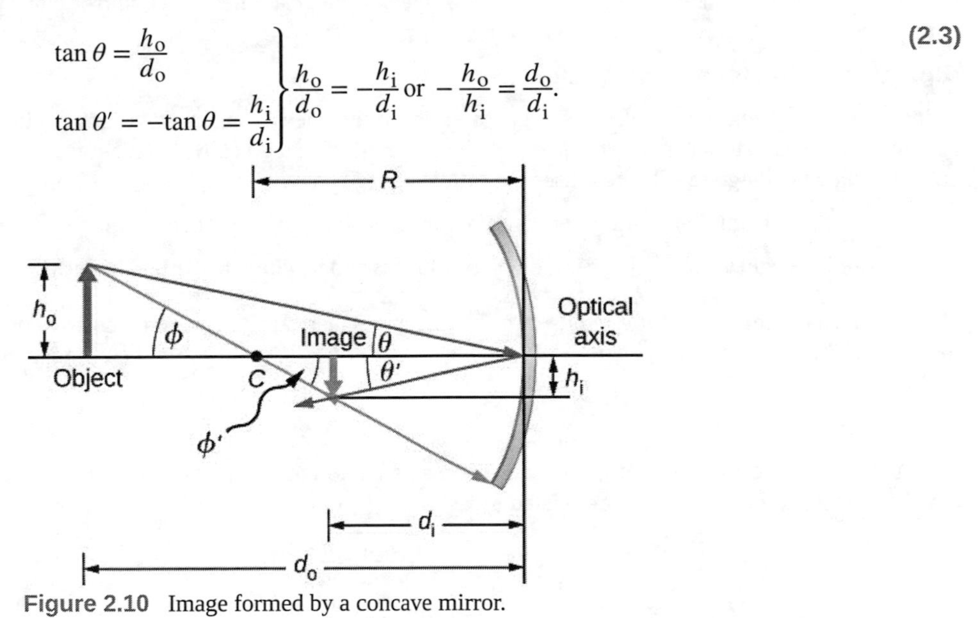

Figure 2.10 Image formed by a concave mirror.

Similarly, taking the tangent of ϕ and ϕ' gives

$$\left.\begin{array}{l}\tan\phi = \dfrac{h_o}{d_o - R}\\[2ex] \tan\phi' = -\tan\phi = \dfrac{h_i}{R - d_i}\end{array}\right\}\frac{h_o}{d_o - R} = -\frac{h_i}{R - d_i} \text{ or } -\frac{h_o}{h_i} = \frac{d_o - R}{R - d_i}.$$

Combining these two results gives

$$\frac{d_o}{d_i} = \frac{d_o - R}{R - d_i}.$$

After a little algebra, this becomes

$$\frac{1}{d_o} + \frac{1}{d_i} = \frac{2}{R}. \tag{2.4}$$

No approximation is required for this result, so it is exact. However, as discussed above, in the small-angle approximation, the focal length of a spherical mirror is one-half the radius of curvature of the mirror, or $f = R/2$. Inserting this into **Equation 2.3** gives the *mirror equation*:

$$\frac{1}{d_o} + \frac{1}{d_i} = \frac{1}{f}. \tag{2.5}$$

The mirror equation relates the image and object distances to the focal distance and is valid only in the small-angle approximation. Although it was derived for a concave mirror, it also holds for convex mirrors (proving this is left as an exercise). We can extend the mirror equation to the case of a plane mirror by noting that a plane mirror has an infinite radius of curvature. This means the focal point is at infinity, so the mirror equation simplifies to

$$d_o = -d_i \tag{2.6}$$

which is the same as **Equation 2.1** obtained earlier.

Notice that we have been very careful with the signs in deriving the mirror equation. For a plane mirror, the image distance has the opposite sign of the object distance. Also, the real image formed by the concave mirror in **Figure 2.10** is on the opposite side of the optical axis with respect to the object. In this case, the image height should have the opposite sign of the object height. To keep track of the signs of the various quantities in the mirror equation, we now introduce a sign convention.

Sign convention for spherical mirrors

Using a consistent sign convention is very important in geometric optics. It assigns positive or negative values for the quantities that characterize an optical system. Understanding the sign convention allows you to describe an image without constructing a ray diagram. This text uses the following sign convention:

1. The focal length f is positive for concave mirrors and negative for convex mirrors.
2. The image distance d_i is positive for real images and negative for virtual images.

Notice that rule 1 means that the radius of curvature of a spherical mirror can be positive or negative. What does it mean to have a negative radius of curvature? This means simply that the radius of curvature for a convex mirror is defined to be negative.

Image magnification

Let's use the sign convention to further interpret the derivation of the mirror equation. In deriving this equation, we found that the object and image heights are related by

$$-\frac{h_o}{h_i} = \frac{d_o}{d_i}. \tag{2.7}$$

See **Equation 2.3**. Both the object and the image formed by the mirror in **Figure 2.10** are real, so the object and image distances are both positive. The highest point of the object is above the optical axis, so the object height is positive. The image, however, is below the optical axis, so the image height is negative. Thus, this sign convention is consistent with our derivation of the mirror equation.

Equation 2.7 in fact describes the **linear magnification** (often simply called "magnification") of the image in terms of the object and image distances. We thus define the dimensionless magnification m as follows:

$$m = \frac{h_i}{h_o}. \tag{2.8}$$

If m is positive, the image is upright, and if m is negative, the image is inverted. If $|m| > 1$, the image is larger than the object, and if $|m| < 1$, the image is smaller than the object. With this definition of magnification, we get the following relation between the vertical and horizontal object and image distances:

$$m = \frac{h_\text{i}}{h_\text{o}} = -\frac{d_\text{i}}{d_\text{o}}. \tag{2.9}$$

This is a very useful relation because it lets you obtain the magnification of the image from the object and image distances, which you can obtain from the mirror equation.

Example 2.1

Solar Electric Generating System

One of the solar technologies used today for generating electricity involves a device (called a parabolic trough or concentrating collector) that concentrates sunlight onto a blackened pipe that contains a fluid. This heated fluid is pumped to a heat exchanger, where the thermal energy is transferred to another system that is used to generate steam and eventually generates electricity through a conventional steam cycle. **Figure 2.11** shows such a working system in southern California. The real mirror is a parabolic cylinder with its focus located at the pipe; however, we can approximate the mirror as exactly one-quarter of a circular cylinder.

Figure 2.11 Parabolic trough collectors are used to generate electricity in southern California. (credit: “kjkolb”/Wikimedia Commons)

a. If we want the rays from the sun to focus at 40.0 cm from the mirror, what is the radius of the mirror?

b. What is the amount of sunlight concentrated onto the pipe, per meter of pipe length, assuming the insolation (incident solar radiation) is 900 W/m^2?

c. If the fluid-carrying pipe has a 2.00-cm diameter, what is the temperature increase of the fluid per meter of pipe over a period of 1 minute? Assume that all solar radiation incident on the reflector is absorbed by the pipe, and that the fluid is mineral oil.

Strategy

First identify the physical principles involved. Part (a) is related to the optics of spherical mirrors. Part (b) involves a little math, primarily geometry. Part (c) requires an understanding of heat and density.

Solution

a. The sun is the object, so the object distance is essentially infinity: $d_\text{o} = \infty$. The desired image distance is $d_\text{i} = 40.0\ \text{cm}$. We use the mirror equation to find the focal length of the mirror:

$$\begin{aligned}\frac{1}{d_o} + \frac{1}{d_i} &= \frac{1}{f} \\ f &= \left(\frac{1}{d_o} + \frac{1}{d_i}\right)^{-1} \\ &= \left(\frac{1}{\infty} + \frac{1}{40.0\ \text{cm}}\right)^{-1} \\ &= 40.0\ \text{cm}\end{aligned}$$

Thus, the radius of the mirror is $R = 2f = 80.0\ \text{cm}$.

b. The insolation is 900 W/m^2. You must find the cross-sectional area *A* of the concave mirror, since the power delivered is 900 $\text{W/m}^2 \times A$. The mirror in this case is a quarter-section of a cylinder, so the area for a length *L* of the mirror is $A = \frac{1}{4}(2\pi R)L$. The area for a length of 1.00 m is then

$$A = \frac{\pi}{2}R(1.00\ \text{m}) = \frac{(3.14)}{2}(0.800\ \text{m})(1.00\ \text{m}) = 1.26\ \text{m}^2.$$

The insolation on the 1.00-m length of pipe is then

$$\left(9.00 \times 10^2 \frac{\text{W}}{\text{m}^2}\right)\left(1.26\ \text{m}^2\right) = 1130\ \text{W}.$$

c. The increase in temperature is given by $Q = mc\Delta T$. The mass *m* of the mineral oil in the one-meter section of pipe is

$$\begin{aligned}m &= \rho V = \rho\pi\left(\frac{d}{2}\right)^2 (1.00\ \text{m}) \\ &= \left(8.00 \times 10^2\ \text{kg/m}^3\right)(3.14)(0.0100\ \text{m})^2(1.00\ \text{m}) \\ &= 0.251\ \text{kg}\end{aligned}$$

Therefore, the increase in temperature in one minute is

$$\begin{aligned}\Delta T &= Q/mc \\ &= \frac{(1130\ \text{W})(60.0\ \text{s})}{(0.251\ \text{kg})(1670\ \text{J} \cdot \text{kg/°C})} \\ &= 162\text{°C}\end{aligned}$$

Significance

An array of such pipes in the California desert can provide a thermal output of 250 MW on a sunny day, with fluids reaching temperatures as high as 400°C. We are considering only one meter of pipe here and ignoring heat losses along the pipe.

Example 2.2

Image in a Convex Mirror

A keratometer is a device used to measure the curvature of the cornea of the eye, particularly for fitting contact lenses. Light is reflected from the cornea, which acts like a convex mirror, and the keratometer measures the magnification of the image. The smaller the magnification, the smaller the radius of curvature of the cornea. If the light source is 12 cm from the cornea and the image magnification is 0.032, what is the radius of curvature of the cornea?

Strategy

If you find the focal length of the convex mirror formed by the cornea, then you know its radius of curvature (it's twice the focal length). The object distance is $d_o = 12\text{ cm}$ and the magnification is $m = 0.032$. First find the image distance d_i and then solve for the focal length *f*.

Solution

Start with the equation for magnification, $m = -d_i/d_o$. Solving for d_i and inserting the given values yields

$$d_i = -md_o = -(0.032)(12\text{ cm}) = -0.384\text{ cm}$$

where we retained an extra significant figure because this is an intermediate step in the calculation. Solve the mirror equation for the focal length *f* and insert the known values for the object and image distances. The result is

$$\begin{aligned} \frac{1}{d_o} + \frac{1}{d_i} &= \frac{1}{f} \\ f &= \left(\frac{1}{d_o} + \frac{1}{d_i}\right)^{-1} \\ &= \left(\frac{1}{12\text{ cm}} + \frac{1}{-0.384\text{ cm}}\right)^{-1} \\ &= -0.40\text{ cm} \end{aligned}$$

The radius of curvature is twice the focal length, so

$$R = 2f = -0.80\text{ cm}$$

Significance

The focal length is negative, so the focus is virtual, as expected for a concave mirror and a real object. The radius of curvature found here is reasonable for a cornea. The distance from cornea to retina in an adult eye is about 2.0 cm. In practice, corneas may not be spherical, which complicates the job of fitting contact lenses. Note that the image distance here is negative, consistent with the fact that the image is behind the mirror. Thus, the image is virtual because no rays actually pass through it. In the problems and exercises, you will show that, for a fixed object distance, a smaller radius of curvature corresponds to a smaller the magnification.

Problem-Solving Strategy: Spherical Mirrors

Step 1. First make sure that image formation by a spherical mirror is involved.

Step 2. Determine whether ray tracing, the mirror equation, or both are required. A sketch is very useful even if ray tracing is not specifically required by the problem. Write symbols and known values on the sketch.

Step 3. Identify exactly what needs to be determined in the problem (identify the unknowns).

Step 4. Make a list of what is given or can be inferred from the problem as stated (identify the knowns).

Step 5. If ray tracing is required, use the ray-tracing rules listed near the beginning of this section.

Step 6. Most quantitative problems require using the mirror equation. Use the examples as guides for using the mirror equation.

Step 7. Check to see whether the answer makes sense. Do the signs of object distance, image distance, and focal length correspond with what is expected from ray tracing? Is the sign of the magnification correct? Are the object and image distances reasonable?

Departure from the Small-Angle Approximation

The small-angle approximation is a cornerstone of the above discussion of image formation by a spherical mirror. When this approximation is violated, then the image created by a spherical mirror becomes distorted. Such distortion is called **aberration**. Here we briefly discuss two specific types of aberrations: spherical aberration and coma.

Spherical aberration

Consider a broad beam of parallel rays impinging on a spherical mirror, as shown in **Figure 2.12**.

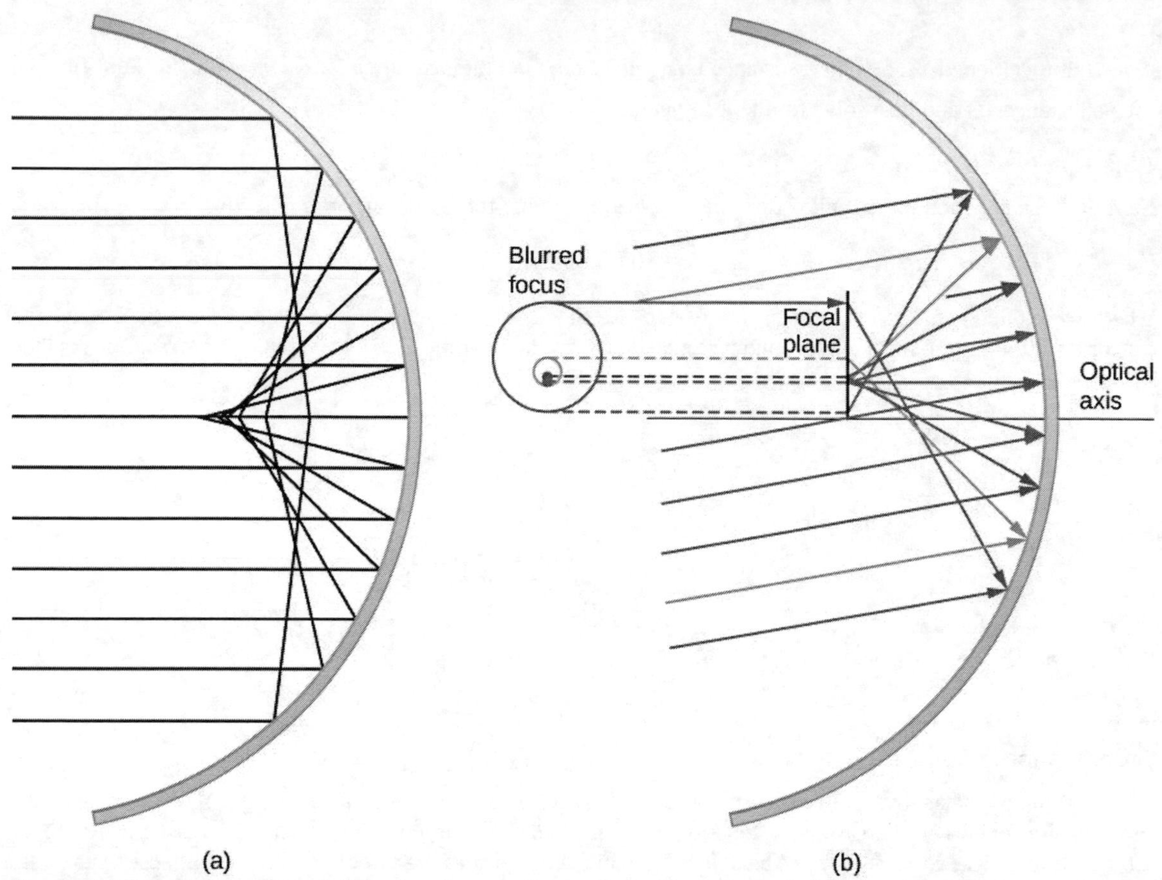

Figure 2.12 (a) With spherical aberration, the rays that are farther from the optical axis and the rays that are closer to the optical axis are focused at different points. Notice that the aberration gets worse for rays farther from the optical axis. (b) For comatic aberration, parallel rays that are not parallel to the optical axis are focused at different heights and at different focal lengths, so the image contains a "tail" like a comet (which is "coma" in Latin). Note that the colored rays are only to facilitate viewing; the colors do not indicate the color of the light.

The farther from the optical axis the rays strike, the worse the spherical mirror approximates a parabolic mirror. Thus, these rays are not focused at the same point as rays that are near the optical axis, as shown in the figure. Because of **spherical aberration**, the image of an extended object in a spherical mirror will be blurred. Spherical aberrations are characteristic of the mirrors and lenses that we consider in the following section of this chapter (more sophisticated mirrors and lenses are needed to eliminate spherical aberrations).

Coma or comatic aberration

Coma is similar to spherical aberration, but arises when the incoming rays are not parallel to the optical axis, as shown in part (b) of Figure 2.12. Recall that the small-angle approximation holds for spherical mirrors that are small compared to their radius. In this case, spherical mirrors are good approximations of parabolic mirrors. Parabolic mirrors focus all rays that are parallel to the optical axis at the focal point. However, parallel rays that are *not* parallel to the optical axis are focused at different heights and at different focal lengths, as show in part (b) of Figure 2.12. Because a spherical mirror is symmetric about the optical axis, the various colored rays in this figure create circles of the corresponding color on the focal plane.

Although a spherical mirror is shown in part (b) of Figure 2.12, comatic aberration occurs also for parabolic mirrors—it does not result from a breakdown in the small-angle approximation. Spherical aberration, however, occurs only for spherical mirrors and is a result of a breakdown in the small-angle approximation. We will discuss both coma and spherical aberration later in this chapter, in connection with telescopes.

2.3 | Images Formed by Refraction

Learning Objectives

By the end of this section, you will be able to:

- Describe image formation by a single refracting surface
- Determine the location of an image and calculate its properties by using a ray diagram
- Determine the location of an image and calculate its properties by using the equation for a single refracting surface

When rays of light propagate from one medium to another, these rays undergo refraction, which is when light waves are bent at the interface between two media. The refracting surface can form an image in a similar fashion to a reflecting surface, except that the law of refraction (Snell's law) is at the heart of the process instead of the law of reflection.

Refraction at a Plane Interface—Apparent Depth

If you look at a straight rod partially submerged in water, it appears to bend at the surface (**Figure 2.13**). The reason behind this curious effect is that the image of the rod inside the water forms a little closer to the surface than the actual position of the rod, so it does not line up with the part of the rod that is above the water. The same phenomenon explains why a fish in water appears to be closer to the surface than it actually is.

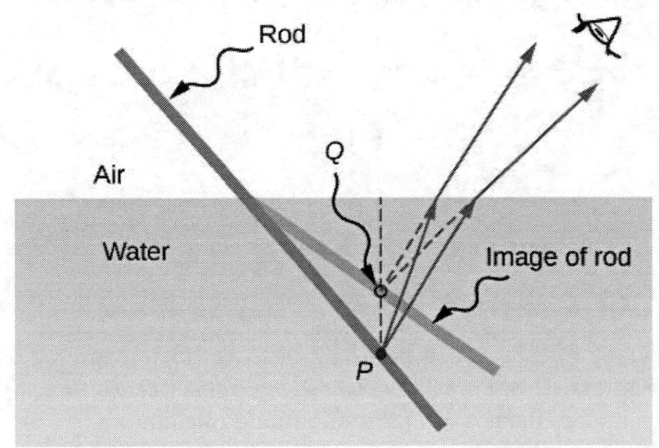

Figure 2.13 Bending of a rod at a water-air interface. Point *P* on the rod appears to be at point *Q*, which is where the image of point *P* forms due to refraction at the air-water interface.

To study image formation as a result of refraction, consider the following questions:

1. What happens to the rays of light when they enter or pass through a different medium?
2. Do the refracted rays originating from a single point meet at some point or diverge away from each other?

To be concrete, we consider a simple system consisting of two media separated by a plane interface (**Figure 2.14**). The object is in one medium and the observer is in the other. For instance, when you look at a fish from above the water surface, the fish is in medium 1 (the water) with refractive index 1.33, and your eye is in medium 2 (the air) with refractive index 1.00, and the surface of the water is the interface. The depth that you "see" is the image height h_i and is called the **apparent depth**. The actual depth of the fish is the object height h_o.

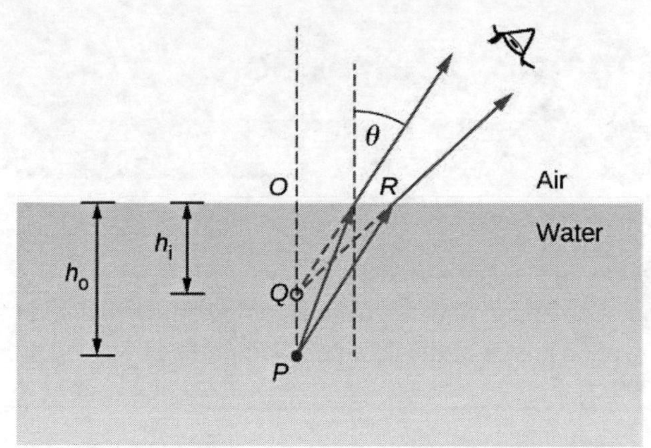

Figure 2.14 Apparent depth due to refraction. The real object at point *P* creates an image at point *Q*. The image is not at the same depth as the object, so the observer sees the image at an "apparent depth."

The apparent depth h_i depends on the angle at which you view the image. For a view from above (the so-called "normal" view), we can approximate the refraction angle θ to be small, and replace sin θ in Snell's law by tan θ. With this approximation, you can use the triangles ΔOPR and ΔOQR to show that the apparent depth is given by

$$h_i = \left(\frac{n_2}{n_1}\right)h_o. \tag{2.10}$$

The derivation of this result is left as an exercise. Thus, a fish appears at 3/4 of the real depth when viewed from above.

Refraction at a Spherical Interface

Spherical shapes play an important role in optics primarily because high-quality spherical shapes are far easier to manufacture than other curved surfaces. To study refraction at a single spherical surface, we assume that the medium with the spherical surface at one end continues indefinitely (a "semi-infinite" medium).

Refraction at a convex surface

Consider a point source of light at point *P* in front of a convex surface made of glass (see **Figure 2.15**). Let *R* be the radius of curvature, n_1 be the refractive index of the medium in which object point *P* is located, and n_2 be the refractive index of the medium with the spherical surface. We want to know what happens as a result of refraction at this interface.

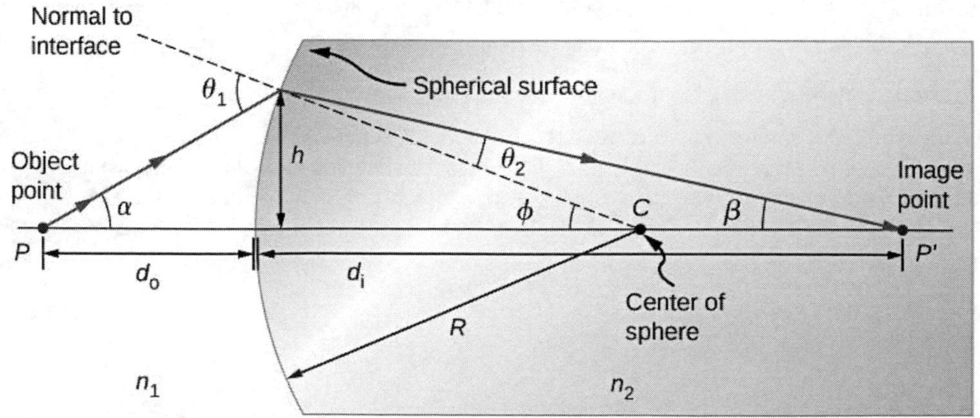

Figure 2.15 Refraction at a convex surface $(n_2 > n_1)$.

Because of the symmetry involved, it is sufficient to examine rays in only one plane. The figure shows a ray of light that starts at the object point *P*, refracts at the interface, and goes through the image point P'. We derive a formula relating the object distance d_o, the image distance d_i, and the radius of curvature *R*.

Applying Snell's law to the ray emanating from point *P* gives $n_1 \sin \theta_1 = n_2 \sin \theta_2$. We work in the small-angle approximation, so $\sin \theta \approx \theta$ and Snell's law then takes the form

$$n_1 \theta_1 \approx n_2 \theta_2.$$

From the geometry of the figure, we see that

$$\theta_1 = \alpha + \phi, \quad \theta_2 = \phi - \beta.$$

Inserting these expressions into Snell's law gives

$$n_1(\alpha + \phi) \approx n_2(\phi - \beta).$$

Using the diagram, we calculate the tangent of the angles α, β, and ϕ:

$$\tan \alpha \approx \frac{h}{d_o}, \quad \tan \beta \approx \frac{h}{d_i}, \quad \tan \phi \approx \frac{h}{R}.$$

Again using the small-angle approximation, we find that $\tan \theta \approx \theta$, so the above relationships become

$$\alpha \approx \frac{h}{d_o}, \quad \beta \approx \frac{h}{d_i}, \quad \phi \approx \frac{h}{R}.$$

Putting these angles into Snell's law gives

$$n_1\left(\frac{h}{d_o} + \frac{h}{R}\right) = n_2\left(\frac{h}{R} - \frac{h}{d_i}\right).$$

We can write this more conveniently as

$$\frac{n_1}{d_o} + \frac{n_2}{d_i} = \frac{n_2 - n_1}{R}. \tag{2.11}$$

If the object is placed at a special point called the **first focus**, or the **object focus** F_1, then the image is formed at infinity, as shown in part (a) of **Figure 2.16**.

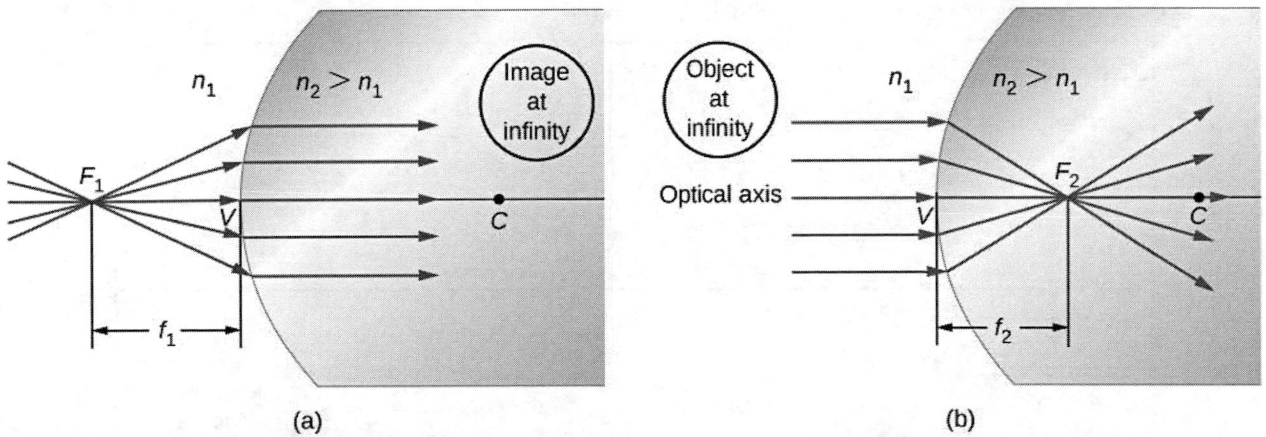

Figure 2.16 (a) First focus (called the "object focus") for refraction at a convex surface. (b) Second focus (called "image focus") for refraction at a convex surface.

We can find the location f_1 of the first focus F_1 by setting $d_i = \infty$ in the preceding equation.

$$\frac{n_1}{f_1} + \frac{n_2}{\infty} = \frac{n_2 - n_1}{R} \tag{2.12}$$

$$f_1 = \frac{n_1 R}{n_2 - n_1} \tag{2.13}$$

Similarly, we can define a **second focus** or **image focus** F_2 where the image is formed for an object that is far away [part (b)]. The location of the second focus F_2 is obtained from **Equation 2.11** by setting $d_o = \infty$:

$$\frac{n_1}{\infty} + \frac{n_2}{f_2} = \frac{n_2 - n_1}{R}$$

$$f_2 = \frac{n_2 R}{n_2 - n_1}.$$

Note that the object focus is at a different distance from the vertex than the image focus because $n_1 \neq n_2$.

Sign convention for single refracting surfaces

Although we derived this equation for refraction at a convex surface, the same expression holds for a concave surface, provided we use the following sign convention:

1. $R > 0$ if surface is convex toward object; otherwise, $R < 0$.
2. $d_i > 0$ if image is real and on opposite side from the object; otherwise, $d_i < 0$.

2.4 | Thin Lenses

Learning Objectives

By the end of this section, you will be able to:

- Use ray diagrams to locate and describe the image formed by a lens
- Employ the thin-lens equation to describe and locate the image formed by a lens

Lenses are found in a huge array of optical instruments, ranging from a simple magnifying glass to a camera's zoom lens to the eye itself. In this section, we use the Snell's law to explore the properties of lenses and how they form images.

The word "lens" derives from the Latin word for a lentil bean, the shape of which is similar to a convex lens. However, not all lenses have the same shape. **Figure 2.17** shows a variety of different lens shapes. The vocabulary used to describe lenses is the same as that used for spherical mirrors: The axis of symmetry of a lens is called the optical axis, where this axis intersects the lens surface is called the vertex of the lens, and so forth.

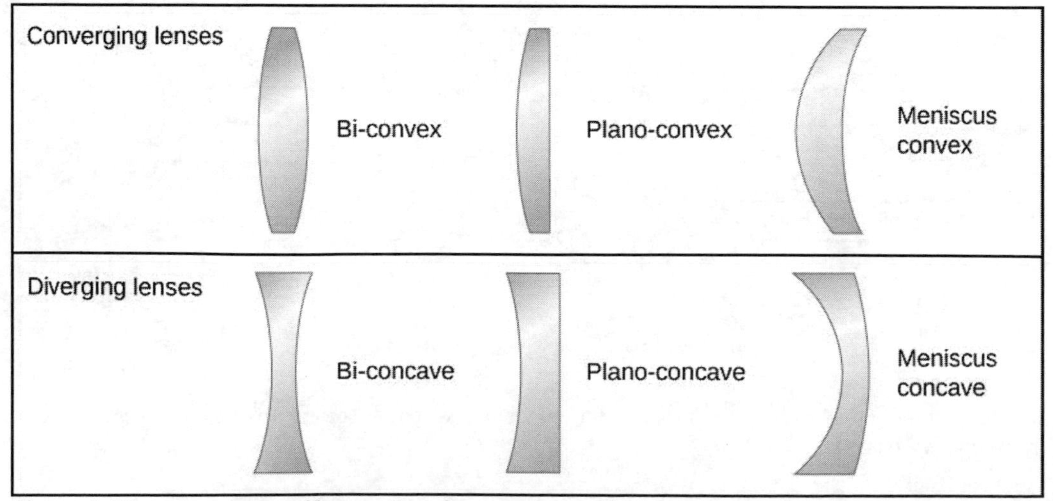

Figure 2.17 Various types of lenses: Note that a converging lens has a thicker "waist," whereas a diverging lens has a thinner waist.

A **convex** or **converging lens** is shaped so that all light rays that enter it parallel to its optical axis intersect (or focus) at a single point on the optical axis on the opposite side of the lens, as shown in part (a) of Figure 2.18. Likewise, a **concave** or **diverging lens** is shaped so that all rays that enter it parallel to its optical axis diverge, as shown in part (b). To understand more precisely how a lens manipulates light, look closely at the top ray that goes through the converging lens in part (a). Because the index of refraction of the lens is greater than that of air, Snell's law tells us that the ray is bent toward the perpendicular to the interface as it enters the lens. Likewise, when the ray exits the lens, it is bent away from the perpendicular. The same reasoning applies to the diverging lenses, as shown in part (b). The overall effect is that light rays are bent toward the optical axis for a converging lens and away from the optical axis for diverging lenses. For a converging lens, the point at which the rays cross is the focal point F of the lens. For a diverging lens, the point from which the rays appear to originate is the (virtual) focal point. The distance from the center of the lens to its focal point is the focal length f of the lens.

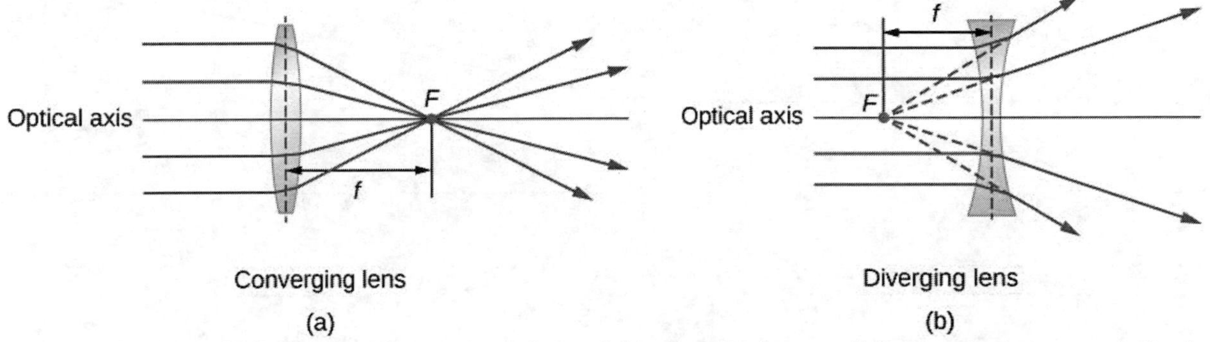

Figure 2.18 Rays of light entering (a) a converging lens and (b) a diverging lens, parallel to its axis, converge at its focal point F. The distance from the center of the lens to the focal point is the lens's focal length f. Note that the light rays are bent upon entering and exiting the lens, with the overall effect being to bend the rays toward the optical axis.

A lens is considered to be thin if its thickness t is much less than the radii of curvature of both surfaces, as shown in Figure 2.19. In this case, the rays may be considered to bend once at the center of the lens. For the case drawn in the figure, light ray 1 is parallel to the optical axis, so the outgoing ray is bent once at the center of the lens and goes through the focal point. Another important characteristic of thin lenses is that light rays that pass through the center of the lens are undeviated, as shown by light ray 2.

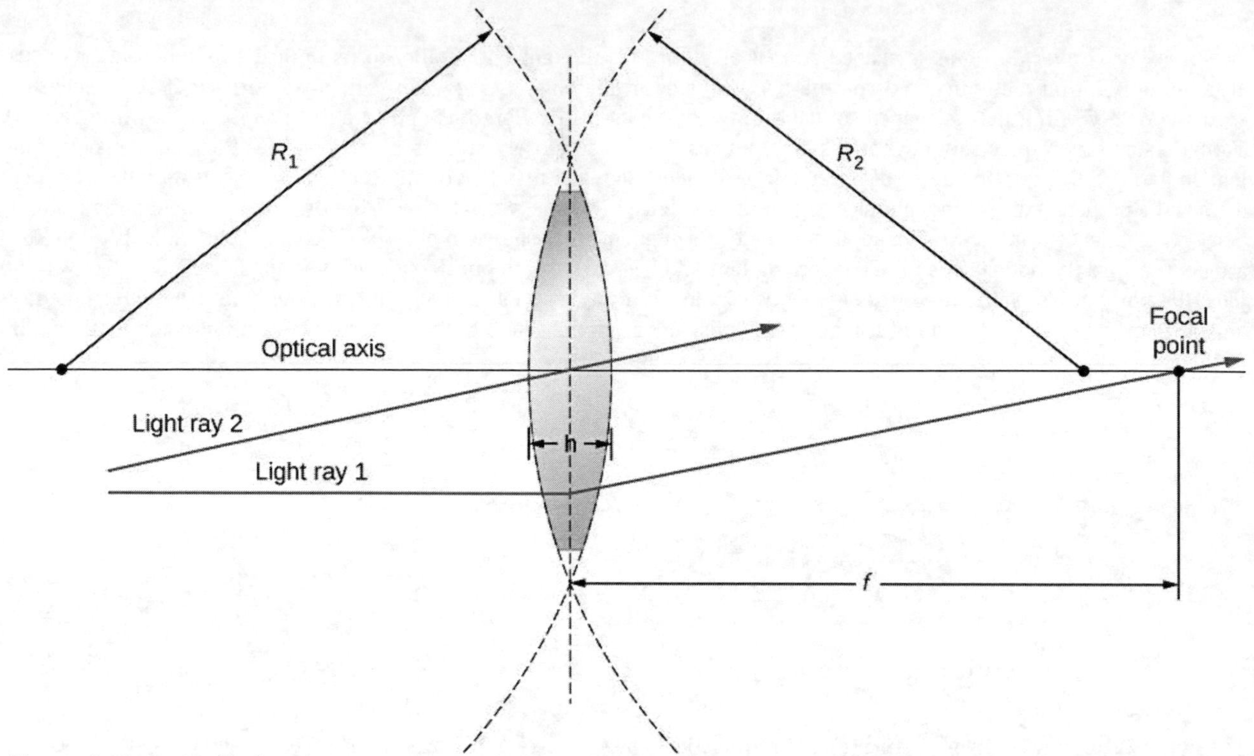

Figure 2.19 In the thin-lens approximation, the thickness d of the lens is much, much less than the radii R_1 and R_2 of curvature of the surfaces of the lens. Light rays are considered to bend at the center of the lens, such as light ray 1. Light ray 2 passes through the center of the lens and is undeviated in the thin-lens approximation.

As noted in the initial discussion of Snell's law, the paths of light rays are exactly reversible. This means that the direction of the arrows could be reversed for all of the rays in **Figure 2.18**. For example, if a point-light source is placed at the focal point of a convex lens, as shown in **Figure 2.20**, parallel light rays emerge from the other side.

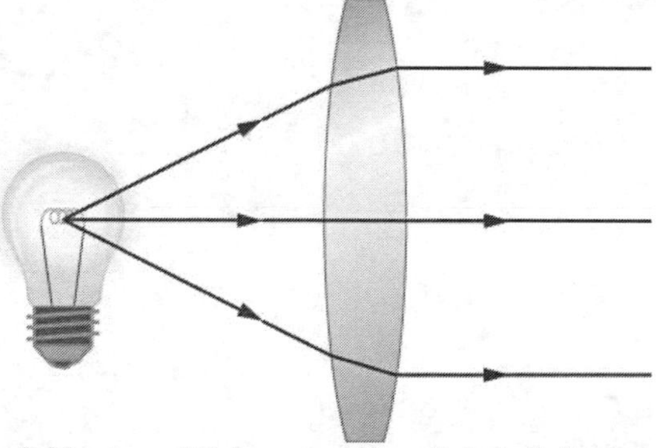

Figure 2.20 A small light source, like a light bulb filament, placed at the focal point of a convex lens results in parallel rays of light emerging from the other side. The paths are exactly the reverse of those shown in **Figure 2.18** in converging and diverging lenses. This technique is used in lighthouses and sometimes in traffic lights to produce a directional beam of light from a source that emits light in all directions.

Ray Tracing and Thin Lenses

Ray tracing is the technique of determining or following (tracing) the paths taken by light rays.

Ray tracing for thin lenses is very similar to the technique we used with spherical mirrors. As for mirrors, ray tracing can accurately describe the operation of a lens. The rules for ray tracing for thin lenses are similar to those of spherical mirrors:

1. A ray entering a converging lens parallel to the optical axis passes through the focal point on the other side of the

lens (ray 1 in part (a) of **Figure 2.21**). A ray entering a diverging lens parallel to the optical axis exits along the line that passes through the focal point on the *same* side of the lens (ray 1 in part (b) of the figure).

2. A ray passing through the center of either a converging or a diverging lens is not deviated (ray 2 in parts (a) and (b)).
3. For a converging lens, a ray that passes through the focal point exits the lens parallel to the optical axis (ray 3 in part (a)). For a diverging lens, a ray that approaches along the line that passes through the focal point on the opposite side exits the lens parallel to the axis (ray 3 in part (b)).

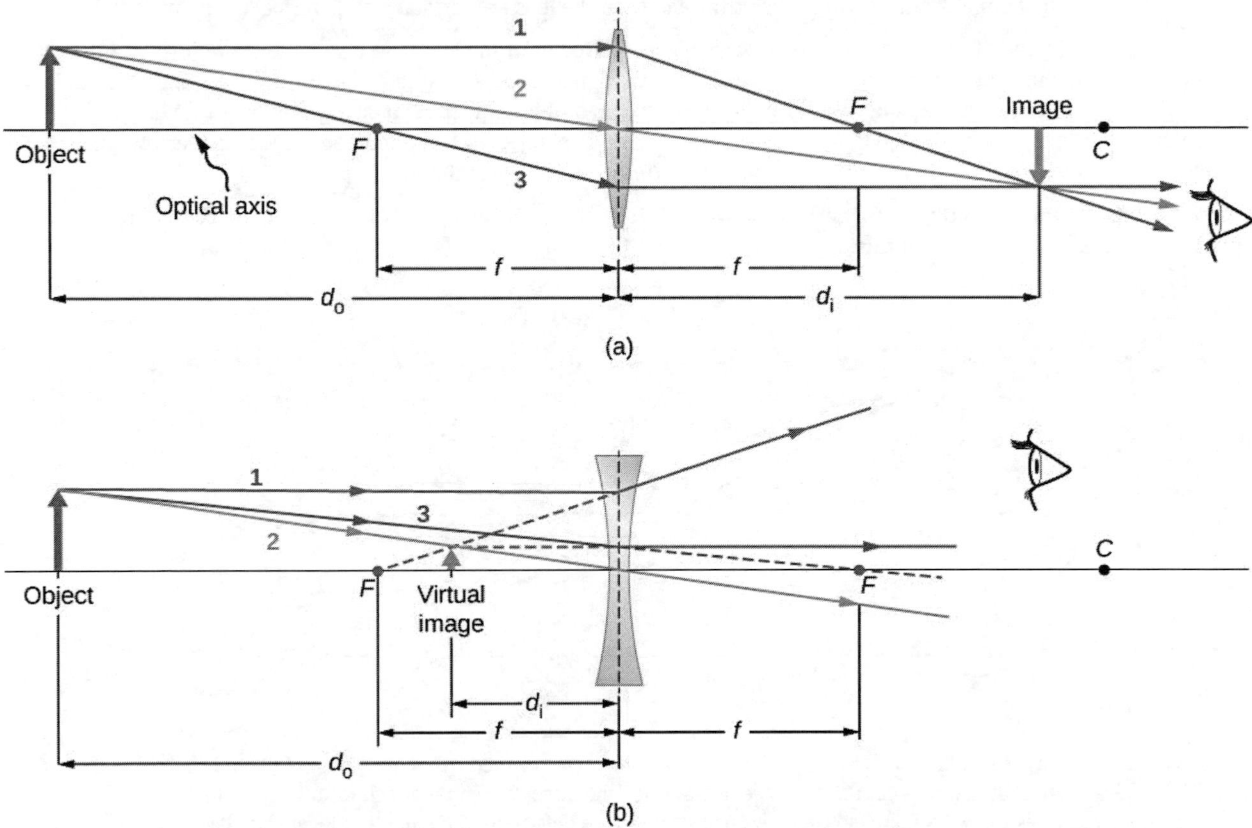

Figure 2.21 Thin lenses have the same focal lengths on either side. (a) Parallel light rays entering a converging lens from the right cross at its focal point on the left. (b) Parallel light rays entering a diverging lens from the right seem to come from the focal point on the right.

Thin lenses work quite well for monochromatic light (i.e., light of a single wavelength). However, for light that contains several wavelengths (e.g., white light), the lenses work less well. The problem is that, as we learned in the previous chapter, the index of refraction of a material depends on the wavelength of light. This phenomenon is responsible for many colorful effects, such as rainbows. Unfortunately, this phenomenon also leads to aberrations in images formed by lenses. In particular, because the focal distance of the lens depends on the index of refraction, it also depends on the wavelength of the incident light. This means that light of different wavelengths will focus at different points, resulting is so-called "chromatic aberrations." In particular, the edges of an image of a white object will become colored and blurred. Special lenses called doublets are capable of correcting chromatic aberrations. A doublet is formed by gluing together a converging lens and a diverging lens. The combined doublet lens produces significantly reduced chromatic aberrations.

Image Formation by Thin Lenses

We use ray tracing to investigate different types of images that can be created by a lens. In some circumstances, a lens forms a real image, such as when a movie projector casts an image onto a screen. In other cases, the image is a virtual image, which cannot be projected onto a screen. Where, for example, is the image formed by eyeglasses? We use ray tracing for thin lenses to illustrate how they form images, and then we develop equations to analyze quantitatively the properties of thin lenses.

Consider an object some distance away from a converging lens, as shown in **Figure 2.22**. To find the location and size of the image, we trace the paths of selected light rays originating from one point on the object, in this case, the tip of the arrow.

The figure shows three rays from many rays that emanate from the tip of the arrow. These three rays can be traced by using the ray-tracing rules given above.

- Ray 1 enters the lens parallel to the optical axis and passes through the focal point on the opposite side (rule 1).
- Ray 2 passes through the center of the lens and is not deviated (rule 2).
- Ray 3 passes through the focal point on its way to the lens and exits the lens parallel to the optical axis (rule 3).

The three rays cross at a single point on the opposite side of the lens. Thus, the image of the tip of the arrow is located at this point. All rays that come from the tip of the arrow and enter the lens are refracted and cross at the point shown.

After locating the image of the tip of the arrow, we need another point of the image to orient the entire image of the arrow. We chose to locate the image base of the arrow, which is on the optical axis. As explained in the section on spherical mirrors, the base will be on the optical axis just above the image of the tip of the arrow (due to the top-bottom symmetry of the lens). Thus, the image spans the optical axis to the (negative) height shown. Rays from another point on the arrow, such as the middle of the arrow, cross at another common point, thus filling in the rest of the image.

Although three rays are traced in this figure, only two are necessary to locate a point of the image. It is best to trace rays for which there are simple ray-tracing rules.

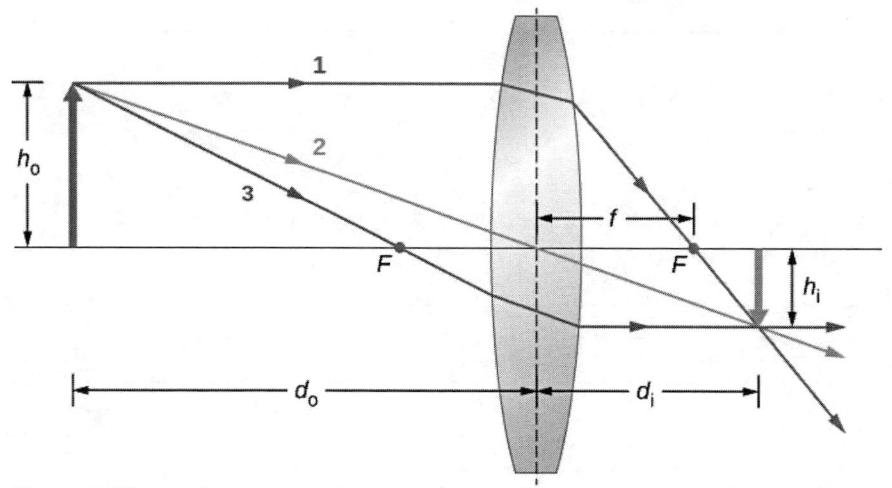

Figure 2.22 Ray tracing is used to locate the image formed by a lens. Rays originating from the same point on the object are traced—the three chosen rays each follow one of the rules for ray tracing, so that their paths are easy to determine. The image is located at the point where the rays cross. In this case, a real image—one that can be projected on a screen—is formed.

Several important distances appear in the figure. As for a mirror, we define d_o to be the object distance, or the distance of an object from the center of a lens. The image distance d_i is defined to be the distance of the image from the center of a lens. The height of the object and the height of the image are indicated by h_o and h_i, respectively. Images that appear upright relative to the object have positive heights, and those that are inverted have negative heights. By using the rules of ray tracing and making a scale drawing with paper and pencil, like that in **Figure 2.22**, we can accurately describe the location and size of an image. But the real benefit of ray tracing is in visualizing how images are formed in a variety of situations.

Oblique Parallel Rays and Focal Plane

We have seen that rays parallel to the optical axis are directed to the focal point of a converging lens. In the case of a diverging lens, they come out in a direction such that they appear to be coming from the focal point on the opposite side of the lens (i.e., the side from which parallel rays enter the lens). What happens to parallel rays that are not parallel to the optical axis (**Figure 2.23**)? In the case of a converging lens, these rays do not converge at the focal point. Instead, they come together on another point in the plane called the **focal plane**. The focal plane contains the focal point and is perpendicular to the optical axis. As shown in the figure, parallel rays focus where the ray through the center of the lens crosses the focal plane.

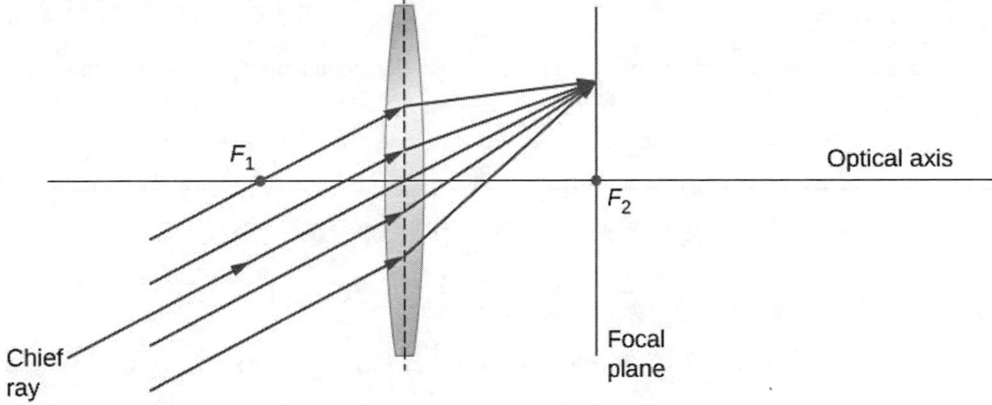

Figure 2.23 Parallel oblique rays focus on a point in a focal plane.

Thin-Lens Equation

Ray tracing allows us to get a qualitative picture of image formation. To obtain numeric information, we derive a pair of equations from a geometric analysis of ray tracing for thin lenses. These equations, called the thin-lens equation and the lens maker's equation, allow us to quantitatively analyze thin lenses.

Consider the thick bi-convex lens shown in **Figure 2.24**. The index of refraction of the surrounding medium is n_1 (if the lens is in air, then $n_1 = 1.00$) and that of the lens is n_2. The radii of curvatures of the two sides are R_1 and R_2. We wish to find a relation between the object distance d_o, the image distance d_i, and the parameters of the lens.

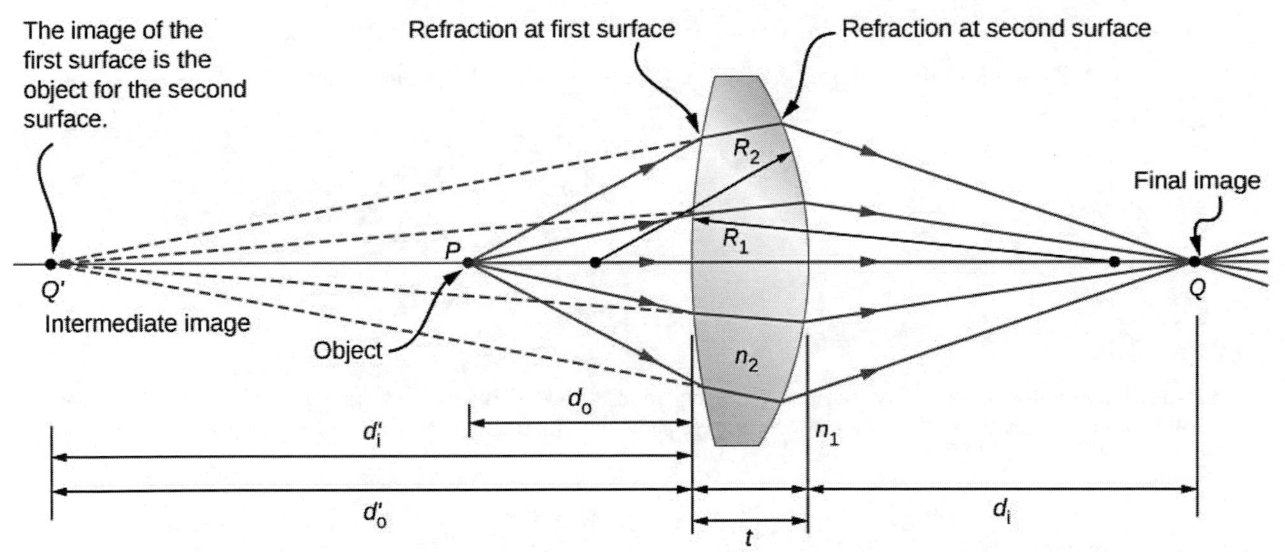

Figure 2.24 Figure for deriving the lens maker's equation. Here, *t* is the thickness of lens, n_1 is the index of refraction of the exterior medium, and n_2 is the index of refraction of the lens. We take the limit of $t \to 0$ to obtain the formula for a thin lens.

To derive the thin-lens equation, we consider the image formed by the first refracting surface (i.e., left surface) and then use this image as the object for the second refracting surface. In the figure, the image from the first refracting surface is Q', which is formed by extending backwards the rays from inside the lens (these rays result from refraction at the first surface). This is shown by the dashed lines in the figure. Notice that this image is virtual because no rays actually pass through the point Q'. To find the image distance d'_i corresponding to the image Q', we use **Equation 2.11**. In this case, the object distance is d_o, the image distance is d'_i, and the radius of curvature is R_1. Inserting these into **Equation 2.3** gives

$$\frac{n_1}{d_o} + \frac{n_2}{d'_i} = \frac{n_2 - n_1}{R_1}. \tag{2.14}$$

The image is virtual and on the same side as the object, so $d'_i < 0$ and $d_o > 0$. The first surface is convex toward the object, so $R_1 > 0$.

To find the object distance for the object Q formed by refraction from the second interface, note that the role of the indices of refraction n_1 and n_2 are interchanged in **Equation 2.11**. In **Figure 2.24**, the rays originate in the medium with index n_2, whereas in **Figure 2.15**, the rays originate in the medium with index n_1. Thus, we must interchange n_1 and n_2 in **Equation 2.11**. In addition, by consulting again **Figure 2.24**, we see that the object distance is d'_o and the image distance is d_i. The radius of curvature is R_2 Inserting these quantities into **Equation 2.11** gives

$$\frac{n_2}{d'_o} + \frac{n_1}{d_i} = \frac{n_1 - n_2}{R_2}. \tag{2.15}$$

The image is real and on the opposite side from the object, so $d_i > 0$ and $d'_o > 0$. The second surface is convex away from the object, so $R_2 < 0$. **Equation 2.15** can be simplified by noting that $d'_o = |d'_i| + t$, where we have taken the absolute value because d'_i is a negative number, whereas both d'_o and t are positive. We can dispense with the absolute value if we negate d'_i, which gives $d'_o = -d'_i + t$. Inserting this into **Equation 2.15** gives

$$\frac{n_2}{-d'_i + t} + \frac{n_1}{d_i} = \frac{n_1 - n_2}{R_2}. \tag{2.16}$$

Summing **Equation 2.14** and **Equation 2.16** gives

$$\frac{n_1}{d_o} + \frac{n_1}{d_i} + \frac{n_2}{d'_i} + \frac{n_2}{-d'_i + t} = (n_2 - n_1)\left(\frac{1}{R_1} - \frac{1}{R_2}\right). \tag{2.17}$$

In the **thin-lens approximation**, we assume that the lens is very thin compared to the first image distance, or $t \ll d'_i$ (or, equivalently, $t \ll R_1$ and R_2). In this case, the third and fourth terms on the left-hand side of **Equation 2.17** cancel, leaving us with

$$\frac{n_1}{d_o} + \frac{n_1}{d_i} = (n_2 - n_1)\left(\frac{1}{R_1} - \frac{1}{R_2}\right).$$

Dividing by n_1 gives us finally

$$\frac{1}{d_o} + \frac{1}{d_i} = \left(\frac{n_2}{n_1} - 1\right)\left(\frac{1}{R_1} - \frac{1}{R_2}\right). \tag{2.18}$$

The left-hand side looks suspiciously like the mirror equation that we derived above for spherical mirrors. As done for spherical mirrors, we can use ray tracing and geometry to show that, for a thin lens,

$$\frac{1}{d_o} + \frac{1}{d_i} = \frac{1}{f} \tag{2.19}$$

where f is the focal length of the thin lens (this derivation is left as an exercise). This is the thin-lens equation. The focal length of a thin lens is the same to the left and to the right of the lens. Combining **Equation 2.18** and **Equation 2.19** gives

$$\frac{1}{f} = \left(\frac{n_2}{n_1} - 1\right)\left(\frac{1}{R_1} - \frac{1}{R_2}\right) \tag{2.20}$$

which is called the lens maker's equation. It shows that the focal length of a thin lens depends only of the radii of curvature and the index of refraction of the lens and that of the surrounding medium. For a lens in air, $n_1 = 1.0$ and $n_2 \equiv n$, so the lens maker's equation reduces to

$$\frac{1}{f} = (n-1)\left(\frac{1}{R_1} - \frac{1}{R_2}\right). \tag{2.21}$$

Sign conventions for lenses

To properly use the thin-lens equation, the following sign conventions must be obeyed:

1. d_i is positive if the image is on the side opposite the object (i.e., real image); otherwise, d_i is negative (i.e., virtual image).
2. f is positive for a converging lens and negative for a diverging lens.
3. R is positive for a surface convex toward the object, and negative for a surface concave toward object.

Magnification

By using a finite-size object on the optical axis and ray tracing, you can show that the magnification m of an image is

$$m \equiv \frac{h_i}{h_o} = -\frac{d_i}{d_o} \tag{2.22}$$

(where the three lines mean "is defined as"). This is exactly the same equation as we obtained for mirrors (see **Equation 2.8**). If $m > 0$, then the image has the same vertical orientation as the object (called an "upright" image). If $m < 0$, then the image has the opposite vertical orientation as the object (called an "inverted" image).

Using the Thin-Lens Equation

The thin-lens equation and the lens maker's equation are broadly applicable to situations involving thin lenses. We explore many features of image formation in the following examples.

Consider a thin converging lens. Where does the image form and what type of image is formed as the object approaches the lens from infinity? This may be seen by using the thin-lens equation for a given focal length to plot the image distance as a function of object distance. In other words, we plot

$$d_i = \left(\frac{1}{f} - \frac{1}{d_o}\right)^{-1}$$

for a given value of f. For $f = 1\ \text{cm}$, the result is shown in part (a) of **Figure 2.25**.

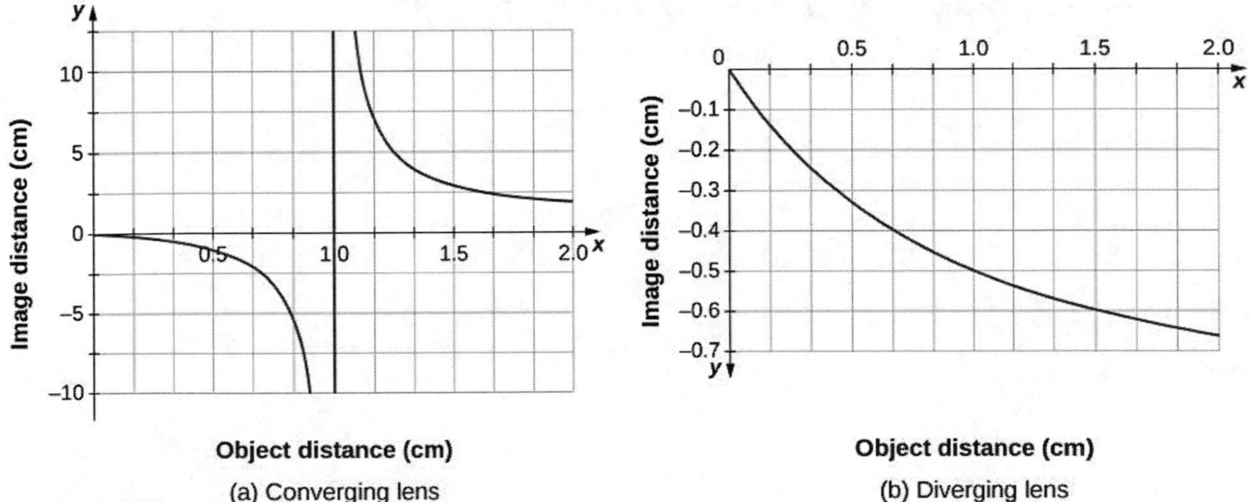

Figure 2.25 (a) Image distance for a thin converging lens with $f = 1.0\ \text{cm}$ as a function of object distance. (b) Same thing but for a diverging lens with $f = -1.0\ \text{cm}$.

An object much farther than the focal length f from the lens should produce an image near the focal plane, because the second term on the right-hand side of the equation above becomes negligible compared to the first term, so we have $d_i \approx f$. This can be seen in the plot of part (a) of the figure, which shows that the image distance approaches asymptotically the focal length of 1 cm for larger object distances. As the object approaches the focal plane, the image distance diverges to positive infinity. This is expected because an object at the focal plane produces parallel rays that form an image at infinity (i.e., very far from the lens). When the object is farther than the focal length from the lens, the image distance is positive, so the image is real, on the opposite side of the lens from the object, and inverted (because $m = -d_i/d_o$). When the object is closer than the focal length from the lens, the image distance becomes negative, which means that the image is virtual, on the same side of the lens as the object, and upright.

For a thin diverging lens of focal length $f = -1.0\text{ cm}$, a similar plot of image distance vs. object distance is shown in part (b). In this case, the image distance is negative for all positive object distances, which means that the image is virtual, on the same side of the lens as the object, and upright. These characteristics may also be seen by ray-tracing diagrams (see **Figure 2.26**).

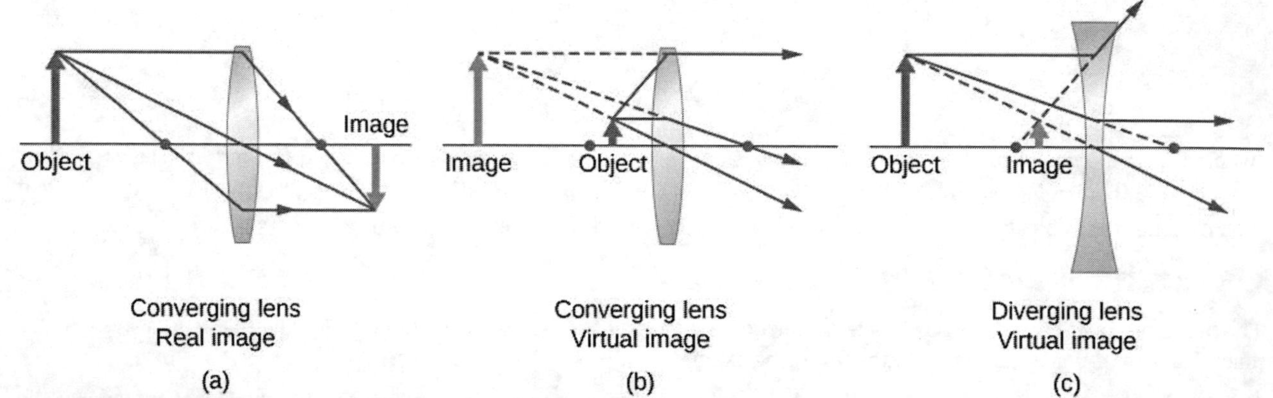

Figure 2.26 The red dots show the focal points of the lenses. (a) A real, inverted image formed from an object that is farther than the focal length from a converging lens. (b) A virtual, upright image formed from an object that is closer than a focal length from the lens. (c) A virtual, upright image formed from an object that is farther than a focal length from a diverging lens.

To see a concrete example of upright and inverted images, look at **Figure 2.27**, which shows images formed by converging lenses when the object (the person's face in this case) is place at different distances from the lens. In part (a) of the figure, the person's face is farther than one focal length from the lens, so the image is inverted. In part (b), the person's face is closer than one focal length from the lens, so the image is upright.

(a) (b)

Figure 2.27 (a) When a converging lens is held farther than one focal length from the man's face, an inverted image is formed. Note that the image is in focus but the face is not, because the image is much closer to the camera taking this photograph than the face. (b) An upright image of the man's face is produced when a converging lens is held at less than one focal length from his face. (credit a: modification of work by "DaMongMan"/Flickr; credit b: modification of work by Casey Fleser)

Work through the following examples to better understand how thin lenses work.

Problem-Solving Strategy: Lenses

Step 1. Determine whether ray tracing, the thin-lens equation, or both would be useful. Even if ray tracing is not used, a careful sketch is always very useful. Write symbols and values on the sketch.

Step 2. Identify what needs to be determined in the problem (identify the unknowns).

Step 3. Make a list of what is given or can be inferred from the problem (identify the knowns).

Step 4. If ray tracing is required, use the ray-tracing rules listed near the beginning of this section.

Step 5. Most quantitative problems require the use of the thin-lens equation and/or the lens maker's equation. Solve these for the unknowns and insert the given quantities or use both together to find two unknowns.

Step 7. Check to see if the answer is reasonable. Are the signs correct? Is the sketch or ray tracing consistent with the calculation?

Example 2.3

Using the Lens Maker's Equation

Find the radius of curvature of a biconcave lens symmetrically ground from a glass with index of refractive 1.55 so that its focal length in air is 20 cm (for a biconcave lens, both surfaces have the same radius of curvature).

Strategy

Use the thin-lens form of the lens maker's equation:

$$\frac{1}{f} = \left(\frac{n_2}{n_1} - 1\right)\left(\frac{1}{R_1} - \frac{1}{R_2}\right)$$

where $R_1 < 0$ and $R_2 > 0$. Since we are making a symmetric biconcave lens, we have $|R_1| = |R_2|$.

Solution

We can determine the radius R of curvature from

$$\frac{1}{f} = \left(\frac{n_2}{n_1} - 1\right)\left(-\frac{2}{R}\right).$$

Solving for R and inserting $f = -20\text{ cm}, n_2 = 1.55,$ and $n_1 = 1.00$ gives

$$R = -2f\left(\frac{n_2}{n_1} - 1\right) = -2(-20\text{ cm})\left(\frac{1.55}{1.00} - 1\right) = 22\text{ cm}.$$

Example 2.4

Converging Lens and Different Object Distances

Find the location, orientation, and magnification of the image for an 3.0 cm high object at each of the following positions in front of a convex lens of focal length 10.0 cm. (a) $d_o = 50.0\text{ cm}$, (b) $d_o = 5.00\text{ cm}$, and (c) $d_o = 20.0\text{ cm}$.

Strategy

We start with the thin-lens equation $\frac{1}{d_i} + \frac{1}{d_o} = \frac{1}{f}$. Solve this for the image distance d_i and insert the given object distance and focal length.

Solution

a. For $d_o = 50\text{ cm}, f = +10\text{ cm}$, this gives

$$\begin{aligned} d_i &= \left(\frac{1}{f} - \frac{1}{d_o}\right)^{-1} \\ &= \left(\frac{1}{10.0\text{ cm}} - \frac{1}{50.0\text{ cm}}\right)^{-1} \\ &= 12.5\text{ cm} \end{aligned}$$

The image is positive, so the image, is real, is on the opposite side of the lens from the object, and is 12.6 cm from the lens. To find the magnification and orientation of the image, use

$$m = -\frac{d_i}{d_o} = -\frac{12.5\text{ cm}}{50.0\text{ cm}} = -0.250.$$

The negative magnification means that the image is inverted. Since $|m| < 1$, the image is smaller than the object. The size of the image is given by

$$|h_i| = |m|h_o = (0.250)(3.0\text{ cm}) = 0.75\text{ cm}$$

b. For $d_o = 5.00\text{ cm}, f = +10.0\text{ cm}$

$$\begin{aligned} d_i &= \left(\frac{1}{f} - \frac{1}{d_o}\right)^{-1} \\ &= \left(\frac{1}{10.0\text{ cm}} - \frac{1}{5.00\text{ cm}}\right)^{-1} \\ &= -10.0\text{ cm} \end{aligned}$$

The image distance is negative, so the image is virtual, is on the same side of the lens as the object, and is 10 cm from the lens. The magnification and orientation of the image are found from

$$m = -\frac{d_i}{d_o} = -\frac{-10.0\text{ cm}}{5.00\text{ cm}} = +2.00.$$

The positive magnification means that the image is upright (i.e., it has the same orientation as the object). Since $|m| > 0$, the image is larger than the object. The size of the image is

$$|h_i| = |m|h_o = (2.00)(3.0\text{ cm}) = 6.0\text{ cm}.$$

c. For $d_o = 20\text{ cm}, f = +10\text{ cm}$

$$\begin{aligned} d_i &= \left(\frac{1}{f} - \frac{1}{d_o}\right)^{-1} \\ &= \left(\frac{1}{10.0\text{ cm}} - \frac{1}{20.0\text{ cm}}\right)^{-1} \\ &= 20.0\text{ cm} \end{aligned}$$

The image distance is positive, so the image is real, is on the opposite side of the lens from the object, and is 20.0 cm from the lens. The magnification is

$$m = -\frac{d_i}{d_o} = -\frac{20.0\text{ cm}}{20.0\text{ cm}} = -1.00.$$

The negative magnification means that the image is inverted. Since $|m| = 1$, the image is the same size as the object.

When solving problems in geometric optics, we often need to combine ray tracing and the lens equations. The following example demonstrates this approach.

Example 2.5

Choosing the Focal Length and Type of Lens

To project an image of a light bulb on a screen 1.50 m away, you need to choose what type of lens to use (converging or diverging) and its focal length (**Figure 2.28**). The distance between the lens and the lightbulb is fixed at 0.75 m. Also, what is the magnification and orientation of the image?

Strategy

The image must be real, so you choose to use a converging lens. The focal length can be found by using the thin-lens equation and solving for the focal length. The object distance is $d_o = 0.75\text{ m}$ and the image distance is $d_i = 1.5\text{ m}$.

Solution

Solve the thin lens for the focal length and insert the desired object and image distances:

$$\begin{aligned} \frac{1}{d_o} + \frac{1}{d_i} &= \frac{1}{f} \\ f &= \left(\frac{1}{d_o} + \frac{1}{d_i}\right)^{-1} \\ &= \left(\frac{1}{0.75\text{ m}} + \frac{1}{1.5\text{ m}}\right)^{-1} \\ &= 0.50\text{ m} \end{aligned}$$

The magnification is

$$m = -\frac{d_i}{d_o} = -\frac{1.5\text{ m}}{0.75\text{ m}} = -2.0.$$

Significance

The minus sign for the magnification means that the image is inverted. The focal length is positive, as expected for a converging lens. Ray tracing can be used to check the calculation (see **Figure 2.28**). As expected, the image is inverted, is real, and is larger than the object.

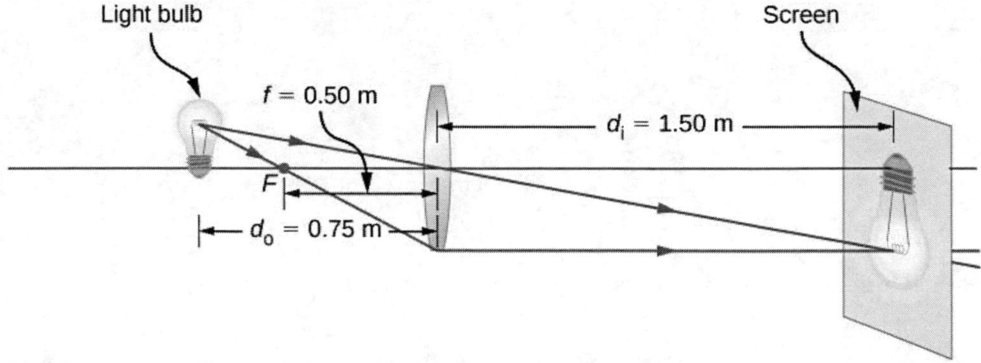

Figure 2.28 A light bulb placed 0.75 m from a lens having a 0.50-m focal length produces a real image on a screen, as discussed in the example. Ray tracing predicts the image location and size.

2.5 | The Eye

Learning Objectives

By the end of this section, you will be able to:

- Understand the basic physics of how images are formed by the human eye
- Recognize several conditions of impaired vision as well as the optics principles for treating these conditions

The human eye is perhaps the most interesting and important of all optical instruments. Our eyes perform a vast number of functions: They allow us to sense direction, movement, colors, and distance. In this section, we explore the geometric optics of the eye.

Physics of the Eye

The eye is remarkable in how it forms images and in the richness of detail and color it can detect. However, our eyes often need some correction to reach what is called "normal" vision. Actually, normal vision should be called "ideal" vision because nearly one-half of the human population requires some sort of eyesight correction, so requiring glasses is by no means "abnormal." Image formation by our eyes and common vision correction can be analyzed with the optics discussed earlier in this chapter.

Figure 2.29 shows the basic anatomy of the eye. The cornea and lens form a system that, to a good approximation, acts as a single thin lens. For clear vision, a real image must be projected onto the light-sensitive retina, which lies a fixed distance from the lens. The flexible lens of the eye allows it to adjust the radius of curvature of the lens to produce an image on the retina for objects at different distances. The center of the image falls on the fovea, which has the greatest density of light receptors and the greatest acuity (sharpness) in the visual field. The variable opening (i.e., the pupil) of the eye, along with chemical adaptation, allows the eye to detect light intensities from the lowest observable to 10^{10} times greater (without damage). This is an incredible range of detection. Processing of visual nerve impulses begins with interconnections in the retina and continues in the brain. The optic nerve conveys the signals received by the eye to the brain.

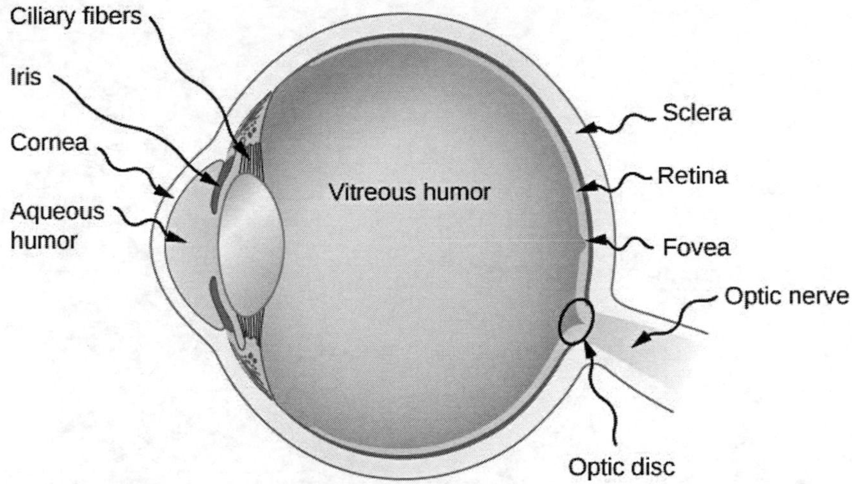

Figure 2.29 The cornea and lens of the eye act together to form a real image on the light-sensing retina, which has its densest concentration of receptors in the fovea and a blind spot over the optic nerve. The radius of curvature of the lens of an eye is adjustable to form an image on the retina for different object distances. Layers of tissues with varying indices of refraction in the lens are shown here. However, they have been omitted from other pictures for clarity.

The indices of refraction in the eye are crucial to its ability to form images. **Table 2.1** lists the indices of refraction relevant to the eye. The biggest change in the index of refraction, which is where the light rays are most bent, occurs at the air-cornea interface rather than at the aqueous humor-lens interface. The ray diagram in **Figure 2.30** shows image formation by the cornea and lens of the eye. The cornea, which is itself a converging lens with a focal length of approximately 2.3 cm, provides most of the focusing power of the eye. The lens, which is a converging lens with a focal length of about 6.4 cm, provides the finer focus needed to produce a clear image on the retina. The cornea and lens can be treated as a single thin lens, even though the light rays pass through several layers of material (such as cornea, aqueous humor, several layers in the lens, and vitreous humor), changing direction at each interface. The image formed is much like the one produced by a single convex lens (i.e., a real, inverted image). Although images formed in the eye are inverted, the brain inverts them once more to make them seem upright.

Material	Index of Refraction
Water	1.33
Air	1.0
Cornea	1.38
Aqueous humor	1.34
Lens	1.41*
Vitreous humor	1.34

Table 2.1 Refractive Indices Relevant to the Eye *This is an average value. The actual index of refraction varies throughout the lens and is greatest in center of the lens.

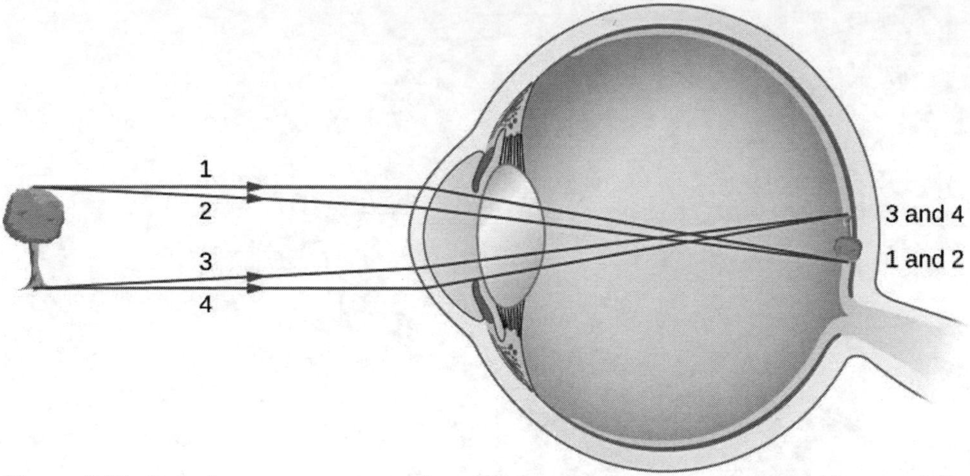

Figure 2.30 In the human eye, an image forms on the retina. Rays from the top and bottom of the object are traced to show how a real, inverted image is produced on the retina. The distance to the object is not to scale.

As noted, the image must fall precisely on the retina to produce clear vision—that is, the image distance d_i must equal the lens-to-retina distance. Because the lens-to-retina distance does not change, the image distance d_i must be the same for objects at all distances. The ciliary muscles adjust the shape of the eye lens for focusing on nearby or far objects. By changing the shape of the eye lens, the eye changes the focal length of the lens. This mechanism of the eye is called **accommodation**.

The nearest point an object can be placed so that the eye can form a clear image on the retina is called the **near point** of the eye. Similarly, the **far point** is the farthest distance at which an object is clearly visible. A person with normal vision can see objects clearly at distances ranging from 25 cm to essentially infinity. The near point increases with age, becoming several meters for some older people. In this text, we consider the near point to be 25 cm.

We can use the thin-lens equations to quantitatively examine image formation by the eye. First, we define the **optical power** of a lens as

$$P = \frac{1}{f} \tag{2.23}$$

with the focal length *f* given in meters. The units of optical power are called "diopters" (D). That is, $1\text{ D} = \frac{1}{\text{m}}$, or 1 m^{-1}.

Optometrists prescribe common eyeglasses and contact lenses in units of diopters. With this definition of optical power, we can rewrite the thin-lens equations as

$$P = \frac{1}{d_o} + \frac{1}{d_i}. \tag{2.24}$$

Working with optical power is convenient because, for two or more lenses close together, the effective optical power of the lens system is approximately the sum of the optical power of the individual lenses:

$$P_{\text{total}} = P_{\text{lens 1}} + P_{\text{lens 2}} + P_{\text{lens 3}} + \cdots \tag{2.25}$$

Example 2.6

Effective Focal Length of the Eye

The cornea and eye lens have focal lengths of 2.3 and 6.4 cm, respectively. Find the net focal length and optical power of the eye.

Strategy

The optical powers of the closely spaced lenses add, so $P_{\text{eye}} = P_{\text{cornea}} + P_{\text{lens}}$.

Solution

Writing the equation for power in terms of the focal lengths gives

$$\frac{1}{f_{\text{eye}}} = \frac{1}{f_{\text{cornea}}} + \frac{1}{f_{\text{lens}}} = \frac{1}{2.3\text{ cm}} + \frac{1}{6.4\text{ cm}}.$$

Hence, the focal length of the eye (cornea and lens together) is

$$f_{\text{eye}} = 1.69\text{ cm}.$$

The optical power of the eye is

$$P_{\text{eye}} = \frac{1}{f_{\text{eye}}} = \frac{1}{0.0169\text{ m}} = 59\text{ D}.$$

For clear vision, the image distance d_{i} must equal the lens-to-retina distance. Normal vision is possible for objects at distances $d_{\text{o}} = 25\text{ cm}$ to infinity. The following example shows how to calculate the image distance for an object placed at the near point of the eye.

Example 2.7

Image of an object placed at the near point

The net focal length of a particular human eye is 1.7 cm. An object is placed at the near point of the eye. How far behind the lens is a focused image formed?

Strategy

The near point is 25 cm from the eye, so the object distance is $d_{\text{o}} = 25\text{ cm}$. We determine the image distance from the lens equation:

$$\frac{1}{d_{\text{i}}} = \frac{1}{f} - \frac{1}{d_{\text{o}}}.$$

Solution

$$\begin{aligned} d_{\text{i}} &= \left(\frac{1}{f} - \frac{1}{d_{\text{o}}}\right)^{-1} \\ &= \left(\frac{1}{1.7\text{ cm}} - \frac{1}{25\text{ cm}}\right)^{-1} \\ &= 1.8\text{ cm} \end{aligned}$$

Therefore, the image is formed 1.8 cm behind the lens.

Significance

From the magnification formula, we find $m = -\frac{1.8\text{ cm}}{25\text{ cm}} = -0.073$. Since $m < 0$, the image is inverted in orientation with respect to the object. From the absolute value of m we see that the image is much smaller than the object; in fact, it is only 7% of the size of the object.

Vision Correction

The need for some type of vision correction is very common. Typical vision defects are easy to understand with geometric optics, and some are simple to correct. Figure 2.31 illustrates two common vision defects. **Nearsightedness**, or **myopia**, is the ability to see near objects, whereas distant objects are blurry. The eye overconverges the nearly parallel rays from a distant object, and the rays cross in front of the retina. More divergent rays from a close object are converged on the retina for a clear image. The distance to the farthest object that can be seen clearly is called the far point of the eye (normally the far point is at infinity). **Farsightedness**, or **hyperopia**, is the ability to see far objects clearly, whereas near objects are blurry. A farsighted eye does not sufficiently converge the rays from a near object to make the rays meet on the retina.

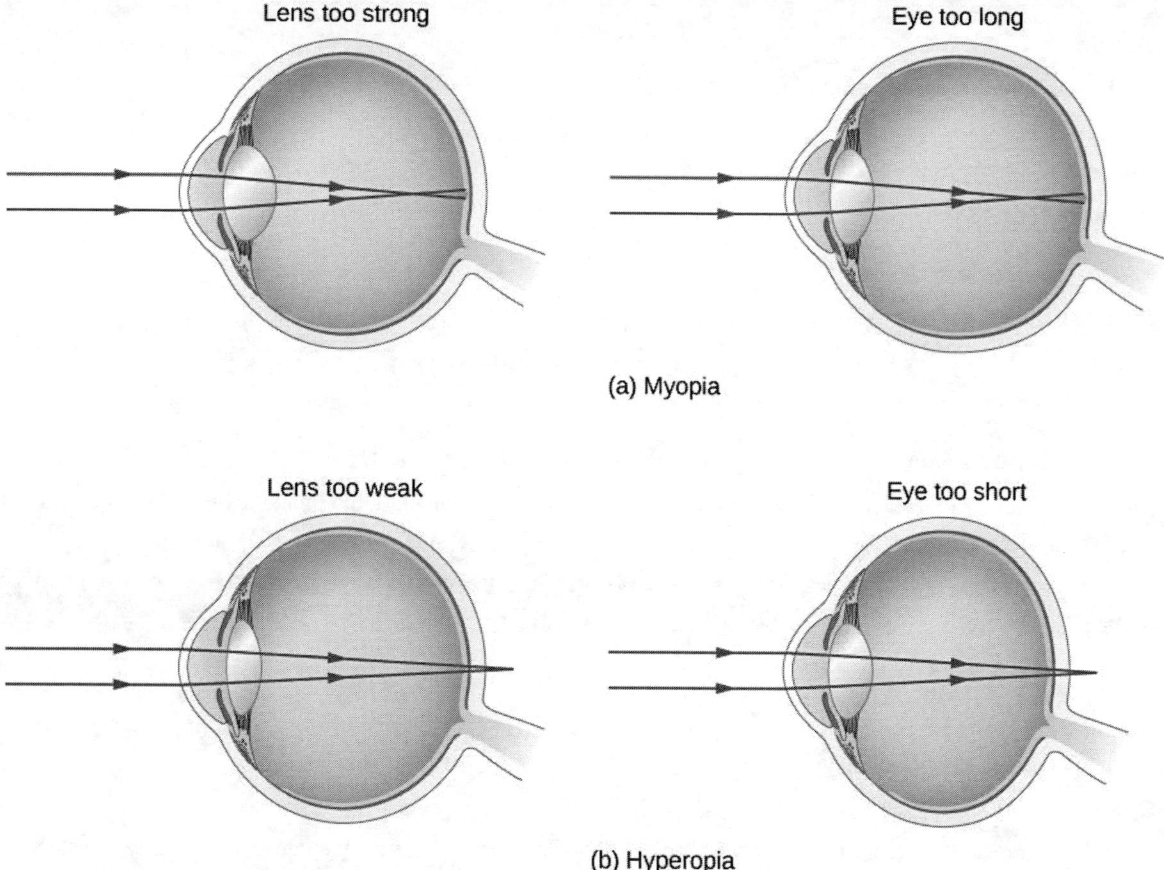

Figure 2.31 (a) The nearsighted (myopic) eye converges rays from a distant object in front of the retina, so they have diverged when they strike the retina, producing a blurry image. An eye lens that is too powerful can cause nearsightedness, or the eye may be too long. (b) The farsighted (hyperopic) eye is unable to converge the rays from a close object on the retina, producing blurry near-field vision. An eye lens with insufficient optical power or an eye that is too short can cause farsightedness.

Since the nearsighted eye overconverges light rays, the correction for nearsightedness consists of placing a diverging eyeglass lens in front of the eye, as shown in Figure 2.32. This reduces the optical power of an eye that is too powerful (recall that the focal length of a diverging lens is negative, so its optical power is negative). Another way to understand this correction is that a diverging lens will cause the incoming rays to diverge more to compensate for the excessive convergence caused by the lens system of the eye. The image produced by the diverging eyeglass lens serves as the (optical) object for the eye, and because the eye cannot focus on objects beyond its far point, the diverging lens must form an image of distant (physical) objects at a point that is closer than the far point.

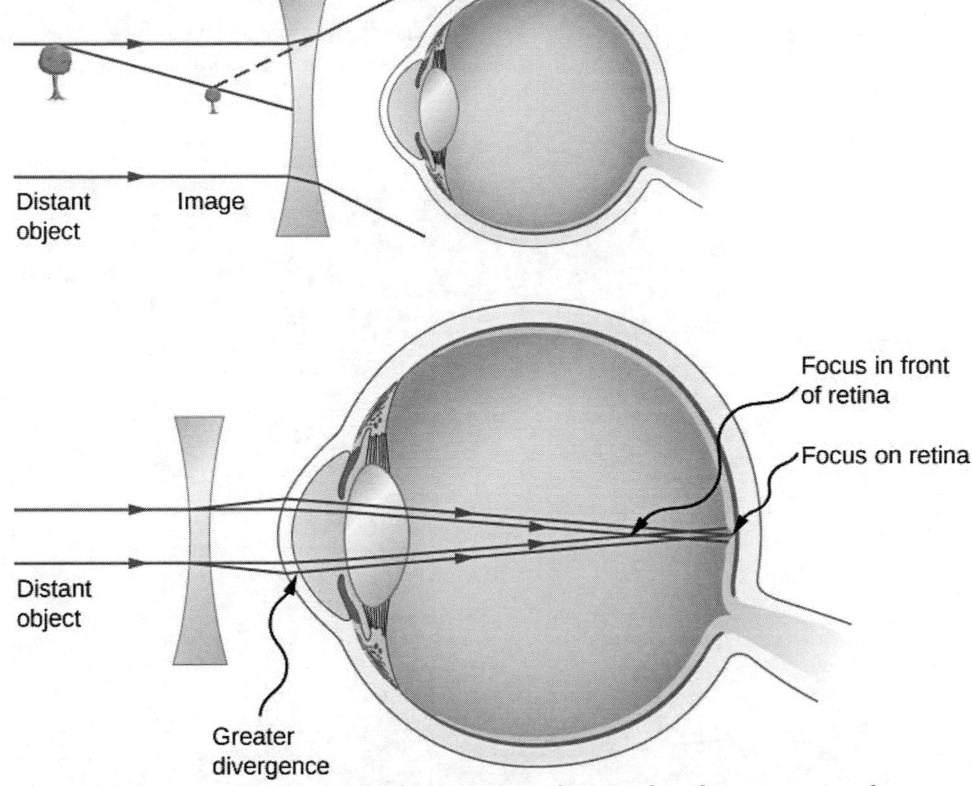

Figure 2.32 Correction of nearsightedness requires a diverging lens that compensates for overconvergence by the eye. The diverging lens produces an image closer to the eye than the physical object. This image serves as the optical object for the eye, and the nearsighted person can see it clearly because it is closer than their far point.

Example 2.8

Correcting Nearsightedness

What optical power of eyeglass lens is needed to correct the vision of a nearsighted person whose far point is 30.0 cm? Assume the corrective lens is fixed 1.50 cm away from the eye.

Strategy

You want this nearsighted person to be able to see distant objects clearly, which means that the eyeglass lens must produce an image 30.0 cm from the eye for an object at infinity. An image 30.0 cm from the eye will be $30.0\,\text{cm} - 1.50\,\text{cm} = 28.5\,\text{cm}$ from the eyeglass lens. Therefore, we must have $d_\text{i} = -28.5\,\text{cm}$ when $d_\text{o} = \infty$. The image distance is negative because it is on the same side of the eyeglass lens as the object.

Solution

Since d_i and d_o are known, we can find the optical power of the eyeglass lens by using **Equation 2.24**:

$$P = \frac{1}{d_\text{o}} + \frac{1}{d_\text{i}} = \frac{1}{\infty} + \frac{1}{-0.285\,\text{m}} = -3.51\text{D}.$$

Significance

The negative optical power indicates a diverging (or concave) lens, as expected. If you examine eyeglasses for nearsighted people, you will find the lenses are thinnest in the center. Additionally, if you examine a prescription for eyeglasses for nearsighted people, you will find that the prescribed optical power is negative and given in units of diopters.

Correcting farsightedness consists simply of using the opposite type of lens as for nearsightedness (i.e., a converging lens), as shown in **Figure 2.33**.

Such a lens will produce an image of physical objects that are closer than the near point at a distance that is between the near point and the far point, so that the person can see the image clearly. To determine the optical power needed for correction, you must therefore know the person's near point, as explained in **Example 2.9**.

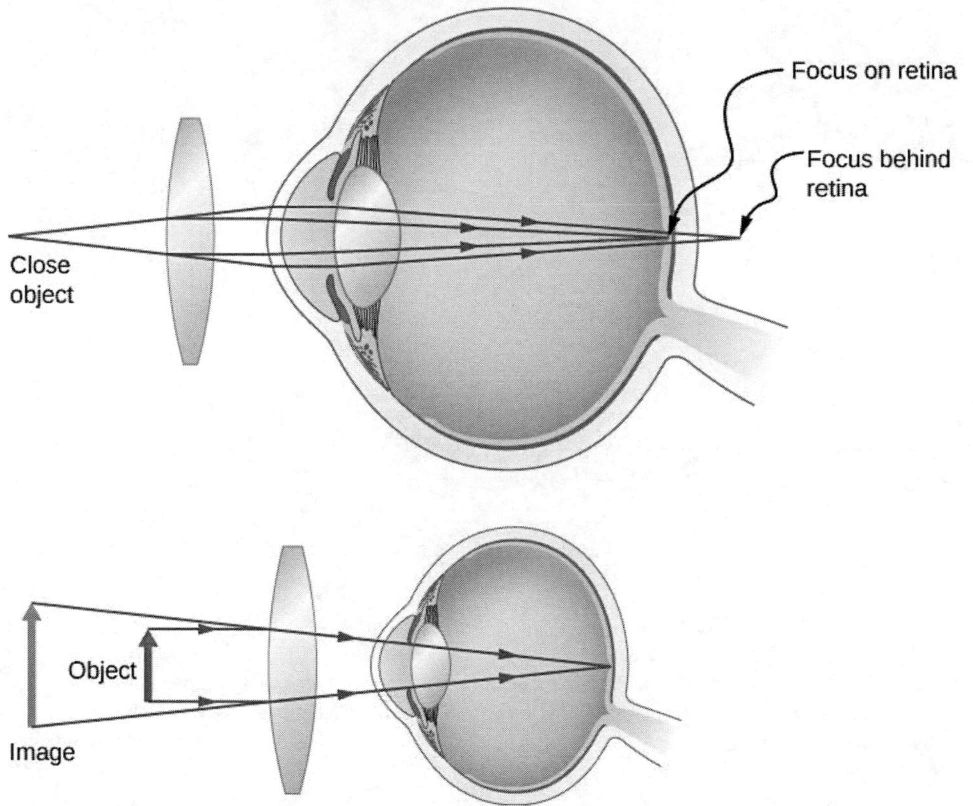

Figure 2.33 Correction of farsightedness uses a converging lens that compensates for the underconvergence by the eye. The converging lens produces an image farther from the eye than the object, so that the farsighted person can see it clearly.

Example 2.9

Correcting Farsightedness

What optical power of eyeglass lens is needed to allow a farsighted person, whose near point is 1.00 m, to see an object clearly that is 25.0 cm from the eye? Assume the corrective lens is fixed 1.5 cm from the eye.

Strategy

When an object is 25.0 cm from the person's eyes, the eyeglass lens must produce an image 1.00 m away (the near point), so that the person can see it clearly. An image 1.00 m from the eye will be $100\ \text{cm} - 1.5\ \text{cm} = 98.5\ \text{cm}$ from the eyeglass lens because the eyeglass lens is 1.5 cm from the eye. Therefore, $d_\text{i} = -98.5\ \text{cm}$, where the minus sign indicates that the image is on the same side of the lens as the object. The object is $25.0\ \text{cm} - 1.5\ \text{cm} = 23.5\ \text{cm}$ from the eyeglass lens, so $d_\text{o} = 23.5\ \text{cm}$.

Solution

Since d_i and d_o are known, we can find the optical power of the eyeglass lens by using **Equation 2.24**:

$$P = \frac{1}{d_\text{o}} + \frac{1}{d_\text{i}} = \frac{1}{0.235\ \text{m}} + \frac{1}{-0.985\ \text{m}} = +3.24\ \text{D}.$$

Significance

The positive optical power indicates a converging (convex) lens, as expected. If you examine eyeglasses of farsighted people, you will find the lenses to be thickest in the center. In addition, prescription eyeglasses for farsighted people have a prescribed optical power that is positive.

2.6 | The Camera

Learning Objectives

By the end of this section, you will be able to:

- Describe the optics of a camera
- Characterize the image created by a camera

Cameras are very common in our everyday life. Between 1825 and 1827, French inventor Nicéphore Niépce successfully photographed an image created by a primitive camera. Since then, enormous progress has been achieved in the design of cameras and camera-based detectors.

Initially, photographs were recorded by using the light-sensitive reaction of silver-based compounds such as silver chloride or silver bromide. Silver-based photographic paper was in common use until the advent of digital photography in the 1980s, which is intimately connected to **charge-coupled device (CCD)** detectors. In a nutshell, a CCD is a semiconductor chip that records images as a matrix of tiny pixels, each pixel located in a "bin" in the surface. Each pixel is capable of detecting the intensity of light impinging on it. Color is brought into play by putting red-, blue-, and green-colored filters over the pixels, resulting in colored digital images (**Figure 2.34**). At its best resolution, one CCD pixel corresponds to one pixel of the image. To reduce the resolution and decrease the size of the file, we can "bin" several CCD pixels into one, resulting in a smaller but "pixelated" image.

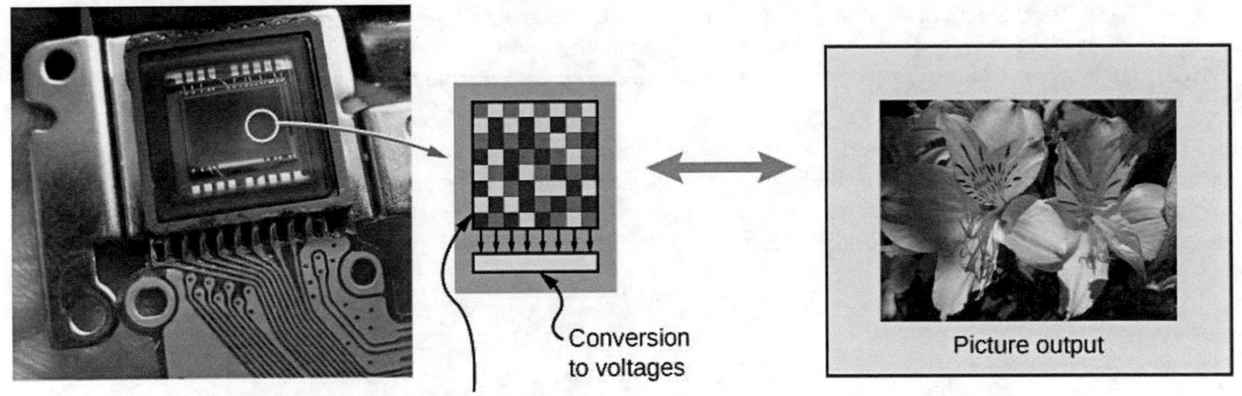

Figure 2.34 A charge-coupled device (CCD) converts light signals into electronic signals, enabling electronic processing and storage of visual images. This is the basis for electronic imaging in all digital cameras, from cell phones to movie cameras. (credit left: modification of work by Bruce Turner)

Clearly, electronics is a big part of a digital camera; however, the underlying physics is basic optics. As a matter of fact, the optics of a camera are pretty much the same as those of a single lens with an object distance that is significantly larger than the lens's focal distance (**Figure 2.35**).

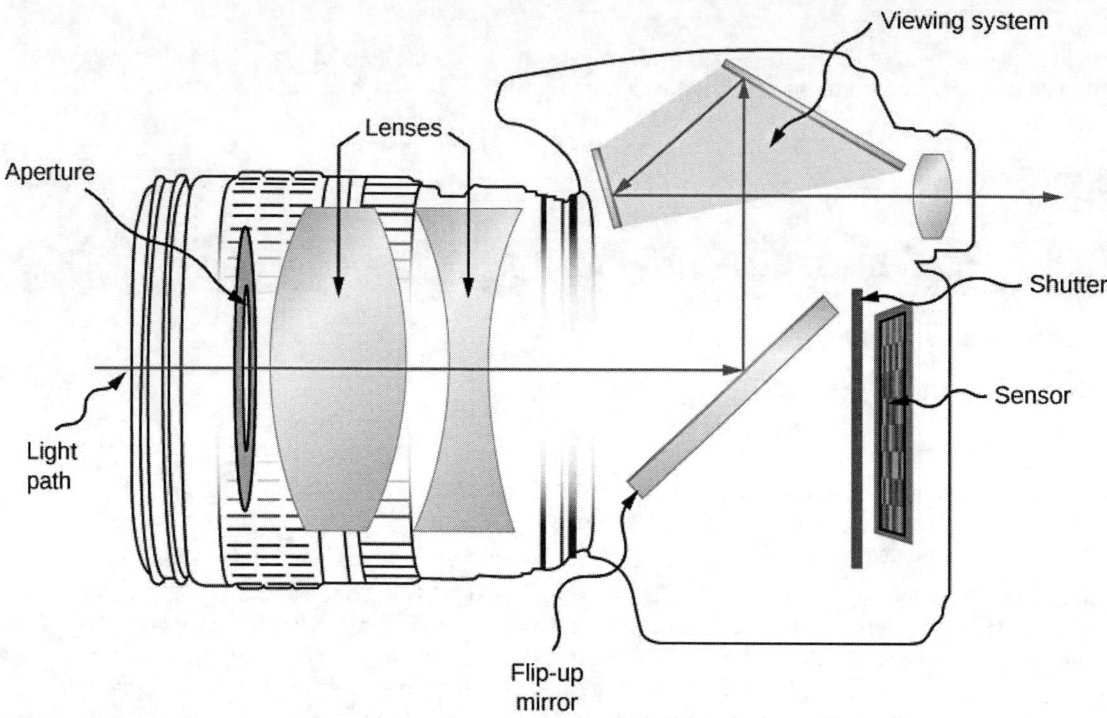

Figure 2.35 Modern digital cameras have several lenses to produce a clear image with minimal aberration and use red, blue, and green filters to produce a color image.

For instance, let us consider the camera in a smartphone. An average smartphone camera is equipped with a stationary wide-angle lens with a focal length of about 4–5 mm. (This focal length is about equal to the thickness of the phone.) The image created by the lens is focused on the CCD detector mounted at the opposite side of the phone. In a cell phone, the lens and the CCD cannot move relative to each other. So how do we make sure that both the images of a distant and a close object are in focus?

Recall that a human eye can accommodate for distant and close images by changing its focal distance. A cell phone camera cannot do that because the distance from the lens to the detector is fixed. Here is where the small focal distance becomes important. Let us assume we have a camera with a 5-mm focal distance. What is the image distance for a selfie? The object distance for a selfie (the length of the hand holding the phone) is about 50 cm. Using the thin-lens equation, we can write

$$\frac{1}{5\text{ mm}} = \frac{1}{500\text{ mm}} + \frac{1}{d_i}$$

We then obtain the image distance:

$$\frac{1}{d_\text{i}} = \frac{1}{5\text{ mm}} - \frac{1}{500\text{ mm}}$$

Note that the object distance is 100 times larger than the focal distance. We can clearly see that the 1/(500 mm) term is significantly smaller than 1/(5 mm), which means that the image distance is pretty much equal to the lens's focal length. An actual calculation gives us the image distance $d_i = 5.05\text{ mm}$. This value is extremely close to the lens's focal distance.

Now let us consider the case of a distant object. Let us say that we would like to take a picture of a person standing about 5 m from us. Using the thin-lens equation again, we obtain the image distance of 5.005 mm. The farther the object is from the lens, the closer the image distance is to the focal distance. At the limiting case of an infinitely distant object, we obtain the image distance exactly equal to the focal distance of the lens.

As you can see, the difference between the image distance for a selfie and the image distance for a distant object is just about 0.05 mm or 50 microns. Even a short object distance such as the length of your hand is two orders of magnitude larger than the lens's focal length, resulting in minute variations of the image distance. (The 50-micron difference is smaller than the thickness of an average sheet of paper.) Such a small difference can be easily accommodated by the same detector, positioned at the focal distance of the lens. Image analysis software can help improve image quality.

Conventional point-and-shoot cameras often use a movable lens to change the lens-to-image distance. Complex lenses of the more expensive mirror reflex cameras allow for superb quality photographic images. The optics of these camera lenses is beyond the scope of this textbook.

2.7 | The Simple Magnifier

Learning Objectives

By the end of this section, you will be able to:

- Understand the optics of a simple magnifier
- Characterize the image created by a simple magnifier

The apparent size of an object perceived by the eye depends on the angle the object subtends from the eye. As shown in Figure 2.36, the object at *A* subtends a larger angle from the eye than when it is position at point *B*. Thus, the object at *A* forms a larger image on the retina (see OA') than when it is positioned at *B* (see OB'). Thus, objects that subtend large angles from the eye appear larger because they form larger images on the retina.

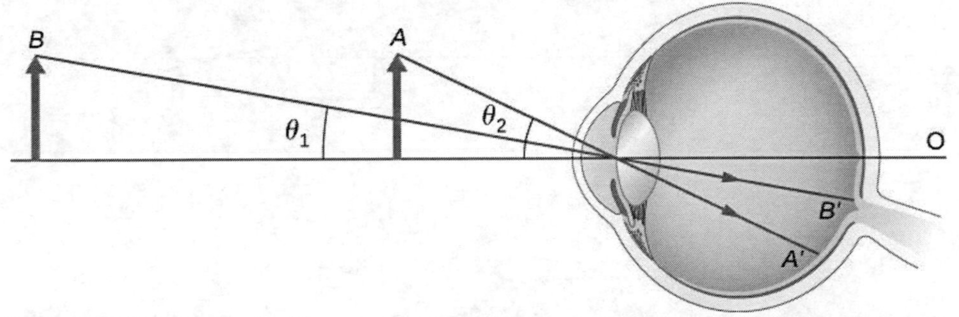

Figure 2.36 Size perceived by an eye is determined by the angle subtended by the object. An image formed on the retina by an object at *A* is larger than an image formed on the retina by the same object positioned at *B* (compared image heights OA' to OB').

We have seen that, when an object is placed within a focal length of a convex lens, its image is virtual, upright, and larger than the object (see part (b) of Figure 2.26). Thus, when such an image produced by a convex lens serves as the object for the eye, as shown in Figure 2.37, the image on the retina is enlarged, because the image produced by the lens subtends a larger angle in the eye than does the object. A convex lens used for this purpose is called a **magnifying glass** or a **simple magnifier**.

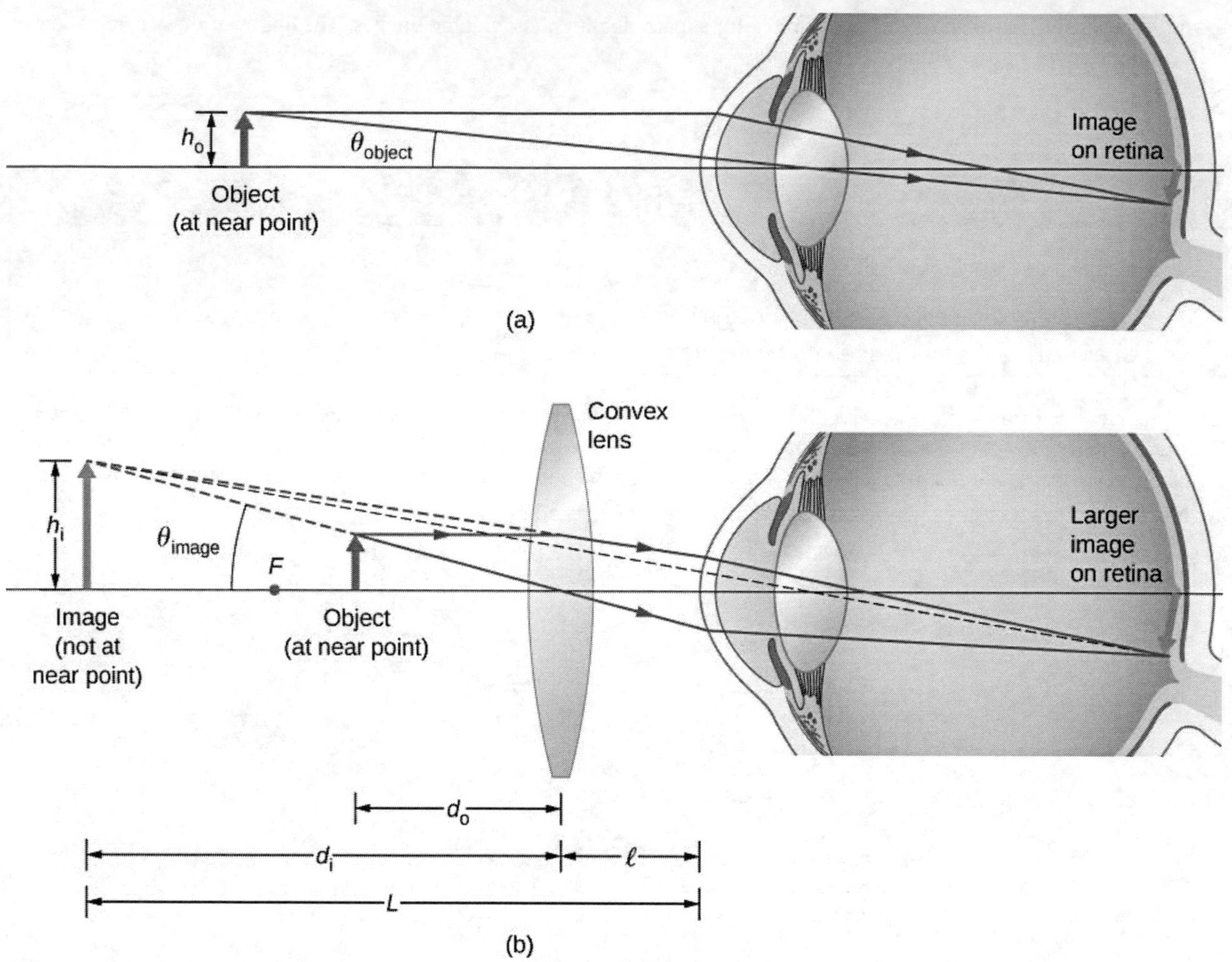

Figure 2.37 The simple magnifier is a convex lens used to produce an enlarged image of an object on the retina. (a) With no convex lens, the object subtends an angle θ_{object} from the eye. (b) With the convex lens in place, the image produced by the convex lens subtends an angle θ_{image} from the eye, with $\theta_{image} > \theta_{object}$. Thus, the image on the retina is larger with the convex lens in place.

To account for the magnification of a magnifying lens, we compare the angle subtended by the image (created by the lens) with the angle subtended by the object (viewed with no lens), as shown in Figure 2.37. We assume that the object is situated at the near point of the eye, because this is the object distance at which the unaided eye can form the largest image on the retina. We will compare the magnified images created by a lens with this maximum image size for the unaided eye. The magnification of an image when observed by the eye is the **angular magnification** M, which is defined by the ratio of the angle θ_{image} subtended by the image to the angle θ_{object} subtended by the object:

$$M = \frac{\theta_{image}}{\theta_{object}}. \tag{2.26}$$

Consider the situation shown in Figure 2.37. The magnifying lens is held a distance ℓ from the eye, and the image produced by the magnifier forms a distance L from the eye. We want to calculate the angular magnification for any arbitrary L and ℓ. In the small-angle approximation, the angular size θ_{image} of the image is h_i/L. The angular size θ_{object} of the object at the near point is $\theta_{object} = h_o/25 \text{ cm}$. The angular magnification is then

$$M = \frac{\theta_{\text{image}}}{\theta_{\text{object}}} = \frac{h_{\text{i}}(25\text{ cm})}{Lh_{\text{o}}}. \tag{2.27}$$

Using **Equation 2.8** for linear magnification

$$m = -\frac{d_{\text{i}}}{d_{\text{o}}} = \frac{h_{\text{i}}}{h_{\text{o}}}$$

and the thin-lens equation

$$\frac{1}{d_{\text{o}}} + \frac{1}{d_{\text{i}}} = \frac{1}{f}$$

in **Equation 2.27**, we arrive at the following expression for the angular magnification of a magnifying lens:

$$\begin{aligned} M &= \left(-\frac{d_{\text{i}}}{d_{\text{o}}}\right)\left(\frac{25\text{ cm}}{L}\right) \\ &= -d_{\text{i}}\left(\frac{1}{f} - \frac{1}{d_{\text{i}}}\right)\left(\frac{25\text{ cm}}{L}\right) \\ &= \left(1 - \frac{d_{\text{i}}}{f}\right)\left(\frac{25\text{ cm}}{L}\right) \end{aligned} \tag{2.28}$$

From part (b) of the figure, we see that the absolute value of the image distance is $|d_{\text{i}}| = L - \ell$. Note that $d_{\text{i}} < 0$ because the image is virtual, so we can dispense with the absolute value by explicitly inserting the minus sign: $-d_{\text{i}} = L - \ell$. Inserting this into **Equation 2.28** gives us the final equation for the angular magnification of a magnifying lens:

$$M = \left(\frac{25\text{ cm}}{L}\right)\left(1 + \frac{L - \ell}{f}\right). \tag{2.29}$$

Note that all the quantities in this equation have to be expressed in centimeters. Often, we want the image to be at the near-point distance ($L = 25\text{ cm}$) to get maximum magnification, and we hold the magnifying lens close to the eye ($\ell = 0$). In this case, **Equation 2.29** gives

$$M = 1 + \frac{25\text{ cm}}{f} \tag{2.30}$$

which shows that the greatest magnification occurs for the lens with the shortest focal length. In addition, when the image is at the near-point distance and the lens is held close to the eye $(\ell = 0)$, then $L = d_{\text{i}} = 25\text{ cm}$ and **Equation 2.27** becomes

$$M = \frac{h_{\text{i}}}{h_{\text{o}}} = m \tag{2.31}$$

where m is the linear magnification (**Equation 2.32**) derived for spherical mirrors and thin lenses. Another useful situation is when the image is at infinity $(L = \infty)$. **Equation 2.29** then takes the form

$$M(L = \infty) = \frac{25\text{ cm}}{f}. \tag{2.32}$$

The resulting magnification is simply the ratio of the near-point distance to the focal length of the magnifying lens, so a lens with a shorter focal length gives a stronger magnification. Although this magnification is smaller by 1 than the magnification obtained with the image at the near point, it provides for the most comfortable viewing conditions, because the eye is relaxed when viewing a distant object.

By comparing **Equation 2.29** with **Equation 2.32**, we see that the range of angular magnification of a given converging lens is

$$\frac{25\text{ cm}}{f} \le M \le 1 + \frac{25\text{ cm}}{f}. \tag{2.33}$$

Example 2.10

Magnifying a Diamond

A jeweler wishes to inspect a 3.0-mm-diameter diamond with a magnifier. The diamond is held at the jeweler's near point (25 cm), and the jeweler holds the magnifying lens close to his eye.

(a) What should the focal length of the magnifying lens be to see a 15-mm-diameter image of the diamond?

(b) What should the focal length of the magnifying lens be to obtain $10\times$ magnification?

Strategy

We need to determine the requisite magnification of the magnifier. Because the jeweler holds the magnifying lens close to his eye, we can use **Equation 2.30** to find the focal length of the magnifying lens.

Solution

a. The required linear magnification is the ratio of the desired image diameter to the diamond's actual diameter (**Equation 2.32**). Because the jeweler holds the magnifying lens close to his eye and the image forms at his near point, the linear magnification is the same as the angular magnification, so

$$M = m = \frac{h_\text{i}}{h_\text{o}} = \frac{15\text{ mm}}{3.0\text{ mm}} = 5.0.$$

The focal length f of the magnifying lens may be calculated by solving **Equation 2.30** for f, which gives

$$M = 1 + \frac{25\text{ cm}}{f}$$

$$f = \frac{25\text{ cm}}{M-1} = \frac{25\text{ cm}}{5.0-1} = 6.3\text{ cm}$$

b. To get an image magnified by a factor of ten, we again solve **Equation 2.30** for f, but this time we use $M = 10$. The result is

$$f = \frac{25\text{ cm}}{M-1} = \frac{25\text{ cm}}{10-1} = 2.8\text{ cm}.$$

Significance

Note that a greater magnification is achieved by using a lens with a smaller focal length. We thus need to use a lens with radii of curvature that are less than a few centimeters and hold it very close to our eye. This is not very convenient. A compound microscope, explored in the following section, can overcome this drawback.

2.8 | Microscopes and Telescopes

Learning Objectives

By the end of this section, you will be able to:

- Explain the physics behind the operation of microscopes and telescopes
- Describe the image created by these instruments and calculate their magnifications

Microscopes and telescopes are major instruments that have contributed hugely to our current understanding of the micro- and macroscopic worlds. The invention of these devices led to numerous discoveries in disciplines such as physics, astronomy, and biology, to name a few. In this section, we explain the basic physics that make these instruments work.

Microscopes

Although the eye is marvelous in its ability to see objects large and small, it obviously is limited in the smallest details it can detect. The desire to see beyond what is possible with the naked eye led to the use of optical instruments. We have seen that a simple convex lens can create a magnified image, but it is hard to get large magnification with such a lens. A magnification greater than $5\times$ is difficult without distorting the image. To get higher magnification, we can combine the simple magnifying glass with one or more additional lenses. In this section, we examine microscopes that enlarge the details that we cannot see with the naked eye.

Microscopes were first developed in the early 1600s by eyeglass makers in The Netherlands and Denmark. The simplest **compound microscope** is constructed from two convex lenses (**Figure 2.38**). The **objective** lens is a convex lens of short focal length (i.e., high power) with typical magnification from $5\times$ to $100\times$. The **eyepiece**, also referred to as the ocular, is a convex lens of longer focal length.

The purpose of a microscope is to create magnified images of small objects, and both lenses contribute to the final magnification. Also, the final enlarged image is produced sufficiently far from the observer to be easily viewed, since the eye cannot focus on objects or images that are too close (i.e., closer than the near point of the eye).

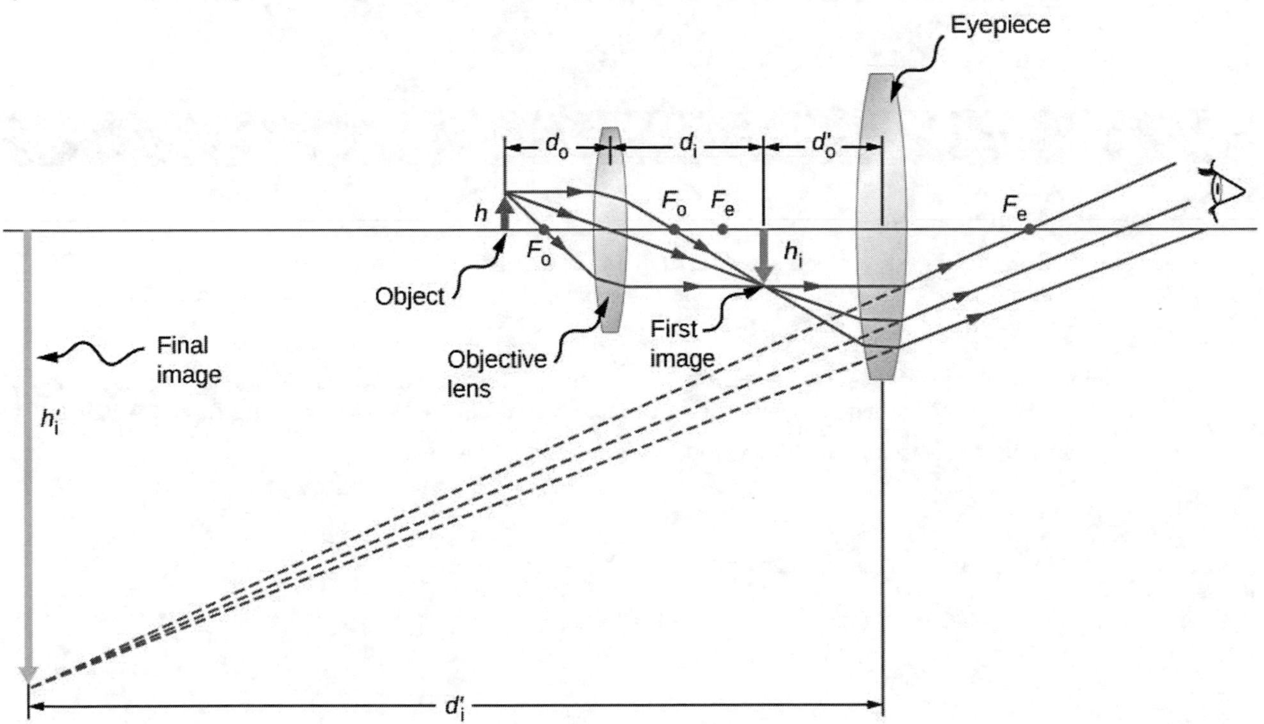

Figure 2.38 A compound microscope is composed of two lenses: an objective and an eyepiece. The objective forms the first image, which is larger than the object. This first image is inside the focal length of the eyepiece and serves as the object for the eyepiece. The eyepiece forms final image that is further magnified.

To see how the microscope in **Figure 2.38** forms an image, consider its two lenses in succession. The object is just beyond the focal length f^{obj} of the objective lens, producing a real, inverted image that is larger than the object. This first image serves as the object for the second lens, or eyepiece. The eyepiece is positioned so that the first image is within its focal length f^{eye}, so that it can further magnify the image. In a sense, it acts as a magnifying glass that magnifies the intermediate image produced by the objective. The image produced by the eyepiece is a magnified virtual image. The final image remains inverted but is farther from the observer than the object, making it easy to view.

The eye views the virtual image created by the eyepiece, which serves as the object for the lens in the eye. The virtual image formed by the eyepiece is well outside the focal length of the eye, so the eye forms a real image on the retina.

The magnification of the microscope is the product of the linear magnification m^{obj} by the objective and the angular magnification M^{eye} by the eyepiece. These are given by

$$m^{\text{obj}} = -\frac{d_{\text{i}}^{\text{obj}}}{d_{\text{o}}^{\text{obj}}} \approx -\frac{d_{\text{i}}^{\text{obj}}}{f^{\text{obj}}} \text{ (linear magnification y objective)}$$

$$M^{\text{eye}} = 1 + \frac{25\text{ cm}}{f^{\text{eye}}} \text{ (angular magnification y eyepiece)}$$

Here, f^{obj} and f^{eye} are the focal lengths of the objective and the eyepiece, respectively. We assume that the final image is formed at the near point of the eye, providing the largest magnification. Note that the angular magnification of the eyepiece is the same as obtained earlier for the simple magnifying glass. This should not be surprising, because the eyepiece is essentially a magnifying glass, and the same physics applies here. The **net magnification** M_{net} of the compound microscope is the product of the linear magnification of the objective and the angular magnification of the eyepiece:

$$M_{\text{net}} = m^{\text{obj}} M^{\text{eye}} = -\frac{d_{\text{i}}^{\text{obj}}\left(f^{\text{eye}} + 25\text{ cm}\right)}{f^{\text{obj}} f^{\text{eye}}}. \tag{2.34}$$

Example 2.11

Microscope Magnification

Calculate the magnification of an object placed 6.20 mm from a compound microscope that has a 6.00 mm-focal length objective and a 50.0 mm-focal length eyepiece. The objective and eyepiece are separated by 23.0 cm.

Strategy

This situation is similar to that shown in **Figure 2.38**. To find the overall magnification, we must know the linear magnification of the objective and the angular magnification of the eyepiece. We can use **Equation 2.34**, but we need to use the thin-lens equation to find the image distance $d_{\text{i}}^{\text{obj}}$ of the objective.

Solution

Solving the thin-lens equation for $d_{\text{i}}^{\text{obj}}$ gives

$$\begin{aligned} d_{\text{i}}^{\text{obj}} &= \left(\frac{1}{f^{\text{obj}}} - \frac{1}{d_{\text{o}}^{\text{obj}}}\right)^{-1} \\ &= \left(\frac{1}{6.00\text{ mm}} - \frac{1}{6.20\text{ mm}}\right)^{-1} = 186\text{ mm} = 18.6\text{ cm} \end{aligned}$$

Inserting this result into **Equation 2.34** along with the known values $f^{\text{obj}} = 6.20\text{ mm} = 0.620\text{ cm}$ and $f^{\text{eye}} = 50.0\text{ mm} = 5.00\text{ cm}$ gives

$$\begin{aligned} M_{\text{net}} &= -\frac{d_{\text{i}}^{\text{obj}}(f^{\text{eye}} + 25\text{ cm})}{f^{\text{obj}} f^{\text{eye}}} \\ &= -\frac{(18.6\text{ cm})(5.00\text{ cm} + 25\text{ cm})}{(0.600\text{ cm})(5.00\text{ cm})} \\ &= -186 \end{aligned}$$

Significance

Both the objective and the eyepiece contribute to the overall magnification, which is large and negative, consistent with **Figure 2.38**, where the image is seen to be large and inverted. In this case, the image is virtual and inverted, which cannot happen for a single element (see **Figure 2.26**).

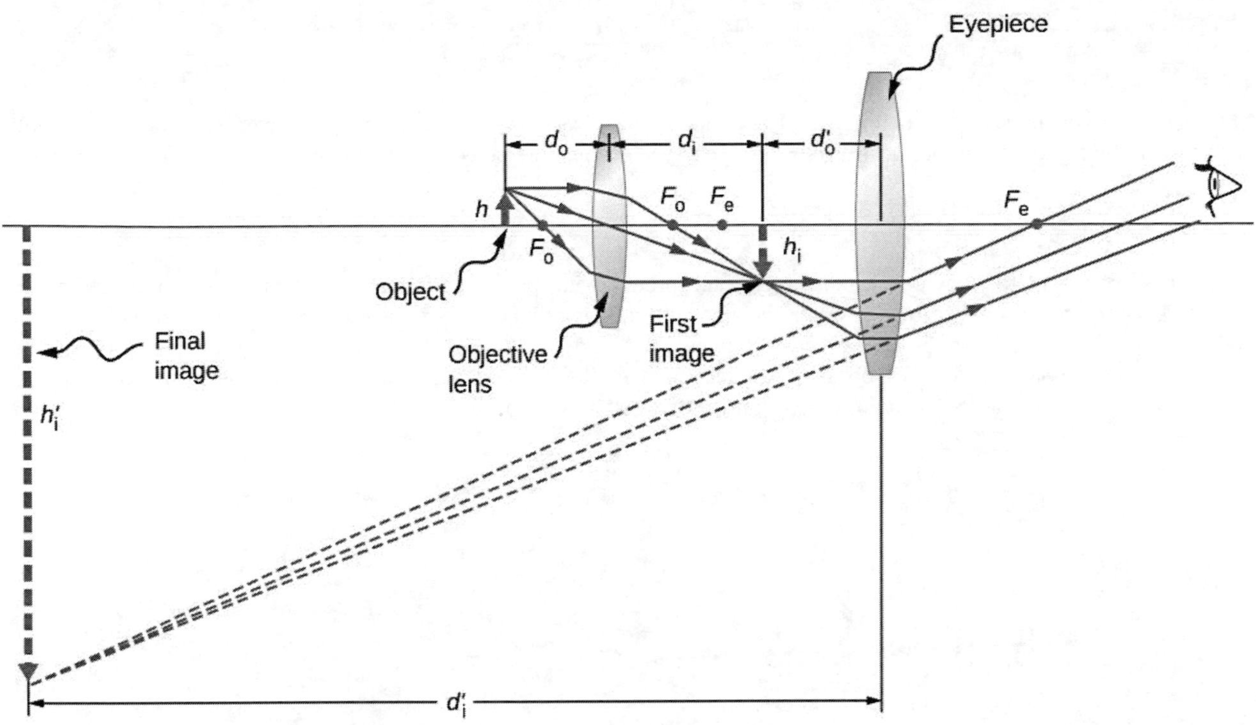

Figure 2.39 A compound microscope with the image created at infinity.

We now calculate the magnifying power of a microscope when the image is at infinity, as shown in **Figure 2.39**, because this makes for the most relaxed viewing. The magnifying power of the microscope is the product of linear magnification m^{obj} of the objective and the angular magnification M^{eye} of the eyepiece. We know that $m^{\text{obj}} = -d_i^{\text{obj}}/d_o^{\text{obj}}$ and from the thin-lens equation we obtain

$$m^{\text{obj}} = -\frac{d_i^{\text{obj}}}{d_o^{\text{obj}}} = 1 - \frac{d_i^{\text{obj}}}{f^{\text{obj}}} = \frac{f^{\text{obj}} - d_i^{\text{obj}}}{f^{\text{obj}}}. \tag{2.35}$$

If the final image is at infinity, then the image created by the objective must be located at the focal point of the eyepiece. This may be seen by considering the thin-lens equation with $d_i = \infty$ or by recalling that rays that pass through the focal point exit the lens parallel to each other, which is equivalent to focusing at infinity. For many microscopes, the distance between the image-side focal point of the objective and the object-side focal point of the eyepiece is standardized at $L = 16\,\text{cm}$. This distance is called the tube length of the microscope. From **Figure 2.39**, we see that $L = f^{\text{obj}} - d_i^{\text{obj}}$. Inserting this into **Equation 2.35** gives

$$m^{\text{obj}} = \frac{L}{f^{\text{obj}}} = \frac{16\,\text{cm}}{f^{\text{obj}}}. \tag{2.36}$$

We now need to calculate the angular magnification of the eyepiece with the image at infinity. To do so, we take the ratio of the angle θ_{image} subtended by the image to the angle θ_{object} subtended by the object at the near point of the eye (this is the closest that the unaided eye can view the object, and thus this is the position where the object will form the largest image on the retina of the unaided eye). Using **Figure 2.39** and working in the small-angle approximation, we have $\theta_{\text{image}} \approx h_i^{\text{obj}}/f^{\text{eye}}$ and $\theta_{\text{object}} \approx h_i^{\text{obj}}/25\,\text{cm}$, where h_i^{obj} is the height of the image formed by the objective, which is the object of the eyepiece. Thus, the angular magnification of the eyepiece is

$$M^{\text{eye}} = \frac{\theta_{\text{image}}}{\theta_{\text{object}}} = \frac{h_i^{\text{obj}}}{f^{\text{eye}}}\frac{25\,\text{cm}}{h_i^{\text{obj}}} = \frac{25\,\text{cm}}{f^{\text{eye}}}. \tag{2.37}$$

The net magnifying power of the compound microscope with the image at infinity is therefore

$$M_{\text{net}} = m^{\text{obj}} M^{\text{eye}} = -\frac{(16\text{ cm})(25\text{ cm})}{f^{\text{obj}} f^{\text{eye}}}. \tag{2.38}$$

The focal distances must be in centimeters. The minus sign indicates that the final image is inverted. Note that the only variables in the equation are the focal distances of the eyepiece and the objective, which makes this equation particularly useful.

Telescopes

Telescopes are meant for viewing distant objects and produce an image that is larger than the image produced in the unaided eye. Telescopes gather far more light than the eye, allowing dim objects to be observed with greater magnification and better resolution. Telescopes were invented around 1600, and Galileo was the first to use them to study the heavens, with monumental consequences. He observed the moons of Jupiter, the craters and mountains on the moon, the details of sunspots, and the fact that the Milky Way is composed of a vast number of individual stars.

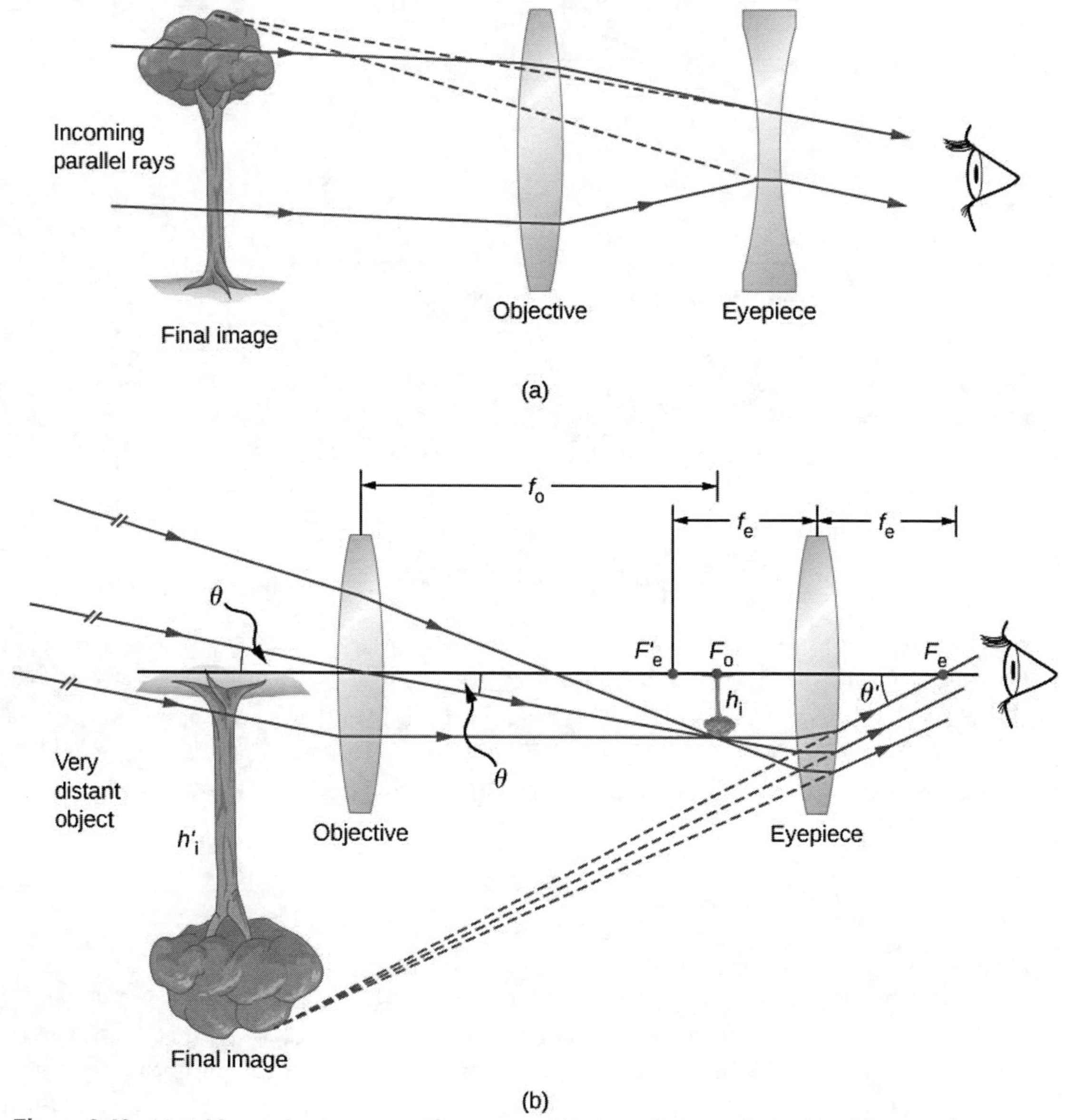

Figure 2.40 (a) Galileo made telescopes with a convex objective and a concave eyepiece. These produce an upright image and are used in spyglasses. (b) Most simple refracting telescopes have two convex lenses. The objective forms a real, inverted image at (or just within) the focal plane of the eyepiece. This image serves as the object for the eyepiece. The eyepiece forms a virtual, inverted image that is magnified.

Part (a) of **Figure 2.40** shows a refracting telescope made of two lenses. The first lens, called the objective, forms a real image within the focal length of the second lens, which is called the eyepiece. The image of the objective lens serves as the object for the eyepiece, which forms a magnified virtual image that is observed by the eye. This design is what Galileo used to observe the heavens.

Although the arrangement of the lenses in a refracting telescope looks similar to that in a microscope, there are important differences. In a telescope, the real object is far away and the intermediate image is smaller than the object. In a microscope, the real object is very close and the intermediate image is larger than the object. In both the telescope and the microscope, the eyepiece magnifies the intermediate image; in the telescope, however, this is the only magnification.

The most common two-lens telescope is shown in part (b) of the figure. The object is so far from the telescope that it is essentially at infinity compared with the focal lengths of the lenses ($d_o^{obj} \approx \infty$), so the incoming rays are essentially parallel and focus on the focal plane. Thus, the first image is produced at $d_i^{obj} = f^{obj}$, as shown in the figure, and is not large compared with what you might see by looking directly at the object. However, the eyepiece of the telescope eyepiece (like the microscope eyepiece) allows you to get nearer than your near point to this first image and so magnifies it (because you are near to it, it subtends a larger angle from your eye and so forms a larger image on your retina). As for a simple magnifier, the angular magnification of a telescope is the ratio of the angle subtended by the image [θ_{image} in part (b)] to the angle subtended by the real object [θ_{object} in part (b)]:

$$M = \frac{\theta_{image}}{\theta_{object}}. \tag{2.39}$$

To obtain an expression for the magnification that involves only the lens parameters, note that the focal plane of the objective lens lies very close to the focal plan of the eyepiece. If we assume that these planes are superposed, we have the situation shown in Figure 2.41.

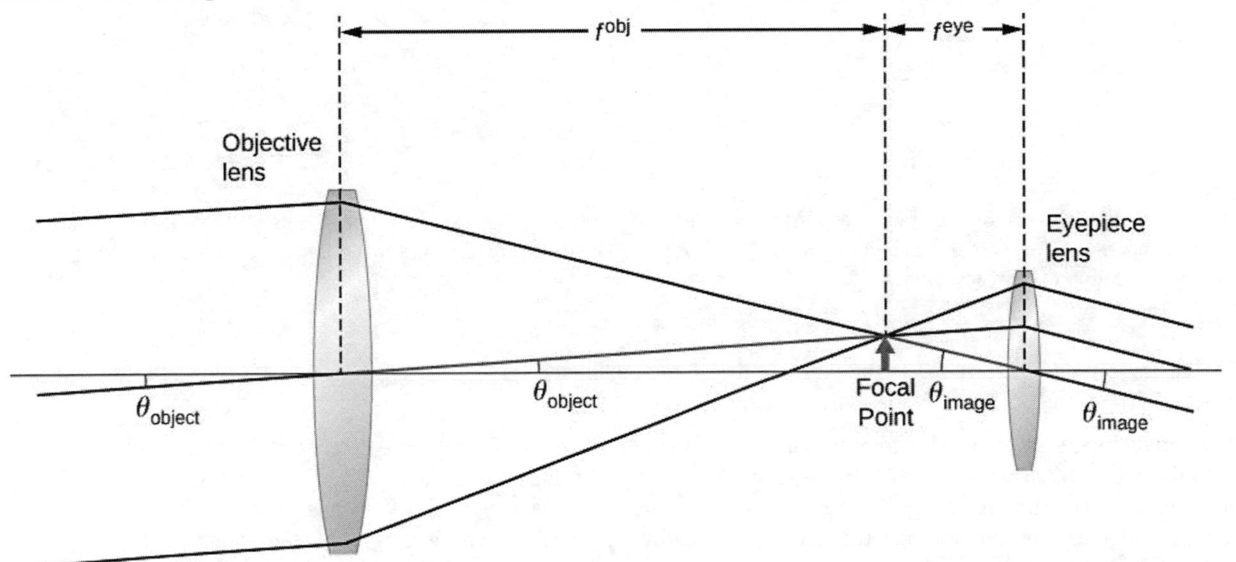

Figure 2.41 The focal plane of the objective lens of a telescope is very near to the focal plane of the eyepiece. The angle θ_{image} subtended by the image viewed through the eyepiece is larger than the angle θ_{object} subtended by the object when viewed with the unaided eye.

We further assume that the angles θ_{object} and θ_{image} are small, so that the small-angle approximation holds ($\tan\theta \approx \theta$). If the image formed at the focal plane has height *h*, then

$$\theta_{object} \approx \tan\theta_{object} = \frac{h}{f^{obj}}$$

$$\theta_{image} \approx \tan\theta_{image} = \frac{-h}{f^{eye}}$$

where the minus sign is introduced because the height is negative if we measure both angles in the counterclockwise direction. Inserting these expressions into **Equation 2.39** gives

$$M = \frac{-h_i}{f^{eye}} \frac{f^{obj}}{h_i} = -\frac{f^{obj}}{f^{eye}}. \tag{2.40}$$

Thus, to obtain the greatest angular magnification, it is best to have an objective with a long focal length and an eyepiece with a short focal length. The greater the angular magnification *M*, the larger an object will appear when viewed through a telescope, making more details visible. Limits to observable details are imposed by many factors, including lens quality and atmospheric disturbance. Typical eyepieces have focal lengths of 2.5 cm or 1.25 cm. If the objective of the telescope has a focal length of 1 meter, then these eyepieces result in magnifications of $40 \times$ and $80 \times$, respectively. Thus, the angular magnifications make the image appear 40 times or 80 times closer than the real object.

The minus sign in the magnification indicates the image is inverted, which is unimportant for observing the stars but is a real problem for other applications, such as telescopes on ships or telescopic gun sights. If an upright image is needed, Galileo's arrangement in part (a) of **Figure 2.40** can be used. But a more common arrangement is to use a third convex lens as an eyepiece, increasing the distance between the first two and inverting the image once again, as seen in **Figure 2.42**.

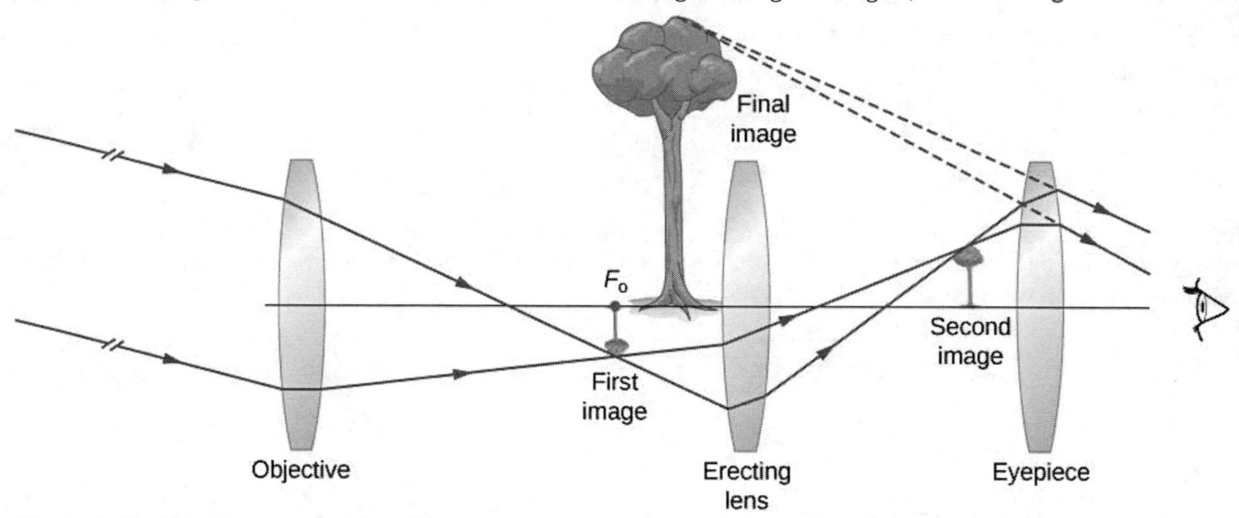

Figure 2.42 This arrangement of three lenses in a telescope produces an upright final image. The first two lenses are far enough apart that the second lens inverts the image of the first. The third lens acts as a magnifier and keeps the image upright and in a location that is easy to view.

The largest refracting telescope in the world is the 40-inch diameter Yerkes telescope located at Lake Geneva, Wisconsin (**Figure 2.43**), and operated by the University of Chicago.

It is very difficult and expensive to build large refracting telescopes. You need large defect-free lenses, which in itself is a technically demanding task. A refracting telescope basically looks like a tube with a support structure to rotate it in different directions. A refracting telescope suffers from several problems. The aberration of lenses causes the image to be blurred. Also, as the lenses become thicker for larger lenses, more light is absorbed, making faint stars more difficult to observe. Large lenses are also very heavy and deform under their own weight. Some of these problems with refracting telescopes are addressed by avoiding refraction for collecting light and instead using a curved mirror in its place, as devised by Isaac Newton. These telescopes are called reflecting telescopes.

Figure 2.43 In 1897, the Yerkes Observatory in Wisconsin (USA) built a large refracting telescope with an objective lens that is 40 inches in diameter and has a tube length of 62 feet. (credit: Yerkes Observatory, University of Chicago)

Reflecting Telescopes

Isaac Newton designed the first reflecting telescope around 1670 to solve the problem of chromatic aberration that happens in all refracting telescopes. In chromatic aberration, light of different colors refracts by slightly different amounts in the lens. As a result, a rainbow appears around the image and the image appears blurred. In the reflecting telescope, light rays from a distant source fall upon the surface of a concave mirror fixed at the bottom end of the tube. The use of a mirror instead of a lens eliminates chromatic aberration. The concave mirror focuses the rays on its focal plane. The design problem is how to observe the focused image. Newton used a design in which the focused light from the concave mirror was reflected to one side of the tube into an eyepiece [part (a) of **Figure 2.44**]. This arrangement is common in many amateur telescopes and is called the **Newtonian design**.

Some telescopes reflect the light back toward the middle of the concave mirror using a convex mirror. In this arrangement, the light-gathering concave mirror has a hole in the middle [part (b) of the figure]. The light then is incident on an eyepiece lens. This arrangement of the objective and eyepiece is called the **Cassegrain design**. Most big telescopes, including the Hubble space telescope, are of this design. Other arrangements are also possible. In some telescopes, a light detector is placed right at the spot where light is focused by the curved mirror.

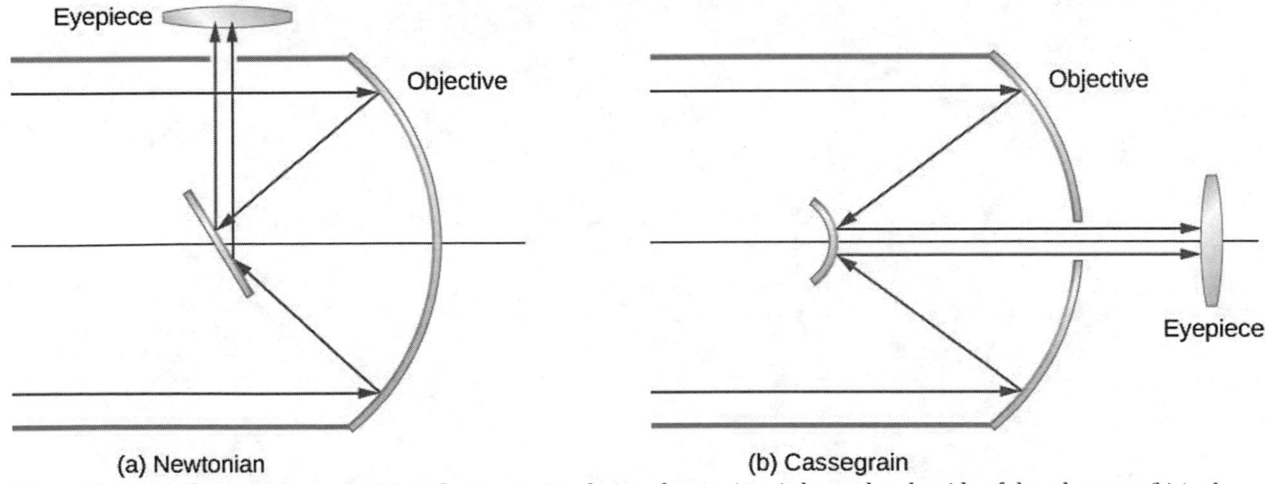

Figure 2.44 Reflecting telescopes: (a) In the Newtonian design, the eyepiece is located at the side of the telescope; (b) in the Cassegrain design, the eyepiece is located past a hole in the primary mirror.

Most astronomical research telescopes are now of the reflecting type. One of the earliest large telescopes of this kind is the Hale 200-inch (or 5-meter) telescope built on Mount Palomar in southern California, which has a 200 inch-diameter mirror. One of the largest telescopes in the world is the 10-meter Keck telescope at the Keck Observatory on the summit of the dormant Mauna Kea volcano in Hawaii. The Keck Observatory operates two 10-meter telescopes. Each is not a single mirror, but is instead made up of 36 hexagonal mirrors. Furthermore, the two telescopes on the Keck can work together, which increases their power to an effective 85-meter mirror. The Hubble telescope (**Figure 2.45**) is another large reflecting telescope with a 2.4 meter-diameter primary mirror. The Hubble was put into orbit around Earth in 1990.

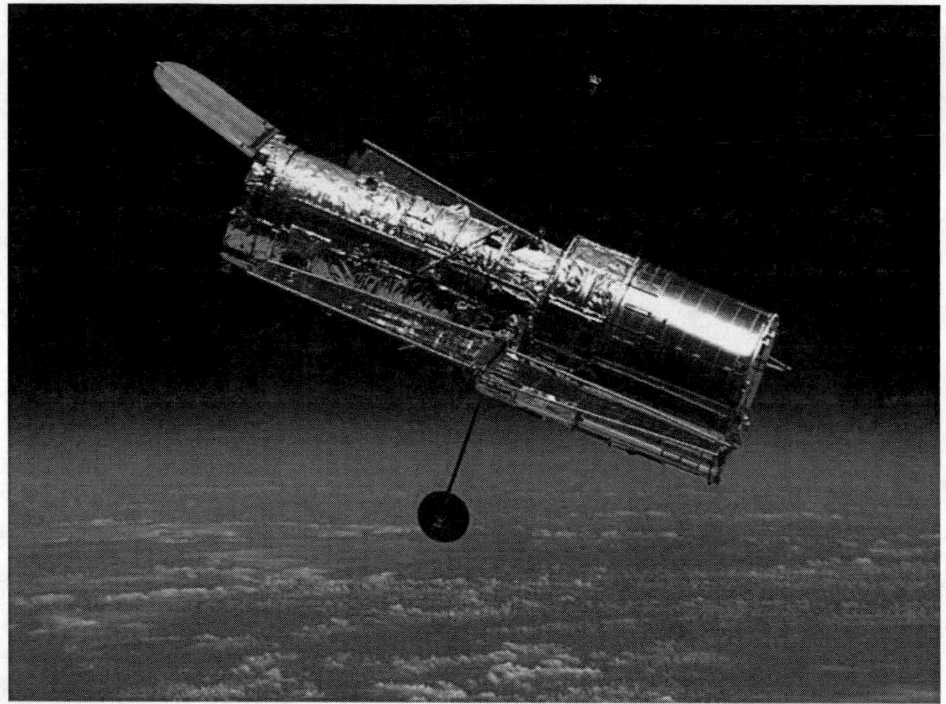

Figure 2.45 The Hubble space telescope as seen from the Space Shuttle Discovery. (credit: modification of work by NASA)

The angular magnification M of a reflecting telescope is also given by **Equation 2.36**. For a spherical mirror, the focal length is half the radius of curvature, so making a large objective mirror not only helps the telescope collect more light but also increases the magnification of the image.

CHAPTER 2 REVIEW

KEY TERMS

aberration distortion in an image caused by departures from the small-angle approximation

accommodation use of the ciliary muscles to adjust the shape of the eye lens for focusing on near or far objects

angular magnification ratio of the angle subtended by an object observed with a magnifier to that observed by the naked eye

apparent depth depth at which an object is perceived to be located with respect to an interface between two media

Cassegrain design arrangement of an objective and eyepiece such that the light-gathering concave mirror has a hole in the middle, and light then is incident on an eyepiece lens

charge-coupled device (CCD) semiconductor chip that converts a light image into tiny pixels that can be converted into electronic signals of color and intensity

coma similar to spherical aberration, but arises when the incoming rays are not parallel to the optical axis

compound microscope microscope constructed from two convex lenses, the first serving as the eyepiece and the second serving as the objective lens

concave mirror spherical mirror with its reflecting surface on the inner side of the sphere; the mirror forms a “cave”

converging (or convex) lens lens in which light rays that enter it parallel converge into a single point on the opposite side

convex mirror spherical mirror with its reflecting surface on the outer side of the sphere

curved mirror mirror formed by a curved surface, such as spherical, elliptical, or parabolic

diverging (or concave) lens lens that causes light rays to bend away from its optical axis

eyepiece lens or combination of lenses in an optical instrument nearest to the eye of the observer

far point furthest point an eye can see in focus

farsightedness (or hyperopia) visual defect in which near objects appear blurred because their images are focused behind the retina rather than on the retina; a farsighted person can see far objects clearly but near objects appear blurred

first focus or object focus object located at this point will result in an image created at infinity on the opposite side of a spherical interface between two media

focal length distance along the optical axis from the focal point to the optical element that focuses the light rays

focal plane plane that contains the focal point and is perpendicular to the optical axis

focal point for a converging lens or mirror, the point at which converging light rays cross; for a diverging lens or mirror, the point from which diverging light rays appear to originate

image distance distance of the image from the central axis of the optical element that produces the image

linear magnification ratio of image height to object height

magnification ratio of image size to object size

near point closest point an eye can see in focus

nearsightedness (or myopia) visual defect in which far objects appear blurred because their images are focused in front of the retina rather than on the retina; a nearsighted person can see near objects clearly but far objects appear blurred

net magnification (M_{net}) of the compound microscope is the product of the linear magnification of the objective and the angular magnification of the eyepiece

Newtonian design arrangement of an objective and eyepiece such that the focused light from the concave mirror was reflected to one side of the tube into an eyepiece

object distance distance of the object from the central axis of the optical element that produces its image

objective lens nearest to the object being examined.

optical axis axis about which the mirror is rotationally symmetric; you can rotate the mirror about this axis without changing anything

optical power (P) inverse of the focal length of a lens, with the focal length expressed in meters. The optical power P of a lens is expressed in units of diopters D; that is, $1\text{D} = 1/\text{m} = 1\text{ m}^{-1}$

plane mirror plane (flat) reflecting surface

ray tracing technique that uses geometric constructions to find and characterize the image formed by an optical system

real image image that can be projected onto a screen because the rays physically go through the image

second focus or image focus for a converging interface, the point where a bundle of parallel rays refracting at a spherical interface; for a diverging interface, the point at which the backward continuation of the refracted rays will converge between two media will focus

simple magnifier (or magnifying glass) converging lens that produces a virtual image of an object that is within the focal length of the lens

small-angle approximation approximation that is valid when the size of a spherical mirror is significantly smaller than the mirror's radius; in this approximation, spherical aberration is negligible and the mirror has a well-defined focal point

spherical aberration distortion in the image formed by a spherical mirror when rays are not all focused at the same point

thin-lens approximation assumption that the lens is very thin compared to the first image distance

vertex point where the mirror's surface intersects with the optical axis

virtual image image that cannot be projected on a screen because the rays do not physically go through the image, they only appear to originate from the image

KEY EQUATIONS

Image distance in a plane mirror	$d_\text{o} = -d_\text{i}$
Focal length for a spherical mirror	$f = \frac{R}{2}$
Mirror equation	$\frac{1}{d_\text{o}} + \frac{1}{d_\text{i}} = \frac{1}{f}$
Magnification of a spherical mirror	$m = \frac{h_\text{i}}{h_\text{o}} = -\frac{d_\text{i}}{d_\text{o}}$
Sign convention for mirrors	
Focal length f	+ for concave mirror − for convex mirror
Object distance d_o	+ for real object − for virtual object
Image distance d_i	+ for real image − for virtual image
Magnification m	+ for upright image − for inverted image
Apparent depth equation	$h_\text{i} = \left(\frac{n_2}{n_1}\right)h_\text{o}$

Spherical interface equation	$\frac{n_1}{d_o} + \frac{n_2}{d_i} = \frac{n_2 - n_1}{R}$
The thin-lens equation	$\frac{1}{d_o} + \frac{1}{d_i} = \frac{1}{f}$
The lens maker's equation	$\frac{1}{f} = \left(\frac{n_2}{n_1} - 1\right)\left(\frac{1}{R_1} - \frac{1}{R_2}\right)$
The magnification *m* of an object	$m \equiv \frac{h_i}{h_o} = -\frac{d_i}{d_o}$
Optical power	$P = \frac{1}{f}$
Optical power of thin, closely spaced lenses	$P_{total} = P_{lens1} + P_{lens2} + P_{lens3} + \cdots$
Angular magnification *M* of a simple magnifier	$M = \frac{\theta_{image}}{\theta_{object}}$
Angular magnification of an object a distance *L* from the eye for a convex lens of focal length *f* held a distance ℓ from the eye	$M = \left(\frac{25\text{ cm}}{L}\right)\left(1 + \frac{L - \ell}{f}\right)$
Range of angular magnification for a given lens for a person with a near point of 25 cm	$\frac{25\text{ cm}}{f} \le M \le 1 + \frac{25\text{ cm}}{f}$
Net magnification of compound microscope	$M_{net} = m^{obj} M^{eye} = -\frac{d_i^{obj}\left(f^{eye} + 25\text{ cm}\right)}{f^{obj} f^{eye}}$

SUMMARY

2.1 Images Formed by Plane Mirrors

- A plane mirror always forms a virtual image (behind the mirror).
- The image and object are the same distance from a flat mirror, the image size is the same as the object size, and the image is upright.

2.2 Spherical Mirrors

- Spherical mirrors may be concave (converging) or convex (diverging).
- The focal length of a spherical mirror is one-half of its radius of curvature: $f = R/2$.
- The mirror equation and ray tracing allow you to give a complete description of an image formed by a spherical mirror.
- Spherical aberration occurs for spherical mirrors but not parabolic mirrors; comatic aberration occurs for both types of mirrors.

2.3 Images Formed by Refraction

This section explains how a single refracting interface forms images.

- When an object is observed through a plane interface between two media, then it appears at an apparent distance h_i that differs from the actual distance h_o: $h_i = (n_2/n_1)h_o$.
- An image is formed by the refraction of light at a spherical interface between two media of indices of refraction n_1 and n_2.

- Image distance depends on the radius of curvature of the interface, location of the object, and the indices of refraction of the media.

2.4 Thin Lenses

- Two types of lenses are possible: converging and diverging. A lens that causes light rays to bend toward (away from) its optical axis is a converging (diverging) lens.
- For a converging lens, the focal point is where the converging light rays cross; for a diverging lens, the focal point is the point from which the diverging light rays appear to originate.
- The distance from the center of a thin lens to its focal point is called the focal length f.
- Ray tracing is a geometric technique to determine the paths taken by light rays through thin lenses.
- A real image can be projected onto a screen.
- A virtual image cannot be projected onto a screen.
- A converging lens forms either real or virtual images, depending on the object location; a diverging lens forms only virtual images.

2.5 The Eye

- Image formation by the eye is adequately described by the thin-lens equation.
- The eye produces a real image on the retina by adjusting its focal length in a process called accommodation.
- Nearsightedness, or myopia, is the inability to see far objects and is corrected with a diverging lens to reduce the optical power of the eye.
- Farsightedness, or hyperopia, is the inability to see near objects and is corrected with a converging lens to increase the optical power of the eye.
- In myopia and hyperopia, the corrective lenses produce images at distances that fall between the person's near and far points so that images can be seen clearly.

2.6 The Camera

- Cameras use combinations of lenses to create an image for recording.
- Digital photography is based on charge-coupled devices (CCDs) that break an image into tiny "pixels" that can be converted into electronic signals.

2.7 The Simple Magnifier

- A simple magnifier is a converging lens and produces a magnified virtual image of an object located within the focal length of the lens.
- Angular magnification accounts for magnification of an image created by a magnifier. It is equal to the ratio of the angle subtended by the image to that subtended by the object when the object is observed by the unaided eye.
- Angular magnification is greater for magnifying lenses with smaller focal lengths.
- Simple magnifiers can produce as great as tenfold ($10\times$) magnification.

2.8 Microscopes and Telescopes

- Many optical devices contain more than a single lens or mirror. These are analyzed by considering each element sequentially. The image formed by the first is the object for the second, and so on. The same ray-tracing and thin-lens techniques developed in the previous sections apply to each lens element.
- The overall magnification of a multiple-element system is the product of the linear magnifications of its individual elements times the angular magnification of the eyepiece. For a two-element system with an objective and an eyepiece, this is

$$M = m^{\text{obj}} M^{\text{eye}}.$$

where m^{obj} is the linear magnification of the objective and M^{eye} is the angular magnification of the eyepiece.

- The microscope is a multiple-element system that contains more than a single lens or mirror. It allows us to see detail that we could not to see with the unaided eye. Both the eyepiece and objective contribute to the magnification. The magnification of a compound microscope with the image at infinity is

$$M_{\text{net}} = -\frac{(16\text{ cm})(25\text{ cm})}{f^{\text{obj}} f^{\text{eye}}}.$$

In this equation, 16 cm is the standardized distance between the image-side focal point of the objective lens and the object-side focal point of the eyepiece, 25 cm is the normal near point distance, f^{obj} and f^{eye} are the focal distances for the objective lens and the eyepiece, respectively.

- Simple telescopes can be made with two lenses. They are used for viewing objects at large distances.
- The angular magnification M for a telescope is given by

$$M = -\frac{f^{\text{obj}}}{f^{\text{eye}}},$$

where f^{obj} and f^{eye} are the focal lengths of the objective lens and the eyepiece, respectively.

CONCEPTUAL QUESTIONS

2.1 Images Formed by Plane Mirrors

1. What are the differences between real and virtual images? How can you tell (by looking) whether an image formed by a single lens or mirror is real or virtual?

2. Can you see a virtual image? Explain your response.

3. Can you photograph a virtual image?

4. Can you project a virtual image onto a screen?

5. Is it necessary to project a real image onto a screen to see it?

6. Devise an arrangement of mirrors allowing you to see the back of your head. What is the minimum number of mirrors needed for this task?

7. If you wish to see your entire body in a flat mirror (from head to toe), how tall should the mirror be? Does its size depend upon your distance away from the mirror? Provide a sketch.

2.2 Spherical Mirrors

8. At what distance is an image always located: at d_o, d_i, or f?

9. Under what circumstances will an image be located at the focal point of a spherical lens or mirror?

10. What is meant by a negative magnification? What is meant by a magnification whose absolute value is less than one?

11. Can an image be larger than the object even though its magnification is negative? Explain.

2.3 Images Formed by Refraction

12. Derive the formula for the apparent depth of a fish in a fish tank using Snell's law.

13. Use a ruler and a protractor to find the image by refraction in the following cases. Assume an air-glass interface. Use a refractive index of 1 for air and of 1.5 for glass. (*Hint*: Use Snell's law at the interface.)

(a) A point object located on the axis of a concave interface located at a point within the focal length from the vertex.

(b) A point object located on the axis of a concave interface located at a point farther than the focal length from the vertex.

(c) A point object located on the axis of a convex interface located at a point within the focal length from the vertex.

(d) A point object located on the axis of a convex interface located at a point farther than the focal length from the vertex.

(e) Repeat (a)–(d) for a point object off the axis.

2.4 Thin Lenses

14. You can argue that a flat piece of glass, such as in a window, is like a lens with an infinite focal length. If so, where does it form an image? That is, how are d_i and d_o related?

15. When you focus a camera, you adjust the distance of the lens from the film. If the camera lens acts like a thin lens, why can it not be a fixed distance from the film for both near and distant objects?

16. A thin lens has two focal points, one on either side of the lens at equal distances from its center, and should behave the same for light entering from either side. Look backward and forward through a pair of eyeglasses and comment on whether they are thin lenses.

17. Will the focal length of a lens change when it is submerged in water? Explain.

2.5 The Eye

18. If the lens of a person's eye is removed because of cataracts (as has been done since ancient times), why would you expect an eyeglass lens of about 16 D to be prescribed?

19. When laser light is shone into a relaxed normal-vision eye to repair a tear by spot-welding the retina to the back of the eye, the rays entering the eye must be parallel. Why?

20. Why is your vision so blurry when you open your eyes while swimming under water? How does a face mask enable clear vision?

21. It has become common to replace the cataract-clouded lens of the eye with an internal lens. This intraocular lens can be chosen so that the person has perfect distant vision. Will the person be able to read without glasses? If the person was nearsighted, is the power of the intraocular lens greater or less than the removed lens?

22. If the cornea is to be reshaped (this can be done surgically or with contact lenses) to correct myopia, should its curvature be made greater or smaller? Explain.

2.8 Microscopes and Telescopes

23. Geometric optics describes the interaction of light with macroscopic objects. Why, then, is it correct to use geometric optics to analyze a microscope's image?

24. The image produced by the microscope in Figure 2.38 cannot be projected. Could extra lenses or mirrors project it? Explain.

25. If you want your microscope or telescope to project a real image onto a screen, how would you change the placement of the eyepiece relative to the objective?

PROBLEMS

2.1 Images Formed by Plane Mirrors

26. Consider a pair of flat mirrors that are positioned so that they form an angle of $120°$. An object is placed on the bisector between the mirrors. Construct a ray diagram as in Figure 2.4 to show how many images are formed.

27. Consider a pair of flat mirrors that are positioned so that they form an angle of $60°$. An object is placed on the bisector between the mirrors. Construct a ray diagram as in Figure 2.4 to show how many images are formed.

28. By using more than one flat mirror, construct a ray diagram showing how to create an inverted image.

2.2 Spherical Mirrors

29. The following figure shows a light bulb between two spherical mirrors. One mirror produces a beam of light with parallel rays; the other keeps light from escaping without being put into the beam. Where is the filament of the light in relation to the focal point or radius of curvature of each mirror?

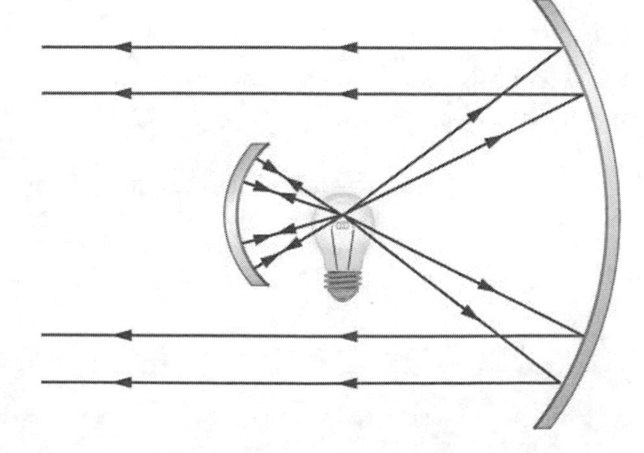

30. Why are diverging mirrors often used for rearview mirrors in vehicles? What is the main disadvantage of using such a mirror compared with a flat one?

31. Some telephoto cameras use a mirror rather than a lens. What radius of curvature mirror is needed to replace a 800 mm-focal length telephoto lens?

32. Calculate the focal length of a mirror formed by the shiny back of a spoon that has a 3.00 cm radius of curvature.

33. Electric room heaters use a concave mirror to reflect infrared (IR) radiation from hot coils. Note that IR radiation follows the same law of reflection as visible light. Given that the mirror has a radius of curvature of 50.0 cm and produces an image of the coils 3.00 m away from the mirror, where are the coils?

34. Find the magnification of the heater element in the previous problem. Note that its large magnitude helps spread out the reflected energy.

35. What is the focal length of a makeup mirror that produces a magnification of 1.50 when a person's face is 12.0 cm away? Explicitly show how you follow the steps in the **Problem-Solving Strategy: Spherical Mirrors**.

36. A shopper standing 3.00 m from a convex security mirror sees his image with a magnification of 0.250. (a) Where is his image? (b) What is the focal length of the mirror? (c) What is its radius of curvature?

37. An object 1.50 cm high is held 3.00 cm from a person's cornea, and its reflected image is measured to be 0.167 cm high. (a) What is the magnification? (b) Where is the image? (c) Find the radius of curvature of the convex mirror formed by the cornea. (Note that this technique is used by optometrists to measure the curvature of the cornea for contact lens fitting. The instrument used is called a keratometer, or curve measurer.)

38. Ray tracing for a flat mirror shows that the image is located a distance behind the mirror equal to the distance of the object from the mirror. This is stated as $d_i = -d_o$, since this is a negative image distance (it is a virtual image). What is the focal length of a flat mirror?

39. Show that, for a flat mirror, $h_i = h_o$, given that the image is the same distance behind the mirror as the distance of the object from the mirror.

40. Use the law of reflection to prove that the focal length of a mirror is half its radius of curvature. That is, prove that $f = R/2$. Note this is true for a spherical mirror only if its diameter is small compared with its radius of curvature.

41. Referring to the electric room heater considered in problem 5, calculate the intensity of IR radiation in W/m^2 projected by the concave mirror on a person 3.00 m away. Assume that the heating element radiates 1500 W and has an area of $100\ cm^2$, and that half of the radiated power is reflected and focused by the mirror.

42. Two mirrors are inclined at an angle of $60°$ and an object is placed at a point that is equidistant from the two mirrors. Use a protractor to draw rays accurately and locate all images. You may have to draw several figures so that that rays for different images do not clutter your drawing.

43. Two parallel mirrors are facing each other and are separated by a distance of 3 cm. A point object is placed between the mirrors 1 cm from one of the mirrors. Find the coordinates of all the images.

2.3 Images Formed by Refraction

44. An object is located in air 30 cm from the vertex of a concave surface made of glass with a radius of curvature 10 cm. Where does the image by refraction form and what is its magnification? Use $n_{air} = 1$ and $n_{glass} = 1.5$.

45. An object is located in air 30 cm from the vertex of a convex surface made of glass with a radius of curvature 80 cm. Where does the image by refraction form and what is its magnification?

46. An object is located in water 15 cm from the vertex of a concave surface made of glass with a radius of curvature 10 cm. Where does the image by refraction form and what is its magnification? Use $n_{water} = 4/3$ and $n_{glass} = 1.5$.

47. An object is located in water 30 cm from the vertex of a convex surface made of Plexiglas with a radius of curvature of 80 cm. Where does the image form by refraction and what is its magnification? $n_{water} = 4/3$ and $n_{Plexiglas} = 1.65$.

48. An object is located in air 5 cm from the vertex of a concave surface made of glass with a radius of curvature 20 cm. Where does the image form by refraction and what is its magnification? Use $n_{air} = 1$ and $n_{glass} = 1.5$.

49. Derive the spherical interface equation for refraction at a concave surface. (*Hint*: Follow the derivation in the text for the convex surface.)

2.4 Thin Lenses

50. How far from the lens must the film in a camera be, if the lens has a 35.0-mm focal length and is being used to photograph a flower 75.0 cm away? Explicitly show how you follow the steps in the **Problem-Solving Strategy: Lenses**.

51. A certain slide projector has a 100 mm-focal length lens. (a) How far away is the screen if a slide is placed 103 mm from the lens and produces a sharp image? (b) If the slide is 24.0 by 36.0 mm, what are the dimensions of the image? Explicitly show how you follow the steps in the **Problem-Solving Strategy: Lenses**.

52. A doctor examines a mole with a 15.0-cm focal length magnifying glass held 13.5 cm from the mole. (a) Where is the image? (b) What is its magnification? (c) How big is the image of a 5.00 mm diameter mole?

53. A camera with a 50.0-mm focal length lens is being used to photograph a person standing 3.00 m away. (a) How far from the lens must the film be? (b) If the film is 36.0 mm high, what fraction of a 1.75-m-tall person will fit on it? (c) Discuss how reasonable this seems, based on your experience in taking or posing for photographs.

54. A camera lens used for taking close-up photographs has a focal length of 22.0 mm. The farthest it can be placed from the film is 33.0 mm. (a) What is the closest object that can be photographed? (b) What is the magnification of this closest object?

55. Suppose your 50.0 mm-focal length camera lens is 51.0 mm away from the film in the camera. (a) How far away is an object that is in focus? (b) What is the height of the object if its image is 2.00 cm high?

56. What is the focal length of a magnifying glass that produces a magnification of 3.00 when held 5.00 cm from an object, such as a rare coin?

57. The magnification of a book held 7.50 cm from a 10.0 cm-focal length lens is 3.00. (a) Find the magnification for the book when it is held 8.50 cm from the magnifier. (b) Repeat for the book held 9.50 cm from the magnifier. (c) Comment on how magnification changes as the object distance increases as in these two calculations.

58. Suppose a 200 mm-focal length telephoto lens is being used to photograph mountains 10.0 km away. (a) Where is the image? (b) What is the height of the image of a 1000 m high cliff on one of the mountains?

59. A camera with a 100 mm-focal length lens is used to photograph the sun. What is the height of the image of the sun on the film, given the sun is 1.40×10^6 km in diameter and is 1.50×10^8 km away?

60. Use the thin-lens equation to show that the magnification for a thin lens is determined by its focal length and the object distance and is given by $m = f/(f - d_o)$.

61. An object of height 3.0 cm is placed 5.0 cm in front of a converging lens of focal length 20 cm and observed from the other side. Where and how large is the image?

62. An object of height 3.0 cm is placed at 5.0 cm in front of a diverging lens of focal length 20 cm and observed from the other side. Where and how large is the image?

63. An object of height 3.0 cm is placed at 25 cm in front of a diverging lens of focal length 20 cm. Behind the diverging lens, there is a converging lens of focal length 20 cm. The distance between the lenses is 5.0 cm. Find the location and size of the final image.

64. Two convex lenses of focal lengths 20 cm and 10 cm are placed 30 cm apart, with the lens with the longer focal length on the right. An object of height 2.0 cm is placed midway between them and observed through each lens from the left and from the right. Describe what you will see, such as where the image(s) will appear, whether they will be upright or inverted and their magnifications.

2.5 The Eye

Unless otherwise stated, the lens-to-retina distance is 2.00 cm.

65. What is the power of the eye when viewing an object 50.0 cm away?

66. Calculate the power of the eye when viewing an object 3.00 m away.

67. The print in many books averages 3.50 mm in height. How high is the image of the print on the retina when the book is held 30.0 cm from the eye?

68. Suppose a certain person's visual acuity is such that he can see objects clearly that form an image $4.00\ \mu m$ high on his retina. What is the maximum distance at which he can read the 75.0-cm-high letters on the side of an airplane?

69. People who do very detailed work close up, such as jewelers, often can see objects clearly at much closer distance than the normal 25 cm. (a) What is the power of the eyes of a woman who can see an object clearly at a distance of only 8.00 cm? (b) What is the image size of a 1.00-mm object, such as lettering inside a ring, held at this distance? (c) What would the size of the image be if the object were held at the normal 25.0 cm distance?

70. What is the far point of a person whose eyes have a relaxed power of 50.5 D?

71. What is the near point of a person whose eyes have an accommodated power of 53.5 D?

72. (a) A laser reshaping the cornea of a myopic patient reduces the power of his eye by 9.00 D, with a $\pm 5.0\ \%$ uncertainty in the final correction. What is the range of diopters for eyeglass lenses that this person might need after this procedure? (b) Was the person nearsighted or farsighted before the procedure? How do you know?

73. The power for normal close vision is 54.0 D. In a vision-correction procedure, the power of a patient's eye is increased by 3.00 D. Assuming that this produces normal close vision, what was the patient's near point before the procedure?

74. For normal distant vision, the eye has a power of 50.0 D. What was the previous far point of a patient who had laser vision correction that reduced the power of her eye by 7.00 D, producing normal distant vision?

75. The power for normal distant vision is 50.0 D. A severely myopic patient has a far point of 5.00 cm. By how many diopters should the power of his eye be reduced in laser vision correction to obtain normal distant vision for him?

76. A student's eyes, while reading the blackboard, have a power of 51.0 D. How far is the board from his eyes?

77. The power of a physician's eyes is 53.0 D while examining a patient. How far from her eyes is the object that is being examined?

78. The normal power for distant vision is 50.0 D. A young woman with normal distant vision has a 10.0% ability to accommodate (that is, increase) the power of her eyes. What is the closest object she can see clearly?

79. The far point of a myopic administrator is 50.0 cm. (a) What is the relaxed power of his eyes? (b) If he has the normal 8.00% ability to accommodate, what is the closest object he can see clearly?

80. A very myopic man has a far point of 20.0 cm. What power contact lens (when on the eye) will correct his distant vision?

81. Repeat the previous problem for eyeglasses held 1.50 cm from the eyes.

82. A myopic person sees that her contact lens prescription is –4.00 D. What is her far point?

83. Repeat the previous problem for glasses that are 1.75 cm from the eyes.

84. The contact lens prescription for a mildly farsighted person is 0.750 D, and the person has a near point of 29.0 cm. What is the power of the tear layer between the cornea and the lens if the correction is ideal, taking the tear layer into account?

2.7 The Simple Magnifier

85. If the image formed on the retina subtends an angle of $30°$ and the object subtends an angle of $5°$, what is the magnification of the image?

86. What is the magnification of a magnifying lens with a focal length of 10 cm if it is held 3.0 cm from the eye and the object is 12 cm from the eye?

87. How far should you hold a 2.1 cm-focal length magnifying glass from an object to obtain a magnification of $10\times$? Assume you place your eye 5.0 cm from the magnifying glass.

88. You hold a 5.0 cm-focal length magnifying glass as close as possible to your eye. If you have a normal near point, what is the magnification?

89. You view a mountain with a magnifying glass of focal length $f = 10\ \text{cm}$. What is the magnification?

90. You view an object by holding a 2.5 cm-focal length magnifying glass 10 cm away from it. How far from your eye should you hold the magnifying glass to obtain a magnification of $10\times$?

91. A magnifying glass forms an image 10 cm on the opposite side of the lens from the object, which is 10 cm away. What is the magnification of this lens for a person with a normal near point if their eye 12 cm from the object?

92. An object viewed with the naked eye subtends a $2°$ angle. If you view the object through a $10\times$ magnifying glass, what angle is subtended by the image formed on your retina?

93. For a normal, relaxed eye, a magnifying glass produces an angular magnification of 4.0. What is the largest magnification possible with this magnifying glass?

94. What range of magnification is possible with a 7.0 cm-focal length converging lens?

95. A magnifying glass produces an angular magnification of 4.5 when used by a young person with a near point of 18 cm. What is the maximum angular magnification obtained by an older person with a near point of 45 cm?

2.8 Microscopes and Telescopes

96. A microscope with an overall magnification of 800 has an objective that magnifies by 200. (a) What is the angular magnification of the eyepiece? (b) If there are two other objectives that can be used, having magnifications of 100 and 400, what other total magnifications are possible?

97. (a) What magnification is produced by a 0.150 cm-focal length microscope objective that is 0.155 cm from the object being viewed? (b) What is the overall magnification if an $8\times$ eyepiece (one that produces an angular magnification of 8.00) is used?

98. Where does an object need to be placed relative to a microscope for its 0.50 cm-focal length objective to produce a magnification of -400?

99. An amoeba is 0.305 cm away from the 0.300 cm-focal length objective lens of a microscope. (a) Where is the image formed by the objective lens? (b) What is this image's magnification? (c) An eyepiece with a 2.00-cm focal length is placed 20.0 cm from the objective. Where is the final image? (d) What angular magnification is produced by the eyepiece? (e) What is the overall magnification? (See **Figure 2.39**.)

100. Unreasonable Results Your friends show you an image through a microscope. They tell you that the microscope has an objective with a 0.500-cm focal length and an eyepiece with a 5.00-cm focal length. The resulting overall magnification is 250,000. Are these viable values for a microscope?

Unless otherwise stated, the lens-to-retina distance is 2.00 cm.

101. What is the angular magnification of a telescope that has a 100 cm-focal length objective and a 2.50 cm-focal length eyepiece?

102. Find the distance between the objective and eyepiece lenses in the telescope in the above problem needed to produce a final image very far from the observer, where vision is most relaxed. Note that a telescope is normally used to view very distant objects.

103. A large reflecting telescope has an objective mirror with a 10.0-m radius of curvature. What angular magnification does it produce when a 3.00 m-focal length eyepiece is used?

104. A small telescope has a concave mirror with a 2.00-m radius of curvature for its objective. Its eyepiece is a 4.00 cm-focal length lens. (a) What is the telescope's angular magnification? (b) What angle is subtended by a 25,000 km-diameter sunspot? (c) What is the angle of its telescopic image?

105. A $7.5\times$ binocular produces an angular magnification of -7.50, acting like a telescope. (Mirrors are used to make the image upright.) If the binoculars have objective lenses with a 75.0-cm focal length, what is the focal length of the eyepiece lenses?

106. Construct Your Own Problem Consider a telescope of the type used by Galileo, having a convex objective and a concave eyepiece as illustrated in part (a) of **Figure 2.40**. Construct a problem in which you calculate the location and size of the image produced. Among the things to be considered are the focal lengths of the lenses and their relative placements as well as the size and location of the object. Verify that the angular magnification is greater than one. That is, the angle subtended at the eye by the image is greater than the angle subtended by the object.

107. Trace rays to find which way the given ray will emerge after refraction through the thin lens in the following figure. Assume thin-lens approximation. (*Hint*: Pick a point *P* on the given ray in each case. Treat that point as an object. Now, find its image *Q*. Use the rule: All rays on the other side of the lens will either go through *Q* or appear to be coming from *Q*.)

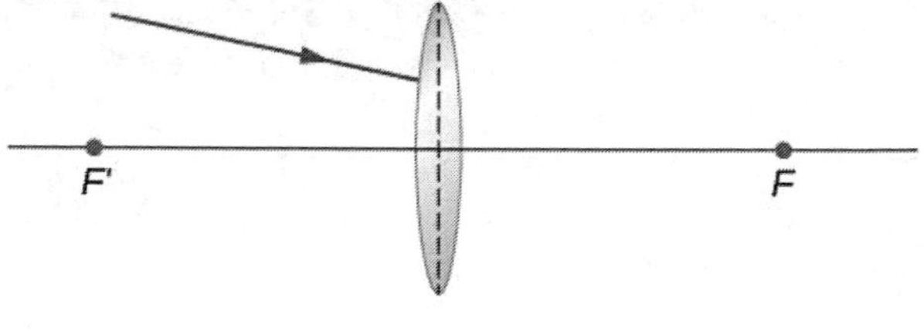

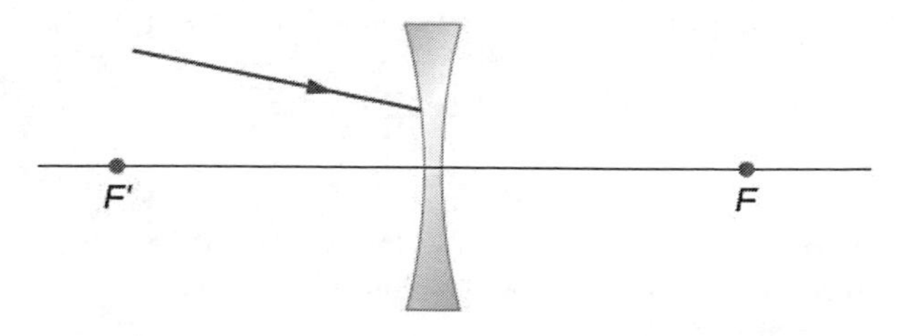

108. Copy and draw rays to find the final image in the following diagram. (*Hint*: Find the intermediate image through lens alone. Use the intermediate image as the object for the mirror and work with the mirror alone to find the final image.)

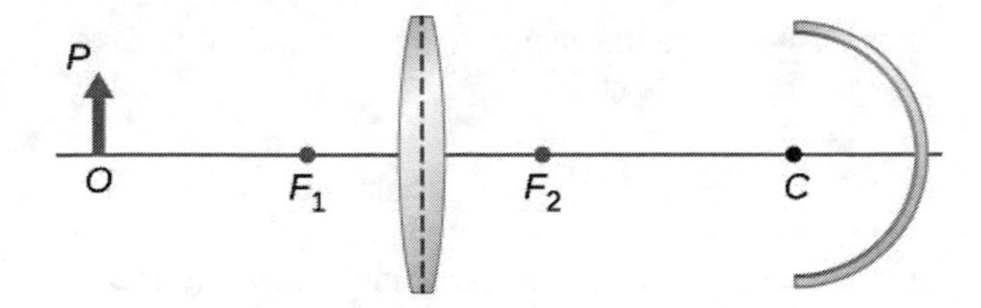

109. A concave mirror of radius of curvature 10 cm is placed 30 cm from a thin convex lens of focal length 15 cm. Find the location and magnification of a small bulb sitting 50 cm from the lens by using the algebraic method.

110. An object of height 3 cm is placed at 25 cm in front of a converging lens of focal length 20 cm. Behind the lens there is a concave mirror of focal length 20 cm. The distance between the lens and the mirror is 5 cm. Find the location, orientation and size of the final image.

111. An object of height 3 cm is placed at a distance of 25 cm in front of a converging lens of focal length 20 cm, to be referred to as the first lens. Behind the lens there is another converging lens of focal length 20 cm placed 10 cm from the first lens. There is a concave mirror of focal length 15 cm placed 50 cm from the second lens. Find the location, orientation, and size of the final image.

112. An object of height 2 cm is placed at 50 cm in front of a diverging lens of focal length 40 cm. Behind the lens, there is a convex mirror of focal length 15 cm placed 30 cm from the converging lens. Find the location, orientation, and size of the final image.

113. Two concave mirrors are placed facing each other. One of them has a small hole in the middle. A penny is placed on the bottom mirror (see the following figure). When you look from the side, a real image of the penny is observed above the hole. Explain how that could happen.

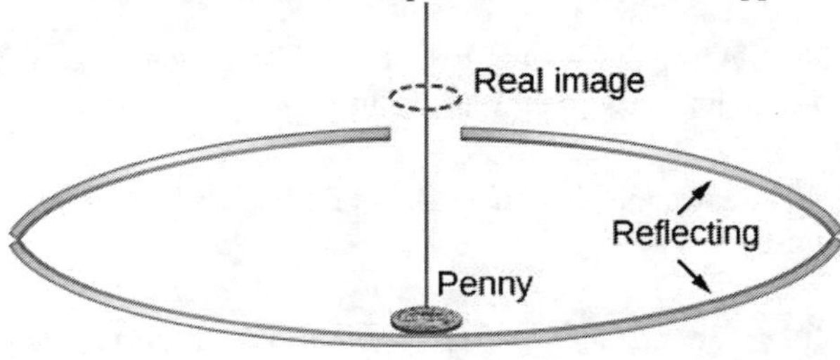

114. A lamp of height 5 cm is placed 40 cm in front of a converging lens of focal length 20 cm. There is a plane mirror 15 cm behind the lens. Where would you find the image when you look in the mirror?

115. Parallel rays from a faraway source strike a converging lens of focal length 20 cm at an angle of 15 degrees with the horizontal direction. Find the vertical position of the real image observed on a screen in the focal plane.

116. Parallel rays from a faraway source strike a diverging lens of focal length 20 cm at an angle of 10 degrees with the horizontal direction. As you look through the lens, where in the vertical plane the image would appear?

117. A light bulb is placed 10 cm from a plane mirror, which faces a convex mirror of radius of curvature 8 cm. The plane mirror is located at a distance of 30 cm from the vertex of the convex mirror. Find the location of two images in the convex mirror. Are there other images? If so, where are they located?

118. A point source of light is 50 cm in front of a converging lens of focal length 30 cm. A concave mirror with a focal length of 20 cm is placed 25 cm behind the lens. Where does the final image form, and what are its orientation and magnification?

119. Copy and trace to find how a horizontal ray from S comes out after the lens. Use $n_{\text{glass}} = 1.5$ for the prism material.

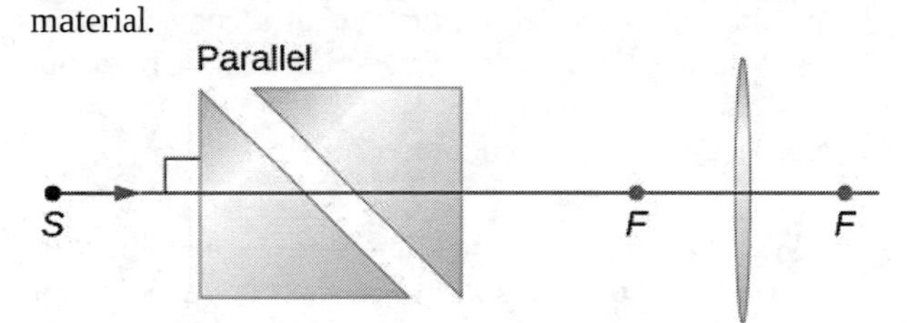

120. Copy and trace how a horizontal ray from S comes out after the lens. Use $n = 1.55$ for the glass.

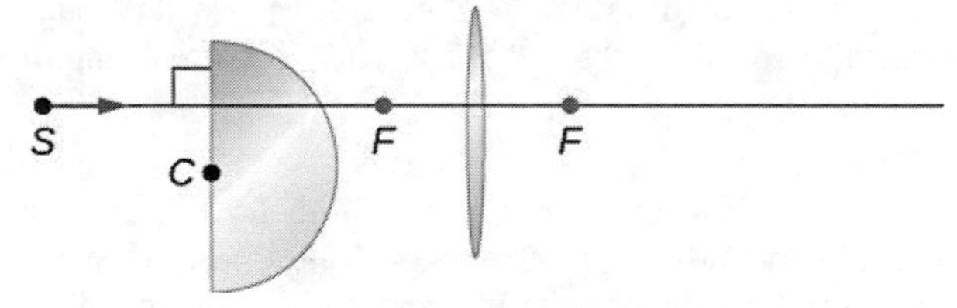

121. Copy and draw rays to figure out the final image.

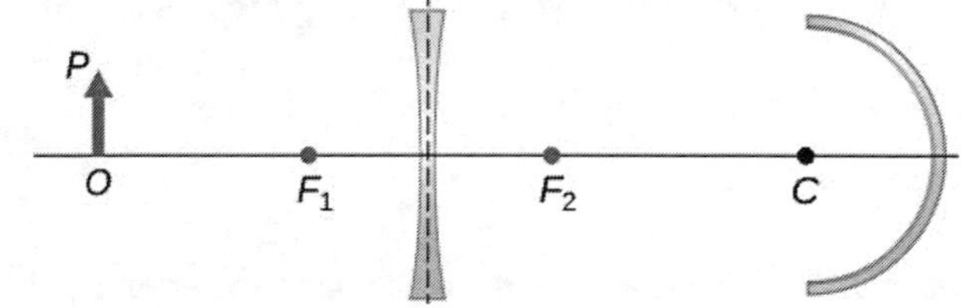

122. By ray tracing or by calculation, find the place inside the glass where rays from S converge as a result of refraction through the lens and the convex air-glass interface. Use a ruler to estimate the radius of curvature.

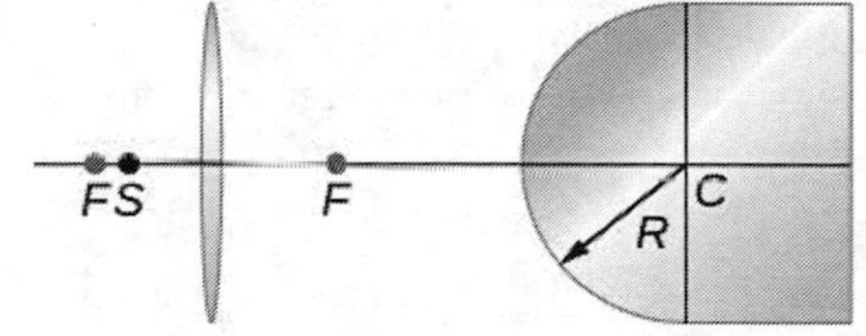

123. A diverging lens has a focal length of 20 cm. What is the power of the lens in diopters?

124. Two lenses of focal lengths of f_1 and f_2 are glued together with transparent material of negligible thickness. Show that the total power of the two lenses simply add.

125. What will be the angular magnification of a convex lens with the focal length 2.5 cm?

126. What will be the formula for the angular magnification of a convex lens of focal length *f* if the eye is very close to the lens and the near point is located a distance *D* from the eye?

ADDITIONAL PROBLEMS

127. Use a ruler and a protractor to draw rays to find images in the following cases.

(a) A point object located on the axis of a concave mirror located at a point within the focal length from the vertex.
(b) A point object located on the axis of a concave mirror located at a point farther than the focal length from the vertex.
(c) A point object located on the axis of a convex mirror located at a point within the focal length from the vertex.
(d) A point object located on the axis of a convex mirror located at a point farther than the focal length from the vertex.
(e) Repeat (a)–(d) for a point object off the axis.

128. Where should a 3 cm tall object be placed in front of a concave mirror of radius 20 cm so that its image is real and 2 cm tall?

129. A 3 cm tall object is placed 5 cm in front of a convex mirror of radius of curvature 20 cm. Where is the image formed? How tall is the image? What is the orientation of the image?

130. You are looking for a mirror so that you can see a four-fold magnified virtual image of an object when the object is placed 5 cm from the vertex of the mirror. What kind of mirror you will need? What should be the radius of curvature of the mirror?

131. Derive the following equation for a convex mirror:

$$\frac{1}{VO} - \frac{1}{VI} = -\frac{1}{VF},$$

where *VO* is the distance to the object *O* from vertex *V*, *VI* the distance to the image *I* from *V*, and *VF* is the distance to the focal point *F* from *V*. (*Hint*: use two sets of similar triangles.)

132. (a) Draw rays to form the image of a vertical object on the optical axis and farther than the focal point from a converging lens. (b) Use plane geometry in your figure and prove that the magnification m is given by $m = \frac{h_i}{h_o} = -\frac{d_i}{d_o}$.

133. Use another ray-tracing diagram for the same situation as given in the previous problem to derive the thin-lens equation, $\frac{1}{d_o} + \frac{1}{d_i} = \frac{1}{f}$.

134. You photograph a 2.0-m-tall person with a camera that has a 5.0 cm-focal length lens. The image on the film must be no more than 2.0 cm high. (a) What is the closest distance the person can stand to the lens? (b) For this distance, what should be the distance from the lens to the film?

135. Find the focal length of a thin plano-convex lens. The front surface of this lens is flat, and the rear surface has a radius of curvature of $R_2 = -35\text{ cm}$. Assume that the index of refraction of the lens is 1.5.

136. Find the focal length of a meniscus lens with $R_1 = 20\text{ cm}$ and $R_2 = 15\text{ cm}$. Assume that the index of refraction of the lens is 1.5.

137. A nearsighted man cannot see objects clearly beyond 20 cm from his eyes. How close must he stand to a mirror in order to see what he is doing when he shaves?

138. A mother sees that her child's contact lens prescription is 0.750 D. What is the child's near point?

139. Repeat the previous problem for glasses that are 2.20 cm from the eyes.

140. The contact-lens prescription for a nearsighted person is −4.00 D and the person has a far point of 22.5 cm. What is the power of the tear layer between the cornea and the lens if the correction is ideal, taking the tear layer into account?

141. Unreasonable Results A boy has a near point of 50 cm and a far point of 500 cm. Will a −4.00 D lens correct his far point to infinity?

142. Find the angular magnification of an image by a magnifying glass of $f = 5.0\text{ cm}$ if the object is placed

$d_o = 4.0\text{ cm}$ from the lens and the lens is close to the eye.

143. Let objective and eyepiece of a compound microscope have focal lengths of 2.5 cm and 10 cm, respectively and be separated by 12 cm. A $70\text{-}\mu\text{m}$ object is placed 6.0 cm from the objective. How large is the virtual image formed by the objective-eyepiece system?

144. Draw rays to scale to locate the image at the retina if the eye lens has a focal length 2.5 cm and the near point is 24 cm. (*Hint*: Place an object at the near point.)

145. The objective and the eyepiece of a microscope have the focal lengths 3 cm and 10 cm respectively. Decide about the distance between the objective and the eyepiece if we need a $10\times$ magnification from the objective/eyepiece compound system.

146. A far-sighted person has a near point of 100 cm. How far in front or behind the retina does the image of an object placed 25 cm from the eye form? Use the cornea to retina distance of 2.5 cm.

147. A near-sighted person has afar point of 80 cm. (a) What kind of corrective lens the person will need if the lens is to be placed 1.5 cm from the eye? (b) What would be the power of the contact lens needed? Assume distance to contact lens from the eye to be zero.

148. In a reflecting telescope the objective is a concave mirror of radius of curvature 2 m and an eyepiece is a convex lens of focal length 5 cm. Find the apparent size of a 25-m tree at a distance of 10 km that you would perceive when looking through the telescope.

149. Two stars that are 10^9 km apart are viewed by a telescope and found to be separated by an angle of 10^{-5} radians. If the eyepiece of the telescope has a focal length of 1.5 cm and the objective has a focal length of 3 meters, how far away are the stars from the observer?

150. What is the angular size of the Moon if viewed from a binocular that has a focal length of 1.2 cm for the eyepiece and a focal length of 8 cm for the objective? Use the radius of the moon $1.74 \times 10^6\text{ m}$ and the distance of the moon from the observer to be $3.8 \times 10^8\text{ m}$.

151. An unknown planet at a distance of 10^{12} m from Earth is observed by a telescope that has a focal length of the eyepiece of 1 cm and a focal length of the objective of 1 m. If the far away planet is seen to subtend an angle of 10^{-5} radian at the eyepiece, what is the size of the planet?

3 | INTERFERENCE

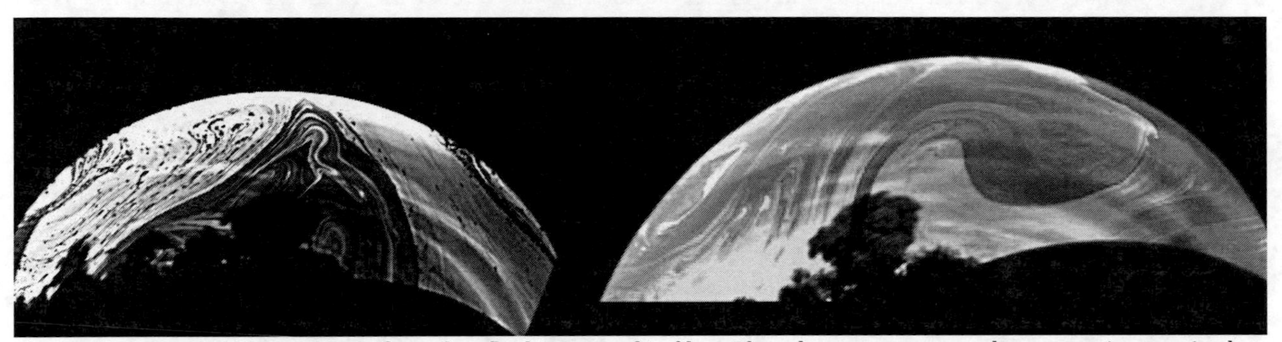

Figure 3.1 Soap bubbles are blown from clear fluid into very thin films. The colors we see are not due to any pigmentation but are the result of light interference, which enhances specific wavelengths for a given thickness of the film.

Chapter Outline

Introduction

The most certain indication of a wave is interference. This wave characteristic is most prominent when the wave interacts with an object that is not large compared with the wavelength. Interference is observed for water waves, sound waves, light waves, and, in fact, all types of waves.

If you have ever looked at the reds, blues, and greens in a sunlit soap bubble and wondered how straw-colored soapy water could produce them, you have hit upon one of the many phenomena that can only be explained by the wave character of light (see **Figure 3.1**). The same is true for the colors seen in an oil slick or in the light reflected from a DVD disc. These and other interesting phenomena cannot be explained fully by geometric optics. In these cases, light interacts with objects and exhibits wave characteristics. The branch of optics that considers the behavior of light when it exhibits wave characteristics is called wave optics (sometimes called physical optics). It is the topic of this chapter.

3.1 | Young's Double-Slit Interference

Learning Objectives

By the end of this section, you will be able to:

- Explain the phenomenon of interference
- Define constructive and destructive interference for a double slit

The Dutch physicist Christiaan Huygens (1629–1695) thought that light was a wave, but Isaac Newton did not. Newton thought that there were other explanations for color, and for the interference and diffraction effects that were observable at the time. Owing to Newton's tremendous reputation, his view generally prevailed; the fact that Huygens's principle worked was not considered direct evidence proving that light is a wave. The acceptance of the wave character of light came many years later in 1801, when the English physicist and physician Thomas Young (1773–1829) demonstrated optical interference with his now-classic double-slit experiment.

If there were not one but two sources of waves, the waves could be made to interfere, as in the case of waves on water (**Figure 3.2**). If light is an electromagnetic wave, it must therefore exhibit interference effects under appropriate circumstances. In Young's experiment, sunlight was passed through a pinhole on a board. The emerging beam fell on two pinholes on a second board. The light emanating from the two pinholes then fell on a screen where a pattern of bright and dark spots was observed. This pattern, called fringes, can only be explained through interference, a wave phenomenon.

Figure 3.2 Photograph of an interference pattern produced by circular water waves in a ripple tank. Two thin plungers are vibrated up and down in phase at the surface of the water. Circular water waves are produced by and emanate from each plunger. The points where the water is calm (corresponding to destructive interference) are clearly visible.

We can analyze double-slit interference with the help of **Figure 3.3**, which depicts an apparatus analogous to Young's. Light from a monochromatic source falls on a slit S_0. The light emanating from S_0 is incident on two other slits S_1 and S_2 that are equidistant from S_0. A pattern of *interference fringes* on the screen is then produced by the light emanating from S_1 and S_2. All slits are assumed to be so narrow that they can be considered secondary point sources for Huygens' wavelets (**The Nature of Light**). Slits S_1 and S_2 are a distance *d* apart ($d \leq 1 \text{ mm}$), and the distance between the screen and the slits is $D(\approx 1 \text{ m})$, which is much greater than *d*.

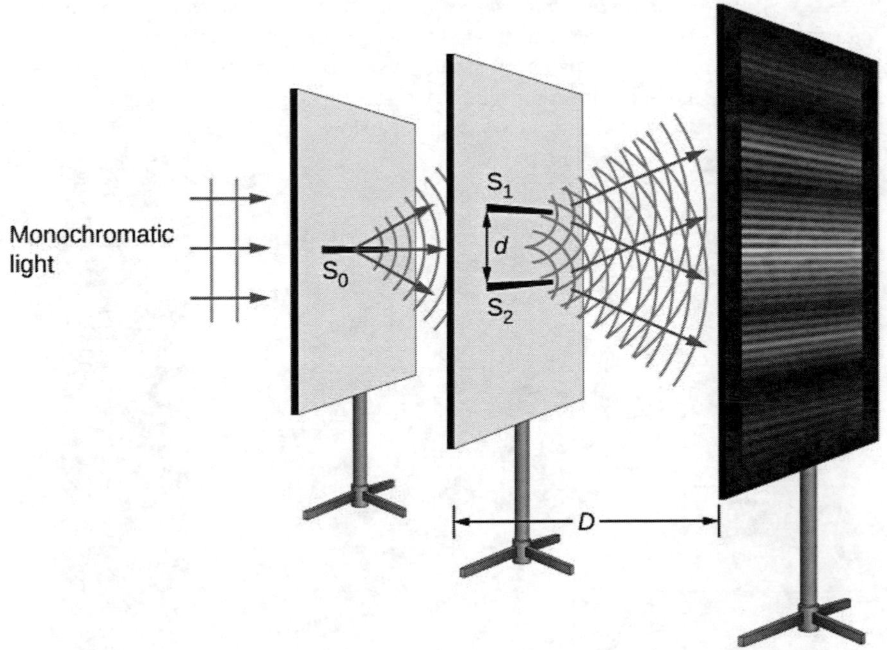

Figure 3.3 The double-slit interference experiment using monochromatic light and narrow slits. Fringes produced by interfering Huygens wavelets from slits S_1 and S_2 are observed on the screen.

Since S_0 is assumed to be a point source of monochromatic light, the secondary Huygens wavelets leaving S_1 and S_2 always maintain a constant phase difference (zero in this case because S_1 and S_2 are equidistant from S_0) and have the same frequency. The sources S_1 and S_2 are then said to be coherent. By **coherent waves**, we mean the waves are in phase or have a definite phase relationship. The term **incoherent** means the waves have random phase relationships, which would be the case if S_1 and S_2 were illuminated by two independent light sources, rather than a single source S_0. Two independent light sources (which may be two separate areas within the same lamp or the Sun) would generally not emit their light in unison, that is, not coherently. Also, because S_1 and S_2 are the same distance from S_0, the amplitudes of the two Huygens wavelets are equal.

Young used sunlight, where each wavelength forms its own pattern, making the effect more difficult to see. In the following discussion, we illustrate the double-slit experiment with **monochromatic** light (single λ) to clarify the effect. Figure 3.4 shows the pure constructive and destructive interference of two waves having the same wavelength and amplitude.

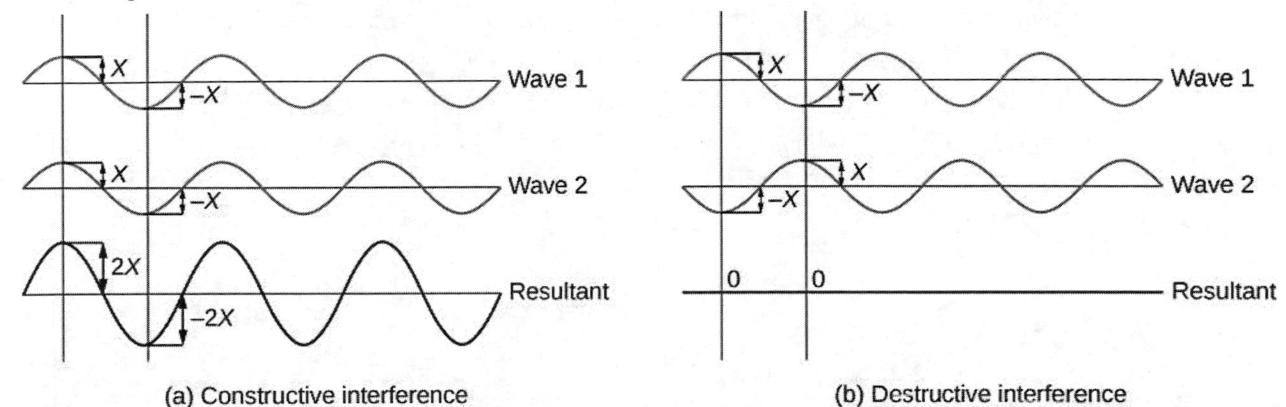

Figure 3.4 The amplitudes of waves add. (a) Pure constructive interference is obtained when identical waves are in phase. (b) Pure destructive interference occurs when identical waves are exactly out of phase, or shifted by half a wavelength.

When light passes through narrow slits, the slits act as sources of coherent waves and light spreads out as semicircular waves, as shown in **Figure 3.5**(a). Pure *constructive interference* occurs where the waves are crest to crest or trough to trough. Pure *destructive interference* occurs where they are crest to trough. The light must fall on a screen and be scattered into our eyes for us to see the pattern. An analogous pattern for water waves is shown in **Figure 3.2**. Note that regions of constructive and destructive interference move out from the slits at well-defined angles to the original beam. These angles depend on wavelength and the distance between the slits, as we shall see below.

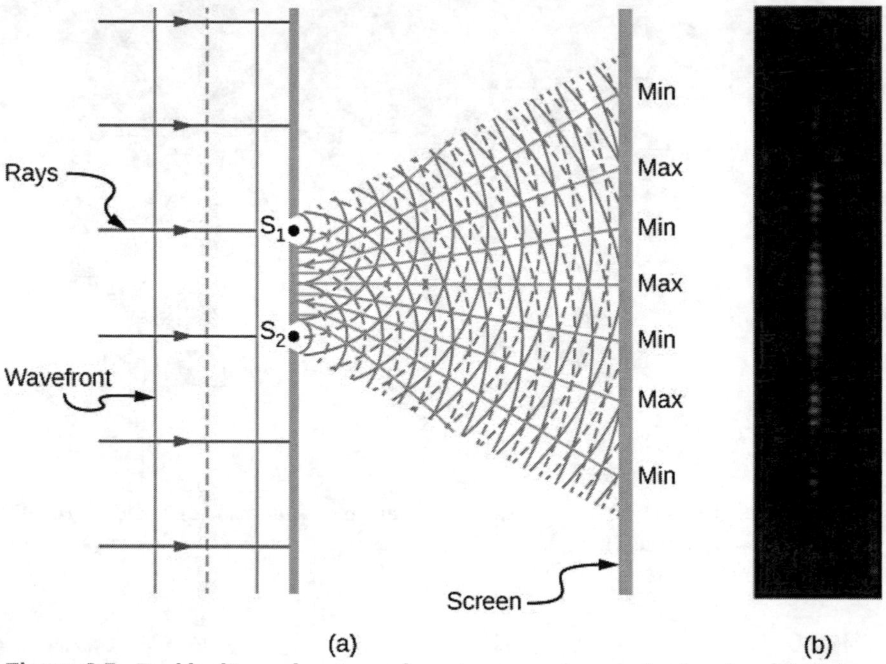

Figure 3.5 Double slits produce two coherent sources of waves that interfere. (a) Light spreads out (diffracts) from each slit, because the slits are narrow. These waves overlap and interfere constructively (bright lines) and destructively (dark regions). We can only see this if the light falls onto a screen and is scattered into our eyes. (b) When light that has passed through double slits falls on a screen, we see a pattern such as this.

To understand the double-slit interference pattern, consider how two waves travel from the slits to the screen (**Figure 3.6**). Each slit is a different distance from a given point on the screen. Thus, different numbers of wavelengths fit into each path. Waves start out from the slits in phase (crest to crest), but they may end up out of phase (crest to trough) at the screen if the paths differ in length by half a wavelength, interfering destructively. If the paths differ by a whole wavelength, then the waves arrive in phase (crest to crest) at the screen, interfering constructively. More generally, if the path length difference Δl between the two waves is any half-integral number of wavelengths [$(1/2)\lambda$, $(3/2)\lambda$, $(5/2)\lambda$, etc.], then destructive interference occurs. Similarly, if the path length difference is any integral number of wavelengths (λ, 2λ, 3λ, etc.), then constructive interference occurs. These conditions can be expressed as equations:

$$\Delta l = m\lambda, \quad \text{for } m = 0, \pm 1, \pm 2, \pm 3 \ \ldots \ \text{(constructive interference)} \tag{3.1}$$

$$\Delta l = \left(m + \frac{1}{2}\right)\lambda, \quad \text{for } m = 0, \pm 1, \pm 2, \pm 3 \ \ldots \ \text{(destructive interference)} \tag{3.2}$$

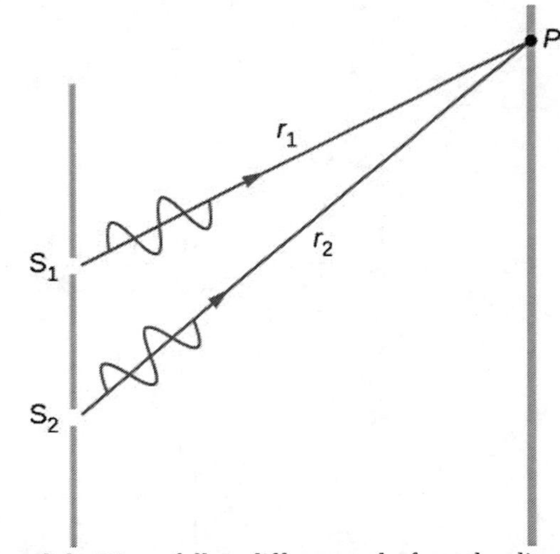

Figure 3.6 Waves follow different paths from the slits to a common point *P* on a screen. Destructive interference occurs where one path is a half wavelength longer than the other—the waves start in phase but arrive out of phase. Constructive interference occurs where one path is a whole wavelength longer than the other—the waves start out and arrive in phase.

3.2 | Mathematics of Interference

Learning Objectives

By the end of this section, you will be able to:

- Determine the angles for bright and dark fringes for double slit interference
- Calculate the positions of bright fringes on a screen

Figure 3.7(a) shows how to determine the path length difference Δl for waves traveling from two slits to a common point on a screen. If the screen is a large distance away compared with the distance between the slits, then the angle θ between the path and a line from the slits to the screen [part (b)] is nearly the same for each path. In other words, r_1 and r_2 are essentially parallel. The lengths of r_1 and r_2 differ by Δl, as indicated by the two dashed lines in the figure. Simple trigonometry shows

$$\Delta l = d \sin \theta \tag{3.3}$$

where *d* is the distance between the slits. Combining this result with **Equation 3.1**, we obtain constructive interference for a double slit when the path length difference is an integral multiple of the wavelength, or

$$d \sin \theta = m\lambda, \quad \text{for } m = 0, \pm 1, \pm 2, \pm 3, \ldots \text{ (constructive interference).} \tag{3.4}$$

Similarly, to obtain destructive interference for a double slit, the path length difference must be a half-integral multiple of the wavelength, or

$$d \sin \theta = \left(m + \frac{1}{2}\right)\lambda, \quad \text{for } m = 0, \pm 1, \pm 2, \pm 3, \ldots \text{ (destructive interference)} \tag{3.5}$$

where λ is the wavelength of the light, *d* is the distance between slits, and θ is the angle from the original direction of the beam as discussed above. We call *m* the **order** of the interference. For example, $m = 4$ is fourth-order interference.

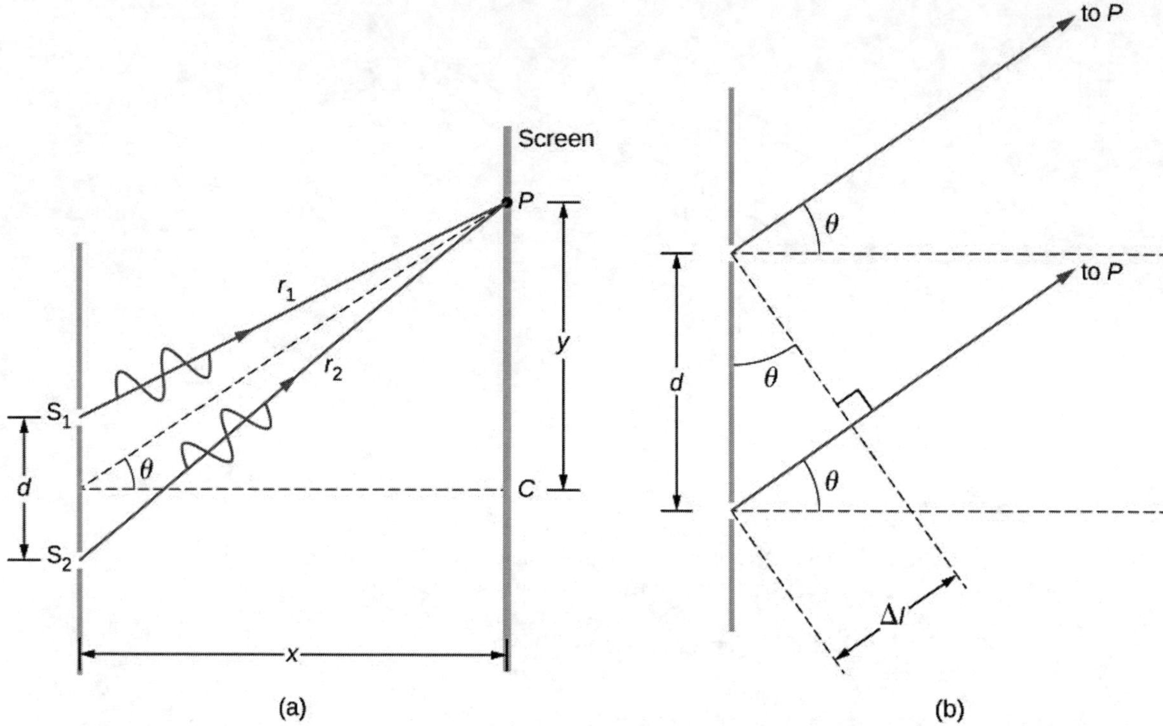

Figure 3.7 (a) To reach *P*, the light waves from S_1 and S_2 must travel different distances. (b) The path difference between the two rays is Δl.

The equations for double-slit interference imply that a series of bright and dark lines are formed. For vertical slits, the light spreads out horizontally on either side of the incident beam into a pattern called interference **fringes** (**Figure 3.8**). The closer the slits are, the more the bright fringes spread apart. We can see this by examining the equation

$d \sin \theta = m\lambda, \text{ for } m = 0, \pm 1, \pm 2, \pm 3 \ldots$. For fixed λ and *m*, the smaller *d* is, the larger θ must be, since $\sin \theta = m\lambda / d$. This is consistent with our contention that wave effects are most noticeable when the object the wave encounters (here, slits a distance *d* apart) is small. Small *d* gives large θ, hence, a large effect.

Referring back to part (a) of the figure, θ is typically small enough that $\sin \theta \approx \tan \theta \approx y_m / D$, where y_m is the distance from the central maximum to the *m*th bright fringe and *D* is the distance between the slit and the screen. **Equation 3.4** may then be written as

$$d \frac{y_m}{D} = m\lambda$$

or

$$y_m = \frac{m\lambda D}{d}. \tag{3.6}$$

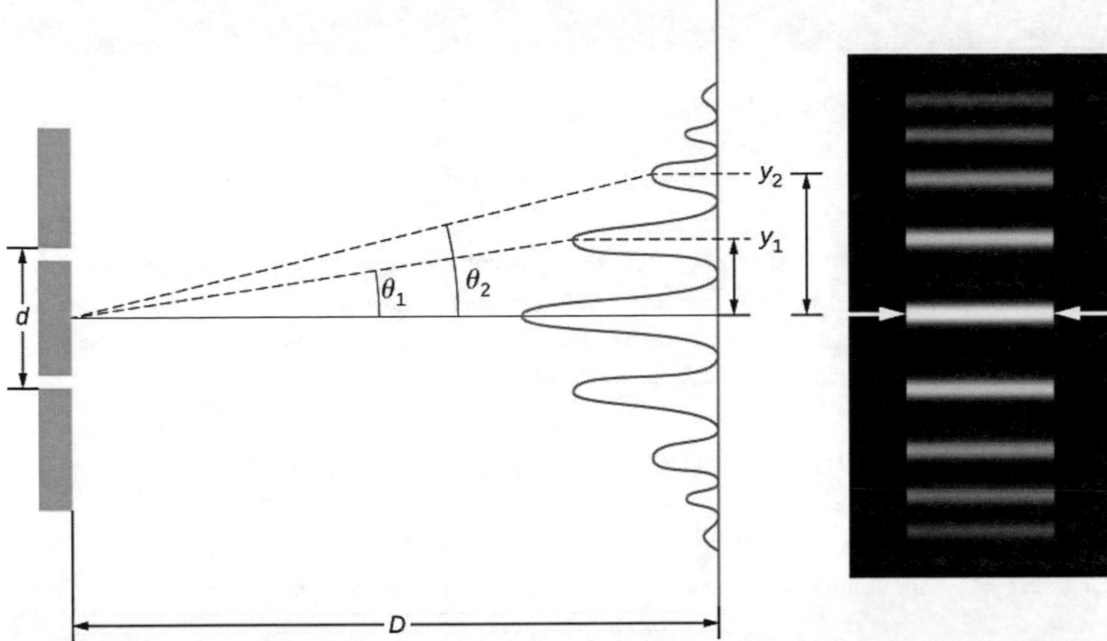

Figure 3.8 The interference pattern for a double slit has an intensity that falls off with angle. The image shows multiple bright and dark lines, or fringes, formed by light passing through a double slit.

Example 3.1

Finding a Wavelength from an Interference Pattern

Suppose you pass light from a He-Ne laser through two slits separated by 0.0100 mm and find that the third bright line on a screen is formed at an angle of $10.95°$ relative to the incident beam. What is the wavelength of the light?

Strategy

The phenomenon is two-slit interference as illustrated in **Figure 3.8** and the third bright line is due to third-order constructive interference, which means that $m = 3$. We are given $d = 0.0100\text{ mm}$ and $\theta = 10.95°$. The wavelength can thus be found using the equation $d \sin \theta = m\lambda$ for constructive interference.

Solution

Solving $d \sin \theta = m\lambda$ for the wavelength λ gives

$$\lambda = \frac{d \sin \theta}{m}.$$

Substituting known values yields

$$\lambda = \frac{(0.0100\text{ mm})(\sin 10.95°)}{3} = 6.33 \times 10^{-4}\text{ mm} = 633\text{ nm}.$$

Significance

To three digits, this is the wavelength of light emitted by the common He-Ne laser. Not by coincidence, this red color is similar to that emitted by neon lights. More important, however, is the fact that interference patterns can be used to measure wavelength. Young did this for visible wavelengths. This analytical techinque is still widely used to measure electromagnetic spectra. For a given order, the angle for constructive interference increases with λ, so that spectra (measurements of intensity versus wavelength) can be obtained.

Example 3.2

Calculating the Highest Order Possible

Interference patterns do not have an infinite number of lines, since there is a limit to how big m can be. What is the highest-order constructive interference possible with the system described in the preceding example?

Strategy

The equation $d \sin \theta = m\lambda$ (for $m = 0, \pm1, \pm2, \pm3\ldots$) describes constructive interference from two slits. For fixed values of d and λ, the larger m is, the larger $\sin \theta$ is. However, the maximum value that $\sin \theta$ can have is 1, for an angle of $90°$. (Larger angles imply that light goes backward and does not reach the screen at all.) Let us find what value of m corresponds to this maximum diffraction angle.

Solution

Solving the equation $d \sin \theta = m\lambda$ for m gives

$$m = \frac{d \sin \theta}{\lambda}.$$

Taking $\sin \theta = 1$ and substituting the values of d and λ from the preceding example gives

$$m = \frac{(0.0100 \text{ mm})(1)}{633 \text{ nm}} \approx 15.8.$$

Therefore, the largest integer m can be is 15, or $m = 15$.

Significance

The number of fringes depends on the wavelength and slit separation. The number of fringes is very large for large slit separations. However, recall (see **The Propagation of Light** and the introduction for this chapter) that wave interference is only prominent when the wave interacts with objects that are not large compared to the wavelength. Therefore, if the slit separation and the sizes of the slits become much greater than the wavelength, the intensity pattern of light on the screen changes, so there are simply two bright lines cast by the slits, as expected, when light behaves like rays. We also note that the fringes get fainter farther away from the center. Consequently, not all 15 fringes may be observable.

3.1 Check Your Understanding In the system used in the preceding examples, at what angles are the first and the second bright fringes formed?

3.3 | Multiple-Slit Interference

Learning Objectives

By the end of this section, you will be able to:

- Describe the locations and intensities of secondary maxima for multiple-slit interference

Analyzing the interference of light passing through two slits lays out the theoretical framework of interference and gives us a historical insight into Thomas Young's experiments. However, much of the modern-day application of slit interference uses not just two slits but many, approaching infinity for practical purposes. The key optical element is called a diffraction grating, an important tool in optical analysis, which we discuss in detail in **Diffraction**. Here, we start the analysis of multiple-slit interference by taking the results from our analysis of the double slit ($N = 2$) and extending it to configurations with three, four, and much larger numbers of slits.

Figure 3.9 shows the simplest case of multiple-slit interference, with three slits, or $N = 3$. The spacing between slits is d, and the path length difference between adjacent slits is $d \sin \theta$, same as the case for the double slit. What is new is that the path length difference for the first and the third slits is $2d \sin \theta$. The condition for constructive interference is the same as for the double slit, that is

$$d \sin \theta = m\lambda.$$

When this condition is met, $2d \sin \theta$ is automatically a multiple of λ, so all three rays combine constructively, and the bright fringes that occur here are called **principal maxima**. But what happens when the path length difference between adjacent slits is only $\lambda/2$? We can think of the first and second rays as interfering destructively, but the third ray remains unaltered. Instead of obtaining a dark fringe, or a minimum, as we did for the double slit, we see a **secondary maximum** with intensity lower than the principal maxima.

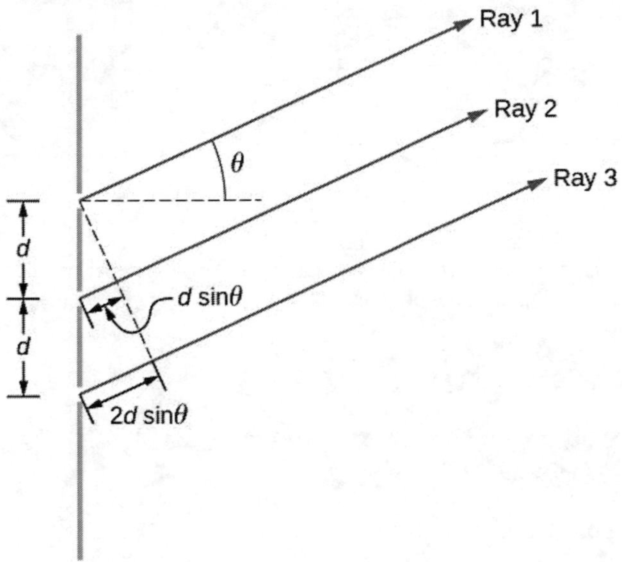

Figure 3.9 Interference with three slits. Different pairs of emerging rays can combine constructively or destructively at the same time, leading to secondary maxima.

In general, for N slits, these secondary maxima occur whenever an unpaired ray is present that does not go away due to destructive interference. This occurs at $(N - 2)$ evenly spaced positions between the principal maxima. The amplitude of the electromagnetic wave is correspondingly diminished to $1/N$ of the wave at the principal maxima, and the light intensity, being proportional to the square of the wave amplitude, is diminished to $1/N^2$ of the intensity compared to the principal maxima. As **Figure 3.10** shows, a dark fringe is located between every maximum (principal or secondary). As N grows larger and the number of bright and dark fringes increase, the widths of the maxima become narrower due to the closely located neighboring dark fringes. Because the total amount of light energy remains unaltered, narrower maxima require that each maximum reaches a correspondingly higher intensity.

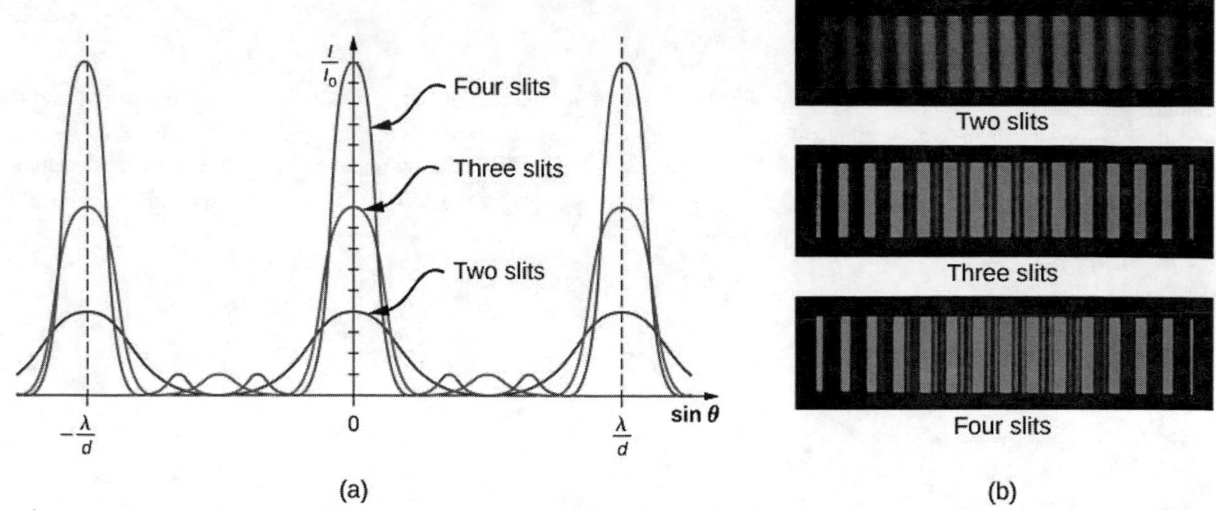

Figure 3.10 Interference fringe patterns for two, three and four slits. As the number of slits increases, more secondary maxima appear, but the principal maxima become brighter and narrower. (a) Graph and (b) photographs of fringe patterns.

3.4 | Interference in Thin Films

Learning Objectives

By the end of this section, you will be able to:

- Describe the phase changes that occur upon reflection
- Describe fringes established by reflected rays of a common source
- Explain the appearance of colors in thin films

The bright colors seen in an oil slick floating on water or in a sunlit soap bubble are caused by interference. The brightest colors are those that interfere constructively. This interference is between light reflected from different surfaces of a thin film; thus, the effect is known as **thin-film interference**.

As we noted before, interference effects are most prominent when light interacts with something having a size similar to its wavelength. A thin film is one having a thickness t smaller than a few times the wavelength of light, λ. Since color is associated indirectly with λ and because all interference depends in some way on the ratio of λ to the size of the object involved, we should expect to see different colors for different thicknesses of a film, as in **Figure 3.11**.

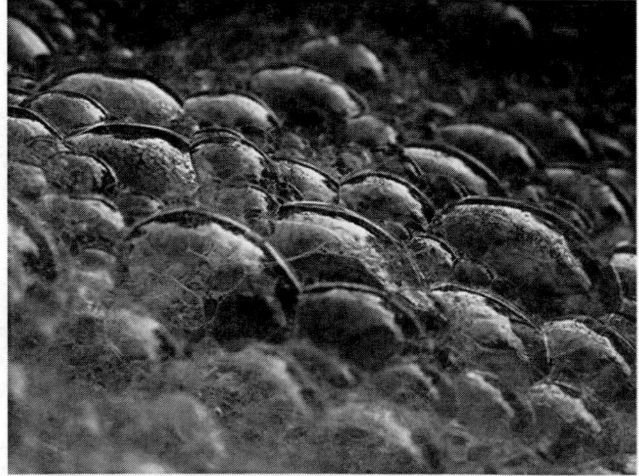

Figure 3.11 These soap bubbles exhibit brilliant colors when exposed to sunlight. (credit: Scott Robinson)

What causes thin-film interference? Figure 3.12 shows how light reflected from the top and bottom surfaces of a film can interfere. Incident light is only partially reflected from the top surface of the film (ray 1). The remainder enters the film and is itself partially reflected from the bottom surface. Part of the light reflected from the bottom surface can emerge from the top of the film (ray 2) and interfere with light reflected from the top (ray 1). The ray that enters the film travels a greater distance, so it may be in or out of phase with the ray reflected from the top. However, consider for a moment, again, the bubbles in Figure 3.11. The bubbles are darkest where they are thinnest. Furthermore, if you observe a soap bubble carefully, you will note it gets dark at the point where it breaks. For very thin films, the difference in path lengths of rays 1 and 2 in Figure 3.12 is negligible, so why should they interfere destructively and not constructively? The answer is that a phase change can occur upon reflection, as discussed next.

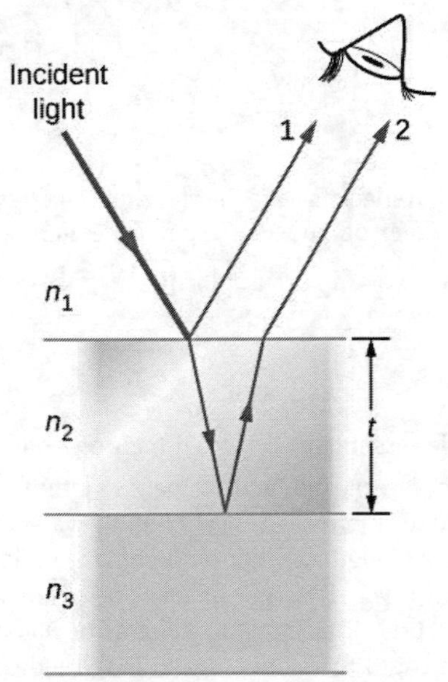

Figure 3.12 Light striking a thin film is partially reflected (ray 1) and partially refracted at the top surface. The refracted ray is partially reflected at the bottom surface and emerges as ray 2. These rays interfere in a way that depends on the thickness of the film and the indices of refraction of the various media.

Changes in Phase due to Reflection

We saw earlier (Waves (http://cnx.org/content/m58367/latest/)) that reflection of mechanical waves can involve a $180°$ phase change. For example, a traveling wave on a string is inverted (i.e., a $180°$ phase change) upon reflection at a boundary to which a heavier string is tied. However, if the second string is lighter (or more precisely, of a lower linear density), no inversion occurs. Light waves produce the same effect, but the deciding parameter for light is the index of refraction. Light waves undergo a $180°$ or π radians phase change upon reflection at an interface beyond which is a medium of higher index of refraction. No phase change takes place when reflecting from a medium of lower refractive index (Figure 3.13). Because of the periodic nature of waves, this phase change or inversion is equivalent to $\pm\lambda/2$ in distance travelled, or path length. Both the path length and refractive indices are important factors in thin-film interference.

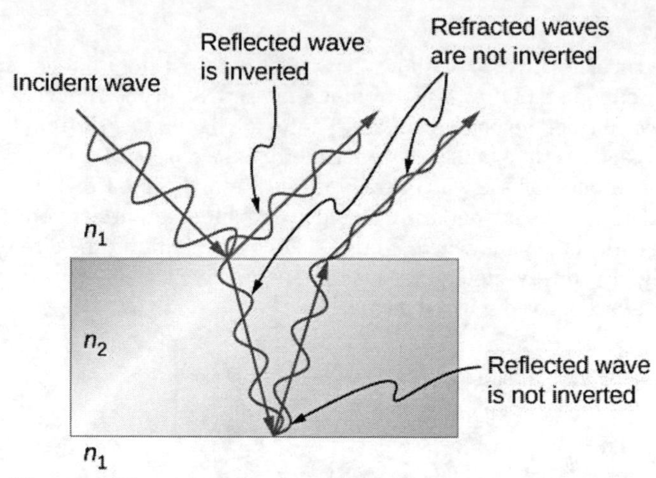

Figure 3.13 Reflection at an interface for light traveling from a medium with index of refraction n_1 to a medium with index of refraction n_2, $n_1 < n_2$, causes the phase of the wave to change by π radians.

If the film in **Figure 3.12** is a **soap bubble** (essentially water with air on both sides), then a phase shift of $\lambda/2$ occurs for ray 1 but not for ray 2. Thus, when the film is very thin and the path length difference between the two rays is negligible, they are exactly out of phase, and destructive interference occurs at all wavelengths. Thus, the soap bubble is dark here. The thickness of the film relative to the wavelength of light is the other crucial factor in thin-film interference. Ray 2 in **Figure 3.12** travels a greater distance than ray 1. For light incident perpendicular to the surface, ray 2 travels a distance approximately $2t$ farther than ray 1. When this distance is an integral or half-integral multiple of the wavelength in the medium ($\lambda_n = \lambda/n$, where λ is the wavelength in vacuum and n is the index of refraction), constructive or destructive interference occurs, depending also on whether there is a phase change in either ray.

Example 3.3

Calculating the Thickness of a Nonreflective Lens Coating

Sophisticated cameras use a series of several lenses. Light can reflect from the surfaces of these various lenses and degrade image clarity. To limit these reflections, lenses are coated with a thin layer of magnesium fluoride, which causes destructive thin-film interference. What is the thinnest this film can be, if its index of refraction is 1.38 and it is designed to limit the reflection of 550-nm light, normally the most intense visible wavelength? Assume the index of refraction of the glass is 1.52.

Strategy

Refer to **Figure 3.12** and use $n_1 = 1.00$ for air, $n_2 = 1.38$, and $n_3 = 1.52$. Both ray 1 and ray 2 have a $\lambda/2$ shift upon reflection. Thus, to obtain destructive interference, ray 2 needs to travel a half wavelength farther than ray 1. For rays incident perpendicularly, the path length difference is $2t$.

Solution

To obtain destructive interference here,

$$2t = \frac{\lambda_{n2}}{2}$$

where λ_{n2} is the wavelength in the film and is given by $\lambda_{n2} = \lambda/n_2$. Thus,

$$2t = \frac{\lambda/n_2}{2}.$$

Solving for t and entering known values yields

$$t = \frac{\lambda/n_2}{4} = \frac{(500\ \text{nm})/1.38}{4} = 90.6\ \text{nm}.$$

Significance

Films such as the one in this example are most effective in producing destructive interference when the thinnest layer is used, since light over a broader range of incident angles is reduced in intensity. These films are called nonreflective coatings; this is only an approximately correct description, though, since other wavelengths are only partially cancelled. Nonreflective coatings are also used in car windows and sunglasses.

Combining Path Length Difference with Phase Change

Thin-film interference is most constructive or most destructive when the path length difference for the two rays is an integral or half-integral wavelength. That is, for rays incident perpendicularly,

$$2t = \lambda_n,\ 2\lambda_n,\ 3\lambda_n, \ldots \text{ or } 2t = \lambda_n/2,\ 3\lambda_n/2,\ 5\lambda_n/2, \ldots.$$

To know whether interference is constructive or destructive, you must also determine if there is a phase change upon reflection. Thin-film interference thus depends on film thickness, the wavelength of light, and the refractive indices. For white light incident on a film that varies in thickness, you can observe rainbow colors of constructive interference for various wavelengths as the thickness varies.

Example 3.4

Soap Bubbles

(a) What are the three smallest thicknesses of a soap bubble that produce constructive interference for red light with a wavelength of 650 nm? The index of refraction of soap is taken to be the same as that of water. (b) What three smallest thicknesses give destructive interference?

Strategy

Use **Figure 3.12** to visualize the bubble, which acts as a thin film between two layers of air. Thus $n_1 = n_3 = 1.00$ for air, and $n_2 = 1.333$ for soap (equivalent to water). There is a $\lambda/2$ shift for ray 1 reflected from the top surface of the bubble and no shift for ray 2 reflected from the bottom surface. To get constructive interference, then, the path length difference ($2t$) must be a half-integral multiple of the wavelength—the first three being $\lambda_n/2,\ 3\lambda_n/2$, and $5\lambda_n/2$. To get destructive interference, the path length difference must be an integral multiple of the wavelength—the first three being 0, λ_n, and $2\lambda_n$.

Solution

a. Constructive interference occurs here when

$$2t_\text{c} = \frac{\lambda_n}{2},\ \frac{3\lambda_n}{2},\ \frac{5\lambda_n}{2},\ \ldots.$$

Thus, the smallest constructive thickness t_c is

$$t_\text{c} = \frac{\lambda_n}{4} = \frac{\lambda/n}{4} = \frac{(650\ \text{nm})/1.333}{4} = 122\ \text{nm}.$$

The next thickness that gives constructive interference is $t'_\text{c} = 3\lambda_n/4$, so that

$$t'_\text{c} = 366\ \text{nm}.$$

Finally, the third thickness producing constructive interference is $t'_\text{c} = 5\lambda_n/4$, so that

$$t'_\text{c} = 610\ \text{nm}.$$

b. For destructive interference, the path length difference here is an integral multiple of the wavelength. The first occurs for zero thickness, since there is a phase change at the top surface, that is,

$$t_d = 0,$$

the very thin (or negligibly thin) case discussed above. The first non-zero thickness producing destructive interference is

$$2t'_d = \lambda_n.$$

Substituting known values gives

$$t'_d = \frac{\lambda}{2} = \frac{\lambda/n}{2} = \frac{(650 \text{ nm})/1.333}{2} = 244 \text{ nm}.$$

Finally, the third destructive thickness is $2t''_d = 2\lambda_n$, so that

$$t''_d = \lambda_n = \frac{\lambda}{n} = \frac{650 \text{ nm}}{1.333} = 488 \text{ nm}.$$

Significance

If the bubble were illuminated with pure red light, we would see bright and dark bands at very uniform increases in thickness. First would be a dark band at 0 thickness, then bright at 122 nm thickness, then dark at 244 nm, bright at 366 nm, dark at 488 nm, and bright at 610 nm. If the bubble varied smoothly in thickness, like a smooth wedge, then the bands would be evenly spaced.

3.2 Check Your Understanding Going further with **Example 3.4**, what are the next two thicknesses of soap bubble that would lead to (a) constructive interference, and (b) destructive interference?

Another example of thin-film interference can be seen when microscope slides are separated (see **Figure 3.14**). The slides are very flat, so that the wedge of air between them increases in thickness very uniformly. A phase change occurs at the second surface but not the first, so a dark band forms where the slides touch. The rainbow colors of constructive interference repeat, going from violet to red again and again as the distance between the slides increases. As the layer of air increases, the bands become more difficult to see, because slight changes in incident angle have greater effects on path length differences. If monochromatic light instead of white light is used, then bright and dark bands are obtained rather than repeating rainbow colors.

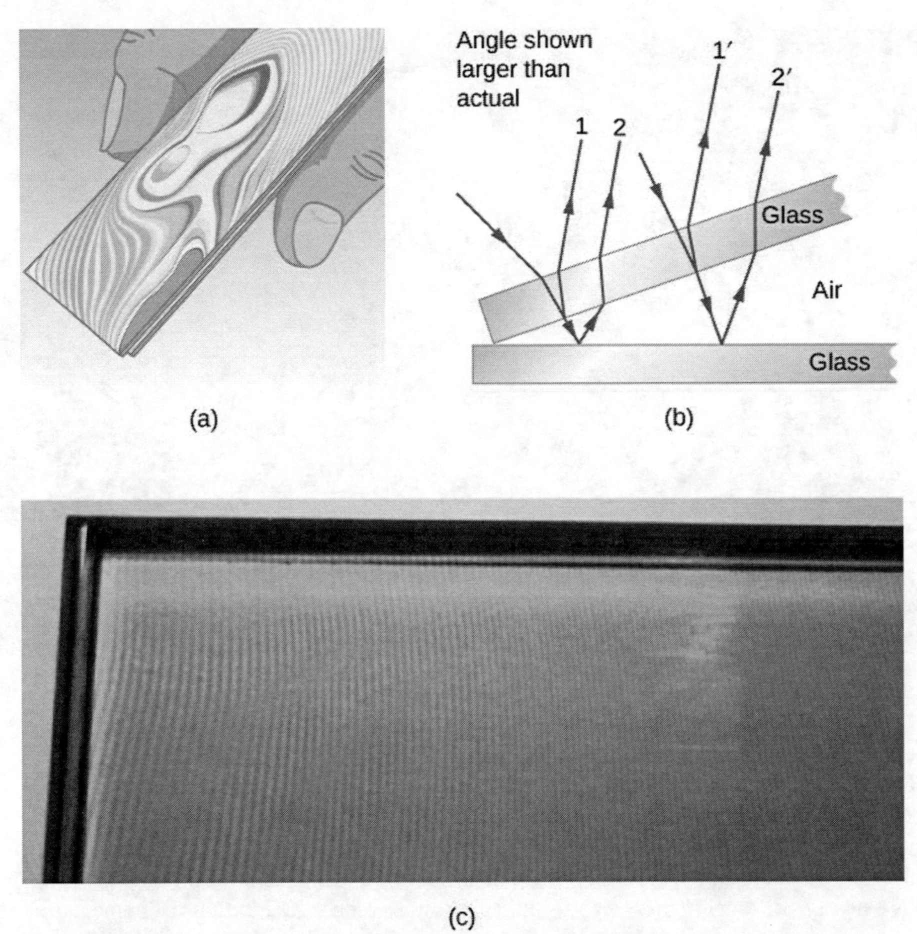

Figure 3.14 (a) The rainbow-color bands are produced by thin-film interference in the air between the two glass slides. (b) Schematic of the paths taken by rays in the wedge of air between the slides. (c) If the air wedge is illuminated with monochromatic light, bright and dark bands are obtained rather than repeating rainbow colors.

An important application of thin-film interference is found in the manufacturing of optical instruments. A lens or mirror can be compared with a master as it is being ground, allowing it to be shaped to an accuracy of less than a wavelength over its entire surface. **Figure 3.15** illustrates the phenomenon called **Newton's rings**, which occurs when the plane surfaces of two lenses are placed together. (The circular bands are called Newton's rings because Isaac Newton described them and their use in detail. Newton did not discover them; Robert Hooke did, and Newton did not believe they were due to the wave character of light.) Each successive ring of a given color indicates an increase of only half a wavelength in the distance between the lens and the blank, so that great precision can be obtained. Once the lens is perfect, no rings appear.

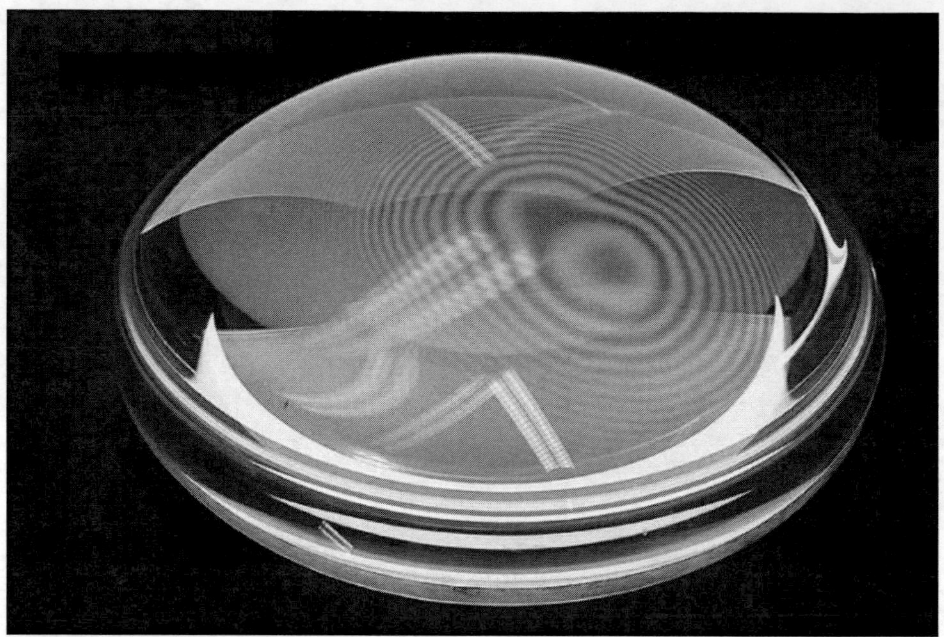

Figure 3.15 "Newton's rings" interference fringes are produced when two plano-convex lenses are placed together with their plane surfaces in contact. The rings are created by interference between the light reflected off the two surfaces as a result of a slight gap between them, indicating that these surfaces are not precisely plane but are slightly convex. (credit: Ulf Seifert)

Thin-film interference has many other applications, both in nature and in manufacturing. The wings of certain moths and butterflies have nearly iridescent colors due to thin-film interference. In addition to pigmentation, the wing's color is affected greatly by constructive interference of certain wavelengths reflected from its film-coated surface. Some car manufacturers offer special paint jobs that use thin-film interference to produce colors that change with angle. This expensive option is based on variation of thin-film path length differences with angle. Security features on credit cards, banknotes, driving licenses, and similar items prone to forgery use thin-film interference, diffraction gratings, or holograms. As early as 1998, Australia led the way with dollar bills printed on polymer with a diffraction grating security feature, making the currency difficult to forge. Other countries, such as Canada, New Zealand, and Taiwan, are using similar technologies, while US currency includes a thin-film interference effect.

3.5 | The Michelson Interferometer

Learning Objectives

By the end of this section, you will be able to:

- Explain changes in fringes observed with a Michelson interferometer caused by mirror movements
- Explain changes in fringes observed with a Michelson interferometer caused by changes in medium

The Michelson **interferometer** (invented by the American physicist Albert A. Michelson, 1852–1931) is a precision instrument that produces interference fringes by splitting a light beam into two parts and then recombining them after they have traveled different optical paths. **Figure 3.16** depicts the interferometer and the path of a light beam from a single point on the extended source S, which is a ground-glass plate that diffuses the light from a monochromatic lamp of wavelength λ_0. The beam strikes the half-silvered mirror M, where half of it is reflected to the side and half passes through the mirror. The reflected light travels to the movable plane mirror M_1, where it is reflected back through M to the observer. The transmitted half of the original beam is reflected back by the stationary mirror M_2 and then toward the observer by M.

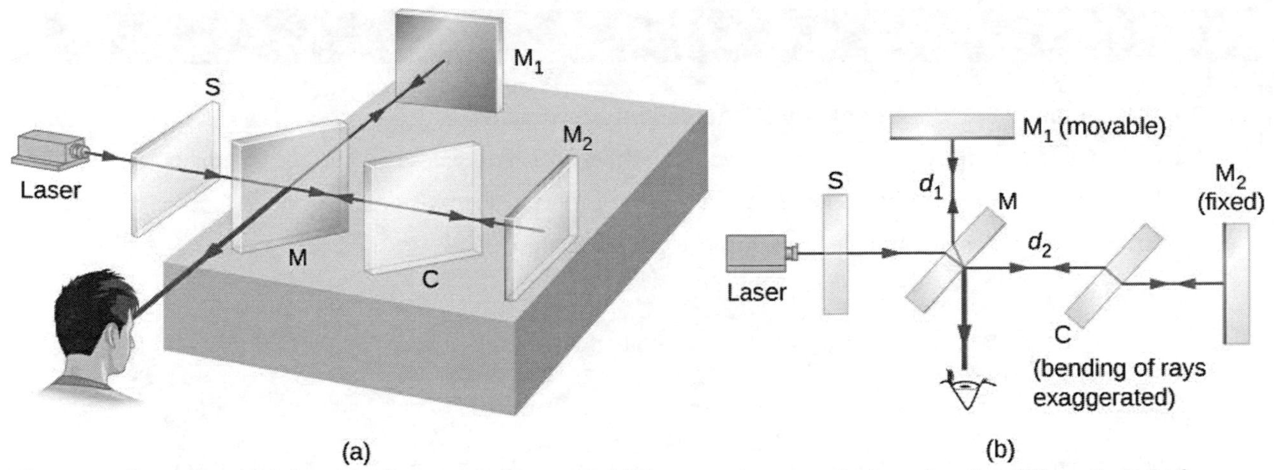

Figure 3.16 (a) The Michelson interferometer. The extended light source is a ground-glass plate that diffuses the light from a laser. (b) A planar view of the interferometer.

Because both beams originate from the same point on the source, they are coherent and therefore interfere. Notice from the figure that one beam passes through M three times and the other only once. To ensure that both beams traverse the same thickness of glass, a compensator plate C of transparent glass is placed in the arm containing M_2. This plate is a duplicate of M (without the silvering) and is usually cut from the same piece of glass used to produce M. With the compensator in place, any phase difference between the two beams is due solely to the difference in the distances they travel.

The path difference of the two beams when they recombine is $2d_1 - 2d_2$, where d_1 is the distance between M and M_1, and d_2 is the distance between M and M_2. Suppose this path difference is an integer number of wavelengths $m\lambda_0$. Then, constructive interference occurs and a bright image of the point on the source is seen at the observer. Now the light from any other point on the source whose two beams have this same path difference also undergoes constructive interference and produces a bright image. The collection of these point images is a bright fringe corresponding to a path difference of $m\lambda_0$ (**Figure 3.17**). When M_1 is moved a distance $\Delta d = \lambda_0/2$, this path difference changes by λ_0, and each fringe moves to the position previously occupied by an adjacent fringe. Consequently, by counting the number of fringes *m* passing a given point as M_1 is moved, an observer can measure minute displacements that are accurate to a fraction of a wavelength, as shown by the relation

$$\Delta d = m\frac{\lambda_0}{2}. \tag{3.7}$$

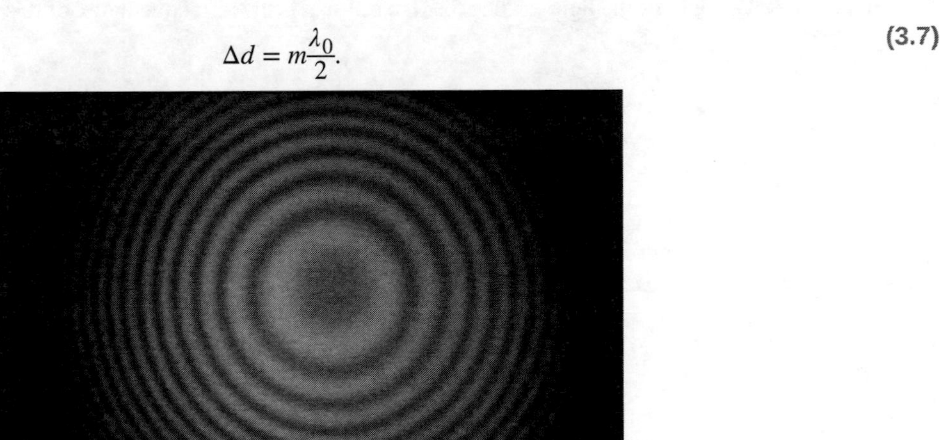

Figure 3.17 Fringes produced with a Michelson interferometer. (credit: "SILLAGESvideos"/YouTube)

Example 3.5

Precise Distance Measurements by Michelson Interferometer

A red laser light of wavelength 630 nm is used in a Michelson interferometer. While keeping the mirror M_1 fixed, mirror M_2 is moved. The fringes are found to move past a fixed cross-hair in the viewer. Find the distance the mirror M_2 is moved for a single fringe to move past the reference line.

Strategy

Refer to **Figure 3.16** for the geometry. We use the result of the Michelson interferometer interference condition to find the distance moved, Δd.

Solution

For a 630-nm red laser light, and for each fringe crossing $(m = 1)$, the distance traveled by M_2 if you keep M_1 fixed is

$$\Delta d = m\frac{\lambda_0}{2} = 1 \times \frac{630\text{ nm}}{2} = 315\text{ nm} = 0.315\ \mu\text{m}.$$

Significance

An important application of this measurement is the definition of the standard meter. As mentioned in **Units and Measurement (http://cnx.org/content/m58268/latest/)**, the length of the standard meter was once defined as the mirror displacement in a Michelson interferometer corresponding to 1,650,763.73 wavelengths of the particular fringe of krypton-86 in a gas discharge tube.

Example 3.6

Measuring the Refractive Index of a Gas

In one arm of a Michelson interferometer, a glass chamber is placed with attachments for evacuating the inside and putting gases in it. The space inside the container is 2 cm wide. Initially, the container is empty. As gas is slowly let into the chamber, you observe that dark fringes move past a reference line in the field of observation. By the time the chamber is filled to the desired pressure, you have counted 122 fringes move past the reference line. The wavelength of the light used is 632.8 nm. What is the refractive index of this gas?

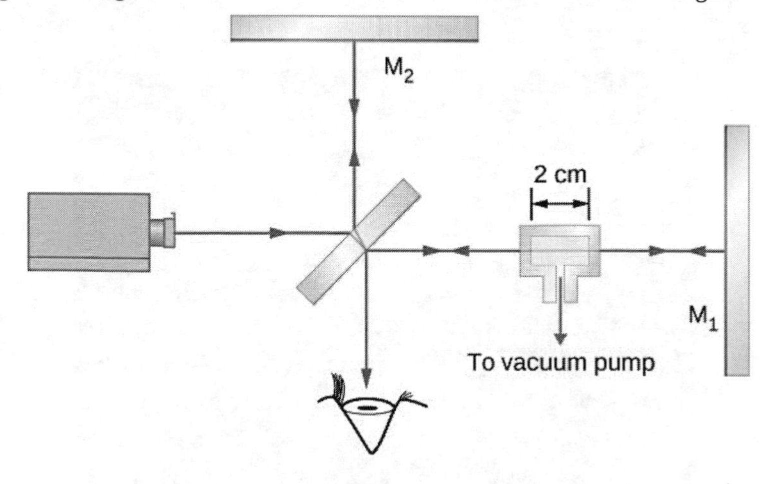

Strategy

The $m = 122$ fringes observed compose the difference between the number of wavelengths that fit within the empty chamber (vacuum) and the number of wavelengths that fit within the same chamber when it is gas-filled. The wavelength in the filled chamber is shorter by a factor of n, the index of refraction.

Solution

The ray travels a distance $t = 2\text{ cm}$ to the right through the glass chamber and another distance t to the left upon reflection. The total travel is $L = 2t$. When empty, the number of wavelengths that fit in this chamber is

$$N_0 = \frac{L}{\lambda_0} = \frac{2t}{\lambda_0}$$

where $\lambda_0 = 632.8\text{ nm}$ is the wavelength in vacuum of the light used. In any other medium, the wavelength is $\lambda = \lambda_0/n$ and the number of wavelengths that fit in the gas-filled chamber is

$$N = \frac{L}{\lambda} = \frac{2t}{\lambda_0/n}.$$

The number of fringes observed in the transition is

$$\begin{aligned} m &= N - N_0, \\ &= \frac{2t}{\lambda_0/n} - \frac{2t}{\lambda_0}, \\ &= \frac{2t}{\lambda_0}(n-1). \end{aligned}$$

Solving for $(n-1)$ gives

$$n - 1 = m\left(\frac{\lambda_0}{2t}\right) = 122\left(\frac{632.8 \times 10^{-9}\text{ m}}{2(2 \times 10^{-2}\text{ m})}\right) = 0.0019$$

and $n = 1.0019$.

Significance

The indices of refraction for gases are so close to that of vacuum, that we normally consider them equal to 1. The difference between 1 and 1.0019 is so small that measuring it requires a correspondingly sensitive technique such as interferometry. We cannot, for example, hope to measure this value using techniques based simply on Snell's law.

3.3 Check Your Understanding Although m, the number of fringes observed, is an integer, which is often regarded as having zero uncertainty, in practical terms, it is all too easy to lose track when counting fringes. In **Example 3.6**, if you estimate that you might have missed as many as five fringes when you reported $m = 122$ fringes, (a) is the value for the index of refraction worked out in **Example 3.6** too large or too small? (b) By how much?

Problem-Solving Strategy: Wave Optics

Step 1. *Examine the situation to determine that interference is involved.* Identify whether slits, thin films, or interferometers are considered in the problem.

Step 2. *If slits are involved,* note that diffraction gratings and double slits produce very similar interference patterns, but that gratings have narrower (sharper) maxima. Single-slit patterns are characterized by a large central maximum and smaller maxima to the sides.

Step 3. *If thin-film interference or an interferometer is involved, take note of the path length difference between the two rays that interfere.* Be certain to use the wavelength in the medium involved, since it differs from the wavelength in vacuum. Note also that there is an additional $\lambda/2$ phase shift when light reflects from a medium with a greater index of refraction.

Step 4. *Identify exactly what needs to be determined in the problem (identify the unknowns).* A written list is useful. Draw a diagram of the situation. Labeling the diagram is useful.

Step 5. *Make a list of what is given or can be inferred from the problem as stated (identify the knowns).*

Step 6. *Solve the appropriate equation for the quantity to be determined (the unknown) and enter the knowns.* Slits, gratings, and the Rayleigh limit involve equations.

Step 7. *For thin-film interference, you have constructive interference for a total shift that is an integral number of wavelengths. You have destructive interference for a total shift of a half-integral number of wavelengths.* Always keep in mind that crest to crest is constructive whereas crest to trough is destructive.

Step 8. *Check to see if the answer is reasonable: Does it make sense?* Angles in interference patterns cannot be greater than $90°$, for example.

CHAPTER 3 REVIEW

KEY TERMS

coherent waves waves are in phase or have a definite phase relationship

fringes bright and dark patterns of interference

incoherent waves have random phase relationships

interferometer instrument that uses interference of waves to make measurements

monochromatic light composed of one wavelength only

Newton's rings circular interference pattern created by interference between the light reflected off two surfaces as a result of a slight gap between them

order integer m used in the equations for constructive and destructive interference for a double slit

principal maximum brightest interference fringes seen with multiple slits

secondary maximum bright interference fringes of intensity lower than the principal maxima

thin-film interference interference between light reflected from different surfaces of a thin film

KEY EQUATIONS

Constructive interference	$\Delta l = m\lambda,$ for m = 0, ±1, ±2, ±3…
Destructive interference	$\Delta l = (m + \frac{1}{2})\lambda,$ for m = 0, ±1, ±2, ±3…
Path length difference for waves from two slits to a common point on a screen	$\Delta l = d \sin \theta$
Constructive interference	$d \sin \theta = m\lambda, \quad \text{for } m = 0, \pm 1, \pm 2, \pm 3, \ldots$
Destructive interference	$d \sin \theta = (m + \frac{1}{2})\lambda, \text{ for } m = 0, \pm 1, \pm 2, \pm 3, \ldots$
Distance from central maximum to the mth bright fringe	$y_m = \frac{m\lambda D}{d}$
Displacement measured by a Michelson interferometer	$\Delta d = m\frac{\lambda_0}{2}$

SUMMARY

3.1 Young's Double-Slit Interference

- Young's double-slit experiment gave definitive proof of the wave character of light.
- An interference pattern is obtained by the superposition of light from two slits.

3.2 Mathematics of Interference

- In double-slit diffraction, constructive interference occurs when $d \sin \theta = m\lambda (\text{for } m = 0, \pm 1, \pm 2, \pm 3\ldots)$, where d is the distance between the slits, θ is the angle relative to the incident direction, and m is the order of the interference.
- Destructive interference occurs when $d \sin \theta = (m + \frac{1}{2})\lambda$ for $m = 0, \pm 1, \pm 2, \pm 3, \ldots$.

3.3 Multiple-Slit Interference

- Interference from multiple slits ($N > 2$) produces principal as well as secondary maxima.
- As the number of slits is increased, the intensity of the principal maxima increases and the width decreases.

3.4 Interference in Thin Films

- When light reflects from a medium having an index of refraction greater than that of the medium in which it is traveling, a $180°$ phase change (or a $\lambda/2$ shift) occurs.
- Thin-film interference occurs between the light reflected from the top and bottom surfaces of a film. In addition to the path length difference, there can be a phase change.

3.5 The Michelson Interferometer

- When the mirror in one arm of the interferometer moves a distance of $\lambda/2$ each fringe in the interference pattern moves to the position previously occupied by the adjacent fringe.

CONCEPTUAL QUESTIONS

3.1 Young's Double-Slit Interference

1. Young's double-slit experiment breaks a single light beam into two sources. Would the same pattern be obtained for two independent sources of light, such as the headlights of a distant car? Explain.

2. Is it possible to create a experimental setup in which there is only destructive interference? Explain.

3. Why won't two small sodium lamps, held close together, produce an interference pattern on a distant screen? What if the sodium lamps were replaced by two laser pointers held close together?

3.2 Mathematics of Interference

4. Suppose you use the same double slit to perform Young's double-slit experiment in air and then repeat the experiment in water. Do the angles to the same parts of the interference pattern get larger or smaller? Does the color of the light change? Explain.

5. Why is monochromatic light used in the double slit experiment? What would happen if white light were used?

3.4 Interference in Thin Films

6. What effect does increasing the wedge angle have on the spacing of interference fringes? If the wedge angle is too large, fringes are not observed. Why?

7. How is the difference in paths taken by two originally in-phase light waves related to whether they interfere constructively or destructively? How can this be affected by reflection? By refraction?

8. Is there a phase change in the light reflected from either surface of a contact lens floating on a person's tear layer? The index of refraction of the lens is about 1.5, and its top surface is dry.

9. In placing a sample on a microscope slide, a glass cover is placed over a water drop on the glass slide. Light incident from above can reflect from the top and bottom of the glass cover and from the glass slide below the water drop. At which surfaces will there be a phase change in the reflected light?

10. Answer the above question if the fluid between the two pieces of crown glass is carbon disulfide.

11. While contemplating the food value of a slice of ham, you notice a rainbow of color reflected from its moist surface. Explain its origin.

12. An inventor notices that a soap bubble is dark at its thinnest and realizes that destructive interference is taking place for all wavelengths. How could she use this knowledge to make a nonreflective coating for lenses that is effective at all wavelengths? That is, what limits would there be on the index of refraction and thickness of the coating? How might this be impractical?

13. A nonreflective coating like the one described in **Example 3.3** works ideally for a single wavelength and for perpendicular incidence. What happens for other wavelengths and other incident directions? Be specific.

14. Why is it much more difficult to see interference fringes for light reflected from a thick piece of glass than from a thin film? Would it be easier if monochromatic light were used?

3.5 The Michelson Interferometer

15. Describe how a Michelson interferometer can be used to measure the index of refraction of a gas (including air).

PROBLEMS

3.2 Mathematics of Interference

16. At what angle is the first-order maximum for 450-nm wavelength blue light falling on double slits separated by 0.0500 mm?

17. Calculate the angle for the third-order maximum of 580-nm wavelength yellow light falling on double slits separated by 0.100 mm.

18. What is the separation between two slits for which 610-nm orange light has its first maximum at an angle of $30.0°$?

19. Find the distance between two slits that produces the first minimum for 410-nm violet light at an angle of $45.0°$.

20. Calculate the wavelength of light that has its third minimum at an angle of $30.0°$ when falling on double slits separated by $3.00\ \mu m$. Explicitly show how you follow the steps from the **Problem-Solving Strategy: Wave Optics**, located at the end of the chapter.

21. What is the wavelength of light falling on double slits separated by $2.00\ \mu m$ if the third-order maximum is at an angle of $60.0°$?

22. At what angle is the fourth-order maximum for the situation in the preceding problem?

23. What is the highest-order maximum for 400-nm light falling on double slits separated by $25.0\ \mu m$?

24. Find the largest wavelength of light falling on double slits separated by $1.20\ \mu m$ for which there is a first-order maximum. Is this in the visible part of the spectrum?

25. What is the smallest separation between two slits that will produce a second-order maximum for 720-nm red light?

26. (a) What is the smallest separation between two slits that will produce a second-order maximum for any visible light? (b) For all visible light?

27. (a) If the first-order maximum for monochromatic light falling on a double slit is at an angle of $10.0°$, at what angle is the second-order maximum? (b) What is the angle of the first minimum? (c) What is the highest-order maximum possible here?

28. Shown below is a double slit located a distance x from a screen, with the distance from the center of the screen given by y. When the distance d between the slits is relatively large, numerous bright spots appear, called fringes. Show that, for small angles (where $\sin\theta \approx \theta$, with θ in radians), the distance between fringes is given by $\Delta y = x\lambda/d$

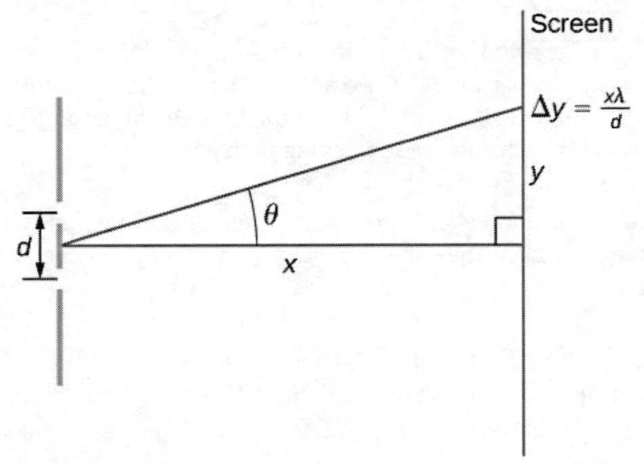

29. Using the result of the preceding problem, (a) calculate the distance between fringes for 633-nm light falling on double slits separated by 0.0800 mm, located 3.00 m from a screen. (b) What would be the distance between fringes if the entire apparatus were submersed in water, whose index of refraction is 1.33?

30. Using the result of the problem two problems prior, find the wavelength of light that produces fringes 7.50 mm apart on a screen 2.00 m from double slits separated by 0.120 mm.

31. In a double-slit experiment, the fifth maximum is 2.8 cm from the central maximum on a screen that is 1.5 m away from the slits. If the slits are 0.15 mm apart, what is the wavelength of the light being used?

32. The source in Young's experiment emits at two wavelengths. On the viewing screen, the fourth maximum for one wavelength is located at the same spot as the fifth maximum for the other wavelength. What is the ratio of the two wavelengths?

33. If 500-nm and 650-nm light illuminates two slits that are separated by 0.50 mm, how far apart are the second-order maxima for these two wavelengths on a screen 2.0 m away?

34. Red light of wavelength of 700 nm falls on a double slit separated by 400 nm. (a) At what angle is the first-order maximum in the diffraction pattern? (b) What is unreasonable about this result? (c) Which assumptions are unreasonable or inconsistent?

3.3 Multiple-Slit Interference

35. Ten narrow slits are equally spaced 0.25 mm apart and illuminated with yellow light of wavelength 580 nm. (a) What are the angular positions of the third and fourth principal maxima? (b) What is the separation of these maxima on a screen 2.0 m from the slits?

36. The width of bright fringes can be calculated as the separation between the two adjacent dark fringes on either side. Find the angular widths of the third- and fourth-order bright fringes from the preceding problem.

37. For a three-slit interference pattern, find the ratio of the peak intensities of a secondary maximum to a principal maximum.

38. What is the angular width of the central fringe of the interference pattern of (a) 20 slits separated by $d = 2.0 \times 10^{-3}\,\text{mm}$? (b) 50 slits with the same separation? Assume that $\lambda = 600\,\text{nm}$.

3.4 Interference in Thin Films

39. A soap bubble is 100 nm thick and illuminated by white light incident perpendicular to its surface. What wavelength and color of visible light is most constructively reflected, assuming the same index of refraction as water?

40. An oil slick on water is 120 nm thick and illuminated by white light incident perpendicular to its surface. What color does the oil appear (what is the most constructively reflected wavelength), given its index of refraction is 1.40?

41. Calculate the minimum thickness of an oil slick on water that appears blue when illuminated by white light perpendicular to its surface. Take the blue wavelength to be 470 nm and the index of refraction of oil to be 1.40.

42. Find the minimum thickness of a soap bubble that appears red when illuminated by white light perpendicular to its surface. Take the wavelength to be 680 nm, and assume the same index of refraction as water.

43. A film of soapy water ($n = 1.33$) on top of a plastic cutting board has a thickness of 233 nm. What color is most strongly reflected if it is illuminated perpendicular to its surface?

44. What are the three smallest non-zero thicknesses of soapy water ($n = 1.33$) on Plexiglas if it appears green (constructively reflecting 520-nm light) when illuminated perpendicularly by white light?

45. Suppose you have a lens system that is to be used primarily for 700-nm red light. What is the second thinnest coating of fluorite (magnesium fluoride) that would be nonreflective for this wavelength?

46. (a) As a soap bubble thins it becomes dark, because the path length difference becomes small compared with the wavelength of light and there is a phase shift at the top surface. If it becomes dark when the path length difference is less than one-fourth the wavelength, what is the thickest the bubble can be and appear dark at all visible wavelengths? Assume the same index of refraction as water. (b) Discuss the fragility of the film considering the thickness found.

47. To save money on making military aircraft invisible to radar, an inventor decides to coat them with a nonreflective material having an index of refraction of 1.20, which is between that of air and the surface of the plane. This, he reasons, should be much cheaper than designing Stealth bombers. (a) What thickness should the coating be to inhibit the reflection of 4.00-cm wavelength radar? (b) What is unreasonable about this result? (c) Which assumptions are unreasonable or inconsistent?

3.5 The Michelson Interferometer

48. A Michelson interferometer has two equal arms. A mercury light of wavelength 546 nm is used for the interferometer and stable fringes are found. One of the arms is moved by $1.5\mu\text{m}$. How many fringes will cross the observing field?

49. What is the distance moved by the traveling mirror of a Michelson interferometer that corresponds to 1500 fringes passing by a point of the observation screen? Assume that the interferometer is illuminated with a 606 nm spectral line of krypton-86.

50. When the traveling mirror of a Michelson interferometer is moved $2.40 \times 10^{-5}\,\text{m}$, 90 fringes pass by a point on the observation screen. What is the wavelength of the light used?

51. In a Michelson interferometer, light of wavelength 632.8 nm from a He-Ne laser is used. When one of the mirrors is moved by a distance *D*, 8 fringes move past the field of view. What is the value of the distance *D*?

52. A chamber 5.0 cm long with flat, parallel windows at the ends is placed in one arm of a Michelson interferometer (see below). The light used has a wavelength of 500 nm in a vacuum. While all the air is being pumped out of the chamber, 29 fringes pass by a point on the observation screen. What is the refractive index of the air?

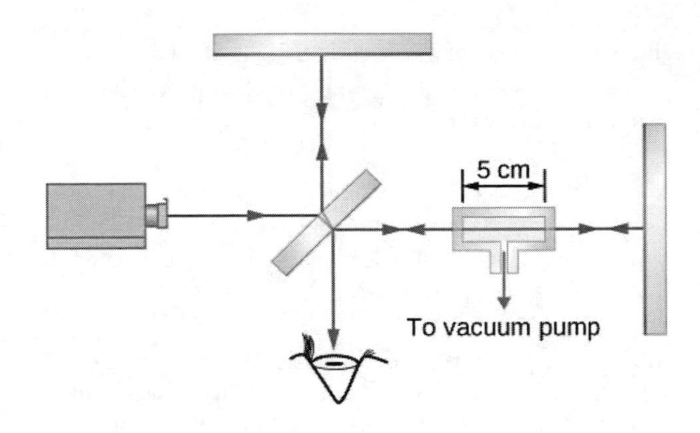

ADDITIONAL PROBLEMS

53. For 600-nm wavelength light and a slit separation of 0.12 mm, what are the angular positions of the first and third maxima in the double slit interference pattern?

54. If the light source in the preceding problem is changed, the angular position of the third maximum is found to be $0.57°$. What is the wavelength of light being used now?

55. Red light ($\lambda = 710.\text{ nm}$) illuminates double slits separated by a distance $d = 0.150\text{ mm}$. The screen and the slits are 3.00 m apart. (a) Find the distance on the screen between the central maximum and the third maximum. (b) What is the distance between the second and the fourth maxima?

56. Two sources as in phase and emit waves with $\lambda = 0.42\text{ m}$. Determine whether constructive or destructive interference occurs at points whose distances from the two sources are (a) 0.84 and 0.42 m, (b) 0.21 and 0.42 m, (c) 1.26 and 0.42 m, (d) 1.87 and 1.45 m, (e) 0.63 and 0.84 m and (f) 1.47 and 1.26 m.

57. Two slits 4.0×10^{-6} m apart are illuminated by light of wavelength 600 nm. What is the highest order fringe in the interference pattern?

58. Suppose that the highest order fringe that can be observed is the eighth in a double-slit experiment where 550-nm wavelength light is used. What is the minimum separation of the slits?

59. The interference pattern of a He-Ne laser light ($\lambda = 632.9\text{ nm}$) passing through two slits 0.031 mm apart is projected on a screen 10.0 m away. Determine the distance between the adjacent bright fringes.

60. Young's double-slit experiment is performed immersed in water ($n = 1.333$). The light source is a He-Ne laser, $\lambda = 632.9\text{ nm}$ in vacuum. (a) What is the wavelength of this light in water? (b) What is the angle for the third order maximum for two slits separated by 0.100 mm.

61. A double-slit experiment is to be set up so that the bright fringes appear 1.27 cm apart on a screen 2.13 m away from the two slits. The light source was wavelength 500 nm. What should be the separation between the two slits?

62. An effect analogous to two-slit interference can occur with sound waves, instead of light. In an open field, two speakers placed 1.30 m apart are powered by a single-function generator producing sine waves at 1200-Hz frequency. A student walks along a line 12.5 m away and parallel to the line between the speakers. She hears an alternating pattern of loud and quiet, due to constructive and destructive interference. What is (a) the wavelength of this sound and (b) the distance between the central maximum and the first maximum (loud) position along this line?

63. A hydrogen gas discharge lamp emits visible light at four wavelengths, $\lambda =$ 410, 434, 486, and 656 nm. (a) If light from this lamp falls on a *N* slits separated by 0.025 mm, how far from the central maximum are the third maxima when viewed on a screen 2.0 m from the slits? (b) By what distance are the second and third maxima separated for $l = 486\text{ nm}$?

64. Monochromatic light of frequency 5.5×10^{14} Hz falls on 10 slits separated by 0.020 mm. What is the separation between the first and third maxima on a screen that is 2.0 m from the slits?

65. Eight slits equally separated by 0.149 mm is uniformly illuminated by a monochromatic light at $\lambda = 523\text{ nm}$. What is the width of the central principal maximum on a screen 2.35 m away?

66. Eight slits equally separated by 0.149 mm is uniformly illuminated by a monochromatic light at $\lambda = 523\text{ nm}$. What is the intensity of a secondary maxima compared to that of the principal maxima?

67. A transparent film of thickness 250 nm and index of refraction of 1.40 is surrounded by air. What wavelength in a beam of white light at near-normal incidence to the film undergoes destructive interference when reflected?

68. An intensity minimum is found for 450 nm light transmitted through a transparent film $(n = 1.20)$ in air. (a) What is minimum thickness of the film? (b) If this wavelength is the longest for which the intensity minimum occurs, what are the next three lower values of λ for which this happens?

69. A thin film with $n = 1.32$ is surrounded by air. What is the minimum thickness of this film such that the reflection of normally incident light with $\lambda = 500\text{ nm}$ is minimized?

70. Repeat your calculation of the previous problem with the thin film placed on a flat glass ($n = 1.50$) surface.

71. After a minor oil spill, a think film of oil ($n = 1.40$) of thickness 450 nm floats on the water surface in a bay. (a) What predominant color is seen by a bird flying overhead? (b) What predominant color is seen by a seal swimming underwater?

72. A microscope slide 10 cm long is separated from a glass plate at one end by a sheet of paper. As shown below, the other end of the slide is in contact with the plate. The slide is illuminated from above by light from a sodium lamp ($\lambda = 589\text{ nm}$), and 14 fringes per centimeter are seen along the slide. What is the thickness of the piece of paper?

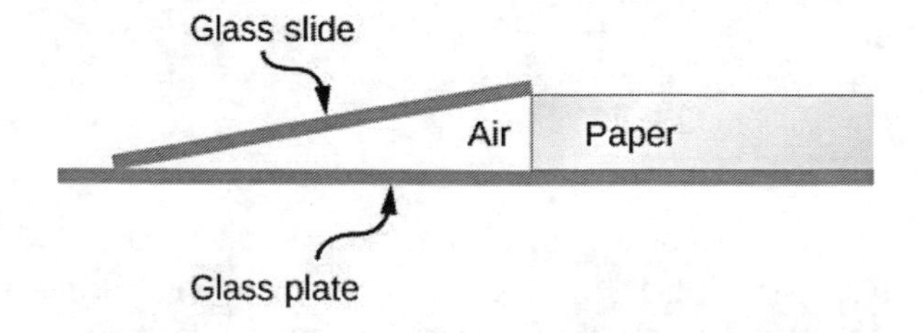

73. Suppose that the setup of the preceding problem is immersed in an unknown liquid. If 18 fringes per centimeter are now seen along the slide, what is the index of refraction of the liquid?

74. A thin wedge filled with air is produced when two flat glass plates are placed on top of one another and a slip of paper is inserted between them at one edge. Interference fringes are observed when monochromatic light falling vertically on the plates are seen in reflection. Is the first fringe near the edge where the plates are in contact a bright fringe or a dark fringe? Explain.

75. Two identical pieces of rectangular plate glass are used to measure the thickness of a hair. The glass plates are in direct contact at one edge and a single hair is placed between them hear the opposite edge. When illuminated with a sodium lamp ($\lambda = 589\text{ nm}$), the hair is seen between the 180th and 181st dark fringes. What are the lower and upper limits on the hair's diameter?

76. Two microscope slides made of glass are illuminated by monochromatic ($\lambda = 589\text{ nm}$) light incident perpendicularly. The top slide touches the bottom slide at one end and rests on a thin copper wire at the other end, forming a wedge of air. The diameter of the copper wire is $29.45\ \mu\text{m}$. How many bright fringes are seen across these slides?

77. A good quality camera "lens" is actually a system of lenses, rather than a single lens, but a side effect is that a reflection from the surface of one lens can bounce around many times within the system, creating artifacts in the photograph. To counteract this problem, one of the lenses in such a system is coated with a thin layer of material ($n = 1.28$) on one side. The index of refraction of the lens glass is 1.68. What is the smallest thickness of the coating that reduces the reflection at 640 nm by destructive interference? (In other words, the coating's effect is to be optimized for $\lambda = 640\text{ nm}$.)

78. Constructive interference is observed from directly above an oil slick for wavelengths (in air) 440 nm and 616 nm. The index of refraction of this oil is $n = 1.54$. What is the film's minimum possible thickness?

79. A soap bubble is blown outdoors. What colors (indicate by wavelengths) of the reflected sunlight are seen enhanced? The soap bubble has index of refraction 1.36 and thickness 380 nm.

80. A Michelson interferometer with a He-Ne laser light source ($\lambda = 632.8\text{ nm}$) projects its interference pattern on a screen. If the movable mirror is caused to move by $8.54\ \mu\text{m}$, how many fringes will be observed shifting through a reference point on a screen?

81. An experimenter detects 251 fringes when the movable mirror in a Michelson interferometer is displaced. The light source used is a sodium lamp, wavelength 589 nm. By what distance did the movable mirror move?

82. A Michelson interferometer is used to measure the wavelength of light put through it. When the movable mirror is moved by exactly 0.100 mm, the number of fringes observed moving through is 316. What is the wavelength of the light?

83. A 5.08-cm-long rectangular glass chamber is inserted into one arm of a Michelson interferometer using a 633-nm light source. This chamber is initially filled with air $(n = 1.000293)$ at standard atmospheric pressure but the air is gradually pumped out using a vacuum pump until a near perfect vacuum is achieved. How many fringes are observed moving by during the transition?

84. Into one arm of a Michelson interferometer, a plastic sheet of thickness $75\ \mu m$ is inserted, which causes a shift in the interference pattern by 86 fringes. The light source has wavelength of 610 nm in air. What is the index of refraction of this plastic?

85. The thickness of an aluminum foil is measured using a Michelson interferometer that has its movable mirror mounted on a micrometer. There is a difference of 27 fringes in the observed interference pattern when the micrometer clamps down on the foil compared to when the micrometer is empty. Calculate the thickness of the foil?

86. The movable mirror of a Michelson interferometer is attached to one end of a thin metal rod of length 23.3 mm. The other end of the rod is anchored so it does not move. As the temperature of the rod changes from $15\ °C$ to $25\ C$, a change of 14 fringes is observed. The light source is a He Ne laser, $\lambda = 632.8\ nm$. What is the change in length of the metal bar, and what is its thermal expansion coefficient?

87. In a thermally stabilized lab, a Michelson interferometer is used to monitor the temperature to ensure it stays constant. The movable mirror is mounted on the end of a 1.00-m-long aluminum rod, held fixed at the other end. The light source is a He Ne laser, $\lambda = 632.8\ nm$. The resolution of this apparatus corresponds to the temperature difference when a change of just one fringe is observed. What is this temperature difference?

88. A 65-fringe shift results in a Michelson interferometer when a $42.0\text{-}\mu m$ film made of an unknown material is placed in one arm. The light source has wavelength 632.9 nm. Identify the material using the indices of refraction found in **Table 1.1**.

CHALLENGE PROBLEMS

89. Determine what happens to the double-slit interference pattern if one of the slits is covered with a thin, transparent film whose thickness is $\lambda/[2(n-1)]$, where λ is the wavelength of the incident light and n is the index of refraction of the film.

90. Fifty-one narrow slits are equally spaced and separated by 0.10 mm. The slits are illuminated by blue light of wavelength 400 nm. What is angular position of the twenty-fifth secondary maximum? What is its peak intensity in comparison with that of the primary maximum?

91. A film of oil on water will appear dark when it is very thin, because the path length difference becomes small compared with the wavelength of light and there is a phase shift at the top surface. If it becomes dark when the path length difference is less than one-fourth the wavelength, what is the thickest the oil can be and appear dark at all visible wavelengths? Oil has an index of refraction of 1.40.

92. **Figure 3.14** shows two glass slides illuminated by monochromatic light incident perpendicularly. The top slide touches the bottom slide at one end and rests on a 0.100-mm-diameter hair at the other end, forming a wedge of air. (a) How far apart are the dark bands, if the slides are 7.50 cm long and 589-nm light is used? (b) Is there any difference if the slides are made from crown or flint glass? Explain.

93. **Figure 3.14** shows two 7.50-cm-long glass slides illuminated by pure 589-nm wavelength light incident perpendicularly. The top slide touches the bottom slide at one end and rests on some debris at the other end, forming a wedge of air. How thick is the debris, if the dark bands are 1.00 mm apart?

94. A soap bubble is 100 nm thick and illuminated by white light incident at a $45°$ angle to its surface. What wavelength and color of visible light is most constructively reflected, assuming the same index of refraction as water?

95. An oil slick on water is 120 nm thick and illuminated by white light incident at a $45°$ angle to its surface. What color does the oil appear (what is the most constructively reflected wavelength), given its index of refraction is 1.40?

4 | DIFFRACTION

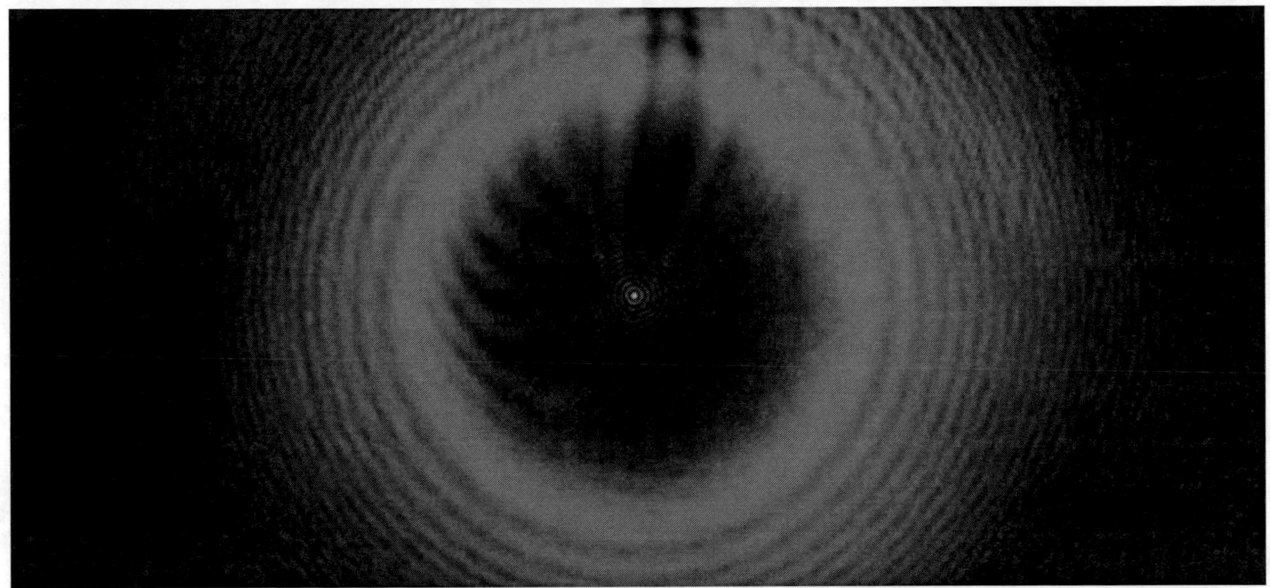

Figure 4.1 A steel ball bearing illuminated by a laser does not cast a sharp, circular shadow. Instead, a series of diffraction fringes and a central bright spot are observed. Known as Poisson's spot, the effect was first predicted by Augustin-Jean Fresnel (1788–1827) as a consequence of diffraction of light waves. Based on principles of ray optics, Siméon-Denis Poisson (1781–1840) argued against Fresnel's prediction. (credit: modification of work by Harvard Natural Science Lecture Demonstrations)

Chapter Outline

Introduction

Imagine passing a monochromatic light beam through a narrow opening—a slit just a little wider than the wavelength of the light. Instead of a simple shadow of the slit on the screen, you will see that an interference pattern appears, even though there is only one slit.

In the chapter on interference, we saw that you need two sources of waves for interference to occur. How can there be an interference pattern when we have only one slit? In **The Nature of Light**, we learned that, due to Huygens's principle, we can imagine a wave front as equivalent to infinitely many point sources of waves. Thus, a wave from a slit can behave not as one wave but as an infinite number of point sources. These waves can interfere with each other, resulting in an interference pattern without the presence of a second slit. This phenomenon is called *diffraction*.

Another way to view this is to recognize that a slit has a small but finite width. In the preceding chapter, we implicitly regarded slits as objects with positions but no size. The widths of the slits were considered negligible. When the slits have finite widths, each point along the opening can be considered a point source of light—a foundation of Huygens's principle. Because real-world optical instruments must have finite apertures (otherwise, no light can enter), diffraction plays a major role in the way we interpret the output of these optical instruments. For example, diffraction places limits on our ability to resolve images or objects. This is a problem that we will study later in this chapter.

4.1 | Single-Slit Diffraction

Learning Objectives

By the end of this section, you will be able to:

- Explain the phenomenon of diffraction and the conditions under which it is observed
- Describe diffraction through a single slit

After passing through a narrow aperture (opening), a wave propagating in a specific direction tends to spread out. For example, sound waves that enter a room through an open door can be heard even if the listener is in a part of the room where the geometry of ray propagation dictates that there should only be silence. Similarly, ocean waves passing through an opening in a breakwater can spread throughout the bay inside. (Figure 4.2). The spreading and bending of sound and ocean waves are two examples of **diffraction**, which is the bending of a wave around the edges of an opening or an obstacle—a phenomenon exhibited by all types of waves.

Figure 4.2 Because of the diffraction of waves, ocean waves entering through an opening in a breakwater can spread throughout the bay. (credit: modification of map data from Google Earth)

The diffraction of sound waves is apparent to us because wavelengths in the audible region are approximately the same size as the objects they encounter, a condition that must be satisfied if diffraction effects are to be observed easily. Since the wavelengths of visible light range from approximately 390 to 770 nm, most objects do not diffract light significantly. However, situations do occur in which apertures are small enough that the diffraction of light is observable. For example, if you place your middle and index fingers close together and look through the opening at a light bulb, you can see a rather clear diffraction pattern, consisting of light and dark lines running parallel to your fingers.

Diffraction through a Single Slit

Light passing through a single slit forms a diffraction pattern somewhat different from those formed by double slits or diffraction gratings, which we discussed in the chapter on interference. Figure 4.3 shows a single-slit diffraction pattern. Note that the central maximum is larger than maxima on either side and that the intensity decreases rapidly on either side. In contrast, a diffraction grating (Diffraction Gratings) produces evenly spaced lines that dim slowly on either side of the center.

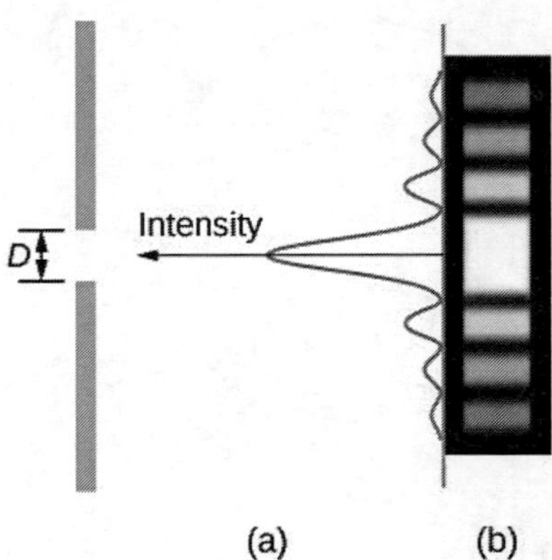

Figure 4.3 Single-slit diffraction pattern. (a) Monochromatic light passing through a single slit has a central maximum and many smaller and dimmer maxima on either side. The central maximum is six times higher than shown. (b) The diagram shows the bright central maximum, and the dimmer and thinner maxima on either side.

The analysis of single-slit diffraction is illustrated in **Figure 4.4**. Here, the light arrives at the slit, illuminating it uniformly and is in phase across its width. We then consider light propagating onwards from different parts of the *same* slit. According to Huygens's principle, every part of the wave front in the slit emits wavelets, as we discussed in **The Nature of Light**. These are like rays that start out in phase and head in all directions. (Each ray is perpendicular to the wave front of a wavelet.) Assuming the screen is very far away compared with the size of the slit, rays heading toward a common destination are nearly parallel. When they travel straight ahead, as in part (a) of the figure, they remain in phase, and we observe a central maximum. However, when rays travel at an angle θ relative to the original direction of the beam, each ray travels a different distance to a common location, and they can arrive in or out of phase. In part (b), the ray from the bottom travels a distance of one wavelength λ farther than the ray from the top. Thus, a ray from the center travels a distance $\lambda/2$ less than the one at the bottom edge of the slit, arrives out of phase, and interferes destructively. A ray from slightly above the center and one from slightly above the bottom also cancel one another. In fact, each ray from the slit interferes destructively with another ray. In other words, a pair-wise cancellation of all rays results in a dark minimum in intensity at this angle. By symmetry, another minimum occurs at the same angle to the right of the incident direction (toward the bottom of the figure) of the light.

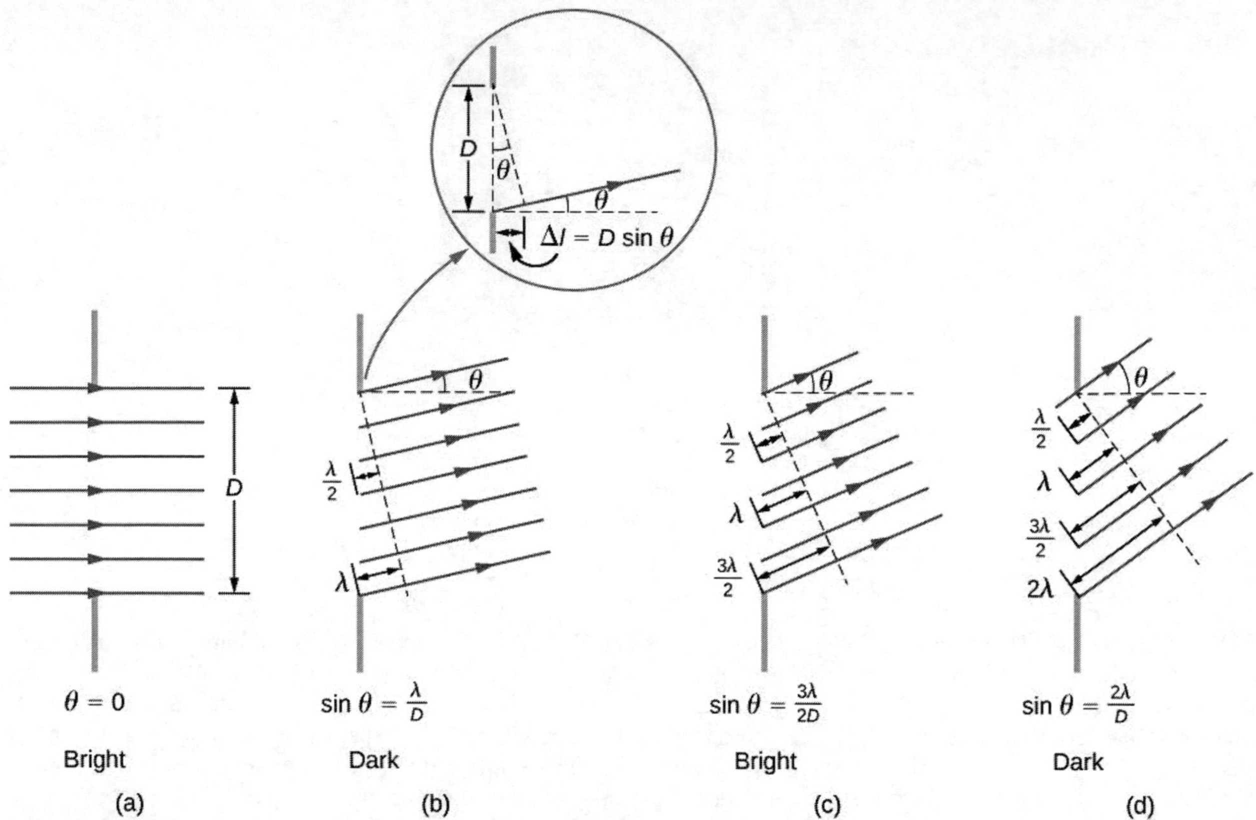

Figure 4.4 Light passing through a single slit is diffracted in all directions and may interfere constructively or destructively, depending on the angle. The difference in path length for rays from either side of the slit is seen to be $D \sin \theta$.

At the larger angle shown in part (c), the path lengths differ by $3\lambda/2$ for rays from the top and bottom of the slit. One ray travels a distance λ different from the ray from the bottom and arrives in phase, interfering constructively. Two rays, each from slightly above those two, also add constructively. Most rays from the slit have another ray to interfere with constructively, and a maximum in intensity occurs at this angle. However, not all rays interfere constructively for this situation, so the maximum is not as intense as the central maximum. Finally, in part (d), the angle shown is large enough to produce a second minimum. As seen in the figure, the difference in path length for rays from either side of the slit is $D \sin \theta$, and we see that a destructive minimum is obtained when this distance is an integral multiple of the wavelength.

Thus, to obtain **destructive interference for a single slit**,

$$D \sin \theta = m\lambda, \quad \text{for } m = \pm 1, \ \pm 2, \ \pm 3, \ \ldots \text{(destructive)}, \tag{4.1}$$

where D is the slit width, λ is the light's wavelength, θ is the angle relative to the original direction of the light, and m is the order of the minimum. **Figure 4.5** shows a graph of intensity for single-slit interference, and it is apparent that the maxima on either side of the central maximum are much less intense and not as wide. This effect is explored in **Double-Slit Diffraction**.

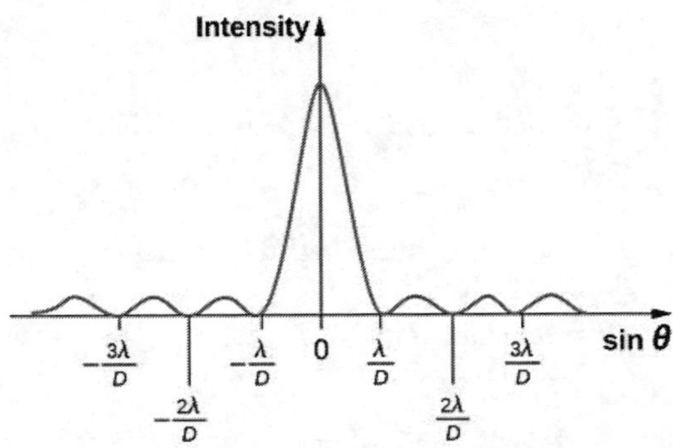

Figure 4.5 A graph of single-slit diffraction intensity showing the central maximum to be wider and much more intense than those to the sides. In fact, the central maximum is six times higher than shown here.

Example 4.1

Calculating Single-Slit Diffraction

Visible light of wavelength 550 nm falls on a single slit and produces its second diffraction minimum at an angle of $45.0°$ relative to the incident direction of the light, as in **Figure 4.6**. (a) What is the width of the slit? (b) At what angle is the first minimum produced?

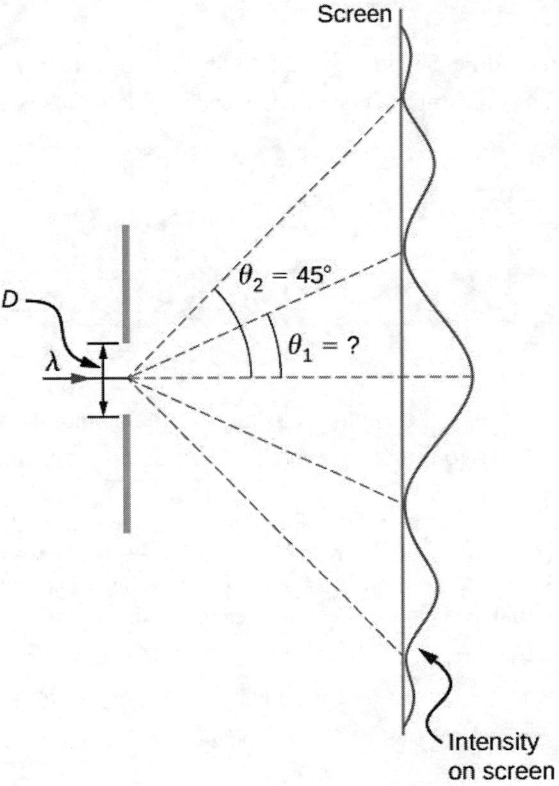

Figure 4.6 In this example, we analyze a graph of the single-slit diffraction pattern.

Strategy

From the given information, and assuming the screen is far away from the slit, we can use the equation $D \sin \theta = m\lambda$ first to find D, and again to find the angle for the first minimum θ_1.

Solution

a. We are given that $\lambda = 550\text{ nm}$, $m = 2$, and $\theta_2 = 45.0°$. Solving the equation $D \sin\theta = m\lambda$ for D and substituting known values gives

$$D = \frac{m\lambda}{\sin\theta_2} = \frac{2(550\text{ nm})}{\sin 45.0°} = \frac{1100 \times 10^{-9}\text{ m}}{0.707} = 1.56 \times 10^{-6}\text{ m}.$$

b. Solving the equation $D \sin\theta = m\lambda$ for $\sin\theta_1$ and substituting the known values gives

$$\sin\theta_1 = \frac{m\lambda}{D} = \frac{1(550 \times 10^{-9}\text{ m})}{1.56 \times 10^{-6}\text{ m}}.$$

Thus the angle θ_1 is

$$\theta_1 = \sin^{-1} 0.354 = 20.7°.$$

Significance

We see that the slit is narrow (it is only a few times greater than the wavelength of light). This is consistent with the fact that light must interact with an object comparable in size to its wavelength in order to exhibit significant wave effects such as this single-slit diffraction pattern. We also see that the central maximum extends $20.7°$ on either side of the original beam, for a width of about $41°$. The angle between the first and second minima is only about $24°$ $(45.0° - 20.7°)$. Thus, the second maximum is only about half as wide as the central maximum.

4.1 Check Your Understanding Suppose the slit width in **Example 4.1** is increased to 1.8×10^{-6} m. What are the new angular positions for the first, second, and third minima? Would a fourth minimum exist?

4.2 | Intensity in Single-Slit Diffraction

Learning Objectives

By the end of this section, you will be able to:

- Calculate the intensity relative to the central maximum of the single-slit diffraction peaks
- Calculate the intensity relative to the central maximum of an arbitrary point on the screen

To calculate the intensity of the diffraction pattern, we follow the phasor method used for calculations with ac circuits in **Alternating-Current Circuits (http://cnx.org/content/m58485/latest/)**. If we consider that there are N Huygens sources across the slit shown in **Figure 4.4**, with each source separated by a distance D/N from its adjacent neighbors, the path difference between waves from adjacent sources reaching the arbitrary point P on the screen is $(D/N)\sin\theta$. This distance is equivalent to a phase difference of $(2\pi D/\lambda N)\sin\theta$. The phasor diagram for the waves arriving at the point whose angular position is θ is shown in **Figure 4.7**. The amplitude of the phasor for each Huygens wavelet is ΔE_0, the amplitude of the resultant phasor is E, and the phase difference between the wavelets from the first and the last sources is

$$\phi = \left(\frac{2\pi}{\lambda}\right) D \sin\theta.$$

With $N \to \infty$, the phasor diagram approaches a circular arc of length $N\Delta E_0$ and radius r. Since the length of the arc is $N\Delta E_0$ for any ϕ, the radius r of the arc must decrease as ϕ increases (or equivalently, as the phasors form tighter spirals).

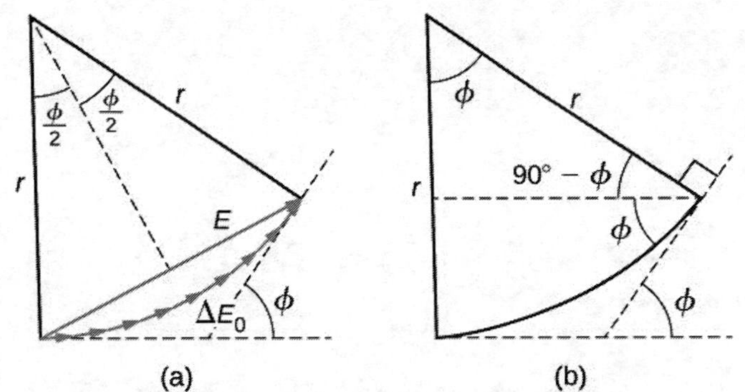

Figure 4.7 (a) Phasor diagram corresponding to the angular position θ in the single-slit diffraction pattern. The phase difference between the wavelets from the first and last sources is $\phi = (2\pi/\lambda)D \sin\theta$. (b) The geometry of the phasor diagram.

The phasor diagram for $\phi = 0$ (the center of the diffraction pattern) is shown in **Figure 4.8**(a) using $N = 30$. In this case, the phasors are laid end to end in a straight line of length $N\Delta E_0$, the radius r goes to infinity, and the resultant has its maximum value $E = N\Delta E_0$. The intensity of the light can be obtained using the relation $I = \frac{1}{2}c\varepsilon_0 E^2$ from **Electromagnetic Waves (http://cnx.org/content/m58495/latest/)**. The intensity of the maximum is then

$$I_0 = \frac{1}{2}c\varepsilon_0 (N\Delta E_0)^2 = \frac{1}{2\mu_0 c}(N\Delta E_0)^2,$$

where $\varepsilon_0 = 1/\mu_0 c^2$. The phasor diagrams for the first two zeros of the diffraction pattern are shown in parts (b) and (d) of the figure. In both cases, the phasors add to zero, after rotating through $\phi = 2\pi$ rad for $m = 1$ and 4π rad for $m = 2$.

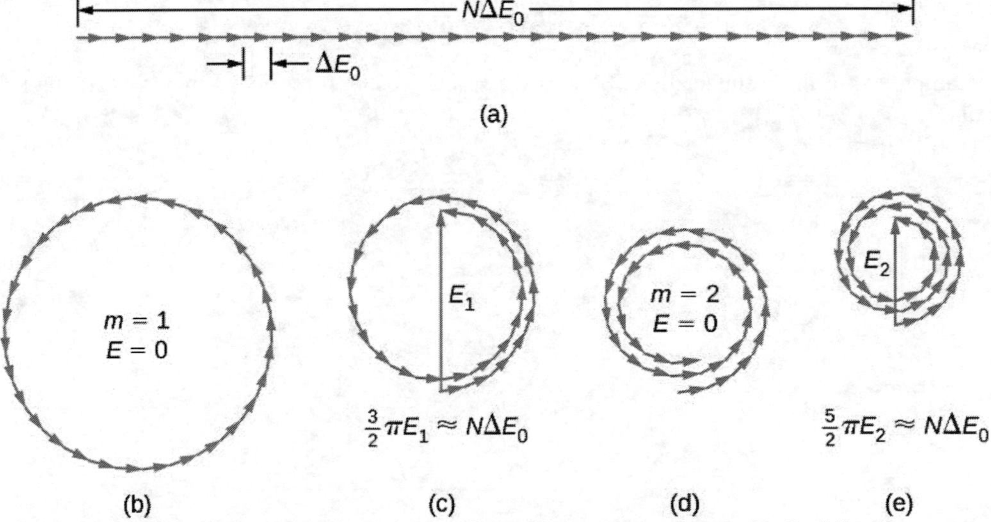

Figure 4.8 Phasor diagrams (with 30 phasors) for various points on the single-slit diffraction pattern. Multiple rotations around a given circle have been separated slightly so that the phasors can be seen. (a) Central maximum, (b) first minimum, (c) first maximum beyond central maximum, (d) second minimum, and (e) second maximum beyond central maximum.

The next two maxima beyond the central maxima are represented by the phasor diagrams of parts (c) and (e). In part (c), the phasors have rotated through $\phi = 3\pi$ rad and have formed a resultant phasor of magnitude E_1. The length of the arc formed by the phasors is $N\Delta E_0$. Since this corresponds to 1.5 rotations around a circle of diameter E_1, we have

$$\frac{3}{2}\pi E_1 \approx N\Delta E_0,$$

so

$$E_1 = \frac{2N\Delta E_0}{3\pi}$$

and

$$I_1 = \frac{1}{2\mu_0 c}E_1^2 = \frac{4(N\Delta E_0)^2}{(9\pi^2)(2\mu_0 c)} \approx 0.045 I_0,$$

where

$$I_0 = \frac{(N\Delta E_0)^2}{2\mu_0 c}.$$

In part (e), the phasors have rotated through $\phi = 5\pi$ rad, corresponding to 2.5 rotations around a circle of diameter E_2 and arc length $N\Delta E_0$. This results in $I_2 \approx 0.016 I_0$. The proof is left as an exercise for the student (**Exercise 4.119**).

These two maxima actually correspond to values of ϕ slightly less than 3π rad and 5π rad. Since the total length of the arc of the phasor diagram is always $N\Delta E_0$, the radius of the arc decreases as ϕ increases. As a result, E_1 and E_2 turn out to be slightly larger for arcs that have not quite curled through 3π rad and 5π rad, respectively. The exact values of ϕ for the maxima are investigated in **Exercise 4.120**. In solving that problem, you will find that they are less than, but very close to, $\phi = 3\pi, 5\pi, 7\pi, \ldots$ rad.

To calculate the intensity at an arbitrary point *P* on the screen, we return to the phasor diagram of **Figure 4.7**. Since the arc subtends an angle ϕ at the center of the circle,

$$N\Delta E_0 = r\phi$$

and

$$\sin\left(\frac{\phi}{2}\right) = \frac{E}{2r}.$$

where *E* is the amplitude of the resultant field. Solving the second equation for *E* and then substituting *r* from the first equation, we find

$$E = 2r\sin\frac{\phi}{2} = 2\frac{N\Delta E_o}{\phi}\sin\frac{\phi}{2}.$$

Now defining

$$\beta = \frac{\phi}{2} = \frac{\pi D\sin\theta}{\lambda} \quad (4.2)$$

we obtain

$$E = N\Delta E_0\frac{\sin\beta}{\beta} \quad (4.3)$$

This equation relates the amplitude of the resultant field at any point in the diffraction pattern to the amplitude $N\Delta E_0$ at the central maximum. The intensity is proportional to the square of the amplitude, so

$$I = I_0 \left(\frac{\sin \beta}{\beta} \right)^2 \tag{4.4}$$

where $I_0 = (N \Delta E_0)^2 / 2\mu_0 c$ is the intensity at the center of the pattern.

For the central maximum, $\phi = 0$, β is also zero and we see from l'Hôpital's rule that $\lim_{\beta \to 0}(\sin \beta / \beta) = 1$, so that $\lim_{\phi \to 0} I = I_0$. For the next maximum, $\phi = 3\pi$ rad, we have $\beta = 3\pi/2$ rad and when substituted into **Equation 4.4**, it yields

$$I_1 = I_0 \left(\frac{\sin 3\pi/2}{3\pi/2} \right)^2 \approx 0.045 I_0,$$

in agreement with what we found earlier in this section using the diameters and circumferences of phasor diagrams. Substituting $\phi = 5\pi$ rad into **Equation 4.4** yields a similar result for I_2.

A plot of **Equation 4.4** is shown in **Figure 4.9** and directly below it is a photograph of an actual diffraction pattern. Notice that the central peak is much brighter than the others, and that the zeros of the pattern are located at those points where $\sin \beta = 0$, which occurs when $\beta = m\pi$ rad. This corresponds to

$$\frac{\pi D \sin \theta}{\lambda} = m\pi,$$

or

$$D \sin \theta = m\lambda,$$

which is **Equation 4.1**.

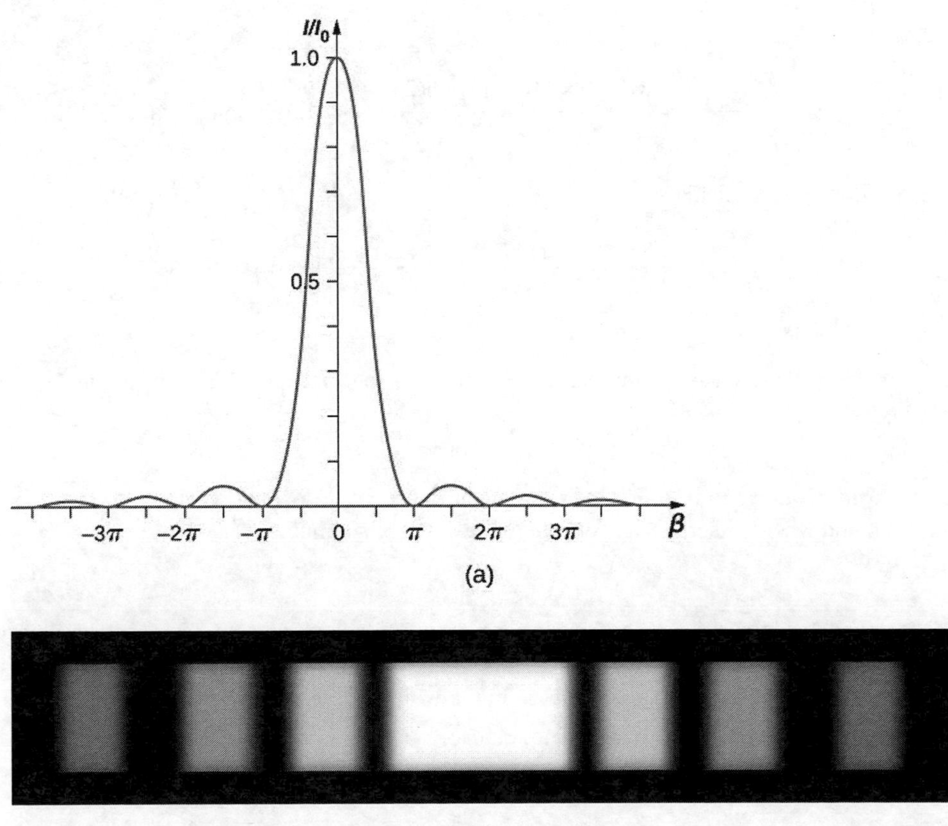

Figure 4.9 (a) The calculated intensity distribution of a single-slit diffraction pattern. (b) The actual diffraction pattern.

Example 4.2

Intensity in Single-Slit Diffraction

Light of wavelength 550 nm passes through a slit of width $2.00\ \mu\text{m}$ and produces a diffraction pattern similar to that shown in Figure 4.9. (a) Find the locations of the first two minima in terms of the angle from the central maximum and (b) determine the intensity relative to the central maximum at a point halfway between these two minima.

Strategy

The minima are given by Equation 4.1, $D \sin \theta = m\lambda$. The first two minima are for $m = 1$ and $m = 2$. Equation 4.4 and Equation 4.2 can be used to determine the intensity once the angle has been worked out.

Solution

a. Solving Equation 4.1 for θ gives us $\theta_m = \sin^{-1}(m\lambda/D)$, so that

$$\theta_1 = \sin^{-1}\left(\frac{(+1)(550 \times 10^{-9}\ \text{m})}{2.00 \times 10^{-6}\ \text{m}}\right) = +16.0°$$

and

$$\theta_2 = \sin^{-1}\left(\frac{(+2)(550 \times 10^{-9}\ \text{m})}{2.00 \times 10^{-6}\ \text{m}}\right) = +33.4°.$$

b. The halfway point between θ_1 and θ_2 is

$$\theta = (\theta_1 + \theta_2)/2 = (16.0° + 33.4°)/2 = 24.7°.$$

Equation 4.2 gives

$$\beta = \frac{\pi D \sin \theta}{\lambda} = \frac{\pi(2.00 \times 10^{-6}\ \text{m})\sin(24.7°)}{(550 \times 10^{-9}\ \text{m})} = 1.52\pi \text{ or } 4.77 \text{ rad}.$$

From Equation 4.4, we can calculate

$$\frac{I}{I_o} = \left(\frac{\sin \beta}{\beta}\right)^2 = \left(\frac{\sin(4.77)}{4.77}\right)^2 = \left(\frac{-0.9985}{4.77}\right)^2 = 0.044.$$

Significance

This position, halfway between two minima, is very close to the location of the maximum, expected near $\beta = 3\pi/2$, or 1.5π.

4.2 Check Your Understanding For the experiment in Example 4.2, at what angle from the center is the third maximum and what is its intensity relative to the central maximum?

If the slit width D is varied, the intensity distribution changes, as illustrated in Figure 4.10. The central peak is distributed over the region from $\sin \theta = -\lambda/D$ to $\sin \theta = +\lambda/D$. For small θ, this corresponds to an angular width $\Delta\theta \approx 2\lambda/D$. Hence, an increase in the slit width results in a decrease in the **width of the central peak**. For a slit with $D \gg \lambda$, the central peak is very sharp, whereas if $D \approx \lambda$, it becomes quite broad.

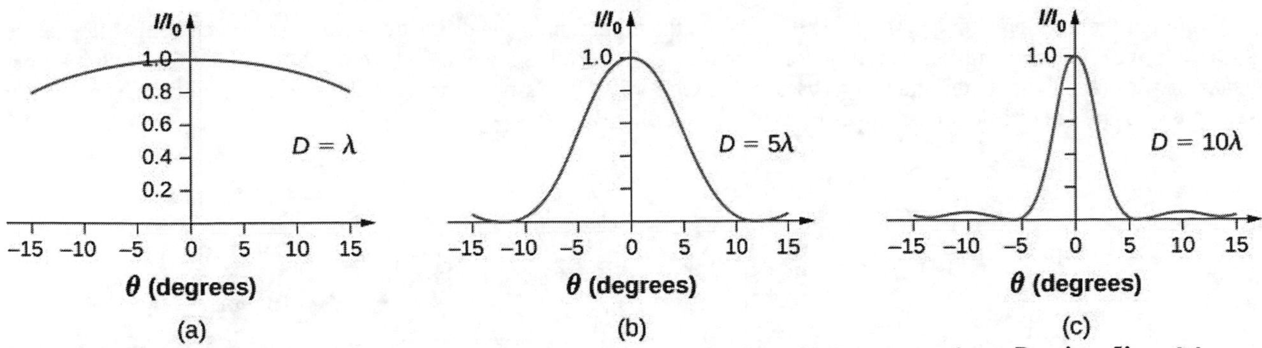

Figure 4.10 Single-slit diffraction patterns for various slit widths. As the slit width D increases from $D = \lambda$ to 5λ and then to 10λ, the width of the central peak decreases as the angles for the first minima decrease as predicted by **Equation 4.1**.

A diffraction experiment in optics can require a lot of preparation but **this simulation (https://openstaxcollege.org/l/21diffrexpoptsi)** by Andrew Duffy offers not only a quick set up but also the ability to change the slit width instantly. Run the simulation and select “Single slit.” You can adjust the slit width and see the effect on the diffraction pattern on a screen and as a graph.

4.3 | Double-Slit Diffraction

Learning Objectives

By the end of this section, you will be able to:

- Describe the combined effect of interference and diffraction with two slits, each with finite width
- Determine the relative intensities of interference fringes within a diffraction pattern
- Identify missing orders, if any

When we studied interference in Young’s double-slit experiment, we ignored the diffraction effect in each slit. We assumed that the slits were so narrow that on the screen you saw only the interference of light from just two point sources. If the slit is smaller than the wavelength, then **Figure 4.10**(a) shows that there is just a spreading of light and no peaks or troughs on the screen. Therefore, it was reasonable to leave out the diffraction effect in that chapter. However, if you make the slit wider, **Figure 4.10**(b) and (c) show that you cannot ignore diffraction. In this section, we study the complications to the double-slit experiment that arise when you also need to take into account the diffraction effect of each slit.

To calculate the diffraction pattern for two (or any number of) slits, we need to generalize the method we just used for a single slit. That is, across each slit, we place a uniform distribution of point sources that radiate Huygens wavelets, and then we sum the wavelets from all the slits. This gives the intensity at any point on the screen. Although the details of that calculation can be complicated, the final result is quite simple:

Two-Slit Diffraction Pattern

The diffraction pattern of two slits of width D that are separated by a distance d is the interference pattern of two point sources separated by d multiplied by the diffraction pattern of a slit of width D.

In other words, the *locations* of the interference fringes are given by the equation $d \sin \theta = m\lambda$, the same as when we considered the slits to be point sources, but the *intensities* of the fringes are now reduced by diffraction effects, according to **Equation 4.4**. [Note that in the chapter on interference, we wrote $d \sin \theta = m\lambda$ and used the integer m to refer to interference fringes. **Equation 4.1** also uses m, but this time to refer to diffraction minima. If both equations are used simultaneously, it is good practice to use a different variable (such as n) for one of these integers in order to keep them distinct.]

Interference and diffraction effects operate simultaneously and generally produce minima at different angles. This gives rise to a complicated pattern on the screen, in which some of the maxima of interference from the two slits are missing if the maximum of the interference is in the same direction as the minimum of the diffraction. We refer to such a missing peak as a **missing order**. One example of a diffraction pattern on the screen is shown in Figure 4.11. The solid line with multiple peaks of various heights is the intensity observed on the screen. It is a product of the interference pattern of waves from separate slits and the diffraction of waves from within one slit.

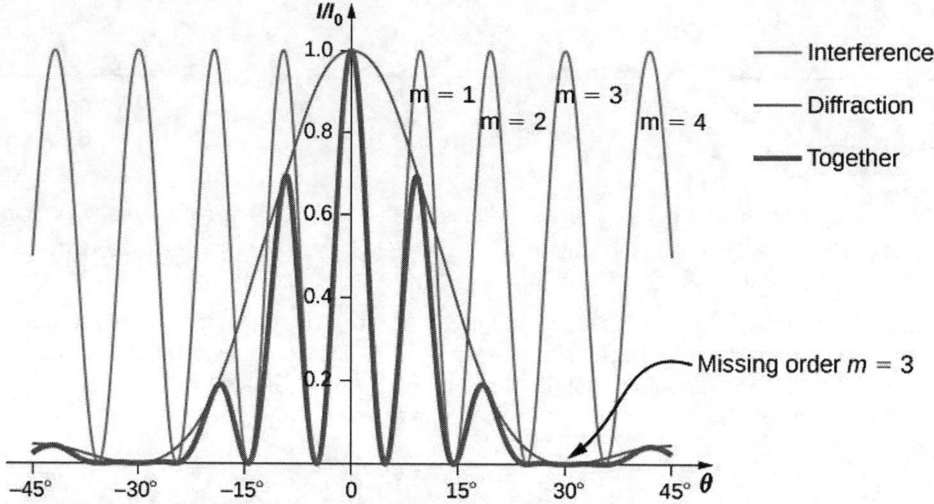

Figure 4.11 Diffraction from a double slit. The purple line with peaks of the same height are from the interference of the waves from two slits; the blue line with one big hump in the middle is the diffraction of waves from within one slit; and the thick red line is the product of the two, which is the pattern observed on the screen. The plot shows the expected result for a slit width $D = 2\lambda$ and slit separation $d = 6\lambda$. The maximum of $m = \pm 3$ order for the interference is missing because the minimum of the diffraction occurs in the same direction.

Example 4.3

Intensity of the Fringes

Figure 4.11 shows that the intensity of the fringe for $m = 3$ is zero, but what about the other fringes? Calculate the intensity for the fringe at $m = 1$ relative to I_0, the intensity of the central peak.

Strategy

Determine the angle for the double-slit interference fringe, using the equation from Interference, then determine the relative intensity in that direction due to diffraction by using Equation 4.4.

Solution

From the chapter on interference, we know that the bright interference fringes occur at $d \sin\theta = m\lambda$, or

$$\sin\theta = \frac{m\lambda}{d}.$$

From Equation 4.4,

$$I = I_0\left(\frac{\sin\beta}{\beta}\right)^2, \text{ where } \beta = \frac{\phi}{2} = \frac{\pi D \sin\theta}{\lambda}.$$

Substituting from above,

$$\beta = \frac{\pi D \sin\theta}{\lambda} = \frac{\pi D}{\lambda} \cdot \frac{m\lambda}{d} = \frac{m\pi D}{d}.$$

For $D = 2\lambda$, $d = 6\lambda$, and $m = 1$,

$$\beta = \frac{(1)\pi(2\lambda)}{(6\lambda)} = \frac{\pi}{3}.$$

Then, the intensity is

$$I = I_0 \left(\frac{\sin \beta}{\beta}\right)^2 = I_0 \left(\frac{\sin (\pi/3)}{\pi/3}\right)^2 = 0.684 I_0.$$

Significance

Note that this approach is relatively straightforward and gives a result that is almost exactly the same as the more complicated analysis using phasors to work out the intensity values of the double-slit interference (thin line in Figure 4.11). The phasor approach accounts for the downward slope in the diffraction intensity (blue line) so that the peak *near* $m = 1$ occurs at a value of θ ever so slightly smaller than we have shown here.

Example 4.4

Two-Slit Diffraction

Suppose that in Young's experiment, slits of width 0.020 mm are separated by 0.20 mm. If the slits are illuminated by monochromatic light of wavelength 500 nm, how many bright fringes are observed in the central peak of the diffraction pattern?

Solution

From Equation 4.1, the angular position of the first diffraction minimum is $\theta \approx \sin \theta = \frac{\lambda}{D} = \frac{5.0 \times 10^{-7}\text{ m}}{2.0 \times 10^{-5}\text{ m}} = 2.5 \times 10^{-2}\text{ rad.}$

Using $\sin \theta = m\lambda$ for $\theta = 2.5 \times 10^{-2}$ rad, we find

$$m = \frac{d \sin \theta}{\lambda} = \frac{(0.20\text{ mm})\left(2.5 \times 10^{-2}\text{ rad}\right)}{\left(5.0 \times 10^{-7}\text{ m}\right)} = 10,$$

which is the maximum interference order that fits inside the central peak. We note that $m = \pm 10$ are missing orders as θ matches exactly. Accordingly, we observe bright fringes for

$$m = -9, -8, -7, -6, -5, -4, -3, -2, -1, 0, +1, +2, +3, +4, +5, +6, +7, +8, \text{ and } +9$$

for a total of 19 bright fringes.

4.3 Check Your Understanding For the experiment in Example 4.4, show that $m = 20$ is also a missing order.

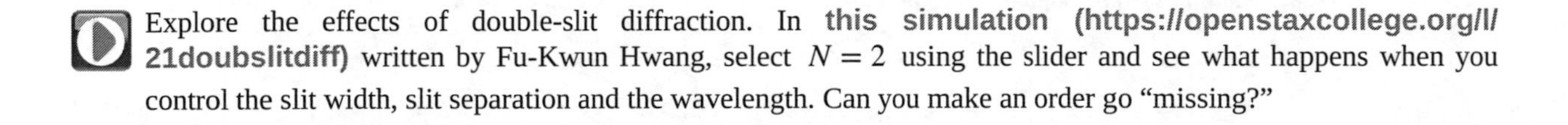

Explore the effects of double-slit diffraction. In this simulation (https://openstaxcollege.org/l/21doubslitdiff) written by Fu-Kwun Hwang, select $N = 2$ using the slider and see what happens when you control the slit width, slit separation and the wavelength. Can you make an order go "missing?"

4.4 | Diffraction Gratings

Learning Objectives

By the end of this section, you will be able to:

- Discuss the pattern obtained from diffraction gratings
- Explain diffraction grating effects

Analyzing the interference of light passing through two slits lays out the theoretical framework of interference and gives us a historical insight into Thomas Young's experiments. However, most modern-day applications of slit interference use not just two slits but many, approaching infinity for practical purposes. The key optical element is called a diffraction grating, an important tool in optical analysis.

Diffraction Gratings: An Infinite Number of Slits

The analysis of multi-slit interference in **Interference** allows us to consider what happens when the number of slits N approaches infinity. Recall that $N - 2$ secondary maxima appear between the principal maxima. We can see there will be an infinite number of secondary maxima that appear, and an infinite number of dark fringes between them. This makes the spacing between the fringes, and therefore the width of the maxima, infinitesimally small. Furthermore, because the intensity of the secondary maxima is proportional to $1/N^2$, it approaches zero so that the secondary maxima are no longer seen. What remains are only the principal maxima, now very bright and very narrow (**Figure 4.12**).

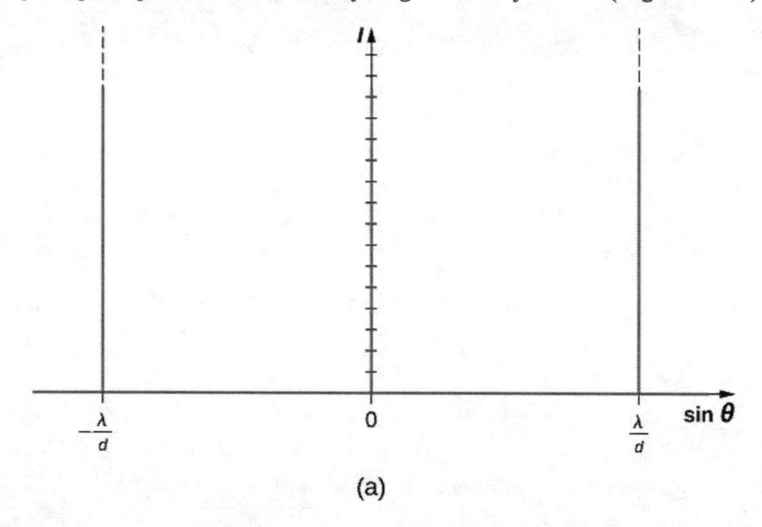

(a)

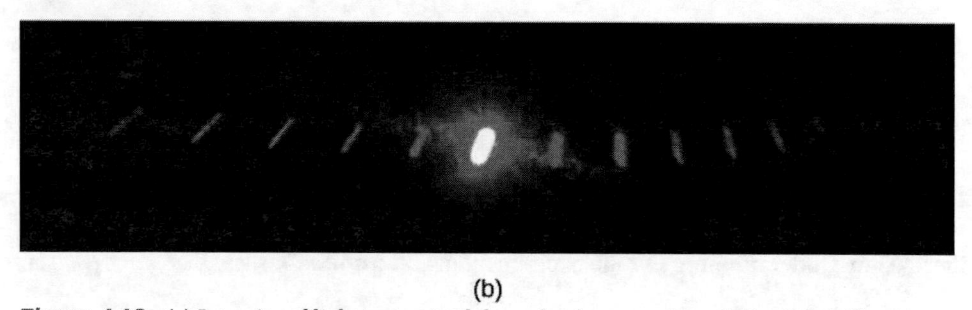

(b)

Figure 4.12 (a) Intensity of light transmitted through a large number of slits. When N approaches infinity, only the principal maxima remain as very bright and very narrow lines. (b) A laser beam passed through a diffraction grating. (credit b: modification of work by Sebastian Stapelberg)

In reality, the number of slits is not infinite, but it can be very large—large enough to produce the equivalent effect. A prime example is an optical element called a **diffraction grating**. A diffraction grating can be manufactured by carving glass with a sharp tool in a large number of precisely positioned parallel lines, with untouched regions acting like slits (**Figure 4.13**). This type of grating can be photographically mass produced rather cheaply. Because there can be over 1000 lines per millimeter across the grating, when a section as small as a few millimeters is illuminated by an incoming ray, the number of illuminated slits is effectively infinite, providing for very sharp principal maxima.

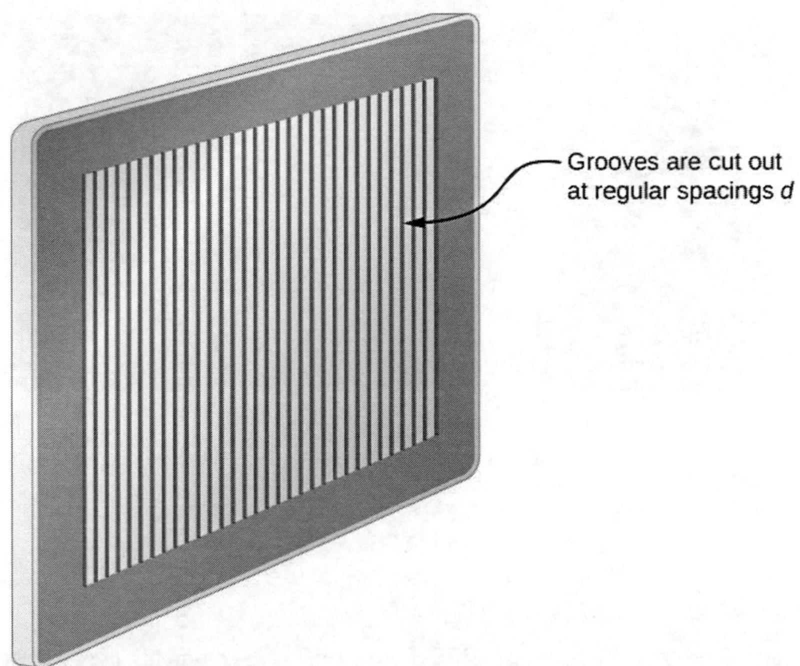

Figure 4.13 A diffraction grating can be manufactured by carving glass with a sharp tool in a large number of precisely positioned parallel lines.

Diffraction gratings work both for transmission of light, as in Figure 4.14, and for reflection of light, as on butterfly wings and the Australian opal in Figure 4.15. Natural diffraction gratings also occur in the feathers of certain birds such as the hummingbird. Tiny, finger-like structures in regular patterns act as reflection gratings, producing constructive interference that gives the feathers colors not solely due to their pigmentation. This is called iridescence.

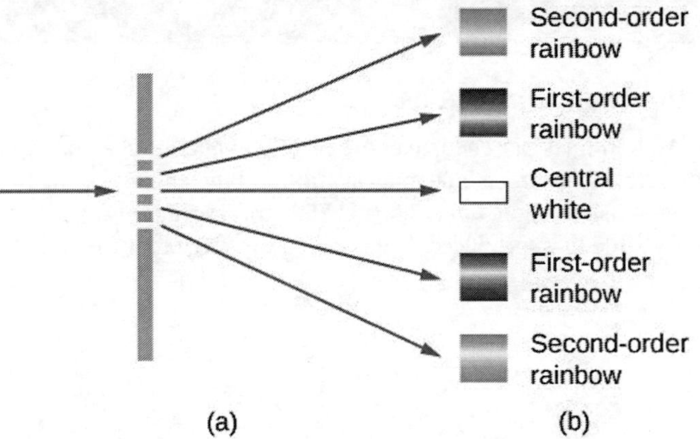

Figure 4.14 (a) Light passing through a diffraction grating is diffracted in a pattern similar to a double slit, with bright regions at various angles. (b) The pattern obtained for white light incident on a grating. The central maximum is white, and the higher-order maxima disperse white light into a rainbow of colors.

(a) (b)

Figure 4.15 (a) This Australian opal and (b) butterfly wings have rows of reflectors that act like reflection gratings, reflecting different colors at different angles. (credit a: modification of work by "Opals-On-Black"/Flickr; credit b: modification of work by “whologwhy”/Flickr)

Applications of Diffraction Gratings

Where are diffraction gratings used in applications? Diffraction gratings are commonly used for spectroscopic dispersion and analysis of light. What makes them particularly useful is the fact that they form a sharper pattern than double slits do. That is, their bright fringes are narrower and brighter while their dark regions are darker. Diffraction gratings are key components of monochromators used, for example, in optical imaging of particular wavelengths from biological or medical samples. A diffraction grating can be chosen to specifically analyze a wavelength emitted by molecules in diseased cells in a biopsy sample or to help excite strategic molecules in the sample with a selected wavelength of light. Another vital use is in optical fiber technologies where fibers are designed to provide optimum performance at specific wavelengths. A range of diffraction gratings are available for selecting wavelengths for such use.

Example 4.5

Calculating Typical Diffraction Grating Effects

Diffraction gratings with 10,000 lines per centimeter are readily available. Suppose you have one, and you send a beam of white light through it to a screen 2.00 m away. (a) Find the angles for the first-order diffraction of the shortest and longest wavelengths of visible light (380 and 760 nm, respectively). (b) What is the distance between the ends of the rainbow of visible light produced on the screen for first-order interference? (See **Figure 4.16**.)

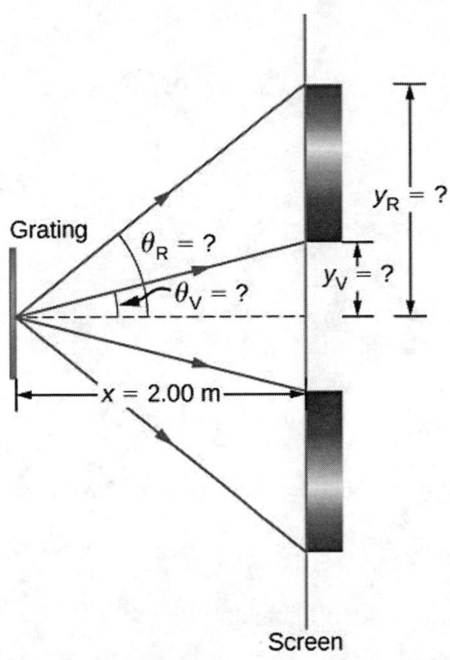

Figure 4.16 (a) The diffraction grating considered in this example produces a rainbow of colors on a screen a distance $x = 2.00 \text{ m}$ from the grating. The distances along the screen are measured perpendicular to the *x*-direction. In other words, the rainbow pattern extends out of the page.
(b) In a bird's-eye view, the rainbow pattern can be seen on a table where the equipment is placed.

Strategy

Once a value for the diffraction grating's slit spacing *d* has been determined, the angles for the sharp lines can be found using the equation

$$d \sin \theta = m\lambda \text{ for } m = 0, \ \pm 1, \ \pm 2, \ \dots .$$

Since there are 10,000 lines per centimeter, each line is separated by 1/10,000 of a centimeter. Once we know the angles, we an find the distances along the screen by using simple trigonometry.

Solution

a. The distance between slits is $d = (1 \text{ cm})/10,000 = 1.00 \times 10^{-4} \text{ cm}$ or $1.00 \times 10^{-6} \text{ m}$. Let us call the two angles θ_V for violet (380 nm) and θ_R for red (760 nm). Solving the equation $d \sin \theta_V = m\lambda$ for $\sin \theta_V$,

$$\sin \theta_V = \frac{m\lambda_V}{d},$$

where $m = 1$ for the first-order and $\lambda_V = 380 \text{ nm} = 3.80 \times 10^{-7} \text{ m}$. Substituting these values gives

$$\sin \theta_V = \frac{3.80 \times 10^{-7} \text{ m}}{1.00 \times 10^{-6} \text{ m}} = 0.380.$$

Thus the angle θ_V is

$$\theta_V = \sin^{-1} 0.380 = 22.33°.$$

Similarly,

$$\sin\theta_R = \frac{7.60 \times 10^{-7}\ \text{m}}{1.00 \times 10^{-6}\ \text{m}} = 0.760.$$

Thus the angle θ_R is

$$\theta_R = \sin^{-1} 0.760 = 49.46°.$$

Notice that in both equations, we reported the results of these intermediate calculations to four significant figures to use with the calculation in part (b).

b. The distances on the secreen are labeled y_V and y_R in **Figure 4.16**. Notice that $\tan\theta = y/x$. We can solve for y_V and y_R. That is,

$$y_V = x\tan\theta_V = (2.00\ \text{m})(\tan 22.33°) = 0.815\ \text{m}$$

and

$$y_R = x\tan\theta_R = (2.00\ \text{m})(\tan 49.46°) = 2.338\ \text{m}.$$

The distance between them is therefore

$$y_R - y_V = 1.523\ \text{m}.$$

Significance

The large distance between the red and violet ends of the rainbow produced from the white light indicates the potential this diffraction grating has as a spectroscopic tool. The more it can spread out the wavelengths (greater dispersion), the more detail can be seen in a spectrum. This depends on the quality of the diffraction grating—it must be very precisely made in addition to having closely spaced lines.

4.4 Check Your Understanding If the line spacing of a diffraction grating d is not precisely known, we can use a light source with a well-determined wavelength to measure it. Suppose the first-order constructive fringe of the H_β emission line of hydrogen $(\lambda = 656.3\ \text{nm})$ is measured at $11.36°$ using a spectrometer with a diffraction grating. What is the line spacing of this grating?

Take **the same simulation (https://openstaxcollege.org/l/21doubslitdiff)** we used for double-slit diffraction and try increasing the number of slits from $N = 2$ to $N = 3, 4, 5...$. The primary peaks become sharper, and the secondary peaks become less and less pronounced. By the time you reach the maximum number of $N = 20$, the system is behaving much like a diffraction grating.

4.5 | Circular Apertures and Resolution

Learning Objectives

By the end of this section, you will be able to:

- Describe the diffraction limit on resolution
- Describe the diffraction limit on beam propagation

Light diffracts as it moves through space, bending around obstacles, interfering constructively and destructively. This can be used as a spectroscopic tool—a diffraction grating disperses light according to wavelength, for example, and is used to produce spectra—but diffraction also limits the detail we can obtain in images.

Figure 4.17(a) shows the effect of passing light through a small circular aperture. Instead of a bright spot with sharp edges, we obtain a spot with a fuzzy edge surrounded by circles of light. This pattern is caused by diffraction, similar to that produced by a single slit. Light from different parts of the circular aperture interferes constructively and destructively. The effect is most noticeable when the aperture is small, but the effect is there for large apertures as well.

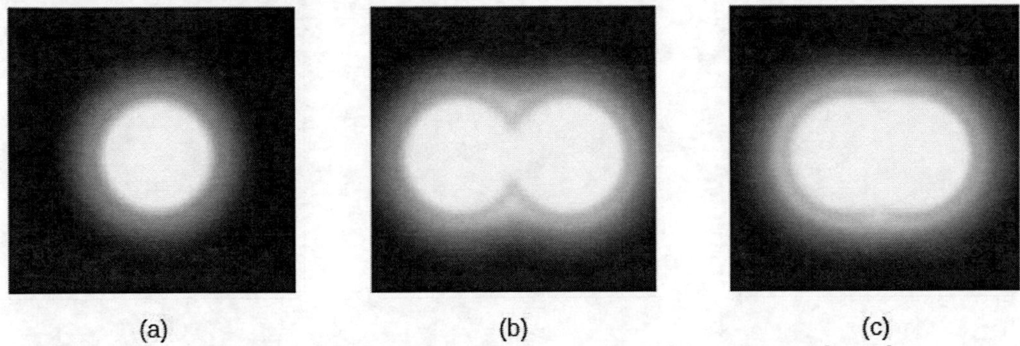

Figure 4.17 (a) Monochromatic light passed through a small circular aperture produces this diffraction pattern. (b) Two point-light sources that are close to one another produce overlapping images because of diffraction. (c) If the sources are closer together, they cannot be distinguished or resolved.

How does diffraction affect the detail that can be observed when light passes through an aperture? Figure 4.17(b) shows the diffraction pattern produced by two point-light sources that are close to one another. The pattern is similar to that for a single point source, and it is still possible to tell that there are two light sources rather than one. If they are closer together, as in Figure 4.17(c), we cannot distinguish them, thus limiting the detail or **resolution** we can obtain. This limit is an inescapable consequence of the wave nature of light.

Diffraction limits the resolution in many situations. The acuity of our vision is limited because light passes through the pupil, which is the circular aperture of the eye. Be aware that the diffraction-like spreading of light is due to the limited diameter of a light beam, not the interaction with an aperture. Thus, light passing through a lens with a diameter D shows this effect and spreads, blurring the image, just as light passing through an aperture of diameter D does. Thus, diffraction limits the resolution of any system having a lens or mirror. Telescopes are also limited by diffraction, because of the finite diameter D of the primary mirror.

Just what is the limit? To answer that question, consider the diffraction pattern for a circular aperture, which has a central maximum that is wider and brighter than the maxima surrounding it (similar to a slit) (Figure 4.18(a)). It can be shown that, for a circular aperture of diameter D, the first minimum in the diffraction pattern occurs at $\theta = 1.22\lambda/D$ (providing the aperture is large compared with the wavelength of light, which is the case for most optical instruments). The accepted criterion for determining the **diffraction limit** to resolution based on this angle is known as the **Rayleigh criterion**, which was developed by Lord Rayleigh in the nineteenth century.

Rayleigh Criterion

The diffraction limit to resolution states that two images are just resolvable when the center of the diffraction pattern of one is directly over the first minimum of the diffraction pattern of the other (Figure 4.18(b)).

The first minimum is at an angle of $\theta = 1.22\lambda/D$, so that two point objects are just resolvable if they are separated by the angle

$$\theta = 1.22\frac{\lambda}{D} \tag{4.5}$$

where λ is the wavelength of light (or other electromagnetic radiation) and D is the diameter of the aperture, lens, mirror, etc., with which the two objects are observed. In this expression, θ has units of radians. This angle is also commonly known as the diffraction limit.

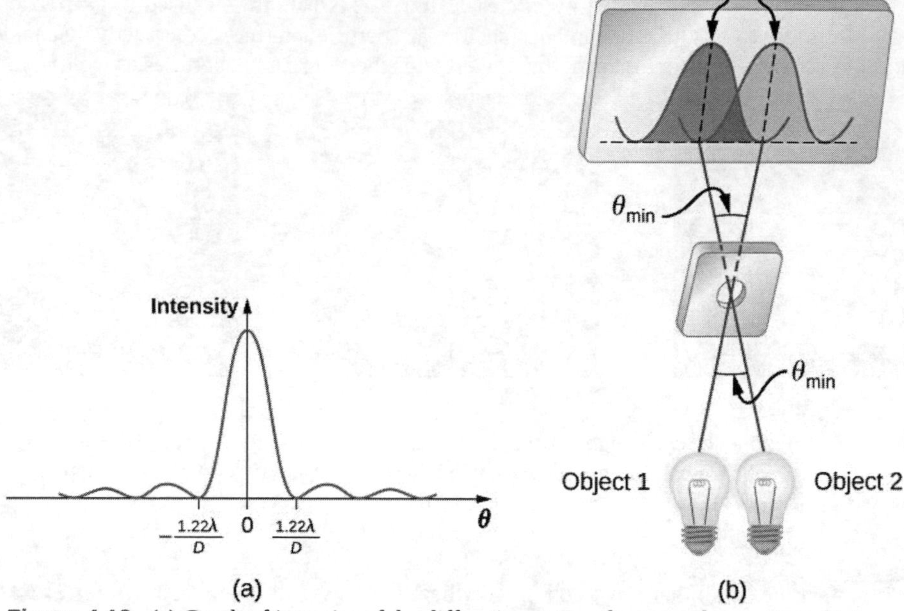

Figure 4.18 (a) Graph of intensity of the diffraction pattern for a circular aperture. Note that, similar to a single slit, the central maximum is wider and brighter than those to the sides. (b) Two point objects produce overlapping diffraction patterns. Shown here is the Rayleigh criterion for being just resolvable. The central maximum of one pattern lies on the first minimum of the other.

All attempts to observe the size and shape of objects are limited by the wavelength of the probe. Even the small wavelength of light prohibits exact precision. When extremely small wavelength probes are used, as with an electron microscope, the system is disturbed, still limiting our knowledge. Heisenberg's uncertainty principle asserts that this limit is fundamental and inescapable, as we shall see in the chapter on quantum mechanics.

Example 4.6

Calculating Diffraction Limits of the Hubble Space Telescope

The primary mirror of the orbiting Hubble Space Telescope has a diameter of 2.40 m. Being in orbit, this telescope avoids the degrading effects of atmospheric distortion on its resolution. (a) What is the angle between two just-resolvable point light sources (perhaps two stars)? Assume an average light wavelength of 550 nm. (b) If these two stars are at a distance of 2 million light-years, which is the distance of the Andromeda Galaxy, how close together can they be and still be resolved? (A light-year, or ly, is the distance light travels in 1 year.)

Strategy

The Rayleigh criterion stated in Equation 4.5, $\theta = 1.22\lambda/D$, gives the smallest possible angle θ between point sources, or the best obtainable resolution. Once this angle is known, we can calculate the distance between the stars, since we are given how far away they are.

Solution

a. The Rayleigh criterion for the minimum resolvable angle is

$$\theta = 1.22\frac{\lambda}{D}.$$

Entering known values gives

$$\theta = 1.22\frac{550 \times 10^{-9}\text{ m}}{2.40\text{ m}} = 2.80 \times 10^{-7}\text{ rad}.$$

b. The distance s between two objects a distance r away and separated by an angle θ is $s = r\theta$.

Substituting known values gives

$$s = \left(2.0 \times 10^6 \text{ ly}\right)\left(2.80 \times 10^{-7} \text{ rad}\right) = 0.56 \text{ ly}.$$

Significance

The angle found in part (a) is extraordinarily small (less than 1/50,000 of a degree), because the primary mirror is so large compared with the wavelength of light. As noticed, diffraction effects are most noticeable when light interacts with objects having sizes on the order of the wavelength of light. However, the effect is still there, and there is a diffraction limit to what is observable. The actual resolution of the Hubble Telescope is not quite as good as that found here. As with all instruments, there are other effects, such as nonuniformities in mirrors or aberrations in lenses that further limit resolution. However, Figure 4.19 gives an indication of the extent of the detail observable with the Hubble because of its size and quality, and especially because it is above Earth's atmosphere.

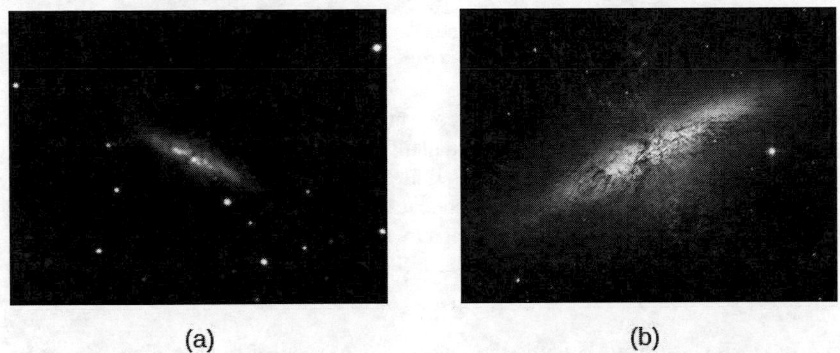

Figure 4.19 These two photographs of the M82 Galaxy give an idea of the observable detail using (a) a ground-based telescope and (b) the Hubble Space Telescope. (credit a: modification of work by "Ricnun"/Wikimedia Commons; credit b: modification of work by NASA, ESA, and The Hubble Heritage Team (STScI/AURA))

The answer in part (b) indicates that two stars separated by about half a light-year can be resolved. The average distance between stars in a galaxy is on the order of five light-years in the outer parts and about one light-year near the galactic center. Therefore, the Hubble can resolve most of the individual stars in Andromeda Galaxy, even though it lies at such a huge distance that its light takes 2 million years to reach us. Figure 4.20 shows another mirror used to observe radio waves from outer space.

Figure 4.20 A 305-m-diameter paraboloid at Arecibo in Puerto Rico is lined with reflective material, making it into a radio telescope. It is the largest curved focusing dish in the world. Although D for Arecibo is much larger than for the Hubble Telescope, it detects radiation of a much longer wavelength and its diffraction limit is significantly poorer than Hubble's. The Arecibo telescope is still very useful, because important information is carried by radio waves that is not carried by visible light. (credit: Jeff Hitchcock)

4.5 Check Your Understanding What is the angular resolution of the Arecibo telescope shown in Figure 4.20 when operated at 21-cm wavelength? How does it compare to the resolution of the Hubble Telescope?

Diffraction is not only a problem for optical instruments but also for the electromagnetic radiation itself. Any beam of light having a finite diameter D and a wavelength λ exhibits diffraction spreading. The beam spreads out with an angle θ given by Equation 4.5, $\theta = 1.22\lambda/D$. Take, for example, a laser beam made of rays as parallel as possible (angles between rays as close to $\theta = 0°$ as possible) instead spreads out at an angle $\theta = 1.22\lambda/D$, where D is the diameter of the beam and λ is its wavelength. This spreading is impossible to observe for a flashlight because its beam is not very parallel to start with. However, for long-distance transmission of laser beams or microwave signals, diffraction spreading can be significant (Figure 4.21). To avoid this, we can increase D. This is done for laser light sent to the moon to measure its distance from Earth. The laser beam is expanded through a telescope to make D much larger and θ smaller.

Figure 4.21 The beam produced by this microwave transmission antenna spreads out at a minimum angle $\theta = 1.22\lambda/D$ due to diffraction. It is impossible to produce a near-parallel beam because the beam has a limited diameter.

In most biology laboratories, resolution is an issue when the use of the microscope is introduced. The smaller the distance x by which two objects can be separated and still be seen as distinct, the greater the resolution. The resolving power of a lens is defined as that distance x. An expression for resolving power is obtained from the Rayleigh criterion. **Figure 4.22**(a) shows two point objects separated by a distance x. According to the Rayleigh criterion, resolution is possible when the minimum angular separation is

$$\theta = 1.22\frac{\lambda}{D} = \frac{x}{d},$$

where d is the distance between the specimen and the objective lens, and we have used the small angle approximation (i.e., we have assumed that x is much smaller than d), so that $\tan\theta \approx \sin\theta \approx \theta$. Therefore, the resolving power is

$$x = 1.22\frac{\lambda d}{D}.$$

Another way to look at this is by the concept of numerical aperture (*NA*), which is a measure of the maximum acceptance angle at which a lens will take light and still contain it within the lens. **Figure 4.22**(b) shows a lens and an object at point *P*. The *NA* here is a measure of the ability of the lens to gather light and resolve fine detail. The angle subtended by the lens at its focus is defined to be $\theta = 2\alpha$. From the figure and again using the small angle approximation, we can write

$$\sin\alpha = \frac{D/2}{d} = \frac{D}{2d}.$$

The *NA* for a lens is $NA = n\sin\alpha$, where n is the index of refraction of the medium between the objective lens and the object at point *P*. From this definition for *NA*, we can see that

$$x = 1.22\frac{\lambda d}{D} = 1.22\frac{\lambda}{2\sin\alpha} = 0.61\frac{\lambda n}{NA}.$$

In a microscope, *NA* is important because it relates to the resolving power of a lens. A lens with a large *NA* is able to resolve finer details. Lenses with larger *NA* are also able to collect more light and so give a brighter image. Another way to describe this situation is that the larger the *NA*, the larger the cone of light that can be brought into the lens, so more of the diffraction modes are collected. Thus the microscope has more information to form a clear image, and its resolving power is higher.

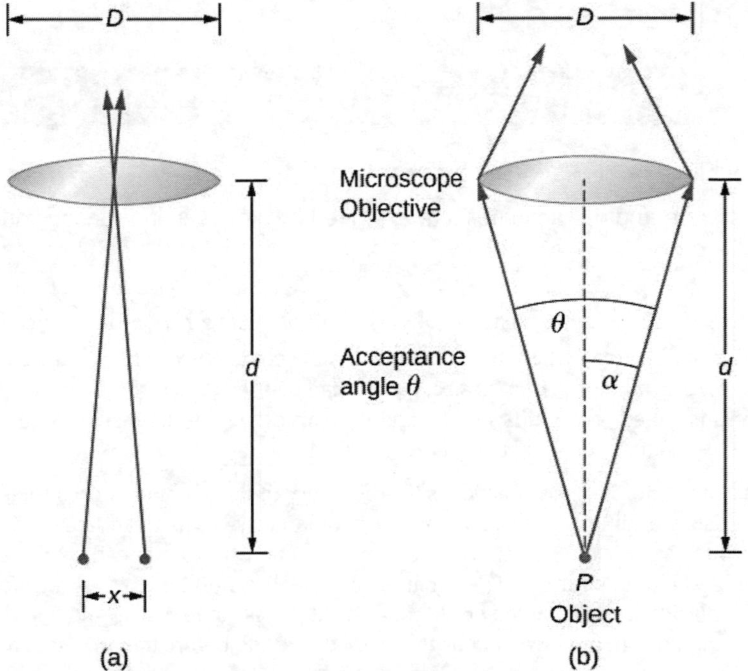

Figure 4.22 (a) Two points separated by a distance x and positioned a distance d away from the objective. (b) Terms and symbols used in discussion of resolving power for a lens and an object at point *P* (credit a: modification of work by "Infopro"/Wikimedia Commons).

One of the consequences of diffraction is that the focal point of a beam has a finite width and intensity distribution. Imagine focusing when only considering geometric optics, as in Figure 4.23(a). The focal point is regarded as an infinitely small point with a huge intensity and the capacity to incinerate most samples, irrespective of the *NA* of the objective lens—an unphysical oversimplification. For wave optics, due to diffraction, we take into account the phenomenon in which the focal point spreads to become a focal spot (Figure 4.23(b)) with the size of the spot decreasing with increasing *NA*. Consequently, the intensity in the focal spot increases with increasing *NA*. The higher the *NA*, the greater the chances of photodegrading the specimen. However, the spot never becomes a true point.

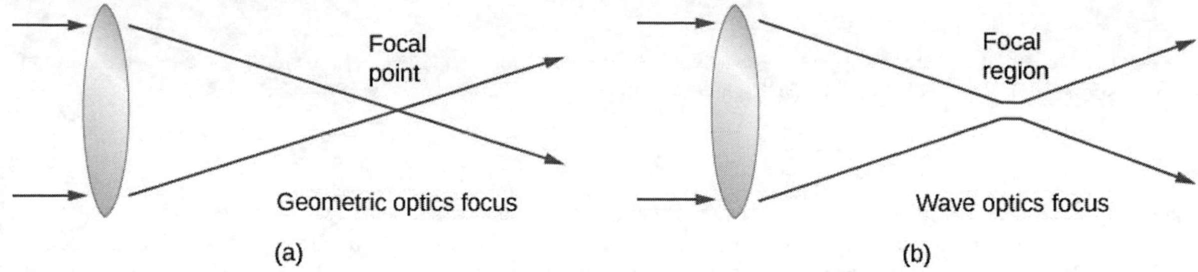

Figure 4.23 (a) In geometric optics, the focus is modelled as a point, but it is not physically possible to produce such a point because it implies infinite intensity. (b) In wave optics, the focus is an extended region.

In a different type of microscope, molecules within a specimen are made to emit light through a mechanism called fluorescence. By controlling the molecules emitting light, it has become possible to construct images with resolution much finer than the Rayleigh criterion, thus circumventing the diffraction limit. The development of super-resolved fluorescence microscopy led to the 2014 Nobel Prize in Chemistry.

In this Optical Resolution Model, two diffraction patterns for light through two circular apertures are shown side by side in this simulation (https://openstaxcollege.org/l/21optresmodsim) by Fu-Kwun Hwang. Watch the patterns merge as you decrease the aperture diameters.

4.6 | X-Ray Diffraction

Learning Objectives

By the end of this section, you will be able to:

- Describe interference and diffraction effects exhibited by X-rays in interaction with atomic-scale structures

Since X-ray photons are very energetic, they have relatively short wavelengths, on the order of 10^{-8} m to 10^{-12} m. Thus, typical X-ray photons act like rays when they encounter macroscopic objects, like teeth, and produce sharp shadows. However, since atoms are on the order of 0.1 nm in size, X-rays can be used to detect the location, shape, and size of atoms and molecules. The process is called **X-ray diffraction**, and it involves the interference of X-rays to produce patterns that can be analyzed for information about the structures that scattered the X-rays.

Perhaps the most famous example of X-ray diffraction is the discovery of the double-helical structure of DNA in 1953 by an international team of scientists working at England's Cavendish Laboratory—American James Watson, Englishman Francis Crick, and New Zealand-born Maurice Wilkins. Using X-ray diffraction data produced by Rosalind Franklin, they were the first to model the double-helix structure of DNA that is so crucial to life. For this work, Watson, Crick, and Wilkins were awarded the 1962 Nobel Prize in Physiology or Medicine. (There is some debate and controversy over the issue that Rosalind Franklin was not included in the prize, although she died in 1958, before the prize was awarded.)

Figure 4.24 shows a diffraction pattern produced by the scattering of X-rays from a crystal. This process is known as X-ray crystallography because of the information it can yield about crystal structure, and it was the type of data Rosalind Franklin supplied to Watson and Crick for DNA. Not only do X-rays confirm the size and shape of atoms, they give information about the atomic arrangements in materials. For example, more recent research in high-temperature superconductors involves complex materials whose lattice arrangements are crucial to obtaining a superconducting material. These can be studied using X-ray crystallography.

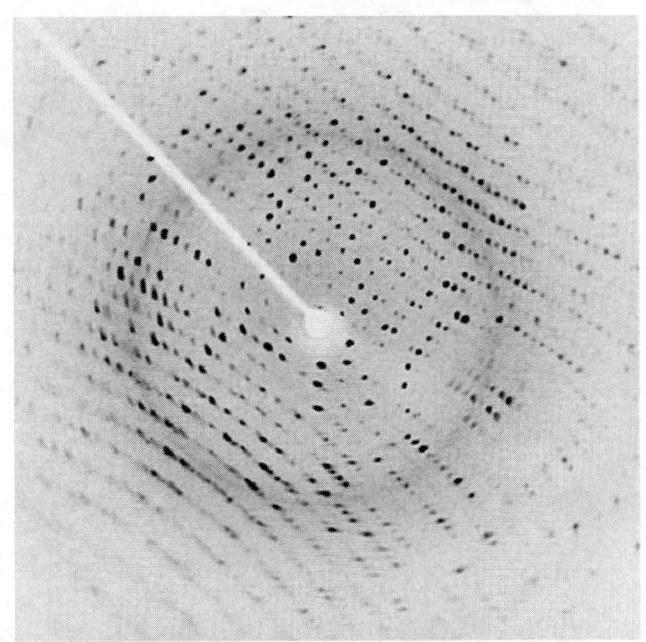

Figure 4.24 X-ray diffraction from the crystal of a protein (hen egg lysozyme) produced this interference pattern. Analysis of the pattern yields information about the structure of the protein. (credit: "Del45"/Wikimedia Commons)

Historically, the scattering of X-rays from crystals was used to prove that X-rays are energetic electromagnetic (EM) waves. This was suspected from the time of the discovery of X-rays in 1895, but it was not until 1912 that the German Max von Laue (1879–1960) convinced two of his colleagues to scatter X-rays from crystals. If a diffraction pattern is obtained, he reasoned, then the X-rays must be waves, and their wavelength could be determined. (The spacing of atoms in various crystals was reasonably well known at the time, based on good values for Avogadro's number.) The experiments were convincing, and the 1914 Nobel Prize in Physics was given to von Laue for his suggestion leading to the proof that X-rays are EM waves. In 1915, the unique father-and-son team of Sir William Henry Bragg and his son Sir William Lawrence Bragg were awarded a joint Nobel Prize for inventing the X-ray spectrometer and the then-new science of X-ray analysis.

In ways reminiscent of thin-film interference, we consider two plane waves at X-ray wavelengths, each one reflecting off a different plane of atoms within a crystal's lattice, as shown in **Figure 4.25**. From the geometry, the difference in path lengths is $2d \sin \theta$. Constructive interference results when this distance is an integer multiple of the wavelength. This condition is captured by the *Bragg equation*,

$$m\lambda = 2d \sin \theta, \ m = 1, \ 2, \ 3 \ldots \tag{4.6}$$

where m is a positive integer and d is the spacing between the planes. Following the Law of Reflection, both the incident and reflected waves are described by the same angle, θ, but unlike the general practice in geometric optics, θ is measured with respect to the surface itself, rather than the normal.

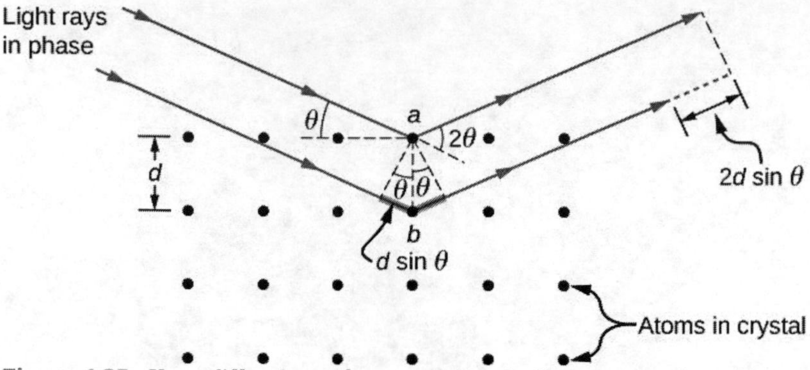

Figure 4.25 X-ray diffraction with a crystal. Two incident waves reflect off two planes of a crystal. The difference in path lengths is indicated by the dashed line.

Example 4.7

X-Ray Diffraction with Salt Crystals

Common table salt is composed mainly of NaCl crystals. In a NaCl crystal, there is a family of planes 0.252 nm apart. If the first-order maximum is observed at an incidence angle of $18.1°$, what is the wavelength of the X-ray scattering from this crystal?

Strategy

Use the Bragg equation, **Equation 4.6**, $m\lambda = 2d \sin\theta$, to solve for θ.

Solution

For first-order, $m = 1,$ and the plane spacing d is known. Solving the Bragg equation for wavelength yields

$$\lambda = \frac{2d \sin\theta}{m} = \frac{2\left(0.252 \times 10^{-9}\ \text{m}\right)\sin(18.1°)}{1} = 1.57 \times 10^{-10}\ \text{m},\ \text{ or } 0.157\ \text{nm}.$$

Significance

The determined wavelength fits within the X-ray region of the electromagnetic spectrum. Once again, the wave nature of light makes itself prominent when the wavelength $(\lambda = 0.157\ \text{nm})$ is comparable to the size of the physical structures $(d = 0.252\ \text{nm})$ it interacts with.

4.6 Check Your Understanding For the experiment described in **Example 4.7**, what are the two other angles where interference maxima may be observed? What limits the number of maxima?

Although **Figure 4.25** depicts a crystal as a two-dimensional array of scattering centers for simplicity, real crystals are structures in three dimensions. Scattering can occur simultaneously from different families of planes at different orientations and spacing patterns known as called **Bragg planes**, as shown in **Figure 4.26**. The resulting interference pattern can be quite complex.

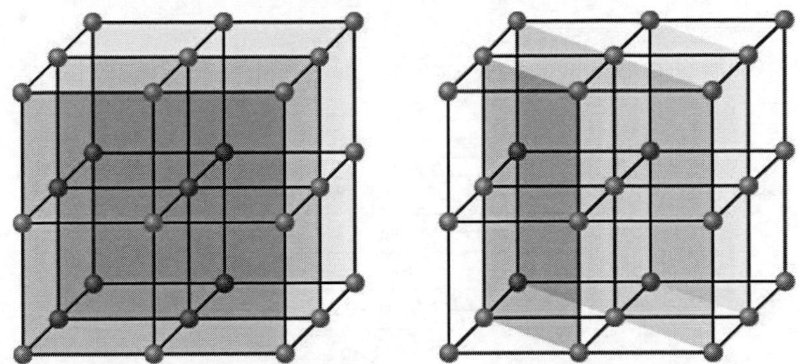

Figure 4.26 Because of the regularity that makes a crystal structure, one crystal can have many families of planes within its geometry, each one giving rise to X-ray diffraction.

4.7 | Holography

Learning Objectives

By the end of this section, you will be able to:

- Describe how a three-dimensional image is recorded as a hologram
- Describe how a three-dimensional image is formed from a hologram

A **hologram**, such as the one in **Figure 4.27**, is a true three-dimensional image recorded on film by lasers. Holograms are used for amusement; decoration on novelty items and magazine covers; security on credit cards and driver's licenses (a laser and other equipment are needed to reproduce them); and for serious three-dimensional information storage. You can see that a hologram is a true three-dimensional image because objects change relative position in the image when viewed from different angles.

Figure 4.27 Credit cards commonly have holograms for logos, making them difficult to reproduce. (credit: Dominic Alves)

The name hologram means "entire picture" (from the Greek *holo*, as in holistic) because the image is three-dimensional. **Holography** is the process of producing holograms and, although they are recorded on photographic film, the process is quite different from normal photography. Holography uses light interference or wave optics, whereas normal photography uses geometric optics. **Figure 4.28** shows one method of producing a hologram. Coherent light from a laser is split by a mirror, with part of the light illuminating the object. The remainder, called the reference beam, shines directly on a piece of film. Light scattered from the object interferes with the reference beam, producing constructive and destructive interference. As a result, the exposed film looks foggy, but close examination reveals a complicated interference pattern stored on it. Where the interference was constructive, the film (a negative actually) is darkened. Holography is sometimes called lens-less photography, because it uses the wave characteristics of light, as contrasted to normal photography, which uses geometric optics and requires lenses.

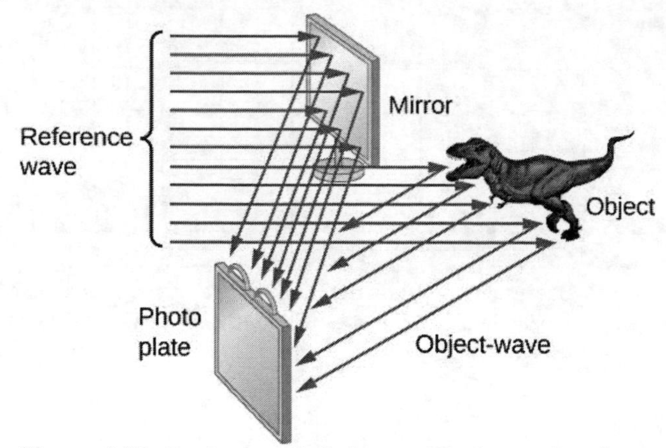

Figure 4.28 Production of a hologram. Single-wavelength coherent light from a laser produces a well-defined interference pattern on a piece of film. The laser beam is split by a partially silvered mirror, with part of the light illuminating the object and the remainder shining directly on the film. (credit: modification of work by Mariana Ruiz Villarreal)

Light falling on a hologram can form a three-dimensional image of the original object. The process is complicated in detail, but the basics can be understood, as shown in Figure 4.29, in which a laser of the same type that exposed the film is now used to illuminate it. The myriad tiny exposed regions of the film are dark and block the light, whereas less exposed regions allow light to pass. The film thus acts much like a collection of diffraction gratings with various spacing patterns. Light passing through the hologram is diffracted in various directions, producing both real and virtual images of the object used to expose the film. The interference pattern is the same as that produced by the object. Moving your eye to various places in the interference pattern gives you different perspectives, just as looking directly at the object would. The image thus looks like the object and is three dimensional like the object.

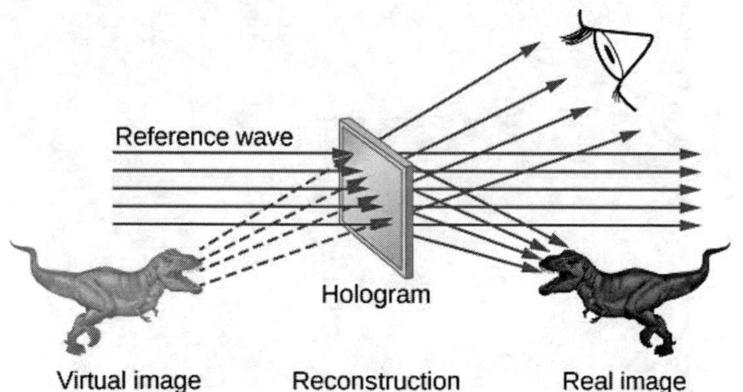

Figure 4.29 A transmission hologram is one that produces real and virtual images when a laser of the same type as that which exposed the hologram is passed through it. Diffraction from various parts of the film produces the same interference pattern that was produced by the object that was used to expose it. (credit: modification of work by Mariana Ruiz Villarreal)

The hologram illustrated in Figure 4.29 is a transmission hologram. Holograms that are viewed with reflected light, such as the white light holograms on credit cards, are reflection holograms and are more common. White light holograms often appear a little blurry with rainbow edges, because the diffraction patterns of various colors of light are at slightly different locations due to their different wavelengths. Further uses of holography include all types of three-dimensional information storage, such as of statues in museums, engineering studies of structures, and images of human organs.

Invented in the late 1940s by Dennis Gabor (1900–1970), who won the 1971 Nobel Prize in Physics for his work, holography became far more practical with the development of the laser. Since lasers produce coherent single-wavelength light, their interference patterns are more pronounced. The precision is so great that it is even possible to record numerous holograms on a single piece of film by just changing the angle of the film for each successive image. This is how the holograms that move as you walk by them are produced—a kind of lens-less movie.

In a similar way, in the medical field, holograms have allowed complete three-dimensional holographic displays of objects from a stack of images. Storing these images for future use is relatively easy. With the use of an endoscope, high-resolution, three-dimensional holographic images of internal organs and tissues can be made.

CHAPTER 4 REVIEW

KEY TERMS

Bragg planes families of planes within crystals that can give rise to X-ray diffraction

destructive interference for a single slit occurs when the width of the slit is comparable to the wavelength of light illuminating it

diffraction bending of a wave around the edges of an opening or an obstacle

diffraction grating large number of evenly spaced parallel slits

diffraction limit fundamental limit to resolution due to diffraction

hologram three-dimensional image recorded on film by lasers; the word hologram means *entire picture* (from the Greek word *holo,* as in holistic)

holography process of producing holograms with the use of lasers

missing order interference maximum that is not seen because it coincides with a diffraction minimum

Rayleigh criterion two images are just-resolvable when the center of the diffraction pattern of one is directly over the first minimum of the diffraction pattern of the other

resolution ability, or limit thereof, to distinguish small details in images

two-slit diffraction pattern diffraction pattern of two slits of width D that are separated by a distance d is the interference pattern of two point sources separated by d multiplied by the diffraction pattern of a slit of width D

width of the central peak angle between the minimum for $m = 1$ and $m = -1$

X-ray diffraction technique that provides the detailed information about crystallographic structure of natural and manufactured materials

KEY EQUATIONS

Destructive interference for a single slit	$D \sin\theta = m\lambda$ for $m = \pm 1, \ \pm 2, \ \pm 3, \ldots$
Half phase angle	$\beta = \frac{\phi}{2} = \frac{\pi D \sin\theta}{\lambda}$
Field amplitude in the diffraction pattern	$E = N\Delta E_0 \frac{\sin\beta}{\beta}$
Intensity in the diffraction pattern	$I = I_0 \left(\frac{\sin\beta}{\beta}\right)^2$
Rayleigh criterion for circular apertures	$\theta = 1.22\frac{\lambda}{D}$
Bragg equation	$m\lambda = 2d \sin\theta, \ m = 1, \ 2, \ 3\ldots$

SUMMARY

4.1 Single-Slit Diffraction

- Diffraction can send a wave around the edges of an opening or other obstacle.
- A single slit produces an interference pattern characterized by a broad central maximum with narrower and dimmer maxima to the sides.

4.2 Intensity in Single-Slit Diffraction

- The intensity pattern for diffraction due to a single slit can be calculated using phasors as

$$I = I_0 \left(\frac{\sin \beta}{\beta} \right)^2,$$

where $\beta = \frac{\phi}{2} = \frac{\pi D \sin \theta}{\lambda}$, D is the slit width, λ is the wavelength, and θ is the angle from the central peak.

4.3 Double-Slit Diffraction

- With real slits with finite widths, the effects of interference and diffraction operate simultaneously to form a complicated intensity pattern.
- Relative intensities of interference fringes within a diffraction pattern can be determined.
- Missing orders occur when an interference maximum and a diffraction minimum are located together.

4.4 Diffraction Gratings

- A diffraction grating consists of a large number of evenly spaced parallel slits that produce an interference pattern similar to but sharper than that of a double slit.
- Constructive interference occurs when $d \sin \theta = m\lambda$ for $m = 0, \ \pm 1, \ \pm 2, \ ...,$ where d is the distance between the slits, θ is the angle relative to the incident direction, and m is the order of the interference.

4.5 Circular Apertures and Resolution

- Diffraction limits resolution.
- The Rayleigh criterion states that two images are just resolvable when the center of the diffraction pattern of one is directly over the first minimum of the diffraction pattern of the other.

4.6 X-Ray Diffraction

- X-rays are relatively short-wavelength EM radiation and can exhibit wave characteristics such as interference when interacting with correspondingly small objects.

4.7 Holography

- Holography is a technique based on wave interference to record and form three-dimensional images.
- Lasers offer a practical way to produce sharp holographic images because of their monochromatic and coherent light for pronounced interference patterns.

CONCEPTUAL QUESTIONS

4.1 Single-Slit Diffraction

1. As the width of the slit producing a single-slit diffraction pattern is reduced, how will the diffraction pattern produced change?

2. Compare interference and diffraction.

3. If you and a friend are on opposite sides of a hill, you can communicate with walkie-talkies but not with flashlights. Explain.

4. What happens to the diffraction pattern of a single slit when the entire optical apparatus is immersed in water?

5. In our study of diffraction by a single slit, we assume that the length of the slit is much larger than the width. What happens to the diffraction pattern if these two dimensions were comparable?

6. A rectangular slit is twice as wide as it is high. Is the central diffraction peak wider in the vertical direction or in the horizontal direction?

4.2 Intensity in Single-Slit Diffraction

7. In Equation 4.4, the parameter β looks like an angle but is not an angle that you can measure with a protractor in the physical world. Explain what β represents.

4.3 Double-Slit Diffraction

8. Shown below is the central part of the interference pattern for a pure wavelength of red light projected onto a double slit. The pattern is actually a combination of single- and double-slit interference. Note that the bright spots are evenly spaced. Is this a double- or single-slit characteristic? Note that some of the bright spots are dim on either side of the center. Is this a single- or double-slit characteristic? Which is smaller, the slit width or the separation between slits? Explain your responses.

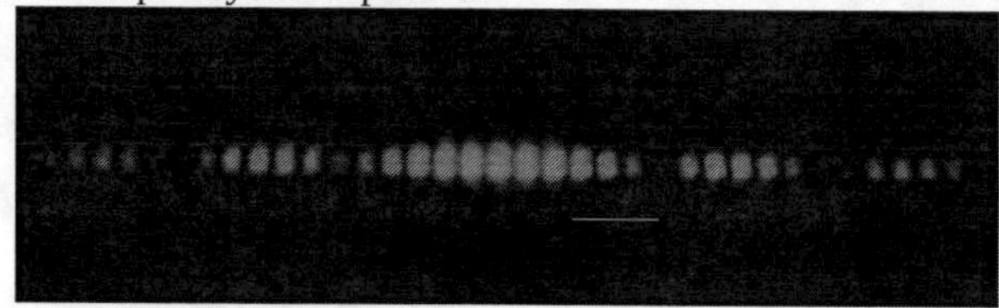

(credit: PASCO)

4.5 Circular Apertures and Resolution

9. Is higher resolution obtained in a microscope with red or blue light? Explain your answer.

10. The resolving power of refracting telescope increases with the size of its objective lens. What other advantage is gained with a larger lens?

11. The distance between atoms in a molecule is about 10^{-8} cm. Can visible light be used to "see" molecules?

12. A beam of light always spreads out. Why can a beam not be created with parallel rays to prevent spreading? Why can lenses, mirrors, or apertures not be used to correct the spreading?

4.6 X-Ray Diffraction

13. Crystal lattices can be examined with X-rays but not UV. Why?

4.7 Holography

14. How can you tell that a hologram is a true three-dimensional image and that those in three-dimensional movies are not?

15. If a hologram is recorded using monochromatic light at one wavelength but its image is viewed at another wavelength, say 10% shorter, what will you see? What if it is viewed using light of exactly half the original wavelength?

16. What image will one see if a hologram is recorded using monochromatic light but its image is viewed in white light? Explain.

PROBLEMS

4.1 Single-Slit Diffraction

17. (a) At what angle is the first minimum for 550-nm light falling on a single slit of width $1.00 \mu m$? (b) Will there be a second minimum?

18. (a) Calculate the angle at which a $2.00\text{-}\mu m$-wide slit produces its first minimum for 410-nm violet light. (b) Where is the first minimum for 700-nm red light?

19. (a) How wide is a single slit that produces its first minimum for 633-nm light at an angle of $28.0°$? (b) At what angle will the second minimum be?

20. (a) What is the width of a single slit that produces its first minimum at $60.0°$ for 600-nm light? (b) Find the wavelength of light that has its first minimum at $62.0°$.

21. Find the wavelength of light that has its third minimum at an angle of $48.6°$ when it falls on a single slit of width $3.00 \mu m$.

22. (a) Sodium vapor light averaging 589 nm in wavelength falls on a single slit of width $7.50 \mu m$. At what angle does it produces its second minimum? (b) What is the highest-order minimum produced?

23. Consider a single-slit diffraction pattern for $\lambda = 589$ nm, projected on a screen that is 1.00 m from a slit of width 0.25 mm. How far from the center of the pattern are the centers of the first and second dark fringes?

24. (a) Find the angle between the first minima for the two sodium vapor lines, which have wavelengths of 589.1 and 589.6 nm, when they fall upon a single slit of width $2.00 \mu m$. (b) What is the distance between these minima if the diffraction pattern falls on a screen 1.00 m from the slit? (c) Discuss the ease or difficulty of measuring such a distance.

25. (a) What is the minimum width of a single slit (in multiples of λ) that will produce a first minimum for a wavelength λ? (b) What is its minimum width if it produces 50 minima? (c) 1000 minima?

26. (a) If a single slit produces a first minimum at $14.5°$, at what angle is the second-order minimum? (b) What is the angle of the third-order minimum? (c) Is there a fourth-order minimum? (d) Use your answers to illustrate how the angular width of the central maximum is about twice the angular width of the next maximum (which is the angle between the first and second minima).

27. If the separation between the first and the second minima of a single-slit diffraction pattern is 6.0 mm, what is the distance between the screen and the slit? The light wavelength is 500 nm and the slit width is 0.16 mm.

28. A water break at the entrance to a harbor consists of a rock barrier with a 50.0-m-wide opening. Ocean waves of 20.0-m wavelength approach the opening straight on. At what angles to the incident direction are the boats inside the harbor most protected against wave action?

29. An aircraft maintenance technician walks past a tall hangar door that acts like a single slit for sound entering the hangar. Outside the door, on a line perpendicular to the opening in the door, a jet engine makes a 600-Hz sound. At what angle with the door will the technician observe the first minimum in sound intensity if the vertical opening is 0.800 m wide and the speed of sound is 340 m/s?

4.2 Intensity in Single-Slit Diffraction

30. A single slit of width $3.0\ \mu m$ is illuminated by a sodium yellow light of wavelength 589 nm. Find the intensity at a $15°$ angle to the axis in terms of the intensity of the central maximum.

31. A single slit of width 0.1 mm is illuminated by a mercury light of wavelength 576 nm. Find the intensity at a $10°$ angle to the axis in terms of the intensity of the central maximum.

32. The width of the central peak in a single-slit diffraction pattern is 5.0 mm. The wavelength of the light is 600 nm, and the screen is 2.0 m from the slit. (a) What is the width of the slit? (b) Determine the ratio of the intensity at 4.5 mm from the center of the pattern to the intensity at the center.

33. Consider the single-slit diffraction pattern for $\lambda = 600\ \text{nm}$, $D = 0.025\ \text{mm}$, and $x = 2.0\ \text{m}$. Find the intensity in terms of I_o at $\theta = 0.5°$, $1.0°$, $1.5°$, $3.0°$, and $10.0°$.

4.3 Double-Slit Diffraction

34. Two slits of width $2\ \mu m$, each in an opaque material, are separated by a center-to-center distance of $6\ \mu m$. A monochromatic light of wavelength 450 nm is incident on the double-slit. One finds a combined interference and diffraction pattern on the screen.

(a) How many peaks of the interference will be observed in the central maximum of the diffraction pattern?

(b) How many peaks of the interference will be observed if the slit width is doubled while keeping the distance between the slits same?

(c) How many peaks of interference will be observed if the slits are separated by twice the distance, that is, $12\ \mu m$, while keeping the widths of the slits same?

(d) What will happen in (a) if instead of 450-nm light another light of wavelength 680 nm is used?

(e) What is the value of the ratio of the intensity of the central peak to the intensity of the next bright peak in (a)?

(f) Does this ratio depend on the wavelength of the light?

(g) Does this ratio depend on the width or separation of the slits?

35. A double slit produces a diffraction pattern that is a combination of single- and double-slit interference. Find the ratio of the width of the slits to the separation between them, if the first minimum of the single-slit pattern falls on the fifth maximum of the double-slit pattern. (This will greatly reduce the intensity of the fifth maximum.)

36. For a double-slit configuration where the slit separation is four times the slit width, how many interference fringes lie in the central peak of the diffraction pattern?

37. Light of wavelength 500 nm falls normally on 50 slits that are 2.5×10^{-3} mm wide and spaced 5.0×10^{-3} mm apart. How many interference fringes lie in the central peak of the diffraction pattern?

38. A monochromatic light of wavelength 589 nm incident on a double slit with slit width $2.5\ \mu m$ and unknown separation results in a diffraction pattern containing nine interference peaks inside the central maximum. Find the separation of the slits.

39. When a monochromatic light of wavelength 430 nm incident on a double slit of slit separation $5\ \mu\text{m}$, there are 11 interference fringes in its central maximum. How many interference fringes will be in the central maximum of a light of wavelength 632.8 nm for the same double slit?

40. Determine the intensities of two interference peaks other than the central peak in the central maximum of the diffraction, if possible, when a light of wavelength 628 nm is incident on a double slit of width 500 nm and separation 1500 nm. Use the intensity of the central spot to be $1\ \text{mW/cm}^2$.

4.4 Diffraction Gratings

41. A diffraction grating has 2000 lines per centimeter. At what angle will the first-order maximum be for 520-nm-wavelength green light?

42. Find the angle for the third-order maximum for 580-nm-wavelength yellow light falling on a difraction grating having 1500 lines per centimeter.

43. How many lines per centimeter are there on a diffraction grating that gives a first-order maximum for 470-nm blue light at an angle of $25.0°$?

44. What is the distance between lines on a diffraction grating that produces a second-order maximum for 760-nm red light at an angle of $60.0°$?

45. Calculate the wavelength of light that has its second-order maximum at $45.0°$ when falling on a diffraction grating that has 5000 lines per centimeter.

46. An electric current through hydrogen gas produces several distinct wavelengths of visible light. What are the wavelengths of the hydrogen spectrum, if they form first-order maxima at angles $24.2°$, $25.7°$, $29.1°$, and $41.0°$ when projected on a diffraction grating having 10,000 lines per centimeter?

47. (a) What do the four angles in the preceding problem become if a 5000-line per centimeter diffraction grating is used? (b) Using this grating, what would the angles be for the second-order maxima? (c) Discuss the relationship between integral reductions in lines per centimeter and the new angles of various order maxima.

48. What is the spacing between structures in a feather that acts as a reflection grating, giving that they produce a first-order maximum for 525-nm light at a $30.0°$ angle?

49. An opal such as that shown in **Figure 4.15** acts like a reflection grating with rows separated by about $8\ \mu\text{m}$. If the opal is illuminated normally, (a) at what angle will red light be seen and (b) at what angle will blue light be seen?

50. At what angle does a diffraction grating produce a second-order maximum for light having a first-order maximum at $20.0°$?

51. (a) Find the maximum number of lines per centimeter a diffraction grating can have and produce a maximum for the smallest wavelength of visible light. (b) Would such a grating be useful for ultraviolet spectra? (c) For infrared spectra?

52. (a) Show that a 30,000 line per centimeter grating will not produce a maximum for visible light. (b) What is the longest wavelength for which it does produce a first-order maximum? (c) What is the greatest number of line per centimeter a diffraction grating can have and produce a complete second-order spectrum for visible light?

53. The analysis shown below also applies to diffraction gratings with lines separated by a distance *d*. What is the distance between fringes produced by a diffraction grating having 125 lines per centimeter for 600-nm light, if the screen is 1.50 m away? (*Hint:* The distance between adjacent fringes is $\Delta y = x\lambda/d$, assuming the slit separation *d* is comparable to λ.)

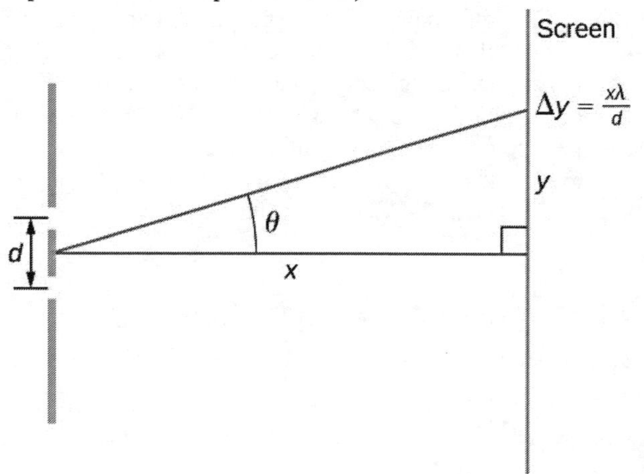

4.5 Circular Apertures and Resolution

54. The 305-m-diameter Arecibo radio telescope pictured in **Figure 4.20** detects radio waves with a 4.00-cm average wavelength. (a) What is the angle between two just-resolvable point sources for this telescope? (b) How close together could these point sources be at the 2 million light-year distance of the Andromeda Galaxy?

55. Assuming the angular resolution found for the Hubble Telescope in **Example 4.6**, what is the smallest detail that could be observed on the moon?

56. Diffraction spreading for a flashlight is insignificant compared with other limitations in its optics, such as spherical aberrations in its mirror. To show this, calculate the minimum angular spreading of a flashlight beam that is originally 5.00 cm in diameter with an average wavelength of 600 nm.

57. (a) What is the minimum angular spread of a 633-nm wavelength He-Ne laser beam that is originally 1.00 mm in diameter? (b) If this laser is aimed at a mountain cliff 15.0 km away, how big will the illuminated spot be? (c) How big a spot would be illuminated on the moon, neglecting atmospheric effects? (This might be done to hit a corner reflector to measure the round-trip time and, hence, distance.)

58. A telescope can be used to enlarge the diameter of a laser beam and limit diffraction spreading. The laser beam is sent through the telescope in opposite the normal direction and can then be projected onto a satellite or the moon. (a) If this is done with the Mount Wilson telescope, producing a 2.54-m-diameter beam of 633-nm light, what is the minimum angular spread of the beam? (b) Neglecting atmospheric effects, what is the size of the spot this beam would make on the moon, assuming a lunar distance of 3.84×10^8 m ?

59. The limit to the eye's acuity is actually related to diffraction by the pupil. (a) What is the angle between two just-resolvable points of light for a 3.00-mm-diameter pupil, assuming an average wavelength of 550 nm? (b) Take your result to be the practical limit for the eye. What is the greatest possible distance a car can be from you if you can resolve its two headlights, given they are 1.30 m apart? (c) What is the distance between two just-resolvable points held at an arm's length (0.800 m) from your eye? (d) How does your answer to (c) compare to details you normally observe in everyday circumstances?

60. What is the minimum diameter mirror on a telescope that would allow you to see details as small as 5.00 km on the moon some 384,000 km away? Assume an average wavelength of 550 nm for the light received.

61. Find the radius of a star's image on the retina of an eye if its pupil is open to 0.65 cm and the distance from the pupil to the retina is 2.8 cm. Assume $\lambda = 550$ nm .

62. (a) The dwarf planet Pluto and its moon, Charon, are separated by 19,600 km. Neglecting atmospheric effects, should the 5.08-m-diameter Palomar Mountain telescope be able to resolve these bodies when they are 4.50×10^9 km from Earth? Assume an average wavelength of 550 nm. (b) In actuality, it is just barely possible to discern that Pluto and Charon are separate bodies using a ground-based telescope. What are the reasons for this?

63. A spy satellite orbits Earth at a height of 180 km. What is the minimum diameter of the objective lens in a telescope that must be used to resolve columns of troops marching 2.0 m apart? Assume $\lambda = 550$ nm.

64. What is the minimum angular separation of two stars that are just-resolvable by the 8.1-m Gemini South telescope, if atmospheric effects do not limit resolution? Use 550 nm for the wavelength of the light from the stars.

65. The headlights of a car are 1.3 m apart. What is the maximum distance at which the eye can resolve these two headlights? Take the pupil diameter to be 0.40 cm.

66. When dots are placed on a page from a laser printer, they must be close enough so that you do not see the individual dots of ink. To do this, the separation of the dots must be less than Raleigh's criterion. Take the pupil of the eye to be 3.0 mm and the distance from the paper to the eye of 35 cm; find the minimum separation of two dots such that they cannot be resolved. How many dots per inch (dpi) does this correspond to?

67. Suppose you are looking down at a highway from a jetliner flying at an altitude of 6.0 km. How far apart must two cars be if you are able to distinguish them? Assume that $\lambda = 550$ nm and that the diameter of your pupils is 4.0 mm.

68. Can an astronaut orbiting Earth in a satellite at a distance of 180 km from the surface distinguish two skyscrapers that are 20 m apart? Assume that the pupils of the astronaut's eyes have a diameter of 5.0 mm and that most of the light is centered around 500 nm.

69. The characters of a stadium scoreboard are formed with closely spaced lightbulbs that radiate primarily yellow light. (Use $\lambda = 600$ nm.) How closely must the bulbs be spaced so that an observer 80 m away sees a display of continuous lines rather than the individual bulbs? Assume that the pupil of the observer's eye has a diameter of 5.0 mm.

70. If a microscope can accept light from objects at angles as large as $\alpha = 70°$, what is the smallest structure that can be resolved when illuminated with light of wavelength 500 nm and (a) the specimen is in air? (b) When the specimen is immersed in oil, with index of refraction of 1.52?

71. A camera uses a lens with aperture 2.0 cm. What is the angular resolution of a photograph taken at 700 nm wavelength? Can it resolve the millimeter markings of a ruler placed 35 m away?

4.6 X-Ray Diffraction

72. X-rays of wavelength 0.103 nm reflects off a crystal and a second-order maximum is recorded at a Bragg angle of $25.5°$. What is the spacing between the scattering planes in this crystal?

73. A first-order Bragg reflection maximum is observed when a monochromatic X-ray falls on a crystal at a $32.3°$ angle to a reflecting plane. What is the wavelength of this X-ray?

74. An X-ray scattering experiment is performed on a crystal whose atoms form planes separated by 0.440 nm. Using an X-ray source of wavelength 0.548 nm, what is the angle (with respect to the planes in question) at which the experimenter needs to illuminate the crystal in order to observe a first-order maximum?

75. The structure of the NaCl crystal forms reflecting planes 0.541 nm apart. What is the smallest angle, measured from these planes, at which X-ray diffraction can be observed, if X-rays of wavelength 0.085 nm are used?

76. On a certain crystal, a first-order X-ray diffraction maximum is observed at an angle of $27.1°$ relative to its surface, using an X-ray source of unknown wavelength. Additionally, when illuminated with a different, this time of known wavelength 0.137 nm, a second-order maximum is detected at $37.3°$. Determine (a) the spacing between the reflecting planes, and (b) the unknown wavelength.

77. Calcite crystals contain scattering planes separated by 0.30 nm. What is the angular separation between first and second-order diffraction maxima when X-rays of 0.130 nm wavelength are used?

78. The first-order Bragg angle for a certain crystal is $12.1°$. What is the second-order angle?

ADDITIONAL PROBLEMS

79. White light falls on two narrow slits separated by 0.40 mm. The interference pattern is observed on a screen 3.0 m away. (a) What is the separation between the first maxima for red light $(\lambda = 700\,\text{nm})$ and violet light $(\lambda = 400\,\text{nm})$? (b) At what point nearest the central maximum will a maximum for yellow light $(\lambda = 600\,\text{nm})$ coincide with a maximum for violet light? Identify the order for each maximum.

80. Microwaves of wavelength 10.0 mm fall normally on a metal plate that contains a slit 25 mm wide. (a) Where are the first minima of the diffraction pattern? (b) Would there be minima if the wavelength were 30.0 mm?

81. *Quasars*, or *quasi-stellar radio sources*, are astronomical objects discovered in 1960. They are distant but strong emitters of radio waves with angular size so small, they were originally unresolved, the same as stars. The quasar 3C405 is actually two discrete radio sources that subtend an angle of 82 arcsec. If this object is studied using radio emissions at a frequency of 410 MHz, what is the minimum diameter of a radio telescope that can resolve the two sources?

82. Two slits each of width 1800 nm and separated by the center-to-center distance of 1200 nm are illuminated by plane waves from a krypton ion laser-emitting at wavelength 461.9 nm. Find the number of interference peaks in the central diffraction peak.

83. A microwave of an unknown wavelength is incident on a single slit of width 6 cm. The angular width of the central peak is found to be $25°$. Find the wavelength.

84. Red light (wavelength 632.8 nm in air) from a Helium-Neon laser is incident on a single slit of width 0.05 mm. The entire apparatus is immersed in water of refractive index 1.333. Determine the angular width of the central peak.

85. A light ray of wavelength 461.9 nm emerges from a 2-mm circular aperture of a krypton ion laser. Due to diffraction, the beam expands as it moves out. How large is the central bright spot at (a) 1 m, (b) 1 km, (c) 1000 km, and (d) at the surface of the moon at a distance of 400,000 km from Earth.

86. How far apart must two objects be on the moon to be distinguishable by eye if only the diffraction effects of the eye's pupil limit the resolution? Assume 550 nm for the wavelength of light, the pupil diameter 5.0 mm, and 400,000 km for the distance to the moon.

87. How far apart must two objects be on the moon to be resolvable by the 8.1-m-diameter Gemini North telescope at Mauna Kea, Hawaii, if only the diffraction effects of the telescope aperture limit the resolution? Assume 550 nm for the wavelength of light and 400,000 km for the distance to the moon.

88. A spy satellite is reputed to be able to resolve objects 10. cm apart while operating 197 km above the surface of Earth. What is the diameter of the aperture of the telescope if the resolution is only limited by the diffraction effects? Use 550 nm for light.

89. Monochromatic light of wavelength 530 nm passes through a horizontal single slit of width $1.5\ \mu\text{m}$ in an opaque plate. A screen of dimensions $2.0\ \text{m} \times 2.0\ \text{m}$ is 1.2 m away from the slit. (a) Which way is the diffraction pattern spread out on the screen? (b) What are the angles of the minima with respect to the center? (c) What are the angles of the maxima? (d) How wide is the central bright fringe on the screen? (e) How wide is the next bright fringe on the screen?

90. A monochromatic light of unknown wavelength is incident on a slit of width $20\ \mu\text{m}$. A diffraction pattern is seen at a screen 2.5 m away where the central maximum is spread over a distance of 10.0 cm. Find the wavelength.

91. A source of light having two wavelengths 550 nm and 600 nm of equal intensity is incident on a slit of width $1.8\ \mu\text{m}$. Find the separation of the $m = 1$ bright spots of the two wavelengths on a screen 30.0 cm away.

92. A single slit of width 2100 nm is illuminated normally by a wave of wavelength 632.8 nm. Find the phase difference between waves from the top and one third from the bottom of the slit to a point on a screen at a horizontal distance of 2.0 m and vertical distance of 10.0 cm from the center.

93. A single slit of width $3.0\ \mu\text{m}$ is illuminated by a sodium yellow light of wavelength 589 nm. Find the intensity at a $15°$ angle to the axis in terms of the intensity of the central maximum.

94. A single slit of width 0.10 mm is illuminated by a mercury lamp of wavelength 576 nm. Find the intensity at a $10°$ angle to the axis in terms of the intensity of the central maximum.

95. A diffraction grating produces a second maximum that is 89.7 cm from the central maximum on a screen 2.0 m away. If the grating has 600 lines per centimeter, what is the wavelength of the light that produces the diffraction pattern?

96. A grating with 4000 lines per centimeter is used to diffract light that contains all wavelengths between 400 and 650 nm. How wide is the first-order spectrum on a screen 3.0 m from the grating?

97. A diffraction grating with 2000 lines per centimeter is used to measure the wavelengths emitted by a hydrogen gas discharge tube. (a) At what angles will you find the maxima of the two first-order blue lines of wavelengths 410 and 434 nm? (b) The maxima of two other first-order lines are found at $\theta_1 = 0.097\ \text{rad}$ and $\theta_2 = 0.132\ \text{rad}$. What are the wavelengths of these lines?

98. For white light $(400\ \text{nm} < \lambda < 700\ \text{nm})$ falling normally on a diffraction grating, show that the second and third-order spectra overlap no matter what the grating constant *d* is.

99. How many complete orders of the visible spectrum $(400\ \text{nm} < \lambda < 700\ \text{nm})$ can be produced with a diffraction grating that contains 5000 lines per centimeter?

100. Two lamps producing light of wavelength 589 nm are fixed 1.0 m apart on a wooden plank. What is the maximum distance an observer can be and still resolve the lamps as two separate sources of light, if the resolution is affected solely by the diffraction of light entering the eye? Assume light enters the eye through a pupil of diameter 4.5 mm.

101. On a bright clear day, you are at the top of a mountain and looking at a city 12 km away. There are two tall towers 20.0 m apart in the city. Can your eye resolve the two towers if the diameter of the pupil is 4.0 mm? If not, what should be the minimum magnification power of the telescope needed to resolve the two towers? In your calculations use 550 nm for the wavelength of the light.

102. Radio telescopes are telescopes used for the detection of radio emission from space. Because radio waves have much longer wavelengths than visible light, the diameter of a radio telescope must be very large to provide good resolution. For example, the radio telescope in Penticton, BC in Canada, has a diameter of 26 m and can be operated at frequencies as high as 6.6 GHz. (a) What is the wavelength corresponding to this frequency? (b) What is the angular separation of two radio sources that can be resolved by this telescope? (c) Compare the telescope's resolution with the angular size of the moon.

Figure 4.30 (credit: modification of work by Jason Nishiyama)

103. Calculate the wavelength of light that produces its first minimum at an angle of $36.9°$ when falling on a single slit of width $1.00\ \mu\text{m}$.

104. (a) Find the angle of the third diffraction minimum for 633-nm light falling on a slit of width $20.0\ \mu\text{m}$. (b) What slit width would place this minimum at $85.0°$?

105. As an example of diffraction by apertures of everyday dimensions, consider a doorway of width 1.0 m. (a) What is the angular position of the first minimum in the diffraction pattern of 600-nm light? (b) Repeat this calculation for a musical note of frequency 440 Hz (A above middle C). Take the speed of sound to be 343 m/s.

106. What are the angular positions of the first and second minima in a diffraction pattern produced by a slit of width 0.20 mm that is illuminated by 400 nm light? What is the angular width of the central peak?

107. How far would you place a screen from the slit of the previous problem so that the second minimum is a distance of 2.5 mm from the center of the diffraction pattern?

108. How narrow is a slit that produces a diffraction pattern on a screen 1.8 m away whose central peak is 1.0 m wide? Assume $\lambda = 589\ \text{nm}$.

109. Suppose that the central peak of a single-slit diffraction pattern is so wide that the first minima can be assumed to occur at angular positions of $\pm 90°$. For this case, what is the ratio of the slit width to the wavelength of the light?

110. The central diffraction peak of the double-slit interference pattern contains exactly nine fringes. What is the ratio of the slit separation to the slit width?

111. Determine the intensities of three interference peaks other than the central peak in the central maximum of the diffraction, if possible, when a light of wavelength 500 nm is incident normally on a double slit of width 1000 nm and separation 1500 nm. Use the intensity of the central spot to be $1\ \text{mW/cm}^2$.

112. The yellow light from a sodium vapor lamp *seems* to be of pure wavelength, but it produces two first-order maxima at $36.093°$ and $36.129°$ when projected on a 10,000 line per centimeter diffraction grating. What are the two wavelengths to an accuracy of 0.1 nm?

113. Structures on a bird feather act like a reflection grating having 8000 lines per centimeter. What is the angle of the first-order maximum for 600-nm light?

114. If a diffraction grating produces a first-order maximum for the shortest wavelength of visible light at $30.0°$, at what angle will the first-order maximum be for the largest wavelength of visible light?

115. (a) What visible wavelength has its fourth-order maximum at an angle of $25.0°$ when projected on a 25,000-line per centimeter diffraction grating? (b) What is unreasonable about this result? (c) Which assumptions are unreasonable or inconsistent?

116. Consider a spectrometer based on a diffraction grating. Construct a problem in which you calculate the distance between two wavelengths of electromagnetic radiation in your spectrometer. Among the things to be considered are the wavelengths you wish to be able to distinguish, the number of lines per meter on the diffraction grating, and the distance from the grating to the screen or detector. Discuss the practicality of the device in terms of being able to discern between wavelengths of interest.

117. An amateur astronomer wants to build a telescope with a diffraction limit that will allow him to see if there are people on the moons of Jupiter. (a) What diameter mirror is needed to be able to see 1.00-m detail on a Jovian moon at a distance of $7.50 \times 10^8\ \text{km}$ from Earth? The wavelength of light averages 600 nm. (b) What is unreasonable about this result? (c) Which assumptions are unreasonable or inconsistent?

CHALLENGE PROBLEMS

118. Blue light of wavelength 450 nm falls on a slit of width 0.25 mm. A converging lens of focal length 20 cm is placed behind the slit and focuses the diffraction pattern on a screen. (a) How far is the screen from the lens? (b) What is the distance between the first and the third minima of the diffraction pattern?

119. (a) Assume that the maxima are halfway between the minima of a single-slit diffraction pattern. The use the diameter and circumference of the phasor diagram, as described in **Intensity in Single-Slit Diffraction**, to determine the intensities of the third and fourth maxima in terms of the intensity of the central maximum. (b) Do the same calculation, using **Equation 4.4**.

120. (a) By differentiating **Equation 4.4**, show that the higher-order maxima of the single-slit diffraction pattern occur at values of β that satisfy $\tan \beta = \beta$. (b) Plot $y = \tan \beta$ and $y = \beta$ versus β and find the intersections of these two curves. What information do they give you about the locations of the maxima? (c) Convince yourself that these points do not appear exactly at $\beta = \left(n + \frac{1}{2}\right)\pi$, where $n = 0,\ 1,\ 2,\ \ldots,$ but are quite close to these values.

121. What is the maximum number of lines per centimeter a diffraction grating can have and produce a complete first-order spectrum for visible light?

122. Show that a diffraction grating cannot produce a second-order maximum for a given wavelength of light unless the first-order maximum is at an angle less than $30.0°$.

123. A He-Ne laser beam is reflected from the surface of a CD onto a wall. The brightest spot is the reflected beam at an angle equal to the angle of incidence. However, fringes are also observed. If the wall is 1.50 m from the CD, and the first fringe is 0.600 m from the central maximum, what is the spacing of grooves on the CD?

124. Objects viewed through a microscope are placed very close to the focal point of the objective lens. Show that the minimum separation x of two objects resolvable through the microscope is given by $x = \frac{1.22\lambda f_0}{D}$, where f_0 is the focal length and D is the diameter of the objective lens as shown below.

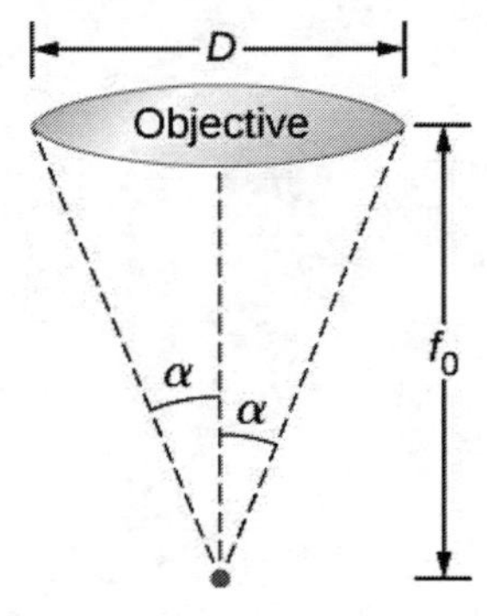

5 | RELATIVITY

Figure 5.1 Special relativity explains how time passes slightly differently on Earth and within the rapidly moving global positioning satellite (GPS). GPS units in vehicles could not find their correct location on Earth without taking this correction into account. (credit: modification of work by U.S. Air Force)

Chapter Outline

Introduction

The special theory of relativity was proposed in 1905 by Albert Einstein (1879–1955). It describes how time, space, and physical phenomena appear in different frames of reference that are moving at constant velocity with respect to each other. This differs from Einstein's later work on general relativity, which deals with any frame of reference, including accelerated frames.

The theory of relativity led to a profound change in the way we perceive space and time. The "common sense" rules that we use to relate space and time measurements in the Newtonian worldview differ seriously from the correct rules at speeds near the speed of light. For example, the special theory of relativity tells us that measurements of length and time intervals are not the same in reference frames moving relative to one another. A particle might be observed to have a lifetime of 1.0×10^{-8} s in one reference frame, but a lifetime of 2.0×10^{-8} s in another; and an object might be measured to be 2.0 m long in one frame and 3.0 m long in another frame. These effects are usually significant only at speeds comparable to the speed of light, but even at the much lower speeds of the global positioning satellite, which requires extremely accurate time measurements to function, the different lengths of the same distance in different frames of reference are significant enough that they need to be taken into account.

Unlike Newtonian mechanics, which describes the motion of particles, or Maxwell's equations, which specify how the electromagnetic field behaves, special relativity is not restricted to a particular type of phenomenon. Instead, its rules on space and time affect all fundamental physical theories.

The modifications of Newtonian mechanics in special relativity do not invalidate classical Newtonian mechanics or require its replacement. Instead, the equations of relativistic mechanics differ meaningfully from those of classical Newtonian mechanics only for objects moving at relativistic speeds (i.e., speeds less than, but comparable to, the speed of light). In the macroscopic world that you encounter in your daily life, the relativistic equations reduce to classical equations, and the predictions of classical Newtonian mechanics agree closely enough with experimental results to disregard relativistic corrections.

5.1 | Invariance of Physical Laws

Learning Objectives

By the end of this section, you will be able to:

- Describe the theoretical and experimental issues that Einstein's theory of special relativity addressed.
- State the two postulates of the special theory of relativity.

Suppose you calculate the hypotenuse of a right triangle given the base angles and adjacent sides. Whether you calculate the hypotenuse from one of the sides and the cosine of the base angle, or from the Pythagorean theorem, the results should agree. Predictions based on different principles of physics must also agree, whether we consider them principles of mechanics or principles of electromagnetism.

Albert Einstein pondered a disagreement between predictions based on electromagnetism and on assumptions made in classical mechanics. Specifically, suppose an observer measures the velocity of a light pulse in the observer's own **rest frame**; that is, in the frame of reference in which the observer is at rest. According to the assumptions long considered obvious in classical mechanics, if an observer measures a velocity $\vec{v}$ in one frame of reference, and that frame of reference is moving with velocity $\vec{u}$ past a second reference frame, an observer in the second frame measures the original velocity as $\vec{v}' = \vec{v} + \vec{u}$. This sum of velocities is often referred to as **Galilean relativity**. If this principle is correct, the pulse of light that the observer measures as traveling with speed c travels at speed $c + u$ measured in the frame of the second observer. If we reasonably assume that the laws of electrodynamics are the same in both frames of reference, then the predicted speed of light (in vacuum) in both frames should be $c = 1/\sqrt{\varepsilon_0 \mu_0}$. Each observer should measure the same speed of the light pulse with respect to that observer's own rest frame. To reconcile difficulties of this kind, Einstein constructed his **special theory of relativity**, which introduced radical new ideas about time and space that have since been confirmed experimentally.

Inertial Frames

All velocities are measured relative to some frame of reference. For example, a car's motion is measured relative to its starting position on the road it travels on; a projectile's motion is measured relative to the surface from which it is launched; and a planet's orbital motion is measured relative to the star it orbits. The frames of reference in which mechanics takes the simplest form are those that are not accelerating. Newton's first law, the law of inertia, holds exactly in such a frame.

Inertial Reference Frame

An **inertial frame of reference** is a reference frame in which a body at rest remains at rest and a body in motion moves at a constant speed in a straight line unless acted upon by an outside force.

For example, to a passenger inside a plane flying at constant speed and constant altitude, physics seems to work exactly the same as when the passenger is standing on the surface of Earth. When the plane is taking off, however, matters are somewhat more complicated. In this case, the passenger at rest inside the plane concludes that a net force F on an object is not equal to the product of mass and acceleration, ma. Instead, F is equal to ma plus a fictitious force. This situation is not as simple as in an inertial frame. The term “special” in “special relativity” refers to dealing only with inertial frames of reference. Einstein’s later theory of general relativity deals with all kinds of reference frames, including accelerating, and therefore non-inertial, reference frames.

Einstein’s First Postulate

Not only are the principles of classical mechanics simplest in inertial frames, but they are the same in all inertial frames. Einstein based the **first postulate** of his theory on the idea that this is true for all the laws of physics, not merely those in mechanics.

First Postulate of Special Relativity

The laws of physics are the same in all inertial frames of reference.

This postulate denies the existence of a special or preferred inertial frame. The laws of nature do not give us a way to endow any one inertial frame with special properties. For example, we cannot identify any inertial frame as being in a state of “absolute rest.” We can only determine the relative motion of one frame with respect to another.

There is, however, more to this postulate than meets the eye. The laws of physics include only those that satisfy this postulate. We will see that the definitions of energy and momentum must be altered to fit this postulate. Another outcome of this postulate is the famous equation $E = mc^2$, which relates energy to mass.

Einstein’s Second Postulate

The second postulate upon which Einstein based his theory of special relativity deals with the speed of light. Late in the nineteenth century, the major tenets of classical physics were well established. Two of the most important were the laws of electromagnetism and Newton’s laws. Investigations such as Young’s double-slit experiment in the early 1800s had convincingly demonstrated that light is a wave. Maxwell’s equations of electromagnetism implied that electromagnetic waves travel at $c = 3.00 \times 10^8$ m/s in a vacuum, but they do not specify the frame of reference in which light has this speed. Many types of waves were known, and all travelled in some medium. Scientists therefore assumed that some medium carried the light, even in a vacuum, and that light travels at a speed c relative to that medium (often called “the aether”).

Starting in the mid-1880s, the American physicist A.A. Michelson, later aided by E.W. Morley, made a series of direct measurements of the speed of light. They intended to deduce from their data the speed v at which Earth was moving through the mysterious medium for light waves. The speed of light measured on Earth should have been $c + v$ when Earth’s motion was opposite to the medium’s flow at speed u past the Earth, and $c - v$ when Earth was moving in the same direction as the medium. The results of their measurements were startling.

Michelson-Morley Experiment

The **Michelson-Morley experiment** demonstrated that the speed of light in a vacuum is independent of the motion of Earth about the Sun.

The eventual conclusion derived from this result is that light, unlike mechanical waves such as sound, does not need a medium to carry it. Furthermore, the Michelson-Morley results implied that the speed of light c is independent of the motion of the source relative to the observer. That is, everyone observes light to move at speed c regardless of how they move relative to the light source or to one another. For several years, many scientists tried unsuccessfully to explain these results within the framework of Newton’s laws.

In addition, there was a contradiction between the principles of electromagnetism and the assumption made in Newton’s laws about relative velocity. Classically, the velocity of an object in one frame of reference and the velocity of that object in a second frame of reference relative to the first should combine like simple vectors to give the velocity seen in the second frame. If that were correct, then two observers moving at different speeds would see light traveling at different speeds. Imagine what a light wave would look like to a person traveling along with it (in vacuum) at a speed c. If such a motion were possible, then the wave would be stationary relative to the observer. It would have electric and magnetic fields whose strengths varied with position but were constant in time. This is not allowed by Maxwell’s equations. So either Maxwell’s equations are different in different inertial frames, or an object with mass cannot travel at speed c. Einstein concluded that the latter is true: An object with mass cannot travel at speed c. Maxwell’s equations are correct, but Newton’s addition of velocities is not correct for light.

Not until 1905, when Einstein published his first paper on special relativity, was the currently accepted conclusion reached. Based mostly on his analysis that the laws of electricity and magnetism would not allow another speed for light, and only slightly aware of the Michelson-Morley experiment, Einstein detailed his **second postulate of special relativity**.

Second Postulate of Special Relativity

Light travels in a vacuum with the same speed c in any direction in all inertial frames.

In other words, the speed of light has the same definite speed for any observer, regardless of the relative motion of the source. This deceptively simple and counterintuitive postulate, along with the first postulate, leave all else open for change. Among the changes are the loss of agreement on the time between events, the variation of distance with speed, and the realization that matter and energy can be converted into one another. We describe these concepts in the following sections.

5.1 Check Your Understanding Explain how special relativity differs from general relativity.

5.2 | Relativity of Simultaneity

Learning Objectives

By the end of this section, you will be able to:

- Show from Einstein's postulates that two events measured as simultaneous in one inertial frame are not necessarily simultaneous in all inertial frames.
- Describe how simultaneity is a relative concept for observers in different inertial frames in relative motion.

Do time intervals depend on who observes them? Intuitively, it seems that the time for a process, such as the elapsed time for a foot race (**Figure 5.2**), should be the same for all observers. In everyday experiences, disagreements over elapsed time have to do with the accuracy of measuring time. No one would be likely to argue that the actual time interval was different for the moving runner and for the stationary clock displayed. Carefully considering just how time is measured, however, shows that elapsed time does depends on the relative motion of an observer with respect to the process being measured.

Figure 5.2 Elapsed time for a foot race is the same for all observers, but at relativistic speeds, elapsed time depends on the motion of the observer relative to the location where the process being timed occurs. (credit: "Jason Edward Scott Bain"/Flickr)

Consider how we measure elapsed time. If we use a stopwatch, for example, how do we know when to start and stop the watch? One method is to use the arrival of light from the event. For example, if you're in a moving car and observe the light arriving from a traffic signal change from green to red, you know it's time to step on the brake pedal. The timing is more accurate if some sort of electronic detection is used, avoiding human reaction times and other complications.

Now suppose two observers use this method to measure the time interval between two flashes of light from flash lamps that are a distance apart (**Figure 5.3**). An observer *A* is seated midway on a rail car with two flash lamps at opposite sides equidistant from her. A pulse of light is emitted from each flash lamp and moves toward observer *A*, shown in frame (a) of the figure. The rail car is moving rapidly in the direction indicated by the velocity vector in the diagram. An observer *B* standing on the platform is facing the rail car as it passes and observes both flashes of light reach him simultaneously, as shown in frame (c). He measures the distances from where he saw the pulses originate, finds them equal, and concludes that the pulses were emitted simultaneously.

However, because of Observer *A*'s motion, the pulse from the right of the railcar, from the direction the car is moving, reaches her before the pulse from the left, as shown in frame (b). She also measures the distances from within her frame of reference, finds them equal, and concludes that the pulses were not emitted simultaneously.

The two observers reach conflicting conclusions about whether the two events at well-separated locations were simultaneous. Both frames of reference are valid, and both conclusions are valid. Whether two events at separate locations are simultaneous depends on the motion of the observer relative to the locations of the events.

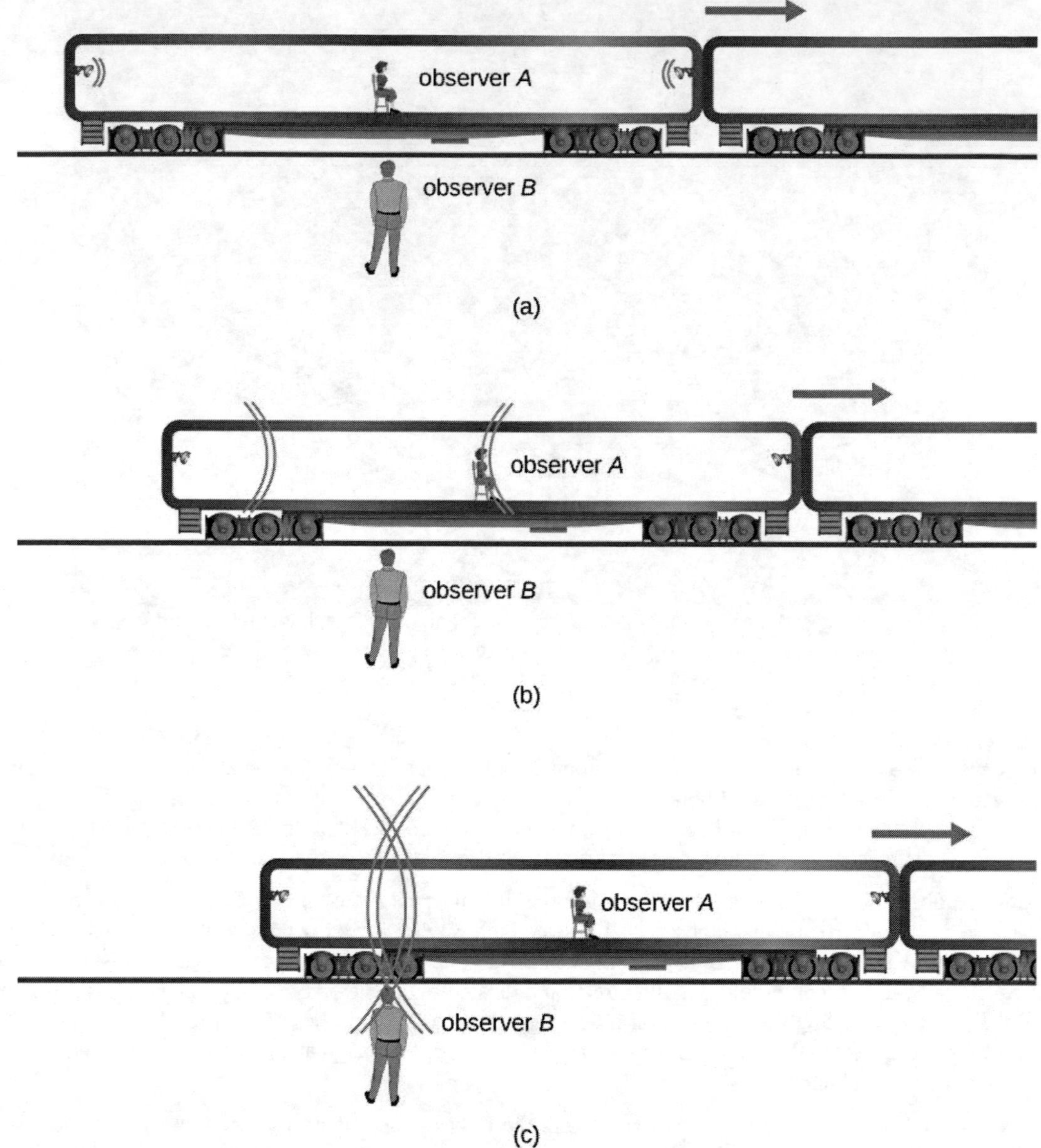

Figure 5.3 (a) Two pulses of light are emitted simultaneously relative to observer *B*. (c) The pulses reach observer *B*'s position simultaneously. (b) Because of *A*'s motion, she sees the pulse from the right first and concludes the bulbs did not flash simultaneously. Both conclusions are correct.

Here, the relative velocity between observers affects whether two events a distance apart are observed to be simultaneous. *Simultaneity is not absolute*. We might have guessed (incorrectly) that if light is emitted simultaneously, then two observers halfway between the sources would see the flashes simultaneously. But careful analysis shows this cannot be the case if the speed of light is the same in all inertial frames.

This type of *thought experiment* (in German, "Gedankenexperiment") shows that seemingly obvious conclusions must be changed to agree with the postulates of relativity. The validity of thought experiments can only be determined by actual observation, and careful experiments have repeatedly confirmed Einstein's theory of relativity.

5.3 | Time Dilation

Learning Objectives

By the end of this section, you will be able to:

- Explain how time intervals can be measured differently in different reference frames.
- Describe how to distinguish a proper time interval from a dilated time interval.
- Describe the significance of the muon experiment.
- Explain why the twin paradox is not a contradiction.
- Calculate time dilation given the speed of an object in a given frame.

The analysis of simultaneity shows that Einstein's postulates imply an important effect: Time intervals have different values when measured in different inertial frames. Suppose, for example, an astronaut measures the time it takes for a pulse of light to travel a distance perpendicular to the direction of his ship's motion (relative to an earthbound observer), bounce off a mirror, and return (**Figure 5.4**). How does the elapsed time that the astronaut measures in the spacecraft compare with the elapsed time that an earthbound observer measures by observing what is happening in the spacecraft?

Examining this question leads to a profound result. The elapsed time for a process depends on which observer is measuring it. In this case, the time measured by the astronaut (within the spaceship where the astronaut is at rest) is smaller than the time measured by the earthbound observer (to whom the astronaut is moving). The time elapsed for the same process is different for the observers, because the distance the light pulse travels in the astronaut's frame is smaller than in the earthbound frame, as seen in **Figure 5.4**. Light travels at the same speed in each frame, so it takes more time to travel the greater distance in the earthbound frame.

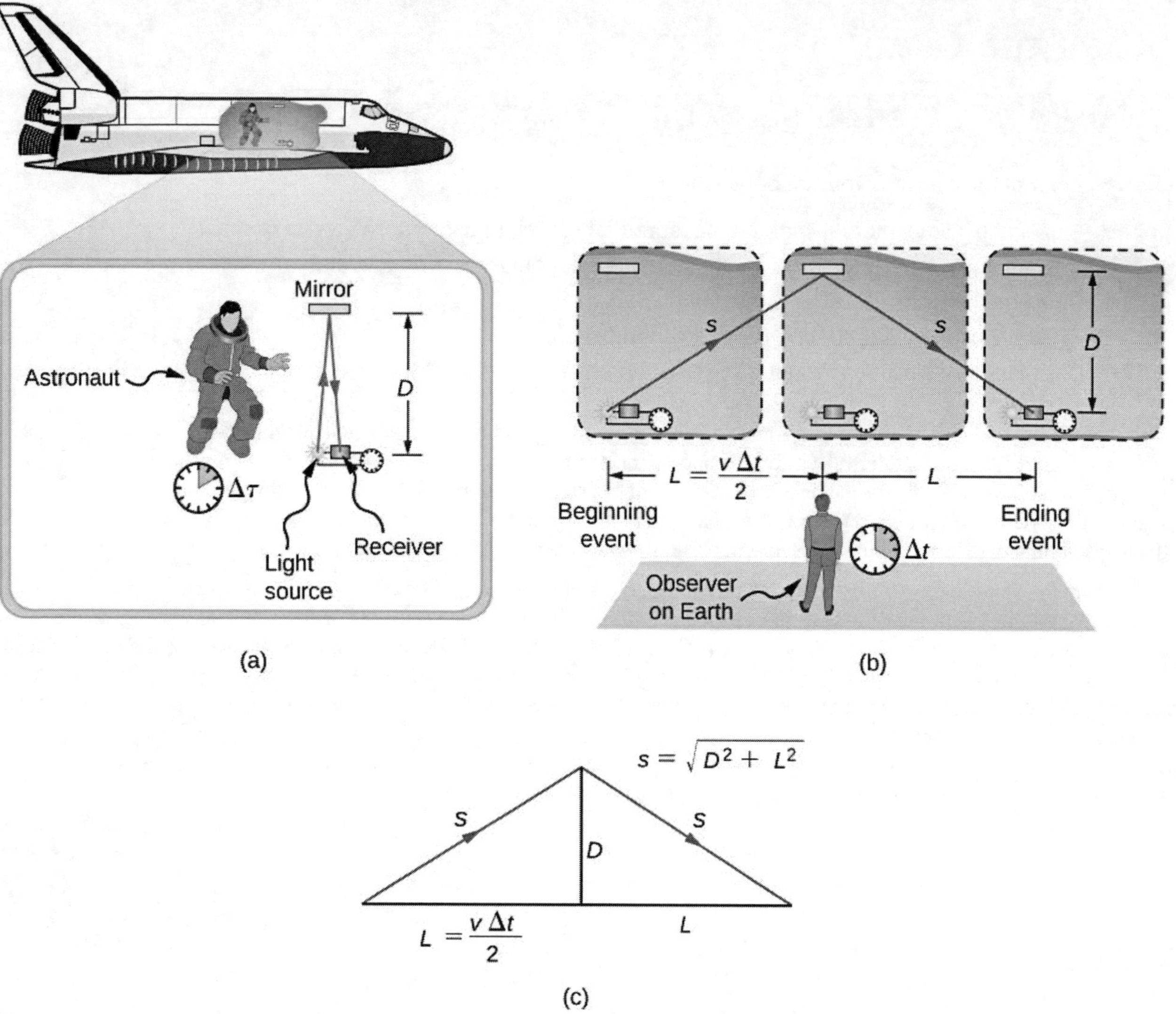

Figure 5.4 (a) An astronaut measures the time $\Delta\tau$ for light to travel distance $2D$ in the astronaut's frame. (b) A NASA scientist on Earth sees the light follow the longer path $2s$ and take a longer time Δt. (c) These triangles are used to find the relationship between the two distances D and s.

Time Dilation

Time dilation is the lengthening of the time interval between two events for an observer in an inertial frame that is moving with respect to the rest frame of the events (in which the events occur at the same location).

To quantitatively compare the time measurements in the two inertial frames, we can relate the distances in **Figure 5.4** to each other, then express each distance in terms of the time of travel (respectively either Δt or $\Delta\tau$) of the pulse in the corresponding reference frame. The resulting equation can then be solved for Δt in terms of $\Delta\tau$.

The lengths D and L in **Figure 5.4** are the sides of a right triangle with hypotenuse s. From the Pythagorean theorem,

$$s^2 = D^2 + L^2.$$

The lengths $2s$ and $2L$ are, respectively, the distances that the pulse of light and the spacecraft travel in time Δt in the earthbound observer's frame. The length D is the distance that the light pulse travels in time $\Delta\tau$ in the astronaut's frame. This gives us three equations:

$$2s = c\Delta t;\ 2L = v\Delta t;\ 2D = c\Delta\tau.$$

Note that we used Einstein's second postulate by taking the speed of light to be c in both inertial frames. We substitute these results into the previous expression from the Pythagorean theorem:

$$\begin{aligned} s^2 &= D^2 + L^2 \\ \left(c\frac{\Delta t}{2}\right)^2 &= \left(c\frac{\Delta\tau}{2}\right)^2 + \left(v\frac{\Delta t}{2}\right)^2. \end{aligned}$$

Then we rearrange to obtain

$$(c\Delta t)^2 - (v\Delta t)^2 = (c\Delta\tau)^2.$$

Finally, solving for Δt in terms of $\Delta\tau$ gives us

$$\Delta t = \frac{\Delta\tau}{\sqrt{1 - (v/c)^2}}. \tag{5.1}$$

This is equivalent to

$$\Delta t = \gamma\Delta\tau,$$

where γ is the relativistic factor (often called the Lorentz factor) given by

$$\gamma = \frac{1}{\sqrt{1 - \frac{v^2}{c^2}}} \tag{5.2}$$

and v and c are the speeds of the moving observer and light, respectively.

Note the asymmetry between the two measurements. Only one of them is a measurement of the time interval between two events—the emission and arrival of the light pulse—at the same position. It is a measurement of the time interval in the rest frame of a single clock. The measurement in the earthbound frame involves comparing the time interval between two events that occur at different locations. The time interval between events that occur at a single location has a separate name to distinguish it from the time measured by the earthbound observer, and we use the separate symbol $\Delta\tau$ to refer to it throughout this chapter.

Proper Time

The **proper time** interval $\Delta\tau$ between two events is the time interval measured by an observer for whom both events occur at the same location.

The equation relating Δt and $\Delta\tau$ is truly remarkable. First, as stated earlier, elapsed time is not the same for different observers moving relative to one another, even though both are in inertial frames. A proper time interval $\Delta\tau$ for an observer who, like the astronaut, is moving with the apparatus, is smaller than the time interval for other observers. It is the smallest possible measured time between two events. The earthbound observer sees time intervals within the moving system as dilated (i.e., lengthened) relative to how the observer moving relative to Earth sees them within the moving system. Alternatively, according to the earthbound observer, less time passes between events within the moving frame. Note that the shortest elapsed time between events is in the inertial frame in which the observer sees the events (e.g., the emission and arrival of the light signal) occur at the same point.

This time effect is real and is not caused by inaccurate clocks or improper measurements. Time-interval measurements of the same event differ for observers in relative motion. The dilation of time is an intrinsic property of time itself. All clocks moving relative to an observer, including biological clocks, such as a person's heartbeat, or aging, are observed to run more slowly compared with a clock that is stationary relative to the observer.

Note that if the relative velocity is much less than the speed of light ($v<<c$), then v^2/c^2 is extremely small, and the elapsed times Δt and $\Delta\tau$ are nearly equal. At low velocities, physics based on modern relativity approaches classical physics—everyday experiences involve very small relativistic effects. However, for speeds near the speed of light, v^2/c^2 is close to one, so $\sqrt{1-v^2/c^2}$ is very small and Δt becomes significantly larger than $\Delta\tau$.

Half-Life of a Muon

There is considerable experimental evidence that the equation $\Delta t = \gamma\Delta\tau$ is correct. One example is found in cosmic ray particles that continuously rain down on Earth from deep space. Some collisions of these particles with nuclei in the upper atmosphere result in short-lived particles called muons. The half-life (amount of time for half of a material to decay) of a muon is 1.52 μs when it is at rest relative to the observer who measures the half-life. This is the proper time interval $\Delta\tau$. This short time allows very few muons to reach Earth's surface and be detected if Newtonian assumptions about time and space were correct. However, muons produced by cosmic ray particles have a range of velocities, with some moving near the speed of light. It has been found that the muon's half-life as measured by an earthbound observer (Δt) varies with velocity exactly as predicted by the equation $\Delta t = \gamma\Delta\tau$. The faster the muon moves, the longer it lives. We on Earth see the muon last much longer than its half-life predicts within its own rest frame. As viewed from our frame, the muon decays more slowly than it does when at rest relative to us. A far larger fraction of muons reach the ground as a result.

Before we present the first example of solving a problem in relativity, we state a strategy you can use as a guideline for these calculations.

Problem-Solving Strategy: Relativity

1. Make a list of what is given or can be inferred from the problem as stated (identify the knowns). Look in particular for information on relative velocity v.
2. Identify exactly what needs to be determined in the problem (identify the unknowns).
3. Make certain you understand the conceptual aspects of the problem before making any calculations (express the answer as an equation). Decide, for example, which observer sees time dilated or length contracted before working with the equations or using them to carry out the calculation. If you have thought about who sees what, who is moving with the event being observed, who sees proper time, and so on, you will find it much easier to determine if your calculation is reasonable.
4. Determine the primary type of calculation to be done to find the unknowns identified above (do the calculation). You will find the section summary helpful in determining whether a length contraction, relativistic kinetic energy, or some other concept is involved.

Note *that you should not round off during the calculation.* As noted in the text, you must often perform your calculations to many digits to see the desired effect. You may round off at the very end of the problem solution, but do not use a rounded number in a subsequent calculation. Also, check the answer to see if it is reasonable: Does it make sense? This may be more difficult for relativity, which has few everyday examples to provide experience with what is reasonable. But you can look for velocities greater than c or relativistic effects that are in the wrong direction (such as a time contraction where a dilation was expected).

Example 5.1

Time Dilation in a High-Speed Vehicle

The Hypersonic Technology Vehicle 2 (HTV-2) is an experimental rocket vehicle capable of traveling at 21,000 km/h (5830 m/s). If an electronic clock in the HTV-2 measures a time interval of exactly 1-s duration, what would observers on Earth measure the time interval to be?

Strategy

Apply the time dilation formula to relate the proper time interval of the signal in HTV-2 to the time interval measured on the ground.

Solution

a. Identify the knowns: $\Delta\tau = 1$ s; $v = 5830$ m/s.

b. Identify the unknown: Δt.

c. Express the answer as an equation:

$$\Delta t = \gamma\Delta\tau = \frac{\Delta\tau}{\sqrt{1 - \frac{v^2}{c^2}}}.$$

d. Do the calculation. Use the expression for γ to determine Δt from $\Delta\tau$:

$$\begin{aligned}\Delta t &= \frac{1\text{ s}}{\sqrt{1 - \left(\frac{5830\text{ m/s}}{3.00 \times 10^8\text{ m/s}}\right)^2}} \\ &= 1.000000000189\text{ s} \\ &= 1\text{ s} + 1.89 \times 10^{-10}\text{ s}.\end{aligned}$$

Significance

The very high speed of the HTV-2 is still only 10^{-5} times the speed of light. Relativistic effects for the HTV-2 are negligible for almost all purposes, but are not zero.

Example 5.2

What Speeds are Relativistic?

How fast must a vehicle travel for 1 second of time measured on a passenger's watch in the vehicle to differ by 1% for an observer measuring it from the ground outside?

Strategy

Use the time dilation formula to find *v/c* for the given ratio of times.

Solution

a. Identify the known:

$$\frac{\Delta\tau}{\Delta t} = \frac{1}{1.01}.$$

b. Identify the unknown: *v/c*.

c. Express the answer as an equation:

$$\begin{aligned}\Delta t &= \gamma\Delta\tau = \frac{1}{\sqrt{1-v^2/c^2}}\Delta\tau \\ \frac{\Delta\tau}{\Delta t} &= \sqrt{1-v^2/c^2} \\ \left(\frac{\Delta\tau}{\Delta t}\right)^2 &= 1-\frac{v^2}{c^2} \\ \frac{v}{c} &= \sqrt{1-(\Delta\tau/\Delta t)^2}.\end{aligned}$$

d. Do the calculation:

$$\begin{aligned}\frac{v}{c} &= \sqrt{1-(1/1.01)^2} \\ &= 0.14.\end{aligned}$$

Significance

The result shows that an object must travel at very roughly 10% of the speed of light for its motion to produce significant relativistic time dilation effects.

Example 5.3

Calculating Δt for a Relativistic Event

Suppose a cosmic ray colliding with a nucleus in Earth's upper atmosphere produces a muon that has a velocity $v = 0.950c$. The muon then travels at constant velocity and lives 2.20 μs as measured in the muon's frame of reference. (You can imagine this as the muon's internal clock.) How long does the muon live as measured by an earthbound observer (**Figure 5.5**)?

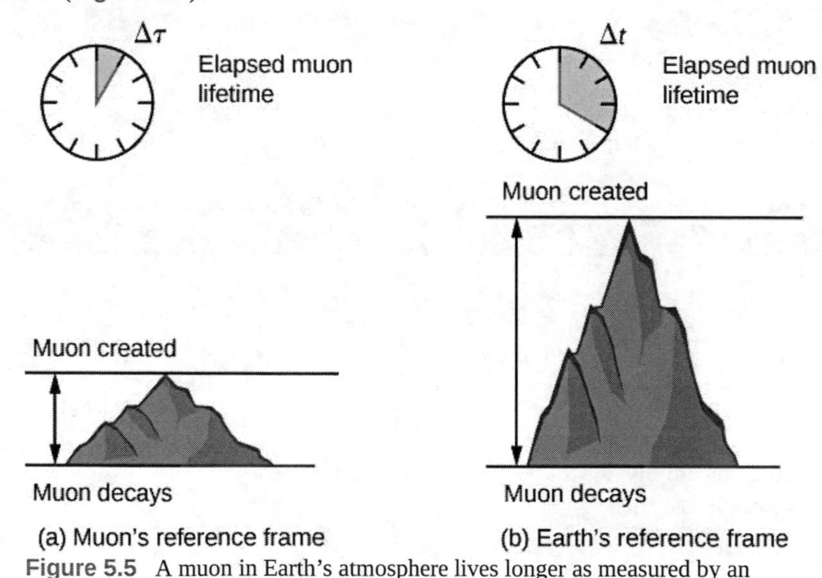

Figure 5.5 A muon in Earth's atmosphere lives longer as measured by an earthbound observer than as measured by the muon's internal clock.

As we will discuss later, in the muon's reference frame, it travels a shorter distance than measured in Earth's reference frame.

Strategy

A clock moving with the muon measures the proper time of its decay process, so the time we are given is $\Delta\tau = 2.20\mu s$. The earthbound observer measures Δt as given by the equation $\Delta t = \gamma\Delta\tau$. Because the velocity is given, we can calculate the time in Earth's frame of reference.

Solution

a. Identify the knowns: $v = 0.950c,\ \Delta\tau = 2.20\mu\text{s}$.

b. Identify the unknown: Δt.

c. Express the answer as an equation. Use:

$$\Delta t = \gamma \Delta\tau$$

with

$$\gamma = \frac{1}{\sqrt{1 - \frac{v^2}{c^2}}}.$$

d. Do the calculation. Use the expression for γ to determine Δt from $\Delta\tau$:

$$\begin{aligned}\Delta t &= \gamma\Delta\tau \\ &= \frac{1}{\sqrt{1 - \frac{v^2}{c^2}}}\Delta\tau \\ &= \frac{2.20\mu\text{s}}{\sqrt{1 - (0.950)^2}} \\ &= 7.05\ \mu\text{s}.\end{aligned}$$

Remember to keep extra significant figures until the final answer.

Significance

One implication of this example is that because $\gamma = 3.20$ at 95.0% of the speed of light $(v = 0.950c)$, the relativistic effects are significant. The two time intervals differ by a factor of 3.20, when classically they would be the same. Something moving at 0.950*c* is said to be highly relativistic.

Example 5.4

Relativistic Television

A non-flat screen, older-style television display (**Figure 5.6**) works by accelerating electrons over a short distance to relativistic speed, and then using electromagnetic fields to control where the electron beam strikes a fluorescent layer at the front of the tube. Suppose the electrons travel at 6.00×10^7 m/s through a distance of 0.200 m from the start of the beam to the screen. (a) What is the time of travel of an electron in the rest frame of the television set? (b) What is the electron’s time of travel in its own rest frame?

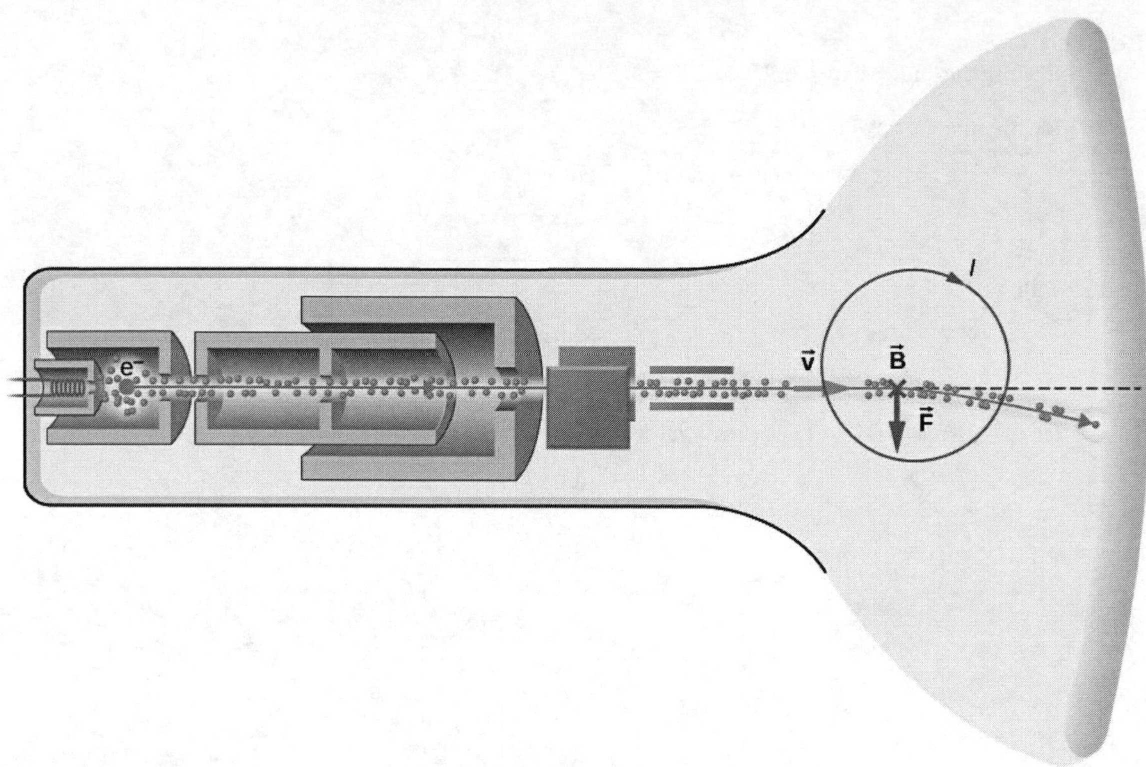

Figure 5.6 The electron beam in a cathode ray tube television display.

Strategy for (a)

(a) Calculate the time from $vt = d$. Even though the speed is relativistic, the calculation is entirely in one frame of reference, and relativity is therefore not involved.

Solution

a. Identify the knowns:

$$v = 6.00 \times 10^7 \text{ m/s}; d = 0.200 \text{ m}.$$

b. Identify the unknown: the time of travel Δt.

c. Express the answer as an equation:

$$\Delta t = \frac{d}{v}.$$

d. Do the calculation:

$$\begin{aligned} t &= \frac{0.200 \text{ m}}{6.00 \times 10^7 \text{ m/s}} \\ &= 3.33 \times 10^{-9} \text{ s}. \end{aligned}$$

Significance

The time of travel is extremely short, as expected. Because the calculation is entirely within a single frame of reference, relativity is not involved, even though the electron speed is close to c.

Strategy for (b)

(b) In the frame of reference of the electron, the vacuum tube is moving and the electron is stationary. The electron-emitting cathode leaves the electron and the front of the vacuum tube strikes the electron with the electron at the same location. Therefore we use the time dilation formula to relate the proper time in the electron rest frame to the time in the television frame.

Solution

a. Identify the knowns (from part a):

$$\Delta t = 3.33 \times 10^{-9}\ \text{s};\ v = 6.00 \times 10^{7}\ \text{m/s};\ d = 0.200\ \text{m}.$$

b. Identify the unknown: τ.

c. Express the answer as an equation:

$$\Delta t = \gamma \Delta\tau = \frac{\Delta\tau}{\sqrt{1 - v^2/c^2}}$$
$$\Delta\tau = \Delta t\sqrt{1 - v^2/c^2}.$$

d. Do the calculation:

$$\Delta\tau = \left(3.33 \times 10^{-9}\ \text{s}\right)\sqrt{1 - \left(\frac{6.00 \times 10^{7}\ \text{m/s}}{3.00 \times 10^{8}\ \text{m/s}}\right)^2}$$
$$= 3.26 \times 10^{-9}\ \text{s}.$$

Significance

The time of travel is shorter in the electron frame of reference. Because the problem requires finding the time interval measured in different reference frames for the same process, relativity is involved. If we had tried to calculate the time in the electron rest frame by simply dividing the 0.200 m by the speed, the result would be slightly incorrect because of the relativistic speed of the electron.

5.2 Check Your Understanding What is γ if $v = 0.650c$?

The Twin Paradox

An intriguing consequence of time dilation is that a space traveler moving at a high velocity relative to Earth would age less than the astronaut's earthbound twin. This is often known as the twin paradox. Imagine the astronaut moving at such a velocity that $\gamma = 30.0$, as in **Figure 5.7**. A trip that takes 2.00 years in her frame would take 60.0 years in the earthbound twin's frame. Suppose the astronaut travels 1.00 year to another star system, briefly explores the area, and then travels 1.00 year back. An astronaut who was 40 years old at the start of the trip would be would be 42 when the spaceship returns. Everything on Earth, however, would have aged 60.0 years. The earthbound twin, if still alive, would be 100 years old.

The situation would seem different to the astronaut in **Figure 5.7**. Because motion is relative, the spaceship would seem to be stationary and Earth would appear to move. (This is the sensation you have when flying in a jet.) Looking out the window of the spaceship, the astronaut would see time slow down on Earth by a factor of $\gamma = 30.0$. Seen from the spaceship, the earthbound sibling will have aged only 2/30, or 0.07, of a year, whereas the astronaut would have aged 2.00 years.

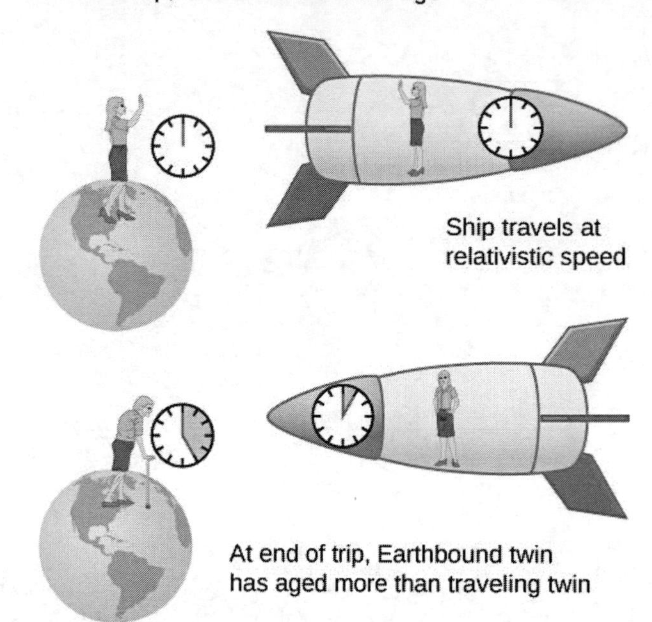

Figure 5.7 The twin paradox consists of the conflicting conclusions about which twin ages more as a result of a long space journey at relativistic speed.

The paradox here is that the two twins cannot both be correct. As with all paradoxes, conflicting conclusions come from a false premise. In fact, the astronaut's motion is significantly different from that of the earthbound twin. The astronaut accelerates to a high velocity and then decelerates to view the star system. To return to Earth, she again accelerates and decelerates. The spacecraft is not in a single inertial frame to which the time dilation formula can be directly applied. That is, the astronaut twin changes inertial references. The earthbound twin does not experience these accelerations and remains in the same inertial frame. Thus, the situation is not symmetric, and it is incorrect to claim that the astronaut observes the same effects as her twin. The lack of symmetry between the twins will be still more evident when we analyze the journey later in this chapter in terms of the path the astronaut follows through four-dimensional space-time.

In 1971, American physicists Joseph Hafele and Richard Keating verified time dilation at low relative velocities by flying extremely accurate atomic clocks around the world on commercial aircraft. They measured elapsed time to an accuracy of a few nanoseconds and compared it with the time measured by clocks left behind. Hafele and Keating's results were within experimental uncertainties of the predictions of relativity. Both special and general relativity had to be taken into account, because gravity and accelerations were involved as well as relative motion.

5.3 Check Your Understanding a. A particle travels at 1.90×10^8 m/s and lives 2.10×10^{-8} s when at rest relative to an observer. How long does the particle live as viewed in the laboratory?

b. Spacecraft *A* and *B* pass in opposite directions at a relative speed of 4.00×10^7 m/s. An internal clock in spacecraft *A* causes it to emit a radio signal for 1.00 s. The computer in spacecraft *B* corrects for the beginning and end of the signal having traveled different distances, to calculate the time interval during which ship *A* was emitting the signal. What is the time interval that the computer in spacecraft *B* calculates?

5.4 | Length Contraction

Learning Objectives

By the end of this section, you will be able to:

- Explain how simultaneity and length contraction are related.
- Describe the relation between length contraction and time dilation and use it to derive the length-contraction equation.

The length of the train car in **Figure 5.8** is the same for all the passengers. All of them would agree on the simultaneous location of the two ends of the car and obtain the same result for the distance between them. But simultaneous events in one inertial frame need not be simultaneous in another. If the train could travel at relativistic speeds, an observer on the ground would see the simultaneous locations of the two endpoints of the car at a different distance apart than observers inside the car. Measured distances need not be the same for different observers when relativistic speeds are involved.

Figure 5.8 People might describe distances differently, but at relativistic speeds, the distances really are different. (credit: "russavia"/Flickr)

Proper Length

Two observers passing each other always see the same value of their relative speed. Even though time dilation implies that the train passenger and the observer standing alongside the tracks measure different times for the train to pass, they still agree that relative speed, which is distance divided by elapsed time, is the same. If an observer on the ground and one on the train measure a different time for the length of the train to pass the ground observer, agreeing on their relative speed means they must also see different distances traveled.

The muon discussed in **Example 5.3** illustrates this concept (**Figure 5.9**). To an observer on Earth, the muon travels at $0.950c$ for 7.05 μs from the time it is produced until it decays. Therefore, it travels a distance relative to Earth of:

$$L_0 = v\Delta t = (0.950)(3.00 \times 10^8 \text{ m/s})(7.05 \times 10^{-6} \text{ s}) = 2.01 \text{ km}.$$

In the muon frame, the lifetime of the muon is 2.20 μs. In this frame of reference, the Earth, air, and ground have only enough time to travel:

$$L = v\Delta\tau = (0.950)(3.00 \times 10^8 \text{ m/s})(2.20 \times 10^{-6} \text{ s}) \text{ km} = 0.627 \text{ km}.$$

The distance between the same two events (production and decay of a muon) depends on who measures it and how they are moving relative to it.

Proper Length

Proper length L_0 is the distance between two points measured by an observer who is at rest relative to both of the points.

The earthbound observer measures the proper length L_0 because the points at which the muon is produced and decays are stationary relative to Earth. To the muon, Earth, air, and clouds are moving, so the distance L it sees is not the proper length.

Figure 5.9 (a) The earthbound observer sees the muon travel 2.01 km. (b) The same path has length 0.627 km seen from the muon's frame of reference. The Earth, air, and clouds are moving relative to the muon in its frame, and have smaller lengths along the direction of travel.

Length Contraction

To relate distances measured by different observers, note that the velocity relative to the earthbound observer in our muon example is given by

$$v = \frac{L_0}{\Delta t}.$$

The time relative to the earthbound observer is $\Delta t,$ because the object being timed is moving relative to this observer. The velocity relative to the moving observer is given by

$$v = \frac{L}{\Delta \tau}.$$

The moving observer travels with the muon and therefore observes the proper time $\Delta \tau.$ The two velocities are identical; thus,

$$\frac{L_0}{\Delta t} = \frac{L}{\Delta \tau}.$$

We know that $\Delta t = \gamma \Delta \tau.$ Substituting this equation into the relationship above gives

$$L = \frac{L_0}{\gamma}. \tag{5.3}$$

Substituting for γ gives an equation relating the distances measured by different observers.

Length Contraction

Length contraction is the decrease in the measured length of an object from its proper length when measured in a reference frame that is moving with respect to the object:

$$L = L_0 \sqrt{1 - \frac{v^2}{c^2}} \tag{5.4}$$

where L_0 is the length of the object in its rest frame, and L is the length in the frame moving with velocity v.

If we measure the length of anything moving relative to our frame, we find its length L to be smaller than the proper length

L_0 that would be measured if the object were stationary. For example, in the muon's rest frame, the distance Earth moves between where the muon was produced and where it decayed is shorter than the distance traveled as seen from the Earth's frame. Those points are fixed relative to Earth but are moving relative to the muon. Clouds and other objects are also contracted along the direction of motion as seen from muon's rest frame.

Thus, two observers measure different distances along their direction of relative motion, depending on which one is measuring distances between objects at rest.

But what about distances measured in a direction perpendicular to the relative motion? Imagine two observers moving along their *x*-axes and passing each other while holding meter sticks vertically in the *y*-direction. **Figure 5.10** shows two meter sticks M and M' that are at rest in the reference frames of two boys S and S', respectively. A small paintbrush is attached to the top (the 100-cm mark) of stick M'. Suppose that S' is moving to the right at a very high speed *v* relative to S, and the sticks are oriented so that they are perpendicular, or transverse, to their relative velocity vector. The sticks are held so that as they pass each other, their lower ends (the 0-cm marks) coincide. Assume that when S looks at his stick M afterwards, he finds a line painted on it, just below the top of the stick. Because the brush is attached to the top of the other boy's stick M', S can only conclude that stick M' is less than 1.0 m long.

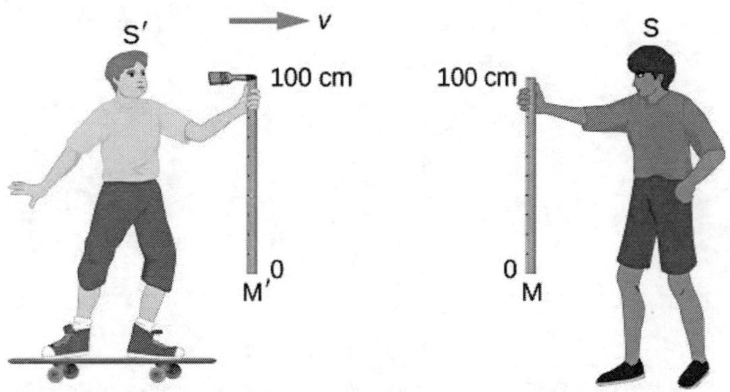

Figure 5.10 Meter sticks M and M' are stationary in the reference frames of observers S and S', respectively. As the sticks pass, a small brush attached to the 100-cm mark of M' paints a line on M.

Now when the boys approach each other, S', like S, sees a meter stick moving toward him with speed *v*. Because their situations are symmetric, each boy must make the same measurement of the stick in the other frame. So, if S measures stick M' to be less than 1.0 m long, S' must measure stick M to be also less than 1.0 m long, and S' must see his paintbrush pass over the top of stick M and not paint a line on it. In other words, after the same event, one boy sees a painted line on a stick, while the other does not see such a line on that same stick!

Einstein's first postulate requires that the laws of physics (as, for example, applied to painting) predict that S and S', who are both in inertial frames, make the same observations; that is, S and S' must either both see a line painted on stick M, or both not see that line. We are therefore forced to conclude our original assumption that S saw a line painted below the top of his stick was wrong! Instead, S finds the line painted right at the 100-cm mark on M. Then both boys will agree that a line is painted on M, and they will also agree that both sticks are exactly 1 m long. We conclude then that measurements of a transverse *length must be the same in different inertial frames*.

Example 5.5

Calculating Length Contraction

Suppose an astronaut, such as the twin in the twin paradox discussion, travels so fast that $\gamma = 30.00$. (a) The astronaut travels from Earth to the nearest star system, Alpha Centauri, 4.300 light years (ly) away as measured by an earthbound observer. How far apart are Earth and Alpha Centauri as measured by the astronaut? (b) In terms of *c*, what is the astronaut's velocity relative to Earth? You may neglect the motion of Earth relative to the sun (**Figure 5.11**).

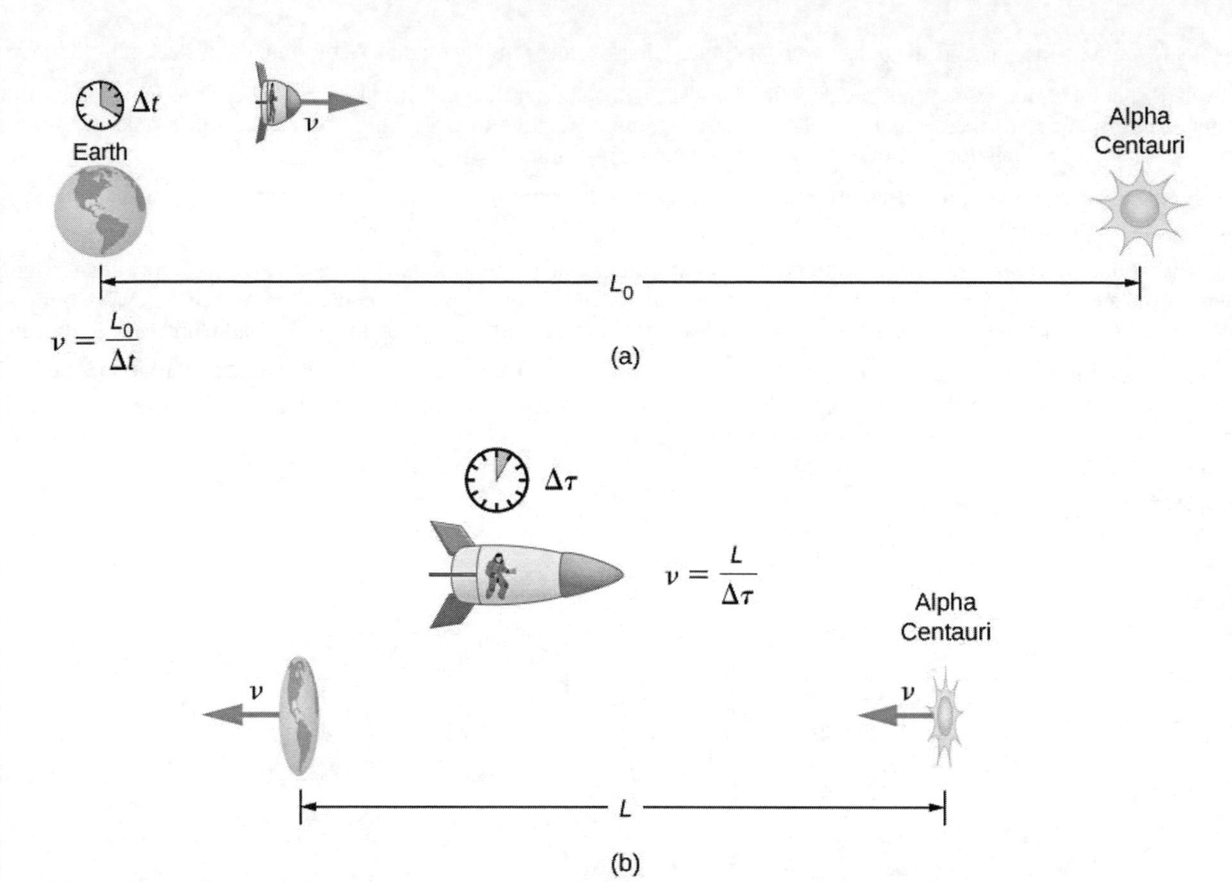

Figure 5.11 (a) The earthbound observer measures the proper distance between Earth and Alpha Centauri. (b) The astronaut observes a length contraction because Earth and Alpha Centauri move relative to her ship. She can travel this shorter distance in a smaller time (her proper time) without exceeding the speed of light.

Strategy

First, note that a light year (ly) is a convenient unit of distance on an astronomical scale—it is the distance light travels in a year. For part (a), the 4.300-ly distance between Alpha Centauri and Earth is the proper distance L_0, because it is measured by an earthbound observer to whom both stars are (approximately) stationary. To the astronaut, Earth and Alpha Centauri are moving past at the same velocity, so the distance between them is the contracted length *L*. In part (b), we are given γ, so we can find *v* by rearranging the definition of γ to express *v* in terms of *c*.

Solution for (a)

For part (a):

a. Identify the knowns: $L_0 = 4.300\text{ ly}; \gamma = 30.00.$

b. Identify the unknown: *L*.

c. Express the answer as an equation: $L = \frac{L_0}{\gamma}.$

d. Do the calculation:

$$\begin{aligned} L &= \frac{L_0}{\gamma} \\ &= \frac{4.300\text{ ly}}{30.00} \\ &= 0.1433\text{ ly}. \end{aligned}$$

Solution for (b)

For part (b):

a. Identify the known: $\gamma = 30.00$.

b. Identify the unknown: v in terms of c.

c. Express the answer as an equation. Start with:

$$\gamma = \frac{1}{\sqrt{1 - \frac{v^2}{c^2}}}.$$

Then solve for the unknown v/c by first squaring both sides and then rearranging:

$$\begin{aligned} \gamma^2 &= \frac{1}{1 - \frac{v^2}{c^2}} \\ \frac{v^2}{c^2} &= 1 - \frac{1}{\gamma^2} \\ \frac{v}{c} &= \sqrt{1 - \frac{1}{\gamma^2}}. \end{aligned}$$

d. Do the calculation:

$$\begin{aligned} \frac{v}{c} &= \sqrt{1 - \frac{1}{\gamma^2}} \\ &= \sqrt{1 - \frac{1}{(30.00)^2}} \\ &= 0.99944 \end{aligned}$$

or

$$v = 0.9994\,c.$$

Significance

Remember not to round off calculations until the final answer, or you could get erroneous results. This is especially true for special relativity calculations, where the differences might only be revealed after several decimal places. The relativistic effect is large here $(\gamma = 30.00)$, and we see that v is approaching (not equaling) the speed of light. Because the distance as measured by the astronaut is so much smaller, the astronaut can travel it in much less time in her frame.

People traveling at extremely high velocities could cover very large distances (thousands or even millions of light years) and age only a few years on the way. However, like emigrants in past centuries who left their home, these people would leave the Earth they know forever. Even if they returned, thousands to millions of years would have passed on Earth, obliterating most of what now exists. There is also a more serious practical obstacle to traveling at such velocities; immensely greater energies would be needed to achieve such high velocities than classical physics predicts can be attained. This will be discussed later in the chapter.

Why don't we notice length contraction in everyday life? The distance to the grocery store does not seem to depend on whether we are moving or not. Examining the equation $L = L_0\sqrt{1 - \frac{v^2}{c^2}}$, we see that at low velocities $(v<<c)$, the lengths are nearly equal, which is the classical expectation. But length contraction is real, if not commonly experienced. For example, a charged particle such as an electron traveling at relativistic velocity has electric field lines that are compressed along the direction of motion as seen by a stationary observer (**Figure 5.12**). As the electron passes a detector, such as a coil of wire, its field interacts much more briefly, an effect observed at particle accelerators such as the 3-km-long Stanford Linear Accelerator (SLAC). In fact, to an electron traveling down the beam pipe at SLAC, the accelerator and Earth are all moving by and are length contracted. The relativistic effect is so great that the accelerator is only 0.5 m long to the electron. It is actually easier to get the electron beam down the pipe, because the beam does not have to be as precisely aimed to get

down a short pipe as it would to get down a pipe 3 km long. This, again, is an experimental verification of the special theory of relativity.

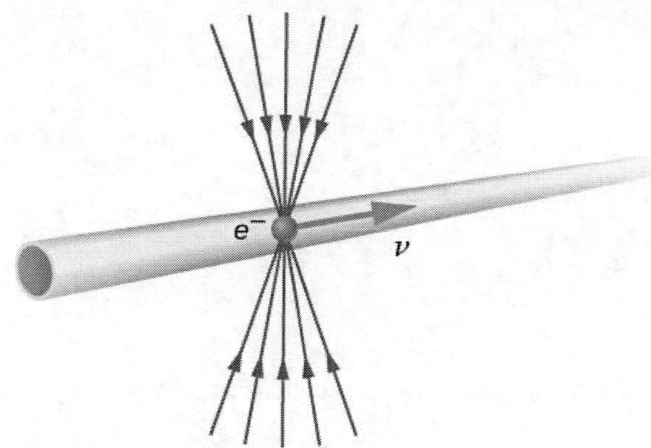

Figure 5.12 The electric field lines of a high-velocity charged particle are compressed along the direction of motion by length contraction, producing an observably different signal as the particle goes through a coil.

5.4 **Check Your Understanding** A particle is traveling through Earth's atmosphere at a speed of $0.750c$. To an earthbound observer, the distance it travels is 2.50 km. How far does the particle travel as viewed from the particle's reference frame?

5.5 | The Lorentz Transformation

Learning Objectives

- Describe the Galilean transformation of classical mechanics, relating the position, time, velocities, and accelerations measured in different inertial frames
- Derive the corresponding Lorentz transformation equations, which, in contrast to the Galilean transformation, are consistent with special relativity
- Explain the Lorentz transformation and many of the features of relativity in terms of four-dimensional space-time

We have used the postulates of relativity to examine, in particular examples, how observers in different frames of reference measure different values for lengths and the time intervals. We can gain further insight into how the postulates of relativity change the Newtonian view of time and space by examining the transformation equations that give the space and time coordinates of events in one inertial reference frame in terms of those in another. We first examine how position and time coordinates transform between inertial frames according to the view in Newtonian physics. Then we examine how this has to be changed to agree with the postulates of relativity. Finally, we examine the resulting Lorentz transformation equations and some of their consequences in terms of four-dimensional space-time diagrams, to support the view that the consequences of special relativity result from the properties of time and space itself, rather than electromagnetism.

The Galilean Transformation Equations

An **event** is specified by its location and time (x, y, z, t) relative to one particular inertial frame of reference S. As an example, (x, y, z, t) could denote the position of a particle at time t, and we could be looking at these positions for many different times to follow the motion of the particle. Suppose a second frame of reference S' moves with velocity v with respect to the first. For simplicity, assume this relative velocity is along the x-axis. The relation between the time and coordinates in the two frames of reference is then

$$x = x' + vt, \quad y = y', \quad z = z'.$$

Implicit in these equations is the assumption that time measurements made by observers in both S and S' are the same. That is,

$$t = t'.$$

These four equations are known collectively as the **Galilean transformation**.

We can obtain the Galilean velocity and acceleration transformation equations by differentiating these equations with respect to time. We use *u* for the velocity of a particle throughout this chapter to distinguish it from *v*, the relative velocity of two reference frames. Note that, for the Galilean transformation, the increment of time used in differentiating to calculate the particle velocity is the same in both frames, $dt = dt'$. Differentiation yields

$$u_x = u'_x + v, \quad u_y = u'_y, \quad u_z = u'_z$$

and

$$a_x = a'_x, \quad a_y = a'_y, \quad a_z = a'_z.$$

We denote the velocity of the particle by *u* rather than *v* to avoid confusion with the velocity *v* of one frame of reference with respect to the other. Velocities in each frame differ by the velocity that one frame has as seen from the other frame. Observers in both frames of reference measure the same value of the acceleration. Because the mass is unchanged by the transformation, and distances between points are uncharged, observers in both frames see the same forces $F = ma$ acting between objects and the same form of Newton's second and third laws in all inertial frames. The laws of mechanics are consistent with the first postulate of relativity.

The Lorentz Transformation Equations

The Galilean transformation nevertheless violates Einstein's postulates, because the velocity equations state that a pulse of light moving with speed *c* along the *x*-axis would travel at speed $c - v$ in the other inertial frame. Specifically, the spherical pulse has radius $r = ct$ at time *t* in the unprimed frame, and also has radius $r' = ct'$ at time t' in the primed frame. Expressing these relations in Cartesian coordinates gives

$$\begin{aligned} x^2 + y^2 + z^2 - c^2t^2 &= 0 \\ x'^2 + y'^2 + z'^2 - c^2t'^2 &= 0. \end{aligned}$$

The left-hand sides of the two expressions can be set equal because both are zero. Because $y = y'$ and $z = z'$, we obtain

$$x^2 - c^2t^2 = x'^2 - c^2t'^2. \qquad (5.5)$$

This cannot be satisfied for nonzero relative velocity *v* of the two frames if we assume the Galilean transformation results in $t = t'$ with $x = x' + vt'$.

To find the correct set of transformation equations, assume the two coordinate systems *S* and S' in **Figure 5.13**. First suppose that an event occurs at $(x',\ 0,\ 0,\ t')$ in S' and at $(x,\ 0,\ 0,\ t)$ in *S*, as depicted in the figure.

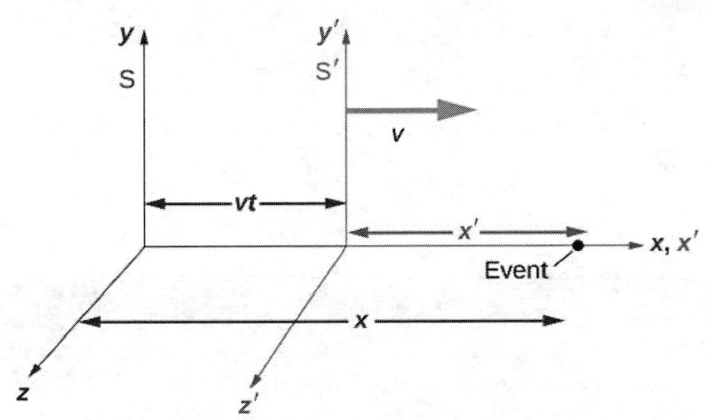

Figure 5.13 An event occurs at (*x*, 0, 0, *t*) in *S* and at $(x',\ 0,\ 0,\ t')$ in S'. The Lorentz transformation equations relate events in the two systems.

Suppose that at the instant that the origins of the coordinate systems in *S* and S' coincide, a flash bulb emits a spherically spreading pulse of light starting from the origin. At time *t*, an observer in *S* finds the origin of S' to be at $x = vt$. With the help of a friend in *S*, the S' observer also measures the distance from the event to the origin of S' and finds it to be

$x'\sqrt{1 - v^2/c^2}$. This follows because we have already shown the postulates of relativity to imply length contraction. Thus the position of the event in S is

$$x = vt + x'\sqrt{1 - v^2/c^2}$$

and

$$x' = \frac{x - vt}{\sqrt{1 - v^2/c^2}}.$$

The postulates of relativity imply that the equation relating distance and time of the spherical wave front:

$$x^2 + y^2 + z^2 - c^2t^2 = 0$$

must apply both in terms of primed and unprimed coordinates, which was shown above to lead to **Equation 5.5**:

$$x^2 - c^2t^2 = x'^2 - c^2t'^2.$$

We combine this with the equation relating x and x' to obtain the relation between t and t' :

$$t' = \frac{t - vx/c^2}{\sqrt{1 - v^2/c^2}}.$$

The equations relating the time and position of the events as seen in S are then

$$\begin{aligned} t &= \frac{t' + vx'/c^2}{\sqrt{1 - v^2/c^2}} \\ x &= \frac{x' + vt'}{\sqrt{1 - v^2/c^2}} \\ y &= y' \\ z &= z'. \end{aligned}$$

This set of equations, relating the position and time in the two inertial frames, is known as the **Lorentz transformation**. They are named in honor of H.A. Lorentz (1853–1928), who first proposed them. Interestingly, he justified the transformation on what was eventually discovered to be a fallacious hypothesis. The correct theoretical basis is Einstein's special theory of relativity.

The reverse transformation expresses the variables in S in terms of those in S'. Simply interchanging the primed and unprimed variables and substituting gives:

$$\begin{aligned} t' &= \frac{t - vx/c^2}{\sqrt{1 - v^2/c^2}} \\ x' &= \frac{x - vt}{\sqrt{1 - v^2/c^2}} \\ y' &= y \\ z' &= z. \end{aligned}$$

Example 5.6

Using the Lorentz Transformation for Time

Spacecraft S' is on its way to Alpha Centauri when Spacecraft S passes it at relative speed $c/2$. The captain of S' sends a radio signal that lasts 1.2 s according to that ship's clock. Use the Lorentz transformation to find the time interval of the signal measured by the communications officer of spaceship S.

Solution

a. Identify the known: $\Delta t' = t_2{}' - t_1{}' = 1.2\text{ s}$; $\Delta x' = x'_2 - x'_1 = 0$.

b. Identify the unknown: $\Delta t = t_2 - t_1$.

c. Express the answer as an equation. The time signal starts as (x', t_1') and stops at (x', t_2'). Note that the x' coordinate of both events is the same because the clock is at rest in S'. Write the first Lorentz transformation equation in terms of $\Delta t = t_2 - t_1$, $\Delta x = x_2 - x_1$, and similarly for the primed coordinates, as:

$$\Delta t = \frac{\Delta t' + v\Delta x'/c^2}{\sqrt{1 - \frac{v^2}{c^2}}}.$$

Because the position of the clock in S' is fixed, $\Delta x' = 0$, and the time interval Δt becomes:

$$\Delta t = \frac{\Delta t'}{\sqrt{1 - \frac{v^2}{c^2}}}.$$

d. Do the calculation.
With $\Delta t' = 1.2\text{ s}$ this gives:

$$\Delta t = \frac{1.2\text{ s}}{\sqrt{1 - \left(\frac{1}{2}\right)^2}} = 1.6\text{ s}.$$

Note that the Lorentz transformation reproduces the time dilation equation.

Example 5.7

Using the Lorentz Transformation for Length

A surveyor measures a street to be $L = 100\text{ m}$ long in Earth frame S. Use the Lorentz transformation to obtain an expression for its length measured from a spaceship S', moving by at speed $0.20c$, assuming the x coordinates of the two frames coincide at time $t = 0$.

Solution

a. Identify the known: $L = 100\text{ m}$; $v = 0.20c$; $\Delta\tau = 0$.

b. Identify the unknown: L'.

c. Express the answer as an equation. The surveyor in frame S has measured the two ends of the stick simultaneously, and found them at rest at x_2 and x_1 a distance $L = x_2 - x_1 = 100\text{ m}$ apart. The spaceship crew measures the simultaneous location of the ends of the sticks in their frame. To relate the lengths recorded by observers in S' and S, respectively, write the second of the four Lorentz transformation equations as:

$$\begin{aligned} x'_2 - x'_1 &= \frac{x_2 - vt}{\sqrt{1 - v^2/c^2}} - \frac{x_1 - vt}{\sqrt{1 - v^2/c^2}} \\ &= \frac{x_2 - x_1}{\sqrt{1 - v^2/c^2}} = \frac{L}{\sqrt{1 - v^2/c^2}}. \end{aligned}$$

d. Do the calculation. Because $x'_2 - x'_1 = 100\text{ m}$, the length of the moving stick is equal to:

$$\begin{aligned} L' &= (100\text{ m})\sqrt{1 - v^2/c^2} \\ &= (100\text{ m})\sqrt{1 - (0.20)^2} \\ &= 98.0\text{ m}. \end{aligned}$$

Note that the Lorentz transformation gave the length contraction equation for the street.

Example 5.8

Lorentz Transformation and Simultaneity

The observer shown in Figure 5.14 standing by the railroad tracks sees the two bulbs flash simultaneously at both ends of the 26 m long passenger car when the middle of the car passes him at a speed of $c/2$. Find the separation in time between when the bulbs flashed as seen by the train passenger seated in the middle of the car.

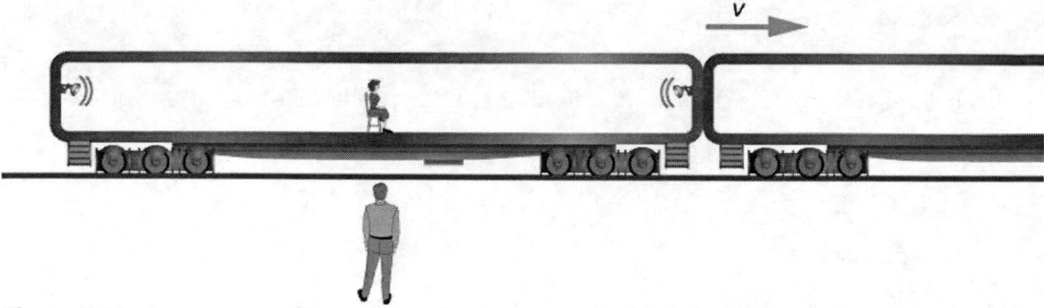

Figure 5.14 An person watching a train go by observes two bulbs flash simultaneously at opposite ends of a passenger car. There is another passenger inside of the car observing the same flashes but from a different perspective.

Solution

a. Identify the known: $\Delta t = 0$.

   Note that the spatial separation of the two events is between the two lamps, not the distance of the lamp to the passenger.

b. Identify the unknown: $\Delta t' = t'_2 - t'_1$.

   Again, note that the time interval is between the flashes of the lamps, not between arrival times for reaching the passenger.

c. Express the answer as an equation:

$$\Delta t = \frac{\Delta t' + v\Delta x'/c^2}{\sqrt{1 - v^2/c^2}}.$$

d. Do the calculation:

$$\begin{aligned} 0 &= \frac{\Delta t' + \frac{c}{2}(26\text{ m})/c^2}{\sqrt{1 - v^2/c^2}} \\ \Delta t' &= -\frac{26\text{ m/s}}{2c} = -\frac{26\text{ m/s}}{2(3.00\times10^8\text{ m/s})} \\ \Delta t' &= -4.33\times10^{-8}\text{ s}. \end{aligned}$$

Significance

The sign indicates that the event with the larger x_2', namely, the flash from the right, is seen to occur first in the S' frame, as found earlier for this example, so that $t_2 < t_1$.

Space-time

Relativistic phenomena can be analyzed in terms of events in a four-dimensional space-time. When phenomena such as the twin paradox, time dilation, length contraction, and the dependence of simultaneity on relative motion are viewed in this way, they are seen to be characteristic of the nature of space and time, rather than specific aspects of electromagnetism.

In three-dimensional space, positions are specified by three coordinates on a set of Cartesian axes, and the displacement of one point from another is given by:

$$(\Delta x,\ \Delta y,\ \Delta z) = (x_2 - x_1,\ y_2 - y_1,\ z_2 - z_1).$$

The distance Δr between the points is

$$\Delta r^2 = (\Delta x)^2 + (\Delta y)^2 + (\Delta z)^2.$$

The distance Δr is invariant under a rotation of axes. If a new set of Cartesian axes rotated around the origin relative to the original axes are used, each point in space will have new coordinates in terms of the new axes, but the distance $\Delta r'$ given by

$$\Delta r'^2 = (\Delta x')^2 + (\Delta y')^2 + (\Delta z')^2.$$

That has the same value that Δr^2 had. Something similar happens with the Lorentz transformation in space-time.

Define the separation between two events, each given by a set of *x, y, z*¸ and *ct* along a four-dimensional Cartesian system of axes in space-time, as

$$(\Delta x,\ \Delta y,\ \Delta z,\ c\Delta t) = (x_2 - x_1,\ y_2 - y_1,\ z_2 - z_1,\ c(t_2 - t_1)).$$

Also define the space-time interval Δs between the two events as

$$\Delta s^2 = (\Delta x)^2 + (\Delta y)^2 + (\Delta z)^2 - (c\Delta t)^2.$$

If the two events have the same value of *ct* in the frame of reference considered, Δs would correspond to the distance Δr between points in space.

The path of a particle through space-time consists of the events (*x, y, z*¸ *ct*) specifying a location at each time of its motion. The path through space-time is called the **world line** of the particle. The world line of a particle that remains at rest at the same location is a straight line that is parallel to the time axis. If the particle moves at constant velocity parallel to the *x*-axis, its world line would be a sloped line $x = vt,$ corresponding to a simple displacement vs. time graph. If the particle accelerates, its world line is curved. The increment of *s* along the world line of the particle is given in differential form as

$$ds^2 = (dx)^2 + (dy)^2 + (dz)^2 - c^2 (dt)^2.$$

Just as the distance Δr is invariant under rotation of the space axes, the space-time interval:

$$\Delta s^2 = (\Delta x)^2 + (\Delta y)^2 + (\Delta z)^2 - (c\Delta t)^2.$$

is invariant under the Lorentz transformation. This follows from the postulates of relativity, and can be seen also by substitution of the previous Lorentz transformation equations into the expression for the space-time interval:

$$\begin{aligned}\Delta s^2 &= (\Delta x)^2 + (\Delta y)^2 + (\Delta z)^2 - (c\Delta t)^2 \\ &= \left(\frac{\Delta x' + v\Delta t'}{\sqrt{1 - v^2/c^2}}\right)^2 + (\Delta y')^2 + (\Delta z')^2 - \left(c\frac{\Delta t' + \frac{v\Delta x'}{c^2}}{\sqrt{1 - v^2/c^2}}\right)^2 \\ &= (\Delta x')^2 + (\Delta y')^2 + (\Delta z')^2 - (c\Delta t')^2 \\ &= \Delta s'^2.\end{aligned}$$

In addition, the Lorentz transformation changes the coordinates of an event in time and space similarly to how a three-dimensional rotation changes old coordinates into new coordinates:

Lorentz transformation	**Axis – rotation around *z*-axis**
(*x, t* coordinates):	(*x, y* coordinates):
$x' = (\gamma)x + (-\beta\gamma)ct$	$x' = (\cos\theta)x + (\sin\theta)y$
$ct' = (-\beta\gamma)x + (\gamma)ct$	$y' = (-\sin\theta)x + (\cos\theta)y$

where $\gamma = \dfrac{1}{\sqrt{1 - \beta^2}};\ \ \beta = v/c.$

Lorentz transformations can be regarded as generalizations of spatial rotations to space-time. However, there are some differences between a three-dimensional axis rotation and a Lorentz transformation involving the time axis, because of differences in how the metric, or rule for measuring the displacements Δr and Δs, differ. Although Δr is invariant under spatial rotations and Δs is invariant also under Lorentz transformation, the Lorentz transformation involving the time axis does not preserve some features, such as the axes remaining perpendicular or the length scale along each axis remaining the same.

Note that the quantity Δs^2 can have either sign, depending on the coordinates of the space-time events involved. For pairs of events that give it a negative sign, it is useful to define $\Delta \tau^2$ as $-\Delta s^2$. The significance of $\Delta \tau$ as just defined follows by noting that in a frame of reference where the two events occur at the same location, we have $\Delta x = \Delta y = \Delta z = 0$ and therefore (from the equation for $\Delta s^2 = -\Delta \tau^2$):

$$\Delta \tau^2 = -\Delta s^2 = (\Delta t)^2.$$

Therefore $\Delta \tau$ is the time interval Δt in the frame of reference where both events occur at the same location. It is the same interval of proper time discussed earlier. It also follows from the relation between Δs and that $\Delta \tau$ that because Δs is Lorentz invariant, the proper time is also Lorentz invariant. All observers in all inertial frames agree on the proper time intervals between the same two events.

5.5 Check Your Understanding Show that if a time increment dt elapses for an observer who sees the particle moving with velocity v, it corresponds to a proper time particle increment for the particle of $d\tau = \gamma dt$.

The light cone

We can deal with the difficulty of visualizing and sketching graphs in four dimensions by imagining the three spatial coordinates to be represented collectively by a horizontal axis, and the vertical axis to be the *ct*-axis. Starting with a particular event in space-time as the origin of the space-time graph shown, the world line of a particle that remains at rest at the initial location of the event at the origin then is the time axis. Any plane through the time axis parallel to the spatial axes contains all the events that are simultaneous with each other and with the intersection of the plane and the time axis, as seen in the rest frame of the event at the origin.

It is useful to picture a light cone on the graph, formed by the world lines of all light beams passing through the origin event *A*, as shown in **Figure 5.15**. The light cone, according to the postulates of relativity, has sides at an angle of $45°$ if the time axis is measured in units of *ct*, and, according to the postulates of relativity, the light cone remains the same in all inertial frames. Because the event *A* is arbitrary, every point in the space-time diagram has a light cone associated with it.

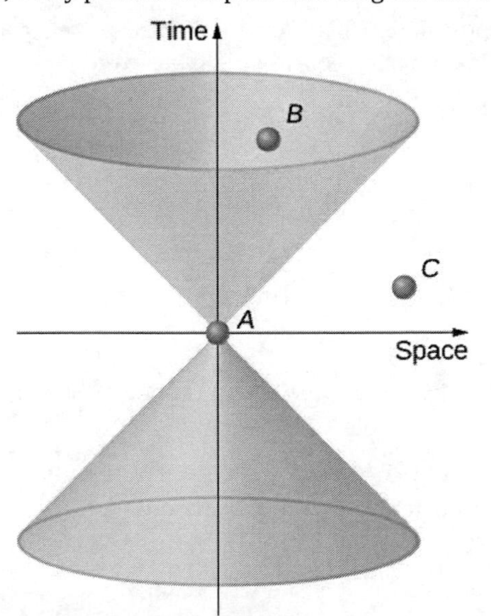

Figure 5.15 The light cone consists of all the world lines followed by light from the event *A* at the vertex of the cone.

Consider now the world line of a particle through space-time. Any world line outside of the cone, such as one passing from *A* through *C*, would involve speeds greater than *c*, and would therefore not be possible. Events such as *C* that lie outside the light cone are said to have a space-like separation from event *A*. They are characterized by:

$$\Delta s^2_{AC} = (x_A - x_B)^2 + (x_A - x_B)^2 + (x_A - x_B)^2 - (c\Delta t)^2 > 0.$$

An event like *B* that lies in the upper cone is reachable without exceeding the speed of light in vacuum, and is characterized by

$$\Delta s^2_{AB} = (x_A - x_B)^2 + (x_A - x_B)^2 + (x_A - x_B)^2 - (c\Delta t)^2 < 0.$$

The event is said to have a time-like separation from *A*. Time-like events that fall into the upper half of the light cone occur at greater values of *t* than the time of the event *A* at the vertex and are in the future relative to *A*. Events that have time-like separation from A and fall in the lower half of the light cone are in the past, and can affect the event at the origin. The region outside the light cone is labeled as neither past nor future, but rather as "elsewhere."

For any event that has a space-like separation from the event at the origin, it is possible to choose a time axis that will make the two events occur at the same time, so that the two events are simultaneous in some frame of reference. Therefore, which of the events with space-like separation comes before the other in time also depends on the frame of reference of the observer. Since space-like separations can be traversed only by exceeding the speed of light; this violation of which event can cause the other provides another argument for why particles cannot travel faster than the speed of light, as well as potential material for science fiction about time travel. Similarly for any event with time-like separation from the event at the origin, a frame of reference can be found that will make the events occur at the same location. Because the relations

$$\Delta s^2_{AC} = (x_A - x_B)^2 + (x_A - x_B)^2 + (x_A - x_B)^2 - (c\Delta t)^2 > 0$$

and

$$\Delta s^2_{AB} = (x_A - x_B)^2 + (x_A - x_B)^2 + (x_A - x_B)^2 - (c\Delta t)^2 < 0.$$

are Lorentz invariant, whether two events are time-like and can be made to occur at the same place or space-like and can be made to occur at the same time is the same for all observers. All observers in different inertial frames of reference agree on whether two events have a time-like or space-like separation.

The twin paradox seen in space-time

The twin paradox discussed earlier involves an astronaut twin traveling at near light speed to a distant star system, and returning to Earth. Because of time dilation, the space twin is predicted to age much less than the earthbound twin. This seems paradoxical because we might have expected at first glance for the relative motion to be symmetrical and naively thought it possible to also argue that the earthbound twin should age less.

To analyze this in terms of a space-time diagram, assume that the origin of the axes used is fixed in Earth. The world line of the earthbound twin is then along the time axis.

The world line of the astronaut twin, who travels to the distant star and then returns, must deviate from a straight line path in order to allow a return trip. As seen in **Figure 5.16**, the circumstances of the two twins are not at all symmetrical. Their paths in space-time are of manifestly different length. Specifically, the world line of the earthbound twin has length $2c\Delta t$, which then gives the proper time that elapses for the earthbound twin as $2\Delta t$. The distance to the distant star system is $\Delta x = v\Delta t$. The proper time that elapses for the space twin is $2\Delta\tau$ where

$$c^2\Delta\tau^2 = -\Delta s^2 = (c\Delta t)^2 - (\Delta x)^2.$$

This is considerably shorter than the proper time for the earthbound twin by the ratio

$$\begin{aligned}\frac{c\Delta\tau}{c\Delta t} &= \sqrt{\frac{(c\Delta t)^2 - (\Delta x)^2}{(c\Delta t)^2}} = \sqrt{\frac{(c\Delta t)^2 - (v\Delta t)^2}{(c\Delta t)^2}} \\ &= \sqrt{1 - \frac{v^2}{c^2}} = \frac{1}{\gamma}.\end{aligned}$$

consistent with the time dilation formula. The twin paradox is therefore seen to be no paradox at all. The situation of the two twins is not symmetrical in the space-time diagram. The only surprise is perhaps that the seemingly longer path on the space-time diagram corresponds to the smaller proper time interval, because of how $\Delta\tau$ and Δs depend on Δx and Δt.

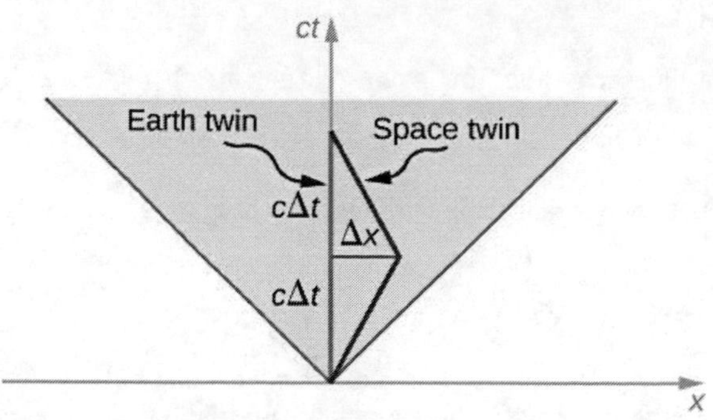

Figure 5.16 The space twin and the earthbound twin, in the twin paradox example, follow world lines of different length through space-time.

Lorentz transformations in space-time

We have already noted how the Lorentz transformation leaves

$$\Delta s^2 = (\Delta x)^2 + (\Delta y)^2 + (\Delta z)^2 - (c\Delta t)^2$$

unchanged and corresponds to a rotation of axes in the four-dimensional space-time. If the S and S' frames are in relative motion along their shared x-direction the space and time axes of S' are rotated by an angle α as seen from S, in the way shown in shown in **Figure 5.17**, where:

$$\tan\alpha = \frac{v}{c} = \beta.$$

This differs from a rotation in the usual three-dimension sense, insofar as the two space-time axes rotate toward each other symmetrically in a scissors-like way, as shown. The rotation of the time and space axes are both through the same angle. The mesh of dashed lines parallel to the two axes show how coordinates of an event would be read along the primed axes. This would be done by following a line parallel to the x' and one parallel to the t' -axis, as shown by the dashed lines. The length scale of both axes are changed by:

$$ct' = ct\sqrt{\frac{1+\beta^2}{1-\beta^2}}; \qquad x' = x\sqrt{\frac{1+\beta^2}{1-\beta^2}}.$$

The line labeled "$v = c$" at $45°$ to the x-axis corresponds to the edge of the light cone, and is unaffected by the Lorentz transformation, in accordance with the second postulate of relativity. The "$v = c$" line, and the light cone it represents, are the same for both the S and S' frame of reference.

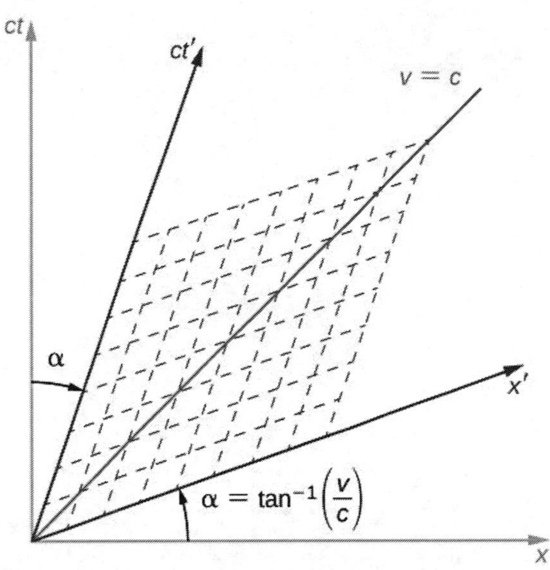

Figure 5.17 The Lorentz transformation results in new space and time axes rotated in a scissors-like way with respect to the original axes.

Simultaneity

Simultaneity of events at separated locations depends on the frame of reference used to describe them, as given by the scissors-like "rotation" to new time and space coordinates as described. If two events have the same t values in the unprimed frame of reference, they need not have the same values measured along the ct'-axis, and would then not be simultaneous in the primed frame.

As a specific example, consider the near-light-speed train in which flash lamps at the two ends of the car have flashed simultaneously in the frame of reference of an observer on the ground. The space-time graph is shown **Figure 5.18**. The flashes of the two lamps are represented by the dots labeled "Left flash lamp" and "Right flash lamp" that lie on the light cone in the past. The world line of both pulses travel along the edge of the light cone to arrive at the observer on the ground simultaneously. Their arrival is the event at the origin. They therefore had to be emitted simultaneously in the unprimed frame, as represented by the point labeled as t(both). But time is measured along the ct'-axis in the frame of reference of the observer seated in the middle of the train car. So in her frame of reference, the emission event of the bulbs labeled as t' (left) and t' (right) were not simultaneous.

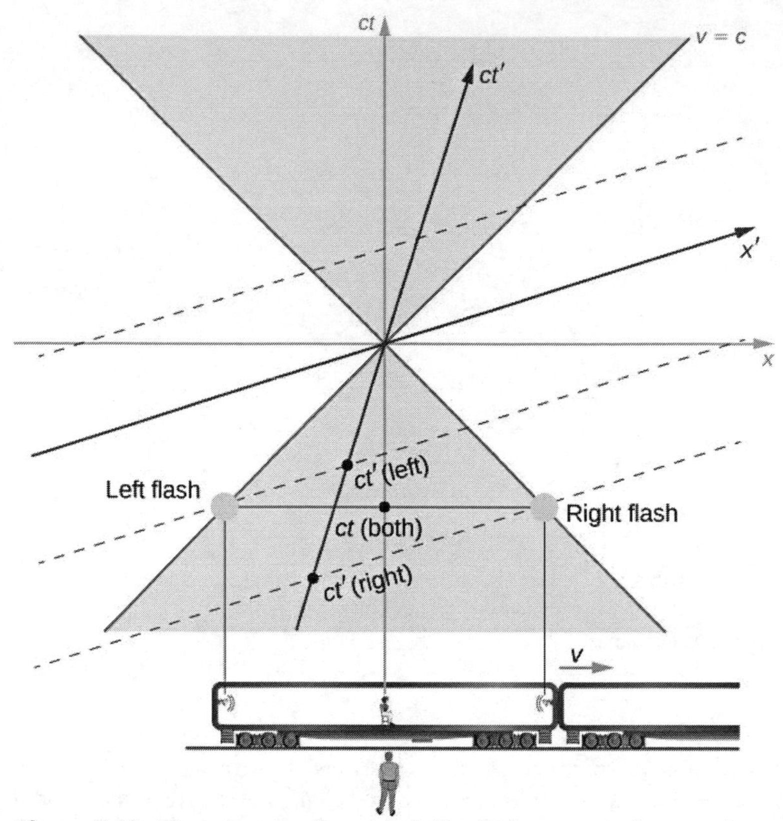

Figure 5.18 The train example revisited. The flashes occur at the same time t(both) along the time axis of the ground observer, but at different times, along the t' time axis of the passenger.

In terms of the space-time diagram, the two observers are merely using different time axes for the same events because they are in different inertial frames, and the conclusions of both observers are equally valid. As the analysis in terms of the space-time diagrams further suggests, the property of how simultaneity of events depends on the frame of reference results from the properties of space and time itself, rather than from anything specifically about electromagnetism.

5.6 | Relativistic Velocity Transformation

Learning Objectives

By the end of this section, you will be able to:

- Derive the equations consistent with special relativity for transforming velocities in one inertial frame of reference into another.
- Apply the velocity transformation equations to objects moving at relativistic speeds.
- Examine how the combined velocities predicted by the relativistic transformation equations compare with those expected classically.

Remaining in place in a kayak in a fast-moving river takes effort. The river current pulls the kayak along. Trying to paddle against the flow can move the kayak upstream relative to the water, but that only accounts for part of its velocity relative to the shore. The kayak's motion is an example of how velocities in Newtonian mechanics combine by vector addition. The kayak's velocity is the vector sum of its velocity relative to the water and the water's velocity relative to the riverbank. However, the relativistic addition of velocities is quite different.

Velocity Transformations

Imagine a car traveling at night along a straight road, as in **Figure 5.19**. The driver sees the light leaving the headlights at speed c within the car's frame of reference. If the Galilean transformation applied to light, then the light from the car's headlights would approach the pedestrian at a speed $u = v + c,$ contrary to Einstein's postulates.

Figure 5.19 According to experimental results and the second postulate of relativity, light from the car's headlights moves away from the car at speed *c* and toward the observer on the sidewalk at speed *c*.

Both the distance traveled and the time of travel are different in the two frames of reference, and they must differ in a way that makes the speed of light the same in all inertial frames. The correct rules for transforming velocities from one frame to another can be obtained from the Lorentz transformation equations.

Relativistic Transformation of Velocity

Suppose an object *P* is moving at constant velocity $\mathbf{u} = \left(u'_x,\, u'_y,\, u'_z\right)$ as measured in the S' frame. The S' frame is moving along its x'-axis at velocity *v*. In an increment of time dt', the particle is displaced by dx' along the x'-axis. Applying the Lorentz transformation equations gives the corresponding increments of time and displacement in the unprimed axes:

$$\begin{aligned} dt &= \gamma\left(dt' + vdx'/c^2\right) \\ dx &= \gamma(dx' + vdt') \\ dy &= dy' \\ dz &= dz'. \end{aligned}$$

The velocity components of the particle seen in the unprimed coordinate system are then

$$\begin{aligned} \frac{dx}{dt} &= \frac{\gamma(dx' + vdt')}{\gamma\left(dt' + vdx'/c^2\right)} = \frac{\frac{dx'}{dt'} + v}{1 + \frac{v}{c^2}\frac{dx'}{dt'}} \\ \frac{dy}{dt} &= \frac{dy'}{\gamma\left(dt' + vdx'/c^2\right)} = \frac{\frac{dy'}{dt'}}{\gamma\left(1 + \frac{v}{c^2}\frac{dx'}{dt'}\right)} \\ \frac{dz}{dt} &= \frac{dz'}{\gamma\left(dt' + vdx'/c^2\right)} = \frac{\frac{dz'}{dt'}}{\gamma\left(1 + \frac{v}{c^2}\frac{dx'}{dt'}\right)}. \end{aligned}$$

We thus obtain the equations for the velocity components of the object as seen in frame *S*:

$$u_x = \left(\frac{u'_x + v}{1 + vu'_x/c^2}\right),\quad u_y = \left(\frac{u'_y/\gamma}{1 + vu'_x/c^2}\right),\quad u_z = \left(\frac{u'_z/\gamma}{1 + vu'_x/c^2}\right).$$

Compare this with how the Galilean transformation of classical mechanics says the velocities transform, by adding simply as vectors:

$$u_x = u'_x + u, \quad u_y = u'_y, \quad u_z = u'_z.$$

When the relative velocity of the frames is much smaller than the speed of light, that is, when $v \ll c$, the special relativity velocity addition law reduces to the Galilean velocity law. When the speed v of S' relative to S is comparable to the speed of light, the **relativistic velocity addition** law gives a much smaller result than the **classical (Galilean) velocity addition** does.

Example 5.9

Velocity Transformation Equations for Light

Suppose a spaceship heading directly toward Earth at half the speed of light sends a signal to us on a laser-produced beam of light (**Figure 5.20**). Given that the light leaves the ship at speed c as observed from the ship, calculate the speed at which it approaches Earth.

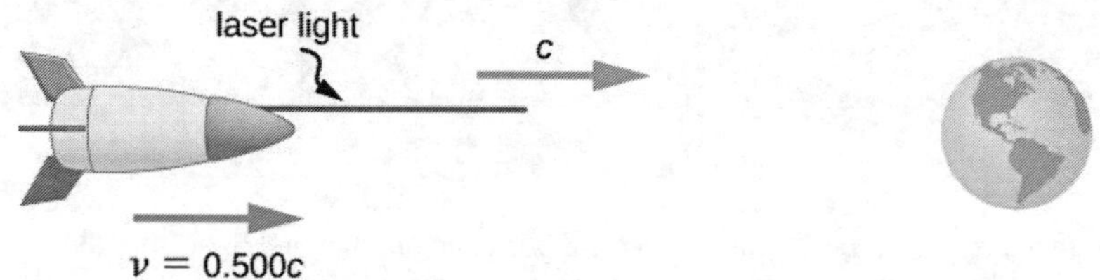

Figure 5.20 How fast does a light signal approach Earth if sent from a spaceship traveling at 0.500c?

Strategy

Because the light and the spaceship are moving at relativistic speeds, we cannot use simple velocity addition. Instead, we determine the speed at which the light approaches Earth using relativistic velocity addition.

Solution

a. Identify the knowns: $v = 0.500c$; $u' = c$.

b. Identify the unknown: u.

c. Express the answer as an equation: $u = \dfrac{v + u'}{1 + \frac{vu'}{c^2}}$.

d. Do the calculation:

$$\begin{aligned} u &= \frac{v + u'}{1 + \frac{vu'}{c^2}} \\ &= \frac{0.500c + c}{1 + \frac{(0.500c)(c)}{c^2}} \\ &= \frac{(0.500 + 1)c}{\left(\frac{c^2 + 0.500c^2}{c^2}\right)} \\ &= c. \end{aligned}$$

Significance

Relativistic velocity addition gives the correct result. Light leaves the ship at speed c and approaches Earth at speed c. The speed of light is independent of the relative motion of source and observer, whether the observer is on the ship or earthbound.

Velocities cannot add to greater than the speed of light, provided that v is less than c and u' does not exceed c. The following example illustrates that relativistic velocity addition is not as symmetric as classical velocity addition.

Example 5.10

Relativistic Package Delivery

Suppose the spaceship in the previous example approaches Earth at half the speed of light and shoots a canister at a speed of $0.750c$ (**Figure 5.21**). (a) At what velocity does an earthbound observer see the canister if it is shot directly toward Earth? (b) If it is shot directly away from Earth?

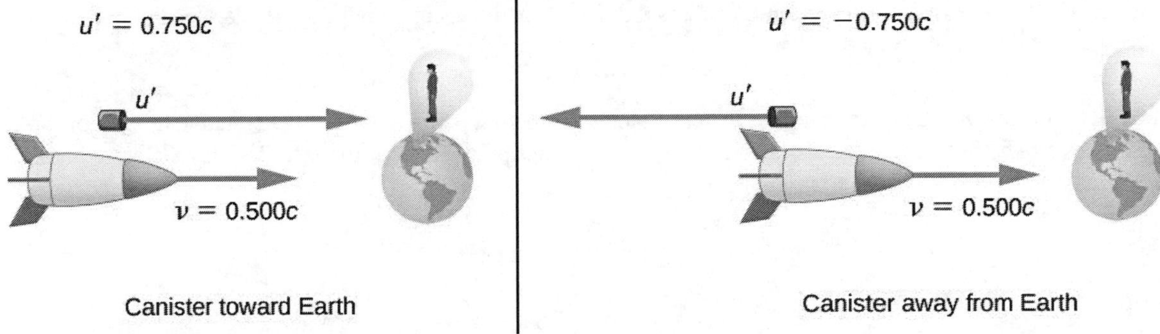

Figure 5.21 A canister is fired at $0.7500c$ toward Earth or away from Earth.

Strategy

Because the canister and the spaceship are moving at relativistic speeds, we must determine the speed of the canister by an earthbound observer using relativistic velocity addition instead of simple velocity addition.

Solution for (a)

a. Identify the knowns: $v = 0.500c$; $u' = 0.750c$.

b. Identify the unknown: u.

c. Express the answer as an equation: $u = \dfrac{v + u'}{1 + \frac{vu'}{c^2}}$.

d. Do the calculation:

$$\begin{aligned} u &= \frac{v + u'}{1 + \frac{vu'}{c^2}} \\ &= \frac{0.500c + 0.750c}{1 + \frac{(0.500c)(0.750c)}{c^2}} \\ &= 0.909c. \end{aligned}$$

Solution for (b)

a. Identify the knowns: $v = 0.500c$; $u' = -0.750c$.

b. Identify the unknown: u.

c. Express the answer as an equation: $u = \dfrac{v + u'}{1 + \frac{vu'}{c^2}}$.

d. Do the calculation:

$$\begin{aligned} u &= \frac{v + u'}{1 + \frac{vu'}{c^2}} \\ &= \frac{0.500c + (-0.750c)}{1 + \frac{(0.500c)(-0.750c)}{c^2}} \\ &= -0.400c. \end{aligned}$$

Significance

The minus sign indicates a velocity away from Earth (in the opposite direction from v), which means the canister is heading toward Earth in part (a) and away in part (b), as expected. But relativistic velocities do not add as simply as they do classically. In part (a), the canister does approach Earth faster, but at less than the vector sum of the velocities, which would give $1.250c$. In part (b), the canister moves away from Earth at a velocity of $-0.400c$, which is *faster* than the $-0.250c$ expected classically. The differences in velocities are not even symmetric: In part (a), an observer on Earth sees the canister and the ship moving apart at a speed of $0.409c$, and at a speed of $0.900c$ in part (b).

5.6 Check Your Understanding Distances along a direction perpendicular to the relative motion of the two frames are the same in both frames. Why then are velocities perpendicular to the x-direction different in the two frames?

5.7 | Doppler Effect for Light

Learning Objectives

By the end of this section, you will be able to:

- Explain the origin of the shift in frequency and wavelength of the observed wavelength when observer and source moved toward or away from each other
- Derive an expression for the relativistic Doppler shift
- Apply the Doppler shift equations to real-world examples

As discussed in the chapter on sound, if a source of sound and a listener are moving farther apart, the listener encounters fewer cycles of a wave in each second, and therefore lower frequency, than if their separation remains constant. For the same reason, the listener detects a higher frequency if the source and listener are getting closer. The resulting Doppler shift in detected frequency occurs for any form of wave. For sound waves, however, the equations for the Doppler shift differ markedly depending on whether it is the source, the observer, or the air, which is moving. Light requires no medium, and the Doppler shift for light traveling in vacuum depends only on the relative speed of the observer and source.

The Relativistic Doppler Effect

Suppose an observer in S sees light from a source in S' moving away at velocity v (**Figure 5.22**). The wavelength of the light could be measured within S'—for example, by using a mirror to set up standing waves and measuring the distance between nodes. These distances are proper lengths with S' as their rest frame, and change by a factor $\sqrt{1 - v^2/c^2}$ when measured in the observer's frame S, where the ruler measuring the wavelength in S' is seen as moving.

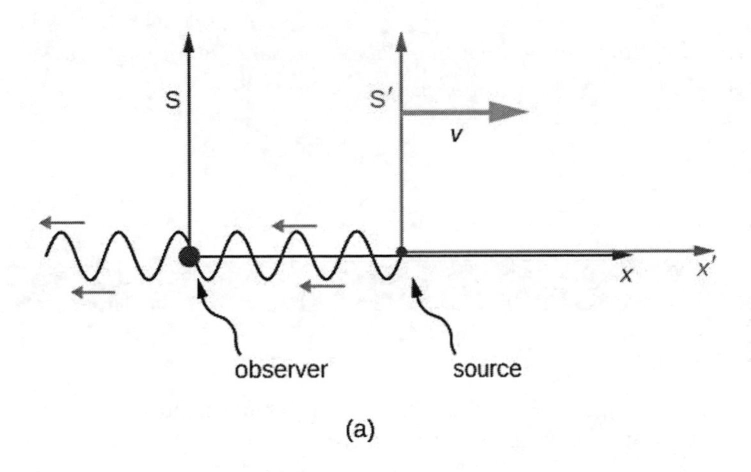

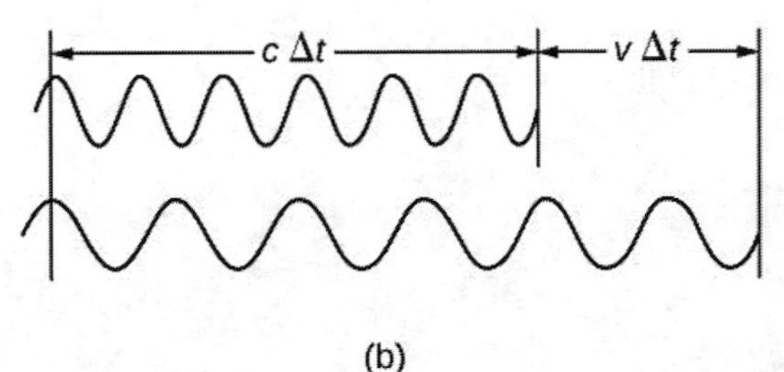

Figure 5.22 (a) When a light wave is emitted by a source fixed in the moving inertial frame S', the observer in *S* sees the wavelength measured in S'. to be shorter by a factor $\sqrt{1 - v^2/c^2}$. (b) Because the observer sees the source moving away within *S*, the wave pattern reaching the observer in *S* is also stretched by the factor $(c\Delta t + v\Delta t)/(c\Delta t) = 1 + v/c$.

If the source were stationary in *S*, the observer would see a length $c\Delta t$ of the wave pattern in time Δt. But because of the motion of S' relative to *S*, considered solely within *S*, the observer sees the wave pattern, and therefore the wavelength, stretched out by a factor of

$$\frac{c\Delta t_{\text{period}} + v\Delta t_{\text{period}}}{c\Delta t_{\text{period}}} = 1 + \frac{v}{c}$$

as illustrated in (b) of **Figure 5.22**. The overall increase from both effects gives

$$\lambda_{\text{obs}} = \lambda_{\text{src}}\left(1 + \frac{v}{c}\right)\sqrt{\frac{1}{1 - \frac{v^2}{c^2}}} = \lambda_{\text{src}}\left(1 + \frac{v}{c}\right)\sqrt{\frac{1}{\left(1 + \frac{v}{c}\right)\left(1 - \frac{v}{c}\right)}} = \lambda_{\text{src}}\sqrt{\frac{\left(1 + \frac{v}{c}\right)}{\left(1 - \frac{v}{c}\right)}}$$

where λ_{src} is the wavelength of the light seen by the source in S' and λ_{obs} is the wavelength that the observer detects within *S*.

Red Shifts and Blue Shifts

The observed wavelength λ_{obs} of electromagnetic radiation is longer (called a "red shift") than that emitted by the source when the source moves away from the observer. Similarly, the wavelength is shorter (called a "blue shift") when the source moves toward the observer. The amount of change is determined by

$$\lambda_{\text{obs}} = \lambda_s\sqrt{\frac{1 + \frac{v}{c}}{1 - \frac{v}{c}}}$$

where λ_s is the wavelength in the frame of reference of the source, and *v* is the relative velocity of the two frames *S* and

S'. The velocity v is positive for motion away from an observer and negative for motion toward an observer. In terms of source frequency and observed frequency, this equation can be written as

$$f_{obs} = f_s\sqrt{\frac{1-\frac{v}{c}}{1+\frac{v}{c}}}.$$

Notice that the signs are different from those of the wavelength equation.

Example 5.11

Calculating a Doppler Shift

Suppose a galaxy is moving away from Earth at a speed 0.825*c*. It emits radio waves with a wavelength of 0.525 m. What wavelength would we detect on Earth?

Strategy

Because the galaxy is moving at a relativistic speed, we must determine the Doppler shift of the radio waves using the relativistic Doppler shift instead of the classical Doppler shift.

Solution

a. Identify the knowns: $u = 0.825c$; $\lambda_s = 0.525\text{ m}$.

b. Identify the unknown: λ_{obs}.

c. Express the answer as an equation:

$$\lambda_{obs} = \lambda_s\sqrt{\frac{1+\frac{v}{c}}{1-\frac{v}{c}}}.$$

d. Do the calculation:

$$\begin{aligned}\lambda_{obs} &= \lambda_s\sqrt{\frac{1+\frac{v}{c}}{1-\frac{v}{c}}} \\ &= (0.525\text{ m})\sqrt{\frac{1+\frac{0.825c}{c}}{1-\frac{0.825c}{c}}} \\ &= 1.70\text{ m}.\end{aligned}$$

Significance

Because the galaxy is moving away from Earth, we expect the wavelengths of radiation it emits to be redshifted. The wavelength we calculated is 1.70 m, which is redshifted from the original wavelength of 0.525 m. You will see in **Particle Physics and Cosmology** that detecting redshifted radiation led to present-day understanding of the origin and evolution of the universe.

5.7 Check Your Understanding Suppose a space probe moves away from Earth at a speed 0.350*c*. It sends a radio-wave message back to Earth at a frequency of 1.50 GHz. At what frequency is the message received on Earth?

The relativistic Doppler effect has applications ranging from Doppler radar storm monitoring to providing information on the motion and distance of stars. We describe some of these applications in the exercises.

5.8 | Relativistic Momentum

Learning Objectives

By the end of this section, you will be able to:

- Define relativistic momentum in terms of mass and velocity
- Show how relativistic momentum relates to classical momentum
- Show how conservation of relativistic momentum limits objects with mass to speeds less than c

Momentum is a central concept in physics. The broadest form of Newton's second law is stated in terms of momentum. Momentum is conserved whenever the net external force on a system is zero. This makes momentum conservation a fundamental tool for analyzing collisions (**Figure 5.23**). Much of what we know about subatomic structure comes from the analysis of collisions of accelerator-produced relativistic particles, and momentum conservation plays a crucial role in this analysis.

Figure 5.23 Momentum is an important concept for these football players from the University of California at Berkeley and the University of California at Davis. A player with the same velocity but greater mass collides with greater impact because his momentum is greater. For objects moving at relativistic speeds, the effect is even greater.

The first postulate of relativity states that the laws of physics are the same in all inertial frames. Does the law of conservation of momentum survive this requirement at high velocities? It can be shown that the momentum calculated as merely $\vec{\mathbf{p}} = m\frac{d\vec{\mathbf{x}}}{dt}$, even if it is conserved in one frame of reference, may not be conserved in another after applying the Lorentz transformation to the velocities. The correct equation for momentum can be shown, instead, to be the classical expression in terms of the increment $d\tau$ of proper time of the particle, observed in the particle's rest frame:

$$\begin{aligned}\vec{\mathbf{p}} &= m\frac{d\vec{\mathbf{x}}}{d\tau} = m\frac{d\vec{\mathbf{x}}}{dt}\frac{dt}{d\tau} \\ &= m\frac{d\vec{\mathbf{x}}}{dt}\frac{1}{\sqrt{1-u^2/c^2}} \\ &= \frac{m\vec{\mathbf{u}}}{\sqrt{1-u^2/c^2}} = \gamma m\vec{\mathbf{u}}.\end{aligned}$$

Relativistic Momentum

Relativistic momentum $\vec{\mathbf{p}}$ is classical momentum multiplied by the relativistic factor γ:

$$\vec{\mathbf{p}} = \gamma m\vec{\mathbf{u}} \tag{5.6}$$

where m is the **rest mass** of the object, $\vec{\mathbf{u}}$ is its velocity relative to an observer, and γ is the relativistic factor:

$$\gamma = \frac{1}{\sqrt{1-\frac{u^2}{c^2}}}. \tag{5.7}$$

Note that we use u for velocity here to distinguish it from relative velocity v between observers. The factor γ that occurs here has the same form as the previous relativistic factor γ except that it is now in terms of the velocity of the particle u instead of the relative velocity v of two frames of reference.

With p expressed in this way, total momentum p_{tot} is conserved whenever the net external force is zero, just as in classical physics. Again we see that the relativistic quantity becomes virtually the same as the classical quantity at low velocities, where u/c is small and γ is very nearly equal to 1. Relativistic momentum has the same intuitive role as classical momentum. It is greatest for large masses moving at high velocities, but because of the factor γ, relativistic momentum approaches infinity as u approaches c (**Figure 5.24**). This is another indication that an object with mass cannot reach the speed of light. If it did, its momentum would become infinite—an unreasonable value.

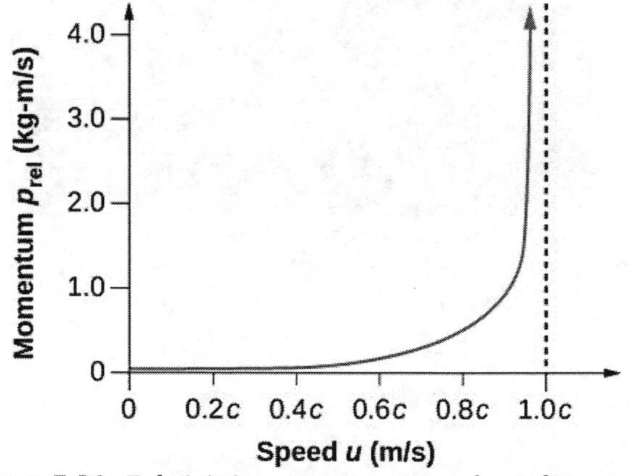

Figure 5.24 Relativistic momentum approaches infinity as the velocity of an object approaches the speed of light.

The relativistically correct definition of momentum as $p = \gamma mu$ is sometimes taken to imply that mass varies with velocity: $m_{\text{var}} = \gamma m$, particularly in older textbooks. However, note that m is the mass of the object as measured by a person at rest relative to the object. Thus, m is defined to be the rest mass, which could be measured at rest, perhaps using gravity. When a mass is moving relative to an observer, the only way that its mass can be determined is through collisions or other means involving momentum. Because the mass of a moving object cannot be determined independently of momentum, the only meaningful mass is rest mass. Therefore, when we use the term "mass," assume it to be identical to "rest mass."

Relativistic momentum is defined in such a way that conservation of momentum holds in all inertial frames. Whenever the net external force on a system is zero, relativistic momentum is conserved, just as is the case for classical momentum. This has been verified in numerous experiments.

5.8 Check Your Understanding What is the momentum of an electron traveling at a speed $0.985c$? The rest mass of the electron is 9.11×10^{-31} kg.

5.9 | Relativistic Energy

Learning Objectives

By the end of this section, you will be able to:

- Explain how the work-energy theorem leads to an expression for the relativistic kinetic energy of an object
- Show how the relativistic energy relates to the classical kinetic energy, and sets a limit on the speed of any object with mass
- Describe how the total energy of a particle is related to its mass and velocity
- Explain how relativity relates to energy-mass equivalence, and some of the practical implications of energy-mass equivalence

The tokamak in **Figure 5.25** is a form of experimental fusion reactor, which can change mass to energy. Nuclear reactors are proof of the relationship between energy and matter.

Conservation of energy is one of the most important laws in physics. Not only does energy have many important forms, but each form can be converted to any other. We know that classically, the total amount of energy in a system remains constant. Relativistically, energy is still conserved, but energy-mass equivalence must now be taken into account, for example, in the reactions that occur within a nuclear reactor. Relativistic energy is intentionally defined so that it is conserved in all inertial frames, just as is the case for relativistic momentum. As a consequence, several fundamental quantities are related in ways not known in classical physics. All of these relationships have been verified by experimental results and have fundamental consequences. The altered definition of energy contains some of the most fundamental and spectacular new insights into nature in recent history.

Figure 5.25 The National Spherical Torus Experiment (NSTX) is a fusion reactor in which hydrogen isotopes undergo fusion to produce helium. In this process, a relatively small mass of fuel is converted into a large amount of energy. (credit: Princeton Plasma Physics Laboratory)

Kinetic Energy and the Ultimate Speed Limit

The first postulate of relativity states that the laws of physics are the same in all inertial frames. Einstein showed that the law of conservation of energy of a particle is valid relativistically, but for energy expressed in terms of velocity and mass in a way consistent with relativity.

Consider first the relativistic expression for the kinetic energy. We again use u for velocity to distinguish it from relative velocity v between observers. Classically, kinetic energy is related to mass and speed by the familiar expression $K = \frac{1}{2}mu^2$. The corresponding relativistic expression for kinetic energy can be obtained from the work-energy theorem. This theorem states that the net work on a system goes into kinetic energy. Specifically, if a force, expressed as $\vec{\mathbf{F}} = \frac{d\vec{\mathbf{p}}}{dt} = m\frac{d(\gamma\vec{\mathbf{u}})}{dt}$, accelerates a particle from rest to its final velocity, the work done on the particle should be equal to its final kinetic energy. In mathematical form, for one-dimensional motion:

$$\begin{aligned} K &= \int F dx = \int m\frac{d}{dt}(\gamma u)dx \\ &= m\int \frac{d(\gamma u)}{dt}\frac{dx}{dt}dt = m\int u\frac{d}{dt}\left(\frac{u}{\sqrt{1-(u/c)^2}}\right)dt. \end{aligned}$$

Integrate this by parts to obtain

$$\begin{aligned} K &= \left.\frac{mu^2}{\sqrt{1-(u/c)^2}}\right|_{0u} - m\int \frac{u}{\sqrt{1-(u/c)^2}}\frac{du}{dt}dt \\ &= \frac{mu^2}{\sqrt{1-(u/c)^2}} - m\int \frac{u}{\sqrt{1-(u/c)^2}}du \\ &= \frac{mu^2}{\sqrt{1-(u/c)^2}} - mc^2\left(\sqrt{1-(u/c)^2}\right)\Big|_0^u \\ &= \frac{mu^2}{\sqrt{1-(u/c)^2}} + \frac{mc^2}{\sqrt{1-(u/c)^2}} - mc^2 \\ &= mc^2\left[\frac{(u^2/c^2) + 1 - (u^2/c^2)}{\sqrt{1-(u/c)^2}}\right] - mc^2 \\ K &= \frac{mc^2}{\sqrt{1-(u/c)^2}} - mc^2. \end{aligned}$$

Relativistic Kinetic Energy

Relativistic kinetic energy of any particle of mass m is

$$K_{\text{rel}} = (\gamma - 1)mc^2. \tag{5.8}$$

When an object is motionless, its speed is $u = 0$ and

$$\gamma = \frac{1}{\sqrt{1-\frac{u^2}{c^2}}} = 1$$

so that $K_{\text{rel}} = 0$ at rest, as expected. But the expression for relativistic kinetic energy (such as total energy and rest energy) does not look much like the classical $\frac{1}{2}mu^2$. To show that the expression for K_{rel} reduces to the classical expression for kinetic energy at low speeds, we use the binomial expansion to obtain an approximation for $(1+\varepsilon)^n$ valid for small ε:

$$(1+\varepsilon)^n = 1 + n\varepsilon + \frac{n(n-1)}{2!}\varepsilon^2 + \frac{n(n-1)(n-2)}{3!}\varepsilon^3 + \cdots \approx 1 + n\varepsilon$$

by neglecting the very small terms in ε^2 and higher powers of ε. Choosing $\varepsilon = -u^2/c^2$ and $n = -\frac{1}{2}$ leads to the conclusion that γ at nonrelativistic speeds, where $\varepsilon = u/c$ is small, satisfies

$$\gamma = \left(1 - u^2/c^2\right)^{-1/2} \approx 1 + \frac{1}{2}\left(\frac{u^2}{c^2}\right).$$

A binomial expansion is a way of expressing an algebraic quantity as a sum of an infinite series of terms. In some cases, as in the limit of small speed here, most terms are very small. Thus, the expression derived here for γ is not exact, but it is a very accurate approximation. Therefore, at low speed:

$$\gamma - 1 = \frac{1}{2}\left(\frac{u^2}{c^2}\right).$$

Entering this into the expression for relativistic kinetic energy gives

$$K_{\text{rel}} = \left[\frac{1}{2}\left(\frac{u^2}{c^2}\right)\right]mc^2 = \frac{1}{2}mu^2 = K_{\text{class}}.$$

That is, relativistic kinetic energy becomes the same as classical kinetic energy when $u << c$.

It is even more interesting to investigate what happens to kinetic energy when the speed of an object approaches the speed of light. We know that γ becomes infinite as *u* approaches *c*, so that K_{rel} also becomes infinite as the velocity approaches the speed of light (**Figure 5.26**). The increase in K_{rel} is far larger than in K_{class} as *v* approaches *c*. An infinite amount of work (and, hence, an infinite amount of energy input) is required to accelerate a mass to the speed of light.

The Speed of Light

No object with mass can attain the **speed of light**.

The speed of light is the ultimate speed limit for any particle having mass. All of this is consistent with the fact that velocities less than *c* always add to less than *c*. Both the relativistic form for kinetic energy and the ultimate speed limit being *c* have been confirmed in detail in numerous experiments. No matter how much energy is put into accelerating a mass, its velocity can only approach—not reach—the speed of light.

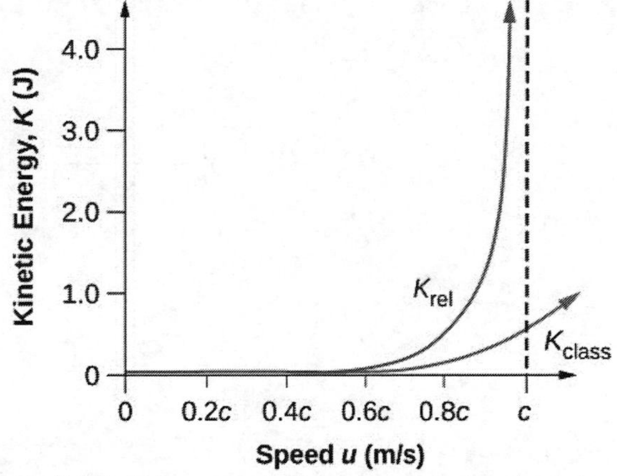

Figure 5.26 This graph of K_{rel} versus velocity shows how kinetic energy increases without bound as velocity approaches the speed of light. Also shown is K_{class}, the classical kinetic energy.

Example 5.12

Comparing Kinetic Energy

An electron has a velocity $v = 0.990c$. (a) Calculate the kinetic energy in MeV of the electron. (b) Compare this with the classical value for kinetic energy at this velocity. (The mass of an electron is 9.11×10^{-31} kg.)

Strategy

The expression for relativistic kinetic energy is always correct, but for (a), it must be used because the velocity is highly relativistic (close to c). First, we calculate the relativistic factor γ, and then use it to determine the relativistic kinetic energy. For (b), we calculate the classical kinetic energy (which would be close to the relativistic value if v were less than a few percent of c) and see that it is not the same.

Solution for (a)

For part (a):

a. Identify the knowns: $v = 0.990c$; $m = 9.11 \times 10^{-31}\,\text{kg}$.

b. Identify the unknown: K_{rel}.

c. Express the answer as an equation: $K_{\text{rel}} = (\gamma - 1)mc^2$ with $\gamma = \frac{1}{\sqrt{1 - u^2/c^2}}$.

d. Do the calculation. First calculate γ. Keep extra digits because this is an intermediate calculation:

$$\begin{aligned} \gamma &= \frac{1}{\sqrt{1 - \frac{u^2}{c^2}}} \\ &= \frac{1}{\sqrt{1 - \frac{(0.990c)^2}{c^2}}} \\ &= 7.0888. \end{aligned}$$

Now use this value to calculate the kinetic energy:

$$\begin{aligned} K_{\text{rel}} &= (\gamma - 1)mc^2 \\ &= (7.0888 - 1)(9.11 \times 10^{-31}\ \text{kg})(3.00 \times 10^8\ \text{m/s}^2) \\ &= 4.9922 \times 10^{-13}\ \text{J}. \end{aligned}$$

e. Convert units:

$$\begin{aligned} K_{\text{rel}} &= (4.9922 \times 10^{-13}\ \text{J})\left(\frac{1\ \text{MeV}}{1.60 \times 10^{-13}\ \text{J}}\right) \\ &= 3.12\ \text{MeV}. \end{aligned}$$

Solution for (b)

For part (b):

a. List the knowns: $v = 0.990c$; $m = 9.11 \times 10^{-31}\,\text{kg}$.

b. List the unknown: K_{rel}.

c. Express the answer as an equation: $K_{\text{class}} = \frac{1}{2}mu^2$.

d. Do the calculation:

$$\begin{aligned} K_{\text{class}} &= \frac{1}{2}mu^2 \\ &= \frac{1}{2}(9.11 \times 10^{-31}\ \text{kg})(0.990)^2(3.00 \times 10^8\ \text{m/s})^2 \\ &= 4.0179 \times 10^{-14}\ \text{J}. \end{aligned}$$

e. Convert units:

$$K_{\text{class}} = 4.0179 \times 10^{-14}\ \text{J}\left(\frac{1\ \text{MeV}}{1.60 \times 10^{-13}\ \text{J}}\right)$$
$$= 0.251\ \text{Mev}.$$

Significance

As might be expected, because the velocity is 99.0% of the speed of light, the classical kinetic energy differs significantly from the correct relativistic value. Note also that the classical value is much smaller than the relativistic value. In fact, $K_{\text{rel}}/K_{\text{class}} = 12.4$ in this case. This illustrates how difficult it is to get a mass moving close to the speed of light. Much more energy is needed than predicted classically. Ever-increasing amounts of energy are needed to get the velocity of a mass a little closer to that of light. An energy of 3 MeV is a very small amount for an electron, and it can be achieved with present-day particle accelerators. SLAC, for example, can accelerate electrons to over $50 \times 10^9\,\text{eV} = 50{,}000\,\text{MeV}$.

Is there any point in getting *v* a little closer to *c* than 99.0% or 99.9%? The answer is yes. We learn a great deal by doing this. The energy that goes into a high-velocity mass can be converted into any other form, including into entirely new particles. In the Large Hadron Collider in **Figure 5.27**, charged particles are accelerated before entering the ring-like structure. There, two beams of particles are accelerated to their final speed of about 99.7% the speed of light in opposite directions, and made to collide, producing totally new species of particles. Most of what we know about the substructure of matter and the collection of exotic short-lived particles in nature has been learned this way. Patterns in the characteristics of these previously unknown particles hint at a basic substructure for all matter. These particles and some of their characteristics will be discussed in a later chapter on particle physics.

Figure 5.27 The European Organization for Nuclear Research (called CERN after its French name) operates the largest particle accelerator in the world, straddling the border between France and Switzerland. (credit: modification of work by NASA)

Total Relativistic Energy

The expression for kinetic energy can be rearranged to:

$$E = \frac{mu^2}{\sqrt{1 - u^2/c^2}} = K + mc^2.$$

Einstein argued in a separate article, also later published in 1905, that if the energy of a particle changes by $\Delta E,$ its mass changes by $\Delta m = \Delta E/c^2$. Abundant experimental evidence since then confirms that mc^2 corresponds to the energy that the particle of mass *m* has when at rest. For example, when a neutral pion of mass *m* at rest decays into two photons, the photons have zero mass but are observed to have total energy corresponding to mc^2 for the pion. Similarly, when a particle of mass m decays into two or more particles with smaller total mass, the observed kinetic energy imparted to the products of the decay corresponds to the decrease in mass. Thus, E is the total relativistic energy of the particle, and mc^2 is its rest energy.

Total Energy

Total energy E of a particle is

$$E = \gamma mc^2 \tag{5.9}$$

where m is mass, c is the speed of light, $\gamma = \frac{1}{\sqrt{1 - \frac{u^2}{c^2}}}$, and u is the velocity of the mass relative to an observer.

Rest Energy

Rest energy of an object is

$$E_0 = mc^2. \tag{5.10}$$

This is the correct form of Einstein's most famous equation, which for the first time showed that energy is related to the mass of an object at rest. For example, if energy is stored in the object, its rest mass increases. This also implies that mass can be destroyed to release energy. The implications of these first two equations regarding relativistic energy are so broad that they were not completely recognized for some years after Einstein published them in 1905, nor was the experimental proof that they are correct widely recognized at first. Einstein, it should be noted, did understand and describe the meanings and implications of his theory.

Example 5.13

Calculating Rest Energy

Calculate the rest energy of a 1.00-g mass.

Strategy

One gram is a small mass—less than one-half the mass of a penny. We can multiply this mass, in SI units, by the speed of light squared to find the equivalent rest energy.

Solution

a. Identify the knowns: $m = 1.00 \times 10^{-3}\,\text{kg};\ \ c = 3.00 \times 10^8\,\text{m/s}$.

b. Identify the unknown: E_0.

c. Express the answer as an equation: $E_0 = mc^2$.

d. Do the calculation:

$$\begin{aligned} E_0 &= mc^2 = (1.00 \times 10^{-3}\ \text{kg})(3.00 \times 10^8\ \text{m/s})^2 \\ &= 9.00 \times 10^{13}\ \text{kg} \cdot \text{m}^2/\text{s}^2. \end{aligned}$$

e. Convert units. Noting that $1\ \text{kg} \cdot \text{m}^2/\text{s}^2 = 1\ \text{J}$, we see the rest energy is:

$$E_0 = 9.00 \times 10^{13}\ \text{J}.$$

Significance

This is an enormous amount of energy for a 1.00-g mass. Rest energy is large because the speed of light c is a large number and c^2 is a very large number, so that mc^2 is huge for any macroscopic mass. The $9.00 \times 10^{13}\,\text{J}$ rest mass energy for 1.00 g is about twice the energy released by the Hiroshima atomic bomb and about 10,000 times the kinetic energy of a large aircraft carrier.

Today, the practical applications of *the conversion of mass into another form of energy*, such as in nuclear weapons and nuclear power plants, are well known. But examples also existed when Einstein first proposed the correct form of relativistic energy, and he did describe some of them. Nuclear radiation had been discovered in the previous decade, and it had been a mystery as to where its energy originated. The explanation was that, in some nuclear processes, a small amount of mass is destroyed and energy is released and carried by nuclear radiation. But the amount of mass destroyed is so small that it is difficult to detect that any is missing. Although Einstein proposed this as the source of energy in the radioactive salts then being studied, it was many years before there was broad recognition that mass could be and, in fact, commonly is, converted to energy (**Figure 5.28**).

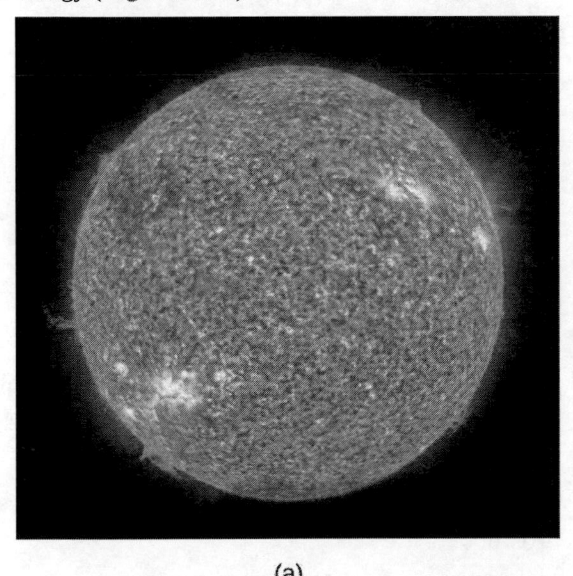

(a) (b)

Figure 5.28 (a) The sun and (b) the Susquehanna Steam Electric Station both convert mass into energy—the sun via nuclear fusion, and the electric station via nuclear fission. (credit a: modification of work by NASA/SDO (AIA))

Because of the relationship of rest energy to mass, we now consider mass to be a form of energy rather than something separate. There had not been even a hint of this prior to Einstein's work. Energy-mass equivalence is now known to be the source of the sun's energy, the energy of nuclear decay, and even one of the sources of energy keeping Earth's interior hot.

Stored Energy and Potential Energy

What happens to energy stored in an object at rest, such as the energy put into a battery by charging it, or the energy stored in a toy gun's compressed spring? The energy input becomes part of the total energy of the object and thus increases its rest mass. All stored and potential energy becomes mass in a system. In seeming contradiction, the principle of conservation of mass (meaning total mass is constant) was one of the great laws verified by nineteenth-century science. Why was it not noticed to be incorrect? The following example helps answer this question.

Example 5.14

Calculating Rest Mass

A car battery is rated to be able to move 600 ampere-hours $(\text{A} \cdot \text{h})$ of charge at 12.0 V. (a) Calculate the increase in rest mass of such a battery when it is taken from being fully depleted to being fully charged, assuming none of the chemical reactants enter or leave the battery. (b) What percent increase is this, given that the battery's mass is 20.0 kg?

Strategy

In part (a), we first must find the energy stored as chemical energy E_{batt} in the battery, which equals the electrical energy the battery can provide. Because $E_{batt} = qV$, we have to calculate the charge q in $600\ \text{A} \cdot \text{h}$, which is the product of the current I and the time t. We then multiply the result by 12.0 V. We can then calculate the battery's increase in mass using $E_{batt} = (\Delta m)c^2$. Part (b) is a simple ratio converted into a percentage.

Solution for (a)

a. Identify the knowns: $I \cdot t = 600\ \text{A} \cdot \text{h}$; $V = 12.0\ \text{V}$; $c = 3.00 \times 10^8\ \text{m/s}$.

b. Identify the unknown: Δm.

c. Express the answer as an equation:

$$\begin{aligned} E_{batt} &= (\Delta m)c^2 \\ \Delta m &= \frac{E_{batt}}{c^2} \\ &= \frac{qV}{c^2} \\ &= \frac{(It)V}{c^2}. \end{aligned}$$

d. Do the calculation:

$$\Delta m = \frac{(600\ \text{A} \cdot \text{h})(12.0\ \text{V})}{(3.00 \times 10^8)^2}.$$

Write amperes A as coulombs per second (C/s), and convert hours into seconds:

$$\begin{aligned} \Delta m &= \frac{(600\ \text{C/s} \cdot \text{h})\left(\frac{3600\ \text{s}}{1\ \text{h}}\right)(12.0\ \text{J/C})}{(3.00 \times 10^8\ \text{m/s})^2} \\ &= 2.88 \times 10^{-10}\ \text{kg}. \end{aligned}$$

where we have used the conversion $1\ \text{kg} \cdot \text{m}^2/\text{s}^2 = 1\ \text{J}$.

Solution for (b)

For part (b):

a. Identify the knowns: $\Delta m = 2.88 \times 10^{-10}\ \text{kg}$; $m = 20.0\ \text{kg}$.

b. Identify the unknown: % change.

c. Express the answer as an equation: $\%\ \text{increase} = \frac{\Delta m}{m} \times 100\%$.

d. Do the calculation:

$$\begin{aligned} \%\ \text{increase} &= \frac{\Delta m}{m} \times 100\% \\ &= \frac{2.88 \times 10^{-10}\ \text{kg}}{20.0\ \text{kg}} \times 100\% \\ &= 1.44 \times 10^{-9}\ \%. \end{aligned}$$

Significance

Both the actual increase in mass and the percent increase are very small, because energy is divided by c^2, a very large number. We would have to be able to measure the mass of the battery to a precision of a billionth of a percent, or 1 part in 10^{11}, to notice this increase. It is no wonder that the mass variation is not readily observed.

In fact, this change in mass is so small that we may question how anyone could verify that it is real. The answer is found in nuclear processes in which the percentage of mass destroyed is large enough to be measured accurately. The mass of the fuel of a nuclear reactor, for example, is measurably smaller when its energy has been used. In that case, stored energy has been released (converted mostly into thermal energy to power electric generators) and the rest mass has decreased. A decrease in mass also occurs from using the energy stored in a battery, except that the stored energy is much greater in nuclear processes, making the change in mass measurable in practice as well as in theory.

Relativistic Energy and Momentum

We know classically that kinetic energy and momentum are related to each other, because:

$$K_{\text{class}} = \frac{p^2}{2m} = \frac{(mu)^2}{2m} = \frac{1}{2}mu^2.$$

Relativistically, we can obtain a relationship between energy and momentum by algebraically manipulating their defining equations. This yields:

$$E^2 = (pc)^2 + (mc^2)^2, \tag{5.11}$$

where E is the relativistic total energy, $E = mc^2/\sqrt{1 - u^2/c^2}$, and p is the relativistic momentum. This relationship between relativistic energy and relativistic momentum is more complicated than the classical version, but we can gain some interesting new insights by examining it. First, total energy is related to momentum and rest mass. At rest, momentum is zero, and the equation gives the total energy to be the rest energy mc^2 (so this equation is consistent with the discussion of rest energy above). However, as the mass is accelerated, its momentum p increases, thus increasing the total energy. At sufficiently high velocities, the rest energy term $(mc^2)^2$ becomes negligible compared with the momentum term $(pc)^2$; thus, $E = pc$ at extremely relativistic velocities.

If we consider momentum p to be distinct from mass, we can determine the implications of the equation $E^2 = (pc)^2 + (mc^2)^2$, for a particle that has no mass. If we take m to be zero in this equation, then $E = pc$, or$p = E/c$. Massless particles have this momentum. There are several massless particles found in nature, including photons (which are packets of electromagnetic radiation). Another implication is that a massless particle must travel at speed c and only at speed c. It is beyond the scope of this text to examine the relationship in the equation $E^2 = (pc)^2 + (mc^2)^2$ in detail, but you can see that the relationship has important implications in special relativity.

5.9 Check Your Understanding What is the kinetic energy of an electron if its speed is $0.992c$?

CHAPTER 5 REVIEW

KEY TERMS

classical (Galilean) velocity addition method of adding velocities when $v<<c$; velocities add like regular numbers in one-dimensional motion: $u = v + u'$, where v is the velocity between two observers, u is the velocity of an object relative to one observer, and u' is the velocity relative to the other observer

event occurrence in space and time specified by its position and time coordinates (x, y, z, t) measured relative to a frame of reference

first postulate of special relativity laws of physics are the same in all inertial frames of reference

Galilean relativity if an observer measures a velocity in one frame of reference, and that frame of reference is moving with a velocity past a second reference frame, an observer in the second frame measures the original velocity as the vector sum of these velocities

Galilean transformation relation between position and time coordinates of the same events as seen in different reference frames, according to classical mechanics

inertial frame of reference reference frame in which a body at rest remains at rest and a body in motion moves at a constant speed in a straight line unless acted on by an outside force

length contraction decrease in observed length of an object from its proper length L_0 to length L when its length is observed in a reference frame where it is traveling at speed v

Lorentz transformation relation between position and time coordinates of the same events as seen in different reference frames, according to the special theory of relativity

Michelson-Morley experiment investigation performed in 1887 that showed that the speed of light in a vacuum is the same in all frames of reference from which it is viewed

proper length L_0; the distance between two points measured by an observer who is at rest relative to both of the points; for example, earthbound observers measure proper length when measuring the distance between two points that are stationary relative to Earth

proper time $\Delta\tau$ is the time interval measured by an observer who sees the beginning and end of the process that the time interval measures occur at the same location

relativistic kinetic energy kinetic energy of an object moving at relativistic speeds

relativistic momentum $\vec{\mathbf{p}}$, the momentum of an object moving at relativistic velocity; $\vec{\mathbf{p}} = \gamma m \vec{\mathbf{u}}$

relativistic velocity addition method of adding velocities of an object moving at a relativistic speeds

rest energy energy stored in an object at rest: $E_0 = mc^2$

rest frame frame of reference in which the observer is at rest

rest mass mass of an object as measured by an observer at rest relative to the object

second postulate of special relativity light travels in a vacuum with the same speed c in any direction in all inertial frames

special theory of relativity theory that Albert Einstein proposed in 1905 that assumes all the laws of physics have the same form in every inertial frame of reference, and that the speed of light is the same within all inertial frames

speed of light ultimate speed limit for any particle having mass

time dilation lengthening of the time interval between two events when seen in a moving inertial frame rather than the rest frame of the events (in which the events occur at the same location)

total energy sum of all energies for a particle, including rest energy and kinetic energy, given for a particle of mass m

and speed u by $E = \gamma mc^2$, where $\gamma = \frac{1}{\sqrt{1 - \frac{u^2}{c^2}}}$

world line path through space-time

KEY EQUATIONS

Time dilation

$$\Delta t = \frac{\Delta\tau}{\sqrt{1 - \frac{v^2}{c^2}}} = \gamma\tau$$

Lorentz factor

$$\gamma = \frac{1}{\sqrt{1 - \frac{v^2}{c^2}}}$$

Length contraction

$$L = L_0\sqrt{1 - \frac{v^2}{c^2}} = \frac{L_0}{\gamma}$$

Galilean transformation

$$x = x' + vt, \quad y = y', \quad z = z', \quad t = t'$$

Lorentz transformation

$$t = \frac{t' + vx'/c^2}{\sqrt{1 - v^2/c^2}}$$

$$x = \frac{x' + vt'}{\sqrt{1 - v^2/c^2}}$$

$$y = y'$$

$$z = z'$$

Inverse Lorentz transformation

$$t' = \frac{t - vx/c^2}{\sqrt{1 - v^2/c^2}}$$

$$x' = \frac{x - vt}{\sqrt{1 - v^2/c^2}}$$

$$y' = y$$

$$z' = z$$

Space-time invariants

$$(\Delta s)^2 = (\Delta x)^2 + (\Delta y)^2 + (\Delta z)^2 - c^2(\Delta t)^2$$

$$(\Delta\tau)^2 = -(\Delta s)^2/c^2 = (\Delta t)^2 - \frac{\left[(\Delta x)^2 + (\Delta y)^2 + (\Delta z)^2\right]}{c^2}$$

Relativistic velocity addition

$$u_x = \left(\frac{u'_x + v}{1 + vu'_x/c^2}\right), \quad u_y = \left(\frac{u'_y/\gamma}{1 + vu'_x/c^2}\right), \quad u_z = \left(\frac{u'_z/\gamma}{1 + vu'_x/c^2}\right)$$

Relativistic Doppler effect for wavelength

$$\lambda_{\text{obs}} = \lambda_s\sqrt{\frac{1 + \frac{v}{c}}{1 - \frac{v}{c}}}$$

Relativistic Doppler effect for frequency

$$f_{\text{obs}} = f_s\sqrt{\frac{1 - \frac{v}{c}}{1 + \frac{v}{c}}}$$

Relativistic momentum

$$\vec{\mathbf{p}} = \gamma m\vec{\mathbf{u}} = \frac{m\vec{\mathbf{u}}}{\sqrt{1 - \frac{u^2}{c}}}$$

Relativistic total energy	$E = \gamma mc^2, \text{ where } \gamma = \frac{1}{\sqrt{1 - \frac{u^2}{c^2}}}$
Relativistic kinetic energy	$K_{\text{rel}} = (\gamma - 1)mc^2, \text{ where } \gamma = \frac{1}{\sqrt{1 - \frac{u^2}{c^2}}}$

SUMMARY

5.1 Invariance of Physical Laws

- Relativity is the study of how observers in different reference frames measure the same event.
- Modern relativity is divided into two parts. Special relativity deals with observers in uniform (unaccelerated) motion, whereas general relativity includes accelerated relative motion and gravity. Modern relativity is consistent with all empirical evidence thus far and, in the limit of low velocity and weak gravitation, gives close agreement with the predictions of classical (Galilean) relativity.
- An inertial frame of reference is a reference frame in which a body at rest remains at rest and a body in motion moves at a constant speed in a straight line unless acted upon by an outside force.
- Modern relativity is based on Einstein's two postulates. The first postulate of special relativity is that the laws of physics are the same in all inertial frames of reference. The second postulate of special relativity is that the speed of light c is the same in all inertial frames of reference, independent of the relative motion of the observer and the light source.
- The Michelson-Morley experiment demonstrated that the speed of light in a vacuum is independent of the motion of Earth about the sun.

5.2 Relativity of Simultaneity

- Two events are defined to be simultaneous if an observer measures them as occurring at the same time (such as by receiving light from the events).
- Two events at locations a distance apart that are simultaneous for an observer at rest in one frame of reference are not necessarily simultaneous for an observer at rest in a different frame of reference.

5.3 Time Dilation

- Two events are defined to be simultaneous if an observer measures them as occurring at the same time. They are not necessarily simultaneous to all observers—simultaneity is not absolute.
- Time dilation is the lengthening of the time interval between two events when seen in a moving inertial frame rather than the rest frame of the events (in which the events occur at the same location).
- Observers moving at a relative velocity v do not measure the same elapsed time between two events. Proper time $\Delta\tau$ is the time measured in the reference frame where the start and end of the time interval occur at the same location. The time interval Δt measured by an observer who sees the frame of events moving at speed v is related to the proper time interval $\Delta\tau$ of the events by the equation:

$$\Delta t = \frac{\Delta\tau}{\sqrt{1 - \frac{v^2}{c^2}}} = \gamma\Delta\tau,$$

where

$$\gamma = \frac{1}{\sqrt{1 - \frac{v^2}{c^2}}}.$$

- The premise of the twin paradox is faulty because the traveling twin is accelerating. The journey is not symmetrical for the two twins.

- Time dilation is usually negligible at low relative velocities, but it does occur, and it has been verified by experiment.
- The proper time is the shortest measure of any time interval. Any observer who is moving relative to the system being observed measures a time interval longer than the proper time.

5.4 Length Contraction

- All observers agree upon relative speed.
- Distance depends on an observer's motion. Proper length L_0 is the distance between two points measured by an observer who is at rest relative to both of the points.
- Length contraction is the decrease in observed length of an object from its proper length L_0 to length L when its length is observed in a reference frame where it is traveling at speed v.
- The proper length is the longest measurement of any length interval. Any observer who is moving relative to the system being observed measures a length shorter than the proper length.

5.5 The Lorentz Transformation

- The Galilean transformation equations describe how, in classical nonrelativistic mechanics, the position, velocity, and accelerations measured in one frame appear in another. Lengths remain unchanged and a single universal time scale is assumed to apply to all inertial frames.
- Newton's laws of mechanics obey the principle of having the same form in all inertial frames under a Galilean transformation, given by

$$x = x' + vt, \quad y = y', \quad z = z', \quad t = t'.$$

  The concept that times and distances are the same in all inertial frames in the Galilean transformation, however, is inconsistent with the postulates of special relativity.
- The relativistically correct Lorentz transformation equations are

Lorentz transformation	Inverse Lorentz transformation
$t = \dfrac{t' + vx'/c^2}{\sqrt{1 - v^2/c^2}}$	$t' = \dfrac{t - vx/c^2}{\sqrt{1 - v^2/c^2}}$
$x = \dfrac{x' + vt'}{\sqrt{1 - v^2/c^2}}$	$x' = \dfrac{x - vt}{\sqrt{1 - v^2/c^2}}$
$y = y'$	$y' = y$
$z = z'$	$z' = z$

  We can obtain these equations by requiring an expanding spherical light signal to have the same shape and speed of growth, c, in both reference frames.
- Relativistic phenomena can be explained in terms of the geometrical properties of four-dimensional space-time, in which Lorentz transformations correspond to rotations of axes.
- The Lorentz transformation corresponds to a space-time axis rotation, similar in some ways to a rotation of space axes, but in which the invariant spatial separation is given by Δs rather than distances Δr, and that the Lorentz transformation involving the time axis does not preserve perpendicularity of axes or the scales along the axes.
- The analysis of relativistic phenomena in terms of space-time diagrams supports the conclusion that these phenomena result from properties of space and time itself, rather than from the laws of electromagnetism.

5.6 Relativistic Velocity Transformation

- With classical velocity addition, velocities add like regular numbers in one-dimensional motion: $u = v + u'$, where v is the velocity between two observers, u is the velocity of an object relative to one observer, and u' is the velocity relative to the other observer.

- Velocities cannot add to be greater than the speed of light.
- Relativistic velocity addition describes the velocities of an object moving at a relativistic velocity.

5.7 Doppler Effect for Light

- An observer of electromagnetic radiation sees relativistic Doppler effects if the source of the radiation is moving relative to the observer. The wavelength of the radiation is longer (called a red shift) than that emitted by the source when the source moves away from the observer and shorter (called a blue shift) when the source moves toward the observer. The shifted wavelength is described by the equation:

$$\lambda_{\text{obs}} = \lambda_s \sqrt{\frac{1 + \frac{v}{c}}{1 - \frac{v}{c}}}.$$

where λ_{obs} is the observed wavelength, λ_s is the source wavelength, and v is the relative velocity of the source to the observer.

5.8 Relativistic Momentum

- The law of conservation of momentum is valid for relativistic momentum whenever the net external force is zero. The relativistic momentum is $p = \gamma m u,$ where m is the rest mass of the object, u is its velocity relative to an observer, and the relativistic factor is $\gamma = \frac{1}{\sqrt{1 - \frac{u^2}{c^2}}}.$
- At low velocities, relativistic momentum is equivalent to classical momentum.
- Relativistic momentum approaches infinity as u approaches c. This implies that an object with mass cannot reach the speed of light.

5.9 Relativistic Energy

- The relativistic work-energy theorem is $W_{\text{net}} = E - E_0 = \gamma mc^2 - mc^2 = (\gamma - 1)mc^2.$
- Relativistically, $W_{\text{net}} = K_{\text{rel}}$ where K_{rel} is the relativistic kinetic energy.
- An object of *mass m* at velocity u has kinetic energy $K_{\text{rel}} = (\gamma - 1)mc^2,$ where $\gamma = \frac{1}{\sqrt{1 - \frac{u^2}{c^2}}}.$
- At low velocities, relativistic kinetic energy reduces to classical kinetic energy.
- No object with mass can attain the speed of light, because an infinite amount of work and an infinite amount of energy input is required to accelerate a mass to the speed of light.
- Relativistic energy is conserved as long as we define it to include the possibility of mass changing to energy.
- The total energy of a particle with mass m traveling at speed u is defined as $E = \gamma mc^2,$ where $\gamma = \frac{1}{\sqrt{1 - \frac{u^2}{c^2}}}$ and u denotes the velocity of the particle.
- The rest energy of an object of mass m is $E_0 = mc^2,$ meaning that mass is a form of energy. If energy is stored in an object, its mass increases. Mass can be destroyed to release energy.
- We do not ordinarily notice the increase or decrease in mass of an object because the change in mass is so small for a large increase in energy. The equation $E^2 = (pc)^2 + (mc^2)^2$ relates the relativistic total energy E and the relativistic momentum p. At extremely high velocities, the rest energy mc^2 becomes negligible, and $E = pc.$

CONCEPTUAL QUESTIONS

5.1 Invariance of Physical Laws

1. Which of Einstein's postulates of special relativity includes a concept that does not fit with the ideas of classical physics? Explain.

2. Is Earth an inertial frame of reference? Is the sun? Justify your response.

3. When you are flying in a commercial jet, it may appear to you that the airplane is stationary and Earth is moving beneath you. Is this point of view valid? Discuss briefly.

5.3 Time Dilation

4. (a) Does motion affect the rate of a clock as measured by an observer moving with it? (b) Does motion affect how an observer moving relative to a clock measures its rate?

5. To whom does the elapsed time for a process seem to be longer, an observer moving relative to the process or an observer moving with the process? Which observer measures the interval of proper time?

6. (a) How could you travel far into the future of Earth without aging significantly? (b) Could this method also allow you to travel into the past?

5.4 Length Contraction

7. To whom does an object seem greater in length, an observer moving with the object or an observer moving relative to the object? Which observer measures the object's proper length?

8. Relativistic effects such as time dilation and length contraction are present for cars and airplanes. Why do these effects seem strange to us?

9. Suppose an astronaut is moving relative to Earth at a significant fraction of the speed of light. (a) Does he observe the rate of his clocks to have slowed? (b) What change in the rate of earthbound clocks does he see? (c) Does his ship seem to him to shorten? (d) What about the distance between two stars that lie in the direction of his motion? (e) Do he and an earthbound observer agree on his velocity relative to Earth?

5.7 Doppler Effect for Light

10. Explain the meaning of the terms "red shift" and "blue shift" as they relate to the relativistic Doppler effect.

11. What happens to the relativistic Doppler effect when relative velocity is zero? Is this the expected result?

12. Is the relativistic Doppler effect consistent with the classical Doppler effect in the respect that λ_{obs} is larger for motion away?

13. All galaxies farther away than about 50×10^6 ly exhibit a red shift in their emitted light that is proportional to distance, with those farther and farther away having progressively greater red shifts. What does this imply, assuming that the only source of red shift is relative motion?

5.8 Relativistic Momentum

14. How does modern relativity modify the law of conservation of momentum?

15. Is it possible for an external force to be acting on a system and relativistic momentum to be conserved? Explain.

5.9 Relativistic Energy

16. How are the classical laws of conservation of energy and conservation of mass modified by modern relativity?

17. What happens to the mass of water in a pot when it cools, assuming no molecules escape or are added? Is this observable in practice? Explain.

18. Consider a thought experiment. You place an expanded balloon of air on weighing scales outside in the early morning. The balloon stays on the scales and you are able to measure changes in its mass. Does the mass of the balloon change as the day progresses? Discuss the difficulties in carrying out this experiment.

19. The mass of the fuel in a nuclear reactor decreases by an observable amount as it puts out energy. Is the same true for the coal and oxygen combined in a conventional power plant? If so, is this observable in practice for the coal and oxygen? Explain.

20. We know that the velocity of an object with mass has an upper limit of c. Is there an upper limit on its momentum? Its energy? Explain.

21. Given the fact that light travels at c, can it have mass? Explain.

22. If you use an Earth-based telescope to project a laser beam onto the moon, you can move the spot across the moon's surface at a velocity greater than the speed of light. Does this violate modern relativity? (Note that light is being sent from the Earth to the moon, not across the surface of the moon.)

PROBLEMS

5.3 Time Dilation

23. (a) What is γ if $v = 0.250c$? (b) If $v = 0.500c$?

24. (a) What is γ if $v = 0.100c$? (b) If $v = 0.900c$?

25. Particles called π-mesons are produced by accelerator beams. If these particles travel at 2.70×10^8 m/s and live 2.60×10^{-8} s when at rest relative to an observer, how long do they live as viewed in the laboratory?

26. Suppose a particle called a kaon is created by cosmic radiation striking the atmosphere. It moves by you at $0.980c$, and it lives 1.24×10^{-8} s when at rest relative to an observer. How long does it live as you observe it?

27. A neutral π-meson is a particle that can be created by accelerator beams. If one such particle lives 1.40×10^{-16} s as measured in the laboratory, and 0.840×10^{-16} s when at rest relative to an observer, what is its velocity relative to the laboratory?

28. A neutron lives 900 s when at rest relative to an observer. How fast is the neutron moving relative to an observer who measures its life span to be 2065 s?

29. If relativistic effects are to be less than 1%, then γ must be less than 1.01. At what relative velocity is $\gamma = 1.01$?

30. If relativistic effects are to be less than 3%, then γ must be less than 1.03. At what relative velocity is $\gamma = 1.03$?

5.4 Length Contraction

31. A spaceship, 200 m long as seen on board, moves by the Earth at $0.970c$. What is its length as measured by an earthbound observer?

32. How fast would a 6.0 m-long sports car have to be going past you in order for it to appear only 5.5 m long?

33. (a) How far does the muon in **Example 5.3** travel according to the earthbound observer? (b) How far does it travel as viewed by an observer moving with it? Base your calculation on its velocity relative to the Earth and the time it lives (proper time). (c) Verify that these two distances are related through length contraction $\gamma = 3.20$.

34. (a) How long would the muon in **Example 5.3** have lived as observed on Earth if its velocity was $0.0500c$? (b) How far would it have traveled as observed on Earth? (c) What distance is this in the muon's frame?

35. **Unreasonable Results** A spaceship is heading directly toward Earth at a velocity of $0.800c$. The astronaut on board claims that he can send a canister toward the Earth at $1.20c$ relative to Earth. (a) Calculate the velocity the canister must have relative to the spaceship. (b) What is unreasonable about this result? (c) Which assumptions are unreasonable or inconsistent?

5.5 The Lorentz Transformation

36. Describe the following physical occurrences as events, that is, in the form (x, y, z, t): (a) A postman rings a doorbell of a house precisely at noon. (b) At the same time as the doorbell is rung, a slice of bread pops out of a toaster that is located 10 m from the door in the east direction from the door. (c) Ten seconds later, an airplane arrives at the airport, which is 10 km from the door in the east direction and 2 km to the south.

37. Describe what happens to the angle $\alpha = \tan(v/c)$, and therefore to the transformed axes in **Figure 5.17**, as the relative velocity v of the S and S′ frames of reference approaches c.

38. Describe the shape of the world line on a space-time diagram of (a) an object that remains at rest at a specific position along the *x*-axis; (b) an object that moves at constant velocity u in the *x*-direction; (c) an object that begins at rest and accelerates at a constant rate of in the positive *x*-direction.

39. A man standing still at a train station watches two boys throwing a baseball in a moving train. Suppose the train is moving east with a constant speed of 20 m/s and one of the boys throws the ball with a speed of 5 m/s with respect to himself toward the other boy, who is 5 m west from him. What is the velocity of the ball as observed by the man on the station?

40. When observed from the sun at a particular instant, Earth and Mars appear to move in opposite directions with speeds 108,000 km/h and 86,871 km/h, respectively. What is the speed of Mars at this instant when observed from Earth?

41. A man is running on a straight road perpendicular to a train track and away from the track at a speed of 12 m/s. The train is moving with a speed of 30 m/s with respect to the track. What is the speed of the man with respect to a passenger sitting at rest in the train?

42. A man is running on a straight road that makes $30°$ with the train track. The man is running in the direction on the road that is away from the track at a speed of 12 m/s. The train is moving with a speed of 30 m/s with respect to the track. What is the speed of the man with respect to a passenger sitting at rest in the train?

43. In a frame at rest with respect to the billiard table, a billiard ball of mass m moving with speed v strikes another billiard ball of mass m at rest. The first ball comes to rest after the collision while the second ball takes off with speed v in the original direction of the motion of the first ball. This shows that momentum is conserved in this frame. (a) Now, describe the same collision from the perspective of a frame that is moving with speed v in the direction of the motion of the first ball. (b) Is the momentum conserved in this frame?

44. In a frame at rest with respect to the billiard table, two billiard balls of same mass m are moving toward each other with the same speed v. After the collision, the two balls come to rest. (a) Show that momentum is conserved in this frame. (b) Now, describe the same collision from the perspective of a frame that is moving with speed v in the direction of the motion of the first ball. (c) Is the momentum conserved in this frame?

45. In a frame S, two events are observed: event 1: a pion is created at rest at the origin and event 2: the pion disintegrates after time τ. Another observer in a frame S' is moving in the positive direction along the positive x-axis with a constant speed v and observes the same two events in his frame. The origins of the two frames coincide at $t = t' = 0$. (a) Find the positions and timings of these two events in the frame S' (a) according to the Galilean transformation, and (b) according to the Lorentz transformation.

5.6 Relativistic Velocity Transformation

46. If two spaceships are heading directly toward each other at $0.800c$, at what speed must a canister be shot from the first ship to approach the other at $0.999c$ as seen by the second ship?

47. Two planets are on a collision course, heading directly toward each other at $0.250c$. A spaceship sent from one planet approaches the second at $0.750c$ as seen by the second planet. What is the velocity of the ship relative to the first planet?

48. When a missile is shot from one spaceship toward another, it leaves the first at $0.950c$ and approaches the other at $0.750c$. What is the relative velocity of the two ships?

49. What is the relative velocity of two spaceships if one fires a missile at the other at $0.750c$ and the other observes it to approach at $0.950c$?

50. Prove that for any relative velocity v between two observers, a beam of light sent from one to the other will approach at speed c (provided that v is less than c, of course).

51. Show that for any relative velocity v between two observers, a beam of light projected by one directly away from the other will move away at the speed of light (provided that v is less than c, of course).

5.7 Doppler Effect for Light

52. A highway patrol officer uses a device that measures the speed of vehicles by bouncing radar off them and measuring the Doppler shift. The outgoing radar has a frequency of 100 GHz and the returning echo has a frequency 15.0 kHz higher. What is the velocity of the vehicle? Note that there are two Doppler shifts in echoes. Be certain not to round off until the end of the problem, because the effect is small.

5.8 Relativistic Momentum

53. Find the momentum of a helium nucleus having a mass of 6.68×10^{-27} kg that is moving at $0.200c$.

54. What is the momentum of an electron traveling at $0.980c$?

55. (a) Find the momentum of a 1.00×10^{9}-kg asteroid heading towards Earth at 30.0 km/s. (b) Find the ratio of this momentum to the classical momentum. (Hint: Use the approximation that $\gamma = 1 + (1/2)v^2/c^2$ at low velocities.)

56. (a) What is the momentum of a 2000-kg satellite orbiting at 4.00 km/s? (b) Find the ratio of this momentum to the classical momentum. (Hint: Use the approximation that $\gamma = 1 + (1/2)v^2/c^2$ at low velocities.)

57. What is the velocity of an electron that has a momentum of 3.04×10^{-21} kg · m/s ? Note that you must calculate the velocity to at least four digits to see the difference from *c*.

58. Find the velocity of a proton that has a momentum of 4.48×10^{-19} kg · m/s.

5.9 Relativistic Energy

59. What is the rest energy of an electron, given its mass is 9.11×10^{-31} kg? Give your answer in joules and MeV.

60. Find the rest energy in joules and MeV of a proton, given its mass is 1.67×10^{-27} kg.

61. If the rest energies of a proton and a neutron (the two constituents of nuclei) are 938.3 and 939.6 MeV, respectively, what is the difference in their mass in kilograms?

62. The Big Bang that began the universe is estimated to have released 10^{68} J of energy. How many stars could half this energy create, assuming the average star's mass is 4.00×10^{30} kg ?

63. A supernova explosion of a 2.00×10^{31} kg star produces 1.00×10^{44} J of energy. (a) How many kilograms of mass are converted to energy in the explosion? (b) What is the ratio $\Delta m/m$ of mass destroyed to the original mass of the star?

64. (a) Using data from Potential Energy of a System (http://cnx.org/content/m58312/latest/#fs-id1165036086155) , calculate the mass converted to energy by the fission of 1.00 kg of uranium. (b) What is the ratio of mass destroyed to the original mass, $\Delta m/m$?

65. (a) Using data from Potential Energy of a System (http://cnx.org/content/m58312/latest/#fs-id1165036086155) , calculate the amount of mass converted to energy by the fusion of 1.00 kg of hydrogen. (b) What is the ratio of mass destroyed to the original mass, $\Delta m/m$? (c) How does this compare with $\Delta m/m$ for the fission of 1.00 kg of uranium?

66. There is approximately 10^{34} J of energy available from fusion of hydrogen in the world's oceans. (a) If 10^{33} J of this energy were utilized, what would be the decrease in mass of the oceans? (b) How great a volume of water does this correspond to? (c) Comment on whether this is a significant fraction of the total mass of the oceans.

67. A muon has a rest mass energy of 105.7 MeV, and it decays into an electron and a massless particle. (a) If all the lost mass is converted into the electron's kinetic energy, find γ for the electron. (b) What is the electron's velocity?

68. A π -meson is a particle that decays into a muon and a massless particle. The π -meson has a rest mass energy of 139.6 MeV, and the muon has a rest mass energy of 105.7 MeV. Suppose the π -meson is at rest and all of the missing mass goes into the muon's kinetic energy. How fast will the muon move?

69. (a) Calculate the relativistic kinetic energy of a 1000-kg car moving at 30.0 m/s if the speed of light were only 45.0 m/s. (b) Find the ratio of the relativistic kinetic energy to classical.

70. Alpha decay is nuclear decay in which a helium nucleus is emitted. If the helium nucleus has a mass of 6.80×10^{-27} kg and is given 5.00 MeV of kinetic energy, what is its velocity?

71. (a) Beta decay is nuclear decay in which an electron is emitted. If the electron is given 0.750 MeV of kinetic energy, what is its velocity? (b) Comment on how the high velocity is consistent with the kinetic energy as it compares to the rest mass energy of the electron.

ADDITIONAL PROBLEMS

72. (a) At what relative velocity is $\gamma = 1.50$? (b) At what relative velocity is $\gamma = 100$?

73. (a) At what relative velocity is $\gamma = 2.00$? (b) At what relative velocity is $\gamma = 10.0$?

74. **Unreasonable Results** (a) Find the value of γ required for the following situation. An earthbound observer measures 23.9 h to have passed while signals from a high-velocity space probe indicate that 24.0 h have passed on board. (b) What is unreasonable about this result? (c) Which assumptions are unreasonable or inconsistent?

75. (a) How long does it take the astronaut in Example 5.5 to travel 4.30 ly at $0.99944c$ (as measured by the earthbound observer)? (b) How long does it take according to the astronaut? (c) Verify that these two times are related through time dilation with $\gamma = 30.00$ as given.

76. (a) How fast would an athlete need to be running for a 100- m race to look 100 yd long? (b) Is the answer consistent with the fact that relativistic effects are difficult to observe in ordinary circumstances? Explain.

77. (a) Find the value of γ for the following situation. An astronaut measures the length of his spaceship to be 100 m, while an earthbound observer measures it to be 25.0 m. (b) What is the speed of the spaceship relative to Earth?

78. A clock in a spaceship runs one-tenth the rate at which an identical clock on Earth runs. What is the speed of the spaceship?

79. An astronaut has a heartbeat rate of 66 beats per minute as measured during his physical exam on Earth. The heartbeat rate of the astronaut is measured when he is in a spaceship traveling at $0.5c$ with respect to Earth by an observer (A) in the ship and by an observer (B) on Earth. (a) Describe an experimental method by which observer B on Earth will be able to determine the heartbeat rate of the astronaut when the astronaut is in the spaceship. (b) What will be the heartbeat rate(s) of the astronaut reported by observers A and B?

80. A spaceship (A) is moving at speed $c/2$ with respect to another spaceship (B). Observers in A and B set their clocks so that the event at (x, y, z, t) of turning on a laser in spaceship B has coordinates (0, 0, 0, 0) in A and also (0, 0, 0, 0) in B. An observer at the origin of B turns on the laser at $t = 0$ and turns it off at $t = \tau$ in his time. What is the time duration between on and off as seen by an observer in A?

81. Same two observers as in the preceding exercise, but now we look at two events occurring in spaceship A. A photon arrives at the origin of A at its time $t = 0$ and another photon arrives at $(x = 1.00\text{ m}, 0, 0)$ at $t = 0$ in the frame of ship A. (a) Find the coordinates and times of the two events as seen by an observer in frame B. (b) In which frame are the two events simultaneous and in which frame are they are not simultaneous?

82. Same two observers as in the preceding exercises. A rod of length 1 m is laid out on the x-axis in the frame of B from origin to $(x = 1.00\text{ m}, 0, 0)$. What is the length of the rod observed by an observer in the frame of spaceship A?

83. An observer at origin of inertial frame S sees a flashbulb go off at $x = 150\text{ km}$, $y = 15.0\text{ km}$, and $z = 1.00\text{ km}$ at time $t = 4.5 \times 10^{-4}\text{ s}$. At what time and position in the S$'$ system did the flash occur, if S$'$ is moving along shared x-direction with S at a velocity $v = 0.6c$?

84. An observer sees two events 1.5×10^{-8} s apart at a separation of 800 m. How fast must a second observer be moving relative to the first to see the two events occur simultaneously?

85. An observer standing by the railroad tracks sees two bolts of lightning strike the ends of a 500-m-long train simultaneously at the instant the middle of the train passes him at 50 m/s. Use the Lorentz transformation to find the time between the lightning strikes as measured by a passenger seated in the middle of the train.

86. Two astronomical events are observed from Earth to occur at a time of 1 s apart and a distance separation of $1.5 \times 10^9\text{ m}$ from each other. (a) Determine whether separation of the two events is space like or time like. (b) State what this implies about whether it is consistent with special relativity for one event to have caused the other?

87. Two astronomical events are observed from Earth to occur at a time of 0.30 s apart and a distance separation of $2.0 \times 10^9\text{ m}$ from each other. How fast must a spacecraft travel from the site of one event toward the other to make the events occur at the same time when measured in the frame of reference of the spacecraft?

88. A spacecraft starts from being at rest at the origin and accelerates at a constant rate g, as seen from Earth, taken to be an inertial frame, until it reaches a speed of $c/2$. (a) Show that the increment of proper time is related to the elapsed time in Earth's frame by: $d\tau = \sqrt{1 - v^2/c^2}dt$.

(b) Find an expression for the elapsed time to reach speed $c/2$ as seen in Earth's frame. (c) Use the relationship in (a) to obtain a similar expression for the elapsed proper time to reach $c/2$ as seen in the spacecraft, and determine the ratio of the time seen from Earth with that on the spacecraft to reach the final speed.

89. (a) All but the closest galaxies are receding from our own Milky Way Galaxy. If a galaxy 12.0×10^9 ly away is receding from us at $0.900c$, at what velocity relative to us must we send an exploratory probe to approach the other galaxy at $0.990c$ as measured from that galaxy? (b) How long will it take the probe to reach the other galaxy as measured from Earth? You may assume that the velocity of the other galaxy remains constant. (c) How long will it then take for a radio signal to be beamed back? (All of this is possible in principle, but not practical.)

90. Suppose a spaceship heading straight toward the Earth at $0.750c$ can shoot a canister at $0.500c$ relative to the ship. (a) What is the velocity of the canister relative to Earth, if it is shot directly at Earth? (b) If it is shot directly away from Earth?

91. Repeat the preceding problem with the ship heading directly away from Earth.

92. If a spaceship is approaching the Earth at $0.100c$ and a message capsule is sent toward it at $0.100c$ relative to Earth, what is the speed of the capsule relative to the ship?

93. (a) Suppose the speed of light were only 3000 m/s. A jet fighter moving toward a target on the ground at 800 m/s shoots bullets, each having a muzzle velocity of 1000 m/s. What are the bullets' velocity relative to the target? (b) If the speed of light was this small, would you observe relativistic effects in everyday life? Discuss.

94. If a galaxy moving away from the Earth has a speed of 1000 km/s and emits 656 nm light characteristic of hydrogen (the most common element in the universe). (a) What wavelength would we observe on Earth? (b) What type of electromagnetic radiation is this? (c) Why is the speed of Earth in its orbit negligible here?

95. A space probe speeding towards the nearest star moves at $0.250c$ and sends radio information at a broadcast frequency of 1.00 GHz. What frequency is received on Earth?

96. Near the center of our galaxy, hydrogen gas is moving directly away from us in its orbit about a black hole. We receive 1900 nm electromagnetic radiation and know that it was 1875 nm when emitted by the hydrogen gas. What is the speed of the gas?

97. (a) Calculate the speed of a 1.00-μg particle of dust that has the same momentum as a proton moving at $0.999c$. (b) What does the small speed tell us about the mass of a proton compared to even a tiny amount of macroscopic matter?

98. (a) Calculate γ for a proton that has a momentum of $1.00\ \text{kg} \cdot \text{m/s}$. (b) What is its speed? Such protons form a rare component of cosmic radiation with uncertain origins.

99. Show that the relativistic form of Newton's second law is (a) $F = m\frac{du}{dt}\frac{1}{\left(1 - u^2/c^2\right)^{3/2}}$; (b) Find the force needed to accelerate a mass of 1 kg by $1\ \text{m/s}^2$ when it is traveling at a velocity of $c/2$.

100. A positron is an antimatter version of the electron, having exactly the same mass. When a positron and an electron meet, they annihilate, converting all of their mass into energy. (a) Find the energy released, assuming negligible kinetic energy before the annihilation. (b) If this energy is given to a proton in the form of kinetic energy, what is its velocity? (c) If this energy is given to another electron in the form of kinetic energy, what is its velocity?

101. What is the kinetic energy in MeV of a π-meson that lives 1.40×10^{-16} s as measured in the laboratory, and 0.840×10^{-16} s when at rest relative to an observer, given that its rest energy is 135 MeV?

102. Find the kinetic energy in MeV of a neutron with a measured life span of 2065 s, given its rest energy is 939.6 MeV, and rest life span is 900s.

103. (a) Show that $(pc)^2/(mc^2)^2 = \gamma^2 - 1$. This means that at large velocities $pc >> mc^2$. (b) Is $E \approx pc$ when $\gamma = 30.0$, as for the astronaut discussed in the twin paradox?

104. One cosmic ray neutron has a velocity of $0.250c$ relative to the Earth. (a) What is the neutron's total energy in MeV? (b) Find its momentum. (c) Is $E \approx pc$ in this situation? Discuss in terms of the equation given in part (a) of the previous problem.

105. What is γ for a proton having a mass energy of 938.3 MeV accelerated through an effective potential of 1.0 TV (teravolt)?

106. (a) What is the effective accelerating potential for electrons at the Stanford Linear Accelerator, if $\gamma = 1.00 \times 10^5$ for them? (b) What is their total energy (nearly the same as kinetic in this case) in GeV?

107. (a) Using data from **Potential Energy of a System (http://cnx.org/content/m58312/latest/#fs-id1165036086155)**, find the mass destroyed when the energy in a barrel of crude oil is released. (b) Given these barrels contain 200 liters and assuming the density of crude oil is 750kg/m^3, what is the ratio of mass destroyed to original mass, $\Delta m/m$?

108. (a) Calculate the energy released by the destruction of 1.00 kg of mass. (b) How many kilograms could be lifted to a 10.0 km height by this amount of energy?

109. A Van de Graaff accelerator utilizes a 50.0 MV potential difference to accelerate charged particles such as protons. (a) What is the velocity of a proton accelerated by such a potential? (b) An electron?

110. Suppose you use an average of $500\,\text{kW}\cdot\text{h}$ of electric energy per month in your home. (a) How long would 1.00 g of mass converted to electric energy with an efficiency of 38.0% last you? (b) How many homes could be supplied at the $500\,\text{kW}\cdot\text{h}$ per month rate for one year by the energy from the described mass conversion?

111. (a) A nuclear power plant converts energy from nuclear fission into electricity with an efficiency of 35.0%. How much mass is destroyed in one year to produce a continuous 1000 MW of electric power? (b) Do you think it would be possible to observe this mass loss if the total mass of the fuel is 10^4 kg?

112. Nuclear-powered rockets were researched for some years before safety concerns became paramount. (a) What fraction of a rocket's mass would have to be destroyed to get it into a low Earth orbit, neglecting the decrease in gravity? (Assume an orbital altitude of 250 km, and calculate both the kinetic energy (classical) and the gravitational potential energy needed.) (b) If the ship has a mass of 1.00×10^5 kg (100 tons), what total yield nuclear explosion in tons of TNT is needed?

113. The sun produces energy at a rate of 3.85×10^{26} W by the fusion of hydrogen. About 0.7% of each kilogram of hydrogen goes into the energy generated by the Sun. (a) How many kilograms of hydrogen undergo fusion each second? (b) If the sun is 90.0% hydrogen and half of this can undergo fusion before the sun changes character, how long could it produce energy at its current rate? (c) How many kilograms of mass is the sun losing per second? (d) What fraction of its mass will it have lost in the time found in part (b)?

114. Show that $E^2 - p^2c^2$ for a particle is invariant under Lorentz transformations.

6 | PHOTONS AND MATTER WAVES

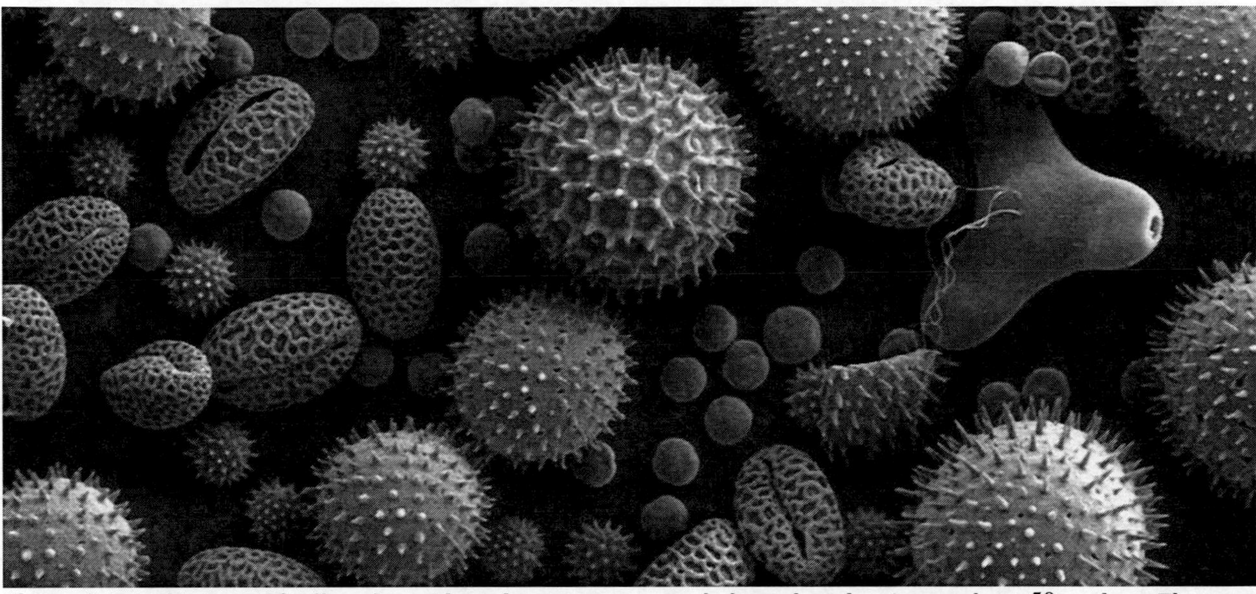

Figure 6.1 In this image of pollen taken with an electron microscope, the bean-shaped grains are about $50 \mu m$ long. Electron microscopes can have a much higher resolving power than a conventional light microscope because electron wavelengths can be 100,000 times shorter than the wavelengths of visible-light photons. (credit: modification of work by Dartmouth College Electron Microscope Facility)

Chapter Outline

Introduction

Two of the most revolutionary concepts of the twentieth century were the description of light as a collection of particles, and the treatment of particles as waves. These wave properties of matter have led to the discovery of technologies such as electron microscopy, which allows us to examine submicroscopic objects such as grains of pollen, as shown above.

In this chapter, you will learn about the energy quantum, a concept that was introduced in 1900 by the German physicist Max Planck to explain blackbody radiation. We discuss how Albert Einstein extended Planck's concept to a quantum of light (a "photon") to explain the photoelectric effect. We also show how American physicist Arthur H. Compton used the photon concept in 1923 to explain wavelength shifts observed in X-rays. After a discussion of Bohr's model of hydrogen, we describe how matter waves were postulated in 1924 by Louis-Victor de Broglie to justify Bohr's model and we examine the experiments conducted in 1923–1927 by Clinton Davisson and Lester Germer that confirmed the existence of de Broglie's matter waves.

6.1 | Blackbody Radiation

Learning Objectives

By the end of this section you will be able to:

- Apply Wien's and Stefan's laws to analyze radiation emitted by a blackbody
- Explain Planck's hypothesis of energy quanta

All bodies emit electromagnetic radiation over a range of wavelengths. In an earlier chapter, we learned that a cooler body radiates less energy than a warmer body. We also know by observation that when a body is heated and its temperature rises, the perceived wavelength of its emitted radiation changes from infrared to red, and then from red to orange, and so forth. As its temperature rises, the body glows with the colors corresponding to ever-smaller wavelengths of the electromagnetic spectrum. This is the underlying principle of the incandescent light bulb: A hot metal filament glows red, and when heating continues, its glow eventually covers the entire visible portion of the electromagnetic spectrum. The temperature (T) of the object that emits radiation, or the **emitter**, determines the wavelength at which the radiated energy is at its maximum. For example, the Sun, whose surface temperature is in the range between 5000 K and 6000 K, radiates most strongly in a range of wavelengths about 560 nm in the visible part of the electromagnetic spectrum. Your body, when at its normal temperature of about 300 K, radiates most strongly in the infrared part of the spectrum.

Radiation that is incident on an object is partially absorbed and partially reflected. At thermodynamic equilibrium, the rate at which an object absorbs radiation is the same as the rate at which it emits it. Therefore, a good **absorber** of radiation (any object that absorbs radiation) is also a good emitter. A perfect absorber absorbs all electromagnetic radiation incident on it; such an object is called a **blackbody**.

Although the blackbody is an idealization, because no physical object absorbs 100% of incident radiation, we can construct a close realization of a blackbody in the form of a small hole in the wall of a sealed enclosure known as a cavity radiator, as shown in Figure 6.2. The inside walls of a cavity radiator are rough and blackened so that any radiation that enters through a tiny hole in the cavity wall becomes trapped inside the cavity. At thermodynamic equilibrium (at temperature T), the cavity walls absorb exactly as much radiation as they emit. Furthermore, inside the cavity, the radiation entering the hole is balanced by the radiation leaving it. The emission spectrum of a blackbody can be obtained by analyzing the light radiating from the hole. Electromagnetic waves emitted by a blackbody are called **blackbody radiation**.

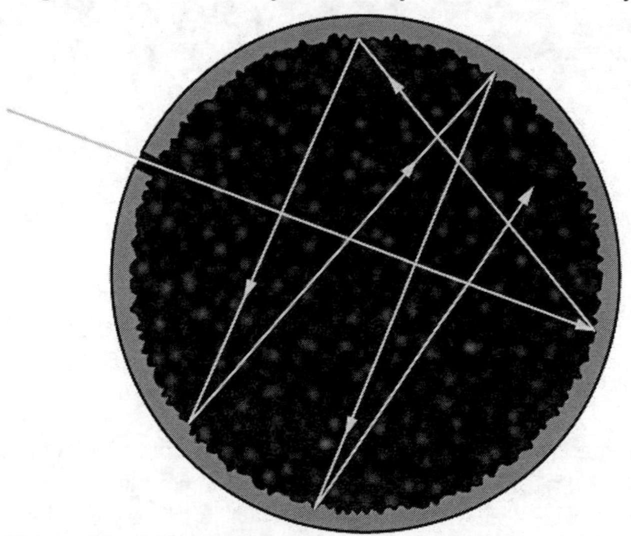

Figure 6.2 A blackbody is physically realized by a small hole in the wall of a cavity radiator.

The intensity $I(\lambda, T)$ of blackbody radiation depends on the wavelength λ of the emitted radiation and on the temperature T of the blackbody (Figure 6.3). The function $I(\lambda, T)$ is the **power intensity** that is radiated per unit wavelength; in other words, it is the power radiated per unit area of the hole in a cavity radiator per unit wavelength. According to this definition, $I(\lambda, T)d\lambda$ is the power per unit area that is emitted in the wavelength interval from λ to $\lambda + d\lambda$. The intensity distribution among wavelengths of radiation emitted by cavities was studied experimentally at the end of the nineteenth century. Generally, radiation emitted by materials only approximately follows the blackbody radiation curve (**Figure 6.4**); however, spectra of common stars do follow the blackbody radiation curve very closely.

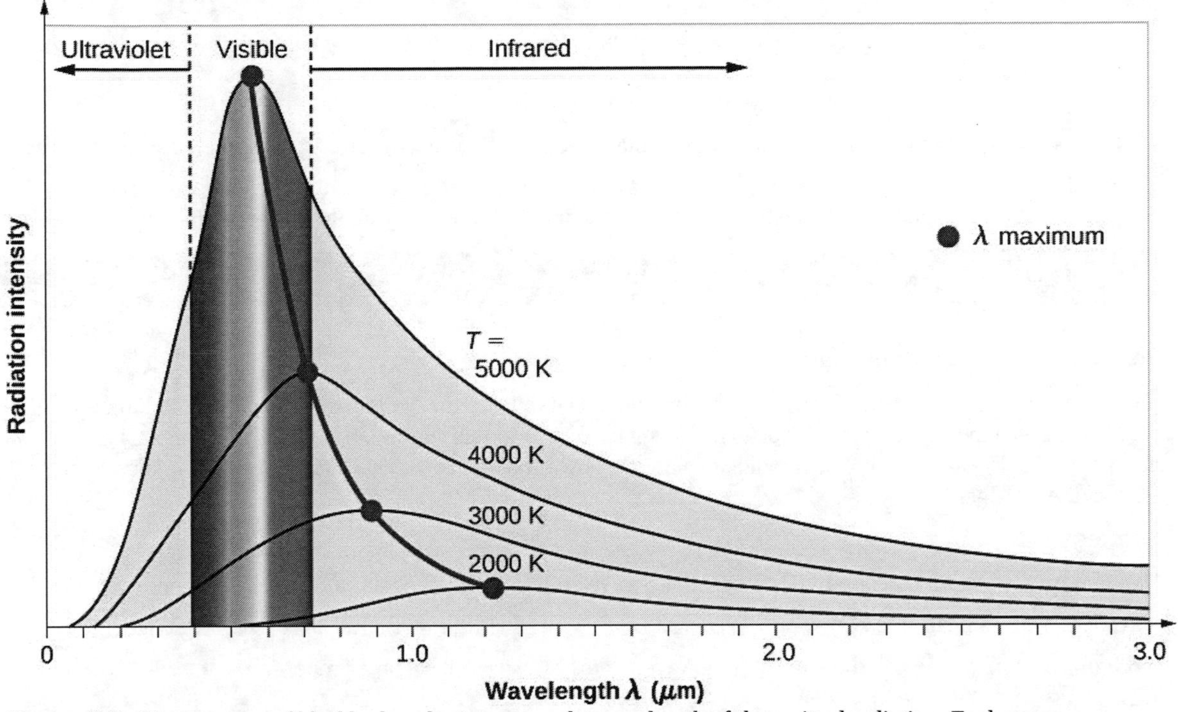

Figure 6.3 The intensity of blackbody radiation versus the wavelength of the emitted radiation. Each curve corresponds to a different blackbody temperature, starting with a low temperature (the lowest curve) to a high temperature (the highest curve).

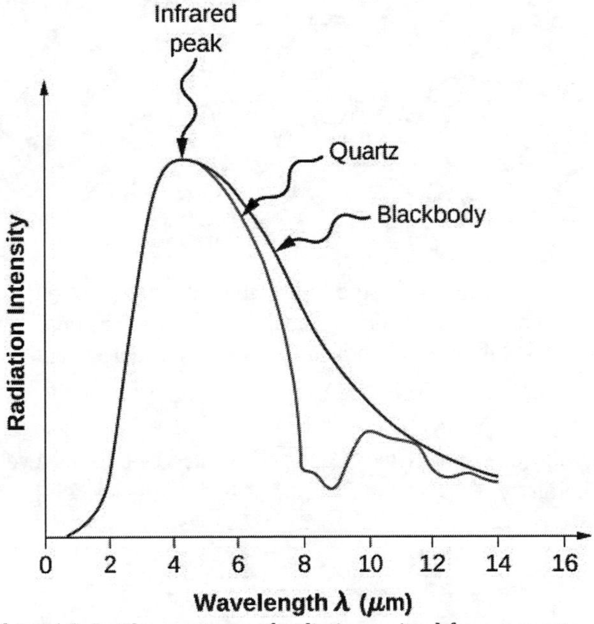

Figure 6.4 The spectrum of radiation emitted from a quartz surface (blue curve) and the blackbody radiation curve (black curve) at 600 K.

Two important laws summarize the experimental findings of blackbody radiation: *Wien's displacement law* and *Stefan's law*. Wien's displacement law is illustrated in **Figure 6.3** by the curve connecting the maxima on the intensity curves. In these curves, we see that the hotter the body, the shorter the wavelength corresponding to the emission peak in the radiation curve. Quantitatively, Wien's law reads

$$\lambda_{max} T = 2.898 \times 10^{-3} \, \text{m} \cdot \text{K} \tag{6.1}$$

where λ_{max} is the position of the maximum in the radiation curve. In other words, λ_{max} is the wavelength at which a blackbody radiates most strongly at a given temperature T. Note that in **Equation 6.1**, the temperature is in kelvins. Wien's displacement law allows us to estimate the temperatures of distant stars by measuring the wavelength of radiation they emit.

Example 6.1

Temperatures of Distant Stars

On a clear evening during the winter months, if you happen to be in the Northern Hemisphere and look up at the sky, you can see the constellation Orion (The Hunter). One star in this constellation, Rigel, flickers in a blue color and another star, Betelgeuse, has a reddish color, as shown in **Figure 6.5**. Which of these two stars is cooler, Betelgeuse or Rigel?

Strategy

We treat each star as a blackbody. Then according to Wien's law, its temperature is inversely proportional to the wavelength of its peak intensity. The wavelength $\lambda_{max}^{(blue)}$ of blue light is shorter than the wavelength $\lambda_{max}^{(red)}$ of red light. Even if we do not know the precise wavelengths, we can still set up a proportion.

Solution

Writing Wien's law for the blue star and for the red star, we have

$$\lambda_{max}^{(red)} T_{(red)} = 2.898 \times 10^{-3} \, \text{m} \cdot \text{K} = \lambda_{max}^{(blue)} T_{(blue)} \tag{6.2}$$

When simplified, **Equation 6.2** gives

$$T_{(red)} = \frac{\lambda_{max}^{(blue)}}{\lambda_{max}^{(red)}} T_{(blue)} < T_{(blue)} \tag{6.3}$$

Therefore, Betelgeuse is cooler than Rigel.

Significance

Note that Wien's displacement law tells us that the higher the temperature of an emitting body, the shorter the wavelength of the radiation it emits. The qualitative analysis presented in this example is generally valid for any emitting body, whether it is a big object such as a star or a small object such as the glowing filament in an incandescent lightbulb.

6.1 Check Your Understanding The flame of a peach-scented candle has a yellowish color and the flame of a Bunsen's burner in a chemistry lab has a bluish color. Which flame has a higher temperature?

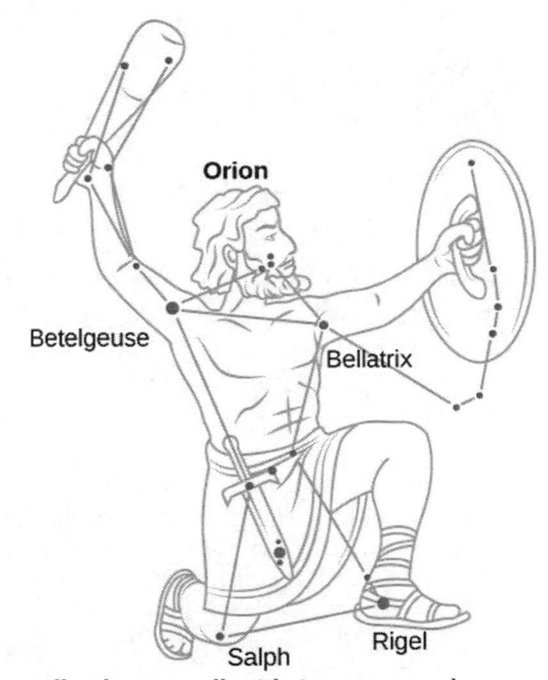

Figure 6.5 In the Orion constellation, the red star Betelgeuse, which usually takes on a yellowish tint, appears as the figure's right shoulder (in the upper left). The giant blue star on the bottom right is Rigel, which appears as the hunter's left foot. (credit left: modification of work by Matthew Spinelli, NASA APOD)

The second experimental relation is Stefan's law, which concerns the total power of blackbody radiation emitted across the entire spectrum of wavelengths at a given temperature. In Figure 6.3, this total power is represented by the area under the blackbody radiation curve for a given T. As the temperature of a blackbody increases, the total emitted power also increases. Quantitatively, Stefan's law expresses this relation as

$$P(T) = \sigma A T^4 \quad (6.4)$$

where A is the surface area of a blackbody, T is its temperature (in kelvins), and σ is the **Stefan–Boltzmann constant**, $\sigma = 5.670 \times 10^{-8}\,\text{W/(m}^2 \cdot \text{K}^4)$. Stefan's law enables us to estimate how much energy a star is radiating by remotely measuring its temperature.

Example 6.2

Power Radiated by Stars

A star such as our Sun will eventually evolve to a "red giant" star and then to a "white dwarf" star. A typical white dwarf is approximately the size of Earth, and its surface temperature is about $2.5 \times 10^4\,\text{K}$. A typical red giant has a surface temperature of $3.0 \times 10^3\,\text{K}$ and a radius ~100,000 times larger than that of a white dwarf. What is the average radiated power per unit area and the total power radiated by each of these types of stars? How do they compare?

Strategy

If we treat the star as a blackbody, then according to Stefan's law, the total power that the star radiates is proportional to the fourth power of its temperature. To find the power radiated per unit area of the surface, we do not need to make any assumptions about the shape of the star because P/A depends only on temperature. However, to compute the total power, we need to make an assumption that the energy radiates through a spherical surface enclosing the star, so that the surface area is $A = 4\pi R^2$, where R is its radius.

Solution

A simple proportion based on Stefan's law gives

$$\frac{P_{\text{dwarf}}/A_{\text{dwarf}}}{P_{\text{giant}}/A_{\text{giant}}} = \frac{\sigma T^4_{\text{dwarf}}}{\sigma T^4_{\text{giant}}} = \left(\frac{T_{\text{dwarf}}}{T_{\text{giant}}}\right)^4 = \left(\frac{2.5 \times 10^4}{3.0 \times 10^3}\right)^4 = 4820 \tag{6.5}$$

The power emitted per unit area by a white dwarf is about 5000 times that the power emitted by a red giant. Denoting this ratio by $a = 4.8 \times 10^3$, **Equation 6.5** gives

$$\frac{P_{\text{dwarf}}}{P_{\text{giant}}} = a\frac{A_{\text{dwarf}}}{A_{\text{giant}}} = a\frac{4\pi R^2_{\text{dwarf}}}{4\pi R^2_{\text{giant}}} = a\left(\frac{R_{\text{dwarf}}}{R_{\text{giant}}}\right)^2 = 4.8 \times 10^3\left(\frac{R_{\text{dwarf}}}{10^5 R_{\text{dwarf}}}\right)^2 = 4.8 \times 10^{-7} \tag{6.6}$$

We see that the total power emitted by a white dwarf is a tiny fraction of the total power emitted by a red giant. Despite its relatively lower temperature, the overall power radiated by a red giant far exceeds that of the white dwarf because the red giant has a much larger surface area. To estimate the absolute value of the emitted power per unit area, we again use Stefan's law. For the white dwarf, we obtain

$$\frac{P_{\text{dwarf}}}{A_{\text{dwarf}}} = \sigma T^4_{\text{dwarf}} = 5.670 \times 10^{-8} \frac{\text{W}}{\text{m}^2 \cdot \text{K}^4}\left(2.5 \times 10^4\,\text{K}\right)^4 = 2.2 \times 10^{10}\,\text{W/m}^2 \tag{6.7}$$

The analogous result for the red giant is obtained by scaling the result for a white dwarf:

$$\frac{P_{\text{giant}}}{A_{\text{giant}}} = \frac{2.2 \times 10^{10}}{4.82 \times 10^3}\frac{\text{W}}{\text{m}^2} = 4.56 \times 10^6 \frac{\text{W}}{\text{m}^2} \cong 4.6 \times 10^6 \frac{\text{W}}{\text{m}^2} \tag{6.8}$$

Significance

To estimate the total power emitted by a white dwarf, in principle, we could use **Equation 6.7**. However, to find its surface area, we need to know the average radius, which is not given in this example. Therefore, the solution stops here. The same is also true for the red giant star.

6.2 Check Your Understanding An iron poker is being heated. As its temperature rises, the poker begins to glow—first dull red, then bright red, then orange, and then yellow. Use either the blackbody radiation curve or Wien's law to explain these changes in the color of the glow.

6.3 Check Your Understanding Suppose that two stars, α and β, radiate exactly the same total power. If the radius of star α is three times that of star β, what is the ratio of the surface temperatures of these stars? Which one is hotter?

The term "blackbody" was coined by Gustav R. Kirchhoff in 1862. The blackbody radiation curve was known experimentally, but its shape eluded physical explanation until the year 1900. The physical model of a blackbody at temperature T is that of the electromagnetic waves enclosed in a cavity (see **Figure 6.2**) and at thermodynamic equilibrium with the cavity walls. The waves can exchange energy with the walls. The objective here is to find the energy density distribution among various modes of vibration at various wavelengths (or frequencies). In other words, we want to know how much energy is carried by a single wavelength or a band of wavelengths. Once we know the energy distribution, we can use standard statistical methods (similar to those studied in a previous chapter) to obtain the blackbody radiation curve, Stefan's law, and Wien's displacement law. When the physical model is correct, the theoretical predictions should be the same as the experimental curves.

In a classical approach to the blackbody radiation problem, in which radiation is treated as waves (as you have studied in previous chapters), the modes of electromagnetic waves trapped in the cavity are in equilibrium and continually exchange their energies with the cavity walls. There is no physical reason why a wave should do otherwise: Any amount of energy can be exchanged, either by being transferred from the wave to the material in the wall or by being received by the wave from the material in the wall. This classical picture is the basis of the model developed by Lord Rayleigh and, independently, by Sir James Jeans. The result of this classical model for blackbody radiation curves is known as the *Rayleigh–Jeans law*.

However, as shown in **Figure 6.6**, the Rayleigh–Jeans law fails to correctly reproduce experimental results. In the limit of short wavelengths, the Rayleigh–Jeans law predicts infinite radiation intensity, which is inconsistent with the experimental results in which radiation intensity has finite values in the ultraviolet region of the spectrum. This divergence between the results of classical theory and experiments, which came to be called the *ultraviolet catastrophe*, shows how classical physics fails to explain the mechanism of blackbody radiation.

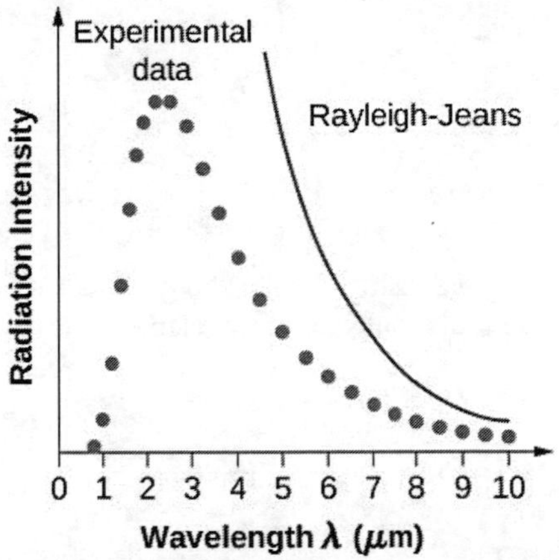

Figure 6.6 The ultraviolet catastrophe: The Rayleigh–Jeans law does not explain the observed blackbody emission spectrum.

The blackbody radiation problem was solved in 1900 by Max Planck. Planck used the same idea as the Rayleigh–Jeans model in the sense that he treated the electromagnetic waves between the walls inside the cavity classically, and assumed that the radiation is in equilibrium with the cavity walls. The innovative idea that Planck introduced in his model is the assumption that the cavity radiation originates from atomic oscillations inside the cavity walls, and that these oscillations can have only *discrete* values of energy. Therefore, the radiation trapped inside the cavity walls can exchange energy with the walls only in discrete amounts. Planck's hypothesis of discrete energy values, which he called *quanta*, assumes that the oscillators inside the cavity walls have **quantized energies**. This was a brand new idea that went beyond the classical physics of the nineteenth century because, as you learned in a previous chapter, in the classical picture, the energy of an oscillator can take on any continuous value. Planck assumed that the energy of an oscillator (E_n) can have only discrete, or quantized, values:

$$E_n = nhf, \quad \text{where } n = 1, 2, 3, \ldots \tag{6.9}$$

In **Equation 6.9**, f is the frequency of Planck's oscillator. The natural number n that enumerates these discrete energies is called a **quantum number**. The physical constant h is called *Planck's constant*:

$$h = 6.626 \times 10^{-34}\,\text{J} \cdot \text{s} = 4.136 \times 10^{-15}\,\text{eV} \cdot \text{s} \tag{6.10}$$

Each discrete energy value corresponds to a **quantum state of a Planck oscillator**. Quantum states are enumerated by quantum numbers. For example, when Planck's oscillator is in its first $n = 1$ quantum state, its energy is $E_1 = hf$; when it is in the $n = 2$ quantum state, its energy is $E_2 = 2hf$; when it is in the $n = 3$ quantum state, $E_3 = 3hf$; and so on.

Note that **Equation 6.9** shows that there are infinitely many quantum states, which can be represented as a sequence $\{hf, 2hf, 3hf, \ldots, (n-1)hf, nhf, (n+1)hf, \ldots\}$. Each two consecutive quantum states in this sequence are separated by an energy jump, $\Delta E = hf$. An oscillator in the wall can receive energy from the radiation in the cavity (absorption), or it can give away energy to the radiation in the cavity (emission). The absorption process sends the oscillator to a higher quantum state, and the emission process sends the oscillator to a lower quantum state. Whichever way this exchange of energy goes, the smallest amount of energy that can be exchanged is hf. There is no upper limit to how much energy can be exchanged, but whatever is exchanged must be an integer multiple of hf. If the energy packet does not have this exact amount, it is neither absorbed nor emitted at the wall of the blackbody.

Planck's Quantum Hypothesis

Planck's hypothesis of energy quanta states that the amount of energy emitted by the oscillator is carried by the quantum of radiation, ΔE :

$$\Delta E = hf$$

Recall that the frequency of electromagnetic radiation is related to its wavelength and to the speed of light by the fundamental relation $f\lambda = c$. This means that we can express Equation 6.10 equivalently in terms of wavelength λ. When included in the computation of the energy density of a blackbody, Planck's hypothesis gives the following theoretical expression for the power intensity of emitted radiation per unit wavelength:

$$I(\lambda, T) = \frac{2\pi hc^2}{\lambda^5} \frac{1}{e^{hc/\lambda k_B T} - 1} \tag{6.11}$$

where c is the speed of light in vacuum and k_B is Boltzmann's constant, $k_B = 1.380 \times 10^{-23}$ J/K. The theoretical formula expressed in Equation 6.11 is called *Planck's blackbody radiation law*. This law is in agreement with the experimental blackbody radiation curve (see Figure 6.7). In addition, Wien's displacement law and Stefan's law can both be derived from Equation 6.11. To derive Wien's displacement law, we use differential calculus to find the maximum of the radiation intensity curve $I(\lambda, T)$. To derive Stefan's law and find the value of the Stefan–Boltzmann constant, we use integral calculus and integrate $I(\lambda, T)$ to find the total power radiated by a blackbody at one temperature in the entire spectrum of wavelengths from $\lambda = 0$ to $\lambda = \infty$. This derivation is left as an exercise later in this chapter.

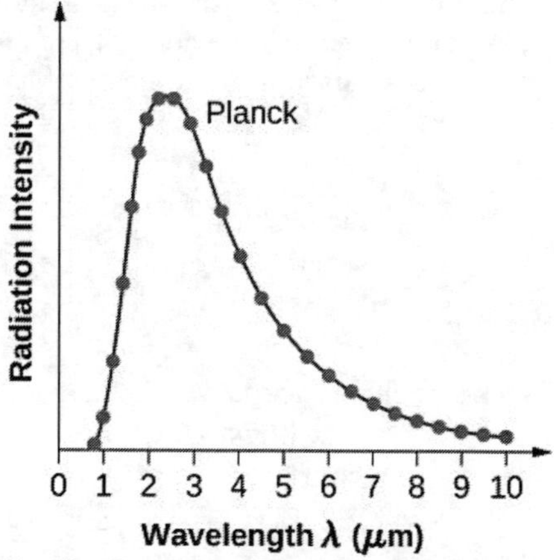

Figure 6.7 Planck's theoretical result (continuous curve) and the experimental blackbody radiation curve (dots).

Example 6.3

Planck's Quantum Oscillator

A quantum oscillator in the cavity wall in Figure 6.2 is vibrating at a frequency of 5.0×10^{14} Hz. Calculate the spacing between its energy levels.

Strategy

Energy states of a quantum oscillator are given by Equation 6.9. The energy spacing ΔE is obtained by finding the energy difference between two adjacent quantum states for quantum numbers $n + 1$ and n.

Solution

We can substitute the given frequency and Planck's constant directly into the equation:

$$\Delta E = E_{n+1} - E_n = (n+1)hf - nhf = hf = (6.626 \times 10^{-34}\,\text{J}\cdot\text{s})(5.0 \times 10^{14}\,\text{Hz}) = 3.3 \times 10^{-19}\,\text{J}$$

Significance

Note that we do not specify what kind of material was used to build the cavity. Here, a quantum oscillator is a theoretical model of an atom or molecule of material in the wall.

6.4 Check Your Understanding A molecule is vibrating at a frequency of $5.0 \times 10^{14}\,\text{Hz}$. What is the smallest spacing between its vibrational energy levels?

Example 6.4

Quantum Theory Applied to a Classical Oscillator

A 1.0-kg mass oscillates at the end of a spring with a spring constant of 1000 N/m. The amplitude of these oscillations is 0.10 m. Use the concept of quantization to find the energy spacing for this classical oscillator. Is the energy quantization significant for macroscopic systems, such as this oscillator?

Strategy

We use **Equation 6.10** as though the system were a quantum oscillator, but with the frequency f of the mass vibrating on a spring. To evaluate whether or not quantization has a significant effect, we compare the quantum energy spacing with the macroscopic total energy of this classical oscillator.

Solution

For the spring constant, $k = 1.0 \times 10^3\,\text{N/m}$, the frequency f of the mass, $m = 1.0\text{kg}$, is

$$f = \frac{1}{2\pi}\sqrt{\frac{k}{m}} = \frac{1}{2\pi}\sqrt{\frac{1.0 \times 10^3\,\text{N/m}}{1.0\text{kg}}} \simeq 5.0\,\text{Hz}$$

The energy quantum that corresponds to this frequency is

$$\Delta E = hf = (6.626 \times 10^{-34}\,\text{J}\cdot\text{s})(5.0\text{Hz}) = 3.3 \times 10^{-33}\,\text{J}$$

When vibrations have amplitude $A = 0.10\text{m}$, the energy of oscillations is

$$E = \frac{1}{2}kA^2 = \frac{1}{2}(1000\text{N/m})(0.1\text{m})^2 = 5.0\text{J}$$

Significance

Thus, for a classical oscillator, we have $\Delta E/E \approx 10^{-34}$. We see that the separation of the energy levels is immeasurably small. Therefore, for all practical purposes, the energy of a classical oscillator takes on continuous values. This is why classical principles may be applied to macroscopic systems encountered in everyday life without loss of accuracy.

6.5 Check Your Understanding Would the result in **Example 6.4** be different if the mass were not 1.0 kg but a tiny mass of 1.0 μg, and the amplitude of vibrations were 0.10 μm?

When Planck first published his result, the hypothesis of energy quanta was not taken seriously by the physics community because it did not follow from any established physics theory at that time. It was perceived, even by Planck himself, as a useful mathematical trick that led to a good theoretical "fit" to the experimental curve. This perception was changed in 1905 when Einstein published his explanation of the photoelectric effect, in which he gave Planck's energy quantum a new meaning: that of a particle of light.

6.2 | Photoelectric Effect

Learning Objectives

By the end of this section you will be able to:

- Describe physical characteristics of the photoelectric effect
- Explain why the photoelectric effect cannot be explained by classical physics
- Describe how Einstein's idea of a particle of radiation explains the photoelectric effect

When a metal surface is exposed to a monochromatic electromagnetic wave of sufficiently short wavelength (or equivalently, above a threshold frequency), the incident radiation is absorbed and the exposed surface emits electrons. This phenomenon is known as the **photoelectric effect**. Electrons that are emitted in this process are called **photoelectrons**.

The experimental setup to study the photoelectric effect is shown schematically in Figure 6.8. The target material serves as the anode, which becomes the emitter of photoelectrons when it is illuminated by monochromatic radiation. We call this electrode the **photoelectrode**. Photoelectrons are collected at the cathode, which is kept at a lower potential with respect to the anode. The potential difference between the electrodes can be increased or decreased, or its polarity can be reversed. The electrodes are enclosed in an evacuated glass tube so that photoelectrons do not lose their kinetic energy on collisions with air molecules in the space between electrodes.

When the target material is not exposed to radiation, no current is registered in this circuit because the circuit is broken (note, there is a gap between the electrodes). But when the target material is connected to the negative terminal of a battery and exposed to radiation, a current is registered in this circuit; this current is called the **photocurrent**. Suppose that we now reverse the potential difference between the electrodes so that the target material now connects with the positive terminal of a battery, and then we slowly increase the voltage. The photocurrent gradually dies out and eventually stops flowing completely at some value of this reversed voltage. The potential difference at which the photocurrent stops flowing is called the **stopping potential**.

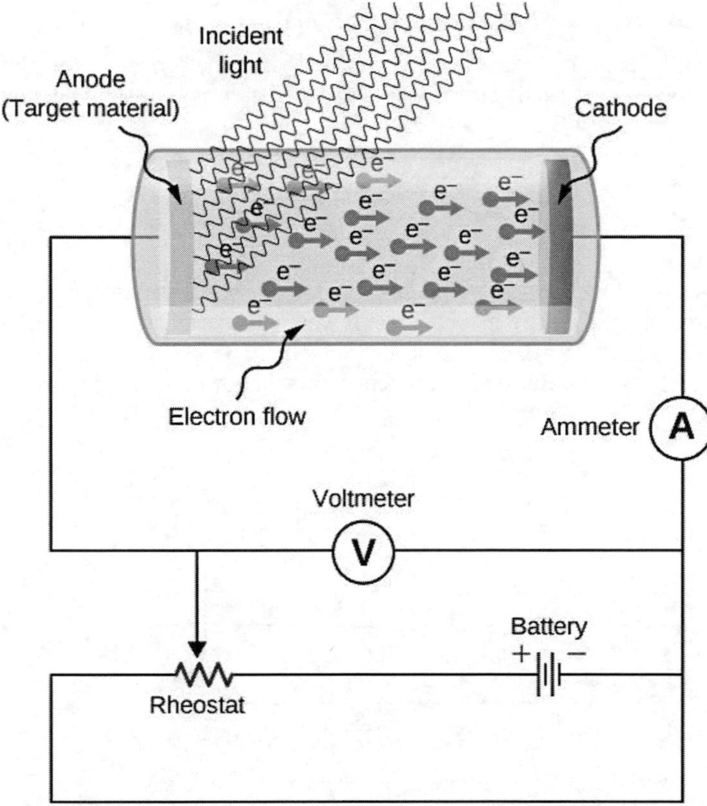

Figure 6.8 An experimental setup to study the photoelectric effect. The anode and cathode are enclosed in an evacuated glass tube. The voltmeter measures the electric potential difference between the electrodes, and the ammeter measures the photocurrent. The incident radiation is monochromatic.

Characteristics of the Photoelectric Effect

The photoelectric effect has three important characteristics that cannot be explained by classical physics: (1) the absence of a lag time, (2) the independence of the kinetic energy of photoelectrons on the intensity of incident radiation, and (3) the presence of a cut-off frequency. Let's examine each of these characteristics.

The absence of lag time

When radiation strikes the target material in the electrode, electrons are emitted almost instantaneously, even at very low intensities of incident radiation. This absence of lag time contradicts our understanding based on classical physics. Classical physics predicts that for low-energy radiation, it would take significant time before irradiated electrons could gain sufficient energy to leave the electrode surface; however, such an energy buildup is not observed.

The intensity of incident radiation and the kinetic energy of photoelectrons

Typical experimental curves are shown in **Figure 6.9**, in which the photocurrent is plotted versus the applied potential difference between the electrodes. For the positive potential difference, the current steadily grows until it reaches a plateau. Furthering the potential increase beyond this point does not increase the photocurrent at all. A higher intensity of radiation produces a higher value of photocurrent. For the negative potential difference, as the absolute value of the potential difference increases, the value of the photocurrent decreases and becomes zero at the stopping potential. For any intensity of incident radiation, whether the intensity is high or low, the value of the stopping potential always stays at one value.

To understand why this result is unusual from the point of view of classical physics, we first have to analyze the energy of photoelectrons. A photoelectron that leaves the surface has kinetic energy K. It gained this energy from the incident electromagnetic wave. In the space between the electrodes, a photoelectron moves in the electric potential and its energy changes by the amount $q\Delta V$, where ΔV is the potential difference and $q = -e$. Because no forces are present but electric force, by applying the work-energy theorem, we obtain the energy balance $\Delta K - e\Delta V = 0$ for the photoelectron, where ΔK is the change in the photoelectron's kinetic energy. When the stopping potential $-\Delta V_s$ is applied, the photoelectron loses its initial kinetic energy K_i and comes to rest. Thus, its energy balance becomes

$(0 - K_i) - e(-\Delta V_s) = 0,$ so that $K_i = e\Delta V_s$. In the presence of the stopping potential, the largest kinetic energy K_{max} that a photoelectron can have is its initial kinetic energy, which it has at the surface of the photoelectrode. Therefore, the largest kinetic energy of photoelectrons can be directly measured by measuring the stopping potential:

$$K_{max} = e\Delta V_s. \tag{6.12}$$

At this point we can see where the classical theory is at odds with the experimental results. In classical theory, the photoelectron absorbs electromagnetic energy in a continuous way; this means that when the incident radiation has a high intensity, the kinetic energy in Equation 6.12 is expected to be high. Similarly, when the radiation has a low intensity, the kinetic energy is expected to be low. But the experiment shows that the maximum kinetic energy of photoelectrons is independent of the light intensity.

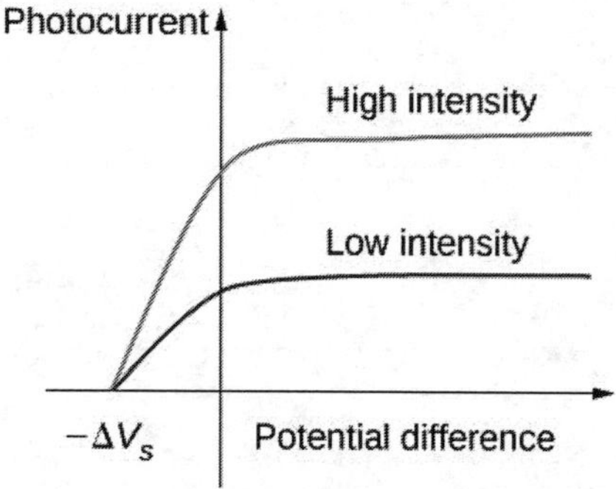

Figure 6.9 The detected photocurrent plotted versus the applied potential difference shows that for any intensity of incident radiation, whether the intensity is high (upper curve) or low (lower curve), the value of the stopping potential is always the same.

The presence of a cut-off frequency

For any metal surface, there is a minimum frequency of incident radiation below which photocurrent does not occur. The value of this **cut-off frequency** for the photoelectric effect is a physical property of the metal: Different materials have different values of cut-off frequency. Experimental data show a typical linear trend (see Figure 6.10). The kinetic energy of photoelectrons at the surface grows linearly with the increasing frequency of incident radiation. Measurements for all metal surfaces give linear plots with one slope. None of these observed phenomena is in accord with the classical understanding of nature. According to the classical description, the kinetic energy of photoelectrons should not depend on the frequency of incident radiation at all, and there should be no cut-off frequency. Instead, in the classical picture, electrons receive energy from the incident electromagnetic wave in a continuous way, and the amount of energy they receive depends only on the intensity of the incident light and nothing else. So in the classical understanding, as long as the light is shining, the photoelectric effect is expected to continue.

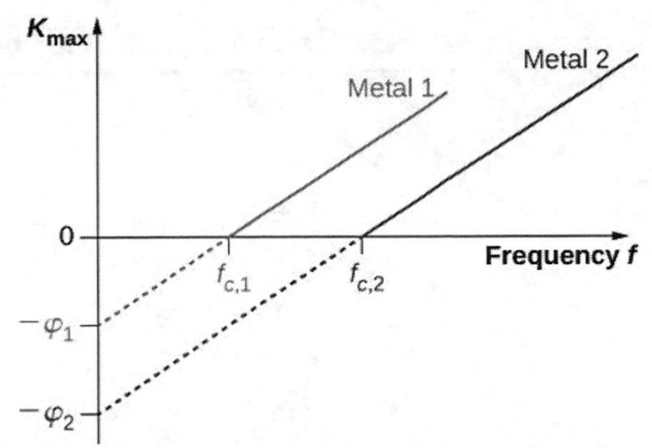

Figure 6.10 Kinetic energy of photoelectrons at the surface versus the frequency of incident radiation. The photoelectric effect can only occur above the cut-off frequency f_c. Measurements for all metal surfaces give linear plots with one slope. Each metal surface has its own cut-off frequency.

The Work Function

The photoelectric effect was explained in 1905 by A. Einstein. Einstein reasoned that if Planck's hypothesis about energy quanta was correct for describing the energy exchange between electromagnetic radiation and cavity walls, it should also work to describe energy absorption from electromagnetic radiation by the surface of a photoelectrode. He postulated that an electromagnetic wave carries its energy in discrete packets. Einstein's postulate goes beyond Planck's hypothesis because it states that the light itself consists of energy quanta. In other words, it states that electromagnetic waves are quantized.

In Einstein's approach, a beam of monochromatic light of frequency *f* is made of photons. A **photon** is a particle of light. Each photon moves at the speed of light and carries an energy quantum E_f. A photon's energy depends only on its frequency *f*. Explicitly, the **energy of a photon** is

$$E_f = hf \tag{6.13}$$

where h is Planck's constant. In the photoelectric effect, photons arrive at the metal surface and each photon gives away *all* of its energy to only *one* electron on the metal surface. This transfer of energy from photon to electron is of the "all or nothing" type, and there are no fractional transfers in which a photon would lose only part of its energy and survive. The essence of a **quantum phenomenon** is either a photon transfers its entire energy and ceases to exist or there is no transfer at all. This is in contrast with the classical picture, where fractional energy transfers are permitted. Having this quantum understanding, the energy balance for an electron on the surface that receives the energy E_f from a photon is

$$E_f = K_{\text{max}} + \phi$$

where K_{max} is the kinetic energy, given by **Equation 6.12**, that an electron has at the very instant it gets detached from the surface. In this energy balance equation, ϕ is the energy needed to detach a photoelectron from the surface. This energy ϕ is called the **work function** of the metal. Each metal has its characteristic work function, as illustrated in **Table 6.1**. To obtain the kinetic energy of photoelectrons at the surface, we simply invert the energy balance equation and use **Equation 6.13** to express the energy of the absorbed photon. This gives us the expression for the kinetic energy of photoelectrons, which explicitly depends on the frequency of incident radiation:

$$K_{\text{max}} = hf - \phi. \tag{6.14}$$

This equation has a simple mathematical form but its physics is profound. We can now elaborate on the physical meaning behind **Equation 6.14**.

Typical Values of the Work Function for Some Common Metals

Metal	ϕ (eV)
Na	2.46
Al	4.08
Pb	4.14
Zn	4.31
Fe	4.50
Cu	4.70
Ag	4.73
Pt	6.35

Table 6.1

In Einstein's interpretation, interactions take place between individual electrons and individual photons. The absence of a lag time means that these one-on-one interactions occur instantaneously. This interaction time cannot be increased by lowering the light intensity. The light intensity corresponds to the number of photons arriving at the metal surface per unit time. Even at very low light intensities, the photoelectric effect still occurs because the interaction is between one electron and one photon. As long as there is at least one photon with enough energy to transfer it to a bound electron, a photoelectron will appear on the surface of the photoelectrode.

The existence of the cut-off frequency f_c for the photoelectric effect follows from **Equation 6.14** because the kinetic energy K_{max} of the photoelectron can take only positive values. This means that there must be some threshold frequency for which the kinetic energy is zero, $0 = hf_c - \phi$. In this way, we obtain the explicit formula for cut-off frequency:

$$f_c = \frac{\phi}{h}. \tag{6.15}$$

Cut-off frequency depends only on the work function of the metal and is in direct proportion to it. When the work function is large (when electrons are bound fast to the metal surface), the energy of the threshold photon must be large to produce a photoelectron, and then the corresponding threshold frequency is large. Photons with frequencies larger than the threshold frequency f_c always produce photoelectrons because they have $K_{\text{max}} > 0$. Photons with frequencies smaller than f_c do not have enough energy to produce photoelectrons. Therefore, when incident radiation has a frequency below the cut-off frequency, the photoelectric effect is not observed. Because frequency f and wavelength λ of electromagnetic waves are related by the fundamental relation $\lambda f = c$ (where c is the speed of light in vacuum), the cut-off frequency has its corresponding **cut-off wavelength** λ_c :

$$\lambda_c = \frac{c}{f_c} = \frac{c}{\phi / h} = \frac{hc}{\phi}. \tag{6.16}$$

In this equation, $hc = 1240\,\text{eV} \cdot \text{nm}$. Our observations can be restated in the following equivalent way: When the incident radiation has wavelengths longer than the cut-off wavelength, the photoelectric effect does not occur.

Example 6.5

Photoelectric Effect for Silver

Radiation with wavelength 300 nm is incident on a silver surface. Will photoelectrons be observed?

Strategy

Photoelectrons can be ejected from the metal surface only when the incident radiation has a shorter wavelength than the cut-off wavelength. The work function of silver is $\phi = 4.73\,\text{eV}$ (**Table 6.1**). To make the estimate, we use **Equation 6.16**.

Solution

The threshold wavelength for observing the photoelectric effect in silver is

$$\lambda_c = \frac{hc}{\phi} = \frac{1240\,\text{eV}\cdot\text{nm}}{4.73\,\text{eV}} = 262\,\text{nm}.$$

The incident radiation has wavelength 300 nm, which is longer than the cut-off wavelength; therefore, photoelectrons are not observed.

Significance

If the photoelectrode were made of sodium instead of silver, the cut-off wavelength would be 504 nm and photoelectrons would be observed.

Equation 6.14 in Einstein's model tells us that the maximum kinetic energy of photoelectrons is a linear function of the frequency of incident radiation, which is illustrated in **Figure 6.10**. For any metal, the slope of this plot has a value of Planck's constant. The intercept with the K_{max} -axis gives us a value of the work function that is characteristic for the metal. On the other hand, K_{max} can be directly measured in the experiment by measuring the value of the stopping potential ΔV_s (see **Equation 6.12**) at which the photocurrent stops. These direct measurements allow us to determine experimentally the value of Planck's constant, as well as work functions of materials.

Einstein's model also gives a straightforward explanation for the photocurrent values shown in **Figure 6.9**. For example, doubling the intensity of radiation translates to doubling the number of photons that strike the surface per unit time. The larger the number of photons, the larger is the number of photoelectrons, which leads to a larger photocurrent in the circuit. This is how radiation intensity affects the photocurrent. The photocurrent must reach a plateau at some value of potential difference because, in unit time, the number of photoelectrons is equal to the number of incident photons and the number of incident photons does not depend on the applied potential difference at all, but only on the intensity of incident radiation. The stopping potential does not change with the radiation intensity because the kinetic energy of photoelectrons (see **Equation 6.14**) does not depend on the radiation intensity.

Example 6.6

Work Function and Cut-Off Frequency

When a 180-nm light is used in an experiment with an unknown metal, the measured photocurrent drops to zero at potential – 0.80 V. Determine the work function of the metal and its cut-off frequency for the photoelectric effect.

Strategy

To find the cut-off frequency f_c, we use **Equation 6.15**, but first we must find the work function ϕ. To find ϕ, we use **Equation 6.12** and **Equation 6.14**. Photocurrent drops to zero at the stopping value of potential, so we identify $\Delta V_s = 0.8\text{V}$.

Solution

We use **Equation 6.12** to find the kinetic energy of the photoelectrons:

$$K_{\text{max}} = e\Delta V_s = e(0.80\text{V}) = 0.80\,\text{eV}.$$

Now we solve **Equation 6.14** for ϕ :

$$\phi = hf - K_{\text{max}} = \frac{hc}{\lambda} - K_{\text{max}} = \frac{1240\,\text{eV}\cdot\text{nm}}{180\,\text{nm}} - 0.80\,\text{eV} = 6.09\,\text{eV}.$$

Finally, we use **Equation 6.15** to find the cut-off frequency:

$$f_c = \frac{\phi}{h} = \frac{6.09\ \text{eV}}{4.136 \times 10^{-15}\ \text{eV} \cdot \text{s}} = 1.47 \times 10^{-15}\ \text{Hz}.$$

Significance

In calculations like the one shown in this example, it is convenient to use Planck's constant in the units of $\text{eV} \cdot \text{s}$ and express all energies in eV instead of joules.

Example 6.7

The Photon Energy and Kinetic Energy of Photoelectrons

A 430-nm violet light is incident on a calcium photoelectrode with a work function of 2.71 eV.

Find the energy of the incident photons and the maximum kinetic energy of ejected electrons.

Strategy

The energy of the incident photon is $E_f = hf = hc/\lambda$, where we use $f\lambda = c$. To obtain the maximum energy of the ejected electrons, we use **Equation 6.16**.

Solution

$$E_f = \frac{hc}{\lambda} = \frac{1240\ \text{eV} \cdot \text{nm}}{430\ \text{nm}} = 2.88\ \text{eV},\ K_{\text{max}} = E_f - \phi = 2.88\ \text{eV} - 2.71\ \text{eV} = 0.17\ \text{eV}$$

Significance

In this experimental setup, photoelectrons stop flowing at the stopping potential of 0.17 V.

6.6 Check Your Understanding A yellow 589-nm light is incident on a surface whose work function is 1.20 eV. What is the stopping potential? What is the cut-off wavelength?

6.7 Check Your Understanding Cut-off frequency for the photoelectric effect in some materials is 8.0×10^{13} Hz. When the incident light has a frequency of 1.2×10^{14} Hz, the stopping potential is measured as – 0.16 V. Estimate a value of Planck's constant from these data (in units $\text{J} \cdot \text{s}$ and $\text{eV} \cdot \text{s}$) and determine the percentage error of your estimation.

6.3 | The Compton Effect

Learning Objectives

By the end of this section, you will be able to:

- Describe Compton's experiment
- Explain the Compton wavelength shift
- Describe how experiments with X-rays confirm the particle nature of radiation

Two of Einstein's influential ideas introduced in 1905 were the theory of special relativity and the concept of a light quantum, which we now call a photon. Beyond 1905, Einstein went further to suggest that freely propagating electromagnetic waves consisted of photons that are particles of light in the same sense that electrons or other massive particles are particles of matter. A beam of monochromatic light of wavelength λ (or equivalently, of frequency f) can be seen either as a classical wave or as a collection of photons that travel in a vacuum with one speed, c (the speed of light), and all carrying the same energy, $E_f = hf$. This idea proved useful for explaining the interactions of light with particles of matter.

Momentum of a Photon

Unlike a particle of matter that is characterized by its rest mass m_0, a photon is massless. In a vacuum, unlike a particle of matter that may vary its speed but cannot reach the speed of light, a photon travels at only one speed, which is exactly the speed of light. From the point of view of Newtonian classical mechanics, these two characteristics imply that a photon should not exist at all. For example, how can we find the linear momentum or kinetic energy of a body whose mass is zero? This apparent paradox vanishes if we describe a photon as a relativistic particle. According to the theory of special relativity, any particle in nature obeys the relativistic energy equation

$$E^2 = p^2c^2 + m_0^2c^4. \tag{6.17}$$

This relation can also be applied to a photon. In **Equation 6.17**, E is the total energy of a particle, p is its linear momentum, and m_0 is its rest mass. For a photon, we simply set $m_0 = 0$ in this equation. This leads to the expression for the momentum p_f of a photon

$$p_f = \frac{E_f}{c}. \tag{6.18}$$

Here the photon's energy E_f is the same as that of a light quantum of frequency f, which we introduced to explain the photoelectric effect:

$$E_f = hf = \frac{hc}{\lambda}. \tag{6.19}$$

The wave relation that connects frequency f with wavelength λ and speed c also holds for photons:

$$\lambda f = c \tag{6.20}$$

Therefore, a photon can be equivalently characterized by either its energy and wavelength, or its frequency and momentum. **Equation 6.19** and **Equation 6.20** can be combined into the explicit relation between a photon's momentum and its wavelength:

$$p_f = \frac{h}{\lambda}. \tag{6.21}$$

Notice that this equation gives us only the magnitude of the photon's momentum and contains no information about the direction in which the photon is moving. To include the direction, it is customary to write the photon's momentum as a vector:

$$\vec{\mathbf{p}}_f = \hbar \vec{\mathbf{k}}. \tag{6.22}$$

In **Equation 6.22**, $\hbar = h/2\pi$ is the **reduced Planck's constant** (pronounced "h-bar"), which is just Planck's constant divided by the factor 2π. Vector $\vec{\mathbf{k}}$ is called the "wave vector" or propagation vector (the direction in which a photon is moving). The **propagation vector** shows the direction of the photon's linear momentum vector. The magnitude of the wave vector is $k = \left| \vec{\mathbf{k}} \right| = 2\pi / \lambda$ and is called the **wave number**. Notice that this equation does not introduce any new physics.

We can verify that the magnitude of the vector in Equation 6.22 is the same as that given by Equation 6.18.

The Compton Effect

The **Compton effect** is the term used for an unusual result observed when X-rays are scattered on some materials. By classical theory, when an electromagnetic wave is scattered off atoms, the wavelength of the scattered radiation is expected to be the same as the wavelength of the incident radiation. Contrary to this prediction of classical physics, observations show that when X-rays are scattered off some materials, such as graphite, the scattered X-rays have different wavelengths from the wavelength of the incident X-rays. This classically unexplainable phenomenon was studied experimentally by Arthur H. Compton and his collaborators, and Compton gave its explanation in 1923.

To explain the shift in wavelengths measured in the experiment, Compton used Einstein's idea of light as a particle. The Compton effect has a very important place in the history of physics because it shows that electromagnetic radiation cannot be explained as a purely wave phenomenon. The explanation of the Compton effect gave a convincing argument to the physics community that electromagnetic waves can indeed behave like a stream of photons, which placed the concept of a photon on firm ground.

The schematics of Compton's experimental setup are shown in Figure 6.11. The idea of the experiment is straightforward: Monochromatic X-rays with wavelength λ are incident on a sample of graphite (the "target"), where they interact with atoms inside the sample; they later emerge as scattered X-rays with wavelength λ'. A detector placed behind the target can measure the intensity of radiation scattered in any direction θ with respect to the direction of the incident X-ray beam. This **scattering angle**, θ, is the angle between the direction of the scattered beam and the direction of the incident beam. In this experiment, we know the intensity and the wavelength λ of the incoming (incident) beam; and for a given scattering angle θ, we measure the intensity and the wavelength λ' of the outgoing (scattered) beam. Typical results of these measurements are shown in Figure 6.12, where the *x*-axis is the wavelength of the scattered X-rays and the *y*-axis is the intensity of the scattered X-rays, measured for different scattering angles (indicated on the graphs). For all scattering angles (except for $\theta = 0°$), we measure two intensity peaks. One peak is located at the wavelength λ, which is the wavelength of the incident beam. The other peak is located at some other wavelength, λ'. The two peaks are separated by $\Delta\lambda$, which depends on the scattering angle θ of the outgoing beam (in the direction of observation). The separation $\Delta\lambda$ is called the **Compton shift**.

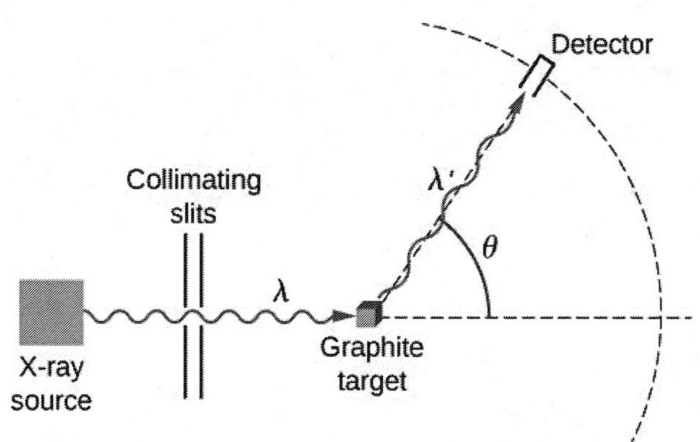

Figure 6.11 Experimental setup for studying Compton scattering.

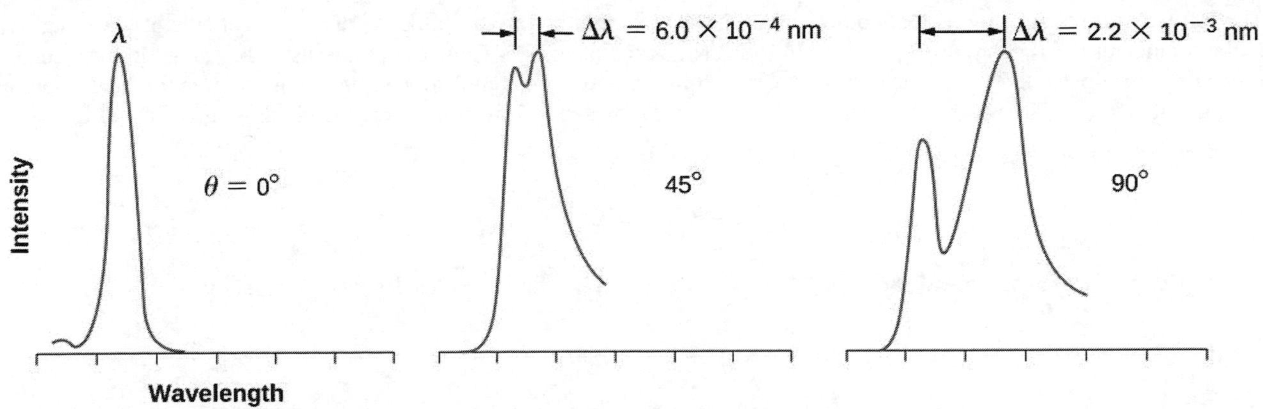

Figure 6.12 Experimental data show the Compton effect for X-rays scattering off graphite at various angles: The intensity of the scattered beam has two peaks. One peak appears at the wavelength λ of the incident radiation and the second peak appears at wavelength λ'. The separation $\Delta\lambda$ between the peaks depends on the scattering angle θ, which is the angular position of the detector in **Figure 6.11**. The experimental data in this figure are plotted in arbitrary units so that the height of the profile reflects the intensity of the scattered beam above background noise.

Compton Shift

As given by Compton, the explanation of the Compton shift is that in the target material, graphite, valence electrons are loosely bound in the atoms and behave like free electrons. Compton assumed that the incident X-ray radiation is a stream of photons. An incoming photon in this stream collides with a valence electron in the graphite target. In the course of this collision, the incoming photon transfers some part of its energy and momentum to the target electron and leaves the scene as a scattered photon. This model explains in qualitative terms why the scattered radiation has a longer wavelength than the incident radiation. Put simply, a photon that has lost some of its energy emerges as a photon with a lower frequency, or equivalently, with a longer wavelength. To show that his model was correct, Compton used it to derive the expression for the Compton shift. In his derivation, he assumed that both photon and electron are relativistic particles and that the collision obeys two commonsense principles: (1) the conservation of linear momentum and (2) the conservation of total relativistic energy.

In the following derivation of the Compton shift, E_f and $\vec{\mathbf{p}}_f$ denote the energy and momentum, respectively, of an incident photon with frequency *f*. The photon collides with a relativistic electron at rest, which means that immediately before the collision, the electron's energy is entirely its rest mass energy, m_0c^2. Immediately after the collision, the electron has energy *E* and momentum $\vec{\mathbf{p}}$, both of which satisfy **Equation 6.19**. Immediately after the collision, the outgoing photon has energy $\tilde{E}_f$, momentum $\vec{\tilde{\mathbf{p}}}_f$, and frequency f'. The direction of the incident photon is horizontal from left to right, and the direction of the outgoing photon is at the angle θ, as illustrated in **Figure 6.11**. The scattering angle θ is the angle between the momentum vectors $\vec{\mathbf{p}}_f$ and $\vec{\tilde{\mathbf{p}}}_f$, and we can write their scalar product:

$$\vec{\mathbf{p}}_f \cdot \vec{\tilde{\mathbf{p}}}_f = p_f \tilde{p}_f \cos\theta. \tag{6.23}$$

Following Compton's argument, we assume that the colliding photon and electron form an isolated system. This assumption is valid for weakly bound electrons that, to a good approximation, can be treated as free particles. Our first equation is the conservation of energy for the photon-electron system:

$$E_f + m_0c^2 = \tilde{E}_f + E. \tag{6.24}$$

The left side of this equation is the energy of the system at the instant immediately before the collision, and the right side of the equation is the energy of the system at the instant immediately after the collision. Our second equation is the conservation of linear momentum for the photon–electron system where the electron is at rest at the instant immediately before the collision:

$$\vec{\mathbf{p}}_f = \vec{\tilde{\mathbf{p}}}_f + \vec{\mathbf{p}}. \tag{6.25}$$

The left side of this equation is the momentum of the system right before the collision, and the right side of the equation is the momentum of the system right after collision. The entire physics of Compton scattering is contained in these three preceding equations—the remaining part is algebra. At this point, we could jump to the concluding formula for the Compton shift, but it is beneficial to highlight the main algebraic steps that lead to Compton's formula, which we give here as follows.

We start with rearranging the terms in **Equation 6.24** and squaring it:

$$\left[\left(E_f - \tilde{E}_f\right) + m_0 c^2\right]^2 = E^2.$$

In the next step, we substitute **Equation 6.19** for E^2, simplify, and divide both sides by c^2 to obtain

$$\left(E_f / c - \tilde{E}_f / c\right)^2 + 2m_0 c\left(E_f / c - \tilde{E}_f / c\right) = p^2.$$

Now we can use **Equation 6.21** to express this form of the energy equation in terms of momenta. The result is

$$\left(p_f - \tilde{p}_f\right)^2 + 2m_0 c\left(p_f - \tilde{p}_f\right) = p^2. \tag{6.26}$$

To eliminate p^2, we turn to the momentum equation **Equation 6.25**, rearrange its terms, and square it to obtain

$$\left(\vec{\mathbf{p}}_f - \vec{\tilde{\mathbf{p}}}_f\right)^2 = p^2 \text{ and} \left(\vec{\mathbf{p}}_f - \vec{\tilde{\mathbf{p}}}_f\right)^2 = p_f^2 + \tilde{p}_f^2 - 2\,\vec{\mathbf{p}}_f \cdot \vec{\tilde{\mathbf{p}}}_f.$$

The product of the momentum vectors is given by **Equation 6.23**. When we substitute this result for p^2 in **Equation 6.26**, we obtain the energy equation that contains the scattering angle θ:

$$\left(p_f - \tilde{p}_f\right)^2 + 2m_0 c\left(p_f - \tilde{p}_f\right) = p_f^2 + \tilde{p}_f^2 - 2p_f \tilde{p}_f \cos\theta.$$

With further algebra, this result can be simplified to

$$\frac{1}{\tilde{p}_f} - \frac{1}{p_f} = \frac{1}{m_0 c}(1 - \cos\theta). \tag{6.27}$$

Now recall **Equation 6.21** and write: $1/\tilde{p}_f = \lambda'/h$ and $1/p_f = \lambda/h$. When these relations are substituted into **Equation 6.27**, we obtain the relation for the Compton shift:

$$\lambda' - \lambda = \frac{h}{m_0 c}(1 - \cos\theta). \tag{6.28}$$

The factor $h/m_0 c$ is called the **Compton wavelength** of the electron:

$$\lambda_c = \frac{h}{m_0 c} = 0.00243 \text{ nm} = 2.43 \text{ pm}. \tag{6.29}$$

Denoting the shift as $\Delta\lambda = \lambda' - \lambda$, the concluding result can be rewritten as

$$\Delta\lambda = \lambda_c(1 - \cos\theta). \tag{6.30}$$

This formula for the Compton shift describes outstandingly well the experimental results shown in **Figure 6.12**. Scattering data measured for molybdenum, graphite, calcite, and many other target materials are in accord with this theoretical result. The nonshifted peak shown in **Figure 6.12** is due to photon collisions with tightly bound inner electrons in the target material. Photons that collide with the inner electrons of the target atoms in fact collide with the entire atom. In this extreme case, the rest mass in **Equation 6.29** must be changed to the rest mass of the atom. This type of shift is four orders of magnitude smaller than the shift caused by collisions with electrons and is so small that it can be neglected.

Compton scattering is an example of **inelastic scattering**, in which the scattered radiation has a longer wavelength than the wavelength of the incident radiation. In today's usage, the term "Compton scattering" is used for the inelastic scattering of photons by free, charged particles. In Compton scattering, treating photons as particles with momenta that can be transferred to charged particles provides the theoretical background to explain the wavelength shifts measured in experiments; this is the evidence that radiation consists of photons.

Example 6.8

Compton Scattering

An incident 71-pm X-ray is incident on a calcite target. Find the wavelength of the X-ray scattered at a $30°$ angle. What is the largest shift that can be expected in this experiment?

Strategy

To find the wavelength of the scattered X-ray, first we must find the Compton shift for the given scattering angle, $\theta = 30°$. We use **Equation 6.30**. Then we add this shift to the incident wavelength to obtain the scattered wavelength. The largest Compton shift occurs at the angle θ when $1 - \cos\theta$ has the largest value, which is for the angle $\theta = 180°$.

Solution

The shift at $\theta = 30°$ is

$$\Delta\lambda = \lambda_c(1 - \cos 30°) = 0.134\lambda_c = (0.134)(2.43)\text{ pm} = 0.325\text{ pm}.$$

This gives the scattered wavelength:

$$\lambda' = \lambda + \Delta\lambda = (71 + 0.325)\text{ pm} = 71.325\text{ pm}.$$

The largest shift is

$$(\Delta\lambda)_{\max} = \lambda_c(1 - \cos 180^0) = 2(2.43\text{ pm}) = 4.86\text{ pm}.$$

Significance

The largest shift in wavelength is detected for the backscattered radiation; however, most of the photons from the incident beam pass through the target and only a small fraction of photons gets backscattered (typically, less than 5%). Therefore, these measurements require highly sensitive detectors.

6.8 Check Your Understanding An incident 71-pm X-ray is incident on a calcite target. Find the wavelength of the X-ray scattered at a $60°$ angle. What is the smallest shift that can be expected in this experiment?

6.4 | Bohr's Model of the Hydrogen Atom

Learning Objectives

By the end of this section, you will be able to:

- Explain the difference between the absorption spectrum and the emission spectrum of radiation emitted by atoms
- Describe the Rutherford gold foil experiment and the discovery of the atomic nucleus
- Explain the atomic structure of hydrogen
- Describe the postulates of the early quantum theory for the hydrogen atom
- Summarize how Bohr's quantum model of the hydrogen atom explains the radiation spectrum of atomic hydrogen

Historically, Bohr's model of the hydrogen atom is the very first model of atomic structure that correctly explained the radiation spectra of atomic hydrogen. The model has a special place in the history of physics because it introduced an early quantum theory, which brought about new developments in scientific thought and later culminated in the development of quantum mechanics. To understand the specifics of Bohr's model, we must first review the nineteenth-century discoveries that prompted its formulation.

When we use a prism to analyze white light coming from the sun, several dark lines in the solar spectrum are observed (Figure 6.13). Solar absorption lines are called **Fraunhofer lines** after Joseph von Fraunhofer, who accurately measured their wavelengths. During 1854–1861, Gustav Kirchhoff and Robert Bunsen discovered that for the various chemical elements, the line **emission spectrum** of an element exactly matches its line **absorption spectrum**. The difference between the absorption spectrum and the emission spectrum is explained in Figure 6.14. An absorption spectrum is observed when light passes through a gas. This spectrum appears as black lines that occur only at certain wavelengths on the background of the continuous spectrum of white light (Figure 6.13). The missing wavelengths tell us which wavelengths of the radiation are absorbed by the gas. The emission spectrum is observed when light is emitted by a gas. This spectrum is seen as colorful lines on the black background (see Figure 6.15 and Figure 6.16). Positions of the emission lines tell us which wavelengths of the radiation are emitted by the gas. Each chemical element has its own characteristic emission spectrum. For each element, the positions of its emission lines are exactly the same as the positions of its absorption lines. This means that atoms of a specific element absorb radiation only at specific wavelengths and radiation that does not have these wavelengths is not absorbed by the element at all. This also means that the radiation emitted by atoms of each element has exactly the same wavelengths as the radiation they absorb.

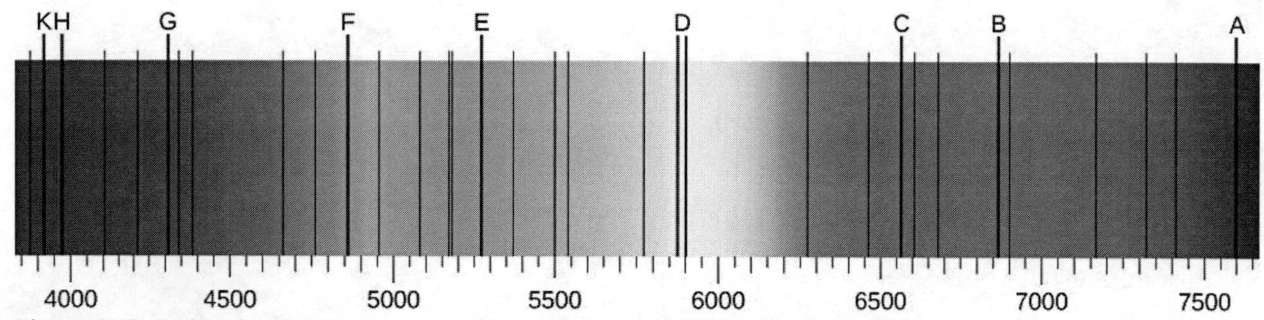

Figure 6.13 In the solar emission spectrum in the visible range from 380 nm to 710 nm, Fraunhofer lines are observed as vertical black lines at specific spectral positions in the continuous spectrum. Highly sensitive modern instruments observe thousands of such lines.

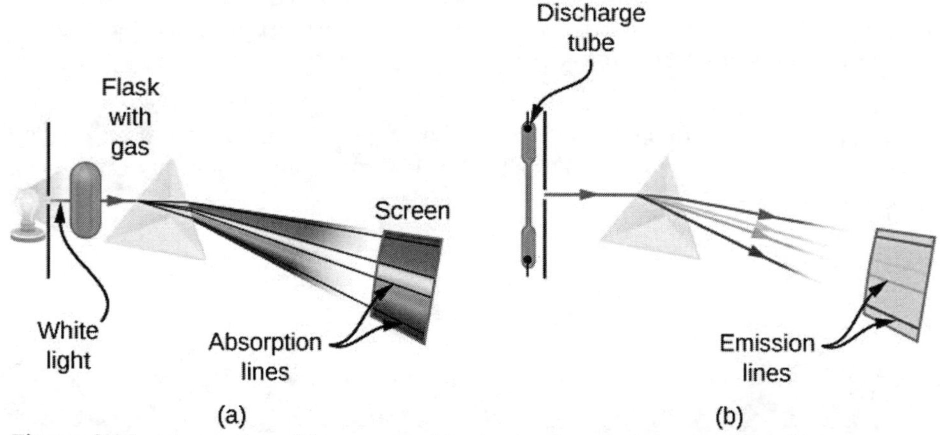

Figure 6.14 Observation of line spectra: (a) setup to observe absorption lines; (b) setup to observe emission lines. (a) White light passes through a cold gas that is contained in a glass flask. A prism is used to separate wavelengths of the passed light. In the spectrum of the passed light, some wavelengths are missing, which are seen as black absorption lines in the continuous spectrum on the viewing screen. (b) A gas is contained in a glass discharge tube that has electrodes at its ends. At a high potential difference between the electrodes, the gas glows and the light emitted from the gas passes through the prism that separates its wavelengths. In the spectrum of the emitted light, only specific wavelengths are present, which are seen as colorful emission lines on the screen.

Figure 6.15 The emission spectrum of atomic hydrogen: The spectral positions of emission lines are characteristic for hydrogen atoms. (credit: "Merikanto"/Wikimedia Commons)

Figure 6.16 The emission spectrum of atomic iron: The spectral positions of emission lines are characteristic for iron atoms.

Emission spectra of the elements have complex structures; they become even more complex for elements with higher atomic numbers. The simplest spectrum, shown in **Figure 6.15**, belongs to the hydrogen atom. Only four lines are visible to the human eye. As you read from right to left in **Figure 6.15**, these lines are: red (656 nm), called the H-α line; aqua (486 nm), blue (434 nm), and violet (410 nm). The lines with wavelengths shorter than 400 nm appear in the ultraviolet part of the spectrum (**Figure 6.15**, far left) and are invisible to the human eye. There are infinitely many invisible spectral lines in the series for hydrogen.

An empirical formula to describe the positions (wavelengths) λ of the hydrogen emission lines in this series was discovered in 1885 by Johann Balmer. It is known as the **Balmer formula**:

$$\frac{1}{\lambda} = R_{\text{H}}\left(\frac{1}{2^2} - \frac{1}{n^2}\right). \tag{6.31}$$

The constant $R_{\text{H}} = 1.09737 \times 10^7 \text{ m}^{-1}$ is called the **Rydberg constant for hydrogen**. In **Equation 6.31**, the positive integer n takes on values $n = 3, 4, 5, 6$ for the four visible lines in this series. The series of emission lines given by the Balmer formula is called the **Balmer series** for hydrogen. Other emission lines of hydrogen that were discovered in the twentieth century are described by the **Rydberg formula**, which summarizes all of the experimental data:

$$\frac{1}{\lambda} = R_{\text{H}}\left(\frac{1}{n_f^2} - \frac{1}{n_i^2}\right), \text{ where } n_i = n_f + 1, n_f + 2, n_f + 3, \ldots \tag{6.32}$$

When $n_f = 1$, the series of spectral lines is called the **Lyman series**. When $n_f = 2$, the series is called the Balmer series, and in this case, the Rydberg formula coincides with the Balmer formula. When $n_f = 3$, the series is called the **Paschen series**. When $n_f = 4$, the series is called the **Brackett series**. When $n_f = 5$, the series is called the **Pfund series**. When $n_f = 6$, we have the **Humphreys series**. As you may guess, there are infinitely many such spectral bands in the spectrum of hydrogen because n_f can be any positive integer number.

The Rydberg formula for hydrogen gives the exact positions of the spectral lines as they are observed in a laboratory; however, at the beginning of the twentieth century, nobody could explain why it worked so well. The Rydberg formula remained unexplained until the first successful model of the hydrogen atom was proposed in 1913.

Example 6.9

Limits of the Balmer Series

Calculate the longest and the shortest wavelengths in the Balmer series.

Strategy

We can use either the Balmer formula or the Rydberg formula. The longest wavelength is obtained when $1/n_i$ is largest, which is when $n_i = n_f + 1 = 3$, because $n_f = 2$ for the Balmer series. The smallest wavelength is obtained when $1/n_i$ is smallest, which is $1/n_i \to 0$ when $n_i \to \infty$.

Solution

The long-wave limit:

$$\frac{1}{\lambda} = R_{\text{H}}\left(\frac{1}{2^2} - \frac{1}{3^2}\right) = (1.09737 \times 10^7)\frac{1}{\text{m}}\left(\frac{1}{4} - \frac{1}{9}\right) \Rightarrow \lambda = 656.3\ \text{nm}$$

The short-wave limit:

$$\frac{1}{\lambda} = R_{\text{H}}\left(\frac{1}{2^2} - 0\right) = (1.09737 \times 10^7)\frac{1}{\text{m}}\left(\frac{1}{4}\right) \Rightarrow \lambda = 364.6\ \text{nm}$$

Significance

Note that there are infinitely many spectral lines lying between these two limits.

6.9 Check Your Understanding What are the limits of the Lyman series? Can you see these spectral lines?

The key to unlocking the mystery of atomic spectra is in understanding atomic structure. Scientists have long known that matter is made of atoms. According to nineteenth-century science, atoms are the smallest indivisible quantities of matter. This scientific belief was shattered by a series of groundbreaking experiments that proved the existence of subatomic particles, such as electrons, protons, and neutrons.

The electron was discovered and identified as the smallest quantity of electric charge by J.J. Thomson in 1897 in his cathode ray experiments, also known as β-ray experiments: A **β-ray** is a beam of electrons. In 1904, Thomson proposed the first model of atomic structure, known as the "plum pudding" model, in which an atom consisted of an unknown positively charged matter with negative electrons embedded in it like plums in a pudding. Around 1900, E. Rutherford, and independently, Paul Ulrich Villard, classified all radiation known at that time as **α-rays**, β-rays, and **γ-rays** (a γ-ray is a beam of highly energetic photons). In 1907, Rutherford and Thomas Royds used spectroscopy methods to show that positively charged particles of α-radiation (called **α-particles**) are in fact doubly ionized atoms of helium. In 1909, Rutherford, Ernest Marsden, and Hans Geiger used α-particles in their famous scattering experiment that disproved Thomson's model (see Linear Momentum and Collisions (http://cnx.org/content/m58317/latest/)).

In the **Rutherford gold foil experiment** (also known as the Geiger–Marsden experiment), α-particles were incident on a thin gold foil and were scattered by gold atoms inside the foil (see Types of Collisions (http://cnx.org/content/m58321/latest/#CNX_UPhysics_09_04_TvsR)). The outgoing particles were detected by a $360°$ scintillation screen surrounding the gold target (for a detailed description of the experimental setup, see Linear Momentum and Collisions (http://cnx.org/content/m58317/latest/)). When a scattered particle struck the screen, a tiny flash of light (scintillation) was observed at that location. By counting the scintillations seen at various angles with respect to the direction of the incident beam, the scientists could determine what fraction of the incident particles were scattered and what fraction were not deflected at all. If the plum pudding model were correct, there would be no back-scattered α-particles. However, the results of the Rutherford experiment showed that, although a sizable fraction of α-particles emerged from the foil not scattered at all as though the foil were not in their way, a significant fraction of α-particles were back-scattered toward the source. This kind of result was possible only when most of the mass and the entire positive charge of the gold atom were concentrated in a tiny space inside the atom.

In 1911, Rutherford proposed a **nuclear model of the atom**. In Rutherford's model, an atom contained a positively charged nucleus of negligible size, almost like a point, but included almost the entire mass of the atom. The atom also contained negative electrons that were located within the atom but relatively far away from the nucleus. Ten years later, Rutherford coined the name *proton* for the nucleus of hydrogen and the name *neutron* for a hypothetical electrically neutral particle that would mediate the binding of positive protons in the nucleus (the neutron was discovered in 1932 by James Chadwick). Rutherford is credited with the discovery of the atomic nucleus; however, the Rutherford model of atomic structure does not explain the Rydberg formula for the hydrogen emission lines.

Bohr's model of the hydrogen atom, proposed by Niels Bohr in 1913, was the first quantum model that correctly explained the hydrogen emission spectrum. Bohr's model combines the classical mechanics of planetary motion with the quantum concept of photons. Once Rutherford had established the existence of the atomic nucleus, Bohr's intuition that the negative electron in the hydrogen atom must revolve around the positive nucleus became a logical consequence of the inverse-square-distance law of electrostatic attraction. Recall that Coulomb's law describing the attraction between two opposite charges has a similar form to Newton's universal law of gravitation in the sense that the gravitational force and the electrostatic force are both decreasing as $1/r^2$, where *r* is the separation distance between the bodies. In the same way as Earth revolves around the sun, the negative electron in the hydrogen atom can revolve around the positive nucleus. However, an accelerating charge radiates its energy. Classically, if the electron moved around the nucleus in a planetary fashion, it would be undergoing centripetal acceleration, and thus would be radiating energy that would cause it to spiral down into the nucleus. Such a planetary hydrogen atom would not be stable, which is contrary to what we know about ordinary hydrogen atoms that do not disintegrate. Moreover, the classical motion of the electron is not able to explain the discrete emission spectrum of hydrogen.

To circumvent these two difficulties, Bohr proposed the following three **postulates of Bohr's model**:

1. The negative electron moves around the positive nucleus (proton) in a circular orbit. All electron orbits are centered at the nucleus. Not all classically possible orbits are available to an electron bound to the nucleus.

2. The allowed electron orbits satisfy the *first quantization condition*: In the *n*th orbit, the angular momentum L_n of the electron can take only discrete values:

$$L_n = n\hbar, \text{ where } n = 1, 2, 3, ... \quad (6.33)$$

   This postulate says that the electron's angular momentum is quantized. Denoted by r_n and v_n, respectively, the radius of the *n*th orbit and the electron's speed in it, the first quantization condition can be expressed explicitly as

$$m_e v_n r_n = n\hbar. \quad (6.34)$$

3. An electron is allowed to make transitions from one orbit where its energy is E_n to another orbit where its energy is E_m. When an atom absorbs a photon, the electron makes a transition to a higher-energy orbit. When an atom emits a photon, the electron transits to a lower-energy orbit. Electron transitions with the simultaneous photon absorption or photon emission take place *instantaneously*. The allowed electron transitions satisfy the *second quantization condition*:

$$hf = |E_n - E_m| \quad (6.35)$$

   where hf is the energy of either an emitted or an absorbed photon with frequency *f*. The second quantization condition states that an electron's change in energy in the hydrogen atom is quantized.

These three postulates of the early quantum theory of the hydrogen atom allow us to derive not only the Rydberg formula, but also the value of the Rydberg constant and other important properties of the hydrogen atom such as its energy levels, its ionization energy, and the sizes of electron orbits. Note that in Bohr's model, along with two nonclassical quantization postulates, we also have the classical description of the electron as a particle that is subjected to the Coulomb force, and its motion must obey Newton's laws of motion. The hydrogen atom, as an isolated system, must obey the laws of conservation of energy and momentum in the way we know from classical physics. Having this theoretical framework in mind, we are ready to proceed with our analysis.

Electron Orbits

To obtain the size r_n of the electron's *n*th orbit and the electron's speed v_n in it, we turn to Newtonian mechanics. As a charged particle, the electron experiences an electrostatic pull toward the positively charged nucleus in the center of its circular orbit. This electrostatic pull is the centripetal force that causes the electron to move in a circle around the nucleus. Therefore, the magnitude of centripetal force is identified with the magnitude of the electrostatic force:

$$\frac{m_e v_n^2}{r_n} = \frac{1}{4\pi\varepsilon_0}\frac{e^2}{r_n^2}. \tag{6.36}$$

Here, e denotes the value of the elementary charge. The negative electron and positive proton have the same value of charge, $|q| = e$. When **Equation 6.36** is combined with the first quantization condition given by **Equation 6.34**, we can solve for the speed, v_n, and for the radius, r_n:

$$v_n = \frac{1}{4\pi\varepsilon_0}\frac{e^2}{\hbar}\frac{1}{n} \tag{6.37}$$

$$r_n = 4\pi\varepsilon_0 \frac{\hbar^2}{m_e e^2} n^2. \tag{6.38}$$

Note that these results tell us that the electron's speed as well as the radius of its orbit depend only on the index *n* that enumerates the orbit because all other quantities in the preceding equations are fundamental constants. We see from **Equation 6.38** that the size of the orbit grows as the square of *n*. This means that the second orbit is four times as large as the first orbit, and the third orbit is nine times as large as the first orbit, and so on. We also see from **Equation 6.37** that the electron's speed in the orbit decreases as the orbit size increases. The electron's speed is largest in the first Bohr orbit, for $n = 1$, which is the orbit closest to the nucleus. The radius of the first Bohr orbit is called the **Bohr radius of hydrogen**, denoted as a_0. Its value is obtained by setting $n = 1$ in **Equation 6.38**:

$$a_0 = 4\pi\varepsilon_0 \frac{\hbar^2}{m_e e^2} = 5.29 \times 10^{-11}\,\text{m} = 0.529\,\text{Å}. \tag{6.39}$$

We can substitute a_0 in **Equation 6.38** to express the radius of the *n*th orbit in terms of a_0:

$$r_n = a_0 n^2. \tag{6.40}$$

This result means that the electron orbits in hydrogen atom are *quantized* because the orbital radius takes on only specific values of a_0, $4a_0$, $9a_0$, $16a_0$, ... given by **Equation 6.40**, and no other values are allowed.

Electron Energies

The total energy E_n of an electron in the *n*th orbit is the sum of its kinetic energy K_n and its electrostatic potential energy U_n. Utilizing **Equation 6.37**, we find that

$$K_n = \frac{1}{2} m_e v_n^2 = \frac{1}{32\pi^2\varepsilon_0^2}\frac{m_e e^4}{\hbar^2}\frac{1}{n^2}. \tag{6.41}$$

Recall that the electrostatic potential energy of interaction between two charges q_1 and q_2 that are separated by a distance r_{12} is $(1/4\pi\varepsilon_0)q_1 q_2/r_{12}$. Here, $q_1 = +e$ is the charge of the nucleus in the hydrogen atom (the charge of the proton), $q_2 = -e$ is the charge of the electron and $r_{12} = r_n$ is the radius of the *n*th orbit. Now we use **Equation 6.38** to find the potential energy of the electron:

$$U_n = -\frac{1}{4\pi\varepsilon_0}\frac{e^2}{r_n} = -\frac{1}{16\pi^2\varepsilon_0^2}\frac{m_e e^4}{\hbar^2}\frac{1}{n^2}. \quad (6.42)$$

The total energy of the electron is the sum of **Equation 6.41** and **Equation 6.42**:

$$E_n = K_n + U_n = -\frac{1}{32\pi^2\varepsilon_0^2}\frac{m_e e^4}{\hbar^2}\frac{1}{n^2}. \quad (6.43)$$

Note that the energy depends only on the index *n* because the remaining symbols in **Equation 6.43** are physical constants. The value of the constant factor in **Equation 6.43** is

$$E_0 = \frac{1}{32\pi^2\varepsilon_0^2}\frac{m_e e^4}{\hbar^2} = \frac{1}{8\varepsilon_0^2}\frac{m_e e^4}{h^2} = 2.17 \times 10^{-18}\,\text{J} = 13.6\,\text{eV}. \quad (6.44)$$

It is convenient to express the electron's energy in the *n*th orbit in terms of this energy, as

$$E_n = -E_0\frac{1}{n^2}. \quad (6.45)$$

Now we can see that the electron energies in the hydrogen atom are *quantized* because they can have only discrete values of $-E_0$, $-E_0/4$, $-E_0/9$, $-E_0/16$, ... given by **Equation 6.45**, and no other energy values are allowed. This set of allowed electron energies is called the **energy spectrum of hydrogen** (**Figure 6.17**). The index *n* that enumerates energy levels in Bohr's model is called the energy **quantum number**. We identify the energy of the electron inside the hydrogen atom with the energy of the hydrogen atom. Note that the smallest value of energy is obtained for $n = 1$, so the hydrogen atom cannot have energy smaller than that. This smallest value of the electron energy in the hydrogen atom is called the **ground state energy of the hydrogen atom** and its value is

$$E_1 = -E_0 = -13.6\,\text{eV}. \quad (6.46)$$

The hydrogen atom may have other energies that are higher than the ground state. These higher energy states are known as **excited energy states of a hydrogen atom**.

There is only one ground state, but there are infinitely many excited states because there are infinitely many values of *n* in **Equation 6.45**. We say that the electron is in the "first exited state" when its energy is E_2 (when $n = 2$), the second excited state when its energy is E_3 (when $n = 3$) and, in general, in the *n*th exited state when its energy is E_{n+1}. There is no highest-of-all excited state; however, there is a limit to the sequence of excited states. If we keep increasing *n* in **Equation 6.45**, we find that the limit is $-\lim_{n\to\infty} E_0/n^2 = 0$. In this limit, the electron is no longer bound to the nucleus but becomes a free electron. An electron remains bound in the hydrogen atom as long as its energy is negative. An electron that orbits the nucleus in the first Bohr orbit, closest to the nucleus, is in the ground state, where its energy has the smallest value. In the ground state, the electron is most strongly bound to the nucleus and its energy is given by **Equation 6.46**. If we want to remove this electron from the atom, we must supply it with enough energy, E_∞, to at least balance out its ground state energy E_1:

$$E_\infty + E_1 = 0 \Rightarrow E_\infty = -E_1 = -(-E_0) = E_0 = 13.6\,\text{eV}. \quad (6.47)$$

The energy that is needed to remove the electron from the atom is called the **ionization energy**. The ionization energy E_∞ that is needed to remove the electron from the first Bohr orbit is called the **ionization limit of the hydrogen atom**. The ionization limit in **Equation 6.47** that we obtain in Bohr's model agrees with experimental value.

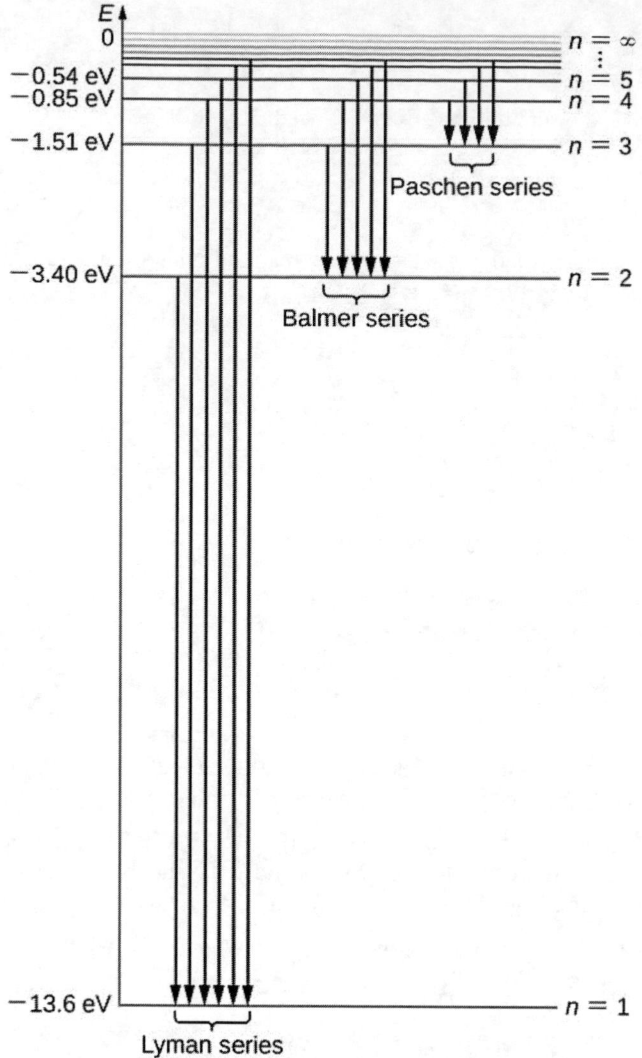

Figure 6.17 The energy spectrum of the hydrogen atom. Energy levels (horizontal lines) represent the bound states of an electron in the atom. There is only one ground state, $n = 1$, and infinite quantized excited states. The states are enumerated by the quantum number $n = 1, 2, 3, 4, \ldots$. Vertical lines illustrate the allowed electron transitions between the states. Downward arrows illustrate transitions with an emission of a photon with a wavelength in the indicated spectral band.

Spectral Emission Lines of Hydrogen

To obtain the wavelengths of the emitted radiation when an electron makes a transition from the *n*th orbit to the *m*th orbit, we use the second of Bohr's quantization conditions and **Equation 6.45** for energies. The emission of energy from the atom can occur only when an electron makes a transition from an excited state to a lower-energy state. In the course of such a transition, the emitted photon carries away the difference of energies between the states involved in the transition. The transition cannot go in the other direction because the energy of a photon cannot be negative, which means that for emission we must have $E_n > E_m$ and $n > m$. Therefore, the third of Bohr's postulates gives

$$hf = \left|E_n - E_m\right| = E_n - E_m = -E_0\frac{1}{n^2} + E_0\frac{1}{m^2} = E_0\left(\frac{1}{m^2} - \frac{1}{n^2}\right). \tag{6.48}$$

Now we express the photon's energy in terms of its wavelength, $hf = hc/\lambda$, and divide both sides of **Equation 6.48** by hc. The result is

$$\frac{1}{\lambda} = \frac{E_0}{hc}\left(\frac{1}{m^2} - \frac{1}{n^2}\right). \tag{6.49}$$

The value of the constant in this equation is

$$\frac{E_0}{hc} = \frac{13.6\,\text{eV}}{(4.136 \times 10^{-15}\,\text{eV}\cdot\text{s})(2.997 \times 10^8\,\text{m/s})} = 1.097 \times 10^7 \frac{1}{\text{m}}. \tag{6.50}$$

This value is exactly the Rydberg constant R_{H} in the Rydberg heuristic formula **Equation 6.32**. In fact, **Equation 6.49** is identical to the Rydberg formula, because for a given m, we have $n = m + 1,\ m + 2,\ ....$ In this way, the Bohr quantum model of the hydrogen atom allows us to derive the experimental Rydberg constant from first principles and to express it in terms of fundamental constants. Transitions between the allowed electron orbits are illustrated in **Figure 6.17**.

We can repeat the same steps that led to **Equation 6.49** to obtain the wavelength of the absorbed radiation; this again gives **Equation 6.49** but this time for the positions of absorption lines in the absorption spectrum of hydrogen. The only difference is that for absorption, the quantum number *m* is the index of the orbit occupied by the electron before the transition (lower-energy orbit) and the quantum number *n* is the index of the orbit to which the electron makes the transition (higher-energy orbit). The difference between the electron energies in these two orbits is the energy of the absorbed photon.

Example 6.10

Size and Ionization Energy of the Hydrogen Atom in an Excited State

If a hydrogen atom in the ground state absorbs a 93.7-nm photon, corresponding to a transition line in the Lyman series, how does this affect the atom's energy and size? How much energy is needed to ionize the atom when it is in this excited state? Give your answers in absolute units, and relative to the ground state.

Strategy

Before the absorption, the atom is in its ground state. This means that the electron transition takes place from the orbit $m = 1$ to some higher *n*th orbit. First, we must determine n for the absorbed wavelength $\lambda = 93.7$ nm. Then, we can use **Equation 6.45** to find the energy E_n of the excited state and its ionization energy $E_{\infty,\,n}$, and use **Equation 6.40** to find the radius r_n of the atom in the excited state. To estimate *n*, we use **Equation 6.49**.

Solution

Substitute $m = 1$ and $\lambda = 93.7\,\text{nm}$ in **Equation 6.49** and solve for n. You should not expect to obtain a perfect integer answer because of rounding errors, but your answer will be close to an integer, and you can estimate *n* by taking the integral part of your answer:

$$\frac{1}{\lambda} = R_{\text{H}}\left(\frac{1}{1^2} - \frac{1}{n^2}\right) \Rightarrow n = \frac{1}{\sqrt{1 - \frac{1}{\lambda R_{\text{H}}}}} = \frac{1}{\sqrt{1 - \frac{1}{(93.7 \times 10^{-9}\,\text{m})(1.097 \times 10^7\,\text{m}^{-1})}}} = 6.07 \Rightarrow n = 6.$$

The radius of the $n = 6$ orbit is

$$r_n = a_0 n^2 = a_0 6^2 = 36 a_0 = 36(0.529 \times 10^{-10}\,\text{m}) = 19.04 \times 10^{-10}\,\text{m} \cong 19.0\,\text{Å}.$$

Thus, after absorbing the 93.7-nm photon, the size of the hydrogen atom in the excited $n = 6$ state is 36 times larger than before the absorption, when the atom was in the ground state. The energy of the fifth excited state ($n = 6$) is:

$$E_n = -\frac{E_0}{n^2} = -\frac{E_0}{6^2} = -\frac{E_0}{36} = -\frac{13.6\,\text{eV}}{36} \cong -0.378\,\text{eV}.$$

After absorbing the 93.7-nm photon, the energy of the hydrogen atom is larger than it was before the absorption. Ionization of the atom when it is in the fifth excited state ($n = 6$) requites 36 times less energy than is needed when the atom is in the ground state:

$$E_{\infty,\,6} = -E_6 = -(-0.378\,\text{eV}) = 0.378\,\text{eV}.$$

Significance

We can analyze any spectral line in the spectrum of hydrogen in the same way. Thus, the experimental measurements of spectral lines provide us with information about the atomic structure of the hydrogen atom.

6.10 Check Your Understanding When an electron in a hydrogen atom is in the first excited state, what prediction does the Bohr model give about its orbital speed and kinetic energy? What is the magnitude of its orbital angular momentum?

Bohr's model of the hydrogen atom also correctly predicts the spectra of some hydrogen-like ions. **Hydrogen-like ions** are atoms of elements with an atomic number Z larger than one ($Z = 1$ for hydrogen) but with all electrons removed except one. For example, an electrically neutral helium atom has an atomic number $Z = 2$. This means it has two electrons orbiting the nucleus with a charge of $q = +Ze$. When one of the orbiting electrons is removed from the helium atom (we say, when the helium atom is singly ionized), what remains is a hydrogen-like atomic structure where the remaining electron orbits the nucleus with a charge of $q = +Ze$. This type of situation is described by the Bohr model. Assuming that the charge of the nucleus is not $+e$ but $+Ze$, we can repeat all steps, beginning with Equation 6.36, to obtain the results for a hydrogen-like ion:

$$r_n = \frac{a_0}{Z} n^2 \tag{6.51}$$

where a_0 is the Bohr orbit of hydrogen, and

$$E_n = -Z^2 E_0 \frac{1}{n^2} \tag{6.52}$$

where E_0 is the ionization limit of a hydrogen atom. These equations are good approximations as long as the atomic number Z is not too large.

The Bohr model is important because it was the first model to postulate the quantization of electron orbits in atoms. Thus, it represents an early quantum theory that gave a start to developing modern quantum theory. It introduced the concept of a quantum number to describe atomic states. The limitation of the early quantum theory is that it cannot describe atoms in which the number of electrons orbiting the nucleus is larger than one. The Bohr model of hydrogen is a semi-classical model because it combines the classical concept of electron orbits with the new concept of quantization. The remarkable success of this model prompted many physicists to seek an explanation for why such a model should work at all, and to seek an understanding of the physics behind the postulates of early quantum theory. This search brought about the onset of an entirely new concept of "matter waves."

6.5 | De Broglie's Matter Waves

Learning Objectives

By the end of this section, you will be able to:

- Describe de Broglie's hypothesis of matter waves
- Explain how the de Broglie's hypothesis gives the rationale for the quantization of angular momentum in Bohr's quantum theory of the hydrogen atom
- Describe the Davisson–Germer experiment
- Interpret de Broglie's idea of matter waves and how they account for electron diffraction phenomena

Compton's formula established that an electromagnetic wave can behave like a particle of light when interacting with matter. In 1924, Louis de Broglie proposed a new speculative hypothesis that electrons and other particles of matter can behave like waves. Today, this idea is known as **de Broglie's hypothesis of matter waves**. In 1926, De Broglie's hypothesis, together with Bohr's early quantum theory, led to the development of a new theory of **wave quantum mechanics** to describe the physics of atoms and subatomic particles. Quantum mechanics has paved the way for new engineering inventions and technologies, such as the laser and magnetic resonance imaging (MRI). These new technologies drive discoveries in other sciences such as biology and chemistry.

According to de Broglie's hypothesis, massless photons as well as massive particles must satisfy one common set of relations that connect the energy E with the frequency f, and the linear momentum p with the wavelength λ. We have discussed these relations for photons in the context of Compton's effect. We are recalling them now in a more general context. Any particle that has energy and momentum is a **de Broglie wave** of frequency f and wavelength λ :

$$E = hf \tag{6.53}$$

$$\lambda = \frac{h}{p}. \tag{6.54}$$

Here, E and p are, respectively, the relativistic energy and the momentum of a particle. De Broglie's relations are usually expressed in terms of the wave vector $\vec{\mathbf{k}}$, $k = 2\pi / \lambda$, and the wave frequency $\omega = 2\pi f$, as we usually do for waves:

$$E = \hbar\omega \tag{6.55}$$

$$\vec{\mathbf{p}} = \hbar \vec{\mathbf{k}} . \tag{6.56}$$

Wave theory tells us that a wave carries its energy with the **group velocity**. For matter waves, this group velocity is the velocity u of the particle. Identifying the energy E and momentum p of a particle with its relativistic energy mc^2 and its relativistic momentum mu, respectively, it follows from de Broglie relations that matter waves satisfy the following relation:

$$\lambda f = \frac{\omega}{k} = \frac{E / \hbar}{p / \hbar} = \frac{E}{p} = \frac{mc^2}{mu} = \frac{c^2}{u} = \frac{c}{\beta} \tag{6.57}$$

where $\beta = u / c$. When a particle is massless we have $u = c$ and **Equation 6.57** becomes $\lambda f = c$.

Example 6.11

How Long Are de Broglie Matter Waves?

Calculate the de Broglie wavelength of: (a) a 0.65-kg basketball thrown at a speed of 10 m/s, (b) a nonrelativistic electron with a kinetic energy of 1.0 eV, and (c) a relativistic electron with a kinetic energy of 108 keV.

Strategy

We use **Equation 6.57** to find the de Broglie wavelength. When the problem involves a nonrelativistic object moving with a nonrelativistic speed u, such as in (a) when $\beta = u/c \ll 1$, we use nonrelativistic momentum p. When the nonrelativistic approximation cannot be used, such as in (c), we must use the relativistic momentum $p = mu = m_0 \gamma u = E_0 \gamma \beta$, where the rest mass energy of a particle is $E_0 = m_0 c^2$ and γ is the Lorentz factor $\gamma = 1/\sqrt{1-\beta^2}$. The total energy E of a particle is given by **Equation 6.53** and the kinetic energy is $K = E - E_0 = (\gamma - 1)E_0$. When the kinetic energy is known, we can invert **Equation 6.18** to find the momentum $p = \sqrt{(E^2 - E_0^2)/c^2} = \sqrt{K(K + 2E_0)}/c$ and substitute in **Equation 6.57** to obtain

$$\lambda = \frac{h}{p} = \frac{hc}{\sqrt{K(K + 2E_0)}}. \tag{6.58}$$

Depending on the problem at hand, in this equation we can use the following values for hc: $hc = (6.626 \times 10^{-34}\,\text{J}\cdot\text{s})(2.998 \times 10^8\,\text{m/s}) = 1.986 \times 10^{-25}\,\text{J}\cdot\text{m} = 1.241\,\text{eV}\cdot\mu\text{m}$

Solution

a. For the basketball, the kinetic energy is

$$K = m_0 u^2/2 = (0.65\text{kg})(10\text{m/s})^2/2 = 32.5\text{J}$$

and the rest mass energy is

$$E_0 = m_0 c^2 = (0.65\text{kg})(2.998 \times 10^8\,\text{m/s})^2 = 5.84 \times 10^{16}\,\text{J}.$$

We see that $K/(K + E_0) \ll 1$ and use $p = m_0 u = (0.65\text{kg})(10\text{m/s}) = 6.5\,\text{J}\cdot\text{s/m}$:

$$\lambda = \frac{h}{p} = \frac{6.626 \times 10^{-34}\,\text{J}\cdot\text{s}}{6.5\text{J}\cdot\text{s/m}} = 1.02 \times 10^{-34}\,\text{m}.$$

b. For the nonrelativistic electron,

$$E_0 = m_0 c^2 = (9.109 \times 10^{-31}\,\text{kg})(2.998 \times 10^8\,\text{m/s})^2 = 511\,\text{keV}$$

and when $K = 1.0\,\text{eV}$, we have $K/(K + E_0) = (1/512) \times 10^{-3} \ll 1$, so we can use the nonrelativistic formula. However, it is simpler here to use **Equation 6.58**:

$$\lambda = \frac{h}{p} = \frac{hc}{\sqrt{K(K + 2E_0)}} = \frac{1.241\,\text{eV}\cdot\mu\text{m}}{\sqrt{(1.0\,\text{eV})[1.0\,\text{eV}+2(511\,\text{keV})]}} = 1.23\,\text{nm}.$$

If we use nonrelativistic momentum, we obtain the same result because 1 eV is much smaller than the rest mass of the electron.

c. For a fast electron with $K = 108\,\text{keV}$, relativistic effects cannot be neglected because its total energy is $E = K + E_0 = 108\,\text{keV} + 511\,\text{keV} = 619\,\text{keV}$ and $K/E = 108/619$ is not negligible:

$$\lambda = \frac{h}{p} = \frac{hc}{\sqrt{K(K + 2E_0)}} = \frac{1.241\,\text{eV}\cdot\mu\text{m}}{\sqrt{108\,\text{keV}[108\,\text{keV} + 2(511\,\text{keV})]}} = 3.55\,\text{pm}.$$

Significance

We see from these estimates that De Broglie's wavelengths of macroscopic objects such as a ball are immeasurably small. Therefore, even if they exist, they are not detectable and do not affect the motion of macroscopic objects.

6.11 Check Your Understanding What is de Broglie's wavelength of a nonrelativistic proton with a kinetic energy of 1.0 eV?

Using the concept of the electron matter wave, de Broglie provided a rationale for the quantization of the electron's angular momentum in the hydrogen atom, which was postulated in Bohr's quantum theory. The physical explanation for the first Bohr quantization condition comes naturally when we assume that an electron in a hydrogen atom behaves not like a particle but like a wave. To see it clearly, imagine a stretched guitar string that is clamped at both ends and vibrates in one of its normal modes. If the length of the string is l (**Figure 6.18**), the wavelengths of these vibrations cannot be arbitrary but must be such that an integer k number of half-wavelengths $\lambda/2$ fit exactly on the distance l between the ends. This is the condition $l = k\lambda/2$ for a standing wave on a string. Now suppose that instead of having the string clamped at the walls, we bend its length into a circle and fasten its ends to each other. This produces a circular string that vibrates in normal modes, satisfying the same standing-wave condition, but the number of half-wavelengths must now be an even number k, $k = 2n$, and the length l is now connected to the radius r_n of the circle. This means that the radii are not arbitrary but must satisfy the following standing-wave condition:

$$2\pi r_n = 2n\frac{\lambda}{2}. \tag{6.59}$$

If an electron in the nth Bohr orbit moves as a wave, by **Equation 6.59** its wavelength must be equal to $\lambda = 2\pi r_n/n$. Assuming that **Equation 6.58** is valid, the electron wave of this wavelength corresponds to the electron's linear momentum, $p = h/\lambda = nh/(2\pi r_n) = n\hbar/r_n$. In a circular orbit, therefore, the electron's angular momentum must be

$$L_n = r_n p = r_n\frac{n\hbar}{r_n} = n\hbar. \tag{6.60}$$

This equation is the first of Bohr's quantization conditions, given by **Equation 6.36**. Providing a physical explanation for Bohr's quantization condition is a convincing theoretical argument for the existence of matter waves.

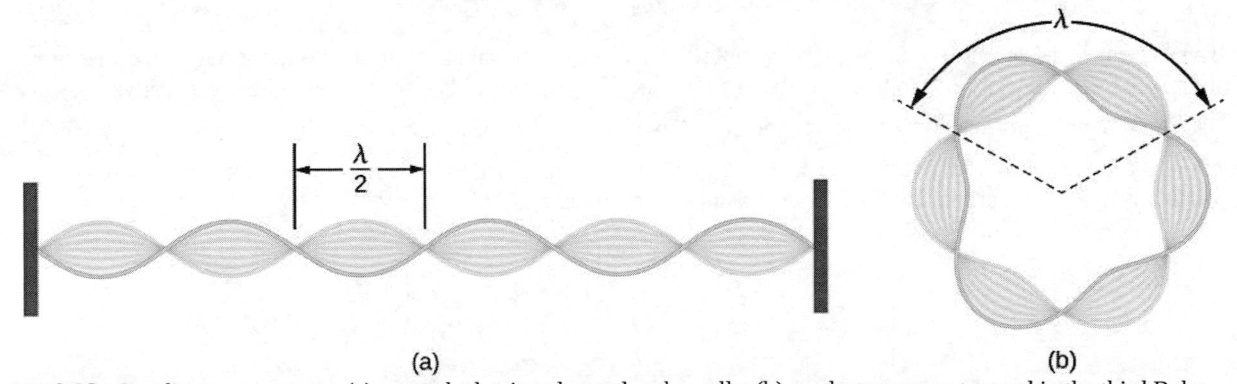

Figure 6.18 Standing-wave pattern: (a) a stretched string clamped at the walls; (b) an electron wave trapped in the third Bohr orbit in the hydrogen atom.

Example 6.12

The Electron Wave in the Ground State of Hydrogen

Find the de Broglie wavelength of an electron in the ground state of hydrogen.

Strategy

We combine the first quantization condition in Equation 6.60 with Equation 6.36 and use Equation 6.38 for the first Bohr radius with $n = 1$.

Solution

When $n = 1$ and $r_n = a_0 = 0.529\ \text{Å}$, the Bohr quantization condition gives $a_0 p = 1 \cdot \hbar \Rightarrow p = \hbar / a_0$. The electron wavelength is:

$$\lambda = h/p = h/\hbar/a_0 = 2\pi a_0 = 2\pi(0.529\ \text{Å}) = 3.324\ \text{Å}.$$

Significance

We obtain the same result when we use Equation 6.58 directly.

6.12 Check Your Understanding Find the de Broglie wavelength of an electron in the third excited state of hydrogen.

Experimental confirmation of matter waves came in 1927 when C. Davisson and L. Germer performed a series of electron-scattering experiments that clearly showed that electrons do behave like waves. Davisson and Germer did not set up their experiment to confirm de Broglie's hypothesis: The confirmation came as a byproduct of their routine experimental studies of metal surfaces under electron bombardment.

In the particular experiment that provided the very first evidence of electron waves (known today as the **Davisson–Germer experiment**), they studied a surface of nickel. Their nickel sample was specially prepared in a high-temperature oven to change its usual polycrystalline structure to a form in which large single-crystal domains occupy the volume. Figure 6.19 shows the experimental setup. Thermal electrons are released from a heated element (usually made of tungsten) in the electron gun and accelerated through a potential difference ΔV, becoming a well-collimated beam of electrons produced by an electron gun. The kinetic energy K of the electrons is adjusted by selecting a value of the potential difference in the electron gun. This produces a beam of electrons with a set value of linear momentum, in accordance with the conservation of energy:

$$e\Delta V = K = \frac{p^2}{2m} \Rightarrow p = \sqrt{2me\Delta V}. \tag{6.61}$$

The electron beam is incident on the nickel sample in the direction normal to its surface. At the surface, it scatters in various directions. The intensity of the beam scattered in a selected direction φ is measured by a highly sensitive detector. The detector's angular position with respect to the direction of the incident beam can be varied from $\varphi = 0°$ to $\varphi = 90°$. The entire setup is enclosed in a vacuum chamber to prevent electron collisions with air molecules, as such thermal collisions would change the electrons' kinetic energy and are not desirable.

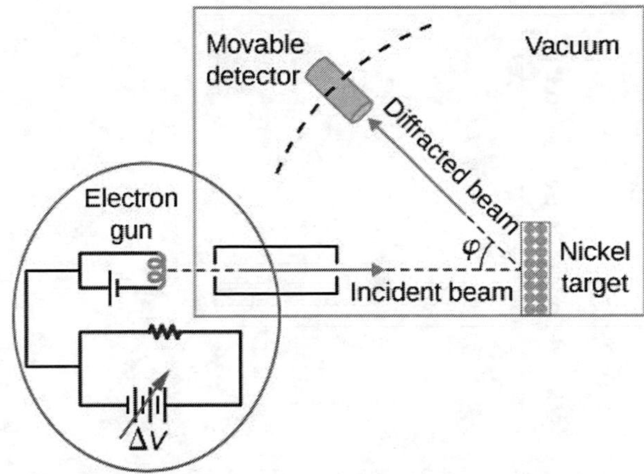

Figure 6.19 Schematics of the experimental setup of the Davisson–Germer diffraction experiment. A well-collimated beam of electrons is scattered off the nickel target. The kinetic energy of electrons in the incident beam is selected by adjusting a variable potential, $\Delta V,$ in the electron gun. Intensity of the scattered electron beam is measured for a range of scattering angles $\varphi,$ whereas the distance between the detector and the target does not change.

When the nickel target has a polycrystalline form with many randomly oriented microscopic crystals, the incident electrons scatter off its surface in various random directions. As a result, the intensity of the scattered electron beam is much the same in any direction, resembling a diffuse reflection of light from a porous surface. However, when the nickel target has a regular crystalline structure, the intensity of the scattered electron beam shows a clear maximum at a specific angle and the results show a clear diffraction pattern (see **Figure 6.20**). Similar diffraction patterns formed by X-rays scattered by various crystalline solids were studied in 1912 by father-and-son physicists William H. Bragg and William L. Bragg. The Bragg law in X-ray crystallography provides a connection between the wavelength λ of the radiation incident on a crystalline lattice, the lattice spacing, and the position of the interference maximum in the diffracted radiation (see **Diffraction**).

The lattice spacing of the Davisson–Germer target, determined with X-ray crystallography, was measured to be $a = 2.15\,\text{Å}.$ Unlike X-ray crystallography in which X-rays penetrate the sample, in the original Davisson–Germer experiment, only the surface atoms interact with the incident electron beam. For the surface diffraction, the maximum intensity of the reflected electron beam is observed for scattering angles that satisfy the condition $n\lambda = a\sin\varphi$ (see **Figure 6.21**). The first-order maximum (for $n = 1$) is measured at a scattering angle of $\varphi \approx 50°$ at $\Delta V \approx 54\text{V},$ which gives the wavelength of the incident radiation as $\lambda = (2.15\,\text{Å})\sin 50° = 1.64\,\text{Å}.$ On the other hand, a 54-V potential accelerates the incident electrons to kinetic energies of $K = 54\,\text{eV}.$ Their momentum, calculated from **Equation 6.61**, is $p = 2.478 \times 10^{-5}\,\text{eV}\cdot\text{s/m}.$ When we substitute this result in **Equation 6.58**, the de Broglie wavelength is obtained as

$$\lambda = \frac{h}{p} = \frac{4.136 \times 10^{-15}\,\text{eV}\cdot\text{s}}{2.478 \times 10^{-5}\,\text{eV}\cdot\text{s/m}} = 1.67\,\text{Å}. \tag{6.62}$$

The same result is obtained when we use $K = 54\,\text{eV}$ in **Equation 6.61**. The proximity of this theoretical result to the Davisson–Germer experimental value of $\lambda = 1.64\,\text{Å}$ is a convincing argument for the existence of de Broglie matter waves.

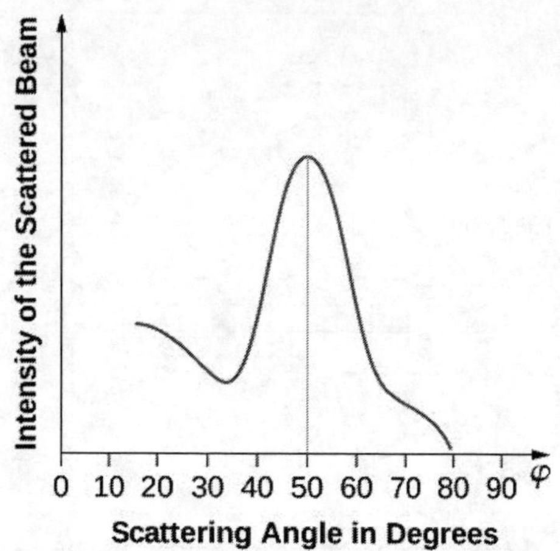

Figure 6.20 The experimental results of electron diffraction on a nickel target for the accelerating potential in the electron gun of about $\Delta V = 54\text{V}$: The intensity maximum is registered at the scattering angle of about $\varphi = 50°$.

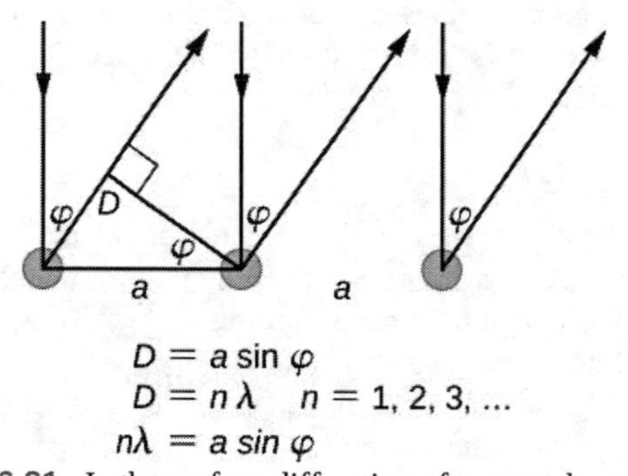

Figure 6.21 In the surface diffraction of a monochromatic electromagnetic wave on a crystalline lattice structure, the in-phase incident beams are reflected from atoms on the surface. A ray reflected from the left atom travels an additional distance $D = a\sin\varphi$ to the detector, where a is the lattice spacing. The reflected beams remain in-phase when D is an integer multiple of their wavelength λ. The intensity of the reflected waves has pronounced maxima for angles φ satisfying $n\lambda = a\sin\varphi$.

Diffraction lines measured with low-energy electrons, such as those used in the Davisson–Germer experiment, are quite broad (see **Figure 6.20**) because the incident electrons are scattered only from the surface. The resolution of diffraction images greatly improves when a higher-energy electron beam passes through a thin metal foil. This occurs because the diffraction image is created by scattering off many crystalline planes inside the volume, and the maxima produced in scattering at Bragg angles are sharp (see **Figure 6.22**).

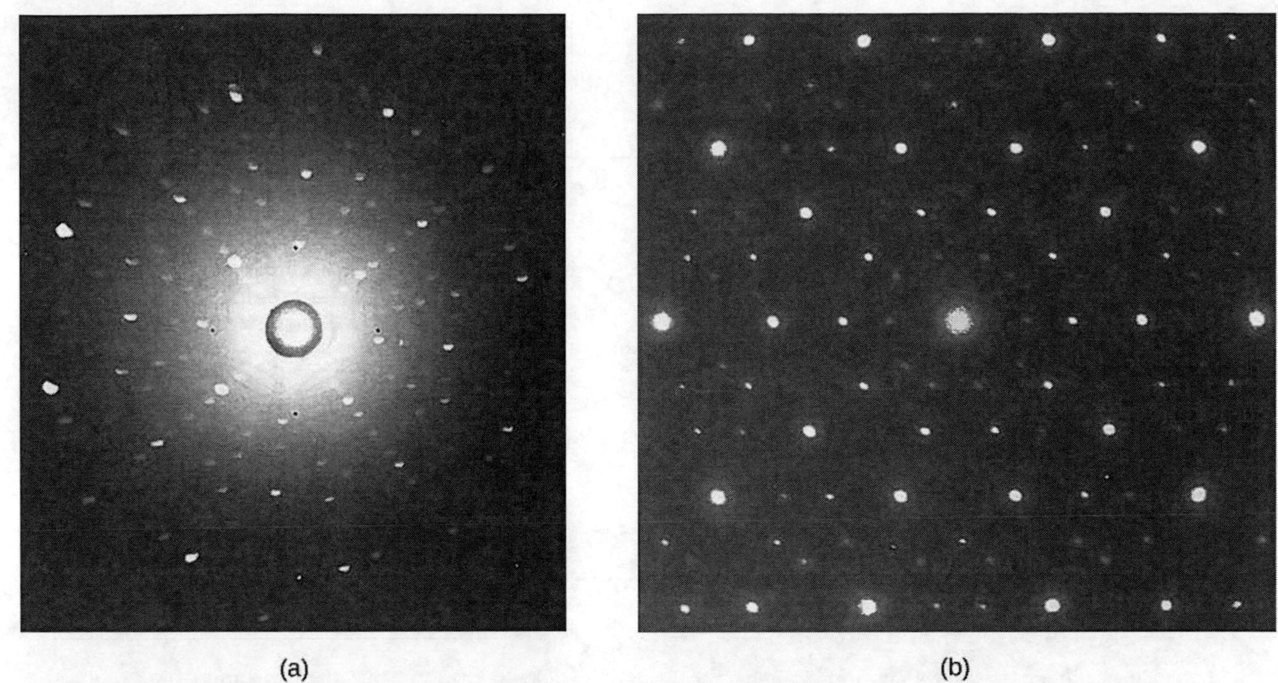

(a) (b)

Figure 6.22 Diffraction patterns obtained in scattering on a crystalline solid: (a) with X-rays, and (b) with electrons. The observed pattern reflects the symmetry of the crystalline structure of the sample.

Since the work of Davisson and Germer, de Broglie's hypothesis has been extensively tested with various experimental techniques, and the existence of de Broglie waves has been confirmed for numerous elementary particles. Neutrons have been used in scattering experiments to determine crystalline structures of solids from interference patterns formed by neutron matter waves. The neutron has zero charge and its mass is comparable with the mass of a positively charged proton. Both neutrons and protons can be seen as matter waves. Therefore, the property of being a matter wave is not specific to electrically charged particles but is true of all particles in motion. Matter waves of molecules as large as carbon C_{60} have been measured. All physical objects, small or large, have an associated matter wave as long as they remain in motion. The universal character of de Broglie matter waves is firmly established.

Example 6.13

Neutron Scattering

Suppose that a neutron beam is used in a diffraction experiment on a typical crystalline solid. Estimate the kinetic energy of a neutron (in eV) in the neutron beam and compare it with kinetic energy of an ideal gas in equilibrium at room temperature.

Strategy

We assume that a typical crystal spacing a is of the order of 1.0 Å. To observe a diffraction pattern on such a lattice, the neutron wavelength λ must be on the same order of magnitude as the lattice spacing. We use **Equation 6.61** to find the momentum p and kinetic energy K. To compare this energy with the energy E_T of ideal gas in equilibrium at room temperature $T = 300\text{K}$, we use the relation $K = \frac{3}{2}k_B T$, where $k_B = 8.62 \times 10^{-5}\,\text{eV/K}$ is the Boltzmann constant.

Solution

We evaluate pc to compare it with the neutron's rest mass energy $E_0 = 940\text{ MeV}$:

$$p = \frac{h}{\lambda} \Rightarrow pc = \frac{hc}{\lambda} = \frac{1.241 \times 10^{-6}\,\text{eV} \cdot \text{m}}{10^{-10}\,\text{m}} = 12.41\text{ keV}.$$

We see that $p^2c^2 \ll E_0^2$ so $K \ll E_0$ and we can use the nonrelativistic kinetic energy:

$$K = \frac{p^2}{2m_n} = \frac{h^2}{2\lambda^2 m_n} = \frac{(6.63 \times 10^{-34}\,\text{J}\cdot\text{s})^2}{(2 \times 10^{-20}\,\text{m}^2)(1.66 \times 10^{-27}\,\text{kg})} = 1.32 \times 10^{-20}\,\text{J} = 82.7\,\text{meV}.$$

Kinetic energy of ideal gas in equilibrium at 300 K is:

$$K_T = \frac{3}{2}k_B T = \frac{3}{2}(8.62 \times 10^{-5}\,\text{eV/K})(300\text{K}) = 38.8\,\text{MeV}.$$

We see that these energies are of the same order of magnitude.

Significance

Neutrons with energies in this range, which is typical for an ideal gas at room temperature, are called "thermal neutrons."

Example 6.14

Wavelength of a Relativistic Proton

In a supercollider at CERN, protons can be accelerated to velocities of $0.75c$. What are their de Broglie wavelengths at this speed? What are their kinetic energies?

Strategy

The rest mass energy of a proton is $E_0 = m_0c^2 = (1.672 \times 10^{-27}\,\text{kg})(2.998 \times 10^8\,\text{m/s})^2 = 938\,\text{MeV}$. When the proton's velocity is known, we have $\beta = 0.75$ and $\beta\gamma = 0.75/\sqrt{1 - 0.75^2} = 1.714$. We obtain the wavelength λ and kinetic energy K from relativistic relations.

Solution

$$\lambda = \frac{h}{p} = \frac{hc}{pc} = \frac{hc}{\beta\gamma E_0} = \frac{1.241\,\text{eV}\cdot\mu\text{m}}{1.714(938\,\text{MeV})} = 0.77\,\text{fm}$$

$$K = E_0(\gamma - 1) = 938\,\text{MeV}(1/\sqrt{1 - 0.75^2} - 1) = 480.1\,\text{MeV}$$

Significance

Notice that because a proton is 1835 times more massive than an electron, if this experiment were performed with electrons, a simple rescaling of these results would give us the electron's wavelength of $(1835)0.77\text{fm} = 1.4\,\text{pm}$ and its kinetic energy of $480.1\,\text{MeV}/1835 = 261.6\,\text{keV}$.

6.13 Check Your Understanding Find the de Broglie wavelength and kinetic energy of a free electron that travels at a speed of $0.75c$.

6.6 | Wave-Particle Duality

Learning Objectives

By the end of this section, you will be able to:

- Identify phenomena in which electromagnetic waves behave like a beam of photons and particles behave like waves
- Describe the physics principles behind electron microscopy
- Summarize the evolution of scientific thought that led to the development of quantum mechanics

The energy of radiation detected by a radio-signal receiving antenna comes as the energy of an electromagnetic wave. The same energy of radiation detected by a photocurrent in the photoelectric effect comes as the energy of individual photon particles. Therefore, the question arises about the nature of electromagnetic radiation: Is a photon a wave or is it a particle? Similar questions may be asked about other known forms of energy. For example, an electron that forms part of an electric current in a circuit behaves like a particle moving in unison with other electrons inside the conductor. The same electron behaves as a wave when it passes through a solid crystalline structure and forms a diffraction image. Is an electron a wave or is it a particle? The same question can be extended to all particles of matter—elementary particles, as well as compound molecules—asking about their true physical nature. At our present state of knowledge, such questions about the true nature of things do not have conclusive answers. All we can say is that **wave-particle duality** exists in nature: Under some experimental conditions, a particle appears to act as a particle, and under different experimental conditions, a particle appears to act a wave. Conversely, under some physical circumstances electromagnetic radiation acts as a wave, and under other physical circumstances, radiation acts as a beam of photons.

This dualistic interpretation is not a new physics concept brought about by specific discoveries in the twentieth century. It was already present in a debate between Isaac Newton and Christiaan Huygens about the nature of light, beginning in the year 1670. According to Newton, a beam of light is a collection of corpuscles of light. According to Huygens, light is a wave. The corpuscular hypothesis failed in 1803, when Thomas Young announced his **double-slit interference experiment** with light (see Figure 6.23), which firmly established light as a wave. In James Clerk Maxwell's theory of electromagnetism (completed by the year 1873), light is an electromagnetic wave. Maxwell's classical view of radiation as an electromagnetic wave is still valid today; however, it is unable to explain blackbody radiation and the photoelectric effect, where light acts as a beam of photons.

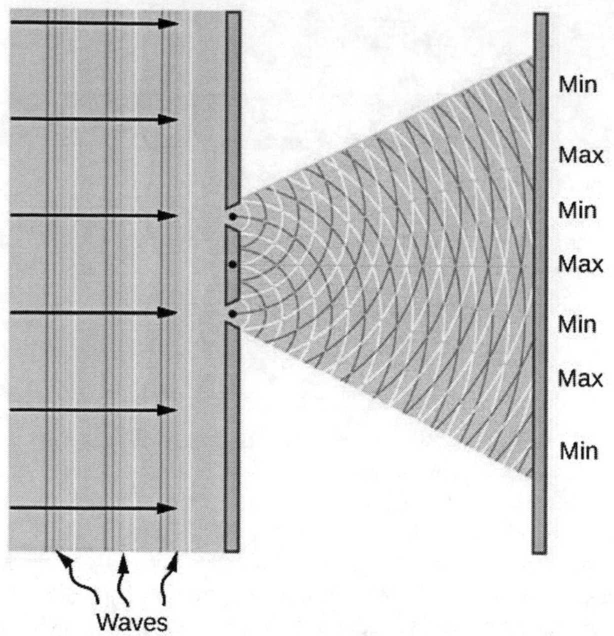

Figure 6.23 Young's double-slit experiment explains the interference of light by making an analogy with the interference of water waves. Two waves are generated at the positions of two slits in an opaque screen. The waves have the same wavelengths. They travel from their origins at the slits to the viewing screen placed to the right of the slits. The waves meet on the viewing screen. At the positions marked "Max" on the screen, the meeting waves are in-phase and the combined wave amplitude is enhanced. At positions marked "Min," the combined wave amplitude is zero. For light, this mechanism creates a bright-and-dark fringe pattern on the viewing screen.

A similar dichotomy existed in the interpretation of electricity. From Benjamin Franklin's observations of electricity in 1751 until J.J. Thomson's discovery of the electron in 1897, electric current was seen as a flow in a continuous electric medium. Within this theory of electric fluid, the present theory of electric circuits was developed, and electromagnetism and electromagnetic induction were discovered. Thomson's experiment showed that the unit of negative electric charge (an electron) can travel in a vacuum without any medium to carry the charge around, as in electric circuits. This discovery changed the way in which electricity is understood today and gave the electron its particle status. In Bohr's early quantum theory of the hydrogen atom, both the electron and the proton are particles of matter. Likewise, in the Compton scattering of X-rays on electrons, the electron is a particle. On the other hand, in electron-scattering experiments on crystalline structures, the electron behaves as a wave.

A skeptic may raise a question that perhaps an electron might always be nothing more than a particle, and that the diffraction images obtained in electron-scattering experiments might be explained within some macroscopic model of a crystal and a macroscopic model of electrons coming at it like a rain of ping-pong balls. As a matter of fact, to investigate this question, we do not need a complex model of a crystal but just a couple of simple slits in a screen that is opaque to electrons. In other words, to gather convincing evidence about the nature of an electron, we need to repeat the Young double-slit experiment with electrons. If the electron is a wave, we should observe the formation of interference patterns typical for waves, such as those described in **Figure 6.23**, even when electrons come through the slits one by one. However, if the electron is a not a wave but a particle, the interference fringes will not be formed.

The very first double-slit experiment with a beam of electrons, performed by Claus Jönsson in Germany in 1961, demonstrated that a beam of electrons indeed forms an interference pattern, which means that electrons collectively behave as a wave. The first double-slit experiments with *single* electrons passing through the slits one-by-one were performed by Giulio Pozzi in 1974 in Italy and by Akira Tonomura in 1989 in Japan. They show that interference fringes are formed gradually, even when electrons pass through the slits individually. This demonstrates conclusively that electron-diffraction images are formed because of the wave nature of electrons. The results seen in double-slit experiments with electrons are illustrated by the images of the interference pattern in **Figure 6.24**.

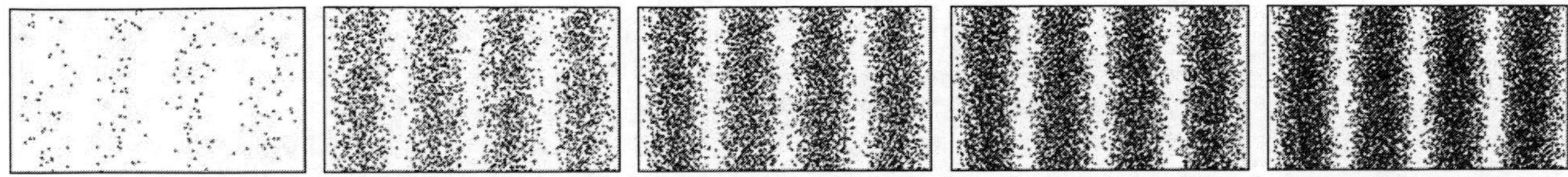

Figure 6.24 Computer-simulated interference fringes seen in the Young double-slit experiment with electrons. One pattern is gradually formed on the screen, regardless of whether the electrons come through the slits as a beam or individually one-by-one.

Example 6.15

Double-Slit Experiment with Electrons

In one experimental setup for studying interference patterns of electron waves, two slits are created in a gold-coated silicon membrane. Each slit is 62-nm wide and 4-μm long, and the separation between the slits is 272 nm. The electron beam is created in an electron gun by heating a tungsten element and by accelerating the electrons across a 600-V potential. The beam is subsequently collimated using electromagnetic lenses, and the collimated beam of electrons is sent through the slits. Find the angular position of the first-order bright fringe on the viewing screen.

Strategy

Recall that the angular position θ of the *n*th order bright fringe that is formed in Young's two-slit interference pattern (discussed in a previous chapter) is related to the separation, *d*, between the slits and to the wavelength, λ, of the incident light by the equation $d\sin\theta = n\lambda$, where $n = 0, \pm 1, \pm 2, ...$ The separation is given and is equal to $d = 272$ nm. For the first-order fringe, we take $n = 1$. The only thing we now need is the wavelength of the incident electron wave.

Since the electron has been accelerated from rest across a potential difference of $\Delta V = 600\text{V}$, its kinetic energy is $K = e\Delta V = 600$ eV. The rest-mass energy of the electron is $E_0 = 511$ keV.

We compute its de Broglie wavelength as that of a nonrelativistic electron because its kinetic energy K is much smaller than its rest energy E_0, $K \ll E_0$.

Solution

The electron's wavelength is

$$\lambda = \frac{h}{p} = \frac{h}{\sqrt{2m_eK}} = \frac{h}{\sqrt{2E_0/c^2K}} = \frac{hc}{\sqrt{2E_0K}} = \frac{1.241 \times 10^{-6}\,\text{eV}\cdot\text{m}}{\sqrt{2(511\,\text{keV})(600\,\text{eV})}} = 0.050\,\text{nm}.$$

This λ is used to obtain the position of the first bright fringe:

$$\sin\theta = \frac{1\cdot\lambda}{d} = \frac{0.050\,\text{nm}}{272\,\text{nm}} = 0.000184 \Rightarrow \theta = 0.010°.$$

Significance

Notice that this is also the angular resolution between two consecutive bright fringes up to about $n = 1000$. For example, between the zero-order fringe and the first-order fringe, between the first-order fringe and the second-order fringe, and so on.

6.14 Check Your Understanding For the situation described in Example 6.15, find the angular position of the fifth-order bright fringe on the viewing screen.

The wave-particle dual nature of matter particles and of radiation is a declaration of our inability to describe physical reality within one unified classical theory because separately neither a classical particle approach nor a classical wave approach can fully explain the observed phenomena. This limitation of the classical approach was realized by the year 1928, and a foundation for a new statistical theory, called quantum mechanics, was put in place by Bohr, Edwin Schrödinger, Werner Heisenberg, and Paul Dirac. Quantum mechanics takes de Broglie's idea of matter waves to be the fundamental property of all particles and gives it a statistical interpretation. According to this interpretation, a wave that is associated with a particle carries information about the probable positions of the particle and about its other properties. A single particle is seen as a moving *wave packet* such as the one shown in **Figure 6.25**. We can intuitively sense from this example that if a particle is a wave packet, we will not be able to measure its exact position in the same sense as we cannot pinpoint a location of a wave packet in a vibrating guitar string. The uncertainty, $\Delta x,$ in measuring the particle's position is connected to the uncertainty, $\Delta p,$ in the simultaneous measuring of its linear momentum by Heisenberg's uncertainty principle:

$$\Delta x \Delta p \geq \frac{1}{2}\hbar. \tag{6.63}$$

Heisenberg's principle expresses the law of nature that, at the quantum level, our perception is limited. For example, if we know the exact position of a body (which means that $\Delta x = 0$ in **Equation 6.63**) at the same time we cannot know its momentum, because then the uncertainty in its momentum becomes infinite (because $\Delta p \geq 0.5\hbar / \Delta x$ in **Equation 6.63**). The **Heisenberg uncertainty principle** sets the limit on the precision of *simultaneous* measurements of position and momentum of a particle; it shows that the best precision we can obtain is when we have an equals sign ($=$) in **Equation 6.63**, and we cannot do better than that, even with the best instruments of the future. Heisenberg's principle is a consequence of the wave nature of particles.

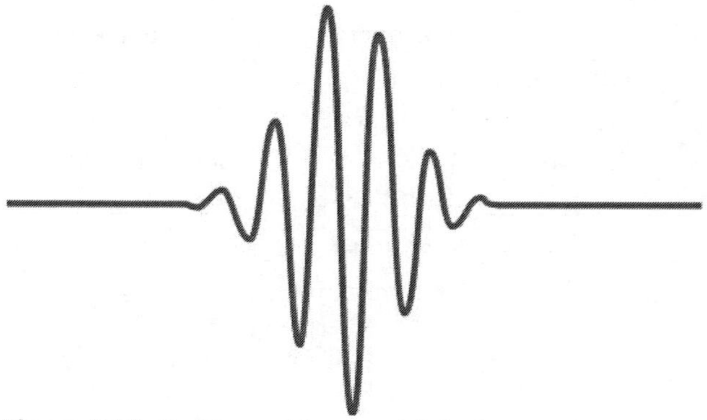

Figure 6.25 In this graphic, a particle is shown as a wave packet and its position does not have an exact value.

We routinely use many electronic devices that exploit wave-particle duality without even realizing the sophistication of the physics underlying their operation. One example of a technology based on the particle properties of photons and electrons is a charge-coupled device, which is used for light detection in any instrumentation where high-quality digital data are required, such as in digital cameras or in medical sensors. An example in which the wave properties of electrons is exploited is an electron microscope.

In 1931, physicist Ernst Ruska—building on the idea that magnetic fields can direct an electron beam just as lenses can direct a beam of light in an optical microscope—developed the first prototype of the electron microscope. This development originated the field of **electron microscopy**. In the transmission electron microscope (TEM), shown in **Figure 6.26**, electrons are produced by a hot tungsten element and accelerated by a potential difference in an electron gun, which gives them up to 400 keV in kinetic energy. After leaving the electron gun, the electron beam is focused by electromagnetic lenses (a system of condensing lenses) and transmitted through a specimen sample to be viewed. The image of the sample is reconstructed from the transmitted electron beam. The magnified image may be viewed either directly on a fluorescent screen or indirectly by sending it, for example, to a digital camera or a computer monitor. The entire setup consisting of the electron gun, the lenses, the specimen, and the fluorescent screen are enclosed in a vacuum chamber to prevent the energy loss from the beam. Resolution of the TEM is limited only by spherical aberration (discussed in a previous chapter). Modern high-resolution models of a TEM can have resolving power greater than 0.5 Å and magnifications higher than 50 million times. For comparison, the best resolving power obtained with light microscopy is currently about 97 nm. A limitation of the TEM is that the samples must be about 100-nm thick and biological samples require a special preparation involving chemical "fixing" to stabilize them for ultrathin slicing.

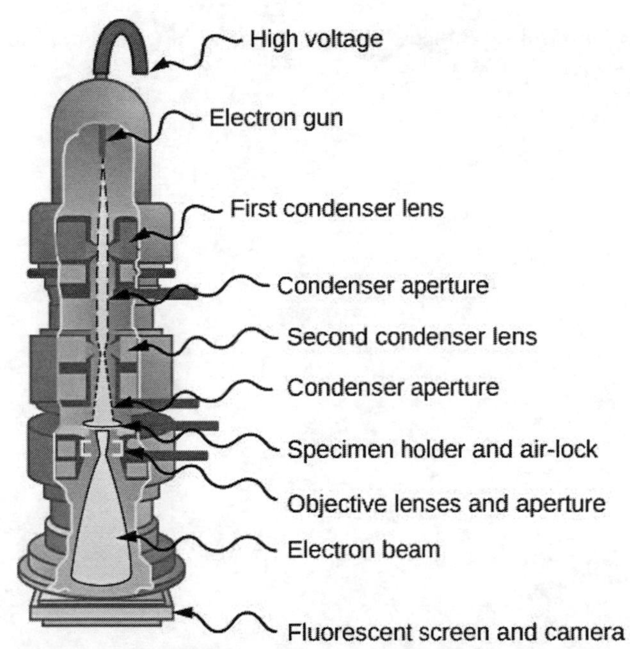

Figure 6.26 TEM: An electron beam produced by an electron gun is collimated by condenser lenses and passes through a specimen. The transmitted electrons are projected on a screen and the image is sent to a camera. (credit: modification of work by Dr. Graham Beards)

Such limitations do not appear in the scanning electron microscope (SEM), which was invented by Manfred von Ardenne in 1937. In an SEM, a typical energy of the electron beam is up to 40 keV and the beam is not transmitted through a sample but is scattered off its surface. Surface topography of the sample is reconstructed by analyzing back-scattered electrons, transmitted electrons, and the emitted radiation produced by electrons interacting with atoms in the sample. The resolving power of an SEM is better than 1 nm, and the magnification can be more than 250 times better than that obtained with a light microscope. The samples scanned by an SEM can be as large as several centimeters but they must be specially prepared, depending on electrical properties of the sample.

High magnifications of the TEM and SEM allow us to see individual molecules. High resolving powers of the TEM and SEM allow us to see fine details, such as those shown in the SEM micrograph of pollen at the beginning of this chapter (**Figure 6.1**).

Example 6.16

Resolving Power of an Electron Microscope

If a 1.0-pm electron beam of a TEM passes through a $2.0\text{-}\mu\text{m}$ circular opening, what is the angle between the two just-resolvable point sources for this microscope?

Solution

We can directly use a formula for the resolving power, $\Delta\theta,$ of a microscope (discussed in a previous chapter) when the wavelength of the incident radiation is $\lambda = 1.0\text{ pm}$ and the diameter of the aperture is $D = 2.0\mu\text{m}$:

$$\Delta\theta = 1.22\frac{\lambda}{D} = 1.22\frac{1.0\text{ pm}}{2.0\mu\text{m}} = 6.10 \times 10^{-7}\text{rad} = 3.50 \times 10^{-5}\text{degree}.$$

Significance

Note that if we used a conventional microscope with a 400-nm light, the resolving power would be only $14°$, which means that all of the fine details in the image would be blurred.

6.15 Check Your Understanding Suppose that the diameter of the aperture in **Example 6.16** is halved. How does it affect the resolving power?

CHAPTER 6 REVIEW

KEY TERMS

absorber any object that absorbs radiation

absorption spectrum wavelengths of absorbed radiation by atoms and molecules

Balmer formula describes the emission spectrum of a hydrogen atom in the visible-light range

Balmer series spectral lines corresponding to electron transitions to/from the $n = 2$ state of the hydrogen atom, described by the Balmer formula

blackbody perfect absorber/emitter

blackbody radiation radiation emitted by a blackbody

Bohr radius of hydrogen radius of the first Bohr's orbit

Bohr's model of the hydrogen atom first quantum model to explain emission spectra of hydrogen

Brackett series spectral lines corresponding to electron transitions to/from the $n = 4$ state

Compton effect the change in wavelength when an X-ray is scattered by its interaction with some materials

Compton shift difference between the wavelengths of the incident X-ray and the scattered X-ray

Compton wavelength physical constant with the value $\lambda_c = 2.43$ pm

cut-off frequency frequency of incident light below which the photoelectric effect does not occur

cut-off wavelength wavelength of incident light that corresponds to cut-off frequency

Davisson–Germer experiment historically first electron-diffraction experiment that revealed electron waves

de Broglie wave matter wave associated with any object that has mass and momentum

de Broglie's hypothesis of matter waves particles of matter can behave like waves

double-slit interference experiment Young's double-slit experiment, which shows the interference of waves

electron microscopy microscopy that uses electron waves to "see" fine details of nano-size objects

emission spectrum wavelengths of emitted radiation by atoms and molecules

emitter any object that emits radiation

energy of a photon quantum of radiant energy, depends only on a photon's frequency

energy spectrum of hydrogen set of allowed discrete energies of an electron in a hydrogen atom

excited energy states of the H atom energy state other than the ground state

Fraunhofer lines dark absorption lines in the continuum solar emission spectrum

ground state energy of the hydrogen atom energy of an electron in the first Bohr orbit of the hydrogen atom

group velocity velocity of a wave, energy travels with the group velocity

Heisenberg uncertainty principle sets the limits on precision in simultaneous measurements of momentum and position of a particle

Humphreys series spectral lines corresponding to electron transitions to/from the $n = 6$ state

hydrogen-like atom ionized atom with one electron remaining and nucleus with charge $+Ze$

inelastic scattering scattering effect where kinetic energy is not conserved but the total energy is conserved

ionization energy energy needed to remove an electron from an atom

ionization limit of the hydrogen atom ionization energy needed to remove an electron from the first Bohr orbit

Lyman series spectral lines corresponding to electron transitions to/from the ground state

nuclear model of the atom heavy positively charged nucleus at the center is surrounded by electrons, proposed by Rutherford

Paschen series spectral lines corresponding to electron transitions to/from the $n = 3$ state

Pfund series spectral lines corresponding to electron transitions to/from the $n = 5$ state

photocurrent in a circuit, current that flows when a photoelectrode is illuminated

photoelectric effect emission of electrons from a metal surface exposed to electromagnetic radiation of the proper frequency

photoelectrode in a circuit, an electrode that emits photoelectrons

photoelectron electron emitted from a metal surface in the presence of incident radiation

photon particle of light

Planck's hypothesis of energy quanta energy exchanges between the radiation and the walls take place only in the form of discrete energy quanta

postulates of Bohr's model three assumptions that set a frame for Bohr's model

power intensity energy that passes through a unit surface per unit time

propagation vector vector with magnitude $2\pi/\lambda$ that has the direction of the photon's linear momentum

quantized energies discrete energies; not continuous

quantum number index that enumerates energy levels

quantum phenomenon in interaction with matter, photon transfers either all its energy or nothing

quantum state of a Planck's oscillator any mode of vibration of Planck's oscillator, enumerated by quantum number

reduced Planck's constant Planck's constant divided by 2π

Rutherford's gold foil experiment first experiment to demonstrate the existence of the atomic nucleus

Rydberg constant for hydrogen physical constant in the Balmer formula

Rydberg formula experimentally found positions of spectral lines of hydrogen atom

scattering angle angle between the direction of the scattered beam and the direction of the incident beam

Stefan–Boltzmann constant physical constant in Stefan's law

stopping potential in a circuit, potential difference that stops photocurrent

wave number magnitude of the propagation vector

wave quantum mechanics theory that explains the physics of atoms and subatomic particles

wave-particle duality particles can behave as waves and radiation can behave as particles

work function energy needed to detach photoelectron from the metal surface

α-particle doubly ionized helium atom

α-ray beam of α-particles (alpha-particles)

β-ray beam of electrons

γ-ray beam of highly energetic photons

KEY EQUATIONS

Wien's displacement law	$\lambda_{max} T = 2.898 \times 10^{-3} \text{m} \cdot \text{K}$
Stefan's law	$P(T) = \sigma A T^4$

Planck's constant	$h = 6.626 \times 10^{-34}\,\text{J} \cdot \text{s} = 4.136 \times 10^{-15}\,\text{eV} \cdot \text{s}$
Energy quantum of radiation	$\Delta E = hf$
Planck's blackbody radiation law	$I(\lambda, T) = \frac{2\pi hc^2}{\lambda^5} \frac{1}{e^{hc/\lambda k_B T} - 1}$
Maximum kinetic energy of a photoelectron	$K_{\text{max}} = e\Delta V_s$
Energy of a photon	$E_f = hf$
Energy balance for photoelectron	$K_{\text{max}} = hf - \phi$
Cut-off frequency	$f_c = \frac{\phi}{h}$
Relativistic invariant energy equation	$E^2 = p^2 c^2 + m_0^2 c^4$
Energy-momentum relation for photon	$p_f = \frac{E_f}{c}$
Energy of a photon	$E_f = hf = \frac{hc}{\lambda}$
Magnitude of photon's momentum	$p_f = \frac{h}{\lambda}$
Photon's linear momentum vector	$\vec{p}_f = \hbar \vec{k}$
The Compton wavelength of an electron	$\lambda_c = \frac{h}{m_0 c} = 0.00243\,\text{nm}$
The Compton shift	$\Delta\lambda = \lambda_c(1 - \cos\theta)$
The Balmer formula	$\frac{1}{\lambda} = R_{\text{H}}\left(\frac{1}{2^2} - \frac{1}{n^2}\right)$
The Rydberg formula	$\frac{1}{\lambda} = R_{\text{H}}\left(\frac{1}{n_f^2} - \frac{1}{n_i^2}\right), n_i = n_f + 1, n_f + 2, \ldots$
Bohr's first quantization condition	$L_n = n\hbar, n = 1, 2, \ldots$
Bohr's second quantization condition	$hf = \lvert E_n - E_m \rvert$
Bohr's radius of hydrogen	$a_0 = 4\pi\varepsilon_0 \frac{\hbar^2}{m_e e^2} = 0.529\text{Å}$
Bohr's radius of the *n*th orbit	$r_n = a_0 n^2$
Ground-state energy value, ionization limit	$E_0 = \frac{1}{8\varepsilon_0^2} \frac{m_e e^4}{h^2} = 13.6\,\text{eV}$
Electron's energy in the *n*th orbit	$E_n = -E_0 \frac{1}{n^2}$
Ground state energy of hydrogen	$E_1 = -E_0 = -13.6\,\text{eV}$

The *n*th orbit of hydrogen-like ion	$r_n = \frac{a_0}{Z} n^2$
The *n*th energy of hydrogen-like ion	$E_n = -Z^2 E_0 \frac{1}{n^2}$
Energy of a matter wave	$E = hf$
The de Broglie wavelength	$\lambda = \frac{h}{p}$
The frequency-wavelength relation for matter waves	$\lambda f = \frac{c}{\beta}$
Heisenberg's uncertainty principle	$\Delta x \Delta p \geq \frac{1}{2}\hbar$

SUMMARY

6.1 Blackbody Radiation

- All bodies radiate energy. The amount of radiation a body emits depends on its temperature. The experimental Wien's displacement law states that the hotter the body, the shorter the wavelength corresponding to the emission peak in the radiation curve. The experimental Stefan's law states that the total power of radiation emitted across the entire spectrum of wavelengths at a given temperature is proportional to the fourth power of the Kelvin temperature of the radiating body.
- Absorption and emission of radiation are studied within the model of a blackbody. In the classical approach, the exchange of energy between radiation and cavity walls is continuous. The classical approach does not explain the blackbody radiation curve.
- To explain the blackbody radiation curve, Planck assumed that the exchange of energy between radiation and cavity walls takes place only in discrete quanta of energy. Planck's hypothesis of energy quanta led to the theoretical Planck's radiation law, which agrees with the experimental blackbody radiation curve; it also explains Wien's and Stefan's laws.

6.2 Photoelectric Effect

- The photoelectric effect occurs when photoelectrons are ejected from a metal surface in response to monochromatic radiation incident on the surface. It has three characteristics: (1) it is instantaneous, (2) it occurs only when the radiation is above a cut-off frequency, and (3) kinetic energies of photoelectrons at the surface do not depend of the intensity of radiation. The photoelectric effect cannot be explained by classical theory.
- We can explain the photoelectric effect by assuming that radiation consists of photons (particles of light). Each photon carries a quantum of energy. The energy of a photon depends only on its frequency, which is the frequency of the radiation. At the surface, the entire energy of a photon is transferred to one photoelectron.
- The maximum kinetic energy of a photoelectron at the metal surface is the difference between the energy of the incident photon and the work function of the metal. The work function is the binding energy of electrons to the metal surface. Each metal has its own characteristic work function.

6.3 The Compton Effect

- In the Compton effect, X-rays scattered off some materials have different wavelengths than the wavelength of the incident X-rays. This phenomenon does not have a classical explanation.
- The Compton effect is explained by assuming that radiation consists of photons that collide with weakly bound electrons in the target material. Both electron and photon are treated as relativistic particles. Conservation laws of the total energy and of momentum are obeyed in collisions.
- Treating the photon as a particle with momentum that can be transferred to an electron leads to a theoretical Compton shift that agrees with the wavelength shift measured in the experiment. This provides evidence that radiation consists of photons.

- Compton scattering is an inelastic scattering, in which scattered radiation has a longer wavelength than that of incident radiation.

6.4 Bohr's Model of the Hydrogen Atom

- Positions of absorption and emission lines in the spectrum of atomic hydrogen are given by the experimental Rydberg formula. Classical physics cannot explain the spectrum of atomic hydrogen.
- The Bohr model of hydrogen was the first model of atomic structure to correctly explain the radiation spectra of atomic hydrogen. It was preceded by the Rutherford nuclear model of the atom. In Rutherford's model, an atom consists of a positively charged point-like nucleus that contains almost the entire mass of the atom and of negative electrons that are located far away from the nucleus.
- Bohr's model of the hydrogen atom is based on three postulates: (1) an electron moves around the nucleus in a circular orbit, (2) an electron's angular momentum in the orbit is quantized, and (3) the change in an electron's energy as it makes a quantum jump from one orbit to another is always accompanied by the emission or absorption of a photon. Bohr's model is semi-classical because it combines the classical concept of electron orbit (postulate 1) with the new concept of quantization (postulates 2 and 3).
- Bohr's model of the hydrogen atom explains the emission and absorption spectra of atomic hydrogen and hydrogen-like ions with low atomic numbers. It was the first model to introduce the concept of a quantum number to describe atomic states and to postulate quantization of electron orbits in the atom. Bohr's model is an important step in the development of quantum mechanics, which deals with many-electron atoms.

6.5 De Broglie's Matter Waves

- De Broglie's hypothesis of matter waves postulates that any particle of matter that has linear momentum is also a wave. The wavelength of a matter wave associated with a particle is inversely proportional to the magnitude of the particle's linear momentum. The speed of the matter wave is the speed of the particle.
- De Broglie's concept of the electron matter wave provides a rationale for the quantization of the electron's angular momentum in Bohr's model of the hydrogen atom.
- In the Davisson–Germer experiment, electrons are scattered off a crystalline nickel surface. Diffraction patterns of electron matter waves are observed. They are the evidence for the existence of matter waves. Matter waves are observed in diffraction experiments with various particles.

6.6 Wave-Particle Duality

- Wave-particle duality exists in nature: Under some experimental conditions, a particle acts as a particle; under other experimental conditions, a particle acts as a wave. Conversely, under some physical circumstances, electromagnetic radiation acts as a wave, and under other physical circumstances, radiation acts as a beam of photons.
- Modern-era double-slit experiments with electrons demonstrated conclusively that electron-diffraction images are formed because of the wave nature of electrons.
- The wave-particle dual nature of particles and of radiation has no classical explanation.
- Quantum theory takes the wave property to be the fundamental property of all particles. A particle is seen as a moving wave packet. The wave nature of particles imposes a limitation on the simultaneous measurement of the particle's position and momentum. Heisenberg's uncertainty principle sets the limits on precision in such simultaneous measurements.
- Wave-particle duality is exploited in many devices, such as charge-couple devices (used in digital cameras) or in the electron microscopy of the scanning electron microscope (SEM) and the transmission electron microscope (TEM).

CONCEPTUAL QUESTIONS

6.1 Blackbody Radiation

1. Which surface has a higher temperature – the surface of a yellow star or that of a red star?

2. Describe what you would see when looking at a body whose temperature is increased from 1000 K to 1,000,000 K.

3. Explain the color changes in a hot body as its temperature is increased.

4. Speculate as to why UV light causes sunburn, whereas visible light does not.

5. Two cavity radiators are constructed with walls made of different metals. At the same temperature, how would their radiation spectra differ?

6. Discuss why some bodies appear black, other bodies appear red, and still other bodies appear white.

7. If everything radiates electromagnetic energy, why can we not see objects at room temperature in a dark room?

8. How much does the power radiated by a blackbody increase when its temperature (in K) is tripled?

6.2 Photoelectric Effect

9. For the same monochromatic light source, would the photoelectric effect occur for all metals?

10. In the interpretation of the photoelectric effect, how is it known that an electron does not absorb more than one photon?

11. Explain how you can determine the work function from a plot of the stopping potential versus the frequency of the incident radiation in a photoelectric effect experiment. Can you determine the value of Planck's constant from this plot?

12. Suppose that in the photoelectric-effect experiment we make a plot of the detected current versus the applied potential difference. What information do we obtain from such a plot? Can we determine from it the value of Planck's constant? Can we determine the work function of the metal?

13. Speculate how increasing the temperature of a photoelectrode affects the outcomes of the photoelectric effect experiment.

14. Which aspects of the photoelectric effect cannot be explained by classical physics?

15. Is the photoelectric effect a consequence of the wave character of radiation or is it a consequence of the particle character of radiation? Explain briefly.

16. The metals sodium, iron, and molybdenum have work functions 2.5 eV, 3.9 eV, and 4.2 eV, respectively. Which of these metals will emit photoelectrons when illuminated with 400 nm light?

6.3 The Compton Effect

17. Discuss any similarities and differences between the photoelectric and the Compton effects.

18. Which has a greater momentum: an UV photon or an IR photon?

19. Does changing the intensity of a monochromatic light beam affect the momentum of the individual photons in the beam? Does such a change affect the net momentum of the beam?

20. Can the Compton effect occur with visible light? If so, will it be detectable?

21. Is it possible in the Compton experiment to observe scattered X-rays that have a shorter wavelength than the incident X-ray radiation?

22. Show that the Compton wavelength has the dimension of length.

23. At what scattering angle is the wavelength shift in the Compton effect equal to the Compton wavelength?

6.4 Bohr's Model of the Hydrogen Atom

24. Explain why the patterns of bright emission spectral lines have an identical spectral position to the pattern of dark absorption spectral lines for a given gaseous element.

25. Do the various spectral lines of the hydrogen atom overlap?

26. The Balmer series for hydrogen was discovered before either the Lyman or the Paschen series. Why?

27. When the absorption spectrum of hydrogen at room temperature is analyzed, absorption lines for the Lyman series are found, but none are found for the Balmer series. What does this tell us about the energy state of most hydrogen atoms at room temperature?

28. Hydrogen accounts for about 75% by mass of the matter at the surfaces of most stars. However, the absorption lines of hydrogen are strongest (of highest intensity) in the spectra of stars with a surface temperature of about 9000 K. They are weaker in the sun spectrum and are essentially nonexistent in very hot (temperatures above 25,000 K) or rather cool (temperatures below 3500 K) stars. Speculate as to why surface temperature affects the hydrogen absorption lines that we observe.

29. Discuss the similarities and differences between

Thomson's model of the hydrogen atom and Bohr's model of the hydrogen atom.

30. Discuss the way in which Thomson's model is nonphysical. Support your argument with experimental evidence.

31. If, in a hydrogen atom, an electron moves to an orbit with a larger radius, does the energy of the hydrogen atom increase or decrease?

32. How is the energy conserved when an atom makes a transition from a higher to a lower energy state?

33. Suppose an electron in a hydrogen atom makes a transition from the $(n+1)$th orbit to the nth orbit. Is the wavelength of the emitted photon longer for larger values of n, or for smaller values of n?

34. Discuss why the allowed energies of the hydrogen atom are negative.

35. Can a hydrogen atom absorb a photon whose energy is greater than 13.6 eV?

36. Why can you see through glass but not through wood?

37. Do gravitational forces have a significant effect on atomic energy levels?

38. Show that Planck's constant has the dimensions of angular momentum.

6.5 De Broglie's Matter Waves

39. Which type of radiation is most suitable for the observation of diffraction patterns on crystalline solids; radio waves, visible light, or X-rays? Explain.

40. Speculate as to how the diffraction patterns of a typical crystal would be affected if γ-rays were used instead of X-rays.

41. If an electron and a proton are traveling at the same speed, which one has the shorter de Broglie wavelength?

42. If a particle is accelerating, how does this affect its de Broglie wavelength?

43. Why is the wave-like nature of matter not observed every day for macroscopic objects?

44. What is the wavelength of a neutron at rest? Explain.

45. Why does the setup of Davisson–Germer experiment need to be enclosed in a vacuum chamber? Discuss what result you expect when the chamber is not evacuated.

6.6 Wave-Particle Duality

46. Give an example of an experiment in which light behaves as waves. Give an example of an experiment in which light behaves as a stream of photons.

47. Discuss: How does the interference of water waves differ from the interference of electrons? How are they analogous?

48. Give at least one argument in support of the matter-wave hypothesis.

49. Give at least one argument in support of the particle-nature of radiation.

50. Explain the importance of the Young double-slit experiment.

51. Does the Heisenberg uncertainty principle allow a particle to be at rest in a designated region in space?

52. Can the de Broglie wavelength of a particle be known exactly?

53. Do the photons of red light produce better resolution in a microscope than blue light photons? Explain.

54. Discuss the main difference between an SEM and a TEM.

PROBLEMS

6.1 Blackbody Radiation

55. A 200-W heater emits a 1.5-μm radiation. (a) What value of the energy quantum does it emit? (b) Assuming that the specific heat of a 4.0-kg body is $0.83 \text{kcal/kg} \cdot \text{K}$, how many of these photons must be absorbed by the body to increase its temperature by 2 K? (c) How long does the heating process in (b) take, assuming that all radiation emitted by the heater gets absorbed by the body?

56. A 900-W microwave generator in an oven generates energy quanta of frequency 2560 MHz. (a) How many energy quanta does it emit per second? (b) How many energy quanta must be absorbed by a pasta dish placed in the radiation cavity to increase its temperature by 45.0 K? Assume that the dish has a mass of 0.5 kg and that its specific heat is $0.9\ \text{kcal/kg}\cdot\text{K}.$ (c) Assume that all energy quanta emitted by the generator are absorbed by the pasta dish. How long must we wait until the dish in (b) is ready?

57. (a) For what temperature is the peak of blackbody radiation spectrum at 400 nm? (b) If the temperature of a blackbody is 800 K, at what wavelength does it radiate the most energy?

58. The tungsten elements of incandescent light bulbs operate at 3200 K. At what frequency does the filament radiate maximum energy?

59. Interstellar space is filled with radiation of wavelength $970\mu\text{m}.$ This radiation is considered to be a remnant of the "big bang." What is the corresponding blackbody temperature of this radiation?

60. The radiant energy from the sun reaches its maximum at a wavelength of about 500.0 nm. What is the approximate temperature of the sun's surface?

6.2 Photoelectric Effect

61. A photon has energy 20 keV. What are its frequency and wavelength?

62. The wavelengths of visible light range from approximately 400 to 750 nm. What is the corresponding range of photon energies for visible light?

63. What is the longest wavelength of radiation that can eject a photoelectron from silver? Is it in the visible range?

64. What is the longest wavelength of radiation that can eject a photoelectron from potassium, given the work function of potassium 2.24 eV? Is it in the visible range?

65. Estimate the binding energy of electrons in magnesium, given that the wavelength of 337 nm is the longest wavelength that a photon may have to eject a photoelectron from magnesium photoelectrode.

66. The work function for potassium is 2.26 eV. What is the cutoff frequency when this metal is used as photoelectrode? What is the stopping potential when for the emitted electrons when this photoelectrode is exposed to radiation of frequency 1200 THz?

67. Estimate the work function of aluminum, given that the wavelength of 304 nm is the longest wavelength that a photon may have to eject a photoelectron from aluminum photoelectrode.

68. What is the maximum kinetic energy of photoelectrons ejected from sodium by the incident radiation of wavelength 450 nm?

69. A 120-nm UV radiation illuminates a gold-plated electrode. What is the maximum kinetic energy of the ejected photoelectrons?

70. A 400-nm violet light ejects photoelectrons with a maximum kinetic energy of 0.860 eV from sodium photoelectrode. What is the work function of sodium?

71. A 600-nm light falls on a photoelectric surface and electrons with the maximum kinetic energy of 0.17 eV are emitted. Determine (a) the work function and (b) the cutoff frequency of the surface. (c) What is the stopping potential when the surface is illuminated with light of wavelength 400 nm?

72. The cutoff wavelength for the emission of photoelectrons from a particular surface is 500 nm. Find the maximum kinetic energy of the ejected photoelectrons when the surface is illuminated with light of wavelength 600 nm.

73. Find the wavelength of radiation that can eject 2.00-eV electrons from calcium electrode. The work function for calcium is 2.71 eV. In what range is this radiation?

74. Find the wavelength of radiation that can eject 0.10-eV electrons from potassium electrode. The work function for potassium is 2.24 eV. In what range is this radiation?

75. Find the maximum velocity of photoelectrons ejected by an 80-nm radiation, if the work function of photoelectrode is 4.73 eV.

6.3 The Compton Effect

76. What is the momentum of a 589-nm yellow photon?

77. What is the momentum of a 4-cm microwave photon?

78. In a beam of white light (wavelengths from 400 to 750 nm), what range of momentum can the photons have?

79. What is the energy of a photon whose momentum is $3.0 \times 10^{-24}\ \text{kg}\cdot\text{m/s}$?

80. What is the wavelength of (a) a 12-keV X-ray photon;

(b) a 2.0-MeV γ -ray photon?

81. Find the momentum and energy of a 1.0-Å photon.

82. Find the wavelength and energy of a photon with momentum 5.00×10^{-29} kg · m/s.

83. A γ -ray photon has a momentum of 8.00×10^{-21} kg · m/s. Find its wavelength and energy.

84. (a) Calculate the momentum of a 2.5-μm photon. (b) Find the velocity of an electron with the same momentum. (c) What is the kinetic energy of the electron, and how does it compare to that of the photon?

85. Show that $p = h/\lambda$ and $E_f = hf$ are consistent with the relativistic formula $E^2 = p^2c^2 + m_0^2c^2$.

86. Show that the energy E in eV of a photon is given by $E = 1.241 \times 10^{-6}\,\text{eV} \cdot \text{m}/\lambda$, where λ is its wavelength in meters.

87. For collisions with free electrons, compare the Compton shift of a photon scattered as an angle of $30°$ to that of a photon scattered at $45°$.

88. X-rays of wavelength 12.5 pm are scattered from a block of carbon. What are the wavelengths of photons scattered at (a) $30°$; (b) $90°$; and, (c) $180°$?

6.4 Bohr's Model of the Hydrogen Atom

89. Calculate the wavelength of the first line in the Lyman series and show that this line lies in the ultraviolet part of the spectrum.

90. Calculate the wavelength of the fifth line in the Lyman series and show that this line lies in the ultraviolet part of the spectrum.

91. Calculate the energy changes corresponding to the transitions of the hydrogen atom: (a) from $n = 3$ to $n = 4$; (b) from $n = 2$ to $n = 1$; and (c) from $n = 3$ to $n = \infty$.

92. Determine the wavelength of the third Balmer line (transition from $n = 5$ to $n = 2$).

93. What is the frequency of the photon absorbed when the hydrogen atom makes the transition from the ground state to the $n = 4$ state?

94. When a hydrogen atom is in its ground state, what are the shortest and longest wavelengths of the photons it can absorb without being ionized?

95. When a hydrogen atom is in its third excided state, what are the shortest and longest wavelengths of the photons it can emit?

96. What is the longest wavelength that light can have if it is to be capable of ionizing the hydrogen atom in its ground state?

97. For an electron in a hydrogen atom in the $n = 2$ state, compute: (a) the angular momentum; (b) the kinetic energy; (c) the potential energy; and (d) the total energy.

98. Find the ionization energy of a hydrogen atom in the fourth energy state.

99. It has been measured that it required 0.850 eV to remove an electron from the hydrogen atom. In what state was the atom before the ionization happened?

100. What is the radius of a hydrogen atom when the electron is in the first excited state?

101. Find the shortest wavelength in the Balmer series. In what part of the spectrum does this line lie?

102. Show that the entire Paschen series lies in the infrared part of the spectrum.

103. Do the Balmer series and the Lyman series overlap? Why? Why not? (Hint: calculate the shortest Balmer line and the longest Lyman line.)

104. (a) Which line in the Balmer series is the first one in the UV part of the spectrum? (b) How many Balmer lines lie in the visible part of the spectrum? (c) How many Balmer lines lie in the UV?

105. A 4.653-μm emission line of atomic hydrogen corresponds to transition between the states $n_f = 5$ and n_i. Find n_i.

6.5 De Broglie's Matter Waves

106. At what velocity will an electron have a wavelength of 1.00 m?

107. What is the de Broglie wavelength of an electron

travelling at a speed of 5.0×10^6 m/s ?

108. What is the de Broglie wavelength of an electron that is accelerated from rest through a potential difference of 20 keV?

109. What is the de Broglie wavelength of a proton whose kinetic energy is 2.0 MeV? 10.0 MeV?

110. What is the de Broglie wavelength of a 10-kg football player running at a speed of 8.0 m/s?

111. (a) What is the energy of an electron whose de Broglie wavelength is that of a photon of yellow light with wavelength 590 nm? (b) What is the de Broglie wavelength of an electron whose energy is that of the photon of yellow light?

112. The de Broglie wavelength of a neutron is 0.01 nm. What is the speed and energy of this neutron?

113. What is the wavelength of an electron that is moving at a 3% of the speed of light?

114. At what velocity does a proton have a 6.0-fm wavelength (about the size of a nucleus)? Give your answer in units of *c*.

115. What is the velocity of a 0.400-kg billiard ball if its wavelength is 7.50 fm?

116. Find the wavelength of a proton that is moving at 1.00% of the speed of light (when $\beta = 0.01$).

6.6 Wave-Particle Duality

117. An AM radio transmitter radiates 500 kW at a frequency of 760 kHz. How many photons per second does the emitter emit?

118. Find the Lorentz factor γ and de Broglie's wavelength for a 50-GeV electron in a particle accelerator.

119. Find the Lorentz factor γ and de Broglie's wavelength for a 1.0-TeV proton in a particle accelerator.

120. What is the kinetic energy of a 0.01-nm electron in a TEM?

121. If electron is to be diffracted significantly by a crystal, its wavelength must be about equal to the spacing, *d*, of crystalline planes. Assuming $d = 0.250$ nm, estimate the potential difference through which an electron must be accelerated from rest if it is to be diffracted by these planes.

122. X-rays form ionizing radiation that is dangerous to living tissue and undetectable to the human eye. Suppose that a student researcher working in an X-ray diffraction laboratory is accidentally exposed to a fatal dose of radiation. Calculate the temperature increase of the researcher under the following conditions: the energy of X-ray photons is 200 keV and the researcher absorbs 4×10^{13} photons per each kilogram of body weight during the exposure. Assume that the specific heat of the student's body is $0.83\text{kcal/kg} \cdot \text{K}$.

123. Solar wind (radiation) that is incident on the top of Earth's atmosphere has an average intensity of 1.3kW/m^2. Suppose that you are building a solar sail that is to propel a small toy spaceship with a mass of 0.1 kg in the space between the International Space Station and the moon. The sail is made from a very light material, which perfectly reflects the incident radiation. To assess whether such a project is feasible, answer the following questions, assuming that radiation photons are incident only in normal direction to the sail reflecting surface. (a) What is the radiation pressure (force per m^2) of the radiation falling on the mirror-like sail? (b) Given the radiation pressure computed in (a), what will be the acceleration of the spaceship when the sail has of an area of 10.0m^2 ? (c) Given the acceleration estimate in (b), how fast will the spaceship be moving after 24 hours when it starts from rest?

124. Treat the human body as a blackbody and determine the percentage increase in the total power of its radiation when its temperature increases from 98.6 ° F to 103 ° F.

125. Show that Wien's displacement law results from Planck's radiation law. (*Hint:* substitute $x = hc/\lambda kT$ and write Planck's law in the form $I(x, T) = Ax^5/(e^x - 1)$, where $A = 2\pi(kT)^5/(h^4c^3)$. Now, for fixed *T*, find the position of the maximum in *I*(*x*,*T*) by solving for *x* in the equation $dI(x, T)/dx = 0.$)

126. Show that Stefan's law results from Planck's radiation law. *Hint:* To compute the total power of blackbody radiation emitted across the entire spectrum of wavelengths at a given temperature, integrate Planck's law over the entire spectrum $P(T) = \int_0^\infty I(\lambda, T)d\lambda$. Use the substitution $x = hc/\lambda kT$ and the tabulated value of the integral $\int_0^\infty dxx^3/(e^x - 1) = \pi^4/15$.

ADDITIONAL PROBLEMS

127. Determine the power intensity of radiation per unit wavelength emitted at a wavelength of 500.0 nm by a blackbody at a temperature of 10,000 K.

128. The HCl molecule oscillates at a frequency of 87.0 THz. What is the difference (in eV) between its adjacent energy levels?

129. A quantum mechanical oscillator vibrates at a frequency of 250.0 THz. What is the minimum energy of radiation it can emit?

130. In about 5 billion years, the sun will evolve to a red giant. Assume that its surface temperature will decrease to about half its present value of 6000 K, while its present radius of $7.0 \times 10^8\,\text{m}$ will increase to $1.5 \times 10^{11}\,\text{m}$ (which is the current Earth-sun distance). Calculate the ratio of the total power emitted by the sun in its red giant stage to its present power.

131. A sodium lamp emits 2.0 W of radiant energy, most of which has a wavelength of about 589 nm. Estimate the number of photons emitted per second by the lamp.

132. Photoelectrons are ejected from a photoelectrode and are detected at a distance of 2.50 cm away from the photoelectrode. The work function of the photoelectrode is 2.71 eV and the incident radiation has a wavelength of 420 nm. How long does it take a photoelectron to travel to the detector?

133. If the work function of a metal is 3.2 eV, what is the maximum wavelength that a photon can have to eject a photoelectron from this metal surface?

134. The work function of a photoelectric surface is 2.00 eV. What is the maximum speed of the photoelectrons emitted from this surface when a 450-nm light falls on it?

135. A 400-nm laser beam is projected onto a calcium electrode. The power of the laser beam is 2.00 mW and the work function of calcium is 2.31 eV. (a) How many photoelectrons per second are ejected? (b) What net power is carried away by photoelectrons?

136. (a) Calculate the number of photoelectrons per second that are ejected from a 1.00-mm^2 area of sodium metal by a 500-nm radiation with intensity 1.30kW/m^2 (the intensity of sunlight above Earth's atmosphere). (b) Given the work function of the metal as 2.28 eV, what power is carried away by these photoelectrons?

137. A laser with a power output of 2.00 mW at a 400-nm wavelength is used to project a beam of light onto a calcium photoelectrode. (a) How many photoelectrons leave the calcium surface per second? (b) What power is carried away by ejected photoelectrons, given that the work function of calcium is 2.31 eV? (c) Calculate the photocurrent. (d) If the photoelectrode suddenly becomes electrically insulated and the setup of two electrodes in the circuit suddenly starts to act like a 2.00-pF capacitor, how long will current flow before the capacitor voltage stops it?

138. The work function for barium is 2.48 eV. Find the maximum kinetic energy of the ejected photoelectrons when the barium surface is illuminated with: (a) radiation emitted by a 100-kW radio station broadcasting at 800 kHz; (b) a 633-nm laser light emitted from a powerful He-Ne laser; and (c) a 434-nm blue light emitted by a small hydrogen gas discharge tube.

139. (a) Calculate the wavelength of a photon that has the same momentum as a proton moving with 1% of the speed of light in a vacuum. (b) What is the energy of this photon in MeV? (c) What is the kinetic energy of the proton in MeV?

140. (a) Find the momentum of a 100-keV X-ray photon. (b) Find the velocity of a neutron with the same momentum. (c) What is the neutron's kinetic energy in eV?

141. The momentum of light, as it is for particles, is exactly reversed when a photon is reflected straight back from a mirror, assuming negligible recoil of the mirror. The change in momentum is twice the photon's incident momentum, as it is for the particles. Suppose that a beam of light has an intensity 1.0kW/m^2 and falls on a -2.0-m^2 area of a mirror and reflects from it. (a) Calculate the energy reflected in 1.00 s. (b) What is the momentum imparted to the mirror? (c) Use Newton's second law to find the force on the mirror. (d) Does the assumption of no-recoil for the mirror seem reasonable?

142. A photon of energy 5.0 keV collides with a stationary electron and is scattered at an angle of $60°$. What is the energy acquired by the electron in the collision?

143. A 0.75-nm photon is scattered by a stationary electron. The speed of the electron's recoil is $1.5 \times 10^6\,\text{m/s}$. (a) Find the wavelength shift of the photon. (b) Find the scattering angle of the photon.

144. Find the maximum change in X-ray wavelength that can occur due to Compton scattering. Does this change depend on the wavelength of the incident beam?

145. A photon of wavelength 700 nm is incident on a hydrogen atom. When this photon is absorbed, the atom becomes ionized. What is the lowest possible orbit that the electron could have occupied before being ionized?

146. What is the maximum kinetic energy of an electron such that a collision between the electron and a stationary hydrogen atom in its ground state is definitely elastic?

147. Singly ionized atomic helium He^{+1} is a hydrogen-like ion. (a) What is its ground-state radius? (b) Calculate the energies of its four lowest energy states. (c) Repeat the calculations for the Li^{2+} ion.

148. A triply ionized atom of beryllium Be^{3+} is a hydrogen-like ion. When Be^{3+} is in one of its excited states, its radius in this *n*th state is exactly the same as the radius of the first Bohr orbit of hydrogen. Find *n* and compute the ionization energy for this state of Be^{3+}.

149. In extreme-temperature environments, such as those existing in a solar corona, atoms may be ionized by undergoing collisions with other atoms. One example of such ionization in the solar corona is the presence of C^{5+} ions, detected in the Fraunhofer spectrum. (a) By what factor do the energies of the C^{5+} ion scale compare to the energy spectrum of a hydrogen atom? (b) What is the wavelength of the first line in the Paschen series of C^{5+} ? (c) In what part of the spectrum are these lines located?

150. (a) Calculate the ionization energy for He^+. (b) What is the minimum frequency of a photon capable of ionizing He^+ ?

151. Experiments are performed with ultracold neutrons having velocities as small as 1.00 m/s. Find the wavelength of such an ultracold neutron and its kinetic energy.

152. Find the velocity and kinetic energy of a 6.0-fm neutron. (Rest mass energy of neutron is $E_0 = 940\text{ MeV}$.)

153. The spacing between crystalline planes in the NaCl crystal is 0.281 nm, as determined by X-ray diffraction with X-rays of wavelength 0.170 nm. What is the energy of neutrons in the neutron beam that produces diffraction peaks at the same locations as the peaks obtained with the X-rays?

154. What is the wavelength of an electron accelerated from rest in a 30.0-kV potential difference?

155. Calculate the velocity of a 1.0-μm electron and a potential difference used to accelerate it from rest to this velocity.

156. In a supercollider at CERN, protons are accelerated to velocities of 0.25*c*. What are their wavelengths at this speed? What are their kinetic energies? If a beam of protons were to gain its kinetic energy in only one pass through a potential difference, how high would this potential difference have to be? (Rest mass energy of a proton is $E_0 = 938\text{ MeV}$).

157. Find the de Broglie wavelength of an electron accelerated from rest in an X-ray tube in the potential difference of 100 keV. (Rest mass energy of an electron is $E_0 = 511\text{ keV}$.)

158. The cutoff wavelength for the emission of photoelectrons from a particular surface is 500 nm. Find the maximum kinetic energy of the ejected photoelectrons when the surface is illuminated with light of wavelength 450 nm.

159. Compare the wavelength shift of a photon scattered by a free electron to that of a photon scattered at the same angle by a free proton.

160. The spectrometer used to measure the wavelengths of the scattered X-rays in the Compton experiment is accurate to $5.0 \times 10^{-4}\text{ nm}$. What is the minimum scattering angle for which the X-rays interacting with the free electrons can be distinguished from those interacting with the atoms?

161. Consider a hydrogen-like ion where an electron is orbiting a nucleus that has charge $q = +Ze$. Derive the formulas for the energy E_n of the electron in *n*th orbit and the orbital radius r_n.

162. Assume that a hydrogen atom exists in the $n = 2$ excited state for 10^{-8} s before decaying to the ground state. How many times does the electron orbit the proton nucleus during this time? How long does it take Earth to orbit the sun this many times?

163. An atom can be formed when a negative muon is captured by a proton. The muon has the same charge as the electron and a mass 207 times that of the electron. Calculate the frequency of the photon emitted when this atom makes the transition from $n = 2$ to the $n = 1$ state. Assume that the muon is orbiting a stationary proton.

7 | QUANTUM MECHANICS

Figure 7.1 A D-wave qubit processor: The brain of a quantum computer that encodes information in quantum bits to perform complex calculations. (credit: modification of work by D-Wave Systems, Inc.)

Chapter Outline

Introduction

Quantum mechanics is a powerful framework for understanding the motions and interactions of particles at small scales, such as atoms and molecules. The ideas behind quantum mechanics often appear quite strange. In many ways, our everyday experience with the macroscopic physical world does not prepare us for the microscopic world of quantum mechanics. The purpose of this chapter is to introduce you to this exciting world.

Pictured above is a quantum-computer processor. This device is the "brain" of a quantum computer that operates at near-absolute zero temperatures. Unlike a digital computer, which encodes information in binary digits (definite states of either zero or one), a quantum computer encodes information in quantum bits or qubits (mixed states of zero *and* one). Quantum computers are discussed in the first section of this chapter.

7.1 | Wave Functions

Learning Objectives

By the end of this section, you will be able to:

- Describe the statistical interpretation of the wave function
- Use the wave function to determine probabilities
- Calculate expectation values of position, momentum, and kinetic energy

In the preceding chapter, we saw that particles act in some cases like particles and in other cases like waves. But what does it mean for a particle to "act like a wave"? What precisely is "waving"? What rules govern how this wave changes and propagates? How is the wave function used to make predictions? For example, if the amplitude of an electron wave is given by a function of position and time, $\Psi(x, t)$, defined for all *x*, *where* exactly is the electron? The purpose of this chapter is to answer these questions.

Using the Wave Function

A clue to the physical meaning of the wave function $\Psi(x, t)$ is provided by the two-slit interference of monochromatic light (**Figure 7.2**). (See also **Electromagnetic Waves (http://cnx.org/content/m58495/latest/)** and **Interference**.) The **wave function** of a light wave is given by *E*(*x*,*t*), and its energy density is given by $|E|^2$, where *E* is the electric field strength. The energy of an individual photon depends only on the frequency of light, $\varepsilon_{\text{photon}} = hf$, so $|E|^2$ is proportional to the number of photons. When light waves from S_1 interfere with light waves from S_2 at the viewing screen (a distance *D* away), an interference pattern is produced (part (a) of the figure). Bright fringes correspond to points of constructive interference of the light waves, and dark fringes correspond to points of destructive interference of the light waves (part (b)).

Suppose the screen is initially unexposed to light. If the screen is exposed to very weak light, the interference pattern appears gradually (**Figure 7.2**(c), left to right). Individual photon hits on the screen appear as dots. The dot density is expected to be large at locations where the interference pattern will be, ultimately, the most intense. In other words, the probability (per unit area) that a single photon will strike a particular spot on the screen is proportional to the square of the total electric field, $|E|^2$ at that point. Under the right conditions, the same interference pattern develops for matter particles, such as electrons.

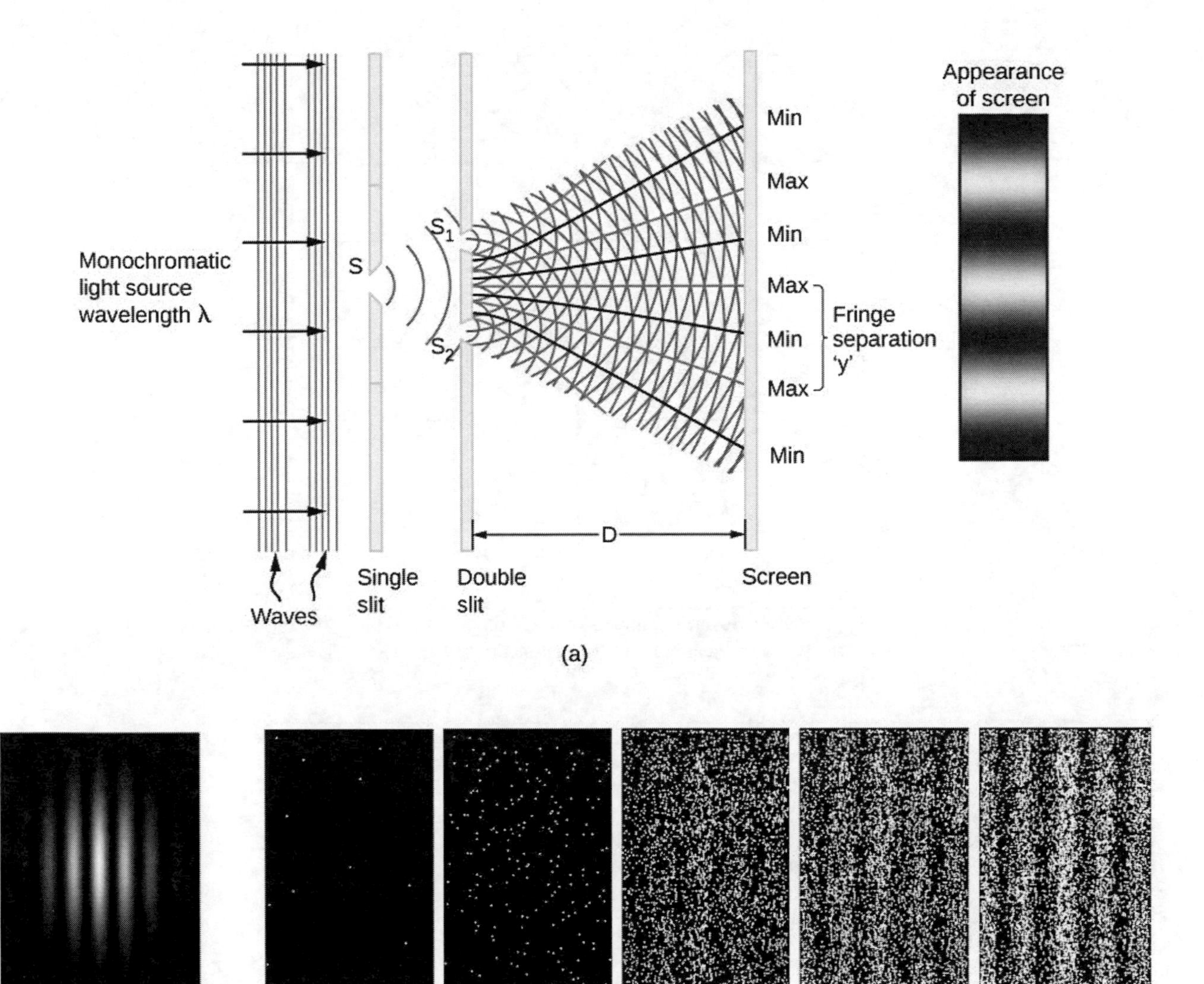

Figure 7.2 Two-slit interference of monochromatic light. (a) Schematic of two-slit interference; (b) light interference pattern; (c) interference pattern built up gradually under low-intensity light (left to right).

Visit this **interactive simulation (https://openstaxcollege.org/l/21intquawavint)** to learn more about quantum wave interference.

The square of the matter wave $|\Psi|^2$ in one dimension has a similar interpretation as the square of the electric field $|E|^2$. It gives the probability that a particle will be found at a particular position and time per unit length, also called the **probability density**. The probability (P) a particle is found in a narrow interval (x, $x + dx$) at time t is therefore

$$P(x, x + dx) = |\Psi(x, t)|^2 dx. \tag{7.1}$$

(Later, we define the magnitude squared for the general case of a function with "imaginary parts.") This probabilistic interpretation of the wave function is called the **Born interpretation**. Examples of wave functions and their squares for a particular time t are given in **Figure 7.3**.

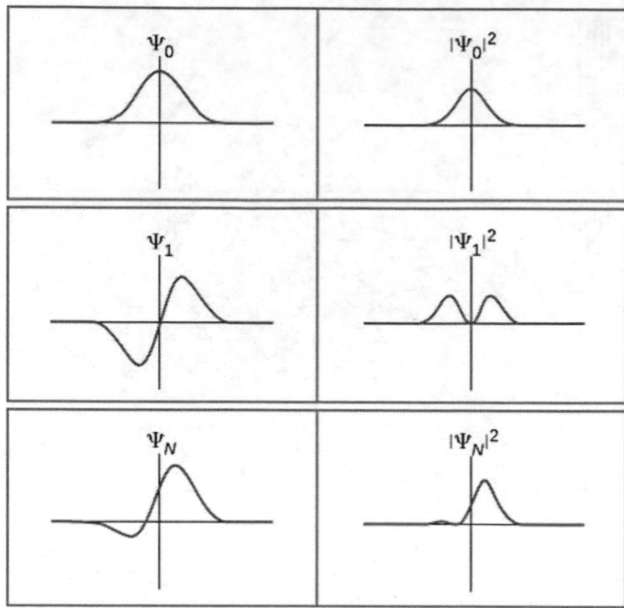

Figure 7.3 Several examples of wave functions and the corresponding square of their wave functions.

If the wave function varies slowly over the interval Δx, the probability a particle is found in the interval is approximately

$$P(x,\ x+\Delta x) \approx |\Psi(x,\ t)|^2 \Delta x. \tag{7.2}$$

Notice that squaring the wave function ensures that the probability is positive. (This is analogous to squaring the electric field strength—which may be positive or negative—to obtain a positive value of intensity.) However, if the wave function does not vary slowly, we must integrate:

$$P(x,\ x+\Delta x) = \int_{x}^{x+\Delta x} |\Psi(x,\ t)|^2 dx. \tag{7.3}$$

This probability is just the area under the function $|\Psi(x,\ t)|^2$ between x and $x+\Delta x$. The probability of finding the particle "somewhere" (the **normalization condition**) is

$$P(-\infty,\ +\infty) = \int_{-\infty}^{\infty} |\Psi(x,\ t)|^2 dx = 1. \tag{7.4}$$

For a particle in two dimensions, the integration is over an area and requires a double integral; for a particle in three dimensions, the integration is over a volume and requires a triple integral. For now, we stick to the simple one-dimensional case.

Example 7.1

Where Is the Ball? (Part I)

A ball is constrained to move along a line inside a tube of length L. The ball is equally likely to be found anywhere in the tube at some time t. What is the probability of finding the ball in the left half of the tube at that time? (The answer is 50%, of course, but how do we get this answer by using the probabilistic interpretation of the quantum mechanical wave function?)

Strategy

The first step is to write down the wave function. The ball is equally like to be found anywhere in the box, so one way to describe the ball with a *constant* wave function (**Figure 7.4**). The normalization condition can be used to find the value of the function and a simple integration over half of the box yields the final answer.

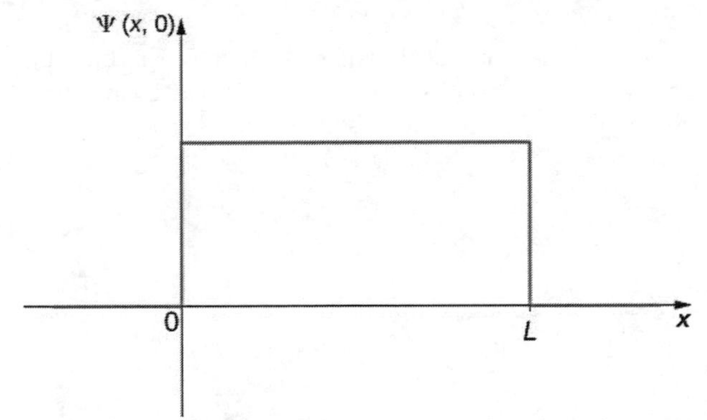

Figure 7.4 Wave function for a ball in a tube of length L.

Solution

The wave function of the ball can be written as $\Psi(x,\, t) = C(0 < x < L)$, where C is a constant, and $\Psi(x,\, t) = 0$ otherwise. We can determine the constant C by applying the normalization condition (we set $t = 0$ to simplify the notation):

$$P(x = -\infty,\, +\infty) = \int_{-\infty}^{\infty} |C|^2 dx = 1.$$

This integral can be broken into three parts: (1) negative infinity to zero, (2) zero to L, and (3) L to infinity. The particle is constrained to be in the tube, so $C = 0$ outside the tube and the first and last integrations are zero. The above equation can therefore be written

$$P(x = 0,\, L) = \int_0^L |C|^2 dx = 1.$$

The value C does not depend on x and can be taken out of the integral, so we obtain

$$|C|^2 \int_0^L dx = 1.$$

Integration gives

$$C = \sqrt{\frac{1}{L}}.$$

To determine the probability of finding the ball in the first half of the box $(0 < x < L)$, we have

$$P(x = 0,\, L/2) = \int_0^{L/2} \left|\sqrt{\frac{1}{L}}\right|^2 dx = \left(\frac{1}{L}\right)\frac{L}{2} = 0.50.$$

Significance

The probability of finding the ball in the first half of the tube is 50%, as expected. Two observations are noteworthy. First, this result corresponds to the area under the constant function from $x = 0$ to $L/2$ (the area of a square left of $L/2$). Second, this calculation requires an integration of the *square* of the wave function. A common mistake in performing such calculations is to forget to square the wave function before integration.

Example 7.2

Where Is the Ball? (Part II)

A ball is again constrained to move along a line inside a tube of length L. This time, the ball is found preferentially in the middle of the tube. One way to represent its wave function is with a simple cosine function (**Figure 7.5**). What is the probability of finding the ball in the last one-quarter of the tube?

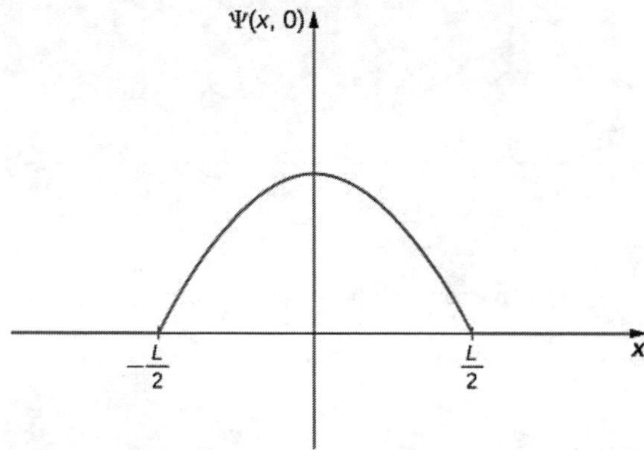

Figure 7.5 Wave function for a ball in a tube of length L, where the ball is preferentially in the middle of the tube.

Strategy

We use the same strategy as before. In this case, the wave function has two unknown constants: One is associated with the wavelength of the wave and the other is the amplitude of the wave. We determine the amplitude by using the boundary conditions of the problem, and we evaluate the wavelength by using the normalization condition. Integration of the square of the wave function over the last quarter of the tube yields the final answer. The calculation is simplified by centering our coordinate system on the peak of the wave function.

Solution

The wave function of the ball can be written

$$\Psi(x,\,0) = A\cos(kx)(-L/2 < x < L/2),$$

where A is the amplitude of the wave function and $k = 2\pi/\lambda$ is its wave number. Beyond this interval, the amplitude of the wave function is zero because the ball is confined to the tube. Requiring the wave function to terminate at the right end of the tube gives

$$\Psi\left(x = \frac{L}{2},\,0\right) = 0.$$

Evaluating the wave function at $x = L/2$ gives

$$A\cos(kL/2) = 0.$$

This equation is satisfied if the argument of the cosine is an integral multiple of $\pi/2,\ 3\pi/2,\ 5\pi/2,$ and so on. In this case, we have

$$\frac{kL}{2} = \frac{\pi}{2},$$

or

$$k = \frac{\pi}{L}.$$

Applying the normalization condition gives $A = \sqrt{2/L}$, so the wave function of the ball is

$$\Psi(x,\,0) = \sqrt{\frac{2}{L}}\cos(\pi x/L), \quad -L/2 < x < L/2.$$

To determine the probability of finding the ball in the last quarter of the tube, we square the function and integrate:

$$P(x = L/4, L/2) = \int_{L/4}^{L/2} \left|\sqrt{\frac{2}{L}}\cos\left(\frac{\pi x}{L}\right)\right|^2 dx = 0.091.$$

Significance

The probability of finding the ball in the last quarter of the tube is 9.1%. The ball has a definite wavelength $(\lambda = 2L)$. If the tube is of macroscopic length $(L = 1\text{ m})$, the momentum of the ball is

$$p = \frac{h}{\lambda} = \frac{h}{2L} \sim 10^{-36}\,\text{m/s}.$$

This momentum is much too small to be measured by any human instrument.

An Interpretation of the Wave Function

We are now in position to begin to answer the questions posed at the beginning of this section. First, for a traveling particle described by $\Psi(x, t) = A\sin(kx - \omega t)$, what is "waving?" Based on the above discussion, the answer is a mathematical function that can, among other things, be used to determine where the particle is likely to be when a position measurement is performed. Second, how is the wave function used to make predictions? If it is necessary to find the probability that a particle will be found in a certain interval, square the wave function and integrate over the interval of interest. Soon, you will learn soon that the wave function can be used to make many other kinds of predictions, as well.

Third, if a matter wave is given by the wave function $\Psi(x, t)$, *where* exactly is the particle? Two answers exist: (1) when the observer *is not* looking (or the particle is not being otherwise detected), the particle is everywhere $(x = -\infty, +\infty)$; and (2) when the observer *is* looking (the particle is being detected), the particle "jumps into" a particular position state $(x, x + dx)$ with a probability given by $P(x, x + dx) = |\Psi(x, t)|^2 dx$ —a process called **state reduction** or **wave function collapse**. This answer is called the **Copenhagen interpretation** of the wave function, or of quantum mechanics.

To illustrate this interpretation, consider the simple case of a particle that can occupy a small container either at x_1 or x_2 (**Figure 7.6**). In classical physics, we assume the particle is located either at x_1 or x_2 when the observer is not looking. However, in quantum mechanics, the particle may exist in a state of indefinite position—that is, it may be located at x_1 *and* x_2 when the observer is not looking. The assumption that a particle can only have one value of position (when the observer is not looking) is abandoned. Similar comments can be made of other measurable quantities, such as momentum and energy.

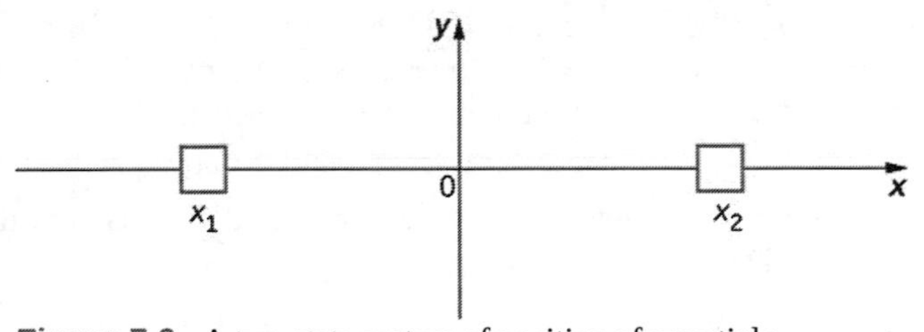

Figure 7.6 A two-state system of position of a particle.

The bizarre consequences of the Copenhagen interpretation of quantum mechanics are illustrated by a creative thought experiment first articulated by Erwin Schrödinger (*National Geographic*, 2013) (**Figure 7.7**):

"A cat is placed in a steel box along with a Geiger counter, a vial of poison, a hammer, and a radioactive substance. When the radioactive substance decays, the Geiger detects it and triggers the hammer to release the poison, which subsequently kills the cat. The radioactive decay is a random [probabilistic] process, and there is no way to predict when it will happen. Physicists say the atom exists in a state known as a superposition—both decayed and not decayed at the same time. Until the box is opened, an observer doesn't know whether the cat is alive or dead—because the cat's fate is intrinsically tied to whether or not the atom has decayed and the cat would [according to the Copenhagen interpretation] be "living and dead ... in equal parts" until it is observed."

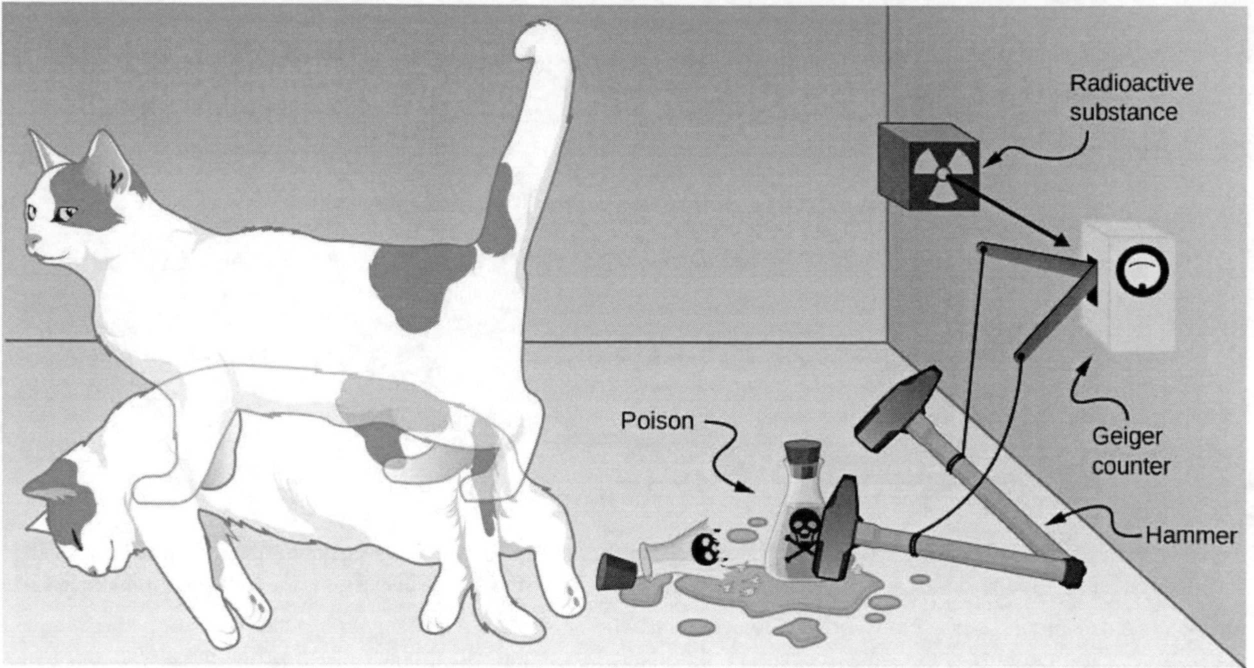

Figure 7.7 Schrödinger's cat.

Schrödinger took the absurd implications of this thought experiment (a cat simultaneously dead and alive) as an argument against the Copenhagen interpretation. However, this interpretation remains the most commonly taught view of quantum mechanics.

Two-state systems (left and right, atom decays and does not decay, and so on) are often used to illustrate the principles of quantum mechanics. These systems find many applications in nature, including electron spin and mixed states of particles, atoms, and even molecules. Two-state systems are also finding application in the quantum computer, as mentioned in the introduction of this chapter. Unlike a digital computer, which encodes information in binary digits (zeroes and ones), a quantum computer stores and manipulates data in the form of quantum bits, or qubits. In general, a qubit is not in a state of zero or one, but rather in a mixed state of zero *and* one. If a large number of qubits are placed in the same quantum state, the measurement of an individual qubit would produce a zero with a probability p, and a one with a probability $q = 1 - p$. Many scientists believe that quantum computers are the future of the computer industry.

Complex Conjugates

Later in this section, you will see how to use the wave function to describe particles that are "free" or bound by forces to other particles. The specific form of the wave function depends on the details of the physical system. A peculiarity of quantum theory is that these functions are usually **complex functions**. A complex function is one that contains one or more imaginary numbers $(i = \sqrt{-1})$. Experimental measurements produce real (nonimaginary) numbers only, so the above procedure to use the wave function must be slightly modified. In general, the probability that a particle is found in the narrow interval $(x, x + dx)$ at time t is given by

$$P(x, x + dx) = |\Psi(x, t)|^2 dx = \Psi^* (x, t)\Psi(x, t)dx, \quad (7.5)$$

where $\Psi^* (x, t)$ is the complex conjugate of the wave function. The complex conjugate of a function is obtaining by replacing every occurrence of $i = \sqrt{-1}$ in that function with $-i$. This procedure eliminates complex numbers in all predictions because the product $\Psi^* (x, t)\Psi(x, t)$ is always a real number.

7.1 Check Your Understanding If $a = 3 + 4i$, what is the product $a^* a$?

Consider the motion of a free particle that moves along the *x*-direction. As the name suggests, a free particle experiences no forces and so moves with a constant velocity. As we will see in a later section of this chapter, a formal quantum mechanical treatment of a free particle indicates that its wave function has real *and* complex parts. In particular, the wave function is given by

$$\Psi(x, t) = A\cos(kx - \omega t) + iA\sin(kx - \omega t),$$

where A is the amplitude, k is the wave number, and ω is the angular frequency. Using Euler's formula, $e^{i\phi} = \cos(\phi) + i\sin(\phi)$, this equation can be written in the form

$$\Psi(x, t) = Ae^{i(kx - \omega t)} = Ae^{i\phi},$$

where ϕ is the phase angle. If the wave function varies slowly over the interval Δx, the probability of finding the particle in that interval is

$$P(x, x + \Delta x) \approx \Psi^*(x, t)\Psi(x, t)\Delta x = \left(Ae^{i\phi}\right)\left(A^* e^{-i\phi}\right)\Delta x = (A^* A)\Delta x.$$

If *A* has real and complex parts $(a + ib$, where *a* and *b* are real constants), then

$$A^* A = (a + ib)(a - ib) = a^2 + b^2.$$

Notice that the complex numbers have vanished. Thus,

$$P(x, x + \Delta x) \approx |A|^2\Delta x$$

is a real quantity. The interpretation of $\Psi^*(x, t)\Psi(x, t)$ as a probability density ensures that the predictions of quantum mechanics can be checked in the "real world."

7.2 Check Your Understanding Suppose that a particle with energy E is moving along the *x*-axis and is confined in the region between 0 and L. One possible wave function is

$$\psi(x, t) = \begin{cases} Ae^{-iEt/\hbar}\sin\frac{\pi x}{L}, & \text{when } 0 \le x \le L \\ 0, & \text{otherwise} \end{cases}.$$

Determine the normalization constant.

Expectation Values

In classical mechanics, the solution to an equation of motion is a function of a measurable quantity, such as *x*(*t*), where *x* is the position and *t* is the time. Note that the particle has one value of position for any time *t*. In quantum mechanics, however, the solution to an equation of motion is a wave function, $\Psi(x, t)$. The particle has many values of position for any time *t*, and only the probability density of finding the particle, $|\Psi(x, t)|^2$, can be known. The average value of position for a large number of particles with the same wave function is expected to be

$$\langle x \rangle = \int_{-\infty}^{\infty} xP(x, t)dx = \int_{-\infty}^{\infty} x\Psi^*(x, t)\Psi(x, t)dx. \tag{7.6}$$

This is called the **expectation value** of the position. It is usually written

$$\langle x \rangle = \int_{-\infty}^{\infty} \Psi^*(x, t)x\Psi(x, t)dx, \tag{7.7}$$

where the *x* is sandwiched between the wave functions. The reason for this will become apparent soon. Formally, *x* is called the **position operator**.

At this point, it is important to stress that a wave function can be written in terms of other quantities as well, such as velocity

(v), momentum (p), and kinetic energy (K). The expectation value of momentum, for example, can be written

$$\langle p \rangle = \int_{-\infty}^{\infty} \Psi^* (p, t) p \Psi(p, t) dp, \tag{7.8}$$

Where dp is used instead of dx to indicate an infinitesimal interval in momentum. In some cases, we know the wave function in position, $\Psi(x, t)$, but seek the expectation of momentum. The procedure for doing this is

$$\langle p \rangle = \int_{-\infty}^{\infty} \Psi^* (x, t)\left(-i\hbar \frac{d}{dx}\right)\Psi(x, t) dx, \tag{7.9}$$

where the quantity in parentheses, sandwiched between the wave functions, is called the **momentum operator** in the x-direction. [The momentum operator in Equation 7.9 is said to be the position-space representation of the momentum operator.] The momentum operator must act (operate) on the wave function to the right, and then the result must be multiplied by the complex conjugate of the wave function on the left, before integration. The momentum operator in the x-direction is sometimes denoted

$$(p_x)_{\text{op}} = -i\hbar \frac{d}{dx}, \tag{7.10}$$

Momentum operators for the y- and z-directions are defined similarly. This operator and many others are derived in a more advanced course in modern physics. In some cases, this derivation is relatively simple. For example, the kinetic energy operator is just

$$(K)_{\text{op}} = \frac{1}{2}m(v_x)^2_{\text{op}} = \frac{(p_x)^2_{\text{op}}}{2m} = \frac{\left(-i\hbar \frac{d}{dx}\right)^2}{2m} = \frac{-\hbar^2}{2m}\left(\frac{d}{dx}\right)\left(\frac{d}{dx}\right). \tag{7.11}$$

Thus, if we seek an expectation value of kinetic energy of a particle in one dimension, two successive ordinary derivatives of the wave function are required before integration.

Expectation-value calculations are often simplified by exploiting the symmetry of wave functions. Symmetric wave functions can be even or odd. An **even function** is a function that satisfies

$$\psi(x) = \psi(-x). \tag{7.12}$$

In contrast, an **odd function** is a function that satisfies

$$\psi(x) = -\psi(-x). \tag{7.13}$$

An example of even and odd functions is shown in Figure 7.8. An even function is symmetric about the y-axis. This function is produced by reflecting $\psi(x)$ for $x > 0$ about the vertical y-axis. By comparison, an odd function is generated by reflecting the function about the y-axis and then about the x-axis. (An odd function is also referred to as an **anti-symmetric function**.)

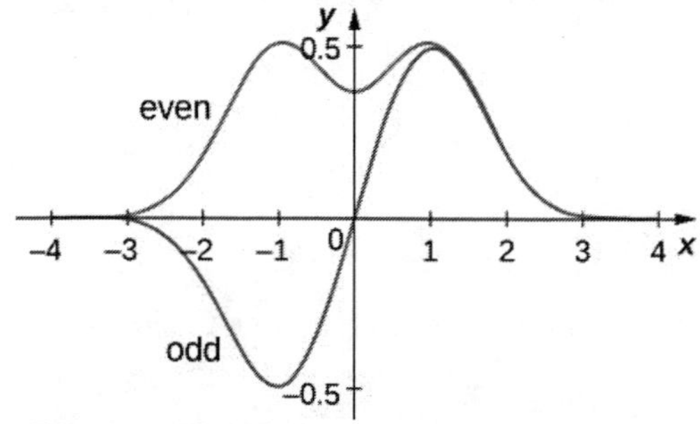

Figure 7.8 Examples of even and odd wave functions.

In general, an even function times an even function produces an even function. A simple example of an even function is the product $x^2 e^{-x^2}$ (even times even is even). Similarly, an odd function times an odd function produces an even function, such as $x \sin x$ (odd times odd is even). However, an odd function times an even function produces an odd function, such as xe^{-x^2} (odd times even is odd). The integral over all space of an odd function is zero, because the total area of the function above the x-axis cancels the (negative) area below it. As the next example shows, this property of odd functions is very useful.

Example 7.3

Expectation Value (Part I)

The normalized wave function of a particle is

$$\psi(x) = e^{-|x|/x_0}/\sqrt{x_0}.$$

Find the expectation value of position.

Strategy

Substitute the wave function into **Equation 7.7** and evaluate. The position operator introduces a multiplicative factor only, so the position operator need not be "sandwiched."

Solution

First multiply, then integrate:

$$\langle x \rangle = \int_{-\infty}^{+\infty} dx x|\psi(x)|^2 = \int_{-\infty}^{+\infty} dx x\left|\frac{e^{-|x|/x_0}}{\sqrt{x_0}}\right|^2 = \frac{1}{x_0}\int_{-\infty}^{+\infty} dx x e^{-2|x|/x_0} = 0.$$

Significance

The function in the integrand ($xe^{-2|x|/x_0}$) is odd since it is the product of an odd function (x) and an even function ($e^{-2|x|/x_0}$). The integral vanishes because the total area of the function about the x-axis cancels the (negative) area below it. The result ($\langle x \rangle = 0$) is not surprising since the probability density function is symmetric about $x = 0$.

Example 7.4

Expectation Value (Part II)

The time-dependent wave function of a particle confined to a region between 0 and L is

$$\psi(x,\, t) = Ae^{-i\omega t}\sin(\pi x/L)$$

where ω is angular frequency and E is the energy of the particle. (*Note:* The function varies as a sine because of the limits (0 to L). When $x = 0$, the sine factor is zero and the wave function is zero, consistent with the boundary conditions.) Calculate the expectation values of position, momentum, and kinetic energy.

Strategy

We must first normalize the wave function to find A. Then we use the operators to calculate the expectation values.

Solution

Computation of the normalization constant:

$$1 = \int_0^L dx \psi^*(x)\psi(x) = \int_0^L dx\left(Ae^{+i\omega t}\sin\frac{\pi x}{L}\right)\left(Ae^{-i\omega t}\sin\frac{\pi x}{L}\right) = A^2\int_0^L dx \sin^2\frac{\pi x}{L} = A^2\frac{L}{2} \Rightarrow A = \sqrt{\frac{2}{L}}.$$

The expectation value of position is

$$\langle x \rangle = \int_0^L dx\psi^*(x)x\psi(x) = \int_0^L dx\left(Ae^{+i\omega t}\sin\frac{\pi x}{L}\right)x\left(Ae^{-i\omega t}\sin\frac{\pi x}{L}\right) = A^2\int_0^L dx x\sin^2\frac{\pi x}{L} = A^2\frac{L^2}{4} = \frac{L}{2}.$$

The expectation value of momentum in the *x*-direction also requires an integral. To set this integral up, the associated operator must— by rule—act to the right on the wave function $\psi(x)$:

$$-i\hbar\frac{d}{dx}\psi(x) = -i\hbar\frac{d}{dx}Ae^{-i\omega t}\sin\frac{\pi x}{L} = -i\frac{Ah}{2L}e^{-i\omega t}\cos\frac{\pi x}{L}.$$

Therefore, the expectation value of momentum is

$$\langle p \rangle = \int_0^L dx\left(Ae^{+i\omega t}\sin\frac{\pi x}{L}\right)\left(-i\frac{Ah}{2L}e^{-i\omega t}\cos\frac{\pi x}{L}\right) = -i\frac{A^2h}{4L}\int_0^L dx\sin\frac{2\pi x}{L} = 0.$$

The function in the integral is a sine function with a wavelength equal to the width of the well, *L*—an odd function about $x = L/2$. As a result, the integral vanishes.

The expectation value of kinetic energy in the *x*-direction requires the associated operator to act on the wave function:

$$-\frac{\hbar^2}{2m}\frac{d^2}{dx^2}\psi(x) = -\frac{\hbar^2}{2m}\frac{d^2}{dx^2}Ae^{-i\omega t}\sin\frac{\pi x}{L} = -\frac{\hbar^2}{2m}Ae^{-i\omega t}\frac{d^2}{dx^2}\sin\frac{\pi x}{L} = \frac{Ah^2}{2mL^2}e^{-i\omega t}\sin\frac{\pi x}{L}.$$

Thus, the expectation value of the kinetic energy is

$$\begin{aligned}\langle K \rangle &= \int_0^L dx\left(Ae^{+i\omega t}\sin\frac{\pi x}{L}\right)\left(\frac{Ah^2}{2mL^2}e^{-i\omega t}\sin\frac{\pi x}{L}\right) \\ &= \frac{A^2h^2}{2mL^2}\int_0^L dx\sin^2\frac{\pi x}{L} = \frac{A^2h^2}{2mL^2}\frac{L}{2} = \frac{h^2}{2mL^2}.\end{aligned}$$

Significance

The average position of a large number of particles in this state is *L*/2. The average momentum of these particles is zero because a given particle is equally likely to be moving right or left. However, the particle is not at rest because its average kinetic energy is not zero. Finally, the probability density is

$$|\psi|^2 = (2/L)\sin^2(\pi x/L).$$

This probability density is largest at location *L*/2 and is zero at $x = 0$ and at $x = L.$ Note that these conclusions do not depend explicitly on time.

7.3 Check Your Understanding For the particle in the above example, find the probability of locating it between positions 0 and *L*/4

Quantum mechanics makes many surprising predictions. However, in 1920, Niels Bohr (founder of the Niels Bohr Institute in Copenhagen, from which we get the term "Copenhagen interpretation") asserted that the predictions of quantum mechanics and classical mechanics must agree for all macroscopic systems, such as orbiting planets, bouncing balls, rocking chairs, and springs. This **correspondence principle** is now generally accepted. It suggests the rules of classical mechanics are an approximation of the rules of quantum mechanics for systems with very large energies. Quantum mechanics describes both the microscopic and macroscopic world, but classical mechanics describes only the latter.

7.2 | The Heisenberg Uncertainty Principle

Learning Objectives

By the end of this section, you will be able to:

- Describe the physical meaning of the position-momentum uncertainty relation
- Explain the origins of the uncertainty principle in quantum theory
- Describe the physical meaning of the energy-time uncertainty relation

Heisenberg's uncertainty principle is a key principle in quantum mechanics. Very roughly, it states that if we know *everything* about where a particle is located (the uncertainty of position is small), we know *nothing* about its momentum (the uncertainty of momentum is large), and vice versa. Versions of the uncertainty principle also exist for other quantities as well, such as energy and time. We discuss the momentum-position and energy-time uncertainty principles separately.

Momentum and Position

To illustrate the momentum-position uncertainty principle, consider a free particle that moves along the x-direction. The particle moves with a constant velocity u and momentum $p = mu$. According to de Broglie's relations, $p = \hbar k$ and $E = \hbar\omega$. As discussed in the previous section, the wave function for this particle is given by

$$\psi_k(x, t) = A[\cos(\omega t - kx) - i\sin(\omega t - kx)] = Ae^{-i(\omega t - kx)} = Ae^{-i\omega t}e^{ikx} \quad (7.14)$$

and the probability density $|\psi_k(x, t)|^2 = A^2$ is *uniform* and independent of time. The particle is equally likely to be found anywhere along the x-axis but has definite values of wavelength and wave number, and therefore momentum. The uncertainty of position is infinite (we are completely uncertain about position) and the uncertainty of the momentum is zero (we are completely certain about momentum). This account of a free particle is consistent with Heisenberg's uncertainty principle.

Similar statements can be made of localized particles. In quantum theory, a localized particle is modeled by a linear superposition of free-particle (or plane-wave) states called a **wave packet**. An example of a wave packet is shown in Figure 7.9. A wave packet contains many wavelengths and therefore by de Broglie's relations many momenta—possible in quantum mechanics! This particle also has many values of position, although the particle is confined mostly to the interval Δx. The particle can be better localized (Δx can be decreased) if more plane-wave states of different wavelengths or momenta are added together in the right way (Δp is increased). According to Heisenberg, these uncertainties obey the following relation.

The Heisenberg Uncertainty Principle

The product of the uncertainty in position of a particle and the uncertainty in its momentum can never be less than one-half of the reduced Planck constant:

$$\Delta x \Delta p \geq \hbar/2. \quad (7.15)$$

This relation expresses Heisenberg's uncertainty principle. It places limits on what we can know about a particle from simultaneous measurements of position and momentum. If Δx is large, Δp is small, and vice versa. Equation 7.15 can be derived in a more advanced course in modern physics. Reflecting on this relation in his work *The Physical Principles of the Quantum Theory*, Heisenberg wrote "Any use of the words 'position' and 'velocity' with accuracy exceeding that given by [the relation] is just as meaningless as the use of words whose sense is not defined."

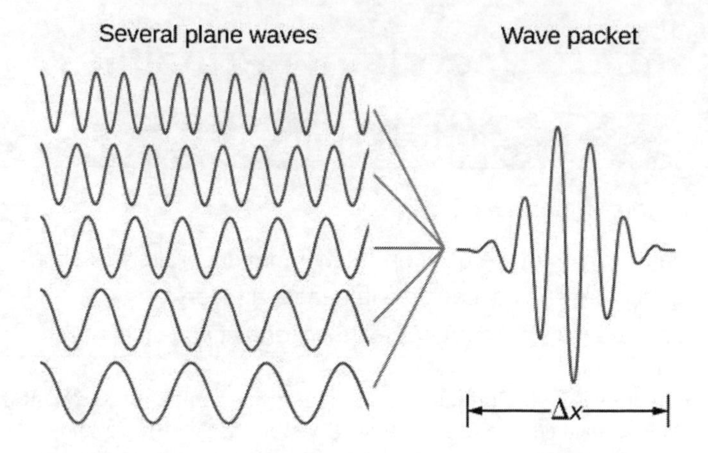

Figure 7.9 Adding together several plane waves of different wavelengths can produce a wave that is relatively localized.

Note that the uncertainty principle has nothing to do with the precision of an experimental apparatus. Even for perfect measuring devices, these uncertainties would remain because they originate in the wave-like nature of matter. The precise value of the product $\Delta x \Delta p$ depends on the specific form of the wave function. Interestingly, the Gaussian function (or bell-curve distribution) gives the minimum value of the uncertainty product: $\Delta x \Delta p = \hbar/2$.

Example 7.5

The Uncertainty Principle Large and Small

Determine the minimum uncertainties in the positions of the following objects if their speeds are known with a precision of $1.0 \times 10^{-3}\,\text{m/s}$: (a) an electron and (b) a bowling ball of mass 6.0 kg.

Strategy

Given the uncertainty in speed $\Delta u = 1.0 \times 10^{-3}\,\text{m/s}$, we have to first determine the uncertainty in momentum $\Delta p = m\Delta u$ and then invert **Equation 7.15** to find the uncertainty in position $\Delta x = \hbar/(2\Delta p)$.

Solution

a. For the electron:

$$\begin{aligned} \Delta p &= m\Delta u = (9.1 \times 10^{-31}\,\text{kg})(1.0 \times 10^{-3}\,\text{m/s}) = 9.1 \times 10^{-34}\,\text{kg}\cdot\text{m/s}, \\ \Delta x &= \frac{\hbar}{2\Delta p} = 5.8\,\text{cm}. \end{aligned}$$

b. For the bowling ball:

$$\begin{aligned} \Delta p &= m\Delta u = (6.0\,\text{kg})(1.0 \times 10^{-3}\,\text{m/s}) = 6.0 \times 10^{-3}\,\text{kg}\cdot\text{m/s}, \\ \Delta x &= \frac{\hbar}{2\Delta p} = 8.8 \times 10^{-33}\,\text{m}. \end{aligned}$$

Significance

Unlike the position uncertainty for the electron, the position uncertainty for the bowling ball is immeasurably small. Planck's constant is very small, so the limitations imposed by the uncertainty principle are not noticeable in macroscopic systems such as a bowling ball.

Example 7.6

Uncertainty and the Hydrogen Atom

Estimate the ground-state energy of a hydrogen atom using Heisenberg's uncertainty principle. (*Hint*: According to early experiments, the size of a hydrogen atom is approximately 0.1 nm.)

Strategy

An electron bound to a hydrogen atom can be modeled by a particle bound to a one-dimensional box of length $L = 0.1$ nm. The ground-state wave function of this system is a half wave, like that given in **Example 7.1**. This is the largest wavelength that can "fit" in the box, so the wave function corresponds to the lowest energy state. Note that this function is very similar in shape to a Gaussian (bell curve) function. We can take the average energy of a particle described by this function (E) as a good estimate of the ground state energy (E_0). This average energy of a particle is related to its average of the momentum squared, which is related to its momentum uncertainty.

Solution

To solve this problem, we must be specific about what is meant by "uncertainty of position" and "uncertainty of momentum." We identify the uncertainty of position (Δx) with the standard deviation of position (σ_x), and the uncertainty of momentum (Δp) with the standard deviation of momentum (σ_p). For the Gaussian function, the uncertainty product is

$$\sigma_x \sigma_p = \frac{\hbar}{2},$$

where

$$\sigma_x^2 = x^2 - \bar{x}^2 \text{ and } \sigma_p^2 = p^2 - p^2.$$

The particle is equally likely to be moving left as moving right, so $\bar{p} = 0$. Also, the uncertainty of position is comparable to the size of the box, so $\sigma_x = L$. The estimated ground state energy is therefore

$$E_0 = E_{\text{Gaussian}} = \frac{\overline{p^2}}{m} = \frac{\sigma_p^2}{2m} = \frac{1}{2m}\left(\frac{\hbar}{2\sigma_x}\right)^2 = \frac{1}{2m}\left(\frac{\hbar}{2L}\right)^2 = \frac{\hbar^2}{8mL^2}.$$

Multiplying numerator and denominator by c^2 gives

$$E_0 = \frac{(\hbar c)^2}{8(mc^2)L^2} = \frac{(197.3 \text{ eV} \cdot \text{nm})^2}{8\left(0.511 \cdot 10^6 \text{eV}\right)(0.1 \text{ nm})^2} = 0.952 \text{ eV} \approx 1 \text{ eV}.$$

Significance

Based on early estimates of the size of a hydrogen atom and the uncertainty principle, the ground-state energy of a hydrogen atom is in the eV range. The ionization energy of an electron in the ground-state energy is approximately 10 eV, so this prediction is roughly confirmed. (*Note:* The product $\hbar c$ is often a useful value in performing calculations in quantum mechanics.)

Energy and Time

Another kind of uncertainty principle concerns uncertainties in simultaneous measurements of the energy of a quantum state and its lifetime,

$$\Delta E \Delta t \geq \frac{\hbar}{2}, \tag{7.16}$$

where ΔE is the uncertainty in the energy measurement and Δt is the uncertainty in the lifetime measurement. The

energy-time uncertainty principle does not result from a relation of the type expressed by **Equation 7.15** for technical reasons beyond this discussion. Nevertheless, the general meaning of the energy-time principle is that a quantum state that exists for only a short time cannot have a definite energy. The reason is that the frequency of a state is inversely proportional to time and the frequency connects with the energy of the state, so to measure the energy with good precision, the state must be observed for many cycles.

To illustrate, consider the excited states of an atom. The finite lifetimes of these states can be deduced from the shapes of spectral lines observed in atomic emission spectra. Each time an excited state decays, the emitted energy is slightly different and, therefore, the emission line is characterized by a *distribution* of spectral frequencies (or wavelengths) of the emitted photons. As a result, all spectral lines are characterized by spectral widths. The average energy of the emitted photon corresponds to the theoretical energy of the excited state and gives the spectral location of the peak of the emission line. Short-lived states have broad spectral widths and long-lived states have narrow spectral widths.

Example 7.7

Atomic Transitions

An atom typically exists in an excited state for about $\Delta t = 10^{-8}\,\text{s}$. Estimate the uncertainty Δf in the frequency of emitted photons when an atom makes a transition from an excited state with the simultaneous emission of a photon with an average frequency of $f = 7.1 \times 10^{14}\ \text{Hz}$. Is the emitted radiation monochromatic?

Strategy

We invert **Equation 7.16** to obtain the energy uncertainty $\Delta E \approx \hbar/2\Delta t$ and combine it with the photon energy $E = hf$ to obtain Δf. To estimate whether or not the emission is monochromatic, we evaluate $\Delta f/f$.

Solution

The spread in photon energies is $\Delta E = h\Delta f$. Therefore,

$$\begin{aligned}\Delta E &\approx \frac{\hbar}{2\Delta t} \Rightarrow h\Delta f \approx \frac{\hbar}{2\Delta t} \Rightarrow \Delta f \approx \frac{1}{4\pi\Delta t} = \frac{1}{4\pi(10^{-8}\,\text{s})} = 8.0 \times 10^{6}\ \text{Hz},\\ \frac{\Delta f}{f} &= \frac{8.0 \times 10^{6}\ \text{Hz}}{7.1 \times 10^{14}\ \text{Hz}} = 1.1 \times 10^{-8}.\end{aligned}$$

Significance

Because the emitted photons have their frequencies within 1.1×10^{-6} percent of the average frequency, the emitted radiation can be considered monochromatic.

7.4 Check Your Understanding A sodium atom makes a transition from the first excited state to the ground state, emitting a 589.0-nm photon with energy 2.105 eV. If the lifetime of this excited state is $1.6 \times 10^{-8}\,\text{s}$, what is the uncertainty in energy of this excited state? What is the width of the corresponding spectral line?

7.3 | The Schrödinger Equation

Learning Objectives

By the end of this section, you will be able to:

- Describe the role Schrödinger's equation plays in quantum mechanics
- Explain the difference between time-dependent and -independent Schrödinger's equations
- Interpret the solutions of Schrödinger's equation

In the preceding two sections, we described how to use a quantum mechanical wave function and discussed Heisenberg's uncertainty principle. In this section, we present a complete and formal theory of quantum mechanics that can be used to make predictions. In developing this theory, it is helpful to review the wave theory of light. For a light wave, the electric field $E(x,t)$ obeys the relation

$$\frac{\partial^2 E}{\partial x^2} = \frac{1}{c^2}\frac{\partial^2 E}{\partial t^2}, \tag{7.17}$$

where c is the speed of light and the symbol ∂ represents a *partial derivative*. (Recall from **Oscillations (http://cnx.org/content/m58360/latest/)** that a partial derivative is closely related to an ordinary derivative, but involves functions of more than one variable. When taking the partial derivative of a function by a certain variable, all other variables are held constant.) A light wave consists of a very large number of photons, so the quantity $|E(x, t)|^2$ can interpreted as a probability density of finding a single photon at a particular point in space (for example, on a viewing screen).

There are many solutions to this equation. One solution of particular importance is

$$E(x, t) = A \sin(kx - \omega t), \tag{7.18}$$

where A is the amplitude of the electric field, k is the wave number, and ω is the angular frequency. Combing this equation with **Equation 7.17** gives

$$k^2 = \frac{\omega^2}{c^2}. \tag{7.19}$$

According to de Broglie's equations, we have $p = \hbar k$ and $E = \hbar\omega$. Substituting these equations in **Equation 7.19** gives

$$p = \frac{E}{c}, \tag{7.20}$$

or

$$E = pc. \tag{7.21}$$

Therefore, according to Einstein's general energy-momentum equation (**Equation 5.11**), **Equation 7.17** describes a particle with a zero rest mass. This is consistent with our knowledge of a photon.

This process can be reversed. We can begin with the energy-momentum equation of a particle and then ask what wave equation corresponds to it. The energy-momentum equation of a nonrelativistic particle in one dimension is

$$E = \frac{p^2}{2m} + U(x, t), \tag{7.22}$$

where p is the momentum, m is the mass, and U is the potential energy of the particle. The wave equation that goes with it turns out to be a key equation in quantum mechanics, called **Schrödinger's time-dependent equation**.

The Schrödinger Time-Dependent Equation

The equation describing the energy and momentum of a wave function is known as the Schrödinger equation:

$$-\frac{\hbar^2}{2m}\frac{\partial^2 \Psi(x, t)}{\partial x^2} + U(x, t)\Psi(x, t) = i\hbar\frac{\partial \Psi(x, t)}{\partial t}. \tag{7.23}$$

As described in **Potential Energy and Conservation of Energy (http://cnx.org/content/m58311/latest/)** , the force on the particle described by this equation is given by

$$F = -\frac{\partial U(x, t)}{\partial x}. \tag{7.24}$$

This equation plays a role in quantum mechanics similar to Newton's second law in classical mechanics. Once the potential energy of a particle is specified—or, equivalently, once the force on the particle is specified—we can solve this differential equation for the wave function. The solution to Newton's second law equation (also a differential equation) in one dimension is a function $x(t)$ that specifies where an object is at any time t. The solution to Schrödinger's time-dependent equation provides a tool—the wave function—that can be used to determine where the particle is *likely* to be. This equation can be also written in two or three dimensions. Solving Schrödinger's time-dependent equation often requires the aid of a computer.

Consider the special case of a free particle. A free particle experiences no force $(F = 0)$. Based on **Equation 7.24**, this requires only that

$$U(x,\, t) = U_0 = \text{constant}. \tag{7.25}$$

For simplicity, we set $U_0 = 0$. Schrödinger's equation then reduces to

$$-\frac{\hbar^2}{2m}\frac{\partial^2 \Psi(x,\, t)}{\partial x^2} = i\hbar\frac{\partial \Psi(x,\, t)}{\partial t}. \tag{7.26}$$

A valid solution to this equation is

$$\Psi(x,\, t) = Ae^{i(kx - \omega t)}. \tag{7.27}$$

Not surprisingly, this solution contains an imaginary number $(i = \sqrt{-1})$ because the differential equation itself contains an imaginary number. As stressed before, however, quantum-mechanical predictions depend only on $|\Psi(x,\, t)|^2$, which yields completely real values. Notice that the real plane-wave solutions, $\Psi(x,\, t) = A\sin(kx - \omega t)$ and $\Psi(x,\, t) = A\cos(kx - \omega t)$, do not obey Schrödinger's equation. The temptation to think that a wave function can be seen, touched, and felt in nature is eliminated by the appearance of an imaginary number. In Schrödinger's theory of quantum mechanics, the wave function is merely a tool for calculating things.

If the potential energy function (*U*) does not depend on time, it is possible to show that

$$\Psi(x,\, t) = \psi(x)e^{-i\omega t} \tag{7.28}$$

satisfies Schrödinger's time-dependent equation, where $\psi(x)$ is a *time*-independent function and $e^{-i\omega t}$ is a *space*-independent function. In other words, the wave function is *separable* into two parts: a space-only part and a time-only part. The factor $e^{-i\omega t}$ is sometimes referred to as a **time-modulation factor** since it modifies the space-only function. According to de Broglie, the energy of a matter wave is given by $E = \hbar\omega$, where *E* is its total energy. Thus, the above equation can also be written as

$$\Psi(x,\, t) = \psi(x)e^{-iEt/\hbar}. \tag{7.29}$$

Any linear combination of such states (mixed state of energy or momentum) is also valid solution to this equation. Such states can, for example, describe a localized particle (see **Figure 7.9**)

7.5 Check Your Understanding A particle with mass *m* is moving along the *x*-axis in a potential given by the potential energy function $U(x) = 0.5m\omega^2 x^2$. Compute the product $\Psi(x,\, t)^*\, U(x)\Psi(x,\, t)$. Express your answer in terms of the time-independent wave function, $\psi(x)$.

Combining **Equation 7.23** and **Equation 7.28**, Schrödinger's time-dependent equation reduces to

$$-\frac{\hbar^2}{2m}\frac{d^2\psi(x)}{dx^2} + U(x)\psi(x) = E\psi(x), \tag{7.30}$$

where *E* is the total energy of the particle (a real number). This equation is called **Schrödinger's time-independent equation**. Notice that we use "big psi" (Ψ) for the time-dependent wave function and "little psi" (ψ) for the time-independent wave function. The wave-function solution to this equation must be multiplied by the time-modulation factor to obtain the time-dependent wave function.

In the next sections, we solve Schrödinger's time-independent equation for three cases: a quantum particle in a box, a simple harmonic oscillator, and a quantum barrier. These cases provide important lessons that can be used to solve more complicated systems. The time-independent wave function $\psi(x)$ solutions must satisfy three conditions:

- $\psi(x)$ must be a continuous function.
- The first derivative of $\psi(x)$ with respect to space, $d\psi(x)/dx$, must be continuous, unless $V(x) = \infty$.
- $\psi(x)$ must not diverge ("blow up") at $x = \pm\infty$.

The first condition avoids sudden jumps or gaps in the wave function. The second condition requires the wave function to be smooth at all points, except in special cases. (In a more advanced course on quantum mechanics, for example, potential spikes of infinite depth and height are used to model solids). The third condition requires the wave function be normalizable. This third condition follows from Born's interpretation of quantum mechanics. It ensures that $|\psi(x)|^2$ is a finite number so we can use it to calculate probabilities.

7.6 Check Your Understanding Which of the following wave functions is a valid wave-function solution for Schrödinger's equation?

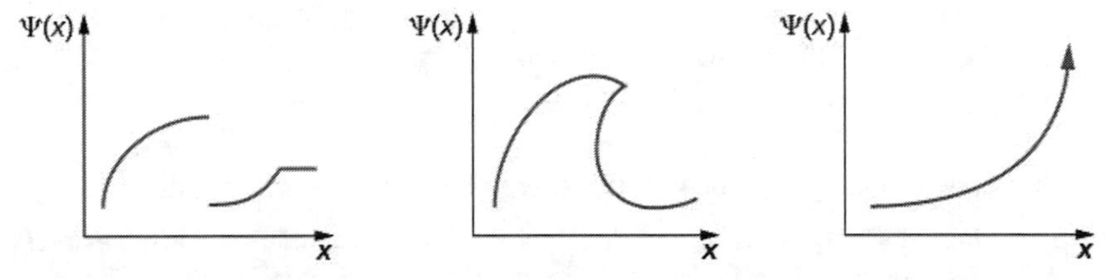

7.4 | The Quantum Particle in a Box

Learning Objectives

By the end of this section, you will be able to:

- Describe how to set up a boundary-value problem for the stationary Schrödinger equation
- Explain why the energy of a quantum particle in a box is quantized
- Describe the physical meaning of stationary solutions to Schrödinger's equation and the connection of these solutions with time-dependent quantum states
- Explain the physical meaning of Bohr's correspondence principle

In this section, we apply Schrödinger's equation to a particle bound to a one-dimensional box. This special case provides lessons for understanding quantum mechanics in more complex systems. The energy of the particle is quantized as a consequence of a standing wave condition inside the box.

Consider a particle of mass m that is allowed to move only along the *x*-direction and its motion is confined to the region between hard and rigid walls located at $x = 0$ and at $x = L$ (**Figure 7.10**). Between the walls, the particle moves freely. This physical situation is called the **infinite square well**, described by the potential energy function

$$U(x) = \begin{cases} 0, & 0 \le x \le L, \\ \infty, & \text{otherwise.} \end{cases} \quad (7.31)$$

Combining this equation with Schrödinger's time-independent wave equation gives

$$\frac{-\hbar^2}{2m}\frac{d^2\psi(x)}{dx^2} = E\psi(x), \text{ for } 0 \le x \le L \quad (7.32)$$

where E is the total energy of the particle. What types of solutions do we expect? The energy of the particle is a positive number, so if the value of the wave function is positive (right side of the equation), the curvature of the wave function is negative, or concave down (left side of the equation). Similarly, if the value of the wave function is negative (right side of the equation), the curvature of the wave function is positive or concave up (left side of equation). This condition is met by an oscillating wave function, such as a sine or cosine wave. Since these waves are confined to the box, we envision standing waves with fixed endpoints at $x = 0$ and $x = L$.

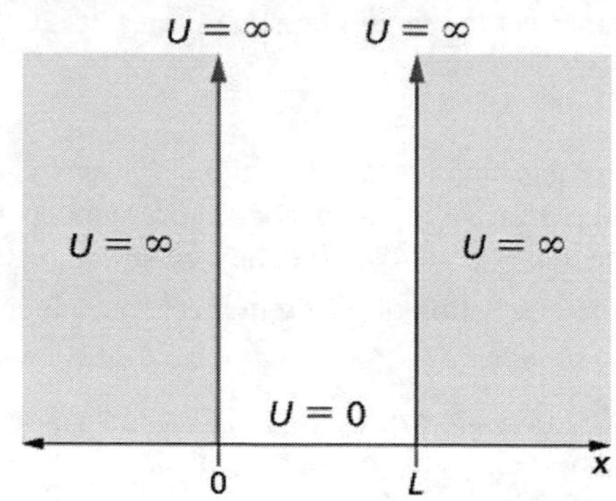

Figure 7.10 The potential energy function that confines the particle in a one-dimensional box.

Solutions $\psi(x)$ to this equation have a probabilistic interpretation. In particular, the square $|\psi(x)|^2$ represents the probability density of finding the particle at a particular location x. This function must be integrated to determine the probability of finding the particle in some interval of space. We are therefore looking for a normalizable solution that satisfies the following normalization condition:

$$\int_0^L dx|\psi(x)|^2 = 1. \tag{7.33}$$

The walls are rigid and impenetrable, which means that the particle is never found beyond the wall. Mathematically, this means that the solution must vanish at the walls:

$$\psi(0) = \psi(L) = 0. \tag{7.34}$$

We expect oscillating solutions, so the most general solution to this equation is

$$\psi_k(x) = A_k \cos kx + B_k \sin kx \tag{7.35}$$

where k is the wave number, and A_k and B_k are constants. Applying the boundary condition expressed by **Equation 7.34** gives

$$\psi_k(0) = A_k \cos(k \cdot 0) + B_k \sin(k \cdot 0) = A_k = 0. \tag{7.36}$$

Because we have $A_k = 0$, the solution must be

$$\psi_k(x) = B_k \sin kx. \tag{7.37}$$

If B_k is zero, $\psi_k(x) = 0$ for all values of x and the normalization condition, **Equation 7.33**, cannot be satisfied. Assuming $B_k \neq 0$, **Equation 7.34** for $x = L$ then gives

$$0 = B_k \sin(kL) \Rightarrow \sin(kL) = 0 \Rightarrow kL = n\pi,\ n = 1,\ 2,\ 3,... \tag{7.38}$$

We discard the $n = 0$ solution because $\psi(x)$ for this quantum number would be zero everywhere—an un-normalizable and therefore unphysical solution. Substituting **Equation 7.37** into **Equation 7.32** gives

$$-\frac{\hbar^2}{2m}\frac{d^2}{dx^2}(B_k \sin(kx)) = E(B_k \sin(kx)). \tag{7.39}$$

Computing these derivatives leads to

$$E = E_k = \frac{\hbar^2 k^2}{2m}. \tag{7.40}$$

According to de Broglie, $p = \hbar k,$ so this expression implies that the total energy is equal to the kinetic energy, consistent with our assumption that the "particle moves freely." Combining the results of **Equation 7.38** and **Equation 7.40** gives

$$E_n = n^2 \frac{\pi^2 \hbar^2}{2mL^2}, \ n = 1, 2, 3, ... \tag{7.41}$$

Strange! A particle bound to a one-dimensional box can only have certain discrete (quantized) values of energy. Further, the particle cannot have a zero kinetic energy—it is impossible for a particle bound to a box to be "at rest."

To evaluate the allowed wave functions that correspond to these energies, we must find the normalization constant B_n. We impose the normalization condition **Equation 7.33** on the wave function

$$\psi_n(x) = B_n \sin n\pi x/L \tag{7.42}$$

$$1 = \int_0^L dx |\psi_n(x)|^2 = \int_0^L dx B_n^2 \sin^2 \frac{n\pi}{L}x = B_n^2 \int_0^L dx \sin^2 \frac{n\pi}{L}x = B_n^2 \frac{L}{2} \Rightarrow B_n = \sqrt{\frac{2}{L}}.$$

Hence, the wave functions that correspond to the energy values given in **Equation 7.41** are

$$\psi_n(x) = \sqrt{\frac{2}{L}} \sin \frac{n\pi x}{L}, \ n = 1, 2, 3, ... \tag{7.43}$$

For the lowest energy state or **ground state energy**, we have

$$E_1 = \frac{\pi^2 \hbar^2}{2mL^2}, \ \psi_1(x) = \sqrt{\frac{2}{L}} \sin\left(\frac{\pi x}{L}\right). \tag{7.44}$$

All other energy states can be expressed as

$$E_n = n^2 E_1, \ \psi_n(x) = \sqrt{\frac{2}{L}} \sin\left(\frac{n\pi x}{L}\right). \tag{7.45}$$

The index n is called the **energy quantum number** or **principal quantum number**. The state for $n = 2$ is the first excited state, the state for $n = 3$ is the second excited state, and so on. The first three quantum states (for $n = 1, 2,$ and 3) of a particle in a box are shown in **Figure 7.11**.

The wave functions in **Equation 7.45** are sometimes referred to as the "states of definite energy." Particles in these states are said to occupy **energy levels**, which are represented by the horizontal lines in **Figure 7.11**. Energy levels are analogous to rungs of a ladder that the particle can "climb" as it gains or loses energy.

The wave functions in **Equation 7.45** are also called **stationary states** and **standing wave states**. These functions are "stationary," because their probability density functions, $|\Psi(x, t)|^2$, do not vary in time, and "standing waves" because their real and imaginary parts oscillate up and down like a standing wave—like a rope waving between two children on a playground. Stationary states are states of definite energy [**Equation 7.45**], but linear combinations of these states, such as $\psi(x) = a\psi_1 + b\psi_2$ (also solutions to Schrödinger's equation) are states of mixed energy.

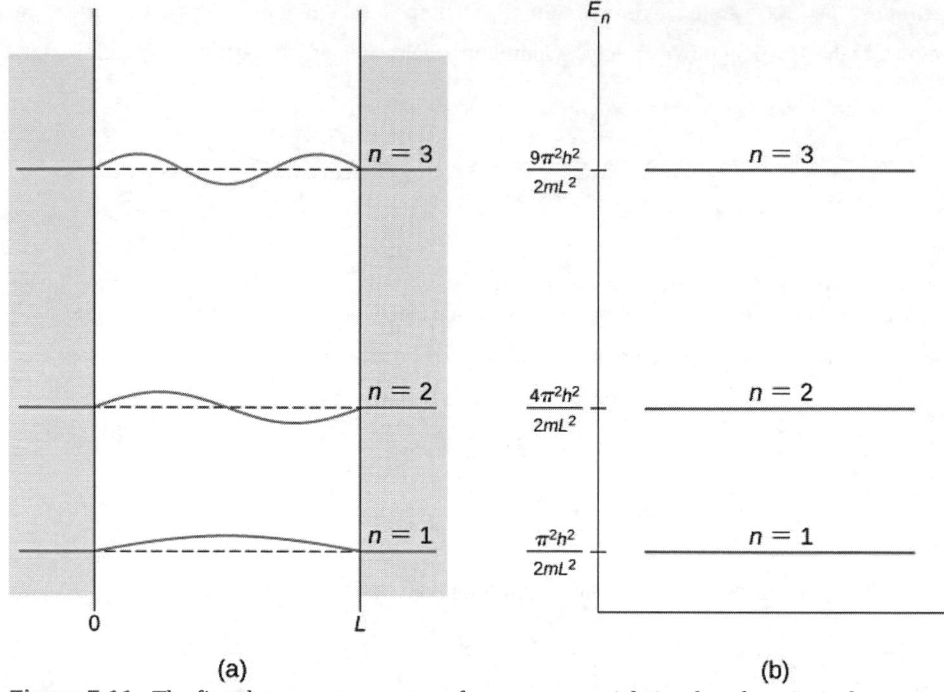

Figure 7.11 The first three quantum states of a quantum particle in a box for principal quantum numbers $n = 1, 2,$ and 3 : (a) standing wave solutions and (b) allowed energy states.

Energy quantization is a consequence of the boundary conditions. If the particle is not confined to a box but wanders freely, the allowed energies are continuous. However, in this case, only certain energies $(E_1, 4E_1, 9E_1, \ldots)$ are allowed. The energy difference between adjacent energy levels is given by

$$\Delta E_{n+1,\, n} = E_{n+1} - E_n = (n+1)^2 E_1 - n^2 E_1 = (2n+1)E_1. \tag{7.46}$$

Conservation of energy demands that if the energy of the system changes, the energy difference is carried in some other form of energy. For the special case of a charged particle confined to a small volume (for example, in an atom), energy changes are often carried away by photons. The frequencies of the emitted photons give us information about the energy differences (spacings) of the system and the volume of containment—the size of the "box" [see **Equation 7.44**].

Example 7.8

A Simple Model of the Nucleus

Suppose a proton is confined to a box of width $L = 1.00 \times 10^{-14}\,\text{m}$ (a typical nuclear radius). What are the energies of the ground and the first excited states? If the proton makes a transition from the first excited state to the ground state, what are the energy and the frequency of the emitted photon?

Strategy

If we assume that the proton confined in the nucleus can be modeled as a quantum particle in a box, all we need to do is to use **Equation 7.41** to find its energies E_1 and E_2. The mass of a proton is $m = 1.76 \times 10^{-27}$ kg. The emitted photon carries away the energy difference $\Delta E = E_2 - E_1$. We can use the relation $E_f = hf$ to find its frequency *f*.

Solution

The ground state:

$$E_1 = \frac{\pi^2 \hbar^2}{2m L^2} = \frac{\pi^2 (1.05 \times 10^{-34}\,\text{J} \cdot \text{s})^2}{2(1.67 \times 10^{-27}\,\text{kg})\,(1.00 \times 10^{-14}\,\text{m})^2} = 3.28 \times 10^{-13}\,\text{J} = 2.05\,\text{MeV}.$$

The first excited state: $E_2 = 2^2 E_1 = 4(2.05\text{ MeV}) = 8.20\text{ MeV}$.

The energy of the emitted photon is $E_f = \Delta E = E_2 - E_1 = 8.20\text{ MeV} - 2.05\text{ MeV} = 6.15\text{ MeV}$.

The frequency of the emitted photon is

$$f = \frac{E_f}{h} = \frac{6.15\text{ MeV}}{4.14 \times 10^{-21}\text{ MeV} \cdot \text{s}} = 1.49 \times 10^{21}\text{ Hz}.$$

Significance

This is the typical frequency of a gamma ray emitted by a nucleus. The energy of this photon is about 10 million times greater than that of a visible light photon.

The expectation value of the position for a particle in a box is given by

$$\langle x \rangle = \int_0^L dx \psi_n^*(x) x \psi_n(x) = \int_0^L dx x |\psi_n^*(x)|^2 = \int_0^L dx x \frac{2}{L} \sin^2 \frac{n\pi x}{L} = \frac{L}{2}. \tag{7.47}$$

We can also find the expectation value of the momentum or average momentum of a large number of particles in a given state:

$$\begin{aligned} \langle p \rangle &= \int_0^L dx \psi_n^*(x)\left[-i\hbar \frac{d}{dx}\psi_n(x)\right] \\ &= -i\hbar \int_0^L dx \sqrt{\frac{2}{L}} \sin \frac{n\pi x}{L}\left[\frac{d}{dx}\sqrt{\frac{2}{L}} \sin \frac{n\pi x}{L}\right] = -i\frac{2\hbar}{L}\int_0^L dx \sin \frac{n\pi x}{L}\left[\frac{n\pi}{L} \cos \frac{n\pi x}{L}\right] \\ &= -i\frac{2n\pi\hbar}{L^2}\int_0^L dx \frac{1}{2} \sin \frac{2n\pi x}{L} = -i\frac{n\pi\hbar}{L^2}\frac{L}{2n\pi}\int_0^{2\pi n} d\varphi \sin \varphi = -i\frac{\hbar}{2L} \cdot 0 = 0. \end{aligned} \tag{7.48}$$

Thus, for a particle in a state of definite energy, the average position is in the middle of the box and the average momentum of the particle is zero—as it would also be for a classical particle. Note that while the minimum energy of a classical particle can be zero (the particle can be at rest in the middle of the box), the minimum energy of a quantum particle is nonzero and given by **Equation 7.44**. The average particle energy in the *nth* quantum state—its expectation value of energy—is

$$E_n = \langle E \rangle = n^2 \frac{\pi^2 \hbar^2}{2m}. \tag{7.49}$$

The result is not surprising because the standing wave state is a state of definite energy. Any energy measurement of this system must return a value equal to one of these allowed energies.

Our analysis of the quantum particle in a box would not be complete without discussing Bohr's correspondence principle. This principle states that for large quantum numbers, the laws of quantum physics must give identical results as the laws of classical physics. To illustrate how this principle works for a quantum particle in a box, we plot the probability density distribution

$$\left|\psi_n(x)\right|^2 = \frac{2}{L}\sin^2(n\pi x/L) \tag{7.50}$$

for finding the particle around location x between the walls when the particle is in quantum state ψ_n. **Figure 7.12** shows these probability distributions for the ground state, for the first excited state, and for a highly excited state that corresponds to a large quantum number. We see from these plots that when a quantum particle is in the ground state, it is most likely to be found around the middle of the box, where the probability distribution has the largest value. This is not so when the particle is in the first excited state because now the probability distribution has the zero value in the middle of the box, so there is no chance of finding the particle there. When a quantum particle is in the first excited state, the probability distribution has two maxima, and the best chance of finding the particle is at positions close to the locations of these maxima. This quantum picture is unlike the classical picture.

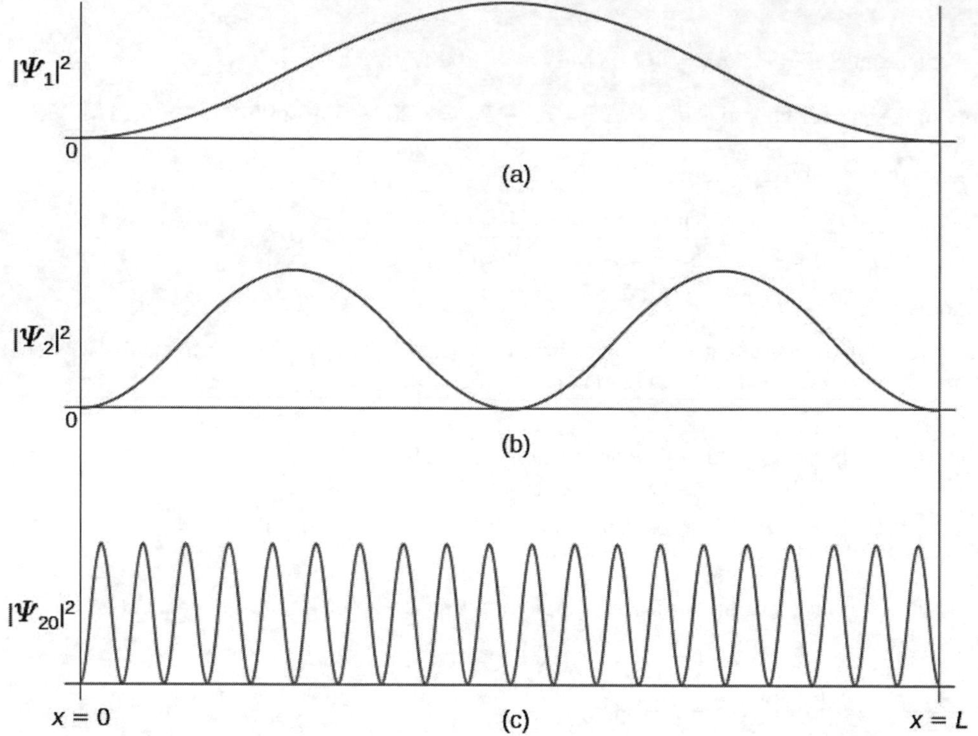

Figure 7.12 The probability density distribution $|\psi_n(x)|^2$ for a quantum particle in a box for: (a) the ground state, $n = 1$; (b) the first excited state, $n = 2$; and, (c) the nineteenth excited state, $n = 20$.

The probability density of finding a classical particle between x and $x + \Delta x$ depends on how much time Δt the particle spends in this region. Assuming that its speed u is constant, this time is $\Delta t = \Delta x/u,$ which is also constant for any location between the walls. Therefore, the probability density of finding the classical particle at x is uniform throughout the box, and there is no preferable location for finding a classical particle. This classical picture is matched in the limit of large quantum numbers. For example, when a quantum particle is in a highly excited state, shown in **Figure 7.12**, the probability density is characterized by rapid fluctuations and then the probability of finding the quantum particle in the interval Δx does not depend on where this interval is located between the walls.

Example 7.9

A Classical Particle in a Box

A small 0.40-kg cart is moving back and forth along an air track between two bumpers located 2.0 m apart. We assume no friction; collisions with the bumpers are perfectly elastic so that between the bumpers, the car maintains a constant speed of 0.50 m/s. Treating the cart as a quantum particle, estimate the value of the principal quantum number that corresponds to its classical energy.

Strategy

We find the kinetic energy K of the cart and its ground state energy E_1 as though it were a quantum particle. The energy of the cart is completely kinetic, so $K = n^2 E_1$ (**Equation 7.45**). Solving for n gives $n = (K/E_1)^{1/2}$.

Solution

The kinetic energy of the cart is

$$K = \frac{1}{2}mu^2 = \frac{1}{2}(0.40\text{ kg})(0.50\text{ m/s})^2 = 0.050\text{ J}.$$

The ground state of the cart, treated as a quantum particle, is

$$E_1 = \frac{\pi^2 \hbar^2}{2mL^2} = \frac{\pi^2 (1.05 \times 10^{-34}\,\mathrm{J \cdot s})^2}{2(0.40\,\mathrm{kg})(2.0\,\mathrm{m})^2} = 1.700 \times 10^{-68}\,\mathrm{J}.$$

Therefore, $n = (K/E_1)^{1/2} = (0.050/1.700 \times 10^{-68})^{1/2} = 1.2 \times 10^{33}$.

Significance

We see from this example that the energy of a classical system is characterized by a very large quantum number. Bohr's correspondence principle concerns this kind of situation. We can apply the formalism of quantum mechanics to any kind of system, quantum or classical, and the results are correct in each case. In the limit of high quantum numbers, there is no advantage in using quantum formalism because we can obtain the same results with the less complicated formalism of classical mechanics. However, we cannot apply classical formalism to a quantum system in a low-number energy state.

7.7 Check Your Understanding (a) Consider an infinite square well with wall boundaries $x = 0$ and $x = L$. What is the probability of finding a quantum particle in its ground state somewhere between $x = 0$ and $x = L/4$? (b) Repeat question (a) for a classical particle.

Having found the stationary states $\psi_n(x)$ and the energies E_n by solving the time-independent Schrödinger equation **Equation 7.32**, we use **Equation 7.28** to write wave functions $\Psi_n(x, t)$ that are solutions of the time-dependent Schrödinger's equation given by **Equation 7.23**. For a particle in a box this gives

$$\Psi_n(x, t) = e^{-i\omega_n t}\psi_n(x) = \sqrt{\frac{2}{L}}e^{-iE_n t/\hbar} \sin\frac{n\pi x}{L},\ n = 1, 2, 3, ... \tag{7.51}$$

where the energies are given by **Equation 7.41**.

The quantum particle in a box model has practical applications in a relatively newly emerged field of optoelectronics, which deals with devices that convert electrical signals into optical signals. This model also deals with nanoscale physical phenomena, such as a nanoparticle trapped in a low electric potential bounded by high-potential barriers.

7.5 | The Quantum Harmonic Oscillator

Learning Objectives

By the end of this section, you will be able to:

- Describe the model of the quantum harmonic oscillator
- Identify differences between the classical and quantum models of the harmonic oscillator
- Explain physical situations where the classical and the quantum models coincide

Oscillations are found throughout nature, in such things as electromagnetic waves, vibrating molecules, and the gentle back-and-forth sway of a tree branch. In previous chapters, we used Newtonian mechanics to study macroscopic oscillations, such as a block on a spring and a simple pendulum. In this chapter, we begin to study oscillating systems using quantum mechanics. We begin with a review of the classic harmonic oscillator.

The Classic Harmonic Oscillator

A simple harmonic oscillator is a particle or system that undergoes harmonic motion about an equilibrium position, such as an object with mass vibrating on a spring. In this section, we consider oscillations in one-dimension only. Suppose a mass moves back-and-forth along the

x-direction about the equilibrium position, $x = 0$. In classical mechanics, the particle moves in response to a linear restoring force given by $F_x = -kx$, where x is the displacement of the particle from its equilibrium position. The motion takes place between two turning points, $x = \pm A$, where A denotes the amplitude of the motion. The position of the object varies periodically in time with angular frequency $\omega = \sqrt{k/m}$, which depends on the mass m of the oscillator and on the force constant k of the net force, and can be written as

$$x(t) = A\cos(\omega t + \phi). \tag{7.52}$$

The total energy E of an oscillator is the sum of its kinetic energy $K = mu^2/2$ and the elastic potential energy of the force $U(x) = kx^2/2$,

$$E = \frac{1}{2}mu^2 + \frac{1}{2}kx^2. \tag{7.53}$$

At turning points $x = \pm A$, the speed of the oscillator is zero; therefore, at these points, the energy of oscillation is solely in the form of potential energy $E = kA^2/2$. The plot of the potential energy $U(x)$ of the oscillator versus its position x is a parabola (**Figure 7.13**). The potential-energy function is a quadratic function of x, measured with respect to the equilibrium position. On the same graph, we also plot the total energy E of the oscillator, as a horizontal line that intercepts the parabola at $x = \pm A$. Then the kinetic energy K is represented as the vertical distance between the line of total energy and the potential energy parabola.

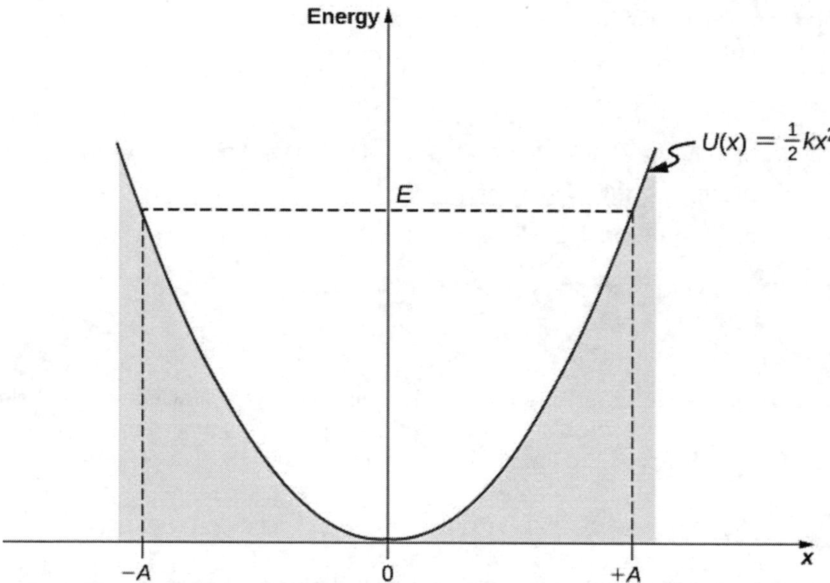

Figure 7.13 The potential energy well of a classical harmonic oscillator: The motion is confined between turning points at $x = -A$ and at $x = +A$. The energy of oscillations is $E = kA^2/2$.

In this plot, the motion of a classical oscillator is confined to the region where its kinetic energy is nonnegative, which is what the energy relation **Equation 7.53** says. Physically, it means that a classical oscillator can never be found beyond its turning points, and its energy depends only on how far the turning points are from its equilibrium position. The energy of a classical oscillator changes in a continuous way. The lowest energy that a classical oscillator may have is zero, which corresponds to a situation where an object is at rest at its equilibrium position. The zero-energy state of a classical oscillator simply means no oscillations and no motion at all (a classical particle sitting at the bottom of the potential well in **Figure 7.13**). When an object oscillates, no matter how big or small its energy may be, it spends the longest time near the turning points, because this is where it slows down and reverses its direction of motion. Therefore, the probability of finding a classical oscillator between the turning points is highest near the turning points and lowest at the equilibrium position. (Note that this is not a statement of preference of the object to go to lower energy. It is a statement about how quickly the object moves through various regions.)

The Quantum Harmonic Oscillator

One problem with this classical formulation is that it is not general. We cannot use it, for example, to describe vibrations of diatomic molecules, where quantum effects are important. A first step toward a quantum formulation is to use the classical expression $k = m\omega^2$ to limit mention of a "spring" constant between the atoms. In this way the potential energy function can be written in a more general form,

$$U(x) = \frac{1}{2}m\omega^2 x^2. \tag{7.54}$$

Combining this expression with the time-independent Schrödinger equation gives

$$-\frac{\hbar}{2m}\frac{d^2\psi(x)}{dx^2} + \frac{1}{2}m\omega^2 x^2 \psi(x) = E\psi(x). \tag{7.55}$$

To solve **Equation 7.55**—that is, to find the allowed energies E and their corresponding wave functions $\psi(x)$ —we require the wave functions to be symmetric about $x = 0$ (the bottom of the potential well) and to be normalizable. These conditions ensure that the probability density $|\psi(x)|^2$ must be finite when integrated over the entire range of x from $-\infty$ to $+\infty$. How to solve **Equation 7.55** is the subject of a more advanced course in quantum mechanics; here, we simply cite the results. The allowed energies are

$$E_n = \left(n + \frac{1}{2}\right)\hbar\omega = \frac{2n+1}{2}\hbar\omega, \quad n = 0, 1, 2, 3, \ldots \tag{7.56}$$

The wave functions that correspond to these energies (the stationary states or states of definite energy) are

$$\psi_n(x) = N_n e^{-\beta^2 x^2/2} H_n(\beta x), \quad n = 0, 1, 2, 3, \ldots \tag{7.57}$$

where $\beta = \sqrt{m\omega/\hbar}$, N_n is the normalization constant, and $H_n(y)$ is a polynomial of degree n called a *Hermite polynomial*. The first four Hermite polynomials are

$$H_0(y) = 1$$
$$H_1(y) = 2y$$
$$H_2(y) = 4y^2 - 2$$
$$H_3(y) = 8y^3 - 12y.$$

A few sample wave functions are given in **Figure 7.14**. As the value of the principal number increases, the solutions alternate between even functions and odd functions about $x = 0$.

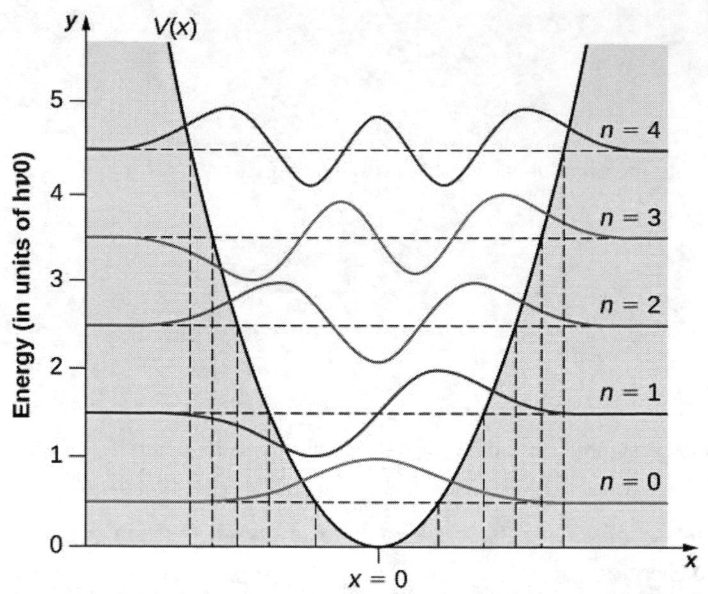

Figure 7.14 The first five wave functions of the quantum harmonic oscillator. The classical limits of the oscillator's motion are indicated by vertical lines, corresponding to the classical turning points at $x = \pm A$ of a classical particle with the same energy as the energy of a quantum oscillator in the state indicated in the figure.

Example 7.10

Classical Region of Harmonic Oscillations

Find the amplitude A of oscillations for a classical oscillator with energy equal to the energy of a quantum oscillator in the quantum state n.

Strategy

To determine the amplitude A, we set the classical energy $E = kx^2/2 = m\omega^2 A^2/2$ equal to E_n given by **Equation 7.56**.

Solution

We obtain

$$E_n = m\omega^2 A_n^2/2 \quad \Rightarrow \quad A_n = \sqrt{\frac{2}{m\omega^2}E_n} = \sqrt{\frac{2}{m\omega^2}\frac{2n+1}{2}\hbar\omega} = \sqrt{(2n+1)\frac{\hbar}{m\omega}}.$$

Significance

As the quantum number n increases, the energy of the oscillator and therefore the amplitude of oscillation increases (for a fixed natural angular frequency. For large n, the amplitude is approximately proportional to the square root of the quantum number.

Several interesting features appear in this solution. Unlike a classical oscillator, the measured energies of a quantum oscillator can have only energy values given by **Equation 7.56**. Moreover, unlike the case for a quantum particle in a box, the allowable energy levels are evenly spaced,

$$\Delta E = E_{n+1} - E_n = \frac{2(n+1)+1}{2}\hbar\omega - \frac{2n+1}{2}\hbar\omega = \hbar\omega = hf. \tag{7.58}$$

When a particle bound to such a system makes a transition from a higher-energy state to a lower-energy state, the smallest-energy quantum carried by the emitted photon is necessarily *hf*. Similarly, when the particle makes a transition from a lower-energy state to a higher-energy state, the smallest-energy quantum that can be absorbed by the particle is *hf*. A quantum oscillator can absorb or emit energy only in multiples of this smallest-energy quantum. This is consistent with Planck's hypothesis for the energy exchanges between radiation and the cavity walls in the blackbody radiation problem.

Example 7.11

Vibrational Energies of the Hydrogen Chloride Molecule

The HCl diatomic molecule consists of one chlorine atom and one hydrogen atom. Because the chlorine atom is 35 times more massive than the hydrogen atom, the vibrations of the HCl molecule can be quite well approximated by assuming that the Cl atom is motionless and the H atom performs harmonic oscillations due to an elastic molecular force modeled by Hooke's law. The infrared vibrational spectrum measured for hydrogen chloride has the lowest-frequency line centered at $f = 8.88 \times 10^{13}$ Hz. What is the spacing between the vibrational energies of this molecule? What is the force constant k of the atomic bond in the HCl molecule?

Strategy

The lowest-frequency line corresponds to the emission of lowest-frequency photons. These photons are emitted when the molecule makes a transition between two adjacent vibrational energy levels. Assuming that energy levels are equally spaced, we use **Equation 7.58** to estimate the spacing. The molecule is well approximated by treating the Cl atom as being infinitely heavy and the H atom as the mass m that performs the oscillations. Treating this molecular system as a classical oscillator, the force constant is found from the classical relation $k = m\omega^2$.

Solution

The energy spacing is

$$\Delta E = hf = (4.14 \times 10^{-15}\,\text{eV} \cdot \text{s})(8.88 \times 10^{13}\text{ Hz}) = 0.368\text{ eV}.$$

The force constant is

$$k = m\omega^2 = m(2\pi f)^2 = (1.67 \times 10^{-27}\text{ kg})(2\pi \times 8.88 \times 10^{13}\text{ Hz})^2 = 520\text{ N/m}.$$

Significance

The force between atoms in an HCl molecule is surprisingly strong. The typical energy released in energy transitions between vibrational levels is in the infrared range. As we will see later, transitions in between vibrational energy levels of a diatomic molecule often accompany transitions between rotational energy levels.

7.8 Check Your Understanding The vibrational frequency of the hydrogen iodide HI diatomic molecule is 6.69×10^{13} Hz. (a) What is the force constant of the molecular bond between the hydrogen and the iodine atoms? (b) What is the energy of the emitted photon when this molecule makes a transition between adjacent vibrational energy levels?

The quantum oscillator differs from the classic oscillator in three ways:

First, the ground state of a quantum oscillator is $E_0 = \hbar\omega/2$, not zero. In the classical view, the lowest energy is zero. The nonexistence of a zero-energy state is common for all quantum-mechanical systems because of omnipresent fluctuations that are a consequence of the Heisenberg uncertainty principle. If a quantum particle sat motionless at the bottom of the potential well, its momentum as well as its position would have to be simultaneously exact, which would violate the Heisenberg uncertainty principle. Therefore, the lowest-energy state must be characterized by uncertainties in momentum and in position, so the ground state of a quantum particle must lie above the bottom of the potential well.

Second, a particle in a quantum harmonic oscillator potential can be found with nonzero probability outside the interval $-A \le x \le +A$. In a classic formulation of the problem, the particle would not have any energy to be in this region. The probability of finding a ground-state quantum particle in the classically forbidden region is about 16%.

Third, the probability density distributions $|\psi_n(x)|^2$ for a quantum oscillator in the ground low-energy state, $\psi_0(x)$, is largest at the middle of the well $(x = 0)$. For the particle to be found with greatest probability at the center of the well, we expect that the particle spends the most time there as it oscillates. This is opposite to the behavior of a classical oscillator, in which the particle spends most of its time moving with relative small speeds near the turning points.

7.9 Check Your Understanding Find the expectation value of the position for a particle in the ground state of a harmonic oscillator using symmetry.

Quantum probability density distributions change in character for excited states, becoming more like the classical distribution when the quantum number gets higher. We observe this change already for the first excited state of a quantum oscillator because the distribution $|\psi_1(x)|^2$ peaks up around the turning points and vanishes at the equilibrium position, as seen in **Figure 7.13**. In accordance with Bohr's correspondence principle, in the limit of high quantum numbers, the quantum description of a harmonic oscillator converges to the classical description, which is illustrated in **Figure 7.15**. The classical probability density distribution corresponding to the quantum energy of the $n = 12$ state is a reasonably good approximation of the quantum probability distribution for a quantum oscillator in this excited state. This agreement becomes increasingly better for highly excited states.

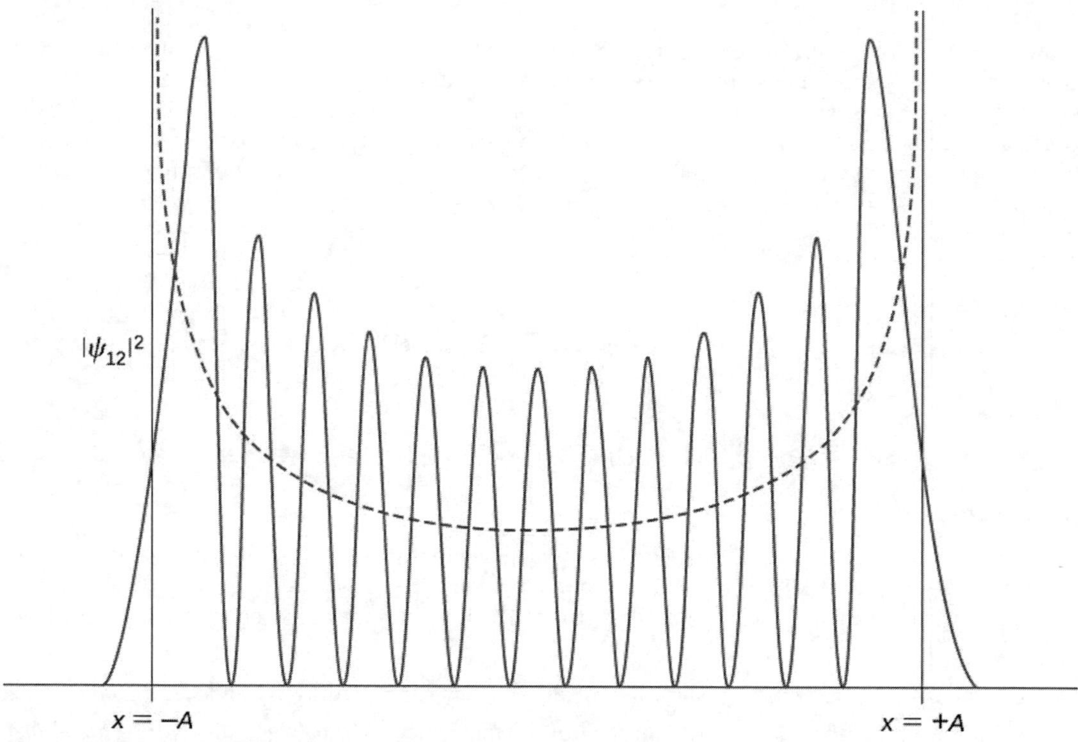

Figure 7.15 The probability density distribution for finding the quantum harmonic oscillator in its $n = 12$ quantum state. The dashed curve shows the probability density distribution of a classical oscillator with the same energy.

7.6 | The Quantum Tunneling of Particles through Potential Barriers

Learning Objectives

By the end of this section, you will be able to:

- Describe how a quantum particle may tunnel across a potential barrier
- Identify important physical parameters that affect the tunneling probability
- Identify the physical phenomena where quantum tunneling is observed
- Explain how quantum tunneling is utilized in modern technologies

Quantum tunneling is a phenomenon in which particles penetrate a potential energy barrier with a height greater than the total energy of the particles. The phenomenon is interesting and important because it violates the principles of classical mechanics. Quantum tunneling is important in models of the Sun and has a wide range of applications, such as the scanning tunneling microscope and the tunnel diode.

Tunneling and Potential Energy

To illustrate quantum tunneling, consider a ball rolling along a surface with a kinetic energy of 100 J. As the ball rolls, it encounters a hill. The potential energy of the ball placed atop the hill is 10 J. Therefore, the ball (with 100 J of kinetic energy) easily rolls over the hill and continues on. In classical mechanics, the probability that the ball passes over the hill is exactly 1—it makes it over every time. If, however, the height of the hill is increased—a ball placed atop the hill has a potential energy of 200 J—the ball proceeds only part of the way up the hill, stops, and returns in the direction it came. The total energy of the ball is converted entirely into potential energy before it can reach the top of the hill. We do not expect, even after repeated attempts, for the 100-J ball to ever be found beyond the hill. Therefore, the probability that the ball passes over the hill is exactly 0, and probability it is turned back or "reflected" by the hill is exactly 1. The ball *never* makes it over the hill. The existence of the ball beyond the hill is an impossibility or "energetically forbidden."

However, according to quantum mechanics, the ball has a wave function and this function is defined over all space. The wave function may be highly localized, but there is always a chance that as the ball encounters the hill, the ball will suddenly be found beyond it. Indeed, this probability is appreciable if the "wave packet" of the ball is wider than the barrier.

View this **interactive simulation (https://openstaxcollege.org/l/21intquatanvid)** for a simulation of tunneling.

In the language of quantum mechanics, the hill is characterized by a **potential barrier**. A finite-height square barrier is described by the following potential-energy function:

$$U(x) = \begin{cases} 0, & \text{when } x < 0 \\ U_0, & \text{when } 0 \le x \le L \\ 0, & \text{when } x > L. \end{cases} \tag{7.59}$$

The potential barrier is illustrated in **Figure 7.16**. When the height U_0 of the barrier is infinite, the wave packet representing an incident quantum particle is unable to penetrate it, and the quantum particle bounces back from the barrier boundary, just like a classical particle. When the width L of the barrier is infinite and its height is finite, a part of the wave packet representing an incident quantum particle can filter through the barrier boundary and eventually perish after traveling some distance inside the barrier.

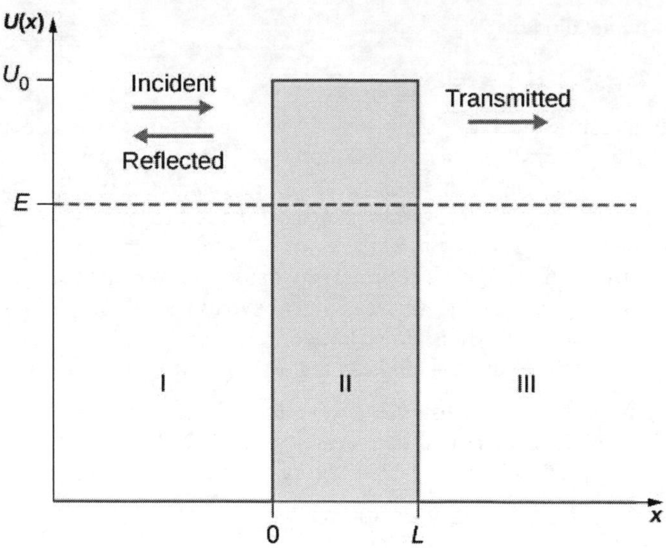

Figure 7.16 A potential energy barrier of height U_0 creates three physical regions with three different wave behaviors. In region I where $x < 0$, an incident wave packet (incident particle) moves in a potential-free zone and coexists with a reflected wave packet (reflected particle). In region II, a part of the incident wave that has not been reflected at $x = 0$ moves as a transmitted wave in a constant potential $U(x) = +U_0$ and tunnels through to region III at $x = L$. In region III for $x > L$, a wave packet (transmitted particle) that has tunneled through the potential barrier moves as a free particle in potential-free zone. The energy *E* of the incident particle is indicated by the horizontal line.

When both the width *L* and the height U_0 are finite, a part of the quantum wave packet incident on one side of the barrier can penetrate the barrier boundary and continue its motion inside the barrier, where it is gradually attenuated on its way to the other side. A part of the incident quantum wave packet eventually emerges on the other side of the barrier in the form of the transmitted wave packet that tunneled through the barrier. How much of the incident wave can tunnel through a barrier depends on the barrier width *L* and its height U_0, and on the energy *E* of the quantum particle incident on the barrier. This is the physics of tunneling.

Barrier penetration by quantum wave functions was first analyzed theoretically by Friedrich Hund in 1927, shortly after Schrödinger published the equation that bears his name. A year later, George Gamow used the formalism of quantum mechanics to explain the radioactive α-decay of atomic nuclei as a quantum-tunneling phenomenon. The invention of the tunnel diode in 1957 made it clear that quantum tunneling is important to the semiconductor industry. In modern nanotechnologies, individual atoms are manipulated using a knowledge of quantum tunneling.

Tunneling and the Wave Function

Suppose a uniform and time-independent beam of electrons or other quantum particles with energy *E* traveling along the *x*-axis (in the positive direction to the right) encounters a potential barrier described by **Equation 7.59**. The question is: What is the probability that an individual particle in the beam will tunnel through the potential barrier? The answer can be found by solving the boundary-value problem for the time-independent Schrödinger equation for a particle in the beam. The general form of this equation is given by **Equation 7.60**, which we reproduce here:

$$-\frac{\hbar^2}{2m}\frac{d^2\psi(x)}{dx^2} + U(x)\psi(x) = E\psi(x), \text{ where } -\infty < x < +\infty. \tag{7.60}$$

In **Equation 7.60**, the potential function *U*(*x*) is defined by **Equation 7.59**. We assume that the given energy *E* of the incoming particle is smaller than the height U_0 of the potential barrier, $E < U_0$, because this is the interesting physical case. Knowing the energy *E* of the incoming particle, our task is to solve **Equation 7.60** for a function $\psi(x)$ that is continuous and has continuous first derivatives for all x. In other words, we are looking for a "smooth-looking" solution (because this is how wave functions look) that can be given a probabilistic interpretation so that $|\psi(x)|^2 = \psi^*(x)\psi(x)$ is the probability density.

We divide the real axis into three regions with the boundaries defined by the potential function in **Equation 7.59** (illustrated in **Figure 7.16**) and transcribe **Equation 7.60** for each region. Denoting by $\psi_{\rm I}(x)$ the solution in region I for $x < 0$, by $\psi_{\rm II}(x)$ the solution in region II for $0 \le x \le L$, and by $\psi_{\rm III}(x)$ the solution in region III for $x > L$, the stationary Schrödinger equation has the following forms in these three regions:

$$-\frac{\hbar^2}{2m}\frac{d^2\psi_{\rm I}(x)}{dx^2} = E\psi_{\rm I}(x), \text{ in region I: } -\infty < x < 0, \tag{7.61}$$

$$-\frac{\hbar^2}{2m}\frac{d^2\psi_{\rm II}(x)}{dx^2} + U_0\psi_{\rm II}(x) = E\psi_{\rm II}(x), \text{ in region II: } 0 \le x \le L, \tag{7.62}$$

$$-\frac{\hbar^2}{2m}\frac{d^2\psi_{\rm III}(x)}{dx^2} = E\psi_{\rm III}(x), \text{ in region III: } L < x < +\infty. \tag{7.63}$$

The continuity condition at region boundaries requires that:

$$\psi_{\rm I}(0) = \psi_{\rm II}(0), \text{ at the boundary between regions I and II and} \tag{7.64}$$

and

$$\psi_{\rm II}(L) = \psi_{\rm III}(L), \text{ at the boundary between regions II and III.} \tag{7.65}$$

The "smoothness" condition requires the first derivative of the solution be continuous at region boundaries:

$$\left.\frac{d\psi_{\rm I}(x)}{dx}\right|_{x=0} = \left.\frac{d\psi_{\rm II}(x)}{dx}\right|_{x=0}, \text{ at the boundary between regions I and II;} \tag{7.66}$$

and

$$\left.\frac{d\psi_{\rm II}(x)}{dx}\right|_{x=L} = \left.\frac{d\psi_{\rm III}(x)}{dx}\right|_{x=L}, \text{ at the boundary between regions II and III.} \tag{7.67}$$

In what follows, we find the functions $\psi_{\rm I}(x)$, $\psi_{\rm II}(x)$, and $\psi_{\rm III}(x)$.

We can easily verify (by substituting into the original equation and differentiating) that in regions I and III, the solutions must be in the following general forms:

$$\psi_{\rm I}(x) = Ae^{+ikx} + Be^{-ikx} \tag{7.68}$$

$$\psi_{\rm III}(x) = Fe^{+ikx} + Ge^{-ikx} \tag{7.69}$$

where $k = \sqrt{2mE}/\hbar$ is a wave number and the complex exponent denotes oscillations,

$$e^{\pm ikx} = \cos kx \pm i \sin kx. \tag{7.70}$$

The constants A, B, F, and G in **Equation 7.68** and **Equation 7.69** may be complex. These solutions are illustrated in **Figure 7.16**. In region I, there are two waves—one is incident (moving to the right) and one is reflected (moving to the left)—so none of the constants A and B in **Equation 7.68** may vanish. In region III, there is only one wave (moving to the right), which is the transmitted wave, so the constant G must be zero in **Equation 7.69**, $G = 0$. We can write explicitly that the incident wave is $\psi_{\rm in}(x) = Ae^{+ikx}$ and that the reflected wave is $\psi_{\rm ref}(x) = Be^{-ikx}$, and that the transmitted wave is $\psi_{\rm tra}(x) = Fe^{+ikx}$. The amplitude of the incident wave is

$$\left|\psi_{\rm in}(x)\right|^2 = \psi_{\rm in}^*(x)\psi_{\rm in}(x) = \left(Ae^{+ikx}\right)^* Ae^{+ikx} = A^*\,e^{-ikx}Ae^{+ikx} = A^*\,A = \left|A\right|^2.$$

Similarly, the amplitude of the reflected wave is $|\psi_{\rm ref}(x)|^2 = |B|^2$ and the amplitude of the transmitted wave is $|\psi_{\rm tra}(x)|^2 = |F|^2$. We know from the theory of waves that the square of the wave amplitude is directly proportional to the wave intensity. If we want to know how much of the incident wave tunnels through the barrier, we need to compute the square of the amplitude of the transmitted wave. The **transmission probability** or **tunneling probability** is the ratio of the transmitted intensity $(|F|^2)$ to the incident intensity $(|A|^2)$, written as

$$T(L, E) = \frac{|\psi_{\text{tra}}(x)|^2}{|\psi_{\text{in}}(x)|^2} = \frac{|F|^2}{|A|^2} = \left|\frac{F}{A}\right|^2 \quad (7.71)$$

where L is the width of the barrier and E is the total energy of the particle. This is the probability an individual particle in the incident beam will tunnel through the potential barrier. Intuitively, we understand that this probability must depend on the barrier height U_0.

In region II, the terms in equation **Equation 7.62** can be rearranged to

$$\frac{d^2\psi_{\text{II}}(x)}{dx^2} = \beta^2\psi_{\text{II}}(x) \quad (7.72)$$

where β^2 is positive because $U_0 > E$ and the parameter β is a real number,

$$\beta^2 = \frac{2m}{\hbar^2}(U_0 - E). \quad (7.73)$$

The general solution to **Equation 7.72** is not oscillatory (unlike in the other regions) and is in the form of exponentials that describe a gradual attenuation of $\psi_{\text{II}}(x)$,

$$\psi_{\text{II}}(x) = Ce^{-\beta x} + De^{+\beta x}. \quad (7.74)$$

The two types of solutions in the three regions are illustrated in **Figure 7.17**.

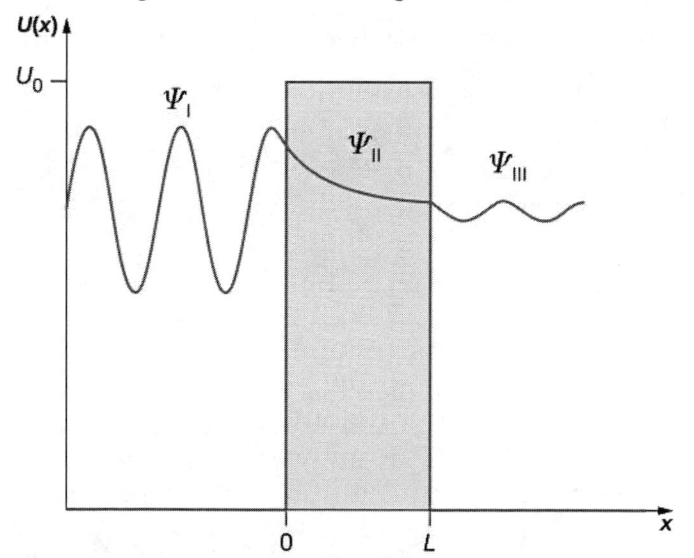

Figure 7.17 Three types of solutions to the stationary Schrödinger equation for the quantum-tunneling problem: Oscillatory behavior in regions I and III where a quantum particle moves freely, and exponential-decay behavior in region II (the barrier region) where the particle moves in the potential U_0.

Now we use the boundary conditions to find equations for the unknown constants. **Equation 7.68** and **Equation 7.74** are substituted into **Equation 7.64** to give

$$A + B = C + D. \tag{7.75}$$

Equation 7.74 and **Equation 7.69** are substituted into **Equation 7.65** to give

$$Ce^{-\beta L} + De^{+\beta L} = Fe^{+ikL}. \tag{7.76}$$

Similarly, we substitute **Equation 7.68** and **Equation 7.74** into **Equation 7.66**, differentiate, and obtain

$$-ik(A - B) = \beta(D - C). \tag{7.77}$$

Similarly, the boundary condition **Equation 7.67** reads explicitly

$$\beta\left(De^{+\beta L} - Ce^{-\beta L}\right) = -ikFe^{+ikL}. \tag{7.78}$$

We now have four equations for five unknown constants. However, because the quantity we are after is the transmission coefficient, defined in **Equation 7.71** by the fraction F/A, the number of equations is exactly right because when we divide each of the above equations by A, we end up having only four unknown fractions: B/A, C/A, D/A, and F/A, three of which can be eliminated to find F/A. The actual algebra that leads to expression for F/A is pretty lengthy, but it can be done either by hand or with a help of computer software. The end result is

$$\frac{F}{A} = \frac{e^{-ikL}}{\cosh(\beta L) + i(\gamma/2)\sinh(\beta L)}. \tag{7.79}$$

In deriving **Equation 7.79**, to avoid the clutter, we use the substitutions $\gamma \equiv \beta/k - k/\beta$,

$$\cosh y = \frac{e^y + e^{-y}}{2}, \text{ and } \sinh y = \frac{e^y - e^{-y}}{2}.$$

We substitute **Equation 7.79** into **Equation 7.71** and obtain the exact expression for the transmission coefficient for the barrier,

$$T(L, E) = \left(\frac{F}{A}\right)^* \frac{F}{A} = \frac{e^{+ikL}}{\cosh(\beta L) - i(\gamma/2)\sinh(\beta L)} \cdot \frac{e^{-ikL}}{\cosh(\beta L) + i(\gamma/2)\sinh(\beta L)}$$

or

$$T(L, E) = \frac{1}{\cosh^2(\beta L) + (\gamma/2)^2 \sinh^2(\beta L)} \tag{7.80}$$

where

$$\left(\frac{\gamma}{2}\right)^2 = \frac{1}{4}\left(\frac{1 - E/U_0}{E/U_0} + \frac{E/U_0}{1 - E/U_0} - 2\right).$$

For a wide and high barrier that transmits poorly, **Equation 7.80** can be approximated by

$$T(L, E) = 16\frac{E}{U_0}\left(1 - \frac{E}{U_0}\right)e^{-2\beta L}. \tag{7.81}$$

Whether it is the exact expression **Equation 7.80** or the approximate expression **Equation 7.81**, we see that the tunneling effect very strongly depends on the width L of the potential barrier. In the laboratory, we can adjust both the potential height U_0 and the width L to design nano-devices with desirable transmission coefficients.

Example 7.12

Transmission Coefficient

Two copper nanowires are insulated by a copper oxide nano-layer that provides a 10.0-eV potential barrier. Estimate the tunneling probability between the nanowires by 7.00-eV electrons through a 5.00-nm thick oxide layer. What if the thickness of the layer were reduced to just 1.00 nm? What if the energy of electrons were increased to 9.00 eV?

Strategy

Treating the insulating oxide layer as a finite-height potential barrier, we use **Equation 7.81**. We identify $U_0 = 10.0\,\text{eV}$, $E_1 = 7.00\,\text{eV}$, $E_2 = 9.00\,\text{eV}$, $L_1 = 5.00\,\text{nm}$, and $L_2 = 1.00\,\text{nm}$. We use **Equation 7.73** to compute the exponent. Also, we need the rest mass of the electron $m = 511\,\text{keV}/c^2$ and Planck's constant $\hbar = 0.1973\text{keV}\cdot\text{nm}/c$. It is typical for this type of estimate to deal with very small quantities that are often not suitable for handheld calculators. To make correct estimates of orders, we make the conversion $e^y = 10^{y/\ln 10}$.

Solution

Constants:

$$\frac{2m}{\hbar^2} = \frac{2(511\,\text{keV}/c^2)}{(0.1973\text{keV}\cdot\text{nm}/c)^2} = 26,254\frac{1}{\text{keV}\cdot(\text{nm})^2},$$

$$\beta = \sqrt{\frac{2m}{\hbar^2}(U_0 - E)} = \sqrt{26,254\frac{(10.0\,\text{eV} - E)}{\text{keV}\cdot(\text{nm})^2}} = \sqrt{26.254(10.0\,\text{eV} - E)/\text{eV}}\frac{1}{\text{nm}}.$$

For a lower-energy electron with $E_1 = 7.00\,\text{eV}$:

$$\beta_1 = \sqrt{26.254(10.00\,\text{eV} - E_1)/\text{eV}}\frac{1}{\text{nm}} = \sqrt{26.254(10.00 - 7.00)}\frac{1}{\text{nm}} = \frac{8.875}{\text{nm}},$$

$$T(L, E_1) = 16\frac{E_1}{U_0}\left(1 - \frac{E_1}{U_0}\right)e^{-2\beta_1 L} = 16\frac{7}{10}\left(1 - \frac{7}{10}\right)e^{-17.75\,L/\text{nm}} = 3.36e^{-17.75\,L/\text{nm}}.$$

For a higher-energy electron with $E_2 = 9.00\,\text{eV}$:

$$\beta_2 = \sqrt{26.254(10.00\,\text{eV} - E_2)/\text{eV}}\frac{1}{\text{nm}} = \sqrt{26.254(10.00 - 9.00)}\frac{1}{\text{nm}} = \frac{5.124}{\text{nm}},$$

$$T(L, E_2) = 16\frac{E_2}{U_0}\left(1 - \frac{E_2}{U_0}\right)e^{-2\beta_2 L} = 16\frac{9}{10}\left(1 - \frac{9}{10}\right)e^{-5.12\,L/\text{nm}} = 1.44e^{-5.12\,L/\text{nm}}.$$

For a broad barrier with $L_1 = 5.00\,\text{nm}$:

$$T(L_1, E_1) = 3.36e^{-17.75\,L_1/\text{nm}} = 3.36e^{-17.75\cdot 5.00\,\text{nm}/\text{nm}} = 3.36e^{-88} = 3.36(6.2\times 10^{-39}) = 2.1\%\times 10^{-36},$$

$$T(L_1, E_2) = 1.44e^{-5.12\,L_1/\text{nm}} = 1.44e^{-5.12\cdot 5.00\,\text{nm}/\text{nm}} = 1.44e^{-25.6} = 1.44(7.62\times 10^{-12}) = 1.1\%\times 10^{-9}.$$

For a narrower barrier with $L_2 = 1.00\,\text{nm}$:

$$T(L_2, E_1) = 3.36e^{-17.75\,L_2/\text{nm}} = 3.36e^{-17.75\cdot 1.00\,\text{nm}/\text{nm}} = 3.36e^{-17.75} = 3.36(5.1\times 10^{-7}) = 1.7\%\times 10^{-4},$$

$$T(L_2, E_2) = 1.44e^{-5.12\,L_2/\text{nm}} = 1.44e^{-5.12\cdot 1.00\,\text{nm}/\text{nm}} = 1.44e^{-5.12} = 1.44(5.98\times 10^{-3}) = 0.86\%.$$

Significance

We see from these estimates that the probability of tunneling is affected more by the width of the potential barrier than by the energy of an incident particle. In today's technologies, we can manipulate individual atoms on metal surfaces to create potential barriers that are fractions of a nanometer, giving rise to measurable tunneling currents. One of many applications of this technology is the scanning tunneling microscope (STM), which we discuss later in this section.

7.10 Check Your Understanding A proton with kinetic energy 1.00 eV is incident on a square potential barrier with height 10.00 eV. If the proton is to have the same transmission probability as an electron of the same energy, what must the width of the barrier be relative to the barrier width encountered by an electron?

Radioactive Decay

In 1928, Gamow identified quantum tunneling as the mechanism responsible for the radioactive decay of atomic nuclei. He observed that some isotopes of thorium, uranium, and bismuth disintegrate by emitting α-particles (which are doubly ionized helium atoms or, simply speaking, helium nuclei). In the process of emitting an α-particle, the original nucleus is transformed into a new nucleus that has two fewer neutrons and two fewer protons than the original nucleus. The α-particles emitted by one isotope have approximately the same kinetic energies. When we look at variations of these energies among isotopes of various elements, the lowest kinetic energy is about 4 MeV and the highest is about 9 MeV, so these energies are of the same order of magnitude. This is about where the similarities between various isotopes end.

When we inspect half-lives (a half-life is the time in which a radioactive sample loses half of its nuclei due to decay), different isotopes differ widely. For example, the half-life of polonium-214 is $160\,\mu\text{s}$ and the half-life of uranium is 4.5 billion years. Gamow explained this variation by considering a 'spherical-box' model of the nucleus, where α-particles can bounce back and forth between the walls as free particles. The confinement is provided by a strong nuclear potential at a spherical wall of the box. The thickness of this wall, however, is not infinite but finite, so in principle, a nuclear particle has a chance to escape this nuclear confinement. On the inside wall of the confining barrier is a high nuclear potential that keeps the α-particle in a small confinement. But when an α-particle gets out to the other side of this wall, it is subject to electrostatic Coulomb repulsion and moves away from the nucleus. This idea is illustrated in **Figure 7.18**. The width *L* of the potential barrier that separates an α-particle from the outside world depends on the particle's kinetic energy *E*. This width is the distance between the point marked by the nuclear radius *R* and the point R_0 where an α-particle emerges on the other side of the barrier, $L = R_0 - R$. At the distance R_0, its kinetic energy must at least match the electrostatic energy of repulsion, $E = (4\pi\varepsilon_0)^{-1} Ze^2/R_0$ (where $+Ze$ is the charge of the nucleus). In this way we can estimate the width of the nuclear barrier,

$$L = \frac{e^2}{4\pi\varepsilon_0}\frac{Z}{E} - R.$$

We see from this estimate that the higher the energy of α-particle, the narrower the width of the barrier that it is to tunnel through. We also know that the width of the potential barrier is the most important parameter in tunneling probability. Thus, highly energetic α-particles have a good chance to escape the nucleus, and, for such nuclei, the nuclear disintegration half-life is short. Notice that this process is highly nonlinear, meaning a small increase in the α-particle energy has a disproportionately large enhancing effect on the tunneling probability and, consequently, on shortening the half-life. This explains why the half-life of polonium that emits 8-MeV α-particles is only hundreds of milliseconds and the half-life of uranium that emits 4-MeV α-particles is billions of years.

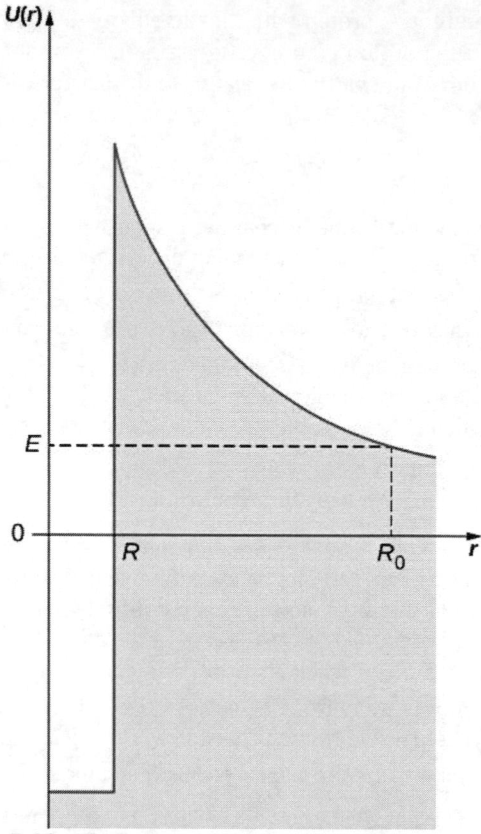

Figure 7.18 The potential energy barrier for an α-particle bound in the nucleus: To escape from the nucleus, an α-particle with energy E must tunnel across the barrier from distance R to distance R_0 away from the center.

Field Emission

Field emission is a process of emitting electrons from conducting surfaces due to a strong external electric field that is applied in the direction normal to the surface (**Figure 7.19**). As we know from our study of electric fields in earlier chapters, an applied external electric field causes the electrons in a conductor to move to its surface and stay there as long as the present external field is not excessively strong. In this situation, we have a constant electric potential throughout the inside of the conductor, including its surface. In the language of potential energy, we say that an electron inside the conductor has a constant potential energy $U(x) = -U_0$ (here, the x means inside the conductor). In the situation represented in **Figure 7.19**, where the external electric field is uniform and has magnitude E_g, if an electron happens to be outside the conductor at a distance x away from its surface, its potential energy would have to be $U(x) = -eE_g x$ (here, x denotes distance to the surface). Taking the origin at the surface, so that $x = 0$ is the location of the surface, we can represent the potential energy of conduction electrons in a metal as the potential energy barrier shown in **Figure 7.20**. In the absence of the external field, the potential energy becomes a step barrier defined by $U(x \le 0) = -U_0$ and by $U(x > 0) = 0$.

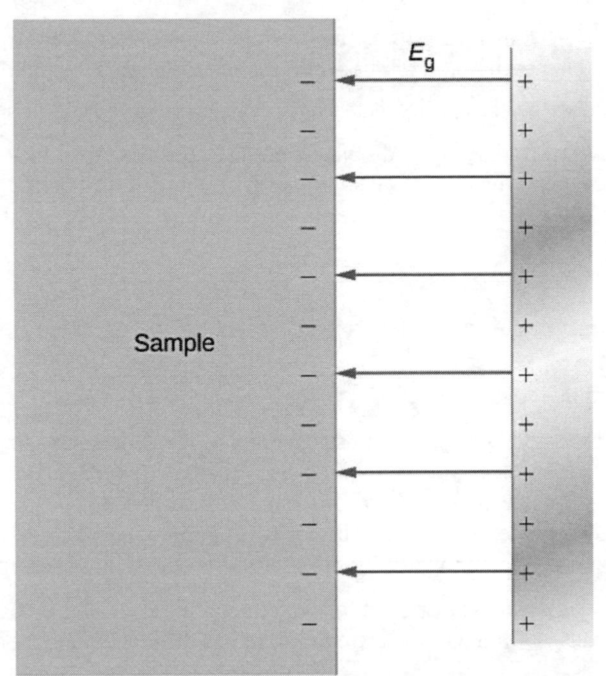

Figure 7.19 A normal-direction external electric field at the surface of a conductor: In a strong field, the electrons on a conducting surface may get detached from it and accelerate against the external electric field away from the surface.

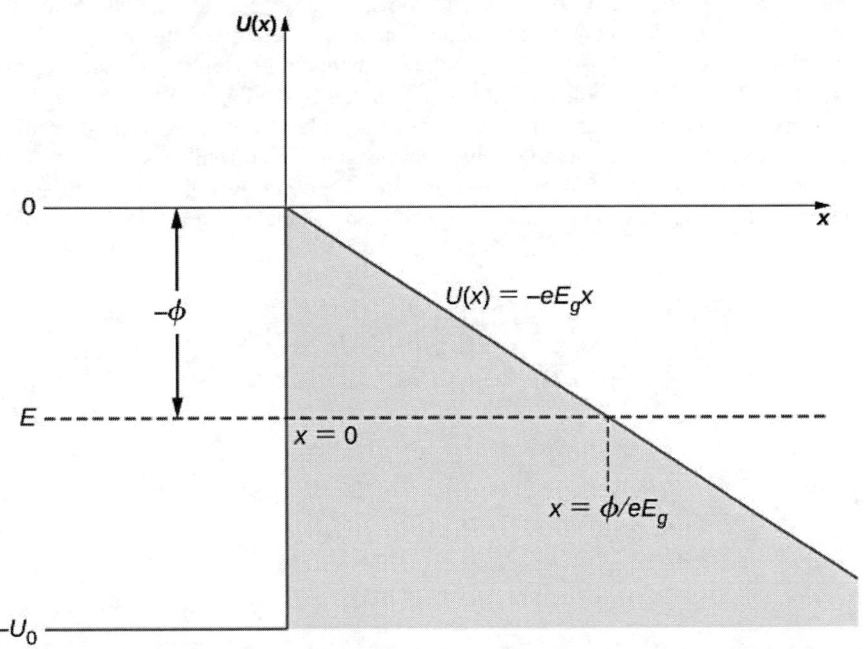

Figure 7.20 The potential energy barrier at the surface of a metallic conductor in the presence of an external uniform electric field E_g normal to the surface: It becomes a step-function barrier when the external field is removed. The work function of the metal is indicated by ϕ.

When an external electric field is strong, conduction electrons at the surface may get detached from it and accelerate along electric field lines in a direction antiparallel to the external field, away from the surface. In short, conduction electrons may escape from the surface. The field emission can be understood as the quantum tunneling of conduction electrons through the potential barrier at the conductor's surface. The physical principle at work here is very similar to the mechanism of α -emission from a radioactive nucleus.

Suppose a conduction electron has a kinetic energy E (the average kinetic energy of an electron in a metal is the work function ϕ for the metal and can be measured, as discussed for the photoelectric effect in **Photons and Matter Waves**), and an external electric field can be locally approximated by a uniform electric field of strength E_g. The width L of the potential barrier that the electron must cross is the distance from the conductor's surface to the point outside the surface where its kinetic energy matches the value of its potential energy in the external field. In **Figure 7.20**, this distance is measured along the dashed horizontal line $U(x) = E$ from $x = 0$ to the intercept with $U(x) = -eE_g x$, so the barrier width is

$$L = \frac{e^{-1}E}{E_g} = \frac{e^{-1}\phi}{E_g}.$$

We see that L is inversely proportional to the strength E_g of an external field. When we increase the strength of the external field, the potential barrier outside the conductor becomes steeper and its width decreases for an electron with a given kinetic energy. In turn, the probability that an electron will tunnel across the barrier (conductor surface) becomes exponentially larger. The electrons that emerge on the other side of this barrier form a current (tunneling-electron current) that can be detected above the surface. The tunneling-electron current is proportional to the tunneling probability. The tunneling probability depends nonlinearly on the barrier width L, and L can be changed by adjusting E_g. Therefore, the tunneling-electron current can be tuned by adjusting the strength of an external electric field at the surface. When the strength of an external electric field is constant, the tunneling-electron current has different values at different elevations L above the surface.

The quantum tunneling phenomenon at metallic surfaces, which we have just described, is the physical principle behind the operation of the **scanning tunneling microscope (STM)**, invented in 1981 by Gerd Binnig and Heinrich Rohrer. The STM device consists of a scanning tip (a needle, usually made of tungsten, platinum-iridium, or gold); a piezoelectric device that controls the tip's elevation in a typical range of 0.4 to 0.7 nm above the surface to be scanned; some device that controls the motion of the tip along the surface; and a computer to display images. While the sample is kept at a suitable voltage bias, the scanning tip moves along the surface (**Figure 7.21**), and the tunneling-electron current between the tip and the surface is registered at each position. The amount of the current depends on the probability of electron tunneling from the surface to the tip, which, in turn, depends on the elevation of the tip above the surface. Hence, at each tip position, the distance from the tip to the surface is measured by measuring how many electrons tunnel out from the surface to the tip. This method can give an unprecedented resolution of about 0.001 nm, which is about 1% of the average diameter of an atom. In this way, we can see individual atoms on the surface, as in the image of a carbon nanotube in **Figure 7.22**.

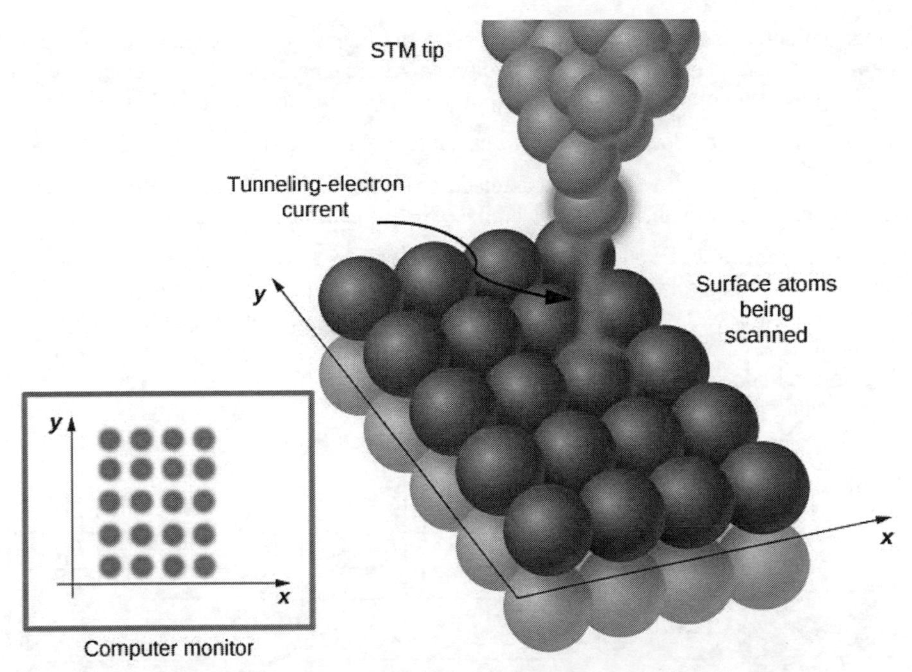

Figure 7.21 In STM, a surface at a constant potential is being scanned by a narrow tip moving along the surface. When the STM tip moves close to surface atoms, electrons can tunnel from the surface to the tip. This tunneling-electron current is continually monitored while the tip is in motion. The amount of current at location (x,y) gives information about the elevation of the tip above the surface at this location. In this way, a detailed topographical map of the surface is created and displayed on a computer monitor.

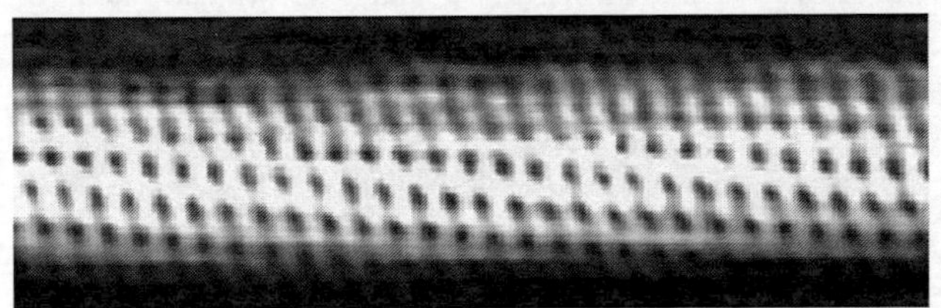

Figure 7.22 An STM image of a carbon nanotube: Atomic-scale resolution allows us to see individual atoms on the surface. STM images are in gray scale, and coloring is added to bring up details to the human eye. (credit: Taner Yildirim, NIST)

Resonant Quantum Tunneling

Quantum tunneling has numerous applications in semiconductor devices such as electronic circuit components or integrated circuits that are designed at nanoscales; hence, the term ‘ **nanotechnology**.’ For example, a diode (an electric-circuit element that causes an electron current in one direction to be different from the current in the opposite direction, when the polarity of the bias voltage is reversed) can be realized by a tunneling junction between two different types of semiconducting materials. In such a **tunnel diode**, electrons tunnel through a single potential barrier at a contact between two different semiconductors. At the junction, tunneling-electron current changes nonlinearly with the applied potential difference across the junction and may rapidly decrease as the bias voltage is increased. This is unlike the Ohm’s law behavior that we are familiar with in household circuits. This kind of rapid behavior (caused by quantum tunneling) is desirable in high-speed electronic devices.

Another kind of electronic nano-device utilizes **resonant tunneling** of electrons through potential barriers that occur in quantum dots. A **quantum dot** is a small region of a semiconductor nanocrystal that is grown, for example, in a silicon or aluminum arsenide crystal. Figure 7.23(a) shows a quantum dot of gallium arsenide embedded in an aluminum arsenide wafer. The quantum-dot region acts as a potential well of a finite height (shown in Figure 7.23(b)) that has two finite-height potential barriers at dot boundaries. Similarly, as for a quantum particle in a box (that is, an infinite potential well), lower-lying energies of a quantum particle trapped in a finite-height potential well are quantized. The difference between the box and the well potentials is that a quantum particle in a box has an infinite number of quantized energies and is trapped in the box indefinitely, whereas a quantum particle trapped in a potential well has a finite number of quantized energy levels and can tunnel through potential barriers at well boundaries to the outside of the well. Thus, a quantum dot of gallium arsenide sitting in aluminum arsenide is a potential well where low-lying energies of an electron are quantized, indicated as E_{dot} in part (b) in the figure. When the energy E_{electron} of an electron in the outside region of the dot does not match its energy E_{dot} that it would have in the dot, the electron does not tunnel through the region of the dot and there is no current through such a circuit element, even if it were kept at an electric voltage difference (bias). However, when this voltage bias is changed in such a way that one of the barriers is lowered, so that E_{dot} and E_{electron} become aligned, as seen in part (c) of the figure, an electron current flows through the dot. When the voltage bias is now increased, this alignment is lost and the current stops flowing. When the voltage bias is increased further, the electron tunneling becomes improbable until the bias voltage reaches a value for which the outside electron energy matches the next electron energy level in the dot. The word 'resonance' in the device name means that the tunneling-electron current occurs only when a selected energy level is matched by tuning an applied voltage bias, such as in the operation mechanism of the **resonant-tunneling diode** just described. Resonant-tunneling diodes are used as super-fast nano-switches.

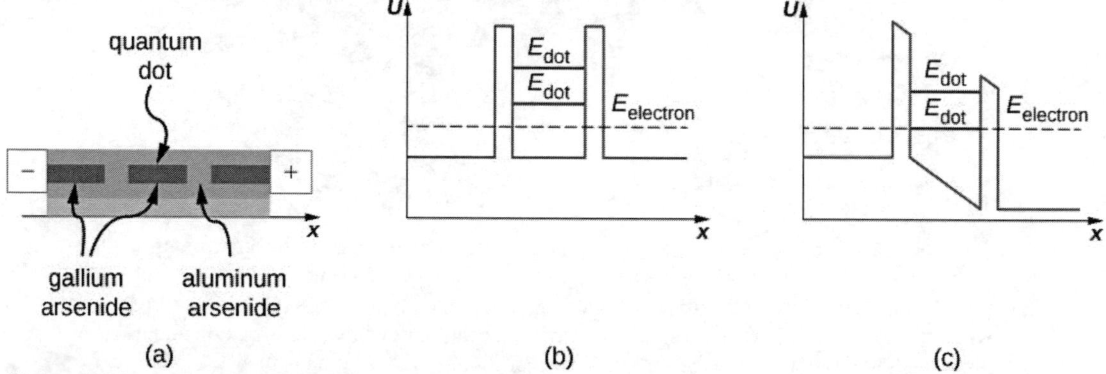

Figure 7.23 Resonant-tunneling diode: (a) A quantum dot of gallium arsenide embedded in aluminum arsenide. (b) Potential well consisting of two potential barriers of a quantum dot with no voltage bias. Electron energies E_{electron} in aluminum arsenide are not aligned with their energy levels E_{dot} in the quantum dot, so electrons do not tunnel through the dot. (c) Potential well of the dot with a voltage bias across the device. A suitably tuned voltage difference distorts the well so that electron-energy levels in the dot are aligned with their energies in aluminum arsenide, causing the electrons to tunnel through the dot.

CHAPTER 7 REVIEW

KEY TERMS

anti-symmetric function odd function

Born interpretation states that the square of a wave function is the probability density

complex function function containing both real and imaginary parts

Copenhagen interpretation states that when an observer *is not* looking or when a measurement is not being made, the particle has many values of measurable quantities, such as position

correspondence principle in the limit of large energies, the predictions of quantum mechanics agree with the predictions of classical mechanics

energy levels states of definite energy, often represented by horizontal lines in an energy "ladder" diagram

energy quantum number index that labels the allowed energy states

energy-time uncertainty principle energy-time relation for uncertainties in the simultaneous measurements of the energy of a quantum state and of its lifetime

even function in one dimension, a function symmetric with the origin of the coordinate system

expectation value average value of the physical quantity assuming a large number of particles with the same wave function

field emission electron emission from conductor surfaces when a strong external electric field is applied in normal direction to conductor's surface

ground state energy lowest energy state in the energy spectrum

Heisenberg's uncertainty principle places limits on what can be known from a simultaneous measurements of position and momentum; states that if the uncertainty on position is small then the uncertainty on momentum is large, and vice versa

infinite square well potential function that is zero in a fixed range and infinitely beyond this range

momentum operator operator that corresponds to the momentum of a particle

nanotechnology technology that is based on manipulation of nanostructures such as molecules or individual atoms to produce nano-devices such as integrated circuits

normalization condition requires that the probability density integrated over the entire physical space results in the number one

odd function in one dimension, a function antisymmetric with the origin of the coordinate system

position operator operator that corresponds to the position of a particle

potential barrier potential function that rises and falls with increasing values of position

principal quantum number energy quantum number

probability density square of the particle's wave function

quantum dot small region of a semiconductor nanocrystal embedded in another semiconductor nanocrystal, acting as a potential well for electrons

quantum tunneling phenomenon where particles penetrate through a potential energy barrier with a height greater than the total energy of the particles

resonant tunneling tunneling of electrons through a finite-height potential well that occurs only when electron energies match an energy level in the well, occurs in quantum dots

resonant-tunneling diode quantum dot with an applied voltage bias across it

scanning tunneling microscope (STM) device that utilizes quantum-tunneling phenomenon at metallic surfaces to obtain images of nanoscale structures

Schrödinger's time-dependent equation equation in space and time that allows us to determine wave functions of a quantum particle

Schrödinger's time-independent equation equation in space that allows us to determine wave functions of a quantum particle; this wave function must be multiplied by a time-modulation factor to obtain the time-dependent wave function

standing wave state stationary state for which the real and imaginary parts of $\Psi(x, t)$ oscillate up and down like a standing wave (often modeled with sine and cosine functions)

state reduction hypothetical process in which an observed or detected particle "jumps into" a definite state, often described in terms of the collapse of the particle's wave function

stationary state state for which the probability density function, $|\Psi(x, t)|^2$, does not vary in time

time-modulation factor factor $e^{-i\omega t}$ that multiplies the time-independent wave function when the potential energy of the particle is time independent

transmission probability also called tunneling probability, the probability that a particle will tunnel through a potential barrier

tunnel diode electron tunneling-junction between two different semiconductors

tunneling probability also called transmission probability, the probability that a particle will tunnel through a potential barrier

wave function function that represents the quantum state of a particle (quantum system)

wave function collapse equivalent to state reduction

wave packet superposition of many plane matter waves that can be used to represent a localized particle

KEY EQUATIONS

Normalization condition in one dimension	$P(x = -\infty, +\infty) = \int_{-\infty}^{\infty} \lvert\Psi(x, t)\rvert^2 dx = 1$
Probability of finding a particle in a narrow interval of position in one dimension $(x, x + dx)$	$P(x, x + dx) = \Psi^* (x, t)\Psi(x, t)dx$
Expectation value of position in one dimension	$\langle x \rangle = \int_{-\infty}^{\infty} \Psi^* (x, t)x\Psi(x, t)dx$
Heisenberg's position-momentum uncertainty principle	$\Delta x \Delta p \geq \frac{\hbar}{2}$
Heisenberg's energy-time uncertainty principle	$\Delta E \Delta t \geq \frac{\hbar}{2}$
Schrödinger's time-dependent equation	$-\frac{\hbar^2}{2m}\frac{\partial^2 \Psi(x, t)}{\partial x^2} + U(x, t)\Psi(x, t) = i\hbar\frac{\partial \Psi(x, t)}{\partial t}$
General form of the wave function for a time-independent potential in one dimension	$\Psi(x, t) = \psi(x)e^{-i\omega t}$
Schrödinger's time-independent equation	$-\frac{\hbar^2}{2m}\frac{d^2 \psi(x)}{dx^2} + U(x)\psi(x) = E\psi(x)$
Schrödinger's equation (free particle)	$-\frac{\hbar^2}{2m}\frac{\partial^2 \psi(x)}{\partial x^2} = E\psi(x)$
Allowed energies (particle in box of length L)	$E_n = n^2 \frac{\pi^2 \hbar^2}{2mL^2}, n = 1, 2, 3, ...$

Stationary states (particle in a box of length L)	$\psi_n(x) = \sqrt{\frac{2}{L}} \sin \frac{n\pi x}{L},\ n = 1, 2, 3, ...$
Potential-energy function of a harmonic oscillator	$U(x) = \frac{1}{2}m\omega^2 x^2$
Stationary Schrödinger equation	$-\frac{\hbar}{2m}\frac{d^2\psi(x)}{dx^2} + \frac{1}{2}m\omega^2 x^2 \psi(x) = E\psi(x)$
The energy spectrum	$E_n = \left(n + \frac{1}{2}\right)\hbar\omega,\ n = 0, 1, 2, 3, ...$
The energy wave functions	$\psi_n(x) = N_n e^{-\beta^2 x^2/2} H_n(\beta x),\ n = 0, 1, 2, 3, ...$
Potential barrier	$U(x) = \begin{cases} 0, & \text{when } x < 0 \\ U_0, & \text{when } 0 \le x \le L \\ 0, & \text{when } x > L \end{cases}$
Definition of the transmission coefficient	$T(L, E) = \frac{\lvert\psi_{\text{tra}}(x)\rvert^2}{\lvert\psi_{\text{in}}(x)\rvert^2}$
A parameter in the transmission coefficient	$\beta^2 = \frac{2m}{\hbar^2}(U_0 - E)$
Transmission coefficient, exact	$T(L, E) = \frac{1}{\cosh^2 \beta L + (\gamma/2)^2 \sinh^2 \beta L}$
Transmission coefficient, approximate	$T(L, E) = 16\frac{E}{U_0}\left(1 - \frac{E}{U_0}\right)e^{-2\beta L}$

SUMMARY

7.1 Wave Functions

- In quantum mechanics, the state of a physical system is represented by a wave function.
- In Born's interpretation, the square of the particle's wave function represents the probability density of finding the particle around a specific location in space.
- Wave functions must first be normalized before using them to make predictions.
- The expectation value is the average value of a quantity that requires a wave function and an integration.

7.2 The Heisenberg Uncertainty Principle

- The Heisenberg uncertainty principle states that it is impossible to simultaneously measure the x-components of position and of momentum of a particle with an arbitrarily high precision. The product of experimental uncertainties is always larger than or equal to $\hbar/2$.
- The limitations of this principle have nothing to do with the quality of the experimental apparatus but originate in the wave-like nature of matter.
- The energy-time uncertainty principle expresses the experimental observation that a quantum state that exists only for a short time cannot have a definite energy.

7.3 The Schrödinger Equation

- The Schrödinger equation is the fundamental equation of wave quantum mechanics. It allows us to make predictions about wave functions.
- When a particle moves in a time-independent potential, a solution of the time-dependent Schrödinger equation is a

product of a time-independent wave function and a time-modulation factor.

- The Schrődinger equation can be applied to many physical situations.

7.4 The Quantum Particle in a Box

- Energy states of a quantum particle in a box are found by solving the time-independent Schrődinger equation.
- To solve the time-independent Schrődinger equation for a particle in a box and find the stationary states and allowed energies, we require that the wave function terminate at the box wall.
- Energy states of a particle in a box are quantized and indexed by principal quantum number.
- The quantum picture differs significantly from the classical picture when a particle is in a low-energy state of a low quantum number.
- In the limit of high quantum numbers, when the quantum particle is in a highly excited state, the quantum description of a particle in a box coincides with the classical description, in the spirit of Bohr's correspondence principle.

7.5 The Quantum Harmonic Oscillator

- The quantum harmonic oscillator is a model built in analogy with the model of a classical harmonic oscillator. It models the behavior of many physical systems, such as molecular vibrations or wave packets in quantum optics.
- The allowed energies of a quantum oscillator are discrete and evenly spaced. The energy spacing is equal to Planck's energy quantum.
- The ground state energy is larger than zero. This means that, unlike a classical oscillator, a quantum oscillator is never at rest, even at the bottom of a potential well, and undergoes quantum fluctuations.
- The stationary states (states of definite energy) have nonzero values also in regions beyond classical turning points. When in the ground state, a quantum oscillator is most likely to be found around the position of the minimum of the potential well, which is the least-likely position for a classical oscillator.
- For high quantum numbers, the motion of a quantum oscillator becomes more similar to the motion of a classical oscillator, in accordance with Bohr's correspondence principle.

7.6 The Quantum Tunneling of Particles through Potential Barriers

- A quantum particle that is incident on a potential barrier of a finite width and height may cross the barrier and appear on its other side. This phenomenon is called 'quantum tunneling.' It does not have a classical analog.
- To find the probability of quantum tunneling, we assume the energy of an incident particle and solve the stationary Schrődinger equation to find wave functions inside and outside the barrier. The tunneling probability is a ratio of squared amplitudes of the wave past the barrier to the incident wave.
- The tunneling probability depends on the energy of the incident particle relative to the height of the barrier and on the width of the barrier. It is strongly affected by the width of the barrier in a nonlinear, exponential way so that a small change in the barrier width causes a disproportionately large change in the transmission probability.
- Quantum-tunneling phenomena govern radioactive nuclear decays. They are utilized in many modern technologies such as STM and nano-electronics. STM allows us to see individual atoms on metal surfaces. Electron-tunneling devices have revolutionized electronics and allow us to build fast electronic devices of miniature sizes.

CONCEPTUAL QUESTIONS

7.1 Wave Functions

1. What is the physical unit of a wave function, $\Psi(x, t)$? What is the physical unit of the square of this wave function?

2. Can the magnitude of a wave function $(\Psi^* (x, t)\, \Psi(x, t))$ be a negative number? Explain.

3. What kind of physical quantity does a wave function of an electron represent?

4. What is the physical meaning of a wave function of a particle?

5. What is the meaning of the expression "expectation value?" Explain.

7.2 The Heisenberg Uncertainty Principle

6. If the formalism of quantum mechanics is 'more exact' than that of classical mechanics, why don't we use quantum mechanics to describe the motion of a leaping frog? Explain.

7. Can the de Broglie wavelength of a particle be known precisely? Can the position of a particle be known precisely?

8. Can we measure the energy of a free localized particle with complete precision?

9. Can we measure both the position and momentum of a particle with complete precision?

7.3 The Schrödinger Equation

10. What is the difference between a wave function $\psi(x, y, z)$ and a wave function $\Psi(x, y, z, t)$ for the same particle?

11. If a quantum particle is in a stationary state, does it mean that it does not move?

12. Explain the difference between time-dependent and -independent Schrödinger's equations.

13. Suppose a wave function is discontinuous at some point. Can this function represent a quantum state of some physical particle? Why? Why not?

7.4 The Quantum Particle in a Box

14. Using the quantum particle in a box model, describe how the possible energies of the particle are related to the size of the box.

15. Is it possible that when we measure the energy of a quantum particle in a box, the measurement may return a smaller value than the ground state energy? What is the highest value of the energy that we can measure for this particle?

16. For a quantum particle in a box, the first excited state (Ψ_2) has zero value at the midpoint position in the box, so that the probability density of finding a particle at this point is exactly zero. Explain what is wrong with the following reasoning: "If the probability of finding a quantum particle at the midpoint is zero, the particle is never at this point, right? How does it come then that the particle can cross this point on its way from the left side to the right side of the box?

7.5 The Quantum Harmonic Oscillator

17. Is it possible to measure energy of $0.75\hbar\omega$ for a quantum harmonic oscillator? Why? Why not? Explain.

18. Explain the connection between Planck's hypothesis of energy quanta and the energies of the quantum harmonic oscillator.

19. If a classical harmonic oscillator can be at rest, why can the quantum harmonic oscillator never be at rest? Does this violate Bohr's correspondence principle?

20. Use an example of a quantum particle in a box or a quantum oscillator to explain the physical meaning of Bohr's correspondence principle.

21. Can we simultaneously measure position and energy of a quantum oscillator? Why? Why not?

7.6 The Quantum Tunneling of Particles through Potential Barriers

22. When an electron and a proton of the same kinetic energy encounter a potential barrier of the same height and width, which one of them will tunnel through the barrier more easily? Why?

23. What decreases the tunneling probability most: doubling the barrier width or halving the kinetic energy of the incident particle?

24. Explain the difference between a box-potential and a potential of a quantum dot.

25. Can a quantum particle 'escape' from an infinite potential well like that in a box? Why? Why not?

26. A tunnel diode and a resonant-tunneling diode both utilize the same physics principle of quantum tunneling. In what important way are they different?

PROBLEMS

7.1 Wave Functions

27. Compute $|\Psi(x, t)|^2$ for the function $\Psi(x, t) = \psi(x) \sin \omega t$, where ω is a real constant.

28. Given the complex-valued function $f(x, y) = (x - iy)/(x + iy)$, calculate $|f(x, y)|^2$.

29. Which one of the following functions, and why, qualifies to be a wave function of a particle that can move along the entire real axis? (a) $\psi(x) = Ae^{-x^2}$; (b) $\psi(x) = Ae^{-x}$; (c) $\psi(x) = A \tan x$; (d) $\psi(x) = A(\sin x)/x$; (e) $\psi(x) = Ae^{-|x|}$.

30. A particle with mass *m* moving along the *x*-axis and its quantum state is represented by the following wave function:

$$\Psi(x, t) = \begin{cases} 0, & x < 0, \\ Axe^{-\alpha x} e^{-iEt/\hbar}, & x \geq 0, \end{cases}$$

where $\alpha = 2.0 \times 10^{10}\,\text{m}^{-1}$. (a) Find the normalization constant. (b) Find the probability that the particle can be found on the interval $0 \leq x \leq L$. (c) Find the expectation value of position. (d) Find the expectation value of kinetic energy.

31. A wave function of a particle with mass *m* is given by

$$\psi(x) = \begin{cases} A \cos \alpha x, & -\frac{\pi}{2\alpha} \leq x \leq +\frac{\pi}{2\alpha}, \\ 0, & \text{otherwise,} \end{cases}$$

where $\alpha = 1.00 \times 10^{10}/\text{m}$. (a) Find the normalization constant. (b) Find the probability that the particle can be found on the interval $0 \leq x \leq 0.5 \times 10^{-10}\,\text{m}$. (c) Find the particle's average position. (d) Find its average momentum. (e) Find its average kinetic energy $-0.5 \times 10^{-10}\,\text{m} \leq x \leq +0.5 \times 10^{-10}\,\text{m}$.

7.2 The Heisenberg Uncertainty Principle

32. A velocity measurement of an α-particle has been performed with a precision of 0.02 mm/s. What is the minimum uncertainty in its position?

33. A gas of helium atoms at 273 K is in a cubical container with 25.0 cm on a side. (a) What is the minimum uncertainty in momentum components of helium atoms? (b) What is the minimum uncertainty in velocity components? (c) Find the ratio of the uncertainties in (b) to the mean speed of an atom in each direction.

34. If the uncertainty in the y-component of a proton's position is 2.0 pm, find the minimum uncertainty in the simultaneous measurement of the proton's y-component of velocity. What is the minimum uncertainty in the simultaneous measurement of the proton's x-component of velocity?

35. Some unstable elementary particle has a rest energy of 80.41 GeV and an uncertainty in rest energy of 2.06 GeV. Estimate the lifetime of this particle.

36. An atom in a metastable state has a lifetime of 5.2 ms. Find the minimum uncertainty in the measurement of energy of the excited state.

37. Measurements indicate that an atom remains in an excited state for an average time of 50.0 ns before making a transition to the ground state with the simultaneous emission of a 2.1-eV photon. (a) Estimate the uncertainty in the frequency of the photon. (b) What fraction of the photon's average frequency is this?

38. Suppose an electron is confined to a region of length 0.1 nm (of the order of the size of a hydrogen atom) and its kinetic energy is equal to the ground state energy of the hydrogen atom in Bohr's model (13.6 eV). (a) What is the minimum uncertainty of its momentum? What fraction of its momentum is it? (b) What would the uncertainty in kinetic energy of this electron be if its momentum were equal to your answer in part (a)? What fraction of its kinetic energy is it?

7.3 The Schrödinger Equation

39. Combine Equation 7.17 and Equation 7.18 to show $k^2 = \frac{\omega^2}{c^2}$.

40. Show that $\Psi(x, t) = Ae^{i(kx - \omega t)}$ is a valid solution to Schrödinger's time-dependent equation.

41. Show that $\Psi(x, t) = A \sin(kx - \omega t)$ and $\Psi(x, t) = A \cos(kx - \omega t)$ do not obey Schrödinger's time-dependent equation.

42. Show that when $\Psi_1(x, t)$ and $\Psi_2(x, t)$ are solutions to the time-dependent Schrödinger equation and *A*,*B* are numbers, then a function $\Psi(x, t)$ that is a superposition of these functions is also a solution: $\Psi(x, t) = A\Psi_1(x, t) + B\Psi_1(x, t)$.

43. A particle with mass m is described by the following wave function: $\psi(x) = A \cos kx + B \sin kx$, where A, B, and k are constants. Assuming that the particle is free, show that this function is the solution of the stationary Schrödinger equation for this particle and find the energy that the particle has in this state.

44. Find the expectation value of the kinetic energy for the particle in the state, $\Psi(x, t) = Ae^{i(kx - \omega t)}$. What conclusion can you draw from your solution?

45. Find the expectation value of the square of the momentum squared for the particle in the state, $\Psi(x, t) = Ae^{i(kx - \omega t)}$. What conclusion can you draw from your solution?

46. A free proton has a wave function given by $\Psi(x, t) = Ae^{i(5.02 \times 10^{11} x - 8.00 \times 10^{15} t)}$.

The coefficient of x is inverse meters (m^{-1}) and the coefficient on t is inverse seconds (s^{-1}). Find its momentum and energy.

7.4 The Quantum Particle in a Box

47. Assume that an electron in an atom can be treated as if it were confined to a box of width 2.0 Å. What is the ground state energy of the electron? Compare your result to the ground state kinetic energy of the hydrogen atom in the Bohr's model of the hydrogen atom.

48. Assume that a proton in a nucleus can be treated as if it were confined to a one-dimensional box of width 10.0 fm. (a) What are the energies of the proton when it is in the states corresponding to $n = 1$, $n = 2$, and $n = 3$? (b) What are the energies of the photons emitted when the proton makes the transitions from the first and second excited states to the ground state?

49. An electron confined to a box has the ground state energy of 2.5 eV. What is the width of the box?

50. What is the ground state energy (in eV) of a proton confined to a one-dimensional box the size of the uranium nucleus that has a radius of approximately 15.0 fm?

51. What is the ground state energy (in eV) of an α-particle confined to a one-dimensional box the size of the uranium nucleus that has a radius of approximately 15.0 fm?

52. To excite an electron in a one-dimensional box from its first excited state to its third excited state requires 20.0 eV. What is the width of the box?

53. An electron confined to a box of width 0.15 nm by infinite potential energy barriers emits a photon when it makes a transition from the first excited state to the ground state. Find the wavelength of the emitted photon.

54. If the energy of the first excited state of the electron in the box is 25.0 eV, what is the width of the box?

55. Suppose an electron confined to a box emits photons. The longest wavelength that is registered is 500.0 nm. What is the width of the box?

56. Hydrogen H_2 molecules are kept at 300.0 K in a cubical container with a side length of 20.0 cm. Assume that you can treat the molecules as though they were moving in a one-dimensional box. (a) Find the ground state energy of the hydrogen molecule in the container. (b) Assume that the molecule has a thermal energy given by $k_B T/2$ and find the corresponding quantum number n of the quantum state that would correspond to this thermal energy.

57. An electron is confined to a box of width 0.25 nm. (a) Draw an energy-level diagram representing the first five states of the electron. (b) Calculate the wavelengths of the emitted photons when the electron makes transitions between the fourth and the second excited states, between the second excited state and the ground state, and between the third and the second excited states.

58. An electron in a box is in the ground state with energy 2.0 eV. (a) Find the width of the box. (b) How much energy is needed to excite the electron to its first excited state? (c) If the electron makes a transition from an excited state to the ground state with the simultaneous emission of 30.0-eV photon, find the quantum number of the excited state?

7.5 The Quantum Harmonic Oscillator

59. Show that the two lowest energy states of the simple harmonic oscillator, $\psi_0(x)$ and $\psi_1(x)$ from **Equation 7.57**, satisfy **Equation 7.55**.

60. If the ground state energy of a simple harmonic oscillator is 1.25 eV, what is the frequency of its motion?

61. When a quantum harmonic oscillator makes a

transition from the $(n+1)$ state to the n state and emits a 450-nm photon, what is its frequency?

62. Vibrations of the hydrogen molecule H_2 can be modeled as a simple harmonic oscillator with the spring constant $k = 1.13 \times 10^3\,\text{N/m}$ and mass $m = 1.67 \times 10^{-27}\,\text{kg}$. (a) What is the vibrational frequency of this molecule? (b) What are the energy and the wavelength of the emitted photon when the molecule makes transition between its third and second excited states?

63. A particle with mass 0.030 kg oscillates back-and-forth on a spring with frequency 4.0 Hz. At the equilibrium position, it has a speed of 0.60 m/s. If the particle is in a state of definite energy, find its energy quantum number.

64. Find the expectation value $\langle x^2 \rangle$ of the square of the position for a quantum harmonic oscillator in the ground state. Note: $\int_{-\infty}^{+\infty} dx x^2 e^{-ax^2} = \sqrt{\pi}(2a^{3/2})^{-1}$.

65. Determine the expectation value of the potential energy for a quantum harmonic oscillator in the ground state. Use this to calculate the expectation value of the kinetic energy.

66. Verify that $\psi_1(x)$ given by **Equation 7.57** is a solution of Schrödinger's equation for the quantum harmonic oscillator.

67. Estimate the ground state energy of the quantum harmonic oscillator by Heisenberg's uncertainty principle. Start by assuming that the product of the uncertainties Δx and Δp is at its minimum. Write Δp in terms of Δx and assume that for the ground state $x \approx \Delta x$ and $p \approx \Delta p$, then write the ground state energy in terms of x. Finally, find the value of x that minimizes the energy and find the minimum of the energy.

68. A mass of 0.250 kg oscillates on a spring with the force constant 110 N/m. Calculate the ground energy level and the separation between the adjacent energy levels. Express the results in joules and in electron-volts. Are quantum effects important?

7.6 The Quantum Tunneling of Particles through Potential Barriers

69. Show that the wave function in (a) **Equation 7.68** satisfies **Equation 7.61**, and (b) **Equation 7.69** satisfies **Equation 7.63**.

70. A 6.0-eV electron impacts on a barrier with height 11.0 eV. Find the probability of the electron to tunnel through the barrier if the barrier width is (a) 0.80 nm and (b) 0.40 nm.

71. A 5.0-eV electron impacts on a barrier of with 0.60 nm. Find the probability of the electron to tunnel through the barrier if the barrier height is (a) 7.0 eV; (b) 9.0 eV; and (c) 13.0 eV.

72. A 12.0-eV electron encounters a barrier of height 15.0 eV. If the probability of the electron tunneling through the barrier is 2.5 %, find its width.

73. A quantum particle with initial kinetic energy 32.0 eV encounters a square barrier with height 41.0 eV and width 0.25 nm. Find probability that the particle tunnels through this barrier if the particle is (a) an electron and, (b) a proton.

74. A simple model of a radioactive nuclear decay assumes that α-particles are trapped inside a well of nuclear potential that walls are the barriers of a finite width 2.0 fm and height 30.0 MeV. Find the tunneling probability across the potential barrier of the wall for α-particles having kinetic energy (a) 29.0 MeV and (b) 20.0 MeV. The mass of the α-particle is $m = 6.64 \times 10^{-27}\,\text{kg}$.

75. A muon, a quantum particle with a mass approximately 200 times that of an electron, is incident on a potential barrier of height 10.0 eV. The kinetic energy of the impacting muon is 5.5 eV and only about 0.10% of the squared amplitude of its incoming wave function filters through the barrier. What is the barrier's width?

76. A grain of sand with mass 1.0 mg and kinetic energy 1.0 J is incident on a potential energy barrier with height 1.000001 J and width 2500 nm. How many grains of sand have to fall on this barrier before, on the average, one passes through?

ADDITIONAL PROBLEMS

77. Show that if the uncertainty in the position of a particle is on the order of its de Broglie's wavelength, then the uncertainty in its momentum is on the order of the value of its momentum.

78. The mass of a ρ-meson is measured to be

$770\ \text{MeV}/c^2$ with an uncertainty of $100\ \text{MeV}/c^2$. Estimate the lifetime of this meson.

79. A particle of mass m is confined to a box of width L. If the particle is in the first excited state, what are the probabilities of finding the particle in a region of width 0.020 L around the given point x: (a) $x = 0.25L$; (b) $x = 0.40L$; (c) $x = 0.75L$; and (d) $x = 0.90L$.

80. A particle in a box [0;L] is in the third excited state. What are its most probable positions?

81. A 0.20-kg billiard ball bounces back and forth without losing its energy between the cushions of a 1.5 m long table. (a) If the ball is in its ground state, how many years does it need to get from one cushion to the other? You may compare this time interval to the age of the universe. (b) How much energy is required to make the ball go from its ground state to its first excited state? Compare it with the kinetic energy of the ball moving at 2.0 m/s.

82. Find the expectation value of the position squared when the particle in the box is in its third excited state and the length of the box is L.

83. Consider an infinite square well with wall boundaries $x = 0$ and $x = L$. Show that the function $\psi(x) = A \sin kx$ is the solution to the stationary Schrödinger equation for the particle in a box only if $k = \sqrt{2mE}/\hbar$. Explain why this is an acceptable wave function only if k is an integer multiple of π/L.

84. Consider an infinite square well with wall boundaries $x = 0$ and $x = L$. Explain why the function $\psi(x) = A \cos kx$ is not a solution to the stationary Schrödinger equation for the particle in a box.

85. Atoms in a crystal lattice vibrate in simple harmonic motion. Assuming a lattice atom has a mass of 9.4×10^{-26} kg, what is the force constant of the lattice if a lattice atom makes a transition from the ground state to first excited state when it absorbs a 525-μm photon?

86. A diatomic molecule behaves like a quantum harmonic oscillator with the force constant 12.0 N/m and mass 5.60×10^{-26} kg. (a) What is the wavelength of the emitted photon when the molecule makes the transition from the third excited state to the second excited state? (b) Find the ground state energy of vibrations for this diatomic molecule.

87. An electron with kinetic energy 2.0 MeV encounters a potential energy barrier of height 16.0 MeV and width 2.00 nm. What is the probability that the electron emerges on the other side of the barrier?

88. A beam of mono-energetic protons with energy 2.0 MeV falls on a potential energy barrier of height 20.0 MeV and of width 1.5 fm. What percentage of the beam is transmitted through the barrier?

CHALLENGE PROBLEMS

89. An electron in a long, organic molecule used in a dye laser behaves approximately like a quantum particle in a box with width 4.18 nm. Find the emitted photon when the electron makes a transition from the first excited state to the ground state and from the second excited state to the first excited state.

90. In STM, an elevation of the tip above the surface being scanned can be determined with a great precision, because the tunneling-electron current between surface atoms and the atoms of the tip is extremely sensitive to the variation of the separation gap between them from point to point along the surface. Assuming that the tunneling-electron current is in direct proportion to the tunneling probability and that the tunneling probability is to a good approximation expressed by the exponential function $e^{-2\beta L}$ with $\beta = 10.0/\text{nm}$, determine the ratio of the tunneling current when the tip is 0.500 nm above the surface to the current when the tip is 0.515 nm above the surface.

91. If STM is to detect surface features with local heights of about 0.00200 nm, what percent change in tunneling-electron current must the STM electronics be able to detect? Assume that the tunneling-electron current has characteristics given in the preceding problem.

92. Use Heisenberg's uncertainty principle to estimate the ground state energy of a particle oscillating on an spring with angular frequency, $\omega = \sqrt{k/m}$, where k is the spring constant and m is the mass.

93. Suppose an infinite square well extends from $-L/2$ to $+L/2$. Solve the time-independent Schrödinger's equation to find the allowed energies and stationary states of a particle with mass m that is confined to this well. Then show that these solutions can be obtained by making the coordinate transformation $x' = x - L/2$ for the solutions obtained for the well extending between 0 and L.

94. A particle of mass m confined to a box of width L is in its first excited state $\psi_2(x)$. (a) Find its average position (which is the expectation value of the position). (b) Where is the particle most likely to be found?

8 | ATOMIC STRUCTURE

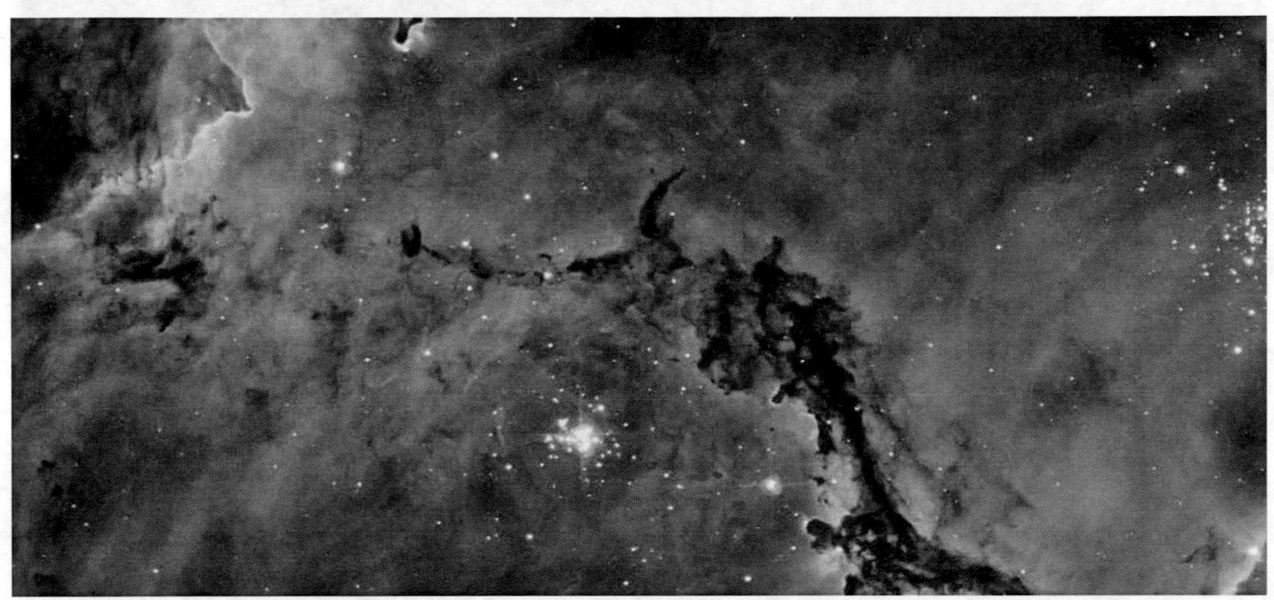

Figure 8.1 NGC1763 is an emission nebula in the Large Magellanic Cloud, which is a satellite galaxy to our Milky Way Galaxy. The colors we see can be explained by applying the ideas of quantum mechanics to atomic structure. (credit: modification of work by NASA, ESA, and Josh Lake)

Chapter Outline

Introduction

In this chapter, we use quantum mechanics to study the structure and properties of atoms. This study introduces ideas and concepts that are necessary to understand more complex systems, such as molecules, crystals, and metals. As we deepen our understanding of atoms, we build on things we already know, such as Rutherford's nuclear model of the atom, Bohr's model of the hydrogen atom, and de Broglie's wave hypothesis.

Figure 8.1 is NGC1763, an emission nebula in the small galaxy known as the Large Magellanic Cloud, which is a satellite of the Milky Way Galaxy. Ultraviolet light from hot stars ionizes the hydrogen atoms in the nebula. As protons and electrons recombine, radiation of different frequencies is emitted. The details of this process can be correctly predicted by quantum mechanics and are examined in this chapter.

8.1 | The Hydrogen Atom

Learning Objectives

By the end of this section, you will be able to:

- Describe the hydrogen atom in terms of wave function, probability density, total energy, and orbital angular momentum
- Identify the physical significance of each of the quantum numbers (n, l, m) of the hydrogen atom
- Distinguish between the Bohr and Schrödinger models of the atom
- Use quantum numbers to calculate important information about the hydrogen atom

The hydrogen atom is the simplest atom in nature and, therefore, a good starting point to study atoms and atomic structure. The hydrogen atom consists of a single negatively charged electron that moves about a positively charged proton (**Figure 8.2**). In Bohr's model, the electron is pulled around the proton in a perfectly circular orbit by an attractive Coulomb force. The proton is approximately 1800 times more massive than the electron, so the proton moves very little in response to the force on the proton by the electron. (This is analogous to the Earth-Sun system, where the Sun moves very little in response to the force exerted on it by Earth.) An explanation of this effect using Newton's laws is given in **Photons and Matter Waves**.

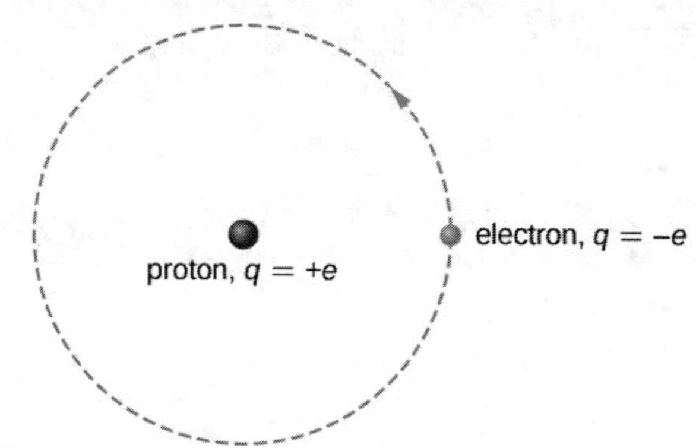

Figure 8.2 A representation of the Bohr model of the hydrogen atom.

With the assumption of a fixed proton, we focus on the motion of the electron.

In the electric field of the proton, the potential energy of the electron is

$$U(r) = -k\frac{e^2}{r}, \tag{8.1}$$

where $k = 1/4\pi\varepsilon_0$ and r is the distance between the electron and the proton. As we saw earlier, the force on an object is equal to the negative of the gradient (or slope) of the potential energy function. For the special case of a hydrogen atom, the force between the electron and proton is an attractive Coulomb force.

Notice that the potential energy function $U(r)$ does not vary in time. As a result, Schrödinger's equation of the hydrogen atom reduces to two simpler equations: one that depends only on space (x, y, z) and another that depends only on time (t). (The separation of a wave function into space- and time-dependent parts for time-independent potential energy functions is discussed in **Quantum Mechanics**.) We are most interested in the space-dependent equation:

$$\frac{-\hbar^2}{2m_e}\left(\frac{\partial^2\psi}{\partial x^2} + \frac{\partial^2\psi}{\partial y^2} + \frac{\partial^2\psi}{\partial z^2}\right) - k\frac{e^2}{r}\psi = E\psi, \tag{8.2}$$

where $\psi = \psi(x, y, z)$ is the three-dimensional wave function of the electron, m_e is the mass of the electron, and E is the total energy of the electron. Recall that the total wave function $\Psi(x, y, z, t),$ is the product of the space-dependent wave function $\psi = \psi(x, y, z)$ and the time-dependent wave function $\varphi = \varphi(t)$.

In addition to being time-independent, $U(r)$ is also spherically symmetrical. This suggests that we may solve Schrödinger's equation more easily if we express it in terms of the spherical coordinates (r, θ, ϕ) instead of rectangular coordinates (x, y, z). A spherical coordinate system is shown in **Figure 8.3**. In spherical coordinates, the variable r is the radial coordinate, θ is the polar angle (relative to the vertical z-axis), and ϕ is the azimuthal angle (relative to the x-axis). The relationship between spherical and rectangular coordinates is $x = r\sin\theta\cos\phi, \quad y = r\sin\theta\sin\phi, \quad z = r\cos\theta.$

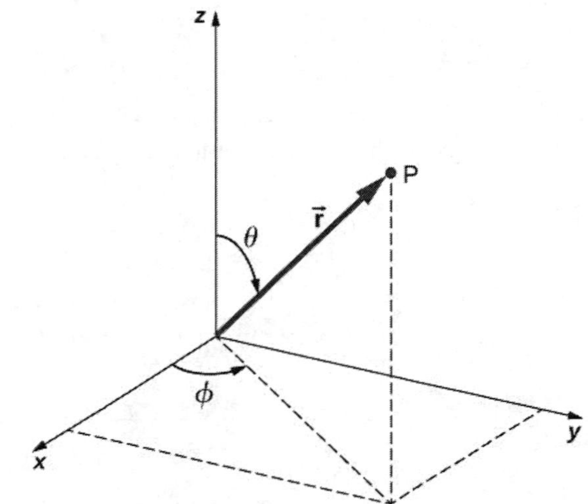

Figure 8.3 The relationship between the spherical and rectangular coordinate systems.

The factor $r\sin\theta$ is the magnitude of a vector formed by the projection of the polar vector onto the xy-plane. Also, the coordinates of x and y are obtained by projecting this vector onto the x- and y-axes, respectively. The inverse transformation gives

$$r = \sqrt{x^2 + y^2 + z^2}, \quad \theta = \cos^{-1}\left(\frac{z}{r}\right), \quad \phi = \cos^{-1}\left(\frac{x}{\sqrt{x^2 + y^2}}\right).$$

Schrödinger's wave equation for the hydrogen atom in spherical coordinates is discussed in more advanced courses in modern physics, so we do not consider it in detail here. However, due to the spherical symmetry of $U(r)$, this equation reduces to three simpler equations: one for each of the three coordinates $(r, \theta, \text{ and } \phi)$. Solutions to the time-independent wave function are written as a product of three functions:

$$\psi(r, \theta, \phi) = R(r)\Theta(\theta)\Phi(\phi),$$

where R is the radial function dependent on the radial coordinate r only; Θ is the polar function dependent on the polar coordinate θ only; and Φ is the phi function of ϕ only. Valid solutions to Schrödinger's equation $\psi(r, \theta, \phi)$ are labeled by the quantum numbers n, l, and m.

n : principal quantum number
l : angular momentum quantum number
m : angular momentum projection quantum number

(The reasons for these names will be explained in the next section.) The radial function R depends only on n and l; the polar function Θ depends only on l and m; and the phi function Φ depends only on m. The dependence of each function on quantum numbers is indicated with subscripts:

$$\psi_{nlm}(r, \theta, \phi) = R_{nl}(r)\Theta_{lm}(\theta)\Phi_m(\phi).$$

Not all sets of quantum numbers (n, l, m) are possible. For example, the orbital angular quantum number l can never be greater or equal to the principal quantum number $n(l < n)$. Specifically, we have

$$\begin{aligned} n &= 1, 2, 3, \ldots \\ l &= 0, 1, 2, \ldots, (n-1) \\ m &= -l, (-l+1), \ldots, 0, \ldots, (+l-1), +l \end{aligned}$$

Notice that for the ground state, $n = 1$, $l = 0$, and $m = 0$. In other words, there is only one quantum state with the wave function for $n = 1$, and it is ψ_{100}. However, for $n = 2$, we have

$$\begin{aligned} l &= 0, \quad m = 0 \\ l &= 1, \quad m = -1, 0, 1. \end{aligned}$$

Therefore, the allowed states for the $n = 2$ state are ψ_{200}, ψ_{21-1}, ψ_{210}, and ψ_{211}. Example wave functions for the hydrogen atom are given in **Table 8.1**. Note that some of these expressions contain the letter *i*, which represents $\sqrt{-1}$. When probabilities are calculated, these complex numbers do not appear in the final answer.

$n = 1, l = 0, m_l = 0$	$\psi_{100} = \frac{1}{\sqrt{\pi}} \frac{1}{a_0^{3/2}} e^{-r/a_0}$
$n = 2, l = 0, m_l = 0$	$\psi_{200} = \frac{1}{4\sqrt{2\pi}} \frac{1}{a_0^{3/2}} \left(2 - \frac{r}{a_0}\right) e^{-r/2a_0}$
$n = 2, l = 1, m_l = -1$	$\psi_{21-1} = \frac{1}{8\sqrt{\pi}} \frac{1}{a_0^{3/2}} \frac{r}{a_0} e^{-r/2a_0} \sin\theta e^{-i\phi}$
$n = 2, l = 1, m_l = 0$	$\psi_{210} = \frac{1}{4\sqrt{2\pi}} \frac{1}{a_0^{3/2}} \frac{r}{a_0} e^{-r/2a_0} \cos\theta$
$n = 2, l = 1, m_l = 1$	$\psi_{211} = \frac{1}{8\sqrt{\pi}} \frac{1}{a_0^{3/2}} \frac{r}{a_0} e^{-r/2a_0} \sin\theta e^{i\phi}$

Table 8.1 Wave Functions of the Hydrogen Atom

Physical Significance of the Quantum Numbers

Each of the three quantum numbers of the hydrogen atom (*n, l, m*) is associated with a different physical quantity. The **principal quantum number** *n* is associated with the total energy of the electron, E_n. According to Schrödinger's equation:

$$E_n = -\left(\frac{m_e k^2 e^4}{2\hbar^2}\right)\left(\frac{1}{n^2}\right) = -E_0\left(\frac{1}{n^2}\right), \quad (8.3)$$

where $E_0 = -13.6\text{ eV}$. Notice that this expression is identical to that of Bohr's model. As in the Bohr model, the electron in a particular state of energy does not radiate.

Example 8.1

How Many Possible States?

For the hydrogen atom, how many possible quantum states correspond to the principal number $n = 3$? What are the energies of these states?

Strategy

For a hydrogen atom of a given energy, the number of allowed states depends on its orbital angular momentum. We can count these states for each value of the principal quantum number, $n = 1, 2, 3$. However, the total energy depends on the principal quantum number only, which means that we can use **Equation 8.3** and the number of states counted.

Solution

If $n = 3$, the allowed values of l are 0, 1, and 2. If $l = 0$, $m = 0$ (1 state). If $l = 1$, $m = -1, 0, +1$ (3 states); and if $l = 2$, $m = -2, -1, 0, +1, +2$ (5 states). In total, there are $1 + 3 + 5 = 9$ allowed states. Because the total energy depends only on the principal quantum number, $n = 3$, the energy of each of these states is

$$E_{n3} = -E_0\left(\frac{1}{n^2}\right) = \frac{-13.6\,\text{eV}}{9} = -1.51\,\text{eV}.$$

Significance

An electron in a hydrogen atom can occupy many different angular momentum states with the very same energy. As the orbital angular momentum increases, the number of the allowed states with the same energy increases.

The **angular momentum orbital quantum number** l is associated with the orbital angular momentum of the electron in a hydrogen atom. Quantum theory tells us that when the hydrogen atom is in the state ψ_{nlm}, the magnitude of its orbital angular momentum is

$$L = \sqrt{l(l+1)}\hbar, \tag{8.4}$$

where

$$l = 0,\ 1,\ 2,\ \ldots,\ (n-1).$$

This result is slightly different from that found with Bohr's theory, which quantizes angular momentum according to the rule $L = n$, where $n = 1, 2, 3, \ldots$.

Quantum states with different values of orbital angular momentum are distinguished using spectroscopic notation (**Table 8.2**). The designations *s*, *p*, *d*, and *f* result from early historical attempts to classify atomic spectral lines. (The letters stand for sharp, principal, diffuse, and fundamental, respectively.) After *f*, the letters continue alphabetically.

The ground state of hydrogen is designated as the 1*s* state, where "1" indicates the energy level $(n = 1)$ and "*s*" indicates the orbital angular momentum state ($l = 0$). When $n = 2$, l can be either 0 or 1. The $n = 2$, $l = 0$ state is designated "2*s*." The $n = 2$, $l = 1$ state is designated "2*p*." When $n = 3$, l can be 0, 1, or 2, and the states are 3*s*, 3*p*, and 3*d*, respectively. Notation for other quantum states is given in **Table 8.3**.

The **angular momentum projection quantum number** m is associated with the azimuthal angle ϕ (see **Figure 8.3**) and is related to the *z*-component of orbital angular momentum of an electron in a hydrogen atom. This component is given by

$$L_z = m\hbar, \tag{8.5}$$

where

$$m = -l,\ -l+1,\ \ldots,\ 0,\ \ldots,\ +l-1,\ l.$$

The *z*-component of angular momentum is related to the magnitude of angular momentum by

$$L_z = L\cos\theta, \tag{8.6}$$

where θ is the angle between the angular momentum vector and the *z*-axis. Note that the direction of the *z*-axis is determined by experiment—that is, along any direction, the experimenter decides to measure the angular momentum. For example, the *z*-direction might correspond to the direction of an external magnetic field. The relationship between L_z and L is given in **Figure 8.4**.

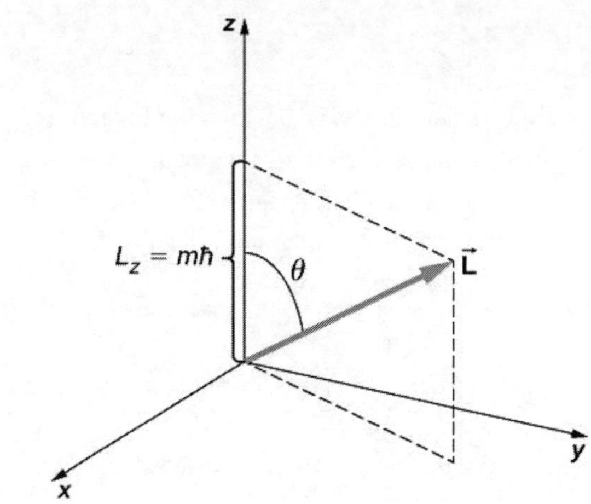

Figure 8.4 The *z*-component of angular momentum is quantized with its own quantum number *m*.

Orbital Quantum Number *l*	Angular Momentum	State	Spectroscopic Name
0	0	*s*	Sharp
1	$\sqrt{2}h$	*p*	Principal
2	$\sqrt{6}h$	*d*	Diffuse
3	$\sqrt{12}h$	*f*	Fundamental
4	$\sqrt{20}h$	*g*	
5	$\sqrt{30}h$	*h*	

Table 8.2 Spectroscopic Notation and Orbital Angular Momentum

	$l = 0$	$l = 1$	$l = 2$	$l = 3$	$l = 4$	$l = 5$
$n = 1$	1*s*					
$n = 2$	2*s*	2*p*				
$n = 3$	3*s*	3*p*	3*d*			
$n = 4$	4*s*	4*p*	4*d*	4*f*		
$n = 5$	5*s*	5*p*	5*d*	5*f*	5*g*	
$n = 6$	6*s*	6*p*	6*d*	6*f*	6*g*	6*h*

Table 8.3 Spectroscopic Description of Quantum States

The quantization of L_z is equivalent to the quantization of θ. Substituting $\sqrt{l(l+1)}\hbar$ for L and m for L_z into this equation, we find

$$m\hbar = \sqrt{l(l+1)}\hbar \cos\theta. \tag{8.7}$$

Thus, the angle θ is quantized with the particular values

$$\theta = \cos^{-1}\left(\frac{m}{\sqrt{l(l+1)}}\right). \tag{8.8}$$

Notice that both the polar angle (θ) and the projection of the angular momentum vector onto an arbitrary *z*-axis (L_z) are quantized.

The quantization of the polar angle for the $l = 3$ state is shown in **Figure 8.5**. The orbital angular momentum vector lies somewhere on the surface of a cone with an opening angle θ relative to the *z*-axis (unless $m = 0,$ in which case $\theta = 90°$ and the vector points are perpendicular to the *z*-axis).

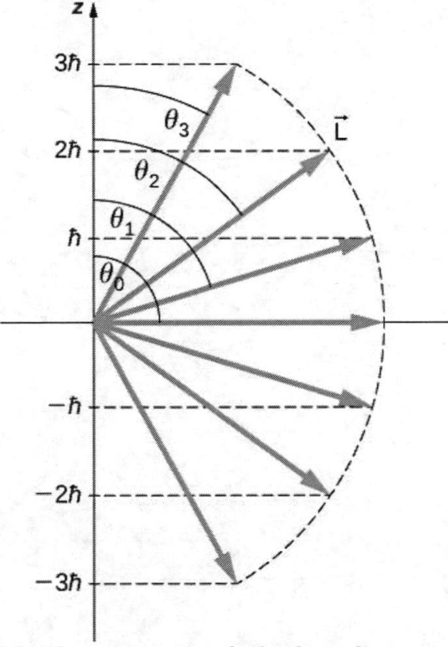

Figure 8.5 The quantization of orbital angular momentum. Each vector lies on the surface of a cone with axis along the *z*-axis.

A detailed study of angular momentum reveals that we cannot know all three components simultaneously. In the previous section, the *z*-component of orbital angular momentum has definite values that depend on the quantum number *m*. This implies that we cannot know both *x*- and *y*-components of angular momentum, L_x and L_y, with certainty. As a result, the precise direction of the orbital angular momentum vector is unknown.

Example 8.2

What Are the Allowed Directions?

Calculate the angles that the angular momentum vector $\vec{\mathbf{L}}$ can make with the *z*-axis for $l = 1$, as shown in **Figure 8.6**.

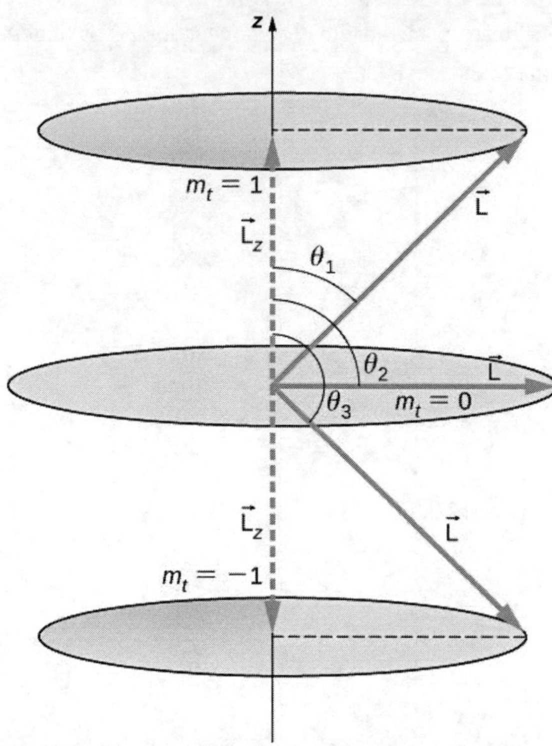

Figure 8.6 The component of a given angular momentum along the *z*-axis (defined by the direction of a magnetic field) can have only certain values. These are shown here for $l = 1$, for which $m = -1, 0, \text{ and} + 1$. The direction of $\vec{\mathbf{L}}$ is quantized in the sense that it can have only certain angles relative to the *z*-axis.

Strategy

The vectors $\vec{\mathbf{L}}$ and $\vec{\mathbf{L}}_z$ (in the *z*-direction) form a right triangle, where $\vec{\mathbf{L}}$ is the hypotenuse and $\vec{\mathbf{L}}_z$ is the adjacent side. The ratio of L_z to $|\vec{\mathbf{L}}|$ is the cosine of the angle of interest. The magnitudes $L = \left|\vec{\mathbf{L}}\right|$ and L_z are given by

$$L = \sqrt{l(l+1)}\hbar \text{ and } L_z = m\hbar.$$

Solution

We are given $l = 1$, so *ml* can be $+1, 0, \text{or } -1$. Thus, *L* has the value given by

$$L = \sqrt{l(l+1)}\hbar = \sqrt{2}\hbar.$$

The quantity L_z can have three values, given by $L_z = m_l\hbar$.

$$L_z = m_l\hbar = \begin{cases} \hbar, & m_l = +1 \\ 0, & m_l = 0 \\ -\hbar, & m_l = -1 \end{cases}$$

As you can see in **Figure 8.6**, $\cos\theta = L_z/L$, so for $m = +1$, we have

$$\cos\theta_1 = \frac{L_Z}{L} = \frac{\hbar}{\sqrt{2}\hbar} = \frac{1}{\sqrt{2}} = 0.707.$$

Thus,

$$\theta_1 = \cos^{-1} 0.707 = 45.0°.$$

Similarly, for $m = 0$, we find $\cos\theta_2 = 0$; this gives

$$\theta_2 = \cos^{-1} 0 = 90.0°.$$

Then for $m_l = -1$:

$$\cos\theta_3 = \frac{L_Z}{L} = \frac{-\hbar}{\sqrt{2}\hbar} = -\frac{1}{\sqrt{2}} = -0.707,$$

so that

$$\theta_3 = \cos^{-1}(-0.707) = 135.0°.$$

Significance

The angles are consistent with the figure. Only the angle relative to the *z*-axis is quantized. *L* can point in any direction as long as it makes the proper angle with the *z*-axis. Thus, the angular momentum vectors lie on cones, as illustrated. To see how the correspondence principle holds here, consider that the smallest angle (θ_1 in the example) is for the maximum value of m_l, namely $m_l = l$. For that smallest angle,

$$\cos\theta = \frac{L_z}{L} = \frac{l}{\sqrt{l(l+1)}},$$

which approaches 1 as l becomes very large. If $\cos\theta = 1$, then $\theta = 0°$. Furthermore, for large l, there are many values of m_l, so that all angles become possible as l gets very large.

8.1 Check Your Understanding Can the magnitude of L_z ever be equal to L?

Using the Wave Function to Make Predictions

As we saw earlier, we can use quantum mechanics to make predictions about physical events by the use of probability statements. It is therefore proper to state, "An electron is located within this volume with this probability at this time," but not, "An electron is located at the position (*x*, *y*, *z*) at this time." To determine the probability of finding an electron in a hydrogen atom in a particular region of space, it is necessary to integrate the probability density $|\psi_{nlm}|^2$ over that region:

$$\text{Probability} = \int_{\text{volume}} |\psi_{nlm}|^2 dV, \tag{8.9}$$

where dV is an infinitesimal volume element. If this integral is computed for all space, the result is 1, because the probability of the particle to be located *somewhere* is 100% (the normalization condition). In a more advanced course on modern physics, you will find that $|\psi_{nlm}|^2 = \psi^*_{nlm}\psi_{nlm}$, where ψ^*_{nlm} is the complex conjugate. This eliminates the occurrences of $i = \sqrt{-1}$ in the above calculation.

Consider an electron in a state of zero angular momentum ($l = 0$). In this case, the electron's wave function depends only on the radial coordinate *r*. (Refer to the states ψ_{100} and ψ_{200} in **Table 8.1**.) The infinitesimal volume element corresponds to a spherical shell of radius *r* and infinitesimal thickness *dr*, written as

$$dV = 4\pi r^2 dr. \tag{8.10}$$

The probability of finding the electron in the region r to $r + dr$ ("at approximately *r*") is

$$P(r)dr = \left|\psi_{n00}\right|^2 4\pi r^2 dr. \tag{8.11}$$

Here $P(r)$ is called the **radial probability density function** (a probability per unit length). For an electron in the ground state of hydrogen, the probability of finding an electron in the region r to $r + dr$ is

$$\left|\psi_{n00}\right|^2 4\pi r^2 dr = (4/a_0^3)r^2 \exp(-2r/a_0)dr, \tag{8.12}$$

where $a_0 = 0.5$ angstroms. The radial probability density function $P(r)$ is plotted in **Figure 8.7**. The area under the curve between any two radial positions, say r_1 and r_2, gives the probability of finding the electron in that radial range. To find the most probable radial position, we set the first derivative of this function to zero ($dP/dr = 0$) and solve for r. The most probable radial position is not equal to the average or expectation value of the radial position because $|\psi_{n00}|^2$ is not symmetrical about its peak value.

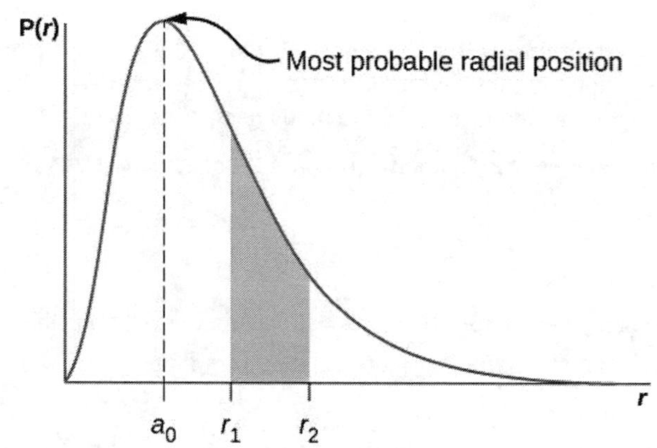

Figure 8.7 The radial probability density function for the ground state of hydrogen.

If the electron has orbital angular momentum ($l \neq 0$), then the wave functions representing the electron depend on the angles θ and ϕ; that is, $\psi_{nlm} = \psi_{nlm}(r, \theta, \phi)$. Atomic orbitals for three states with $n = 2$ and $l = 1$ are shown in **Figure 8.8**. An **atomic orbital** is a region in space that encloses a certain percentage (usually 90%) of the electron probability. (Sometimes atomic orbitals are referred to as "clouds" of probability.) Notice that these distributions are pronounced in certain directions. This directionality is important to chemists when they analyze how atoms are bound together to form molecules.

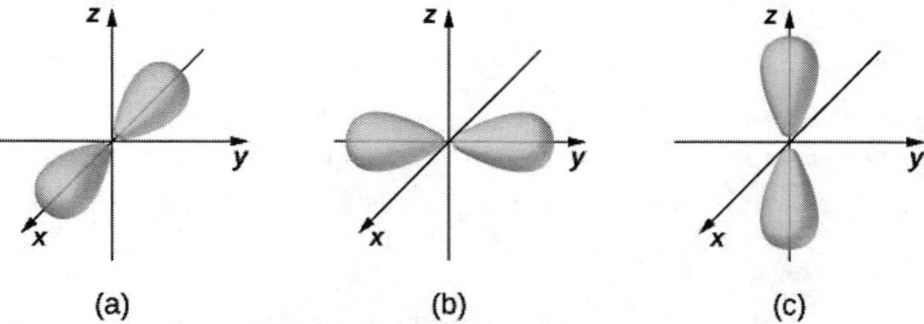

Figure 8.8 The probability density distributions for three states with $n = 2$ and $l = 1$. The distributions are directed along the (a) x-axis, (b) y-axis, and (c) z-axis.

A slightly different representation of the wave function is given in **Figure 8.9**. In this case, light and dark regions indicate locations of relatively high and low probability, respectively. In contrast to the Bohr model of the hydrogen atom, the electron does not move around the proton nucleus in a well-defined path. Indeed, the uncertainty principle makes it impossible to know how the electron gets from one place to another.

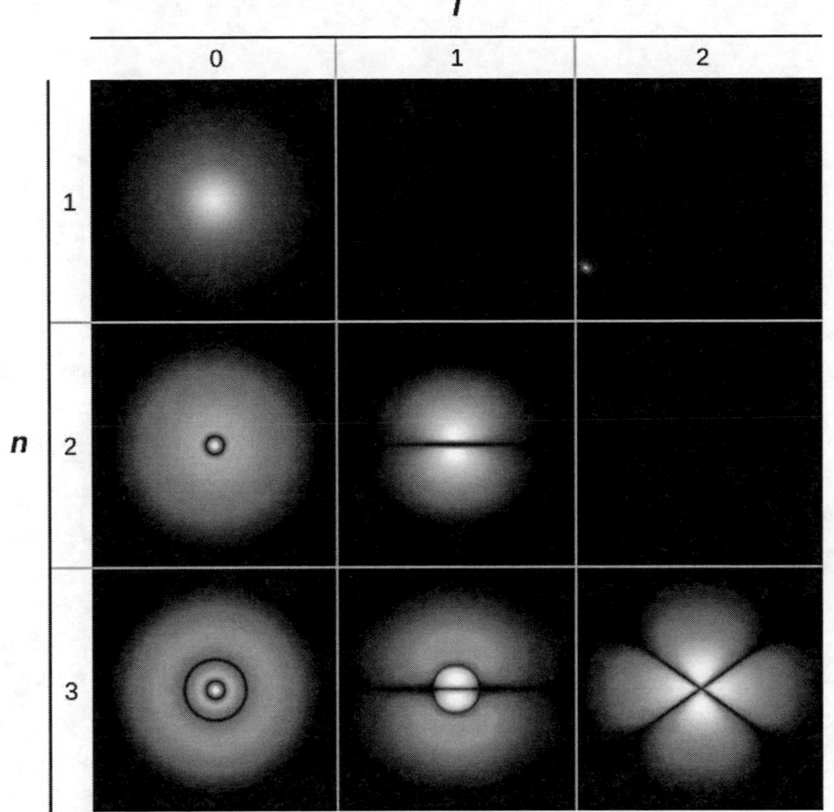

Figure 8.9 Probability clouds for the electron in the ground state and several excited states of hydrogen. The probability of finding the electron is indicated by the shade of color; the lighter the coloring, the greater the chance of finding the electron.

8.2 | Orbital Magnetic Dipole Moment of the Electron

Learning Objectives

By the end of this section, you will be able to:

- Explain why the hydrogen atom has magnetic properties
- Explain why the energy levels of a hydrogen atom associated with orbital angular momentum are split by an external magnetic field
- Use quantum numbers to calculate the magnitude and direction of the orbital magnetic dipole moment of a hydrogen atom

In Bohr's model of the hydrogen atom, the electron moves in a circular orbit around the proton. The electron passes by a particular point on the loop in a certain time, so we can calculate a current $I = Q/t$. An electron that orbits a proton in a hydrogen atom is therefore analogous to current flowing through a circular wire (**Figure 8.10**). In the study of magnetism, we saw that a current-carrying wire produces magnetic fields. It is therefore reasonable to conclude that the hydrogen atom produces a magnetic field and interacts with other magnetic fields.

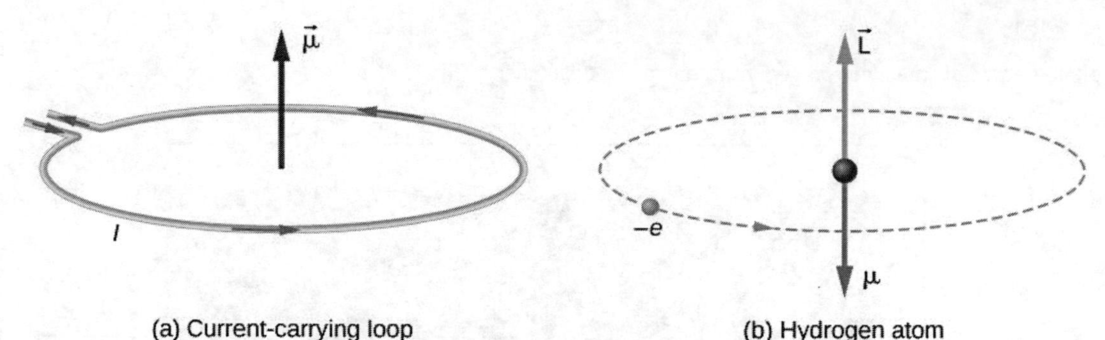

Figure 8.10 (a) Current flowing through a circular wire is analogous to (b) an electron that orbits a proton in a hydrogen atom.

The **orbital magnetic dipole moment** is a measure of the strength of the magnetic field produced by the orbital angular momentum of an electron. From **Force and Torque on a Current Loop (http://cnx.org/content/m58743/latest/#fs-id1171360245659)** , the magnitude of the orbital magnetic dipole moment for a current loop is

$$\mu = IA, \tag{8.13}$$

where I is the current and A is the area of the loop. (For brevity, we refer to this as the magnetic moment.) The current I associated with an electron in orbit about a proton in a hydrogen atom is

$$I = \frac{e}{T}, \tag{8.14}$$

where e is the magnitude of the electron charge and T is its orbital period. If we assume that the electron travels in a perfectly circular orbit, the orbital period is

$$T = \frac{2\pi r}{v}, \tag{8.15}$$

where r is the radius of the orbit and v is the speed of the electron in its orbit. Given that the area of a circle is πr^2, the absolute magnetic moment is

$$\mu = IA = \frac{e}{\left(\frac{2\pi r}{v}\right)}\pi r^2 = \frac{evr}{2}. \tag{8.16}$$

It is helpful to express the magnetic momentum μ in terms of the orbital angular momentum ($\vec{\mathbf{L}} = \vec{\mathbf{r}} \times \vec{\mathbf{p}}$). Because the electron orbits in a circle, the position vector $\vec{\mathbf{r}}$ and the momentum vector $\vec{\mathbf{p}}$ form a right angle. Thus, the magnitude of the orbital angular momentum is

$$L = \left|\vec{\mathbf{L}}\right| = \left|\vec{\mathbf{r}} \times \vec{\mathbf{p}}\right| = rp\sin\theta = rp = rmv. \tag{8.17}$$

Combining these two equations, we have

$$\mu = \left(\frac{e}{2m_e}\right)L. \tag{8.18}$$

In full vector form, this expression is written as

$$\vec{\mu} = -\left(\frac{e}{2m_e}\right)\vec{L}. \tag{8.19}$$

The negative sign appears because the electron has a negative charge. Notice that the direction of the magnetic moment of the electron is antiparallel to the orbital angular momentum, as shown in **Figure 8.10**(b). In the Bohr model of the atom, the relationship between $\vec{\mu}$ and $\vec{\mathbf{L}}$ in **Equation 8.19** is independent of the radius of the orbit.

The magnetic moment μ can also be expressed in terms of the orbital angular quantum number l. Combining **Equation**

8.18 and Equation 8.15, the magnitude of the magnetic moment is

$$\mu = \left(\frac{e}{2m_e}\right)L = \left(\frac{e}{2m_e}\right)\sqrt{l(l+1)}\hbar = \mu_B\sqrt{l(l+1)}. \quad (8.20)$$

The z-component of the magnetic moment is

$$\mu_z = -\left(\frac{e}{2m_e}\right)L_z = -\left(\frac{e}{2m_e}\right)m\hbar = -\mu_B m. \quad (8.21)$$

The quantity μ_B is a fundamental unit of magnetism called the **Bohr magneton**, which has the value 9.3×10^{-24} joule/tesla (J/T) or 5.8×10^{-5} eV/T. Quantization of the magnetic moment is the result of quantization of the orbital angular momentum.

As we will see in the next section, the total magnetic dipole moment of the hydrogen atom is due to both the orbital motion of the electron and its intrinsic spin. For now, we ignore the effect of electron spin.

Example 8.3

Orbital Magnetic Dipole Moment

What is the magnitude of the orbital dipole magnetic moment μ of an electron in the hydrogen atom in the (a) *s* state, (b) *p* state, and (c) *d* state? (Assume that the spin of the electron is zero.)

Strategy

The magnetic momentum of the electron is related to its orbital angular momentum L. For the hydrogen atom, this quantity is related to the orbital angular quantum number l. The states are given in spectroscopic notation, which relates a letter (*s*, *p*, *d*, etc.) to a quantum number.

Solution

The magnitude of the magnetic moment is given in Equation 8.20:

$$\mu = \left(\frac{e}{2m_e}\right)L = \left(\frac{e}{2m_e}\right)\sqrt{l(l+1)}\hbar = \mu_B\sqrt{l(l+1)}.$$

a. For the *s* state, $l = 0$ so we have $\mu = 0$ and $\mu_z = 0$.

b. For the *p* state, $l = 1$ and we have

$$\mu = \mu_B\sqrt{1(1+1)} = \sqrt{2}\mu_B$$
$$\mu_z = -\mu_B m, \text{ where } m = (-1, 0, 1), \text{ so}$$
$$\mu_z = \mu_B, 0, -\mu_B.$$

c. For the *d* state, $l = 2$ and we obtain

$$\mu = \mu_B\sqrt{2(2+1)} = \sqrt{6}\mu_B$$
$$\mu_z = -\mu_B m, \text{ where } m = (-2, -1, 0, 1, 2), \text{ so}$$
$$\mu_z = 2\mu_B, \mu_B, 0, -\mu_B, -2\mu_B.$$

Significance

In the *s* state, there is no orbital angular momentum and therefore no magnetic moment. This does not mean that the electron is at rest, just that the overall motion of the electron does not produce a magnetic field. In the *p* state, the electron has a magnetic moment with three possible values for the z-component of this magnetic moment; this means that magnetic moment can point in three different polar directions—each antiparallel to the orbital angular momentum vector. In the *d* state, the electron has a magnetic moment with five possible values for the z-component of this magnetic moment. In this case, the magnetic moment can point in five different polar directions.

A hydrogen atom has a magnetic field, so we expect the hydrogen atom to interact with an external magnetic field—such as the push and pull between two bar magnets. From **Force and Torque on a Current Loop (http://cnx.org/content/m58743/latest/#fs-id1171360288680)** , we know that when a current loop interacts with an external magnetic field $\vec{\mathbf{B}}$, it experiences a torque given by

$$\vec{\tau} = I\left(\vec{\mathbf{A}} \times \vec{\mathbf{B}}\right) = \vec{\mu} \times \vec{\mathbf{B}}, \tag{8.22}$$

where I is the current, $\vec{\mathbf{A}}$ is the area of the loop, $\vec{\mu}$ is the magnetic moment, and $\vec{\mathbf{B}}$ is the external magnetic field. This torque acts to rotate the magnetic moment vector of the hydrogen atom to align with the external magnetic field. Because mechanical work is done by the external magnetic field on the hydrogen atom, we can talk about energy transformations in the atom. The potential energy of the hydrogen atom associated with this magnetic interaction is given by **Equation 8.23**:

$$U = -\vec{\mu} \cdot \vec{B}. \tag{8.23}$$

If the magnetic moment is antiparallel to the external magnetic field, the potential energy is large, but if the magnetic moment is parallel to the field, the potential energy is small. Work done on the hydrogen atom to rotate the atom's magnetic moment vector in the direction of the external magnetic field is therefore associated with a drop in potential energy. The energy of the system is conserved, however, because a drop in potential energy produces radiation (the emission of a photon). These energy transitions are quantized because the magnetic moment can point in only certain directions.

If the external magnetic field points in the positive z-direction, the potential energy associated with the orbital magnetic dipole moment is

$$U(\theta) = -\mu B \cos\theta = -\mu_z B = -(-\mu_{\mathrm{B}} m)B = m\mu_{\mathrm{B}} B, \tag{8.24}$$

where μ_B is the Bohr magneton and m is the angular momentum projection quantum number (or **magnetic orbital quantum number**), which has the values

$$m = -l, -l+1, \ldots, 0, \ldots, l-1, l. \tag{8.25}$$

For example, in the $l = 1$ electron state, the total energy of the electron is split into three distinct energy levels corresponding to $U = -\mu_{\mathrm{B}} B, 0, \mu_{\mathrm{B}} B$.

The splitting of energy levels by an external magnetic field is called the **Zeeman effect**. Ignoring the effects of electron spin, transitions from the $l = 1$ state to a common lower energy state produce three closely spaced spectral lines (**Figure 8.11**, left column). Likewise, transitions from the $l = 2$ state produce five closely spaced spectral lines (right column). The separation of these lines is proportional to the strength of the external magnetic field. This effect has many applications. For example, the splitting of lines in the hydrogen spectrum of the Sun is used to determine the strength of the Sun's magnetic field. Many such magnetic field measurements can be used to make a map of the magnetic activity at the Sun's surface called a **magnetogram** (**Figure 8.12**).

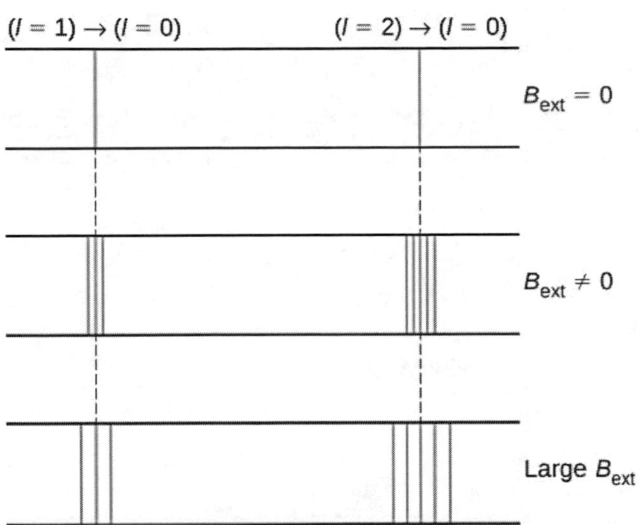

Figure 8.11 The Zeeman effect refers to the splitting of spectral lines by an external magnetic field. In the left column, the energy splitting occurs due to transitions from the state $(n = 2,\ l = 1)$ to a lower energy state; and in the right column, energy splitting occurs due to transitions from the state $(n = 2, l = 2)$ to a lower-energy state. The separation of these lines is proportional to the strength of the external magnetic field.

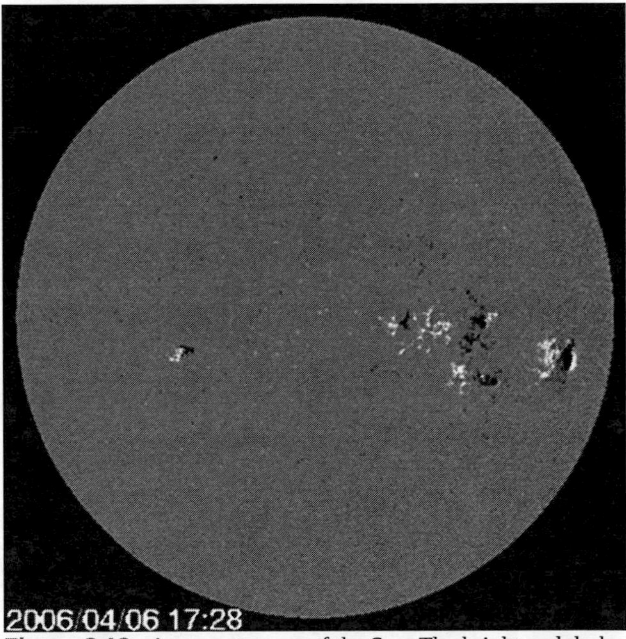

Figure 8.12 A magnetogram of the Sun. The bright and dark spots show significant magnetic activity at the surface of the Sun. (credit: NASA, SDO)

8.3 | Electron Spin

Learning Objectives

By the end of this section, you will be able to:

- Express the state of an electron in a hydrogen atom in terms of five quantum numbers
- Use quantum numbers to calculate the magnitude and direction of the spin and magnetic moment of an electron
- Explain the fine and hyperfine structure of the hydrogen spectrum in terms of magnetic interactions inside the hydrogen atom

In this section, we consider the effects of electron spin. Spin introduces two additional quantum numbers to our model of the hydrogen atom. Both were discovered by looking at the fine structure of atomic spectra. Spin is a fundamental characteristic of all particles, not just electrons, and is analogous to the intrinsic spin of extended bodies about their own axes, such as the daily rotation of Earth.

Spin is quantized in the same manner as orbital angular momentum. It has been found that the magnitude of the intrinsic spin angular momentum S of an electron is given by

$$S = \sqrt{s(s+1)}\hbar, \quad (8.26)$$

where s is defined to be the **spin quantum number**. This is similar to the quantization of L given in **Equation 8.4**, except that the only value allowed for s for an electron is $s = 1/2$. The electron is said to be a "spin-half particle." The **spin projection quantum number** m_s is associated with the z-components of spin, expressed by

$$S_z = m_s \hbar. \quad (8.27)$$

In general, the allowed quantum numbers are

$$m_s = -s, -s+1, \ldots, 0, \ldots, +s-1, s. \quad (8.28)$$

For the special case of an electron ($s = 1/2$),

$$m_s = -\frac{1}{2}, \frac{1}{2}. \quad (8.29)$$

Directions of intrinsic spin are quantized, just as they were for orbital angular momentum. The $m_s = -1/2$ state is called the "spin-down" state and has a z-component of spin, $s_z = -1/2$; the $m_s = +1/2$ state is called the "spin-up" state and has a z-component of spin, $s_z = +1/2$. These states are shown in **Figure 8.13**.

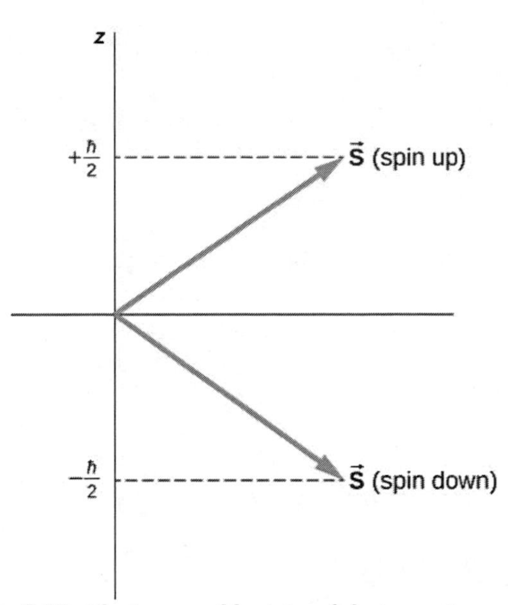

Figure 8.13 The two possible states of electron spin.

The intrinsic magnetic dipole moment of an electron μ_e can also be expressed in terms of the spin quantum number. In analogy to the orbital angular momentum, the magnitude of the electron magnetic moment is

$$\mu_s = \left(\frac{e}{2m_e}\right)S. \tag{8.30}$$

According to the special theory of relativity, this value is low by a factor of 2. Thus, in vector form, the spin magnetic moment is

$$\vec{\mu} = \left(\frac{e}{m_e}\right)\vec{S}. \tag{8.31}$$

The z-component of the magnetic moment is

$$\mu_z = -\left(\frac{e}{m_e}\right)S_z = -\left(\frac{e}{m_e}\right)m_s\,\hbar. \tag{8.32}$$

The spin projection quantum number has just two values $(m_s = \pm 1/2)$, so the z-component of the magnetic moment also has just two values:

$$\mu_z = \pm\left(\frac{e}{2m_e}\right) = \pm\,\mu_\mathrm{B}\,\hbar, \tag{8.33}$$

where μ_B is one Bohr magneton. An electron is magnetic, so we expect the electron to interact with other magnetic fields. We consider two special cases: the interaction of a free electron with an external (nonuniform) magnetic field, and an electron in a hydrogen atom with a magnetic field produced by the orbital angular momentum of the electron.

Example 8.4

Electron Spin and Radiation

A hydrogen atom in the ground state is placed in an external uniform magnetic field ($B = 1.5\ \mathrm{T}$). Determine the frequency of radiation produced in a transition between the spin-up and spin-down states of the electron.

Strategy

The spin projection quantum number is $m_s = \pm 1/2$, so the z-component of the magnetic moment is

$$\mu_z = \pm\left(\frac{e}{2m_e}\right) = \pm \mu_B \hbar.$$

The potential energy associated with the interaction between the electron magnetic moment and the external magnetic field is

$$U = -\mu_z B = \mp \mu_B B.$$

The frequency of light emitted is proportional to the energy (ΔE) difference between these two states.

Solution

The energy difference between these states is $\Delta E = 2\mu_B B$, so the frequency of radiation produced is

$$f = \frac{\Delta E}{h} = \frac{2\mu_B B}{h} = \frac{2\left(5.79 \times \frac{10^{-5}\ \text{eV}}{\text{T}}\right)(1.5\text{T})}{4.136 \times 10^{-15}\ \text{eV} \cdot \text{s}} = 4.2 \times 10^{10} \frac{\text{cycles}}{\text{s}}.$$

Significance

The electron magnetic moment couples with the external magnetic field. The energy of this system is different whether the electron is aligned or not with the proton. The frequency of radiation produced by a transition between these states is proportional to the energy difference. If we double the strength of the magnetic field, holding all other things constant, the frequency of the radiation doubles and its wavelength is cut in half.

In a hydrogen atom, the electron magnetic moment can interact with the magnetic field produced by the orbital angular momentum of the electron, a phenomenon called **spin-orbit coupling**. The orbital angular momentum ($\vec{L}$), orbital magnetic moment ($\vec{\mu}$), spin angular momentum ($\vec{S}$), and spin magnetic moment ($\vec{\mu}_s$) vectors are shown together in **Figure 8.14**.

Just as the energy levels of a hydrogen atom can be split by an *external* magnetic field, so too are the energy levels of a hydrogen atom split by *internal* magnetic fields of the atom. If the magnetic moment of the electron and orbital magnetic moment of the electron are antiparallel, the potential energy from the magnetic interaction is relatively high, but when these moments are parallel, the potential energy is relatively small. Transition from each of these two states to a lower-energy level results in the emission of a photon of slightly different frequency. That is, the spin-orbit coupling "splits" the spectral line expected from a spin-less electron. The **fine structure** of the hydrogen spectrum is explained by spin-orbit coupling.

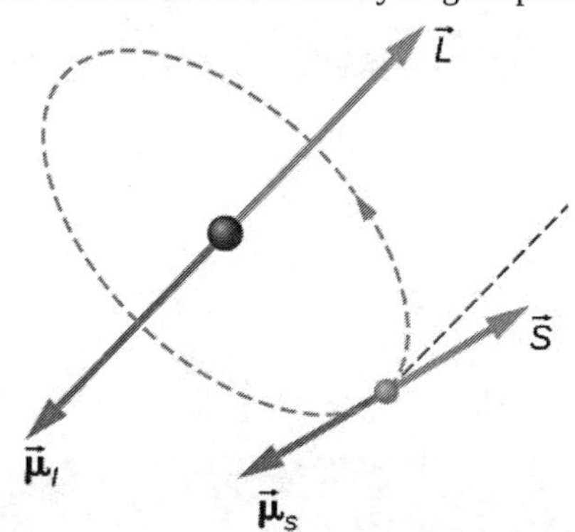

Figure 8.14 Spin-orbit coupling is the interaction of an electron's spin magnetic moment $\vec{\mu}_s$ with its orbital magnetic moment $\vec{\mu}_l$.

The Stern-Gerlach experiment provides experimental evidence that electrons have spin angular momentum. The experiment passes a stream of silver (Ag) atoms through an external, nonuniform magnetic field. The Ag atom has an orbital angular momentum of zero and contains a single unpaired electron in the outer shell. Therefore, the total angular momentum of the Ag atom is due entirely to the spin of the outer electron ($s = 1/2$) . Due to electron spin, the Ag atoms act as tiny magnets as they pass through the magnetic field. These "magnets" have two possible orientations, which correspond to the spin-up and -down states of the electron. The magnetic field diverts the spin up atoms in one direction and the spin-down atoms in another direction. This produces two distinct bands on a screen (**Figure 8.15**).

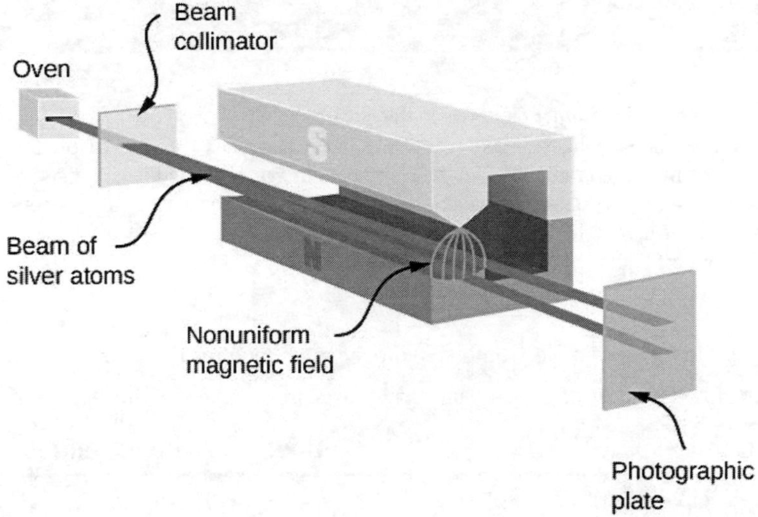

Figure 8.15 In the Stern-Gerlach experiment, an external, nonuniform magnetic field diverts a beam of electrons in two different directions. This result is due to the quantization of spin angular momentum.

According to classical predictions, the angular momentum (and, therefore, the magnetic moment) of the Ag atom can point in any direction, so one expects, instead, a continuous smudge on the screen. The resulting two bands of the Stern-Gerlach experiment provide startling support for the ideas of quantum mechanics.

Visit **PhET Explorations: Stern-Gerlach Experiment (https://openstaxcollege.org/l/21sterngerlach)** to learn more about the Stern-Gerlach experiment.

8.2 Check Your Understanding If the Stern-Gerlach experiment yielded four distinct bands instead of two, what might be concluded about the spin quantum number of the charged particle?

Just like an electron, a proton is spin 1/2 and has a magnetic moment. (According to nuclear theory, this moment is due to the orbital motion of quarks within the proton.) The **hyperfine structure** of the hydrogen spectrum is explained by the interaction between the magnetic moment of the proton and the magnetic moment of the electron, an interaction known as spin-spin coupling. The energy of the electron-proton system is different depending on whether or not the moments are aligned. Transitions between these states (**spin-flip transitions**) result in the emission of a photon with a wavelength of $\lambda \approx 21$ cm (in the radio range). The 21-cm line in atomic spectroscopy is a "fingerprint" of hydrogen gas. Astronomers exploit this spectral line to map the spiral arms of galaxies, which are composed mostly of hydrogen (**Figure 8.16**).

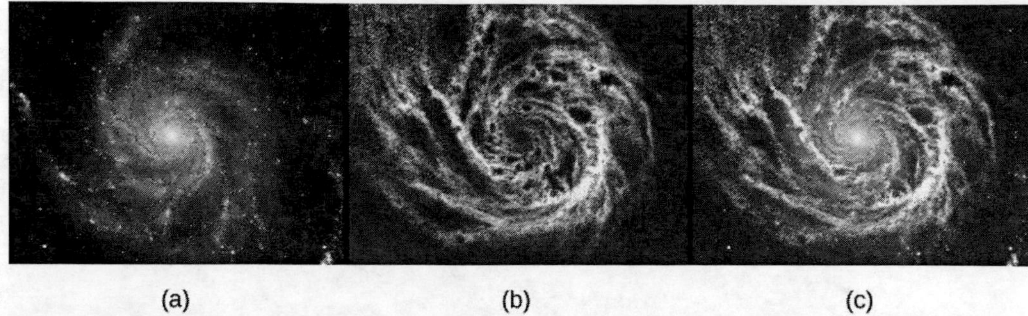

Figure 8.16 The magnetic interaction between the electron and proton in the hydrogen atom is used to map the spiral arms of the Pinwheel Galaxy (NGC 5457). (a) The galaxy seen in visible light; (b) the galaxy seen in 21-cm hydrogen radiation; (c) the composite image of (a) and (b). Notice how the hydrogen emission penetrates dust in the galaxy to show the spiral arms very clearly, whereas the galactic nucleus shows up better in visible light (credit a: modification of work by ESA & NASA; credit b: modification of work by Fabian Walter).

A complete specification of the state of an electron in a hydrogen atom requires five quantum numbers: n, l, m, s, and m_s. The names, symbols, and allowed values of these quantum numbers are summarized in Table 8.4.

Name	Symbol	Allowed values
Principal quantum number	n	1, 2, 3, …
Angular momentum	l	0, 1, 2, … $n-1$
Angular momentum projection	m	$0, \pm 1, \pm 2, ... \pm l$
Spin	s	1/2 (electrons)
Spin projection	m_s	$-½, +½$

Table 8.4 Summary of Quantum Numbers of an Electron in a Hydrogen Atom

Note that the intrinsic quantum numbers introduced in this section (s and m_s) are valid for many particles, not just electrons. For example, quarks within an atomic nucleus are also spin-half particles. As we will see later, quantum numbers help to classify subatomic particles and enter into scientific models that attempt to explain how the universe works.

8.4 | The Exclusion Principle and the Periodic Table

Learning Objectives

By the end of this section, you will be able to:

- Explain the importance of Pauli's exclusion principle to an understanding of atomic structure and molecular bonding
- Explain the structure of the periodic table in terms of the total energy, orbital angular momentum, and spin of individual electrons in an atom
- Describe the electron configuration of atoms in the periodic table

So far, we have studied only hydrogen, the simplest chemical element. We have found that an electron in the hydrogen atom can be completely specified by five quantum numbers:

$$
\begin{aligned}
&n: && \text{principal quantum number}\\
&l: && \text{angular momentum quantum number}\\
&m: && \text{angular momentum projection quantum number}\\
&s: && \text{spin quantum number}\\
&m_s: && \text{spin projection quantum number}
\end{aligned}
\tag{8.34}
$$

To construct the ground state of a neutral multi-electron atom, imagine starting with a nucleus of charge *Ze* (that is, a nucleus of atomic number *Z*) and then adding *Z* electrons one by one. Assume that each electron moves in a spherically symmetrical electric field produced by the nucleus and all other electrons of the atom. The assumption is valid because the electrons are distributed randomly around the nucleus and produce an average electric field (and potential) that is spherically symmetrical. The electric potential *U*(*r*) for each electron does not follow the simple $-1/r$ form because of interactions between electrons, but it turns out that we can still label each individual electron state by quantum numbers, (n, l, m, s, m_s). (The spin quantum number *s* is the same for all electrons, so it will not be used in this section.)

The structure and chemical properties of atoms are explained in part by **Pauli's exclusion principle**: No two electrons in an atom can have the same values for all four quantum numbers (n, l, m, m_s). This principle is related to two properties of electrons: All electrons are identical ("when you've seen one electron, you've seen them all") and they have half-integral spin $(s = 1/2)$. Sample sets of quantum numbers for the electrons in an atom are given in **Table 8.5**. Consistent with Pauli's exclusion principle, no two rows of the table have the exact same set of quantum numbers.

n	*l*	*m*	m_s	Subshell symbol	No. of electrons: subshell	No. of electrons: shell
1	0	0	½	1*s*	2	2
1	0	0	–½			
2	0	0	½	2*s*	2	8
2	0	0	–½			
2	1	–1	½			
2	1	–1	–½			
2	1	0	½	2*p*	6	
2	1	0	–½			
2	1	1	½			
2	1	1	–½			
3	0	0	½	3*s*	2	
3	0	0	–½			
3	1	–1	½			
3	1	–1	–½			
3	1	0	½	3*p*	6	
3	1	0	–½			18
3	1	1	½			
3	1	1	–½			
3	2	–2	½			
3	2	–2	–½	3*d*	10	
3	2	–1	½			

Table 8.5 Electron States of Atoms Because of Pauli's exclusion principle, no two electrons in an atom have the same set of four quantum numbers.

n	l	m	m_s	Subshell symbol	No. of electrons: subshell	No. of electrons: shell
3	2	–1	–½			
3	2	0	½			
3	2	0	–½			
3	2	1	½			
3	2	1	–½			
3	2	2	½			
3	2	2	–½			

Table 8.5 Electron States of Atoms Because of Pauli's exclusion principle, no two electrons in an atom have the same set of four quantum numbers.

Electrons with the same principal quantum number n are said to be in the same shell, and those that have the same value of l are said to occupy the same subshell. An electron in the $n = 1$ state of a hydrogen atom is denoted 1*s*, where the first digit indicates the shell $(n = 1)$ and the letter indicates the subshell $(s, p, d, f\ldots$ correspond to $l = 0, 1, 2, 3\ldots)$. Two electrons in the $n = 1$ state are denoted as $1s^2$, where the superscript indicates the number of electrons. An electron in the $n = 2$ state with $l = 1$ is denoted 2*p*. The combination of two electrons in the $n = 2$ and $l = 0$ state, and three electrons in the $n = 2$ and $l = 1$ state is written as $2s^2 2p^3$, and so on. This representation of the electron state is called the **electron configuration** of the atom. The electron configurations for several atoms are given in Table 8.6. Electrons in the outer shell of an atom are called **valence electrons**. Chemical bonding between atoms in a molecule are explained by the transfer and sharing of valence electrons.

Element	Electron Configuration	Spin Alignment
H	$1s^1$	$(\uparrow)$
He	$1s^2$	$(\uparrow\downarrow)$
Li	$1s^2 2s^1$	$(\uparrow)$
Be	$1s^2 2s^2$	$(\uparrow\downarrow)$
B	$1s^2 2s^2 2p^1$	$(\uparrow\downarrow)(\uparrow)$
C	$1s^2 2s^2 2p^2$	$(\uparrow\downarrow)(\uparrow)(\uparrow)$
N	$1s^2 2s^2 2p^3$	$(\uparrow\downarrow)(\uparrow)(\uparrow)(\uparrow)$
O	$1s^2 2s^2 2p^4$	$(\uparrow\downarrow)(\uparrow\downarrow)(\uparrow)(\uparrow)$
F	$1s^2 2s^2 2p^5$	$(\uparrow\downarrow)(\uparrow\downarrow)(\uparrow\downarrow)(\uparrow)$
Ne	$1s^2 2s^2 2p^6$	$(\uparrow\downarrow)(\uparrow\downarrow)(\uparrow\downarrow)(\uparrow\downarrow)$
Na	$1s^2 2s^2 2p^6 3s^1$	$(\uparrow)$

Table 8.6 Electron Configurations of Electrons in an Atom The symbol $(\uparrow)$ indicates an unpaired electron in the outer shell, whereas the symbol $(\uparrow\downarrow)$ indicates a pair of spin-up and -down electrons in an outer shell.

Element	Electron Configuration	Spin Alignment
Mg	$1s^2 2s^2 2p^6 3s^2$	(↑↓)
Al	$1s^2 2s^2 2p^6 3s^2 3p^1$	(↑↓)(↑)

Table 8.6 Electron Configurations of Electrons in an Atom The symbol (↑) indicates an unpaired electron in the outer shell, whereas the symbol (↑↓) indicates a pair of spin-up and -down electrons in an outer shell.

The maximum number of electrons in a subshell depends on the value of the angular momentum quantum number, l. For a given a value l, there are $2l + 1$ orbital angular momentum states. However, each of these states can be filled by two electrons (spin up and down, ↑↓). Thus, the maximum number of electrons in a subshell is

$$N = 2(2l + 1) = 4l + 2. \tag{8.35}$$

In the 2*s* $(l = 0)$ subshell, the maximum number of electrons is 2. In the 2*p* $(l = 1)$ subshell, the maximum number of electrons is 6. Therefore, the total maximum number of electrons in the $n = 2$ shell (including both the $l = 0$ and 1 subshells) is $2 + 6$ or 8. In general, the maximum number of electrons in the *n*th shell is $2n^2$.

Example 8.5

Subshells and Totals for $n = 3$

How many subshells are in the $n = 3$ shell? Identify each subshell and calculate the maximum number of electrons that will fill each. Show that the maximum number of electrons that fill an atom is $2n^2$.

Strategy

Subshells are determined by the value of l; thus, we first determine which values of l are allowed, and then we apply the equation "maximum number of electrons that can be in a subshell $= 2(2l + 1)$" to find the number of electrons in each subshell.

Solution

Because $n = 3$, we know that l can be 0, 1, or 2; thus, there are three possible subshells. In standard notation, they are labeled the 3*s*, 3*p*, and 3*d* subshells. We have already seen that two electrons can be in an *s* state, and six in a *p* state, but let us use the equation "maximum number of electrons that can be in a subshell $= 2(2l + 1)$" to calculate the maximum number in each:

$$\begin{aligned}
&3s \text{ has } l = 0;\ \text{thus, } 2(2l + 1) = 2(0 + 1) = 2 \\
&3p \text{ has } l = 1;\ \text{thus, } 2(2l + 1) = 2(2 + 1) = 6 \\
&3d \text{ has } l = 2;\ \text{thus, } 2(2l + 1) = 2(4 + 1) = 10 \\
&\text{Total} = 18 \\
&(\text{in the } n = 3 \text{ shell}).
\end{aligned}$$

The equation "maximum number of electrons that can be in a shell $= 2n^2$" gives the maximum number in the $n = 3$ shell to be

$$\text{Maximum number of electrons} = 2n^2 = 2(3)^2 = 2(9) = 18.$$

Significance

The total number of electrons in the three possible subshells is thus the same as the formula $2n^2$. In standard (spectroscopic) notation, a filled $n = 3$ shell is denoted as $3s^2 3p^6 3d^{10}$. Shells do not fill in a simple manner. Before the $n = 3$ shell is completely filled, for example, we begin to find electrons in the $n = 4$ shell.

The structure of the periodic table (**Figure 8.17**) can be understood in terms of shells and subshells, and, ultimately, the total energy, orbital angular momentum, and spin of the electrons in the atom. A detailed discussion of the periodic table is left to a chemistry course—we sketch only its basic features here. In this discussion, we assume that the atoms are electrically neutral; that is, they have the same number of electrons and protons. (Recall that the total number of protons in an atomic nucleus is called the atomic number, *Z*.)

First, the periodic table is arranged into columns and rows. The table is read left to right and top to bottom in the order of increasing atomic number *Z*. Atoms that belong to the same column or **chemical group** share many of the same chemical properties. For example, the Li and Na atoms (in the first column) bond to other atoms in a similar way. The first row of the table corresponds to the $1s$ ($l = 0$) shell of an atom.

Consider the hypothetical procedure of adding electrons, one by one, to an atom. For hydrogen (H) (upper left), the $1s$ shell is filled with either a spin up or down electron ($\uparrow$ or $\downarrow$). This lone electron is easily shared with other atoms, so hydrogen is chemically active. For helium (He) (upper right), the $1s$ shell is filled with both a spin up and a spin down ($\uparrow\downarrow$) electron. This "fills" the $1s$ shell, so a helium atom tends not to share electrons with other atoms. The helium atom is said to be chemically inactive, inert, or noble; likewise, helium gas is said to be an inert gas or noble gas.

Build an atom by adding and subtracting protons, neutrons, and electrons. How does the element, charge, and mass change? Visit **PhET Explorations: Build an Atom (https://openstaxcollege.org/l/21buildanatom)** to explore the answers to these questions.

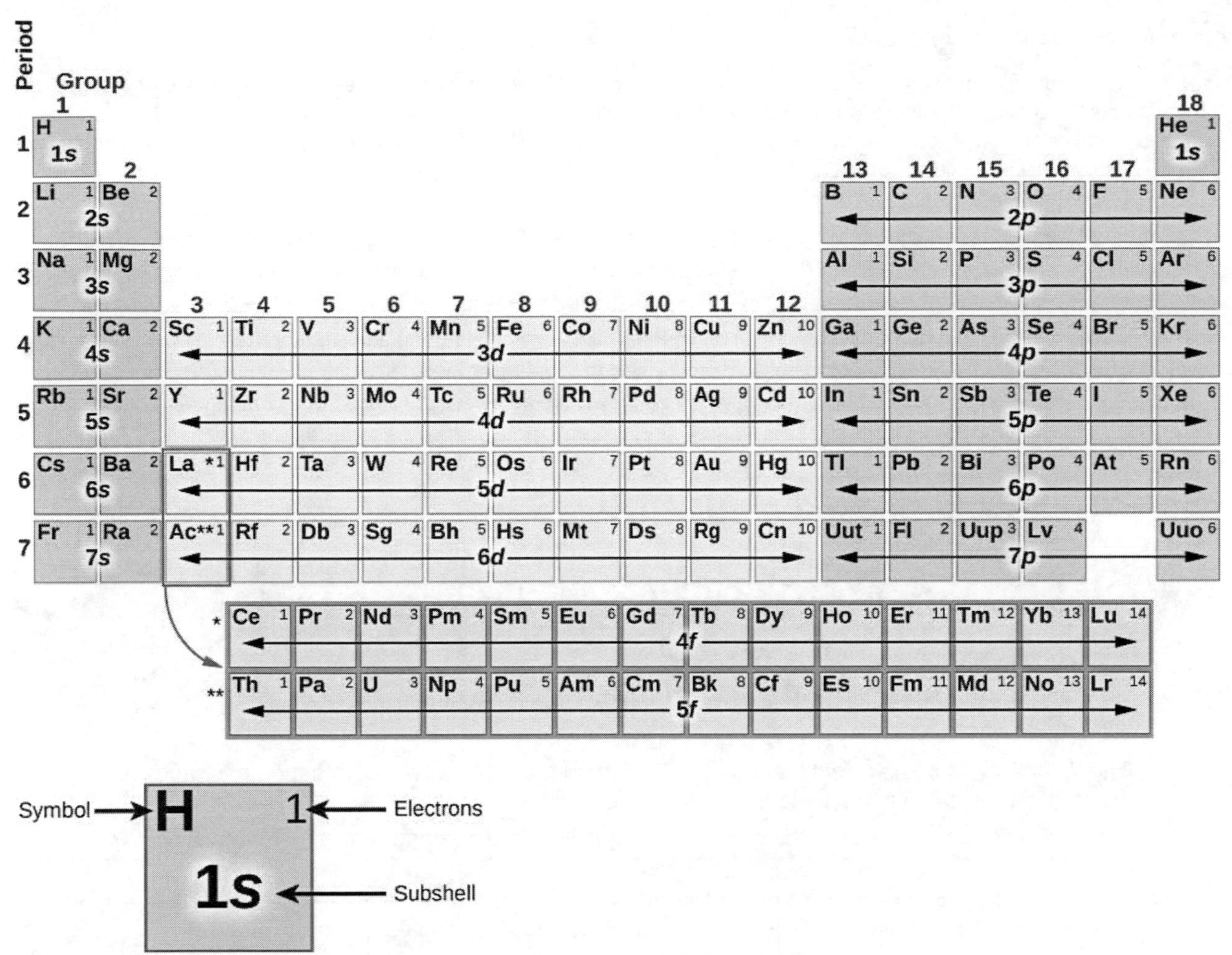

Figure 8.17 The periodic table of elements, showing the structure of shells and subshells.

The second row corresponds to the 2*s* and 2*p* subshells. For lithium (Li) (upper left), the 1*s* shell is filled with a spin-up *and* spin-down electron ($\uparrow\downarrow$) and the 2*s* shell is filled with either a spin-up or -down electron ($\uparrow \text{or} \downarrow$). Its electron configuration is therefore $1s^2 2s^1$ or [He]2*s*, where [He] indicates a helium core. Like hydrogen, the lone electron in the outermost shell is easily shared with other atoms. For beryllium (Be), the 2*s* shell is filled with a spin-up and -down electron ($\uparrow\downarrow$), and has the electron configuration [He] $2s^2$.

Next, we look at the right side of the table. For boron (B), the 1*s* and 2*s* shells are filled and the 2*p* ($l = 1$) shell contains either a spin up or down electron ($\uparrow \text{or} \downarrow$). From carbon (C) to neon (N), we the fill the 2*p* shell. The maximum number of electrons in the 2*p* shells is $4l + 2 = 4(2) + 2 = 6$. For neon (Ne), the 1*s* shell is filled with a spin-up and spin-down electron ($\uparrow\downarrow$), and the 2*p* shell is filled with six electrons ($\uparrow\downarrow\ \uparrow\downarrow\ \uparrow\downarrow$) . This "fills" the 1*s*, 2*s*, and 2*p* subshells, so like helium, the neon atom tends not to share electrons with other atoms.

The process of electron filling repeats in the third row. However, beginning in the fourth row, the pattern is broken. The actual order of order of electron filling is given by

1*s*, 2*s*, 2*p*, 3*s*, 3*p*, 4*s*, ***3d***, 4*p*, 5*s*, ***4d***, 5*p*, 6*s*, ***4f***, ***5d***, 6*p*, 7*s*,...

Notice that the 3*d*, 4*d*, 4*f*, and 5*d* subshells (in bold) are filled out of order; this occurs because of interactions between electrons in the atom, which so far we have neglected. The **transition metals** are elements in the gap between the first two columns and the last six columns that contain electrons that fill the *d* ($l = 1$) subshell. As expected, these atoms are arranged in $4l + 2 = 4(2) + 2 = 10$ columns. The structure of the periodic table can be understood in terms of the quantization of the total energy (*n*), orbital angular momentum (*l*), and spin (*s*). The first two columns correspond to the *s* ($l = 0$) subshell, the next six columns correspond to the *p* ($l = 1$) subshell, and the gap between these columns corresponds to the d ($l = 2$) subshell.

The periodic table also gives information on molecular bonding. To see this, consider atoms in the left-most column (the so-called alkali metals including: Li, Na, and K). These atoms contain a single electron in the 2*s* subshell, which is easily donated to other atoms. In contrast, atoms in the second-to-right column (the halogens: for example, Cl, F, and Br) are relatively stingy in sharing electrons. These atoms would much rather accept an electron, because they are just one electron shy of a filled shell ("of being noble").

Therefore, if a Na atom is placed in close proximity to a Cl atom, the Na atom freely donates its 2*s* electron and the Cl atom eagerly accepts it. In the process, the Na atom (originally a neutral charge) becomes positively charged and the Cl (originally a neutral charge) becomes negatively charged. Charged atoms are called ions. In this case, the ions are Na^+ and Cl^-, where the superscript indicates charge of the ion. The electric (Coulomb) attraction between these atoms forms a NaCl (salt) molecule. A chemical bond between two ions is called an **ionic bond**. There are many kinds of chemical bonds. For example, in an oxygen molecule O_2 electrons are equally shared between the atoms. The bonding of oxygen atoms is an example of a **covalent bond**.

8.5 | Atomic Spectra and X-rays

Learning Objectives

By the end of this section, you will be able to:

- Describe the absorption and emission of radiation in terms of atomic energy levels and energy differences
- Use quantum numbers to estimate the energy, frequency, and wavelength of photons produced by atomic transitions in multi-electron atoms
- Explain radiation concepts in the context of atomic fluorescence and X-rays

The study of atomic spectra provides most of our knowledge about atoms. In modern science, atomic spectra are used to identify species of atoms in a range of objects, from distant galaxies to blood samples at a crime scene.

The theoretical basis of atomic spectroscopy is the transition of electrons between energy levels in atoms. For example, if an electron in a hydrogen atom makes a transition from the $n = 3$ to the $n = 2$ shell, the atom emits a photon with a wavelength

$$\lambda = \frac{c}{f} = \frac{h \cdot c}{h \cdot f} = \frac{hc}{\Delta E} = \frac{hc}{E_3 - E_2}, \quad (8.36)$$

where $\Delta E = E_3 - E_2$ is energy carried away by the photon and $hc = 1940\,\text{eV} \cdot \text{nm}$. After this radiation passes through a spectrometer, it appears as a sharp spectral line on a screen. The Bohr model of this process is shown in **Figure 8.18**. If the electron later absorbs a photon with energy ΔE, the electron returns to the $n = 3$ shell. (We examined the Bohr model earlier, in **Photons and Matter Waves**.)

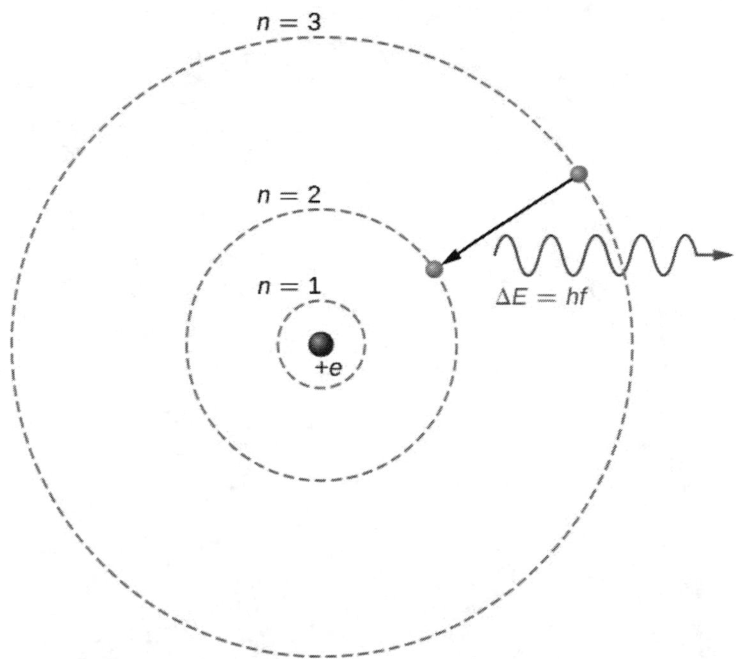

Figure 8.18 An electron transition from the $n = 3$ to the $n = 2$ shell of a hydrogen atom.

To understand atomic transitions in multi-electron atoms, it is necessary to consider many effects, including the Coulomb repulsion between electrons and internal magnetic interactions (spin-orbit and spin-spin couplings). Fortunately, many properties of these systems can be understood by neglecting interactions between electrons and representing each electron by its own single-particle wave function ψ_{nlm}.

Atomic transitions must obey **selection rules**. These rules follow from principles of quantum mechanics and symmetry. Selection rules classify transitions as either allowed or forbidden. (Forbidden transitions do occur, but the probability of the typical forbidden transition is very small.) For a hydrogen-like atom, atomic transitions that involve electromagnetic interactions (the emission and absorption of photons) obey the following selection rule:

$$\Delta l = \pm 1, \tag{8.37}$$

where l is associated with the magnitude of orbital angular momentum,

$$L = \sqrt{l(l+1)}\hbar. \tag{8.38}$$

For multi-electron atoms, similar rules apply. To illustrate this rule, consider the observed atomic transitions in hydrogen (H), sodium (Na), and mercury (Hg) (**Figure 8.19**). The horizontal lines in this diagram correspond to atomic energy levels, and the transitions allowed by this selection rule are shown by lines drawn between these levels. The energies of these states are on the order of a few electron volts, and photons emitted in transitions are in the visible range. Technically, atomic transitions can violate the selection rule, but such transitions are uncommon.

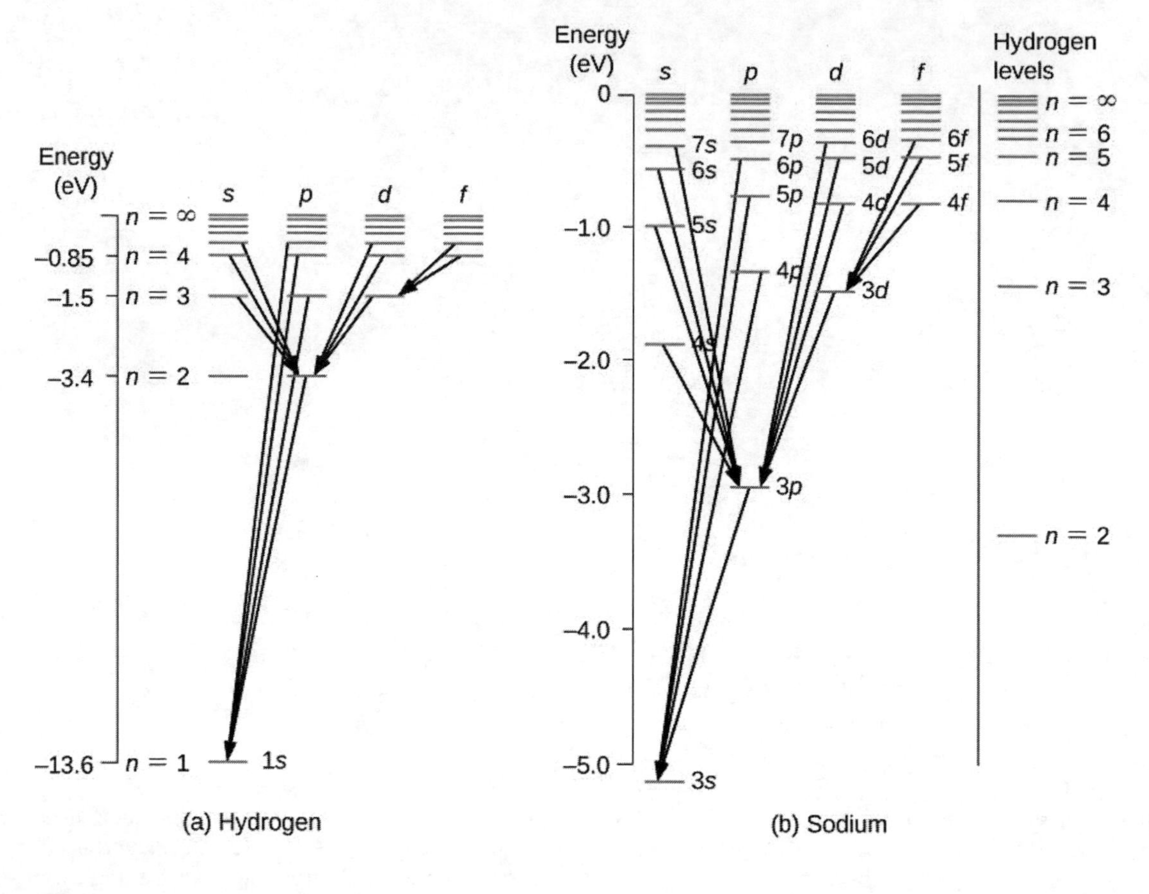

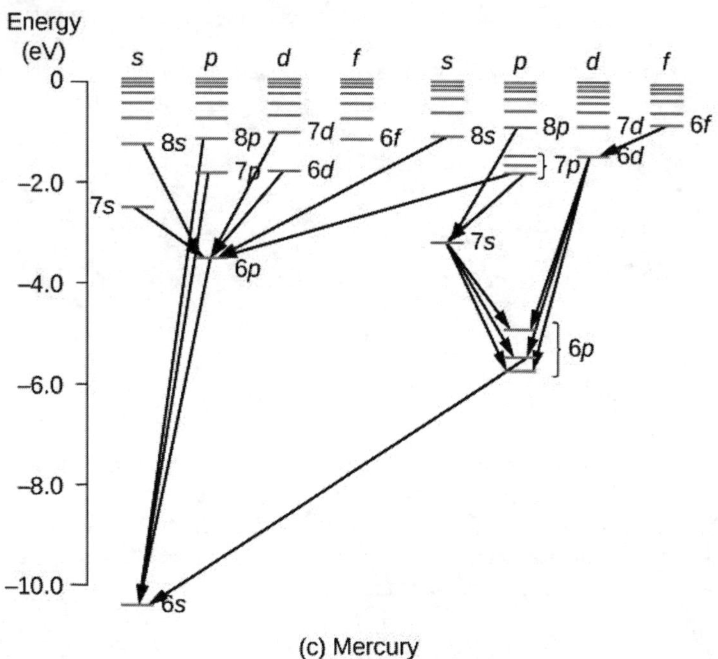

Figure 8.19 Energy-level diagrams for (a) hydrogen, (b) sodium, and (c) mercury. For comparison, hydrogen energy levels are shown in the sodium diagram.

The hydrogen atom has the simplest energy-level diagram. If we neglect electron spin, all states with the same value of n have the same total energy. However, spin-orbit coupling splits the $n = 2$ states into two angular momentum states (s and p) of slightly different energies. (These levels are not vertically displaced, because the energy splitting is too small to show up in this diagram.) Likewise, spin-orbit coupling splits the $n = 3$ states into three angular momentum states (s, p, and d).

The energy-level diagram for hydrogen is similar to sodium, because both atoms have one electron in the outer shell. The valence electron of sodium moves in the electric field of a nucleus shielded by electrons in the inner shells, so it does not experience a simple $1/r$ Coulomb potential and its total energy depends on both n and l. Interestingly, mercury has two separate energy-level diagrams; these diagrams correspond to two net spin states of its 6*s* (valence) electrons.

Example 8.6

The Sodium Doublet

The spectrum of sodium is analyzed with a spectrometer. Two closely spaced lines with wavelengths 589.00 nm and 589.59 nm are observed. (a) If the doublet corresponds to the excited (valence) electron that transitions from some excited state down to the 3*s* state, what was the original electron angular momentum? (b) What is the energy difference between these two excited states?

Strategy

Sodium and hydrogen belong to the same column or chemical group of the periodic table, so sodium is "hydrogen-like." The outermost electron in sodium is in the 3*s* ($l = 0$) subshell and can be excited to higher energy levels. As for hydrogen, subsequent transitions to lower energy levels must obey the selection rule:

$$\Delta l = \pm 1.$$

We must first determine the quantum number of the initial state that satisfies the selection rule. Then, we can use this number to determine the magnitude of orbital angular momentum of the initial state.

Solution

a. Allowed transitions must obey the selection rule. If the quantum number of the initial state is $l = 0$, the transition is forbidden because $\Delta l = 0$. If the quantum number of the initial state is $l = 2, 3, 4, \ldots$the transition is forbidden because $\Delta l > 1$. Therefore, the quantum of the initial state must be $l = 1$. The orbital angular momentum of the initial state is

$$L = \sqrt{l(l+1)}\hbar = 1.41\hbar.$$

b. Because the final state for both transitions is the same (3*s*), the difference in energies of the photons is equal to the difference in energies of the two excited states. Using the equation

$$\Delta E = hf = h\left(\frac{c}{\lambda}\right),$$

we have

$$\begin{aligned}\Delta E &= hc\left(\frac{1}{\lambda_1} - \frac{1}{\lambda_2}\right) \\ &= \left(4.14 \times 10^{-15}\ \text{eVs}\right)\left(3.00 \times 10^8\ \text{m/s}\right) \times \left(\frac{1}{589.00 \times 10^{-9}\ \text{m}} - \frac{1}{589.59 \times 10^{-9}\ \text{m}}\right) \\ &= 2.11 \times 10^{-3}\ \text{eV}.\end{aligned}$$

Significance

To understand the difficulty of measuring this energy difference, we compare this difference with the average energy of the two photons emitted in the transition. Given an average wavelength of 589.30 nm, the average energy of the photons is

$$E = \frac{hc}{\lambda} = \frac{(4.14 \times 10^{-15}\ \text{eVs})(3.00 \times 10^8\ \text{m/s})}{589.30 \times 10^{-9}\ \text{m}} = 2.11\ \text{eV}.$$

The energy difference ΔE is about 0.1% (1 part in 1000) of this average energy. However, a sensitive spectrometer can measure the difference.

Atomic Fluorescence

Fluorescence occurs when an electron in an atom is excited several steps above the ground state by the absorption of a high-energy ultraviolet (UV) photon. Once excited, the electron "de-excites" in two ways. The electron can drop back to the ground state, emitting a photon of the same energy that excited it, or it can drop in a series of smaller steps, emitting several low-energy photons. Some of these photons may be in the visible range. Fluorescent dye in clothes can make colors seem brighter in sunlight by converting UV radiation into visible light. Fluorescent lights are more efficient in converting electrical energy into visible light than incandescent filaments (about four times as efficient). Figure 8.20 shows a scorpion illuminated by a UV lamp. Proteins near the surface of the skin emit a characteristic blue light.

Figure 8.20 A scorpion glows blue under a UV lamp. (credit: Ken Bosma)

X-rays

The study of atomic energy transitions enables us to understand X-rays and X-ray technology. Like all electromagnetic radiation, X-rays are made of photons. X-ray photons are produced when electrons in the outermost shells of an atom drop to the inner shells. (Hydrogen atoms do not emit X-rays, because the electron energy levels are too closely spaced together to permit the emission of high-frequency radiation.) Transitions of this kind are normally forbidden because the lower states are already filled. However, if an inner shell has a vacancy (an inner electron is missing, perhaps from being knocked away by a high-speed electron), an electron from one of the outer shells can drop in energy to fill the vacancy. The energy gap for such a transition is relatively large, so wavelength of the radiated X-ray photon is relatively short.

X-rays can also be produced by bombarding a metal target with high-energy electrons, as shown in Figure 8.21. In the figure, electrons are boiled off a filament and accelerated by an electric field into a tungsten target. According to the classical theory of electromagnetism, *any* charged particle that accelerates emits radiation. Thus, when the electron strikes the tungsten target, and suddenly slows down, the electron emits **braking radiation**. (Braking radiation refers to radiation produced by any charged particle that is slowed by a medium.) In this case, braking radiation contains a continuous range of frequencies, because the electrons will collide with the target atoms in slightly different ways.

Braking radiation is not the only type of radiation produced in this interaction. In some cases, an electron collides with another inner-shell electron of a target atom, and knocks the electron out of the atom—billiard ball style. The empty state is filled when an electron in a higher shell drops into the state (drop in energy level) and emits an X-ray photon.

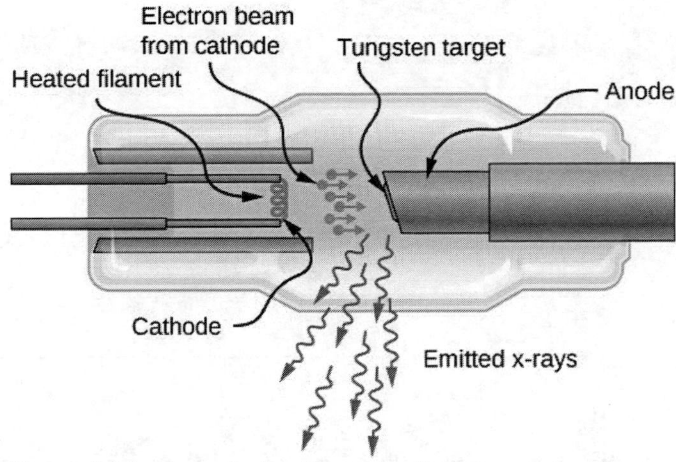

Figure 8.21 A sketch of an X-ray tube. X-rays are emitted from the tungsten target.

Historically, X-ray spectral lines were labeled with letters (*K*, *L*, *M*, *N*, …). These letters correspond to the atomic shells ($n = 1, 2, 3, 4, \ldots$). X-rays produced by a transition from any higher shell to the *K* ($n = 1$) shell are labeled as *K* X-rays. X-rays produced in a transition from the *L* ($n = 2$) shell are called K_α X-rays; X-rays produced in a transition from the *M* ($n = 3$) shell are called K_β X-rays; X-rays produced in a transition from the *N* ($n = 4$) shell are called K_γ X-rays; and so forth. Transitions from higher shells to *L* and *M* shells are labeled similarly. These transitions are represented by an energy-level diagram in **Figure 8.22**.

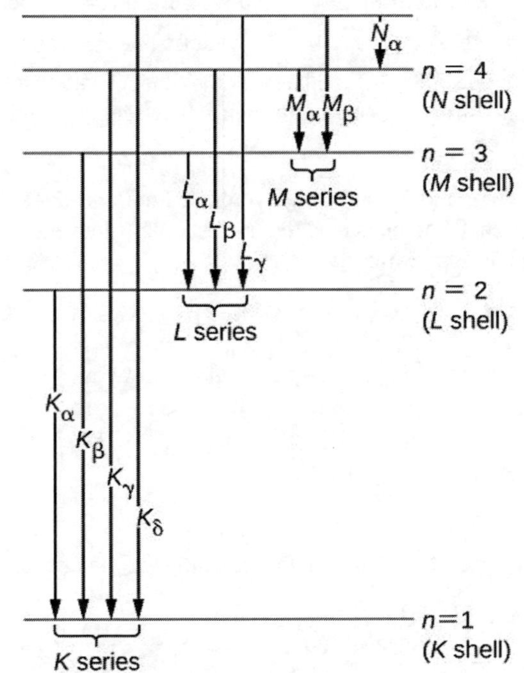

Figure 8.22 X-ray transitions in an atom.

The distribution of X-ray wavelengths produced by striking metal with a beam of electrons is given in **Figure 8.23**. X-ray transitions in the target metal appear as peaks on top of the braking radiation curve. Photon frequencies corresponding to the spikes in the X-ray distribution are called characteristic frequencies, because they can be used to identify the target metal. The sharp cutoff wavelength (just below the K_γ peak) corresponds to an electron that loses all of its energy to a single photon. Radiation of shorter wavelengths is forbidden by the conservation of energy.

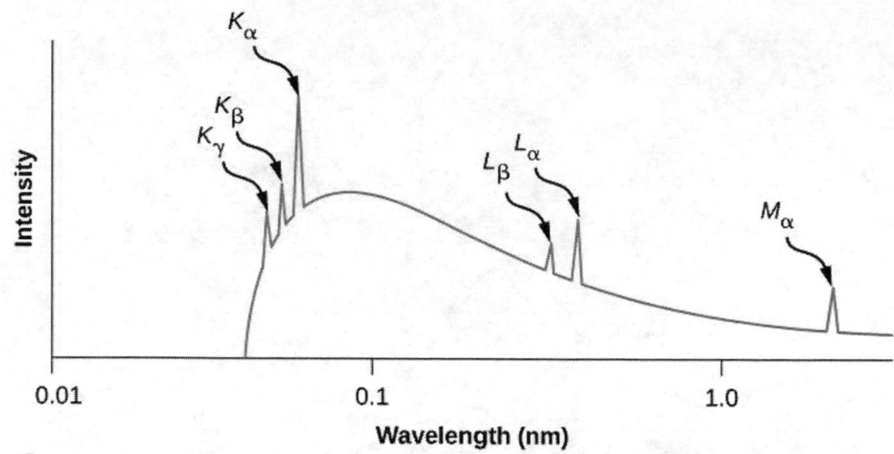

Figure 8.23 X-ray spectrum from a silver target. The peaks correspond to characteristic frequencies of X-rays emitted by silver when struck by an electron beam.

Example 8.7

X-Rays from Aluminum

Estimate the characteristic energy and frequency of the K_α X-ray for aluminum ($Z = 13$).

Strategy

A K_α X-ray is produced by the transition of an electron in the L ($n = 2$) shell to the K ($n = 1$) shell. An electron in the L shell "sees" a charge $Z = 13 - 1 = 12,$ because one electron in the K shell shields the nuclear charge. (Recall, two electrons are not in the K shell because the other electron state is vacant.) The frequency of the emitted photon can be estimated from the energy difference between the L and K shells.

Solution

The energy difference between the L and K shells in a hydrogen atom is 10.2 eV. Assuming that other electrons in the L shell or in higher-energy shells do not shield the nuclear charge, the energy difference between the L and K shells in an atom with $Z = 13$ is approximately

$$\Delta E_{L \to K} \approx (Z - 1)^2 (10.2 \text{ eV}) = (13 - 1)^2 (10.2 \text{ eV}) = 1.47 \times 10^3 \text{eV}. \tag{8.39}$$

Based on the relationship $f = (\Delta E_{L \to K})/h$, the frequency of the X-ray is

$$f = \frac{1.47 \times 10^3 \text{ eV}}{4.14 \times 10^{-15} \text{ eV} \cdot \text{s}} = 3.55 \times 10^{17} \text{ Hz}.$$

Significance

The wavelength of the typical X-ray is 0.1–10 nm. In this case, the wavelength is:

$$\lambda = \frac{c}{f} = \frac{3.0 \times 10^8 \text{ m/s}}{3.55 \times 10^{17} \text{ Hz}} = 8.5 \times 10^{-10} = 0.85 \text{ nm}.$$

Hence, the transition $L \to K$ in aluminum produces X-ray radiation.

X-ray production provides an important test of quantum mechanics. According to the Bohr model, the energy of a K_α X-ray depends on the nuclear charge or atomic number, Z. If Z is large, Coulomb forces in the atom are large, energy differences (ΔE) are large, and, therefore, the energy of radiated photons is large. To illustrate, consider a single electron in a multi-electron atom. Neglecting interactions between the electrons, the allowed energy levels are

$$E_n = -\frac{Z^2 (13.6 \text{ eV})}{n^2}, \tag{8.40}$$

where $n = 1, 2, \ldots$and Z is the atomic number of the nucleus. However, an electron in the L ($n = 2$) shell "sees" a charge $Z - 1$, because one electron in the K shell shields the nuclear charge. (Recall that there is only one electron in the K shell because the other electron was "knocked out.") Therefore, the approximate energies of the electron in the L and K shells are

$$E_L \approx -\frac{(Z-1)^2(13.6\,\text{eV})}{2^2}$$
$$E_K \approx -\frac{(Z-1)^2(13.6\,\text{eV})}{1^2}.$$

The energy carried away by a photon in a transition from the L shell to the K shell is therefore

$$\begin{aligned}\Delta E_{L\to K} &= (Z-1)^2(13.6\,\text{eV})\left(\frac{1}{1^2}-\frac{1}{2^2}\right)\\ &= (Z-1)^2(10.2\,\text{eV}),\end{aligned}$$

where Z is the atomic number. In general, the X-ray photon energy for a transition from an outer shell to the K shell is

$$\Delta E_{L\to K} = hf = \text{constant} \times (Z-1)^2,$$

or

$$(Z-1) = \text{constant}\sqrt{f}, \quad (8.41)$$

where f is the frequency of a K_α X-ray. This equation is **Moseley's law**. For large values of Z, we have approximately

$$Z \approx \text{constant}\sqrt{f}.$$

This prediction can be checked by measuring f for a variety of metal targets. This model is supported if a plot of Z versus $\sqrt{f}$ data (called a **Moseley plot**) is linear. Comparison of model predictions and experimental results, for both the K and L series, is shown in Figure 8.24. The data support the model that X-rays are produced when an outer shell electron drops in energy to fill a vacancy in an inner shell.

8.3 Check Your Understanding X-rays are produced by bombarding a metal target with high-energy electrons. If the target is replaced by another with two times the atomic number, what happens to the frequency of X-rays?

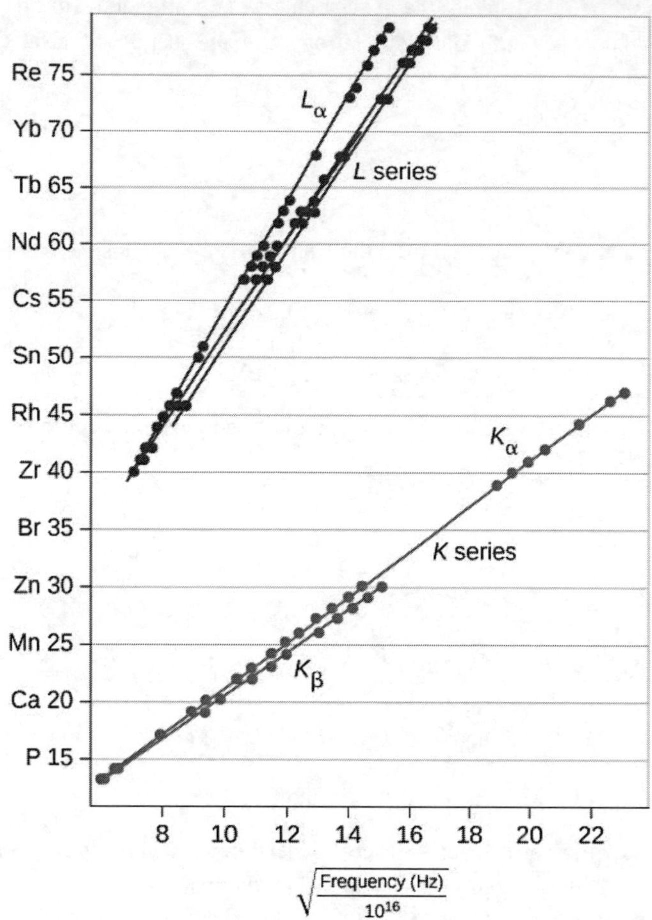

Figure 8.24 A Moseley plot. These data were adapted from Moseley's original data (H. G. J. Moseley, *Philos. Mag.* (6) 77:703, 1914).

Example 8.8

Characteristic X-Ray Energy

Calculate the approximate energy of a K_α X-ray from a tungsten anode in an X-ray tube.

Strategy

Two electrons occupy a filled *K* shell. A vacancy in this shell would leave one electron, so the effective charge for an electron in the *L* shell would be $Z - 1$ rather than *Z*. For tungsten, $Z = 74,$ so the effective charge is 73. This number can be used to calculate the energy-level difference between the *L* and *K* shells, and, therefore, the energy carried away by a photon in the transition $L \to K.$

Solution

The effective *Z* is 73, so the K_α X-ray energy is given by

$$E_{K_\alpha} = \Delta E = E_\text{i} - E_\text{f} = E_2 - E_1,$$

where

$$E_1 = -\frac{Z^2}{1^2}E_0 = -\frac{73^2}{1}(13.6\text{ eV}) = -72.5\text{ keV}$$

and

$$E_2 = -\frac{Z^2}{2^2}E_0 = -\frac{73^2}{4}(13.6\,\text{eV}) = -18.1\,\text{keV}.$$

Thus,

$$E_{K_\alpha} = -18.1\,\text{keV} - (-72.5\,\text{keV}) = 54.4\,\text{keV}.$$

Significance

This large photon energy is typical of X-rays. X-ray energies become progressively larger for heavier elements because their energy increases approximately as Z^2. An acceleration voltage of more than 50,000 volts is needed to "knock out" an inner electron from a tungsten atom.

X-ray Technology

X-rays have many applications, such as in medical diagnostics (**Figure 8.25**), inspection of luggage at airports (**Figure 8.26**), and even detection of cracks in crucial aircraft components. The most common X-ray images are due to shadows. Because X-ray photons have high energy, they penetrate materials that are opaque to visible light. The more energy an X-ray photon has, the more material it penetrates. The depth of penetration is related to the density of the material, as well as to the energy of the photon. The denser the material, the fewer X-ray photons get through and the darker the shadow. X-rays are effective at identifying bone breaks and tumors; however, overexposure to X-rays can damage cells in biological organisms.

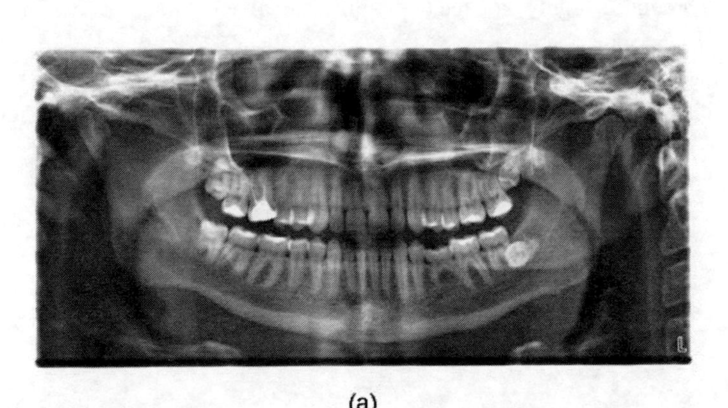

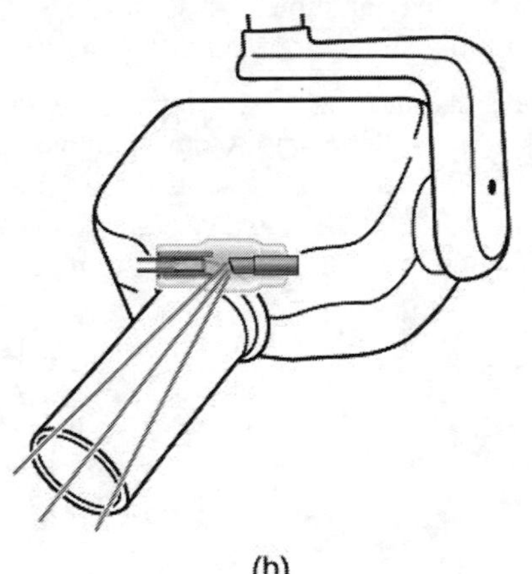

(a) (b)

Figure 8.25 (a) An X-ray image of a person's teeth. (b) A typical X-ray machine in a dentist's office produces relatively low-energy radiation to minimize patient exposure. (credit a: modification of work by "Dmitry G"/Wikimedia Commons)

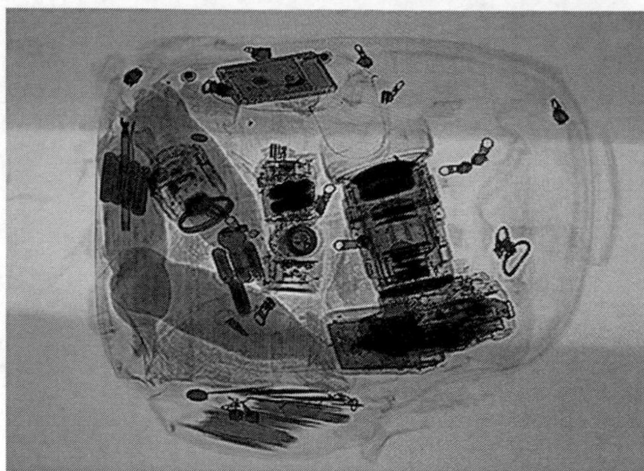

Figure 8.26 An X-ray image of a piece of luggage. The denser the material, the darker the shadow. Object colors relate to material composition—metallic objects show up as blue in this image. (credit: “IDuke”/Wikimedia Commons)

A standard X-ray image provides a two-dimensional view of the object. However, in medical applications, this view does not often provide enough information to draw firm conclusions. For example, in a two-dimensional X-ray image of the body, bones can easily hide soft tissues or organs. The CAT (computed axial tomography) scanner addresses this problem by collecting numerous X-ray images in “slices” throughout the body. Complex computer-image processing of the relative absorption of the X-rays, in different directions, can produce a highly detailed three-dimensional X-ray image of the body.

X-rays can also be used to probe the structures of atoms and molecules. Consider X-rays incident on the surface of a crystalline solid. Some X-ray photons reflect at the surface, and others reflect off the “plane” of atoms just below the surface. Interference between these photons, for different angles of incidence, produces a beautiful image on a screen (**Figure 8.27**). The interaction of X-rays with a solid is called X-ray diffraction. The most famous example using X-ray diffraction is the discovery of the double-helix structure of DNA.

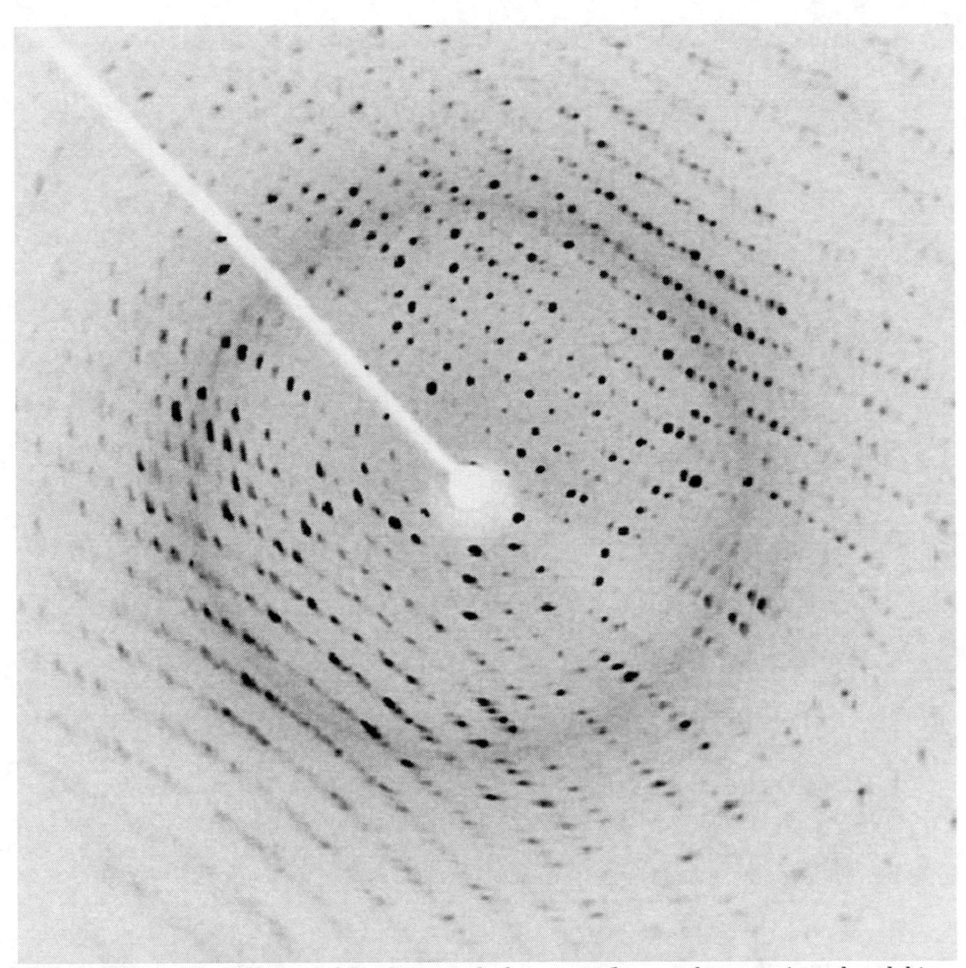

Figure 8.27 X-ray diffraction from the crystal of a protein (hen egg lysozyme) produced this interference pattern. Analysis of the pattern yields information about the structure of the protein. (credit: “Del45”/Wikimedia Commons)

8.6 | Lasers

Learning Objectives

By the end of this section, you will be able to:

- Describe the physical processes necessary to produce laser light
- Explain the difference between coherent and incoherent light
- Describe the application of lasers to a CD and Blu-Ray player

A **laser** is device that emits coherent and monochromatic light. The light is coherent if photons that compose the light are in-phase, and **monochromatic** if the photons have a single frequency (color). When a gas in the laser absorbs radiation, electrons are elevated to different energy levels. Most electrons return immediately to the ground state, but others linger in what is called a **metastable state**. It is possible to place a majority of these atoms in a metastable state, a condition called a **population inversion**.

When a photon of energy disturbs an electron in a metastable state (Figure 8.28), the electron drops to the lower-energy level and emits an addition photon, and the two photons proceed off together. This process is called **stimulated emission**. It occurs with relatively high probability when the energy of the incoming photon is equal to the energy difference between the excited and “de-excited” energy levels of the electron ($\Delta E = hf$). Hence, the incoming photon and the photon produced by de-excitation have the same energy, *hf*. These photons encounter more electrons in the metastable state, and the process repeats. The result is a cascade or chain reaction of similar de-excitations. Laser light is coherent because all light waves in laser light share the same frequency (color) and the same phase (any two points of along a line perpendicular to the direction of motion are on the “same part” of the wave”). A schematic diagram of coherent and incoherent light wave pattern is given in **Figure 8.29**.

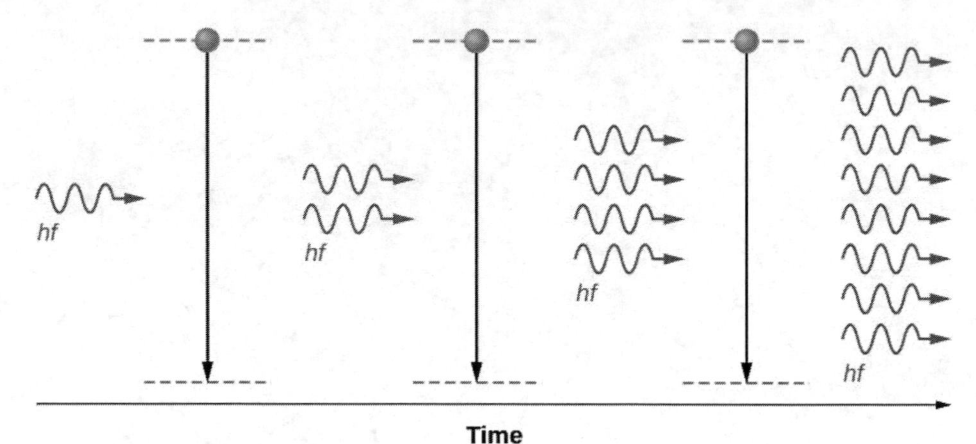

Figure 8.28 The physics of a laser. An incident photon of frequency *f* causes a cascade of photons of the same frequency.

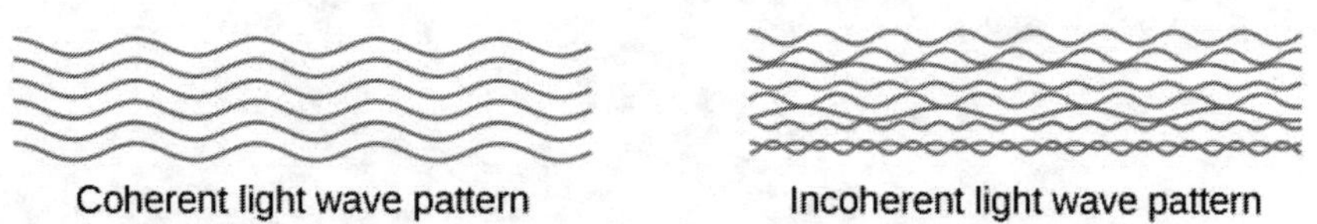

Figure 8.29 A coherent light wave pattern contains light waves of the same frequency and phase. An incoherent light wave pattern contains light waves of different frequencies and phases.

Lasers are used in a wide range of applications, such as in communication (optical fiber phone lines), entertainment (laser light shows), medicine (removing tumors and cauterizing vessels in the retina), and in retail sales (bar code readers). Lasers can also be produced by a large range of materials, including solids (for example, the ruby crystal), gases (helium-gas mixture), and liquids (organic dyes). Recently, a laser was even created using gelatin—an edible laser! Below we discuss two practical applications in detail: CD players and Blu-Ray Players.

CD Player

A CD player reads digital information stored on a compact disc (CD). A CD is 6-inch diameter disc made of plastic that contains small “bumps” and “pits” nears its surface to encode digital or binary data (**Figure 8.30**). The bumps and pits appear along a very thin track that spirals outwards from the center of the disc. The width of the track is smaller than 1/20th the width of a human hair, and the heights of the bumps are even smaller yet.

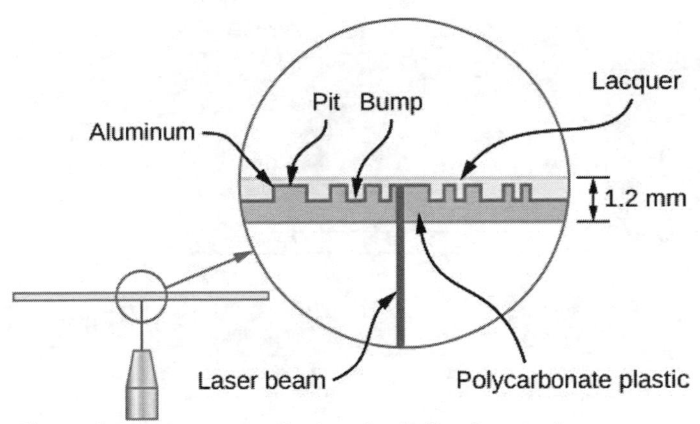

Figure 8.30 A compact disc is a plastic disc that uses bumps near its surface to encode digital information. The surface of the disc contains multiple layers, including a layer of aluminum and one of polycarbonate plastic.

A CD player uses a laser to read this digital information. Laser light is suited to this purpose, because coherent light can be focused onto an incredibly small spot and therefore distinguish between bumps and pits in the CD. After processing by player components (including a diffraction grating, polarizer, and collimator), laser light is focused by a lens onto the CD surface. Light that strikes a bump ("land") is merely reflected, but light that strikes a "pit" destructively interferes, so no light returns (the details of this process are not important to this discussion). Reflected light is interpreted as a "1" and unreflected light is interpreted as a "0." The resulting digital signal is converted into an analog signal, and the analog signal is fed into an amplifier that powers a device such as a pair of headphones. The laser system of a CD player is shown in Figure 8.31.

Figure 8.31 A CD player and its laser component.

Blu-Ray Player

Like a CD player, a Blu-Ray player reads digital information (video or audio) stored on a disc, and a laser is used to record this information. The pits on a Blu-Ray disc are much smaller and more closely packed together than for a CD, so much more information can be stored. As a result, the resolving power of the laser must be greater. This is achieved using short wavelength $(\lambda = 405 \text{ nm})$ blue laser light—hence, the name "Blu-" Ray. (CDs and DVDs use red laser light.) The different pit sizes and player-hardware configurations of a CD, DVD, and Blu-Ray player are shown in Figure 8.32. The pit sizes of a Blu-Ray disk are more than twice as small as the pits on a DVD or CD. Unlike a CD, a Blu-Ray disc store data on a polycarbonate layer, which places the data closer to the lens and avoids readability problems. A hard coating is used to protect the data since it is so close to the surface.

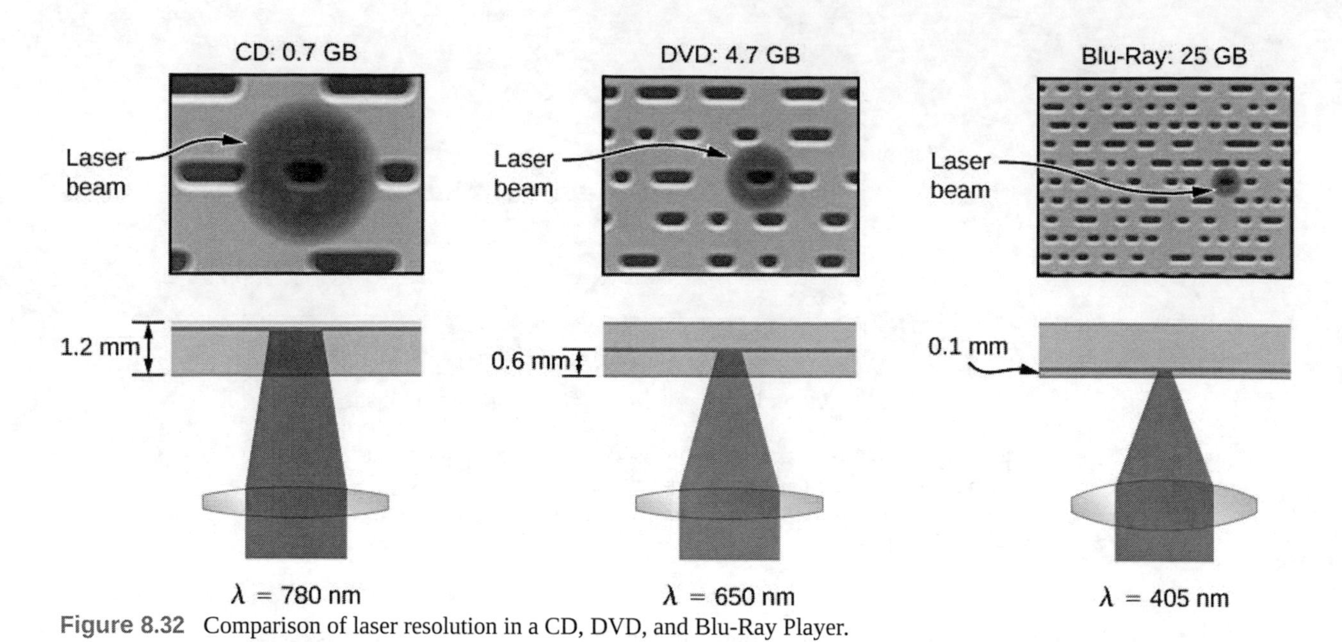

Figure 8.32 Comparison of laser resolution in a CD, DVD, and Blu-Ray Player.

CHAPTER 8 REVIEW

KEY TERMS

angular momentum orbital quantum number (*l*) quantum number associated with the orbital angular momentum of an electron in a hydrogen atom

angular momentum projection quantum number (*m*) quantum number associated with the *z*-component of the orbital angular momentum of an electron in a hydrogen atom

atomic orbital region in space that encloses a certain percentage (usually 90%) of the electron probability

Bohr magneton magnetic moment of an electron, equal to 9.3×10^{-24} J/T or 5.8×10^{-5} eV/T

braking radiation radiation produced by targeting metal with a high-energy electron beam (or radiation produced by the acceleration of any charged particle in a material)

chemical group group of elements in the same column of the periodic table that possess similar chemical properties

coherent light light that consists of photons of the same frequency and phase

covalent bond chemical bond formed by the sharing of electrons between two atoms

electron configuration representation of the state of electrons in an atom, such as $1s^2 2s^1$ for lithium

fine structure detailed structure of atomic spectra produced by spin-orbit coupling

fluorescence radiation produced by the excitation and subsequent, gradual de-excitation of an electron in an atom

hyperfine structure detailed structure of atomic spectra produced by spin-orbit coupling

ionic bond chemical bond formed by the electric attraction between two oppositely charged ions

laser coherent light produced by a cascade of electron de-excitations

magnetic orbital quantum number another term for the angular momentum projection quantum number

magnetogram pictoral representation, or map, of the magnetic activity at the Sun's surface

metastable state state in which an electron "lingers" in an excited state

monochromatic light that consists of photons with the same frequency

Moseley plot plot of the atomic number versus the square root of X-ray frequency

Moseley's law relationship between the atomic number and X-ray photon frequency for X-ray production

orbital magnetic dipole moment measure of the strength of the magnetic field produced by the orbital angular momentum of the electron

Pauli's exclusion principle no two electrons in an atom can have the same values for all four quantum numbers (n, l, m, m_s)

population inversion condition in which a majority of atoms contain electrons in a metastable state

principal quantum number (*n*) quantum number associated with the total energy of an electron in a hydrogen atom

radial probability density function function use to determine the probability of a electron to be found in a spatial interval in *r*

selection rules rules that determine whether atomic transitions are allowed or forbidden (rare)

spin projection quantum number (m_s) quantum number associated with the *z*-component of the spin angular momentum of an electron

spin quantum number (*s*) quantum number associated with the spin angular momentum of an electron

spin-flip transitions atomic transitions between states of an electron-proton system in which the magnetic moments are aligned and not aligned

spin-orbit coupling interaction between the electron magnetic moment and the magnetic field produced by the orbital angular momentum of the electron

stimulated emission when a photon of energy triggers an electron in a metastable state to drop in energy emitting an additional photon

transition metal element that is located in the gap between the first two columns and the last six columns of the table of elements that contains electrons that fill the *d* subshell

valence electron electron in the outer shell of an atom that participates in chemical bonding

Zeeman effect splitting of energy levels by an external magnetic field

KEY EQUATIONS

Orbital angular momentum	$L = \sqrt{l(l+1)}\hbar$
z-component of orbital angular momentum	$L_z = m\hbar$
Radial probability density function	$P(r)dr = \left\vert\psi_{n00}\right\vert^2 4\pi r^2 dr$
Spin angular momentum	$S = \sqrt{s(s+1)}\hbar$
z-component of spin angular momentum	$S_z = m_s \hbar$
Electron spin magnetic moment	$\vec{\mu}_s = \left(\frac{e}{m_e}\right)\vec{\mathbf{S}}$
Electron orbital magnetic dipole moment	$\vec{\mu} = -\left(\frac{e}{2m_e}\right)\vec{\mathbf{L}}$
Potential energy associated with the magnetic interaction between the orbital magnetic dipole moment and an external magnetic field $\vec{\mathbf{B}}$	$U(\theta) = -\mu_z B = m\mu_B B$
Maximum number of electrons in a subshell of a hydrogen atom	$N = 4l + 2$
Selection rule for atomic transitions in a hydrogen-like atom	$\Delta l = \pm 1$
Moseley's law for X-ray production	$(Z-1) = \text{constant}\sqrt{f}$

SUMMARY

8.1 The Hydrogen Atom

- A hydrogen atom can be described in terms of its wave function, probability density, total energy, and orbital angular momentum.
- The state of an electron in a hydrogen atom is specified by its quantum numbers (n, l, m).
- In contrast to the Bohr model of the atom, the Schrödinger model makes predictions based on probability statements.
- The quantum numbers of a hydrogen atom can be used to calculate important information about the atom.

8.2 Orbital Magnetic Dipole Moment of the Electron

- A hydrogen atom has magnetic properties because the motion of the electron acts as a current loop.
- The energy levels of a hydrogen atom associated with orbital angular momentum are split by an external magnetic field because the orbital angular magnetic moment interacts with the field.
- The quantum numbers of an electron in a hydrogen atom can be used to calculate the magnitude and direction of the

orbital magnetic dipole moment of the atom.

8.3 Electron Spin

- The state of an electron in a hydrogen atom can be expressed in terms of five quantum numbers.
- The spin angular momentum quantum of an electron is $= +½$. The spin angular momentum projection quantum number is $m_s = +½$ or $-½$ (spin up or spin down).
- The fine and hyperfine structures of the hydrogen spectrum are explained by magnetic interactions within the atom.

8.4 The Exclusion Principle and the Periodic Table

- Pauli's exclusion principle states that no two electrons in an atom can have all the same quantum numbers.
- The structure of the periodic table of elements can be explained in terms of the total energy, orbital angular momentum, and spin of electrons in an atom.
- The state of an atom can be expressed by its electron configuration, which describes the shells and subshells that are filled in the atom.

8.5 Atomic Spectra and X-rays

- Radiation is absorbed and emitted by atomic energy-level transitions.
- Quantum numbers can be used to estimate the energy, frequency, and wavelength of photons produced by atomic transitions.
- Atomic fluorescence occurs when an electron in an atom is excited several steps above the ground state by the absorption of a high-energy ultraviolet (UV) photon.
- X-ray photons are produced when a vacancy in an inner shell of an atom is filled by an electron from the outer shell of the atom.
- The frequency of X-ray radiation is related to the atomic number Z of an atom.

8.6 Lasers

- Laser light is coherent (monochromatic and "phase linked") light.
- Laser light is produced by population inversion and subsequent de-excitation of electrons in a material (solid, liquid, or gas).
- CD and Blu-Ray players uses lasers to read digital information stored on discs.

CONCEPTUAL QUESTIONS

8.1 The Hydrogen Atom

1. Identify the physical significance of each of the quantum numbers of the hydrogen atom.

2. Describe the ground state of hydrogen in terms of wave function, probability density, and atomic orbitals.

3. Distinguish between Bohr's and Schrödinger's model of the hydrogen atom. In particular, compare the energy and orbital angular momentum of the ground states.

8.2 Orbital Magnetic Dipole Moment of the Electron

4. Explain why spectral lines of the hydrogen atom are split by an external magnetic field. What determines the number and spacing of these lines?

5. A hydrogen atom is placed in a magnetic field. Which of the following quantities are affected? (a) total energy; (b) angular momentum; (c) z-component of angular momentum; (d) polar angle.

6. On what factors does the orbital magnetic dipole moment of an electron depend?

8.3 Electron Spin

7. Explain how a hydrogen atom in the ground state $(l = 0)$ can interact magnetically with an external magnetic field.

8. Compare orbital angular momentum with spin angular momentum of an electron in the hydrogen atom.

9. List all the possible values of s and m_s for an electron. Are there particles for which these values are different?

10. Are the angular momentum vectors $\vec{\mathbf{L}}$ and $\vec{\mathbf{S}}$ necessarily aligned?

11. What is spin-orbit coupling?

8.4 The Exclusion Principle and the Periodic Table

12. What is Pauli's exclusion principle? Explain the importance of this principle for the understanding of atomic structure and molecular bonding.

13. Compare the electron configurations of the elements in the same column of the periodic table.

14. Compare the electron configurations of the elements that belong in the same row of the periodic table of elements.

8.5 Atomic Spectra and X-rays

15. Atomic and molecular spectra are discrete. What does discrete mean, and how are discrete spectra related to the quantization of energy and electron orbits in atoms and molecules?

16. Discuss the process of the absorption of light by matter in terms of the atomic structure of the absorbing medium.

17. NGC1763 is an emission nebula in the Large Magellanic Cloud just outside our Milky Way Galaxy. Ultraviolet light from hot stars ionize the hydrogen atoms in the nebula. As protons and electrons recombine, light in the visible range is emitted. Compare the energies of the photons involved in these two transitions.

18. Why are X-rays emitted only for electron transitions to inner shells? What type of photon is emitted for transitions between outer shells?

19. How do the allowed orbits for electrons in atoms differ from the allowed orbits for planets around the sun?

8.6 Lasers

20. Distinguish between coherent and monochromatic light.

21. Why is a metastable state necessary for the production of laser light?

22. How does light from an incandescent light bulb differ from laser light?

23. How is a Blu-Ray player able to read more information that a CD player?

24. What are the similarities and differences between a CD player and a Blu-Ray player?

PROBLEMS

8.1 The Hydrogen Atom

25. The wave function is evaluated at rectangular coordinates $(x, y, z) = (2, 1, 1)$ in arbitrary units. What are the spherical coordinates of this position?

26. If an atom has an electron in the $n = 5$ state with $m = 3$, what are the possible values of l?

27. What are the possible values of m for an electron in the $n = 4$ state?

28. What, if any, constraints does a value of $m = 1$ place on the other quantum numbers for an electron in an atom?

29. What are the possible values of m for an electron in the $n = 4$ state?

30. (a) How many angles can L make with the z-axis for an $l = 2$ electron? (b) Calculate the value of the smallest angle.

31. The force on an electron is "negative the gradient of the potential energy function." Use this knowledge and **Equation 8.1** to show that the force on the electron in a hydrogen atom is given by Coulomb's force law.

32. What is the total number of states with orbital angular momentum $l = 0$? (Ignore electron spin.)

33. The wave function is evaluated at spherical coordinates $(r, \theta, \phi) = (\sqrt{3}, 45°, 45°)$, where the value of the radial coordinate is given in arbitrary units. What are the rectangular coordinates of this position?

34. Coulomb's force law states that the force between two charged particles is:

$F = k\frac{Qq}{r^2}$. Use this expression to determine the potential energy function.

35. Write an expression for the total number of states with orbital angular momentum *l*.

36. Consider hydrogen in the ground state, ψ_{100}. (a) Use the derivative to determine the radial position for which the probability density, *P*(*r*), is a maximum.

(b) Use the integral concept to determine the average radial position. (This is called the expectation value of the electron's radial position.) Express your answers into terms of the Bohr radius, a_o. Hint: The expectation value is the just average value. (c) Why are these values different?

37. What is the probability that the 1*s* electron of a hydrogen atom is found outside the Bohr radius?

38. How many polar angles are possible for an electron in the $l = 5$ state?

39. What is the maximum number of orbital angular momentum electron states in the $n = 2$ shell of a hydrogen atom? (Ignore electron spin.)

40. What is the maximum number of orbital angular momentum electron states in the $n = 3$ shell of a hydrogen atom? (Ignore electron spin.)

8.2 Orbital Magnetic Dipole Moment of the Electron

41. Find the magnitude of the orbital magnetic dipole moment of the electron in in the 3*p* state. (Express your answer in terms of μ_B.)

42. A current of $I = 2\text{A}$ flows through a square-shaped wire with 2-cm side lengths. What is the magnetic moment of the wire?

43. Estimate the ratio of the electron magnetic moment to the *muon* magnetic moment for the same state of orbital angular momentum. (*Hint:* $m_\mu = 105.7\ \text{MeV}/c^2$)

44. Find the magnitude of the orbital magnetic dipole moment of the electron in in the 4*d* state. (Express your answer in terms of μ_B.)

45. For a 3*d* electron in an external magnetic field of $2.50 \times 10^{-3}\ \text{T}$, find (a) the current associated with the orbital angular momentum, and (b) the maximum torque.

46. An electron in a hydrogen atom is in the $n = 5$, $l = 4$ state. Find the smallest angle the magnetic moment makes with the *z*-axis. (Express your answer in terms of μ_B.)

47. Find the minimum torque magnitude $|\vec{\tau}|$ that acts on the orbital magnetic dipole of a 3*p* electron in an external magnetic field of $2.50 \times 10^{-3}\ \text{T}$.

48. An electron in a hydrogen atom is in 3*p* state. Find the smallest angle the magnetic moment makes with the *z*-axis. (Express your answer in terms of μ_B.)

49. Show that $U = -\vec{\mu} \cdot \vec{\mathbf{B}}$.

(*Hint*: An infinitesimal amount of work is done to align the magnetic moment with the external field. This work rotates the magnetic moment vector through an angle $-d\theta$ (toward the positive *z*-direction), where $d\theta$ is a positive angle change.)

8.3 Electron Spin

50. What is the magnitude of the spin momentum of an electron? (Express you answer in terms of $\hbar$.)

51. What are the possible polar orientations of the spin momentum vector for an electron?

52. For $n = 1$, write all the possible sets of quantum numbers (n, l, m, m_s).

53. A hydrogen atom is placed in an external uniform magnetic field ($B = 200\ \text{T}$). Calculate the wavelength of light produced in a transition from a spin up to spin down state.

54. If the magnetic field in the preceding problem is quadrupled, what happens to the wavelength of light produced in a transition from a spin up to spin down state?

55. If the magnetic moment in the preceding problem is doubled, what happens to the frequency of light produced in a transition from a spin-up to spin-down state?

56. For $n = 2$, write all the possible sets of quantum numbers (n, l, m, m_s).

8.4 The Exclusion Principle and the Periodic Table

57. (a) How many electrons can be in the $n = 4$ shell?

(b) What are its subshells, and how many electrons can be in each?

58. (a) What is the minimum value of l for a subshell that contains 11 electrons?

(b) If this subshell is in the $n = 5$ shell, what is the spectroscopic notation for this atom?

59. **Unreasonable result.** Which of the following spectroscopic notations are not allowed? (a) $5s^1$ (b) $1d^1$ (c) $4s^3$ (d) $3p^7$ (e) $5g^{15}$. State which rule is violated for each notation that is not allowed.

60. Write the electron configuration for potassium.

61. Write the electron configuration for iron.

62. The valence electron of potassium is excited to a 5d state. (a) What is the magnitude of the electron's orbital angular momentum? (b) How many states are possible along a chosen direction?

63. (a) If one subshell of an atom has nine electrons in it, what is the minimum value of l? (b) What is the spectroscopic notation for this atom, if this subshell is part of the $n = 3$ shell?

64. Write the electron configuration for magnesium.

65. Write the electron configuration for carbon.

66. The magnitudes of the resultant spins of the electrons of the elements B through Ne when in the ground state are: $\sqrt{3}\hbar/2$, $\sqrt{2}\hbar$, $\sqrt{15}\hbar/2$, $\sqrt{2}\hbar$, $\sqrt{3}\hbar/2$, and 0, respectively. Argue that these spins are consistent with Hund's rule.

8.5 Atomic Spectra and X-rays

67. What is the minimum frequency of a photon required to ionize: (a) a He^+ ion in its ground state? (b) A Li^{2+} ion in its first excited state?

68. The ion Li^{2+} makes an atomic transition from an $n = 4$ state to an $n = 2$ state. (a) What is the energy of the photon emitted during the transition? (b) What is the wavelength of the photon?

69. The red light emitted by a ruby laser has a wavelength of 694.3 nm. What is the difference in energy between the initial state and final state corresponding to the emission of the light?

70. The yellow light from a sodium-vapor street lamp is produced by a transition of sodium atoms from a 3p state to a 3s state. If the difference in energies of those two states is 2.10 eV, what is the wavelength of the yellow light?

71. Estimate the wavelength of the K_α X-ray from calcium.

72. Estimate the frequency of the K_α X-ray from cesium.

73. X-rays are produced by striking a target with a beam of electrons. Prior to striking the target, the electrons are accelerated by an electric field through a potential energy difference:

$$\Delta U = -e\Delta V,$$

where e is the charge of an electron and ΔV is the voltage difference. If $\Delta V = 15{,}000$ volts, what is the minimum wavelength of the emitted radiation?

74. For the preceding problem, what happens to the minimum wavelength if the voltage across the X-ray tube is doubled?

75. Suppose the experiment in the preceding problem is conducted with muons. What happens to the minimum wavelength?

76. An X-ray tube accelerates an electron with an applied voltage of 50 kV toward a metal target. (a) What is the shortest-wavelength X-ray radiation generated at the target? (b) Calculate the photon energy in eV. (c) Explain the relationship of the photon energy to the applied voltage.

77. A color television tube generates some X-rays when its electron beam strikes the screen. What is the shortest wavelength of these X-rays, if a 30.0-kV potential is used to accelerate the electrons? (Note that TVs have shielding to prevent these X-rays from exposing viewers.)

78. An X-ray tube has an applied voltage of 100 kV. (a) What is the most energetic X-ray photon it can produce? Express your answer in electron volts and joules. (b) Find the wavelength of such an X-ray.

79. The maximum characteristic X-ray photon energy comes from the capture of a free electron into a K shell vacancy. What is this photon energy in keV for tungsten, assuming that the free electron has no initial kinetic energy?

80. What are the approximate energies of the K_α and K_β X-rays for copper?

81. Compare the X-ray photon wavelengths for copper and gold.

82. The approximate energies of the K_α and K_β X-rays for copper are $E_{K_\alpha} = 8.00\,\text{keV}$ and $E_{K_\beta} = 9.48\,\text{keV}$, respectively. Determine the ratio of X-ray frequencies of gold to copper, then use this value to estimate the corresponding energies of K_α and K_β X-rays for gold.

8.6 Lasers

83. A carbon dioxide laser used in surgery emits infrared radiation with a wavelength of $10.6\,\mu\text{m}$. In 1.00 ms, this laser raised the temperature of $1.00\,\text{cm}^3$ of flesh to $100\,°\text{C}$ and evaporated it. (a) How many photons were required? You may assume that flesh has the same heat of vaporization as water. (b) What was the minimum power output during the flash?

84. An excimer laser used for vision correction emits UV radiation with a wavelength of 193 nm. (a) Calculate the photon energy in eV. (b) These photons are used to evaporate corneal tissue, which is very similar to water in its properties. Calculate the amount of energy needed per molecule of water to make the phase change from liquid to gas. That is, divide the heat of vaporization in kJ/kg by the number of water molecules in a kilogram. (c) Convert this to eV and compare to the photon energy. Discuss the implications.

ADDITIONAL PROBLEMS

85. For a hydrogen atom in an excited state with principal quantum number *n*, show that the smallest angle that the orbital angular momentum vector can make with respect to the *z*-axis is $\theta = \cos^{-1}\left(\sqrt{\frac{n-1}{n}}\right)$.

86. What is the probability that the 1*s* electron of a hydrogen atom is found between $r = 0$ and $r = \infty$?

87. Sketch the potential energy function of an electron in a hydrogen atom. (a) What is the value of this function at $r = 0$? in the limit that $r = \infty$? (b) What is unreasonable or inconsistent with the former result?

88. Find the value of l, the orbital angular momentum quantum number, for the Moon around Earth.

89. Show that the maximum number of orbital angular momentum electron states in the *n*th shell of an atom is n^2. (Ignore electron spin.) (*Hint:* Make a table of the total number of orbital angular momentum states for each shell and find the pattern.)

90. What is the magnitude of an electron magnetic moment?

91. What is the maximum number of electron states in the $n = 5$ shell?

92. A ground-state hydrogen atom is placed in a uniform magnetic field, and a photon is emitted in the transition from a spin-up to spin-down state. The wavelength of the photon is $168\,\mu\text{m}$. What is the strength of the magnetic field?

93. Show that the maximum number of electron states in the *n*th shell of an atom is $2n^2$.

94. The valence electron of chlorine is excited to a 3*p* state. (a) What is the magnitude of the electron's orbital angular momentum? (b) What are possible values for the *z*-component of angular measurement?

95. Which of the following notations are allowed (that is, which violate none of the rules regarding values of quantum numbers)? (a) $1s^1$; (b) $1d^3$; (c) $4s^2$; (d) $3p^7$; (e) $6h^{20}$

96. The ion Be^{3+} makes an atomic transition from an $n = 3$ state to an $n = 2$ state. (a) What is the energy of the photon emitted during the transition? (b) What is the wavelength of the photon?

97. The maximum characteristic X-ray photon energy comes from the capture of a free electron into a *K* shell vacancy. What is this photon frequency for tungsten, assuming that the free electron has no initial kinetic energy?

98. Derive an expression for the ratio of X-ray photon

frequency for two elements with atomic numbers Z_1 and Z_2.

99. Compare the X-ray photon wavelengths for copper and silver.

100. (a) What voltage must be applied to an X-ray tube to obtain 0.0100-fm-wavelength X-rays for use in exploring the details of nuclei? (b) What is unreasonable about this result? (c) Which assumptions are unreasonable or inconsistent?

101. A student in a physics laboratory observes a hydrogen spectrum with a diffraction grating for the purpose of measuring the wavelengths of the emitted radiation. In the spectrum, she observes a yellow line and finds its wavelength to be 589 nm. (a) Assuming that this is part of the Balmer series, determine n_i, the principal quantum number of the initial state. (b) What is unreasonable about this result? (c) Which assumptions are unreasonable or inconsistent?

9 | CONDENSED MATTER PHYSICS

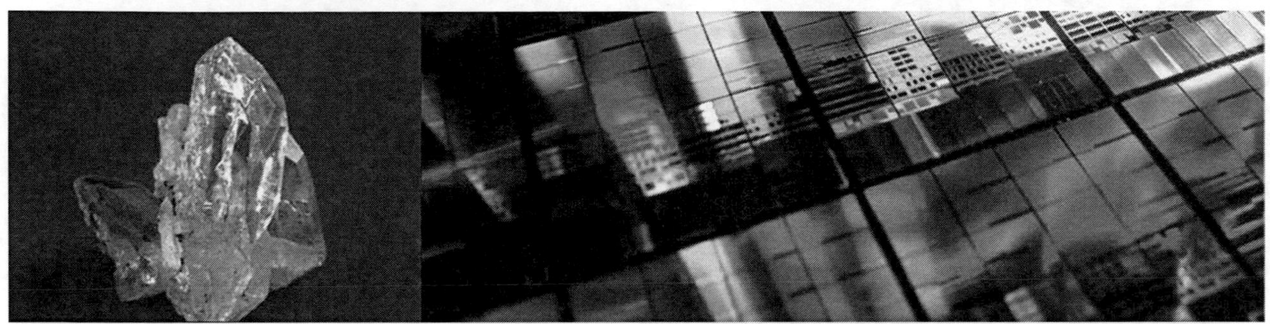

Figure 9.1 The crystalline structure of quartz allows it to cleave into smooth planes that refract light, making it suitable for jewelry. Silicon, the main element in quartz, also forms crystals in its pure form, and these crystals form the basis for the worldwide semiconductor electronics industry. (credit left: modification of work by the United States Geological Survey)

Chapter Outline

Introduction

In this chapter, we examine applications of quantum mechanics to more complex systems, such as molecules, metals, semiconductors, and superconductors. We review and develop concepts of the previous chapters, including wave functions, orbitals, and quantum states. We also introduce many new concepts, including covalent bonding, rotational energy levels, Fermi energy, energy bands, doping, and Cooper pairs.

The main topic in this chapter is the crystal structure of solids. For centuries, crystalline solids have been prized for their beauty, including gems like diamonds and emeralds, as well as geological crystals of quartz and metallic ores. But the crystalline structures of semiconductors such as silicon have also made possible the electronics industry of today. In this chapter, we study how the structures of solids give them properties from strength and transparency to electrical conductivity.

9.1 | Types of Molecular Bonds

Learning Objectives

By the end of this section, you will be able to:

- Distinguish between the different types of molecular bonds
- Determine the dissociation energy of a molecule using the concepts ionization energy, electron affinity, and Coulomb force
- Describe covalent bonding in terms of exchange symmetry
- Explain the physical structure of a molecule in terms of the concept of hybridization

Quantum mechanics has been extraordinarily successful at explaining the structure and bonding in molecules, and is therefore the foundation for all of chemistry. Quantum chemistry, as it is sometimes called, explains such basic questions as why H_2O molecules exist, why the bonding angle between hydrogen atoms in this molecule is precisely $104.5°$, and why these molecules bind together to form liquid water at room temperature. Applying quantum mechanics to molecules can be very difficult mathematically, so our discussion will be qualitative only.

As we study molecules and then solids, we will use many different scientific models. In some cases, we look at a molecule or crystal as a set of point nuclei with electrons whizzing around the outside in well-defined trajectories, as in the Bohr model. In other cases, we employ our full knowledge of quantum mechanics to study these systems using wave functions and the concept of electron spin. It is important to remember that we study modern physics with models, and that different models are useful for different purposes. We do not always use the most powerful model, when a less-powerful, easier-to-use model will do the job.

Types of Bonds

Chemical units form by many different kinds of chemical bonds. An **ionic bond** forms when an electron transfers from one atom to another. A **covalent bond** occurs when two or more atoms share electrons. A **van der Waals bond** occurs due to the attraction of charge-polarized molecules and is considerably weaker than ionic or covalent bonds. Many other types of bonding exist as well. Often, bonding occurs via more than one mechanism. The focus of this section is ionic and covalent bonding.

Ionic bonds

The ionic bond is perhaps the easiest type of bonding to understand. It explains the formation of salt compounds, such as sodium chloride, NaCl. The sodium atom (symbol Na) has the same electron arrangement as a neon atom plus one 3*s* electron. Only 5.14 eV of energy is required to remove this one electron from the sodium atom. Therefore, Na can easily give up or donate this electron to an adjacent (nearby) atom, attaining a more stable arrangement of electrons. Chlorine (symbol Cl) requires just one electron to complete its valence shell, so it readily accepts this electron if it is near the sodium atom. We therefore say that chlorine has a large **electron affinity**, which is the energy associated with an accepted electron. The energy given up by the chlorine atom in this process is 3.62 eV. After the electron transfers from the sodium atom to the chlorine atom, the sodium atom becomes a positive ion and the chlorine atom becomes a negative ion. The total energy required for this transfer is given by

$$E_{\text{transfer}} = 5.14\,\text{eV} - 3.62\,\text{eV} = 1.52\,\text{eV}.$$

The positive sodium ion and negative chloride ion experience an attractive Coulomb force. The potential energy associated with this force is given by

$$U_{\text{coul}} = -\frac{ke^2}{r_0}, \tag{9.1}$$

where $ke^2 = 1.440\,\text{eV-nm}$ and r_0 is the distance between the ions.

As the sodium and chloride ions move together ("descend the potential energy hill"), the force of attraction between the ions becomes stronger. However, if the ions become too close, core-electron wave functions in the two ions begin to overlap.

Due to the exclusion principle, this action promotes the core electrons—and therefore the entire molecule—into a higher energy state. The **equilibrium separation distance** (or bond length) between the ions occurs when the molecule is in its lowest energy state. For diatomic NaCl, this distance is 0.236 nm. Figure 9.2 shows the total energy of NaCl as a function of the distance of separation between ions.

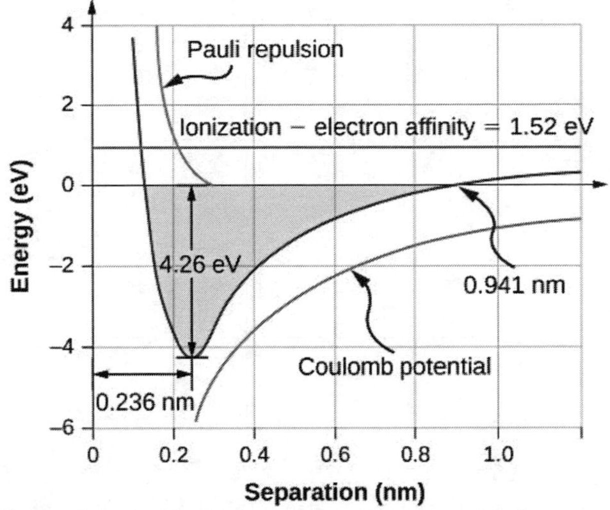

Figure 9.2 Graph of energy versus ionic separation for sodium chloride. Equilibrium separation occur when the total energy is a minimum $(-4.36\ \text{eV})$.

The total energy required to form a single salt unit is

$$U_{\text{form}} = E_{\text{transfer}} + U_{\text{coul}} + U_{\text{ex}}, \tag{9.2}$$

where U_{ex} is the energy associated with the repulsion between core electrons due to Pauli's exclusion principle. The value of U_{form} must be negative for the bond to form spontaneously. The **dissociation energy** is defined as the energy required to separate the unit into its constituent ions, written

$$U_{\text{diss}} = -U_{\text{form}} \tag{9.3}$$

Every diatomic formula unit has its own characteristic dissociation energy and equilibrium separation length. Sample values are given in Table 9.1.

Molecule	Dissociation Energy (eV)	Equilibrium Separation (nm) (Bond length)
NaCl	4.26	0.236
NaF	4.99	0.193
NaBr	3.8	0.250
NaI	3.1	0.271
NaH	2.08	0.189
LiCl	4.86	0.202
LiH	2.47	0.239

Table 9.1 Bond Length

Molecule	Dissociation Energy (eV)	Equilibrium Separation (nm) (Bond length)
LiI	3.67	0.238
KCl	4.43	0.267
KBr	3.97	0.282
RbF	5.12	0.227
RbCl	4.64	0.279
CsI	3.57	0.337
H-H	4.5	0.075
N-N	9.8	0.11
O-O	5.2	0.12
F-F	1.6	0.14
Cl-Cl	2.5	0.20

Table 9.1 Bond Length

Example 9.1

The Energy of Salt

What is the dissociation energy of a salt formula unit (NaCl)?

Strategy

Sodium chloride (NaCl) is a salt formed by ionic bonds. The energy change associated with this bond depends on three main processes: the ionization of Na; the acceptance of the electron from a Na atom by a Cl atom; and Coulomb attraction of the resulting ions (Na^+ and Cl^-). If the ions get too close, they repel due to the exclusion principle (0.32 eV). The equilibrium separation distance is $r_0 = 0.236\ \text{nm}$.

Solution

The energy change associated with the transfer of an electron from Na to Cl is 1.52 eV, as discussed earlier in this section. At equilibrium separation, the atoms are $r_0 = 0.236\ \text{nm}$ apart. The electrostatic potential energy of the atoms is

$$U_{\text{coul}} = -\frac{ke^2}{r_0} = -\frac{1.44\ \text{eV}\cdot\text{nm}}{0.236\ \text{nm}} = -6.10\ \text{eV}.$$

The total energy difference associated with the formation of a NaCl formula unit is

$$E_{\text{form}} = E_{\text{xfr}} + U_{\text{coul}} + U_{\text{ex}} = 1.52\ \text{eV} + (-6.10\ \text{eV}) + 0.32\ \text{eV} = -4.26\ \text{eV}.$$

Therefore, the dissociated energy of NaCl is 4.26 eV.

Significance

The formation of a NaCl formula unit by ionic bonding is energetically favorable. The dissociation energy, or energy required to separate the NaCl unit into Na^+ and Cl^- ions is 4.26 eV, consistent with **Figure 9.2**.

9.1 Check Your Understanding Why is the potential energy associated with the exclusion principle positive in **Example 9.1**?

For a sodium ion in an ionic NaCl crystal, the expression for Coulomb potential energy U_{coul} must be modified by a factor known as the **Madelung constant**. This factor takes into account the interaction of the sodium ion with all nearby chloride and sodium ions. The Madelung constant for a NaCl crystal is about 1.75. This value implies an equilibrium separation distance between Na^+ and Cl^- ions of 0.280 nm—slightly larger than for diatomic NaCl. We will return to this point again later.

Covalent bonds

In an ionic bond, an electron transfers from one atom to another. However, in a covalent bond, an electron is shared between two atoms. The ionic bonding mechanism cannot explain the existence of such molecules as $H_2, O_2,$ and CO, since no separation distance exists for which the negative potential energy of attraction is greater in magnitude than the energy needed to create ions. Understanding precisely how such molecules are covalently bonded relies on a deeper understanding of quantum mechanics that goes beyond the coverage of this book, but we will qualitatively describe the mechanisms in the following section.

Covalent bonds can be understood using the simple example of a H_2^+ molecule, which consists of one electron in the electric field of two protons. This system can be modeled by an electron in a double square well (Figure 9.3). The electron is equally likely to be found in each well, so the wave function is either symmetric or antisymmetric about a point midway between the wells.

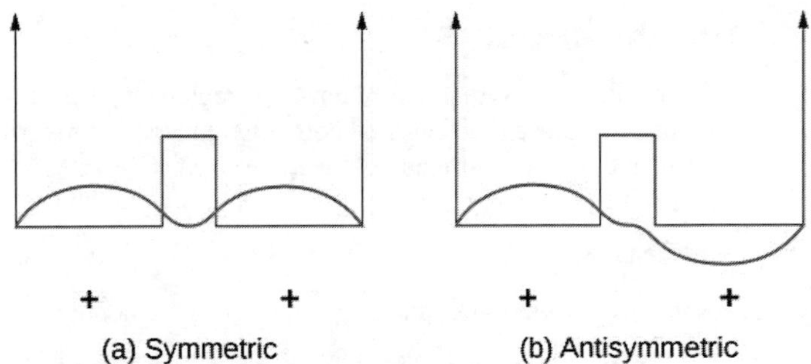

Figure 9.3 A one-dimensional model of covalent bonding in a H_2^+ molecule. (a) The symmetric wave function of the electron shared by the two positively charged protons (represented by the two finite square wells). (b) The corresponding antisymmetric wave function.

Now imagine that the two wells are separated by a large distance. In the ground state, the wave function exists in one of two possible states: either a single positive peak (a sine wave-like "hump") in both wells (symmetric case), or a positive peak in one well and a negative peak in the other (antisymmetric case). These states have the same energy. However, when the wells are brought together, the symmetric wave function becomes the ground state and the antisymmetric state becomes the first excited state—in other words, the energy level of the electron is split. Notice, the space-symmetric state becomes the energetically favorable (lower energy) state.

The same analysis is appropriate for an electron bound to two hydrogen atoms. Here, the shapes of the ground-state wave functions have the form e^{-r/a_0} or $e^{(-|x|/a_0)}$ in one dimension. The energetically favorable, space-symmetric state implies a high charge density midway between the protons where the electrons are likely to pull the positively charged protons together.

If a second electron is added to this system to form a H_2 molecule, the wave function must describe both particles, including their spatial relationship and relative spins. This wave function must also respect the indistinguishability of electrons. ("If you've seen one electron, you've seen them all.") In particular, switching or exchanging the electrons should *not* produce an observable effect, a property called **exchange symmetry**. Exchange symmetry can be *symmetric*, producing no change in the wave function, or *antisymmetric*, producing an overall change in the sign of the wave function—neither of which is observable.

As we discuss later, the total wave function of two electrons must be antisymmetric on exchange. For example, two electrons bound to a hydrogen molecule can be in a space-symmetric state with antiparallel spins $(\uparrow\downarrow)$ or space-antisymmetric state with parallel spins $(\uparrow\uparrow)$. The state with antiparallel spins is energetically favorable and therefore used in covalent bonding. If the protons are drawn too closely together, however, repulsion between the protons becomes important. (In other molecules, this effect is supplied by the exclusion principle.) As a result, H_2 reaches an equilibrium separation of about 0.074 nm with a binding energy is 4.52 eV.

Visit this **PBS Learning Media tutorial and interactive simulation (https://openstaxcollege.org/l/21covalentbond)** to explore the attractive and repulsive forces that act on atomic particles and covalent bonding in a H_2 molecule.

Quantum mechanics excludes many types of molecules. For example, the molecule H_3 does not form, because if a third H atom approaches diatomic hydrogen, the wave function of the electron in this atom overlaps the electrons in the other two atoms. If all three electrons are in the ground states of their respective atoms, one pair of electrons shares all the same quantum numbers, which is forbidden by the exclusion principle. Instead, one of the electrons is forced into a higher energy state. No separation between three protons exists for which the total energy change of this process is negative—that is, where bonding occurs spontaneously. Similarly, He_2 is not covalently bonded under normal conditions, because these atoms have no valence electrons to share. As the atoms are brought together, the wave functions of the core electrons overlap, and due to the exclusion principle, the electrons are forced into a higher energy state. No separation exists for which such a molecule is energetically favorable.

Bonding in Polyatomic Molecules

A **polyatomic molecule** is a molecule made of more than two atoms. Examples range from a simple water molecule to a complex protein molecule. The structures of these molecules can often be understood in terms of covalent bonding and **hybridization**. Hybridization is a change in the energy structure of an atom in which mixed states (states that can be written as a linear superposition of others) participate in bonding.

To illustrate hybridization, consider the bonding in a simple water molecule, H_2O. The electron configuration of oxygen is $1s^2 2s^2 2p^4$. The 1*s* and 2*s* electrons are in "closed shells" and do not participate in bonding. The remaining four electrons are the valence electrons. These electrons can fill six possible states ($l = 1$, $m = 0$, ± 1, plus spin up and down). The energies of these states are the same, so the oxygen atom can exploit any linear combination of these states in bonding with the hydrogen atoms. These linear combinations (which you learned about in the chapter on atomic structure) are called atomic orbitals, and they are denoted by p_x, p_y, and p_z. The electron charge distributions for these orbitals are given in **Figure 9.4**.

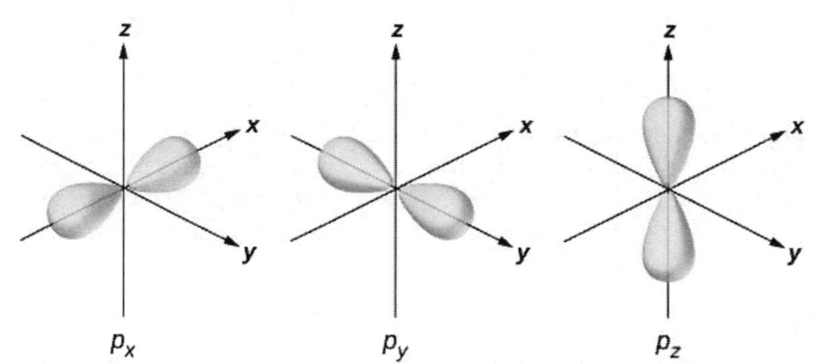

Figure 9.4 Oxygen has four valence electrons. In the context of a water molecule, two valence electrons fill the p_z orbital and one electron fills each of the p_x and p_y orbitals. The p_x and p_y orbitals are used in bonding with hydrogen atoms to form H_2O. Without repulsion of H atoms, the bond angle between hydrogen atoms would be 90 degrees.

The transformation of the electron wave functions of oxygen to p_x, p_y, and p_z orbitals in the presence of the hydrogen atoms is an example of hybridization. Two electrons are found in the p_z orbital with paired spins $(\uparrow \downarrow)$. One electron is found in each of the p_x and p_y orbitals, with unpaired spins. The latter orbitals participate in bonding with the hydrogen atoms. Based on **Figure 9.4**, we expect the bonding angle for H—O—H to be $90°$. However, if we include the effects of repulsion between atoms, the bond angle is $104.5°$. The same arguments can be used to understand the tetrahedral shape of methane (CH_4) and other molecules.

9.2 | Molecular Spectra

Learning Objectives

By the end of this section, you will be able to:

- Use the concepts of vibrational and rotational energy to describe energy transitions in a diatomic molecule
- Explain key features of a vibrational-rotational energy spectrum of a diatomic molecule
- Estimate allowed energies of a rotating molecule
- Determine the equilibrium separation distance between atoms in a diatomic molecule from the vibrational-rotational absorption spectrum

Molecular energy levels are more complicated than atomic energy levels because molecules can also vibrate and rotate. The energies associated with such motions lie in different ranges and can therefore be studied separately. Electronic transitions are of order 1 eV, vibrational transitions are of order 10^{-2} eV, and rotational transitions are of order 10^{-3} eV. For complex molecules, these energy changes are difficult to characterize, so we begin with the simple case of a diatomic molecule.

According to classical mechanics, the energy of rotation of a diatomic molecule is given by

$$E_r = \frac{L^2}{2I}, \tag{9.4}$$

where I is the moment of inertia and L is the angular momentum. According to quantum mechanics, the rotational angular momentum is quantized:

$$L = \sqrt{l(l+1)}\hbar \, (l = 0,\ 1,\ 2,\ 3,...), \tag{9.5}$$

where l is the orbital angular quantum number. The allowed **rotational energy level** of a diatomic molecule is therefore

$$E_r = l(l+1)\frac{\hbar^2}{2I} = l(l+1)E_{0r} \quad (l = 0,\ 1,\ 2,\ 3,...), \tag{9.6}$$

where the characteristic rotational energy of a molecule is defined as

$$E_{0r} = \frac{\hbar^2}{2I}. \tag{9.7}$$

For a diatomic molecule, the moment of inertia with reduced mass μ is

$$I = \mu r_0^2, \tag{9.8}$$

where r_0 is the total distance between the atoms. The energy difference between rotational levels is therefore

$$\Delta E_r = E_{l+1} - E_l = 2(l+1)\,E_{0r}. \tag{9.9}$$

A detailed study of transitions between rotational energy levels brought about by the absorption or emission of radiation (a so-called **electric dipole transition**) requires that

$$\Delta l = \pm 1. \quad (9.10)$$

This rule, known as a **selection rule**, limits the possible transitions from one quantum state to another. Equation 9.10 is the selection rule for rotational energy transitions. It applies only to diatomic molecules that have an electric dipole moment. For this reason, symmetric molecules such as H_2 and N_2 do not experience rotational energy transitions due to the absorption or emission of electromagnetic radiation.

Example 9.2

The Rotational Energy of HCl

Determine the lowest three rotational energy levels of a hydrogen chloride (HCl) molecule.

Strategy

Hydrogen chloride (HCl) is a diatomic molecule with an equilibrium separation distance of 0.127 nm. Rotational energy levels depend only on the momentum of inertia I and the orbital angular momentum quantum number l (in this case, $l = 0$, 1, and 2). The momentum of inertia depends, in turn, on the equilibrium separation distance (which is given) and the reduced mass, which depends on the masses of the H and Cl atoms.

Solution

First, we compute the reduced mass. If Particle 1 is hydrogen and Particle 2 is chloride, we have

$$\mu = \frac{m_1 m_2}{m_1 + m_2} = \frac{(1.0\,\text{u})(35.4\,\text{u})}{1.0\,\text{u} + 35.4\,\text{u}} = 0.97\,\text{u} = 0.97\,\text{u}\left(\frac{931.5\frac{\text{MeV}}{c^2}}{1\,\text{u}}\right) = 906\frac{\text{MeV}}{c^2}.$$

The corresponding rest mass energy is therefore

$$\mu c^2 = 9.06 \times 10^8\ \text{eV}.$$

This allows us to calculate the characteristic energy:

$$E_{0r} = \frac{\hbar^2}{2I} = \frac{\hbar^2}{2\left(\mu r_0^2\right)} = \frac{(\hbar c)^2}{2\left(\mu c^2\right)r_0^2} = \frac{(197.3\,\text{eV}\cdot\text{nm})^2}{2\left(9.06 \times 10^8\ \text{eV}\right)(0.127\,\text{nm})^2} = 1.33 \times 10^{-3}\ \text{eV}.$$

(Notice how this expression is written in terms of the rest mass energy. This technique is common in modern physics calculations.) The rotational energy levels are given by

$$E_r = l(l+1)\frac{\hbar^2}{2I} = l(l+1)E_{0r},$$

where l is the orbital quantum number. The three lowest rotational energy levels of an HCl molecule are therefore

$$l = 0;\ E_r = 0\,\text{eV (no rotation)},$$

$$l = 1;\ E_r = 2\,E_{0r} = 2.66 \times 10^{-3}\ \text{eV},$$

$$l = 2;\ E_r = 6\,E_{0r} = 7.99 \times 10^{-3}\ \text{eV}.$$

Significance

The rotational spectrum is associated with weak transitions (1/1000 to 1/100 of an eV). By comparison, the energy of an electron in the ground state of hydrogen is $-13.6\,\text{eV}$.

9.2 Check Your Understanding What does the energy separation between absorption lines in a rotational spectrum of a diatomic molecule tell you?

The **vibrational energy level**, which is the energy level associated with the vibrational energy of a molecule, is more difficult to estimate than the rotational energy level. However, we can estimate these levels by assuming that the two atoms in the diatomic molecule are connected by an ideal spring of spring constant *k*. The potential energy of this spring system is

$$U_{\text{osc}} = \frac{1}{2}k\,\Delta r^2, \tag{9.11}$$

Where Δr is a change in the "natural length" of the molecule along a line that connects the atoms. Solving Schrödinger's equation for this potential gives

$$E_n = \left(n + \frac{1}{2}\right)\hbar\omega \ (n = 0,\ 1,\ 2,\ \ldots), \tag{9.12}$$

Where ω is the natural angular frequency of vibration and *n* is the vibrational quantum number. The prediction that vibrational energy levels are evenly spaced $(\Delta E = \hbar\omega)$ turns out to be good at lower energies.

A detailed study of transitions between vibrational energy levels induced by the absorption or emission of radiation (and the specifically so-called electric dipole transition) requires that

$$\Delta n = \pm 1. \tag{9.13}$$

Equation 9.13 represents the selection rule for vibrational energy transitions. As mentioned before, this rule applies only to diatomic molecules that have an electric dipole moment. Symmetric molecules do not experience such transitions.

Due to the selection rules, the absorption or emission of radiation by a diatomic molecule involves a transition in vibrational and rotational states. Specifically, if the vibrational quantum number (*n*) changes by one unit, then the rotational quantum number (*l*) changes by one unit. An energy-level diagram of a possible transition is given in Figure 9.5. The absorption spectrum for such transitions in hydrogen chloride (HCl) is shown in Figure 9.6. The absorption peaks are due to transitions from the $n = 0$ to $n = 1$ vibrational states. Energy differences for the band of peaks at the left and right are, respectively, $\Delta E_{l \to l+1} = \hbar\omega + 2(l+1)E_{0r} = \hbar\omega + 2E_{0r},\ \hbar\omega + 4E_{0r},\ \hbar\omega + 6E_{0r},\ \ldots$ (right band) and $\Delta E_{l \to l-1} = \hbar\omega - 2lE_{0r} = \hbar\omega - 2E_{0r},\ \hbar\omega - 4E_{0r},\ \hbar\omega - 6E_{0r},\ \ldots$ (left band).

The moment of inertia can then be determined from the energy spacing between individual peaks $(2E_{0r})$ or from the gap between the left and right bands $(4E_{0r})$. The frequency at the center of this gap is the frequency of vibration.

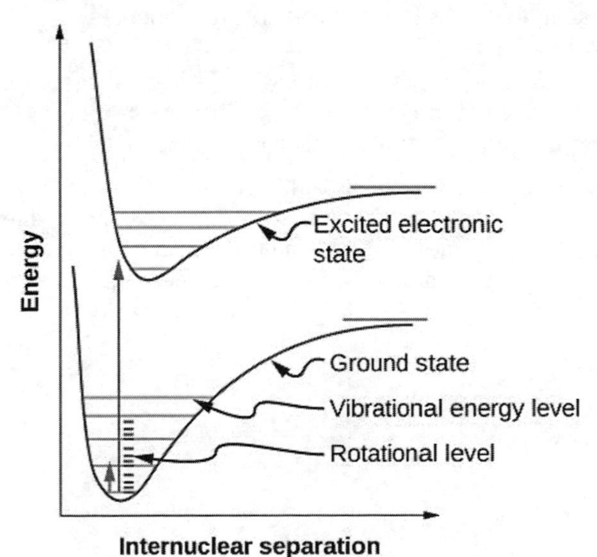

Figure 9.5 Three types of energy levels in a diatomic molecule: electronic, vibrational, and rotational. If the vibrational quantum number (*n*) changes by one unit, then the rotational quantum number (*l*) changes by one unit.

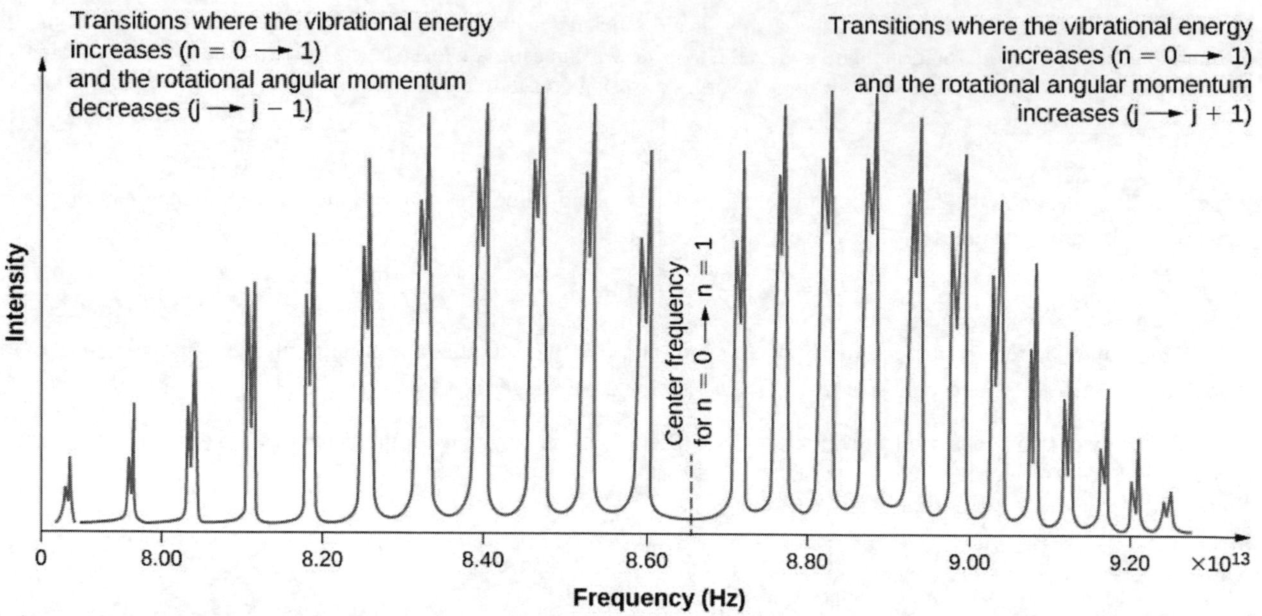

Figure 9.6 Absorption spectrum of hydrogen chloride (HCl) from the $n = 0$ to $n = 1$ vibrational levels. The discrete peaks indicate a quantization of the angular momentum of the molecule. The bands to the left indicate a decrease in angular momentum, whereas those to the right indicate an increase in angular momentum.

9.3 | Bonding in Crystalline Solids

Learning Objectives

By the end of this section, you will be able to:

- Describe the packing structures of common solids
- Explain the difference between bonding in a solid and in a molecule
- Determine the equilibrium separation distance given crystal properties
- Determine the dissociation energy of a salt given crystal properties

Beginning in this section, we study crystalline solids, which consist of atoms arranged in an extended regular pattern called a **lattice**. Solids that do not or are unable to form crystals are classified as amorphous solids. Although amorphous solids (like glass) have a variety of interesting technological applications, the focus of this chapter will be on crystalline solids.

Atoms arrange themselves in a lattice to form a crystal because of a net attractive force between their constituent electrons and atomic nuclei. The crystals formed by the bonding of atoms belong to one of three categories, classified by their bonding: ionic, covalent, and metallic. Molecules can also bond together to form crystals; these bonds, not discussed here, are classified as molecular. Early in the twentieth century, the atomic model of a solid was speculative. We now have direct evidence of atoms in solids (**Figure 9.7**).

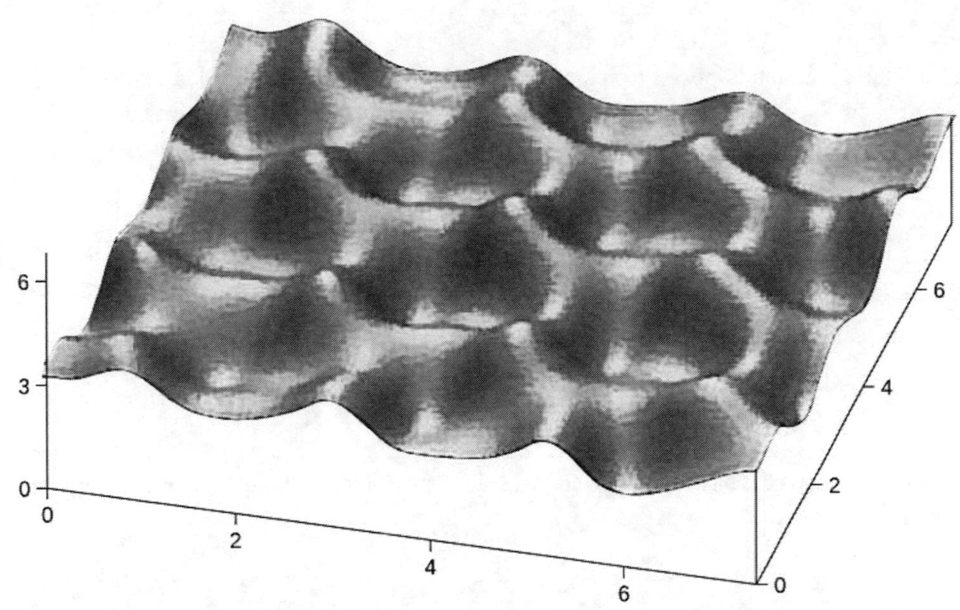

Figure 9.7 An image made with a scanning tunneling microscope of the surface of graphite. The peaks represent the atoms, which are arranged in hexagons. The scale is in angstroms.

Ionic Bonding in Solids

Many solids form by ionic bonding. A prototypical example is the sodium chloride crystal, as we discussed earlier. Electrons transfer from sodium atoms to adjacent chlorine atoms, since the valence electrons in sodium are loosely bound and chlorine has a large electron affinity. The positively charged sodium ions and negatively charged chlorine (chloride) ions organize into an extended regular array of atoms (Figure 9.8).

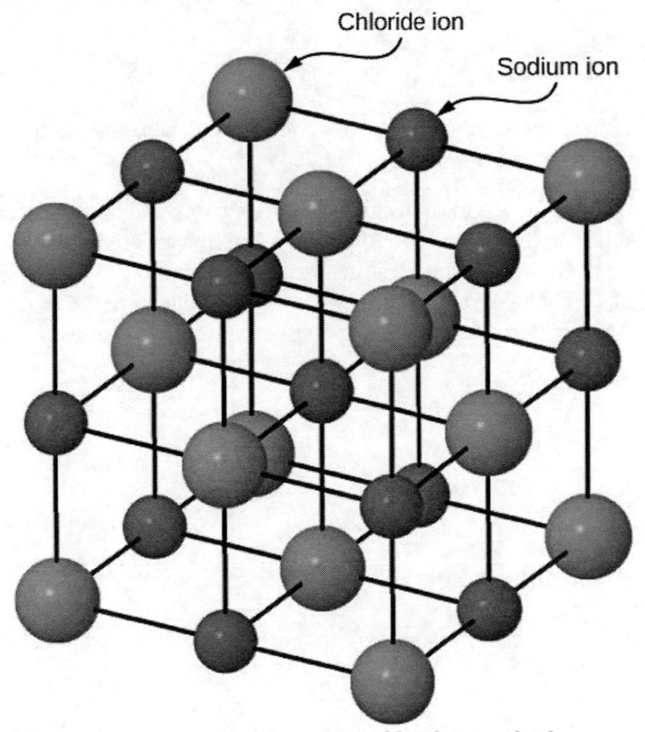

Figure 9.8 Structure of the sodium chloride crystal. The sodium and chloride ions are arranged in a face-centered cubic (FCC) structure.

The charge distributions of the sodium and chloride ions are spherically symmetric, and the chloride ion is about two times the diameter of the sodium ion. The lowest energy arrangement of these ions is called the **face-centered cubic (FCC)** structure. In this structure, each ion is closest to six ions of the other species. The unit cell is a cube—an atom occupies the center and corners of each "face" of the cube. The attractive potential energy of the Na^+ ion due to the fields of these six Cl^- ions is written

$$U_1 = -6\frac{e^2}{4\pi\varepsilon_0 r} \tag{9.14}$$

where the minus sign designates an attractive potential (and we identify $k = 1/4\pi\varepsilon_0$). At a distance $\sqrt{2}r$ are its next-nearest neighbors: twelve Na^+ ions of the same charge. The total repulsive potential energy associated with these ions is

$$U_2 = 12\frac{e^2}{4\pi\varepsilon_0 \sqrt{2}r}. \tag{9.15}$$

Next closest are eight Cl^- ions a distance $\sqrt{3}r$ from the Na^+ ion. The potential energy of the Na^+ ion in the field of these eight ions is

$$U_3 = -8\frac{e^2}{4\pi\varepsilon_0 \sqrt{3}r}. \tag{9.16}$$

Continuing in the same manner with alternate sets of Cl^- and Na^+ ions, we find that the net attractive potential energy U_A of the single Na^+ ion can be written as

$$U_{coul} = -\alpha\frac{e^2}{4\pi\varepsilon_0 r} \tag{9.17}$$

where α is the Madelung constant, introduced earlier. From this analysis, we can see that this constant is the infinite converging sum

$$\alpha = 6 - \frac{12}{\sqrt{2}} + \frac{8}{\sqrt{3}} + \cdots. \tag{9.18}$$

Distant ions make a significant contribution to this sum, so it converges slowly, and many terms must be used to calculate α accurately. For all FCC ionic solids, α is approximately 1.75.

Other possible packing arrangements of atoms in solids include **simple cubic** and **body-centered cubic (BCC)**. These three different packing structures of solids are compared in **Figure 9.9**. The first row represents the location, but not the size, of the ions; the second row indicates the unit cells of each structure or lattice; and the third row represents the location and size of the ions. The BCC structure has eight nearest neighbors, with a Madelung constant of about 1.76—only slightly different from that for the FCC structure. Determining the Madelung constant for specific solids is difficult work and the subject of current research.

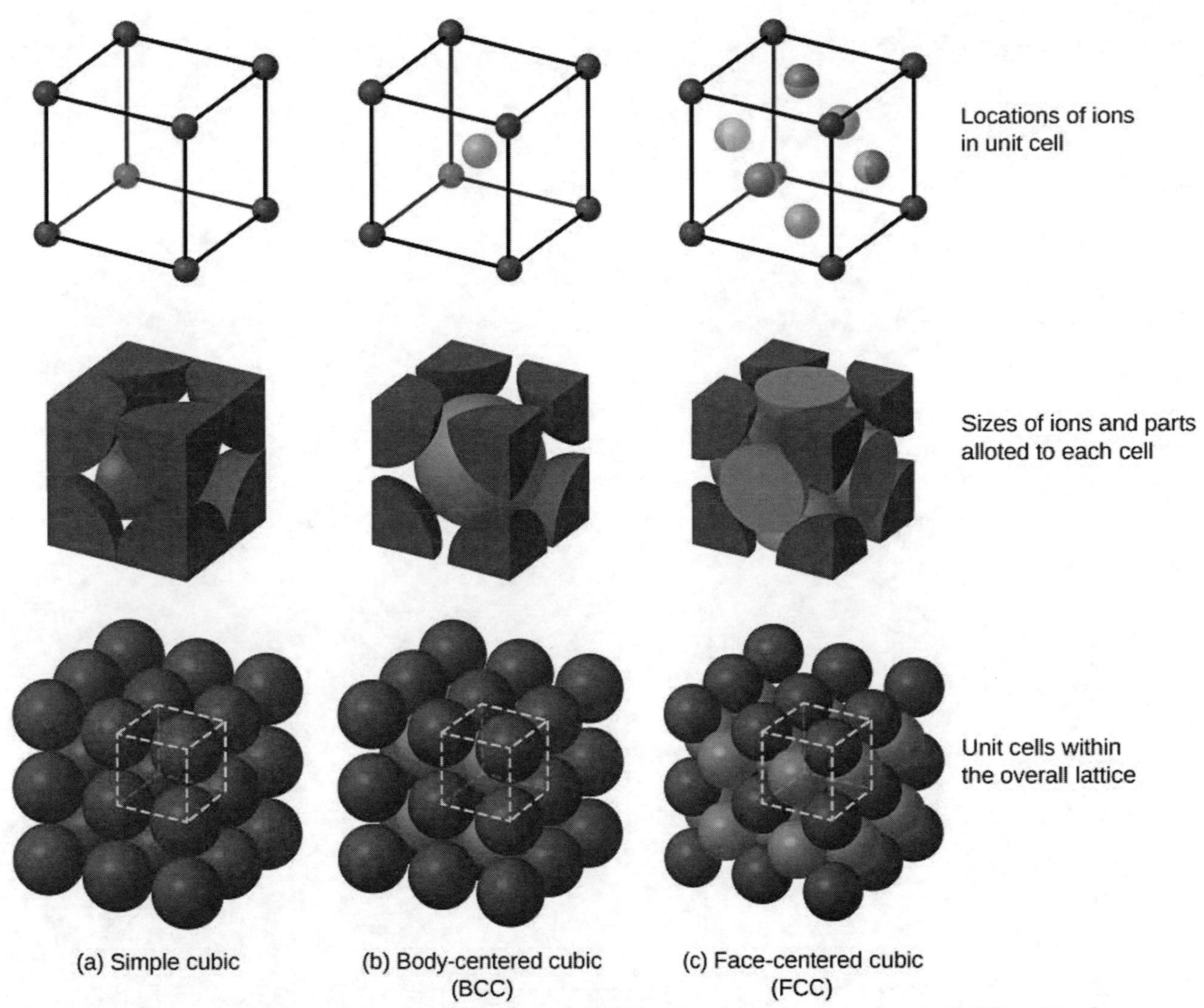

Figure 9.9 Packing structures for solids from left to right: (a) simple cubic, (b) body-centered cubic (BCC), and (c) face-centered cubic (FCC). Each crystal structure minimizes the energy of the system.

The energy of the sodium ions is not entirely due to attractive forces between oppositely charged ions. If the ions are bought too close together, the wave functions of core electrons of the ions overlap, and the electrons repel due to the exclusion principle. The total potential energy of the Na^+ ion is therefore the sum of the attractive Coulomb potential (U_{coul}) and the repulsive potential associated with the exclusion principle (U_{ex}). Calculating this repulsive potential requires powerful computers. Fortunately, however, this energy can be described accurately by a simple formula that contains adjustable parameters:

$$U_{ex} = \frac{A}{r^n} \tag{9.19}$$

where the parameters A and n are chosen to give predictions consistent with experimental data. For the problem at the end of this chapter, the parameter n is referred to as the **repulsion constant**. The total potential energy of the Na^+ ion is therefore

$$U = -\alpha\frac{e^2}{4\pi\varepsilon_0 r} + \frac{A}{r^n}. \tag{9.20}$$

At equilibrium, there is no net force on the ion, so the distance between neighboring Na^+ and Cl^- ions must be the value

r_0 for which U is a minimum. Setting $\frac{dU}{dr} = 0$, we have

$$0 = \frac{\alpha e^2}{4\pi\varepsilon_0 {r_0}^2} - \frac{nA}{{r_0}^{n+1}}. \tag{9.21}$$

Thus,

$$A = \frac{\alpha e^2 {r_0}^{n-1}}{4\pi\varepsilon_0 n}. \tag{9.22}$$

Inserting this expression into the expression for the total potential energy, we have

$$U = -\frac{\alpha e^2}{4\pi\varepsilon_0 r_0}\left[\frac{r_0}{r} - \frac{1}{n}\left(\frac{r_0}{r}\right)^n\right]. \tag{9.23}$$

Notice that the total potential energy now has only one adjustable parameter, *n*. The parameter *A* has been replaced by a function involving r_0, the equilibrium separation distance, which can be measured by a diffraction experiment (you learned about diffraction in a previous chapter). The total potential energy is plotted in **Figure 9.10** for $n = 8$, the approximate value of *n* for NaCl.

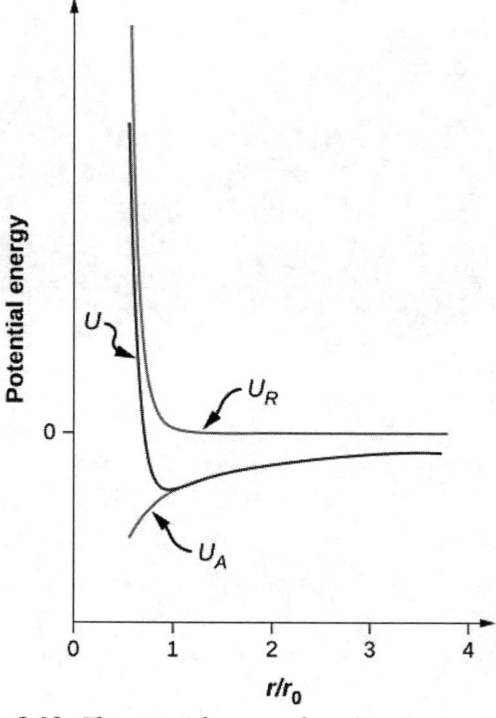

Figure 9.10 The potential energy of a sodium ion in a NaCl crystal for $n = 8$. The equilibrium bond length occurs when the energy is a minimized.

As long as $n > 1$, the curve for *U* has the same general shape: *U* approaches infinity as $r \to 0$ and *U* approaches zero as $r \to \infty$. The minimum value of the potential energy is given by

$$U_{\min}(r = r_0) = -\alpha\frac{ke^2}{r_0}\left(1 - \frac{1}{n}\right). \tag{9.24}$$

The energy per ion pair needed to separate the crystal into ions is therefore

$$U_{\text{diss}} = \alpha \frac{ke^2}{r_0}\left(1 - \frac{1}{n}\right). \tag{9.25}$$

This is the **dissociation energy** of the solid. The dissociation energy can also be used to describe the total energy needed to break a mole of a solid into its constituent ions, often expressed in kJ/mole. The dissociation energy can be determined experimentally using the latent heat of vaporization. Sample values are given in the following table.

	F^-	Cl^-	Br^-	I^-
Li^+	1036	853	807	757
Na^+	923	787	747	704
K^+	821	715	682	649
Rb^+	785	689	660	630
Cs^+	740	659	631	604

Table 9.2 Lattice Energy for Alkali Metal Halides

Thus, we can determine the Madelung constant from the crystal structure and n from the lattice energy. For NaCl, we have $r_0 = 2.81\ \text{Å}$, $n \approx 8$, and $U_{\text{diss}} = 7.84$ eV/ion pair. This dissociation energy is relatively large. The most energetic photon from the visible spectrum, for example, has an energy of approximately

$$hf = (4.14 \times 10^{-15}\ \text{eV} \cdot \text{s})(7.5 \times 10^{14}\ \text{Hz}) = 3.1\ \text{eV}.$$

Because the ions in crystals are so tightly bound, ionic crystals have the following general characteristics:

1. They are fairly hard and stable.
2. They vaporize at relatively high temperatures (1000 to 2000 K).
3. They are transparent to visible radiation, because photons in the visible portion of the spectrum are not energetic enough to excite an electron from its ground state to an excited state.
4. They are poor electrical conductors, because they contain effectively no free electrons.
5. They are usually soluble in water, because the water molecule has a large dipole moment whose electric field is strong enough to break the electrostatic bonds between the ions.

Example 9.3

The Dissociation Energy of Salt

Determine the dissociation energy of sodium chloride (NaCl) in kJ/mol. (*Hint:* The repulsion constant n of NaCl is approximately 8.)

Strategy

A sodium chloride crystal has an equilibrium separation of 0.282 nm. (Compare this value with 0.236 nm for a free diatomic unit of NaCl.) The dissociation energy depends on the separation distance, repulsion constant, and Madelung constant for an FCC structure. The separation distance depends in turn on the molar mass and measured density. We can determine the separation distance, and then use this value to determine the dissociation energy for one mole of the solid.

Solution

The atomic masses of Na and Cl are 23.0 u and 58.4 u, so the molar mass of NaCl is 58.4 g/mol. The density of NaCl is $2.16\ \text{g/cm}^3$. The relationship between these quantities is

$$\rho = \frac{M}{V} = \frac{M}{2N_A r_0^3},$$

where M is the mass of one mole of salt, N_A is Avogadro's number, and r_0 is the equilibrium separation distance. The factor 2 is needed since both the sodium and chloride ions represent a cubic volume r_0^3. Solving for the distance, we get

$$r_0^3 = \frac{M}{2N_A \rho} = \frac{58.4\text{g/mol}}{2\left(6.03 \times 10^{23}\right)\left(2.160\text{g/cm}^3\right)} = 2.23 \times 10^{-23}\ \text{cm}^3,$$

or

$$r_0 = 2.80 \times 10^{-8}\ \text{cm} = 0.280\ \text{nm}.$$

The potential energy of one ion pair $\left(\text{Na}^+\ \text{Cl}^-\right)$ is

$$U = -\alpha\frac{ke^2}{r_0}\left(1 - \frac{1}{n}\right),$$

where α is the Madelung constant, r_0 is the equilibrium separation distance, and n is the repulsion constant. NaCl is FCC, so the Madelung constant is $\alpha = 1.7476$. Substituting these values, we get

$$U = -1.75\frac{1.44\ \text{eV}\cdot\text{nm}}{0.280\ \text{nm}}\left(1 - \frac{1}{8}\right) = -7.88\frac{\text{eV}}{\text{ion pair}}.$$

The dissociation energy of one mole of sodium chloride is therefore

$$D = \left(\frac{7.88\ \text{eV}}{\text{ion pair}}\right)\left(\frac{\frac{23.052\ \text{kcal}}{1\ \text{mol}}}{\frac{1\ \text{eV}}{\text{ion pair}}}\right) = 182\ \text{kcal/mol} = 760\ \text{kJ/mol}.$$

Significance

This theoretical value of the dissociation energy of 766 kJ/mol is close to the accepted experimental value of 787 kJ/mol. Notice that for larger density, the equilibrium separation distance between ion pairs is smaller, as expected. This small separation distance drives up the force between ions and therefore the dissociation energy. The conversion at the end of the equation took advantage of the conversion factor $1\ \text{kJ} = 0.239\ \text{kcal}$.

9.3 Check Your Understanding If the dissociation energy were larger, would that make it easier or more difficult to break the solid apart?

Covalent Bonding in Solids

Crystals can also be formed by covalent bonding. For example, covalent bonds are responsible for holding carbon atoms together in diamond crystals. The electron configuration of the carbon atom is $1s^2 2s^2 2p^2$—a He core plus four valence electrons. This electron configuration is four electrons short of a full shell, so by sharing these four electrons with other carbon atoms in a covalent bond, the shells of all carbon atoms are filled. Diamond has a more complicated structure than most ionic crystals (**Figure 9.11**). Each carbon atom is the center of a regular tetrahedron, and the angle between the bonds is $110°$. This angle is a direct consequence of the directionality of the p orbitals of carbon atoms.

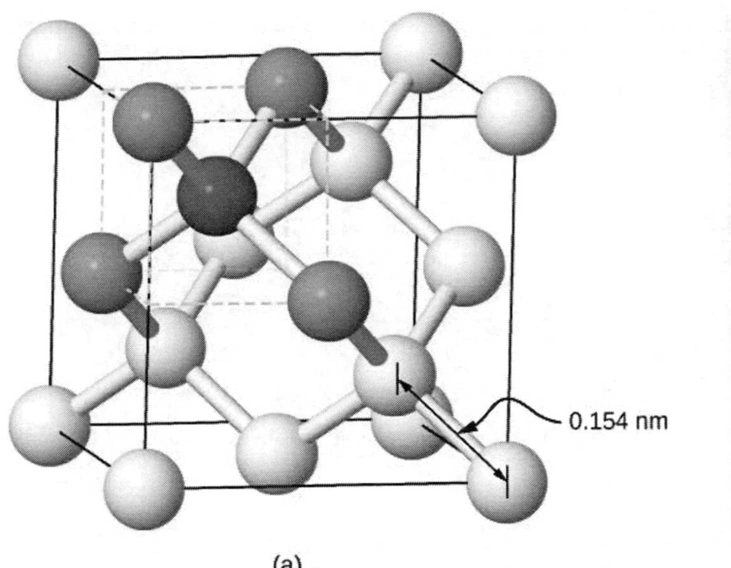

Figure 9.11 Structure of the diamond crystal. (a) The single carbon atom represented by the dark blue sphere is covalently bonded to the four carbon atoms represented by the light blue spheres. (b) Gem-quality diamonds can be cleaved along smooth planes, which gives a large number of angles that cause total internal reflection of incident light, and thus gives diamonds their prized brilliance.

Covalently bonded crystals are not as uniform as ionic crystals but are reasonably hard, difficult to melt, and are insoluble in water. For example, diamond has an extremely high melting temperature (4000 K) and is transparent to visible light. In comparison, covalently bonded tin (also known as alpha-tin, which is nonmetallic) is relatively soft, melts at 600 K, and reflects visible light. Two other important examples of covalently bonded crystals are silicon and germanium. Both of these solids are used extensively in the manufacture of diodes, transistors, and integrated circuits. We will return to these materials later in our discussion of semiconductors.

Metallic Bonding in Solids

As the name implies, metallic bonding is responsible for the formation of metallic crystals. The valence electrons are essentially free of the atoms and are able to move relatively easily throughout the metallic crystal. Bonding is due to the attractive forces between the positive ions and the conduction electrons. Metallic bonds are weaker than ionic or covalent bonds, with dissociation energies in the range $1 - 3\,\text{eV}$.

9.4 | Free Electron Model of Metals

Learning Objectives

By the end of this section, you will be able to:

- Describe the classical free electron model of metals in terms of the concept electron number density
- Explain the quantum free-electron model of metals in terms of Pauli's exclusion principle
- Calculate the energy levels and energy-level spacing of a free electron in a metal

Metals, such as copper and aluminum, are held together by bonds that are very different from those of molecules. Rather than sharing and exchanging electrons, a metal is essentially held together by a system of free electrons that wander throughout the solid. The simplest model of a metal is the **free electron model**. This model views electrons as a gas. We first consider the simple one-dimensional case in which electrons move freely along a line, such as through a very thin metal rod. The potential function $U(x)$ for this case is a one-dimensional infinite square well where the walls of the well correspond to the edges of the rod. This model ignores the interactions between the electrons but respects the exclusion principle. For the special case of $T = 0\,\text{K}$, N electrons fill up the energy levels, from lowest to highest, two at a time (spin up and spin down), until the highest energy level is filled. The highest energy filled is called the **Fermi energy**.

The one-dimensional free electron model can be improved by considering the three-dimensional case: electrons moving freely in a three-dimensional metal block. This system is modeled by a three-dimensional infinite square well. Determining the allowed energy states requires us to solve the time-independent Schrödinger equation

$$-\frac{h^2}{2m_e}\left(\frac{\partial^2}{\partial x^2}+\frac{\partial^2}{\partial y^2}+\frac{\partial^2}{\partial z^2}\right)\psi(x, y, z) = E\,\psi(x, y, z), \quad (9.26)$$

where we assume that the potential energy inside the box is zero and infinity otherwise. The allowed wave functions describing the electron's quantum states can be written as

$$\psi(x, y, z) = \left(\sqrt{\frac{2}{L_x}}\sin\frac{n_x \pi x}{L_x}\right)\left(\sqrt{\frac{2}{L_y}}\sin\frac{n_y \pi y}{L_y}\right)\left(\sqrt{\frac{2}{L_z}}\sin\frac{n_z \pi z}{L_z}\right), \quad (9.27)$$

where $n_x, n_y,$ and n_z are positive integers representing quantum numbers corresponding to the motion in the *x*-, *y*-, and *z*-directions, respectively, and $L_x, L_y,$ and L_z are the dimensions of the box in those directions. **Equation 9.27** is simply the product of three one-dimensional wave functions. The allowed energies of an electron in a cube $(L = L_x = L_y = L_z)$ are

$$E = \frac{\pi^2 \hbar^2}{2mL^2}\left(n_1^2 + n_2^2 + n_3^2\right). \quad (9.28)$$

Associated with each set of quantum numbers (n_x, n_y, n_z) are two quantum states, spin up and spin down. In a real material, the number of filled states is enormous. For example, in a cubic centimeter of metal, this number is on the order of 10^{22}. Counting how many particles are in which state is difficult work, which often requires the help of a powerful computer. The effort is worthwhile, however, because this information is often an effective way to check the model.

Example 9.4

Energy of a Metal Cube

Consider a solid metal cube of edge length 2.0 cm. (a) What is the lowest energy level for an electron within the metal? (b) What is the spacing between this level and the next energy level?

Strategy

An electron in a metal can be modeled as a wave. The lowest energy corresponds to the largest wavelength and smallest quantum number: $n_x, n_y, n_z = (1, 1, 1)$. **Equation 9.28** supplies this "ground state" energy value.

Since the energy of the electron increases with the quantum number, the next highest level involves the smallest increase in the quantum numbers, or $(n_x, n_y, n_z) = (2, 1, 1), (1, 2, 1),$ or (1, 1, 2).

Solution

The lowest energy level corresponds to the quantum numbers $n_x = n_y = n_z = 1.$ From **Equation 9.28**, the energy of this level is

$$\begin{aligned} E(1, 1, 1) &= \frac{\pi^2 h^2}{2m_e L^2}(1^2 + 1^2 + 1^2) \\ &= \frac{3\pi^2\,(1.05 \times 10 - 34\,\text{J}\cdot\text{s})^2}{2\,(9.11 \times 10^{-31}\,\text{kg})\,(2.00 \times 10^{-2}\,\text{m})^2} \\ &= 4.48 \times 10^{-34}\,\text{J} = 2.80 \times 10^{-15}\,\text{eV}. \end{aligned}$$

The next-higher energy level is reached by increasing any one of the three quantum numbers by 1. Hence, there are actually three quantum states with the same energy. Suppose we increase n_x by 1. Then the energy becomes

$$\begin{aligned}E(2,\ 1,\ 1) &= \frac{\pi^2 h^2}{2m_e L^2}(2^2+1^2+1^2)\\ &= \frac{6\pi^2(1.05\times 10-34\,\text{J}\cdot\text{s})^2}{2(9.11\times 10^{-31}\ \text{kg})(2.00\times 10^{-2}\ \text{m})^2}\\ &= 8.96\times 10^{-34}\ \text{J} = 5.60\times 10^{-15}\ \text{eV}.\end{aligned}$$

The energy spacing between the lowest energy state and the next-highest energy state is therefore

$$\text{E}(2,\ 1,\ 1)-\text{E}(1,\ 1,\ 1) = 2.80\times 10^{-15}\ \text{eV}.$$

Significance

This is a very small energy difference. Compare this value to the average kinetic energy of a particle, $k_\text{B}T$, where k_B is Boltzmann's constant and *T* is the temperature. The product $k_\text{B}T$ is about 1000 times greater than the energy spacing.

9.4 Check Your Understanding What happens to the ground state energy of an electron if the dimensions of the solid increase?

Often, we are not interested in the total number of particles in all states, but rather the number of particles *dN* with energies in a narrow energy interval. This value can be expressed by

$$dN = n(E)dE = g(E)dE\cdot F$$

where *n*(*E*) is the **electron number density**, or the number of electrons per unit volume; *g*(*E*) is the **density of states**, or the number of allowed quantum states per unit energy; *dE* is the size of the energy interval; and *F* is the **Fermi factor**. The Fermi factor is the probability that the state will be filled. For example, if *g*(*E*)*dE* is 100 available states, but *F* is only 5%, then the number of particles in this narrow energy interval is only five. Finding *g*(*E*) requires solving Schrödinger's equation (in three dimensions) for the allowed energy levels. The calculation is involved even for a crude model, but the result is simple:

$$g(E) = \frac{\pi V}{2}\left(\frac{8m_e}{h^2}\right)^{3/2} E^{1/2}, \tag{9.29}$$

where *V* is the volume of the solid, m_e is the mass of the electron, and *E* is the energy of the state. Notice that the density of states increases with the square root of the energy. More states are available at high energy than at low energy. This expression does *not* provide information of the density of the electrons in physical space, but rather the density of energy levels in "energy space." For example, in our study of the atomic structure, we learned that the energy levels of a hydrogen atom are much more widely spaced for small energy values (near than ground state) than for larger values.

This equation tells us how many electron states are available in a three-dimensional metallic solid. However, it does not tell us how likely these states will be filled. Thus, we need to determine the Fermi factor, *F*. Consider the simple case of $T = 0\,\text{K}$. From classical physics, we expect that all the electrons ($\sim 10^{22}\ /\ \text{cm}^3$) would simply go into the ground state to achieve the lowest possible energy. However, this violates Pauli's exclusion principle, which states that no two electrons can be in the same quantum state. Hence, when we begin filling the states with electrons, the states with lowest energy become occupied first, then states with progressively higher energies. The *last electron* we put in has the highest energy. This energy is the Fermi energy E_F of the free electron gas. A state with energy $E < E_\text{F}$ is occupied by a single electron, and a state with energy $E > E_\text{F}$ is unoccupied. To describe this in terms of a probability *F*(*E*) that a state of energy *E* is occupied, we write for $T = 0\,\text{K}$:

$$\begin{aligned}F(E) &= 1 \quad (E < E_\text{F})\\ F(E) &= 0 \quad (E > E_\text{F}).\end{aligned} \tag{9.30}$$

The density of states, Fermi factor, and electron number density are plotted against energy in Figure 9.12.

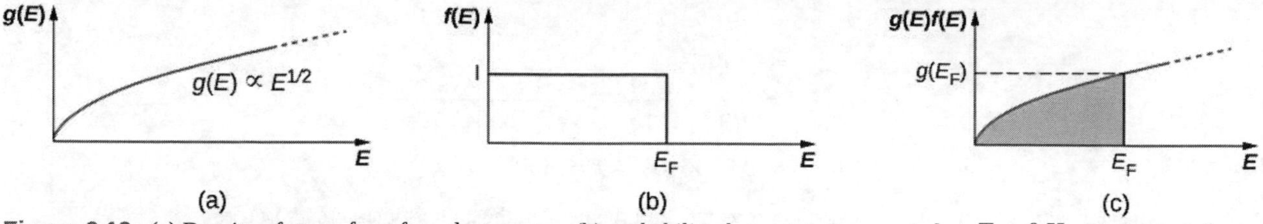

Figure 9.12 (a) Density of states for a free electron gas; (b) probability that a state is occupied at $T = 0\,\text{K}$; (c) density of occupied states at $T = 0\,\text{K}$.

A few notes are in order. First, the electron number density (last row) distribution drops off sharply at the Fermi energy. According to the theory, this energy is given by

$$E_{\text{F}} = \frac{h^2}{8m_e}\left(\frac{3N}{\pi V}\right)^{2/3}. \tag{9.31}$$

Fermi energies for selected materials are listed in the following table.

Element	Conduction Band Electron Density $\left(10^{28}\ \text{m}^{-3}\right)$	Free-Electron Model Fermi Energy (eV)
Al	18.1	11.7
Ba	3.15	3.64
Cu	8.47	7.00
Au	5.90	5.53
Fe	17.0	11.1
Ag	5.86	5.49

Table 9.3 Conduction Electron Densities and Fermi Energies for Some Metals

Note also that only the graph in part (c) of the figure, which answers the question, “How many particles are found in the energy range?” is checked by experiment. The **Fermi temperature** or effective “temperature” of an electron at the Fermi energy is

$$T_{\text{F}} = \frac{E_{\text{F}}}{k_{\text{B}}}. \tag{9.32}$$

Example 9.5

Fermi Energy of Silver

Metallic silver is an excellent conductor. It has 5.86×10^{28} conduction electrons per cubic meter. (a) Calculate its Fermi energy. (b) Compare this energy to the thermal energy $k_{\text{B}}T$ of the electrons at a room temperature of 300 K.

Solution

a. From **Equation 9.31**, the Fermi energy is

$$\begin{aligned} E_F &= \frac{h^2}{2m_e}(3\pi^2 n_e)^{2/3} \\ &= \frac{(1.05 \times 10^{-34}\ \text{J}\cdot\text{s})^2}{2(9.11 \times 10^{-31}\ \text{kg})} \times [(3\pi^2 (5.86 \times 10^{28}\ \text{m}^{-3})]^{2/3} \\ &= 8.79 \times 10^{-19}\ \text{J} = 5.49\ \text{eV}. \end{aligned}$$

This is a typical value of the Fermi energy for metals, as can be seen from **Table 9.3**.

b. We can associate a Fermi temperature T_F with the Fermi energy by writing $k_B T_F = E_F$. We then find for the Fermi temperature

$$T_F = \frac{8.79 \times 10^{-19}\ \text{J}}{1.38 \times 10^{-23}\ \text{J/K}} = 6.37 \times 10^4\ \text{K},$$

which is much higher than room temperature and also the typical melting point ($\sim 10^3$ K) of a metal. The ratio of the Fermi energy of silver to the room-temperature thermal energy is

$$\frac{E_F}{k_B T} = \frac{T_F}{T} \approx 210.$$

To visualize how the quantum states are filled, we might imagine pouring water slowly into a glass, such as that of **Figure 9.13**. The first drops of water (the electrons) occupy the bottom of the glass (the states with lowest energy). As the level rises, states of higher and higher energy are occupied. Furthermore, since the glass has a wide opening and a narrow stem, more water occupies the top of the glass than the bottom. This reflects the fact that the density of states $g(E)$ is proportional to $E^{1/2}$, so there is a relatively large number of higher energy electrons in a free electron gas. Finally, the level to which the glass is filled corresponds to the Fermi energy.

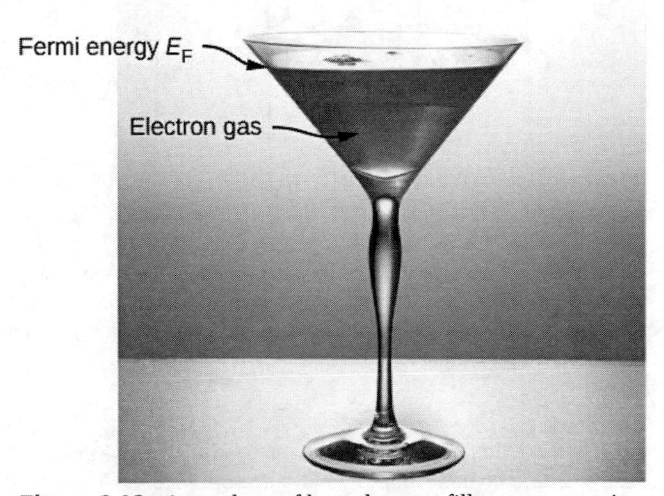

Figure 9.13 An analogy of how electrons fill energy states in a metal. As electrons fill energy states, lowest to highest, the number of available states increases. The highest energy state (corresponding to the water line) is the Fermi energy. (credit: modification of work by "Didriks"/Flickr)

Suppose that at $T = 0\ \text{K}$, the number of conduction electrons per unit volume in our sample is n_e. Since each field state has one electron, the number of filled states per unit volume is the same as the number of electrons per unit volume.

9.5 | Band Theory of Solids

Learning Objectives

By the end of this section, you will be able to:

- Describe two main approaches to determining the energy levels of an electron in a crystal
- Explain the presence of energy bands and gaps in the energy structure of a crystal
- Explain why some materials are good conductors and others are good insulators
- Differentiate between an insulator and a semiconductor

The free electron model explains many important properties of conductors but is weak in at least two areas. First, it assumes a constant potential energy within the solid. (Recall that a constant potential energy is associated with no forces.) **Figure 9.14** compares the assumption of a constant potential energy (dotted line) with the periodic Coulomb potential, which drops as $-1/r$ at each lattice point, where r is the distance from the ion core (solid line). Second, the free electron model assumes an impenetrable barrier at the surface. This assumption is not valid, because under certain conditions, electrons can escape the surface—such as in the photoelectric effect. In addition to these assumptions, the free electron model does not explain the dramatic differences in electronic properties of conductors, semiconductors, and insulators. Therefore, a more complete model is needed.

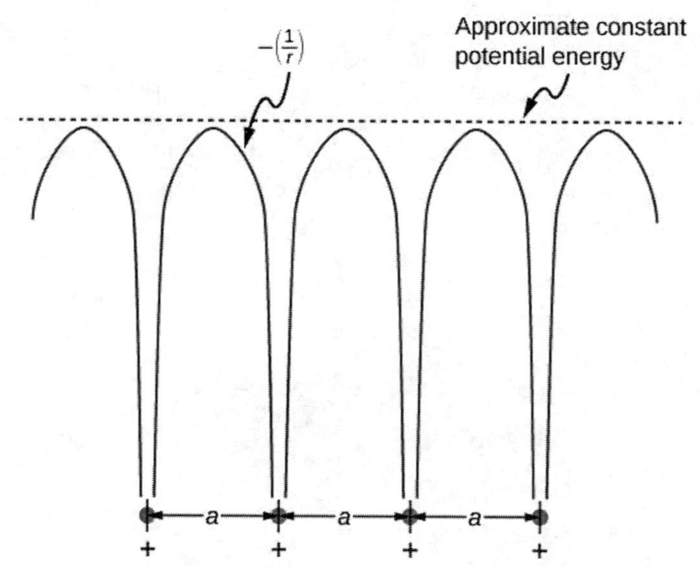

Figure 9.14 The periodic potential used to model electrons in a conductor. Each ion in the solid is the source of a Coulomb potential. Notice that the free electron model is productive because the average of this field is approximately constant.

We can produce an improved model by solving Schrödinger's equation for the periodic potential shown in **Figure 9.14**. However, the solution requires technical mathematics far beyond our scope. We again seek a qualitative argument based on quantum mechanics to find a way forward.

We first review the argument used to explain the energy structure of a covalent bond. Consider two identical hydrogen atoms so far apart that there is no interaction whatsoever between them. Further suppose that the electron in each atom is in the same ground state: a 1*s* electron with an energy of $-13.6\,\text{eV}$ (ignore spin). When the hydrogen atoms are brought closer together, the individual wave functions of the electrons overlap and, by the exclusion principle, can no longer be in the same quantum state, which splits the original equivalent energy levels into two different energy levels. The energies of these levels depend on the interatomic distance, α (**Figure 9.15**).

If four hydrogen atoms are brought together, four levels are formed from the four possible symmetries—a single sine wave "hump" in each well, alternating up and down, and so on. In the limit of a very large number N of atoms, we expect a spread of nearly continuous bands of electronic energy levels in a solid (see Figure 9.15(c)). Each of these bands is known as an **energy band**. (The allowed states of energy and wave number are still technically quantized, but for large numbers of atoms, these states are so close together that they are consider to be continuous or "in the continuum.")

Energy bands differ in the number of electrons they hold. In the 1s and 2s energy bands, each energy level holds up to two electrons (spin up and spin down), so this band has a maximum occupancy of 2N electrons. In the 2p energy band, each energy level holds up to six electrons, so this band has a maximum occupancy of 6N electrons (Figure 9.16).

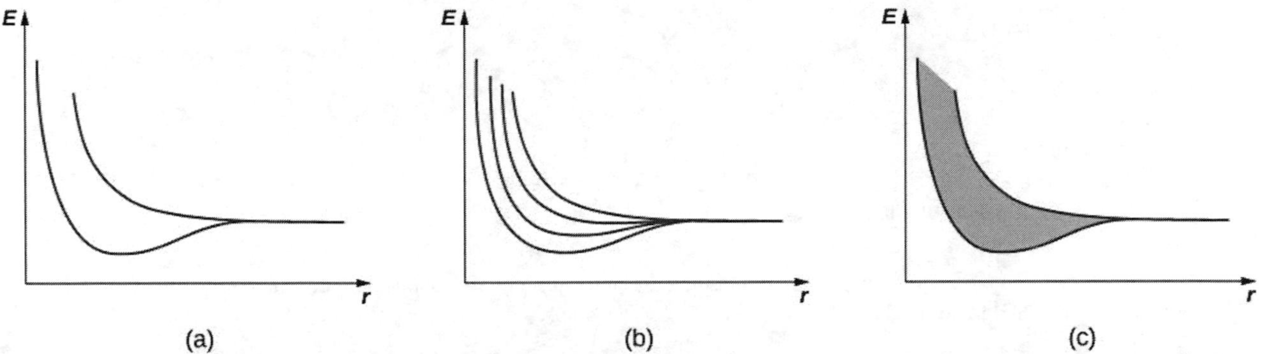

Figure 9.15 The dependence of energy-level splitting on the average distance between (a) two atoms, (b) four atoms, and (c) a large number of atoms. For a large number of electrons, a continuous band of energies is produced.

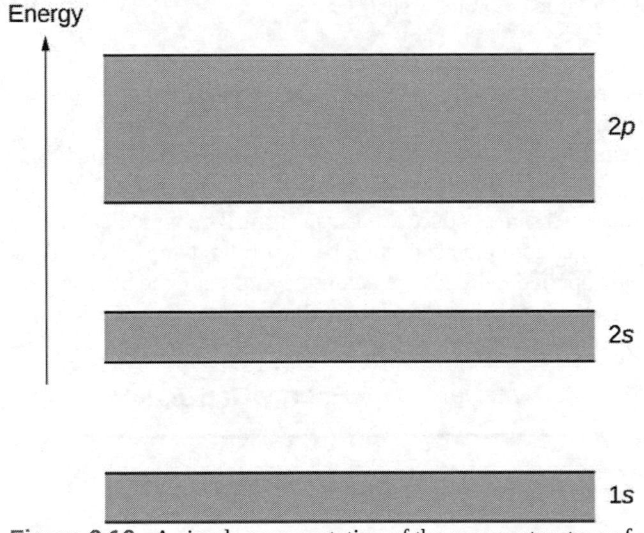

Figure 9.16 A simple representation of the energy structure of a solid. Electrons belong to energy bands separated by energy gaps.

Each energy band is separated from the other by an **energy gap**. The electrical properties of conductors and insulators can be understood in terms of energy bands and gaps. The highest energy band that is filled is known as a **valence band**. The next available band in the energy structure is known as a **conduction band**. In a conductor, the highest energy band that contains electrons is partially filled, whereas in an insulator, the highest energy band containing electrons is completely filled. The difference between a conductor and insulator is illustrated in Figure 9.17.

A conductor differs from an insulator in how its electrons respond to an applied electric field. If a significant number of electrons are set into motion by the field, the material is a conductor. In terms of the band model, electrons in the partially filled conduction band gain kinetic energy from the electric field by filling higher energy states in the conduction band. By contrast, in an insulator, electrons belong to completely filled bands. When the field is applied, the electrons cannot make such transitions (acquire kinetic energy from the electric field) due to the exclusion principle. As a result, the material does not conduct electricity.

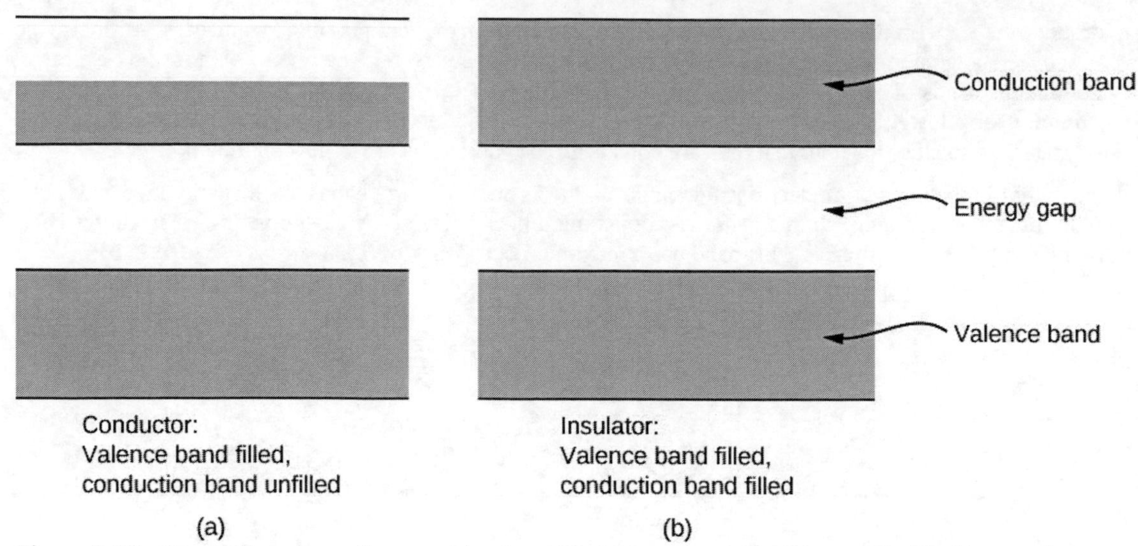

Figure 9.17 Comparison of a conductor and insulator. The highest energy band is partially filled in a conductor but completely filled in an insulator.

Visit this **simulation (https://openstaxcollege.org/l/21bandstructure)** to learn about the origin of energy bands in crystals of atoms and how the structure of bands determines how a material conducts electricity. Explore how band structure creates a lattice of many wells.

A **semiconductor** has a similar energy structure to an insulator except it has a relatively small energy gap between the lowest completely filled band and the next available unfilled band. This type of material forms the basis of modern electronics. At $T = 0\,\text{K}$, the semiconductor and insulator both have completely filled bands. The only difference is in the size of the energy gap (or *band gap*) E_g between the highest energy band that is filled (the valence band) and the next-higher empty band (the conduction band). In a semiconductor, this gap is small enough that a substantial number of electrons from the valence band are thermally excited into the conduction band at room temperature. These electrons are then in a nearly empty band and can respond to an applied field. As a general rule of thumb, the band gap of a semiconductor is about 1 eV. (See **Table 9.4** for silicon.) A band gap of greater than approximately 1 eV is considered an insulator. For comparison, the energy gap of diamond (an insulator) is several electron-volts.

Material	Energy Gap E_g (eV)
Si	1.14
Ge	0.67
GaAs	1.43
GaP	2.26
GaSb	0.69
InAs	0.35
InP	1.35
InSb	0.16
C (diamond)	5.48

Table 9.4 Energy Gap for Various Materials at 300 K Note: Except for diamond, the materials listed are all semiconductors.

9.6 | Semiconductors and Doping

Learning Objectives

By the end of this section, you will be able to:

- Describe changes to the energy structure of a semiconductor due to doping
- Distinguish between an n-type and p-type semiconductor
- Describe the Hall effect and explain its significance
- Calculate the charge, drift velocity, and charge carrier number density of a semiconductor using information from a Hall effect experiment

In the preceding section, we considered only the contribution to the electric current due to electrons occupying states in the conduction band. However, moving an electron from the valence band to the conduction band leaves an unoccupied state or **hole** in the energy structure of the valence band, which a nearby electron can move into. As these holes are filled by other electrons, new holes are created. The electric current associated with this filling can be viewed as the collective motion of many negatively charged electrons or the motion of the positively charged electron holes.

To illustrate, consider the one-dimensional lattice in Figure 9.18. Assume that each lattice atom contributes one valence electron to the current. As the hole on the right is filled, this hole moves to the left. The current can be interpreted as the flow of positive charge to the left. The density of holes, or the number of holes per unit volume, is represented by p. Each electron that transitions into the conduction band leaves behind a hole. If the conduction band is originally empty, the conduction electron density p is equal to the hole density, that is, $n = p$.

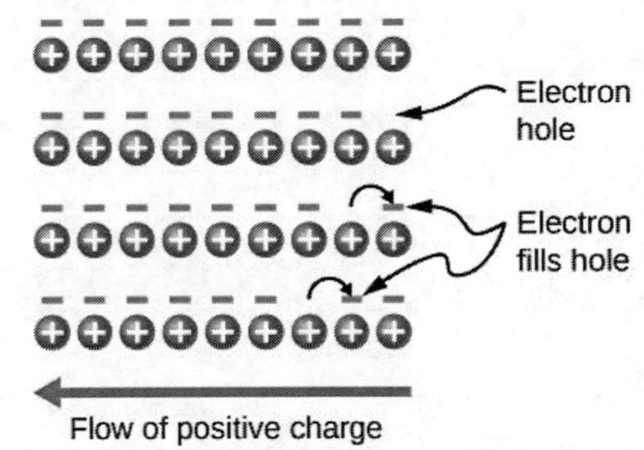

Figure 9.18 The motion of holes in a crystal lattice. As electrons shift to the right, an electron hole moves to the left.

As mentioned, a semiconductor is a material with a filled valence band, an unfilled conduction band, and a relatively small energy gap between the bands. Excess electrons or holes can be introduced into the material by the substitution into the crystal lattice of an **impurity atom**, which is an atom of a slightly different valence number. This process is known as **doping**. For example, suppose we add an arsenic atom to a crystal of silicon (Figure 9.19(a)).

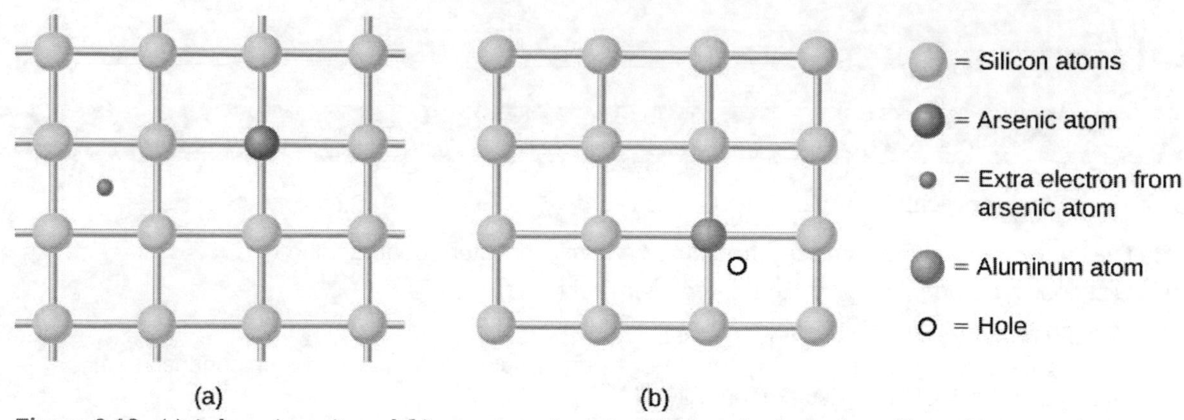

Figure 9.19 (a) A donor impurity and (b) an acceptor impurity. The introduction to impurities and acceptors into a semiconductor significantly changes the electronic properties of this material.

Arsenic has five valence electrons, whereas silicon has only four. This extra electron must therefore go into the conduction band, since there is no room in the valence band. The arsenic ion left behind has a net positive charge that weakly binds the delocalized electron. The binding is weak because the surrounding atomic lattice shields the ion's electric field. As a result, the binding energy of the extra electron is only about 0.02 eV. In other words, the energy level of the impurity electron is in the band gap below the conduction band by 0.02 eV, a much smaller value than the energy of the gap, 1.14 eV. At room temperature, this impurity electron is easily excited into the conduction band and therefore contributes to the conductivity (Figure 9.20(a)). An impurity with an extra electron is known as a **donor impurity**, and the doped semiconductor is called an ***n*-type semiconductor** because the primary carriers of charge (electrons) are negative.

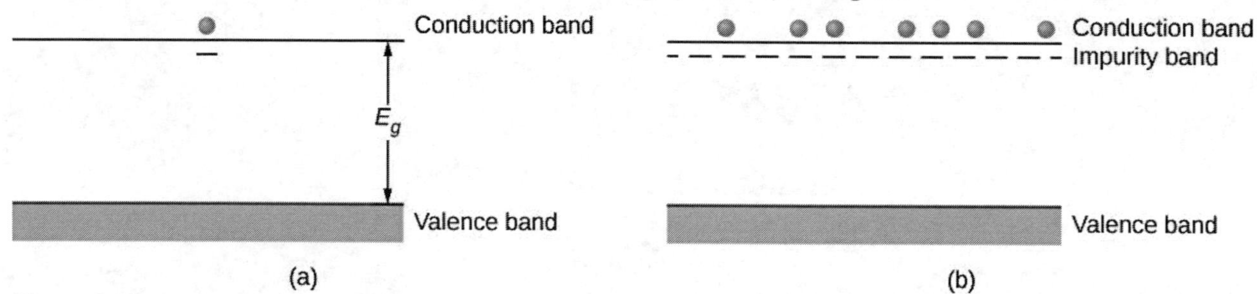

Figure 9.20 (a) The extra electron from a donor impurity is excited into the conduction band; (b) formation of an impurity band in an *n*-type semiconductor.

By adding more donor impurities, we can create an **impurity band**, a new energy band created by semiconductor doping, as shown in Figure 9.20(b). The Fermi level is now between this band and the conduction band. At room temperature, many impurity electrons are thermally excited into the conduction band and contribute to the conductivity. Conduction can then also occur in the impurity band as vacancies are created there. Note that changes in the energy of an electron correspond to a change in the motion (velocities or kinetic energy) of these charge carriers with the semiconductor, but not the bulk motion of the semiconductor itself.

Doping can also be accomplished using impurity atoms that typically have one *fewer* valence electron than the semiconductor atoms. For example, Al, which has three valence electrons, can be substituted for Si, as shown in Figure 9.19(b). Such an impurity is known as an **acceptor impurity**, and the doped semiconductor is called a ***p*-type semiconductor**, because the primary carriers of charge (holes) are positive. If a hole is treated as a positive particle weakly bound to the impurity site, then an empty electron state is created in the band gap just above the valence band. When this state is filled by an electron thermally excited from the valence band (Figure 9.21(a)), a mobile hole is created in the valence band. By adding more acceptor impurities, we can create an impurity band, as shown in Figure 9.21(b).

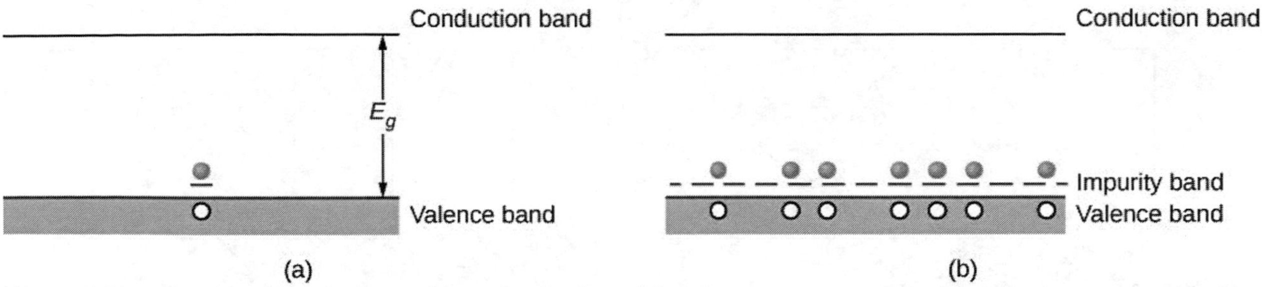

Figure 9.21 (a) An electron from the conduction band is excited into the empty state resulting from the acceptor impurity; (b) formation of an impurity band in a *p*-type semiconductor.

The electric current of a doped semiconductor can be due to the motion of a **majority carrier**, in which holes are contributed by an impurity atom, or due to a **minority carrier**, in which holes are contributed purely by thermal excitations of electrons across the energy gap. In an *n*-type semiconductor, majority carriers are free electrons contributed by impurity atoms, and minority carriers are free electrons produced by thermal excitations from the valence to the conduction band. In a *p*-type semiconductor, the majority carriers are free holes contributed by impurity atoms, and minority carriers are free holes left by the filling of states due to thermal excitation of electrons across the gap. In general, the number of majority carriers far exceeds the minority carriers. The concept of a majority and minority carriers will be used in the next section to explain the operation of diodes and transistors.

In studying *p*- and *n*-type doping, it is natural to ask: Do "electron holes" really act like particles? The existence of holes in a doped *p*-type semiconductor is demonstrated by the Hall effect. The Hall effect is the production of a potential difference due to the motion of a conductor through an external magnetic field (see **The Hall Effect (http://cnx.org/content/m58744/latest/)**). A schematic of the Hall effect is shown in **Figure 9.22**(a). A semiconductor strip is bathed in a uniform magnetic field (which points into the paper). As the electron holes move from left to right through the semiconductor, a Lorentz force drives these charges toward the upper end of the strip. (Recall that the motion of the positively charged carriers is determined by the right-hand rule.) Positive charge continues to collect on the upper edge of the strip until the force associated with the downward electric field between the upper and lower edges of the strip $(F_E = Eq)$ just balances the upward magnetic force $(F_B = qvB)$. Setting these forces equal to each other, we have $E = vB$. The voltage that develops across the strip is therefore

$$V_{\text{H}} = vBw, \tag{9.33}$$

where V_{H} is the Hall voltage; v is the hole's **drift velocity**, or average velocity of a particle that moves in a partially random fashion; B is the magnetic field strength; and w is the width of the strip. Note that the Hall voltage is transverse to the voltage that initially produces current through the material. A measurement of the sign of this voltage (or potential difference) confirms the collection of holes on the top side of the strip. The magnitude of the Hall voltage yields the drift velocity (v) of the majority carriers.

Additional information can also be extracted from the Hall voltage. Note that the electron current density (the amount of current per unit cross-sectional area of the semiconductor strip) is

$$j = nqv, \tag{9.34}$$

where q is the magnitude of the charge, n is the number of charge carriers per unit volume, and v is the drift velocity. The current density is easily determined by dividing the total current by the cross-sectional area of the strip, q is charge of the hole (the magnitude of the charge of a single electron), and u is determined by the Hall effect **Equation 9.34**. Hence, the above expression for the electron current density gives the number of charge carriers per unit volume, n. A similar analysis can be conducted for negatively charged carriers in an *n*-type material (see **Figure 9.22**).

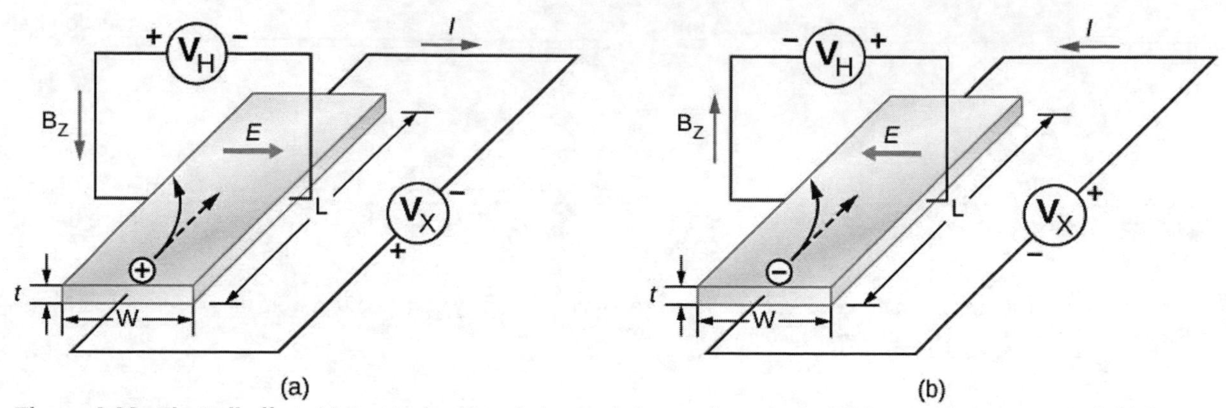

Figure 9.22 The Hall effect. (a) Positively charged electron holes are drawn to the left by a uniform magnetic field that points downward. An electric field is generated to the right. (b) Negative charged electrons are drawn to the left by a magnetic field that points up. An electric field is generated to the left.

9.7 | Semiconductor Devices

Learning Objectives

By the end of this section, you will be able to:

- Describe what occurs when n- and p-type materials are joined together using the concept of diffusion and drift current (zero applied voltage)
- Explain the response of a p-n junction to a forward and reverse bias voltage
- Describe the function of a transistor in an electric circuit
- Use the concept of a p-n junction to explain its applications in audio amplifiers and computers

Semiconductors have many applications in modern electronics. We describe some basic semiconductor devices in this section. A great advantage of using semiconductors for circuit elements is the fact that many thousands or millions of semiconductor devices can be combined on the same tiny piece of silicon and connected by conducting paths. The resulting structure is called an integrated circuit (ic), and ic chips are the basis of many modern devices, from computers and smartphones to the internet and global communications networks.

Diodes

Perhaps the simplest device that can be created with a semiconductor is a diode. A diode is a circuit element that allows electric current to flow in only one direction, like a one-way valve (see **Model of Conduction in Metals (http://cnx.org/content/m58730/latest/)**). A diode is created by joining a *p*-type semiconductor to an *n*-type semiconductor (**Figure 9.23**). The junction between these materials is called a ***p-n* junction**. A comparison of the energy bands of a silicon-based diode is shown in **Figure 9.23**(b). The positions of the valence and conduction bands are the same, but the impurity levels are quite different. When a *p-n* junction is formed, electrons from the conduction band of the *n*-type material diffuse to the *p*-side, where they combine with holes in the valence band. This migration of charge leaves positive ionized donor ions on the *n*-side and negative ionized acceptor ions on the *p*-side, producing a narrow double layer of charge at the *p-n* junction called the **depletion layer**. The electric field associated with the depletion layer prevents further diffusion. The potential energy for electrons across the *p-n* junction is given by **Figure 9.24**.

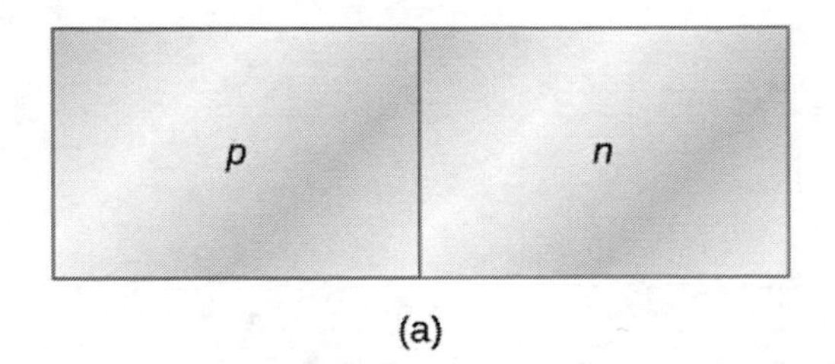

(a)

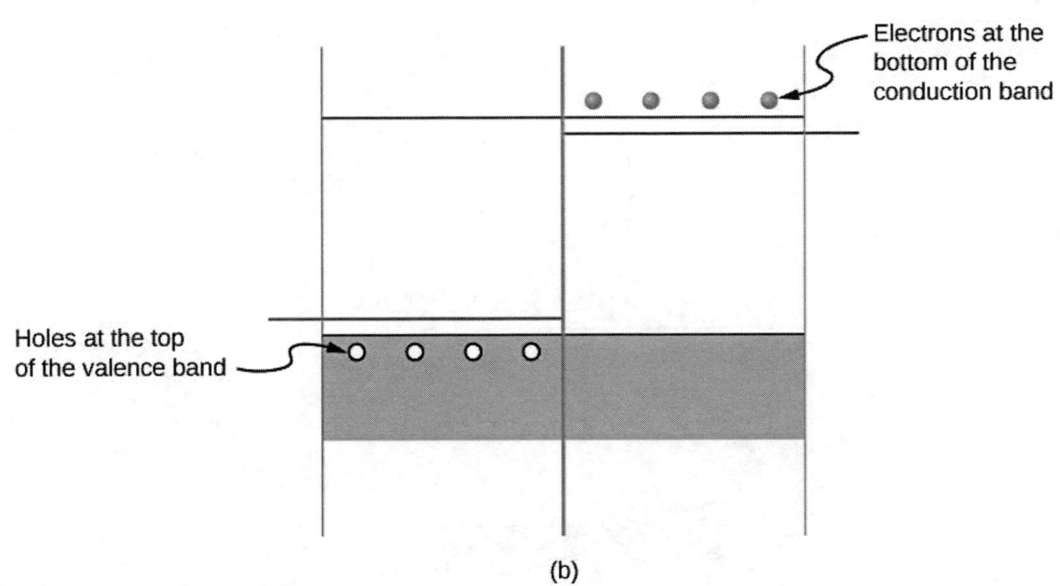

(b)

Figure 9.23 (a) Representation of a *p*-*n* junction. (b) A comparison of the energy bands of *p*-type and *n*-type silicon prior to equilibrium.

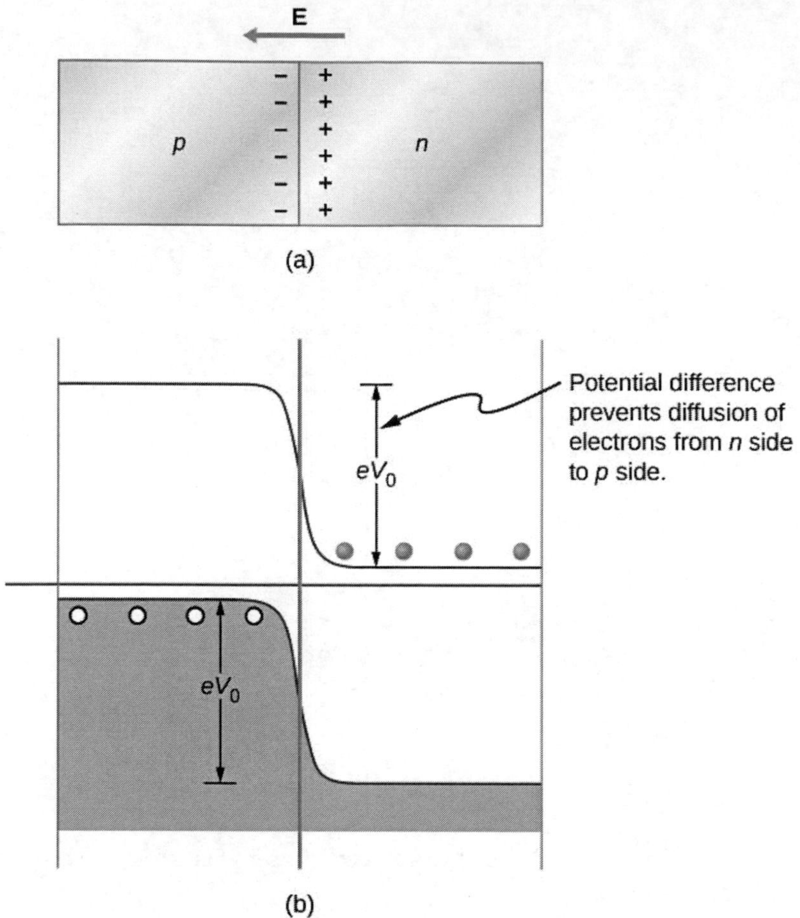

Figure 9.24 At equilibrium, (a) excess charge resides near the interface and the net current is zero, and (b) the potential energy difference for electrons (in light blue) prevents further diffusion of electrons into the *p*-side.

The behavior of a semiconductor diode can now be understood. If the positive side of the battery is connected to the *n*-type material, the depletion layer is widened, and the potential energy difference across the *p*-*n* junction is increased. Few or none of the electrons (holes) have enough energy to climb the potential barrier, and current is significantly reduced. This is called the **reverse bias configuration**. On the other hand, if the positive side of a battery is connected to the *p*-type material, the depletion layer is narrowed, the potential energy difference across the *p*-*n* junction is reduced, and electrons (holes) flow easily. This is called the **forward bias configuration** of the diode. In sum, the diode allows current to flow freely in one direction but prevents current flow in the opposite direction. In this sense, the semiconductor diode is a one-way valve.

We can estimate the mathematical relationship between the current and voltage for a diode using the electric potential concept. Consider N negatively charged majority carriers (electrons donated by impurity atoms) in the *n*-type material and a potential barrier V across the *p*-*n* junction. According to the Maxwell-Boltzmann distribution, the fraction of electrons that have enough energy to diffuse across the potential barrier is $Ne^{-eV/k_\text{B}T}$. However, if a battery of voltage V_b is applied in the forward-bias configuration, this fraction improves to $Ne^{-e(V-V_b)/k_\text{B}T}$. The electric current due to the majority carriers from the *n*-side to the *p*-side is therefore

$$I = Ne^{-eV/k_\text{B}T}e^{eV_b/k_\text{B}T} = I_0 e^{eV_b/k_\text{B}T}, \tag{9.35}$$

where I_0 is the current with no applied voltage and T is the temperature. Current due to the minority carriers (thermal excitation of electrons from the valence band to the conduction band on the *p*-side and subsequent attraction to the *n*-side) is $-I_0$, independent of the bias voltage. The net current is therefore

$$I_{\text{net}} = I_0\left(e^{eV_b/k_B T} - 1\right). \tag{9.36}$$

A sample graph of the current versus bias voltage is given in **Figure 9.25**. In the forward bias configuration, small changes in the bias voltage lead to large changes in the current. In the reverse bias configuration, the current is $I_{\text{net}} \approx -I_0$. For extreme values of reverse bias, the atoms in the material are ionized which triggers an avalanche of current. This case occurs at the **breakdown voltage**.

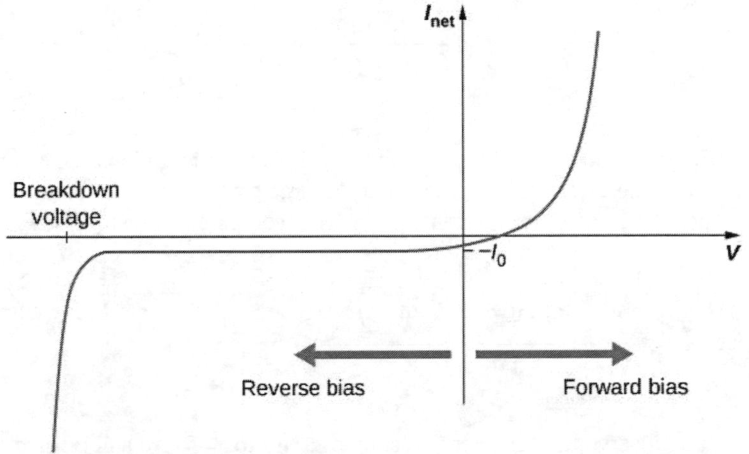

Figure 9.25 Current versus voltage across a *p-n* junction (diode). In the forward bias configuration, electric current flows easily. However, in the reverse bias configuration, electric current flow very little.

Example 9.6

Diode Current

Attaching the positive end of a battery to the *p*-side and the negative end to the *n*-side of a semiconductor diode produces a current of 4.5×10^{-1} A. The reverse saturation current is 2.2×10^{-8} A. (The reverse saturation current is the current of a diode in a reverse bias configuration such as this.) The battery voltage is 0.12 V. What is the diode temperature?

Strategy

The first arrangement is a forward bias configuration, and the second is the reverse bias configuration. In either case, **Equation 9.2** gives the current.

Solution

The current in the forward and reverse bias configurations is given by

$$I_{\text{net}} = I_0\left(e^{eV_b/k_B T} - 1\right).$$

The current with no bias is related to the reverse saturation current by

$$I_0 \approx -I_{\text{sat}} = 2.2 \times 10^{-8}.$$

Therefore

$$\frac{I_{\text{net}}}{I_0} = \frac{4.5 \times 10^{-1}\ \text{A}}{2.2 \times 10^{-8}\ \text{A}} = 2.0 \times 10^{8}.$$

Equation 9.2 can be written as

$$\frac{I_{\text{net}}}{I_0} + 1 = e^{eV_b/k_B T}.$$

This ratio is much greater than one, so the second term on the left-hand side of the equation vanishes. Taking the natural log of both sides gives

$$\frac{eV_b}{k_B T} = 19.$$

The temperature is therefore

$$T = \frac{eV_b}{k_B}\left(\frac{1}{19}\right) = \frac{e(0.12\text{ V})}{8.617 \times 10^{-5}\text{ eV/K}}\left(\frac{1}{19}\right) = 73\text{ K}.$$

Significance

The current moving through a diode in the forward and reverse bias configuration is sensitive to the temperature of the diode. If the potential energy supplied by the battery is large compared to the thermal energy of the diode's surroundings, $k_B T$, then the forward bias current is very large compared to the reverse saturation current.

9.5 Check Your Understanding How does the magnitude of the forward bias current compare with the reverse bias current?

Create a *p-n* junction and observe the behavior of a simple circuit for forward and reverse bias voltages. Visit this **site (https://openstaxcollege.org/l/21semiconductor)** to learn more about semiconductor diodes.

Junction Transistor

If diodes are one-way valves, transistors are one-way valves that can be carefully opened and closed to control current. A special kind of transistor is a junction transistor. A **junction transistor** has three parts, including an *n*-type semiconductor, also called the emitter; a thin *p*-type semiconductor, which is the base; and another *n*-type semiconductor, called the collector (**Figure 9.26**). When a positive terminal is connected to the *p*-type layer (the base), a small current of electrons, called the **base current** I_B, flows to the terminal. This causes a large **collector current** I_c to flow through the collector. The base current can be adjusted to control the large collector current. The current gain is therefore

$$I_c = \beta I_B. \tag{9.37}$$

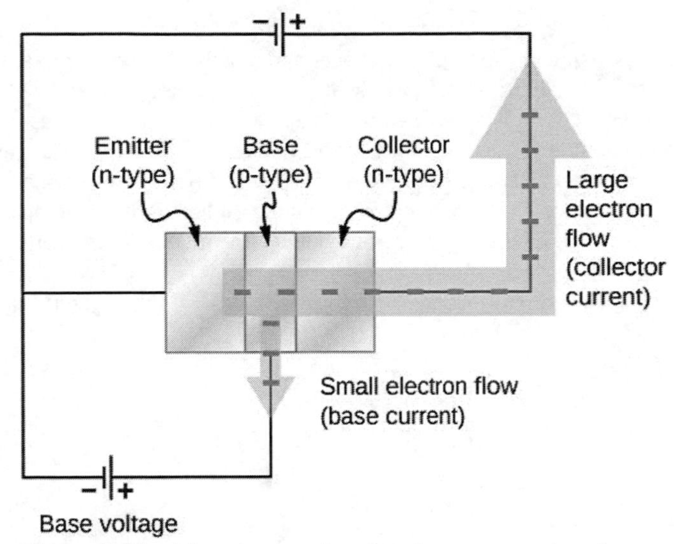

Figure 9.26 A junction transistor has three parts: emitter, base, and collector. Voltage applied to the base acts as a valve to control electric current from the emitter to the collector.

A junction transistor can be used to amplify the voltage from a microphone to drive a loudspeaker. In this application, sound waves cause a diaphragm inside the microphone to move in and out rapidly (Figure 9.27). When the diaphragm is in the "in" position, a tiny positive voltage is applied to the base of the transistor. This opens the transistor "valve" and allows a large electrical current flow to the loudspeaker. When the diaphragm is in the "out" position, a tiny negative voltage is applied to the base of the transistor, which shuts off the transistor valve so that no current flows to the loudspeaker. This shuts the transistor "valve" off so no current flows to the loudspeaker. In this way, current to the speaker is controlled by the sound waves, and the sound is amplified. Any electric device that amplifies a signal is called an **amplifier**.

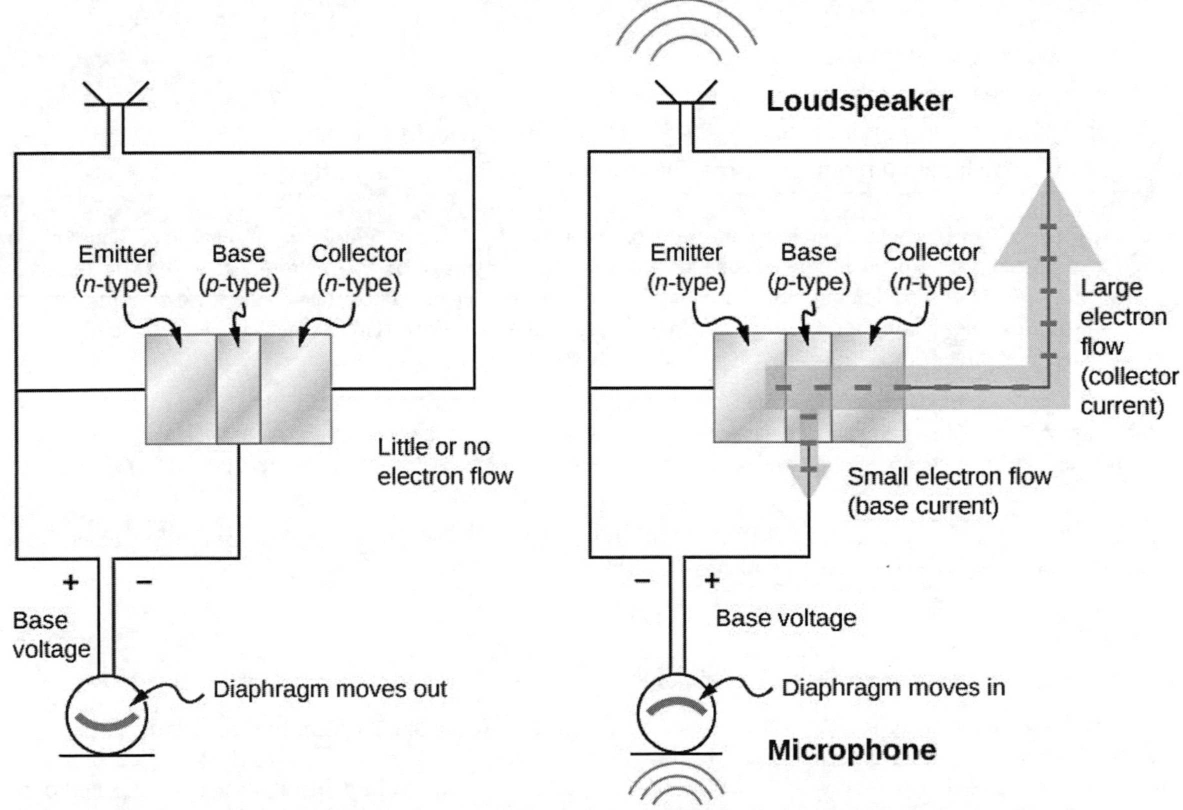

Figure 9.27 An audio amplifier based on a junction transistor. Voltage applied to the base by a microphone acts as a valve to control a larger electric current that passes through a loudspeaker.

In modern electronic devices, digital signals are used with diodes and transistors to perform tasks such as data manipulation. Electric circuits carry two types of electrical signals: analog and digital (**Figure 9.28**). An analog signal varies continuously, whereas a digital signal switches between two fixed voltage values, such as plus 1 volt and zero volts. In digital circuits like those found in computers, a transistor behaves like an on-off switch. The transistor is either on, meaning the valve is completely open, or it is off, meaning the valve is completely closed. Integrated circuits contain vast collections of transistors on a single piece of silicon. They are designed to handle digital signals that represent ones and zeroes, which is also known as binary code. The invention of the ic helped to launch the modern computer revolution.

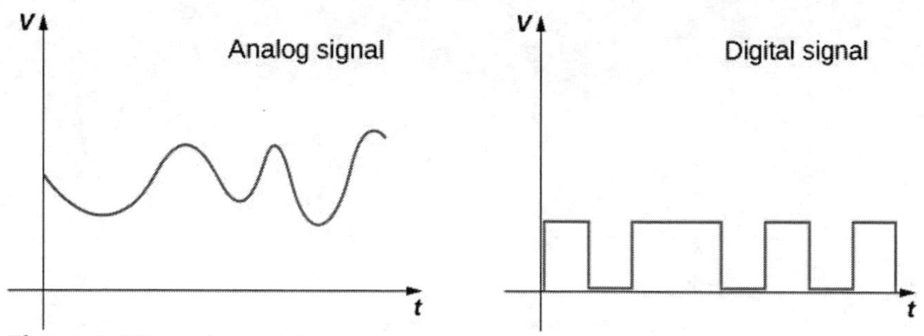

Figure 9.28 Real-world data are often analog, meaning data can vary continuously. Intensity values of sound or visual images are usually analog. These data are converted into digital signals for electronic processing in recording devices or computers. The digital signal is generated from the analog signal by requiring certain voltage cut-off value.

9.8 | Superconductivity

Learning Objectives

By the end of this section, you will be able to:

- Describe the main features of a superconductor
- Describe the BCS theory of superconductivity
- Determine the critical magnetic field for T = 0 K from magnetic field data
- Calculate the maximum emf or current for a wire to remain superconducting

Electrical resistance can be considered as a measure of the frictional force in electrical current flow. Thus, electrical resistance is a primary source of energy dissipation in electrical systems such as electromagnets, electric motors, and transmission lines. Copper wire is commonly used in electrical wiring because it has one of the lowest room-temperature electrical resistivities among common conductors. (Actually, silver has a lower resistivity than copper, but the high cost and limited availability of silver outweigh its savings in energy over copper.)

Although our discussion of conductivity seems to imply that all materials must have electrical resistance, we know that this is not the case. When the temperature decreases below a critical value for many materials, their electrical resistivity drops to zero, and the materials become superconductors (see **Superconductors (http://cnx.org/content/m58735/latest/)**).

Watch this **NOVA video (https://openstaxcollege.org/l/21NOVA)** excerpt, Making Stuff Colder, as an introduction to the topic of superconductivity and its many applications.

Properties of Superconductors

In addition to zero electrical resistance, superconductors also have perfect diamagnetism. In other words, in the presence of an applied magnetic field, the net magnetic field within a superconductor is always zero (**Figure 9.29**). Therefore, any magnetic field lines that pass through a superconducting sample when it is in its normal state are expelled once the sample becomes superconducting. These are manifestations of the Meissner effect, which you learned about in the chapter on current and resistance.

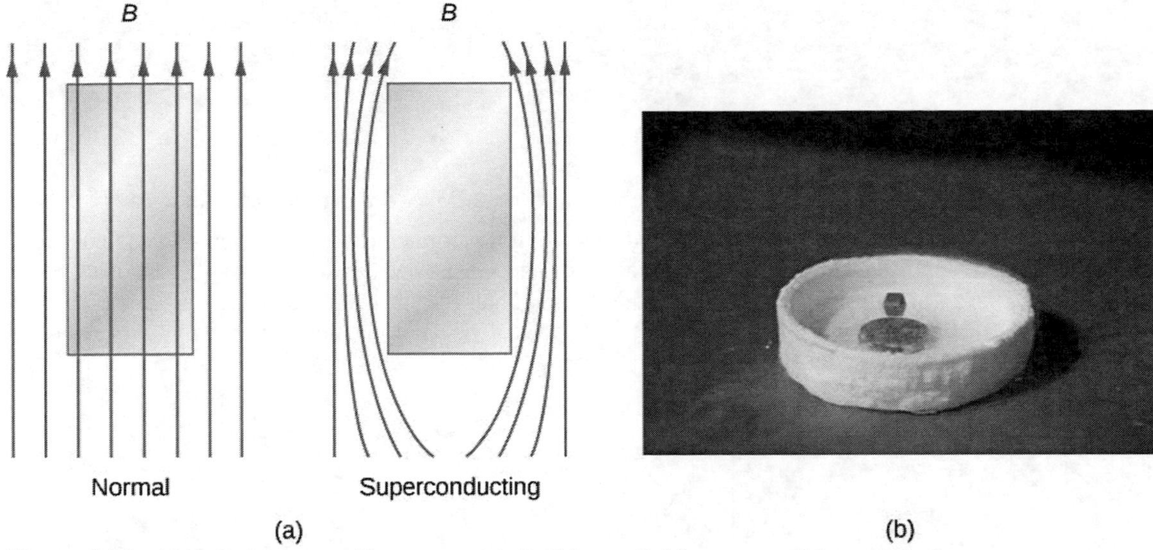

Figure 9.29 (a) In the Meissner effect, a magnetic field is expelled from a material once it becomes superconducting. (b) A magnet can levitate above a superconducting material, supported by the force expelling the magnetic field. (credit b: modification of work by Kevin Jarrett)

Interestingly, the Meissner effect is not a consequence of the resistance being zero. To see why, suppose that a sample placed in a magnetic field undergoes a transition in which its resistance drops to zero. From Ohm's law, the current density, j, in the sample is related to the net internal electric field, E, and the resistivity ρ by $j = E/\rho$. If ρ is zero, E must also be zero so that j can remain finite. Now E and the magnetic flux Φ_m through the sample are related by Faraday's law as

$$\oint E dl = -\frac{d\Phi_m}{dt}. \tag{9.38}$$

If E is zero, $d\Phi_m/dt$ is also zero, that is, the magnetic flux through the sample cannot change. The magnetic field lines within the sample should therefore not be expelled when the transition occurs. Hence, it does not follow that a material whose resistance goes to zero has to exhibit the Meissner effect. Rather, the Meissner effect is a special property of superconductors.

Another important property of a superconducting material is its **critical temperature**, T_c, the temperature below which the material is superconducting. The known range of critical temperatures is from a fraction of 1 K to slightly above 100 K. Superconductors with critical temperatures near this higher limit are commonly known as "high-temperature" superconductors. From a practical standpoint, superconductors for which $T_c \gg 77\text{ K}$ are very important. At present, applications involving superconductors often still require that superconducting materials be immersed in liquid helium (4.2 K) in order to keep them below their critical temperature. The liquid helium baths must be continually replenished because of evaporation, and cooling costs can easily outweigh the savings in using a superconductor. However, 77 K is the temperature of liquid nitrogen, which is far more abundant and inexpensive than liquid helium. It would be much more cost-effective if we could easily fabricate and use high-temperature superconductor components that only need to be kept in liquid nitrogen baths to maintain their superconductivity.

High-temperature superconducting materials are presently in use in various applications. An example is the production of magnetic fields in some particle accelerators. The ultimate goal is to discover materials that are superconducting at room temperature. Without any cooling requirements, the bulk of electronic components and transmission lines could be superconducting, resulting in dramatic and unprecedented increases in efficiency and performance.

Another important property of a superconducting material is its **critical magnetic field** $B_c(T)$, which is the maximum applied magnetic field at a temperature T that will allow a material to remain superconducting. An applied field that is greater than the critical field will destroy the superconductivity. The critical field is zero at the critical temperature and increases as the temperature decreases. Plots of the critical field versus temperature for several superconducting materials are shown in **Figure 9.30**. The temperature dependence of the critical field can be described approximately by

$$B_c(T) = B_c(0)\left[1 - \left(\frac{T}{T_c}\right)^2\right] \tag{9.39}$$

where $B_c(0)$ is the critical field at absolute zero temperature. **Table 9.5** lists the critical temperatures and fields for two classes of superconductors: **type I superconductor** and **type II superconductor**. In general, type I superconductors are elements, such as aluminum and mercury. They are perfectly diamagnetic below a critical field $B_C(T)$, and enter the normal non-superconducting state once that field is exceeded. The critical fields of type I superconductors are generally quite low (well below one tesla). For this reason, they cannot be used in applications requiring the production of high magnetic fields, which would destroy their superconducting state.

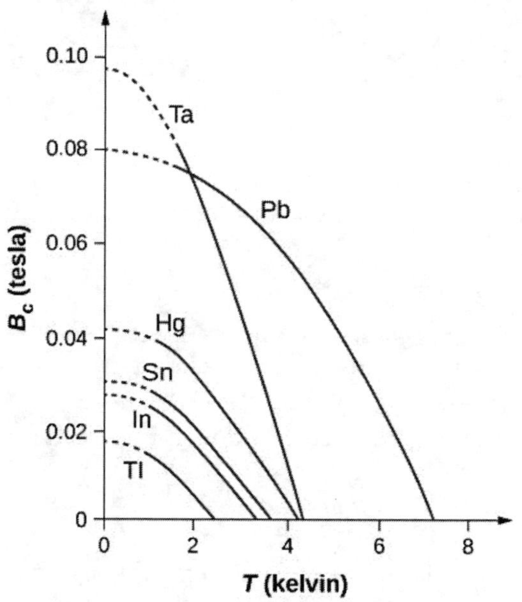

Figure 9.30 The temperature dependence of the critical field for several superconductors. Superconductivity occurs for magnetic fields and temperatures below the curves shown.

Material	Critical Temperature (K)	Critical Magnetic Field (T)
Type I		
Al	1.2	0.011
Ga	1.1	0.0051
Hg(α)	4.2	0.041
In	3.4	0.029
Nb	9.3	0.20
Pb	7.2	0.080
Sn	3.7	0.031
Th	1.4	0.00016
Zn	0.87	0.0053

Table 9.5 Critical Temperature and Critical Magnetic Field at $T = 0\,\text{K}$ for Various Superconductors

Material	Critical Temperature (K)	Critical Magnetic Field (T)
Type II		
Nb_3Al	18	32
Nb_3Ge	23	38
Nb_3Sn	18	25
NbTi	9.3	15
$YBa_2Cu_3O_7$	92	>100

Table 9.5 Critical Temperature and Critical Magnetic Field at $T = 0\ \text{K}$ for Various Superconductors

Type II superconductors are generally compounds or alloys involving transition metals or actinide series elements. Almost all superconductors with relatively high critical temperatures are type II. They have two critical fields, represented by $B_{c1}(T)$ and $B_{c2}(T)$. When the field is below $B_{c1}(T)$, type II superconductors are perfectly diamagnetic, and no magnetic flux penetration into the material can occur. For a field exceeding $B_{c2}(T)$, they are driven into their normal state. When the field is greater than $B_{c1}(T)$ but less than $B_{c2}(T)$, type II superconductors are said to be in a mixed state. Although there is some magnetic flux penetration in the mixed state, the resistance of the material is zero. Within the superconductor, filament-like regions exist that have normal electrical and magnetic properties interspersed between regions that are superconducting with perfect diamagnetism. A representation of this state is given in **Figure 9.31**. The magnetic field is expelled from the superconducting regions but exists in the normal regions. In general, $B_{c2}(T)$ is very large compared with the critical fields of type I superconductors, so wire made of type II superconducting material is suitable for the windings of high-field magnets.

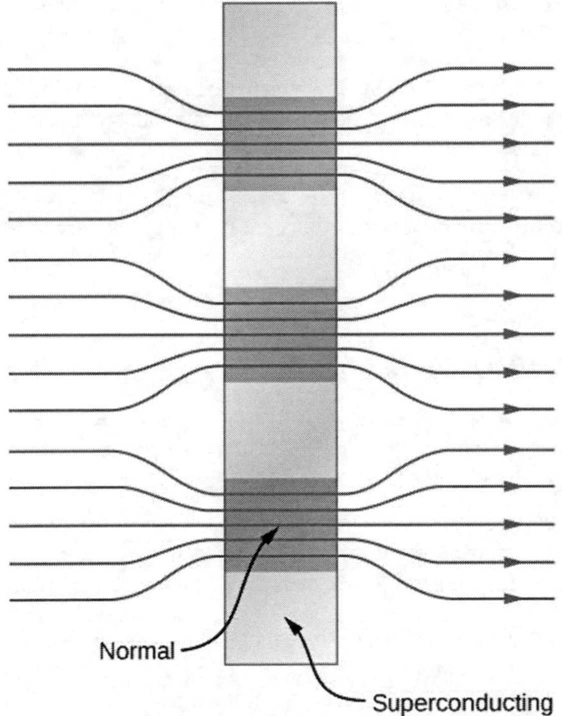

Figure 9.31 A schematic representation of the mixed state of a type II superconductor. Superconductors (the gray squares) expel magnetic fields in their vicinity.

Example 9.7

Niobium Wire

In an experiment, a niobium (Nb) wire of radius 0.25 mm is immersed in liquid helium ($T = 4.2\text{ K}$) and required to carry a current of 300 A. Does the wire remain superconducting?

Strategy

The applied magnetic field can be determined from the radius of the wire and current. The critical magnetic field can be determined from **Equation 9.1**, the properties of the superconductor, and the temperature. If the applied magnetic field is greater than the critical field, then superconductivity in the Nb wire is destroyed.

Solution

At $T = 4.2\text{ K}$, the critical field for Nb is, from **Equation 9.1** and **Table 9.5**,

$$B_c(4.2\text{ K}) = B_c(0)\left[1 - \left(\frac{4.2\text{ K}}{9.3\text{ K}}\right)^2\right] = (0.20\text{ T})(0.80) = 0.16\text{ T}.$$

In an earlier chapter, we learned the magnetic field inside a current-carrying wire of radius a is given by

$$B = \frac{\mu_0 I}{2\pi a},$$

where r is the distance from the central axis of the wire. Thus, the field at the surface of the wire is $\frac{\mu_0 I_r}{2\pi a}$. For the niobium wire, this field is

$$B = \frac{(4\pi \times 10^{-7}\text{ T m/A})(300\text{ A})}{2\pi(2.5 \times 10^{-4}\text{ m})} = 0.24\text{ T}.$$

Since this exceeds the critical 0.16 T, the wire does not remain superconducting.

Significance

Superconductivity requires low temperatures and low magnetic fields. These simultaneous conditions are met less easily for Nb than for many other metals. For example, aluminum superconducts at temperatures 7 times lower and magnetic fields 18 times lower.

9.6 Check Your Understanding What conditions are necessary for superconductivity?

Theory of Superconductors

A successful theory of superconductivity was developed in the 1950s by John Bardeen, Leon Cooper, and J. Robert Schrieffer, for which they received the Nobel Prize in 1972. This theory is known as the **BCS theory**. BCS theory is complex, so we summarize it qualitatively below.

In a normal conductor, the electrical properties of the material are due to the most energetic electrons near the Fermi energy. In 1956, Cooper showed that if there is any attractive interaction between two electrons at the Fermi level, then the electrons can form a bound state in which their total energy is less than $2E_F$. Two such electrons are known as a **Cooper pair**.

It is hard to imagine two electrons attracting each other, since they have like charge and should repel. However, the proposed interaction occurs only in the context of an atomic lattice. A depiction of the attraction is shown in **Figure 9.32**. Electron 1 slightly displaces the positively charged atomic nuclei toward itself as it travels past because of the Coulomb attraction. Electron 2 "sees" a region with a higher density of positive charge relative to the surroundings and is therefore attracted into this region and, therefore indirectly, to electron 1. Because of the exclusion principle, the two electrons of a Cooper pair must have opposite spin.

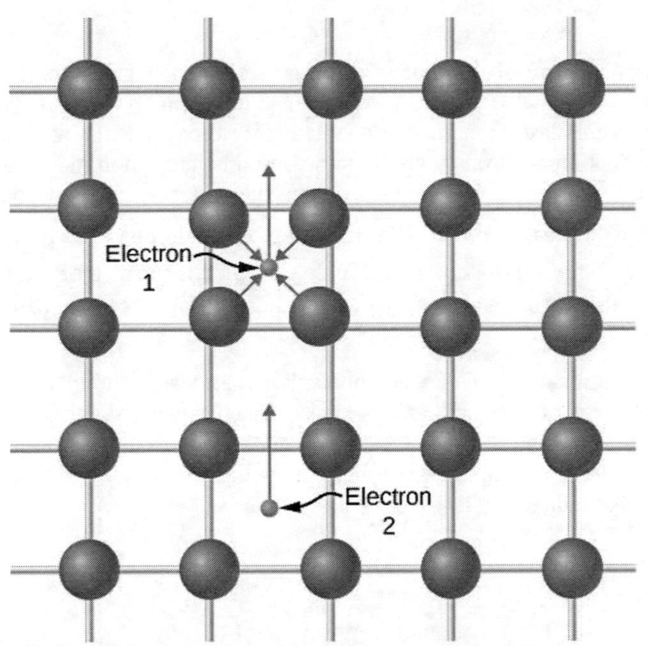

Figure 9.32 A Cooper pair can form as a result of the displacement of positive atomic nuclei. Electron 1 slightly displaces the positively charged atomic nuclei toward itself as it travels past because of the Coulomb attraction. Electron 2 “sees” a region with a higher density of positive charge relative to the surroundings and is therefore attracted into this region.

The BCS theory extends Cooper’s ideas, which are for a single pair of electrons, to the entire free electron gas. When the transition to the superconducting state occurs, all the electrons pair up to form Cooper pairs. On an atomic scale, the distance between the two electrons making up a Cooper pair is quite large. Between these electrons are typically about 10^6 other electrons, each also pairs with a distant electron. Hence, there is considerable overlap between the wave functions of the individual Cooper pairs, resulting in a strong correlation among the motions of the pairs. They all move together “in step,” like the members of a marching band. In the superconducting transition, the density of states becomes drastically changed near the Fermi level. As shown in **Figure 9.33**, an energy gap appears around E_F because the collection of Cooper pairs has lower ground state energy than the Fermi gas of noninteracting electrons. The appearance of this gap characterizes the superconducting state. If this state is destroyed, then the gap disappears, and the density of states reverts to that of the free electron gas.

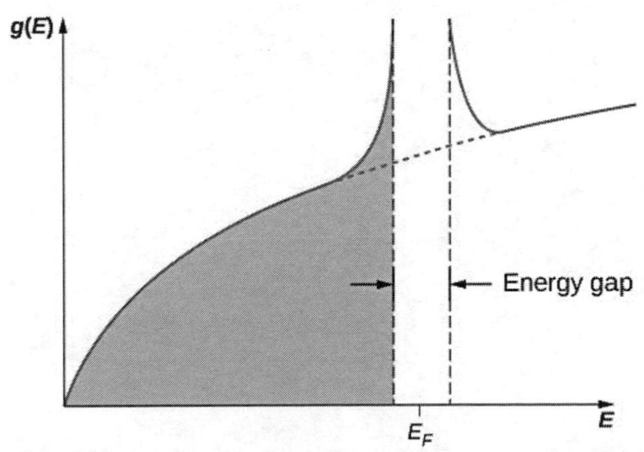

Figure 9.33 A relatively large energy gap is formed around the Fermi energy when a material becomes superconducting. If this state is destroyed, then the gap disappears, and the density of states reverts to that of the free electron gas.

The BCS theory is able to predict many of the properties observed in superconductors. Examples include the Meissner effect, the critical temperature, the critical field, and, perhaps most importantly, the resistivity becoming zero at a critical temperature. We can think about this last phenomenon qualitatively as follows. In a normal conductor, resistivity results from the interaction of the conduction electrons with the lattice. In this interaction, the energy exchanged is on the order of $k_B T,$ the thermal energy. In a superconductor, electric current is carried by the Cooper pairs. The only way for a lattice to scatter a Cooper pair is to break it up. The destruction of one pair then destroys the collective motion of all the pairs. This destruction requires energy on the order of $10^{-3}\,\text{eV}$, which is the size of the energy gap. Below the critical temperature, there is not enough thermal energy available for this process, so the Cooper pairs travel unimpeded throughout the superconductor.

Finally, it is interesting to note that no evidence of superconductivity has been found in the best normal conductors, such as copper and silver. This is not unexpected, given the BCS theory. The basis for the formation of the superconducting state is an interaction between the electrons and the lattice. In the best conductors, the electron-lattice interaction is weakest, as evident from their minimal resistivity. We might expect then that in these materials, the interaction is so weak that Cooper pairs cannot be formed, and superconductivity is therefore precluded.

CHAPTER 9 REVIEW

KEY TERMS

acceptor impurity atom substituted for another in a semiconductor that results in a free electron

amplifier electrical device that amplifies an electric signal

base current current drawn from the base *n*-type material in a transistor

BCS theory theory of superconductivity based on electron-lattice-electron interactions

body-centered cubic (BCC) crystal structure in which an ion is surrounded by eight nearest neighbors located at the corners of a unit cell

breakdown voltage in a diode, the reverse bias voltage needed to cause an avalanche of current

collector current current drawn from the collector *p*-type material

conduction band above the valence band, the next available band in the energy structure of a crystal

Cooper pair coupled electron pair in a superconductor

covalent bond bond formed by the sharing of one or more electrons between atoms

critical magnetic field maximum field required to produce superconductivity

critical temperature maximum temperature to produce superconductivity

density of states number of allowed quantum states per unit energy

depletion layer region near the *p-n* junction that produces an electric field

dissociation energy amount of energy needed to break apart a molecule into atoms; also, total energy per ion pair to separate the crystal into isolated ions

donor impurity atom substituted for another in a semiconductor that results in a free electron hole

doping alteration of a semiconductor by the substitution of one type of atom with another

drift velocity average velocity of a randomly moving particle

electric dipole transition transition between energy levels brought by the absorption or emission of radiation

electron affinity energy associated with an accepted (bound) electron

electron number density number of electrons per unit volume

energy band nearly continuous band of electronic energy levels in a solid

energy gap gap between energy bands in a solid

equilibrium separation distance distance between atoms in a molecule

exchange symmetry how a total wave function changes under the exchange of two electrons

face-centered cubic (FCC) crystal structure in which an ion is surrounded by six nearest neighbors located at the faces at the faces of a unit cell

Fermi energy largest energy filled by electrons in a metal at $T = 0\,\text{K}$

Fermi factor number that expresses the probability that a state of given energy will be filled

Fermi temperature effective temperature of electrons with energies equal to the Fermi energy

forward bias configuration diode configuration that results in high current

free electron model model of a metal that views electrons as a gas

hole unoccupied states in an energy band

hybridization change in the energy structure of an atom in which energetically favorable mixed states participate in bonding

impurity atom acceptor or donor impurity atom

impurity band new energy band create by semiconductor doping

ionic bond bond formed by the Coulomb attraction of a positive and negative ions

junction transistor electrical valve based on a *p-n-p* junction

lattice regular array or arrangement of atoms into a crystal structure

Madelung constant constant that depends on the geometry of a crystal used to determine the total potential energy of an ion in a crystal

majority carrier free electrons (or holes) contributed by impurity atoms

minority carrier free electrons (or holes) produced by thermal excitations across the energy gap

***n*-type semiconductor** doped semiconductor that conducts electrons

***p-n* junction** junction formed by joining *p*- and *n*-type semiconductors

***p*-type semiconductor** doped semiconductor that conducts holes

polyatomic molecule molecule formed of more than one atom

repulsion constant experimental parameter associated with a repulsive force between ions brought so close together that the exclusion principle is important

reverse bias configuration diode configuration that results in low current

rotational energy level energy level associated with the rotational energy of a molecule

selection rule rule that limits the possible transitions from one quantum state to another

semiconductor solid with a relatively small energy gap between the lowest completely filled band and the next available unfilled band

simple cubic basic crystal structure in which each ion is located at the nodes of a three-dimensional grid

type I superconductor superconducting element, such as aluminum or mercury

type II superconductor superconducting compound or alloy, such as a transition metal or an actinide series element

valence band highest energy band that is filled in the energy structure of a crystal

van der Waals bond bond formed by the attraction of two electrically polarized molecules

vibrational energy level energy level associated with the vibrational energy of a molecule

KEY EQUATIONS

Electrostatic energy for equilibrium separation distance between atoms	$U_{\text{coul}} = -\frac{ke^2}{r_0}$
Energy change associated with ionic bonding	$U_{\text{form}} = E_{\text{transfer}} + U_{\text{coul}} + U_{\text{ex}}$
Critical magnetic field of a superconductor	$B_c(T) = B_c(0)\left[1 - \left(\frac{T}{T_c}\right)^2\right]$
Rotational energy of a diatomic molecule	$E_r = l(l+1)\frac{\hbar^2}{2I}$
Characteristic rotational energy of a molecule	$E_{0r} = \frac{\hbar^2}{2I}$
Potential energy associated with the exclusion principle	$U_{\text{ex}} = \frac{A}{r^n}$
Dissociation energy of a solid	$U_{\text{diss}} = \alpha\frac{ke^2}{r_0}\left(1 - \frac{1}{n}\right)$

Moment of inertia of a diatomic molecule with reduced mass μ	$I = \mu r_0^2$
Electron energy in a metal	$E = \frac{\pi^2 \hbar^2}{2mL^2}\left(n_1^2 + n_2^2 + n_3^2\right)$
Electron density of states of a metal	$g(E) = \frac{\pi V}{2}\left(\frac{8m_e}{h^2}\right)^{3/2} E^{1/2}$
Fermi energy	$E_F = \frac{h^2}{8m_e}\left(\frac{3N}{\pi V}\right)^{2/3}$
Fermi temperature	$T_F = \frac{E_F}{k_B}$
Hall effect	$V_H = uBw$
Current versus bias voltage across *p-n* junction	$I_{net} = I_0\left(e^{eV_b/k_B T} - 1\right)$
Current gain	$I_c = \beta I_B$
Selection rule for rotational energy transitions	$\Delta l = \pm 1$
Selection rule for vibrational energy transitions	$\Delta n = \pm 1$

SUMMARY

9.1 Types of Molecular Bonds

- Molecules form by two main types of bonds: the ionic bond and the covalent bond. An ionic bond transfers an electron from one atom to another, and a covalent bond shares the electrons.
- The energy change associated with ionic bonding depends on three main processes: the ionization of an electron from one atom, the acceptance of the electron by the second atom, and the Coulomb attraction of the resulting ions.
- Covalent bonds involve space-symmetric wave functions.
- Atoms use a linear combination of wave functions in bonding with other molecules (hybridization).

9.2 Molecular Spectra

- Molecules possess vibrational and rotational energy.
- Energy differences between adjacent vibrational energy levels are larger than those between rotational energy levels.
- Separation between peaks in an absorption spectrum is inversely related to the moment of inertia.
- Transitions between vibrational and rotational energy levels follow selection rules.

9.3 Bonding in Crystalline Solids

- Packing structures of common ionic salts include FCC and BCC.
- The density of a crystal is inversely related to the equilibrium constant.
- The dissociation energy of a salt is large when the equilibrium separation distance is small.
- The densities and equilibrium radii for common salts (FCC) are nearly the same.

9.4 Free Electron Model of Metals

- Metals conduct electricity, and electricity is composed of large numbers of randomly colliding and approximately free electrons.

- The allowed energy states of an electron are quantized. This quantization appears in the form of very large electron energies, even at $T = 0\,\mathrm{K}$.
- The allowed energies of free electrons in a metal depend on electron mass and on the electron number density of the metal.
- The density of states of an electron in a metal increases with energy, because there are more ways for an electron to fill a high-energy state than a low-energy state.
- Pauli's exclusion principle states that only two electrons (spin up and spin down) can occupy the same energy level. Therefore, in filling these energy levels (lowest to highest at $T = 0\,\mathrm{K}$), the last and largest energy level to be occupied is called the Fermi energy.

9.5 Band Theory of Solids

- The energy levels of an electron in a crystal can be determined by solving Schrödinger's equation for a periodic potential and by studying changes to the electron energy structure as atoms are pushed together from a distance.
- The energy structure of a crystal is characterized by continuous energy bands and energy gaps.
- The ability of a solid to conduct electricity relies on the energy structure of the solid.

9.6 Semiconductors and Doping

- The energy structure of a semiconductor can be altered by substituting one type of atom with another (doping).
- Semiconductor *n*-type doping creates and fills new energy levels just below the conduction band.
- Semiconductor *p*-type doping creates new energy levels just above the valence band.
- The Hall effect can be used to determine charge, drift velocity, and charge carrier number density of a semiconductor.

9.7 Semiconductor Devices

- A diode is produced by an *n*-*p* junction. A diode allows current to move in just one direction. In forward biased configuration of a diode, the current increases exponentially with the voltage.
- A transistor is produced by an *n*-*p*-*n* junction. A transistor is an electric valve that controls the current in a circuit.
- A transistor is a critical component in audio amplifiers, computers, and many other devices.

9.8 Superconductivity

- A superconductor is characterized by two features: the conduction of electrons with zero electrical resistance and the repelling of magnetic field lines.
- A minimum temperature is required for superconductivity to occur.
- A strong magnetic field destroys superconductivity.
- Superconductivity can be explain in terms of Cooper pairs.

CONCEPTUAL QUESTIONS

9.1 Types of Molecular Bonds

1. What is the main difference between an *ionic bond*, a *covalent bond*, and a *van der Waals bond*?

2. For the following cases, what type of bonding is expected? (a) KCl molecule; (b) N_2 molecule.

3. Describe three steps to ionic bonding.

4. What prevents a positive and negative ion from having a zero separation?

5. For the H_2 molecule, why must the spins the electron spins be antiparallel?

9.2 Molecular Spectra

6. Does the absorption spectrum of the diatomic molecule HCl depend on the isotope of chlorine contained in the molecule? Explain your reasoning.

7. Rank the energy spacing (ΔE) of the following transitions from least to greatest: an electron energy transition in an atom (atomic energy), the rotational energy of a molecule, or the vibrational energy of a molecule?

8. Explain key features of a vibrational-rotation energy spectrum of the diatomic molecule.

9.3 Bonding in Crystalline Solids

9. Why is the equilibrium separation distance between K^+ and Cl^- different for a diatomic molecule than for solid KCl?

10. Describe the difference between a face-centered cubic structure (FCC) and a body-centered cubic structure (BCC).

11. In sodium chloride, how many Cl^- atoms are "nearest neighbors" of Na^+ ? How many Na^+ atoms are "nearest neighbors" of Cl^- ?

12. In cesium iodide, how many Cl^- atoms are "nearest neighbors" of Cs^+ ? How many Cs^+ atoms are "nearest neighbors" of Cl^- ?

13. The NaCl crystal structure is FCC. The equilibrium spacing is $r_0 = 0.282\,\text{nm}$. If each ion occupies a cubic volume of r_0^3, estimate the distance between "nearest neighbor" Na^+ ions (center-to-center)?

9.4 Free Electron Model of Metals

14. Why does the Fermi energy (E_F) increase with the number of electrons in a metal?

15. If the electron number density (*N/V*) of a metal increases by a factor 8, what happens to the Fermi energy (E_F)?

16. Why does the horizontal line in the graph in **Figure 9.12** suddenly stop at the Fermi energy?

17. Why does the graph in **Figure 9.12** increase gradually from the origin?

18. Why are the sharp transitions at the Fermi energy "smoothed out" by increasing the temperature?

9.5 Band Theory of Solids

19. What are the two main approaches used to determine the energy levels of electrons in a crystal?

20. Describe two features of energy levels for an electron in a crystal.

21. How does the number of energy levels in a band correspond to the number, *N*, of atoms.

22. Why are some materials very good conductors and others very poor conductors?

23. Why are some materials semiconductors?

24. Why does the resistance of a semiconductor decrease as the temperature increases?

9.6 Semiconductors and Doping

25. What kind of semiconductor is produced if germanium is doped with (a) arsenic, and (b) gallium?

26. What kind of semiconductor is produced if silicon is doped with (a) phosphorus, and (b) indium?

27. What is the Hall effect and what is it used for?

28. For an *n*-type semiconductor, how do impurity atoms alter the energy structure of the solid?

29. For a *p*-type semiconductor, how do impurity atoms alter the energy structure of the solid?

9.7 Semiconductor Devices

30. When *p*- and *n*-type materials are joined, why is a uniform electric field generated near the junction?

31. When *p*- and *n*-type materials are joined, why does the depletion layer not grow indefinitely?

32. How do you know if a diode is in the *forward biased* configuration?

33. Why does the reverse bias configuration lead to a very small current?

34. What happens in the extreme case that where the *n*- and *p*-type materials are heavily doped?

35. Explain how an audio amplifier works, using the transistor concept.

9.8 Superconductivity

36. Describe two main features of a superconductor.

37. How does BCS theory explain superconductivity?

38. What is the Meissner effect?

39. What impact does an increasing magnetic field have on the critical temperature of a semiconductor?

PROBLEMS

9.1 Types of Molecular Bonds

40. The electron configuration of carbon is $1s^2 2s^2 2p^2$. Given this electron configuration, what other element might exhibit the same type of hybridization as carbon?

41. Potassium chloride (KCl) is a molecule formed by an ionic bond. At equilibrium separation the atoms are $r_0 = 0.279\ \text{nm}$ apart. Determine the electrostatic potential energy of the atoms.

42. The electron affinity of Cl is 3.89 eV and the ionization energy of K is 4.34 eV. Use the preceding problem to find the dissociation energy. (Neglect the energy of repulsion.)

43. The measured energy dissociated energy of KCl is 4.43 eV. Use the results of the preceding problem to determine the energy of repulsion of the ions due to the exclusion principle.

9.2 Molecular Spectra

44. In a physics lab, you measure the vibrational-rotational spectrum of HCl. The estimated separation between absorption peaks is $\Delta f \approx 5.5 \times 10^{11}\ \text{Hz}$. The central frequency of the band is $f_0 = 9.0 \times 10^{13}\ \text{Hz}$. (a) What is the moment of inertia (*I*)? (b) What is the energy of vibration for the molecule?

45. For the preceding problem, find the equilibrium separation of the H and Cl atoms. Compare this with the actual value.

46. The separation between oxygen atoms in an O_2 molecule is about 0.121 nm. Determine the characteristic energy of rotation in eV.

47. The characteristic energy of the N_2 molecule is $2.48 \times 10^{-4}\ \text{eV}$. Determine the separation distance between the nitrogen atoms

48. The characteristic energy for KCl is 1.4×10^{-5} eV. (a) Determine μ for the KCl molecule. (b) Find the separation distance between the K and Cl atoms.

49. A diatomic F_2 molecule is in the $l = 1$ state. (a) What is the energy of the molecule? (b) How much energy is radiated in a transition from a $l = 2$ to a $l = 1$ state?

50. In a physics lab, you measure the vibrational-rotational spectrum of potassium bromide (KBr). The estimated separation between absorption peaks is $\Delta f \approx 5.35 \times 10^{10}\ \text{Hz}$. The central frequency of the band is $f_0 = 8.75 \times 10^{12}\ \text{Hz}$. (a) What is the moment of inertia (*I*)? (b) What is the energy of vibration for the molecule?

9.3 Bonding in Crystalline Solids

51. The CsI crystal structure is BCC. The equilibrium spacing is approximately $r_0 = 0.46\ \text{nm}$. If Cs^+ ion occupies a cubic volume of r_0^3, what is the distance of this ion to its "nearest neighbor" I^+ ion?

52. The potential energy of a crystal is $-8.10\ \text{eV}$/ion pair. Find the dissociation energy for four moles of the crystal.

53. The measured density of a NaF crystal is $2.558\ \text{g/cm}^3$. What is the equilibrium separate distance of Na^+ and Fl^- ions?

54. What value of the repulsion constant, *n*, gives the measured dissociation energy of 221 kcal/mole for NaF?

55. Determine the dissociation energy of 12 moles of sodium chloride (NaCl). (*Hint:* the repulsion constant *n* is approximately 8.)

56. The measured density of a KCl crystal is $1.984\ \text{g/cm}^3$. What is the equilibrium separation distance of K^+ and Cl^- ions?

57. What value of the repulsion constant, *n*, gives the measured dissociation energy of 171 kcal/mol for KCl?

58. The measured density of a CsCl crystal is $3.988\ \text{g/cm}^3$. What is the equilibrium separate distance of Cs^+ and Cl^- ions?

9.4 Free Electron Model of Metals

59. What is the difference in energy between the $n_x = n_y = n_z = 4$ state and the state with the next higher energy? What is the percentage change in the energy between the $n_x = n_y = n_z = 4$ state and the state with the next higher energy? (b) Compare these with the difference in energy and the percentage change in the energy between the $n_x = n_y = n_z = 400$ state and the state with the next higher energy.

60. An electron is confined to a metal cube of $l = 0.8\ \text{cm}$ on each side. Determine the density of states at (a) $E = 0.80\ \text{eV}$; (b) $E = 2.2\ \text{eV}$; and (c) $E = 5.0\ \text{eV}$.

61. What value of energy corresponds to a density of states of $1.10 \times 10^{24}\ \text{eV}^{-1}$?

62. Compare the density of states at 2.5 eV and 0.25 eV.

63. Consider a cube of copper with edges 1.50 mm long. Estimate the number of electron quantum states in this cube whose energies are in the range 3.75 to 3.77 eV.

64. If there is one free electron per atom of copper, what is the electron number density of this metal?

65. Determine the Fermi energy and temperature for copper at $T = 0\ \text{K}$.

9.5 Band Theory of Solids

66. For a one-dimensional crystal, write the lattice spacing (a) in terms of the electron wavelength.

67. What is the main difference between an insulator and a semiconductor?

68. What is the longest wavelength for a photon that can excite a valence electron into the conduction band across an energy gap of 0.80 eV?

69. A valence electron in a crystal absorbs a photon of wavelength, $\lambda = 0.300\ \text{nm}$. This is just enough energy to allow the electron to jump from the valence band to the conduction band. What is the size of the energy gap?

9.6 Semiconductors and Doping

70. An experiment is performed to demonstrate the Hall effect. A thin rectangular strip of semiconductor with width 10 cm and length 30 cm is attached to a battery and immersed in a 1.50-*T* field perpendicular to its surface. This produced a Hall voltage of 12 V. What is the drift velocity of the charge carriers?

71. Suppose that the cross-sectional area of the strip (the area of the face perpendicular to the electric current) presented to the in the preceding problem is $1\ \text{mm}^2$ and the current is independently measured to be 2 mA. What is the number density of the charge carriers?

72. A current-carrying copper wire with cross-section $\sigma = 2\ \text{mm}^2$ has a drift velocity of 0.02 cm/s. Find the total current running through the wire.

73. The Hall effect is demonstrated in the laboratory. A thin rectangular strip of semiconductor with width 5 cm and cross-sectional area $2\ \text{mm}^2$ is attached to a battery and immersed in a field perpendicular to its surface. The Hall voltage reads 12.5 V and the measured drift velocity is 50 m/s. What is the magnetic field?

9.7 Semiconductor Devices

74. Show that for *V* less than zero, $I_{\text{net}} \approx -I_0$.

75. A *p-n* diode has a reverse saturation current $1.44 \times 10^{-8}\ \text{A}$. It is forward biased so that it has a current of $6.78 \times 10^{-1}\ \text{A}$ moving through it. What bias voltage is being applied if the temperature is 300 K?

76. The collector current of a transistor is 3.4 A for a base current of 4.2 mA. What is the current gain?

77. Applying the positive end of a battery to the *p*-side and the negative end to the *n*-side of a *p-n* junction, the measured current is $8.76 \times 10^{-1}\ \text{A}$. Reversing this polarity give a reverse saturation current of $4.41 \times 10^{-8}\ \text{A}$. What is the temperature if the bias voltage is 1.2 V?

78. The base current of a transistor is 4.4 A, and its current gain 1126. What is the collector current?

9.8 Superconductivity

79. At what temperature, in terms of T_C, is the critical field of a superconductor one-half its value at $T = 0\ \text{K}$?

80. What is the critical magnetic field for lead at $T = 2.8\text{ K}$?

81. A Pb wire wound in a tight solenoid of diameter of 4.0 mm is cooled to a temperature of 5.0 K. The wire is connected in series with a 50-Ω resistor and a variable source of emf. As the emf is increased, what value does it have when the superconductivity of the wire is destroyed?

82. A tightly wound solenoid at 4.0 K is 50 cm long and is constructed from Nb wire of radius 1.5 mm. What maximum current can the solenoid carry if the wire is to remain superconducting?

ADDITIONAL PROBLEMS

83. Potassium fluoride (KF) is a molecule formed by an ionic bond. At equilibrium separation the atoms are $r_0 = 0.255\text{ nm}$ apart. Determine the electrostatic potential energy of the atoms. The electron affinity of F is 3.40 eV and the ionization energy of K is 4.34 eV. Determine dissociation energy. (Neglect the energy of repulsion.)

84. For the preceding problem, sketch the potential energy versus separation graph for the bonding of K^+ and Fl^- ions. (a) Label the graph with the energy required to transfer an electron from K to Fl. (b) Label the graph with the dissociation energy.

85. The separation between hydrogen atoms in a H_2 molecule is about 0.075 nm. Determine the characteristic energy of rotation in eV.

86. The characteristic energy of the Cl_2 molecule is $2.95 \times 10^{-5}\text{ eV}$. Determine the separation distance between the nitrogen atoms.

87. Determine the lowest three rotational energy levels of H_2.

88. A carbon atom can hybridize in the sp^2 configuration. (a) What is the angle between the hybrid orbitals?

89. List five main characteristics of ionic crystals that result from their high dissociation energy.

90. Why is bonding in ${H_2}^+$ favorable? Express your answer in terms of the symmetry of the electron wave function.

91. Astronomers claim to find evidence of He_2 from light spectra of a distant star. Do you believe them?

92. Show that the moment of inertia of a diatomic molecule is $I = \mu r_0^2$, where μ is the reduced mass, and r_0 is the distance between the masses.

93. Show that the average energy of an electron in a one-dimensional metal is related to the Fermi energy by $\bar{E} = \frac{1}{2}E_F$.

94. Measurements of a superconductor's critical magnetic field (in *T*) at various temperatures (in K) are given below. Use a line of best fit to determine $B_c(0)$. Assume $T_c = 9.3\text{ K}$.

T (in K)	$B_c(T)$
3.0	0.18
4.0	0.16
5.0	0.14
6.0	0.12
7.0	0.09
8.0	0.05
9.0	0.01

Table 9.6

95. Estimate the fraction of Si atoms that must be replaced by As atoms in order to form an impurity band.

96. Transition in the rotation spectrum are observed at ordinary room temperature ($T = 300\text{ K}$). According to your lab partner, a peak in the spectrum corresponds to a transition from the $l = 4$ to the $l = 1$ state. Is this possible? If so, determine the momentum of inertia of the molecule.

97. Determine the Fermi energies for (a) Mg, (b) Na, and (c) Zn.

98. Find the average energy of an electron in a Zn wire.

99. What value of the repulsion constant, *n*, gives the measured dissociation energy of 158 kcal/mol for CsCl?

100. A physical model of a diamond suggests a BCC packing structure. Why is this not possible?

CHALLENGE PROBLEMS

101. For an electron in a three-dimensional metal, show that the average energy is given by

$$\bar{E} = \frac{1}{N}\int_0^{E_F} Eg(E)dE = \frac{3}{5}E_F,$$

Where N is the total number electrons in the metal.

10 | NUCLEAR PHYSICS

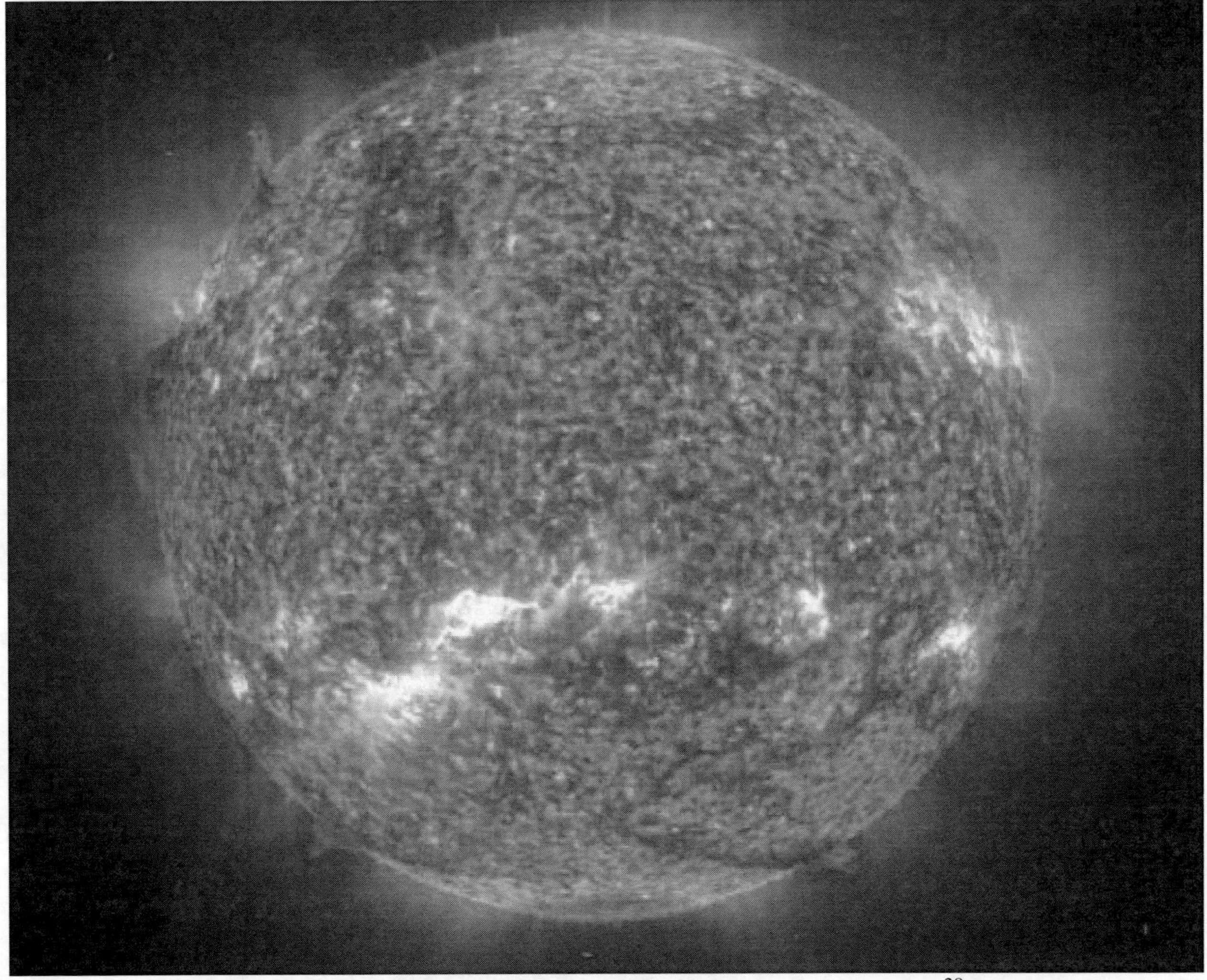

Figure 10.1 The Sun is powered by nuclear fusion in its core. The core converts approximately 10^{38} protons/second into helium at a temperature of 14 million K. This process releases energy in the form of photons, neutrinos, and other particles. (credit: modification of work by EIT SOHO Consortium, ESA, NASA)

Chapter Outline

Introduction

In this chapter, we study the composition and properties of the atomic nucleus. The nucleus lies at the center of an atom, and consists of protons and neutrons. A deep understanding of the nucleus leads to numerous valuable technologies, including devices to date ancient rocks, map the galactic arms of the Milky Way, and generate electrical power.

The Sun is the main source of energy in the solar system. The Sun is 109 Earth diameters across, and accounts for more than 99% of the total mass of the solar system. The Sun shines by fusing hydrogen nuclei—protons—deep inside its interior. Once this fuel is spent, the Sun will burn helium and, later, other nuclei. Nuclear fusion in the Sun is discussed toward the end of this chapter. In the meantime, we will investigate nuclear properties that govern all nuclear processes, including fusion.

10.1 | Properties of Nuclei

Learning Objectives

By the end of this section, you will be able to:

- Describe the composition and size of an atomic nucleus
- Use a nuclear symbol to express the composition of an atomic nucleus
- Explain why the number of neutrons is greater than protons in heavy nuclei
- Calculate the atomic mass of an element given its isotopes

The **atomic nucleus** is composed of **protons** and **neutrons** (Figure 10.2). Protons and neutrons have approximately the same mass, but protons carry one unit of positive charge $(+e)$, and neutrons carry no charge. These particles are packed together into an extremely small space at the center of an atom. According to scattering experiments, the nucleus is spherical or ellipsoidal in shape, and about 1/100,000th the size of a hydrogen atom. If an atom were the size of a major league baseball stadium, the nucleus would be roughly the size of the baseball. Protons and neutrons within the nucleus are called **nucleons**.

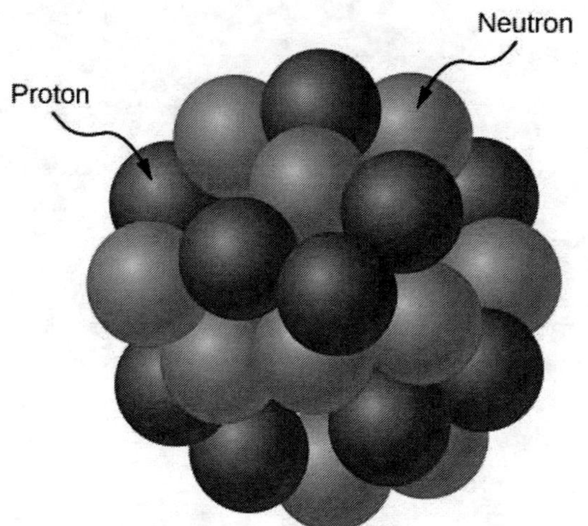

Figure 10.2 The atomic nucleus is composed of protons and neutrons. Protons are shown in blue, and neutrons are shown in red.

Counts of Nucleons

The number of protons in the nucleus is given by the **atomic number**, Z. The number of neutrons in the nucleus is the **neutron number**, N. The total number of nucleons is the **mass number**, A. These numbers are related by

$$A = Z + N. \tag{10.1}$$

A nucleus is represented symbolically by

$$^{A}_{Z}X, \tag{10.2}$$

where X represents the chemical element, A is the mass number, and Z is the atomic number. For example, $^{12}_{6}C$ represents the carbon nucleus with six protons and six neutrons (or 12 nucleons).

A graph of the number N of neutrons versus the number Z of protons for a range of stable nuclei (**nuclides**) is shown in Figure 10.3. For a given value of Z, multiple values of N (blue points) are possible. For small values of Z, the number of neutrons equals the number of protons $(N = P)$, and the data fall on the red line. For large values of Z, the number of neutrons is greater than the number of protons $(N > P)$, and the data points fall above the red line. The number of neutrons is generally greater than the number of protons for $Z > 15$.

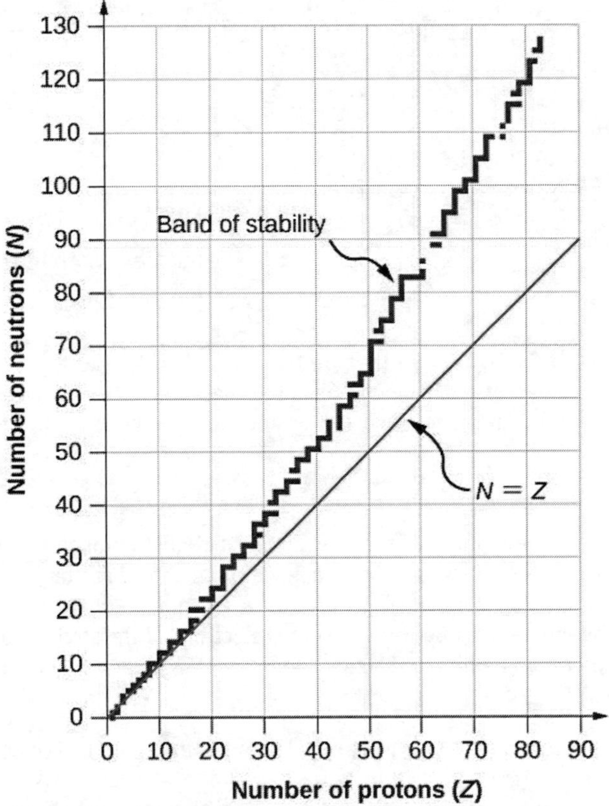

Figure 10.3 This graph plots the number of neutrons N against the number of protons Z for stable atomic nuclei. Larger nuclei, have more neutrons than protons.

A chart based on this graph that provides more detailed information about each nucleus is given in Figure 10.4. This chart is called a **chart of the nuclides**. Each cell or tile represents a separate nucleus. The nuclei are arranged in order of ascending Z (along the horizontal direction) and ascending N (along the vertical direction).

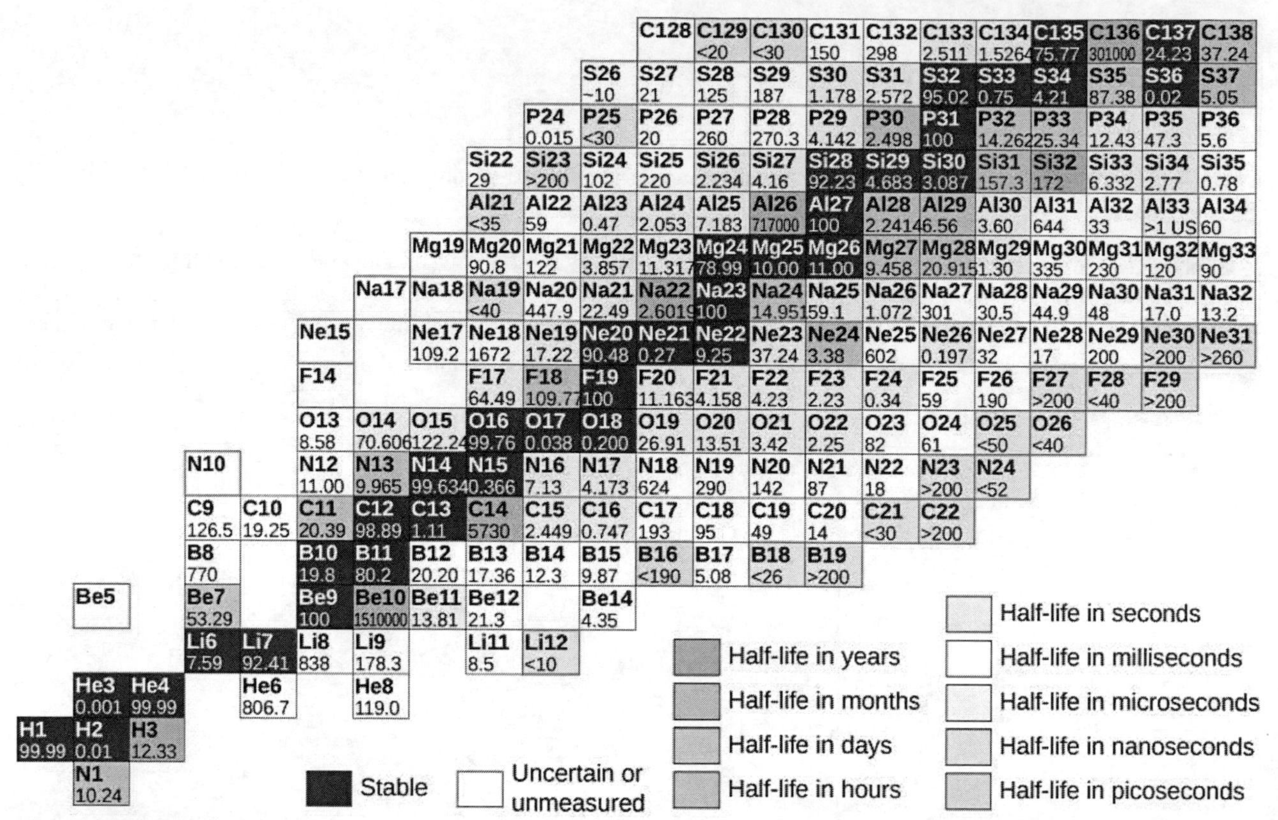

Figure 10.4 Partial chart of the nuclides. For stable nuclei (dark blue backgrounds), cell values represent the percentage of nuclei found on Earth with the same atomic number (percent abundance). For the unstable nuclei, the number represents the half-life.

Atoms that contain nuclei with the same number of protons (Z) and different numbers of neutrons (N) are called **isotopes**. For example, hydrogen has three isotopes: normal hydrogen (1 proton, no neutrons), deuterium (one proton and one neutron), and tritium (one proton and two neutrons). Isotopes of a given atom share the same chemical properties, since these properties are determined by interactions between the outer electrons of the atom, and not the nucleons. For example, water that contains deuterium rather than hydrogen ("heavy water") looks and tastes like normal water. The following table shows a list of common isotopes.

Element	Symbol	Mass Number	Mass (Atomic Mass Units)	Percent Abundance*	Half-life**
Hydrogen	H	1	1.0078	99.99	stable
	^{2}H or D	2	2.0141	0.01	stable
	^{3}H	3	3.0160	–	12.32 y
Carbon	^{12}C	12	12.0000	98.91	stable
	^{13}C	13	13.0034	1.1	stable
	^{14}C	14	14.0032	–	5730 y
Nitrogen	^{14}N	14	14.0031	99.6	stable

Table 10.1 Common Isotopes *No entry if less than 0.001 (trace amount).
**Stable if half-life > 10 seconds.

Element	Symbol	Mass Number	Mass (Atomic Mass Units)	Percent Abundance*	Half-life**
	^{15}N	15	15.0001	0.4	stable
	^{16}N	16	16.0061	–	7.13 s
Oxygen	^{16}O	16	15.9949	99.76	stable
	^{17}O	17	16.9991	0.04	stable
	^{18}O	18	17.9992	0.20	stable
	^{19}O	19	19.0035	–	26.46 s

Table 10.1 Common Isotopes *No entry if less than 0.001 (trace amount).
**Stable if half-life > 10 seconds.

Why do neutrons outnumber protons in heavier nuclei (**Figure 10.5**)? The answer to this question requires an understanding of forces inside the nucleus. Two types of forces exist: (1) the long-range electrostatic (Coulomb) force that makes the positively charged protons repel one another; and (2) the short-range **strong nuclear force** that makes all nucleons in the nucleus attract one another. You may also have heard of a "weak" nuclear force. This force is responsible for some nuclear decays, but as the name implies, it does not play a role in stabilizing the nucleus against the strong Coulomb repulsion it experiences. We discuss strong nuclear force in more detail in the next chapter when we cover particle physics. Nuclear stability occurs when the attractive forces between nucleons compensate for the repulsive, long-range electrostatic forces between all protons in the nucleus. For heavy nuclei $(Z > 15)$, excess neutrons are necessary to keep the electrostatic interactions from breaking the nucleus apart, as shown in **Figure 10.3**.

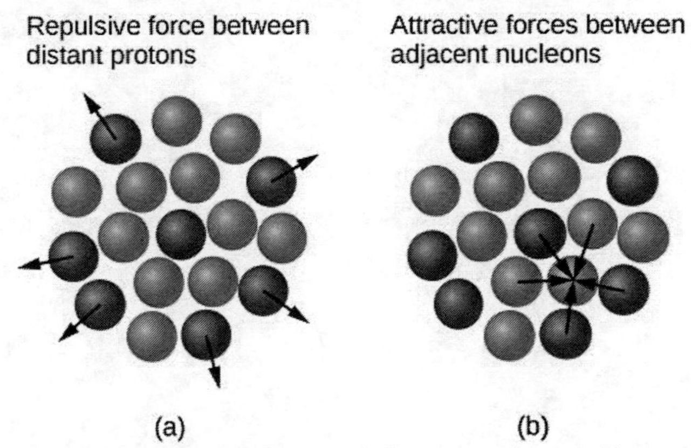

Figure 10.5 (a) The electrostatic force is repulsive and has long range. The arrows represent outward forces on protons (in blue) at the nuclear surface by a proton (also in blue) at the center. (b) The strong nuclear force acts between neighboring nucleons. The arrows represent attractive forces exerted by a neutron (in red) on its nearest neighbors.

Because of the existence of stable isotopes, we must take special care when quoting the mass of an element. For example, Copper (Cu) has two stable isotopes:

$$^{63}_{29}\text{Cu}\left(62.929595\ \text{g/mol}\right)\ \text{with an abundance of } 69.09\%$$

$$^{65}_{29}\text{Cu}\left(64.927786\ \text{g/mol}\right)\ \text{with an abundance of } 30.91\%$$

Given these two "versions" of Cu, what is the mass of this element? The **atomic mass** of an element is defined as the weighted average of the masses of its isotopes. Thus, the atomic mass of Cu is

$m_{Cu} = (62.929595)(0.6909) + (64.927786)(0.3091) = 63.55\ \text{g/mol}$. The mass of an individual nucleus is often expressed in **atomic mass units** (u), where $u = 1.66054 \times 10^{-27}\ \text{kg}$. (An atomic mass unit is defined as 1/12th the mass of a ^{12}C nucleus.) In atomic mass units, the mass of a helium nucleus ($A = 4$) is approximately 4 u. A helium nucleus is also called an alpha (α) particle.

Nuclear Size

The simplest model of the nucleus is a densely packed sphere of nucleons. The volume V of the nucleus is therefore proportional to the number of nucleons A, expressed by

$$V = \frac{4}{3}\pi r^3 = kA,$$

where r is the **radius of a nucleus** and k is a constant with units of volume. Solving for r, we have

$$r = r_0 A^{1/3} \tag{10.3}$$

where r_0 is a constant. For hydrogen ($A = 1$), r_0 corresponds to the radius of a single proton. Scattering experiments support this general relationship for a wide range of nuclei, and they imply that neutrons have approximately the same radius as protons. The experimentally measured value for r_0 is approximately 1.2 femtometer (recall that $1\ \text{fm} = 10^{-15}\ \text{m}$).

Example 10.1

The Iron Nucleus

Find the radius (r) and approximate density (ρ) of a Fe-56 nucleus. Assume the mass of the Fe-56 nucleus is approximately 56 u.

Strategy

(a) Finding the radius of ^{56}Fe is a straightforward application of $r = r_0 A^{1/3}$, given $A = 56$. (b) To find the approximate density of this nucleus, assume the nucleus is spherical. Calculate its volume using the radius found in part (a), and then find its density from $\rho = m/V$.

Solution

a. The radius of a nucleus is given by

$$r = r_0 A^{1/3}.$$

Substituting the values for r_0 and A yields

$$\begin{aligned} r &= (1.2\ \text{fm})(56)^{1/3} = (1.2\ \text{fm})(3.83) \\ &= 4.6\ \text{fm}. \end{aligned}$$

b. Density is defined to be $\rho = m/V$, which for a sphere of radius r is

$$\rho = \frac{m}{V} = \frac{m}{(4/3)\pi r^3}.$$

Substituting known values gives

$$\rho = \frac{56\ \text{u}}{(1.33)(3.14)(4.6\ \text{fm})^3} = 0.138\ \text{u/fm}^3.$$

Converting to units of kg/m^3, we find

$$\rho = (0.138\ \text{u/fm}^3)(1.66 \times 10^{-27}\ \text{kg/u})\left(\frac{1\ \text{fm}}{10^{-15}\ \text{m}}\right) = 2.3 \times 10^{17}\ \text{kg/m}^3.$$

Significance

a. The radius of the Fe-56 nucleus is found to be approximately 5 fm, so its diameter is about 10 fm, or 10^{-14} m. In previous discussions of Rutherford's scattering experiments, a light nucleus was estimated to be 10^{-15} m in diameter. Therefore, the result shown for a mid-sized nucleus is reasonable.

b. The density found here may seem incredible. However, it is consistent with earlier comments about the nucleus containing nearly all of the mass of the atom in a tiny region of space. One cubic meter of nuclear matter has the same mass as a cube of water 61 km on each side.

10.1 Check Your Understanding Nucleus X is two times larger than nucleus Y. What is the ratio of their atomic masses?

10.2 | Nuclear Binding Energy

Learning Objectives

By the end of this section, you will be able to:

- Calculate the mass defect and binding energy for a wide range of nuclei
- Use a graph of binding energy per nucleon (BEN) versus mass number (A) graph to assess the relative stability of a nucleus
- Compare the binding energy of a nucleon in a nucleus to the ionization energy of an electron in an atom

The forces that bind nucleons together in an atomic nucleus are much greater than those that bind an electron to an atom through electrostatic attraction. This is evident by the relative sizes of the atomic nucleus and the atom (10^{-15} and 10^{-10} m, respectively). The energy required to pry a nucleon from the nucleus is therefore much larger than that required to remove (or ionize) an electron in an atom. In general, all nuclear changes involve large amounts of energy per particle undergoing the reaction. This has numerous practical applications.

Mass Defect

According to nuclear particle experiments, the total mass of a nucleus (m_{nuc}) is *less* than the sum of the masses of its constituent nucleons (protons and neutrons). The mass difference, or **mass defect**, is given by

$$\Delta m = Zm_p + (A - Z)m_n - m_{\text{nuc}} \tag{10.4}$$

where Zm_p is the total mass of the protons, $(A - Z)m_n$ is the total mass of the neutrons, and m_{nuc} is the mass of the nucleus. According to Einstein's special theory of relativity, mass is a measure of the total energy of a system ($E = mc^2$). Thus, the total energy of a nucleus is less than the sum of the energies of its constituent nucleons. The formation of a nucleus from a system of isolated protons and neutrons is therefore an exothermic reaction—meaning that it releases energy. The energy emitted, or radiated, in this process is $(\Delta m)c^2$.

Now imagine this process occurs in reverse. Instead of forming a nucleus, energy is put into the system to break apart the nucleus (Figure 10.6). The amount of energy required is called the total **binding energy (BE)**, E_b.

Binding Energy

The binding energy is equal to the amount of energy released in forming the nucleus, and is therefore given by

$$E_b = (\Delta m)c^2. \quad (10.5)$$

Experimental results indicate that the binding energy for a nucleus with mass number $A > 8$ is roughly proportional to the total number of nucleons in the nucleus, *A*. The binding energy of a magnesium nucleus (^{24}Mg), for example, is approximately two times greater than for the carbon nucleus (^{12}C).

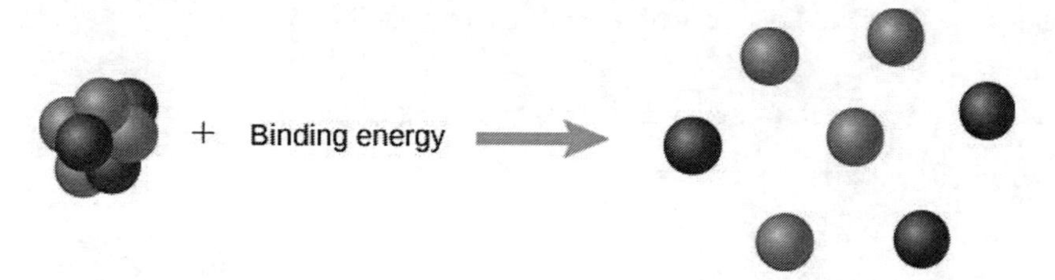

Figure 10.6 The binding energy is the energy required to break a nucleus into its constituent protons and neutrons. A system of separated nucleons has a greater mass than a system of bound nucleons.

Example 10.2

Mass Defect and Binding Energy of the Deuteron

Calculate the mass defect and the binding energy of the deuteron. The mass of the deuteron is $m_D = 3.34359 \times 10^{-27}\,\text{kg}$ or $1875.61\,\text{MeV}/c^2$.

Solution

From **Equation 10.4**, the mass defect for the deuteron is

$$\begin{aligned} \Delta m &= m_p + m_n - m_D \\ &= 938.28\,\text{MeV}/c^2 + 939.57\,\text{MeV}/c^2 - 1875.61\,\text{MeV}/c^2 \\ &= 2.24\,\text{MeV}/c^2. \end{aligned}$$

The binding energy of the deuteron is then

$$E_b = (\Delta m)c^2 = \left(2.24\,\text{MeV}/c^2\right)\left(c^2\right) = 2.24\,\text{MeV}.$$

Over two million electron volts are needed to break apart a deuteron into a proton and a neutron. This very large value indicates the great strength of the nuclear force. By comparison, the greatest amount of energy required to liberate an electron bound to a hydrogen atom by an attractive Coulomb force (an electromagnetic force) is about 10 eV.

Graph of Binding Energy per Nucleon

In nuclear physics, one of the most important experimental quantities is the **binding energy per nucleon (BEN)**, which is defined by

$$BEN = \frac{E_b}{A} \quad (10.6)$$

This quantity is the average energy required to remove an individual nucleon from a nucleus—analogous to the ionization energy of an electron in an atom. If the BEN is relatively large, the nucleus is relatively stable. BEN values are estimated from nuclear scattering experiments.

A graph of binding energy per nucleon versus atomic number *A* is given in **Figure 10.7**. This graph is considered by many physicists to be one of the most important graphs in physics. Two notes are in order. First, typical BEN values range from 6–10 MeV, with an average value of about 8 MeV. In other words, it takes several million electron volts to pry a nucleon from a typical nucleus, as compared to just 13.6 eV to ionize an electron in the ground state of hydrogen. This is why nuclear force is referred to as the "strong" nuclear force.

Second, the graph rises at low *A*, peaks very near iron $(\text{Fe}, A = 56)$, and then tapers off at high *A*. The peak value suggests that the iron nucleus is the most stable nucleus in nature (it is also why nuclear fusion in the cores of stars ends with Fe). The reason the graph rises and tapers off has to do with competing forces in the nucleus. At low values of *A*, attractive nuclear forces between nucleons dominate over repulsive electrostatic forces between protons. But at high values of *A*, repulsive electrostatic forces between forces begin to dominate, and these forces tend to break apart the nucleus rather than hold it together.

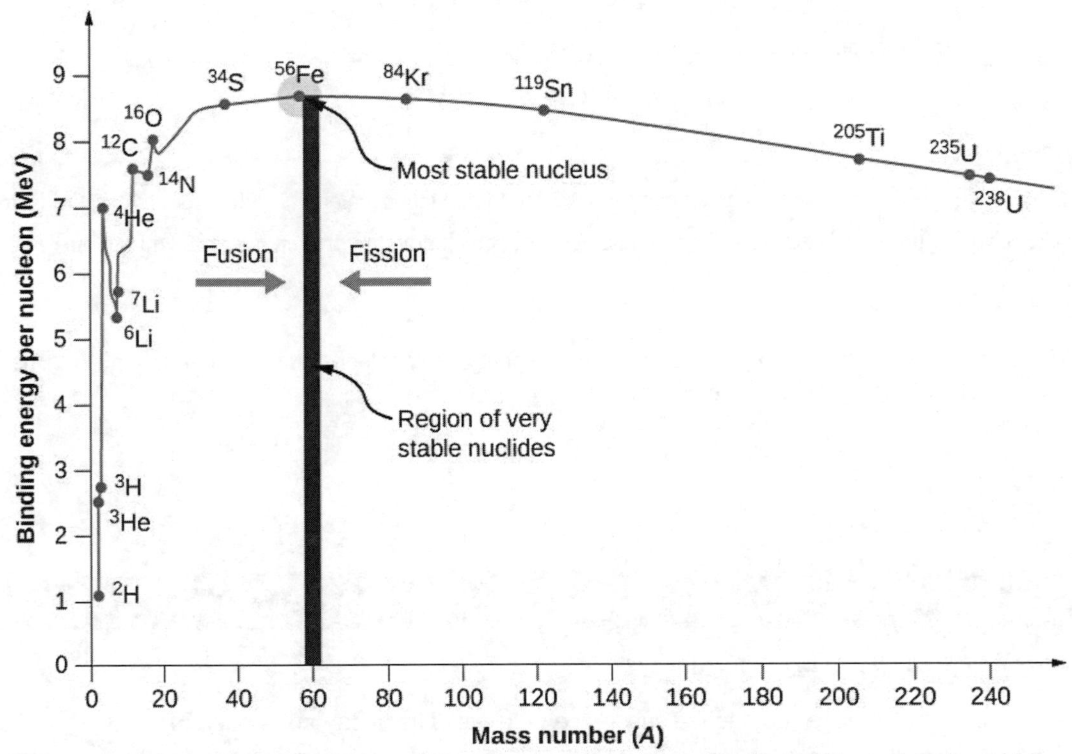

Figure 10.7 In this graph of binding energy per nucleon for stable nuclei, the BEN is greatest for nuclei with a mass near ^{56}Fe. Therefore, fusion of nuclei with mass numbers much less than that of Fe, and fission of nuclei with mass numbers greater than that of Fe, are exothermic processes.

As we will see, the BEN-versus-*A* graph implies that nuclei divided or combined release an enormous amount of energy. This is the basis for a wide range of phenomena, from the production of electricity at a nuclear power plant to sunlight.

Example 10.3

Tightly Bound Alpha Nuclides

Calculate the binding energy per nucleon of an $^{4}\text{He}\,(\alpha\text{ particle})$.

Strategy

Determine the total binding energy (BE) using the equation $\text{BE} = (\Delta m)c^2$, where Δm is the mass defect. The binding energy per nucleon (BEN) is BE divided by *A*.

Solution

For ^4He, we have $Z = N = 2$. The total binding energy is

$$\text{BE} = \{[2m_p + 2m_n] - m(^4\text{He})\}c^2.$$

These masses are $m(^4\text{He}) = 4.002602\text{ u}$, $m_p = 1.007825\text{ u}$, and $m_n = 1.008665\text{ u}$. Thus we have,

$$\text{BE} = (0.030378\text{ u})c^2.$$

Noting that $1\text{ u} = 931.5\text{ MeV}/c^2$, we find

$$\begin{aligned}\text{BE} &= (0.030378)(931.5\text{ MeV}/c^2)c^2\\ &= 28.3\text{ MeV}.\end{aligned}$$

Since $A = 4$, the total binding energy per nucleon is

$$\text{BEN} = 7.07\text{ MeV/nucleon}.$$

Significance

Notice that the binding energy per nucleon for ^4He is much greater than for the hydrogen isotopes (only $\approx 3\text{ MeV/nucleon}$). Therefore, helium nuclei cannot break down hydrogen isotopes without energy being put into the system.

10.2 Check Your Understanding If the binding energy per nucleon is large, does this make it harder or easier to strip off a nucleon from a nucleus?

10.3 | Radioactive Decay

Learning Objectives

By the end of this section, you will be able to:

- Describe the decay of a radioactive substance in terms of its decay constant and half-life
- Use the radioactive decay law to estimate the age of a substance
- Explain the natural processes that allow the dating of living tissue using ^{14}C

In 1896, Antoine Becquerel discovered that a uranium-rich rock emits invisible rays that can darken a photographic plate in an enclosed container. Scientists offer three arguments for the nuclear origin of these rays. First, the effects of the radiation do not vary with chemical state; that is, whether the emitting material is in the form of an element or compound. Second, the radiation does not vary with changes in temperature or pressure—both factors that in sufficient degree can affect electrons in an atom. Third, the very large energy of the invisible rays (up to hundreds of eV) is not consistent with atomic electron transitions (only a few eV). Today, this radiation is explained by the conversion of mass into energy deep within the nucleus of an atom. The spontaneous emission of radiation from nuclei is called nuclear **radioactivity** (Figure 10.8).

Figure 10.8 The international ionizing radiation symbol is universally recognized as the warning symbol for nuclear radiation.

Radioactive Decay Law

When an individual nucleus transforms into another with the emission of radiation, the nucleus is said to **decay**. Radioactive decay occurs for all nuclei with $Z > 82,$ and also for some unstable isotopes with $Z < 83.$ The decay rate is proportional to the number of original (undecayed) nuclei *N* in a substance. The number of nuclei lost to decay, $-dN$ in time interval *dt*, is written

$$-\frac{dN}{dt} = \lambda N \tag{10.7}$$

where λ is called the **decay constant**. (The minus sign indicates the number of original nuclei decreases over time.) In other words, the more nuclei available to decay, the more that do decay (in time *dt*). This equation can be rewritten as

$$\frac{dN}{N} = -\lambda dt. \tag{10.8}$$

Integrating both sides of the equation, and defining N_0 to be the number of nuclei at $t = 0$, we obtain

$$\int_{N_0}^{N} \frac{dN'}{N} = -\int_0^t \lambda dt'. \tag{10.9}$$

This gives us

$$\ln \frac{N}{N_0} = -\lambda t. \tag{10.10}$$

Taking the left and right sides of the equation as a power of *e*, we have the **radioactive decay law**.

Radioactive Decay Law

The total number *N* of radioactive nuclei remaining after time *t* is

$$N = N_0 e^{-\lambda t} \tag{10.11}$$

where λ is the decay constant for the particular nucleus.

The total number of nuclei drops very rapidly at first, and then more slowly (**Figure 10.9**).

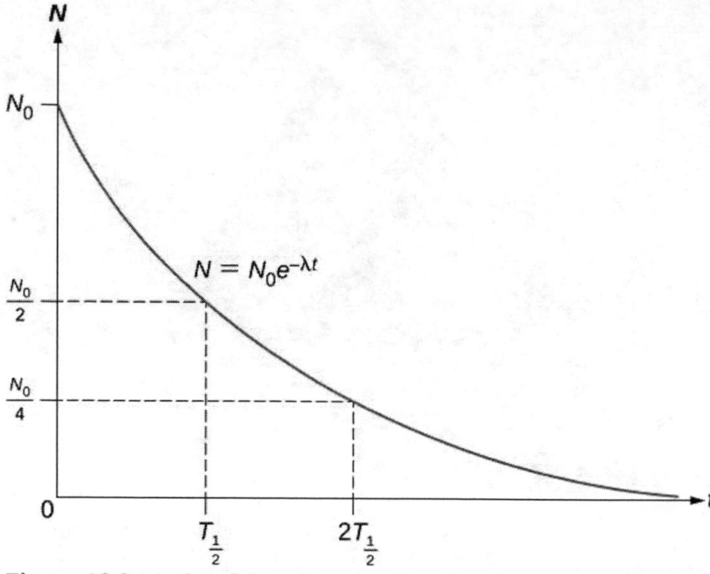

Figure 10.9 A plot of the radioactive decay law demonstrates that the number of nuclei remaining in a decay sample drops dramatically during the first moments of decay.

The **half-life** $(T_{1/2})$ of a radioactive substance is defined as the time for half of the original nuclei to decay (or the time at which half of the original nuclei remain). The half-lives of unstable isotopes are shown in the chart of nuclides in **Figure 10.4**. The number of radioactive nuclei remaining after an integer (n) number of half-lives is therefore

$$N = \frac{N_0}{2^n} \tag{10.12}$$

If the decay constant (λ) is large, the half-life is small, and vice versa. To determine the relationship between these quantities, note that when $t = T_{1/2}$, then $N = N_0/2$. Thus, **Equation 10.10** can be rewritten as

$$\frac{N_0}{2} = N_0 e^{-\lambda T_{1/2}}. \tag{10.13}$$

Dividing both sides by N_0 and taking the natural logarithm yields

$$\ln\frac{1}{2} = \ln e^{-\lambda T_{1/2}} \tag{10.14}$$

which reduces to

$$\lambda = \frac{0.693}{T_{1/2}}. \tag{10.15}$$

Thus, if we know the half-life $T_{1/2}$ of a radioactive substance, we can find its decay constant. The **lifetime** $\bar{T}$ of a radioactive substance is defined as the average amount of time that a nucleus exists before decaying. The lifetime of a substance is just the reciprocal of the decay constant, written as

$$\bar{T} = \frac{1}{\lambda}. \tag{10.16}$$

The **activity** A is defined as the magnitude of the decay rate, or

$$A = -\frac{dN}{dt} = \lambda N = \lambda N_0 e^{-\lambda t}. \quad (10.17)$$

The infinitesimal change dN in the time interval dt is negative because the number of parent (undecayed) particles is decreasing, so the activity (A) is positive. Defining the initial activity as $A_0 = \lambda N_0$, we have

$$A = A_0 e^{-\lambda t}. \quad (10.18)$$

Thus, the activity A of a radioactive substance decreases exponentially with time (**Figure 10.10**).

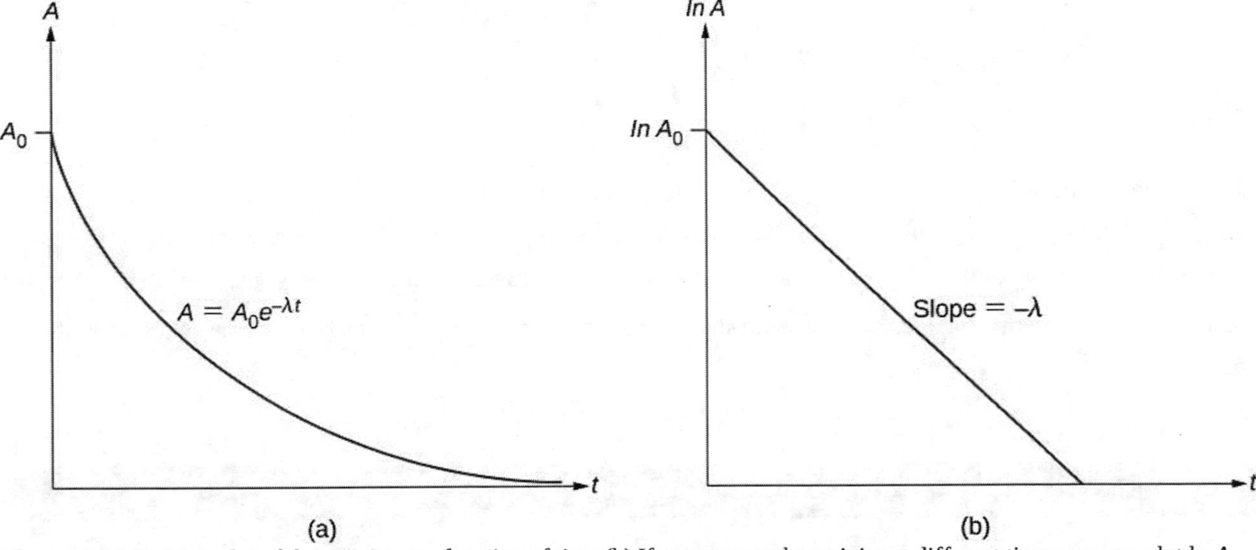

Figure 10.10 (a) A plot of the activity as a function of time (b) If we measure the activity at different times, we can plot ln A versus t, and obtain a straight line.

Example 10.4

Decay Constant and Activity of Strontium-90

The half-life of strontium-90, ${}^{90}_{38}\text{Sr}$, is 28.8 y. Find (a) its decay constant and (b) the initial activity of 1.00 g of the material.

Strategy

We can find the decay constant directly from **Equation 10.15**. To determine the activity, we first need to find the number of nuclei present.

Solution

a. The decay constant is found to be

$$\lambda = \frac{0.693}{T_{1/2}} = \left(\frac{0.693}{T_{1/2}}\right)\left(\frac{1 \text{ yr}}{3.16 \times 10^7 \text{ s}}\right) = 7.61 \times 10^{-10} \text{ s}^{-1}.$$

b. The atomic mass of ${}^{90}_{38}\text{Sr}$ is 89.91 g. Using Avogadro's number $N_A = 6.022 \times 10^{23}$ atoms/mol, we find the initial number of nuclei in 1.00 g of the material:

$$N_0 = \frac{1.00 \text{ g}}{89.91 \text{ g}}(N_A) = 6.70 \times 10^{21} \text{ nuclei}.$$

From this, we find that the activity A_0 at $t = 0$ for 1.00 g of strontium-90 is

$$\begin{aligned} A_0 &= \lambda N_0 \\ &= (7.61 \times 10^{-10}\ \text{s}^{-1})(6.70 \times 10^{21}\ \text{nuclei}) \\ &= 5.10 \times 10^{12}\ \text{decays/s}. \end{aligned}$$

Expressing λ in terms of the half-life of the substance, we get

$$A = A_0 e^{-(0.693/T_{1/2})T_{1/2}} = A_0 e^{-0.693} = A_0/2. \quad (10.19)$$

Therefore, the activity is halved after one half-life. We can determine the decay constant λ by measuring the activity as a function of time. Taking the natural logarithm of the left and right sides of **Equation 10.17**, we get

$$\ln A = -\lambda t + \ln A_0. \quad (10.20)$$

This equation follows the linear form $y = mx + b$. If we plot ln A versus t, we expect a straight line with slope $-\lambda$ and y-intercept $\ln A_0$ (**Figure 10.10**(b)). Activity A is expressed in units of **becquerels** (Bq), where one $1\ \text{Bq} = 1$ decay per second. This quantity can also be expressed in decays per minute or decays per year. One of the most common units for activity is the **curie (Ci)**, defined to be the activity of 1 g of ^{226}Ra. The relationship between the Bq and Ci is

$$1\ \text{Ci} = 3.70 \times 10^{10}\ \text{Bq}.$$

Example 10.5

What is ^{14}C Activity in Living Tissue?

Approximately 20% of the human body by mass is carbon. Calculate the activity due to ^{14}C in 1.00 kg of carbon found in a living organism. Express the activity in units of Bq and Ci.

Strategy

The activity of ^{14}C is determined using the equation $A_0 = \lambda N_0$, where λ is the decay constant and N_0 is the number of radioactive nuclei. The number of ^{14}C nuclei in a 1.00-kg sample is determined in two steps. First, we determine the number of ^{12}C nuclei using the concept of a mole. Second, we multiply this value by 1.3×10^{-12} (the known abundance of ^{14}C in a carbon sample from a living organism) to determine the number of ^{14}C nuclei in a living organism. The decay constant is determined from the known half-life of ^{14}C (available from **Figure 10.4**).

Solution

One mole of carbon has a mass of 12.0 g, since it is nearly pure ^{12}C. Thus, the number of carbon nuclei in a kilogram is

$$N(^{12}\text{C}) = \frac{6.02 \times 10^{23}\ \text{mol}^{-1}}{12.0\ \text{g/mol}} \times (1000\ \text{g}) = 5.02 \times 10^{25}.$$

The number of ^{14}C nuclei in 1 kg of carbon is therefore

$$N(^{14}\text{C}) = (5.02 \times 10^{25})(1.3 \times 10^{-12}) = 6.52 \times 10^{13}.$$

Now we can find the activity A by using the equation $A = \frac{0.693\,N}{t_{1/2}}$. Entering known values gives us

$$A = \frac{0.693\left(6.52 \times 10^{13}\right)}{5730\text{ y}} = 7.89 \times 10^{9}\text{ y}^{-1}$$

or 7.89×10^{9} decays per year. To convert this to the unit Bq, we simply convert years to seconds. Thus,

$$A = \left(7.89 \times 10^{9}\text{ y}^{-1}\right)\frac{1.00\text{ y}}{3.16 \times 10^{7}\text{ s}} = 250\text{ Bq},$$

or 250 decays per second. To express A in curies, we use the definition of a curie,

$$A = \frac{250\text{ Bq}}{3.7 \times 10^{10}\text{ Bq/Ci}} = 6.76 \times 10^{-9}\text{ Ci}.$$

Thus,

$$A = 6.76\text{ nCi}.$$

Significance

Approximately 20% of the human body by weight is carbon. Hundreds of ^{14}C decays take place in the human body every second. Carbon-14 and other naturally occurring radioactive substances in the body compose a person's background exposure to nuclear radiation. As we will see later in this chapter, this activity level is well below the maximum recommended dosages.

Radioactive Dating

Radioactive dating is a technique that uses naturally occurring radioactivity to determine the age of a material, such as a rock or an ancient artifact. The basic approach is to estimate the original number of nuclei in a material and the present number of nuclei in the material (after decay), and then use the known value of the decay constant λ and **Equation 10.10** to calculate the total time of the decay, t.

An important method of radioactive dating is **carbon-14 dating**. Carbon-14 nuclei are produced when high-energy solar radiation strikes ^{14}N nuclei in the upper atmosphere and subsequently decay with a half-life of 5730 years. Radioactive carbon has the same chemistry as stable carbon, so it combines with the ecosphere and eventually becomes part of every living organism. Carbon-14 has an abundance of 1.3 parts per trillion of normal carbon. Therefore, if you know the number of carbon nuclei in an object, you multiply that number by 1.3×10^{-12} to find the number of ^{14}C nuclei in that object. When an organism dies, carbon exchange with the environment ceases, and ^{14}C is not replenished as it decays.

By comparing the abundance of ^{14}C in an artifact, such as mummy wrappings, with the normal abundance in living tissue, it is possible to determine the mummy's age (or the time since the person's death). Carbon-14 dating can be used for biological tissues as old as 50,000 years, but is generally most accurate for younger samples, since the abundance of ^{14}C nuclei in them is greater. Very old biological materials contain no ^{14}C at all. The validity of carbon dating can be checked by other means, such as by historical knowledge or by tree-ring counting.

Example 10.6

An Ancient Burial Cave

In an ancient burial cave, your team of archaeologists discovers ancient wood furniture. Only 80% of the original ^{14}C remains in the wood. How old is the furniture?

Strategy

The problem statement implies that $N/N_0 = 0.80$. Therefore, the equation $N = N_0 e^{-\lambda t}$ can be used to find the product, λt. We know the half-life of ^{14}C is 5730 y, so we also know the decay constant, and therefore the total decay time *t*.

Solution

Solving the equation $N = N_0 e^{-\lambda t}$ for N/N_0 gives us

$$\frac{N}{N_0} = e^{-\lambda t}.$$

Thus,

$$0.80 = e^{-\lambda t}.$$

Taking the natural logarithm of both sides of the equation yields

$$\ln 0.80 = -\lambda t,$$

so that

$$-0.223 = -\lambda t.$$

Rearranging the equation to isolate *t* gives us

$$t = \frac{0.223}{\lambda},$$

where

$$\lambda = \frac{0.693}{t_{1/2}} = \frac{0.693}{5730 \text{ y}}.$$

Combining this information yields

$$t = \frac{0.223}{\left(\frac{0.693}{5730 \text{ y}}\right)} = 1844 \text{ y}.$$

Significance

The furniture is almost 2000 years old—an impressive discovery. The typical uncertainty on carbon-14 dating is about 5%, so the furniture is anywhere between 1750 and 1950 years old. This date range must be confirmed by other evidence, such as historical records.

10.3 Check Your Understanding A radioactive nuclide has a high decay rate. What does this mean for its half-life and activity?

Visit the **Radioactive Dating Game (https://openstaxcollege.org/l/21raddatgame)** to learn about the types of radiometric dating and try your hand at dating some ancient objects.

10.4 | Nuclear Reactions

Learning Objectives

By the end of this section, you will be able to:

- Describe and compare three types of nuclear radiation
- Use nuclear symbols to describe changes that occur during nuclear reactions
- Describe processes involved in the decay series of heavy elements

Early experiments revealed three types of nuclear "rays" or radiation: **alpha (α) rays**, **beta (β) rays**, and **gamma (γ) rays**. These three types of radiation are differentiated by their ability to penetrate matter. Alpha radiation is barely able to pass through a thin sheet of paper. Beta radiation can penetrate aluminum to a depth of about 3 mm, and gamma radiation can penetrate lead to a depth of 2 or more centimeters (Figure 10.11).

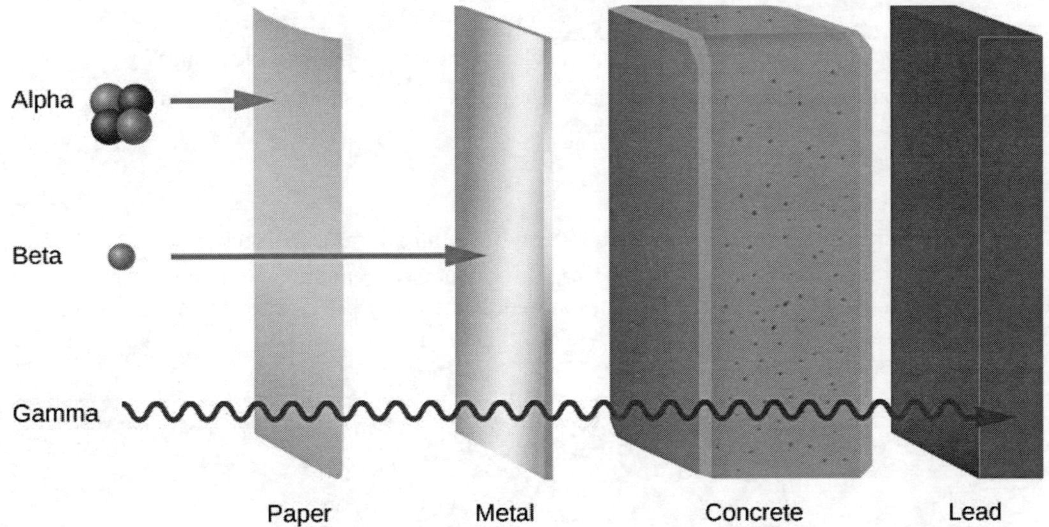

Figure 10.11 A comparison of the penetration depths of alpha (α), beta (β), and gamma (γ) radiation through various materials.

The electrical properties of these three types of radiation are investigated by passing them through a uniform magnetic field, as shown in Figure 10.12. According to the magnetic force equation $\vec{\mathbf{F}} = q\vec{\mathbf{v}} \times \vec{\mathbf{B}}$, positively charged particles are deflected upward, negatively charged particles are deflected downward, and particles with no charge pass through the magnetic field undeflected. Eventually, α rays were identified with helium nuclei $\left({}^4\text{He}\right)$, β rays with electrons and **positrons** (positively charged electrons or **antielectrons**), and γ rays with high-energy photons. We discuss alpha, beta, and gamma radiation in detail in the remainder of this section.

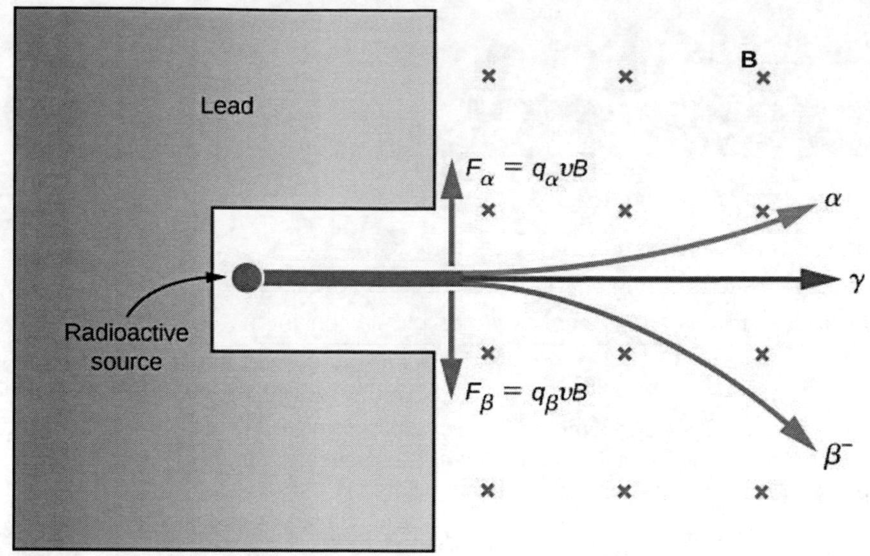

Figure 10.12 The effect of a magnetic field on alpha (α), beta (β), and gamma (γ) radiation. This figure is a schematic only. The relative paths of the particles depend on their masses and initial kinetic energies.

Alpha Decay

Heavy unstable nuclei emit α radiation. In α-particle decay (or **alpha decay**), the nucleus loses two protons and two neutrons, so the atomic number decreases by two, whereas its mass number decreases by four. Before the decay, the nucleus is called the **parent nucleus**. The nucleus or nuclei produced in the decay are referred to as the **daughter nucleus** or daughter nuclei. We represent an α decay symbolically by

$$ {}^{A}_{Z}\mathrm{X} \to {}^{A-4}_{Z-2}\mathrm{X} + {}^{4}_{2}\mathrm{He} \qquad (10.21)$$

where ${}^{A}_{Z}\mathrm{X}$ is the parent nucleus, ${}^{A-4}_{Z-2}\mathrm{X}$ is the daughter nucleus, and ${}^{4}_{2}\mathrm{He}$ is the α particle. In α decay, a nucleus of atomic number Z decays into a nucleus of atomic number $Z-2$ and atomic mass $A-4$. Interestingly, the dream of the ancient alchemists to turn other metals into gold is scientifically feasible through the alpha-decay process. The efforts of the alchemists failed because they relied on chemical interactions rather than nuclear interactions.

Watch alpha particles escape from a polonium nucleus, causing radioactive alpha decay. See how random decay times relate to the half-life. To try a simulation of alpha decay, visit **alpha particles (https://openstaxcollege.org/l/21alphaparvid)**

An example of alpha decay is uranium-238:

$$ {}^{238}_{92}\mathrm{U} \to {}^{234}_{90}\mathrm{X} + {}^{4}_{2}\mathrm{He}.$$

The atomic number has dropped from 92 to 90. The chemical element with $Z = 90$ is thorium. Hence, Uranium-238 has decayed to Thorium-234 by the emission of an α particle, written

$$ {}^{238}_{92}\mathrm{U} \to {}^{234}_{90}\mathrm{Th} + {}^{4}_{2}\mathrm{He}.$$

Subsequently, ${}^{234}_{90}\mathrm{Th}$ decays by β emission with a half-life of 24 days. The energy released in this alpha decay takes the form of kinetic energies of the thorium and helium nuclei, although the kinetic energy of thorium is smaller than helium due to its heavier mass and smaller velocity.

Example 10.7

Plutonium Alpha Decay

Find the energy emitted in the α decay of ^{239}Pu.

Strategy

The energy emitted in the α decay of ^{239}Pu can be found using the equation $E = (\Delta m)c^2$. We must first find $\Delta m,$ the difference in mass between the parent nucleus and the products of the decay.

Solution

The decay equation is

$$^{239}\text{Pu} \rightarrow {}^{235}\text{U} + {}^{4}\text{He}.$$

Thus, the pertinent masses are those of ^{239}Pu, ^{235}U, and the α particle or ^{4}He, all of which are known. The initial mass was $m(^{239}\text{Pu}) = 239.052157\text{ u}$. The final mass is the sum

$$\begin{aligned} m(^{235}\text{U}) + m(^{4}\text{He}) &= 235.043924\text{ u} + 4.002602\text{ u} \\ &= 239.046526\text{ u}. \end{aligned}$$

Thus,

$$\begin{aligned} \Delta m &= m(^{239}\text{Pu}) - \left[m(^{235}\text{U}) + m(^{4}\text{He})\right] \\ &= 239.052157\text{ u} - 239.046526\text{ u} \\ &= 0.0005631\text{ u}. \end{aligned}$$

Now we can find E by entering Δm into the equation:

$$E = (\Delta m)c^2 = (0.005631\text{ u})c^2.$$

We know $1\text{ u} = 931.5\text{ MeV}/c^2,$ so we have

$$\begin{aligned} E &= (0.005631)(931.5\text{ MeV}/c^2)(c^2) \\ &= 5.25\text{ MeV}. \end{aligned}$$

Significance

The energy released in this α decay is in the MeV range, many times greater than chemical reaction energies. Most of this energy becomes kinetic energy of the α particle (or ^{4}He nucleus), which moves away at high speed. The energy carried away by the recoil of the ^{235}U nucleus is much smaller due to its relatively large mass. The ^{235}U nucleus can be left in an excited state to later emit photons (γ rays).

Beta Decay

In most β particle decays (or **beta decay**), either an electron (β^-) or positron (β^+) is emitted by a nucleus. A positron has the same mass as the electron, but its charge is $+e$. For this reason, a positron is sometimes called an antielectron. How does β decay occur? A possible explanation is the electron (positron) is confined to the nucleus prior to the decay and somehow escapes. To obtain a rough estimate of the escape energy, consider a simplified model of an electron trapped in a box (or in the terminology of quantum mechanics, a one-dimensional square well) that has the width of a typical nucleus (10^{-14} m). According to the Heisenberg uncertainty principle in **Quantum Mechanics**, the uncertainty of the momentum of the electron is:

$$\Delta p > \frac{h}{\Delta x} = \frac{6.6 \times 10^{-34}\ \text{m}^2 \cdot \text{kg/s}}{10^{-14}\,\text{m}} = 6.6 \times 10^{-20}\,\text{kg} \cdot \text{m/s}.$$

Taking this momentum value (an underestimate) to be the "true value," the kinetic energy of the electron on escape is approximately

$$\frac{(\Delta p)^2}{2m_e} = \frac{\left(6.6 \times 10^{-20}\ \text{kg} \cdot \text{m/s}\right)^2}{2\left(9.1 \times 10^{-31}\,\text{kg}\right)} = 2.0 \times 10^{-9}\,\text{J} = 12{,}400\,\text{MeV}.$$

Experimentally, the electrons emitted in β^- decay are found to have kinetic energies of the order of only a few MeV. We therefore conclude that the electron is somehow produced in the decay rather than escaping the nucleus. Particle production (annihilation) is described by theories that combine quantum mechanics and relativity, a subject of a more advanced course in physics.

Nuclear beta decay involves the conversion of one nucleon into another. For example, a neutron can decay to a proton by the emission of an electron (β^-) and a nearly massless particle called an **antineutrino** ($\bar{\nu}$):

$${}^{1}_{0}\text{n} \rightarrow {}^{1}_{1}\text{p} + {}^{\;\;0}_{-1}\text{e} + \bar{\nu}\,.$$

The notation ${}^{\;\;0}_{-1}\text{e}$ is used to designate the electron. Its mass number is 0 because it is not a nucleon, and its atomic number is -1 to signify that it has a charge of $-e$. The proton is represented by ${}^{1}_{1}\text{p}$ because its mass number and atomic number are 1. When this occurs within an atomic nucleus, we have the following equation for beta decay:

$${}^{A}_{Z}\text{X} \rightarrow {}_{Z+1}^{\;\;\;\;A}\text{X} + {}^{\;\;0}_{-1}\text{e} + \bar{\nu}\,. \tag{10.22}$$

As discussed in another chapter, this process occurs due to the weak nuclear force.

Watch **beta decay (https://openstaxcollege.org/l/21betadecayvid)** occur for a collection of nuclei or for an individual nucleus.

As an example, the isotope ${}^{234}_{\;\;90}\text{Th}$ is unstable and decays by β^- emission with a half-life of 24 days. Its decay can be represented as

$${}^{234}_{\;\;90}\text{Th} \rightarrow {}^{234}_{\;\;91}\text{X} + {}^{\;\;0}_{-1}\text{e} + \bar{\nu}\,.$$

Since the chemical element with atomic number 91 is protactinium (Pa), we can write the β^- decay of thorium as

$${}^{234}_{\;\;90}\text{Th} \rightarrow {}^{234}_{\;\;91}\text{Pa} + {}^{\;\;0}_{-1}\text{e} + \bar{\nu}\,.$$

The reverse process is also possible: A proton can decay to a neutron by the emission of a positron (β^+) and a nearly massless particle called a **neutrino** (ν). This reaction is written as ${}^{1}_{1}\text{p} \rightarrow {}^{1}_{0}\text{n} + {}^{\;\;0}_{+1}\text{e} + \nu$.

The positron ${}^{\;\;0}_{+1}\text{e}$ is emitted with the neutrino ν, and the neutron remains in the nucleus. (Like β^- decay, the positron does not precede the decay but is produced in the decay.) For an isolated proton, this process is impossible because the neutron is heavier than the proton. However, this process is possible within the nucleus because the proton can receive energy from other nucleons for the transition. As an example, the isotope of aluminum ${}^{26}_{13}\text{Al}$ decays by β^+ emission with a half-life of $7.40 \times 10^5\,\text{y}$. The decay is written as

$${}^{26}_{13}\text{Al} \rightarrow {}^{26}_{12}\text{X} + {}^{\;\;0}_{+1}\text{e} + \nu.$$

The atomic number 12 corresponds to magnesium. Hence,

$$^{26}_{13}\text{Al} \rightarrow ^{26}_{12}\text{Mg} + ^{0}_{+1}\text{e} + \nu.$$

As a nuclear reaction, positron emission can be written as

$$^{A}_{Z}\text{X} \rightarrow _{Z-1}^{A}\text{X} + ^{0}_{+1}\text{e} + \nu. \quad (10.23)$$

The neutrino was not detected in the early experiments on β decay. However, the laws of energy and momentum seemed to require such a particle. Later, neutrinos were detected through their interactions with nuclei.

Example 10.8

Bismuth Alpha and Beta Decay

The $^{211}_{83}\text{Bi}$ nucleus undergoes both α and β^- decay. For each case, what is the daughter nucleus?

Strategy

We can use the processes described by **Equation 10.21** and **Equation 10.22**, as well as the Periodic Table, to identify the resulting elements.

Solution

The atomic number and the mass number for the α particle are 2 and 4, respectively. Thus, when a bismuth-211 nucleus emits an α particle, the daughter nucleus has an atomic number of 81 and a mass number of 207. The element with an atomic number of 81 is thallium, so the decay is given by

$$^{211}_{83}\text{Bi} \rightarrow ^{207}_{81}\text{Ti} + ^{4}_{2}\text{He}.$$

In β^- decay, the atomic number increases by 1, while the mass number stays the same. The element with an atomic number of 84 is polonium, so the decay is given by

$$^{211}_{83}\text{Bi} \rightarrow ^{211}_{84}\text{Po} + ^{0}_{-1}\text{e} + \bar{\nu}.$$

10.4 Check Your Understanding In radioactive beta decay, does the atomic mass number, *A*, increase or decrease?

Gamma Decay

A nucleus in an excited state can decay to a lower-level state by the emission of a "gamma-ray" photon, and this is known as **gamma decay**. This is analogous to de-excitation of an atomic electron. Gamma decay is represented symbolically by

$$^{A}_{Z}\text{X}^* \rightarrow ^{A}_{Z}\text{X} + \gamma \quad (10.24)$$

where the asterisk (*) on the nucleus indicates an excited state. In γ decay, neither the atomic number nor the mass number changes, so the type of nucleus does not change.

Radioactive Decay Series

Nuclei with $Z > 82$ are unstable and decay naturally. Many of these nuclei have very short lifetimes, so they are not found in nature. Notable exceptions include $^{232}_{90}\text{Th}$ (or Th-232) with a half-life of 1.39×10^{10} years, and $^{238}_{92}\text{U}$ (or U-238) with a half-life of 7.04×10^{8} years. When a heavy nucleus decays to a lighter one, the lighter daughter nucleus can become the parent nucleus for the next decay, and so on. This process can produce a long series of nuclear decays called a **decay series**. The series ends with a stable nucleus.

To illustrate the concept of a decay series, consider the decay of Th-232 series (**Figure 10.13**). The neutron number, *N*, is plotted on the vertical *y*-axis, and the atomic number, *Z*, is plotted on the horizontal *x*-axis, so Th-232 is found at the coordinates $(N, Z) = (142, 90)$. Th-232 decays by α emission with a half-life of 1.39×10^{10} years. Alpha decay decreases the atomic number by 2 and the mass number by 4, so we have

$$^{232}_{90}\text{Th} \rightarrow {}^{228}_{88}\text{Ra} + {}^{4}_{2}\text{He}.$$

The neutron number for Radium-228 is 140, so it is found in the diagram at the coordinates $(N, Z) = (140, 88)$. Radium-228 is also unstable and decays by β^- emission with a half-life of 5.76 years to Actinum-228. The atomic number increases by 1, the mass number remains the same, and the neutron number decreases by 1. Notice that in the graph, α emission appears as a line sloping downward to the left, with both *N* and *Z* decreasing by 2. Beta emission, on the other hand, appears as a line sloping downward to the right with *N* decreasing by 1, and *Z* increasing by 1. After several additional alpha and beta decays, the series ends with the stable nucleus Pb-208.

The relative frequency of different types of radioactive decays (alpha, beta, and gamma) depends on many factors, including the strength of the forces involved and the number of ways a given reaction can occur without violating the conservation of energy and momentum. How often a radioactive decay occurs often depends on a sensitive balance of the strong and electromagnetic forces. These forces are discussed in **Particle Physics and Cosmology**.

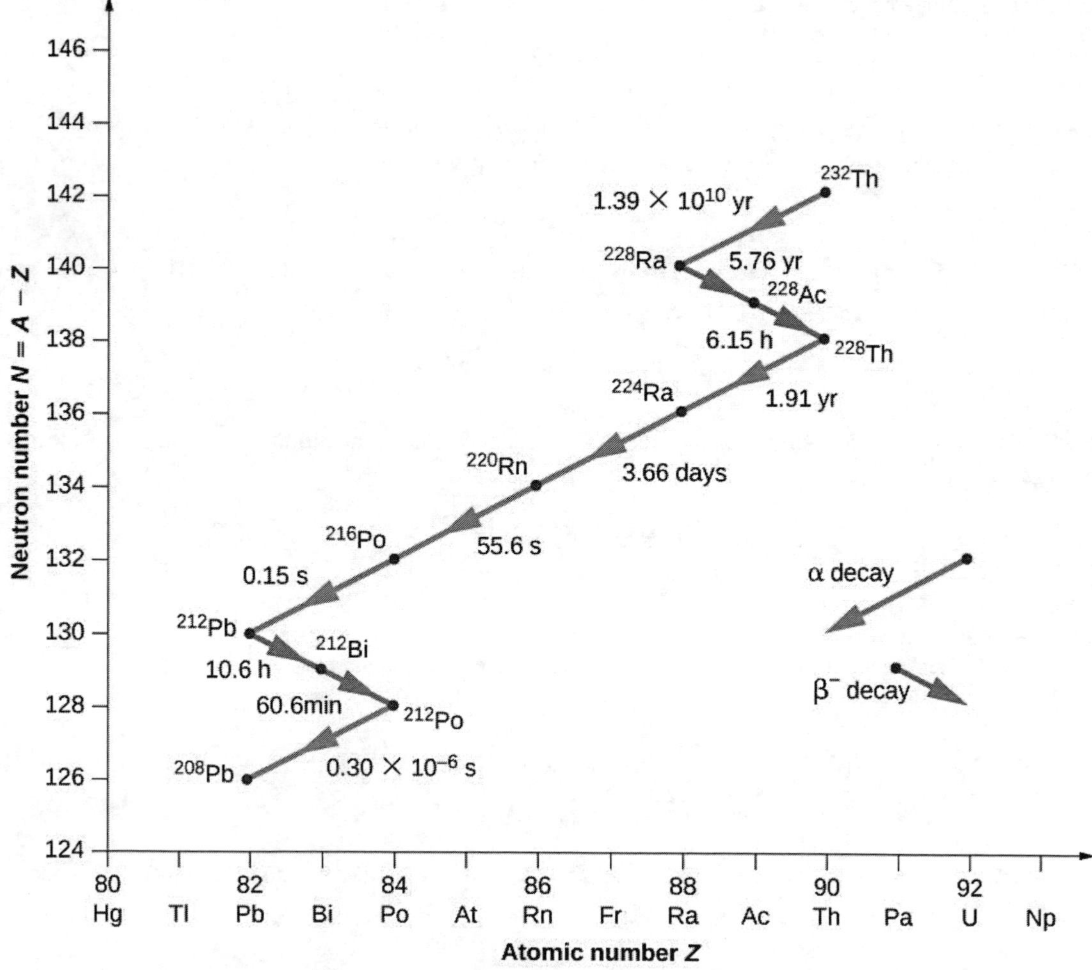

Figure 10.13 In the thorium $^{232}_{90}\text{Th}$ decay series, alpha (α) decays reduce the atomic number, as indicated by the red arrows. Beta (β^-) decays increase the atomic number, as indicated by the blue arrows. The series ends at the stable nucleus Pb-208.

As another example, consider the U-238 decay series shown in **Figure 10.14**. After numerous alpha and beta decays, the series ends with the stable nucleus Pb-206. An example of a decay whose parent nucleus no longer exists naturally is shown in **Figure 10.15**. It starts with Neptunium-237 and ends in the stable nucleus Bismuth-209. Neptunium is called a **transuranic element** because it lies beyond uranium in the periodic table. Uranium has the highest atomic number $(Z = 92)$ of any element found in nature. Elements with $Z > 92$ can be produced only in the laboratory. They most probably also existed in nature at the time of the formation of Earth, but because of their relatively short lifetimes, they have completely decayed. There is nothing fundamentally different between naturally occurring and artificial elements.

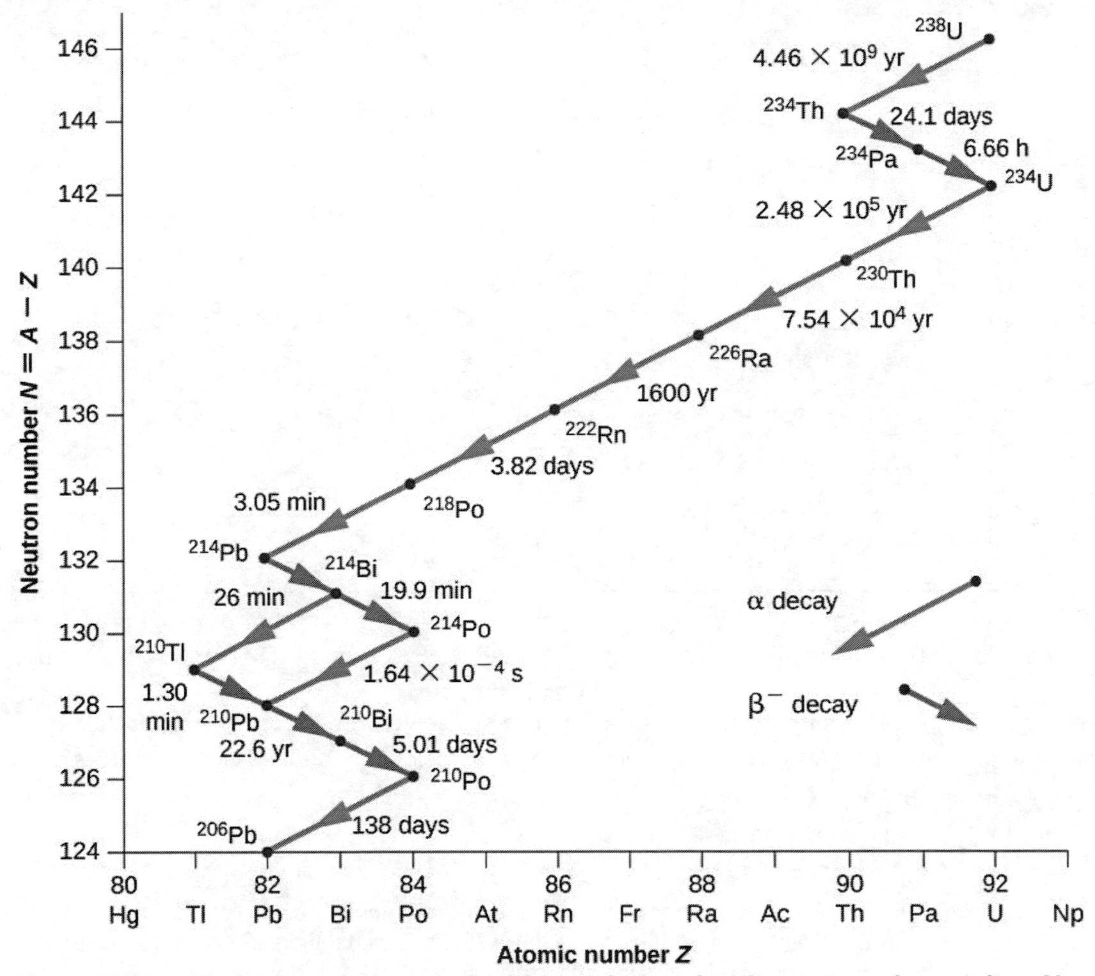

Figure 10.14 In the Uranium-238 decay series, alpha (α) decays reduce the atomic number, as indicated by the red arrows. Beta (β^-) decays increase the atomic number, as indicated by the blue arrows. The series ends at the stable nucleus Pb-206.

Notice that for Bi (21), the decay may proceed through either alpha or beta decay.

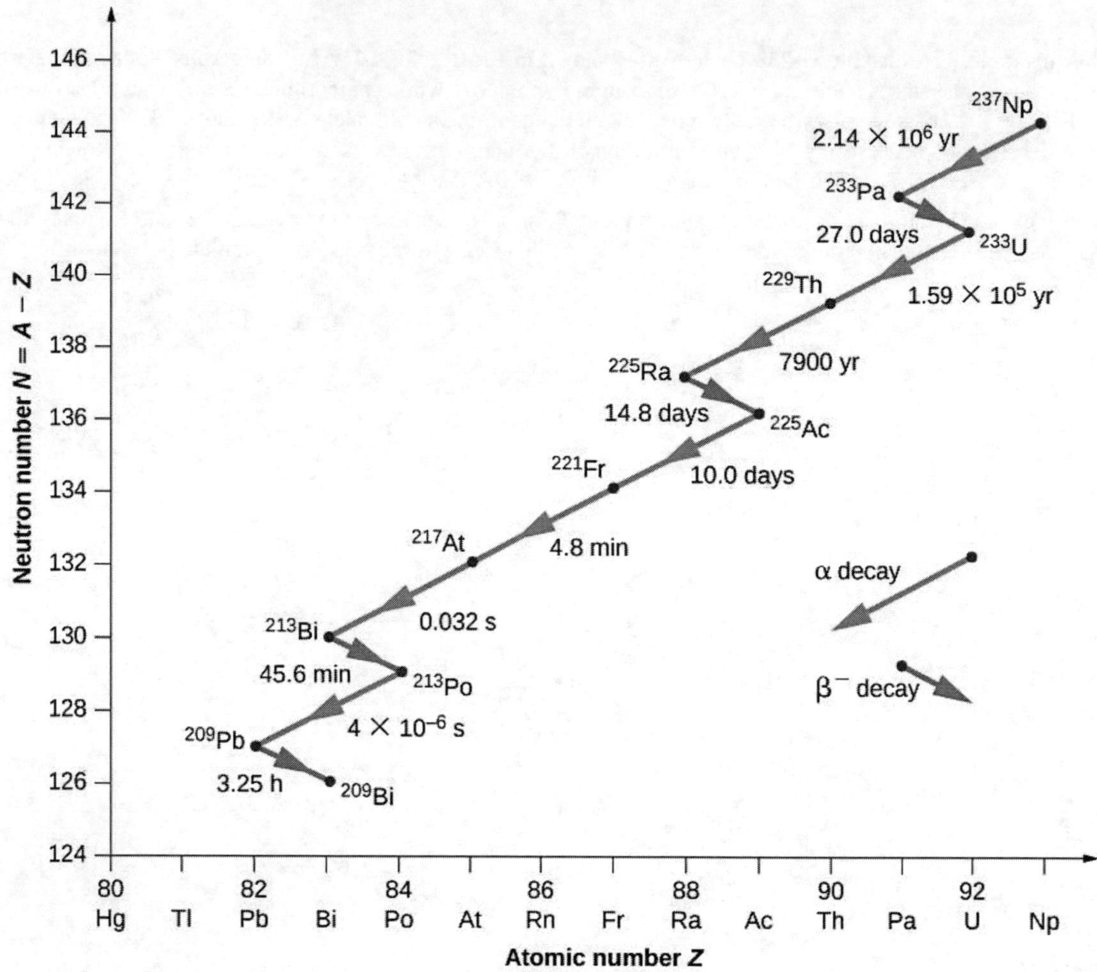

Figure 10.15 In the Neptunium-237 decay series, alpha (α) decays reduce the atomic number, as indicated by the red arrows. Beta (β^-) decays increase the atomic number, as indicated by the blue arrows. The series ends at the stable nucleus Bi-209.

Radioactivity in the Earth

According to geologists, if there were no heat source, Earth should have cooled to its present temperature in no more than 1 billion years. Yet, Earth is more than 4 billion years old. Why is Earth cooling so slowly? The answer is nuclear radioactivity, that is, high-energy particles produced in radioactive decays heat Earth from the inside (**Figure 10.16**).

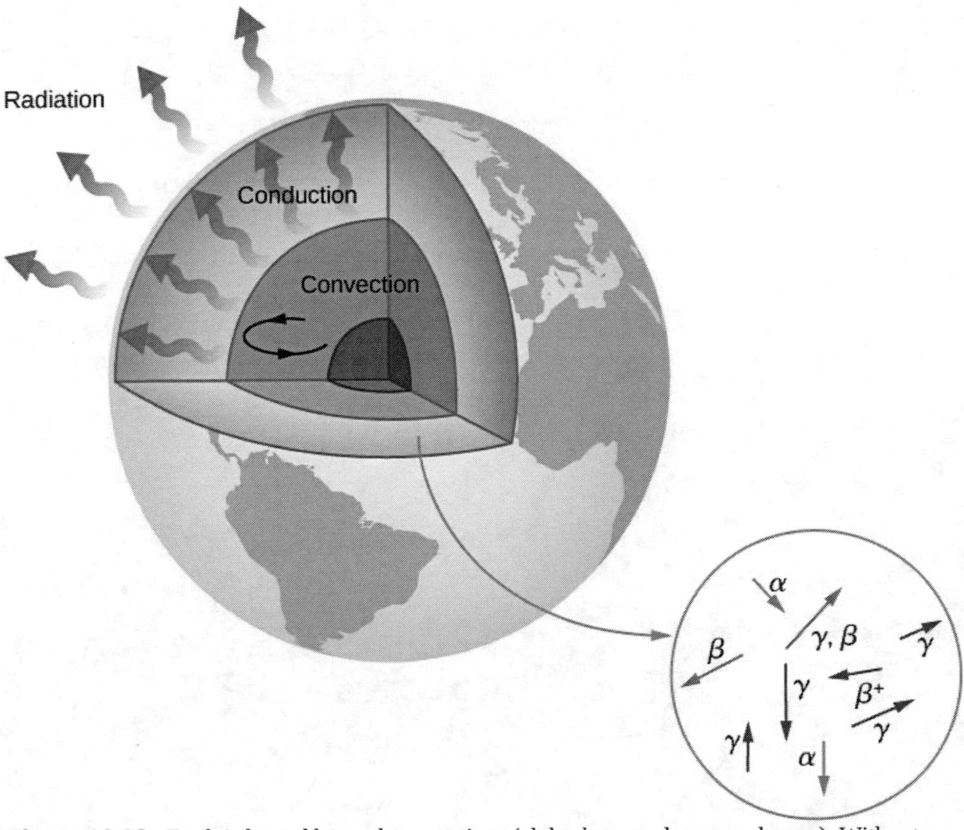

Figure 10.16 Earth is heated by nuclear reactions (alpha, beta, and gamma decays). Without these reactions, Earth's surface would be much cooler than it is now.

Candidate nuclei for this heating model are ^{238}U and ^{40}K, which possess half-lives similar to or longer than the age of Earth. The energy produced by these decays (per second per cubic meter) is small, but the energy cannot escape easily, so Earth's core is very hot. Thermal energy in Earth's core is transferred to Earth's surface and away from it through the processes of convection, conduction, and radiation.

10.5 | Fission

Learning Objectives

By the end of this section, you will be able to:

- Describe the process of nuclear fission in terms of its product and reactants
- Calculate the energies of particles produced by a fission reaction
- Explain the fission concept in the context of fission bombs and nuclear reactions

In 1934, Enrico Fermi bombarded chemical elements with neutrons in order to create isotopes of other elements. He assumed that bombarding uranium with neutrons would make it unstable and produce a new element. Unfortunately, Fermi could not determine the products of the reaction. Several years later, Otto Hahn and Fritz Strassman reproduced these experiments and discovered that the products of these reactions were smaller nuclei. From this, they concluded that the uranium nucleus had split into two smaller nuclei.

The splitting of a nucleus is called **fission**. Interestingly, U-235 fission does not always produce the same fragments. Example fission reactions include:

$$
\begin{aligned}
{}^{1}_{0}\text{n} + {}^{235}_{92}\text{U} &\to {}^{141}_{56}\text{Ba} + {}^{92}_{36}\text{Kr} + 3\,{}^{1}_{0}\text{n} + Q, \\
{}^{1}_{0}\text{n} + {}^{235}_{92}\text{U} &\to {}^{140}_{54}\text{Xe} + {}^{94}_{38}\text{Sr} + 2\,{}^{1}_{0}\text{n} + Q, \\
{}^{1}_{0}\text{n} + {}^{235}_{92}\text{U} &\to {}^{132}_{50}\text{Sn} + {}^{101}_{42}\text{Mo} + 3\,{}^{1}_{0}\text{n} + Q.
\end{aligned}
$$

In each case, the sum of the masses of the product nuclei are less than the masses of the reactants, so the fission of uranium is an exothermic process $(Q > 0)$. This is the idea behind the use of fission reactors as sources of energy (**Figure 10.17**).

The energy carried away by the reaction takes the form of particles with kinetic energy. The percent yield of fragments from a U-235 fission is given in **Figure 10.18**.

Figure 10.17 The Phillipsburg Nuclear Power Plant in Germany uses a fission reactor to generate electricity.

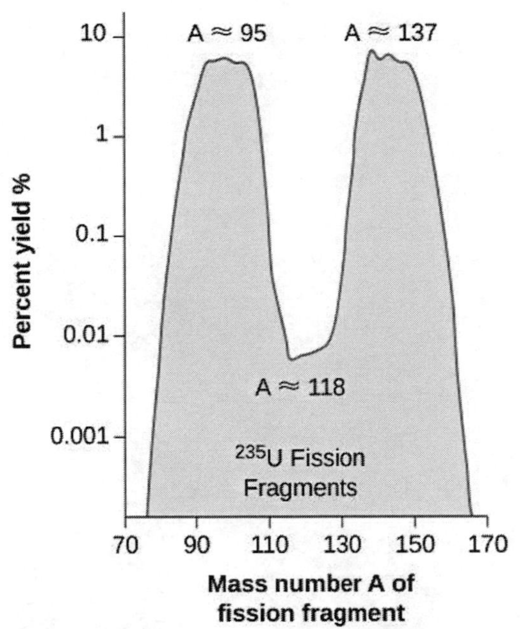

Figure 10.18 In this graph of fission fragments from U-235, the peaks in the graph indicate nuclei that are produced in the greatest abundance by the fission process.

Energy changes in a nuclear fission reaction can be understood in terms of the binding energy per nucleon curve (Figure 10.7). The BEN value for uranium $(A = 236)$ is slightly lower than its daughter nuclei, which lie closer to the iron (Fe) peak. This means that nucleons in the nuclear fragments are more tightly bound than those in the U-235 nucleus. Therefore, a fission reaction results in a drop in the average energy of a nucleon. This energy is carried away by high-energy neutrons.

Niels Bohr and John Wheeler developed the **liquid drop model** to understand the fission process. According to this model, firing a neutron at a nucleus is analogous to disturbing a droplet of water (Figure 10.19). The analogy works because short-range forces between nucleons in a nucleus are similar to the attractive forces between water molecules in a water droplet. In particular, forces between nucleons at the surface of the nucleus result in a surface tension similar to that of a water droplet. A neutron fired into a uranium nucleus can set the nucleus into vibration. If this vibration is violent enough, the nucleus divides into smaller nuclei and also emits two or three individual neutrons.

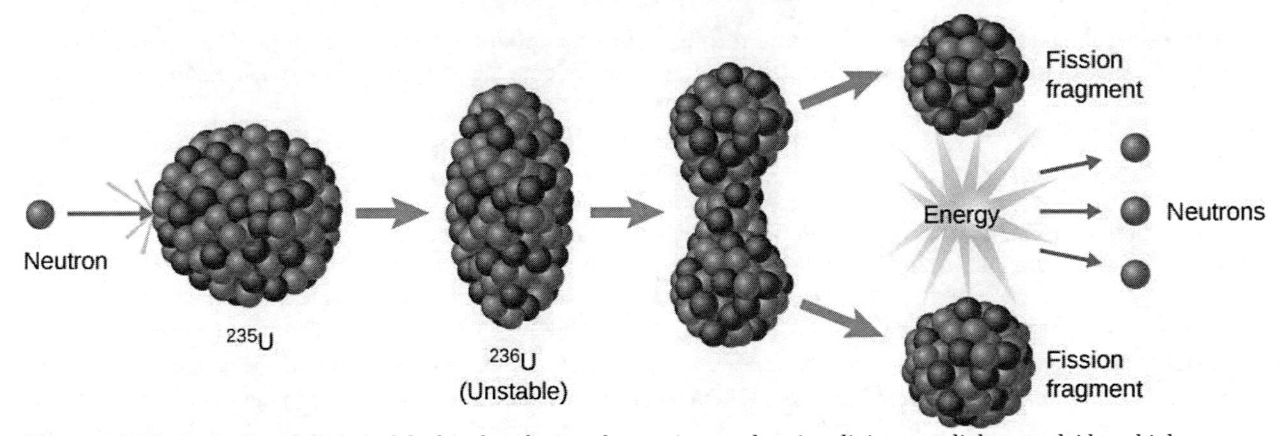

Figure 10.19 In the liquid drop model of nuclear fission, the uranium nucleus is split into two lighter nuclei by a high-energy neutron.

U-235 fission can produce a chain reaction. In a compound consisting of many U-235 nuclei, neutrons in the decay of one U-235 nucleus can initiate the fission of additional U-235 nuclei (Figure 10.20). This chain reaction can proceed in a controlled manner, as in a nuclear reactor at a power plant, or proceed uncontrollably, as in an explosion.

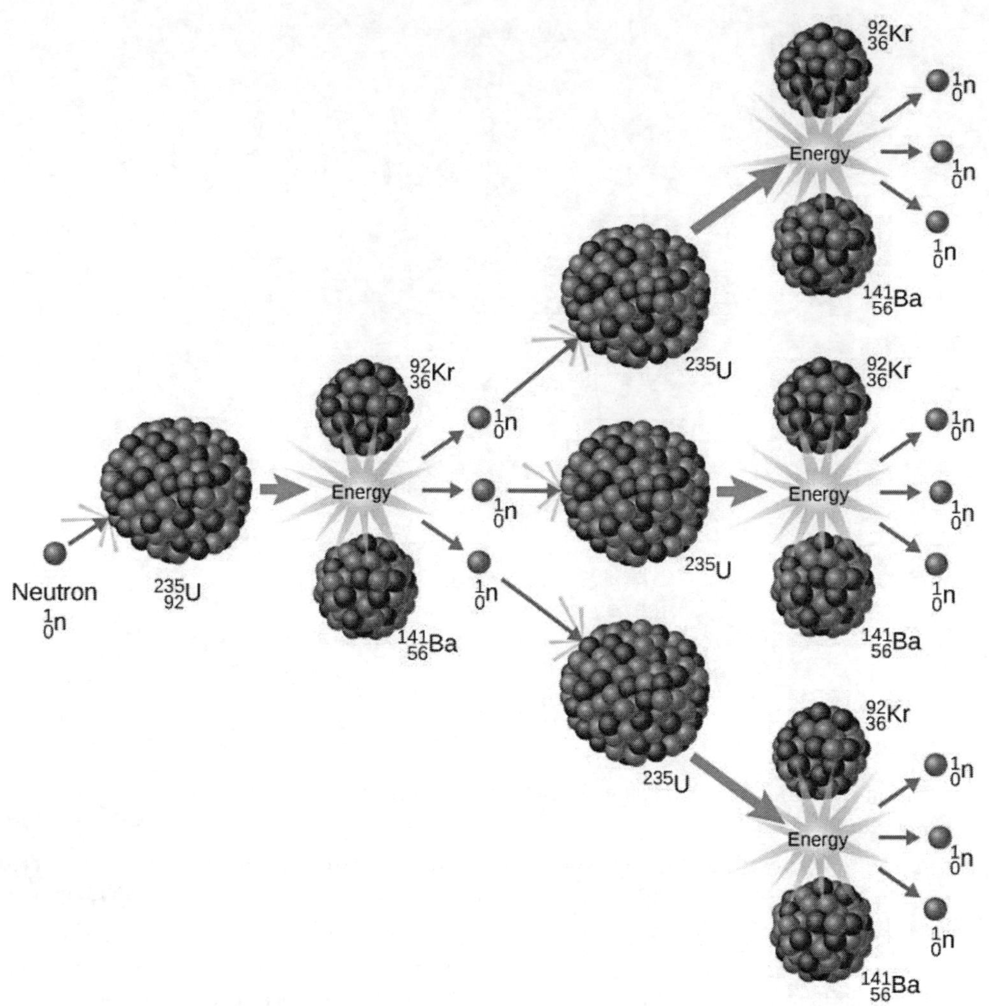

Figure 10.20 In a U-235 fission chain reaction, the fission of the uranium nucleus produces high-energy neutrons that go on to split more nuclei. The energy released in this process can be used to produce electricity.

View a simulation on **nuclear fission (https://openstaxcollege.org/l/21nuclrfissvid)** to start a chain reaction, or introduce nonradioactive isotopes to prevent one. Control energy production in a nuclear reactor.

The Atomic Bomb

The possibility of a chain reaction in uranium, with its extremely large energy release, led nuclear scientists to conceive of making a bomb—an atomic bomb. (These discoveries were taking place in the years just prior to the Second World War and many of the European physicists involved in these discoveries came from countries that were being overrun.) Natural uranium contains 99.3% U-238 and only 0.7% U-235, and does not produce a chain reaction. To produce a controlled, sustainable chain reaction, the percentage of U-235 must be increased to about 50% . In addition, the uranium sample must be massive enough so a typical neutron is more likely to induce fission than it is to escape. The minimum mass needed for the chain reaction to occur is called the **critical mass**. When the critical mass reaches a point at which the chain reaction becomes self-sustaining, this is a condition known as **criticality**. The original design required two pieces of U-235 below the critical mass. When one piece in the form of a bullet is fired into the second piece, the critical mass is exceeded and a chain reaction is produced.

An important obstacle to the U-235 bomb is the production of a critical mass of fissionable material. Therefore, scientists developed a plutonium-239 bomb because Pu-239 is more fissionable than U-235 and thus requires a smaller critical mass. The bomb was made in the form of a sphere with pieces of plutonium, each below the critical mass, at the edge of the sphere. A series of chemical explosions fired the plutonium pieces toward the center of the sphere simultaneously. When all these pieces of plutonium came together, the combination exceeded the critical mass and produced a chain reaction. Both the U-235 and Pu-239 bombs were used in World War II. Whether to develop and use atomic weapons remain two of the most important questions faced by human civilization.

Example 10.9

Calculating Energy Released by Fission

Calculate the energy released in the following spontaneous fission reaction:

$$^{238}\text{U} \rightarrow {}^{95}\text{Sr} + {}^{140}\text{Xe} + 3\text{n},$$

The atomic masses are $m\left(^{238}\text{U}\right) = 238.050784\ \text{u}$, $m\left(^{95}\text{Sr}\right) = 94.919388\ \text{u}$, $m\left(^{140}\text{Xe}\right) = 139.921610\ \text{u}$, and $m(\text{n}) = 1.008665\ \text{u}$.

Strategy

As always, the energy released is equal to the mass destroyed times c^2, so we must find the difference in mass between the parent ^{238}U and the fission products.

Solution

The products have a total mass of

$$\begin{aligned} m_{\text{products}} &= 94.919388\ \text{u} + 139.921610\ \text{u} + 3(1.008665\ \text{u}) \\ &= 237.866993\ \text{u}. \end{aligned}$$

The mass lost is the mass of $^{238}\text{U} - m_{\text{products}}$ or

$$\Delta m = 238.050784\ \text{u} - 237.8669933\ \text{u} = 0.183791\ \text{u}.$$

Therefore, the energy released is

$$E = (\Delta m)c^2 = (0.183791\ \text{u})\frac{931.5\ \text{MeV}/c^2}{\text{u}}c^2 = 171.2\ \text{MeV}.$$

Significance

Several important things arise in this example. The energy release is large but less than it would be if the nucleus split into two equal parts, since energy is carried away by neutrons. However, this fission reaction produces neutrons and does not split the nucleus into two equal parts. Fission of a given nuclide, such as ^{238}U, does not always produce the same products. Fission is a statistical process in which an entire range of products are produced with various probabilities. Most fission produces neutrons, although the number varies. This is an extremely important aspect of fission, because *neutrons can induce more fission*, enabling self-sustaining chain reactions.

Fission Nuclear Reactors

The first nuclear reactor was built by Enrico Fermi on a squash court on the campus of the University of Chicago on December 2, 1942. The reactor itself contained U-238 enriched with 3.6% U-235. Neutrons produced by the chain reaction move too fast to initiate fission reactions. One way to slow them down is to enclose the entire reactor in a water bath under high pressure. The neutrons collide with the water molecules and are slowed enough to be used in the fission process. The slowed neutrons split more U-235 nuclei and a chain reaction occurs. The rate at which the chain reaction proceeds is controlled by a series of "control" rods made of cadmium inserted into the reactor. Cadmium is capable of absorbing a large number of neutrons without becoming unstable.

A nuclear reactor design, called a pressurized water reactor, can also be used to generate electricity (**Figure 10.21**). A pressurized water reactor (on the left in the figure) is designed to control the fission of large amounts of ^{235}U. The energy released in this process is absorbed by water flowing through pipes in the system (the "primary loop") and steam is produced. Cadmium control rods adjust the neutron flux (the rate of flow of neutrons passing through the system) and therefore control the reaction. In case the reactor overheats and the water boils away, the chain reaction terminates, because water is used to thermalize the neutrons. (This safety feature can be overwhelmed in extreme circumstances.) The hot, high-pressure water then passes through a pipe to a second tank of water at normal pressure in the steam generator. The steam produced at one end of the steam generator fills a chamber that contains a turbine. This steam is at a very high pressure. Meanwhile, a steam condenser connected to the other side of the turbine chamber maintains steam at low pressure. The pressure differences force steam through the chamber, which turns the turbine. The turbine, in turn, powers an electric generator.

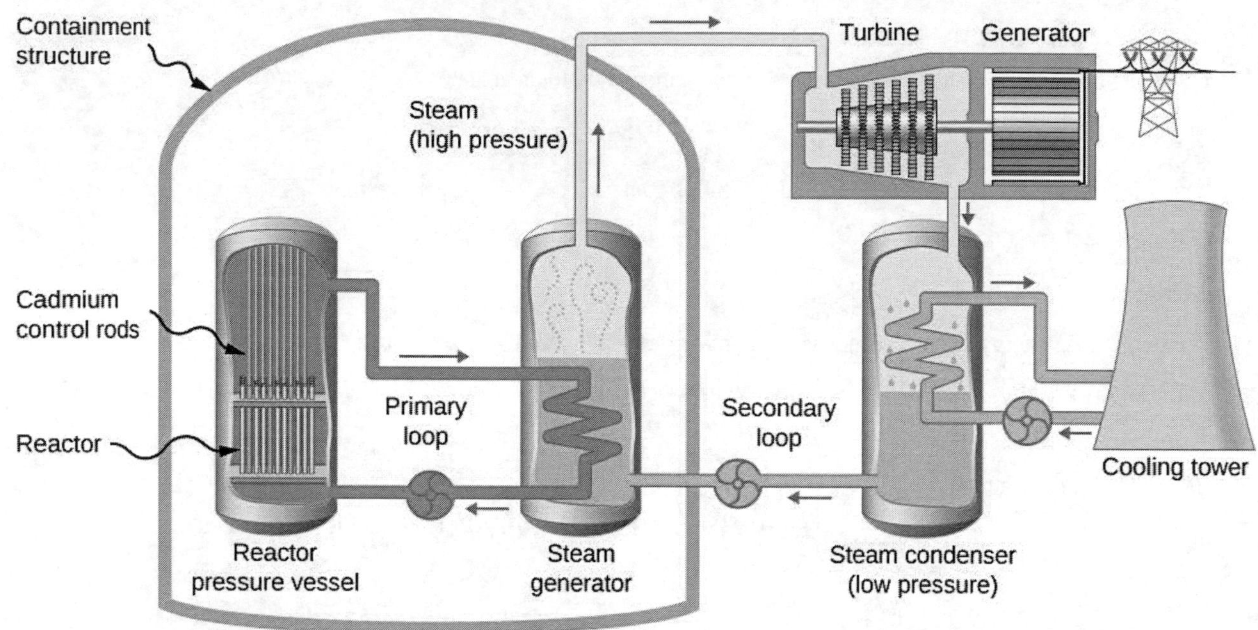

Figure 10.21 A nuclear reactor uses the energy produced in the fission of U-235 to produce electricity. Energy from a nuclear fission reaction produces hot, high-pressure steam that turns a turbine. As the turbine turns, electricity is produced.

The major drawback to a fission reactor is nuclear waste. U-235 fission produces nuclei with long half-lives such as ^{236}U that must be stored. These products cannot be dumped into oceans or left in any place where they will contaminate the environment, such as through the soil, air, or water. Many scientists believe that the best place to store nuclear waste is the bottom of old salt mines or inside of stable mountains.

Many people are fearful that a nuclear reactor may explode like an atomic bomb. However, a nuclear reactor does not contain enough U-235 to do this. Also, a nuclear reactor is designed so that failure of any mechanism of the reactor causes the cadmium control rods to fall fully into the reactor, stopping the fission process. As evidenced by the Fukushima and Chernobyl disasters, such systems can fail. Systems and procedures to avoid such disasters is an important priority for advocates of nuclear energy.

If all electrical power were produced by nuclear fission of U-235, Earth's known reserves of uranium would be depleted in less than a century. However, Earth's supply of fissionable material can be expanded considerably using a **breeder reactor**. A breeder reactor operates for the first time using the fission of U-235 as just described for the pressurized water reactor. But in addition to producing energy, some of the fast neutrons originating from the fission of U-235 are absorbed by U-238, resulting in the production of Pu-239 via the set of reactions

$$^{1}_{0}\text{n} + {}^{238}_{92}\text{U} \rightarrow {}^{239}_{92}\text{U} \xrightarrow{\beta} {}^{239}_{93}\text{Np} \xrightarrow{\beta} {}^{239}_{94}\text{Pu}.$$

The Pu-239 is itself highly fissionable and can therefore be used as a nuclear fuel in place of U-235. Since 99.3% of naturally occurring uranium is the U-238 isotope, the use of breeder reactors should increase our supply of nuclear fuel by roughly a factor of 100. Breeder reactors are now in operation in Great Britain, France, and Russia. Breeder reactors also have drawbacks. First, breeder reactors produce plutonium, which can, if leaked into the environment, produce serious public health problems. Second, plutonium can be used to build bombs, thus increasing significantly the risk of nuclear proliferation.

Example 10.10

Calculating Energy of Fissionable Fuel

Calculate the amount of energy produced by the fission of 1.00 kg of ^{235}U given that the average fission reaction of ^{235}U produces 200 MeV.

Strategy

The total energy produced is the number of ^{235}U atoms times the given energy per ^{235}U fission. We should therefore find the number of ^{235}U atoms in 1.00 kg.

Solution

The number of ^{235}U atoms in 1.00 kg is Avogadro's number times the number of moles. One mole of ^{235}U has a mass of 235.04 g; thus, there are $(1000\text{ g})/(235.04\text{ g/mol}) = 4.25\text{ mol}$. The number of ^{235}U atoms is therefore

$$(4.25\text{ mol})\left(6.02 \times 10^{23}\ ^{235}\text{U/mol}\right) = 2.56 \times 10^{24}\ ^{235}\text{U}.$$

Thus, the total energy released is

$$E = \left(2.56 \times 10^{24}\ ^{235}\text{U}\right)\left(\frac{200\text{ MeV}}{^{235}\text{U}}\right)\left(\frac{1.60 \times 10^{-13}\text{ J}}{\text{MeV}}\right) = 8.21 \times 10^{13}\text{ J}.$$

Significance

This is another impressively large amount of energy, equivalent to about 14,000 barrels of crude oil or 600,000 gallons of gasoline. However, it is only one-fourth the energy produced by the fusion of a kilogram mixture of deuterium and tritium. Even though each fission reaction yields about 10 times the energy of a fusion reaction, the energy per kilogram of fission fuel is less, because there are far fewer moles per kilogram of the heavy nuclides. Fission fuel is also much scarcer than fusion fuel, and less than 1% of uranium (the ^{235}U) is readily usable.

10.5 Check Your Understanding Which has a larger energy yield per fission reaction, a large or small sample of pure ^{235}U?

10.6 | Nuclear Fusion

Learning Objectives

By the end of this section, you will be able to:

- Describe the process of nuclear fusion in terms of its product and reactants
- Calculate the energies of particles produced by a fusion reaction
- Explain the fission concept in the context of fusion bombs, the production of energy by the Sun, and nucleosynthesis

The process of combining lighter nuclei to make heavier nuclei is called **nuclear fusion**. As with fission reactions, fusion reactions are exothermic—they release energy. Suppose that we fuse a carbon and helium nuclei to produce oxygen:

$$^{12}_{6}\text{C} + {}^{4}_{2}\text{He} \rightarrow {}^{16}_{8}\text{O} + \gamma.$$

The energy changes in this reaction can be understood using a graph of binding energy per nucleon (**Figure 10.7**). Comparing the binding energy per nucleon for oxygen, carbon, and helium, the oxygen nucleus is much more tightly bound than the carbon and helium nuclei, indicating that the reaction produces a drop in the energy of the system. This energy is released in the form of gamma radiation. Fusion reactions are said to be exothermic when the amount of energy released (known as the *Q value*) in each reaction is greater than zero $(Q > 0)$.

An important example of nuclear fusion in nature is the production of energy in the Sun. In 1938, Hans Bethe proposed that the Sun produces energy when hydrogen nuclei (^1H) fuse into stable helium nuclei $\left(^4\text{He}\right)$ in the Sun's core (**Figure 10.22**). This process, called the **proton-proton chain**, is summarized by three reactions:

$$\begin{aligned} &{}^1_1\text{H} + {}^1_1\text{H} \rightarrow {}^2_1\text{H} + {}^{\;\,0}_{+1}\text{e} + \nu + Q, \\ &{}^1_1\text{H} + {}^2_1\text{H} \rightarrow {}^3_2\text{He} + \gamma + Q, \\ &{}^3_2\text{He} + {}^3_2\text{He} \rightarrow {}^4_2\text{He} + {}^1_1\text{H} + {}^1_1\text{H} + Q. \end{aligned}$$

Thus, a stable helium nucleus is formed from the fusion of the nuclei of the hydrogen atom. These three reactions can be summarized by

$$4\,{}^1_1\text{H} \rightarrow {}^4_2\text{He} + 2\,{}^{\;\,0}_{+1}\text{e} + 2\gamma + 2\nu + Q.$$

The net Q value is about 26 MeV. The release of this energy produces an outward thermal gas pressure that prevents the Sun from gravitational collapse. Astrophysicists find that hydrogen fusion supplies the energy stars require to maintain energy balance over most of a star's life span.

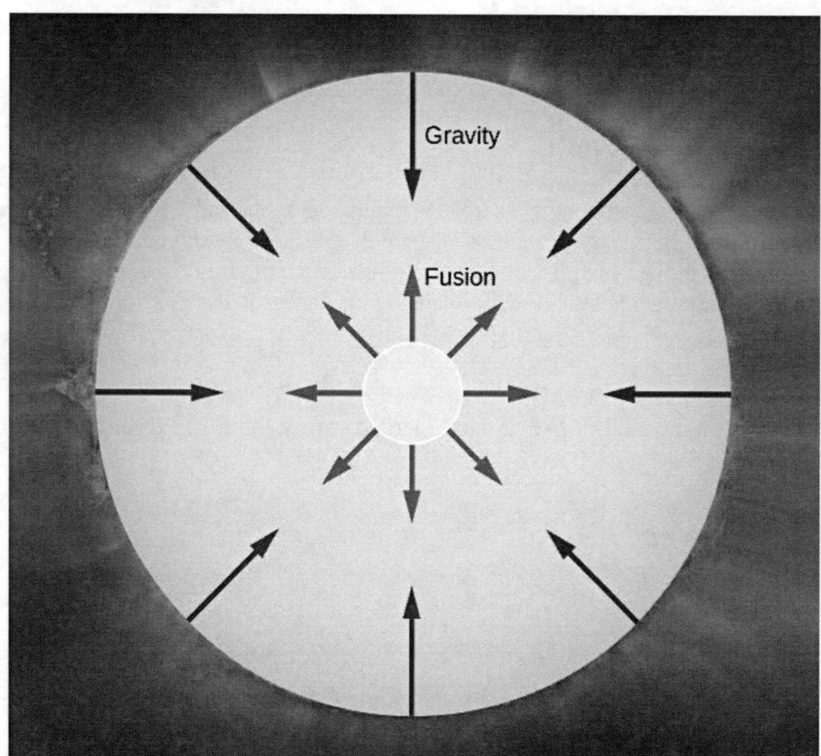

Figure 10.22 The Sun produces energy by fusing hydrogen into helium at the Sun's core. The red arrows show outward pressure due to thermal gas, which tends to make the Sun expand. The blue arrows show inward pressure due to gravity, which tends to make the Sun contract. These two influences balance each other.

Nucleosynthesis

Scientist now believe that many heavy elements found on Earth and throughout the universe were originally synthesized by fusion within the hot cores of the stars. This process is known as **nucleosynthesis**. For example, in lighter stars, hydrogen combines to form helium through the proton-proton chain. Once the hydrogen fuel is exhausted, the star enters the next stage of its life and fuses helium. An example of a nuclear reaction chain that can occur is:

$$\begin{aligned} {}^{4}_{2}\text{He} + {}^{4}_{2}\text{He} &\rightarrow {}^{8}_{4}\text{Be} + \gamma, \\ {}^{8}_{4}\text{Be} + {}^{4}_{2}\text{He} &\rightarrow {}^{12}_{6}\text{C} + \gamma, \\ {}^{12}_{6}\text{C} + {}^{4}_{2}\text{He} &\rightarrow {}^{16}_{8}\text{O} + \gamma. \end{aligned}$$

Carbon and oxygen nuclei produced in such processes eventually reach the star's surface by convection. Near the end of its lifetime, the star loses its outer layers into space, thus enriching the interstellar medium with the nuclei of heavier elements (**Figure 10.23**).

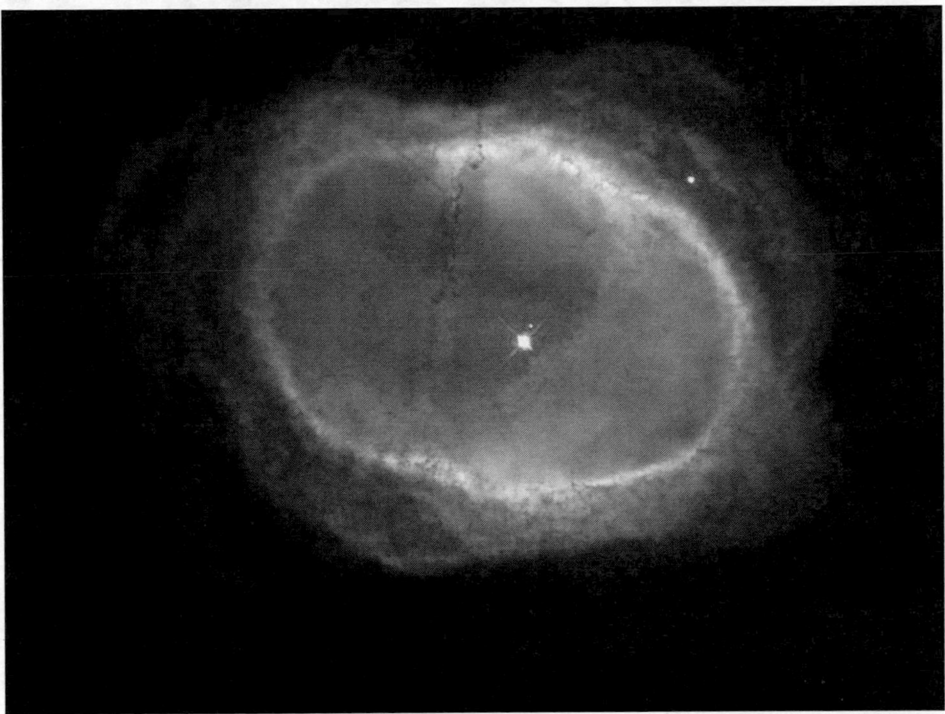

Figure 10.23 A planetary nebula is produced at the end of the life of a star. The greenish color of this planetary nebula comes from oxygen ions. (credit: Hubble Heritage Team (STScI/AURA/NASA/ESA))

Stars similar in mass to the Sun do not become hot enough to fuse nuclei as heavy (or heavier) than oxygen nuclei. However, in massive stars whose cores become much hotter $\left(T > 6 \times 10^{8}\ \text{K}\right)$, even more complex nuclei are produced. Some representative reactions are

$$\begin{aligned} {}^{12}_{6}\text{C} + {}^{12}_{6}\text{C} &\rightarrow {}^{23}_{11}\text{Na} + {}^{1}_{1}\text{H}, \\ {}^{12}_{6}\text{C} \rightarrow {}^{12}_{6}\text{C} &\rightarrow {}^{24}_{12}\text{Mg} + \gamma, \\ {}^{12}_{6}\text{C} + {}^{16}_{8}\text{O} &\rightarrow {}^{28}_{14}\text{Si} + \gamma. \end{aligned}$$

Nucleosynthesis continues until the core is primarily iron-nickel metal. Now, iron has the peculiar property that any fusion or fission reaction involving the iron nucleus is endothermic, meaning that energy is absorbed rather than produced. Hence, nuclear energy cannot be generated in an iron-rich core. Lacking an outward pressure from fusion reactions, the star begins to contract due to gravity. This process heats the core to a temperature on the order of $5 \times 10^{9}\ \text{K}$. Expanding shock waves generated within the star due to the collapse cause the star to quickly explode. The luminosity of the star can increase temporarily to nearly that of an entire galaxy. During this event, the flood of energetic neutrons reacts with iron and the other nuclei to produce elements heavier than iron. These elements, along with much of the star, are ejected into space by the explosion. Supernovae and the formation of planetary nebulas together play a major role in the dispersal of chemical elements into space.

Eventually, much of the material lost by stars is pulled together through the gravitational force, and it condenses into a new generation of stars and accompanying planets. Recent images from the Hubble Space Telescope provide a glimpse of this magnificent process taking place in the constellation Serpens (**Figure 10.24**). The new generation of stars begins the nucleosynthesis process anew, with a higher percentage of heavier elements. Thus, stars are "factories" for the chemical elements, and many of the atoms in our bodies were once a part of stars.

Figure 10.24 This image taken by NASA's Spitzer Space Telescope and the Two Micron All Sky Survey (2MASS), shows the Serpens Cloud Core, a star-forming region in the constellation Serpens (the "Serpent"). Located about 750 light-years away, this cluster of stars is formed from cooling dust and gases. Infrared light has been used to reveal the youngest stars in orange and yellow. (credit: NASA/JPL-Caltech/2MASS)

Example 10.11

Energy of the Sun

The power output of the Sun is approximately 3.8×10^{26} J/s. Most of this energy is produced in the Sun's core by the proton-proton chain. This energy is transmitted outward by the processes of convection and radiation. (a) How many of these fusion reactions per second must occur to supply the power radiated by the Sun? (b) What is the rate at which the mass of the Sun decreases? (c) In about five billion years, the central core of the Sun will be depleted of hydrogen. By what percentage will the mass of the Sun have decreased from its present value when the core is depleted of hydrogen?

Strategy

The total energy output per second is given in the problem statement. If we know the energy released in each fusion reaction, we can determine the rate of the fusion reactions. If the mass loss per fusion reaction is known, the mass loss rate is known. Multiplying this rate by five billion years gives the total mass lost by the Sun. This value is divided by the original mass of the Sun to determine the percentage of the Sun's mass that has been lost when the hydrogen fuel is depleted.

Solution

a. The decrease in mass for the fusion reaction is

$$\begin{aligned}\Delta m &= 4m\left({}^{1}_{1}\mathrm{H}\right) - m\left({}^{4}_{2}\mathrm{He}\right) - 2m\left({}^{\;\,0}_{+1}\mathrm{e}\right)\\ &= 4(1.007825\,\mathrm{u}) - 4.002603\,\mathrm{u} - 2(0.000549\,\mathrm{u})\\ &= 0.0276\,\mathrm{u}.\end{aligned}$$

The energy released per fusion reaction is

$$Q = (0.0276\,\mathrm{u})(931.49\,\mathrm{MeV/u}) = 25.7\,\mathrm{MeV}.$$

Thus, to supply $3.8 \times 10^{26}\ \mathrm{J/s} = 2.38 \times 10^{39}\ \mathrm{MeV/s},$ there must be

$$\frac{2.38 \times 10^{39}\ \mathrm{MeV/s}}{25.7\ \mathrm{MeV/reaction}} = 9.26 \times 10^{37}\ \mathrm{reaction/s}.$$

b. The Sun's mass decreases by $0.0276\,\text{u} = 4.58 \times 10^{-29}\,\text{kg}$ per fusion reaction, so the rate at which its mass decreases is

$$\left(9.26 \times 10^{37}\ \text{reaction/s}\right)\left(4.58 \times 10^{-29}\ \text{kg/reaction}\right) = 4.24 \times 10^{9}\ \text{kg/s}.$$

c. In $5 \times 10^{9}\ \text{y} = 1.6 \times 10^{17}\ \text{s},$ the Sun's mass will therefore decrease by

$$\Delta M = \left(4.24 \times 10^{9}\ \text{kg/s}\right)\left(1.6 \times 10^{17}\ \text{s}\right) = 6.8 \times 10^{26}\ \text{kg}.$$

The current mass of the Sun is about $2.0 \times 10^{30}\ \text{kg},$ so the percentage decrease in its mass when its hydrogen fuel is depleted will be

$$\left(\frac{6.8 \times 10^{26}\ \text{kg}}{2.0 \times 10^{30}\ \text{kg}}\right) \times 100\% = 0.034\%.$$

Significance

After five billion years, the Sun is very nearly the same mass as it is now. Hydrogen burning does very little to change the mass of the Sun. This calculation assumes that only the proton-proton decay change is responsible for the power output of the Sun.

10.6 Check Your Understanding Where does the energy from the Sun originate?

The Hydrogen Bomb

In 1942, Robert Oppenheimer suggested that the extremely high temperature of an atomic bomb could be used to trigger a fusion reaction between deuterium and tritium, thus producing a fusion (or hydrogen) bomb. The reaction between deuterium and tritium, both isotopes of hydrogen, is given by

$${}_{1}^{2}\text{H} + {}_{1}^{3}\text{H} \rightarrow {}_{2}^{4}\text{He} + {}_{0}^{1}\text{n} + 17.6\,\text{MeV}.$$

Deuterium is relatively abundant in ocean water but tritium is scarce. However, tritium can be generated in a nuclear reactor through a reaction involving lithium. The neutrons from the reactor cause the reaction

$${}_{0}^{1}\text{n} + {}_{3}^{7}\text{Li} \rightarrow {}_{2}^{4}\text{He} + {}_{1}^{3}\text{H} + {}_{0}^{1}\text{n},$$

to produce the desired tritium. The first hydrogen bomb was detonated in 1952 on the remote island of Eniwetok in the Marshall Islands. A hydrogen bomb has never been used in war. Modern hydrogen bombs are approximately 1000 times more powerful than the fission bombs dropped on Hiroshima and Nagasaki in World War II.

The Fusion Reactor

The fusion chain believed to be the most practical for use in a **nuclear fusion reactor** is the following two-step process:

$${}_{1}^{2}\text{H} + {}_{1}^{2}\text{H} \rightarrow {}_{1}^{3}\text{H} + {}_{1}^{1}\text{H},$$
$${}_{1}^{2}\text{H} + {}_{1}^{3}\text{H} \rightarrow {}_{2}^{4}\text{He} + {}_{0}^{1}\text{n}.$$

This chain, like the proton-proton chain, produces energy without any radioactive by-product. However, there is a very difficult problem that must be overcome before fusion can be used to produce significant amounts of energy: Extremely high temperatures $\left(\sim 10^{7}\,\text{K}\right)$ are needed to drive the fusion process. To meet this challenge, test fusion reactors are being developed to withstand temperatures 20 times greater than the Sun's core temperature. An example is the Joint European Torus (JET) shown in **Figure 10.25**. A great deal of work still has to be done on fusion reactor technology, but many scientists predict that fusion energy will power the world's cities by the end of the twentieth century.

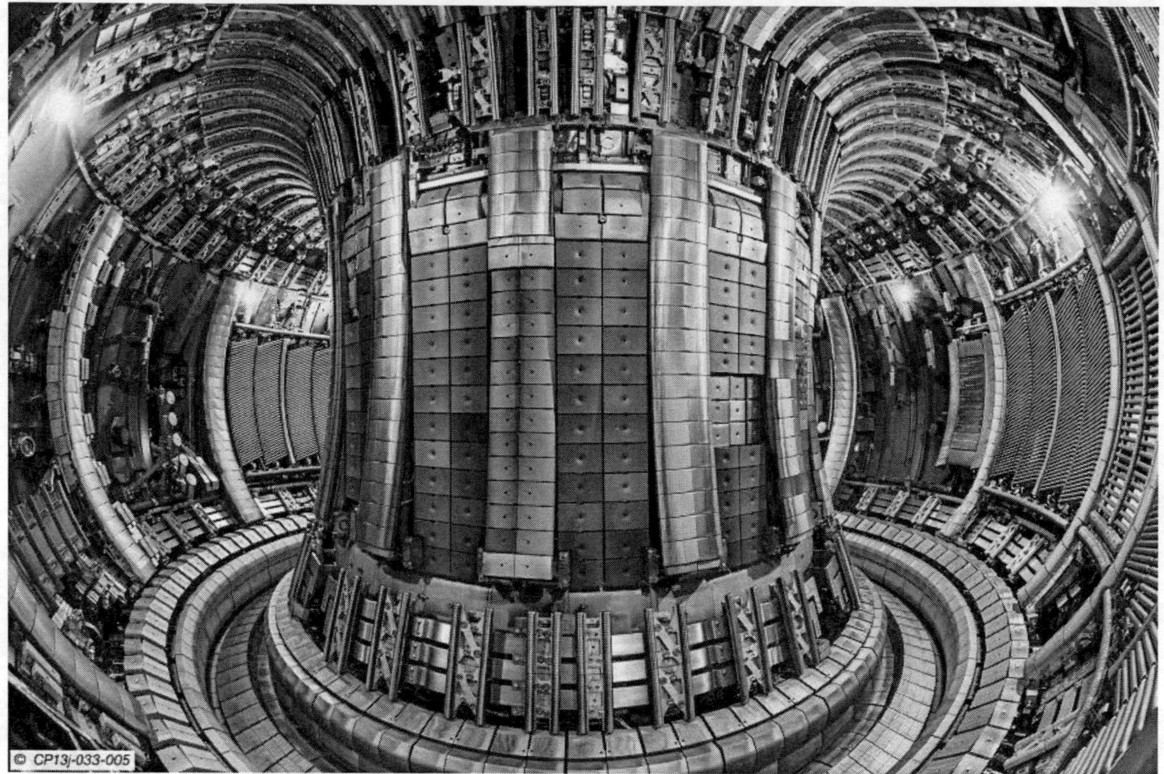

Figure 10.25 The Joint European Torus (JET) tokamak fusion detector uses magnetic fields to fuse deuterium and tritium nuclei (credit: EUROfusion).

10.7 | Medical Applications and Biological Effects of Nuclear Radiation

Learning Objectives

By the end of this section, you will be able to:

- Describe two medical uses of nuclear technology
- Explain the origin of biological effects due to nuclear radiation
- List common sources of radiation and their effects
- Estimate exposure for nuclear radiation using common dosage units

Nuclear physics is an integral part of our everyday lives (**Figure 10.26**). Radioactive compounds are used in to identify cancer, study ancient artifacts, and power our cities. Nuclear fusion also powers the Sun, the primary source of energy on Earth. The focus of this chapter is nuclear radiation. In this section, we ask such questions as: How is nuclear radiation used to benefit society? What are its health risks? How much nuclear radiation is the average person exposed to in a lifetime?

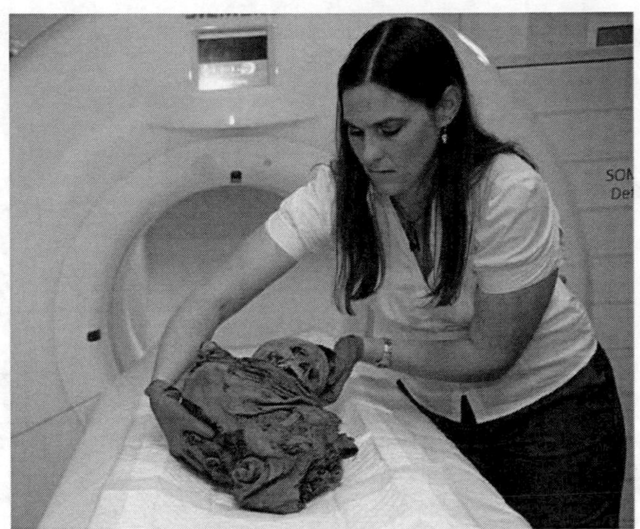

Figure 10.26 Dr. Tori Randall, a curator at the San Diego Museum of Man, uses nuclear radiation to study a 500-year-old Peruvian child mummy. The origin of this radiation is the transformation of one nucleus to another. (credit: Samantha A. Lewis, U.S. Navy)

Medical Applications

Medical use of nuclear radiation is quite common in today's hospitals and clinics. One of the most important uses of nuclear radiation is the location and study of diseased tissue. This application requires a special drug called a **radiopharmaceutical**. A radiopharmaceutical contains an unstable radioactive isotope. When the drug enters the body, it tends to concentrate in inflamed regions of the body. (Recall that the interaction of the drug with the body does not depend on whether a given nucleus is replaced by one of its isotopes, since this interaction is determined by chemical interactions.) Radiation detectors used outside the body use nuclear radiation from the radioisotopes to locate the diseased tissue. Radiopharmaceuticals are called **radioactive tags** because they allow doctors to track the movement of drugs in the body. Radioactive tags are for many purposes, including the identification of cancer cells in the bones, brain tumors, and Alzheimer's disease (Figure 10.27). Radioactive tags are also used to monitor the function of body organs, such as blood flow, heart muscle activity, and iodine uptake in the thyroid gland.

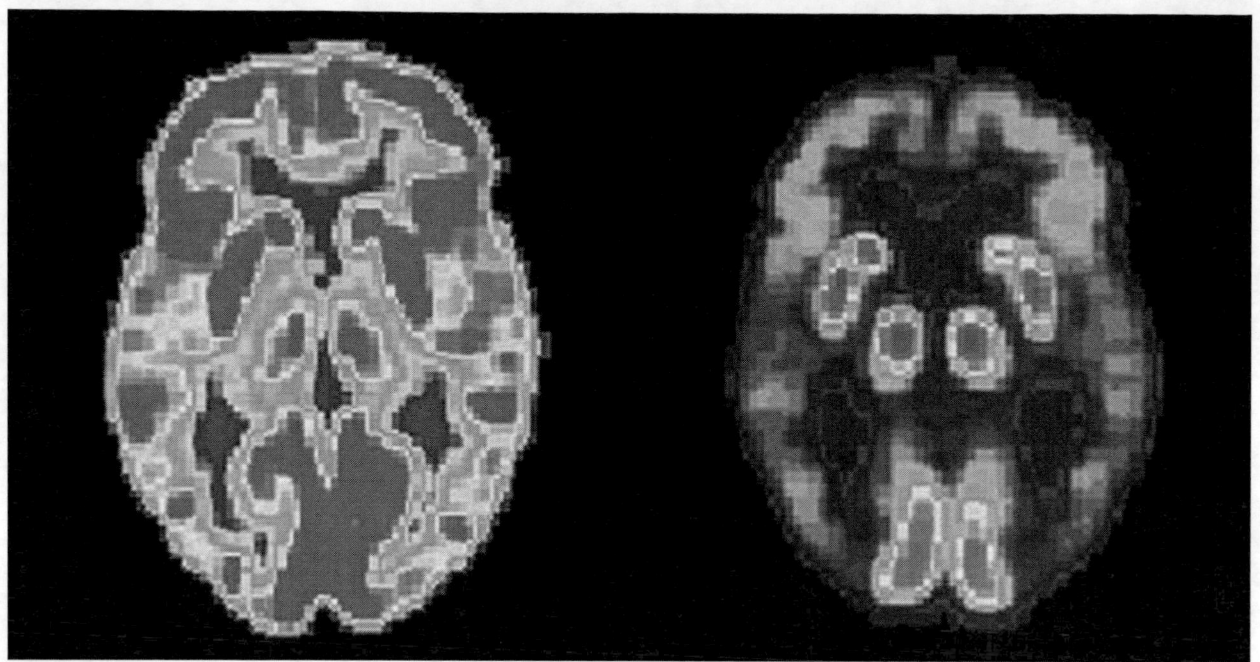

Figure 10.27 These brain images are produced using a radiopharmaceutical. The colors indicate relative metabolic or biochemical activity (red indicates high activity and blue indicates low activity). The figure on the left shows the normal brain of an individual and the figure on the right shows the brain of someone diagnosed with Alzheimer's disease. The brain image of the normal brain indicates much greater metabolic activity (a larger fraction of red and orange areas). (credit: modification of works by National Institutes of Health)

Table 10.2 lists some medical diagnostic uses of radiopharmaceuticals, including isotopes and typical activity (*A*) levels. One common diagnostic test uses iodine to image the thyroid, since iodine is concentrated in that organ. Another common nuclear diagnostic is the thallium scan for the cardiovascular system, which reveals blockages in the coronary arteries and examines heart activity. The salt TlCl can be used because it acts like NaCl and follows the blood. Note that **Table 10.2** lists many diagnostic uses for ^{99m}Tc, where "m" stands for a metastable state of the technetium nucleus. This isotope is used in many compounds to image the skeleton, heart, lungs, and kidneys. About 80% of all radiopharmaceuticals employ ^{99m}Tc because it produces a single, easily identified, 0.142-MeV γ ray and has a short 6.0-h half-life, which reduces radiation exposure.

Procedure, Isotope	Activity (mCi), where $1\,\text{mCi} = 3.7 \times 10^7\,\text{Bq}$	Procedure, Isotope	Activity (mCi), where $1\,\text{mCi} = 3.7 \times 10^7\,\text{Bq}$
Brain scan		*Thyroid scan*	
^{99m}Tc	7.5	^{131}I	0.05
^{15}O (PET)	50	^{123}I	0.07
Lung scan		*Liver scan*	
^{13}Xe	7.5	^{198}Au (colloid)	0.1
^{99m}Tc	2	^{99m}Tc (colloid)	2
Cardiovascular blood pool		*Bone scan*	

Table 10.2 Diagnostic Uses of Radiopharmaceuticals

Procedure, Isotope	Activity (mCi), where $1\ \text{mCi} = 3.7 \times 10^7\ \text{Bq}$	Procedure, Isotope	Activity (mCi), where $1\ \text{mCi} = 3.7 \times 10^7\ \text{Bq}$
^{131}I	0.2	^{85}Sr	0.1
$^{99\text{m}}\text{Tc}$	2	$^{99\text{m}}\text{Tc}$	10
Cardiovascular arterial flow		*Kidney scan*	
^{201}Tl	3	^{197}Hg	0.1
^{24}Na	7.5	$^{99\text{m}}\text{Tc}$	1.5

Table 10.2 Diagnostic Uses of Radiopharmaceuticals

The first radiation detectors produced two-dimensional images, like a photo taken from a camera. However, a circular array of detectors that can be rotated can be used to produce three-dimensional images. This technique is similar to that used in X-ray computed tomography (CT) scans. One application of this technique is called **single-photon-emission CT (SPECT)** (Figure 10.28). The spatial resolution of this technique is about 1 cm.

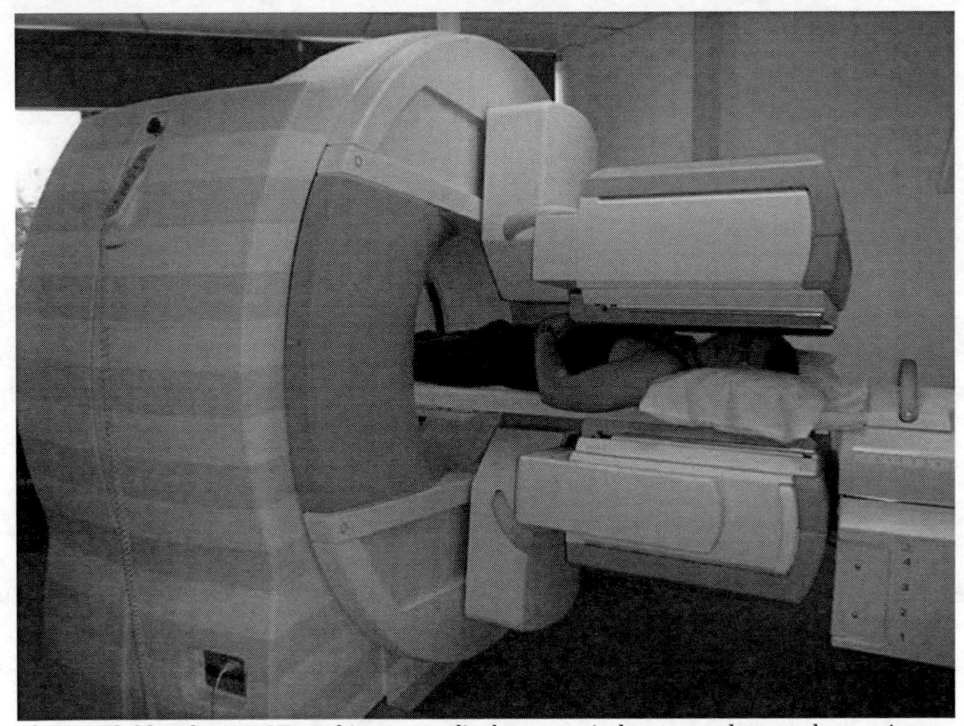

Figure 10.28 The SPECT machine uses radiopharmaceutical compounds to produce an image of the human body. The machine takes advantage of the physics of nuclear beat decays and electron-positron collisions. (credit: "Woldo"/Wikimedia Commons)

Improved image resolution is achieved by a technique known as **positron emission tomography (PET)**. This technique use radioisotopes that decay by β^+ radiation. When a positron encounters an electron, these particle annihilate to produce two gamma-ray photons. This reaction is represented by

$$e^+ + e^- \rightarrow 2\gamma.$$

These γ-ray photons have identical 0.511-MeV energies and move directly away from one another (Figure 10.29). This easily identified decay signature can be used to identify the location of the radioactive isotope. Examples of β^+-emitting isotopes used in PET include ^{11}C, ^{13}N, ^{15}O, and ^{18}F. The nuclei have the advantage of being able to function as tags for natural body compounds. Its resolution of 0.5 cm is better than that of SPECT.

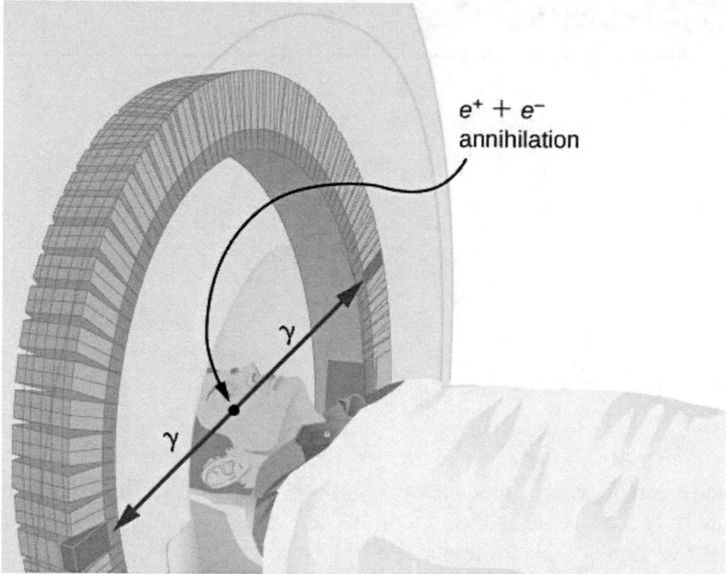

Figure 10.29 A PET system takes advantage of the two identical γ -ray photons produced by positron-electron annihilation. These γ rays are emitted in opposite directions, so that the line along which each pair is emitted is determined.

PET scans are especially useful to examine the brain's anatomy and function. For example, PET scans can be used to monitor the brain's use of oxygen and water, identify regions of decreased metabolism (linked to Alzheimer's disease), and locate different parts of the brain responsible for sight, speech, and fine motor activity

Is it a tumor? View an **animation (https://openstaxcollege.org/l/21simmagresimg)** of simplified magnetic resonance imaging (MRI) to see if you can tell. Your head is full of tiny radio transmitters (the nuclear spins of the hydrogen nuclei of your water molecules). In an MRI unit, these little radios can be made to broadcast their positions, giving a detailed picture of the inside of your head.

Biological Effects

Nuclear radiation can have both positive and negative effects on biological systems. However, it can also be used to treat and even cure cancer. How do we understand these effects? To answer this question, consider molecules within cells, particularly DNA molecules.

Cells have long, double-helical DNA molecules containing chemical codes that govern the function and processes of the cell. Nuclear radiation can alter the structural features of the DNA chain, leading to changes in the genetic code. In human cells, we can have as many as a million individual instances of damage to DNA per cell per day. DNA contains codes that check whether the DNA is damaged and can repair itself. This repair ability of DNA is vital for maintaining the integrity of the genetic code and for the normal functioning of the entire organism. It should be constantly active and needs to respond rapidly. The rate of DNA repair depends on various factors such as the type and age of the cell. If nuclear radiation damages the ability of the cell to repair DNA, the cell can

1. Retreat to an irreversible state of dormancy (known as senescence);
2. Commit suicide (known as programmed cell death); or
3. Progress into unregulated cell division, possibly leading to tumors and cancers.

Nuclear radiation can harm the human body is many other ways as well. For example, high doses of nuclear radiation can cause burns and even hair loss.

Biological effects of nuclear radiation are expressed by many different physical quantities and in many different units. A common unit to express the biological effects of nuclear radiation is the **rad** or **radiation dose unit**. One rad is equal to 1/100 of a joule of nuclear energy deposited per kilogram of tissue, written:

$$1 \text{ rad} = 0.01 \text{ J/kg}.$$

For example, if a 50.0-kg person is exposed to nuclear radiation over her entire body and she absorbs 1.00 J, then her whole-body radiation dose is

$$(1.00 \text{ J})/(50.0 \text{ kg}) = 0.0200 \text{ J/kg} = 2.00 \text{ rad}.$$

Nuclear radiation damages cells by ionizing atoms in the cells as they pass through the cells (Figure 10.30). The effects of ionizing radiation depend on the dose in rads, but also on the type of radiation (alpha, beta, gamma, or X-ray) and the type of tissue. For example, if the range of the radiation is small, as it is for α rays, then the ionization and the damage created is more concentrated and harder for the organism to repair. To account for such affects, we define the **relative biological effectiveness** (RBE). Sample RBE values for several types of ionizing nuclear radiation are given in Table 10.3.

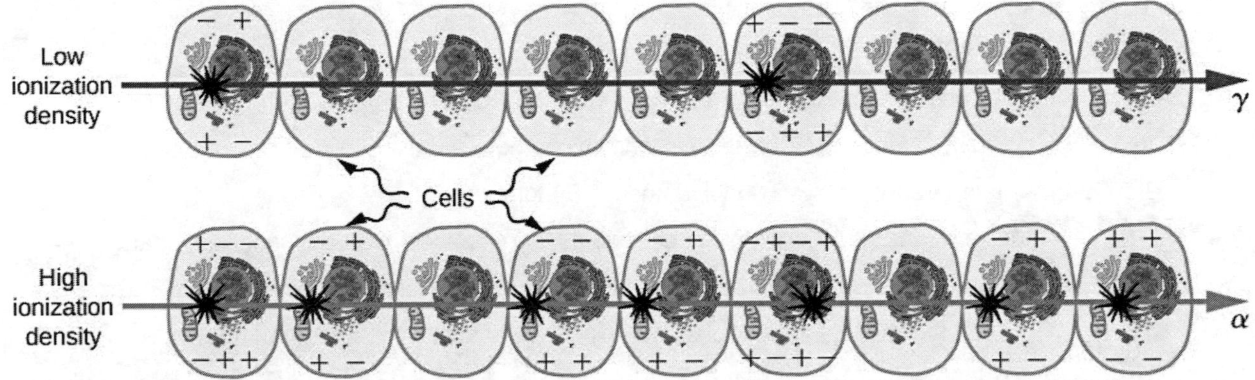

Figure 10.30 The image shows ionization created in cells by α and γ radiation. Because of its shorter range, the ionization and damage created by α rays is more concentrated and harder for the organism to repair. Thus, the RBE for α rays is greater than the RBE for γ rays, even though they create the same amount of ionization at the same energy.

Type and Energy of Radiation	RBE[1]
X-rays	1
γ rays	1
β rays greater than 32 keV	1
β rays less than 32 keV	1.7
Neutrons, thermal to slow (<20 keV)	2–5
Neutrons, fast (1–10 MeV)	10 (body), 32 (eyes)
Protons (1–10 MeV)	10 (body), 32 (eyes)
α rays from radioactive decay	10–20
Heavy ions from accelerators	10–20

Table 10.3 Relative Biological Effectiveness [1] Values approximate. Difficult to determine.

A dose unit more closely related to effects in biological tissue is called the **roentgen equivalent man (rem)** and is defined to be the dose (in rads) multiplied by the relative biological effectiveness (RBE). Thus, if a person had a whole-body dose of 2.00 rad of γ radiation, the dose in rem would be $(2.00 \text{ rad})(1) = 2.00$ rem for the whole body. If the person had a whole-body dose of 2.00 rad of α radiation, then the dose in rem would be $(2.00 \text{ rad})(20) = 40.0$ rem for the whole body. The α rays would have 20 times the effect on the person than the γ rays for the same deposited energy. The SI equivalent of the rem, and the more standard term, is the **sievert (Sv)** is

$$1 \text{ Sv} = 100 \text{ rem}.$$

The RBEs given in Table 10.3 are approximate but reflect an understanding of nuclear radiation and its interaction with living tissue. For example, neutrons are known to cause more damage than γ rays, although both are neutral and have large ranges, due to secondary radiation. Any dose less than 100 mSv (10 rem) is called a **low dose**, 0.1 Sv to 1 Sv (10 to 100 rem) is called a **moderate dose**, and anything greater than 1 Sv (100 rem) is called a **high dose**. It is difficult to determine if a person has been exposed to less than 10 mSv.

Biological effects of different levels of nuclear radiation on the human body are given in **Table 10.4**. The first clue that a person has been exposed to radiation is a change in blood count, which is not surprising since blood cells are the most rapidly reproducing cells in the body. At higher doses, nausea and hair loss are observed, which may be due to interference with cell reproduction. Cells in the lining of the digestive system also rapidly reproduce, and their destruction causes nausea. When the growth of hair cells slows, the hair follicles become thin and break off. High doses cause significant cell death in all systems, but the lowest doses that cause fatalities do so by weakening the immune system through the loss of white blood cells.

Dose in Sv[1]	Effect
0–0.10	No observable effect.
0.1–1	Slight to moderate decrease in white blood cell counts.
0.5	Temporary sterility; 0.35 for women, 0.50 for men.
1–2	Significant reduction in blood cell counts, brief nausea and vomiting. Rarely fatal.
2–5	Nausea, vomiting, hair loss, severe blood damage, hemorrhage, fatalities.
4.5	Lethal to 50% of the population within 32 days after exposure if not treated.
5–20	Worst effects due to malfunction of small intestine and blood systems. Limited survival.
>20	Fatal within hours due to collapse of central nervous system.

Table 10.4 Immediate Effects of Radiation (Adults, Whole-Body, Single Exposure) [1] Multiply by 100 to obtain dose in rem.

Sources of Radiation

Human are also exposed to many sources of nuclear radiation. A summary of average radiation doses for different sources by country is given in **Table 10.5**. Earth emits radiation due to the isotopes of uranium, thorium, and potassium. Radiation levels from these sources depend on location and can vary by a factor of 10. Fertilizers contain isotopes of potassium and uranium, which we digest in the food we eat. Fertilizers have more than 3000 Bq/kg radioactivity, compared to just 66 Bq/kg for Carbon-14.

Source	Dose (mSv/y)[1]			
	Australia	Germany	US	World
Natural radiation – external				
Cosmic rays	0.30	0.28	0.30	0.39
Soil, building materials	0.40	0.40	0.30	0.48
Radon gas	0.90	1.1	2.0	1.2
Natural radiation – internal				
${}^{40}\text{K}$, ${}^{14}\text{C}$, ${}^{226}\text{Ra}$	0.24	0.28	0.40	0.29
Artificial radiation				
Medical and dental	0.80	0.90	0.53	0.40
TOTAL	2.6	3.0	3.5	2.8

Table 10.5 Background Radiation Sources and Average Doses [1] Multiply by 100 to obtain does in mrem/y.

Medical visits are also a source of nuclear radiation. A sample of common nuclear radiation doses is given in **Table 10.6**.

These doses are generally low and can be lowered further with improved techniques and more sensitive detectors. With the possible exception of routine dental X-rays, medical use of nuclear radiation is used only when the risk-benefit is favorable. Chest X-rays give the lowest doses—about 0.1 mSv to the tissue affected, with less than 5% scattering into tissues that are not directly imaged. Other X-ray procedures range upward to about 10 mSv in a CT scan, and about 5 mSv (0.5 rem) per dental X-ray, again both only affecting the tissue imaged. Medical images with radiopharmaceuticals give doses ranging from 1 to 5 mSv, usually localized.

Procedure	Effective Dose (mSv)
Chest	0.02
Dental	0.01
Skull	0.07
Leg	0.02
Mammogram	0.40
Barium enema	7.0
Upper GI	3.0
CT head	2.0
CT abdomen	10.0

Table 10.6 Typical Doses Received During Diagnostic X-Ray Exams

Example 10.12

What Mass of ^{137}Cs Escaped Chernobyl?

The Chernobyl accident in Ukraine (formerly in the Soviet Union) exposed the surrounding population to a large amount of radiation through the decay of ^{137}Cs. The initial radioactivity level was approximately $A = 6.0\,\text{MCi}$. Calculate the total mass of ^{137}Cs involved in this accident.

Strategy

The total number of nuclei, N, can be determined from the known half-life and activity of ^{137}Cs (30.2 y). The mass can be calculated from N using the concept of a mole.

Solution

Solving the equation $A = \dfrac{0.693\,N}{t_{1/2}}$ for N gives

$$N = \frac{A\,t_{1/2}}{0.693}.$$

Entering the given values yields

$$N = \frac{(6.0\,\text{MCi})(30.2\,\text{y})}{0.693}.$$

To convert from curies to becquerels and years to seconds, we write

$$N = \frac{\left(6.0 \times 10^{6}\ \text{Ci}\right)\left(3.7 \times 10^{10}\ \text{Bq/Ci}\right)(30.2\ \text{y})\left(3.16 \times 10^{7}\ \text{s/y}\right)}{0.693} = 3.1 \times 10^{26}.$$

One mole of a nuclide ^{A}X has a mass of A grams, so that one mole of ^{137}Cs has a mass of 137 g. A mole has 6.02×10^{23} nuclei. Thus the mass of ^{137}Cs released was

$$m = \left(\frac{137\ \text{g}}{6.02 \times 10^{23}}\right)(3.1 \times 10^{26}) = 70 \times 10^{3}\ \text{g} = 70\ \text{kg}.$$

Significance

The mass of ^{137}Cs involved in the Chernobyl accident is a small material compared to the typical amount of fuel used in a nuclear reactor. However, approximately 250 people were admitted to local hospitals immediately after the accident, and diagnosed as suffering acute radiation syndrome. They received external radiation dosages between 1 and 16 Sv. Referring to biological effects in **Table 10.4**, these dosages are extremely hazardous. The eventual death toll is estimated to be around 4000 people, primarily due to radiation-induced cancer.

10.7 Check Your Understanding Radiation propagates in all directions from its source, much as electromagnetic radiation from a light bulb. Is *activity* concept more analogous to power, intensity, or brightness?

CHAPTER 10 REVIEW

KEY TERMS

activity magnitude of the decay rate for radioactive nuclides

alpha (α) rays one of the types of rays emitted from the nucleus of an atom as alpha particles

alpha decay radioactive nuclear decay associated with the emission of an alpha particle

antielectrons another term for positrons

antineutrino antiparticle of an electron's neutrino in β^- decay

atomic mass total mass of the protons, neutrons, and electrons in a single atom

atomic mass unit unit used to express the mass of an individual nucleus, where $1\text{u} = 1.66054 \times 10^{-27}$ kg

atomic nucleus tightly packed group of nucleons at the center of an atom

atomic number number of protons in a nucleus

becquerel (Bq) SI unit for the decay rate of a radioactive material, equal to 1 decay/second

beta (β) rays one of the types of rays emitted from the nucleus of an atom as beta particles

beta decay radioactive nuclear decay associated with the emission of a beta particle

binding energy (BE) energy needed to break a nucleus into its constituent protons and neutrons

binding energy per nucleon (BEN) energy need to remove a nucleon from a nucleus

breeder reactor reactor that is designed to make plutonium

carbon-14 dating method to determine the age of formerly living tissue using the ratio $^{14}\text{C}/^{12}\text{C}$

chart of the nuclides graph comprising stable and unstable nuclei

critical mass minimum mass required of a given nuclide in order for self-sustained fission to occur

criticality condition in which a chain reaction easily becomes self-sustaining

curie (Ci) unit of decay rate, or the activity of 1 g of ^{226}Ra, equal to 3.70×10^{10} Bq

daughter nucleus nucleus produced by the decay of a parent nucleus

decay process by which an individual atomic nucleus of an unstable atom loses mass and energy by emitting ionizing particles

decay constant quantity that is inversely proportional to the half-life and that is used in equation for number of nuclei as a function of time

decay series series of nuclear decays ending in a stable nucleus

fission splitting of a nucleus

gamma (γ) rays one of the types of rays emitted from the nucleus of an atom as gamma particles

gamma decay radioactive nuclear decay associated with the emission of gamma radiation

half-life time for half of the original nuclei to decay (or half of the original nuclei remain)

high dose dose of radiation greater than 1 Sv (100 rem)

isotopes nuclei having the same number of protons but different numbers of neutrons

lifetime average time that a nucleus exists before decaying

liquid drop model model of nucleus (only to understand some of its features) in which nucleons in a nucleus act like atoms in a drop

low dose dose of radiation less than 100 mSv (10 rem)

mass defect difference between the mass of a nucleus and the total mass of its constituent nucleons

mass number number of nucleons in a nucleus

moderate dose dose of radiation from 0.1 Sv to 1 Sv (10 to 100 rem)

neutrino subatomic elementary particle which has no net electric charge

neutron number number of neutrons in a nucleus

nuclear fusion process of combining lighter nuclei to make heavier nuclei

nuclear fusion reactor nuclear reactor that uses the fusion chain to produce energy

nucleons protons and neutrons found inside the nucleus of an atom

nucleosynthesis process of fusion by which all elements on Earth are believed to have been created

nuclide nucleus

parent nucleus original nucleus before decay

positron electron with positive charge

positron emission tomography (PET) tomography technique that uses β^+ emitters and detects the two annihilation γ rays, aiding in source localization

proton-proton chain combined reactions that fuse hydrogen nuclei to produce He nuclei

radiation dose unit (rad) ionizing energy deposited per kilogram of tissue

radioactive dating application of radioactive decay in which the age of a material is determined by the amount of radioactivity of a particular type that occurs

radioactive decay law describes the exponential decrease of parent nuclei in a radioactive sample

radioactive tags special drugs (radiopharmaceuticals) that allow doctors to track movement of other drugs in the body

radioactivity spontaneous emission of radiation from nuclei

radiopharmaceutical compound used for medical imaging

radius of a nucleus radius of a nucleus is defined as $r = r_0 A^{1/3}$

relative biological effectiveness (RBE) number that expresses the relative amount of damage that a fixed amount of ionizing radiation of a given type can inflict on biological tissues

roentgen equivalent man (rem) dose unit more closely related to effects in biological tissue

sievert (Sv) SI equivalent of the rem

single-photon-emission computed tomography (SPECT) tomography performed with γ-emitting radiopharmaceuticals

strong nuclear force force that binds nucleons together in the nucleus

transuranic element element that lies beyond uranium in the periodic table

KEY EQUATIONS

Atomic mass number	$A = Z + N$
Standard format for expressing an isotope	${}^{A}_{Z}\mathrm{X}$
Nuclear radius, where r_0 is the radius of a single proton	$r = r_0 A^{1/3}$
Mass defect	$\Delta m = Zm_p + (A - Z)m_n - m_{\text{nuc}}$

Binding energy	$E = (\Delta m)c^2$
Binding energy per nucleon	$BEN = \frac{E_b}{A}$
Radioactive decay rate	$-\frac{dN}{dt} = \lambda N$
Radioactive decay law	$N = N_0 e^{-\lambda t}$
Decay constant	$\lambda = \frac{0.693}{T_{1/2}}$
Lifetime of a substance	$\bar{T} = \frac{1}{\lambda}$
Activity of a radioactive substance	$A = A_0 e^{-\lambda t}$
Activity of a radioactive substance (linear form)	$\ln A = -\lambda t + \ln A_0$
Alpha decay	${}^{A}_{Z}\text{X} \rightarrow {}^{A-4}_{Z-2}\text{X} + {}^{4}_{2}\text{He}$
Beta decay	${}^{A}_{Z}\text{X} \rightarrow {}_{Z+1}{}^{A}\text{X} + {}_{-1}^{0}\text{e} + \bar{\nu}$
Positron emission	${}^{A}_{Z}\text{X} \rightarrow {}_{Z-1}{}^{A}\text{X} + {}_{+1}^{0}\text{e} + \nu$
Gamma decay	${}^{A}_{Z}\text{X}^* \rightarrow {}^{A}_{Z}\text{X} + \gamma$

SUMMARY

10.1 Properties of Nuclei

- The atomic nucleus is composed of protons and neutrons.
- The number of protons in the nucleus is given by the atomic number, *Z*. The number of neutrons in the nucleus is the neutron number, *N*. The number of nucleons is mass number, *A*.
- Atomic nuclei with the same atomic number, *Z*, but different neutron numbers, *N*, are isotopes of the same element.
- The atomic mass of an element is the weighted average of the masses of its isotopes.

10.2 Nuclear Binding Energy

- The mass defect of a nucleus is the difference between the total mass of a nucleus and the sum of the masses of all its constituent nucleons.
- The binding energy (BE) of a nucleus is equal to the amount of energy released in forming the nucleus, or the mass defect multiplied by the speed of light squared.
- A graph of binding energy per nucleon (BEN) versus atomic number *A* implies that nuclei divided or combined release an enormous amount of energy.
- The binding energy of a nucleon in a nucleus is analogous to the ionization energy of an electron in an atom.

10.3 Radioactive Decay

- In the decay of a radioactive substance, if the decay constant (λ) is large, the half-life is small, and vice versa.
- The radioactive decay law, $N = N_0 e^{-\lambda t}$, uses the properties of radioactive substances to estimate the age of a substance.
- Radioactive carbon has the same chemistry as stable carbon, so it mixes into the ecosphere and eventually becomes

part of every living organism. By comparing the abundance of ^{14}C in an artifact with the normal abundance in living tissue, it is possible to determine the artifact's age.

10.4 Nuclear Reactions

- The three types of nuclear radiation are alpha (α) rays, beta (β) rays, and gamma (γ) rays.
- We represent α decay symbolically by ${}^{A}_{Z}X \rightarrow {}^{A-4}_{Z-2}X + {}^{4}_{2}He$. There are two types of β decay: either an electron (β^-) or a positron (β^+) is emitted by a nucleus. γ decay is represented symbolically by ${}^{A}_{Z}X^* \rightarrow {}^{A}_{Z}X + \gamma$.
- When a heavy nucleus decays to a lighter one, the lighter daughter nucleus can become the parent nucleus for the next decay, and so on, producing a decay series.

10.5 Fission

- Nuclear fission is a process in which the sum of the masses of the product nuclei are less than the masses of the reactants.
- Energy changes in a nuclear fission reaction can be understood in terms of the binding energy per nucleon curve.
- The production of new or different isotopes by nuclear transformation is called breeding, and reactors designed for this purpose are called breeder reactors.

10.6 Nuclear Fusion

- Nuclear fusion is a reaction in which two nuclei are combined to form a larger nucleus; energy is released when light nuclei are fused to form medium-mass nuclei.
- The amount of energy released by a fusion reaction is known as the Q value.
- Nuclear fusion explains the reaction between deuterium and tritium that produces a fusion (or hydrogen) bomb; fusion also explains the production of energy in the Sun, the process of nucleosynthesis, and the creation of the heavy elements.

10.7 Medical Applications and Biological Effects of Nuclear Radiation

- Nuclear technology is used in medicine to locate and study diseased tissue using special drugs called radiopharmaceuticals. Radioactive tags are used to identify cancer cells in the bones, brain tumors, and Alzheimer's disease, and to monitor the function of body organs, such as blood flow, heart muscle activity, and iodine uptake in the thyroid gland.
- The biological effects of ionizing radiation are due to two effects it has on cells: interference with cell reproduction and destruction of cell function.
- Common sources of radiation include that emitted by Earth due to the isotopes of uranium, thorium, and potassium; natural radiation from cosmic rays, soils, and building materials, and artificial sources from medical and dental diagnostic tests.
- Biological effects of nuclear radiation are expressed by many different physical quantities and in many different units, including the rad or radiation dose unit.

CONCEPTUAL QUESTIONS

10.1 Properties of Nuclei

1. Define and make clear distinctions between the terms neutron, nucleon, nucleus, and nuclide.

2. What are isotopes? Why do isotopes of the same atom share the same chemical properties?

10.2 Nuclear Binding Energy

3. Explain why a bound system should have less mass than its components. Why is this not observed traditionally, say, for a building made of bricks?

4. Why is the number of neutrons greater than the number of protons in stable nuclei that have an A greater than about 40? Why is this effect more pronounced for the heaviest nuclei?

5. To obtain the most precise value of the binding energy per nucleon, it is important to take into account forces between nucleons at the surface of the nucleus. Will surface effects increase or decrease estimates of BEN?

10.3 Radioactive Decay

6. How is the initial activity rate of a radioactive substance related to its half-life?

7. For the carbon dating described in this chapter, what important assumption is made about the time variation in the intensity of cosmic rays?

10.4 Nuclear Reactions

8. What is the key difference and the key similarity between beta (β^-) decay and alpha decay?

9. What is the difference between γ rays and characteristic X-rays and visible light?

10. What characteristics of radioactivity show it to be nuclear in origin and not atomic?

11. Consider Figure 10.12. If the magnetic field is replaced by an electric field pointed in toward the page, in which directions will the α -, β^+ -, and γ rays bend?

12. Why is Earth's core molten?

10.5 Fission

13. Should an atomic bomb really be called *nuclear* bomb?

14. Why does a chain reaction occur during a fission reaction?

15. In what way is an atomic nucleus like a liquid drop?

10.6 Nuclear Fusion

16. Explain the difference between nuclear fission and nuclear fusion.

17. Why does the fusion of light nuclei into heavier nuclei release energy?

10.7 Medical Applications and Biological Effects of Nuclear Radiation

18. Why is a PET scan more accurate than a SPECT scan?

19. Isotopes that emit α radiation are relatively safe outside the body and exceptionally hazardous inside. Explain why.

20. Ionizing radiation can impair the ability of a cell to repair DNA. What are the three ways the cell can respond?

PROBLEMS

10.1 Properties of Nuclei

21. Find the atomic numbers, mass numbers, and neutron numbers for (a) $^{58}_{29}\text{Cu}$, (b) $^{24}_{11}\text{Na}$, (c) $^{210}_{84}\text{Po}$, (d) $^{45}_{20}\text{Ca}$, and (e) $^{206}_{82}\text{Pb}$.

22. Silver has two stable isotopes. The nucleus, $^{107}_{47}\text{Ag}$, has atomic mass 106.905095 g/mol with an abundance of 51.83%; whereas $^{109}_{47}\text{Ag}$ has atomic mass 108.904754 g/mol with an abundance of 48.17%. Find the atomic mass of the element silver.

23. The mass (*M*) and the radius (*r*) of a nucleus can be expressed in terms of the mass number, *A*. (a) Show that the density of a nucleus is independent of *A*. (b) Calculate the density of a gold (Au) nucleus. Compare your answer to that for iron (Fe).

24. A particle has a mass equal to 10 u. If this mass is converted completely into energy, how much energy is released? Express your answer in mega-electron volts (MeV). (Recall that $1\text{ eV} = 1.6 \times 10^{-19}\text{ J}$.)

25. Find the length of a side of a cube having a mass of 1.0 kg and the density of nuclear matter.

26. The detail that you can observe using a probe is limited by its wavelength. Calculate the energy of a particle that has a wavelength of $1 \times 10^{-16}\text{ m}$, small enough to detect details about one-tenth the size of a nucleon.

10.2 Nuclear Binding Energy

27. How much energy would be released if six hydrogen

atoms and six neutrons were combined to form ${}^{12}_{6}C$?

28. Find the mass defect and the binding energy for the helium-4 nucleus.

29. ${}^{56}Fe$ is among the most tightly bound of all nuclides. It makes up more than 90% of natural iron. Note that ${}^{56}Fe$ has even numbers of protons and neutrons. Calculate the binding energy per nucleon for ${}^{56}Fe$ and compare it with the approximate value obtained from the graph in **Figure 10.7**.

30. ${}^{209}Bi$ is the heaviest stable nuclide, and its BEN is low compared with medium-mass nuclides. Calculate BEN for this nucleus and compare it with the approximate value obtained from the graph in **Figure 10.7**.

31. (a) Calculate BEN for ${}^{235}U$, the rarer of the two most common uranium isotopes; (b) Calculate BEN for ${}^{238}U$. (Most of uranium is ${}^{238}U$.)

32. The fact that BEN peaks at roughly $A = 60$ implies that the *range* of the strong nuclear force is about the diameter of this nucleus.

(a) Calculate the diameter of $A = 60$ nucleus.

(b) Compare BEN for ${}^{58}Ni$ and ${}^{90}Sr$. The first is one of the most tightly bound nuclides, whereas the second is larger and less tightly bound.

10.3 Radioactive Decay

33. A sample of radioactive material is obtained from a very old rock. A plot ln*A* verses *t* yields a slope value of $-10^{-9}\,s^{-1}$ (see **Figure 10.10**(b)). What is the half-life of this material?

34. Show that: $\bar{T} = \frac{1}{\lambda}$.

35. The half-life of strontium-91, ${}^{91}_{38}Sr$ is 9.70 h. Find (a) its decay constant and (b) for an initial 1.00-g sample, the activity after 15 hours.

36. A sample of pure carbon-14 $(T_{1/2} = 5730\,y)$ has an activity of $1.0\,\mu Ci$. What is the mass of the sample?

37. A radioactive sample initially contains 2.40×10^{-2} mol of a radioactive material whose half-life is 6.00 h. How many moles of the radioactive material remain after 6.00 h? After 12.0 h? After 36.0 h?

38. An old campfire is uncovered during an archaeological dig. Its charcoal is found to contain less than 1/1000 the normal amount of ${}^{14}C$. Estimate the minimum age of the charcoal, noting that $2^{10} = 1024$.

39. Calculate the activity R, in curies of 1.00 g of ${}^{226}Ra$. (b) Explain why your answer is not exactly 1.00 Ci, given that the curie was originally supposed to be exactly the activity of a gram of radium.

40. Natural uranium consists of ${}^{235}U$ (percent abundance $= 0.7200\%$, $\lambda = 3.12 \times 10^{-17}/s$) and ${}^{238}U$ (percent abundance $= 99.27\%$, $\lambda = 4.92 \times 10^{-18}/s$). What were the values for percent abundance of ${}^{235}U$ and ${}^{238}U$ when Earth formed 4.5×10^{9} years ago?

41. World War II aircraft had instruments with glowing radium-painted dials. The activity of one such instrument was 1.0×10^{5} Bq when new. (a) What mass of ${}^{226}Ra$ was present? (b) After some years, the phosphors on the dials deteriorated chemically, but the radium did not escape. What is the activity of this instrument 57.0 years after it was made?

42. The ${}^{210}Po$ source used in a physics laboratory is labeled as having an activity of $1.0\,\mu Ci$ on the date it was prepared. A student measures the radioactivity of this source with a Geiger counter and observes 1500 counts per minute. She notices that the source was prepared 120 days before her lab. What fraction of the decays is she observing with her apparatus?

43. Armor-piercing shells with depleted uranium cores are fired by aircraft at tanks. (The high density of the uranium makes them effective.) The uranium is called depleted because it has had its ${}^{235}U$ removed for reactor use and is nearly pure ${}^{238}U$. Depleted uranium has been erroneously called nonradioactive. To demonstrate that this is wrong: (a) Calculate the activity of 60.0 g of pure ${}^{238}U$. (b) Calculate the activity of 60.0 g of natural uranium, neglecting the ${}^{234}U$ and all daughter nuclides.

10.4 Nuclear Reactions

44. ^{249}Cf undergoes alpha decay. (a) Write the reaction equation. (b) Find the energy released in the decay.

45. (a) Calculate the energy released in the α decay of ^{238}U. (b) What fraction of the mass of a single ^{238}U is destroyed in the decay? The mass of ^{234}Th is 234.043593 u. (c) Although the fractional mass loss is large for a single nucleus, it is difficult to observe for an entire macroscopic sample of uranium. Why is this?

46. The β^- particles emitted in the decay of ^3H (tritium) interact with matter to create light in a glow-in-the-dark exit sign. At the time of manufacture, such a sign contains 15.0 Ci of ^3H. (a) What is the mass of the tritium? (b) What is its activity 5.00 y after manufacture?

47. (a) Write the complete β^- decay equation for ^{90}Sr, a major waste product of nuclear reactors. (b) Find the energy released in the decay.

48. Write a nuclear β^- decay reaction that produces the ^{90}Y nucleus. (*Hint:* The parent nuclide is a major waste product of reactors and has chemistry similar to calcium, so that it is concentrated in bones if ingested.)

49. Write the complete decay equation in the complete $^A_Z\text{X}_N$ notation for the beta (β^-) decay of ^3H (tritium), a manufactured isotope of hydrogen used in some digital watch displays, and manufactured primarily for use in hydrogen bombs.

50. If a 1.50-cm-thick piece of lead can absorb 90.0% of the rays from a radioactive source, how many centimeters of lead are needed to absorb all but 0.100% of the rays?

51. An electron can interact with a nucleus through the beta-decay process:

$^A_Z\text{X} + e^- \rightarrow Y + \nu_e$.

(a) Write the complete reaction equation for electron capture by ^7Be.

(b) Calculate the energy released.

52. (a) Write the complete reaction equation for electron capture by ^{15}O.

(b) Calculate the energy released.

53. A rare decay mode has been observed in which ^{222}Ra emits a ^{14}C nucleus. (a) The decay equation is $^{222}\text{Ra} \rightarrow {}^A\text{X} + {}^{14}\text{C}$. Identify the nuclide ^AX. (b) Find the energy emitted in the decay. The mass of ^{222}Ra is 222.015353 u.

10.5 Fission

54. A large power reactor that has been in operation for some months is turned off, but residual activity in the core still produces 150 MW of power. If the average energy per decay of the fission products is 1.00 MeV, what is the core activity?

55. (a) Calculate the energy released in the neutron-induced fission $n + {}^{238}\text{U} \rightarrow {}^{96}\text{Sr} + {}^{140}\text{Xe} + 3n$, given $m(^{96}\text{Sr}) = 95.921750\ \text{u}$ and $m(^{140}\text{Xe}) = 139.92164$.

(b) This result is about 6 MeV greater than the result for spontaneous fission. Why?

(c) Confirm that the total number of nucleons and total charge are conserved in this reaction.

56. (a) Calculate the energy released in the neutron-induced fission reaction $n + {}^{235}\text{U} \rightarrow {}^{92}\text{Kr} + {}^{142}\text{Ba} + 2n$, given $m(^{92}\text{Kr}) = 91.926269\ \text{u}$ and $m(^{142}\text{Ba}) = 141.916361\ \text{u}$. (b) Confirm that the total number of nucleons and total charge are conserved in this reaction.

57. The electrical power output of a large nuclear reactor facility is 900 MW. It has a 35.0% efficiency in converting nuclear power to electrical power.

(a) What is the thermal nuclear power output in megawatts?

(b) How many ^{235}U nuclei fission each second, assuming the average fission produces 200 MeV?

(c) What mass of ^{235}U is fissioned in 1 year of full-power operation?

58. Find the total energy released if 1.00 kg of $^{235}_{92}\text{U}$ were to undergo fission.

10.6 Nuclear Fusion

59. Verify that the total number of nucleons, and total charge are conserved for each of the following fusion reactions in the proton-proton chain.

(i) $^1\text{H} + {}^1\text{H} \to {}^2\text{H} + e^+ + \nu_e$,

(ii) $^1\text{H} + {}^2\text{H} \to {}^3\text{He} + \gamma$, and (iii) $^3\text{He} + {}^3\text{He} \to {}^4\text{He} + {}^1\text{H} + {}^1\text{H}$.

(List the value of each of the conserved quantities before and after each of the reactions.)

60. Calculate the energy output in each of the fusion reactions in the proton-proton chain, and verify the values determined in the preceding problem.

61. Show that the total energy released in the proton-proton chain is 26.7 MeV, considering the overall effect in $^1\text{H} + {}^1\text{H} \to {}^2\text{H} + e^+ + \nu_e$, $^1\text{H} + {}^2\text{H} \to {}^3\text{He} + \gamma$, and $^3\text{He} + {}^3\text{He} \to {}^4\text{He} + {}^1\text{H} + {}^1\text{H}$. Be sure to include the annihilation energy.

62. Two fusion reactions mentioned in the text are $n + {}^3\text{He} \to {}^4\text{He} + \gamma$ and $n + {}^1\text{H} \to {}^2\text{H} + \gamma$. Both reactions release energy, but the second also creates more fuel. Confirm that the energies produced in the reactions are 20.58 and 2.22 MeV, respectively. Comment on which product nuclide is most tightly bound, ^4He or ^2H.

63. The power output of the Sun is $4 \times 10^{26}\,\text{W}$. (a) If 90% of this energy is supplied by the proton-proton chain, how many protons are consumed per second? (b) How many neutrinos per second should there be per square meter at the surface of Earth from this process?

64. Another set of reactions that fuses hydrogen into helium in the Sun and especially in hotter stars is called the CNO cycle:

$$^{12}\text{C} + {}^1\text{H} \to {}^{13}\text{N} + \gamma$$

$$^{13}\text{N} \to {}^{13}\text{C} + e^+ + \nu_e$$

$$^{13}\text{C} + {}^1\text{H} \to {}^{14}\text{N} + \gamma$$

$$^{14}\text{N} + {}^1\text{H} \to {}^{15}\text{O} + \gamma$$

$$^{15}\text{O} \to {}^{15}\text{N} + e^+ + \nu_e$$

$$^{15}\text{N} + {}^1\text{H} \to {}^{12}\text{C} + {}^4\text{He}$$

This process is a “cycle” because ^{12}C appears at the beginning and end of these reactions. Write down the overall effect of this cycle (as done for the proton-proton chain in $2e^- + 4{}^1\text{H} \to {}^4\text{He} + 2\nu_e + 6\gamma$). Assume that the positrons annihilate electrons to form more γ rays.

65. (a) Calculate the energy released by the fusion of a 1.00-kg mixture of deuterium and tritium, which produces helium. There are equal numbers of deuterium and tritium nuclei in the mixture.

(b) If this process takes place continuously over a period of a year, what is the average power output?

10.7 Medical Applications and Biological Effects of Nuclear Radiation

66. What is the dose in mSv for: (a) a 0.1-Gy X-ray? (b) 2.5 mGy of neutron exposure to the eye? (c) 1.5m Gy of α exposure?

67. Find the radiation dose in Gy for: (a) A 10-mSv fluoroscopic X-ray series. (b) 50 mSv of skin exposure by an α emitter. (c) 160 mSv of β^- and γ rays from the ^{40}K in your body.

68. Find the mass of ^{239}Pu that has an activity of $1.00\,\mu\text{Ci}$.

69. In the 1980s, the term picowave was used to describe food irradiation in order to overcome public resistance by playing on the well-known safety of microwave radiation. Find the energy in MeV of a photon having a wavelength of a picometer.

70. What is the dose in Sv in a cancer treatment that exposes the patient to 200 Gy of γ rays?

71. One half the γ rays from ^{99m}Tc are absorbed by a 0.170-mm-thick lead shielding. Half of the γ rays that pass through the first layer of lead are absorbed in a second layer of equal thickness. What thickness of lead will absorb all but one in 1000 of these γ rays?

72. How many Gy of exposure is needed to give a cancerous tumor a dose of 40 Sv if it is exposed to α activity?

73. A plumber at a nuclear power plant receives a whole-body dose of 30 mSv in 15 minutes while repairing a crucial valve. Find the radiation-induced yearly risk of death from cancer and the chance of genetic defect from this maximum allowable exposure.

74. Calculate the dose in rem/y for the lungs of a weapons plant employee who inhales and retains an activity of $1.00\mu\text{Ci}$ ^{239}Pu in an accident. The mass of affected lung tissue is 2.00 kg and the plutonium decays by emission of a

5.23-MeV α particle. Assume a RBE value of 20.

ADDITIONAL PROBLEMS

75. The wiki-phony site states that the atomic mass of chlorine is 40 g/mol. Check this result. *Hint:* The two, most common stable isotopes of chlorine are: ${}^{35}_{17}\text{Cl}$ and ${}^{37}_{17}\text{Cl}$. (The abundance of Cl-35 is 75.8%, and the abundance of Cl-37 is 24.2%.)

76. A particle physicist discovers a neutral particle with a mass of 2.02733 u that he assumes is two neutrons bound together.

(a) Find the binding energy.

(b) What is unreasonable about this result?

77. A nuclear physicist finds $1.0\,\mu g$ of ${}^{236}\text{U}$ in a piece of uranium ore ($T_{1/2} = 2.348 \times 10^7\,\text{y}$). (a) Use the decay law to determine how much ${}^{236}\text{U}$ would had to have been on Earth when it formed $4.543 \times 10^9\,\text{y}$ ago for $1.0\,\mu g$ to be left today. (b) What is unreasonable about this result? (c) How is this unreasonable result resolved?

78. A group of scientists use carbon dating to date a piece of wood to be 3 billion years old. Why doesn't this make sense?

79. According to your lab partner, a 2.00-cm-thick sodium-iodide crystal absorbs all but 10% of rays from a radioactive source and a 4.00-cm piece of the same material absorbs all but 5%? Is this result reasonable?

80. In the science section of the newspaper, an article reports the efforts of a group of scientists to create a new nuclear reactor based on the fission of iron (Fe). Is this a good idea?

81. The ceramic glaze on a red-orange "Fiestaware" plate is U_2O_3 and contains 50.0 grams of ${}^{238}\text{U}$, but very little ${}^{235}\text{U}$. (a) What is the activity of the plate? (b) Calculate the total energy that will be released by the ${}^{238}\text{U}$ decay. (c) If energy is worth 12.0 cents per $\text{kW} \cdot \text{h}$, what is the monetary value of the energy emitted? (These brightly-colored ceramic plates went out of production some 30 years ago, but are still available as collectibles.)

82. Large amounts of depleted uranium $\left({}^{238}\text{U}\right)$ are available as a by-product of uranium processing for reactor fuel and weapons. Uranium is very dense and makes good counter weights for aircraft. Suppose you have a 4000-kg block of ${}^{238}\text{U}$. (a) Find its activity. (b) How many calories per day are generated by thermalization of the decay energy? (c) Do you think you could detect this as heat? Explain.

83. A piece of wood from an ancient Egyptian tomb is tested for its carbon-14 activity. It is found to have an activity per gram of carbon of $A = 10\,\text{decay/min} \cdot \text{g}$. What is the age of the wood?

CHALLENGE PROBLEMS

84. This problem demonstrates that the binding energy of the electron in the ground state of a hydrogen atom is much smaller than the rest mass energies of the proton and electron.

(a) Calculate the mass equivalent in u of the 13.6-eV binding energy of an electron in a hydrogen atom, and compare this with the known mass of the hydrogen atom.

(b) Subtract the known mass of the proton from the known mass of the hydrogen atom.

(c) Take the ratio of the binding energy of the electron (13.6 eV) to the energy equivalent of the electron's mass (0.511 MeV).

(d) Discuss how your answers confirm the stated purpose of this problem.

85. The *Galileo* space probe was launched on its long journey past Venus and Earth in 1989, with an ultimate goal of Jupiter. Its power source is 11.0 kg of ${}^{238}\text{Pu}$, a by-product of nuclear weapons plutonium production. Electrical energy is generated thermoelectrically from the heat produced when the 5.59-MeV α particles emitted in each decay crash to a halt inside the plutonium and its shielding. The half-life of ${}^{238}\text{Pu}$ is 87.7 years.

(a) What was the original activity of the ${}^{238}\text{Pu}$ in becquerels?

(b) What power was emitted in kilowatts?

(c) What power was emitted 12.0 y after launch? You may neglect any extra energy from daughter nuclides and any losses from escaping γ rays.

86. Find the energy emitted in the β^- decay of ^{60}Co.

87. Engineers are frequently called on to inspect and, if necessary, repair equipment in nuclear power plants. Suppose that the city lights go out. After inspecting the nuclear reactor, you find a leaky pipe that leads from the steam generator to turbine chamber. (a) How do the pressure readings for the turbine chamber and steam condenser compare? (b) Why is the nuclear reactor *not* generating electricity?

88. If two nuclei are to fuse in a nuclear reaction, they must be moving fast enough so that the repulsive Coulomb force between them does not prevent them for getting within $R \approx 10^{-14}\,\text{m}$ of one another. At this distance or nearer, the attractive nuclear force can overcome the Coulomb force, and the nuclei are able to fuse.

(a) Find a simple formula that can be used to estimate the minimum kinetic energy the nuclei must have if they are to fuse. To keep the calculation simple, assume the two nuclei are identical and moving toward one another with the same speed *v*. (b) Use this minimum kinetic energy to estimate the minimum temperature a gas of the nuclei must have before a significant number of them will undergo fusion. Calculate this minimum temperature first for hydrogen and then for helium. (*Hint:* For fusion to occur, the minimum kinetic energy when the nuclei are far apart must be equal to the Coulomb potential energy when they are a distance *R* apart.)

89. For the reaction, $n + {}^{3}\text{He} \rightarrow {}^{4}\text{He} + \gamma$, find the amount of energy transfers to ^{4}He and γ (on the right side of the equation). Assume the reactants are initially at rest. (*Hint:* Use conservation of momentum principle.)

90. Engineers are frequently called on to inspect and, if necessary, repair equipment in medical hospitals. Suppose that the PET system malfunctions. After inspecting the unit, you suspect that one of the PET photon detectors is misaligned. To test your theory you position one detector at the location $(r, \theta, \varphi) = (1.5, 45, 30)$ relative to a radioactive test sample at the center of the patient bed. (a) If the second photon detector is properly aligned where should it be located? (b) What energy reading is expected?

11 | PARTICLE PHYSICS AND COSMOLOGY

Figure 11.1 The Large Hadron Collider (LHC) is located over 150 meters (500 feet) underground on the border of Switzerland and France near Geneva, Switzerland. The LHC is the most powerful machine ever developed to test our understanding of elementary particle interactions. Shown here is the ATLAS detector, which helps identify new particles formed in collisions. (credit: modification of work by Maximilien Brice, CERN)

Chapter Outline

Introduction

At the very beginning of this text we discussed the wide range of scales that physics encompasses, from the very smallest particles to the largest scale possible—the universe itself. In this final chapter we examine some of the frontiers of research at these extreme scales. Particle physics deals with the most basic building blocks of matter and the forces that hold them together. Cosmology is the study of the stars, galaxies, and galactic structures that populate our universe, as well as their past history and future evolution.

These two areas of physics are not as disconnected as you might think. The study of elementary particles requires enormous energies to produce isolated particles, involving some of the largest machines humans have ever built. But such high energies were present in the earliest stages of the universe and the universe we see around us today was shaped in part by the nature and interactions of the elementary particles created then. Bear in mind that particle physics and cosmology are both areas of intense current research, subject to much speculation on the part of physicists (as well science-fiction writers). In this chapter we try to emphasize what is known on the basis of deductions from observational evidence, and identify ideas that are conjectured but still unproven.

11.1 | Introduction to Particle Physics

Learning Objectives

By the end of this section, you will be able to:

- Describe the four fundamental forces and what particles participate in them
- Identify and describe fermions and bosons
- Identify and describe the quark and lepton families
- Distinguish between particles and antiparticles, and describe their interactions

Elementary particle physics is the study of fundamental particles and their interactions in nature. Those who study elementary particle physics—the particle physicists—differ from other physicists in the scale of the systems that they study. A particle physicist is not content to study the microscopic world of cells, molecules, atoms, or even atomic nuclei. They are interested in physical processes that occur at scales even smaller than atomic nuclei. At the same time, they engage the most profound mysteries in nature: How did the universe begin? What explains the pattern of masses in the universe? Why is there more matter than antimatter in the universe? Why are energy and momentum conserved? How will the universe evolve?

Four Fundamental Forces

An important step to answering these questions is to understand particles and their interactions. Particle interactions are expressed in terms of four **fundamental forces**. In order of decreasing strength, these forces are the **strong nuclear force**, the electromagnetic force, the **weak nuclear force**, and the gravitational force.

1. **Strong nuclear force.** The strong nuclear force is a very strong attractive force that acts only over very short distances (about 10^{-15} m). The strong nuclear force is responsible for binding protons and neutrons together in atomic nuclei. Not all particles participate in the strong nuclear force; for instance, electrons and neutrinos are not affected by it. As the name suggests, this force is much stronger than the other forces.
2. **Electromagnetic force.** The electromagnetic force can act over very large distances (it has an infinite range) but is only 1/100 the strength of the strong nuclear force. Particles that interact through this force are said to have "charge." In the classical theory of static electricity (Coulomb's law), the electric force varies as the product of the charges of the interacting particles, and as the inverse square of the distances between them. In contrast to the strong force, the electromagnetic force can be attractive or repulsive (opposite charges attract and like charges repel). The magnetic force depends in a more complicated way on the charges and their motions. The unification of the electric and magnetic force into a single electromagnetic force (an achievement of James Clerk Maxwell) stands as one of the greatest intellectual achievements of the nineteenth century. This force is central to scientific models of atomic structure and molecular bonding.
3. **Weak nuclear force.** The weak nuclear force acts over very short distances $\left(10^{-15}\text{ m}\right)$ and, as its name suggest, is very weak. It is roughly 10^{-6} the strength of the strong nuclear force. This force is manifested most notably in decays of elementary particles and neutrino interactions. For example, the neutron can decay to a proton, electron, and electron neutrino through the weak force. The weak force is vitally important because it is essential for understanding stellar nucleosynthesis—the process that creates new atomic nuclei in the cores of stars.
4. **Gravitational force.** Like the electromagnetic force, the gravitational force can act over infinitely large distances; however, it is only 10^{-38} as strong as the strong nuclear force. In Newton's classical theory of gravity, the force of gravity varies as the product of the masses of the interacting particles and as the inverse square of the distance between them. This force is an attractive force that acts between all particles with mass. In modern theories of gravity, this force behavior is considered a special case for low-energy macroscopic interactions. Compared with the other forces of nature, gravity is by far the weakest.

The fundamental forces may not be truly "fundamental" but may actually be different aspects of the same force. Just as the electric and magnetic forces were unified into an electromagnetic force, physicists in the 1970s unified the electromagnetic force with the weak nuclear force into an **electroweak force**. Any scientific theory that attempts to unify the electroweak force and strong nuclear force is called a **grand unified theory**, and any theory that attempts to unify all four forces is called a **theory of everything**. We will return to the concept of unification later in this chapter.

Classifications of Elementary Particles

A large number of subatomic particles exist in nature. These particles can be classified in two ways: the property of spin and participation in the four fundamental forces. Recall that the spin of a particle is analogous to the rotation of a macroscopic object about its own axis. These types of classification are described separately below.

Classification by spin

Particles of matter can be divided into **fermions** and **bosons**. Fermions have half-integral spin $\left(\frac{1}{2}\hbar,\ \frac{3}{2}\hbar,\ \ldots\right)$ and bosons have integral spin $(0\hbar,\ 1\hbar,\ 2\hbar,\ \ldots)$. Familiar examples of fermions are electrons, protons, and neutrons. A familiar example of a boson is a photon. Fermions and bosons behave very differently in groups. For example, when electrons are confined to a small region of space, Pauli's exclusion principle states that no two electrons can occupy the same quantum-mechanical state. However, when photons are confined to a small region of space, there is no such limitation.

The behavior of fermions and bosons in groups can be understood in terms of the property of indistinguishability. Particles are said to be "indistinguishable" if they are identical to one another. For example, electrons are indistinguishable because every electron in the universe has exactly the same mass and spin as all other electrons—"when you've seen one electron, you've seen them all." If you switch two indistinguishable particles in the same small region of space, the square of the wave function that describes this system and can be measured $\left(|\psi|^2\right)$ is unchanged. If this were not the case, we could tell whether or not the particles had been switched and the particle would not be truly indistinguishable. Fermions and bosons differ by whether the sign of the wave function (ψ)— not directly observable—flips:

$$\psi \rightarrow -\psi \text{ (indistinguishable fermions)},$$
$$\psi \rightarrow +\psi \text{ (indistinguishable bosons)}.$$

Fermions are said to be "antisymmetric on exchange" and bosons are "symmetric on exchange." Pauli's exclusion principle is a consequence of **exchange symmetry** of fermions—a connection developed in a more advanced course in modern physics. The electronic structure of atoms is predicated on Pauli's exclusion principle and is therefore directly related to the indistinguishability of electrons.

Classification by force interactions

Fermions can be further divided into **quarks** and **leptons**. The primary difference between these two types of particles is that quarks interact via the strong force and leptons do not. Quarks and leptons (as well as bosons to be discussed later) are organized in **Figure 11.2**. The upper two rows (first three columns in purple) contain six quarks. These quarks are arranged into two particle families: up, charm, and top (u, c, t), and down, strange, and bottom (d, s, b). Members of the same particle family share the same properties but differ in mass (given in MeV/c^2). For example, the mass of the top quark is much greater than the charm quark, and the mass of the charm quark is much greater than the up quark. All quarks interact with one another through the strong nuclear force.

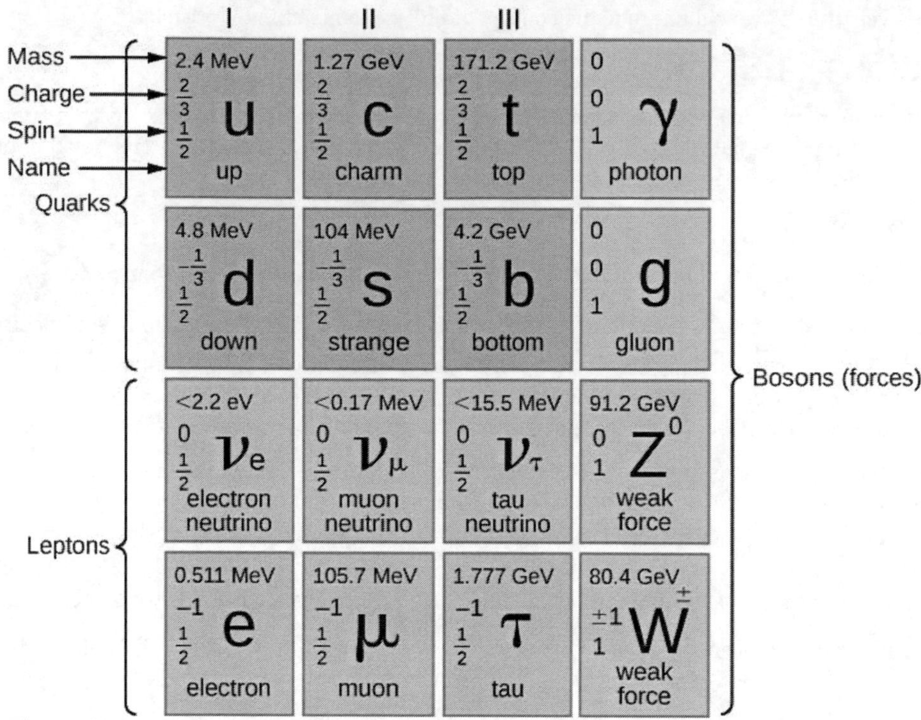

Figure 11.2 The families of subatomic particles, categorized by the types of forces with which they interact. (credit: modification of work by "MissMJ"/Wikimedia Commons)

Ordinary matter consists of two types of quarks: the up quark (elementary charge, $q = +2/3$) and the down quark ($q = -1/3$). Heavier quarks are unstable and quickly decay to lighter ones via the weak force. Quarks bind together in groups of twos and threes called **hadrons** via the strong force. Hadrons that consist of two quarks are called **mesons**, and those that consist of three quarks are called **baryons**. Examples of mesons include the pion and kaon, and examples of baryons include the familiar proton and neutron. A proton is two up quarks and a down quark $(\mathrm{p} = uud,\ q = +1)$ and a neutron is one up quark and two down quarks $(\mathrm{n} = udd,\ q = 0)$. Properties of sample mesons and baryons are given in **Table 11.1**. Quarks participate in all four fundamental forces: strong, weak, electromagnetic, and gravitational.

The lower two rows in the figure (in green) contain six leptons arranged into two particle families: electron, muon, and tau $(e,\ \mu,\ \tau)$, and electron neutrino, muon neutrino, and tau neutrino $(\upsilon_e,\ \upsilon_\mu,\ \upsilon_\tau)$. The muon is over 200 times heavier than an electron, but is otherwise similar to the electron. The tau is about 3500 times heavier than the electron, but is otherwise similar to the muon and electron. Once created, the muon and tau quickly decay to lighter particles via the weak force. Leptons do not participate in the strong force. Quarks and leptons will be discussed later in this chapter. Leptons participate in the weak, electromagnetic, and gravitational forces, but do not participate in the strong force.

Bosons (shown in red) are the force carriers of the fermions. In this model, leptons and quarks interact with each other by sending and receiving bosons. For example, Coulombic interaction occurs when two positively charged particles send and receive (exchange) photons. The photons are said to "carry" the force between charged particles. Likewise, attraction between two quarks in an atomic nucleus occurs when two quarks send and receive **gluons**. Additional examples include **W and Z bosons** (which carry weak nuclear force) and gravitons (which carry gravitational force). The Higgs boson is a special particle: When it interacts with other particles, it endows them not with force but with mass. In other words, the Higgs boson helps to explains *why* particles have mass. These assertions are part of a tentative but very productive scientific model (the Standard Model) discussed later.

Particles and Antiparticles

In the late 1920s, the special theory of relativity and quantum mechanics were combined into a relativistic quantum theory of the electron. A surprising result of this theory was the prediction of two energy states for each electron: One is associated with the electron, and the other is associated with another particle with the same mass of an electron but with a charge of e^+. This particle is called the antielectron or **positron**. The positron was discovered experimentally in the 1930s.

Soon it was discovered that for every particle in nature, there is a corresponding **antiparticle**. An antiparticle has the same mass and lifetime as its associated particle, and the opposite sign of electric charge. These particles are produced in high-energy reactions. Examples of high-energy particles include the antimuon (μ^+), anti-up quark ($\bar{u}$), and anti-down quark ($\bar{d}$). (Note that antiparticles for quarks are designated with an over-bar.) Many mesons and baryons contain antiparticles. For example, the antiproton ($\bar{\text{p}}$) is $\bar{u}\bar{u}\bar{d}$ and the positively charged pion (π^+) is $u\bar{d}$. Some neutral particles, such as the photon and the π^0 meson, are their own antiparticles. Sample particles, antiparticles, and their properties are listed in **Table 11.1**.

	Particle name	Symbol	Antiparticle	Mass (MeV/c^2)	Average lifetime (s)
			Leptons		
	Electron	e^-	e^+	0.511	Stable
	Electron neutrino	υ_e	$\overline{\upsilon_e}$	≈ 0	Stable
	Muon	μ^-	μ^+	105.7	2.20×10^{-6}
	Muon neutrino	υ_μ	$\overline{\upsilon_\mu}$	≈ 0	Stable
	Tau	τ^-	τ^+	1784	$< 4 \times 10^{-13}$
	Tau neutrino	υ_τ	$\overline{\upsilon_\tau}$	≈ 0	Stable
			Hadrons		
Baryons	Proton	p	$\bar{\text{p}}$	938.3	Stable
	Neutron	n	$\bar{\text{n}}$	939.6	920
	Lambda	Λ^0	$\overline{\Lambda^0}$	1115.6	2.6×10^{-10}
	Sigma	Σ^+	Σ^-	1189.4	0.80×10^{-10}
	Xi	Ξ^+	Ξ^-	1315	2.9×10^{-10}
	Omega	Ω^+	Ω^-	1672	0.82×10^{-10}
Mesons	Pion	π^+	π^-	139.6	2.60×10^{-8}
	π -Zero	π^0	π^0	135.0	0.83×10^{-16}
	Kaon	K^+	K^-	493.7	1.24×10^{-8}
	k-Short	K_S^0	$\overline{K_S^0}$	497.7	0.89×10^{-10}
	k-Long	K_L^0	$\overline{K_L^0}$	497.0	5.2×10^{-8}
	J/ψ	J/ψ	J/ψ	3100	7.1×10^{-21}
	Upsilon	Υ	Υ	9460	1.2×10^{-20}

Table 11.1 Particles and their Properties

The same forces that hold ordinary matter together also hold antimatter together. Under the right conditions, it is possible to create antiatoms such as antihydrogen, antioxygen, and even antiwater. In antiatoms, positrons orbit a negatively charged nucleus of antiprotons and antineutrons. **Figure 11.3** compares atoms and antiatoms.

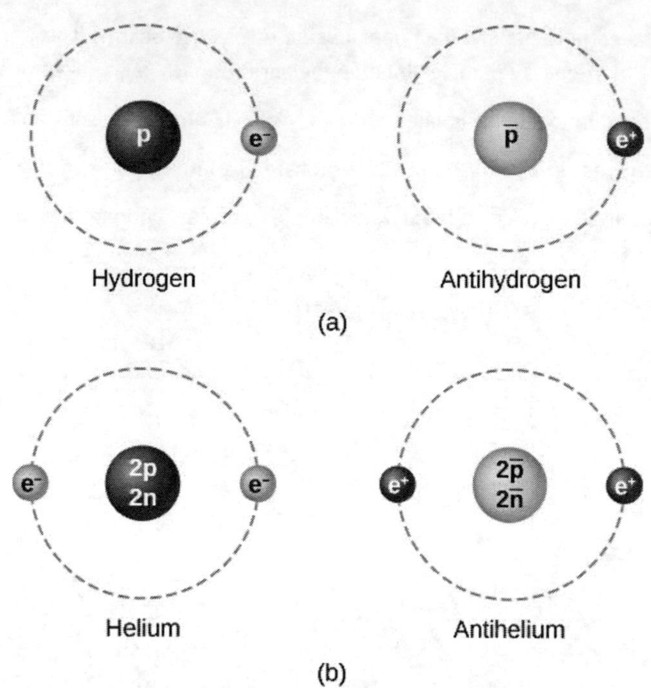

Figure 11.3 A comparison of the simplest atoms of matter and antimatter. (a) In the Bohr model, an antihydrogen atom consists of a positron that orbits an antiproton. (b) An antihelium atom consists of two positrons that orbit a nucleus of two antiprotons and two antineutrons.

Antimatter cannot exist for long in nature because particles and antiparticles annihilate each other to produce high-energy radiation. A common example is electron-positron annihilation. This process proceeds by the reaction

$$e^- + e^+ \rightarrow 2\gamma.$$

The electron and positron vanish completely and two photons are produced in their place. (It turns out that the production of a single photon would violate conservation of energy and momentum.) This reaction can also proceed in the reverse direction: Two photons can annihilate each other to produce an electron and positron pair. Or, a single photon can produce an electron-positron pair in the field of a nucleus, a process called pair production. Reactions of this kind are measured routinely in modern particle detectors. The existence of antiparticles in nature is not science fiction.

Watch this **video (https://openstaxcollege.org/l/21matter)** to learn more about matter and antimatter particles.

11.2 | Particle Conservation Laws

Learning Objectives

By the end of this section, you will be able to:

- Distinguish three conservation laws: baryon number, lepton number, and strangeness
- Use rules to determine the total baryon number, lepton number, and strangeness of particles before and after a reaction
- Use baryon number, lepton number, and strangeness conservation to determine if particle reactions or decays occur

Conservation laws are critical to an understanding of particle physics. Strong evidence exists that energy, momentum, and angular momentum are all conserved in all particle interactions. The annihilation of an electron and positron at rest, for example, cannot produce just one photon because this violates the conservation of linear momentum. As discussed in **Relativity**, the special theory of relativity modifies definitions of momentum, energy, and other familiar quantities. In particular, the relativistic momentum of a particle differs from its classical momentum by a factor $\gamma = 1/\sqrt{1-(v/c)^2}$ that varies from 1 to ∞, depending on the speed of the particle.

In previous chapters, we encountered other conservation laws as well. For example, charge is conserved in all electrostatic phenomena. Charge lost in one place is gained in another because charge is carried by particles. No known physical processes violate charge conservation. In the next section, we describe three less-familiar conservation laws: baryon number, lepton number, and strangeness. These are by no means the only conservation laws in particle physics.

Baryon Number Conservation

No conservation law considered thus far prevents a neutron from decaying via a reaction such as

$$\mathrm{n} \rightarrow \mathrm{e}^{+} + \mathrm{e}^{-}.$$

This process conserves charge, energy, and momentum. However, it does not occur because it violates the law of baryon number conservation. This law requires that the total baryon number of a reaction is the same before and after the reaction occurs. To determine the total baryon number, every elementary particle is assigned a **baryon number** *B*. The baryon number has the value $B = +1$ for baryons, –1 for antibaryons, and 0 for all other particles. Returning to the above case (the decay of the neutron into an electron-positron pair), the neutron has a value $B = +1$, whereas the electron and the positron each has a value of 0. Thus, the decay does not occur because the total baryon number changes from 1 to 0. However, the proton-antiproton collision process

$$\mathrm{p} + \bar{\mathrm{p}} \rightarrow \mathrm{p} + \mathrm{p} + \bar{\mathrm{p}} + \bar{\mathrm{p}},$$

does satisfy the law of conservation of baryon number because the baryon number is zero before and after the interaction. The baryon number for several common particles is given in **Table 11.2**.

Particle name	Symbol	Lepton number (L_e)	Lepton number (L_μ)	Lepton number (L_τ)	Baryon number (*B*)	Strangeness number
Electron	e^-	1	0	0	0	0
Electron neutrino	υ_e	1	0	0	0	0
Muon	μ^-	0	1	0	0	0
Muon neutrino	υ_μ	0	1	0	0	0
Tau	τ^-	0	0	1	0	0
Tau neutrino	υ_τ	0	0	1	0	0
Pion	π^+	0	0	0	0	0
Positive kaon	K^+	0	0	0	0	1
Negative kaon	K^-	0	0	0	0	–1
Proton	p	0	0	0	1	0
Neutron	n	0	0	0	1	0
Lambda zero	Λ^0	0	0	0	1	–1

Table 11.2 Conserved Properties of Particles

Particle name	Symbol	Lepton number (L_e)	Lepton number (L_μ)	Lepton number (L_τ)	Baryon number (*B*)	Strange-ness number
Positive sigma	Σ^+	0	0	0	1	–1
Negative sigma	Σ^-	0	0	0	1	–1
Xi zero	Ξ^0	0	0	0	1	–2
Negative xi	Ξ^-	0	0	0	1	–2
Omega	Ω^-	0	0	0	1	–3

Table 11.2 Conserved Properties of Particles

Example 11.1

Baryon Number Conservation

Based on the law of conservation of baryon number, which of the following reactions can occur?

$$\text{(a)}\ \pi^- + \text{p} \to \pi^0 + \text{n} + \pi^- + \pi^+$$
$$\text{(b)}\ \text{p} + \bar{\text{p}} \to \text{p} + \text{p} + \bar{\text{p}}$$

Strategy

Determine the total baryon number for the reactants and products, and require that this value does not change in the reaction. **Solution**

For reaction (a), the net baryon number of the two reactants is $0 + 1 = 1$ and the net baryon number of the four products is $0 + 1 + 0 + 0 = 1$. Since the net baryon numbers of the reactants and products are equal, this reaction is allowed on the basis of the baryon number conservation law.

For reaction (b), the net baryon number of the reactants is $1 + (-1) = 0$ and the net baryon number of the proposed products is $1 + 1 + (-1) = 1$. Since the net baryon numbers of the reactants and proposed products are not equal, this reaction cannot occur.

Significance

Baryon number is conserved in the first reaction, but not in the second. Baryon number conservation constrains what reactions can and cannot occur in nature.

11.1 Check Your Understanding What is the baryon number of a hydrogen nucleus?

Lepton Number Conservation

Lepton number conservation states that the sum of lepton numbers before and after the interaction must be the same. There are three different **lepton numbers**: the electron-lepton number L_e, the muon-lepton number L_μ, and the tau-lepton number L_τ. In any interaction, each of these quantities must be conserved *separately*. For electrons and electron neutrinos, $L_e = 1$; for their antiparticles, $L_e = -1$; all other particles have $L_e = 0$. Similarly, $L_\mu = 1$ for muons and muon neutrinos, $L_\mu = -1$ for their antiparticles, and $L_\mu = 0$ for all other particles. Finally, $L_\tau = 1, -1$, or 0, depending on whether we have a tau or tau neutrino, their antiparticles, or any other particle, respectively. Lepton number conservation guarantees that the number of electrons and positrons in the universe stays relatively constant. (*Note:* The total lepton number is, as far as we know, conserved in nature. However, observations have shown variations of family lepton number (for example, L_e) in a phenomenon called *neutrino oscillations*.)

To illustrate the lepton number conservation law, consider the following known two-step decay process:

$$\pi^+ \rightarrow \mu^+ + \nu_\mu$$
$$\mu^+ \rightarrow \mathrm{e}^+ + \nu_c + \overline{\nu}_\mu.$$

In the first decay, all of the lepton numbers for π^+ are 0. For the products of this decay, $L_\mu = -1$ for μ^+ and $L_\mu = 1$ for ν_μ. Therefore, muon-lepton number is conserved. Neither electrons nor tau are involved in this decay, so $L_\mathrm{e} = 0$ and $L_\tau = 0$ for the initial particle and all decay products. Thus, electron-lepton and tau-lepton numbers are also conserved. In the second decay, μ^+ has a muon-lepton number $L_\mu = -1,$ whereas the net muon-lepton number of the decay products is $0 + 0 + (-1) = -1$. Thus, the muon-lepton number is conserved. Electron-lepton number is also conserved, as $L_\mathrm{e} = 0$ for μ^+, whereas the net electron-lepton number of the decay products is $(-1) + 1 + 0 = 0$. Finally, since no taus or tau-neutrons are involved in this decay, the tau-lepton number is also conserved.

Example 11.2

Lepton Number Conservation

Based on the law of conservation of lepton number, which of the following decays can occur?

$$\text{(a) } \mathrm{n} \rightarrow \mathrm{p} + \mathrm{e}^- + \overline{\nu}_e$$
$$\text{(b) } \pi^- \rightarrow \mu^- + \nu_\mu + \overline{\nu}_\mu$$

Strategy

Determine the total lepton number for the reactants and products, and require that this value does not change in the reaction.

Solution

For decay (a), the electron-lepton number of the neutron is 0, and the net electron-lepton number of the decay products is $0 + 1 + (-1) = 0$. Since the net electron-lepton numbers before and after the decay are the same, the decay is possible on the basis of the law of conservation of electron-lepton number. Also, since there are no muons or taus involved in this decay, the muon-lepton and tauon-lepton numbers are conserved.

For decay (b), the muon-lepton number of the π^- is 0, and the net muon-lepton number of the proposed decay products is $1 + 1 + (-1) = 1$. Thus, on the basis of the law of conservation of muon-lepton number, this decay cannot occur.

Significance

Lepton number is conserved in the first reaction, but not in the second. Lepton number conservation constrains what reactions can and cannot occur in nature.

11.2 Check Your Understanding What is the lepton number of an electron-positron pair?

Strangeness Conservation

In the late 1940s and early 1950s, cosmic-ray experiments revealed the existence of particles that had never been observed on Earth. These particles were produced in collisions of pions with protons or neutrons in the atmosphere. Their production and decay were unusual. They were produced in the strong nuclear interactions of pions and nucleons, and were therefore inferred to be hadrons; however, their decay was mediated by the much more slowly acting weak nuclear interaction. Their lifetimes were on the order of 10^{-10} to 10^{-8} s, whereas a typical lifetime for a particle that decays via the strong nuclear reaction is 10^{-23} s. These particles were also unusual because they were always produced in pairs in the pion-nucleon collisions. For these reasons, these newly discovered particles were described as *strange*. The production and subsequent decay of a pair of strange particles is illustrated in Figure 11.4 and follows the reaction

$$\pi^- + p \to \Lambda^0 + K^0.$$

The lambda particle then decays through the weak nuclear interaction according to

$$\Lambda^0 \to \pi^- + p,$$

and the kaon decays via the weak interaction

$$K^0 \to \pi^+ + \pi^-.$$

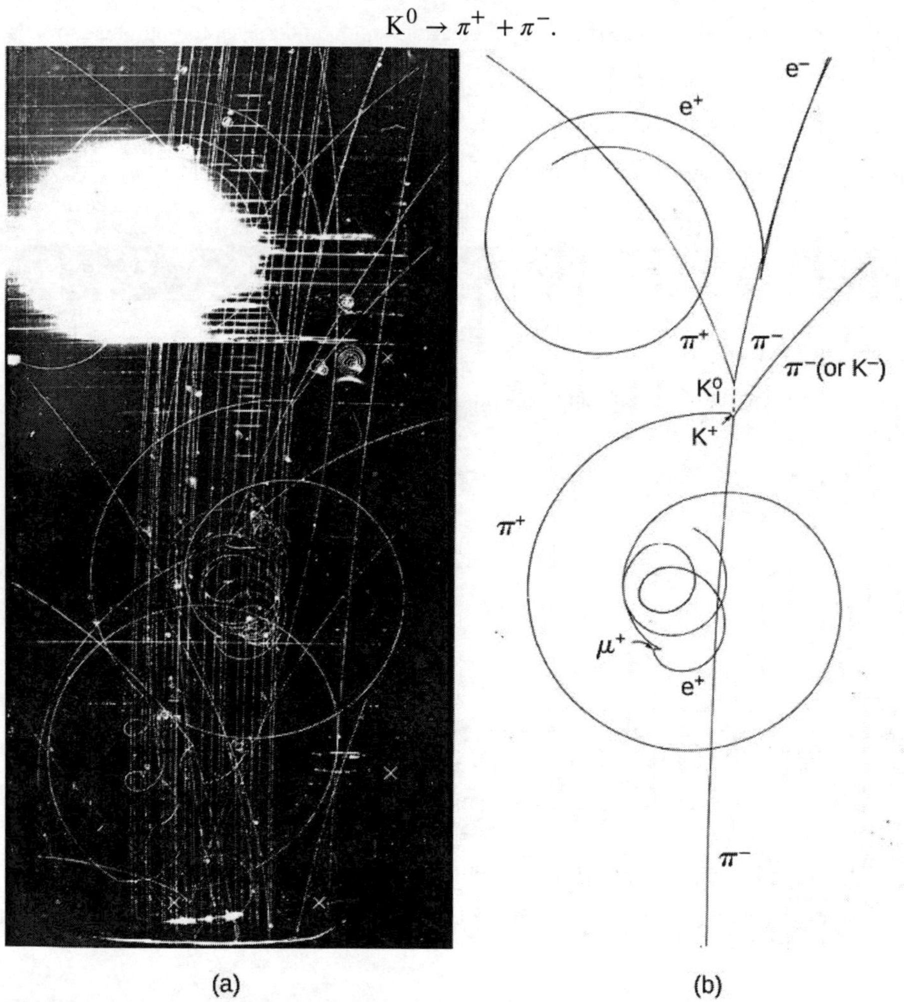

Figure 11.4 The interactions of hadrons. (a) Bubble chamber photograph; (b) sketch that represents the photograph.

To rationalize the behavior of these strange particles, particle physicists invented a particle property conserved in strong interactions but not in weak interactions. This property is called **strangeness** and, as the name suggests, is associated with the presence of a strange quark. The strangeness of a particle is equal to the number of strange quarks of the particle. Strangeness conservation requires the total strangeness of a reaction or decay (summing the strangeness of all the particles) is the same before and after the interaction. Strangeness conservation is not absolute: It is conserved in strong interactions and electromagnetic interactions but not in weak interactions. The strangeness number for several common particles is given in Table 11.2.

Example 11.3

Strangeness Conservation

(a) Based on the conservation of strangeness, can the following reaction occur?

$$\pi^- + \mathrm{p} \to \mathrm{K}^+ + \mathrm{K}^- + \mathrm{n}.$$

(b) The following decay is mediated by the weak nuclear force:

$$\mathrm{K}^+ \to \pi^+ + \pi^0.$$

Does the decay conserve strangeness? If not, can the decay occur?

Strategy

Determine the strangeness of the reactants and products and require that this value does not change in the reaction.

Solution

a. The net strangeness of the reactants is $0 + 0 = 0,$ and the net strangeness of the products is $1 + (-1) + 0 = 0.$ Thus, the strong nuclear interaction between a pion and a proton is not forbidden by the law of conservation of strangeness. Notice that baryon number is also conserved in the reaction.

b. The net strangeness before and after this decay is 1 and 0, so the decay does not conserve strangeness. However, the decay may still be possible, because the law of conservation of strangeness does not apply to weak decays.

Significance

Strangeness is conserved in the first reaction, but not in the second. Strangeness conservation constrains what reactions can and cannot occur in nature.

11.3 Check Your Understanding What is the strangeness number of a muon?

11.3 | Quarks

Learning Objectives

By the end of this section, you will be able to:

- Compare and contrast the six known quarks
- Use quark composition of hadrons to determine the total charge of these particles
- Explain the primary evidence for the existence of quarks

In the 1960s, particle physicists began to realize that hadrons are not elementary particles but are made of particles called *quarks*. (The name 'quark' was coined by the physicist Murray Gell-Mann, from a phrase in the James Joyce novel *Finnegans Wake*.) Initially, it was believed there were only three types of quarks, called *up* (*u*), *down* (*d*), and *strange* (*s*). However, this number soon grew to six—interestingly, the same as the number of leptons—to include *charmed* (*c*), *bottom* (*b*), and *top* (*t*).

All quarks are spin-half fermions $(s = 1/2),$ have a fractional charge $(1/3 \text{ or } 2/3e)$, and have baryon number $B = 1/3.$ Each quark has an antiquark with the same mass but opposite charge and baryon number. The names and properties of the six quarks are listed in **Table 11.3**.

Quark	Charge (units of *e*)	Spin (*s*)	Baryon number	Strangeness number
Down (*d*)	$-1/3$	1/2	1/3	0
Up (*u*)	$+2/3$	1/2	1/3	0
Strange (*s*)	$-1/3$	1/2	1/3	-1
Charm (*c*)	$+2/3$	1/2	1/3	0
Bottom (*b*)	$-1/3$	1/2	1/3	0
Top (*t*)	$+2/3$	1/2	1/3	0

Table 11.3 Quarks

Quark Combinations

As mentioned earlier, quarks bind together in groups of two or three to form hadrons. Baryons are formed from three quarks. Sample baryons, including quark content and properties, are given in **Table 11.4**. Interestingly, the delta plus (Δ^+) baryon is formed from the same three quarks as the proton, but the total spin of the particle is 3/2 rather than 1/2. Similarly, the mass of Δ^+ with spin 3/2 is 1.3 times the mass of the proton, and the delta zero (Δ^0) baryon with a spin 3/2 is 1.3 times the neutron mass. Evidently, the energy associated with the spin (or angular momentum) of the particle contributes to its mass energy. It is also interesting that no baryons are believed to exist with top quarks, because top quarks decay too quickly to bind to the other quarks in their production.

Name	Symbol	Quarks	Charge (unit of *e*)	Spin (*s*)	Mass (GeV/c^2)
Proton	p	*u u d*	1	1/2	0.938
Neutron	n	*u d d*	0	1/2	0.940
Delta plus plus	Δ^{++}	*u u u*	2	3/2	1.232
Delta plus	Δ^+	*u u d*	1	3/2	1.232
Delta zero	Δ^0	*u d d*	0	3/2	1.232
Delta minus	Δ^-	*d d d*	-1	3/2	1.232
Lambda zero	Λ^0	*u d s*	0	1/2	1.116
Positive sigma	Σ^+	*u u s*	1	1/2	1.189
Neutral sigma	Σ^0	*u d s*	0	1/2	1.192
Negative xi	Ξ^-	*s d s*	-1	1/2	1.321
Neutral xi	Ξ^0	*s u s*	0	1/2	1.315
Omega minus	Ω^-	*s s s*	-1	3/2	1.672
Charmed lambda	Λ_{C+}	*u d c*	1	1/2	2.281
Charmed bottom	Λ_{b0}	*u d b*	0	1/2	5.619

Table 11.4 Baryon Quarks

Mesons are formed by two quarks—a quark-antiquark pair. Sample mesons, including quark content and properties, are given in **Table 11.5**. Consider the formation of the pion ($\pi^+ = u\bar{d}$). Based on its quark content, the charge of the pion is

$$\frac{2}{3}e + \frac{1}{3}e = e.$$

Both quarks are spin-half ($s = ½$), so the resultant spin is either 0 or 1. The spin of the π^+ meson is 0. The same quark-antiquark combination gives the rho (ρ) meson with spin 1. This meson has a mass approximately 5.5 times that of the π^+ meson.

Example 11.4

Quark Structure

Show that the quark composition given in **Table 11.5** for Ξ^0 is consistent with the known charge, spin, and strangeness of this baryon.

Strategy

Ξ^0 is composed of two strange quarks and an up quark (*s u s*). We can add together the properties of quarks to predict the resulting properties of the Ξ^0 baryon.

Solution

The charge of the *s* quark is $-e/3$ and the charge of the *u* quark is 2*e*/3. Thus, the combination (*s u s*) has no net charge, in agreement with the known charge of Ξ^0. Since three spin $-1/2$ quarks can combine to produce a particle with spin of either 1/2 or 3/2, the quark composition is consistent with the known spin ($s = 1/2$) of Ξ^0. Finally, the net strangeness of the (*s u s*) combination is $(-1) + 0 + (-1) = -2,$ which also agrees with experiment.

Significance

The charge, spin, and strangeness of the Ξ^0 particle can be determined from the properties of its constituent quarks. The great diversity of baryons and mesons can be traced to the properties of just six quarks: up, down, charge, strange, top, and bottom.

11.4 Check Your Understanding What is the baryon number of a pion?

Name	Symbol	Quarks	Charge (*e*)	Spin	Mass (GeV/c^2)
Positive pion	π^+	$u\bar{d}$	1	0	0.140
Positive rho	ρ^+	$u\bar{d}$	1	1	0.768
Negative pion	π^-	$\bar{u}d$	−1	0	0.140
Negative rho	ρ^-	$\bar{u}d$	−1	1	0.768
Neutral Pion	π^0	$\bar{u}u$ or $\bar{d}d$	0	0	0.135
Neutral eta	η^0	$\bar{u}u$, $\bar{d}d$ or $\bar{s}s$	0	0	0.547
Positive kaon	K^+	$u\bar{s}$	1	0	0.494
Neutral kaon	K^0	$d\bar{s}$	0	0	0.498
Negative kaon	K^-	$\bar{u}s$	−1	0	0.494
J/Psi	J/ψ	$\bar{c}c$	0	1	3.10

Table 11.5 Meson Quarks

Name	Symbol	Quarks	Charge (*e*)	Spin	Mass (GeV/c^2)
Charmed eta	$\eta 0$	$c\bar{c}$	0	0	2.98
Neutral D	D^0	$\bar{u}c$	0	0	1.86
Neutral D	D^{*0}	$\bar{u}c$	0	1	2.01
Positive D	D^+	$\bar{d}c$	1	0	1.87
Neutral B	B^0	$\bar{d}b$	0	0	5.26
Upsilon	Υ	$b\bar{b}$	0	1	9.46

Table 11.5 Meson Quarks

Color

Quarks are fermions that obey Pauli's exclusion principle, so it might be surprising to learn that three quarks can bind together within a nucleus. For example, how can two up quarks exist in the same small region of space within a proton? The solution is to invent a third new property to distinguish them. This property is called **color**, and it plays the same role in the strong nuclear interaction as charge does in electromagnetic interactions. For this reason, quark color is sometimes called "strong charge."

Quarks come in three colors: red, green, and blue. (These are just labels—quarks are not actually colored.) Each type of quark (u, d, c, s, b, t) can possess any other colors. For example, three strange quarks exist: a red strange quark, a green strange quark, and a blue strange quark. Antiquarks have anticolor. Quarks that bind together to form hadrons (baryons and mesons) must be color neutral, colorless, or "white." Thus, a baryon must contain a red, blue, and green quark. Likewise, a meson contains either a red-antired, blue-antiblue, or green-antigreen quark pair. Thus, two quarks can be found in the same spin state in a hadron, without violating Pauli's exclusion principle, because their colors are different.

Quark Confinement

The first strong evidence for the existence of quarks came from a series of experiments performed at the Stanford Linear Accelerator Center (SLAC) and at CERN around 1970. This experiment was designed to probe the structure of the proton, much like Rutherford studied structure inside the atom with his α-particle scattering experiments. Electrons were collided with protons with energy in excess of 20 GeV. At this energy, $E \approx pc$, so the de Broglie wavelength of an electron is

$$\lambda = \frac{h}{p} = \frac{hc}{E} \approx 6 \times 10^{-17} \text{ m}. \tag{11.1}$$

The wavelength of the electron is much smaller than the diameter of the proton (about 10^{-15} m). Thus, like an automobile traveling through a rocky mountain range, electrons can be used to probe the structure of the nucleus.

The SLAC experiments found that some electrons were deflected at very large angles, indicating small scattering centers within the proton. The scattering distribution was consistent with electrons being scattered from sites with spin 1/2, the spin of quarks. The experiments at CERN used neutrinos instead of electrons. This experiment also found evidence for the tiny scattering centers. In both experiments, the results suggested that the charges of the scattering particles were either $+2/3e$ or $-1/3e$, in agreement with the quark model.

Watch this **video (https://openstaxcollege.org/l/21quarks)** to learn more about quarks.

The quark model has been extremely successful in organizing the complex world of subatomic particles. Interestingly, however, no experiment has ever produced an isolated quark. All quarks have fractional charge and should therefore be easily distinguishable from the known elementary particles, whose charges are all an integer multiple of *e*. Why are isolated quarks not observed? In current models of particle interactions, the answer is expressed in terms of quark confinement. Quark confinement refers to the confinement of quarks in groups of two or three in a small region of space. The quarks are completely free to move about in this space, and send and receive gluons (the carriers of the strong force). However, if these quarks stray too far from one another, the strong force pulls them back it. This action is likened to a bola, a weapon used for hunting (**Figure 11.5**). The stones are tied to a central point by a string, so none of the rocks can move too far from the others. The bola corresponds to a baryon, the stones correspond to quarks, and the string corresponds to the gluons that hold the system together.

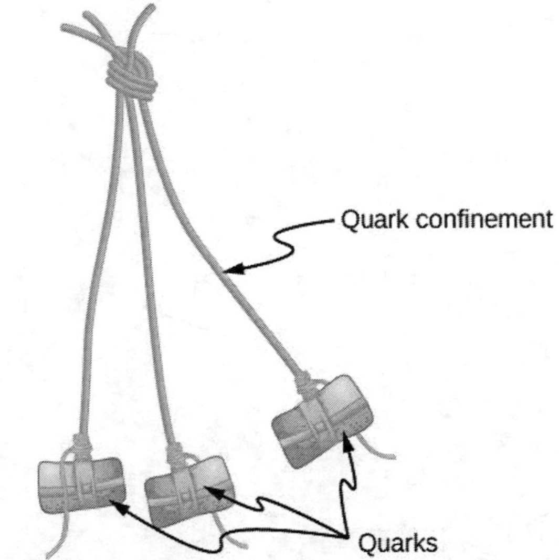

Figure 11.5 A baryon is analogous to a bola, a weapon used for hunting. The rocks in this image correspond to the baryon quarks. The quarks are free to move about but must remain close to the other quarks.

11.4 | Particle Accelerators and Detectors

Learning Objectives

By the end of this section, you will be able to:

- Compare and contrast different types of particle accelerators
- Describe the purpose, components, and function of a typical colliding beam machine
- Explain the role of each type of subdetector of a typical multipurpose particle detector
- Use the curvature of a charge track to determine the momentum of a particle

The goal of experimental particle physics is to accurately measure elementary particles. The primary method used to achieve this end is to produce these particles in high-energy collisions and then measure the products of using highly sensitive particle detectors. These experiments are used to test and revise scientific models of particle interactions. The purpose of this section is to describe particle accelerators and detectors. Modern machines are based on earlier ones, so it is helpful to present a brief history of accelerators and detectors.

Early Particle Accelerators

A **particle accelerator** is a machine designed to accelerate charged particles. This acceleration is usually achieved with strong electric fields, magnetic fields, or both. A simple example of a particle accelerator is the Van de Graaff accelerator (see **Electric Potential (http://cnx.org/content/m58427/latest/)**). This type of accelerator collects charges on a hollow metal sphere using a moving belt. When the electrostatic potential difference of the sphere is sufficiently large, the field is used to accelerate particles through an evacuated tube. Energies produced by a Van de Graaff accelerator are not large enough to create new particles, but the machine was important for early exploration of the atomic nucleus.

Larger energies can be produced by a linear accelerator (called a "linac"). Charged particles produced at the beginning of the linac are accelerated by a continuous line of charged hollow tubes. The voltage between a given pair of tubes is set to draw the charged particle in, and once the particle arrives, the voltage between the next pair of tubes is set to push the charged particle out. In other words, voltages are applied in such a way that the tubes deliver a series of carefully synchronized electric kicks (**Figure 11.6**). Modern linacs employ radio frequency (RF) cavities that set up oscillating electromagnetic fields, which propel the particle forward like a surfer on an ocean wave. Linacs can accelerate electrons to over 100 MeV. (Electrons with kinetic energies greater than 2 MeV are moving very close to the speed of light.) In modern particle research, linear accelerators are often used in the first stage of acceleration.

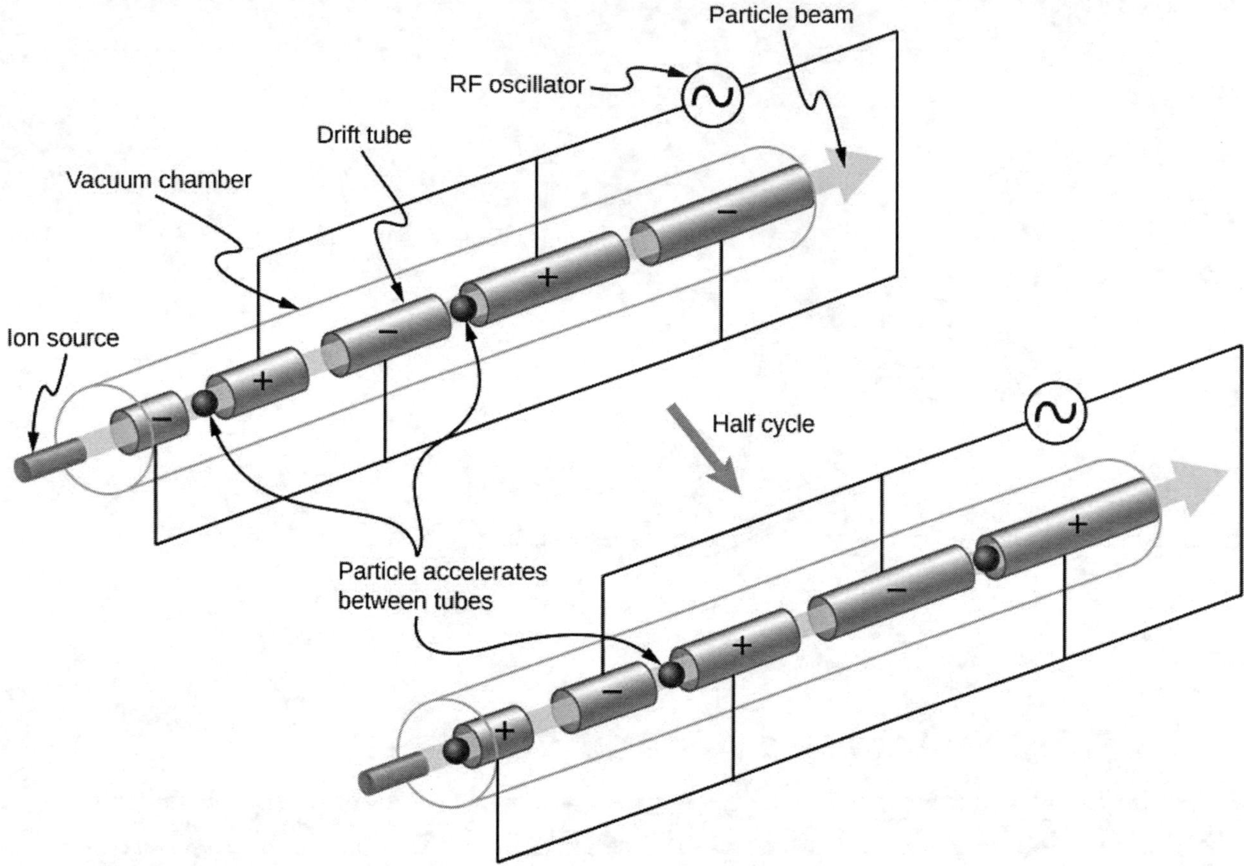

Figure 11.6 In a linear accelerator, charged tubes accelerate particles in a series of electromagnetic kicks. Each tube is longer than the preceding tube because the particle is moving faster as it accelerates.

Example 11.5

Accelerating Tubes

A linear accelerator designed to produce a beam of 800-MeV protons has 2000 accelerating tubes separated by gaps. What average voltage must be applied between tubes to achieve the desired energy? (*Hint*: $U = qV$.)

Strategy

The energy given to the proton in each gap between tubes is $U = qV,$ where q is the proton's charge and V is the potential difference (voltage) across the gap. Since $q = q_e = 1.6 \times 10^{-19}\text{C}$ and $1 \text{ eV} = (1 \text{ V})\left(1.6 \times 10^{-19} \text{ C}\right),$ the proton gains 1 eV in energy for each volt across the gap that it passes through. The ac voltage applied to the tubes is timed so that it adds to the energy in each gap. The effective voltage is the sum of the gap voltages and equals 800 MV to give each proton an energy of 800 MeV.

Solution

There are 2000 gaps and the sum of the voltages across them is 800 MV. Therefore, the average voltage applied is 0.4 MV or 400 kV.

Significance

A voltage of this magnitude is not difficult to achieve in a vacuum. Much larger gap voltages would be required for higher energy, such as those at the 50-GeV SLAC facility. Synchrotrons are aided by the circular path of the accelerated particles, which can orbit many times, effectively multiplying the number of accelerations by the number of orbits. This makes it possible to reach energies greater than 1 TeV.

11.5 Check Your Understanding How much energy does an electron receive in accelerating through a 1-V potential difference?

The next-generation accelerator after the linac is the cyclotron (**Figure 11.7**). A cyclotron uses alternating electric fields and fixed magnets to accelerate particles in a circular spiral path. A particle at the center of the cyclotron is first accelerated by an electric field in a gap between two D-shaped magnets (Dees). As the particle crosses over the D-shaped magnet, the particle is bent into a circular path by a Lorentz force. (The Lorentz force was discussed in **Magnetic Forces and Fields (http://cnx.org/content/m58737/latest/)** .) Assuming no energy losses, the momentum of the particle is related to its radius of curvature by

$$p = 0.3Br \tag{11.2}$$

where p is the momentum in GeV/c, B is in teslas, and r is the radius of the trajectory ("orbit") in meters. This expression is valid to classical and relativistic velocities. The circular trajectory returns the particle to the electric field gap, the electric field is reversed, and the process continues. As the particle is accelerated, the radius of curvature gets larger and larger—spirally outward—until the electrons leave the device.

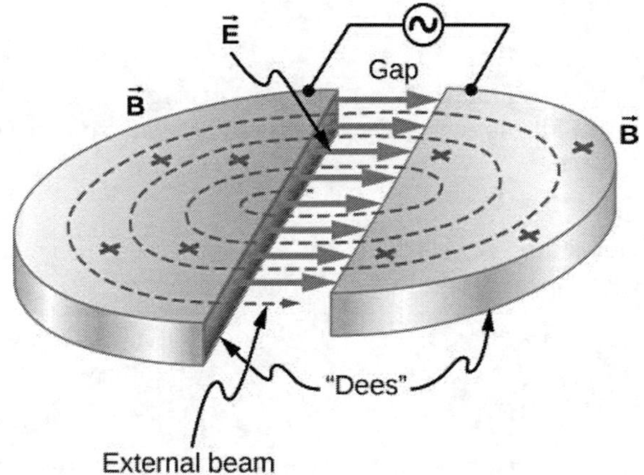

Figure 11.7 Cyclotrons use a magnetic field to cause particles to move in circular orbits. As the particles pass between the plates of the "Dees," the voltage across the gap is reversed so the particles are accelerated twice in each orbit.

Watch this **video (https://openstaxcollege.org/l/21cyclotron)** to learn more about cyclotrons.

A **synchrotron** is a circular accelerator that uses alternating voltage and increasing magnetic field strength to accelerate particles to higher energies. Charged particles are accelerated by RF cavities, and steered and focused by magnets. RF cavities are *synchronized* to deliver "kicks" to the particles as they pass by, hence the name. Steering high-energy particles requires strong magnetic fields, so superconducting magnets are often used to reduce heat losses. As the charged particles move in a circle, they radiate energy: According to classical theory, any charged particle that accelerates (and circular motion is an accelerated motion) also radiates. In a synchrotron, such radiation is called **synchrotron radiation**. This radiation is useful for many other purposes, such as medical and materials research.

Example 11.6

The Energy of an Electron in a Cyclotron

An electron is accelerated using a cyclotron. If the magnetic field is 1.5 T and the radius of the "Dees" is 1.2 m, what is the kinetic energy of the outgoing particle?

Strategy

If the radius of orbit of the electron exceeds the radius of the "Dees," the electron exits the device. So, the radius of the "Dees" places an upper limit on the radius and, therefore, the momentum and energy of the accelerated particle. The exit momentum of the particle is determined using the radius of orbit and strength of the magnetic field. The exit energy of the particle can be determined the particle momentum (**Relativity**).

Solution

Assuming no energy losses, the momentum of the particle in the cyclotron is

$$p = 0.3Br = 0.3(1.5\,\text{T})(1.2\,\text{m}) = 0.543\,\text{GeV}/c.$$

The momentum energy $pc^2 = 0.543\,\text{GeV} = 543\,\text{MeV}$ is much larger than the rest mass energy of the electron, $mc^2 = 0.511\,\text{MeV},$ so relativistic expression for the energy of the electron must be used (see **Relativity**). The total energy of the electron is

$$E_{\text{total}} = \sqrt{(pc)^2 + (mc^2)^2} = \sqrt{(543)^2 + (0.511)^2} \approx 543\,\text{MeV and}$$
$$K = E_{total} - mc^2 = 543\,\text{GeV} - 0.511\,\text{GeV} \approx 543\,\text{MeV}.$$

Significance

The total energy of the electron is much larger than its rest mass energy. In other words, the total energy of the electron is almost all in the form of kinetic energy. Cyclotrons can be used to conduct nuclear physics experiments or in particle therapy to treat cancer.

11.6 Check Your Understanding A charged particle of a certain momentum travels in an arc through a uniform magnetic field. What happens if the magnetic field is doubled?

Colliding Beam Machines

New particles can be created by colliding particles at high energies. According to Einstein's mass-energy relation, the energies of the colliding particles are converted into mass energy of the created particle. The most efficient way to do this is with particle-colliding beam machines. A colliding beam machine creates two counter-rotating beams in a circular accelerator, stores the beams at constant energy, and then at the desired moment, focuses the beams on one another at the center of a sensitive detector.

The prototypical colliding beam machine is the Cornell Electron Storage Ring, located in Ithaca, New York (**Figure 11.8**). Electrons (e^-) and positrons (e^+) are created at the beginning of the linear accelerator and are accelerated up to 150 MeV. The particles are then injected into the inner synchrotron ring, where they are accelerated by RF cavities to 4.5 to 6 GeV. When the beams are up to speed, they are transferred and "stored" in an outer storage ring at the same energy. The two counter-rotating beams travel through the same evacuated pipe, but are kept apart until collisions are desired. The electrons and positrons circle the machine in bunches 390,000 times every second.

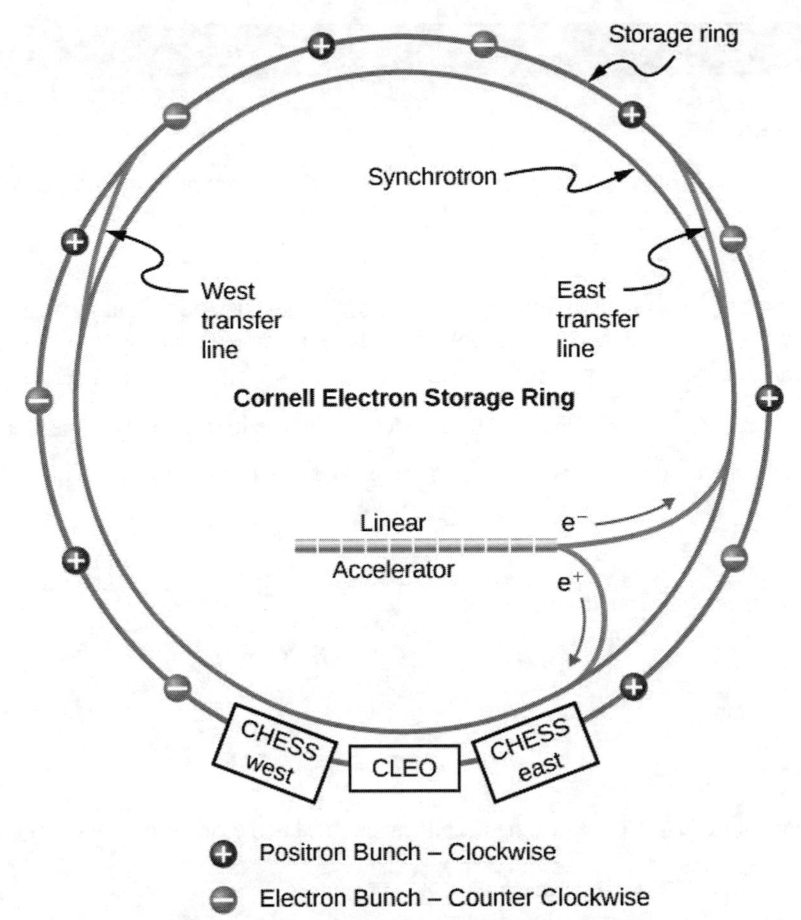

Figure 11.8 The Cornell Electron Storage Ring uses a linear accelerator and a synchrotron to accelerate electrons and positrons to 4.5–6 GeV. The particles are held in the outer storage ring at that energy until they are made to collide in a particle detector. (credit: modification of work by Laboratory of Nuclear Studies, Cornell Electron Storage Ring)

When an electron and positron collide, they annihilate each other to produce a photon, which exists for too short a time to be detected. The photon produces either a lepton pair (e.g., an electron and position, muon or antimuon, or tau and antitau) or a quark pair. If quarks are produced, mesons form, such as $c\bar{c}$ and $b\bar{b}$. These mesons are created nearly at rest since the initial total momentum of the electron-positron system is zero. Note, mesons cannot be created at just any colliding energy but only at "resonant" energies that correspond to the unique masses of the mesons (**Table 11.5**). The mesons created in this way are highly unstable and decay quickly into lighter particles, such as electrons, protons, and photons. The collision "fragments" provide valuable information about particle interactions.

As the field of particle physics advances, colliding beam machines are becoming more powerful. The Large Hadron Collider (LHC), currently the largest accelerator in the world, collides protons at beam energies exceeding 6 TeV. The center-of-mass energy (W) refers to the total energy available to create new particles in a colliding machine, or the total energy of incoming particles in the center-of-mass frame. (The concept of a center-of-mass frame of reference is discussed in **Linear Momentum and Collisions (http://cnx.org/content/m58317/latest/)** .) Therefore, the LHC is able to produce one or more particles with a total mass exceeding 12 TeV. The center-of-mass energy is given by:

$$W^2 = 2[E_1 E_2 + (p_1 c)(p_2 c)] + (m_1 c^2)^2 + (m_2 c^2)^2, \quad (11.3)$$

where E_1 and E_2 are the total energies of the incoming particles (1 and 2), p_1 and p_2 are the magnitudes of their momenta, and m_1 and m_2 are their rest masses.

Example 11.7

Creating a New Particle

The mass of the upsilon (Υ) meson ($b\bar{b}$) is created in a symmetric electron-positron collider. What beam energy is required?

Strategy

The Particle Data Group (https://openstaxcollege.org/l/21particledata) has stated that the rest mass energy of this meson is approximately 10.58 GeV. The above expression for the center-of-mass energy can be simplified because a symmetric collider implies $\vec{p}_1 = -\vec{p}_2$. Also, the rest masses of the colliding electrons and positrons are identical $\left(m_e c^2 = 0.511 \text{ MeV}\right)$ and much smaller than the mass of the energy particle created. Thus, the center-of-mass energy (*W*) can be expressed completely in terms of the beam energy, $E_{\text{beam}} = E_1 = E_2$.

Solution

Based on the above assumptions, we have

$$W^2 \approx 2[E_1 E_2 + E_1 E_2] = 4E_1 E_2 = 4E_1^2.$$

The beam energy is therefore

$$E_{\text{beam}} \approx E_1 = \frac{W}{2}.$$

The rest mass energy of the particle created in the collision is equal to the center-of-mass energy, so

$$E_{\text{beam}} \approx \frac{10.58 \text{ GeV}}{2} = 5.29 \text{ GeV}.$$

Significance

Given the energy scale of this problem, the rest mass energy of the upsilon (Υ) meson is due almost entirely due to the initial kinetic energies of the electron and positrons. This meson is highly unstable and quickly decays to lighter and more stable particles. The existence of the upsilon (Υ) particle appears as a dramatic increase of such events at 5.29 GeV.

11.7 Check Your Understanding Why is a symmetric collider "symmetric?"

Higher beam energies require larger accelerators, so modern colliding beam machines are very large. The LHC, for example, is 17 miles in circumference (**Figure 5.27**). (In the 1940s, Enrico Fermi envisioned an accelerator that encircled all of Earth!) An important scientific challenge of the twenty-first century is to reduce the size of particle accelerators.

Particle Detectors

The purpose of a **particle detector** is to accurately measure the outcome of collisions created by a particle accelerator. The detectors are multipurpose. In other words, the detector is divided into many subdetectors, each designed to measure a different aspect of the collision event. For example, one detector might be designed to measure photons and another might be designed to measure muons. To illustrate how subdetectors contribute to an understanding of an entire collision event, we describe the subdetectors of the Compact Muon Solenoid (CMS), which was used to discover the Higgs Boson at the LHC (**Figure 11.9**).

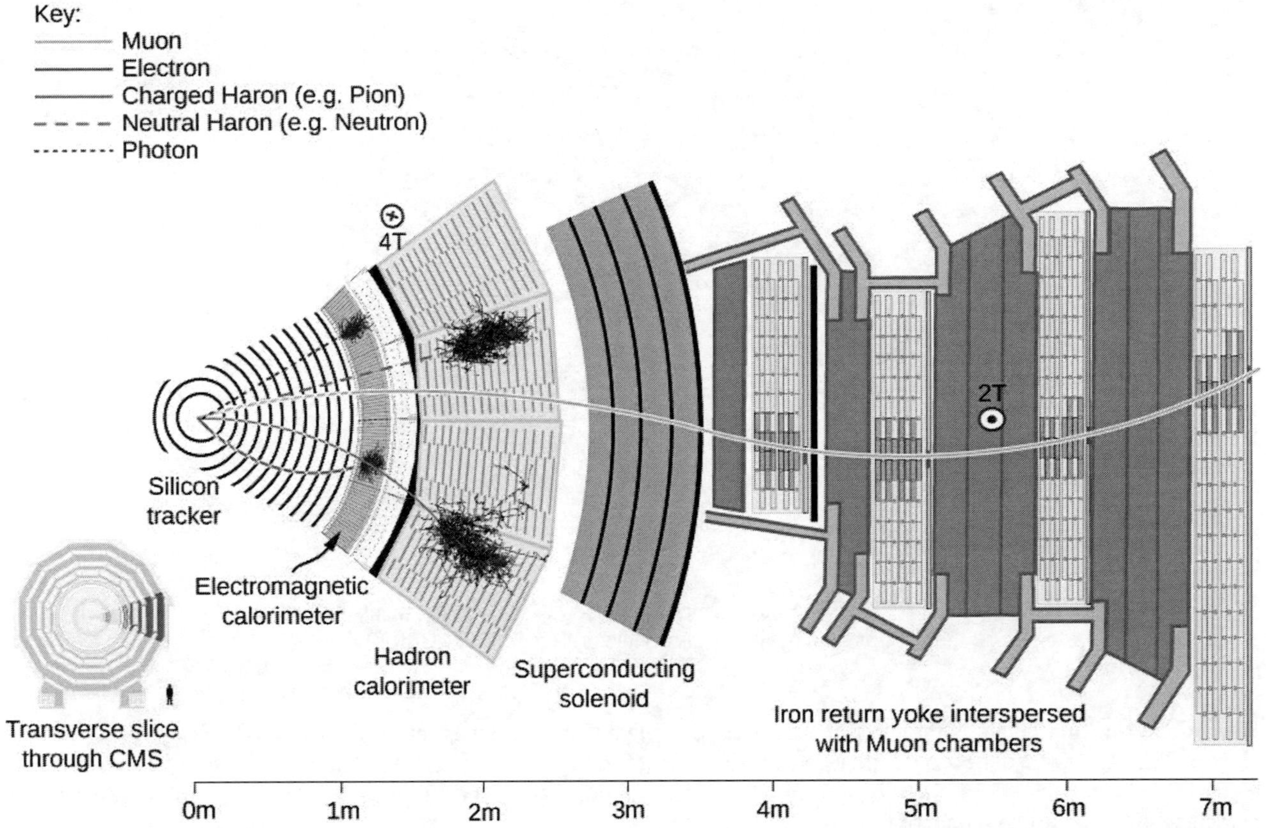

Figure 11.9 Compact Muon Solenoid detector. The detector consists of several layers, each responsible for measuring different types of particles. (credit: modification of work by David Barney/CERN)

The beam pipe of the detector is out of (and into) the page at the left. Particles produced by *pp* collisions (the "collision fragments") stream out of the detector in all directions. These particles encounter multiple layers of subdetectors. A subdetector is a particle detector within a larger system of detectors designed to measure certain types of particles. There are several main types of subdetectors. Tracking devices determine the path and therefore momentum of a particle; calorimeters measure a particle's energy; and particle-identification detectors determine a particle's identity (mass).

The first set of subdetectors that particles encounter is the silicon tracking system. This system is designed to measure the momentum of charged particles (such as electrons and protons). The detector is bathed in a uniform magnetic field, so the charged particles are bent in a circular path by a Lorentz force (as for the cyclotron). If the momentum of the particle is large, the radius of the trajectory is large, and the path is almost straight. But if the momentum is small, the radius of the trajectory is small, and the path is tightly curved. As the particles pass through the detector, they interact with silicon microstrip detectors at multiple points. These detectors produce small electrical signals as the charged particles pass near the detector elements. The signals are then amplified and recorded. A series of electrical "hits" is used to determine the trajectory of the particle in the tracking system. A computer-generated "best fit" to this trajectory gives the track radius and therefore the particle momentum. At the LHC, a large number of tracks are recorded for the same collision event. Fits to the tracks are shown by the blue and green lines in **Figure 11.10**.

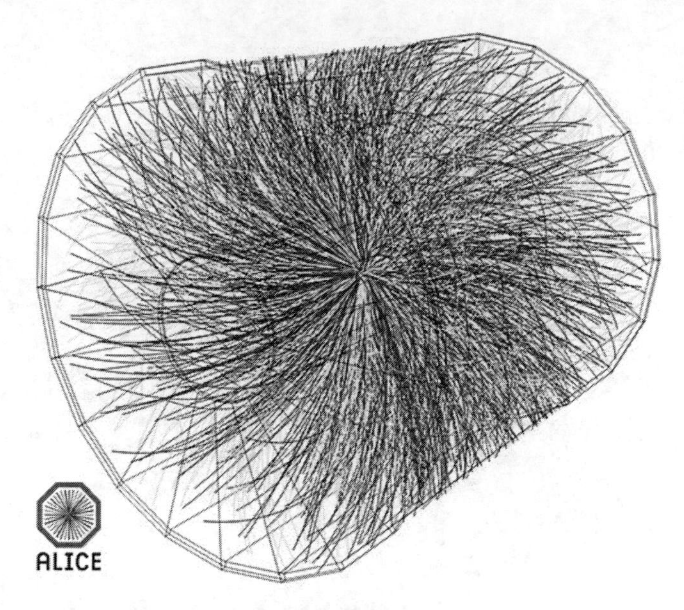

Figure 11.10 A three-dimensional view of particle fragments in the LHC as seen by the ATLAS detector. (credit: LHC/CERN)

Beyond the tracking layers is the electromagnetic calorimeter. This detector is made of clear, lead-based crystals. When electrons interact with the crystals, they radiate high-energy photons. The photons interact with the crystal to produce electron-positron pairs. Then, these particles radiate more photons. The process repeats, producing a particle shower (the crystal "glows"). A crude model of this process is as follows.

An electron with energy E_0 strikes the crystal and loses half of its energy in the form of a photon. The photon produces an electron-positron pair, and each particle proceeds away with half the energy of the photon. Meanwhile, the original electron radiates again. So, we are left with four particles: two electrons, one positron, and one photon, each with an energy $E_0/4$.

The number of particles in the shower increases geometrically. After *n* radiation events, there are $N = 2^n$ particles. Hence, the total energy per particle after *n* radiation events is

$$E(t) = \frac{E_0}{2^n},$$

where E_0 is the incident energy and $E(t)$ is the amount of energy per particle after *n* events. An incoming photon triggers a similar chain of events (**Figure 11.11**). If the energy per particle drops below a particular threshold value, other types of radiative processes become important and the particle shower ceases. Eventually, the total energy of the incoming particle is absorbed and converted into an electrical signal.

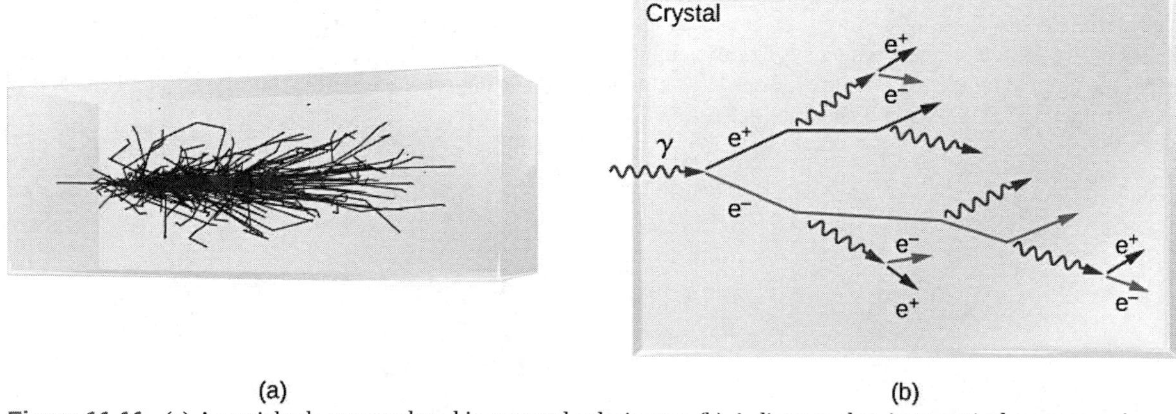

Figure 11.11 (a) A particle shower produced in a crystal calorimeter. (b) A diagram showing a typical sequence of reactions in a particle shower.

Beyond the crystal calorimeter is the hadron calorimeter. As the name suggests, this subdetector measures hadrons such as protons and pions. The hadron calorimeter consists of layers of brass and steel separated by plastic scintillators. Its purpose is to absorb the particle energy and convert it into an electronic signal. Beyond this detector is a large magnetic coil used to produce a uniform field for tracking.

The last subdetector is the muon detector, which consists of slabs of iron that only muons (and neutrinos) can penetrate. Between the iron slabs are multiple types of muon-tracking elements that accurately measure the momentum of the muon. The muon detectors are important because the Higgs boson (discussed soon) can be detected through its decays to four muons—hence the name of the detector.

Once data is collected from each of the particle subdetectors, the entire collision event can be assessed. The energy of the *i*th particle is written

$$E_i = \sqrt{(p_i c)^2 + (m_i c^2)^2},$$

where p_i is the absolute magnitude of the momentum of the *i*th particle, and m_i is its rest mass.

The total energy of all particles is therefore

$$E_{\text{total}} = \sum_i E_i.$$

If all particles are detected, the total energy should be equal to the center-of-mass energy of the colliding beam machine (*W*). In practice, not all particles are identified, either because these particles are too difficult to detect (neutrinos) or because these particles "slip through." In many cases, whole chains of decays can be "reconstructed," like putting back together a watch that has been smashed to pieces. Information about these decay chains are critical to the evaluation of models of particle interactions.

11.5 | The Standard Model

Learning Objectives

By the end of this section, you will be able to:

- Describe the Standard Model in terms of the four fundamental forces and exchange particles
- Draw a Feynman diagram for a simple particle interaction
- Use Heisenberg's uncertainty principle to determine the range of forces described by the Standard Model
- Explain the rationale behind grand unification theories

The chief intellectual activity of any scientist is the development and revision of scientific models. A particle physicist seeks to develop models of particle interactions. This work builds directly on work done on gravity and electromagnetism in the seventeenth, eighteenth, and nineteenth centuries. The ultimate goal of physics is a unified "theory of everything" that describes all particle interactions in terms of a single elegant equation and a picture. The equation itself might be complex, but many scientists suspect the *idea* behind the equation will make us exclaim: "How could we have missed it? It was so obvious!"

In this section, we introduce the Standard Model, which is the best current model of particle interactions. We describe the Standard Model in detail in terms of electromagnetic, weak nuclear, and strong forces. At the end of this section, we review unification theories in particle physics.

Introduction to the Standard Model

The **Standard Model** of particle interactions contains two ideas: *electroweak theory* and **quantum chromodynamics (QCD)** (the force acting between color charges). Electroweak theory unifies the theory of **quantum electrodynamics (QED)**, the modern equivalent of classical electromagnetism, and the theory of weak nuclear interactions. The Standard Model combines the theory of relativity and quantum mechanics.

In the Standard Model, particle interactions occur through the exchange of bosons, the "force carriers." For example, the electrostatic force is communicated between two positively charged particles by sending and receiving massless photons.

This can occur at a theoretical infinite range. The result of these interactions is Coulomb repulsion (or attraction). Similarly, quarks bind together through the exchange of massless gluons. Leptons scatter off other leptons (or decay into lighter particles) through the exchange of massive W and Z bosons. A summary of forces as described by the Standard Model is given in Table 11.6. The gravitational force, mediated by the exchange of massless gravitations, is added in this table for completeness but is not part of the Standard Model.

Force	Relative strength	Exchange particle (bosons)	Particles acted upon	Range
Strong	1	Gluon	Quarks	10^{-15} m
Electromagnetic	1/137	photon	Charged particles	∞
Weak	10^{-10}	W^+, W^-, Z bosons	Quarks, leptons, neutrinos	10^{-18} m
Gravitational	10^{-38}	graviton	All particles	∞

Table 11.6 Four Forces and the Standard Model

The Standard Model can be expressed in terms of equations and diagrams. The equations are complex and are usually covered in a more advanced course in modern physics. However, the essence of the Standard Model can be captured using **Feynman diagrams**. A Feynman diagram, invented by American physicist Richard Feynman (1918–1988), is a space-time diagram that describes how particles move and interact. Different symbols are used for different particles. Particle interactions in one dimension are shown as a time-position graph (not a position-time graph). As an example, consider the scattering of an electron and electron-neutrino (Figure 11.12). The electron moves toward positive values of x (to the right) and collides with an electron neutrino moving to the left. The electron exchanges a Z boson (charge zero). The electron scatters to the left and the neutrino scatters to the right. This exchange is not instantaneous. The Z boson travels from one particle to the other over a short period of time. The interaction of the electron and neutrino is said to occur via the weak nuclear force. This force cannot be explained by classical electromagnetism because the charge of the neutrino is zero. The weak nuclear force is discussed again later in this section.

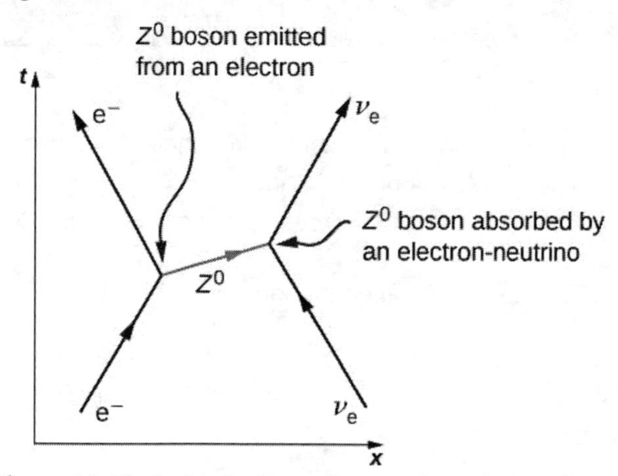

Figure 11.12 In this Feynman diagram, the exchange of a virtual Z^0 carries the weak nuclear force between an electron and a neutrino.

Electromagnetic Force

According to QED, the electromagnetic force is transmitted between charged particles through the exchange of photons. The theory is based on three basic processes: An electron travels from one place to the next, emits or absorbs a photon, and travels from one place to another again. When two electrons interact, one electron emits the photon and the other receives it (Figure 11.13). Photons transfer energy and momentum from one electron to the other. The net result in this case is a repulsive force. The photons exchanged are virtual. A **virtual particle** is a particle that exists for too short a time to be observable. Virtual photons may violate the law of conservation of energy. To see this, consider that if the photon transit time Δt is extremely small, then Heisenberg's uncertainty principle states that the uncertainly in the photon's energy, ΔE, may be very large.

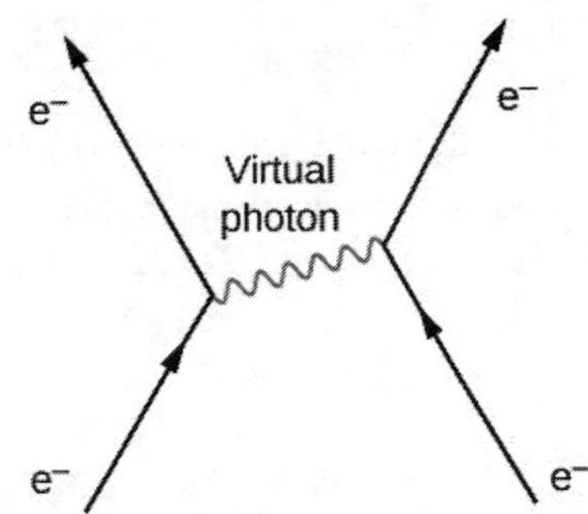

Figure 11.13 Feynman diagram of two electrons interacting through the exchange of a photon.

To estimate the range of the electromagnetic interaction, assume that the uncertainty on the energy is comparable to the energy of the photon itself, written

$$\Delta E \approx E. \tag{11.4}$$

The Heisenberg uncertainly principle states that

$$\Delta E \approx \frac{h}{\Delta t}. \tag{11.5}$$

Combining these equations, we have

$$\Delta t \approx \frac{h}{E}. \tag{11.6}$$

The energy of a photon is given by $E = hf$, so

$$\Delta t \approx \frac{h}{hf} \approx \frac{1}{f} = \frac{\lambda}{c}. \tag{11.7}$$

The distance d that the photon can move in this time is therefore

$$d = c\,\Delta t \approx c\left(\frac{\lambda}{c}\right) = \lambda. \tag{11.8}$$

The energy of the virtual photon can be arbitrarily small, so its wavelength can be arbitrarily large—in principle, even infinitely large. The electromagnetic force is therefore a long-range force.

Weak Nuclear Force

The weak nuclear force is responsible for radioactive decay. The range of the weak nuclear force is very short (only about 10^{-18} m) and like the other forces in the Standard Model, the weak force can be described in terms of particle exchange. (There is no simple function like the Coulomb force to describe these interactions.) The particle exchanged is one of three bosons: W^+, W^-, and Z^0. The Standard Model predicts the existence of these spin-1 particles and also predicts their specific masses. In combination with previous experiments, the mass of the charged W bosons was predicted to be $81\,\mathrm{GeV}/c^2$ and that of the Z^0 was predicted to be $90\,\mathrm{GeV}/c^2$. A CERN experiment discovered particles in the 1980s with precisely these masses—an impressive victory for the model.

The weak nuclear force is most frequently associated with scattering and decays of unstable particles to light particles. For example, neutrons decay to protons through the weak nuclear force. This reaction is written

$$\mathrm{n} \rightarrow \mathrm{p} + \mathrm{e}^- + \nu_\mathrm{e},$$

where n is the neutron, p is a proton, e^- is an electron, and ν_e is a nearly massless electron neutrino. This process, called beta decay, is important in many physical processes. A Feynman diagram of beta decay is given in **Figure 11.14**(a). The neutron emits a W^- and becomes a proton, then the W^- produces an electron and an antineutrino. This process is similar to the scattering event

$$e^- + p \rightarrow n + \nu_e,$$

In this process, the proton emits a W^+ and is converted into a neutron (b). The W^+ then combines with the electron, forming a neutrino. Other electroweak interactions are considered in the exercises.

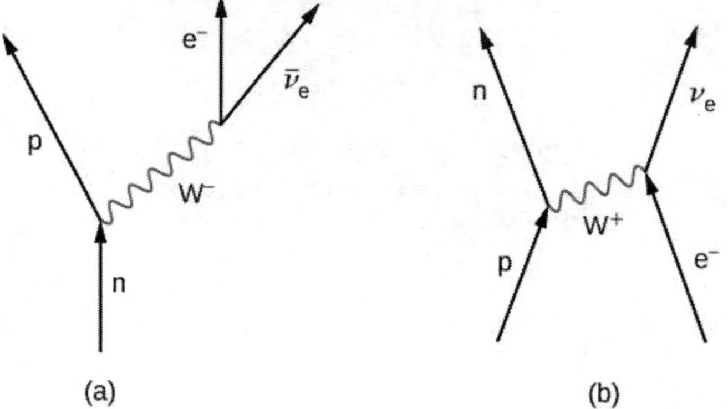

Figure 11.14 Feynman diagram of particles interacting through the exchange of a W boson: (a) beta decay; (b) conversion of a proton into a neutron.

The range of the weak nuclear force can be estimated with an argument similar to the one before. Assuming the uncertainty on the energy is comparable to the energy of the exchange particle by $(E \approx mc^2)$, we have

$$\Delta t \approx \frac{h}{mc^2}. \tag{11.9}$$

The maximum distance d that the exchange particle can travel (assuming it moves at a speed close to c) is therefore

$$d \approx c\Delta t = \frac{h}{mc}. \tag{11.10}$$

For one of the charged vector bosons with $mc^2 \approx 80\,\text{GeV} = 1.28 \times 10^{-8}\,\text{J}$, we obtain $mc = 4.27 \times 10^{-17}\,\text{J} \cdot \text{s/m}$. Hence, the range of the force mediated by this boson is

$$d \approx \frac{1.05 \times 10^{-34}\,\text{J} \cdot \text{s}}{4.27 \times 10^{-17}\,\text{J} \cdot \text{s/m}} \approx 2 \times 10^{-18}\,\text{m}. \tag{11.11}$$

Strong Nuclear Force

Strong nuclear interactions describe interactions between quarks. Details of these interactions are described by QCD. According to this theory, quarks bind together by sending and receiving gluons. Just as quarks carry electric charge [either $(+2/3)e$ or $(-1/3)e$] that determines the strength of electromagnetic interactions between the quarks, quarks also carry "color charge" (either red, blue, or green) that determines the strength of strong nuclear interactions. As discussed before, quarks bind together in groups in color neutral (or "white") combinations, such as red-blue-green and red-antired.

Interestingly, the gluons themselves carry color charge. Eight known gluons exist: six that carry a color and anticolor, and two that are color neutral (**Figure 11.15**(a)). To illustrate the interaction between quarks through the exchange of charged gluons, consider the Feynman diagram in part (b). As time increases, a red down quark moves right and a green strange quark moves left. (These appear at the lower edge of the graph.) The up quark exchanges a red-antigreen gluon with the strange quark. (Anticolors are shown as secondary colors. For example, antired is represented by cyan because cyan mixes with red to form white light.) According to QCD, all interactions in this process—identified with the vertices—must be color neutral. Therefore, the down quark transforms from red to green, and the strange quark transforms from green to red.

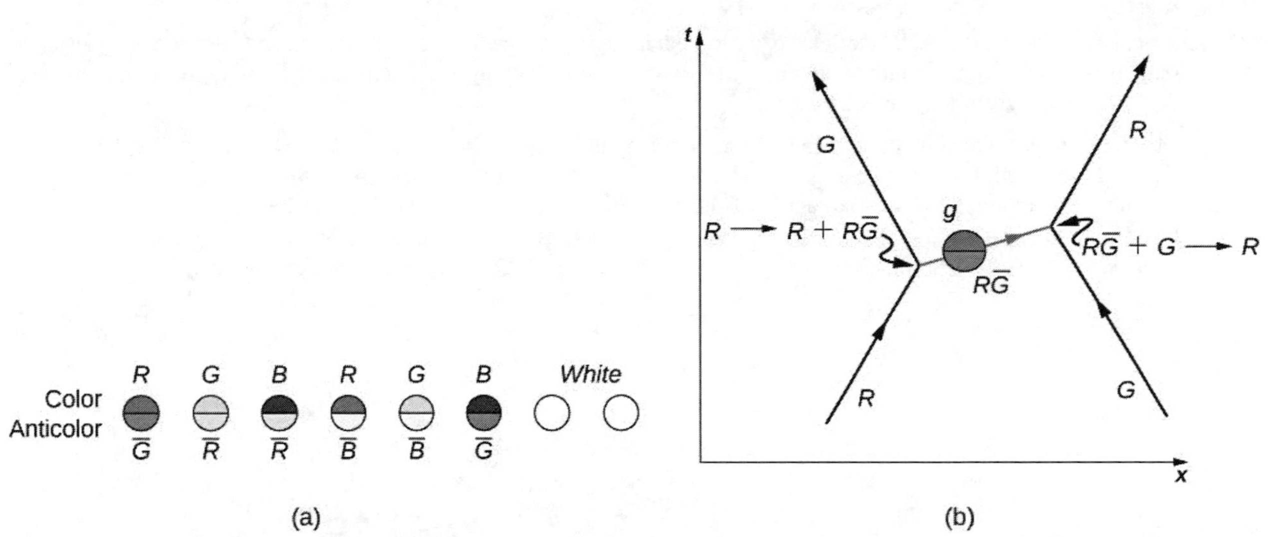

Figure 11.15 (a) Eight types of gluons carry the strong nuclear force. The white gluons are mixtures of color-anticolor pairs. (b) An interaction between two quarks through the exchange of a gluon.

As suggested by this example, the interaction between quarks in an atomic nucleus can be very complicated. **Figure 11.16** shows the interaction between a proton and neutron. Notice that the proton converts into a neutron and the neutron converts into a proton during the interaction. The presence of quark-antiquark pairs in the exchange suggest that bonding between nucleons can be modeled as an exchange of pions.

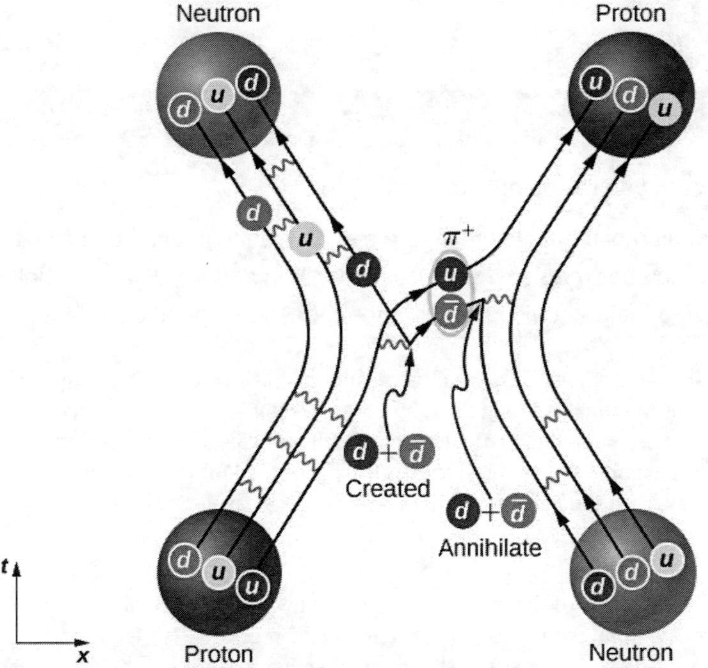

Figure 11.16 A Feynman diagram that describes a strong nuclear interaction between a proton and a neutron.

In practice, QCD predictions are difficult to produce. This difficulty arises from the inherent strength of the force and the inability to neglect terms in the equations. Thus, QCD calculations are often performed with the aid of supercomputers. The existence of gluons is supported by electron-nucleon scattering experiments. The estimated quark momenta implied by these scattering events are much smaller than we would expect without gluons because the gluons carry away some of the momentum of each collision.

Unification Theories

Physicists have long known that the strength of an interaction between particles depends on the distance of the interaction.

For example, two positively charged particles experience a larger repulsive force at a short distance then at a long distance. In scattering experiments, the strength of an interaction depends on the energy of the interacting particle, since larger energy implies both closer and stronger interactions.

Particle physicists now suspect that the strength of all particle interactions (the four forces) merge at high energies, and the details of particle interactions at these energies can be described in terms of a single force (**Figure 11.17**). A unified theory describes what these interactions are like and explains why this description breaks down at low-energy scales. A grand unified theory is a theory that attempts to describe strong and electroweak interaction in terms of just one force. A theory of everything (TOE) takes the unification concept one step further. A TOE combines all four fundamental forces (including gravity) into one theory.

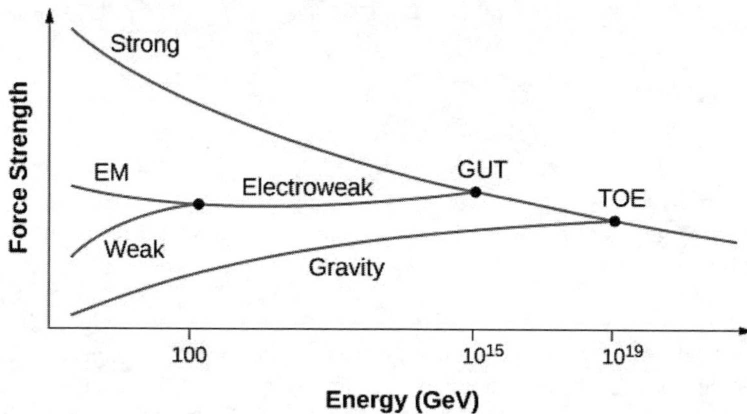

Figure 11.17 Grand unification of forces at high energies.

11.6 | The Big Bang

Learning Objectives

By the end of this section, you will be able to:

- Explain the expansion of the universe in terms of a Hubble graph and cosmological redshift
- Describe the analogy between cosmological expansion and an expanding balloon
- Use Hubble's law to make predictions about the measured speed of distant galaxies

We have been discussing elementary particles, which are some of the smallest things we can study. Now we are going to examine what we know about the universe, which is the biggest thing we can study. The link between these two topics is high energy: The study of particle interactions requires very high energies, and the highest energies we know about existed during the early evolution of the universe. Some physicists think that the unified force theories we described in the preceding section may actually have governed the behavior of the universe in its earliest moments.

Hubble's Law

In 1929, Edwin Hubble published one of the most important discoveries in modern astronomy. Hubble discovered that (1) galaxies appear to move away from Earth and (2) the velocity of recession (v) is proportional to the distance (d) of the galaxy from Earth. Both v and d can be determined using stellar light spectra. A best fit to the sample illustrative data is given in **Figure 11.18**. (Hubble's original plot had a considerable scatter but a general trend was still evident.)

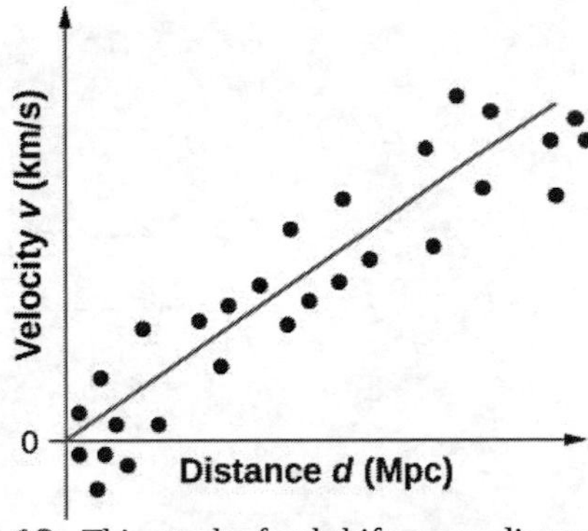

Figure 11.18 This graph of red shift versus distance for galaxies shows a linear relationship, with larger red shifts at greater distances, implying an expanding universe. The slope gives an approximate value for the expansion rate. (credit: John Cub)

The trend in the data suggests the simple proportional relationship:

$$v = H_0 d, \tag{11.12}$$

where $H_0 = 70 \text{ km / s / Mpc}$ is known as **Hubble's constant**. (*Note:* 1 Mpc is one megaparsec or one million parsecs, where one parsec is 3.26 light-years.) This relationship, called **Hubble's law**, states that distant stars and galaxies recede away from us at a speed of 70 km/s for every one megaparsec of distance from us. Hubble's constant corresponds to the slope of the line in **Figure 11.18**. Hubble's constant is a bit of a misnomer, because it varies with time. The value given here is only its value *today*.

Watch this **video (https://openstaxcollege.org/l/21hubble)** to learn more about the history of Hubble's constant.

Hubble's law describes an average behavior of all but the closest galaxies. For example, a galaxy 100 Mpc away (as determined by its size and brightness) typically moves away from us at a speed of

$$v = \left(\left(70\frac{\text{km}}{\text{s}}\right)/\text{Mpc}\right)(100 \text{ Mpc}) = 7000 \text{ km/s}.$$

This speed may vary due to interactions with neighboring galaxies. Conversely, if a galaxy is found to be moving away from us at speed of 100,000 km/s based on its red shift, it is at a distance

$$d = v/H_0 = (10{,}000 \text{ km/s})/\left(\left(70\frac{\text{km}}{\text{s}}\right)/\text{Mpc}\right) = 143 \text{ Mpc}.$$

This last calculation is approximate because it assumes the expansion rate was the same 5 billion years ago as it is now.

Big Bang Model

Scientists who study the origin, evolution, and ultimate fate of the universe (**cosmology**) believe that the universe began in an explosion, called the **Big Bang**, approximately 13.7 billion years ago. This explosion was not an explosion of particles through space, like fireworks, but a rapid expansion of space itself. The distances and velocities of the outward-going stars and galaxies permit us to estimate when all matter in the universe was once together—at the beginning of time.

Scientists often explain the Big Bang expansion using an inflated-balloon model (**Figure 11.19**). Dots marked on the surface of the balloon represent galaxies, and the balloon skin represents four-dimensional space-time (**Relativity**). As the balloon is inflated, every dot "sees" the other dots moving away. This model yields two insights. First, the expansion is observed by all observers in the universe, no matter where they are located. The "center of expansion" does not exist, so Earth does not reside at the "privileged" center of the expansion (see **Exercise 11.24**).

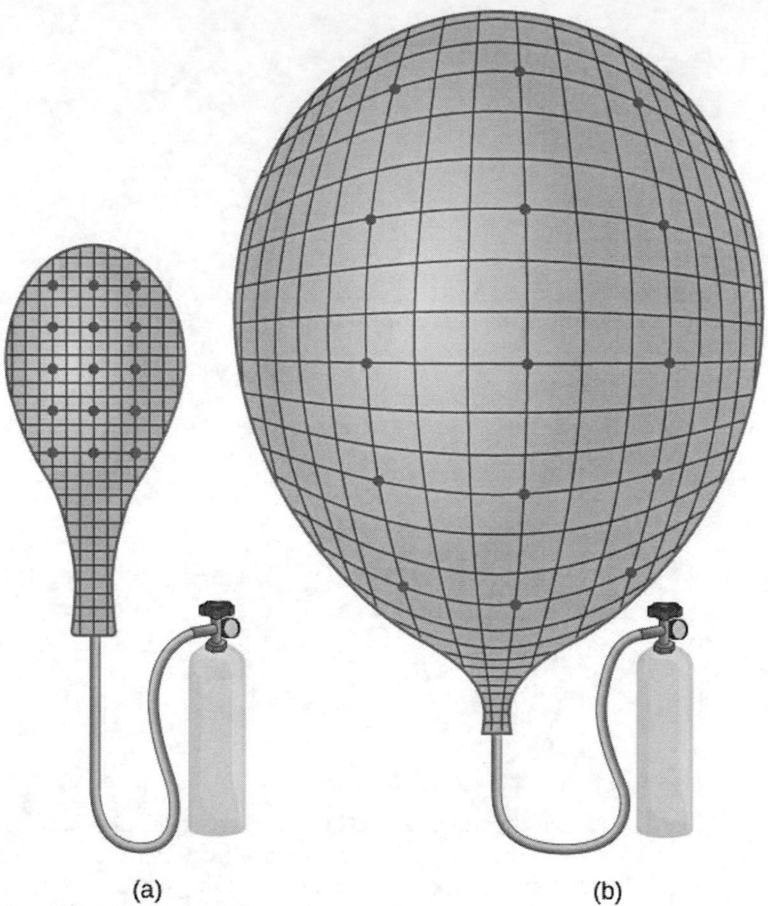

Figure 11.19 An analogy to the expanding universe: The dots move away from each other as the balloon expands; compare (a) to (b) after expansion.

Second, as mentioned already, the Big Bang expansion is due to the expansion of space, not the increased separation of galaxies in ordinary (static) three-dimensional space. This cosmological expansion affects all things: dust, stars, planets, and even light. Thus, the wavelength of light (λ) emitted by distant galaxies is "stretched" out. This makes the light appear "redder" (lower energy) to the observer—a phenomenon called cosmological **redshift**. Cosmological redshift is measurable only for galaxies farther away than 50 million light-years.

Example 11.8

Calculating Speeds and Galactic Distances

A galaxy is observed to have a redshift:

$$z = \frac{\lambda_{\text{obs}} - \lambda_{\text{emit}}}{\lambda_{\text{emit}}} = 4.5.$$

This value indicates a galaxy moving close to the speed of light. Using the relativistic redshift formula (given in **Relativity**), determine (a) How fast is the galaxy receding with respect to Earth? (b) How far away is the galaxy?

Strategy

We need to use the relativistic Doppler formula to determine speed from redshift and then use Hubble's law to find the distance from the speed.

Solution

a. According to the relativistic redshift formula:

$$z = \sqrt{\frac{1+\beta}{1-\beta}} - 1,$$

where $\beta = v/c$. Substituting the value for z and solving for β, we get $\beta = 0.93$. This value implies that the speed of the galaxy is 2.8×10^8 m/s.

b. Using Hubble's law, we can find the distance to the galaxy if we know its recession velocity:

$$d = \frac{v}{H_0} = \frac{2.8 \times 10^8 \text{ m/s}}{73.8 \times 10^3 \text{ m/s per Mpc}} = 3.8 \times 10^3 \text{ Mpc}.$$

Significance

Distant galaxies appear to move very rapidly away from Earth. The redshift of starlight from these galaxies can be used to determine the precise speed of recession, over 90% of the speed of light in this case. This motion is not due to the motion of galaxy through space but by the expansion of space itself.

11.8 Check Your Understanding The light of a galaxy that moves away from us is "redshifted." What occurs to the light of a galaxy that moves toward us?

View this **video (https://openstaxcollege.org/l/21expansion)** to learn more about the cosmological expansion.

Structure and Dynamics of the Universe

At large scales, the universe is believed to be both isotropic and homogeneous. The universe is believed to isotropic because it appears to be the same in all directions, and homogeneous because it appears to be the same in all places. A universe that is isotropic and homogeneous is said to be smooth. The assumption of a smooth universe is supported by the Automated Plate Measurement Galaxy Survey conducted in the 1980s and 1900s (**Figure 11.20**). However, even before these data were collected, the assumption of a smooth universe was used by theorists to simplify models of the expansion of the universe. This assumption of a smooth universe is sometimes called the cosmological principle.

Figure 11.20 The Automated Plate Measurement (APM) Galaxy Survey. Over 2 million galaxies are depicted in a region 100 degrees across centered toward the Milky Way's south pole. (credit: 2MASS/T. H. Jarrett, J. Carpenter, & R. Hurt)

The fate of this expanding and smooth universe is an open question. According to the general theory of relativity, an important way to characterize the state of the universe is through the space-time metric:

$$ds^2 = c^2 dt^2 - a(t)^2 d\Sigma^2, \quad (11.13)$$

where c is the speed of light, a is a scale factor (a function of time), and $d\Sigma$ is the length element of the space. In spherical coordinates (r, θ, ϕ), this length element can be written

$$d\Sigma^2 = \frac{dr^2}{1 - kr^2} + r^2\left(d\theta^2 + \sin^2\theta d\varphi^2\right), \quad (11.14)$$

where k is a constant with units of inverse area that describes the curvature of space. This constant distinguishes between open, closed, and flat universes:

- $k = 0$ (flat universe)
- $k > 0$ (closed universe, such as a sphere)
- $k < 0$ (open universe, such as a hyperbola)

In terms of the scale factor a, this metric also distinguishes between static, expanding, and shrinking universes:

- $a = 1$ (static universe)
- $da/dt > 0$ (expanding universe)
- $da/dt < 0$ (shrinking universe)

The scale factor a and the curvature k are determined from Einstein's general theory of relativity. If we treat the universe as a gas of galaxies of density ρ and pressure p, and assume $k = 0$ (a flat universe), than the scale factor a is given by

$$\frac{d^2 a}{dt^2} = -\frac{4\pi G}{3}(\rho + 3p)a, \quad (11.15)$$

where G is the universal gravitational constant. (For ordinary matter, we expect the quantity $\rho + 3p$ to be greater than zero.) If the scale factor is positive ($a > 0$), the value of the scale factor "decelerates" ($d^2 a/dt^2 < 0$), and the expansion of the universe slows down over time. If the numerator is less than zero (somehow, the pressure of the universe is negative), the value of the scale factor "accelerates," and the expansion of the universe speeds up over time. According to recent cosmological data, the universe appears to be expanding. Many scientists explain the current state of the universe in terms of a very rapid expansion in the early universe. This expansion is called inflation.

11.7 | Evolution of the Early Universe

Learning Objectives

By the end of this section, you will be able to:

- Describe the evolution of the early universe in terms of the four fundamental forces
- Use the concept of gravitational lensing to explain astronomical phenomena
- Provide evidence of the Big Bang in terms of cosmic background radiation
- Distinguish between dark matter and dark energy

In the previous section, we discussed the structure and dynamics of universe. In particular, the universe appears to be expanding and even accelerating. But what was the universe like at the beginning of time? In this section, we discuss what evidence scientists have been able to gather about the early universe and its evolution to present time.

The Early Universe

Before the short period of cosmic inflation, cosmologists believe that all matter in the universe was squeezed into a space much smaller than an atom. Cosmologists further believe that the universe was extremely dense and hot, and interactions between particles were governed by a single force. In other words, the four fundamental forces (strong nuclear, electromagnetic, weak nuclear, and gravitational) merge into one at these energies (**Figure 11.21**). How and why this "unity" breaks down at lower energies is an important unsolved problem in physics.

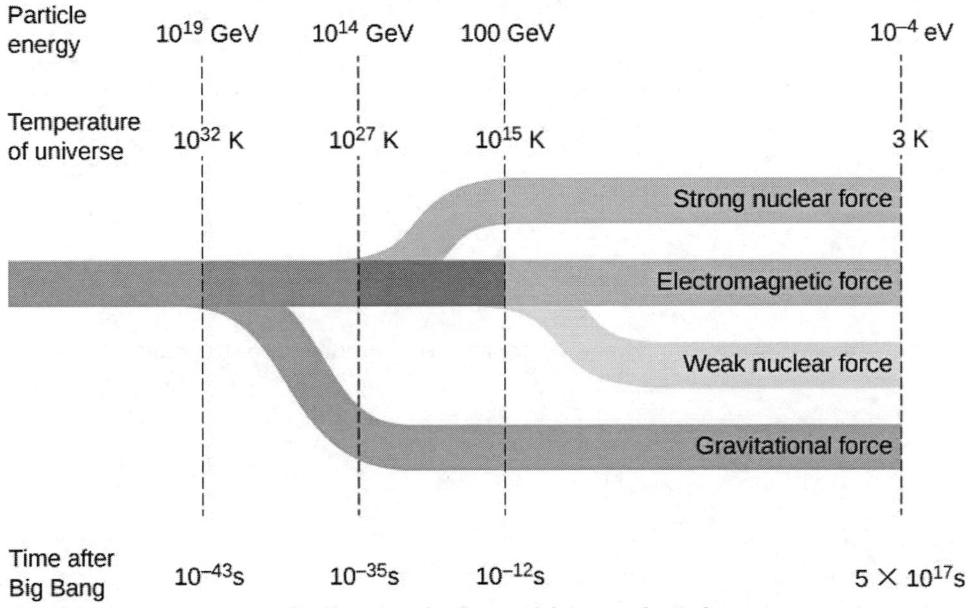

Figure 11.21 The separation of the four fundamental forces in the early universe.

Scientific models of the early universe are highly speculative. **Figure 11.22** shows a sketch of one possible timeline of events.

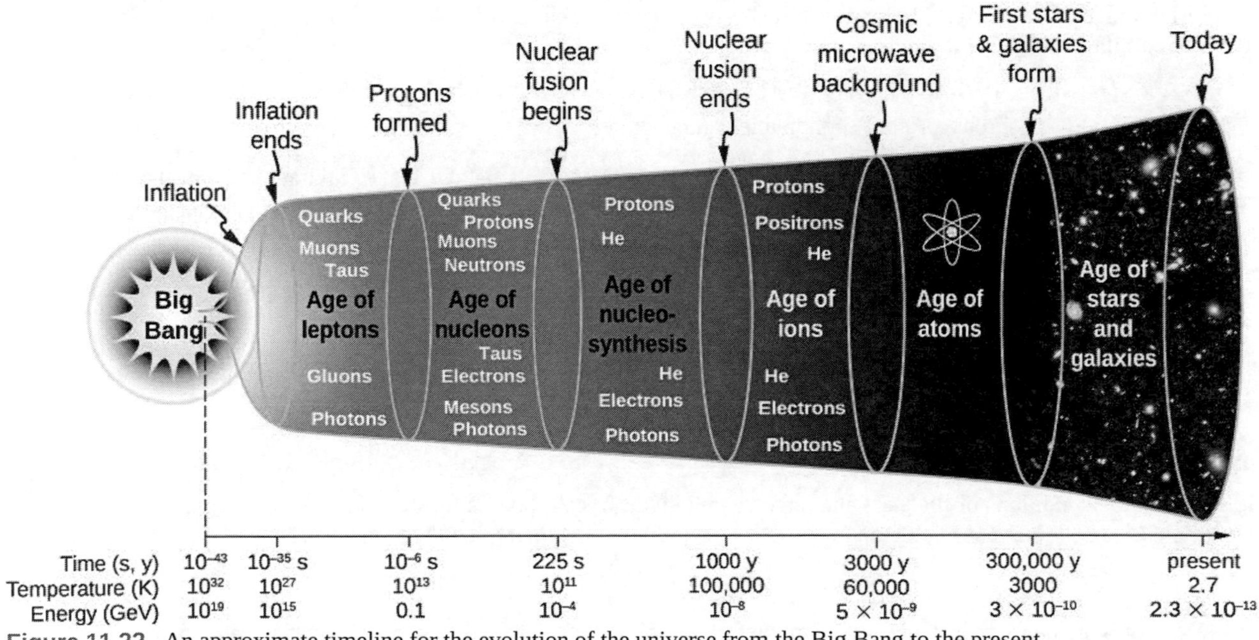

Figure 11.22 An approximate timeline for the evolution of the universe from the Big Bang to the present.

1. *Big Bang* $\left(t < 10^{-43}\,\text{s}\right)$: The current laws of physics break down. At the end of the initial Big Bang event, the temperature of the universe is approximately $T = 10^{32}\,\text{K}$.

2. *Inflationary phase* $(t = 10^{-43} \text{ to } 10^{-35} \text{ s})$: The universe expands exponentially, and gravity separates from the other forces. The universe cools to approximately $T = 10^{27}$ K.
3. *Age of leptons* $(t = 10^{-35} \text{ to } 10^{-6} \text{ s})$: As the universe continues to expand, the strong nuclear force separates from the electromagnetic and weak nuclear forces (or electroweak force). Soon after, the weak nuclear force separates from the electromagnetic force. The universe is a hot soup of quarks, leptons, photons, and other particles.
4. *Age of nucleons* $(t = 10^{-6} \text{ to } 225 \text{ s})$: The universe consists of leptons and hadrons (such as protons, neutrons, and mesons) in thermal equilibrium. Pair production and pair annihilation occurs with equal ease, so photons remain in thermal equilibrium:

$$\gamma + \gamma \leftrightarrow e^- + e^+$$
$$\gamma + \gamma \leftrightarrow p + \bar{p}$$
$$\gamma + \gamma \leftrightarrow n + \bar{n}.$$

The number of protons is approximately equal to the number of neutrons through interactions with neutrinos:

$$\nu_e + n \leftrightarrow e^- + p$$
$$\bar{\nu}_e + p \leftrightarrow e^+ + n.$$

The temperature of the universe settles to approximately 10^{11} K —much too cool for the continued production of nucleon-antinucleon pairs. The numbers of protons and neutrons begin to dominate over their anti-particles, so proton-antiproton $(p\bar{p})$ and neutron-antineutron ($n\bar{n}$) annihilations decline. Deuterons (proton-neutron pairs) begin to form.
5. *Age of nucleosynthesis* ($t = 225$ s to 1000 years): As the universe continues to expand, deuterons react with protons and neutrons to form larger nuclei; these larger nuclei react with protons and neutrons to form still larger nuclei. At the end of this period, about 1/4 of the mass of the universe is helium. (This explains the current amount of helium in the universe.) Photons lack the energy to continue electron-positron production, so electrons and positrons annihilate each other to photons only.
6. *Age of ions* ($t = 1000$ to 3000 years): The universe is hot enough to ionize any atoms formed. The universe consists of electrons, positrons, protons, light nuclei, and photons.
7. *Age of atoms* ($t = 3000$ to 300,000 years): The universe cools below 10^5 K and atoms form. Photons do not interact strongly with neutral atoms, so they "decouple" (separate) from atoms. These photons constitute the **cosmic microwave background radiation** to be discussed later.
8. *Age of stars and galaxies* ($t = 300{,}000$ years to present): The atoms and particles are pulled together by gravity and form large lumps. The atoms and particles in stars undergo nuclear fusion reaction.

Watch this **video (https://openstaxcollege.org/l/21bigbang)** to learn more about Big Bang cosmology.

To describe the conditions of the early universe quantitatively, recall the relationship between the average thermal energy of particle (*E*) in a system of interacting particles and equilibrium temperature (*T*) of that system:

$$E = k_B T, \qquad (11.16)$$

where k_B is Boltzmann's constant. In the hot conditions of the early universe, particle energies were unimaginably large.

Example 11.9

What Was the Average Thermal Energy of a Particle just after the Big Bang?

Strategy

The average thermal energy of a particle in a system of interacting particles depends on the equilibrium temperature of that system Equation 11.1. We are given this approximate temperature in the above timeline.

Solution

Cosmologists think the temperature of the universe just after the Big Bang was approximately $T = 10^{32}\,\text{K}$. Therefore, the average thermal energy of a particle would have been

$$k_B T \approx (10^{-4}\ \text{eV/K})(10^{32}\,\text{K}) = 10^{28}\ \text{eV} = 10^{19}\ \text{GeV}.$$

Significance

This energy is many orders of magnitude larger than particle energies produced by human-made particle accelerators. Currently, these accelerators operate at energies less than 10^4 GeV.

11.9 Check Your Understanding Compare the abundance of helium by mass 10,000 years after the Big Bang and now.

Nucleons form at energies approximately equal to the rest mass of a proton, or 1000 MeV. The temperature corresponding to this energy is therefore

$$T = \frac{1000\ \text{MeV}}{8.62 \times 10^{11}\ \text{MeV} \cdot \text{K}^{-1}} = 1.2 \times 10^{13}\ \text{K}.$$

Temperatures of this value or higher existed within the first second of the early universe. A similar analysis can be done for atoms. Atoms form at an energy equal to the ionization energy of ground-state hydrogen (13 eV). The effective temperature for atom formation is therefore

$$T = \frac{13\ \text{eV}}{8.62 \times 10^{5}\ \text{eV} \cdot \text{K}^{-1}} = 1.6 \times 10^{5}\ \text{K}.$$

This occurs well after the four fundamental forces have separated, including forces necessary to bind the protons and neutrons in the nucleus (strong nuclear force), and bind electrons to the nucleus (electromagnetic force).

Nucleosynthesis of Light Elements

The relative abundances of the light elements hydrogen, helium, lithium, and beryllium in the universe provide key evidence for the Big Bang. The data suggest that much of the helium in the universe is primordial. For instance, it turns out that that 25% of the matter in the universe is helium, which is too high an abundance and cannot be explained based on the production of helium in stars.

How much of the elements in the universe were created in the Big Bang? If you run the clock backward, the universe becomes more and more compressed, and hotter and hotter. Eventually, temperatures are reached that permit **nucleosynthesis**, the period of formation of nuclei, similar to what occurs at the core of the Sun. Big Bang nucleosynthesis is believed to have occurred within a few hundred seconds of the Big Bang.

How did Big Bang nucleosynthesis occur? At first, protons and neutrons combined to form deuterons, ^2H. The deuteron captured a neutron to form triton, ^3H —the nucleus of the radioactive hydrogen called tritium. Deuterons also captured protons to make helium ^3He. When ^3H captures a proton or ^3He captures a neutron, helium ^4He results. At this stage in the Big Bang, the ratio of protons to neutrons was about 7:1. Thus, the process of conversion to ^4He used up almost all neutrons. The process lasted about 3 minutes and almost 25% of all the matter turned into ^4He, along with small percentages of ^2H, ^3H, and ^3He. Tiny amounts of ^7Li and ^7Be were also formed. The expansion during this time cooled the universe enough that the nuclear reactions stopped. The abundances of the light nuclei ^2H, ^4He, and ^7Li created after the Big Bang are very dependent on the matter density.

The predicted abundances of the elements in the universe provide a stringent test of the Big Bang and the Big Bang nucleosynthesis. Recent experimental estimates of the matter density from the Wilkinson Microwave Anisotropy Probe (WMAP) agree with model predictions. This agreement provides convincing evidence of the Big Bang model.

Cosmic Microwave Background Radiation

According to cosmological models, the Big Bang event should have left behind thermal radiation called the cosmic microwave background radiation (CMBR). The intensity of this radiation should follow the blackbody radiation curve (**Photons and Matter Waves**). Wien's law states that the wavelength of the radiation at peak intensity is

$$\lambda_{\text{max}} = \frac{2.898 \times 10^{-3} \text{ m-K}}{T}, \quad (11.17)$$

where T is temperature in kelvins. Scientists expected the expansion of the universe to "stretch the light," and the temperature to be very low, so cosmic background radiation should be long-wavelength and low energy.

In the 1960s, Arno Penzias and Robert Wilson of Bell Laboratories noticed that no matter what they did, they could not get rid of a faint background noise in their satellite communication system. The noise was due to radiation with wavelengths in the centimeter range (the microwave region). Later, this noise was associated with the cosmic background radiation. An intensity map of the cosmic background radiation appears in **Figure 11.23**. The thermal spectrum is modeled well by a blackbody curve that corresponds to a temperature $T = 2.7\text{K}$ (**Figure 11.24**).

Figure 11.23 This map of the sky uses color to show fluctuations, or wrinkles, in the cosmic microwave background observed with the WMAP spacecraft. The Milky Way has been removed for clarity. Red represents higher temperature and higher density, whereas blue indicates lower temperature and density. This map does not contradict the earlier claim of smoothness because the largest fluctuations are only one part in one million. (credit: NASA/WMAP Science Team)

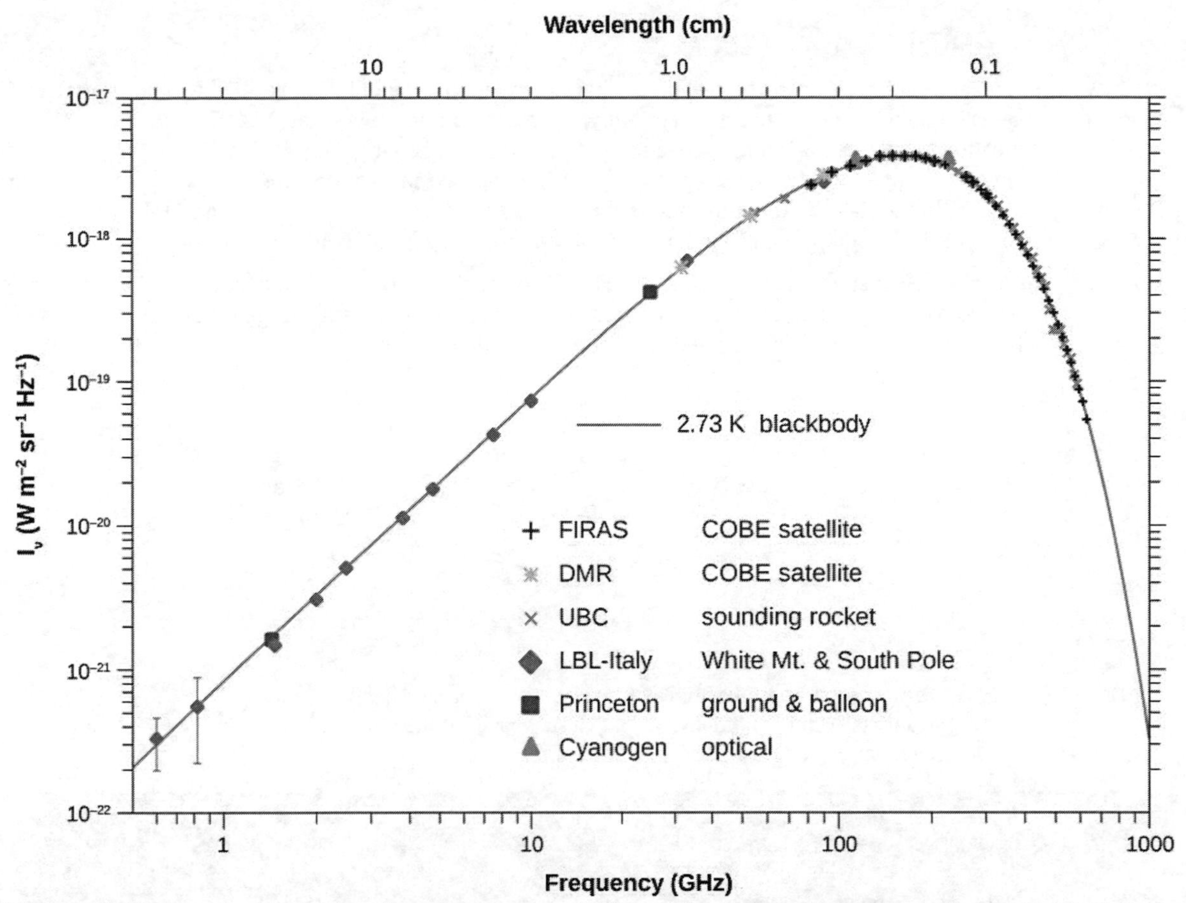

Figure 11.24 Intensity distribution of cosmic microwave background radiation. The model predictions (the line) agree extremely well with the experimental results (the dots). Frequency and brightness values are shown on a log axis. (credit: modification of work by George Smoot/NASA COBE Project)

The formation of atoms in the early universe makes these atoms less likely to interact with light. Therefore, photons that belong to the cosmic background radiation must have separated from matter at a temperature T associated with 1 eV (the approximate ionization energy of an atom) . The temperature of the universe at this point was

$$\mathrm{k_B T} \sim 1\text{ eV} \Rightarrow T = \frac{1\text{ eV}}{8.617 \times 10^5\text{ eV/K}} \sim 10^4\text{ K}.$$

According to cosmological models, the time when photons last scattered off charged particles was approximately 380,000 years after the Big Bang. Before that time, matter in the universe was in the plasma form and the photons were "thermalized."

Antimatter and Matter

We know from direct observation that antimatter is rare. Earth and the solar system are nearly pure matter, and most of the universe also seems dominated by matter. This is proven by the lack of annihilation radiation coming to us from space, particularly the relative absence of 0.511-MeV γ rays created by the mutual annihilation of electrons and positrons. (Antimatter in nature is created in particle collisions and in β^+ decays, but only in small amounts that quickly annihilate, leaving almost pure matter surviving.)

Despite the observed dominance of matter over antimatter in the universe, the Standard Model of particle interactions and experimental measurement suggests only small differences in the ways that matter and antimatter interact. For example, neutral kaon decays produce only slightly more matter than antimatter. Yet, if through such decay, slightly more matter than antimatter was produced in the early universe, the rest could annihilate pair by pair, leaving mostly ordinary matter to form the stars and galaxies. In this way, the vast number of stars we observe may be only a tiny remnant of the original matter created in the Big Bang.

Dark Matter and Dark Energy

In the last two decades, new and more powerful techniques have revealed that the universe is filled with **dark matter**. This type of matter is interesting and important because, currently, scientists do not know what it is! However, we can infer its existence by the deflection of distant starlight. For example, if light from a distant galaxy is bent by the gravitational field of a clump of dark matter between us and the galaxy, it is possible that two images of the same galaxy can be produced (**Figure 11.25**). The bending of light by the gravitational field of matter is called gravitational lensing. In some cases, the starlight travels to an observer by multiple paths around the galaxy, producing a ring (**Figure 11.26**).

Based on current research, scientist know only that dark matter is cold, slow moving, and interacts weakly with ordinary matter. Dark matter candidates include neutralinos (partners of Z bosons, photons, and Higgs bosons in "supersymmetry theory") and particles that circulate in tiny rings set up by extra spatial dimensions.

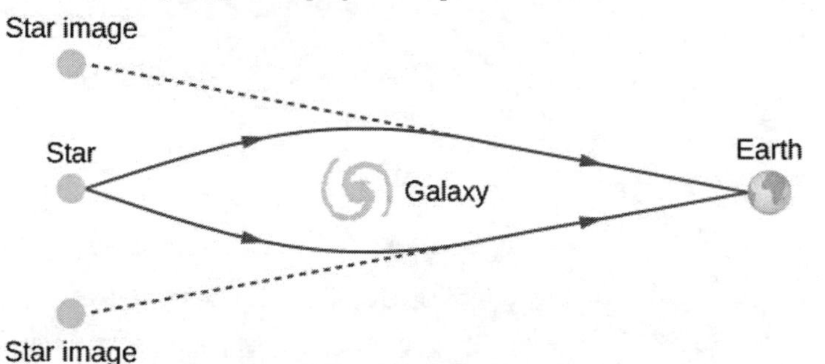

Figure 11.25 Light from a distant star is bent around a galaxy. Under the right conditions, two duplicate images of the same star can be seen.

Figure 11.26 Light from a distant star is bent around a galaxy. Under the right conditions, we can see a ring of light instead of a single star. (credit: modification of work by ESA/Hubble & NASA)

Increasingly precise astronomical measurements of the expanding universe also reveal the presence of a new form of energy called **dark energy**. This energy is thought to explain larger-than-expected values for the observed galactic redshifts for distant galaxies. These redshifts suggest that the universe is not only expanding, but expanding at an increasing rate. Virtually nothing is known about the nature and properties of dark energy. Together, dark energy and dark matter represent two of the most interesting and unsolved puzzles of modern physics. Scientists attribute 68.3% of the energy of the universe to dark energy, 26.8% to dark matter, and just 4.9% to the mass-energy of ordinary particles (**Figure 11.27**). Given the current great mystery over the nature of dark matter and dark energy, Isaac Newton's humble words are as true now as they were centuries ago:

"I do not know what I may appear to the world, but to myself I seem to have been only like a boy playing on the sea-shore, and diverting myself in now and then finding a smoother pebble or a prettier shell than ordinary, whilst the great ocean of truth lay all undiscovered before me."

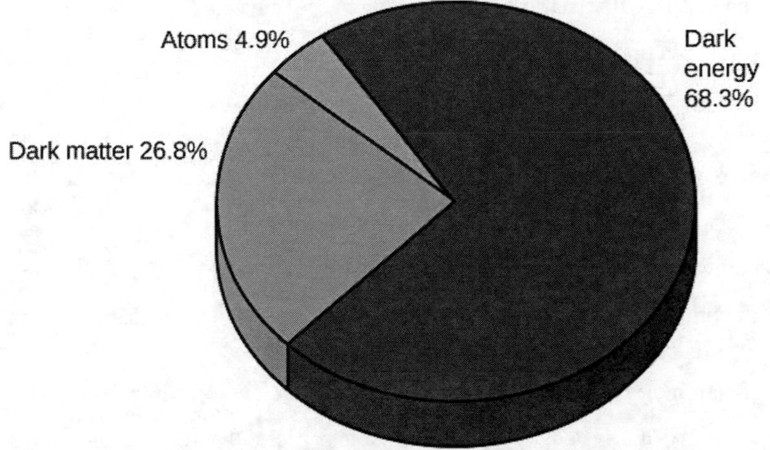

Figure 11.27 Estimated distribution of matter and energy in the universe. (credit: NASA/WMAP Science Team)

CHAPTER 11 REVIEW

KEY TERMS

antiparticle subatomic particle with the same mass and lifetime as its associated particle, but opposite electric charge

baryon number baryon number has the value $B = +1$ for baryons, -1 for antibaryons, and 0 for all other particles and is conserved in particle interactions

baryons group of three quarks

Big Bang rapid expansion of space that marked the beginning of the universe

boson particle with integral spin that are symmetric on exchange

color property of particles and that plays the same role in strong nuclear interactions as electric charge does in electromagnetic interactions

cosmic microwave background radiation (CMBR) thermal radiation produced by the Big Bang event

cosmology study of the origin, evolution, and ultimate fate of the universe

dark energy form of energy believed to be responsible for the observed acceleration of the universe

dark matter matter in the universe that does not interact with other particles but that can be inferred by deflection of distance star light

electroweak force unification of electromagnetic force and weak-nuclear force interactions

exchange symmetry property of a system of indistinguishable particles that requires the exchange of any two particles to be unobservable

fermion particle with half-integral spin that is antisymmetric on exchange

Feynman diagram space-time diagram that describes how particles move and interact

fundamental force one of four forces that act between bodies of matter: the strong nuclear, electromagnetic, weak nuclear, and gravitational forces

gluon particle that that carry the strong nuclear force between quarks within an atomic nucleus

grand unified theory theory of particle interactions that unifies the strong nuclear, electromagnetic, and weak nuclear forces

hadron a meson or baryon

Hubble's constant constant that relates speed and distance in Hubble's law

Hubble's law relationship between the speed and distance of stars and galaxies

lepton a fermion that participates in the electroweak force

lepton number electron-lepton number L_e, the muon-lepton number L_μ, and the tau-lepton number L_τ are conserved separately in every particle interaction

mesons a group of two quarks

nucleosynthesis creation of heavy elements, occurring during the Big Bang

particle accelerator machine designed to accelerate charged particles; this acceleration is usually achieved with strong electric fields, magnetic fields, or both

particle detector detector designed to accurately measure the outcome of collisions created by a particle accelerator; particle detectors are hermetic and multipurpose

positron antielectron

quantum chromodynamics (QCD) theory that describes strong interactions between quarks

quantum electrodynamics (QED) theory that describes the interaction of electrons with photons

quark a fermion that participates in the electroweak and strong nuclear force

redshift lengthening of the wavelength of light (or reddening) due to cosmological expansion

Standard Model model of particle interactions that contains the electroweak theory and quantum chromodynamics (QCD)

strangeness particle property associated with the presence of a strange quark

strong nuclear force relatively strong attractive force that acts over short distances (about 10^{-15} m) responsible for binding protons and neutrons together in atomic nuclei

synchrotron circular accelerator that uses alternating voltage and increasing magnetic field strengths to accelerate particles to higher and higher energies

synchrotron radiation high-energy radiation produced in a synchrotron accelerator by the circular motion of a charged beam

theory of everything a theory of particle interactions that unifies all four fundamental forces

virtual particle particle that exists for too short of time to be observable

W and Z boson particle with a relatively large mass that carries the weak nuclear force between leptons and quarks

weak nuclear force relative weak force (about 10^{-6} the strength of the strong nuclear force) responsible for decays of elementary particles and neutrino interactions

KEY EQUATIONS

Momentum of a charged particle in a cyclotron	$p = 0.3Br$
Center-of-mass energy of a colliding beam machine	$W^2 = 2[E_1 E_2 + (p_1 c)(p_2 c)] + (m_1 c^2)^2 + (m_2 c^2)^2$
Approximate time for exchange of a virtual particle between two other particles	$\Delta t = \frac{h}{E}$
Hubble's law	$v = H_0 d$
Cosmological space-time metric	$ds^2 = c^2 dt^2 - a(t)^2 d\Sigma^2$

SUMMARY

11.1 Introduction to Particle Physics

- The four fundamental forces of nature are, in order of strength: strong nuclear, electromagnetic, weak nuclear, and gravitational. Quarks interact via the strong force, but leptons do not. Both quark and leptons interact via the electromagnetic, weak, and gravitational forces.
- Elementary particles are classified into fermions and boson. Fermions have half-integral spin and obey the exclusion principle. Bosons have integral spin and do not obey this principle. Bosons are the force carriers of particle interactions.
- Quarks and leptons belong to particle families composed of three members each. Members of a family share many properties (charge, spin, participation in forces) but not mass.
- All particles have antiparticles. Particles share the same properties as their antimatter particles, but carry opposite charge.

11.2 Particle Conservation Laws

- Elementary particle interactions are governed by particle conservation laws, which can be used to determine what particle reactions and decays are possible (or forbidden).
- The baryon number conservation law and the three lepton number conversation law are valid for all physical

processes. However, conservation of strangeness is valid only for strong nuclear interactions and electromagnetic interactions.

11.3 Quarks

- Six known quarks exist: up (*u*), down (*d*), charm (*c*), strange (*s*), top (*t*), and bottom (*b*). These particles are fermions with half-integral spin and fractional charge.
- Baryons consist of three quarks, and mesons consist of a quark-antiquark pair. Due to the strong force, quarks cannot exist in isolation.
- Evidence for quarks is found in scattering experiments.

11.4 Particle Accelerators and Detectors

- Many types of particle accelerators have been developed to study particles and their interactions. These include linear accelerators, cyclotrons, synchrotrons, and colliding beams.
- Colliding beam machines are used to create massive particles that decay quickly to lighter particles.
- Multipurpose detectors are used to design all aspects of high-energy collisions. These include detectors to measure the momentum and energies of charge particles and photons.
- Charged particles are measured by bending these particles in a circle by a magnetic field.
- Particles are measured using calorimeters that absorb the particles.

11.5 The Standard Model

- The Standard Model describes interactions between particles through the strong nuclear, electromagnetic, and weak nuclear forces.
- Particle interactions are represented by Feynman diagrams. A Feynman diagram represents interactions between particles on a space-time graph.
- Electromagnetic forces act over a long range, but strong and weak forces act over a short range. These forces are transmitted between particles by sending and receiving bosons.
- Grand unified theories seek an understanding of the universe in terms of just one force.

11.6 The Big Bang

- The universe is expanding like a balloon—every point is receding from every other point.
- Distant galaxies move away from us at a velocity proportional to its distance. This rate is measured to be approximately 70 km/s/Mpc. Thus, the farther galaxies are from us, the greater their speeds. These "recessional velocities" can be measure using the Doppler shift of light.
- According to current cosmological models, the universe began with the Big Bang approximately 13.7 billion years ago.

11.7 Evolution of the Early Universe

- The early universe was hot and dense.
- The universe is isotropic and expanding.
- Cosmic background radiation is evidence for the Big Bang.
- The vast portion of the mass and energy of the universe is not well understood.

CONCEPTUAL QUESTIONS

11.1 Introduction to Particle Physics

1. What are the four fundamental forces? Briefly describe them.

2. Distinguish fermions and bosons using the concepts of indistiguishability and exchange symmetry.

3. List the quark and lepton families

4. Distinguish between elementary particles and antiparticles. Describe their interactions.

11.2 Particle Conservation Laws

5. What are six particle conservation laws? Briefly describe them.

6. In general, how do we determine if a particle reaction or decay occurs?

7. Why might the detection of particle interaction that violates an established particle conservation law be considered a *good* thing for a scientist?

11.3 Quarks

8. What are the six known quarks? Summarize their properties.

9. What is the general quark composition of a baryon? Of a meson?

10. What evidence exists for the existence of quarks?

11. Why do baryons with the same quark composition sometimes differ in their rest mass energies?

11.4 Particle Accelerators and Detectors

12. Briefly compare the Van de Graaff accelerator, linear accelerator, cyclotron, and synchrotron accelerator.

13. Describe the basic components and function of a typical colliding beam machine.

14. What are the subdetectors of the Compact Muon Solenoid experiment? Briefly describe them.

15. What is the advantage of a colliding-beam accelerator over one that fires particles into a fixed target?

16. An electron appears in the muon detectors of the CMS. How is this possible?

11.5 The Standard Model

17. What is the Standard Model? Express your answer in terms of the four fundamental forces and exchange particles.

18. Draw a Feynman diagram to represents annihilation of an electron and positron into a photon.

19. What is the motivation behind grand unification theories?

20. If a theory is developed that unifies all four forces, will it still be correct to say that the orbit of the Moon is determined by the gravitational force? Explain why.

21. If the Higgs boson is discovered and found to have mass, will it be considered the ultimate carrier of the weak force? Explain your response.

22. One of the common decay modes of the Λ^0 is $\Lambda^0 \rightarrow \pi^- + \text{p}$. Even though only hadrons are involved in this decay, it occurs through the weak nuclear force. How do we know that this decay does not occur through the strong nuclear force?

11.6 The Big Bang

23. What is meant by cosmological expansion? Express your answer in terms of a Hubble graph and the red shift of distant starlight.

24. Describe the balloon analogy for cosmological expansion. Explain why it only *appears* that we are at the center of expansion of the universe.

25. Distances to local galaxies are determined by measuring the brightness of stars, called Cepheid variables, that can be observed individually and that have absolute brightnesses at a standard distance that are well known. Explain how the measured brightness would vary with distance, as compared with the absolute brightness.

11.7 Evolution of the Early Universe

26. What is meant by a "cosmological model of the early universe?" Briefly describe this model in terms of the four fundamental forces.

27. Describe two pieces of evidence that support the Big Bang model.

28. In what sense are we, as Newton once said, "a boy playing on the sea-shore"? Express your answer in terms of the concepts of dark matter and dark energy.

29. If some unknown cause of redshift—such as light becoming "tired" from traveling long distances through empty space—is discovered, what effect would that have on cosmology?

30. In the past, many scientists believed the universe to be infinite. However, if the universe is infinite, then any line of sight should eventually fall on a star's surface and the night sky should be very bright. How is this paradox resolved in modern cosmology?

PROBLEMS

11.1 Introduction to Particle Physics

31. How much energy is released when an electron and a positron at rest annihilate each other? (For particle masses, see **Table 11.1**.)

32. If 1.0×10^{30} MeV of energy is released in the annihilation of a sphere of matter and antimatter, and the spheres are equal mass, what are the masses of the spheres?

33. When both an electron and a positron are at rest, they can annihilate each other according to the reaction

$e^- + e^+ \rightarrow \gamma + \gamma.$

In this case, what are the energy, momentum, and frequency of each photon?

34. What is the *total kinetic energy* carried away by the particles of the following decays?

(a) $\pi^0 \rightarrow \gamma + \gamma$

(b) $\mathrm{K}^0 \rightarrow \pi^+ + \pi^-$

(c) $\Sigma^+ \rightarrow n + \pi^+$

(d) $\Sigma^0 \rightarrow \Lambda^0 + \gamma.$

11.2 Particle Conservation Laws

35. Which of the following decays cannot occur because the law of conservation of lepton number is violated?

(a) $\mathrm{n} \rightarrow \mathrm{p} + \mathrm{e}^-$

(b) $\mu^+ \rightarrow \mathrm{e}^+ + \upsilon_\mathrm{e}$

(c) $\pi^+ \rightarrow \mathrm{e}^+ + \upsilon_\mathrm{e} + \bar{\upsilon}_\mu$

(d) $\mathrm{p} \rightarrow \mathrm{n} + \mathrm{e}^+ + \upsilon_\mathrm{e}$

(e) $\pi^- \rightarrow \mathrm{e}^- + \bar{\upsilon}_\mathrm{e}$

(f) $\mu^- \rightarrow \mathrm{e}^- + \bar{\upsilon}_\mathrm{e} + \upsilon_\mu$

(g) $\Lambda^0 \rightarrow \pi^- + \mathrm{p}$

(h) $\mathrm{K}^+ \rightarrow \mu^+ + \upsilon_\mu$

36. Which of the following reactions cannot because the law of conservation of strangeness is violated?

(a) $\mathrm{p} + \mathrm{n} \rightarrow \mathrm{p} + \mathrm{p} + \pi^-$

(b) $\mathrm{p} + \mathrm{n} \rightarrow \mathrm{p} + \mathrm{p} + \mathrm{K}^-$

(c) $\mathrm{K}^- + \mathrm{p} \rightarrow \mathrm{K}^- + \Sigma^+$

(d) $\pi^- + \mathrm{p} \rightarrow \mathrm{K}^+ + \Sigma^-$

(e) $\mathrm{K}^- + \mathrm{p} \rightarrow \Xi^0 + \mathrm{K}^+ + \pi^-$

(f) $\mathrm{K}^- + \mathrm{p} \rightarrow \Xi^0 + \pi^- + \pi^-$

(g) $\pi^+ + \mathrm{p} \rightarrow \Sigma^+ + \mathrm{K}^+$

(h) $\pi^- + \mathrm{n} \rightarrow \mathrm{K}^- + \Lambda^0$

37. Identify one possible decay for each of the following antiparticles:

(a) $\bar{n}$, (b) $\overline{\Lambda^0}$, (c) Ω^+, (d) K^-, and (e) $\bar{\Sigma}$.

38. Each of the following strong nuclear reactions is forbidden. Identify a conservation law that is violated for each one.

(a) $\mathrm{p} + \bar{\mathrm{p}} \rightarrow \mathrm{p} + \mathrm{n} + \bar{\mathrm{p}}$

(b) $\mathrm{p} + \mathrm{n} \rightarrow \mathrm{p} + \bar{\mathrm{p}} + \mathrm{n} + \pi^+$

(c) $\pi^- + \mathrm{p} \rightarrow \Sigma^+ + \mathrm{K}^-$

(d) $\mathrm{K}^- + \mathrm{p} \rightarrow \Lambda^0 + \mathrm{n}$

11.3 Quarks

39. Based on quark composition of a proton, show that its charge is $+1$.

40. Based on the quark composition of a neutron, show that is charge is 0.

41. Argue that the quark composition given in **Table 11.5** for the positive kaon is consistent with the known charge, spin, and strangeness of this baryon.

42. Mesons are formed from the following combinations of quarks (subscripts indicate color and $AR =$ antired): $(d_\mathrm{R}, \bar{d}_\mathrm{AR})$, $(s_\mathrm{G}, \bar{u}_\mathrm{AG})$, and $(s_\mathrm{R}, \bar{s}_\mathrm{AR})$.

(a) Determine the charge and strangeness of each combination. (*b*) Identify one or more mesons formed by each quark-antiquark combination.

43. Why can't either set of quarks shown below form a hadron?

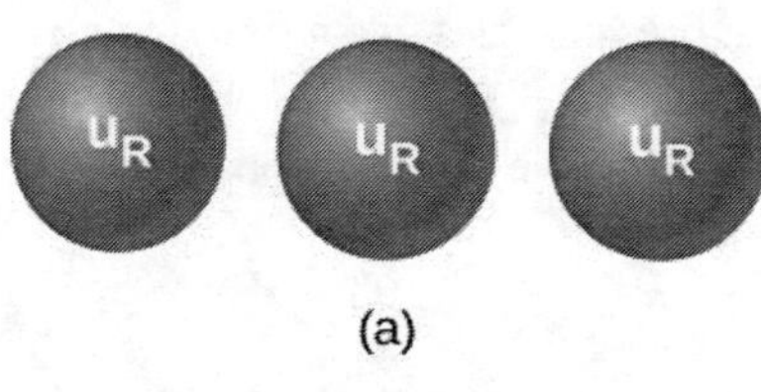

(a)

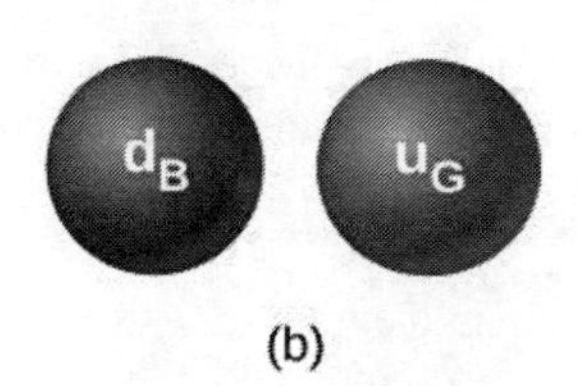

(b)

44. Experimental results indicate an isolate particle with charge $+2/3$—an isolated quark. What quark could this be? Why would this discovery be important?

45. Express the β decays $n \rightarrow p + e^- + \bar{\nu}$ and $p \rightarrow n + e^+ + \nu$ in terms of β decays of quarks. Check to see that the conservation laws for charge, lepton number, and baryon number are satisfied by the quark β decays.

11.4 Particle Accelerators and Detectors

46. A charged particle in a 2.0-T magnetic field is bent in a circle of radius 75 cm. What is the momentum of the particle?

47. A proton track passes through a magnetic field with radius of 50 cm. The magnetic field strength is 1.5 T. What is the total energy of the proton?

48. Derive the equation $p = 0.3Br$ using the concepts of centripetal acceleration (**Motion in Two and Three Dimensions (http://cnx.org/content/m58288/latest/)**) and relativistic momentum (**Relativity**)

49. Assume that beam energy of an electron-positron collider is approximately 4.73 GeV. What is the total mass (*W*) of a particle produced in the annihilation of an electron and positron in this collider? What meson might be produced?

50. At full energy, protons in the 2.00-km-diameter Fermilab synchrotron travel at nearly the speed of light, since their energy is about 1000 times their rest mass energy. (a) How long does it take for a proton to complete one trip around? (b) How many times per second will it pass through the target area?

51. Suppose a W^- created in a particle detector lives for 5.00×10^{-25} s. What distance does it move in this time if it is traveling at 0.900*c*? (Note that the time is longer than the given W^- lifetime, which can be due to the statistical nature of decay or time dilation.)

52. What length track does a π^+ traveling at 0.100*c* leave in a bubble chamber if it is created there and lives for 2.60×10^{-8} s? (Those moving faster or living longer may escape the detector before decaying.)

53. The 3.20-km-long SLAC produces a beam of 50.0-GeV electrons. If there are 15,000 accelerating tubes, what average voltage must be across the gaps between them to achieve this energy?

11.5 The Standard Model

54. Using the Heisenberg uncertainly principle, determine the range of the weak force if this force is produced by the exchange of a Z boson.

55. Use the Heisenberg uncertainly principle to estimate the range of a weak nuclear decay involving a graviton.

56. (a) The following decay is mediated by the electroweak force:

$$\text{p} \rightarrow \text{n} + \text{e}^+ + \upsilon_\text{e}.$$

Draw the Feynman diagram for the decay.

(b) The following scattering is mediated by the electroweak force:

$$\upsilon_e + \text{e}^- \rightarrow \upsilon_e + \text{e}^-.$$

Draw the Feynman diagram for the scattering.

57. Assuming conservation of momentum, what is the energy of each γ ray produced in the decay of a neutral pion at rest, in the reaction $\pi^0 \rightarrow \gamma + \gamma$?

58. What is the wavelength of a 50-GeV electron, which is produced at SLAC? This provides an idea of the limit to the detail it can probe.

59. The primary decay mode for the negative pion is $\pi^- \rightarrow \mu^- + \bar{\nu}_\mu$. (a) What is the energy release in MeV in this decay? (b) Using conservation of momentum, how much energy does each of the decay products receive, given the π^- is at rest when it decays? You may assume the muon antineutrino is massless and has momentum $p = E/c$, just like a photon.

60. Suppose you are designing a proton decay experiment and you can detect 50 percent of the proton decays in a tank of water. (a) How many kilograms of water would you need to see one decay per month, assuming a lifetime of 10^{31} y? (b) How many cubic meters of water is this? (c) If the actual lifetime is 10^{33} y, how long would you have to wait on an average to see a single proton decay?

11.6 The Big Bang

61. If the speed of a distant galaxy is 0.99*c*, what is the distance of the galaxy from an Earth-bound observer?

62. The distance of a galaxy from our solar system is 10 Mpc. (a) What is the recessional velocity of the galaxy? (b) By what fraction is the starlight from this galaxy redshifted (that is, what is its z value)?

63. If a galaxy is 153 Mpc away from us, how fast do we expect it to be moving and in what direction?

64. On average, how far away are galaxies that are moving away from us at 2.0% of the speed of light?

65. Our solar system orbits the center of the Milky Way Galaxy. Assuming a circular orbit 30,000 ly in radius and an orbital speed of 250 km/s, how many years does it take for one revolution? Note that this is approximate, assuming constant speed and circular orbit, but it is representative of the time for our system and local stars to make one revolution around the galaxy.

66. (a) What is the approximate velocity relative to us of a galaxy near the edge of the known universe, some 10 Gly away? (b) What fraction of the speed of light is this? Note that we have observed galaxies moving away from us at greater than 0.9*c*.

67. (a) Calculate the approximate age of the universe from the average value of the Hubble constant, $H_0 = 20\,\text{km/s} \cdot \text{Mly}$. To do this, calculate the time it would take to travel 0.307 Mpc at a constant expansion rate of 20 km/s. (b) If somehow acceleration occurs, would the actual age of the universe be greater or less than that found here? Explain.

68. The Andromeda Galaxy is the closest large galaxy and is visible to the naked eye. Estimate its brightness relative to the Sun, assuming it has luminosity 10^{12} times that of the Sun and lies 0.613 Mpc away.

69. Show that the velocity of a star orbiting its galaxy in a circular orbit is inversely proportional to the square root of its orbital radius, assuming the mass of the stars inside its orbit acts like a single mass at the center of the galaxy. You may use an equation from a previous chapter to support your conclusion, but you must justify its use and define all terms used.

ADDITIONAL PROBLEMS

70. Experimental results suggest that a muon decays to an electron and photon. How is this possible?

71. Each of the following reactions is missing a single particle. Identify the missing particle for each reaction.

(a) $\text{p} + \bar{\text{p}} \rightarrow \text{n} + ?$

(b) $\text{p} + \text{p} \rightarrow \text{p} + \Lambda^0 + ?$

(c) $\pi^? + \text{p} \rightarrow \Sigma^- + ?$

(d) $\text{K}^- + \text{n} \rightarrow \Lambda^0 + ?$

(e) $\tau^+ \rightarrow \text{e}^+ + \nu_\text{e} + ?$

(f) $\bar{\nu}_\text{e} + \text{p} \rightarrow \text{n} + ?$

72. Because of energy loss due to synchrotron radiation in the LHC at CERN, only 5.00 MeV is added to the energy of each proton during each revolution around the main ring. How many revolutions are needed to produce 7.00-TeV (7000 GeV) protons, if they are injected with an initial energy of 8.00 GeV?

73. A proton and an antiproton collide head-on, with each having a kinetic energy of 7.00 TeV (such as in the LHC at CERN). How much collision energy is available, taking into account the annihilation of the two masses? (Note that this is not significantly greater than the extremely relativistic kinetic energy.)

74. When an electron and positron collide at the SLAC facility, they each have 50.0-GeV kinetic energies. What is the total collision energy available, taking into account the annihilation energy? Note that the annihilation energy is insignificant, because the electrons are highly relativistic.

75. The core of a star collapses during a supernova, forming a neutron star. Angular momentum of the core is conserved, so the neutron star spins rapidly. If the initial core radius is 5.0×10^5 km and it collapses to 10.0 km, find the neutron star's angular velocity in revolutions per second, given the core's angular velocity was originally 1 revolution per 30.0 days.

76. Using the solution from the previous problem, find the increase in rotational kinetic energy, given the core's mass is 1.3 times that of our Sun. Where does this increase in kinetic energy come from?

77. (a) What Hubble constant corresponds to an approximate age of the universe of 10^{10} y? To get an approximate value, assume the expansion rate is constant and calculate the speed at which two galaxies must move apart to be separated by 1 Mly (present average galactic separation) in a time of 10^{10} y. (b) Similarly, what Hubble constant corresponds to a universe approximately 2×10^{10} years old?

CHALLENGE PROBLEMS

78. Electrons and positrons are collided in a circular accelerator. Derive the expression for the center-of-mass energy of the particle.

79. The intensity of cosmic ray radiation decreases rapidly with increasing energy, but there are occasionally extremely energetic cosmic rays that create a shower of radiation from all the particles they create by striking a nucleus in the atmosphere. Suppose a cosmic ray particle having an energy of 10^{10} GeV converts its energy into particles with masses averaging $200\text{MeV}/c^2$.

(a) How many particles are created? (b) If the particles rain down on a 1.00-km^2 area, how many particles are there per square meter?

80. (a) Calculate the relativistic quantity $\gamma = \frac{1}{\sqrt{1 - v^2/c^2}}$ for 1.00-TeV protons produced at Fermilab. (b) If such a proton created a π^+ having the same speed, how long would its life be in the laboratory? (c) How far could it travel in this time?

81. Plans for an accelerator that produces a secondary beam of K mesons to scatter from nuclei, for the purpose of studying the strong force, call for them to have a kinetic energy of 500 MeV. (a) What would the relativistic quantity $\gamma = \frac{1}{\sqrt{1 - v^2/c^2}}$ be for these particles? (b) How long would their average lifetime be in the laboratory? (c) How far could they travel in this time?

82. In supernovae, neutrinos are produced in huge amounts. They were detected from the 1987A supernova in the Magellanic Cloud, which is about 120,000 light-years away from Earth (relatively close to our Milky Way Galaxy). If neutrinos have a mass, they cannot travel at the speed of light, but if their mass is small, their velocity would be almost that of light. (a) Suppose a neutrino with a $7\text{-eV}/c^2$ mass has a kinetic energy of 700 keV. Find the relativistic quantity $\gamma = \frac{1}{\sqrt{1 - v^2/c^2}}$ for it. (b) If the neutrino leaves the 1987A supernova at the same time as a photon and both travel to Earth, how much sooner does the photon arrive? This is not a large time difference, given that it is impossible to know which neutrino left with which photon and the poor efficiency of the neutrino detectors. Thus, the fact that neutrinos were observed within hours of the brightening of the supernova only places an upper limit on the neutrino's mass. (*Hint:* You may need to use a series expansion to find v for the neutrino, since its γ is so large.)

83. Assuming a circular orbit for the Sun about the center of the Milky Way Galaxy, calculate its orbital speed using the following information: The mass of the galaxy is equivalent to a single mass 1.5×10^{11} times that of the Sun (or 3×10^{41} kg), located 30,000 ly away.

84. (a) What is the approximate force of gravity on a 70-kg person due to the Andromeda Galaxy, assuming its total mass is 10^{13} that of our Sun and acts like a single mass 0.613 Mpc away? (b) What is the ratio of this force to the person's weight? Note that Andromeda is the closest large galaxy.

85. (a) A particle and its antiparticle are at rest relative to an observer and annihilate (completely destroying both masses), creating two γ rays of equal energy. What is the characteristic γ-ray energy you would look for if searching for evidence of proton-antiproton annihilation? (The fact that such radiation is rarely observed is evidence that there is very little antimatter in the universe.) (b) How does this compare with the 0.511-MeV energy associated with electron-positron annihilation?

86. The peak intensity of the CMBR occurs at a wavelength of 1.1 mm. (a) What is the energy in eV of a 1.1-mm photon? (b) There are approximately 10^9 photons for each massive particle in deep space. Calculate the energy of 10^9 such photons. (c) If the average massive particle in space has a mass half that of a proton, what energy would be created by converting its mass to energy? (d) Does this imply that space is "matter dominated"? Explain briefly.

87. (a) Use the Heisenberg uncertainty principle to calculate the uncertainty in energy for a corresponding time interval of 10^{-43} s. (b) Compare this energy with the 10^{19} GeV unification-of-forces energy and discuss why they are similar.

APPENDIX A | UNITS

Quantity	Common Symbol	Unit	Unit in Terms of Base SI Units
Acceleration	$\vec{\mathbf{a}}$	m/s^2	m/s^2
Amount of substance	n	**mole**	mol
Angle	θ, ϕ	radian (rad)	
Angular acceleration	$\vec{\alpha}$	rad/s^2	s^{-2}
Angular frequency	ω	rad/s	s^{-1}
Angular momentum	$\vec{\mathbf{L}}$	$\text{kg} \cdot \text{m}^2/\text{s}$	$\text{kg} \cdot \text{m}^2/\text{s}$
Angular velocity	$\vec{\omega}$	rad/s	s^{-1}
Area	A	m^2	m^2
Atomic number	Z		
Capacitance	C	farad (F)	$\text{A}^2 \cdot \text{s}^4/\text{kg} \cdot \text{m}^2$
Charge	q, Q, e	coulomb (C)	$\text{A} \cdot \text{s}$
Charge density:			
Line	λ	C/m	$\text{A} \cdot \text{s/m}$
Surface	σ	C/m^2	$\text{A} \cdot \text{s/m}^2$
Volume	ρ	C/m^3	$\text{A} \cdot \text{s/m}^3$
Conductivity	σ	$1/\Omega \cdot \text{m}$	$\text{A}^2 \cdot \text{s}^3/\text{kg} \cdot \text{m}^3$
Current	I	**ampere**	A
Current density	$\vec{\mathbf{J}}$	A/m^2	A/m^2
Density	ρ	kg/m^3	kg/m^3
Dielectric constant	κ		
Electric dipole moment	$\vec{\mathbf{p}}$	$\text{C} \cdot \text{m}$	$\text{A} \cdot \text{s} \cdot \text{m}$
Electric field	$\vec{\mathbf{E}}$	N/C	$\text{kg} \cdot \text{m/A} \cdot \text{s}^3$
Electric flux	Φ	$\text{N} \cdot \text{m}^2/\text{C}$	$\text{kg} \cdot \text{m}^3/\text{A} \cdot \text{s}^3$
Electromotive force	ε	volt (V)	$\text{kg} \cdot \text{m}^2/\text{A} \cdot \text{s}^3$
Energy	E, U, K	joule (J)	$\text{kg} \cdot \text{m}^2/\text{s}^2$
Entropy	S	J/K	$\text{kg} \cdot \text{m}^2/\text{s}^2 \cdot \text{K}$

Table A1 Units Used in Physics (Fundamental units in bold)

Quantity	Common Symbol	Unit	Unit in Terms of Base SI Units
Force	$\vec{\mathbf{F}}$	newton (N)	$kg \cdot m/s^2$
Frequency	*f*	hertz (Hz)	s^{-1}
Heat	*Q*	joule (J)	$kg \cdot m^2/s^2$
Inductance	*L*	henry (H)	$kg \cdot m^2/A^2 \cdot s^2$
Length:	ℓ, L	**meter**	m
Displacement	$\Delta x, \Delta \vec{\mathbf{r}}$		
Distance	*d*, *h*		
Position	$x, y, z, \vec{\mathbf{r}}$		
Magnetic dipole moment	$\vec{\mu}$	$N \cdot J/T$	$A \cdot m^2$
Magnetic field	$\vec{\mathbf{B}}$	$\text{tesla(T)} = \left(Wb/m^2\right)$	$kg/A \cdot s^2$
Magnetic flux	Φ_m	weber (Wb)	$kg \cdot m^2/A \cdot s^2$
Mass	*m*, *M*	**kilogram**	kg
Molar specific heat	*C*	$J/mol \cdot K$	$kg \cdot m^2/s^2 \cdot mol \cdot K$
Moment of inertia	*I*	$kg \cdot m^2$	$kg \cdot m^2$
Momentum	$\vec{\mathbf{p}}$	$kg \cdot m/s$	$kg \cdot m/s$
Period	*T*	s	s
Permeability of free space	μ_0	$N/A^2 = (H/m)$	$kg \cdot m/A^2 \cdot s^2$
Permittivity of free space	ε_0	$C^2/N \cdot m^2 = (F/m)$	$A^2 \cdot s^4/kg \cdot m^3$
Potential	*V*	$\text{volt(V)} = (J/C)$	$kg \cdot m^2/A \cdot s^3$
Power	*P*	$\text{watt(W)} = (J/s)$	$kg \cdot m^2/s^3$
Pressure	*p*	$\text{pascal(Pa)} = \left(N/m^2\right)$	$kg/m \cdot s^2$
Resistance	*R*	$\text{ohm}(\Omega) = (V/A)$	$kg \cdot m^2/A^2 \cdot s^3$
Specific heat	*c*	$J/kg \cdot K$	$m^2/s^2 \cdot K$
Speed	v	m/s	m/s
Temperature	*T*	**kelvin**	K
Time	*t*	**second**	s
Torque	$\vec{\tau}$	$N \cdot m$	$kg \cdot m^2/s^2$

Table A1 Units Used in Physics (Fundamental units in bold)

Quantity	Common Symbol	Unit	Unit in Terms of Base SI Units
Velocity	$\vec{v}$	m/s	m/s
Volume	V	m^3	m^3
Wavelength	λ	m	m
Work	W	$\text{joule(J)} = (\text{N} \cdot \text{m})$	$\text{kg} \cdot \text{m}^2/\text{s}^2$

Table A1 Units Used in Physics (Fundamental units in bold)

APPENDIX B | CONVERSION FACTORS

	m	cm	km
1 meter	1	10^2	10^{-3}
1 centimeter	10^{-2}	1	10^{-5}
1 kilometer	10^3	10^5	1
1 inch	2.540×10^{-2}	2.540	2.540×10^{-5}
1 foot	0.3048	30.48	3.048×10^{-4}
1 mile	1609	1.609×10^4	1.609
1 angstrom	10^{-10}		
1 fermi	10^{-15}		
1 light-year			9.460×10^{12}
	in.	**ft**	**mi**
1 meter	39.37	3.281	6.214×10^{-4}
1 centimeter	0.3937	3.281×10^{-2}	6.214×10^{-6}
1 kilometer	3.937×10^4	3.281×10^3	0.6214
1 inch	1	8.333×10^{-2}	1.578×10^{-5}
1 foot	12	1	1.894×10^{-4}
1 mile	6.336×10^4	5280	1

Table B1 Length

Area

$1\ \text{cm}^2 = 0.155\ \text{in.}^2$

$1\ \text{m}^2 = 10^4\ \text{cm}^2 = 10.76\ \text{ft}^2$

$1\ \text{in.}^2 = 6.452\ \text{cm}^2$

$1\ \text{ft}^2 = 144\ \text{in.}^2 = 0.0929\ \text{m}^2$

Volume

$1\ \text{liter} = 1000\ \text{cm}^3 = 10^{-3}\ \text{m}^3 = 0.03531\ \text{ft}^3 = 61.02\ \text{in.}^3$

$1\ \text{ft}^3 = 0.02832\ \text{m}^3 = 28.32\ \text{liters} = 7.477\ \text{gallons}$

$1\ \text{gallon} = 3.788\ \text{liters}$

	s	min	h	day	yr
1 second	1	1.667×10^{-2}	2.778×10^{-4}	1.157×10^{-5}	3.169×10^{-8}
1 minute	60	1	1.667×10^{-2}	6.944×10^{-4}	1.901×10^{-6}
1 hour	3600	60	1	4.167×10^{-2}	1.141×10^{-4}
1 day	8.640×10^{4}	1440	24	1	2.738×10^{-3}
1 year	3.156×10^{7}	5.259×10^{5}	8.766×10^{3}	365.25	1

Table B2 Time

	m/s	cm/s	ft/s	mi/h
1 meter/second	1	10^{2}	3.281	2.237
1 centimeter/second	10^{-2}	1	3.281×10^{-2}	2.237×10^{-2}
1 foot/second	0.3048	30.48	1	0.6818
1 mile/hour	0.4470	44.70	1.467	1

Table B3 Speed

Acceleration

$1 \text{ m/s}^2 = 100 \text{ cm/s}^2 = 3.281 \text{ ft/s}^2$

$1 \text{ cm/s}^2 = 0.01 \text{ m/s}^2 = 0.03281 \text{ ft/s}^2$

$1 \text{ ft/s}^2 = 0.3048 \text{ m/s}^2 = 30.48 \text{ cm/s}^2$

$1 \text{ mi/h} \cdot \text{s} = 1.467 \text{ ft/s}^2$

	kg	g	slug	u
1 kilogram	1	10^{3}	6.852×10^{-2}	6.024×10^{26}
1 gram	10^{-3}	1	6.852×10^{-5}	6.024×10^{23}
1 slug	14.59	1.459×10^{4}	1	8.789×10^{27}
1 atomic mass unit	1.661×10^{-27}	1.661×10^{-24}	1.138×10^{-28}	1
1 metric ton	1000			

Table B4 Mass

	N	dyne	lb
1 newton	1	10^{5}	0.2248
1 dyne	10^{-5}	1	2.248×10^{-6}
1 pound	4.448	4.448×10^{5}	1

Table B5 Force

	Pa	dyne/cm^2	atm	cmHg	lb/in.^{2}
1 pascal	1	10	9.869×10^{-6}	7.501×10^{-4}	1.450×10^{-4}
1 dyne/ centimeter^2	10^{-1}	1	9.869×10^{-7}	7.501×10^{-5}	1.450×10^{-5}
1 atmosphere	1.013×10^5	1.013×10^6	1	76	14.70
1 centimeter mercury*	1.333×10^3	1.333×10^4	1.316×10^{-2}	1	0.1934
1 pound/inch^2	6.895×10^3	6.895×10^4	6.805×10^{-2}	5.171	1
1 bar	10^5				
1 torr				1 (mmHg)	

***Where the acceleration due to gravity is $9.80665\ \text{m/s}^2$ and the temperature is $0°\text{C}$**

Table B6 Pressure

	J	erg	ft.lb
1 joule	1	10^7	0.7376
1 erg	10^{-7}	1	7.376×10^{-8}
1 foot-pound	1.356	1.356×10^7	1
1 electron-volt	1.602×10^{-19}	1.602×10^{-12}	1.182×10^{-19}
1 calorie	4.186	4.186×10^7	3.088
1 British thermal unit	1.055×10^3	1.055×10^{10}	7.779×10^2
1 kilowatt-hour	3.600×10^6		
	eV	**cal**	**Btu**
1 joule	6.242×10^{18}	0.2389	9.481×10^{-4}
1 erg	6.242×10^{11}	2.389×10^{-8}	9.481×10^{-11}
1 foot-pound	8.464×10^{18}	0.3239	1.285×10^{-3}
1 electron-volt	1	3.827×10^{-20}	1.519×10^{-22}
1 calorie	2.613×10^{19}	1	3.968×10^{-3}
1 British thermal unit	6.585×10^{21}	2.520×10^2	1

Table B7 Work, Energy, Heat

Power

$1\ \text{W} = 1\ \text{J/s}$

$1\ \text{hp} = 746\ \text{W} = 550\ \text{ft} \cdot \text{lb/s}$

$1\ \text{Btu/h} = 0.293\ \text{W}$

Angle

$1 \text{ rad} = 57.30° = 180°/\pi$

$1° = 0.01745 \text{ rad} = \pi/180 \text{ rad}$

$1 \text{ revolution} = 360° = 2\pi \text{ rad}$

$1 \text{ rev/min(rpm)} = 0.1047 \text{ rad/s}$

APPENDIX C | FUNDAMENTAL CONSTANTS

Quantity	Symbol	Value
Atomic mass unit	u	$1.660\ 538\ 782\ (83) \times 10^{-27}$ kg $931.494\ 028\ (23)$ MeV/c^2
Avogadro's number	N_A	$6.022\ 141\ 79\ (30) \times 10^{23}$ particles/mol
Bohr magneton	$\mu_B = \frac{e\hbar}{2m_e}$	$9.274\ 009\ 15\ (23) \times 10^{-24}$ J/T
Bohr radius	$a_0 = \frac{\hbar^2}{m_e e^2 k_e}$	$5.291\ 772\ 085\ 9\ (36) \times 10^{-11}$ m
Boltzmann's constant	$k_B = \frac{R}{N_A}$	$1.380\ 650\ 4\ (24) \times 10^{-23}$ J/K
Compton wavelength	$\lambda_C = \frac{h}{m_e c}$	$2.426\ 310\ 217\ 5\ (33) \times 10^{-12}$ m
Coulomb constant	$k_e = \frac{1}{4\pi\varepsilon_0}$	$8.987\ 551\ 788... \times 10^9\ \text{N} \cdot \text{m}^2/\text{C}^2$ (exact)
Deuteron mass	m_d	$3.343\ 583\ 20\ (17) \times 10^{-27}$ kg $2.013\ 553\ 212\ 724(78)$ u $1875.612\ 859$ MeV/c^2
Electron mass	m_e	$9.109\ 382\ 15\ (45) \times 10^{-31}$ kg $5.485\ 799\ 094\ 3(23) \times 10^{-4}$ u $0.510\ 998\ 910\ (13)$ MeV/c^2
Electron volt	eV	$1.602\ 176\ 487\ (40) \times 10^{-19}$ J
Elementary charge	e	$1.602\ 176\ 487\ (40) \times 10^{-19}$ C
Gas constant	R	$8.314\ 472\ (15)$ J/mol · K
Gravitational constant	G	$6.674\ 28\ (67) \times 10^{-11}\ \text{N} \cdot \text{m}^2/\text{kg}^2$

Table C1 Fundamental Constants *Note:* These constants are the values recommended in 2006 by CODATA, based on a least-squares adjustment of data from different measurements. The numbers in parentheses for the values represent the uncertainties of the last two digits.

Quantity	Symbol	Value
Neutron mass	m_n	$1.674\ 927\ 211\ (84) \times 10^{-27}$ kg $1.008\ 664\ 915\ 97\ (43)$ u $939.565\ 346\ (23)\ \text{MeV}/c^2$
Nuclear magneton	$\mu_n = \dfrac{e\hbar}{2m_p}$	$5.050\ 783\ 24\ (13) \times 10^{-27}$ J/T
Permeability of free space	μ_0	$4\pi \times 10^{-7}\ \text{T} \cdot \text{m/A(exact)}$
Permittivity of free space	$\varepsilon_0 = \dfrac{1}{\mu_0 c^2}$	$8.854\ 187\ 817... \times 10^{-12}\ \text{C}^2/\text{N} \cdot \text{m}^2$ (exact)
Planck's constant	h $\hbar = \dfrac{h}{2\pi}$	$6.626\ 068\ 96\ (33) \times 10^{-34}\ \text{J} \cdot \text{s}$ $1.054\ 571\ 628\ (53) \times 10^{-34}\ \text{J} \cdot \text{s}$
Proton mass	m_p	$1.672\ 621\ 637\ (83) \times 10^{-27}$ kg $1.007\ 276\ 466\ 77\ (10)$ u $938.272\ 013\ (23)\ \text{MeV}/c^2$
Rydberg constant	R_H	$1.097\ 373\ 156\ 852\ 7\ (73) \times 10^7\ \text{m}^{-1}$
Speed of light in vacuum	c	$2.997\ 924\ 58 \times 10^8$ m/s (exact)

Table C1 Fundamental Constants *Note:* These constants are the values recommended in 2006 by CODATA, based on a least-squares adjustment of data from different measurements. The numbers in parentheses for the values represent the uncertainties of the last two digits.

Useful combinations of constants for calculations:

$hc = 12{,}400\ \text{eV} \cdot \text{Å} = 1240\ \text{eV} \cdot \text{nm} = 1240\ \text{MeV} \cdot \text{fm}$

$\hbar c = 1973\ \text{eV} \cdot \text{Å} = 197.3\ \text{eV} \cdot \text{nm} = 197.3\ \text{MeV} \cdot \text{fm}$

$k_e e^2 = 14.40\ \text{eV} \cdot \text{Å} = 1.440\ \text{eV} \cdot \text{nm} = 1.440\ \text{MeV} \cdot \text{fm}$

$k_\text{B} T = 0.02585\ \text{eV at}\ T = 300\ \text{K}$

APPENDIX D | ASTRONOMICAL DATA

Celestial Object	Mean Distance from Sun (million km)	Period of Revolution (d = days) (y = years)	Period of Rotation at Equator	Eccentricity of Orbit
Sun	–	–	27 d	–
Mercury	57.9	88 d	59 d	0.206
Venus	108.2	224.7 d	243 d	0.007
Earth	149.6	365.26 d	23 h 56 min 4 s	0.017
Mars	227.9	687 d	24 h 37 min 23 s	0.093
Jupiter	778.4	11.9 y	9 h 50 min 30 s	0.048
Saturn	1426.7	29.5 6	10 h 14 min	0.054
Uranus	2871.0	84.0 y	17 h 14 min	0.047
Neptune	4498.3	164.8 y	16 h	0.009
Earth's Moon	149.6 (0.386 from Earth)	27.3 d	27.3 d	0.055
Celestial Object	**Equatorial Diameter (km)**	**Mass (Earth = 1)**	**Density (g/cm^3)**	
Sun	1,392,000	333,000.00	1.4	
Mercury	4879	0.06	5.4	
Venus	12,104	0.82	5.2	
Earth	12,756	1.00	5.5	
Mars	6794	0.11	3.9	
Jupiter	142,984	317.83	1.3	
Saturn	120,536	95.16	0.7	
Uranus	51,118	14.54	1.3	
Neptune	49,528	17.15	1.6	
Earth's Moon	3476	0.01	3.3	

Table D1 Astronomical Data

Other Data:

Mass of Earth: 5.97×10^{24} kg

Mass of the Moon: 7.36×10^{22} kg

Mass of the Sun: 1.99×10^{30} kg

APPENDIX E | MATHEMATICAL FORMULAS

Quadratic formula

If $ax^2 + bx + c = 0$, then $x = \dfrac{-b \pm \sqrt{b^2 - 4ac}}{2a}$

Triangle of base b and height h	Area $= \frac{1}{2}bh$	
Circle of radius r	Circumference $= 2\pi r$	Area $= \pi r^2$
Sphere of radius r	Surface area $= 4\pi r^2$	Volume $= \frac{4}{3}\pi r^3$
Cylinder of radius r and height h	Area of curved surface $= 2\pi rh$	Volume $= \pi r^2 h$

Table E1 Geometry

Trigonometry

Trigonometric Identities

1. $\sin\theta = 1/\csc\theta$
2. $\cos\theta = 1/\sec\theta$
3. $\tan\theta = 1/\cot\theta$
4. $\sin(90^0 - \theta) = \cos\theta$
5. $\cos(90^0 - \theta) = \sin\theta$
6. $\tan(90^0 - \theta) = \cot\theta$
7. $\sin^2\theta + \cos^2\theta = 1$
8. $\sec^2\theta - \tan^2\theta = 1$
9. $\tan\theta = \sin\theta/\cos\theta$
10. $\sin(\alpha \pm \beta) = \sin\alpha\cos\beta \pm \cos\alpha\sin\beta$
11. $\cos(\alpha \pm \beta) = \cos\alpha\cos\beta \mp \sin\alpha\sin\beta$
12. $\tan(\alpha \pm \beta) = \dfrac{\tan\alpha \pm \tan\beta}{1 \mp \tan\alpha\tan\beta}$
13. $\sin 2\theta = 2\sin\theta\cos\theta$
14. $\cos 2\theta = \cos^2\theta - \sin^2\theta = 2\cos^2\theta - 1 = 1 - 2\sin^2\theta$

15. $\sin\alpha + \sin\beta = 2\sin\frac{1}{2}(\alpha+\beta)\cos\frac{1}{2}(\alpha-\beta)$

16. $\cos\alpha + \cos\beta = 2\cos\frac{1}{2}(\alpha+\beta)\cos\frac{1}{2}(\alpha-\beta)$

Triangles

1. Law of sines: $\frac{a}{\sin\alpha} = \frac{b}{\sin\beta} = \frac{c}{\sin\gamma}$

2. Law of cosines: $c^2 = a^2 + b^2 - 2ab\cos\gamma$

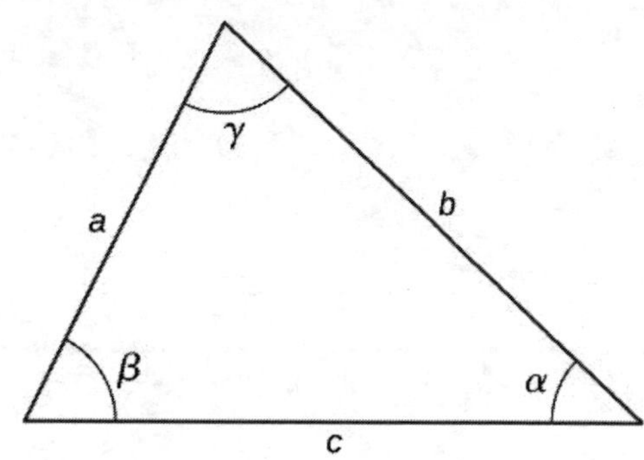

3. Pythagorean theorem: $a^2 + b^2 = c^2$

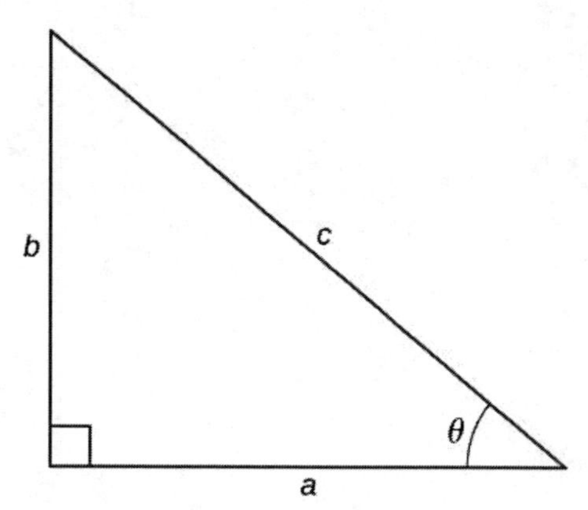

Series expansions

1. Binomial theorem: $(a+b)^n = a^n + na^{n-1}b + \frac{n(n-1)a^{n-2}b^2}{2!} + \frac{n(n-1)(n-2)a^{n-3}b^3}{3!} + \cdots$

2. $(1 \pm x)^n = 1 \pm \frac{nx}{1!} + \frac{n(n-1)x^2}{2!} \pm \cdots \left(x^2 < 1\right)$

3. $(1 \pm x)^{-n} = 1 \mp \frac{nx}{1!} + \frac{n(n+1)x^2}{2!} \mp \cdots \left(x^2 < 1\right)$

4. $\sin x = x - \frac{x^3}{3!} + \frac{x^5}{5!} - \cdots$

5. $\cos x = 1 - \frac{x^2}{2!} + \frac{x^4}{4!} - \cdots$

6. $\tan x = x + \frac{x^3}{3} + \frac{2x^5}{15} + \cdots$

7. $e^x = 1 + x + \frac{x^2}{2!} + \cdots$

8. $\ln(1+x) = x - \frac{1}{2}x^2 + \frac{1}{3}x^3 - \cdots(|x| < 1)$

Derivatives

1. $\frac{d}{dx}[af(x)] = a\frac{d}{dx}f(x)$

2. $\frac{d}{dx}[f(x) + g(x)] = \frac{d}{dx}f(x) + \frac{d}{dx}g(x)$

3. $\frac{d}{dx}[f(x)g(x)] = f(x)\frac{d}{dx}g(x) + g(x)\frac{d}{dx}f(x)$

4. $\frac{d}{dx}f(u) = \left[\frac{d}{du}f(u)\right]\frac{du}{dx}$

5. $\frac{d}{dx}x^m = mx^{m-1}$

6. $\frac{d}{dx}\sin x = \cos x$

7. $\frac{d}{dx}\cos x = -\sin x$

8. $\frac{d}{dx}\tan x = \sec^2 x$

9. $\frac{d}{dx}\cot x = -\csc^2 x$

10. $\frac{d}{dx}\sec x = \tan x \sec x$

11. $\frac{d}{dx}\csc x = -\cot x \csc x$

12. $\frac{d}{dx}e^x = e^x$

13. $\frac{d}{dx}\ln x = \frac{1}{x}$

14. $\frac{d}{dx}\sin^{-1} x = \frac{1}{\sqrt{1 - x^2}}$

15. $\frac{d}{dx}\cos^{-1} x = -\frac{1}{\sqrt{1 - x^2}}$

16. $\frac{d}{dx}\tan^{-1} x = -\frac{1}{1 + x^2}$

Integrals

1. $\int af(x)dx = a\int f(x)dx$

2. $\int [f(x) + g(x)]dx = \int f(x)dx + \int g(x)dx$

3. $\int x^m\, dx = \frac{x^{m+1}}{m+1} (m \neq -1)$
   $= \ln x (m = -1)$

4. $\int \sin x\, dx = -\cos x$

5. $\int \cos x\, dx = \sin x$

6. $\int \tan x\, dx = \ln|\sec x|$

7. $\int \sin^2 ax\, dx = \frac{x}{2} - \frac{\sin 2ax}{4a}$

8. $\int \cos^2 ax\, dx = \frac{x}{2} + \frac{\sin 2ax}{4a}$

9. $\int \sin ax \cos ax\, dx = -\frac{\cos 2ax}{4a}$

10. $\int e^{ax}\, dx = \frac{1}{a} e^{ax}$

11. $\int x e^{ax}\, dx = \frac{e^{ax}}{a^2}(ax - 1)$

12. $\int \ln ax\, dx = x \ln ax - x$

13. $\int \frac{dx}{a^2 + x^2} = \frac{1}{a} \tan^{-1} \frac{x}{a}$

14. $\int \frac{dx}{a^2 - x^2} = \frac{1}{2a} \ln \left| \frac{x + a}{x - a} \right|$

15. $\int \frac{dx}{\sqrt{a^2 + x^2}} = \sinh^{-1} \frac{x}{a}$

16. $\int \frac{dx}{\sqrt{a^2 - x^2}} = \sin^{-1} \frac{x}{a}$

17. $\int \sqrt{a^2 + x^2}\, dx = \frac{x}{2}\sqrt{a^2 + x^2} + \frac{a^2}{2} \sinh^{-1} \frac{x}{a}$

18. $\int \sqrt{a^2 - x^2}\, dx = \frac{x}{2}\sqrt{a^2 - x^2} + \frac{a^2}{2} \sin^{-1} \frac{x}{a}$

APPENDIX F | CHEMISTRY

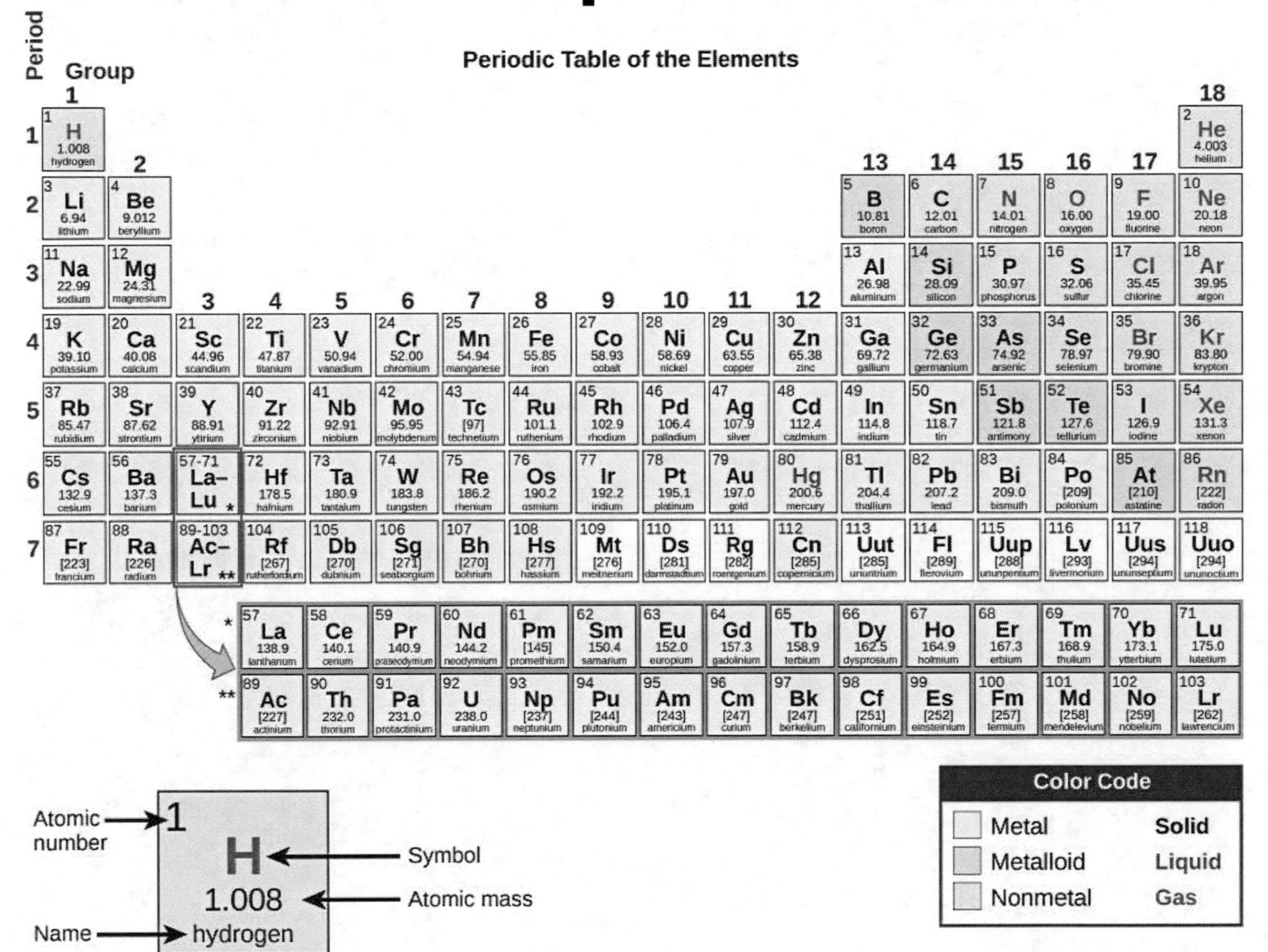

APPENDIX G | THE GREEK ALPHABET

Name	Capital	Lowercase	Name	Capital	Lowercase
Alpha	A	α	Nu	N	ν
Beta	B	β	Xi	Ξ	ξ
Gamma	Γ	γ	Omicron	O	o
Delta	Δ	δ	Pi	Π	π
Epsilon	E	ε	Rho	P	ρ
Zeta	Z	ζ	Sigma	Σ	σ
Eta	H	η	Tau	T	τ
Theta	Θ	θ	Upsilon	Υ	υ
Iota	I	ι	Phi	Φ	ϕ
Kappa	K	κ	Chi	X	χ
Lambda	Λ	λ	Psi	Ψ	ψ
Mu	M	μ	Omega	Ω	ω

Table G1 The Greek Alphabet

ANSWER KEY

CHAPTER 1

CHECK YOUR UNDERSTANDING

1.1. 2.1% (to two significant figures)
1.2. $15.1°$
1.3. air to water, because the condition that the second medium must have a smaller index of refraction is not satisfied
1.4. 9.3 cm
1.5. AA' becomes longer, $A'B'$ tilts further away from the surface, and the refracted ray tilts away from the normal.
1.6. also 90.0%
1.7. There will be only refraction but no reflection.

CONCEPTUAL QUESTIONS

1. Light can be modeled as a ray when devices are large compared to wavelength, and as a wave when devices are comparable or small compared to wavelength.
3. This fact simply proves that the speed of light is greater than that of sound. If one knows the distance to the location of the lightning and the speed of sound, one could, in principle, determine the speed of light from the data. In practice, because the speed of light is so great, the data would have to be known to impractically high precision.
5. Powder consists of many small particles with randomly oriented surfaces. This leads to diffuse reflection, reducing shine.
7. "toward" when increasing *n* (air to water, water to glass); "away" when decreasing *n* (glass to air)
9. A ray from a leg emerges from water after refraction. The observer in air perceives an apparent location for the source, as if a ray traveled in a straight line. See the dashed ray below.

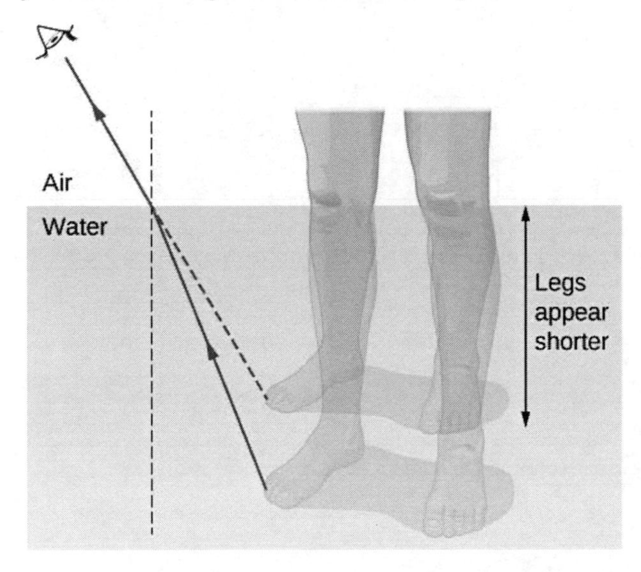

11. The gemstone becomes invisible when its index of refraction is the same, or at least similar to, the water surrounding it. Because diamond has a particularly high index of refraction, it can still sparkle as a result of total internal reflection, not invisible.
13. One can measure the critical angle by looking for the onset of total internal reflection as the angle of incidence is varied. Equation 1.14 can then be applied to compute the index of refraction.
15. In addition to total internal reflection, rays that refract into and out of diamond crystals are subject to dispersion due to varying values of n across the spectrum, resulting in a sparkling display of colors.
17. yes
19. No. Sound waves are not transverse waves.
21. Energy is absorbed into the filters.
23. Sunsets are viewed with light traveling straight from the Sun toward us. When blue light is scattered out of this path, the remaining red light dominates the overall appearance of the setting Sun.
25. The axis of polarization for the sunglasses has been rotated $90°$.

PROBLEMS

27. 2.99705×10^8 m/s; 1.97×10^8 m/s
29. ice at $0°C$

31. 1.03 ns
33. 337 m
35. proof
37. proof
39. reflection, $70°$; refraction, $45°$
41. $42°$
43. 1.53
45. a. 2.9 m; b. 1.4 m
47. a. $24.42°$; b. $31.33°$
49. $79.11°$
51. a. 1.43, fluorite; b. $44.2°$
53. a. $48.2°$; b. $27.3°$
55. $46.5°$ for red, $46.0°$ for violet
57. a. $0.04°$; b. 1.3 m
59. $72.8°$
61. $53.5°$ for red, $55.2°$ for violet
63. 0.500
65. 0.125 or 1/8
67. $84.3°$
69. $0.250\,I_0$
71. a. 0.500; b. 0.250; c. 0.187
73. $67.54°$
75. $53.1°$

ADDITIONAL PROBLEMS

77. 114 radian/s
79. 3.72 mm
81. $41.2°$
83. a. 1.92. The gem is not a diamond (it is zircon). b. $55.2°$
85. a. 0.898; b. We cannot have $n < 1.00$, since this would imply a speed greater than *c*. c. The refracted angle is too big relative to the angle of incidence.
87. $0.707\,B_1$
89. a. $1.69 \times 10^{-2}\,°\text{C/s}$; b. yes

CHALLENGE PROBLEMS

91. First part: $88.6°$. The remainder depends on the complexity of the solution the reader constructs.
93. proof; 1.33
95. a. 0.750; b. 0.563; c. 1.33

CHAPTER 2

CONCEPTUAL QUESTIONS

1. Virtual image cannot be projected on a screen. You cannot distinguish a real image from a virtual image simply by judging from the image perceived with your eye.
3. Yes, you can photograph a virtual image. For example, if you photograph your reflection from a plane mirror, you get a photograph of a virtual image. The camera focuses the light that enters its lens to form an image; whether the source of the light is a real object or a reflection from mirror (i.e., a virtual image) does not matter.
5. No, you can see the real image the same way you can see the virtual image. The retina of your eye effectively serves as a screen.
7. The mirror should be half your size and its top edge should be at the level of your eyes. The size does not depend on your distance from the mirror.
9. when the object is at infinity; see the mirror equation
11. Yes, negative magnification simply means that the image is upside down; this does not prevent the image from being larger than the object. For instance, for a concave mirror, if distance to the object is larger than one focal distance but smaller than two focal distances the image will be inverted and magnified.
13. answers may vary

15. The focal length of the lens is fixed, so the image distance changes as a function of object distance.
17. Yes, the focal length will change. The lens maker's equation shows that the focal length depends on the index of refraction of the medium surrounding the lens. Because the index of refraction of water differs from that of air, the focal length of the lens will change when submerged in water.
19. A relaxed, normal-vision eye will focus parallel rays of light onto the retina.
21. A person with an internal lens will need glasses to read because their muscles cannot distort the lens as they do with biological lenses, so they cannot focus on near objects. To correct nearsightedness, the power of the intraocular lens must be less than that of the removed lens.
23. Microscopes create images of macroscopic size, so geometric optics applies.
25. The eyepiece would be moved slightly farther from the objective so that the image formed by the objective falls just beyond the focal length of the eyepiece.

PROBLEMS

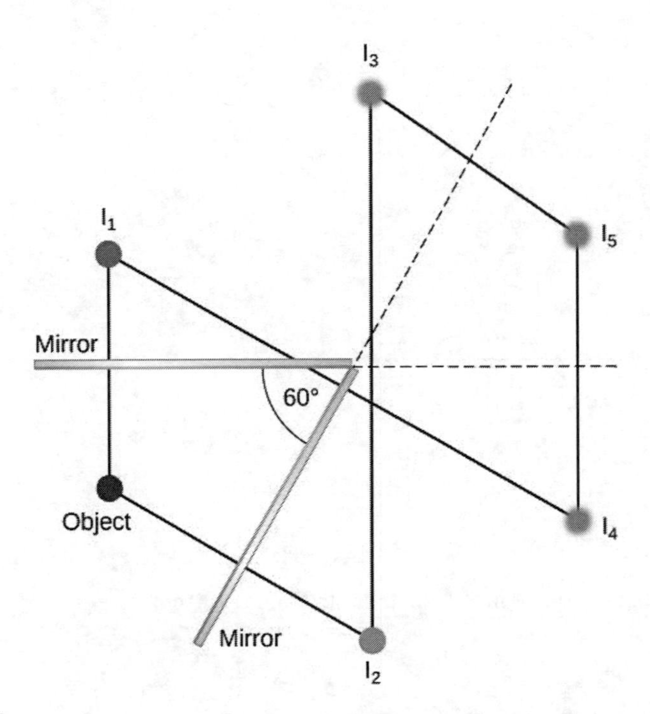

27.
29. It is in the focal point of the big mirror and at the center of curvature of the small mirror.
31. $f = \frac{R}{2} \Rightarrow R = +1.60 \text{ m}$
33. $d_o = 27.3 \text{ cm}$
35. Step 1: Image formation by a mirror is involved.
Step 2: Draw the problem set up when possible.
Step 3: Use thin-lens equations to solve this problem.
Step 4: Find f.
Step 5: Given: $m = 1.50, d_o = 0.120 \text{ m}$.
Step 6: No ray tracing is needed.
Step 7: Using $m = \frac{d_i}{d_o}$, $d_i = -0.180 \text{ m}$. Then, $f = 0.360 \text{ m}$.
Step 8: The image is virtual because the image distance is negative. The focal length is positive, so the mirror is concave.
37. a. for a convex mirror $d_i < 0 \Rightarrow m > 0$. $m = +0.111$; b. $d_i = -0.334 \text{ cm}$ (behind the cornea);
c. $f = -0.376 \text{ cm}$, so that $R = -0.752 \text{ cm}$
39. $m = \frac{h_i}{h_o} = -\frac{d_i}{d_o} = -\frac{-d_o}{d_o} = \frac{d_o}{d_o} = 1 \Rightarrow h_i = h_o$

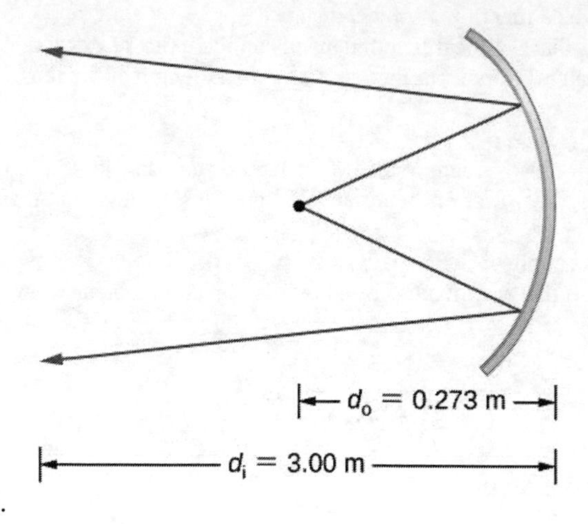

41.

$$m = -11.0$$
$$A' = 0.110\,\text{m}^2$$
$$I = 6.82\,\text{kW/m}^2$$

43. $$x_{2m} = -x_{2m-1}, \quad (m = 1, 2, 3, ...),$$ $$x_{2m+1} = b - x_{2m}, \quad (m = 0, 1, 2, ...), \text{ with } x_0 = a.$$

45. $d_i = -55$ cm; $m = +1.8$

47. $d_i = -41$ cm, $m = 1.4$

49. proof

51. a. $\frac{1}{d_i} + \frac{1}{d_o} = \frac{1}{f} \Rightarrow d_i = 3.43\,\text{m}$;

b. $m = -33.33$, so that $$(2.40 \times 10^{-2}\,\text{m})(33.33) = 80.0\,\text{cm, and}$$ $$(3.60 \times 10^{-2}\,\text{m})(33.33) = 1.20\,\text{m} \Rightarrow 0.800\,\text{m} \times 1.20\,\text{m or } 80.0\,\text{cm} \times 120\,\text{cm}$$

53. a. $$\frac{1}{d_o} + \frac{1}{d_i} = \frac{1}{f};$$ $$d_i = 5.08\,\text{cm}$$

b. $m = -1.695 \times 10^{-2}$, so the maximum height is $\frac{0.036\,\text{m}}{1.695 \times 10^{-2}} = 2.12\,\text{m} \Rightarrow 100\%$;

c. This seems quite reasonable, since at 3.00 m it is possible to get a full length picture of a person.

55. a. $\frac{1}{d_o} + \frac{1}{d_i} = \frac{1}{f} \Rightarrow d_o = 2.55\,\text{m}$;

b. $\frac{h_i}{h_o} = -\frac{d_i}{d_o} \Rightarrow h_o = 1.00\,\text{m}$

57. a. Using $\frac{1}{d_o} + \frac{1}{d_i} = \frac{1}{f}$, $d_i = -56.67\,\text{cm}$. Then we can determine the magnification, $m = 6.67$. b. $d_i = -190\,\text{cm}$ and $m = +20.0$; c. The magnification m increases rapidly as you increase the object distance toward the focal length.

59.

$$\frac{1}{d_o} + \frac{1}{d_i} = \frac{1}{f}$$
$$d_i = \frac{1}{(1/f) - (1/d_o)}$$
$$\frac{d_i}{d_o} = 6.667 \times 10^{-13} = \frac{h_i}{h_o}$$
$$h_i = -0.933\,\text{mm}$$

61. $d_i = -6.7$ cm

$h_i = 4.0$ cm

63. 83 cm to the right of the converging lens, $m = -2.3$, $h_i = 6.9$ cm

65. $P = 52.0\text{ D}$

67. $\frac{h_i}{h_o} = -\frac{d_i}{d_o} \Rightarrow h_i = -h_o\left(\frac{d_i}{d_o}\right) = -(3.50\text{ mm})\left(\frac{2.00\text{ cm}}{30.0\text{ cm}}\right) = -0.233\text{ mm}$

69. a. $P = +62.5\text{ D}$;

b. $\frac{h_i}{h_o} = -\frac{d_i}{d_o} \Rightarrow h_i = -0.250\text{ mm}$;

c. $h_i = -0.0800\text{ mm}$

71. $P = \frac{1}{d_o} + \frac{1}{d_i} \Rightarrow d_o = 28.6\text{ cm}$

73. Originally, the close vision was 51.0 D. Therefore, $P = \frac{1}{d_o} + \frac{1}{d_i} \Rightarrow d_o = 1.00\text{ m}$

75. originally, $P = 70.0\text{ D}$; because the power for normal distant vision is 50.0 D, the power should be decreased by 20.0 D

77. $P = \frac{1}{d_o} + \frac{1}{d_i} \Rightarrow d_o = 0.333\text{ m}$

79. a. $P = 52.0\text{ D}$;

$P' = 56.16\text{ D}$

b. $\frac{1}{d_o} + \frac{1}{d_i} = P \Rightarrow d_o = 16.2\text{ cm}$

81. We need $d_i = -18.5\text{ cm}$ when $d_o = \infty$, so

$P = -5.41\text{ D}$

83. Let x = far point

$\Rightarrow P = \frac{1}{-(x - 0.0175\text{ m})} + \frac{1}{\infty} \Rightarrow -xP + (0.0175\text{ m})P = 1$

$\Rightarrow x = 26.8\text{ cm}$

85. $M = 6\times$

87.
$$\begin{aligned} M &= \left(\frac{25\text{ cm}}{L}\right)\left(1 + \frac{L - \ell}{f}\right) \\ L - \ell &= d_o \\ d_o &= 13\text{ cm} \end{aligned}$$

89. $M = 2.5\times$

91. $M = -2.1\times$

93.
$$\begin{aligned} M &= \frac{25\text{ cm}}{f} \\ M_{max} &= 5 \end{aligned}$$

95.
$$\begin{aligned} M_{max}^{young} &= 1 + \frac{18\text{ cm}}{f} \Rightarrow f = \frac{18\text{ cm}}{M_{max}^{young} - 1} \\ M_{max}^{old} &= 9.8\times \end{aligned}$$

97. a.
$$\begin{aligned} \frac{1}{d_o} + \frac{1}{d_i} &= \frac{1}{f} \Rightarrow d_i = 4.65\text{ cm} \\ &\Rightarrow m = -30.0 \end{aligned}$$;

b. $M_{net} = -240$

99. a. $\frac{1}{d_o^{obj}} + \frac{1}{d_i^{obj}} = \frac{1}{f^{obj}} \Rightarrow d_i^{obj} = 18.3\text{ cm}$ behind the objective lens;

b. $m^{obj} = -60.0$;

c.
$$\begin{aligned} d_o^{eye} &= 1.70\text{ cm} \\ d_i^{eye} &= -11.3\text{ cm} \end{aligned}$$

in front of the eyepiece; d. $M^{eye} = 13.5$;

e. $M_{\text{net}} = -810$

101. $M = -40.0$

103. $f^{\text{obj}} = \frac{R}{2}, M = -1.67$

105. $M = -\frac{f^{\text{obj}}}{f^{\text{eye}}}, f^{\text{eye}} = +10.0\,\text{cm}$

107. Answers will vary.

109. 12 cm to the left of the mirror, $m = 3/5$

111. 27 cm in front of the mirror, $m = 0.6$, $h_i = 1.76\,\text{cm}$, orientation upright

113. The following figure shows three successive images beginning with the image Q_1 in mirror M_1. Q_1 is the image in mirror M_1, whose image in mirror M_2 is Q_{12} whose image in mirror M_1 is the real image Q_{121}.

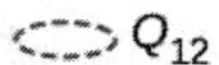

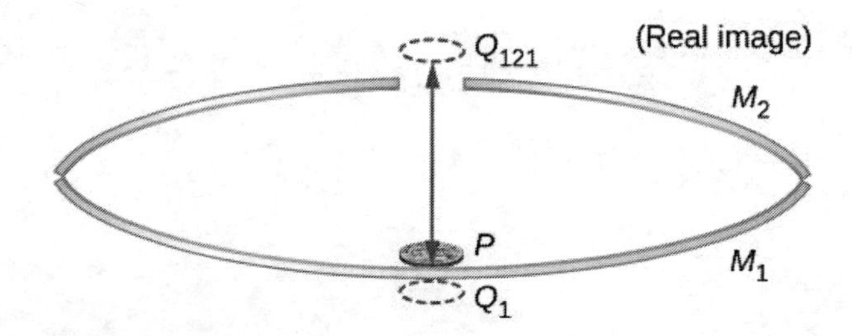

115. 5.4 cm from the axis

117. Let the vertex of the concave mirror be the origin of the coordinate system. Image 1 is at −10/3 cm (−3.3 cm), image 2 is at −40/11 cm (−3.6 cm). These serve as objects for subsequent images, which are at −310/83 cm (−3.7 cm), −9340/2501 cm (−3.7 cm), −140,720/37,681 cm (−3.7 cm). All remaining images are at approximately −3.7 cm.

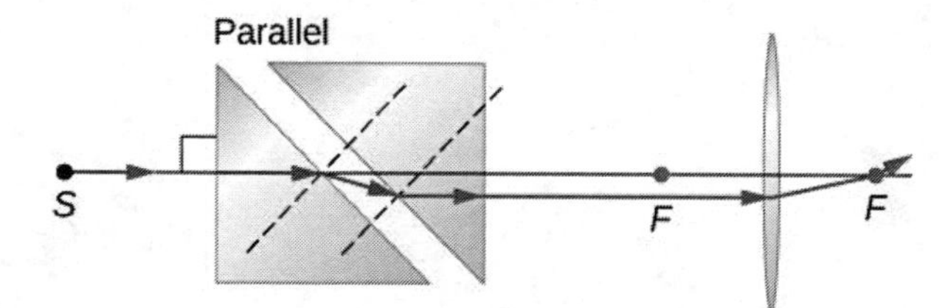

119.

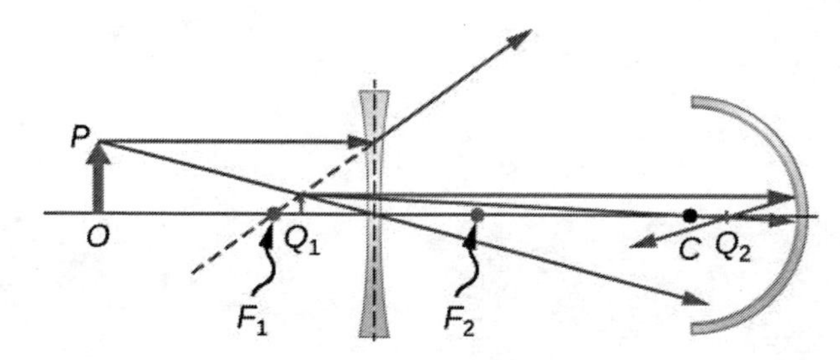

121.

123. −5 D

125. 11

ADDITIONAL PROBLEMS

127. a.

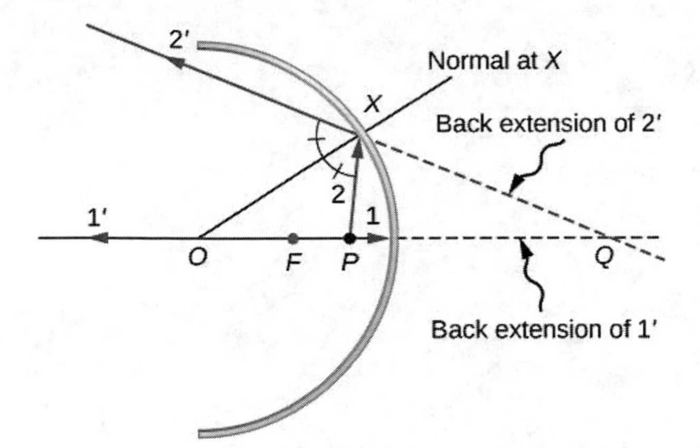

b.

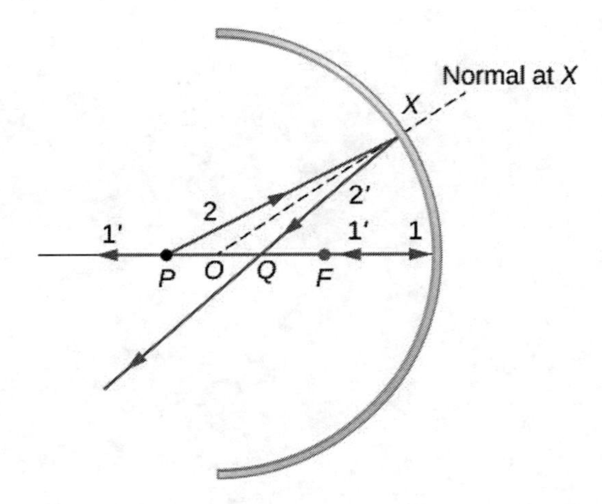

c.

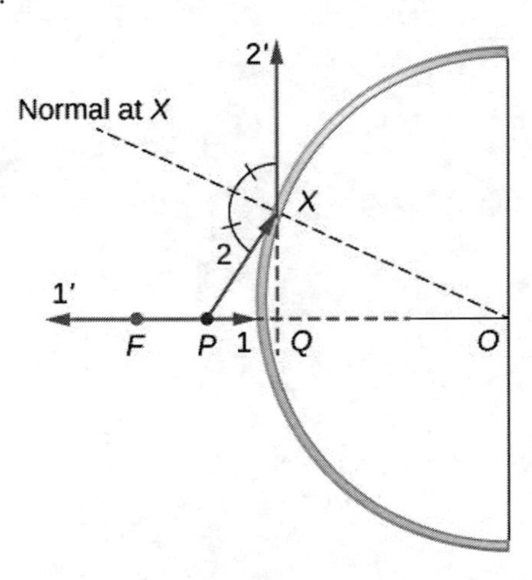

d. similar to the previous picture but with point P outside the focal length; e. Repeat (a)–(d) for a point object off the axis. For a point object placed off axis in front of a concave mirror corresponding to parts (a) and (b), the case for convex mirror left as exercises.

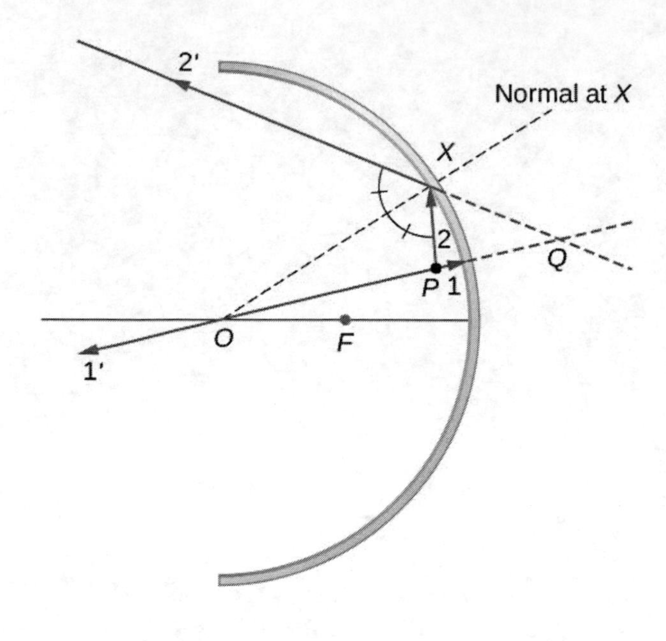

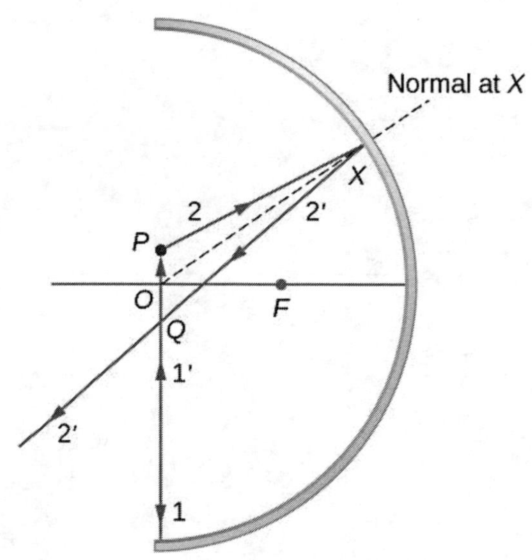

129. $d_i = -10/3\ \text{cm},\ h_i = 2\ \text{cm}$, upright

131. proof

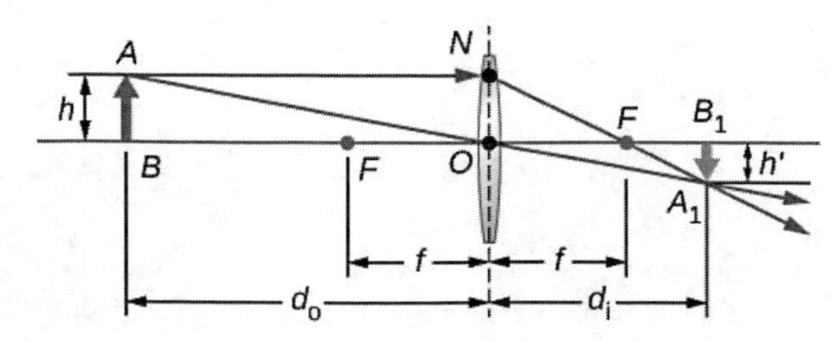

133.

Triangles BAO and B_1A_1O are similar triangles. Thus, $\frac{A_1B_1}{AB} = \frac{d_i}{d_o}$.Triangles NOF and B_1A_1F are similar triangles. Thus, $\frac{NO}{f} = \frac{A_1B_1}{d_i - f}$. Noting that $NO = AB$ gives $\frac{AB}{f} = \frac{A_1B_1}{d_i - f}$ or $\frac{AB}{A_1B_1} = \frac{f}{d_i - f}$. Inverting this gives $\frac{A_1B_1}{AB} = \frac{d_i - f}{f}$. Equating the two expressions for the ratio $\frac{A_1B_1}{AB}$ gives $\frac{d_i}{d_o} = \frac{d_i - f}{f}$. Dividing through by d_i gives $\frac{1}{d_o} = \frac{1}{f} - \frac{1}{d_i}$ or

$\frac{1}{d_o}+\frac{1}{d_i}=\frac{1}{f}$.

135. 70 cm

137. The plane mirror has an infinite focal point, so that $d_i = -d_o$. The total apparent distance of the man in the mirror will be his actual distance, plus the apparent image distance, or $d_o + (-d_i) = 2d_o$. If this distance must be less than 20 cm, he should stand at $d_o = 10\text{ cm}$.

139. Here we want $d_o = 25\text{ cm} - 2.20\text{ cm} = 0.228\text{ m}$. If $x =$ near point, $d_i = -(x - 0.0220\text{ m})$. Thus, $P = \frac{1}{d_o} + \frac{1}{d_i} = \frac{1}{0.228\text{ m}} + \frac{1}{x - 0.0220\text{ m}}$. Using $P = 0.75\text{ D}$ gives $x = 0.253\text{ m}$, so the near point is 25.3 cm.

141. Assuming a lens at 2.00 cm from the boy's eye, the image distance must be $d_i = -(500\text{ cm} - 2.00\text{ cm}) = -498\text{ cm}$. For an infinite-distance object, the required power is $P = \frac{1}{d_i} = -0.200\text{ D}$. Therefore, the -4.00 D lens will correct the nearsightedness.

143. $87\ \mu\text{m}$

145. Use, $M_{\text{net}} = -\frac{d_i^{\text{obj}}\left(f^{\text{eye}} + 25\text{ cm}\right)}{f^{\text{obj}} f^{\text{eye}}}$. The image distance for the objective is $d_i^{\text{obj}} = -\frac{M_{\text{net}} f^{\text{obj}} f^{\text{eye}}}{f^{\text{eye}} + 25\text{ cm}}$. Using $f^{\text{obj}} = 3.0\text{ cm}$, $f^{\text{eye}} = 10\text{ cm}$, and $M = -10$ gives $d_i^{\text{obj}} = 8.6\text{ cm}$. We want this image to be at the focal point of the eyepiece so that the eyepiece forms an image at infinity for comfortable viewing. Thus, the distance *d* between the lenses should be $d = f^{\text{eye}} + d_i^{\text{obj}} = 10\text{ cm} + 8.6\text{ cm} = 19\text{ cm}$.

147. a. focal length of the corrective lens $f_c = -80\text{ cm}$; b. −1.25 D

149. $2 \times 10^{16}\text{ km}$

151. 10^5 m

CHAPTER 3

CHECK YOUR UNDERSTANDING

3.1. $3.63°$ and $7.27°$, respectively

3.2. a. 853 nm, 1097 nm; b. 731 nm, 975 nm

3.3. a. too small; b. up to 8×10^{-5}

CONCEPTUAL QUESTIONS

1. No. Two independent light sources do not have coherent phase.

3. Because both the sodium lamps are not coherent pairs of light sources. Two lasers operating independently are also not coherent so no interference pattern results.

5. Monochromatic sources produce fringes at angles according to $d \sin\theta = m\lambda$. With white light, each constituent wavelength will produce fringes at its own set of angles, blending into the fringes of adjacent wavelengths. This results in rainbow patterns.

7. Differing path lengths result in different phases at destination resulting in constructive or destructive interference accordingly. Reflection can cause a $180°$ phase change, which also affects how waves interfere. Refraction into another medium changes the wavelength inside that medium such that a wave can emerge from the medium with a different phase compared to another wave that travelled the same distance in a different medium.

9. Phase changes occur upon reflection at the top of glass cover and the top of glass slide only.

11. The surface of the ham being moist means there is a thin layer of fluid, resulting in thin-film interference. Because the exact thickness of the film varies across the piece of ham, which is illuminated by white light, different wavelengths produce bright fringes at different locations, resulting in rainbow colors.

13. Other wavelengths will not generally satisfy $t = \frac{\lambda/n}{4}$ for the same value of *t* so reflections will result in completely destructive interference. For an incidence angle θ, the path length inside the coating will be increased by a factor $1/\cos\theta$ so the new condition for destructive interference becomes $\frac{t}{\cos\theta} = \frac{\lambda/n}{4}$.

15. In one arm, place a transparent chamber to be filled with the gas. See **Example 3.6**.

PROBLEMS

17. $0.997°$
19. $0.290\ \mu m$
21. $5.77 \times 10^{-7}\ m = 577\ nm$
23. 62.5; since m must be an integer, the highest order is then $m = 62$.
25. $1.44\ \mu m$
27. a. $20.3°$; b. $4.98°$; c. 5.76, the highest order is $m = 5$.
29. a. 2.37 cm; b. 1.78 cm
31. 560 nm
33. 1.2 mm
35. a. $0.40°, 0.53°$; b. $4.6 \times 10^{-3}\ m$
37. 1:9
39. 532 nm (green)
41. $8.39 \times 10^{-8}\ m = 83.9\ nm$
43. 620 nm (orange)
45. 380 nm
47. a. Assuming n for the plane is greater than 1.20, then there are two phase changes: 0.833 cm. b. It is too thick, and the plane would be too heavy. c. It is unreasonable to think the layer of material could be any thickness when used on a real aircraft.
49. $4.55 \times 10^{-4}\ m$
51. $D = 2.53 \times 10^{-6}\ m$

ADDITIONAL PROBLEMS

53. $0.29°$ and $0.86°$
55. a. 4.26 cm; b. 2.84 cm
57. 6
59. 0.20 m
61. 0.0839 mm
63. a. 9.8, 10.4, 11.7, and 15.7 cm; b. 3.9 cm
65. $0.0575°$
67. 700 nm
69. 189 nm
71. a. green (504 nm); b. magenta (white minus green)
73. 1.29
75. $52.7\ \mu m$ and $53.0\ \mu m$
77. 160 nm
79. 413 nm and 689 nm
81. $73.9\ \mu m$
83. 47
85. $8.5\ \mu m$
87. $0.013°C$

CHALLENGE PROBLEMS

89. Bright and dark fringes switch places.
91. The path length must be less than one-fourth of the shortest visible wavelength in oil. The thickness of the oil is half the path length, so it must be less than one-eighth of the shortest visible wavelength in oil. If we take 380 nm to be the shortest visible wavelength in air, 33.9 nm.
93. $4.42 \times 10^{-5}\ m$
95. for one phase change: 950 nm (infrared); for three phase changes: 317 nm (ultraviolet); Therefore, the oil film will appear black, since the reflected light is not in the visible part of the spectrum.

CHAPTER 4

CHECK YOUR UNDERSTANDING

4.1. $17.8°$, $37.7°$, $66.4°$; no

4.2. $74.3°$, $0.0083 I_0$
4.3. From $d \sin \theta = m\lambda$, the interference maximum occurs at $2.87°$ for $m = 20$. From **Equation 4.1**, this is also the angle for the second diffraction minimum. (*Note:* Both equations use the index *m* but they refer to separate phenomena.)
4.4. 3.332×10^{-6} m or 300 lines per millimeter
4.5. 8.4×10^{-4} rad, 3000 times broader than the Hubble Telescope
4.6. $38.4°$ and $68.8°$; Between $\theta = 0° \rightarrow 90°$, orders 1, 2, and 3, are all that exist.

CONCEPTUAL QUESTIONS

1. The diffraction pattern becomes wider.
3. Walkie-talkies use radio waves whose wavelengths are comparable to the size of the hill and are thus able to diffract around the hill. Visible wavelengths of the flashlight travel as rays at this size scale.
5. The diffraction pattern becomes two-dimensional, with main fringes, which are now spots, running in perpendicular directions and fainter spots in intermediate directions.
7. The parameter $\beta = \phi/2$ is the arc angle shown in the phasor diagram in **Figure 4.7**. The phase difference between the first and last Huygens wavelet across the single slit is 2β and is related to the curvature of the arc that forms the resultant phasor that determines the light intensity.
9. blue; The shorter wavelength of blue light results in a smaller angle for diffraction limit.
11. No, these distances are three orders of magnitude smaller than the wavelength of visible light, so visible light makes a poor probe for atoms.
13. UV wavelengths are much larger than lattice spacings in crystals such that there is no diffraction. The Bragg equation implies a value for $\sin \theta$ greater than unity, which has no solution.
15. Image will appear at slightly different location and/or size when viewed using 10% shorter wavelength but at exactly half the wavelength, a higher-order interference reconstructs the original image, different color.

PROBLEMS

17. a. $33.4°$; b. no
19. a. 1.35×10^{-6} m; b. $69.9°$
21. 750 nm
23. 2.4 mm, 4.7 mm
25. a. 1.00λ; b. 50.0λ; c. 1000λ
27. 1.92 m
29. $45.1°$
31. $I/I_0 = 2.2 \times 10^{-5}$
33. $0.63I_0$, $0.11I_0$, $0.0067I_0$, $0.0062I_0$, $0.00088I_0$
35. 0.200
37. 3
39. 9
41. $5.97°$
43. 8.99×10^3
45. 707 nm
47. a. $11.8°$, $12.5°$, $14.1°$, $19.2°$; b. $24.2°$, $25.7°$, $29.1°$, $41.0°$; c. Decreasing the number of lines per centimeter by a factor of *x* means that the angle for the *x*-order maximum is the same as the original angle for the first-order maximum.
49. a. using $\lambda = 700$ nm, $\theta = 5.0°$; b. using $\lambda = 460$ nm, $\theta = 3.3°$
51. a. 26,300 lines/cm; b. yes; c. no
53. 1.13×10^{-2} m
55. 107 m
57. a. 7.72×10^{-4} rad; b. 23.2 m; c. 590 km
59. a. 2.24×10^{-4} rad; b. 5.81 km; c. 0.179 mm; d. can resolve details 0.2 mm apart at arm's length
61. $2.9\ \mu m$
63. 6.0 cm
65. 7.71 km
67. 1.0 m
69. 1.2 cm or closer

71. no
73. 0.120 nm
75. $4.51°$
77. $13.2°$

ADDITIONAL PROBLEMS

79. a. 2.2 mm; b. $0.172°$, second-order yellow and third-order violet coincide
81. 2.2 km
83. 1.3 cm
85. a. 0.28 mm; b. 0.28 m; c. 280 m; d. 113 km
87. 33 m
89. a. vertically; b. $\pm 20°$, $\pm 44°$; c. 0, $\pm 31°$, $\pm 60°$; d. 89 cm; e. 71 cm
91. 0.98 cm
93. $I/I_0 = 0.041$
95. 340 nm
97. a. 0.082 rad and 0.087 rad; b. 480 nm and 660 nm
99. two orders
101. yes and N/A
103. 600 nm
105. a. $3.4 \times 10^{-5}{}°$; b. $51°$
107. 0.63 m
109. 1
111. 0.17 mW/cm^2 for $m = 1$ only, no higher orders
113. $28.7°$
115. a. 42.3 nm; b. This wavelength is not in the visible spectrum. c. The number of slits in this diffraction grating is too large. Etching in integrated circuits can be done to a resolution of 50 nm, so slit separations of 400 nm are at the limit of what we can do today. This line spacing is too small to produce diffraction of light.
117. a. 549 km; b. This is an unreasonably large telescope. c. Unreasonable to assume diffraction limit for optical telescopes unless in space due to atmospheric effects.

CHALLENGE PROBLEMS

119. a. $\text{I} = 0.00500\,\text{I}_0,\ 0.00335\,\text{I}_0$; b. $\text{I} = 0.00500\,\text{I}_0,\ 0.00335\,\text{I}_0$
121. 12,800
123. 1.58×10^{-6} m

CHAPTER 5

CHECK YOUR UNDERSTANDING

5.1. Special relativity applies only to objects moving at constant velocity, whereas general relativity applies to objects that undergo acceleration.

5.2.
$$\gamma = \frac{1}{\sqrt{1 - \frac{v^2}{c^2}}} = \frac{1}{\sqrt{1 - \frac{(0.650c)^2}{c^2}}} = 1.32$$

5.3. a.
$$\Delta t = \frac{\Delta\tau}{\sqrt{1 - \frac{v^2}{c^2}}} = \frac{2.10 \times 10^{-8}\,\text{s}}{\sqrt{1 - \frac{(1.90 \times 10^8\ \text{m/s})^2}{(3.00 \times 10^8\ \text{m/s})^2}}} = 2.71 \times 10^{-8}\ \text{s}.$$

5.3. b. Only the relative speed of the two spacecraft matters because there is no absolute motion through space. The signal is emitted from a fixed location in the frame of reference of *A*, so the proper time interval of its emission is $\tau = 1.00$ s. The duration of the signal measured from frame of reference *B* is then
$$\Delta t = \frac{\Delta\tau}{\sqrt{1 - \frac{v^2}{c^2}}} = \frac{1.00\ \text{s}}{\sqrt{1 - \frac{(4.00 \times 10^7\ \text{m/s})^2}{(3.00 \times 10^8\ \text{m/s})^2}}} = 1.01\ \text{s}.$$

5.4. $L = L_0\sqrt{1 - \frac{v^2}{c^2}} = (2.50\text{ km})\sqrt{1 - \frac{(0.750c)^2}{c^2}} = 1.65\text{ km}$

5.5. Start with the definition of the proper time increment:

$d\tau = \sqrt{-(ds)^2/c^2} = \sqrt{dt^2 - \left(dx^2 + dx^2 + dx^2\right)/c^2}.$

where (dx, dy, dx, cdt) are measured in the inertial frame of an observer who does not necessarily see that particle at rest. This therefore becomes

$$\begin{aligned} d\tau &= \sqrt{-(ds)^2/c^2} = \sqrt{dt^2 - \left[(dx)^2 + (dy)^2 + (dz)^2\right]/c^2} \\ &= dt\sqrt{1 - \left[\left(\frac{dx}{dt}\right)^2 + \left(\frac{dy}{dt}\right)^2 + \left(\frac{dz}{dt}\right)^2\right]/c^2} \\ &= dt\sqrt{1 - v^2/c^2} \\ dt &= \gamma d\tau. \end{aligned}$$

5.6. Although displacements perpendicular to the relative motion are the same in both frames of reference, the time interval between events differ, and differences in dt and dt' lead to different velocities seen from the two frames.

5.7. We can substitute the data directly into the equation for relativistic Doppler frequency:

$$f_{\text{obs}} = f_s\sqrt{\frac{1 - \frac{v}{c}}{1 + \frac{v}{c}}} = (1.50\text{ GHz})\sqrt{\frac{1 - \frac{0.350c}{c}}{1 + \frac{0.350c}{c}}} = 1.04\text{ GHz}.$$

5.8. Substitute the data into the given equation:

$$p = \gamma mu = \frac{mu}{\sqrt{1 - \frac{u^2}{c^2}}} = \frac{(9.11 \times 10^{-31}\text{ kg})(0.985)(3.00 \times 10^8\text{ m/s})}{\sqrt{1 - \frac{(0.985c)^2}{c^2}}} = 1.56 \times 10^{-21}\text{ kg-m/s}.$$

5.9.

$$\begin{aligned} K_{\text{rel}} &= (\gamma - 1)mc^2 = \left(\frac{1}{\sqrt{1 - \frac{u^2}{c^2}}} - 1\right)mc^2 \\ &= \left(\frac{1}{\sqrt{1 - \frac{(0.992c)^2}{c^2}}} - 1\right)(9.11 \times 10^{-31}\text{ kg})(3.00 \times 10^8\text{ m/s})^2 = 5.67 \times 10^{-13}\text{ J} \end{aligned}$$

CONCEPTUAL QUESTIONS

1. the second postulate, involving the speed of light; classical physics already included the idea that the laws of mechanics, at least, were the same in all inertial frames, but the velocity of a light pulse was different in different frames moving with respect to each other

3. yes, provided the plane is flying at constant velocity relative to the Earth; in that case, an object with no force acting on it within the plane has no change in velocity relative to the plane and no change in velocity relative to the Earth; both the plane and the ground are inertial frames for describing the motion of the object

5. The observer moving with the process sees its interval of proper time, which is the shortest seen by any observer.

7. The length of an object is greatest to an observer who is moving with the object, and therefore measures its proper length.

9. a. No, not within the astronaut's own frame of reference. b. He sees Earth clocks to be in their rest frame moving by him, and therefore sees them slowed. c. No, not within the astronaut's own frame of reference. d. Yes, he measures the distance between the two stars to be shorter. e. The two observers agree on their relative speed.

11. There is no measured change in wavelength or frequency in this case. The relativistic Doppler effect depends only on the relative velocity of the source and the observer, not any speed relative to a medium for the light waves.

13. It shows that the stars are getting more distant from Earth, that the universe is expanding, and doing so at an accelerating rate, with greater velocity for more distant stars.]

15. Yes. This can happen if the external force is balanced by other externally applied forces, so that the net external force is zero.

17. Because it loses thermal energy, which is the kinetic energy of the random motion of its constituent particles, its mass decreases by an extremely small amount, as described by energy-mass equivalence.

19. Yes, in principle there would be a similar effect on mass for any decrease in energy, but the change would be so small for the energy changes in a chemical reaction that it would be undetectable in practice.

21. Not according to special relativity. Nothing with mass can attain the speed of light.

PROBLEMS

23. a. 1.0328; b. 1.15

25. 5.96×10^{-8} s

27. 0.800*c*

29. 0.140*c*

31. 48.6 m

33. Using the values given in **Example 5.3**: a. 1.39 km; b. 0.433 km; c. 0.433 km

35. a. 10.0*c*; b. The resulting speed of the canister is greater than c, an impossibility. c. It is unreasonable to assume that the canister will move toward the earth at 1.20*c*.

37. The angle α approaches $45°$, and the t'- and x'-axes rotate toward the edge of the light cone.

39. 15 m/s east

41. 32 m/s

43. a. The second ball approaches with velocity $-v$ and comes to rest while the other ball continues with velocity $-v$; b. This conserves momentum.

45. a. $t_1{}' = 0;\ x_1{}' = 0;\ t_2{}' = \tau;\ x_2{}' = 0$; b. $t_1{}' = 0;\ x_1{}' = 0;\ t_2{}' = \dfrac{\tau}{\sqrt{1 - v^2/c^2}};\ x_2{}' = \dfrac{-v\tau}{\sqrt{1 - v^2/c^2}}$

47. 0.615*c*

49. 0.696*c*

51. (Proof)

53. 4.09×10^{-19} kg · m/s

55. a. $3.000000015 \times 10^{13}$ kg · m/s; b. 1.000000005

57. 2.988×10^{8} m/s

59. 0.512 MeV according to the number of significant figures stated. The exact value is closer to 0.511 MeV.

61. 2.3×10^{-30} kg; to two digits because the difference in rest mass energies is found to two digits

63. a. 1.11×10^{27} kg; b. 5.56×10^{-5}

65. a. 7.1×10^{-3} kg; b. $7.1 \times 10^{-3} = 7.1 \times 10^{-3}$; c. $\frac{\Delta m}{m}$ is greater for hydrogen

67. a. 208; b. 0.999988*c*; six digits used to show difference from c

69. a. 6.92×10^{5} J; b. 1.54

71. a. 0.914*c*; b. The rest mass energy of an electron is 0.511 MeV, so the kinetic energy is approximately 150% of the rest mass energy. The electron should be traveling close to the speed of light.

ADDITIONAL PROBLEMS

73. a. 0.866*c*; b. 0.995*c*

75. a. 4.303 y to four digits to show any effect; b. 0.1434 y; c. $1/\sqrt{(1 - v^2/c^2)} = 29.88.$

77. a. 4.00; b. $v = 0.867c$

79. a. A sends a radio pulse at each heartbeat to B, who knows their relative velocity and uses the time dilation formula to calculate the proper time interval between heartbeats from the observed signal. b. $(66 \text{ beats/min})\sqrt{1 - v^2/c^2} = 57.1 \text{ beats/min}$

81. a. first photon: $(0,\ 0,\ 0)$ at $t = t'$; second photon:

$$t' = \frac{-vx/c^2}{\sqrt{1 - v^2/c^2}} = \frac{-(c/2)(1.00\text{ m})/c^2}{\sqrt{0.75}} = -\frac{0.577\text{ m}}{c} = 1.93 \times 10^{-9}\text{ s}$$

$$x' = \frac{x}{\sqrt{1 - v^2/c^2}} = \frac{1.00\text{ m}}{\sqrt{0.75}} = 1.15\text{ m}$$

b. simultaneous in A, not simultaneous in B

$$\begin{aligned} t' &= \frac{t - vx/c^2}{\sqrt{1 - v^2/c^2}} = \frac{\left(4.5 \times 10^{-4}\,\text{s}\right) - (0.6c)\left(\frac{150 \times 10^3\,\text{m}}{c^2}\right)}{\sqrt{1 - (0.6)^2}} \\ &= 1.88 \times 10^{-4}\,\text{s} \end{aligned}$$

83.

$$\begin{aligned} x' &= \frac{x - vt}{\sqrt{1 - v^2/c^2}} = \frac{150 \times 10^3\,\text{m} - (0.60)\left(3.00 \times 10^8\,\text{m/s}\right)\left(4.5 \times 10^{-4}\,\text{s}\right)}{\sqrt{1 - (0.6)^2}} \\ &= -1.01 \times 10^5\,\text{m} = -101\,\text{km} \\ y &= y' = 15\,\text{km} \\ z &= z' = 1\,\text{km} \end{aligned}$$

85.

$$\begin{aligned} \Delta t &= \frac{\Delta t' + v\Delta x'/c^2}{\sqrt{1 - v^2/c^2}} \\ 0 &= \frac{\Delta t' + v(500\,\text{m})/c^2}{\sqrt{1 - v^2/c^2}}; \end{aligned}$$

since $v \ll c,$ we can ignore the term v^2/c^2 and find

$$\Delta t' = -\frac{(50\,\text{m/s})(500\,\text{m})}{\left(3.00 \times 10^8\,\text{m/s}\right)^2} = -2.78 \times 10^{-13}\,\text{s}$$

The breakdown of Newtonian simultaneity is negligibly small, but not exactly zero, at realistic train speeds of 50 m/s.

87.

$$\begin{aligned} \Delta t' &= \frac{\Delta t - v\Delta x/c^2}{\sqrt{1 - v^2/c^2}} \\ 0 &= \frac{(0.30\,\text{s}) - \frac{(v)\left(2.0 \times 10^9\,\text{m}\right)}{\left(3.00 \times 10^8\,\text{m/s}\right)^2}}{\sqrt{1 - v^2/c^2}} \\ v &= \frac{(0.30\,\text{s})}{\left(2.0 \times 10^9\,\text{m}\right)}\left(3.00 \times 10^8\,\text{m/s}\right)^2 \\ v &= 1.35 \times 10^7\,\text{m/s} \end{aligned}$$

89. Note that all answers to this problem are reported to five significant figures, to distinguish the results. a. 0.99947*c*; b. 1.2064×10^{11} y; c. 1.2058×10^{11} y

91. a. –0.400*c*; b. –0.909*c*

93. a. 1.65 km/s; b. Yes, if the speed of light were this small, speeds that we can achieve in everyday life would be larger than 1% of the speed of light and we could observe relativistic effects much more often.

95. 775 MHz

97. a. 1.12×10^{-8} m/s; b. The small speed tells us that the mass of a protein is substantially smaller than that of even a tiny amount of macroscopic matter.

99. a.

$$\begin{aligned} F &= \frac{dp}{dt} = \frac{d}{dt}\left(\frac{mu}{\sqrt{1 - u^2/c^2}}\right) \\ &= \frac{du}{dt}\left(\frac{m}{\sqrt{1 - u^2/c^2}}\right) - \frac{1}{2}\frac{mu^2}{\left(1 - u^2/c^2\right)^{3/2}} 2\frac{du}{dt}; \\ &= \frac{m}{\left(1 - u^2/c^2\right)^{3/2}}\frac{du}{dt} \end{aligned}$$

b.

$$F = \frac{m}{\left(1 - u^2/c^2\right)^{3/2}} \frac{du}{dt}$$
$$= \frac{1\ \text{kg}}{\left(1 - \left(\frac{1}{2}\right)^2\right)^{3/2}} \left(1\ \text{m/s}^2\right)$$
$$= 1.53\ \text{N}$$

101. 90.0 MeV

103. a. $\gamma^2 - 1$; b. yes

105. 1.07×10^3

107. a. 6.56×10^{-8} kg; b. $m = (200\ \text{L})\left(1\ \text{m}^3/1000\ \text{L}\right)\left(750\ \text{kg/m}^3\right) = 150\ \text{kg}$; therefore, $\frac{\Delta m}{m} = 4.37 \times 10^{-10}$

109. a. $0.314c$; b. $0.99995c$ (Five digits used to show difference from c)

111. a. 1.00 kg; b. This much mass would be measurable, but probably not observable just by looking because it is 0.01% of the total mass.

113. a. 6.06×10^{11} kg/s; b. 4.67×10^{10} y; c. 4.27×10^9 kg; d. 0.32%

CHAPTER 6

CHECK YOUR UNDERSTANDING

6.1. Bunsen's burner

6.2. The wavelength of the radiation maximum decreases with increasing temperature.

6.3. $T_\alpha / T_\beta = 1/\sqrt{3} \cong 0.58,$ so the star β is hotter.

6.4. 3.3×10^{-19} J

6.5. No, because then $\Delta E/E \approx 10^{-21}$

6.6. -0.91 V; 1040 nm

6.7. $h = 6.40 \times 10^{-34}\ \text{J} \cdot \text{s} = 4.0 \times 10^{-15}\ \text{eV} \cdot \text{s}; -3.5\ \%$

6.8. $(\Delta\lambda)_{\text{min}} = 0\text{m}$ at a $0°$ angle; $71.0\ \text{pm} + 0.5\lambda_c = 72.215\ \text{pm}$

6.9. 121.5 nm and 91.1 nm; no, these spectral bands are in the ultraviolet

6.10. $v_2 = 1.1 \times 10^6\ \text{m/s} \cong 0.0036c$; $L_2 = 2\hbar\ K_2 = 3.4\ \text{eV}$

6.11. 29 pm

6.12. $\lambda = 2\pi n a_0 = 2(3.324\ \text{Å}) = 6.648\ \text{Å}$

6.13. $\lambda = 2.14\ \text{pm}$; $K = 261.56\ \text{keV}$

6.14. $0.052°$

6.15. doubles it

CONCEPTUAL QUESTIONS

1. yellow

3. goes from red to violet through the rainbow of colors

5. would not differ

7. human eye does not see IR radiation

9. No

11. from the slope

13. Answers may vary

15. the particle character

17. Answers may vary

19. no; yes

21. no

23. right angle

25. no

27. They are at ground state.

29. Answers may vary

31. increase

33. for larger n

35. Yes, the excess of 13.6 eV will become kinetic energy of a free electron.
37. no
39. X-rays, best resolving power
41. proton
43. negligibly small de Broglie's wavelengths
45. to avoid collisions with air molecules
47. Answers may vary
49. Answers may vary
51. yes
53. yes

PROBLEMS

55. a. 0.81 eV; b. 2.1×10^{23}; c. 2 min 20 sec
57. a. 7245 K; b. 3.62 μm
59. about 3 K
61. 4.835×10^{18} Hz; 0.620 Å
63. 263 nm; no
65. 3.68 eV
67. 4.09 eV
69. 5.54 eV
71. a. 1.89 eV; b. 459 THz; c. 1.21 V
73. 264 nm; UV
75. 1.95×10^6 m/s
77. 1.66×10^{-32} kg · m/s
79. 56.21 eV
81. 6.63×10^{-23} kg · m/s; 124 keV
83. 82.9 fm; 15 MeV
85. (Proof)
87. $\Delta\lambda_{30}/\Delta\lambda_{45} = 45.74\%$
89. 121.5 nm
91. a. 0.661 eV; b. –10.2 eV; c. 1.511 eV
93. 3038 THz
95. 97.33 nm
97. a. h/ π; b. 3.4 eV; c. – 6.8 eV; d. – 3.4 eV
99. $n = 4$
101. 365 nm; UV
103. no
105. 7
107. 145.5 pm
109. 20 fm; 9 fm
111. a. 2.103 eV; b. 0.846 nm
113. 80.9 pm
115. 2.21×10^{-19} m/s
117. 9.929×10^{32}
119. $\gamma = 1060$; 0.00124 fm
121. 24.11 V
123. a. $P = 2I/c = 8.67 \times 10^{-6}\,\text{N/m}^2$; b. $a = PA/m = 8.67 \times 10^{-4}\,\text{m/s}^2$; c. 74.91 m/s
125. $x = 4.965$

ADDITIONAL PROBLEMS

127. 7.124×10^{16} W/m^3
129. 1.034 eV
131. 5.93×10^{18}
133. 387.8 nm

135. a. 4.02×10^{15}; b. 0.533 mW

137. a. 4.02×10^{15}; b. 0.533 mW; c. 0.644 mA; d. 2.57 ns

139. a. 0.132 pm; b. 9.39 MeV; c. 0.047 MeV

141. a. 2 kJ; b. 1.33×10^{-5} kg · m/s; c. 1.33×10^{-5} N; d. yes

143. a. 0.003 nm; b. $105.56°$

145. $n = 3$

147. a. $a_0/2$; b. $-54.4\,\text{eV}/n^2$; c. $a_0/3, \; -122.4\,\text{eV}/n^2$

149. a. 36; b. 18.2 nm; c. UV

151. 396 nm; 5.23 neV

153. 7.3 keV

155. 728 m/s; $1.5\mu\text{V}$

157. $\lambda = hc/\sqrt{K(2E_0 + K)} = 3.705 \times 10^{-12}\text{ m}, K = 100\,\text{keV}$

159. $\Delta\lambda_c^{(\text{electron})}/\Delta\lambda_c^{(\text{proton})} = m_p/m_e = 1836$

161. (Proof)

163. $5.1 \times 10^{17}\,\text{Hz}$

CHAPTER 7

CHECK YOUR UNDERSTANDING

7.1. $(3 + 4i)(3 - 4i) = 9 - 16i^2 = 25$

7.2. $A = \sqrt{2/L}$

7.3. $(1/2 - 1/\pi)/2 = 9\%$

7.4. $4.1 \times 10^{-8}\,\text{eV}$; $1.1 \times 10^{-5}\,\text{nm}$

7.5. $0.5m\omega^2 x^2 \psi(x)^* \, \psi(x)$

7.6. None. The first function has a discontinuity; the second function is double-valued; and the third function diverges so is not normalizable.

7.7. a. 9.1%; b. 25%

7.8. a. 295 N/m; b. 0.277 eV

7.9. $\langle x \rangle = 0$

7.10. $L_{\text{proton}}/L_{\text{electron}} = \sqrt{m_e/m_p} = 2.3\%$

CONCEPTUAL QUESTIONS

1. $1/\sqrt{L}$, where $L = \text{length}$; $1/L$, where $L = \text{length}$

3. The wave function does not correspond directly to any measured quantity. It is a tool for predicting the values of physical quantities.

5. The average value of the physical quantity for a large number of particles with the same wave function.

7. Yes, if its position is completely unknown. Yes, if its momentum is completely unknown.

9. No. According to the uncertainty principle, if the uncertainty on the particle's position is small, the uncertainty on its momentum is large. Similarly, if the uncertainty on the particle's position is large, the uncertainty on its momentum is small.

11. No, it means that predictions about the particle (expressed in terms of probabilities) are time-independent.

13. No, because the probability of the particle existing in a narrow (infinitesimally small) interval at the discontinuity is undefined.

15. No. For an infinite square well, the spacing between energy levels increases with the quantum number n. The *smallest* energy measured corresponds to the transition from $n = 2$ to 1, which is three times the ground state energy. The largest *energy* measured corresponds to a transition from $n = \infty$ to 1, which is infinity. (Note: Even particles with extremely large energies remain bound to an infinite square well—they can never "escape")

17. No. This energy corresponds to $n = 0.25$, but n must be an integer.

19. Because the smallest allowed value of the quantum number n for a simple harmonic oscillator is 0. No, because quantum mechanics and classical mechanics agree only in the limit of large n.

21. Yes, within the constraints of the uncertainty principle. If the oscillating particle is localized, the momentum and therefore energy of the oscillator are distributed.

23. doubling the barrier width

25. No, the restoring force on the particle at the walls of an infinite square well is infinity.

PROBLEMS

27. $|\psi(x)|^2 \sin^2 \omega t$

29. (a) and (e), can be normalized

31. a. $A = \sqrt{2\alpha/\pi}$; b. probability $= 29.3\%$; c. $\langle x \rangle = 0$; d. $\langle p \rangle = 0$; e. $\langle K \rangle = \alpha^2 \hbar^2/2m$

33. a. $\Delta p \geq 2.11 \times 10^{-34}\,\text{N}\cdot\text{s}$; b. $\Delta v \geq 6.31 \times 10^{-8}\,\text{m}$; c. $\Delta v/\sqrt{k_B T/m_\alpha} = 5.94 \times 10^{-11}$

35. $\Delta\tau \geq 1.6 \times 10^{-25}\,\text{s}$

37. a. $\Delta f \geq 1.59\,\text{MHz}$; b. $\Delta\omega/\omega_0 = 3.135 \times 10^{-9}$

39. Carrying out the derivatives yields $k^2 = \frac{\omega^2}{c^2}$.

41. Carrying out the derivatives (as above) for the sine function gives a cosine on the right side the equation, so the equality fails. The same occurs for the cosine solution.

43. $E = \hbar^2 k^2/2m$

45. $\hbar^2 k^2$; The particle has definite momentum and therefore definite momentum squared.

47. 9.4 eV, 64%

49. 0.38 nm

51. 1.82 MeV

53. 24.7 nm

55. 6.03 Å

57. a.

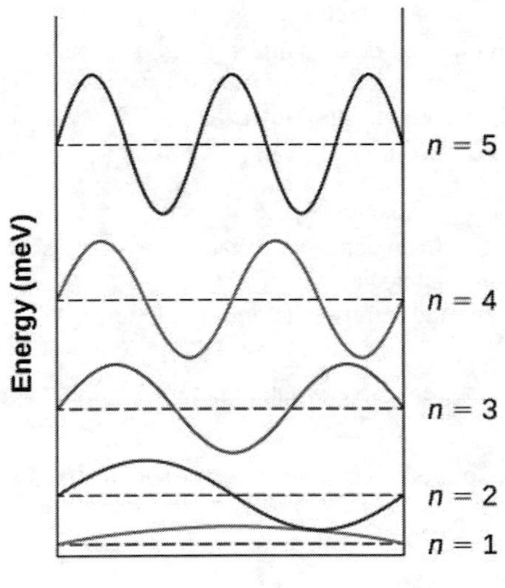

;

b. $\lambda_{5\to3} = 12.9\,\text{nm}$, $\lambda_{3\to1} = 25.8\,\text{nm}$, $\lambda_{4\to3} = 29.4\,\text{nm}$

59. proof

61. $6.662 \times 10^{14}\,\text{Hz}$

63. $n \approx 2.037 \times 10^{30}$

65. $\langle x \rangle = 0.5m\omega^2 \langle x^2 \rangle = \hbar\omega/4$; $\langle K \rangle = \langle E \rangle - \langle U \rangle = \hbar\omega/4$

67. proof

69. A complex function of the form, $Ae^{i\phi}$, satisfies Schrödinger's time-independent equation. The operators for kinetic and total energy are linear, so any linear combination of such wave functions is also a valid solution to Schrödinger's equation. Therefore, we conclude that **Equation 7.113** satisfies **Equation 7.106**, and **Equation 7.114** satisfies **Equation 7.108**.

71. a. 4.21%; b. 0.84%; c. 0.06%

73. a. 0.13%; b. close to 0%

75. 0.38 nm

ADDITIONAL PROBLEMS

77. proof
79. a. 4.0 %; b. 1.4 %; c. 4.0%; d. 1.4%
81. a. $t = mL^2/h = 2.15 \times 10^{26}$ years ; b. $E_1 = 1.46 \times 10^{-66}$ J,$K = 0.4$ J
83. proof
85. 1.2 N/m
87. 0

CHALLENGE PROBLEMS

89. 19.2 μm; 11.5 μm
91. 3.92%
93. proof

CHAPTER 8

CHECK YOUR UNDERSTANDING

8.1. No. The quantum number $m = -l, -l+1, \ldots, 0, \ldots, l-1, l$. Thus, the magnitude of L_z is always less than L because $< \sqrt{l(l+1)}$
8.2. $s = 3/2 <$
8.3. frequency quadruples

CONCEPTUAL QUESTIONS

1. n (principal quantum number) $\rightarrow$ total energy
l (orbital angular quantum number) $\rightarrow$ total absolute magnitude of the orbital angular momentum
m (orbital angular projection quantum number) $\rightarrow$ z-component of the orbital angular momentum
3. The Bohr model describes the electron as a particle that moves around the proton in well-defined orbits. Schrödinger's model describes the electron as a wave, and knowledge about the position of the electron is restricted to probability statements. The total energy of the electron in the ground state (and all excited states) is the same for both models. However, the orbital angular momentum of the ground state is different for these models. In Bohr's model, $L(\text{ground state}) = 1$, and in Schrödinger's model, $L(\text{ground state}) = 0$.
5. a, c, d; The total energy is changed (Zeeman splitting). The work done on the hydrogen atom rotates the atom, so the z-component of angular momentum and polar angle are affected. However, the angular momentum is not affected.
7. Even in the ground state ($l = 0$), a hydrogen atom has magnetic properties due the intrinsic (internal) electron spin. The magnetic moment of an electron is proportional to its spin.
9. For all electrons, $s = ½$ and $m_s = \pm ½$. As we will see, not all particles have the same spin quantum number. For example, a photon as a spin 1 ($s = 1$), and a Higgs boson has spin 0 ($s = 0$).
11. An electron has a magnetic moment associated with its intrinsic (internal) spin. Spin-orbit coupling occurs when this interacts with the magnetic field produced by the orbital angular momentum of the electron.
13. Elements that belong in the same column in the periodic table of elements have the same fillings of their outer shells, and therefore the same number of valence electrons. For example:
Li: $1s^2 2s^1$ (one valence electron in the $n = 2$ shell)
Na: $1s^2 2s 2p^6 3s^1$ (one valence electron in the $n = 2$ shell)
Both, Li and Na belong to first column.
15. Atomic and molecular spectra are said to be "discrete," because only certain spectral lines are observed. In contrast, spectra from a white light source (consisting of many photon frequencies) are continuous because a continuous "rainbow" of colors is observed.
17. UV light consists of relatively high frequency (short wavelength) photons. So the energy of the absorbed photon and the energy transition (ΔE) in the atom is relatively large. In comparison, visible light consists of relatively lower-frequency photons. Therefore, the energy transition in the atom and the energy of the emitted photon is relatively small.
19. For macroscopic systems, the quantum numbers are very large, so the energy difference (ΔE) between adjacent energy levels (orbits) is very small. The energy released in transitions between these closely space energy levels is much too small to be detected.
21. Laser light relies on the process of stimulated emission. In this process, electrons must be prepared in an excited (upper) metastable state such that the passage of light through the system produces de-excitations and, therefore, additional light.
23. A Blu-Ray player uses blue laser light to probe the bumps and pits of the disc and a CD player uses red laser light. The

relatively short-wavelength blue light is necessary to probe the smaller pits and bumps on a Blu-ray disc; smaller pits and bumps correspond to higher storage densities.

PROBLEMS

25. $(r, \theta, \phi) = (\sqrt{6}, 66°, 27°)$.

27. $\pm 3, \ \pm 2, \ \pm 1, \ 0$ are possible

29. $\pm 3, \ \pm 2, \ \pm 1, \ 0$ are possible

31. $F = -k\frac{Qq}{r^2}$

33. (1, 1, 1)
35. For the orbital angular momentum quantum number, *l*, the allowed values of:
$m = -l, \ -l + 1, ... \ 0, ... \ l - 1, \ l$.
With the exception of $m = 0$, the total number is just 2*l* because the number of states on either side of $m = 0$ is just *l*. Including $m = 0$, the total number of orbital angular momentum states for the orbital angular momentum quantum number, *l*, is: $2l + 1$. Later, when we consider electron spin, the total number of angular momentum states will be found to twice this value because each orbital angular momentum states is associated with two states of electron spin: spin up and spin down).

37. The probability that the 1*s* electron of a hydrogen atom is found outside of the Bohr radius is $\int_{a_0}^{\infty} P(r)dr \approx 0.68$

39. For $n = 2$, $l = 0$ (1 state), and $l = 1$ (3 states). The total is 4.

41. The 3*p* state corresponds to $n = 3$, $l = 2$. Therefore, $\mu = \mu_B \sqrt{6}$

43. The ratio of their masses is 1/207, so the ratio of their magnetic moments is 207. The electron's magnetic moment is more than 200 times larger than the muon.
45. a. The 3*d* state corresponds to $n = 3$, $l = 2$. So,
$I = 4.43 \times 10^{-7}$ A.
b. The maximum torque occurs when the magnetic moment and external magnetic field vectors are at right angles ($\sin\theta = 1$) . In this case:
$|\vec{\tau}| = \mu B.$
$\tau = 5.70 \times 10^{-26}$ N · m.
47. A 3*p* electron is in the state $n = 3$ and $l = 1$. The minimum torque magnitude occurs when the magnetic moment and external magnetic field vectors are most parallel (antiparallel). This occurs when $m = \pm 1$.The torque magnitude is given by
$|\vec{\tau}| = \mu B \sin\theta,$
Where
$\mu = (1.31 \times 10^{-24}$ J/T).
For $m = \pm 1$, we have:
$|\vec{\tau}| = 2.32 \times 10^{21}$ N · m.
49. An infinitesimal work *dW* done by a magnetic torque τ to rotate the magnetic moment through an angle $-d\theta$:
$dW = \tau(-d\theta)$,
where $\tau = |\vec{\mu} \times \vec{\mathbf{B}}|$. Work done is interpreted as a drop in potential energy *U*, so
$dW = -dU.$
The total energy change is determined by summing over infinitesimal changes in the potential energy:
$U = -\mu B \cos\theta$
$U = -\vec{\mu} \cdot \vec{\mathbf{B}}$.
51. Spin up (relative to positive *z*-axis):
$\theta = 55°$.
Spin down (relative to positive *z*-axis):

$$\theta = \cos^{-1}\left(\frac{S_z}{S}\right) = \cos^{-1}\left(\frac{-\frac{1}{2}}{\frac{\sqrt{3}}{2}}\right) = \cos^{-1}\left(\frac{-1}{\sqrt{3}}\right) = 125°.$$

53. The spin projection quantum number is $m_s = \pm ½$, so the z-component of the magnetic moment is
$\mu_z = \pm \mu_B$.

The potential energy associated with the interaction between the electron and the external magnetic field is
$U = \mp \mu_B B$.

The energy difference between these states is $\Delta E = 2\mu_B B$, so the wavelength of light produced is

$\lambda = 8.38 \times 10^{-5}\ \text{m} \approx 84\ \mu\text{m}$

55. It is increased by a factor of 2.
57. a. 32; b.

ℓ		$2(2\ell + 1)$		
0	s	$2(0 + 1)$	=	2
1	p	$2(2 + 1)$	=	6
2	d	$2(4 + 1)$	=	10
3	f	$2(6 + 1)$	=	14
				32

59. a. and e. are allowed; the others are not allowed.
b. $l = 3$ not allowed for $n = 1,\ l \leq (n - 1)$.

c. Cannot have three electrons in s subshell because $3 > 2(2l + 1) = 2$.

d. Cannot have seven electrons in p subshell (max of 6) $2(2l + 1) = 2(2 + 1) = 6$.

61. $[\text{Ar}]\,4s^2 3d^6$

63. a. The minimum value of ℓ is $l = 2$ to have nine electrons in it.

b. $3d^9$.

65. $[\text{He}]\,2s^2 2p^2$

67. For He^+, one electron "orbits" a nucleus with two protons and two neutrons ($Z = 2$). Ionization energy refers to the energy required to remove the electron from the atom. The energy needed to remove the electron in the ground state of He^+ ion to infinity is negative the value of the ground state energy, written:
$E = -54.4\ \text{eV}$.

Thus, the energy to ionize the electron is $+54.4\ \text{eV}$.

Similarly, the energy needed to remove an electron in the first excited state of Li^{2+} ion to infinity is negative the value of the first excited state energy, written:
$E = -30.6\ \text{eV}$.

The energy to ionize the electron is 30.6 eV.
69. The wavelength of the laser is given by:

$$\lambda = \frac{hc}{-\Delta E},$$

where E_γ is the energy of the photon and ΔE is the magnitude of the energy difference. Solving for the latter, we get:

$\Delta E = -2.795\ \text{eV}$.

The negative sign indicates that the electron lost energy in the transition.

71. $\Delta E_{L \to K} \approx (Z - 1)^2 (10.2\ \text{eV}) = 3.68 \times 10^3\ \text{eV}$.

73. According to the conservation of the energy, the potential energy of the electron is converted completely into kinetic energy. The initial kinetic energy of the electron is zero (the electron begins at rest). So, the kinetic energy of the electron just before it strikes the target is:
$K = e\Delta V$.

If *all* of this energy is converted into braking radiation, the frequency of the emitted radiation is a maximum, therefore:

$$f_{\text{max}} = \frac{e\Delta V}{h}.$$

When the emitted frequency is a maximum, then the emitted wavelength is a minimum, so:
$\lambda_{\text{min}} = 0.1293\ \text{nm}$.

75. A muon is 200 times heavier than an electron, but the minimum wavelength does not depend on mass, so the result is unchanged.

77. $4.13 \times 10^{-11}\ \text{m}$

79. 72.5 keV

81. The atomic numbers for Cu and Au are $Z = 29$ and 79, respectively. The X-ray photon frequency for gold is greater than copper by a factor:

$$\left(\frac{f_{\text{Au}}}{f_{\text{Cu}}}\right)^2 = \left(\frac{79-1}{29-1}\right)^2 \approx 8.$$

Therefore, the X-ray wavelength of Au is about eight times shorter than for copper.

83. a. If flesh has the same density as water, then we used 1.34×10^{23} photons. b. 2.52 MW

ADDITIONAL PROBLEMS

85. The smallest angle corresponds to $l = n - 1$ and $m = l = n - 1$. Therefore $\theta = \cos^{-1}\left(\sqrt{\frac{n-1}{n}}\right)$.

87. a. According to **Equation 8.1**, when $r = 0$, $U(r) = -\infty$, and when $r = +\infty$, $U(r) = 0$. b. The former result suggests that the electron can have an infinite negative potential energy. The quantum model of the hydrogen atom avoids this possibility because the probability density at $r = 0$ is zero.

89. A formal solution using sums is somewhat complicated. However, the answer easily found by studying the mathematical pattern between the principal quantum number and the total number of orbital angular momentum states.
For $n = 1$, the total number of orbital angular momentum states is 1; for $n = 2$, the total number is 4; and, when $n = 3$, the total number is 9, and so on. The pattern suggests the total number of orbital angular momentum states for the *n*th shell is n^2. (Later, when we consider electron spin, the total number of angular momentum states will be found to be $2n^2$, because each orbital angular momentum states is associated with two states of electron spin; spin up and spin down).

91. 50

93. The maximum number of orbital angular momentum electron states in the *n*th shell of an atom is n^2. Each of these states can be filled by a spin up and spin down electron. So, the maximum number of electron states in the *n*th shell is $2n^2$.

95. a., c., and e. are allowed; the others are not allowed. b. $l > n$ is not allowed.
d. $7 > 2(2l + 1)$

97. $f = 1.8 \times 10^9$ Hz

99. The atomic numbers for Cu and Ag are $Z = 29$ and 47, respectively. The X-ray photon frequency for silver is greater than copper by the following factor:

$$\left(\frac{f_{\text{Ag}}}{f_{\text{Cu}}}\right)^2 = 2.7.$$

Therefore, the X-ray wavelength of Ag is about three times shorter than for copper.

101. a. 3.24; b. n_i is not an integer. c. The wavelength must not be correct. Because $n_i > 2,$ the assumption that the line was from the Balmer series is possible, but the wavelength of the light did not produce an integer value for n_i. If the wavelength is correct, then the assumption that the gas is hydrogen is not correct; it might be sodium instead.

CHAPTER 9

CHECK YOUR UNDERSTANDING

9.1. It corresponds to a repulsive force between core electrons in the ions.

9.2. the moment of inertia

9.3. more difficult

9.4. It decreases.

9.5. The forward bias current is much larger. To a good approximation, diodes permit current flow in only one direction.

9.6. a low temperature and low magnetic field

CONCEPTUAL QUESTIONS

1. An ionic bond is formed by the attraction of a positive and negative ion. A covalent bond is formed by the sharing of one or more electrons between atoms. A van der Waals bond is formed by the attraction of two electrically polarized molecules.

3. 1. An electron is removed from one atom. The resulting atom is a positive ion. 2. An electron is absorbed from another atom. The result atom is a negative ion. 3. The positive and negative ions are attracted together until an equilibrium separation is reached.

5. Bonding is associated with a spatial function that is symmetric under exchange of the two electrons. In this state, the electron density is largest between the atoms. The total function must be antisymmetric (since electrons are fermions), so the spin function must be antisymmetric. In this state, the spins of the electrons are antiparallel.

7. rotational energy, vibrational energy, and atomic energy

9. Each ion is in the field of multiple ions of the other opposite charge.
11. 6, 6
13. 0.399 nm
15. increases by a factor of $\sqrt[3]{8^2} = 4$
17. For larger energies, the number of accessible states increases.
19. (1) Solve Schrödinger's equation for the allowed states and energies. (2) Determine energy levels for the case of a very large lattice spacing and then determine the energy levels as this spacing is reduced.
21. For *N* atoms spaced far apart, there are *N* different wave functions, all with the same energy (similar to the case of an electron in the double well of H_2). As the atoms are pushed together, the energies of these *N* different wave functions are split. By the exclusion principle, each electron must each have a unique set of quantum numbers, so the *N* atoms bringing *N* electrons together must have at least *N* states.
23. For a semiconductor, there is a relatively large energy gap between the lowest completely filled band and the next available unfilled band. Typically, a number of electrons traverse the gap and therefore the electrical conductivity is small. The properties of a semiconductor are sensitivity to temperature: As the temperature is increased, thermal excitations promote charge carriers from the valence band across the gap and into the conduction band.
25. a. Germanium has four valence electrons. If germanium doped with *arsenic* (five valence electrons), four are used in bonding and one electron will be left for conduction. This produces an *n*-type material. b. If germanium is doped with *gallium* (three valence electrons), all three electrons are used in bonding, leaving one hole for conduction. This results in a *p*-type material.
27. The Hall effect is the production of a potential difference due to motion of a conductor through an external magnetic field. This effect can be used to determine the drift velocity of the charge carriers (electrons or hole). If the current density is measured, this effect can also determine the number of charge carriers per unit volume.
29. It produces new unfilled energy levels just above the filled valence band. These levels accept electrons from the valence band.
31. The electric field produced by the uncovered ions reduces further diffusion. In equilibrium, the diffusion and drift currents cancel so the net current is zero. Therefore, the resistance of the depletion region is large.
33. The positive terminal is applied to the *n*-side, which uncovers more ions near the junction (widens the depletion layer), increases the junction voltage difference, and therefore reduces the diffusion of holes across the junction.
35. Sound moves a diaphragm in and out, which varies the input or base current of the transistor circuit. The transistor amplifies this signal (*p*-*n*-*p* semiconductor). The output or collector current drives a speaker.
37. BSC theory explains superconductivity in terms of the interactions between electron pairs (Cooper pairs). One electron in a pair interacts with the lattice, which interacts with the second electron. The combine electron-lattice-electron interaction binds the electron pair together in a way that overcomes their mutual repulsion.
39. As the magnitude of the magnetic field is increased, the critical temperature decreases.

PROBLEMS

41. $U = -5.16\,\text{eV}$
43. $-4.43\,\text{eV} = -4.69\,\text{eV} + U_{\text{ex}},\ U_{\text{ex}} = 0.26\,\text{eV}$
45. The measured value is 0.484 nm, and the actual value is close to 0.127 nm. The laboratory results are the same order of magnitude, but a factor 4 high.
47. 0.110 nm
49. a. $E = 2.2 \times 10^{-4}$ eV ; b. $\Delta E = 4.4 \times 10^{-4}$ eV
51. 0.65 nm
53. $r_0 = 0.240\,\text{nm}$
55. 2196 kcal
57. 11.5
59. a. 4% ; b. $4.2 \times 10^{-4}\,\%$; for very large values of the quantum numbers, the spacing between adjacent energy levels is very small ("in the continuum"). This is consistent with the expectation that for large quantum numbers, quantum and classical mechanics give approximately the same predictions.
61. 10.0 eV
63. 4.55×10^9
65. Fermi energy, $E_F = 7.03\,\text{eV}$, Temperature, $T_F = 8.2 \times 10^4\ \text{K}$
67. For an insulator, the energy gap between the valence band and the conduction band is larger than for a semiconductor.
69. 4.13 keV
71. $n = 1.56 \times 10^{19}$ holes/m^3
73. 5 T
75. $V_b = 0.458\,\text{V}$
77. $T = 829\,\text{K}$

79. $T = 0.707\, T_c$

81. 61 kV

ADDITIONAL PROBLEMS

83.
$$\begin{aligned} U_{\text{coul}} &= -5.65\text{ eV} \\ E_{\text{form}} &= -4.71\text{ eV},\ E_{\text{diss}} = 4.71\text{ eV} \end{aligned}$$

85. $E_{0r} = 7.43 \times 10^{-3}$ eV

87. $E_{0r} = 7.43 \times 10^{-3}$ eV ; $l = 0;\ E_r = 0$ eV (no rotation);

$l = 1;\ E_r = 1.49 \times 10^{-2}$ eV ; $l = 2;\ E_r = 4.46 \times 10^{-2}$ eV

89.

i. They are fairly hard and stable.
ii. They vaporize at relatively high temperatures (1000 to 2000 K).
iii. They are transparent to visible radiation, because photons in the visible portion of the spectrum are not energetic enough to excite an electron from its ground state to an excited state.
iv. They are poor electrical conductors because they contain effectively no free electrons.
v. They are usually soluble in water, because the water molecule has a large dipole moment whose electric field is strong enough to break the electrostatic bonds between the ions.

91. No, He atoms do not contain valence electrons that can be shared in the formation of a chemical bond.

93. $\sum_{1}^{N/2} n^2 = \frac{1}{3}\left(\frac{N}{2}\right)^3$, so $\bar{E} = \frac{1}{3}E_F$

95. An impurity band will be formed when the density of the donor atoms is high enough that the orbits of the extra electrons overlap. We saw earlier that the orbital radius is about 50 Angstroms, so the maximum distance between the impurities for a band to form is 100 Angstroms. Thus if we use 1 Angstrom as the interatomic distance between the Si atoms, we find that 1 out of 100 atoms along a linear chain must be a donor atom. And in a three-dimensional crystal, roughly 1 out of 10^6 atoms must be replaced by a donor atom in order for an impurity band to form.

97. a. $E_F = 7.11$ eV ; b. $E_F = 3.24$ eV ; c. $E_F = 9.46$ eV

99. $9.15 \approx 9$

CHALLENGE PROBLEMS

101. In three dimensions, the energy of an electron is given by:
$E = R^2 E_1$, where $R^2 = n_1^2 + n_2^2 + n_3^2$. Each allowed energy state corresponds to node in *N* space (n_1, n_2, n_3). The number of particles corresponds to the number of states (nodes) in the first octant, within a sphere of radius, *R*. This number is given by: $N = 2\left(\frac{1}{8}\right)\left(\frac{4}{3}\right)\pi R^3$, where the factor 2 accounts for two states of spin. The density of states is found by differentiating this expression by energy:
$g(E) = \frac{\pi V}{2}\left(\frac{8m_e}{h^2}\right)^{3/2} E^{1/2}$. Integrating gives: $\bar{E} = \frac{3}{5}E_F$.

CHAPTER 10

CHECK YOUR UNDERSTANDING

10.1. eight
10.2. harder
10.3. Half-life is inversely related to decay rate, so the half-life is short. Activity depends on both the number of decaying particles and the decay rate, so the activity can be great or small.
10.4. Neither; it stays the same.
10.5. the same
10.6. the conversion of mass to energy
10.7. power

CONCEPTUAL QUESTIONS

1. The nucleus of an atom is made of one or more nucleons. A nucleon refers to either a proton or neutron. A nuclide is a stable nucleus.

3. A bound system should have less mass than its components because of energy-mass equivalence $\left(E = mc^2\right)$. If the energy of a system is reduced, the total mass of the system is reduced. If two bricks are placed next to one another, the attraction between them is purely gravitational, assuming the bricks are electrically neutral. The gravitational force between the bricks is relatively small (compared to the strong nuclear force), so the mass defect is much too small to be observed. If the bricks are glued together with cement, the mass defect is likewise small because the electrical interactions between the electrons involved in the bonding are still relatively small.
5. Nucleons at the surface of a nucleus interact with fewer nucleons. This reduces the binding energy per nucleon, which is based on an average over all the nucleons in the nucleus.
7. That it is constant.
9. Gamma (γ) rays are produced by nuclear interactions and X-rays and light are produced by atomic interactions. Gamma rays are typically shorter wavelength than X-rays, and X-rays are shorter wavelength than light.
11. Assume a rectangular coordinate system with an *xy*-plane that corresponds to the plane of the paper. α bends into the page (trajectory parabolic in the *xz*-plane); β^+ bends into the page (trajectory parabolic in the *xz*-plane); and γ is unbent.
13. Yes. An atomic bomb is a fission bomb, and a fission bomb occurs by splitting the *nucleus* of atom.
15. Short-range forces between nucleons in a nucleus are analogous to the forces between water molecules in a water droplet. In particular, the forces between nucleons at the surface of the nucleus produce a surface tension similar to that of a water droplet.
17. The nuclei produced in the fusion process have a larger binding energy per nucleon than the nuclei that are fused. That is, nuclear fusion decreases average energy of the nucleons in the system. The energy difference is carried away as radiation.
19. Alpha particles do not penetrate materials such as skin and clothes easily. (Recall that alpha radiation is barely able to pass through a thin sheet of paper.) However, when produce inside the body, neighboring cells are vulnerable.

PROBLEMS

21. Use the rule $A = Z + N$.

	Atomic Number (*Z*)	Neutron Number (*N*)	Mass Number (*A*)
(a)	29	29	58
(b)	11	13	24
(c)	84	126	210
(d)	20	25	45
(e)	82	124	206

23. a. $r = r_0 A^{1/3}$, $\rho = \frac{3\text{ u}}{4\pi r_0^{\ 3}}$;

b. $\rho = 2.3 \times 10^{17}\ \text{kg/m}^3$

25. side length $= 1.6\ \mu\text{m}$

27. 92.4 MeV
29. $8.790\ \text{MeV} \approx \text{graph's value}$

31. a. 7.570 MeV; b. $7.591\ \text{MeV} \approx \text{graph's value}$

33. The decay constant is equal to the negative value of the slope or $10^{-9}\ \text{s}^{-1}$. The half-life of the nuclei, and thus the material, is $T_{1/2} = 693$ million years.

35. a. The decay constant is $\lambda = 1.99 \times 10^{-5}\ \text{s}^{-1}$. b. Since strontium-91 has an atomic mass of 90.90 g, the number of nuclei in a 1.00-g sample is initially
$N_0 = 6.63 \times 10^{21}$ nuclei.
The initial activity for strontium-91 is

$$\begin{aligned} A_0 &= \lambda N_0 \\ &= 1.32 \times 10^{17}\ \text{decays/s} \end{aligned}$$

The activity at $t = 15.0\ \text{h} = 5.40 \times 10^4\ \text{s}$ is
$A = 4.51 \times 10^{16}$ decays/s.

37. 1.20×10^{-2} mol; 6.00×10^{-3} mol; 3.75×10^{-4} mol

39. a. 0.988 Ci; b. The half-life of ^{226}Ra is more precisely known than it was when the Ci unit was established.

41. a. $2.73 \mu g$; b. 9.76×10^4 Bq

43. a. 7.46×10^5 Bq ; b. 7.75×10^5 Bq

45. a. 4.273 MeV; b. 1.927×10^{-5} ; c. Since ^{238}U is a slowly decaying substance, only a very small number of nuclei decay on human timescales; therefore, although those nuclei that decay lose a noticeable fraction of their mass, the change in the total mass of the sample is not detectable for a macroscopic sample.

47. a. $^{90}_{38}Sr_{52} \rightarrow ^{90}_{39}Y_{51} + \beta^{-1} + \bar{\nu}_e$; b. 0.546 MeV

49. $^{3}_{1}H_2 \rightarrow ^{3}_{2}He_1 + \beta^- + \bar{\nu}_e$

51. a. $^{7}_{4}Be_3 + e^- \rightarrow ^{7}_{3}Li_4 + \nu_e$; b. 0.862 MeV

53. a. $X = ^{208}_{82}Pb_{126}$; b. 33.05 MeV

55. a. 177.1 MeV; b. This value is approximately equal to the average BEN for heavy nuclei. c. $n + ^{238}_{92}U_{146} \rightarrow ^{96}_{38}Sr_{58} + ^{140}_{54}Xe_{86} + 3n,$

$$\begin{aligned} A_i &= 239 = A_f, \\ Z_i &= 92 = 38 + 54 = Z_f \end{aligned}$$

57. a. 2.57×10^3 MW ; b. 8.04×10^{19} fissions/ ; c. 991 kg

59. i.

$$\begin{aligned} ^1_1H + ^1_1H &\rightarrow ^2_1H + e^+ + \nu_e \\ A_i &= 1 + 1 = 2;\ A_f = 2\ Z_i = 1 + 1 = 2; \\ Z_f &= 1 + 1 = 2 \end{aligned}$$

ii.

$$\begin{aligned} ^1_1H + ^2_1H &\rightarrow ^3_2H + \gamma \\ A_i &= 1 + 2 = 3;\ A_f = 3 + 0 = 3\ Z_i = 1 + 1 = 2; \\ Z_E &= 1 + 1 = 2 \end{aligned}$$

iii.

$$\begin{aligned} ^3_2H + ^3_2H &\rightarrow ^4_2H + ^1_1H + ^1_1H \\ A_i &= 3 + 3 = 6;\ A_f = 4 + 1 + 1 = 6\ Z_i = 2 + 2 = 4 \\ Z_f &= 2 + 1 + 1 = 4 \end{aligned}$$

61. 26.73 MeV

63. a. 3×10^{38} protons/s ; b. 6×10^{14} neutrinos/m$^2 \cdot$ s ;

This huge number is indicative of how rarely a neutrino interacts, since large detectors observe very few per day.

65. a. The atomic mass of deuterium (^2H) is 2.014102 u, while that of tritium (^3H) is 3.016049 u, for a total of 5.032151 u per reaction. So a mole of reactants has a mass of 5.03 g, and in 1.00 kg, there are $(1000\ g)/(5.03\ g/mol) = 198.8\ mol$ of reactants. The number of reactions that take place is therefore

$$(198.8\ mol)(6.02 \times 10^{23}\ mol^{-1}) = 1.20 \times 10^{26}\ \text{reactions}.$$

The total energy output is the number of reactions times the energy per reaction:

$E = 3.37 \times 10^{14}$ J;

b. Power is energy per unit time. One year has 3.16×10^7 s, so

$P = 10.7$ MW.

We expect nuclear processes to yield large amounts of energy, and this is certainly the case here. The energy output of 3.37×10^{14} J from fusing 1.00 kg of deuterium and tritium is equivalent to 2.6 million gallons of gasoline and about eight times the energy output of the bomb that destroyed Hiroshima. Yet the average backyard swimming pool has about 6 kg of deuterium in it, so that fuel is plentiful if it can be utilized in a controlled manner.

67. $Gy = \frac{Sv}{RBE}$: a. 0.01 Gy; b. 0.0025 Gy; c. 0.16 Gy

69. 1.24 MeV

71. 1.69 mm

73. For cancer: $(3\ rem)\left(\frac{10}{10^6\ rem \cdot y}\right) = \frac{30}{10^6\ y}$, The risk each year of dying from induced cancer is 30 in a million. For genetic defect: $(3\text{ rem})\left(\frac{3.3}{10^6\text{ rem}\cdot\text{y}}\right) = \frac{9.9}{10^6\text{ y}}$, The chance each year of an induced genetic defect is 10 in a million.

ADDITIONAL PROBLEMS

75. atomic mass (Cl) = 35.5 g/mol

77. a. 1.71×10^{58} kg ; b. This mass is impossibly large; it is greater than the mass of the entire Milky Way galaxy. c. ^{236}U is not produced through natural processes operating over long times on Earth, but through artificial processes in a nuclear reactor.
79. If 10% of rays are left after 2.00 cm, then only $(0.100)^2 = 0.01 = 1\%$ are left after 4.00 cm. This is much smaller than your lab partner's result (5%).

81. a. 1.68×10^{-5} Ci ; (b) From **Appendix B**, the energy released per decay is 4.27 MeV, so 8.65×10^{10} J ; (c) The monetary value of the energy is $\$2.9 \times 10^3$

83. We know that $\lambda = 3.84 \times 10^{-12}\text{ s}^{-1}$ and $A_0 = 0.25\text{ decays/s}\cdot\text{g} = 15\text{ decays/min}\cdot\text{g}$.
Thus, the age of the tomb is

$$t = -\frac{1}{3.84 \times 10^{-12}\text{ s}^{-1}}\ln\frac{10\text{ decays/ min}\cdot\text{g}}{15\text{ decays/ min}\cdot\text{g}} = 1.06 \times 10^{11}\text{ s} \approx 3350\text{ y}.$$

CHALLENGE PROBLEMS

85. a. 6.97×10^{15} Bq ; b. 6.24 kW; c. 5.67 kW

87. a. Due to the leak, the pressure in the turbine chamber has dropped significantly. The pressure difference between the turbine chamber and steam condenser is now very low. b. A large pressure difference is required for steam to pass through the turbine chamber and turn the turbine.
89. The energies are

$$\begin{aligned} E_\gamma &= 20.6\text{ MeV} \\ E_{^4\text{He}} &= 5.68 \times 10^{-2}\text{ MeV} \end{aligned}$$

. Notice that most of the energy goes to the γ ray.

CHAPTER 11

CHECK YOUR UNDERSTANDING

11.1. 1
11.2. 0
11.3. 0
11.4. 0
11.5. 1 eV
11.6. The radius of the track is cut in half.
11.7. The colliding particles have identical mass but opposite vector momenta.
11.8. blueshifted
11.9. about the same

CONCEPTUAL QUESTIONS

1. Strong nuclear force: interaction between quarks, mediated by gluons. Electromagnetic force: interaction between charge particles, mediated photons. Weak nuclear force: interactions between fermions, mediated by heavy bosons. Gravitational force: interactions between material (massive) particle, mediate by hypothetical gravitons.
3. electron, muon, tau; electron neutrino, muon neutrino, tau neutrino; down quark, strange quark, bottom quark; up quark, charm quark, top quark
5. Conservation energy, momentum, and charge (familiar to classical and relativistic mechanics). Also, conservation of baryon number, lepton number, and strangeness—numbers that do not change before and after a collision or decay.
7. It means that the theory that requires the conservation law is not understood. The failure of a long-established theory often leads to a deeper understanding of nature.
9. 3 quarks, 2 quarks (a quark-antiquark pair)
11. Baryons with the same quark composition differ in rest energy because this energy depends on the internal energy of the quarks $\left(m = E/c^2\right)$. So, a baryon that contains a quark with a large angular momentum is expected to be more massive than the same baryon with less angular momentum.
13. the "linac" to accelerate the particles in a straight line, a synchrotron to accelerate and store the moving particles in a circular

ring, and a detector to measure the products of the collisions
15. In a colliding beam experiment, the energy of the colliding particles goes into the rest mass energy of the new particle. In a fix-target experiment, some of this energy is lost to the momentum of the new particle since the center-of-mass of colliding particles is not fixed.
17. The Standard Model is a model of elementary particle interactions. This model contains the electroweak theory and quantum chromodynamics (QCD). It describes the interaction of leptons and quarks though the exchange of photons (electromagnetism) and bosons (weak theory), and the interaction of quark through the exchange of gluons (QCD). This model does not describe gravitational interactions.
19. To explain particle interactions that involve the strong nuclear, electromagnetic, and weak nuclear forces in a unified way.
21. No, however it will explain why the W and Z bosons are massive (since the Higgs "imparts" mass to these particles), and therefore why the weak force is short ranged.
23. Cosmological expansion is an expansion of space. This expansion is different than the explosion of a bomb where particles pass rapidly *through* space. A plot of the recessional speed of a galaxy is proportional to its distance. This speed is measured using the red shift of distant starlight.
25. With distance, the absolute brightness is the same, but the apparent brightness is inversely proportional to the square of its distance (or by Hubble's law recessional velocity).
27. The observed expansion of the universe and the cosmic background radiation spectrum.
29. If light slow down, it takes long to reach Earth than expected. We conclude that the object is much closer than it really is. Thus, for every recessional velocity (based on the frequency of light, which we assume is not disturbed by the slowing), the distance is smaller than the "true" value, Hubble's constant is larger than the "true" value, and the age of the universe is smaller than the "true" value.

PROBLEMS

31. 1.022 MeV
33. 0.511 MeV, $2.73 \times 10^{-22}\ \text{kg} \cdot \text{m/s}$, 1.23×10^{20} Hz
35. a, b, and c
37. a. $\bar{p}_e{}^+\ ve$; b. $\bar{p}\pi^+$ or $\bar{p}\pi^0$; c. $\overline{\Xi^0}\pi^0$ or $\overline{\Lambda^0}\text{K}^+$; d. $\mu^-\ \bar{v}_\mu$ or $\pi^-\pi^0$; e. $\bar{p}\pi^0$ or $\bar{n}\pi^-$
39. A proton consists of two up quarks and one down quark. The total charge of a proton is therefore $+\frac{2}{3} + \frac{2}{3} + -\frac{1}{3} = +1$.
41. The K^+ meson is composed of an up quark and a strange antiquark ($u\bar{s}$). Since the changes of this quark and antiquark are 2*e*/3 and *e*/3, respectively, the net charge of the K^+ meson is *e*, in agreement with its known value. Two spin $-1/2$ particles can combine to produce a particle with spin of either 0 or 1, consistent with the K^+ meson's spin of 0. The net strangeness of the up quark and strange antiquark is $0 + 1 = 1$, in agreement with the measured strangeness of the K^+ meson.
43. a. color; b. quark-antiquark
45. $d \to u + e^- + \bar{v}_e;\ u \to d + e^+ + v_e$
47. 965 GeV
49. According to **Example 11.7**,
$W = 2E_{\text{beam}} = 9.46\ \text{GeV}$,

$M = 9.46\ \text{GeV}/c^2$.
This is the mass of the upsilon (1S) meson first observed at Fermi lab in 1977. The upsilon meson consists of a bottom quark and its antiparticle $\left(b\bar{b}\right)$.
51. 0.135 fm; Since this distance is too short to make a track, the presence of the W^- must be inferred from its decay products.
53. 3.33 MV
55. The graviton is massless, so like the photon is associated with a force of infinite range.
57. 67.5 MeV
59. a. 33.9 MeV; b. By conservation of momentum, $|p_\mu| = |p_\nu| = p$. By conservation of energy, $E_\nu = 29.8\ \text{MeV}$, $E_\mu = 4.1\ \text{MeV}$
61. $(0.99)(299792\ \text{km/s}) = \left(\left(70\frac{\text{km}}{\text{s}}\right)/\ \text{Mpc}\right)(d),\ d = 4240\ \text{Mpc}$
63. 1.0×10^4 km/s away from us.
65. 2.26×10^8 y
67. a. $1.5 \times 10^{10}\ \text{y} = 15$ billion years; b. Greater, since if it was moving slower in the past it would take less more to travel the distance.

69. $v = \sqrt{\frac{GM}{r}}$

ADDITIONAL PROBLEMS

71. a. $\bar{n}$; b. K^+ ; c. K^+ ; d. π^- ; e. $\bar{\nu}_\tau$; f. e^+

73. $14.002 \text{ TeV} \approx 14.0 \text{ TeV}$

75. 964 rev/s

77. a. $H_0 = \frac{30 \text{ km/s}}{1 \text{ Mly}} = 30 \text{km/s} \cdot \text{Mly}$; b. $H_0 = \frac{15 \text{ km/s}}{1 \text{ Mly}} = 15 \text{km/s} \cdot \text{Mly}$

CHALLENGE PROBLEMS

79. a. 5×10^{10} ; b. divide the number of particles by the area they hit: $5 \times 10^4 \text{ particles/m}^2$

81. a. 2.01; b. 2.50×10^{-8} s ; c. 6.50 m

83.

$$\frac{mv^2}{r} = \frac{GMm}{r^2} \Rightarrow$$

$$v = \left(\frac{GM}{r}\right)^{1/2} = \left[\frac{(6.67 \times 10^{-11} \text{ N} \cdot \text{m}^2/\text{kg}^2)(3 \times 10^{41} \text{ kg})}{(30{,}000 \text{ ly})(9.46 \times 10^{15} \text{ m/ly})}\right] = 2.7 \times 10^5 \text{ m/s}$$

85. a. 938.27 MeV; b. 1.84×10^3

87. a. $3.29 \times 10^{18} \text{ GeV} \approx 3 \times 10^{18} \text{ GeV}$; b. 0.3; Unification of the three forces breaks down shortly after the separation of gravity from the unification force (near the Planck time interval). The uncertainty in time then becomes greater. Hence the energy available becomes less than the needed unification energy.

INDEX

Symbols

A

B

C

D

Q

R

S

T